SOMETHING ABOUT THE AUTHOR®

Something about
the Author *was named
an*"**Outstanding
Reference Source,**"
*the highest honor given
by the American
Library Association
Reference and Adult
Services Division.*

ISSN 0276-816X

SOMETHING ABOUT THE AUTHOR®

**Facts and Pictures about Authors
and Illustrators of Books for Young People**

volume 215

GALE
CENGAGE Learning™

Detroit • New York • San Francisco • New Haven, Conn • Waterville, Maine • London

LSL
ReF
PN
451
.S6
v.215

Something about the Author, Volume 215

Project Editor: Lisa Kumar

Editorial: Laura Avery, Pamela Bow, Jim Craddock, Amy Fuller, Andrea Henderson, Margaret Mazurkiewicz, Tracie Moy, Jeff Muhr, Kathy Nemeh, Mary Ruby, Mike Tyrkus

Permissions: Jacqueline Flowers, Savannah Gignac, Jhanay Williams

Imaging and Multimedia: Savannah Gignac, John Watkins

Composition and Electronic Capture: Amy Darga

Manufacturing: Drew Kalasky

Product Manager: Janet Witalec

© 2010 Gale, Cengage Learning

For product information and technology assistance, contact us at **Gale Customer Support, 1-800-877-4253.** For permission to use material from this text or product, submit all requests online at **www.cengage.com/permissions.** Further permissions questions can be emailed to **permissionrequest@cengage.com**

Gale
27500 Drake Rd.
Farmington Hills, MI, 48331-3535

LIBRARY OF CONGRESS CATALOG CARD NUMBER 62-52046

ISBN-13: 978-1-4144-4789-6
ISBN-10: 1-4144-4789-2

ISSN 0276-816X

This title is also available as an e-book.
ISBN-13: 978-1-4144-6447-3
ISBN-10: 1-4144-6447-9
Contact your Gale sales representative for ordering information.

Printed in the United States of America
1 2 3 4 5 6 7 14 13 12 11 10

Contents

Authors in Forthcoming Volumes ix

Introduction xi

SATA Product Advisory Board xiii

Illustrations Index 211

Author Index 245

A

Alarcón, Francisco X. 1954- 1

Alarcón, Franciso Xavier
   See Alarcón, Francisco X. 1

Anelli, Melissa 1979- 6

Atkinson, Elizabeth 7

B

Bang, Garrett
   See Bang, Molly 9

Bang, Molly 1943- 9

Bang, Molly Garrett
   See Bang, Molly 9

Bayrock, Fiona 17

Bell, Krista 1950- 18

Bradford, Chris 1974- 21

Buzzeo, Toni 1951- 22

C

Carlstrom, Nancy White 1948- 27

Carpenter, Nancy 33

Carpenter, Nancy Sippel
   See Carpenter, Nancy 33

Cepeda, Joe 37

Chorao, Kay 1936- 41

Clarke, Greg 1959- 46

Clover, Peter 1952- 47

Cochrane, Hamilton E.
   See Cochrane, Mick 49

Cochrane, Mick 1956- 49

Cohen, Santiago 1954- 51

D

Dean, Claire 54

Delano, Marfé Ferguson 55

Dewin, Howie
   See Howie, Betsy 93

Dugger, Elizabeth L.
   See Kanell, Beth 101

DuPrau, Jeanne 1944- 57

Durango, Julia 1967- 60

F

Forman, Mark L.
   See Forman, M.L. 62

Forman, M.L. 1964- 62

Furlonger, Patricia
   See Wrightson, Patricia 209

G

Gentry, Marita 63

Giraudon, David 1975- 63

Gold, August 1955- 64

H

Haas, Jessie 1959- 67

Handler, Daniel
   See Snicket, Lemony 166

Haworth-Attard, Barbara 1953- . . . .

Hesse, Karen 1952- 72

Hoose, Phillip 1947- 81

Hoose, Phillip M.
   See Hoose, Phillip 81

Hopkins, Lee Bennett 1938- 84

Howie, Betsy 1962- 93

I

Ives, Penny 1956- 95

J

Jennewein, James 96

Jennewein, Jim
  See Jennewein, James 96

Johnson, Gillian 1963- 98

K

Kanell, Beth 101

Kelly, Katy 1955- 102

Kendall, Gideon 1966- 104

Koralek, Jenny 1934- 105

L

Labatt, Mary 1944- 109

Lane, Alison Hoffman 111

Lee, Jared 1943- 112

Lee, Jared D.
  See Lee, Jared 112

Lerman, Josh 114

Levchuk, Lisa 116

Lodge, Bernard 1933- 117

M

Markey, Kevin 1965- 121

Mendez, Simon 1975- 122

Michaelis, Antonia 1979- 123

Miller Brothers
  See Miller, Christopher 124

Miller, Christopher 1976- 124

Milway, Alex 1978- 125

Molski, Carol 126

N

Nahoko, Uehashi
  See Uehashi, Nahoko 196

Nelson, D.A. 1970- 127

Nelson, Dawn Ann
  See Nelson, D.A. 127

Nichols, Michael 1952- 128

Nichols, Michael "Nick"
  See Nichols, Michael 128

Nolan, Lucy 130

Novgorodoff, Danica 1980- 132

O

Osborn, Jacob 1981(?)- 134

Osborne, Linda Barrett 1949- 134

P

Parker, Tom S. 135

Paver, Michelle 1960- 136

Peterson, Mary 139

Phelan, Matt 1970- 139

R

Reed, Lynn Rowe 143

Rhue, Morton
  See Strasser, Todd 175

Ripken, Cal, Jr. 1960- 146

Ripken, Calvin Edward, Jr.
  See Ripken, Cal, Jr. 146

Ritter, John H. 1951- 149

Ruurs, Margriet 1952- 153

S

Sarcone-Roach, Julia 158

Scaletta, Kurtis 1968- 159

Shipton, Jonathan 1948- 160

Shore, Diane Z. 160

Shore, Diane ZuHone
  See Shore, Diane Z. 160

Smith, Cynthia Leitich 1967- 162

Smith, Emily Wing 1980- 165

Snicket, Lemony 1970- 166

Spires, Elizabeth 1952- 172

Squires, Janet 175

Strasser, Todd 1950- 175

Swarner, Kristina 1965- 183

T

Tanaka, Yoko 1947- 186

Thaler, Michael C.
  See Thaler, Mike 188

Thaler, Mike 1936- 188

Thomason, Mark 194

U

Uehashi, Nahoko 1962- 196

Urdahl, Catherine 198

V

Vamos, Samantha R. 199

Vess, Charles 1951- 200

Vivian, Siobhan 1979(?)- 203

Authors in Forthcoming Volumes

Below are some of the authors and illustrators that will be featured in upcoming volumes of *SATA*. These include new entries on the swiftly rising stars of the field, as well as completely revised and updated entries (indicated with *) on some of the most notable and best-loved creators of books for children.

*Sandy Asher ▌ Incorporating memories and characters from her childhood, Asher has earned critical praise and numerous awards for for her prose works for young readers. In addition to picture books like *Princess Bee and the Royal Good-Night Story* and *Too Many Frogs!*, Her young-adult novels include *Just like Jenny, Things Are Seldom What They Seem*, and *Everything Is Not Enough*. A playwright and anthologist as well as a children's author, Asher is editor of the award-winning *With All My Heart, with All My Mind: Thirteen Stories about Growing up Jewish*, and also inspires other writers in *Writing It Right: How Successful Children's Authors Revise and Sell Their Stories*.

Jen Calonita ▌ Calonita turned to writing teen fiction after a career as an entertainment journalist and senior editor of a teen publisher imprint. As a reporter, she had the chance to interview a number of top Hollywood celebrities, and she drew from the best characteristics of this exclusive group in crafting the teen heroine in her popular novel series "Secrets of My Hollywood Life," which includes *On Location, Family Affairs, Paparazzi Princess, Broadway Lights*, and *There's No Place like Home*.

*Michael Foreman ▌ Foreman, an acclaimed children's author and graphic artist, is best known for creating artwork for the texts of such beloved authors as Rudyard Kipling, Oscar Wilde, Michael Morpurgo, and Terry Jones. He has also produced a number of original self-illustrated works, including *Seal Surfer, Jack's Fantastic Voyage, Michael Foreman's Mother Goose*, and the award-winning *War Boy: A Country Childhood,* and has collaborated with his son, Jack Foreman, on the engaging picture book *Say Hello*.

Jacqueline Kelly ▌ Born in New Zealand, Kelly was raised in Texas, where she graduated from medical school and then earned a law degree. While working as a physician, Kelly also cultivated her love of writing and published short fiction. Her middle-grade novel *The Evolution of Calpurnia Tate* was inspired by both the Texas landscape and Kelly's fascination with nature and science.

James Lovegrove ▌ After one of his short stories won a college prize while Lovegrove was at Oxford University, he gave himself two years to write and successfully market a novel upon graduation, and he accomplished this goal with *The Hope*. Spanning genres including science fiction, fantasy, and horror, Lovegrove writes for a broad audience, from adults to preteens, and his books have been praised for their entertaining plots, compelling characters, and strong research.

*Asthma Mobin-Uddin ▌ An American of Pakistani descent, writer and pediatrician Mobin-Uddin made her publishing debut with *My Name Is Bilal*, in which she inspires young readers to be true to themselves and cherish their unique cultural identity. Other books have followed, including *The Best Eid Ever* and *A Party in Ramadan,* both of which share the traditions surrounding major Muslim holy days with children of other cultures.

*Olga Cossi ▌ Cossi focuses her picture books, teen novels, and nonfiction titles on travel and environmental topics, and she shares her Italian heritage and her California upbringing in such books as *Orlanda and the Contest of Thieves* and *Adventure on the Graveyard of the Wrecks*. Her empathy for young people—from preschoolers to high schoolers—is reflected in a number of her issue-oriented books: *The Magic Box* addresses the relationship between smoking and teen sports, while *Pemba Sherpa* includes an exposition of cultural expectations and gender roles.

James Rollins ▌ Rollins, a veterinarian-turned-writer, is the author of such best-selling adventure novels as *Sandstorm, The Doomsday Key,* and other works in the "Sigma Force" series. Rollins, whose real name is James Czajkowski, is also the creator of the "Jake Ransom" series for young readers, and he writes fantasy novels under the pseudonym James Clemens.

Laura Purdie Salas ▌ A prolific writer who has been praised for her engaging use of rhyme, Salas is the author of poetry collections such as *Y Is for Yowl!: A Scary Alphabet, Stampede!: Poems to Celebrate the Wild Side of School,* and *A Fuzzy-fast Blur: Poems about Pets*. The natural world figures prominently in many of Salas's picture-book texts, which cover a range of scientific subjects, including animals and weather. *And Then There Were Eight,* which focuses on astronomy, is characteristic of Salas's work in its use of a variety of poetic forms, such as limerick, free verse, cinquain, and acrostic.

Shaoli Wang ▌ Born in the People's Republic of China, Wang grew up under the strictures of the Cultural Revolution, where her artistic talents were recognized early on. Now living in British Columbia, Canada, Wang continues to teach and exhibit her award-winning art. She has also illustrated several picture books for noted Canadian children's author Paul Yee, among them *Bamboo* and *Shu-Li and Tamara*.

Introduction

Something about the Author (*SATA*) is an ongoing reference series that examines the lives and works of authors and illustrators of books for children. *SATA* includes not only well-known writers and artists but also less prominent individuals whose works are just coming to be recognized. This series is often the only readily available information source on emerging authors and illustrators. You'll find *SATA* informative and entertaining, whether you are a student, a librarian, an English teacher, a parent, or simply an adult who enjoys children's literature.

What's Inside *SATA*

SATA provides detailed information about authors and illustrators who span the full time range of children's literature, from early figures like John Newbery and L. Frank Baum to contemporary figures like Judy Blume and Richard Peck. Authors in the series represent primarily English-speaking countries, particularly the United States, Canada, and the United Kingdom. Also included, however, are authors from around the world whose works are available in English translation. The writings represented in *SATA* include those created intentionally for children and young adults as well as those written for a general audience and known to interest younger readers. These writings cover the entire spectrum of children's literature, including picture books, humor, folk and fairy tales, animal stories, mystery and adventure, science fiction and fantasy, historical fiction, poetry and nonsense verse, drama, biography, and nonfiction. Obituaries are also included in *SATA* and are intended not only as death notices but also as concise overviews of people's lives and work. Additionally, each edition features newly revised and updated entries for a selection of *SATA* listees who remain of interest to today's readers and who have been active enough to require extensive revisions of their earlier biographies.

Autobiography Feature

Beginning with Volume 103, many volumes of *SATA* feature one or more specially commissioned autobiographical essays. These unique essays, averaging about ten thousand words in length and illustrated with an abundance of personal photos, present an entertaining and informative first-person perspective on the lives and careers of prominent authors and illustrators profiled in *SATA*.

Two Convenient Indexes

In response to suggestions from librarians, *SATA* indexes no longer appear in every volume but are included in alternate (odd-numbered) volumes of the series, beginning with Volume 57.

SATA continues to include two indexes that cumulate with each alternate volume: the Illustrations Index, arranged by the name of the illustrator, gives the number of the volume and page where the illustrator's work appears in the current volume as well as all preceding volumes in the series; the Author Index gives the number of the volume in which a person's biographical sketch, autobiographical essay, or obituary appears in the current volume as well as all preceding volumes in the series.

These indexes also include references to authors and illustrators who appear in *Gale's Yesterday's Authors of Books for Children, Children's Literature Review,* and *Something about the Author Autobiography Series.*

Easy-to-Use Entry Format

Whether you're already familiar with the *SATA* series or just getting acquainted, you will want to be aware of the kind of information that an entry provides. In every *SATA* entry the editors attempt to give as complete a picture of the person's life and work as possible. A typical entry in *SATA* includes the following clearly labeled information sections:

PERSONAL: date and place of birth and death, parents' names and occupations, name of spouse, date of marriage, names of children, educational institutions attended, degrees received, religious and political affiliations, hobbies and other interests.

ADDRESSES: complete home, office, electronic mail, and agent addresses, whenever available.

CAREER: name of employer, position, and dates for each career post; art exhibitions; military service; memberships and offices held in professional and civic organizations.

MEMBER: professional, civic, and other association memberships and any official posts held.

AWARDS, HONORS: literary and professional awards received.

WRITINGS: title-by-title chronological bibliography of books written and/or illustrated, listed by genre when known; lists of other notable publications, such as plays, screenplays, and periodical contributions.

ADAPTATIONS: a list of films, television programs, plays, CD-ROMs, recordings, and other media presentations that have been adapted from the author's work.

WORK IN PROGRESS: description of projects in progress.

SIDELIGHTS: a biographical portrait of the author or illustrator's development, either directly from the biographee—and often written specifically for the *SATA* entry—or gathered from diaries, letters, interviews, or other published sources.

BIOGRAPHICAL AND CRITICAL SOURCES: cites sources quoted in "Sidelights" along with references for further reading.

EXTENSIVE ILLUSTRATIONS: photographs, movie stills, book illustrations, and other interesting visual materials supplement the text.

How a *SATA* Entry Is Compiled

SATA editors examine a wide variety of published sources to gather information for an entry. Biographical and bibliographic sources are consulted, as are book reviews, feature articles, published interviews, and material sometimes obtained from the biographee's family, publishers, agent, or other associates. Whenever possible, the author or illustrator is sent a copy of the entry to check for accuracy and completeness.

Entries that have not been verified by the biographees or their representatives are marked with an asterisk (*).

Contact the Editor

We encourage our readers to examine the entire *SATA* series. Please write and tell us if we can make *SATA* even more helpful to you. Give your comments and suggestions to the editor:

Editor
Something about the Author
Gale, Cengage Learning
27500 Drake Rd.
Farmington Hills MI 48331-3535

Toll-free: 800-877-GALE
Fax: 248-699-8070

Something about the Author Product Advisory Board

The editors of *Something about the Author* are dedicated to maintaining a high standard of excellence by publishing comprehensive, accurate, and highly readable entries on a wide array of writers for children and young adults. In addition to the quality of the content, the editors take pride in the graphic design of the series, which is intended to be orderly yet inviting, allowing readers to utilize the pages of *SATA* easily and with efficiency. Despite the longevity of the *SATA* print series, and the success of its format, we are mindful that the vitality of a literary reference product is dependent on its ability to serve its users over time. As literature, and attitudes about literature, constantly evolve, so do the reference needs of students, teachers, scholars, journalists, researchers, and book club members. To be certain that we continue to keep pace with the expectations of our customers, the editors of *SATA* listen carefully to their comments regarding the value, utility, and quality of the series. Librarians, who have firsthand knowledge of the needs of library users, are a valuable resource for us. The *Something about the Author* Product Advisory Board, made up of school, public, and academic librarians, is a forum to promote focused feedback about *SATA* on a regular basis. The nine-member advisory board includes the following individuals, whom the editors wish to thank for sharing their expertise:

Eva M. Davis
Director,
Canton Public Library,
Canton, Michigan

Joan B. Eisenberg
Lower School Librarian,
Milton Academy,
Milton, Massachusetts

Francisca Goldsmith
Teen Services Librarian,
Berkeley Public Library,
Berkeley, California

Susan Dove Lempke
Children's Services Supervisor,
Niles Public Library District,
Niles, Illinois

Robyn Lupa
Head of Children's Services,
Jefferson County Public Library,
Lakewood, Colorado

Victor L. Schill
Assistant Branch Librarian/Children's Librarian,
Harris County Public Library/Fairbanks Branch,
Houston, Texas

Caryn Sipos
Community Librarian,
Three Creeks Community Library,
Vancouver, Washington

Steven Weiner
Director,
Maynard Public Library,
Maynard, Massachusetts

something ABOUT the AUThOR

ALARCÓN, Francisco X. 1954-
  (Franciso Xavier Alarcón)

Personal

Born February 21, 1954, in Wilmington, CA; son of Jesus Pastor and Consuelo Vargas Alarcón. *Education:* Attended East Los Angeles College, 1973-74; California State University, Long Beach, B.A., 1977; Stanford University, M.A., 1979, A.B.D., 1990; attended Universidad Nacional Autónoma de México, 1982.

Addresses

Home—Davis, CA. *Office*—Department of Spanish and Portuguese, 604 Sproul Hall, University of California, Davis, One Shields Ave., Davis, CA 95616. *E-mail*—fjalarcon@ucdavis.edu.

Career

Writer and educator. Worked as a dishwasher and grape harvester, c. early 1970s; Milagro Books, Oakland, CA, program director, 1981-82; Computer Curriculum Corporation, Palo Alto, CA, translator, 1984; Golden Gate National Recreation Area, CA, park ranger, 1984; University of California, Santa Cruz, lecturer, 1985-92; Monterey Institute of International Studies, lecturer, 1988; University of California, Davis, lecturer and program director for Spanish for Native Speakers, beginning 1992. Mission Cultural Center, former board member, president, 1986-89; San Francisco Poetry Center,

Francisco X. Alarcón (Photograph by Francisco Dominguez. Reproduced by permission.)

1

former board member; Familia Center, board member, 1990-92, secretary, 1990; La Raza/Galéria Posada, board member, 1993-98, co-coordinator of El Taller Literario, 1993—; Children's Book Press, San Francisco, CA, board member, beginning 1998. Member, Arts Education and Outreach Committee of the Sacramento Metropolitan Arts Commission, 1993-94.

Member

National Poetry Association (former board member), El Centro Chicano de Escritores (former president), PEN West-New Mexico (former advisory board member), American Council on the Teaching of Foreign Languages (ACTFL)-New York (co-chair, Spanish for Native Speakers special interest group).

Awards, Honors

Fulbright fellowship, 1982-83; second prize, *Palabra nueva* contest, University of Texas at El Paso, 1983, for "Los repatriaciones de noviembre"; named Distinguished Alumnus of California State University, Long Beach, 1984; first prize, Chicano Literary Contest, University of California—Irvine, 1984; Prisma Award, CURAS, 1987; California Arts Council fellowship in poetry, 1989-90; Josephine Miles Literary Award, PEN Oakland, 1993; American Book Award, 1993; Pura Belpré Honor Award for Poetry, American Library Association (ALA), 1998, for *Laughing Tomatoes, and Other Spring Poems*, 2000, for *From the Bellybutton of the Moon, and Other Summer Poems*, 2002, for *Iguanas in the Snow, and Other Winter Poems;* Pellicer-Frost Poetry Prize second honor mention, Third Binational Border Poetry Contest, 1998; Fred Cody Lifetime Achievement Award, Bay Area Book Reviewers Association, 2002; Jane Addams Children's Book Award Honor designation, Jane Addams Peace Association, Children's Books of the Year selection, Bank Street College of Education, and Notable Children's Book designation, ALA, all c. 2005, all for *Poems to Dream Together;* finalist for state poet laureate of California.

Writings

POETRY; FOR CHILDREN

Snake Poems: An Aztec Invocation, Chronicle Books (San Francisco, CA), 1992.
Laughing Tomatoes, and Other Spring Poems/Jitomates risueños y otros poemas de primavera, illustrated by Maya Christina Gonzalez, Children's Book Press (San Francisco, CA), 1997.
From the Bellybutton of the Moon, and Other Summer Poems/Del ombligo de la luna y otros poemas de verano, illustrated by Maya Christina Gonzalez, Children's Book Press (San Francisco, CA), 1998.
Angels Ride Bikes, and Other Fall Poems/Los ángeles andan en bicicleta y otros poemas de otoño, illustrated by Maya Christina Gonzalez, Children's Book Press (San Francisco, CA), 1999.

Iguanas in the Snow, and Other Winter Poems/Iguanas en la nieve y otros poemas de invierno, illustrated by Maya Christina Gonzalez, Children's Book Press (San Francisco, CA), 2001.
Poems to Dream Together/Poemas para soñar juntos, illustrated by Paula Barragán, Lee & Low (New York, NY), 2005.
Animal Poems of the Iguazú/Animalario del Iguazú, illustrated by Maya Christina Gonzalez, Children's Book Press (San Francisco, CA), 2008.

Contributor to anthologies, including *I Feel a Little Jumpy around You: A Book of Her Poems and His Poems Collected in Pairs,* edited by Noami Shihab Nye and Paul B. Janezko, Simon & Schuster (New York, NY), 1997, and *Love to Mamá: A Tribute to Mothers,* edited by Pat Mora, Lee & Low (New York, NY), 2001.

POETRY FOR ADULTS

Tattoos, Nomad (Oakland, CA), 1985.
(With Rodrigo Reyes and Juan Pablo Gutiérrez) *Ya vas, carnal* (title means "Right on, Brother"), Humanizarte (San Francisco, CA), 1985.
(Coeditor) *Quarry West 26: Chicanas y chicanos en dialogo* (anthology), University of California, Santa Cruz (Santa Cruz, CA), 1989.
Quake Poems, We Press (Santa Cruz, CA), 1989.
Body in Flames/Cuerpo en llamas, translated by Francisco Aragón, Chronicle Books (San Francisco, CA), 1990.
Loma Prieta, photographs by Frank Balthis, We Press (Santa Cruz, CA), 1990.
De amor oscuro (title means "Of Dark Love"), translated by Adrienne Rich and Francisco Aragón, illustrated by Ray Rice, Moving Parts Press (Santa Cruz, CA), 1991.
Poemas Zurdos, Editorial Factor (Mexico City, Mexico), 1992.
No Golden Gate for Us, Pennywhistle Press (Tesuque, NM), 1993.
Sonnets to Madness and Other Misfortunes/Sonetos a la locura y otras penas, Creative Arts Book Company (Berkeley, CA), 2001.
From the Other Side of Night/Del otro lado de la noche: New and Selected Poems, translated by Francisco Aragón, University of Arizona Press (Tucson, AZ), 2002.

Poems anthologized in *Palabra Nueva: Cuentos Chicanos,* edited by Ricardo Aguilar, Armando Armengol, and Sergio Elizondo, Texas Western Press (El Paso, TX), 1984; *Lenguas Sueltas: Poemas,* Moving Parts Press (Santa Cruz, CA), 1994; *Lighthouse Point: An Anthology of Santa Cruz Writers,* edited by Patrice Vecchione and Steve Wiesinger, M. Press Soquel (Santa Cruz, CA), 1987; *Best New Chicano Literature 1989,* edited by Julian Palley, Bilingual Press (Tempe, AZ), 1989; *New Chicana/Chicano Writing 1,* edited by Charles M. Tatum, University of Arizona Press, 1992; *After Aztlan: Latino Poets of the Nineties,* edited by Ray González, David R. Godine (Boston, MA), 1992; *Catch a Sunflake,* Macmillan/McGraw-Hill, 1993;

Voices from the Fields: Children of Migrant Farmworkers Tell Their Stories, Little, Brown (Boston, MA), 1993; *Currents from the Dancing River: Contemporary Latino Fiction, Nonfiction, and Poetry,* edited by González, Harcourt Brace (New York, NY), 1994; *La poesía actual en español (decada 1983-1992),* Asociación Prometeo de Poesía (Madrid, Spain), 1994; *Del otro lado,* Fondo Nacional para la Cultura y las Artes; *Supplemento de Blanco Movil,* edited by Eduardo Mosches, [Mexico City, Mexico,] 1994; *An Introduction to Poetry,* edited by X.J. Kennedy and Dana Gioia, HarperCollins (New York, NY), 1994; *Saludos! Poemas de Nuevo Mexico/Poems of New Mexico,* Pennywhistle Press (Tesuque, NM), 1995; *Letters to America: Contemporary American Poetry on Race,* edited by Jim Daniels, Wayne State University Press (Detroit, MI), 1995; *Paper Dance: Fifty-five Latino Poets,* edited by Victor Hernández Cruz, Leroy V. Quintana, and Virgil Suárez, Persea Books, 1995; *Strange Attraction: The Best of Ten Years of ZYZZYVA,* edited by Howard Junker, University of Nevada Press, 1995; *The Name of Love: Classic Gay Love Poems,* edited by Michael Lassell, St. Martin's Press (New York, NY), 1995; *POESidA: A Bilingual Anthology of AIDS Poetry from the United States, Latin America, and Spain,* edited by Carlos A. Rodriguez, Ollantay Press, 1995; *La voz urgente: Antología de literatura chicana en español,* edited by Manuel M. Martín-Rodríguez, Editorial Fundamentos, 1995; *Poemcrazy,* edited by Susan G. Wooldridge, Clarkson Potter, 1996; *Goddess of the Americas/La diosa de las Américas: Writings on the Virgin of Guadalupe,* edited by Ana Castillo, Riverhead Books (New York, NY), 1996; and *Under the Pomegranate Tree: The Best New Latino Erotica,* edited by González, Washington Square Books, 1996.

Author's works have been translated into Gaelic and Swedish.

OTHER

(Author of introduction) Otto René Castillo, *Tomorrow Triumphant,* Night Horn (San Francisco, CA), 1984.

(With Fabián A. Samaniego and Nelson Rojas) *Mundo 21* (textbook), Houghton Mifflin (Boston, MA), 1995.

(Editor, with M. Cecilia Colombi) *La enseñanza del Español a Hispanohablantes: praxis y teoría* (college textbook), Houghton Mifflin (Boston, MA), 1996.

(Translator) Carmen L. Garza, *In My Family (En mi familia)* (picture book), Children's Book Press (San Francisco, CA), 1996.

(Translator) Lynn Moroney and Te Ata, *Viborita de Cascabel* (picture book), illustrated by Mira Reisberg, Children's Book Press (San Francisco, CA), 1996.

(With Fabián Samaniego and Ricardo Otherguy) *Tu mundo* (textbook), Houghton Mifflin (Boston, MA), 1997.

(With Fabián Samaniego and Nelson Rojas) *Nuestro Mundo* (textbook), Houghton Mifflin, 1997.

(Translator) Carmen L. Garza, *Magic Windows* (picture book), Children's Book Press (San Francisco, CA), 1999.

Contributor of essay to *Without Discovery: A Native Response to Columbus,* edited by Ray González, Broken Moon Press (Seattle, WA), 1992. Contributor to periodicals, including *Alcatraz, Américas Review, Andelas, Before Columbus Review, Berkeley Poetry Review, Bloomsbury Review, Compost 8, Confluencia, Five Fingers Review, Guadalupe Review, James White Review, La Opinión, Metamorfosis, Mocking Bird, Plural, Poetry Flash, Poetry Now, Puerto del Sol, Revista Mujeres, SIC: Vice & Verse, Wild Duck,* and *ZYZZYVA, the Last Word.*

Sidelights

As a writer, performer, professor, and activist raised in both Mexico and the United States, Francisco X. Alarcón shares his multicultural upbringing and rich Mexican heritage with younger audiences through verse collections that include *Snake Poems: An Aztec Invocation, From the Bellybutton of the Moon, and Other Summer Poems/Del ombligo de la luna y otros poemas de verano,* and *Poems to Dream Together/Poemas para soñar juntos.* "I write both in English and Spanish," the prolific Alarcón remarked in a *¡Colorín Colorado!* online interview. "My work as a poet reflects this life. Now, . . . this is interesting because it's not just me; I think this life reflects the lives of millions of Americans that . . . have this bilingual background." Noting that there are tens of millions of Latino Americans, Alarcón continued, "I think the majority of those Latinos at this moment are bilingual, they have this connection with the Spanish language, and I want to keep that, to me it's very important."

Born in Wilmington, California, in 1954, Alarcón was raised in both Mexico and the United States because his family moved frequently. Named after his grandfather, he was mesmerized by the elderly man's tales of old Mexico and the country's early-twentieth-century revolutionary movements. As a teen, Alarcón moved to California, arriving with only five dollars to his name, and worked a series of low-paying jobs that included a stint as a migrant laborer. In order to earn a U.S. high-school diploma, he began an educational journey that started in a Los Angeles adult-education program and culminated in three college degrees, including a Master of Arts degree from Stanford University.

Alarcón first began writing poetry during his college years. While at Stanford he worked for a bilingual newspaper in a job that helped him become involved with the surrounding community and awakened him to the political realities of being Hispanic in the United States. Much of Alarcón's early poetry, taut verses written in Spanish and geared for adults, is a reflection of his mixed heritage and his growing awareness of the social and political implications of the barrio. He lived in a San Francisco neighborhood that was a diverse blend of Latin and Central American peoples with strong ties to their homelands; solidarity with this Hispanic community played an integral role in shaping his voice as a

poet. He began reading his work in the numerous hospitable venues for poetry in the Bay Area, enjoying a reputation as a rising young voice on the literary scene.

After he received his graduate degree, Alarcón returned to Mexico as a Fulbright fellow and from there took a trip to Cuba; these experiences introduced him to such prominent Latin-American writers as Elíeas Nandino and helped shape the direction of Alarcón's poetry. His encounter with Nandino—an openly gay writer then in his eighties and finally achieving critical recognition—solidified Alarcón's commitment to maintain honesty about his own sexual orientation in his poetry.

The trip marked another turning point in Alarcón's career, helping to shape the young writer's literary voice and bringing wider recognition to his work. He now became involved with a theater group and appeared frequently in local media coverage of the literary scene in Mexico City. Following his return to California he won several awards for his work, which by then had expanded to include prose and essays, and joined the faculty of the University of California at Santa Cruz as a lecturer in Chicano literature.

While most of Alarcón's early works are for older readers, he turned to young adults in *Snake Poems*. For this work he drew upon a seventeenth-century manuscript written by a Spanish priest—also named Alarcón—who had traveled to what is now Mexico. The priest chronicled the powerful rituals and beliefs of the Aztecs in their original language in order to provide concrete evidence of their heathenism. The poet Alarcón uses this historic text to highlight the complexity and beauty of Mexico's indigenous people and their spirituality. Supplementing the translated manuscript of the priest, he inserts original lyrical and narrative pieces plus his impressions of contemporary Mexican-American culture. Calling *Snake Poems* "unusual" and "powerful" in *Booklist,* Pat Monaghan appreciated the way Alarcón "reveals and revels in his heritage."

Alarcón connects with an even younger audience—primary graders—with *Laughing Tomatoes, and Other Spring Poems/Jitomates risueños y otros poemas de primavera,* the first of four titles done in collaboration with illustrator Maya Christina Gonzalez. With its bilingual Spanish/English text, the book contains a collection of short poems, or "quick snapshots of moments in life," according to *School Library Journal* contributor Ann Welton. As the title indicates, Alarcón's energetic, colorful poems describe various signs of spring to readers as if they were seeing them for the first time. Janice M. Del Negro, writing in the *Bulletin of the Center for*

Alarcón's poetry collection Laughing Tomatoes, and Other Spring Poems *features artwork by Maya Christina Gonzalez.* (Illustration copyright © 1997 by Maya Christina Gonzalez. All rights reserved. Reproduced by permission of the publisher, Children's Book Press, San Francisco, CA., www.childrensbookpress.org.)

Alarcón focuses on the animals of Argentina's Iguazú National Park in* Animal Poems of the Iguazú, *a book illustrated by Gonzalez.

Children's Books, noted that each poem "seems to have something to shout about," while a *Kirkus Reviews* critic called *Laughing Tomatoes, and Other Spring Poems* an "accessible, open-hearted collection."

In *From the Bellybutton of the Moon, and Other Summer Poems,* a companion volume to *Laughing Tomatoes, and Other Spring Poems,* Alarcón shares a lyrical reminiscence of his childhood in Mexico. Annie Ayres, reviewing the bilingual collection in *Booklist,* praised its "sunny sensations, tangy tastes, and warm memories of a loving Latino family life." In *Angels Ride Bikes, and Other Fall Poems/Los ángeles andan en bicicleta y otros poemas de otoño,* Alarcón explores a variety of subjects, including family, school, and the city of Los Angeles. Ayres noted that here Gonzales's "colorful and expressive paintings provide a vibrantly visual response to the poetry." Winter in Northern California is the fo-

cus of the fourth seasonal collection, *Iguanas in the Snow, and Other Winter Poems/Iguanas en la nieve y otros poemas de invierno.* "The selections are short of line and long on meter, with a rhythmic roll that begs reading aloud," Welton remarked in her review of the collection for *School Library Journal.*

Another work for younger readers, *Poems to Dream Together,* finds Alarcón expressing his hopes for humankind, focusing on themes of peace, cooperation, and altruism. In an interview on the Lee & Low Books Web site, the poet stated that his overall message in the book is: "Let's all act out our dreams for a better world, a world where there's no word for war and all living creatures share the bounties of this earth." According to *Booklist* contributor Stella Clark, *Poems to Dream Together* "delivers a strong message with a very gentle touch," and Welton observed that the "poetic images

are at once accessible and inspiring." According to a critic in *Kirkus Reviews*, the illustrations by Paula Barragan provide a successful counterpoint to the text by "embody[ing] Alarcón's utopian longings."

In *Animal Poems of the Iguazú/Animalario del Iguazú*, Alarcón once again joins forces with Gonzalez in a collection that extols the virtues of Argentina's Iguazú National Park, renowned for its cascading waterfalls and diverse wildlife. He "writes with a kind of bubbly reverence, avoiding the sententiousness that characterizes much save-the-rain forest literature," a reviewer stated in *Publishers Weekly*. In *Kirkus Reviews* a contributor observed that the blend of "brilliant illustrations and eloquently crafted bilingual poems" in *Animal Poems of the Iguazú* celebrates the animal life and natural beauty of the rainforest."

Discussing his literary career and its relationship with his Hispanic heritage in the *Dictionary of Literary Biography*, Alarcón explained: "I'm sort of in the Latin tradition of the poet. There's no difference between the political and the personal, the social and the intimate. . . . It's very common in Latin America to have poets as the collective voice and the person who takes on a certain responsibility in the community."

Biographical and Critical Sources

BOOKS

Dictionary of Literary Biography, Volume 122: *Chicano Writers*, Gale (Detroit, MI), 1992.

PERIODICALS

Booklist, March 1, 1992, Pat Monaghan, review of *Snake Poems: An Aztec Invocation*, p. 1191; October 15, 1998, Annie Ayres, review of *From the Bellybutton of the Moon, and Other Summer Poems/Del ombligo de la luna y otros poemas de verano*, p. 423; December 1, 1999, Annie Ayres, review of *Angels Ride Bikes, and Other Fall Poems/Los ángeles andan en bicicleta y otros poemas de otoño*, p. 707; August, 2000, Isabel Schon, review of *Angels Ride Bikes, and Other Fall Poems*, p. 2154; July, 2005, Stella Clark, review of *Poems to Dream Together/Poemas para soñar juntos*, p. 1918.
Bulletin of the Center for Children's Books, June, 1997, Janice M. Del Negro, review of *Laughing Tomatoes, and Other Spring Poems*, p. 349.
Instructor, October, 2001, Alice Quiocho, review of *From the Bellybutton of the Moon, and Other Summer Poems*, p. 16.
Kirkus Reviews, March 15, 1997, review of *Laughing Tomatoes, and Other Spring Poems*, p. 458; May 1, 2005, review of *Poems to Dream Together*, p. 533; July 1, 2008, review of *Animal Poems of the Iguazú/Animalario del Iguazú*.

Publishers Weekly, September 24, 2001, review of *Sonnets to Madness, and Other Misfortunes/Sonetos a la locura y otras penas*, p. 91; February 25, 2002, review of *From the Other Side of the Night*, p. 57; June 23, 2008, review of *Animal Poems of the Iguazú*, p. 54.
School Library Journal, May, 1997, Ann Welton, review of *Laughing Tomatoes, and Other Spring Poems*, p. 118; August, 2001, Ann Welton, review of *Iguanas in the Snow, and Other Winter Poems*, p. 166; October, 2005, Ann Welton, review of *Poems to Dream Together*, p. 148.

ONLINE

¡Colorín Colorado! Web site, http://www.colorincolorado. org/ (March 1, 2010), interview with Alarcón.
Lee & Low Books Web site, http://www.leeandlow.com/ (March 1, 2010), "Booktalk with Francisco Alarcón."
University of California, Davis Web site, http://www.uc davis.edu/ (March 1, 2010), "Francisco X. Alarcón."*

*   *   *

ALARCÓN, Franciso Xavier
See ALARCÓN, Francisco X.

*   *   *

ANELLI, Melissa 1979-

Personal

Born December 27, 1979. *Education:* Georgetown University, degree (journalism), c. 2001. *Hobbies and other interests:* Attending the theatre.

Addresses

Home—Brooklyn, NY. *E-mail*—melissa@penbitten. com.

Career

MTV Networks, former editorial assistant; *Staten Island Advance*, former reporter; freelance writer.

Writings

Harry, a History: The True Story of a Boy Wizard, His Fans, and Life inside the Harry Potter Phenomenon, Pocket Books (New York, NY), 2008.

Sidelights

A journalist based in Brooklyn, New York, Melissa Anelli began covering the phenomenal popularity of the "Harry Potter" fantasy novels in 2001, contributing to

the burgeoning print and electronic media that has focused on the seven books written by British novelist J.K. Rowling. With a decade of author interviews, podcasts, news reports, and even Potter-related rock concerts under her belt, Anelli has become something of an expert in all things Potter, and her expertise continues to grow as Web mistress of The Leaky Cauldron (http://www.the-leaky-cauldron.org), a site credited by *USA Today* contributor Deirdre Donahue as "the second-largest English-language Potter fan website." Anelli's work for The Leaky Cauldron ultimately won the approval of Potter's creator, and when she compiled her collected knowledge into book form as *Harry, a History: The True Story of a Boy Wizard, His Fans, and Life inside the Harry Potter Phenomenon*, Rowling graciously agreed to contribute the book's foreword.

In *Harry, a History* Anelli explores the seven novels—*Harry Potter and the Philosopher's Stone, Harry Potter and the Chamber of Secrets,* and *Harry Potter and the Half-Blood Prince* among them—that have frequently been credited with sparking the late-twentieth-century fantasy-writing boom. In addition to recounting the history of Rowling's series and the varied response to it, Anelli threads her history with personal comments regarding her own love of the Potter subculture. Describing the book as "a revealing, delicious insider's view" of Rowling's most passionate online fans, a *Kirkus Reviews* writer added that *Harry, a History* "vividly captures the exhilaration of being part of [both] . . . a community and a movement," while *Booklist* contributor Michael Cart dubbed Anelli's work "painstakingly detailed." In prose featuring what a *Publishers Weekly* contributor characterized as an "infectious, at times frenetic, excitement," the book serves as "a love letter" to Potter fans, while also sharing "sweet scenes of meeting Rowling and the actors" in the films based on the "Potter" novels. Anelli's "excitement never falters," noted Audrey Snowden in a review of *Harry, a History* for *Library Journal,* "and Potter fans will find much to like here."

Biographical and Critical Sources

PERIODICALS

Booklist, November 15, 2008, Michael Cart, review of *Harry, a History: The True Story of a Boy Wizard, His Fans, and Life inside the Harry Potter Phenomenon,* p. 13.

Globe & Mail (Toronto, Ontario, Canada), February 7, 2009, review of *Harry, a History,* p. F12.

Kirkus Reviews, October 15, 2008, review of *Harry, a History.*

Library Journal, January 1, 2009, Audrey Snowden, review of *Harry, a History,* p. 89.

Publishers Weekly, October 6, 2008, review of *Harry, a History,* p. 49.

Toronto Star, December 28, 2008, Nathan Whitlock, *Living for the Boy Who Didn't Die,* p. ID4.

USA Today, November 11, 2009, Dierde Donahue, review of *Harry, a History,* p. D1.

ONLINE

Extreme Tech Web site, http://www.extremetech.com/ (July 18, 2007), "Harry Potter Spawns Parallel Internet World."

Leaky Cauldron Web site, http://www.the-leaky-cauldron.org/ (April 15, 2010), "Melissa Anelli."

Melissa Anelli Home Page, http://www.penbitten.com (March 15, 2010).

Simon & Schuster Web site, http://www.authors.simonandschuster.com/ (April 15, 2010), "Melissa Anelli."*

*   *   *

ATKINSON, Elizabeth

Personal

Born in MA; married; children. *Education:* Hobart & William Smith Colleges, B.A. (anthropology), 1983; Dartmouth College, M.A. (liberal studies), 1995.

Addresses

Home—Newbury, MA. *E-mail*—eeames@comcast.net.

Career

Educator, librarian, and author. Former teacher of English literature; former children's librarian; co-executive director of local arts foundation.

Awards, Honors

Best Children's Book designation, Bank Street College of Education, 2009, for *From Alice to Zen and Everyone in Between.*

Writings

MIDDLE-GRADE NOVELS

From Alice to Zen and Everyone in Between, Carolrhoda Books (Minneapolis, MN), 2008.

I, Emma Freke, Carolrhoda Books (Minneapolis, MN), 2010.

OTHER

Monster Vehicles, Capstone Press (Mankato, MN), 1991.

GLEE!: An Easy Guide to Gluten-free Independence, Clan Thompson, 2009.

Biographical and Critical Sources

PERIODICALS

Booklist, May 1, 2008, Francisca Goldsmith, review of *From Alice to Zen and Everyone in Between,* p. 87.

School Library Journal, September, 2008, Erin Schirota, review of *From Alice to Zen and Everyone in Between,* p. 172.

ONLINE

Elizabeth Atkinson Home Page, http://www.elizabethatkinson.com (March 15, 2010).*

B

BANG, Garrett
See BANG, Molly

* * *

BANG, Molly 1943-
(Garrett Bang, Molly Garrett Bang)

Personal
Born December 29, 1943, in Princeton, NJ; daughter of Frederik Barry (a research physician) and Betsy (an author, translator, and scientist) Bang; married Richard H. Campbell (an acoustics engineer), September 27, 1974; children: Monika. *Education:* Wellesley College, B.A. (French), 1965; University of Arizona, M.A. (Far Eastern languages and literatures), 1969; Harvard University, M.A. (Far Eastern languages and literatures), 1971.

Addresses
Home—89 Water St., Woods Hole, MA 02543. *E-mail*—mgbbooks@aol.com.

Career
Author, illustrator, and translator. Doshisha University, Kyoto, Japan, teacher of English, 1965-67; Asahi Shimbun, New York, NY, interpreter of Japanese, 1969; Baltimore *Sun* (newspaper), Baltimore, MD, reporter, 1970. Illustrator and consultant for UNICEF, Johns Hopkins Center for Medical Research and Training, and Harvard Institute for International Development.

Awards, Honors
Notable Book designation, American Library Association (ALA), 1977, for *Wiley and the Hairy Man* by Betsy Bang, and 1980, for *The Grey Lady and the Strawberry Snatcher;* Illustration Honor designation, *Boston Globe/Horn Book* Award, 1980, for *The Grey Lady and the Strawberry Snatcher,* 1984, for *Dawn,* and

Molly Bang (Reproduced by permission.)

1986, for *The Paper Crane;* Caldecott Honor Book designation, 1981, for *The Grey Lady and the Strawberry Snatcher,* 1983, for *Ten, Nine, Eight,* and 2000, for *When Sophie Gets Angry—Really, Really Angry . . . ;* Kate Greenaway Medal Honor designation, 1983, for *Ten, Nine, Eight;* Illustration Honor designation, *Boston Globe/Horn Book* Award, 1986, Hans Christian Andersen Award nomination, 1988, and illustration award, International Board on Books for Young People, all for *The Paper Crane;* Giverny Award for Best Science Picture Book for Children, 1998, for *Common Ground;* Charlotte Zolotow Award, 2000, for *When Sophie Gets Angry—Really, Really Angry . . . ; Boston Globe/Horn Book* Honor Award in picture-book category (with Monika Bang-Campbell), 2002, for *Little Rat Sets Sail;* New England Book Award, New England Booksellers

Association, 2004, and Notable Book designation, ALA, and Massachusetts Book Award, both 2005, both for *My Light;* (with Penny Chisholm) AAAS/Subaru SB & F Prize for Excellence in Children's Science Picture Book, 2010, for *Living Sunlight.*

Writings

FOR CHILDREN; SELF-ILLUSTRATED

(Compiler) *The Goblins Giggle, and Other Stories* (folktales), Scribner (New York, NY), 1973.

(Translator and compiler, under name Garrett Bang) *Men from the Village Deep in the Mountains, and Other Japanese Folk Tales,* Macmillan (New York, NY), 1973.

(Editor) Betsy Bang, adaptor, *Wiley and the Hairy Man,* Macmillan (New York, NY), 1976.

(Compiler) *The Buried Moon and Other Stories* (folktales), Scribner (New York, NY), 1977.

The Grey Lady and the Strawberry Snatcher, Four Winds Press (New York, NY), 1980.

(Adaptor) *Tye May and the Magic Brush* (Chinese folktale), Greenwillow (New York, NY), 1981.

Ten, Nine, Eight, Greenwillow (New York, NY), 1983.

(Adaptor) *Dawn* (Japanese folktale), Morrow (New York, NY), 1983.

(Adaptor) *The Paper Crane* (Chinese folktale), Greenwillow (New York, NY), 1985.

Delphine, Morrow (New York, NY), 1988.

Yellow Ball, Morrow (New York, NY), 1991.

One Fall Day, Greenwillow (New York, NY), 1994.

Chattanooga Sludge, Harcourt (San Diego, CA), 1996.

Goose, Blue Sky Press (New York, NY), 1996.

Common Ground: The Water, Earth, and Air We Share, Blue Sky Press (New York, NY), 1997.

When Sophie Gets Angry—Really, Really Angry . . . , Blue Sky Press (New York, NY), 1999.

Picture This: How Pictures Work, SeaStar Books (New York, NY), 2000.

Nobody Particular: One Woman's Fight to Save the Bays, Holt (New York, NY), 2000.

Tiger's Fall, Holt (New York, NY), 2001.

My Light, Blue Sky Press (New York, NY), 2004.

In My Heart, Little, Brown (New York, NY), 2005.

All of Me!: A Book of Thanks, Blue Sky Press (New York, NY), 2009.

(With Penny Chisholm) *Living Sunlight: How Plants Bring the Earth to Life,* Blue Sky Press (New York, NY), 2009.

Also author and illustrator of numerous health care manuals.

Several of Bang's works have been translated into Spanish.

ILLUSTRATOR

Betsy Bang, translator and adaptor, *The Old Woman and the Red Pumpkin: A Bengali Folk Tale,* Macmillan (New York, NY), 1975.

Betsy Bang, adaptor, *The Old Woman and the Rice Thief* (Bengali folktale), Greenwillow (New York, NY), 1978.

Betsy Bang, adaptor, *Tuntuni, the Tailor Bird* (Bengali folktale), Greenwillow (New York, NY), 1978.

Betsy Bang, translator and adaptor, *The Demons of Rajpur: Five Tales from Bengal,* Greenwillow (New York, NY), 1980.

Judith Benet Richardson, *David's Landing,* Woods Hole Historical Collection (Woods Hole, MA), 1984.

Sylvia Cassedy and Kunihiro Suetake, translators, *Red Dragonfly on My Shoulder: Haiku,* HarperCollins (New York, NY), 1992.

Amy L. Cohn, compiler, *From Sea to Shining Sea: A Treasury of American Folklore and Folk Songs,* Scholastic, Inc. (New York, NY), 1993.

Star Livingstone, *Harley,* SeaStar Books (New York, NY), 2001.

Monika Bang-Campbell, *Little Rat Sets Sail,* Harcourt (San Diego, CA), 2002.

Monika Bang-Campbell, *Little Rat Rides,* Harcourt (San Diego, CA), 2004.

Monika Bang-Campbell, *Little Rat Makes Music,* Harcourt (San Diego, CA), 2007.

Victoria Miles, *Old Mother Bear,* Chronicle Books (San Francisco, CA), 2007.

Robie H. Harris, *The Day Leo Said I Hate You!,* Little, Brown (New York, NY), 2008.

OTHER

Picture This: Perception and Composition (nonfiction for adults), Little, Brown (Boston, MA), 1991.

Adaptations

The Grey Lady and the Strawberry Snatcher, Ten, Nine, Eight, Dawn, and *The Paper Crane* were adapted for filmstrip by Random House; *When Sophie Gets Angry—Really, Really Angry. . .* was also adapted for filmstrip.

Sidelights

Molly Bang is a talented, prolific author and illustrator of many popular and award-winning books for children. Well traveled and worldly wise, Bang weaves her interest in foreign lands, people, and folklore into her many works. While she has published a number of unique adaptations of traditional legends from all over the world, she is perhaps most well known for creating original tales, steeped in mystery and branded with her unique sense of humor. Among her best-known books are *The Paper Crane,* which won the 1986 *Boston Globe/Horn Book* award for illustration, and 1999's *When Sophie Gets Angry—Really, Really Angry. . . .* In addition to creating artwork for her original stories, Bang had also illustrated tales by Robie H. Harris, Amy Cohn, and Judith Bennett Richardson, among other authors, and has also worked with her mother, writer Betsy Bang, and daughter, Monica Bang-Campbell.

Born in Princeton, New Jersey, in 1943, Bang gained a love for books early in her childhood. Her mother, Betsy Bang—who, like her daughter, is fluent in several lan-

Sophie is a volcano, ready to explode.

Bang captures the energy fueling a young child's temper in her self-illustrated picture book When Sophie Gets Angry—Really, Really Angry. . . . (Copyright © 1999 by Molly Bang. Reproduced by permission of Scholastic, Inc.)

guages—adapted and translated several folktales, five of which daughter Molly would eventually illustrate. Bang's parents also maintained an extensive library and presented each other with copies of nineteenth-century artist Arthur Rackham's handsomely illustrated books on special occasions, such as birthdays and anniversaries. Rackham's illustrations fascinated Bang and inspired her to think that illustration might someday be her profession.

For years Bang kept her dreams of illustrating books in the back of her mind while she pursued a variety of subjects and interests in high school and college. After graduating from Wellesley College with a degree in French, she went to Japan to teach English at Doshisha University in Kyoto for eighteen months. She returned to the United States to work on master's degrees in Far Eastern languages and literatures at the University of Arizona and Harvard University. Bang then returned to travel, going overseas once more to illustrate health manuals for rural health projects organized by UNICEF, the Johns Hopkins Center for Medical Research and Training, and the Harvard Institute for International Research in such cities as Calcutta, India; Dacca, Bangladesh; and the West-African republic of Mali.

While working overseas, Bang also began her career as an author and illustrator of books for children, gathering the tales she would illustrate in her first book. Published in 1973, *The Goblins Giggle, and Other Stories* was the first of many books that successfully incorpo-

rate Bang's fascination with international folklore and legends with her love of mystery and suspense. In a *School Library Journal* review of *The Goblins Giggle, and Other Stories,* Margaret A. Dorsey commented that the "five spooky folk tales" included "are smoothly told and greatly enhanced by full or double-page black-and-white illustrations," making the book "a charming collection in which humans triumph over supernatural adversaries after a few suitably chilling thrills." A critic for the *New York Times Book Review* also praised the book, concluding of *The Goblins Giggle, and Other Stories:* "Bang has a splendid feeling for general chill, and her choices are all scary but end comfortably so as not to keep anyone awake for long. Her illustrations are unique and intriguing."

As she did in her first book, Bang has continued to showcase her talent for interpreting folktales that are rich in mystery and suspense. In such popular and award-winning books as *Wiley and the Hairy Man, The Grey Lady and the Strawberry Snatcher, Dawn,* and *The Paper Crane* she either breathes new life into traditional fables or creates original stories through her skill as a gifted and sensitive writer and a versatile illustrator.

In *Wiley and the Hairy Man,* published in 1976, Bang retells an African-American folktale she discovered in B.A. Botkin's *Treasury of American Folklore,* basing her illustrations on thing she saw while traveling in the southern United States. Set in Alabama, *Wiley and the Hairy Man* tells of a young boy and his mother, who are terrorized by a scary swamp monster. After several frightful encounters, the pair resourcefully fend off the monster. "The tale has all the best elements of entertainment—humor, suspense, action, and ethnic color—with the stylistic simplicity befitting an easy reader," wrote Judith Goldberger in *Booklist.* Goldberger also noted that "flourishes are accomplished via illustrations in moss-grey, black, and white. . . . It is hard to imagine a reader unaffected by this book's punch."

Another of Bang's books to capture the attention of readers and critics alike is *The Grey Lady and the Strawberry Snatcher.* The first book by Bang to earn its author a Caldecott Honor Book designation, *The Grey Lady and the Strawberry Snatcher* recounts the tale of an old woman who is relentlessly pursued by a bizarre, strawberry-stealing creature. Patricia Jean Cianciolo remarked in *Picture Books for Children* that, despite the absence of text, Bang's story "is filled with surprises, lively humor, and suspense," while "its unusual colors and its characters are . . . strongly suggestive of a folktale from India. The skillfully executed, impressionistic illustrations, so full of meticulous, often startling details, offer an exciting visual treat to the readers of this wordless book." Denise M. Wilms commented in her review for *Booklist* that "Bang's art is a sum of disparate colors, patterns, and spreads of gray that unexpectedly blend. None of her figures is conventional: the tropical-type setting is peopled by warm brown faces

and hot colors," and "backgrounds point to a variety of ethnic motifs." According to Wilms, *The Grey Lady and the Strawberry Snatcher* is "a visual jigsaw that somehow balances and holds beyond the story line."

In both *Dawn* and *The Paper Crane* Bang casts classic Asian folktales in contemporary settings. Published in 1983, *Dawn* updates the traditional Japanese tale of "The Crane Wife," a yarn about a young man who rescues an injured bird, and sets the tale in nineteenth-century New England. After nursing a wild goose back to health, the man releases it and watches it transform into a beautiful young woman. The two ultimately marry and have a daughter, Dawn. After the man breaks a promise to his wife, she transforms back into a goose and flies away amid a passing flock of geese. The story continues as, years later, Dawn attempts to search for her mother. Reviewing *Dawn, Bulletin of the Center for Children's Books* contributor Zena Sutherland wrote that Bang "has made a touching and effective tale . . . and has illustrated it handsomely." Michael Dirda had particular praise for the illustrations in *Dawn,* writing in the *Washington Post Book World* that "Bang's. . . . watercolors alternate with pencil and charcoal drawings . . . and the whole book [is] pleasingly designed. . . . This is a haunting picture book, as affecting to adults as it is entrancing for children."

Based on a classic Chinese legend and featuring intricate cut-paper collage illustrations, *The Paper Crane* shows an act of kindness being rewarded by a magical gift. In Bang's retelling, a patronless restaurant loses business when it is bypassed by a new highway. When a poor stranger enters the restaurant, he is treated to a delicious meal by the owner and his son. In thanks, the stranger crafts a crane out of a paper napkin and presents it to the two with the instructions that the bird will come to life and dance for them when they clap their hands. When word spreads about the dancing crane, customers once again flock to the restaurant, saving the business from closing. "Here is that very rare treat, a contemporary folk tale that feels just right," concluded Patricia Dooley in her review of *The Paper Crane* for *School Library Journal.* Hanna B. Zeiger declared in a *Horn Book* that, "in a world in which we use the word 'gentle' to describe everything from laxatives to scouring powder, Molly Bang has restored dignity to the word with her truly gentle tale of *The Paper Crane,*" a story that "successfully blends Asian folklore themes with contemporary Western characterization."

With *One Fall Day,* Bang explores three-dimensional art, using collage to bring to life her story about the quiet events of a typical fall day. In the story, a group of toys—including a doll, a gray stuffed cat, an origami crane, and a yellow ball—join a child in a typical day.

Bang's concern for Earth's environment inspired her self-illustrated picture book **Common Ground.** (Illustration copyright © 1997 by Molly Bang. Reproduced by permission of Scholastic, Inc.)

After breakfast, they play and rake leaves outside until a surprise shower sends them running for cover. Inside again, they read books, draw pictures, and finally curl up cozily in bed. While noting the sophisticated illustrations—a *Publishers Weekly* contributor likened each one to "a stage set, complete with props"—a critic for *Kirkus Reviews* commented of *One Fall Day* that the "crisp images and primary colors that dominate the art are all perfect for very young children." Noting the "surreal" sense of "isolation and loneliness" in Bang's images, Elizabeth Bush added in her *Bulletin of the Center for Children's Books* review that "the varied angles and distances from which [Bang's] . . . compositions are photographed give the book character and interest."

When Sophie Gets Angry—Really, Really Angry. . . goes to the heart of a major challenge of growing up: learning to control one's temper. In Bang's vividly colored picture book, Sophie reacts poorly when it is her sister's turn to play with a favorite toy: a stuffed gorilla. After kicking, screaming, and crying, Sophie runs out of the house and into the woods where some quiet time spent in a tree listening to the sounds of nature calms her down. Praising the book for its focus, *New York Times Book Review* contributor Jeanne B. Pinder added that *When Sophie Gets Angry—Really, Really Angry* . . . "is perfect for sparking conversations about feelings: what causes anger . . . and how different people cope with it." In *Riverbank Review,* Susan Marie Swanson commented positively on Bang's text, noting that its simple rhythms and alliterations make it "rich in gentle sound-effects."

Bang's concerns regarding the preservation of Earth's environment are addressed in the picture books *Common Ground: The Water, Earth, and Air We Share* and *Chattanooga Sludge.* In *Common Ground* she uses clear, brilliant colors to "sound . . . a sober warning about increasing demands on earth's dwindling resources," according to a reviewer in *Publishers Weekly.* Framing her lesson within the day-to-day activities of a simple farming village, Bang shows how increased grazing of livestock, overpopulation, and poor land use can cause problems within the village, within society, and, ultimately, upon the earth as a whole if not addressed. With its introduction to basic ecology, *Common Ground* contains "a timely, provocative message, housed in a small, weighty book," maintained a *Kirkus Reviews* commentator.

Written for slightly older readers, the true story in *Chattanooga Sludge* relates the efforts of scientist John Todd to clean up one of the most polluted waterways in the United States. Using an experimental program involving "Living Machines"—greenhouse-grown plants and pollution-eating bacteria—Todd attempted to remove industrial toxins from the water, with only partial success. His results "provide . . . readers with a sobering view of the pollution problem and the encouraging but limited ability of science to combat it," according to

The efforts of a woman to save an endangered portion of U.S. coastline is the focus of Bang's large-format picture book **Nobody Particular.** (Copyright © 2001 by Molly Bang. Reprinted by arrangement with Henry Holt & Company, LLC.)

Bush in her *Bulletin of the Center for Children's Books* review. A discussion of microbiology as it pertains to Todd's experiments is also included, amid brightly colored collages and cartoon frogs that provide background information on each page. "Bringing this subject to life and making it comprehensible to a lay audience of any age is an impressive feat," concluded *School Library Journal* contributor Melissa Hudak. In *Chattanooga Sludge* "Bang pulls it off nicely," the critics asserted.

Environmental themes also figure in *Nobody Particular: One Woman's Fight to Save the Bays,* the story of Diane Wilson, who fought both a giant corporation and the Environmental Protection Agency to save the bays along the Texas coast. The bay area was popular with commercial shrimp fishermen, and when Wilson discovered that these fishing grounds were dangerously polluted, she mounted a campaign to save them. Bang's book tells two parallel stories: the frame of each page depicts the natural history of the Texas bays region, while the center areas follow Wilson's efforts to battle the region's pollution. A *Horn Book* critic called *Nobody Particular* a "complex and visually stunning picture book." Leonard P. Rivard, writing in *Science Activities,* deemed the book "a wonderful testament to democratic action by a concerned individual," while Michael Cart described it in *Booklist* as "a riveting, emotional story of how single individuals can make a difference in a world of bewildering complexity."

In *My Light* Bang explores the many ways sunlight is transformed into energy. In one sequence, the book explains how the sun's rays are responsible for the water cycle that creates rain, then river water, and then the moving waters that are captured at dams and made to turn generators to create electricity. Other topics include how sunlight creates plant life through photosynthesis, thus creating coal and oil once those plants die and decay, and how it creates the winds that power windmills. The book showcases Bang's "carefully honed prose and wholly original visual imagination," asserted a critic for *Publishers Weekly,* and Jennifer Mattson wrote in *Booklist* that *My Light* is "a lovely and illuminating book that presents sound science while expressing the wonder of flipping a switch and flooding a room with light."

A sequel to *My Light, Living Sunlight: How Plants Bring the Earth to Life* finds Bang working with ecology professor Penny Chisholm to introduce the concept of photosynthesis to younger readers. Narrated in a rhyming text by the sun itself, *Living Sunlight* shows how daylight is transformed into the energy that fuels growth in both plants and animals. "Beautiful illustration light up the pages" of the picture-book collaboration, asserted Carolyn Janssen in *School Library Journal,* and *Booklist* contributor Carolyn Phelan dubbed *Living Sunlight* "an outstanding book to read and absorb" due to its "simple yet precise" text and "vibrant images."

A terrible accident is the focus of Bang's book *Tiger's Fall.* Eleven-year-old Lupe accepts a dare from her

Bang pairs her colorful art with a gentle, child-centered text in **All of Me!: A Book of Thanks.** (Copyright © 2009 by Molly Bang. Reproduced by permission of Scholastic, Inc.)

cousin to climb the old, supposedly haunted fig tree. On the way down, she loses her balance and falls to the ground. Now paralyzed from the waist down, Lupe is operated on, but the surgery leaves her battling a life-threatening infection and her parents drowning in debt. Unable to help her at home, her parents take an angry and depressed Lupe to PROJIMO, the Project of Rehabilitation Organized by Disabled Youth of Western Mexico, which is a center run by and for the disabled. Here Lupe learns to tend and heal the wounds of others and discovers she can still be useful, especially when she heals enough to be in her wheelchair.

Bang was inspired to write *Tiger's Fall* after visiting the real PROJIMO center. Claire Martin, writing in the *Denver Post,* found that "Bang sketches a vivid, honest picture of how stupendously a life (many lives, really, including her family and friends) can change with one misstep." Hazel Rochman, writing in *Booklist,* believed that "the disabled and those who love them will appreciate the truth of Lupe's anger and depression and her struggle to find her own kindness and courage."

In *All of Me!: A Book of Thanks* Bang once again demonstrates her understanding of the emotions of small children. In the story, a child expresses appreciation for his body, feelings, and place in the world through both a simple, rhythmic text and naïf-style collage illustrations crafted of kraft paper, crayon, and paint. Bang concludes her story by describing how she created her illustrations and encouraging children to create a Thank-you story of their own. Praising the upbeat narrator, and the cat that follows him through his day of appreciation, Julie Roach added in *School Library Journal* that "homey details abound" in Bang's celebratory story, and a *Kirkus Reviews* writer dubbed the book "joyous" and "an earnest" depiction of "all toddlers' most fascinating subject (themselves)." Noting that the picture book "feels like a game for parent and child," a *Publishers Weekly* critic added that *All of Me!* treats readers to "a joyful, grateful prayer."

Bang teams with her daughter, Monika Bang-Campbell, on a series of beginning readers that include *Little Rat Sets Sail, Little Rat Rides,* and *Little Rat Makes Music. Little Rat Sets Sail* follows Little Rat as she learns how to sail a boat, even though she is scared of the water. Then she attends sailing lessons and her class, taught by Buzzy Bear, includes a raccoon who is even more scared of the water than is Little Rat. Together, the two students help each other learn the basics of sailing, and they both grow to enjoy the sport. A critic for *Kirkus Reviews* noted that "Little Rat is a brave little sailor with her own shy appeal and Bang's charming illustrations are impossible to resist," while *School Library Journal* critic Lynda S. Poling found Bang's illustrations to be "charming and sweet." In a review of *Little Rat Sets Sail* for *Horn Book,* Martha V. Parravano concluded that "Bang brings her extraordinary picture book-making skills to a fine text by her daughter."

The adventures of Little Rat continue in *Little Rat Rides,* as the young rodent decides to learn to ride a horse, only to realize that sitting atop a strong, large animal can be rather frightening. Fortunately, her teacher encourages Little Rat to overcome her fears, even after she falls off the back of Pee Wee the pony. The challenge of learning to play the violin is attempted by the determined Little Rat in *Little Rat Makes Music,* and this time the youngster triumphs over frustration, squeaky strings, and discouragement. Noting that Bang-Campbell "skillfully captures a young child's perspective" in her text for *Little Rat Rides,* Joy Fleishhacker added in her *School Library Journal* review that Bang's water color, gouache, and pencil illustrations capture "humor" and "a lot of genuine affection." Her pictures of Little Rat also "emphasize and add to the charm and vibrancy" of her daughter's text in *Little Rat Makes Music,* noted a *Kirkus Reviews* writer, the critic recommending the book for children "in transition from beginning readers to chapter books."

In addition to her many picture books, Bang has also written the adult work *Picture This: Perception and Composition,* which, according to an essayist in the *St. James Guide to Children's Writers* "provides an insightful key to Bang's work in picture books." In *Picture This* she takes artists through the steps of creating an illustration by making them aware of the elements of shape, color, and size, and by showing how different combinations of these elements create differing emotional responses from viewers.

While she is gratified that so many young readers have been delighted and sometimes even inspired by her books, Bang has also expressed concern that many children have minimal access to the enormous variety of books published yearly for young readers. "Ways need to be found to get books to children beyond the privileged class," Bang declared to Robert D. Hale in *Horn Book.* She cited the budget restrictions of both public and school libraries as one of the reasons lower-income children often find reading a difficult skill to master. "Too many children don't know how to use a book, because they aren't given the chance to learn," Bang added. "If they only have flimsy paperbacks, they never experience the feel of a real book. Because they are less available to people who are poor, books become less relevant. In the midst of all this self-congratulation we have to think about that."

Biographical and Critical Sources

BOOKS

Children's Books and Their Creators, Houghton (Boston, MA), 1995, pp. 45-46.
Children's Literature Review, Volume 8, Gale (Detroit, MI), 1985, pp. 17-24.

Picture Books for Children, American Library Association, 1981, p. 151.

St. James Guide to Children's Writers, 5th edition, St. James Press (Detroit, MI), 1999.

PERIODICALS

Booklist, July 15, 1976, Judith Goldberger, review of *Wiley and the Hairy Man,* p. 1601; July 15, 1980, Denise M. Wilms, review of *The Grey Lady and the Strawberry Snatcher,* pp. 1673-1674; October 1, 1997, Susan Dove Lempke, review of *Common Ground: The Water, Earth, and Air We Share,* p. 330; February 1, 1999, Stephanie Zvirin, review of *When Sophie Gets Angry—Really, Really Angry . . . ,* p. 978; February 1, 2001, Michael Cart, review of *Nobody Particular: One Woman's Fight to Save the Bays,* p. 1050; November 1, 2001, Hazel Rochman, review of *Tiger's Fall,* p. 474; April 1, 2002, Kathy Broderick, review of *Little Rat Sets Sail,* p. 1326; February 1, 2004, Jennifer Mattson, review of *My Light,* p. 974; April 15, 2007, Hazel Rochman, review of *Old Mother Bear,* p. 49; September 1, 2008, Daniel Kraus, review of *The Day Leo Said I Hate You!,* p. 102; December 1, 2008, Carolyn Phelan, review of *Living Sunlight: How Plants Bring the Earth to Life,* p. 67.

Bulletin of the Center for Children's Books, January, 1984, Zena Sutherland, review of *Dawn,* pp. 82-83; October, 1994, Elizabeth Bush, review of *One Fall Day,* p. 37; April, 1996, Elizabeth Bush, review of *Chattanooga Sludge,* pp. 256-257.

Denver Post, February 17, 2002, Claire Martin, review of *Tiger's Fall,* p. EE2.

Horn Book, January, 1986, Hanna B. Zeiger, review of *The Paper Crane,* p. 45; November-December, 1989, Robert D. Hale, "Musings," pp. 806-807; November-December, 1997, Ellen Fader, review of *Common Ground,* p. 692; January, 2001, review of *Nobody Particular,* p. 106; July, 2001, review of *Harley,* p. 456; July-August, 2002, Martha V. Parravano, review of *Little Rat Sets Sail,* p. 452; May-June, 2004, Jennifer M. Brabander, review of *Little Rat Rides,* p. 325, Ruth Ketchum, review of *My Light,* p. 341; March-April, 2006, Martha V. Parravano, review of *In My Heart,* p. 169; November-December, 2007, Lolly Robinson, review of *Little Rat Makes Music,* p. 673; May-June, 2009, Betty Carter, review of *Living Sunlight,* p. 320.

Kirkus Reviews, August 15, 1994, review of *One Fall Day,* p. 1120; August 15, 1997, review of *Common Ground,* pp. 1302-1303; September 15, 2001, review of *Tiger's Fall,* p. 1352; February 1, 2002, review of *Little Rat Sets Sail,* p. 176; March 1, 2004, review of *My Light,* p. 218; July 1, 2007, review of *Little Rat Makes Music;* August 15, 2009, review of *All of Me!: A Book of Thanks.*

National Fisherman, May, 2002, Linc Bedrosian, *Nobody Particular,* p. 9.

New York Times, June 27, 2004, Eric Nagourney, review of *My Light,* p. 15.

New York Times Book Review, January 13, 1974, review of *The Goblins Giggle, and Other Stories,* p. 8; May 16, 1999, Jeanne B. Pinder, "It's a Mad, Mad, Mad, Mad Girl," p. 27; April 12, 2009, review of *Living Sunlight,* p. L15.

Publishers Weekly, August 8, 1994, review of *One Fall Day,* p. 428; September 22, 1997, review of *Common Ground,* p. 81; January 18, 1999, review of *When Sophie Gets Angry—Really, Really Angry . . . ,* p. 337; December 11, 2000, review of *Nobody Particular,* p. 86; February 26, 2001, review of *Harley,* p. 87; August 25, 2003, review of *Little Rat Sets Sail,* p. 67; February 23, 2004, review of *My Light,* p. 75; December 5, 2005, review of *In My Heart,* p. 53; July 7, 2008, review of *The Day Leo Said I Hate You!,* p. 58; September 14, 2009, review of *All of Me!,* p. 46.

Riverbank Review, spring, 1999, Susan Marie Swanson, review of *When Sophie Gets Angry—Really, Really Angry . . . ,* pp. 33-34.

School Arts, December, 2000, Kent Anderson, review of *Picture This: How Pictures Work,* p. 56.

School Library Journal, January, 1974, Margaret A. Dorsey, review of *The Goblins Giggle, and Other Stories,* p. 45; December, 1985, Patricia Dooley, review of *The Paper Crane,* p. 66; August, 1996, Melissa Hudak, review of *Chattanooga Sludge,* p. 148; July, 2000, Ginny Harrell, review of *Wiley and the Hairy Man,* p. 55; January, 2001, Kathy Piehl, review of *Nobody Particular,* p. 138; June, 2001, Kathleen Kelly MacMillan, review of *Harley,* p. 125; December, 2001, Caroline Ward, review of *Tiger's Fall,* p. 132; June, 2002, Lynda S. Poling, review of *Little Rat Sets Sail,* p. 80; February, 2003, Lee Bock, reviews of *Goose* and *When Sophie Gets Angry—Really, Really Angry . . . ,* p. 95; October, 2003, Jennifer Ralston, review of *When Sophie Gets Angry—Really, Really Angry . . . ,* p. 97; April, 2004, Wendy Lukehart, review of *Picture This,* p. 63, and Dona Ratterre, review of *My Light,* p. 128; May, 2004, Joy Fleishhacker, review of *Little Rat Rides,* p. 101; June, 2007, June Wolfe, review of *Old Mother Bear,* p. 116; August, 2008, Wendy Lukehart, review of *The Day Leo Said I Hate You!,* p. 92; February, 2009, Carolyn Janssen, review of *Living Sunlight,* p. 89; October, 2009, Julie Roach, review of *All of Me!,* p. 86.

Science Activities, spring, 2003, Leonard P. Rivard, review of *Nobody Particular,* p. 446.

Washington Post Book World, October 9, 1983, Michael Dirda, review of *Dawn,* pp. 10-11.

Whole Earth, winter, 2002, review of *Little Rat Sets Sail,* p. 105.

ONLINE

Molly Bang Home Page, http://www.mollybang.com (April 15, 2010).*

* * *

BANG, Molly Garrett
See BANG, Molly

BAYROCK, Fiona

Personal

Born in Canada; married; children. *Education:* University of British Columbia, B.A. (commerce); studied science at the college level. *Hobbies and other interests:* Acting in community theatre, reading, spending time with family.

Addresses

Home—Chilliwack, British Columbia, Canada. *E-mail*—fiona@fionabayrock.com.

Career

Author. Presenter at schools and conferences.

Member

Canadian Society of Children's Authors, Illustrators, and Performers, Society of Children's Book Writers and Illustrators, Children's Writers and Illustrators of British Columbia (secretary), Vancouver Children's Literature Roundtable, Yellowknife Children's Literature Roundtable.

Awards, Honors

National Science Teachers Association Recommended Title designation, 2006, for *Sound*.

Writings

Hop! Spring! Leap!: Animals That Jump, Scholastic Canada (Markham, Ontario, Canada), 2005.
What Am I?, illustrated by Réjean Roy, Scholastic Canada (Markham, Ontario, Canada), 2005.
How Do Polar Bears Stay Warm?, Scholastic Canada (Markham, Ontario, Canada), 2005.
The Ocean Explorer's Handbook, Scholastic, Inc. (New York, NY), 2005.
Sound: A Question-and-Answer Book, Capstone Press (Mankato, MN), 2006.
States of Matter: A Question-and-Answer Book, Capstone Press (Mankato, MN), 2006.
Icebergs!, Scholastic Canada (Markham, Ontario, Canada), 2007.
Extreme Animals!, Scholastic Canada (Markham, Ontario, Canada), 2007.
Bubble Homes and Fish Farts, illustrated by Carolyn Conahan, Charlesbridge (Watertown, MA), 2009.

Author, under a pseudonym, of six books in the "Physical Sciences Q&A" series. Contributor to periodicals, including *Yes, Know, Wild, Odyssey,* and *Highlights for Children.* Contributor to print and electronic educational resources.

Sidelights

Although Fiona Bayrock began her writing career by producing elementary-grade nonfiction books dealing with subjects selected by her publishing-house editor,

Bubble Homes and Fish Farts was different. This picture book, with its giggle-inducing title, was inspired by the spittle bugs that made their homes in Bayrock's garden. Her own curiosity about other bubbles that might have a purpose in the natural world led her through several months of research and writing, as well as interviews with several scientists. Along the way, Bayrock learned about sixteen different animals, insects, or fish that utilize bubbles in various ways. She also learned that some fish really do make a funny noise that scientists term a Fast Repetitive Tick, or FaRT.

In reviewing *Bubble Homes and Fish Farts* for *School Library Journal,* Frances E. Millhouser described Bayrock's text as "enjoyable and engaging," the critic adding that the "corny" captions accompanying artist Carolyn Conahan's pastel-toned water-color illustrations "infuse the information with fun." According to *Booklist* critic Carolyn Phelan, the author's "intriguing" text draws readers into a factual work that is "attractive" and "illustrated with finesse." "Bayrock's love of 'way cool science' bubbles over in this surprisingly substantial book," concluded a *Kirkus Reviews* writer in reviewing *Bubble Homes and Fish Farts.*

"I like to add sensory details, and find ways to help kids connect emotionally with the material," Bayrock told interviewer Jennifer Feinberg in discussing her work as a science writer for British Columbia's *Chilli-*

Fiona Bayrock's quirky nature book Bubble Homes and Fish Farts *features artwork by Carolyn Conahan.* (Illustration copyright © 2009 by Carolyn Conahan. Used with permission by Charlesbridge Publishing, Inc. All rights reserved.)

wack Progress newspaper. "That makes it more fun, because science really is fun." "My goal is to inspire kids to ask questions about their world, to have them make connections and create their own 'Eureka!' moments by 'checking stuff out,'" she added on her home page. "My writing is peppered with hands-on activities and simulations to make complicated concepts kid-friendly and easily understood."

Biographical and Critical Sources

PERIODICALS

Booklist, June 1, 2009, Carolyn Phelan, review of *Bubble Homes and Fish Farts,* p. 53.

Bulletin of the Center for Children's Books, March, 2009, Elizabeth Bush, review of *Bubble Homes and Fish Farts,* p. 277.

Chilliwack Progress (Chilliwack, British Columbia, Canada), March 26, 2009, Jennifer Feinberg, review of *Bubble Homes and Fish Farts,* p. 27.

Kirkus Reviews, November, 2009, review of *Bubble Homes and Fish Farts.*

School Library Journal, March, 2009, Frances E. Millhouser, review of *Bubble Homes and Fish Farts,* p. 131.

ONLINE

Fiona Bayrock Home Page, http://www.fionabayrock.com (March 15, 2010).*

*   *   *

BELL, Krista 1950-

Personal

Born January 27, 1950, in Sydney, New South Wales, Australia; daughter of John Spencer (an engineer) and Lurline Joyce Blakeney; married Douglas Bell (a transport planner), July 16, 1983; children: Ben, Damien, Henry. *Education:* Attended St. Vincent's College (Potts Point, Sydney, New South Wales, Australia), Catholic Ladies College (Melbourne, Victoria, Australia), and Monash University. *Hobbies and other interests:* Watercolor painting, recycled book and clothing shops, books, music, gardening, Asian food, tennis, animals and birds.

Addresses

Home—Kooyong, Victoria, Australia. *E-mail*—krista@ kristabell.com.

Career

Writer. Australian Broadcasting Commission (ABC) Radio, book reviewer, 1984-96; freelance book reviewer for newspapers and literary magazines, 1985-2000; full-

Krista Bell (Reproduced by permission.)

time writer, beginning 2000. Radio for the Print Handicapped, Melbourne, Victoria, Australia, writer, producer, and presenter of *The Children's Hour,* 1990-95; presents workshops and talks at libraries and schools; coordinator of Virtuoso Literary Weekends, 1997-99.

Member

Australian Society of Authors, Children's Book Council of Australia, Dromkeen Society, Actor's Equity.

Awards, Honors

Young Australians Best Book Awards (YABBA) shortlist, 1992, for *Jezza*; Australia Publishers Education Excellence Awards shortlist, and Children's Book Council of Australia Notable Book designation, both 1997, both for *Where Do You Get Your Ideas?*; Australian Family Therapist's Award for Children's Literature, 2004, for *Who Dares?*; New South Wales Premier's History Award shortlist, and (with David Miller) Young People's History Prize, both 2008, both for *Lofty's Mission.*

Writings

FICTION FOR CHILDREN

Jezza, illustrated by Kym Lardner, Macmillan (South Melbourne, Victoria, Australia), 1991.

That's Our Henry, illustrated by Mike Johnson, Era Publications (Flinders Park, South Australia, Australia), 1996.

Pidge, illustrated by Ann James, Allen & Unwin (St. Leonards, New South Wales, Australia), 1997.

The Kindest Family (picture book), Nelson, 2001.

Rory's Big Chance (picture book), Nelson, 2001.

Sniffy the Sniffer Dog, illustrated by Craig Smith, Lothian Books (Port Melbourne, Victoria, Australia), 2003.

That's the Trick, illustrated by Sarah Dunk, Lothian Books (Port Melbourne, Victoria, Australia), 2006.

Flying Feet (chapter book), illustrated by Beth Norling, Puffin (Camberwell, Victoria, Australia), 2006.

If the Shoe Fits (chapter book), illustrated by Craig Smith, Lothian Books (Port Melbourne, Victoria, Australia), 2006, Charlesbridge (Watertown, MA), 2008.

Lofty's Mission, illustrated by David Miller, Lothian (Port Melbourne, Victoria, Australia), 2007.

Peeking Ducks, illustrated by Sally Rippin, Windy Hollow Books (Kew East, Victoria, Australia), 2010.

Author's work has been translated into Korean.

"TOP SHOTS" CHAPTER-BOOK SERIES

The Slammers, illustrated by Kevin Burgemeestre, Allen & Unwin (St. Leonards, New South Wales, Australia), 1995.

Star Rookie, illustrated by Kevin Burgemeestre, Allen & Unwin (St. Leonards, New South Wales, Australia), 1995.

Camp Phantom, illustrated by Kevin Burgemeestre, Allen & Unwin (St. Leonards, New South Wales, Australia), 1996.

Nothing but Net, illustrated by Kevin Burgemeestre, Allen & Unwin (St. Leonards, New South Wales, Australia), 1996.

"TAKEAWAYS" YOUNG-ADULT NOVEL SERIES

Read My Mind!, Lothian Books (Port Melbourne, Victoria, Australia), 2000.

Get a Life!, Lothian Books (Port Melbourne, Victoria, Australia), 2001.

No Regrets, Lothian Books (Port Melbourne, Victoria, Australia), 2002.

Who Cares?, Lothian Books (Port Melbourne, Victoria, Australia), 2003.

No Strings, Lothian Books (Port Melbourne, Victoria, Australia), 2004.

Who Dares?, Lothian Books (Port Melbourne, Victoria, Australia), 2005.

No Tears, Lothian Books (Port Melbourne, Victoria, Australia), 2007.

OTHER

Where Do You Get Your Ideas?: Interviews with Australian Authors of Children's Books, Reed Library, Cardigan Street (Port Melbourne, Victoria, Australia), 1996.

(With Anna Healey) *Why Not Me?: My Journey with MS,* Pan Macmillan (Sydney, New South Wales, Australia), 2002.

Contributor of stories to anthologies, including *Saddle Up Again: More Australian Horse Stories,* compiled by Mary Small, Blue Gum Press, 1995; and *Thrillogy: Cliff Hangers,* Longman, 2001. Contributor of book reviews to periodicals, including *Classroom Magazine, Author, Magpies, Literature Base, Australian Book Review, Herald Sun* (Melbourne, Victoria, Australia), *Pets and Vets Australia,* and *Writing Australia.*

Sidelights

The writings of Australian author Krista Bell range from the award-winning picture book *Lofty's Mission* to the humorous chapter book *If the Shoe Fits* and her "Takeaways" young-adult novels. In *That's the Trick!* Bell also plays with language while presenting an illustrated introduction to homonyms: words that sound the same even though they are spelled differently and mean different things. "Bell has a love of words which is obvious in this little offering," concluded *Aussie Reviews Online* contributor Sally Murphy in discussing *That's the Trick!*

If the Shoe Fits, *Bell's chapter book about an enthusiastic young dancer, features artwork by Craig Smith.* (Illustration copyright © 2008 by Craig Smith. All rights reserved. Reproduced by permission of the illustrator.)

Set in Bell's native Melbourne during World War II, *Lofty's Mission* focuses on Harley McNamara's concern after his six-week-old trained racing pigeon, Lofty, is requisitioned by the Australian Army and trained to be a messenger pigeon. Readers follow the young bird as it leaves its young owner and goes to Queensland for training before being shipped to New Guinea, where Australian forces are fighting. While Lofty bravely carries an important message through a barrage of enemy gunfire, Harley suffers from infantile paralysis but has no will to recover because of his sadness over the loss of his bird. Praised by Margaret Hamilton as a "heart-warming story" in her review for the *Australian Bookseller and Publisher, Lofty's Mission* is enhanced by "stunningly detailed paper sculptures" by David Miller that add "an almost tactile . . . realism" to the story. An *Adelaide Advertiser* critic predicted that Bell's story will appeal to "junior primary students and any reader who enjoys Australian history."

Geared for reluctant elementary-grade readers, Bell's "Top Shots" books play off the growing popularity of basketball among young Australians. In this series of four novels, she centers on a team of youngsters called the Slammers. In *The Slammers* members of the team go from fans of the sport to experienced players, all with the help of a former professional basketball player. "When the Slammers finally face their opponents, the tension builds sharply, players have to leave the court, and the chance of victory seems certain to slip from their fingers," remarked Russ Merrin in a review of the book for *Magpies*. In *Top Shots,* the second novel in the series, the Slammers must raise money for new uniforms and shoes but the injury of the team's best player puts its ability to win against the Mighty Mixtures in doubt. "It is action and fun all the way," Merrin stated. The use of basketball as the sport at the center of the series give the books a built-in audience, Merrin noted in her review of *Top Shots,* and Bell's "story-telling captures the modern idiom well, and cleverly manages to describe tips, hints, strategies and rules of the game."

Bell's chapter books *If the Shoe Fits* and *Flying Feet* also combine high energy and humor. In the first book, Cassie dreams of becoming a dancer but finds that shyness will keep her off the stage unless she can conquer it, while in *Flying Feet* Henry discovers that tap dancing is the perfect way to channel his toe-tapping energy. In *Kirkus Reviews* a critic dubbed *If the Shoe Fits* "a winner for the reader ready for a step beyond early readers," and Murphy dubbed it "a delightful story of dancing and self-confidence."

In her "Takeaways" novels for teen readers, Bell also focuses on young people attempting to deal with problems in constructive ways. In *No Strings,* for example, thirteen-year-old Felix is a talented saxophone player, but outside the school band room his life is made miserable by a bully. Two boys with seemingly little in common become fast friends in *Who Cares?* and find their surfing vacation cut short by an act of theft in

Who Dares? Because teen sports are the focus of several books in the "Takeaways" series, Bell makes sure the action is realistic by talking with expert skateboarders, surfers, and the like. In her review of *Who Dares?* for *Aussiereviews.com,* Murphy wrote that the novel's "mix of surfing, skateboarding and mystery . . . is a blend sure to appeal . . . to young male readers."

Bell drew upon her years producing and hosting the radio program *The Children's Hour* in writing *Where Do You Get Your Ideas?: Interviews with Australian Authors of Children's Books.* Here, thirty-one of the children's book authors and illustrators she interviewed for the program are showcased with brief biographical information and a selection of between three and five questions and answers from the original interviews. Each subject gets a two-page spread with a photograph and an illustration or two from their books. The subject matter dealt with is almost entirely devoted to the writing of picture books, noted Joan Zahnleiter in *Magpies.* While it is difficult to pinpoint the intended audience for *Where Do You Get Great Ideas?,* the critic added that "teachers and teacher-librarians would find it useful for extension work."

Bell once told *SATA:* "I was a bookseller, and then a publicist before reviewing books on radio for about fifteen years, as well as being a critic for literary magazines and newspapers. When I finally started to write fiction for children, I was terrified that no one would take my writing seriously—but luckily they did.

"Since 2000 I've been writing fiction full time, and it's been like 'coming home.' My one career regret is that I didn't become an author before I was forty—so many books to write, and so little time! If I had attended Bennington College, Vermont, in 1970, as I originally intended, while my parents were living in New York, perhaps my career would have taken off far earlier. But I returned to Australia instead!

"My advice to would-be writers is to do it *now*—there's no 'right time to write,' just as there's no 'right way to write.' Write now, do it your way and find your own unique voice.

"When I give writing workshops, I tell children that I write not fiction, but 'fibtion.' To create my stories, I take my own experiences and stories that I've been told, or overheard, and then I use a portion of truth, mixed with a large dollop of imaginative fibs. That's fibtion!"

Biographical and Critical Sources

PERIODICALS

Adelaide Advertiser, March 11, 2008, review of *Lofty's Mission.*
Age, March 27, 2004, Lorien Kaye, review of *No Strings.*

Australian Bookseller & Publisher, February, 2008, Margaret Hamilton, review of *Lofty's Mission.*

Kirkus Reviews, June 15, 2008, review of *If the Shoe Fits.*

Magpies, September, 1995, Russ Merrin, reviews of *The Slammers* and *Star Rookie,* both p. 24; September, 1996, Joan Zahnleiter, review of *Where Do You Get Your Ideas?: Interviews with Australian Authors of Children's Books,* p. 43; November, 2000, Debbie Mulligan, review of *Read My Mind,* p. 37.

Melbourne Herald Sun, April 9, 2005, review of *Who Dares?*

Reading Time, Volume 44, number 4, 2000, review of *Read My Mind,* p. 24.

ONLINE

Aussie Reviews Online, http://www.ausiereviews.com/ (April 15, 2010), Sally Murphy, reviews of *Who Dares?, That's the Trick,* and *If the Shoe Fits.*

Krista Bell Home Page, http://www.kristabell.com (April 20, 2010).*

*   *   *

BRADFORD, Chris 1974-

Personal

Born 1974, in England. *Hobbies and other interests:* Karate, kickboxing, samurai swordsmanship.

Addresses

Home—England. *Agent*—Viney Agency, 23 Erlanger Rd., Telegraph Hill, London SE14 5TF, England. *E-mail*—fanmail@youngsamurai.com.

Career

Writer, martial artist, and musician.

Awards, Honors

Fighting Spirit Awards Book of the Year designation, and Great Britain Sasakawa Award, both 2008, Carnegie Medal nomination, and Red House Children's Book Award shortlist, both 2009, and several other award nominations, all for "Young Samurai" series.

Writings

"YOUNG SAMURAI" NOVEL SERIES

The Way of the Warrior, Puffin (London, England), 2008, Hyperion Books for Children (New York, NY), 2009.

The Way of the Sword, Puffin (London, England), 2009, Hyperion Books for Children (New York, NY), 2010.

The Way of the Dragon, Puffin (London, England), 2010, Hyperion Books for Children (New York, NY), 2011.

The Ring of Earth, Puffin (London, England), 2010.

Author's work has been translated into more than sixteen languages.

OTHER

Heart and Soul: Revealing the Craft of Songwriting, Sanctuary, 2005.

Record Deals Outloud, Music Sales, 2006.

Artist Management Outloud, Music Sales, 2006.

Music Publishing Outloud, Music Sales, 2006.

Virtual Kombat, Puffin (London, England), 2010.

Also author of *Crash Course: Songwriting.*

Sidelights

In his "Young Samurai" series, which includes *The Way of the Warrior, The Way of the Sword,* and *The Way of the Dragon,* British writer and musician Chris Bradford taps his interest in the martial arts and adventure. In addition to learning kickboxing and karate, Bradford has studied samurai swordsmanship and holds a black belt in Zen Kyo Shin Taijutsu, a martial art used by the ninja.

Cover of Chris Bradford's middle-grade novel Young Samurai: The Way of the Warrior, *featuring artwork by Greg Weiner.* (Hyperion Books, 2008. Cover photograph by Greg Weiner. Reproduced by permission of Hyperion Books for Children.)

Set in 1611, *The Way of the Warrior* finds twelve-year-old Jack Fletcher shipwrecked off the coast of Japan, where his pilot father and the crew of the *Alexandria* have fallen victim to pirates. With no hope of ever returning to his native England, Jack becomes the student of legendary swordsman Masamoto Takeshi and trains to become a samurai warrior. Although he is befriended by Akiko, a fellow student, the boy is also tormented due to his Caucasian appearance and runs afoul of Kazuki and his gang of toughs. *The Way of the Sword* finds Jack a year older and anticipating a test of courage known as the Circle of Three. Still attracting the ire of Kazuki, Jack also awaits the coming of Dragon Eye, an evil ninja who wants the thirteen year old dead once he acquires the special maps Jack's father had entrusted to his son's care. War looms in *The Way of the Dragon,* and a battle with Dragon Eye also seems to be in Jack's future, unless he can master Takeshi's secret fighting technique: the Two Heavens.

Writing in *School Library Journal,* Bethany Isaacson praised *The Way of the Warrior* for treating readers to a look at life in seventeenth-century Japan and described the novel as an "a detailed story full of riveting elements: instant enemies, sworn friends, unfortunate misunderstandings, and ultimate forgiveness." The regimen Jack follows during his training to be a samurai is "conveyed with clarity and plenty of bravura," noted Ian Chipman in his *Booklist* review, and the author's use of Japanese terms reflects his "genuine respect for the subject." Although a *Kirkus Reviews* writer maintained that Branford alternates "exciting scenes" with "length lessons" and language that does not fit with the story's seventeenth-century setting, an enthusiastic reviewer for *Publishers Weekly* dubbed *The Way of the Warrior* "a page-turner" that "earns the literary equivalent of a black belt."

Biographical and Critical Sources

PERIODICALS

Booklist, January 1, 2009, Ian Chipman, review of *The Way of the Warrior,* p. 74.

Bulletin of the Center for Children's Books, July-August, 2009, Elizabeth Bush, review of *The Way of the Warrior,* p. 435.

Kirkus Reviews, January 15, 2009, review of *The Way of the Warrior.*

Publishers Weekly, January 12, 2009, review of *The Way of the Warrior,* p. 48.

School Library Journal, April, 2009, Bethany Isaacson, review of *The Way of the Warrior,* p. 129.

ONLINE

Chris Bradford Home Page, http://www.chrisbradford.co.uk (April 20, 2010).

BUZZEO, Toni 1951-

Personal

Born 1951, in Dearborn, MI; daughter of Anthony and Jeanne Buzzeo; married Kenneth Cyll; children: Christopher. *Education:* University of Michigan—Dearborn, B.A. (English), 1976; University of Michigan, M.A. (English), 1978; University of Rhode Island, M.L.I.S., 1990.

Addresses

Home—Buxton, ME. *E-mail*—tonibuzzeo@tonibuzzeo.com.

Career

Educator, library media specialist, and author. Baxter Memorial Library, Gorham, ME, children's librarian, beginning 1988; Margaret Chase Smith School, Sanford, ME, library media specialist, beginning 1990; Longfellow Elementary School, Portland, ME, library media specialist, 1993-2004. Visiting author at schools; keynote speaker at state, regional, nationa, and international conferences; conducts workshops and training sessions at conferences and in school districts.

Member

American Library Association, American Association of School Librarians, Society of Children's Book Writers and Illustrators, Maine Writers and Publishers Alliance, Maine Association of School Libraries, International Library Science Honor Society (Beta Phi Mu).

Awards, Honors

Named Maine Library Media Specialist of the Year, Maine Association of School Libraries, 1999; Barbara Karlin grant, Society of Children's Book Writers and Illustrators, 2000, Oppenheim Toy Portfolio Gold Award, Maine Lupine Honor designation, Young Hoosier Book Award nominee, Maine Raising Readers selection, Best Children's Books of the Year designation, Bank Street College of Education, and Best Books for the Classroom selection, Virginia Center for Children's Books, all 2002, and Children's Crown Gallery Award, 2004-05, all for *The Sea Chest;* named School of Education Alumnus of the Year, University of Michigan—Dearborn, 2004; New Jersey State Library Pick of the Decade listee, Maine Raising Readers selection, all 2003, all for *Dawdle Duckling;* Maine Raising Readers anthology selection, and Bank Street College Best Children's Books of the Year designation, both 2004, both for *Little Loon and Papa;* Maine Literary Award honor designation for forthcoming middle-grade novel, 2010.

Writings

FICTION

The Sea Chest, illustrated by Mary GrandPré, Dial (New York, NY), 2002.

Toni Buzzeo (Reproduced by permission.)

Dawdle Duckling, illustrated by Margaret Spengler, Dial (New York, NY), 2003.

Little Loon and Papa, illustrated by Margaret Spengler, Dial (New York, NY), 2004.

Ready or Not, Dawdle Duckling, illustrated by Margaret Spengler, Dial (New York, NY), 2005.

Our Librarian Won't Tell Us Anything!, illustrated by Sachiko Yoshikawa, UpstartBooks (Fort Atkinson, WI), 2006.

Fire Up with Reading!, illustrated by Sachiko Yoshikawa, UpstartBooks (Fort Atkinson, WI), 2007.

"R" Is for Research, illustrated by Nicole Wong, UpstartBooks (Fort Atkinson, WI), 2008.

The Library Doors, illustrated by Nadine Bernard Westcott, UpstartBooks (Fort Atkinson, WI), 2008.

Adventure Annie Goes to Work, illustrated by Amy Wummer, Dial (New York, NY), 2009.

The Great Dewey Hunt, illustrated by Sachiko Yoshikawa, UpstartBooks (Janesville, WI), 2009.

Adventure Annie Goes to Kindergarten, illustrated by Amy Wummer, Dial (New York, NY), 2010.

No T. Rex in the Library, illustrated by Sachiko Yoshikawa, Margaret K. McElderry Books (New York, NY), 2010.

Penelope Popper, Book Doctor, illustrated by Jana Christie, Upstart (Janesville, WI), 2011.

A Lighthouse Christmas, illustrated by Nancy Carpenter, Dial (New York, NY), 2011.

NONFICTION

(With Jane Kurtz) *Terrific Connections with Authors, Illustrators, and Storytellers: Real Space and Virtual Links,* Libraries Unlimited (Englewood, CO), 1999.

(With Jane Kurtz) *Thirty-five Best Books for Teaching U.S. Regions: Using Fiction to Help Students Explore the Geography, History, and Cultures of the Seven U.S. Regions—And Link to Social Studies,* Scholastic Professional (New York, NY), 1999.

Collaborating to Meet Standards: Teacher/Librarian Partnerships for K-6, Linworth Publishing (Worthington, OH), 2002, 2nd edition, 2007.

Collaborating to Meet Standards: Teacher/Librarian Partnerships for 7-12, Linworth Publishing (Worthington, OH), 2002.

Toni Buzzeo and You, Libraries Unlimited (Westport, CT), 2005.

Read! Perform! Learn!: Ten Reader's Theater Programs for Literacy Enhancement, UpstartBooks (Fort Atkinson, WI), 2006.

Read! Perform! Learn! Two: Ten More Reader's Theater Programs for Literacy Enhancement, UpstartBooks (Fort Atkinson, WI), 2007.

Collaborating to Meet Literacy Standards: Teacher/Librarian Partnerships for K-2, Linworth Publishing (Worthington, OH), 2007.

The Collaboration Handbook, Linworth Publishing (Columbus, OH), 2008.

ABC Read to Me: Teaching Letter of the Week in the Library and the Classroom, UpstartBooks (Fort Atkinson, WI), 2009.

Contributor of articles to *Library Sparks, Library Media Connection, School Library Journal,* and *Children's Writer.*

Sidelights

A library media specialist, Toni Buzzeo is well known for her work in bringing young children together with authors and illustrators through her work as both a librarian and as a writer of professional books and articles. In addition, Buzzeo has released more than a dozen picture books, among them *The Sea Chest, Our Librarian Won't Tell Us Anything!,* and *Adventure Annie Goes to Work.* As Buzzeo noted in an interview on the Ravenstone Press Web site, "my work with children and children's literature definitely influenced me as a writer. I am so knowledgeable about what is out there—what is being published for kids—that it influences what I write, I am sure."

Born and raised in Dearborn, Michigan, Buzzeo attended Sacred Heart School and was a frequent visitor to the Dearborn Public Library as a child. As a teen she began what she considers her writing apprenticeship by copying favorite poems into spiral notebooks, then rereading them to learn the cadences of the poems and develop a love and a habit for lyrical language. In high school Buzzeo continued to frequent libraries, shelving books as a library page, and at age eighteen working as a full-time library clerk to earn money for college tuition. While attending the University of Michigan, she had several of her own poems published in the school's literary magazine. It was at this point, as she noted on her home page, that she "began to think of myself as a *real* writer. Since then I have always written, in one way or another."

Buzzeo's first published book, *Terrific Connections with Authors, Illustrators, and Storytellers: Real Space and Virtual Links,* was coauthored with Jane Kurtz and con-

tains information for educators desiring to host author and illustrator visits. Noting the book's wealth of "common sense" and "practical hints," *Booklist* contributor Todd Morning had special praise for Buzzeo and Kurtz's inclusion of "the section on 'virtual visits,' which explores ways in which students and authors can communicate online or via television/satellite links."

Buzzeo's first story for children, *The Sea Chest*, features artwork by Mary GrandPré and centers on the tender relationship between a young girl and her great-aunt Maita, who is the daughter of a Maine lighthouse keeper and his wife. While anxiously awaiting the arrival of her newly adopted sister, the youngster is treated to Maita's telling of an amazing episode from her own childhood. "Buzzeo uses heightened language with great

clarity and emotional precision," a contributor stated in a *Kirkus Reviews* appraisal of *The Sea Chest*. "Poignant, poetic and movingly illustrated, this story resonates with sisterly love," stated a *Publishers Weekly* critic in reviewing the same book.

Buzzeo focuses on an easily distracted waterfowl in a pair of books that includes *Dawdle Duckling* and *Ready or Not, Dawdle Duckling*. In *Dawdle Duckling* the free-spirited duckling fails to heed Mama Duck's warnings about straying from her side until it is confronted by a hungry predator. According to Joy Fleishhacker in *School Library Journal*, "Buzzeo mixes a comfortingly repetitive text with fresh and evocative imagery," and a *Kirkus Reviews* contributor called the "gentle lesson" "just right for the preschool set." In *Ready or Not,*

Buzzeo's imaginative story in* The Sea Chest *is captured in dramatic paintings by Mary GrandPré. (Illustration copyright © 2002 by Mary GrandPré. Reproduced by permission of Dial Books for Young Readers, a division of Penguin Putnam Books for Young Readers.)

Buzzeo's library-centered alphabet book "R" Is for Research *is brought to life in Nicole Wong's engaging art.* (Illustration © 2008 by Nicole Wong. Reproduced by permission.)

Dawdle Duckling the duckling youngster makes a host of aquatic friends while playing hide-and-seek with its mother. Susan Weitz, writing in *School Library Journal,* praised Buzzeo's "vigorous text" for the story and described *Ready or Not, Dawdle Duckling* as "tailor-made for preschoolers."

In *Little Loon and Papa* Buzzeo centers her young readers' focus on a little bird that is determined to learn how to dive beneath the water. Paired with engaging illustrations by Margaret Spengler, the book's "staccato text is filled with alliteration and rhythmic sound effects," observed Linda Staskus in *School Library Journal.*

Buzzeo employs her experiences as a librarian in *"R" Is for Research,* a rhyming abecedarian in which "the concept of research is charmingly introduced," according to Maura Bresnahan in *School Library Journal.* In *Our Librarian Won't Tell Us Anything!,* the first of a se-

ries of books, a new student timidly approaches his first meeting with the dreaded Mrs. Skorupski, the school's wiley librarian. "This amusing story . . . can be used to launch research units," advised *School Library Journal* critic Gloria Koster. Second and third in the series are *Fire up with Reading* and *The Great Dewey Hunt.*

One of two books sharing Buzzeo's likeable young heroine, *Adventure Annie Goes to Work* finds energetic young Annie on her way to her mother's office to help recover a missing school report. The author's "uplifting selection is full of everyday fun," a *Kirkus Reviews* critic wrote of the book, which is part of a series illustrated by Amy Wummer that also includes *Adventure Annie Goes to Kindergarten.*

In *No T. Rex in the Library,* a spunky young heroine whose mother puts her in time-out at the public library for her unruly behavior brings a T. Rex to life. "Buzzeo and [illustrator] Yoshikawa make it obvious how chil-

dren are supposed to behave in a library while giving sneak peeks at some of the different sections and exciting possibilities that they might encounter on a visit," observed Tanya Boudreau in a review of the book for *School Library Journal.*

Buzzeo told *SATA:* "My life has been devoted to words, both spoken and written. I began my career as a teacher of writing, both at the high school and college level, a path that ultimately led me to librarianship. As a teaching librarian for sixteen years in elementary schools, I added to my storehouse of knowledge about children's literature and engaged my own desire to add to that body of work by writing and publishing children's books.

"As a published author and nationally known speaker, I am able to share my passions for teaching and for children's books from a unique vantage point, as a teacher, as a librarian, and as a children's book creator. As a visiting author in schools, I have the opportunity to regularly engage with my young readers, to share my journey from book-loving child to published author, and to encourage them to hone their work as writers and illustrators through hard work and openness to revision. As I often tell students, 'Anyone can write a first draft. The real work of writing comes in the revision, the willingness to remain open to a new vision, to hear the comments and criticism of others with an open heart and open mind.'"

Biographical and Critical Sources

PERIODICALS

Booklist, March 15, 2000, Todd Morning, review of *Terrific Connections with Authors, Illustrators, and Storytellers: Real Space and Virtual Links,* p. 1391;

March 1, 2005, Connie Fletcher, review of *Ready or Not, Dawdle Duckling,* p. 1202; Hazel Rochman, review of *Adventure Annie Goes to Work,* p. 45.

Kirkus Reviews, July 1, 2002, review of *The Sea Chest,* p. 949; November 15, 2002, review of *Dawdle Duckling,* p. 1689; January 15, 2009, review of *Adventure Annie Goes to Work;* February 15, 2010, review of *No T. Rex in the Library.*

Publishers Weekly, August 5, 2002, review of *The Sea Chest,* p. 72; November 18, 2002, review of *Dawdle Duckling,* p. 58; May 17, 2004, review of *Little Loon and Papa,* p. 49.

School Library Journal, August, 2002, Barbara Buckley, review of *The Sea Chest,* p. 147; Joy Fleishhacker, review of *Dawdle Duckling,* p. 116; June, 2004, Linda Staskus, review of *Little Loon and Papa,* p. 103; March, 2005, Susan Weitz, review of *Ready or Not, Dawdle Duckling,* p. 168; February, 2007, Gloria Koster, review of *Our Librarian Won't Tell Us Anything!,* p. 85; September, 2008, Maura Bresnahan, review of *"R" Is for Research,* p. 164; April, 2008, Jane Barrer, review of *Collaborating to Meet Standards: Teacher/Librarian Partnerships for Grades K-6,* p. 176; May, 2009, Marcia Kochel, review of *The Collaboration Handbook,* p. 143; January, 2010, Tanya Boudreau, review of *No T. Rex in the Library,* p. 69.

ONLINE

Cynsations Web log, http://cynthialeitichsmith.blogspot.com/ (April 6, 2006), Cynthia Leitich Smith, "Toni Buzzeo."

Ravenstone Press Web site, http://ravenstonepress.com/ (March 1, 2010), "Toni Buzzeo."

Toni Buzzeo Home Page, http://www.tonibuzzeo.com (March 1, 2010).

C

CARLSTROM, Nancy White 1948-

Personal

Born August 4, 1948, in Washington, PA; daughter of William J. (a steel mill worker) and Eva White; married David R. Carlstrom, September 7, 1974; children: Jesse David, Joshua White. *Education:* Wheaton College, B.A., 1970; studied at Harvard Extension and Radcliffe College, 1974-76. *Religion:* Christian. *Hobbies and other interests:* Birding, international travel, reading.

Addresses

Home—Seattle, WA. *E-mail*—nancy@nancywhitecarl strom.com.

Career

Educator and author. A. Leo Weil Elementary School, Pittsburgh, PA, teacher, 1970-72; Plum Cove Elementary School, Gloucester, MA, teacher, 1972-74; Secret Garden Children's Bookshop, Seattle, WA, owner and manager, 1977-83; freelance writer, beginning 1983. Worked with children in West Africa and the West Indies; worked at school for children with Down's syndrome in Merida, Yucatán, Mexico.

Member

Society of Children's Book Writers and Illustrators.

Awards, Honors

Editor's Choice designation, *Booklist,* 1986, and Children's Choice designation, International Reading Association/Children's Book Council (IRA/CBC), 1987, both for *Jesse Bear, What Will You Wear?;* American Booksellers Pick of the List selection, and Notable Book designation, National Council of Teachers of English (NCTE), both 1987, both for *Wild Wild Sunflower Child Anna;* Best Book designation, *Parents'* magazine, 1990, for *Where Does the Night Hide?;* NCTE Notable Book

Nancy White Carlstrom

designation, 1991, for *Goodbye Geese;* IRA/CBC Children's Choice selection, and Parents' Choice designation, *Booklist,* both 1991, both for *Blow Me a Kiss, Miss Lilly;* CBC Multicultural Book listee, and Georgia State Book Award nomination. both 1991, both for *Light; Publishers Weekly* Best Books designation, 1992, and Gold Medal, Society of Illustrators, both for *North-*

ern Lullaby illustrated by Leo and Diane Dillon; Parent Council Outstanding Book selection, 1993, for *Does God Know How to Tie Shoes?;* Tennessee Book Award nomination, 1993, for *Grandpappy;* Parents' Choice designation, 1994, for *Baby-0;* National Outdoor Book Award, 2001 and Independent Publishers Book Award, both for *What Does the Sky Say?; Booklist* Top Ten Religious Books selection, 2001, for *Glory; ForeWord* magazine Book of the Year Award finalist, 2002, for *Before You Were Born.*

Writings

FOR CHILDREN

Jesse Bear, What Will You Wear?, illustrated by Bruce Degen, Macmillan (New York, NY), 1986, board book edition, Little Simon (New York, NY), 1996, original book reprinted, Aladdin (New York, NY), 2005.

The Moon Came, Too, illustrated by Stella Ormai, Macmillan (New York, NY), 1987.

Wild Wild Sunflower Child Anna, illustrated by Jerry Pinkney, Macmillan (New York, NY), 1987.

Better Not Get Wet, Jesse Bear, illustrated by Bruce Degen, Macmillan (New York, NY), 1988.

Where Does the Night Hide?, illustrated by Thomas B. Allen and Laura Allen, Macmillan (New York, NY), 1988.

Graham Cracker Animals 1-2-3, illustrated by John Sandford, Macmillan (New York, NY), 1989.

Blow Me a Kiss, Miss Lilly, illustrated by Amy Schwartz, Harper (New York, NY), 1990.

Heather Hiding, illustrated by Dennis Nolan, Macmillan (New York, NY), 1990.

It's about Time, Jesse Bear, and Other Rhymes, illustrated by Bruce Degen, Macmillan (New York, NY), 1990.

I'm Not Moving, Mama!, illustrated by Thor Wickstrom, Macmillan (New York, NY), 1990.

Grandpappy, illustrated by Laurel Molk, Little, Brown (Boston, MA), 1990.

No Nap for Benjamin Badger, illustrated by Dennis Nolan, Macmillan (New York, NY), 1990.

Light: Stories of a Small Kindness, illustrated by Lisa Desimini, Little, Brown (Boston, MA), 1990.

Moose in the Garden, illustrated by Lisa Desimini, Harper (New York, NY), 1990.

Goodbye Geese, illustrated by Ed Young, Philomel (New York, NY), 1991.

Who Gets the Sun out of Bed?, illustrated by David McPhail, Little, Brown (Boston, MA), 1992.

Northern Lullaby, illustrated by Leo and Diane Dillon, Philomel (New York, NY), 1992.

Kiss Your Sister, Rose Marie!, illustrated by Thor Wickstrom, Macmillan (New York, NY), 1992.

How Do You Say It Today, Jesse Bear?, illustrated by Bruce Degen, Macmillan (New York, NY), 1992.

Baby-O, illustrated by Suçie Stevenson, Little, Brown (Boston, MA), 1992.

The Snow Speaks, illustrated by Jane Dyer, Little, Brown (Boston, MA), 1993.

What Does the Rain Play?, illustrated by Henri Sorensen, Macmillan (New York, NY), 1993.

Swim the Silver Sea, Joshie Otter, illustrated by Ken Kuori, Philomel (New York, NY), 1993.

Rise and Shine, illustrated by Dominic Catalano, HarperCollins (New York, NY), 1993.

How Does the Wind Walk?, illustrated by Deborah K. Ray, Macmillan (New York, NY), 1993.

Fish and Flamingo, illustrated by Lisa Desimini, Little, Brown (Boston, MA), 1993.

Wishing at Dawn in Summer, illustrated by Diane Wolfolk Allison, Little, Brown (Boston, MA), 1993.

Does God Know How to Tie Shoes?, illustrated by Lori McElrath-Eslick, Eerdmans (Grand Rapids, MI), 1993, board-book edition, 2010.

What Would You Do If You Lived at the Zoo?, illustrated by Lizi Boyd, Little, Brown (Boston, MA), 1994.

Jesse Bear's Yum-Yum Crumble, Aladdin Books (New York, NY), 1994.

Jesse Bear's Wiggle-Jiggle Jump-Up, Aladdin Books (New York, NY), 1994.

Jesse Bear's Tum Tum Tickle, Aladdin Books (New York, NY), 1994.

Jesse Bear's Tra-La Tub, Aladdin Books (New York, NY), 1994.

Happy Birthday, Jesse Bear!, illustrated by Bruce Degen, Macmillan (New York, NY), 1994.

Barney Is Best, illustrated by James G. Hale, HarperCollins (New York, NY), 1994.

Who Said Boo?: Halloween Poems for the Very Young, illustrated by R.W. Alley, Simon & Schuster (New York, NY), 1995.

I Am Christmas, illustrated by Lori McElrath-Eslick, Eerdmans (Grand Rapids, MI), 1995.

Let's Count It out, Jesse Bear, illustrated by Bruce Degen, Simon & Schuster (New York, NY), 1996.

Ten Christmas Sheep, illustrated by Cynthia Fisher, Eerdmans (Grand Rapids, MI), 1996.

Raven and River, illustrated by Jon Van Zyle, Little, Brown (Boston, MA), 1997.

I Love You, Papa, in All Kinds of Weather, illustrated by Bruce Degen, Little Simon (New York, NY), 1997.

I Love You, Mama, Any Time of Year, illustrated by Bruce Degen, Little Simon (New York, NY), 1997.

Hooray for Me, Hooray for You, Hooray for Blue: Jesse Bear's Colors, illustrated by Bruce Degen, Little Simon (New York, NY), 1997.

Bizz Buzz Chug-a-Chug: Jesse Bear's Sounds, illustrated by Bruce Degen, Little Simon (New York, NY), 1997.

Guess Who's Coming, Jesse Bear?, illustrated by Bruce Degen, Simon & Schuster (New York, NY), 1998.

Midnight Dance of the Snowshoe Hare: Poems of Alaska, illustrated by Ken Kuori, Philomel (New York, NY), 1998.

What a Scare, Jesse Bear!, illustrated by Bruce Degen, Simon & Schuster (New York, NY), 1999.

Thanksgiving Day at Our House: Thanksgiving Poems for the Very Young, illustrated by R.W. Alley, Simon & Schuster (New York, NY), 1999.

Where Is Christmas, Jesse Bear?, illustrated by Bruce Degen, Simon & Schuster (New York, NY), 2000.

The Way to Wyatt's House, illustrated by Mary Morgan, Walker & Co. (New York, NY), 2000.

What Does the Sky Say?, illustrated by Tim Ladwig, Eerdmans (Grand Rapids, MI), 2001.

Glory, illustrated by Debra Reid Jenkins, Eerdmans (Grand Rapids, MI), 2001.

Before You Were Born, illustrated by Linda Saport, Eerdmans (Grand Rapids, MI), 2002.

Giggle-Wiggle Wake-up!, illustrated by Melissa Sweet, Knopf (New York, NY), 2003.

Climb the Family Tree, Jesse Bear!, illustrated by Bruce Degen, Simon & Schuster (New York, NY), 2004.

It's Your First Day of School, Annie Claire, illustrated by Margie Moore, Abrams Books for Young Readers (New York, NY), 2009.

Mama, Will It Snow Tonight?, illustrated by Paul Tong, Boyds Mills Press (Honesdale, PA), 2009.

This Is the Day!, illustrated by Richard Cowdrey, Zonderkidz (Grand Rapids, MI), 2009.

Sidelights

Nancy White Carlstrom is the author of many books for young children, among them the popular "Jesse Bear"

Carlstrom's family-themed picture book **Before You Were Born** *is brought to life in artwork by Linda Saport.* (Eerdmans Books for Young Readers, 2002. Illustration © 2002 by Linda Saport. Reproduced by permission.)

series, which is illustrated by Bruce Degen and features such titles as *Where Is Christmas, Jesse Bear?*, *Jesse Bear, What Will You Wear?*, and *Climb the Family Tree, Jesse Bear!* Known for crafting compact rhyming texts filled with vivid description and evocations of the every day, Carlstrom creates hopeful and humorous picture and board books for very young readers. Her stories are known for their simple vocabulary and subjects ranging from counting and colors to more sophisticated topics like intergenerational and multicultural relationships.

Carlstrom's concerns with society and her love of nature are a reflection of her own upbringing and world view. Growing up without television, she learned to create her own fantasies and to entertain herself. Carlstrom decided to become a writer of children's books at an early age; she worked in the children's department of her local library during her high-school years, and "that's where my dream of writing children's books was born," as she once told *SATA*. After earning a B.A. in education from Wheaton College, she taught primary school in Pittsburgh while working summers with children in the West Indies and in West Africa. She also studied art and children's literature, then moved with her husband to the Yucatán where she worked at a school for children with Down's syndrome. Upon their return to the United States, the couple moved to Seattle, where Carlstrom became proprietor of The Secret Garden, a children's bookstore, and promoted quality children's books via book fairs and public presentations.

In 1981 Carlstrom participated in a two-week writer's workshop led by noted children's-book author Jane Yolen. During that workshop she wrote the poem that would eventually become the text of *Wild Wild Sunflower Child Anna*. During the several years that it took for this text to find a publisher, Carlstrom wrote *Jesse Bear, What Will You Wear?*, a book that has proved so popular that it has remained in continually in print since publication. "My husband and I often called our son Jesse Bear," the author once recalled to *SATA*, "and the book . . . began as a little song I sang while dressing him. I finished the picture book text for Jesse's first birthday."

Jesse Bear, What Will You Wear? progresses through a single day as little Jesse dresses and then messes and must dress again. Liza Bliss, writing in *School Library Journal*, noted in particular that Carlstrom's "rhymes, besides having a charming lilt to them, are clean and catchy and beg to be recited." A *Bulletin of the Center for Children's Books* reviewer drew attention to the book's lyrics, as well, noting that, "without crossing the line into sentimentality, this [story] offers a happy, humorous soundfest that will associate reading aloud with a sense of play."

Carlstrom continues to chronicle the adventures of Jesse Bear in a number of other books. *Better Not Get Wet, Jesse Bear* is a "winsome picture book," according to a *Publishers Weekly* reviewer. The critic also cited the

story's "lilting, strongly rhymed text," while Ellen Fader wrote in *Horn Book* that *Better Not Get Wet, Jesse Bear* "never loses its claim to the sensibility of young children, who will be won over by Jesse Bear's delight in water play and his final triumphant splash." Clocks and telling time are at the heart of *It's about Time, Jesse Bear, and Other Rhymes,* a book that "children are sure to enjoy," according to Patricia Pearl in *School Library Journal. How Do You Say It Today, Jesse Bear?* celebrates the holidays of the year, from Independence Day to Halloween and Christmas. Carolyn Phelan commented in *Booklist* that this work provides a "good way to learn about the months and holidays, or read it just for fun."

Let's Count It out, Jesse Bear finds the playful bear "in a high-impact counting game," according to a *Publishers Weekly* reviewer. *Where Is Christmas, Jesse Bear?* proves that "there's no hibernating for this little bear," as *Booklist* reviewer Shelley Townsend-Hudson noted. Praising Carlstrom's "child-centered focus," Townsend-Hudson also dubbed the holiday-themed picture book "infectiously jubilant," while in *School Library Journal* Marian Drabkin noted that *Where Is Christmas, Jesse Bear?* calls forth the "sights . . . that traditionally shout Christmas." The "Jesse Bear" series has also prompted spin-off board books and a stuffed bear, as well as a loyal following among readers.

Surprisingly, although Carlstrom has also written many books outside of the "Jesse Bear" series, her first, *Wild Wild Sunflower Child Anna,* remains among her favorite self-authored stories. Reviewing this story, about a child's exploration and discovery of the natural world around her, Denise M. Wilms maintained in *Booklist* that "audiences young and old will find [Anna's] pleasure in the day most contagious." Ellen Fader concluded in *Horn Book* that "an exceptional treat awaits the parent and child who lose themselves in" *Wild Wild Sunflower Child Anna.*

Carlstrom further celebrates the lives of preschoolers in books such as *Heather Hiding,* the tale of a hide-and-seek game; *Blow Me a Kiss, Miss Lilly,* which deals with the death of a loved one; and *It's Your First Day of School, Annie-Claire,* about a young puppy's first day of preschool. *Light: Stories of a Small Kindness* draws somewhat on Carlstrom's time spent in Mexico in that the gathered tales all have Hispanic settings and all deal with small but significant gestures of affection. "Tender, thought-provoking, moving are just a few of the words to describe these seven short stories," commented Ilene Cooper in a *Booklist* review of the work. Featuring lovingly crafted illustrations by Margie Moore, *It's Your First Day of School, Annie Claire* depicts a conversation between a mother and daughter that crystallizes, "in comforting words," the affectionate relationship between the two, according to *Booklist* contributor Diane Foote. Reflecting the qualities characteristic of Carlstrom's work, the picture book was de-

Carlstrom's paean to the wonders of nature teams with Richard Cowdrey's detailed paintings in **This Is the Day!** (Illustration copyright © 2009 by Richard Cowdrey. All rights reserved. Reproduced by permission.)

scribed by *School Library Journal* contributor Anne Beier as "a charming story for parent-child sharing."

In another rhythmic tale for toddlers, *Baby-O,* the rhythms of the West Indies are celebrated in a rhyming cumulative story about a family on its way to market to sell its garden produce. "Sing it, chant it, clap it, or stamp it," Jane Marino suggested in her upbeat review of the book for *School Library Journal.* "Just don't miss it." Carlstrom deals with topics as various as the relationship between a young boy and his grandfather in *Grandpappy,* unlikely friendships in *Fish and Flamingo,* a child's fears of a trip to the hospital in *Barney Is Best,* and the possibilities that life holds at the start of a brand new week in *Giggle-Wiggle Wake-up!,* the last in which Carlstrom's "infectiously singsong text dances in readers' ears," according to a *Publishers Weekly* reviewer.

A move to Alaska in 1987 provided Carlstrom with new settings and themes for her writing: "freely wandering moose, northern lights, and extreme seasonal changes to name a few," as she once told *SATA.* Books such as *Moose in the Garden, The Snow Speaks, Northern Lullaby,* and *Goodbye Geese* have all been inspired by the wilderness and wildlife of the far north. "A first-rate choice for toddlers" is how *School Library Journal* contributor Ellen Fader described *Moose in the Garden,* which tells of a moose invading a family vegetable garden and—to the delight of the young boy of the fam-

ily—eating all the vegetables the boy does not like. The northern winter is lovingly examined in *Goodbye Geese* through the question-and-answer exchange between a father and his curious child. In *Booklist* Phelan found *Goodbye Geese* to be "an effective mood book for story hour" and "a vivid introduction to personification." In *Northern Lullaby* Carlstrom also personifies the natural elements such as the moon and stars, along with wild creatures to conjure up a vision of the vastness of the far north. "The end effect," commented *Bulletin of the Center for Children's Books* reviewer Betsy Hearne, "is both simple and sophisticated." A *Kirkus Reviews* critic noted the book's "gently cadenced verse," and a *Publishers Weekly* reviewer praised *Northern Lullaby* as a "stunning, seamlessly executed work."

Wintertime in Alaska also inspired Carlstrom's *The Snow Speaks,* in which two children experience the first snowfall of the season. Phelan noted that Carlstrom used "lyrical language to turn down-to-earth experiences into something more," and Jane Marino asserted in *School Library Journal* that *The Snow Speaks* is "a book to be enjoyed all winter, long after the decorations have been packed away."

Natural phenomena form the core of many of Carlstrom's books, among them *Where Does the Night Hide?, Who Gets the Sun out of Bed?, What Does the Rain Play?, How Does the Wind Walk?,* and *Mama, Will It Snow Tonight?* With *Who Gets the Sun out of*

Bed? the author reverses the goodnight story, relating instead a tale about waking up. *School Library Journal* contributor Ruth K. MacDonald found this work to be "an altogether successful story about the coming of the day," noting that "the persistent gentle patterns of questions and answers leads up to a climax that is warm but not boisterous—a fitting, final ending to a story that . . . functions as an appropriate bedtime tale." The sounds of rain take center stage in *What Does the Rain Play?*, which focuses on a little boy who loves the various noises rain makes, even at night. Emily Melton noted in *Booklist* that "the gently calming writing and softly lulling rhythms of the rain sounds make this book a perfect bedtime choice."

In *How Does the Wind Walk?* another little boy observes the varied moods of the wind in different seasons, his reflections captured by Carlstrom in a question-and-answer format. A critic in *Kirkus Reviews* noted that Carlstrom's text for the book includes "lots of alliteration and some subtle internal rhymes" to produce "wonderfully evocative effects." In *Mama, Will It Snow Tonight?* a small child asks the same question over and over, while a variety of animals are depicted in Paul Tong's illustrations, their winter preparations made. Carlstrom's "simple, beautiful portrayal of antici-

Tim Ladwig captures the wonder experienced by a small child in his artwork for Carlstrom's **What Does the Sky Say?** (Illustration copyright 2001 by Tim Ladwig. Reproduced by permission.)

pation answers young children's desire for reassurance [and] . . . information," concluded Diane Foote in her appraisal of *Mama, Will It Snow Tonight?*

Harkening back to her own childhood enjoyment of the Bible and her Christian roots, Carlstrom has also created several faith-based books for young readers. She encourages a child's questions about God in *Does God Know How to Tie Shoes?*, and has also authored several nativity tales, including *I Am Christmas* and *Ten Christmas Sheep.* Her picture book *Glory* contains a prayer that recounts how all the creatures on Earth are connected to God in one way or another, while *This Is the Day!* reflects on a well-known bible verse by celebrating the many joys to be found in the natural world. Praising Debra Reid Jenkins for creating the colorful illustrations in *Glory, School Library Journal* reviewer Gay Lynn van Vleck wrote that Carlstrom's book reinforces "how good it feels to be alive," and will serve as a special treat for young animal lovers.

In *This Is the Day!* the author utilizes "active verbs and sensory details to draw" in young readers, according to a *Kirkus Reviews* writer, while artist Richard Cowdrey contributes "realistic paintings [that] capture the intriguing" cast of animal characters. "After living in Fairbanks, Alaska, for eighteen year my husband and I moved back to Seattle where we continue to live," Carlstrom told *SATA.* "We also spend time in Friday Harbor, San Juan Island, Washington, which is the setting for *This Is the Day.* The book is a celebration of God's creation and in it, I try to encourage readers to be surprised by wonder in the natural world."

Carlstrom draws from Psalm 139 in her book *Before You Were Born,* which describes how life changes with the birth of a new child. Dubbing the book a "beautiful portrayal of the transformation of a couple into a family," a *Kirkus Reviews* critic added that the text of *Before You Were Born* contains "effulgent imagery" that reassuringly shows that parents hold children to be central to their lives.

Carlstrom practices the craft of writing with care and intelligence. "A picture book, like a poem, is what I call a bare bones kind of writing," she once explained to *SATA.* "Usually I start with many more words than I need or want. I keep cutting away until I am down to the bare bones of what I want to say. It is then up to the illustrator to create pictures that will enlarge and enhance the text. . . . Often a title of a story will come first. I write it down and tend to think about it for a long time before actually sitting down to work on it. Sometimes I just get a few pieces of the story and they have to simmer on the back burner, like a good pot of soup. When the time is right, the writing of the story comes easily." In *Books That Invite Talk, Wonder, and Play,* she also noted that she often sings her words to get the correct rhythm. "Language is a musical experience for me. Rhythm, rhyme, and cadence all become an important part of the process. I love the way a young

child, just learning the language, rolls a word around on her tongue and, if she likes the sound of it, may chant it over and over."

All of Carlstrom's books share the common denominator of humor and hope. "No matter how bad things get, in this world or in my life," Carlstrom commented in a *Speaking of Poets* interview, "I do believe in joy and hope because I believe there's someone greater than myself in charge. It is my own religious faith that affects both the way I live my life and the way I write." "I can't always explain exactly why my poems come out the way they do," she later added, "but there is a joy that I have that I do want to express. And for me, writing is my way of celebrating."

Biographical and Critical Sources

BOOKS

Books That Invite Talk, Wonder, and Play, edited by Amy A. McClure and Janice V. Kristo, National Council of Teachers of English, 1996, pp. 236-238.
Speaking of Poets, Volume 2, edited by Jeffrey S. Copeland and Vicky L. Copeland, National Council of Teachers of English, 1994, pp. 194-202.

PERIODICALS

Booklist, October 1, 1987, Denise M. Wilms, review of *Wild Wild Sunflower Child Anna,* p. 257; December 15, 1990, Ilene Cooper, review of *Light: Stories of a Small Kindness,* pp. 855, 860; November 15, 1991, Carolyn Phelan, review of *Goodbye Geese,* p. 628; September 15, 1992, Carolyn Phelan, reviews of *The Snow Speaks* and *How Do You Say It Today, Jesse Bear?,* both p. 154; April 1, 1993, Emily Melton, review of *What Does the Rain Play?,* p. 1436; February 15, 1998, Lauren Peterson, review of *Guess Who's Coming, Jesse Bear?;* September, 2000, Lauren Peterson, review of *The Way to Wyatt's House,* p. 121; November 15, 2000, Shelley Townsend-Hudson, review of *Where Is Christmas, Jesse Bear?,* p. 646; July, 2001, Denise Wilms, review of *What Does the Sky Say?,* p. 2017; October 1, 2002, Ilene Cooper, review of *Glory,* p. 344; September 1, 2009, Diane Foote, review of *It's Your First Day of School, Annie-Claire,* p. 98; September 15, 2009, Diane Foote, review of *Mama, Will It Snow Tonight?,* p. 65.
Bulletin of the Center for Children's Books, May, 1986, review of *Jesse Bear, What Will You Wear?,* p. 162; October, 1992, Betsy Hearne, review of *Northern Lullaby,* p. 40.
Horn Book, November-December, 1987, Ellen Fader, review of *Wild Wild Sunflower Child Anna,* pp. 721-722; May-June, 1988, Ellen Fader, review of *Better Not Get Wet, Jesse Bear,* pp. 338-339.
Kirkus Reviews, February 15, 1986, review of *Jesse Bear, What Will You Wear?,* p. 300; October 15, 1992, review of *Northern Lullaby,* p. 1307; September 1, 1993,

review of *How Does the Wind Walk?,* p. 1141; December 15, 2001, review of *Before You Were Born,* p. 1755; October 1, 2003, review of *Giggle-Wiggle Wake-up!,* p. 1221; January 15, 2009, review of *This Is the Day!;* June 15, 2009, review of *It's Your First Day of School, Annie-Claire.*
Publishers Weekly, March 11, 1988, review of *Better Not Get Wet, Jesse Bear,* p. 102; October 19, 1992, review of *Northern Lullaby,* p. 75; June 17, 1996, review of *Let's Count It out, Jesse Bear,* p. 63; November 15, 1999, review of *I'm Not Moving Mama!,* p. 69; February 14, 2000, review of *Happy Birthday, Jesse Bear!,* p. 203; September 25, 2000, review of *The Way to Wyatt's House,* p. 115; November 24, 2003, review of *Giggle-Wiggle Wake-up!,* p. 62.
School Library Journal, April, 1986, Liza Bliss, review of *Jesse Bear, What Will You Wear?,* pp. 68-69; April, 1990, Patricia Pearl, review of *It's about Time, Jesse Bear, and Other Rhymes,* p. 87; October, 1990, Ellen Fader, review of *Moose in the Garden,* p. 86; April, 1992, Jane Marino, review of *Baby-O,* p. 89; September, 1992, Ruth K. MacDonald, review of *Who Gets the Sun out of Bed?,* p. 199; October, 1992, Jane Marino, review of *The Snow Speaks,* p. 38; October, 1999, Anne Parker, review of *What a Scare, Jesse Bear!;* October, 2000, Marian Drabkin, reviews of *Where Is Christmas, Jesse Bear?,* p. 57, and *The Way to Wyatt's House,* p. 119; December, 2001, Be Astengo, review of *What Does the Sky Say?,* p. 118; December, 2001, Gay Lynn van Vleck, review of *Glory,* p. 118; June, 2002, Martha Topol, review of *Before You Were Born,* p. 90; August, 2004, Wendy Woodfill, review of *Climb the Family Tree, Jesse Bear!,* p. 84; August, 2009, Anne Beier, review of *It's Your First Day of School, Annie-Claire,* p. 72.

ONLINE

Nancy White Carlstrom Home Page, http://www.nancy whitecarlstrom.com (April 25, 2010).

*   *   *

CARPENTER, Nancy (Nancy Sippel Carpenter)

Personal

Married; children: Maeve.

Addresses

Home—Brooklyn, NY.

Career

Children's book illustrator, 1990—. Has also worked as a graphic reporter for Associated Press, an illustrator for the *New York Times,* and an illustrator of greeting cards.

Awards, Honors

Notable Children's Book selection, American Library Association (ALA), Jane Addams Children's Book Award, and Notable Children's Book in Social Studies, National Council for the Social Studies/Children's Book Council, all for *Sitti's Secrets;* Notable Children's Book selection, ALA, One Hundred Titles for Reading and Sharing selection, New York Public Library, and Golden Kite Award, Society of Children's Book Writers and Illustrators, all 2004, all for *Apples to Oregon.*

Illustrator

Sharon Phillips Denslow, *At Taylor's Place,* Bradbury Press (New York, NY), 1990.

Dorothy Hoobler and Thomas Hoobler, *Treasure in the Stream: The Story of a Gold Rush Girl,* Silver Burdett Press (Englewood Cliffs, NJ), 1991.

Jimmy Allder, Corey Allder, and Ellen Harvey Showell, *Our Mountain,* Bradbury Press (New York, NY), 1991.

Sharon Phillips Denslow, *Riding with Aunt Lucy,* Bradbury Press (New York, NY), 1991.

Virginia Kroll, *Masai and I,* Four Winds Press (New York, NY), 1992.

Anna Quindlen, *The Tree That Came to Stay,* Crown (New York, NY), 1992.

Karen Hesse, *Lester's Dog,* Crown (New York, NY), 1993.

Sharon Phillips Denslow, *Bus Riders,* Four Winds Press (New York, NY), 1993.

(As Nancy Sippel Carpenter) James Howe, *The Secret Garden* (adapted from the book of the same name by Frances Hodgson Burnett), Random House (New York, NY), 1993.

Naomi Shihab Nye, *Sitti's Secrets,* Four Winds Press (New York, NY), 1994.

Jacqueline Briggs Martin, *Washing the Willow Tree Loon,* Simon & Schuster (New York, NY), 1995.

Margery Facklam, *Only a Star,* Eerdmans (Grand Rapids, MI), 1996.

Virginia Kroll, *Can You Dance, Dalila?,* Simon & Schuster (New York, NY), 1996.

Kate Jacobs, *A Sister's Wish,* Hyperion (New York, NY), 1996.

(As Nancy Sippel Carpenter) Jane Yolen, *Sing Noel: Christmas Carols,* musical arrangements by Adam Stemple, Boyds Mills Press (Honesdale, PA), 1996.

Eve Bunting, *Twinnies,* Harcourt Brace (San Diego, CA), 1997.

Alexis O'Neill, *Loud Emily,* Simon & Schuster (New York, NY), 1998.

Kathi Appelt, *Someone's Come to Our House,* Eerdmans (Grand Rapids, MI), 1999.

Darleen Bailey Beard, *Twister,* Farrar, Straus, & Giroux (New York, NY), 1999.

Eve Bunting, *A Picnic in October,* Harcourt Brace (San Diego, CA), 1999.

Lynea Bowdish, *Brooklyn, Bugsy, and Me,* Farrar, Straus, & Giroux (New York, NY), 2000.

Barbara Ann Porte, *If You Ever Get Lost: The Adventures of Julia and Evan,* Greenwillow Books (New York, NY), 2000.

Deborah Hopkinson, *Fannie in the Kitchen: The Whole Story from Soup to Nuts of How Fannie Farmer Invented Recipes with Precise Measurements,* Atheneum (New York, NY), 2001.

Karin Cates, *A Far-fetched Story,* Greenwillow Books (New York, NY), 2002.

Eve Bunting, *Little Bear's Little Boat,* Clarion Books (New York, NY), 2003.

Naomi Shihab Nye, *Baby Radar,* Greenwillow Books (New York, NY), 2003.

Kay Winters, *Abe Lincoln: The Boy Who Loved Books,* Simon & Schuster (New York, NY), 2003.

Deborah Hopkinson, *Apples to Oregon: Being the (Slightly) True Narrative of How a Brave Pioneer Father Brought Apples, Peaches, Pears, Plums, Grapes, and Cherries (and Children) across the Plains,* Atheneum (New York, NY), 2004.

Linda Arms White, *I Could Do That! Esther Morris Gets Women the Vote,* Farrar, Straus, & Giroux (New York, NY), 2005.

Jenny Offill, *Seventeen Things I'm Not Allowed to Do Anymore,* Schwartz & Wade Books (New York, NY), 2007.

Linda Ashman, *M Is for Mischief: An A to Z of Naughty Children,* Dutton (New York, NY), 2008.

Sidelights

Nancy Carpenter is an award-winning illustrator of books for young readers that include works by such acclaimed authors as Naomi Shihab Nye, Jane Yolen, Virginia Kroll, Karen Hesse, and Jenny Offill. A former illustrator for the *New York Times,* Carpenter made her picture-book debut in 1990, providing the artwork for Sharon Phillips Denslow's *At Taylor's Place.* Carpenter has garnered praise from critics for her ability to work in a variety of mediums; her illustrations incorporate oil paint, colored pencil, pen and ink, and digital imagery. "I'm not sure I'm capable of doing one style," Carpenter told Joy Bean in a *Publishers Weekly Online* interview. "I gravitate to manuscripts that challenge me so I can try something new each time. It keeps me fresh."

Carpenter served as the illustrator for Anna Quindlen's debut picture book *The Tree That Came to Stay,* a tale about the perfect Christmas tree. According to *Publishers Weekly* contributor Elizabeth Devereaux, "Carpenter's tranquil, dreamy pictures radiate goodwill." In *Masai and I,* a title by Kroll, an African-American schoolgirl wonders about life in East Africa, where the Masai tribe lives. "The artwork, realistic and warm, portrays a joyful girl who feels 'the tingle of kinship' with the Masai culture," observed another *Publishers Weekly* reviewer.

In *Lester's Dog,* a work by Hesse, a young boy must overcome his fear of a vicious neighborhood dog to rescue a stray kitten. With the help of a hearing-impaired friend, Corey musters the necessary courage to complete the good deed and brighten the day of a lonely widower. Carpenter's "ability to capture expressions infuses the pictures with vitality," wrote Mary M. Burns

in *Horn Book.* When their regular bus driver undergoes surgery, a group of schoolchildren are treated to a host of wacky substitutes in Sharon Phillips Denslow's *Bus Riders.* Here Carpenter's artwork, done in oils and pencil, again drew notice; the illustrator "has a command of page design and perspective, allowing the reader both to ride inside the bus and to view it from the outside," Bush noted.

In a more serious work, Nye's *Sitti's Secrets,* a young Arab-American girl recalls fond memories of a family visit to her grandmother's Palestinian village. Maeve Visser Knoth, writing in *Horn Book,* noted that the author's "simple sentences are dotted with imagery that is often picked up in the illustrations." According to *Booklist* contributor Hazel Rochman, Carpenter's "pictures flow with soft curving lines of clothes and hills, birds and sky, all part of the circle of the rolling earth." Carpenter and Nye have also collaborated on *Baby Radar,* a rhyming tale about a toddler who can only view the world from his stroller. "Carpenter's loose-line watercolor-and-ink illustrations are the high point of this playfully conceived picture book," a *Publishers Weekly* critic wrote, and a contributor in *Kirkus Reviews* noted that in *Baby Radar* the illustrator offers a child's-eye view of the sights "from low angles in sketchy, wonderfully accurate lines and vigorously brushed watercolors."

Jacqueline Briggs Martin looks at the aftereffects of an ecological disaster—an oil spill—in *Washing the Willow Tree Loon.* Carpenter's "lovely double-page oil paintings" for this book "make fine use of color to cast changing light on sky and water," remarked Bush. In Kroll's *Can You Dance, Dalila?* an active young girl grows frustrated after she fails in her attempts to perform a fox-trot, a jig, and a ballet. When Dalila attends a performance of a West African dance troupe, however, she finds her true calling. Carpenter's "joyful oil paintings express the movement and playfulness of all the dancing," Rochman stated. Sibling rivalry is the subject of *Twinnies,* a work by Eve Bunting. Although a youngster at first finds herself overshadowed by her twin baby sisters, she slowly warms to the new additions to her family. "Carpenter's oil paintings of butter yellow and sky blue have a timeless quality," observed a contributor in *Publishers Weekly.* Carpenter has more-recently teamed with Bunting on *Little Bear's Little Boat,* a tale about a gentle creature that outgrows his favorite sailing vessel. Writing in *Booklist,* Gillian Engberg noted that Carpenter's "charming ink-and-paint illustrations . . . echo the spare clarity of the words."

Set in 1850s New England, *Loud Emily,* a tall tale by Alexis O'Neill, centers on a little girl with a booming voice. After running away from Miss Meekmeister's School for Soft-spoken Girls, Emily proves her worth by saving a ship's crew during a storm. "Carpenter's exuberant oil paintings are in the folk-art styles of the period," Rochman stated, and a *Publishers Weekly* critic noted that "the compositions also integrate a crackled

paint effect that make them look authentically aged." In Kathi Appelt's *Someone's Come to Our House,* a work told in verse, a family throws a special homecoming celebration for a new baby. A *Publishers Weekly* reviewer commented that Carpenter's "robust art" prevents the tale from becoming too sentimental. "Bustling with energy, the illustrations convey a host of lifelike scenarios unfolding throughout the party," the critic stated.

After spotting a funnel cloud, a rural family seeks shelter from the storm in Darleen Bailey Beard's *Twister.* Here "Carpenter's stormy chalklike illustrations are filled with wild movement against the dark sky as the people fight the wind and shout and scream and see one another through," Rochman wrote, and a *Publishers Weekly* critic stated that her illustrations of the family members "have an emotional pull, showing the kids' move from playful to fearful to thankful as the ordeal begins and ends." A young boy learns a valuable lesson about patriotism in Bunting's *A Picnic in October.* Although at first Tony grumbles about spending his grandma's birthday on blustery Ellis Island, he forms a different opinion after spotting a new immigrant family making a visit to the Statue of Liberty. Ilene Cooper, writing in *Booklist,* complimented Carpenter's illustrations for *A Picnic in October,* calling them "vibrant with sea and sky blues," and a reviewer in *Publishers Weekly* noted that the illustrator "captures a touch of the 'huddled masses' as she depicts crowds" in New York City.

In *Brooklyn, Bugsy, and Me,* a work of historical fiction by Lynea Bowdish, nine-year-old Sam moves with his widowed mother from West Virginia to Brooklyn. Once there, Sam must adjust to living with his sometimes grouchy grandfather, known as Bugsy to his neighbors. According to *Booklist* reviewer Connie Fletcher, Carpenter's pictures "add a nice touch to this funny and touching chapter-book retake on Brooklyn in the 1950s." Barbara Ann Porte's chapter book *If You Ever Get Lost: The Adventures of Julia and Evan* collects nine short tales about a pair of energetic siblings. Carpenter's "playful black-and-white sketches" for Porte's stories earned applause from *School Library Journal* critic Linda L. Plevak.

Deborah Hopkinson offers a humorous take on a celebrated nineteenth-century cook in *Fannie in the Kitchen: The Whole Story from Soup to Nuts of How Fannie Farmer Invented Recipes with Precise Measurements.* In the story, a spunky youngster who is a disaster in the kitchen learns how to prepare meals under the tutelage of Miss Farmer. To create the illustrations, Carpenter digitally combined her own pen-and-ink drawings with period engravings. "Her scenes wittily spoof Victorian decorum," wrote a *Publishers Weekly* critic, and in the opinion of *Booklist* reviewer Shelle Rosenfeld, "the collage artwork is exceptional—elegant as well as whimsical." Inspired by the life of Oregon nursery owner Henderson Luelling, Hopkinson's *Apples to*

Oregon: Being the (Slightly) True Narrative of How a Brave Pioneer Father Brought Apples, Peaches, Pears, Plums, Grapes, and Cherries (and Children) across the Plains follows the often comic adventures of a pioneer family traveling the Oregon Trail. "Amusing details abound," commented Roxanne Burg in her School Library Journal review of the book, and the slightly exaggerated humor of the pictures is in perfect balance with the tone of the text."

In A Far-fetched Story, a picture book by Karin Cates, the members of Grandmother's family fail to convince her that gathering wood can be a dangerous task. Carpenter's original pen, ink, and watercolor drawings were ironed onto white linen; according to a contributor in Kirkus Reviews, "the coloration and patterns in paisleys and plaids piece together this cozy and fetching story, one that is a delightful fabrication."

In a biographical work, Abe Lincoln: The Boy Who Loved Books by Kay Winters, the author depicts events from the sixteenth president's childhood and adolescence, highlighting his love of literature. "Frontier life unfolds in warm earth-toned shades," observed a Publishers Weekly critic, who added that in Abe Lincoln Carpenter "sets a brisk pace by interspersing smaller vignettes with full-bleed vistas." Another biography, Linda Arms White's I Could Do That! Esther Morris Gets Women the Vote, tells the story of the Wyoming suffragist who became the first woman to hold public office in the United States. According to Lucinda Snyder Whitehurst, writing in School Library Journal, "Carpenter's bright, lively chalk illustrations contribute to the cheerful, fast-paced tone of the story."

In Seventeen Things I'm Not Allowed to Do Anymore, Offill's first book for young readers, a seemingly repentant young girl offers a list of her past transgressions, including stapling her brother's hair to his pillow and dropping flies in the ice cube tray. Carpenter's mixed-media illustrations, a collage of pen-and-ink drawings and photographic elements, bring "depth and texture to each spread," Catherine Threadgill stated in School Library Journal. "Kids will be intrigued by the pictures' playful sense of composition," predicted a Publishers Weekly critic.

Biographical and Critical Sources

PERIODICALS

Booklist, March 15, 1994, Hazel Rochman, review of Sitti's Secrets, p. 1374; October 15, 1996, Ilene Cooper, review of Only a Star, p. 426; November 15, 1996, Hazel Rochman, review of Can You Dance, Dalila?, p. 594; September 15, 1997, Ilene Cooper, review of Twinnies, p. 240; October 15, 1998, Hazel Rochman, review of Loud Emily, p. 428; October 15, 1999, Ilene Cooper, review of A Picnic in October, p. 450; Febru-

ary 15, 2000, Connie Fletcher, review of Brooklyn, Bugsy, and Me, p. 1110; February 1, 1999, Hazel Rochman, review of Twister, p. 979; June 1, 2000, Carolyn Phelan, review of If You Ever Get Lost: The Adventures of Julia and Evan, p. 1897; May 15, 2001, Shelle Rosenfeld, review of Fannie in the Kitchen: The Whole Story from Soup to Nuts of How Fannie Farmer Invented Recipes with Precise Measurements, p. 1751; February 15, 2002, Ilene Cooper, review of A Far-fetched Story, p. 1019; January 1, 2003, Kay Weisman, review of Abe Lincoln: The Boy Who Loved Books, p. 901; August, 2003, Gillian Engberg, review of Little Bear's Little Boat, p. 1987; September 15, 2003, Hazel Rochman, review of Baby Radar, p. 239; September 1, 2004, Kay Weisman, review of Apples to Oregon: Being the (Slightly) True Narrative of How a Brave Pioneer Father Brought Apples, Peaches, Pears, Plums, Grapes, and Cherries (and Children) across the Plains, p. 132; September 15, 2005, Jennifer Mattson, review of I Could Do That! Esther Morris Gets Women the Vote, p. 63.

Horn Book, May-June, 1993, Margaret A. Bush, review of Bus Riders, p. 315; March-April, 1994, Mary M. Burns, review of Lester's Dog, p. 190; May-June, 1994, Maeve Visser Knoth, review of Sitti's Secrets, p. 317; September-October, 1995, Margaret A. Bush, review of Washing the Willow Tree Loon, p. 591.

Kirkus Reviews, December 1, 2001, review of A Far-fetched Story, p. 1682; November 15, 2002, review of Abe Lincoln, p. 1703; May 15, 2003, review of Little Bear's Little Boat, p. 747; August 1, 2003, review of Baby Radar, p. 1021; August 15, 2004, review of Apples to Oregon, p. 807; August 15, 2005, review of I Could Do That!, p. 924; December 1, 2006, review of Seventeen Things I'm not Allowed to Do Anymore, p. 1224

Publishers Weekly, June 29, 1992, review of Masai and I, p. 62; September 7, 1992, Elizabeth Devereaux, review of The Tree That Came to Stay, p. 68; August 30, 1993, review of Lester's Dog, p. 95; September 30, 1996, review of Only a Star, p. 89; July 21, 1997, review of Twinnies, p. 201; September 28, 1998, review of Loud Emily, p. 100; May 31, 1999, review of Someone's Come to Our House, p. 86; November 29, 1999, review of A Picnic in October, p. 70; April 23, 2001, review of Fannie in the Kitchen, p. 77; December 10, 2001, review of A Far-fetched Story, p. 70; November 25, 2002, review of Abe Lincoln, p. 67; April 21, 2003, review of Little Bear's Little Boat, p. 61; September 29, 2003, review of Baby Radar, p. 63; August 30, 2004, review of Apples to Oregon, p. 53; October 30, 2006, review of Seventeen Things I'm Not Allowed to Do Anymore, p. 60.

School Library Journal, June, 2000, Pat Leach, review of Brooklyn, Bugsy, and Me, p. 102; July, 2000, Linda L. Plevak, review of If You Ever Get Lost, p. 86; May, 2001, Genevieve Ceraldi, review of Fannie in the Kitchen, p. 143; January, 2002, Susan Hepler, review of A Far-fetched Story, p. 95; August, 2003, Be Astengo, review of Little Bear's Little Boat, p. 124; September, 2003, Diane S. Marton, review of Baby Radar, p. 186; September, 2004, Roxanne Burg, review of Apples to Oregon, p. 162; September, 2005, Lu-

cinda Snyder Whitehurst, review of *I Could Do That!*, p. 197; November, 2006, Catherine Threadgill, review of *Seventeen Things I'm Not Allowed to Do Anymore*, p. 107.

ONLINE

Houghton Mifflin Reading, http://www.eduplace.com/kids/hmr/ (March 1, 2008), "Meet the Illustrator: Nancy Carpenter."

Monster.com, http://midcareer.monster.com/qanda/bookillustrator/ (March 1, 2008), Eileen O'Reilly, "Job Q&A: Nancy Carpenter."

Powells.com, http://www.powells.com/ (March 1, 2008), "Powells.com Ink Q&A: Jenny Offill and Nancy Carpenter."

Publishers Weekly Online, http://www.publishersweekly.com/ (November 16, 2006), Joy Bean, "Children's Bookshelf Talks with Nancy Carpenter."*

*   *   *

CARPENTER, Nancy Sippel
See CARPENTER, Nancy

*   *   *

CEPEDA, Joe

Personal

Born in Los Angeles, CA; married; children: one son. *Education:* California State University, Long Beach, B.F.A. (illustration), 1992; attended Cornell University.

Addresses

Home—Whittier, CA. *E-mail*—joe@joecepeda.com.

Career

Commercial artist and illustrator. Clients include Health Net, Hilton Hotels, Land's End, and Unocal. Lecturer at schools. Presenter at schools and conferences. *Exhibitions:* Works included in exhibitions at Every Picture Tells a Story, Los Angeles, CA, and at Society of Illustrators shows in New York, NY, and Los Angeles.

Member

Graphic Artist's Guild.

Awards, Honors

American Bookseller Pick of the Lists selection, 1996, for *Gracias, the Thanksgiving Turkey* by Joy Cowley; *Family Life* Top Ten Best Books selection, *Family Fun* magazine Critic's Choice designation, and *Bulletin of the Center for Children's Books* Blue Ribbon selection, all 1999, all for *What a Truly Cool World* by Julius

Lester; Recognition of Merit Award, George G. Stone Center for Children's Books, 2000; Pura Belpré Honor Award, 2002, for *Juan Bobo Goes to Work* by Marisa Montes.

Writings

SELF-ILLUSTRATED

The Swing, Arthur A. Levine Books (New York, NY), 2006.

ILLUSTRATOR

Gary Soto, *The Cat's Meow,* Scholastic, Inc. (New York, NY), 1995.

Gary Soto, *The Old Man and His Door,* G.P. Putnam's Sons (New York, NY), 1996.

Joy Cowley, *Gracias, the Thanksgiving Turkey,* Scholastic Press (New York, NY), 1996.

Carolivia Herron, *Nappy Hair,* Knopf (New York, NY), 1997.

Caryn Yacowitz, *Pumpkin Fiesta,* HarperCollins (New York, NY), 1998.

Gary Soto, *Big Bushy Mustache,* Knopf (New York, NY), 1998.

Liesel Moak Skorpen, *We Were Tired of Living in a House,* G.P. Putnam's Sons (New York, NY), 1999.

Verna Aardema, *Koi and the Kola Nuts: A Tale from Liberia,* Atheneum Books for Young Readers (New York, NY), 1999.

Julius Lester, *What a Truly Cool World,* Scholastic, Inc. (New York, NY), 1999.

Marisa Montes, *Juan Bobo Goes to Work: A Puerto Rican Folktale,* Morrow Junior Books (New York, NY), 2000.

Kristi T. Butler, *Rip's Secret Spot,* Green Light Readers/Harcourt (San Diego, CA), 2000.

John Coy, *Vroomaloom Zoom,* Crown Publishers (New York, NY), 2000.

Judy Giglio, *The Tapping Tale,* Green Light Readers/Harcourt (San Diego, CA), 2000.

Roni Schotter, *Captain Bob Sets Sail,* Atheneum Books for Young Readers (New York, NY), 2000.

Arnold Adoff, *Daring Dog and Captain Cat,* Simon & Schuster Books for Young Readers (New York, NY), 2001.

Pam Muñoz Ryan, *Mice and Beans,* Scholastic, Inc. (New York, NY), 2001.

Julius Lester, *Why Heaven Is Far Away,* Scholastic, Inc. (New York, NY), 2002.

Elizabeth Swados, *Hey You! Come Here!,* Arthur A. Levine Books (New York, NY), 2002.

Darcy Pattison, *The Journey of Oliver K. Woodman,* Harcourt (San Diego, CA), 2003.

Roni Schotter, *Captain Bob Takes Flight,* Atheneum Books for Young Readers (New York, NY), 2003.

Eliza Thomas, *The Red Blanket,* Scholastic, Inc. (New York, NY), 2004.

Robert L. McKissack, *Try Your Best,* Harcourt (Orlando, FL), 2004.

Darcy Pattison, *Searching for Oliver K. Woodman,* Harcourt (Orlando, FL), 2005.

Gail Gauthier, *A Girl, a Boy, and a Monster Cat,* G.P. Putnam's Sons (New York, NY), 2007.

Susan Middleton Elya and Merry Banks, *N Is for Navidad,* Chronicle Books (San Francisco, CA), 2007.

Gail Gauthier, *A Girl, a Boy, and Three Robbers,* G.P. Putnam's Sons (New York, NY), 2008.

Toni Morrison and Slade Morrison, *Peeny Butter Fudge,* Simon & Schuster Books for Young Readers (New York, NY), 2009.

Contributor of illustrations to periodicals, including *American Prospect, Latina, Buzz, Los Angeles Times,* and *Hispanic Business.*

ILLUSTRATOR; "GOLDEN HAMSTER SAGA" SERIES BY DIETLOF REICHE

I, Freddy, translated by John Brownjohn, Scholastic, Inc. (New York, NY), 2003.

Freddy in Peril, translated by John Brownjohn, Scholastic, Inc. (New York, NY), 2004.

Julius Lester's unusual porquoi story is enhanced by Joe Cepeda's artwork in **Why Heaven Is Far Away.** (Illustration copyright © 2002 by Joe Cepeda. Reproduced by permission of Scholastic, Inc.)

Freddy to the Rescue, translated by John Brownjohn, Scholastic, Inc. (New York, NY), 2005.

The Haunting of Freddy, translated by John Brownjohn, Scholastic Press (New York, NY), 2006.

Freddy's Final Quest, translated by John Brownjohn, Scholastic Press (New York, NY), 2007.

ILLUSTRATOR; "GET READY FOR GABI!" SERIES BY MARISA MONTES

A Crazy Mixed-up Spanglish Day, Scholastic, Inc. (New York, NY), 2003.

Who's That Girl?, Scholastic, Inc. (New York, NY), 2003.

Please Don't Go!, Scholastic, Inc. (New York, NY), 2004.

No More Spanish, Scholastic, Inc. (New York, NY), 2004.

Sidelights

A California-based commercial artist whose work has appeared in numerous magazines and client publications, Joe Cepeda has also established himself as a respected picture-book illustrator by contributing to books by authors such as Gary Soto, Darcy Pattison, Robert L. McKissack, Julius Lester, and Toni Morrison. Using oils, water color, and acrylics, he also enlivens German writer Dietlof Reiche's multi-volume "Golden Hamster Saga" and brings to life the adventures of a spunky Puerto Rican-American heroine in Marisa Montes' upbeat chapter-book series "Get Ready for Gabi!" The versatile artist also creates pen-and-ink cartoons for Gail Gauthier's *A Girl, a Boy, and a Monster Cat,* "add[ing] just the right touch" to the chapter book, according to *Horn Book* critic Robin L. Smith. In addition, Cepeda also illustrates his own story in *The Swing,* introducing an absent-minded family and a little girl's surprising discovery in a picture book that *School Library Journal* contributor Catherine Threadgill dubbed a "kid-friendly flight of fancy."

Notable among Cepeda's picture-book works are Soto's *Big Bushy Mustache* and Lester's *What a Truly Cool World,* the latter which presents a version of the creation tale about how God created the world. Based on a narrative collected by Zora Neale Hurston, the story first appeared in Lester's 1969 book *Black Folktales,* but the author's fresh spin and Cepeda's brightly colored illustrations update it for a new generation of readers. Praising his "vivid palette" and inclusion of "hip" elements, a *Publishers Weekly* contributor wrote that the illustrator adds "a funky dimension to [Lester's] . . . playfully outlandish depiction of how the world came to be." Cepeda's depiction of "soaring vistas and wonderful pinks, purples, greens and golds" in *What a Truly Cool World* might cause readers to "almost believe they were seeing colors for the first time," added Ilene Cooper in *Booklist.* Praising the illustrations Cepeda creates for Soto's *Big Bushy Mustache,* Michael Cart noted in *Booklist* that the artist's "vibrantly colored" works "find and expand the heart and the humor" of Soto's text.

Cepeda creates the colorful acrylic paintings that highlight Carolivia Herron's picture book **Nappy Hair.** (Illustration copyright © 1997 by Joe Cepeda. Used by permission of Alfred A. Knopf, an imprint of Random House Children's Books, a division of Random House, Inc.)

In addition to working with well-known writers such as Lester and Soto, Cepeda has been paired with first-time picture-book writers such as Carolivia Herron, whose *Nappy Hair* he illustrated in 1997. A rhythmic tale about a young black girl named Brenda, who has amazingly curly hair, Herron's book contains several story threads that a *Publishers Weekly* contributor noted could confuse some readers. According to the critic, the illustrator's "vibrant paintings help pull together the text's disparate strands" and reinforce the personality of the main character, Brenda. "Cepeda's vibrant, folk-art style paintings in *Nappy Hair* have a strong sense of color, form, and design," added *Booklist* reviewer Julie Corsaro.

Many of Cepeda's picture-book credits reference texts with Latino themes. In *Pumpkin Fiesta,* for example, Caryn Yacowitz's story about Old Juana's success at growing the largest pumpkin in town despite a neighbor's efforts to sabotage her success is enlivened by what a *Publishers Weekly* contributor described as Cepeda's "festive palette" and his creation of "energetic, slightly skewed characters" that encourage readers to turn the page. In *Mice and Beans,* a story by Pam Muñoz Ryan about Rosa Maria's preparations for her grandchild's seventh birthday and the mice who take their small share, "Cepeda adds detail and expression to the smallest objects," according to Mary Elam in *School*

Library Journal. In *Kirkus Reviews* a critic noted that the artist's "color-drenched scenes stuffed with detail make Rosa Maria's world a pleasure-giving place." Cepeda's "lively paintings take a colorful, dynamic look at a warm Latino neighborhood celebration," asserted Anne Connor in her *School Library Journal* review of Susan Middleton Elya and Merry Banks' bilingual picture book *N Is for Navidad.*

Cepeda's contribution to Montes' picture book *Juan Bobo Goes to Work: A Puerto Rican Folktale* earned critical praise as well as the 2002 Pura Belpré honor award for illustration. *Juan Bobo Goes to Work* finds a clumsy young man unable to hold a job for long, and when he does find work, he ultimately loses the day's pay. When his foolish antics cause a wealthy man's daughter to laugh, Juan discovers his true talent and receives a lasting payment—in the form of a large ham that will not slip through his fingers. "Cepeda's illustrations steal the show," announced *School Library Journal* reviewer Grace Oliff, the critic adding that the title character in *Juan Bobo Goes to Work* comes alive as "endearing" rather than foolish.

A Crazy Mixed-up Spanglish Day, Who's That Girl?, Please Don't Go!, and *No More Spanish* treat readers to the company of the engaging young girl that stars in Montes' "Get Ready for Gabi" series. *A Crazy Mixed-up Spanglish Day* finds Gabi switching from English to Spanish between school and home, resulting in both humor and confusion, while in *Who's That Girl?* Gabi befriends a new girl in her neighborhood. "Cepeda's pen-and-ink drawings" for *A Crazy Mixed-up Spanglish Day* "have the same energy" as Montes' upbeat story, asserted Cooper in *Booklist,* and a *Kirkus Reviews* writer described the artwork for *Who's That Girl?* as "wry, emotive, and . . . a bit exaggerated," all in keeping with the imaginative Gabi.

Beginning with *I, Freddy,* Reiche's quick-typing hamster protagonist tells the story of his life cohabiting with a succession of humans, his friendships with a household cat named Sir William and the sometimes annoying pet guinea pigs Enrico and Caruso, and his desire to read and write. Describing Cepeda's illustrations for *I, Freddy* as "spare yet comical," a *Publishers Weekly* reviewer added that the illustrator's "line art reveals endearing views of Freddy and some inventive shots of his surroundings."

Pattison's picture books *The Journey of Oliver K. Woodman* and its sequel, *Searching for Oliver K. Woodman,* allow Cepeda a great deal of creative latitude. In the first volume, the text is composed entirely of the letters and postcards sent by the many people who help a wooden doll travel from a North Carolina woodworker named Uncle Ray to Ray's twelve-year-old niece, Tameka Schwarz, in California. Beginning with a map of the United States, Cepeda follows the doll's journey as it is aided by what *Horn Book* reviewer Barbara Bader dubbed a series of "good-natured caricatures"

Gail Gauthier's middle-grade novel **A Girl, a Boy, and Three Robbers** *is brought to life in Cepeda's cartoon art.* (Illustration copyright © 2008 by Joe Cepeda. Reproduced by permission of G.P. Putnam's Sons, a division of Penguin Putnam Books for Young Readers.)

ranging from elderly tourists to farmers to teen travelers. In *Booklist* Shelle Rosenfeld called Cepeda's oil-over-acrylic paintings "vibrant, textured, rainbow-hued, with a mostly cheerful multicultured cast," and Bader praised the artistry in *The Journey of Oliver K. Woodman* as "virtuoso narrative illustration." The doll's disappearance is the focus of *Searching for Oliver K. Woodman*, as Uncle Ray and a private investigator attempt to locate the missing Oliver. Here Cepeda's paintings "fairly fizz with energy and good humor," according to a *Kirkus Reviews* writer.

In an interview for the Harcourt Web site, Cepeda discussed his illustration technique and his characteristic use of bold, saturated colors. "I begin by preparing an illustration board by applying an acrylic gesso, then a light umber mid-tone, then transferring my drawing," he explained. "Then I paint all the shapes and images in arbitrary color, in acrylic. Next, when I begin to use oil paint, I will purposely allow some of that acrylic to show through. As an example, on the jacket [of *The Journey of Oliver K. Woodman*] there is an ochre color in the sky and around the clouds that I let come through.

The blue lines that delineate Oliver are actually the blue acrylic under-painting that's allowed to show through in the form of line. The texture just develops with the several layers of paint and my brush handling."

"I paint color in a very responsive way. I try and plan as little as possible. When I do the under-paintings in arbitrary color I see some very unusual combinations, blue trees, purple faces, orange mountains, etc. As I start to apply the oils there are unexpected colors all over the place. I respond to that by trying make the 'logical' color I might be applying be in harmony with whatever is random. Most of the time it's bright and vibrant!"

Biographical and Critical Sources

PERIODICALS

Booklist, February 1, 1997, Julie Corsaro, review of *Nappy Hair,* p. 946; June 1, 1998, Michael Cart, review of *Big Bushy Mustache,* p. 1784; February 15, 1999, Ilene Cooper, review of *What a Truly Cool World,* p. 1076; March 15, 1999, Carolyn Phelan, review of *We Were Tired of Living in a House,* p. 1334; October 15, 1999, Linda Perkins, review of *Koi and the Kola Nuts: A Tale from Liberia,* p. 447; December 1, 2000, Ilene Cooper, review of *Vroomaloom Zoom,* p. 717; February 1, 2001, Linda Perkins, review of *Juan Bobo Goes to Work: A Puerto Rican Folktale,* p. 1057; October 1, 2002, John Green, review of *Why Heaven Is Far Away,* p. 345; April 1, 2003, Shelle Rosenfeld, review of *The Journey of Oliver K. Woodman,* p. 1403; April 1, 2003, Kay Weisman, review of *I, Freddy,* p. 1398; September 1, 2003, Ilene Cooper, review of *A Crazy Mixed-up Spanglish Day,* p. 121; May 15, 2004, Hazel Rochman, review of *The Red Blanket,* p. 1627; July 1, 2009, Daniel Kraus, review of *Peeny Butter Fudge,* p. 68.

Childhood Education, spring, 2002, Jeanie Burnett, review of *Mice and Beans,* p. 173.

Horn Book, March, 1999, Margaret A. Bush, review of *What a Truly Cool World,* p. 196; November-December, 2002, Joanna Rudge Long, review of *Why Heaven Is Far Away,* p. 735; May-June, 2003, Barbara Bader, review of *The Journey of Oliver K. Woodman,* p. 333; November-December, 2007, Jennifer M. Brabander, review of *N Is for Navidad,* p. 628; September-October, 2008, Robin Smith, review of *A Girl, a Boy, and Three Robbers,* p. 582.

Kirkus Reviews, August 1, 2001, review of *Mice and Beans,* p. 1131; August 15, 2001, review of *Daring Dog and Captain Cat,* p. 1206; February 1, 2002, review of *Hey You! C'mere: A Poetry Slam,* p. 190; March 1, 2003, review of *The Journey of Oliver K. Woodman,* p. 394; March 15, 2003, review of *Captain Bob Takes Flight,* p. 478; March 15, 2003, review of *A Crazy Mixed-up Spanglish Day,* p. 473; May 15, 2003, review of *I, Freddy,* p. 756; August 1, 2003, review of *Who's That Girl?,* p. 1020; November, 2003,

Terrie Dorio, review of *A Crazy Mixed-up Spanglish Day,* p. 110; March 15, 2004, review of *Try Your Best,* p. 274; April 1, 2004, review of *Freddy in Peril,* p. 336; January 15, 2005, review of *Searching for Oliver K. Woodman,* p. 124; August 15, 2006, review of *The Swing,* p. 837.

Newsweek, December 1, 1997, Malcolm Jones, Jr., review of *Nappy Hair,* p. 78.

Publishers Weekly, January 6, 1997, review of *Nappy Hair,* p. 72; July 13, 1998, review of *Pumpkin Fiesta,* p. 76; January 4, 1999, review of *What a Truly Cool World,* p. 89; April 12, 1999, review of *We Were Tired of Living in a House,* p. 73; May 8, 2000, review of *Captain Bob Sets Sail,* p. 220; November 6, 2000, review of *Vroomaloom Zoom,* p. 90; September 24, 2001, review of *Daring Dog and Captain Cat,* p. 93; February 18, 2002, review of *Hey You! C'mere,* p. 97; November 25, 2002, review of *Koi and the Kola Nuts,* p. 71; January 20, 2003, Darcy Patitson, review of *The Journey of Oliver K. Woodman,* p. 82; April 7, 2003, review of *A Crazy Mixed-up Spanglish Day,* p. 66; May 26, 2003, review of *I, Freddy,* p. 70; May 31, 2004, review of *The Red Blanket,* p. 73; January 17, 2005, review of *Searching for Oliver K. Woodman,* p. 55.

School Library Journal, August, 2000, Nancy J. Fuster, review of *The Tapping Tale,* p. 154; October, 2000, Grace Oliff, review of *Juan Bobo Goes to Work: A Puerto Rican Folktale,* p. 150; October, 2000, Sheilah Kosco, review of *Vroomaloom Zoom,* p. 119; October, 2000, Joyce Rice, review of *Rip's Secret Spot,* p. 112; September, 2001, Nina Lindsay, review of *Daring Dog and Captain Cat,* p. 182; October, 2001, Mary Elam, review of *Mice and Beans,* p. 130; April, 2002, Nina Lindsay, review of *Hey You! C'Mere,* p. 141; October, 2002, Miriam Lang Budin, review of *Why Heaven Is Far Away,* p. 118; April, 2003, Kathleen Simonetta, review of *The Journey of Oliver K. Woodman,* p. 134; May, 2003, Nancy A. Gifford, review of *Captain Bob Takes Flight,* p. 129; November, 2003, Elaine E. Knight, review of *I, Freddy,* p. 113; May, 2004, Kristina Aaronson, review of *Try Your Best,* p. 119; May, 2005, Maryann H. Owen, review of *Searching for Oliver K. Woodman,* p. 94; September, 2005, Elizabeth Bird, review of *Freddy to the Rescue,* p. 185; October, 2006, Catherine Threadgill, review of *The Swing,* p. 103; October, 2007, Anne Connor, review of *N Is for Navidad,* p. 97; November, 2008, Sharon R. Pearce, review of *A Girl, a Boy, and Three Robbers,* p. 88; September, 2009, Meg Smith, review of *Peeny Butter Fudge,* p. 130.

ONLINE

Harcourt Web site, http://www.harcourtbooks.com/ (April 25, 2010), interview with Cepeda.

Joe Cepeda Web site, http://www.joecepeda.com (April 25, 2010).

Scholastic Web site, http://www2.scholastic.com/ (April 25, 2010).*

CHORAO, Kay 1936-

Personal

Surname pronounced "shoe-row"; born January 7, 1936, in Elkhart, IN; daughter of James McKay (a lawyer) and Elizabeth Sproat; married Ernesto A.K. Chorao (an artist), June 10, 1960; children: Jamie, Peter, Ian. *Education:* Wheaton College, B.A., 1958; graduate study at Chelsea School of Art, 1958-59; studied book illustration at School of Visual Arts, 1966-68.

Addresses

Home—New York, NY; (summer) Box 644, Jamesport, NY 11947.

Career

Artist, illustrator, and author of children's books. Freelance art work includes educational filmstrips and a television commercial. *Exhibitions:* Work exhibited at Montclair Museum, 1991-92; Art Association of Jacksonville/ David Strawn Art Gallery, 1993; and in several American Institute of Graphic Arts and Society of Illustrators exhibitions.

Awards, Honors

Best Book citation, *School Library Journal,* 1973, for *A Magic Eye for Ida;* certificate of excellence, American Institute of Graphic Arts, 1974, for *Ralph and the Queen's Bathtub;* American Library Association Notable Book citation, and Society of Illustrators Certificate of Merit, both 1974, and Children's Book Showcase title, 1975, all for *Albert's Toothache;* Communicating with Children Award, 1976, for *Henrietta, the Wild Woman of Borneo;* Society of Illustrators Certificate of Merit, 1976, for *Clyde Monster;* Christopher Award, 1979, for *Chester Chipmunk's Thanksgiving,* and 1988, for *The Good-bye Book;* Ten Best Books inclusion, *New York Times,* 1988, for *Cathedral Mouse;* Notable Books for Children citation, *Smithsonian* magazine, 1998, for *Little Farm by the Sea;* numerous other writing awards.

Writings

SELF-ILLUSTRATED; FOR CHILDREN

The Repair of Uncle Toe, Farrar, Straus (New York, NY), 1972.

A Magic Eye for Ida, Seabury Press (New York, NY), 1973.

Ralph and the Queen's Bathtub, Farrar, Straus (New York, NY), 1974.

Ida Makes a Movie, Seabury Press (New York, NY), 1974.

Maudie's Umbrella, Dutton (New York, NY), 1975.

Molly's Moe, Seabury Press (New York, NY), 1976.

Lester's Overnight, Dutton (New York, NY), 1977.

(Adapter) *The Baby's Lap Book* (nursery rhymes), Dutton (New York, NY), 1977, with color illustrations, 1990.

Molly's Lies, Seabury Press (New York, NY), 1979.

Oink and Pearl, Harper (New York, NY), 1981.

Kate's Car, Dutton (New York, NY), 1982.

Kate's Box, Dutton (New York, NY), 1982.

Kate's Quilt, Dutton (New York, NY), 1982.

Kate's Snowman, Dutton (New York, NY), 1982.

Lemon Moon, Holiday House (New York, NY), 1983.

(Compiler) *The Baby's Bedtime Book* (poems and rhymes), Dutton (New York, NY), 1984.

(Adapter) *The Baby's Story Book,* Dutton (New York, NY), 1985.

Ups and Downs with Oink and Pearl, Harper (New York, NY), 1985.

(Compiler) *The Baby's Good Morning Book* (poems and rhymes), Dutton (New York, NY), 1986.

George Told Kate, Dutton (New York, NY), 1987.

(Adapter) *The Child's Story Book* (fairy tales), Dutton (New York, NY), 1987.

Cathedral Mouse, Dutton (New York, NY), 1988.

The Cherry Pie Baby, Dutton (New York, NY), 1989.

(Adapter) *The Child's Fairy Tale Book,* Dutton (New York, NY), 1990.

(Compiler) *Baby's Christmas Treasury* (poems, stories, and songs), Random House (New York, NY), 1991.

Ida and Betty and the Secret Eggs, Clarion Books (New York, NY), 1991.

(Compiler) *Mother Goose Magic,* Dutton (New York, NY), 1992.

Annie and Cousin Precious, Dutton (New York, NY), 1994.

Rock, Rock, My Baby, Random House (New York, NY), 1994.

Peekaboo! Was It You?, Random House (New York, NY), 1994.

Carousel Round and Round, Clarion Books (New York, NY), 1995.

(Editor) *The Book of Giving: Poems of Thanks, Praise, and Celebration,* Dutton (New York, NY), 1995.

Number One Number Fun, Holiday House (New York, NY), 1995.

(Adapter) *Christmas Story,* Holiday House (New York, NY), 1996.

(Compiler) *Jumpety-Bumpety Hop: A Parade of Animal Poems,* Dutton (New York, NY), 1997.

The Cats Kids, Holiday House (New York, NY), 1998.

Little Farm by the Sea, Holt (New York, NY), 1998.

Knock at the Door and Other Baby Action Rhymes, Dutton (New York, NY), 1999.

Pig and Crow, Holt (New York, NY), 2000.

Here Comes Kate, Dutton (New York, NY), 2000.

Shadow Night: A Picture Book with Shadow Play, Dutton (New York, NY), 2001.

Up and down with Kate, Dutton (New York, NY), 2002.

Grayboy, Holt (New York, NY), 2002.

The Baby's Book of Baby Animals, Dutton (New York, NY), 2004.

D Is for Drum: A Colonial Williamsburg ABC, Harry Abrams (New York, NY), 2004.

(Compiler) *The Baby's Playtime Book,* Dutton Children's Books (New York, NY), 2006.

(Compiler) *Rhymes 'round the World,* Dutton Children's Books (New York, NY), 2009.

ILLUSTRATOR

Judith Viorst, *My Mama Says There Aren't Any Zombies, Ghosts, Vampires, Creatures, Demons, Monsters, Fiends, Goblins, or Things,* Atheneum (New York, NY), 1973.

Madeline Edmonson, *The Witch's Egg,* Seabury Press (New York, NY), 1974.

Barbara Williams, *Albert's Toothache,* Dutton (New York, NY), 1974.

Barbara Williams, *Kevin's Grandma,* Dutton (New York, NY), 1975.

Winifred Rosen, *Henrietta, the Wild Woman of Borneo,* Four Winds Press (New York, NY), 1975.

Ann Schweninger, *The Hunt for Rabbit's Galosh,* Doubleday (New York, NY), 1976.

Barbara Williams, *Someday, Said Mitchell,* Dutton (New York, NY), 1976.

Daisy Wallace, editor, *Monster Poems,* Holiday House (New York, NY), 1976.

Robert Crowe, *Clyde Monster,* Dutton (New York, NY), 1976.

Marjorie Sharmat, *I'm Terrific,* Holiday House (New York, NY), 1977.

Jan Wahl, *Frankenstein's Dog* (also see below), Prentice-Hall (Englewood Cliffs, NJ), 1977.

Susan Pearson, *That's Enough for One Day, J.P.,* Dial (New York, NY), 1977.

Jan Wahl, *Dracula's Cat* (also see below), Prentice-Hall (Englewood Cliffs, NJ), 1978.

Barbara Williams, *Chester Chipmunk's Thanksgiving,* Dutton (New York, NY), 1978.

Winifred Rosen, *Henrietta and the Day of the Iguana,* Four Winds Press (New York, NY), 1978.

Marjorie Sharmat, *Thornton the Worrier,* Holiday House (New York, NY), 1978.

Norma Klein, *Visiting Pamela,* Dial (New York, NY), 1979.

A.E. Hoffman, *The Nutcracker,* Dutton (New York, NY), 1979.

Barbara Williams, *A Valentine for Cousin Archie,* Dutton (New York, NY), 1980.

Marjorie Sharmat, *Sometimes Mama and Papa Fight,* Harper (New York, NY), 1980.

Robert Crowe, *Tyler Toad and the Thunder,* Dutton (New York, NY), 1980.

Marjorie Sharmat, *Grumley the Grouch,* Holiday House (New York, NY), 1980.

Winifred Rosen, *Henrietta and the Gong from Hong Kong,* Four Winds Press (New York, NY), 1981.

Steven Kroll, *Giant Journey,* Holiday House (New York, NY), 1981.

Barbara Joosse, *The Thinking Place,* Pantheon (New York, NY), 1981.

Phyllis Naylor, *The Boy with the Helium Head,* Atheneum (New York, NY), 1982.

Barbara Joosse, *Spiders in the Fruit Cellar,* Pantheon (New York, NY), 1983.

Charlotte Zolotow, *But Not Billy,* Harper (New York, NY), 1983.

Shirley Rousseau Murphy, *Valentine for a Dragon,* Atheneum (New York, NY), 1984.

Maggie Davis, *Rickety Witch,* Holiday House (New York, NY), 1984.

Judith Viorst, *The Good-bye Book,* Atheneum (New York, NY), 1988.

Lois Duncan, *Songs from Dreamland: Original Lullabies,* Random House (New York, NY), 1989.

Jan Wahl, *Dracula's Cat and Frankenstein's Dog,* Simon & Schuster (New York, NY), 1990.

Riki Levinson, *Country Dawn to Dusk,* Dutton (New York, NY), 1992.

Nancy Abraham Hall and Jill Syverson-Stork, editors, *Los Pollitos dicen: juegos, rimas y canciones infantiles de países de habla hispaña/The Baby Chicks Sing: Traditional Games, Nursery Rhymes, and Lullabies from Spanish-speaking Countries,* Little, Brown (Boston, MA), 1994.

Jandelyn Southwell, *The Little Country Town,* Holt (New York, NY), 2000.

Bethany Roberts, *Ruby to the Rescue,* Holt (New York, NY), 2002.

Bethany Roberts, *Rosie to the Rescue,* Holt (New York, NY), 2003.

Barbara Seuling, *Whose House?,* Harcourt (Orlando, FL), 2004.

Jane Yolen, *Grandma's Hurrying Child,* Harcourt (Orlando, FL), 2005.

Jo Harper, *I Could Eat You Up!,* Holiday House (New York, NY), 2007.

Lezlie Evans, *The Bunnies' Picnic,* Hyperion Books for Children (New York, NY), 2007.

Lezlie Evans, *The Bunnies' Trip,* Hyperion Books for Children (New York, NY), 2008.

David A. Adler, *It's Time to Sleep, It's Time to Dream,* Holiday House (New York, NY), 2009.

Deborah Lee Rose, *Through All the Seasons of the Year,* Abrams Books for Young Readers (New York, NY), 2010.

Debra Sartell, *Time for Bed, Baby Ted,* Holiday House (New York, NY), 2010.

OTHER

Contributor of stories and essays to magazines.

Adaptations

The Baby's Lap Book, The Baby's Bedtime Book, The Baby's Story Book, and *The Baby's Good Morning Book* were adapted as video cassettes and book/cassette packages.

Sidelights

An award-winning creator of self-illustrated children's books such as *The Baby's Playtime Book, Ida and Betty and the Secret Eggs,* and *Cathedral Mouse,* Kay Chorao has also contributed her colorful artwork to books by authors such as Jane Yolen, Judith Viorst, Jan Wahl, David A. Adler, and Marjorie Sharmat. In her own work, Chorao frequently uses gentle humor to address familiar childhood situations such as losing a toy, taking an overnight trip, or being caught in a lie. Populated by characters such as piglets, elephants, and whimsical monsters, Chorao's lighthearted picture books have gained widespread appeal, and she has been repeatedly praised by critics as a skillful and imaginative illustrator whose drawings suitably express the accompanying text.

In *Little Farm by the Sea,* which was selected by *Smithsonian* magazine as one of its notable books for 1998, Chorao presents a view of Small-holdings Farm on Long Island, New York, a place not far from her own summer home. Here Farmer Brown and his family tend crops and animals through all four seasons of the year. As a *Publishers Weekly* reviewer noted, the author/illustrator's "sprawling, good-humored illustrations gracefully depict the colors and signs of the changing seasons." Of special appeal to children, the reviewer observed, are the book's "endearing glimpses of animal mothers and their babies snoozing in unexpected spots." Maeve Visser Knoth, writing in *Horn Book,* dubbed the picture book a "loving look at one family farm," and described Chorao's gouache and pen-and-ink illustrations in *Little Farm by the Sea* as "soft and almost sketchy. An abundance of spring flowers and fall vegetables fills the pages and even runs off the edges. The style . . . is well-suited to the earthy setting."

Kay Chorao's detailed, fun-filled drawings capture the interest of pre-readers in D Is for Drums. *(Illustration copyright © 2004 by Kay Chorao. Reproduced by permission.)*

Toddlers are introduced to the family-centered traditions of a beloved holiday and Chorao's self-illustrated Baby's Christmas Treasury.

Similarly positive reviews greeted Chorao's *Pig and Crow,* a gentle fable about a too-clever crow that exchanges "magic" gifts for the delicious desserts Pig bakes to ease his own loneliness. The magic seeds only grow into ordinary pumpkins, however, and when a magic worm turns into a beautiful butterfly, the creature breaks Pig's heart when it flies away. Finally, however, a magic egg hatches, introducing a stay-at-home goose that becomes a companion and makes Pig's loneliness vanish. A *Horn Book* reviewer commended Chorao's story, noting that "its original and engaging plot [is] built around three natural wonders of genuine interest to young children." Kathleen Kelly MacMillan, writing in *School Library Journal,* dubbed *Pig and Crow* a "delightful tale" in which Chorao's "vivid . . . illustrations capture the characters perfectly, from Pig's dejection to Crow's tricky grin." As *Booklist* contributor Lauren Petersen wrote, "Chorao's illustrations are so wonderfully expressive that the joy on Pig's face when the butterfly hatches and the horror as it flies away tell the story as effectively as the words."

Other books by Chorao include *Grayboy,* which follows the efforts of two children to aid a wounded seagull discovered near their summer home on Peconic Bay, Long Island, and *Up and down with Kate,* a beginning reader in which a loving grandmother helps encourage a young girl's art even though the woman has to move away. "More than an ecological plea," wrote *Booklist* reviewer Kathy Broderick, *Grayboy* is a "dramatic tale" that includes a tense episode in which a boy and his father are

lost during a storm at sea as well as a loving reflection on an endangered landscape that is dear to Chorao's heart. While some children may enjoy the author's depiction of nature, Helen Foster James noted in *School Library Journal* that *Grayboy* will also be appreciated by "children grappling with the death of a beloved pet."

The Baby's Book of Baby Animals is one of several books Chorao has created for laptime sharing; others include *The Baby's Bedtime Book, Baby's Christmas Treasury, The Baby's Playtime Book,* and *Rhymes 'round the World.* In *The Baby's Book of Baby Animals* the editor/illustrator collects poems, songs, and other short works by authors ranging from William Wordsworth and Alfred, Lord Tennyson, to Mother Goose, each of which he brings to life in her colorful artwork. In *School Library Journal* Andrea Tarr deemed the book "a treasure of a treasury." Praising Chorao for crafting a "compelling mixture" of prose and verse, a *Kirkus Reviews* writer added that she "sprinkles her illustrations with sly humor" and a "winsome assortment of cuddlesome creatures [that] adds to the overall appeal." In *Booklist* Karin Snelson also had praise for Chorao's artwork in *The Baby's Book of Baby Animals,* which she described as a "charmingly expressive" and "old-fashioned" menagerie of puppies, bunnies, piglets, ducklings, and toddlers.

The Baby's Playtime Book also pairs Chorao's engaging art with selected poems and song lyrics that capture the playful aspects of toddler life. "Anyone looking for material for lapsit programs need search no further," asserted Kathleen Whalin in a *School Library Journal* review of the work, while in *Kirkus Reviews* a contributor cites the classic selections by writers ranging from William Shakespeare to Myra Cohn Livingston as well as Chorao's characteristic cast of animal characters, which are depicted in a "sentimental, sometimes old-fashioned" manner. *Rhymes 'round the World* takes a similar approach, but this time Chorao spans the globe in search of engaging poems and songs that "are so short they can be used with very young children," according to *Booklist* contributor Ilene Cooper. The artwork for this book includes Chorao's "trademark joyful, round-faced tots in a variety of dynamic scenarios and landscapes," according to a *Kirkus Reviews* writer.

Chorao's engaging artwork is also a feature of many books written by others. In *Grandma's Hurrying Child* Yolen's story about a child's curiosity about the day of her birth is enhanced by softly toned illustrations that *School Library Journal* contributor Lauralyn Persson described as "pretty and accessible," while Phelan noted of Lezlie Evans' *The Bunnies' Picnic* that the artist's "washes of color create sunny scenes that brim with activity and winsome details." Jo Harper's *I Could Eat You Up!,* a picture book that captures the affection between parents and children of several animal species, benefits from colored pencil-and-gouache images that "feature realistically detailed animals with added anthropomorphic touches," according to a *Kirkus Reviews*

Chorao contributes her whimsical art to Barbara Williams' picture book **Albert's Toothache.** (Illustration copyright © 1974 by Kay Sproat Chorao. All rights reserved. Used by permission of Dutton Children's Books, an imprint of Penguin Putnam Books for Young Readers, a division of Penguin Putnam, Inc.)

writer. In *School Library Journal* Laura Scott predicted that Chorao's detailed images for *I Could Eat You Up!* will "invite repeated study" from storytime audiences.

Commenting in *Horn Book,* Chorao wrote of her work for children: "I hope my drawings and those of many other illustrators offer new ways of seeing and arouse the curiosity of the young."

Biographical and Critical Sources

PERIODICALS

Booklist, December 1, 1992, Hazel Rochman, review of *Country Dawn to Dusk,* p. 676; January 1, 1994, Ilene Cooper, review of *Mother Goose Magic,* p. 830; June 1, 1994, Isabel Schon, review of *The Baby Chicks Sing,* p. 1849; June 1, 1994, Mary Harris Veeder, review of *Annie and Cousin Precious,* p. 1836; November 15, 1995, Susan Dove Lempke, review of *The Book of Giving: Poems of Thanks, Praise, and Celebration,* p. 561; September 1, 1996, Susan Dove Lempke, review of *The Christmas Story,* p. 135; May 15, 1998, Carolyn Phelan, review of *Little Farm by the Sea,* p. 1630; November 1, 1998, Shelley Townsend-Hudson, review of *The Cats Kids,* p. 501; July, 1999, GraceAnne DeCandido, review of *Knock at the Door and Other Baby Action Rhymes,* p. 1948; July, 2000, Lauren Peterson, review of *Pig and Crow,* p. 2032; January 1, 2001, Connie Fletcher, review of *The Little Country Town,* p. 974; August, 2002, Kathy

Broderick, review of *Grayboy,* p. 1969; January 1, 2004, Karin Snelson, review of *The Baby's Book of Baby Animals,* p. 864; May 1, 2004, Ilene Cooper, review of *Who's House?,* p. 1564; December 1, 2006, Carolyn Phelan, review of *The Bunnies' Picnic,* p. 51; April 1, 2008, Ilene Cooper, review of *The Bunnies' Trip,* p. 58; March 1, 2009, Julie Cummins, review of *It's Time to Sleep, It's Time to Dream,* p. 50, and Ilene Cooper, review of *Rhymes 'round the World,* p. 52.

Horn Book, August, 1979, Kay Chorao, "A Delayed Reply: Illustration and the Imagination," pp. 463-469; November-December, 1997, Liza Woodruff, review of *Jumpety-Bumpety Hop: A Parade of Animal Poems,* p. 692; March-April, 1998, Maeve Visser Knoth, review of *Little Farm by the Sea,* p. 211; May, 2000, review of *Pig and Crow,* p. 291.

Kirkus Reviews, December 15, 2003, review of *The Baby's Book of Baby Animals,* p. 1448; August, 2004, review of *D Is for Drum: A Colonial ABC,* p. 739; August 1, 2004, review of *D Is for Drum,* p. 739; April 15, 2005, review of *Grandma's Hurrying Child,* p. 485; February 15, 2006, review of *The Baby's Playtime Book,* p. 180; April 1, 2007, review of *I Could Eat You Up!;* February 15, 2009, review of *Rhymes 'round the World.*

Publishers Weekly, May 25, 1998, review of *Little Farm by the Sea,* p. 90.

School Library Journal, January, 1993, Kathleen Odean, review of *Country Dawn to Dusk,* p. 80; March, 1994, Mary Lou Budd, review of *Mother Goose Magic,* p. 218; July, 1994, Virginia Opocensky, review of *Annie and Cousin Precious,* p. 74; March, 1994, Heide Piehler, review of *Number One Number Fun,* p. 178; April, 1995, Linda Wicher, review of *Peekaboo! Was It You?,* p. 100; June, 1995, Virginia E. Jeschelnig, review of *Carousel Round and Round,* p. 78; January, 1996, Sally R. Dow, review of *The Book of Giving,* p. 100; October, 1996, Jane Marino, review of *The Christmas Story,* p. 34; November, 1997, Sarabeth Kalajian, review of *Jumpety-Bumpety Hop,* p. 105; June, 1998, Lee Bock, review of *Little Farm by the Sea,* p. 97; November 1, 1998, Marty Abbott Goodman, review of *The Cats Kids,* p. 77; October, 1999, Jane Marino, review of *Knock at the Door and Other Baby Action Rhymes,* p. 135; June, 2000, Kathleen Kelly MacMillan, review of *Pig and Crow,* p. 104; January, 2001, Carolyn Janssen, review of *The Little Country Town,* p. 108; February, 2001, Lisa Smith, review of *Here Comes Kate,* p. 93; May, 2001, Olga R. Kuharets, review of *Shadow Night: A Picture Book with Shadow Play,* p. 113; July, 2002, Helen Foster James, review of *Grayboy,* p. 85; January, 2004, Andrea Tarr, review of *The Baby's Book of Baby Animals,* p. 112; August, 2004, Elaine Lesh Morgan, review of *Who's House?,* p. 93; November, 2004, Gay Lynn Van Vleck, review of *D Is for Drum,* p. 123; April, 2005, Lauralyn Persson, review of *Grandma's Hurrying Child,* p. 116; March, 2006, Kathleen Whalin, review of *The Baby's Playtime Book,* p. 207; January, 2007, Julie Roach, review of *The Bunnies' Picnic,* p. 92; April, 2007, Laura Scott, review of *I Could Eat You Up!,* p. 106; April, 2008, Linda M. Kenton, review of *The Bunnies' Trip,* p. 106; April, 2009, Laura Butler, review of *It's Time to Sleep, It's Time to Dream,* p. 99.

ONLINE

Macmillan Web site, http://us.macmillan.com/ (April 25, 2010), "Kay Chorao."*

Chorao contributes her gentle illustrations to Lezlie Evans' book series that includes **The Bunnies' Picnic.** (Illustration © 2007 by Kay Sproat Chorao. All rights reserved. Reproduced by permission of Hyperion Books for Children.)

* * *

CLARKE, Greg 1959-

Personal

Born 1959; married; two children. *Education:* University of California—Los Angeles, B.A. (fine art).

Addresses

Home—Metro Los Angeles, CA. *E-mail*—greg@greg clarke.com.

Career

Illustrator and graphic artist. Formerly worked as an art director and graphic designer.

Awards, Honors

Awards from periodicals *American Illustration, Graphis, Print,* and *Communication Arts;* three awards from Society of Illustrators—New York.

Illustrator

Judith Herbst, *The Mystery of UFOs,* Atheneum Books for Young Readers (New York, NY), 1997.

Golf Rules Illustrated, Callaway (New York, NY), 2000.

Allan Wolf, *The Blood-hungry Spleen, and Other Poems about Our Parts,* Candlewick Press (Cambridge, MA), 2003.

Gary Soto, *Worlds Apart: Traveling with Fernie and Me* (poems), G.P. Putnam's Sons (New York, NY), 2005.

Josh Lerman, *How to Raise Mom and Dad: Instructions from Someone Who Figured It Out,* Dutton Children's Books (New York, NY), 2009.

Contributor to periodicals, including *Atlantic Monthly, New Yorker, Rolling Stone,* and *Time.*

Sidelights

After graduating with a degree in fine art, Greg Clarke spent several year working as a graphic designer and art director. In 1990 he shifted his focus to illustration, creating images for books and periodicals. In addition to appearing in such high-profile magazines as the *Atlantic Monthly* and the *New Yorker,* Clarke's artwork is a feature of books by poets Allan Wolf and Gary Soto, as well as of Josh Lerman's humorous picture book *How to Raise Mom and Dad: Instructions from Someone Who Figured It Out.* Discussing the artist's contribution to Soto's *Worlds Apart: Traveling with Fernie and Me,* *Horn Book* reviewer Roger Sutton wrote that Clarke's "scattered pen-and-ink drawings honor both the humor and amity" of Soto's free-verse, world-spanning poems, while a *Kirkus Reviews* writer noted that his "comical, cartoonish illustrations contribute to the sense of exuberance and discovery" in the poet's "disarming tribute to boyhood friendship."

The tongue-in-cheek humor in Lerman's text for the picture-book guide *How to Raise Mom and Dad* is geared more for adults, according to *Booklist* contributor Hazel Rochman, but Clarke's "colorful cartoon pictures . . . will draw kids," according to the critic. In the story, a young girl dispenses practical advice to her little brother, explaining how nagging, whining, refusing to eat green vegetables, and polling both parents to get the best answer to a question are all helpful for the adults, who are hoping to develop parental skills. Noting the "easy flow" of Lerman's text, a *Kirkus Reviews* writer added that the accompanying renderings of the four-member family "are all fine examples of the bug-eyed, pumpkin-head school" that feature "clear line work and nostalgic colors." Reviewing the book for *School Library Journal,* Ieva Bates wrote that in *How to Raise Mom and Dad* Clarke's "gouache illustrations are as joyful as the text."

Biographical and Critical Sources

PERIODICALS

Booklist, December 1, 1997, John Peters, review of *The Mystery of UFOs,* p. 620; March 1, 2009, Hazel Rochman, review of *How to Raise Mom and Dad: Instructions from Someone Who Figured It Out,* p. 50.

Horn Book, May-June, 2005, Roger Sutton, review of *Worlds Apart: Traveling with Fernie and Me,* p. 344.

Kirkus Reviews, July 1, 2003, review of *The Blood-hungry Spleen, and Other Poems about Our Parts,* p. 917; February 15, 2005, review of *Worlds Apart,* p. 235; January 15, 2009, review of *How to Raise Mom and Dad.*

Publishers Weekly, November 17, 1997, review of *The Mystery of UFOs,* p. 62; August 4, 2003, review of *The Blood-hungry Spleen, and Other Poems about Our Parts,* p. 80.

School Library Journal, October, 2003, Dona Ratterree, review of *The Blood-hungry Spleen, and Other Poems about Our Parts,* p. 206; March, 2005, Nina Lindsay, review of *Worlds Apart,* p. 234; February, 2009, Ieva Bates, review of *How to Raise Mom and Dad,* p. 78.

ONLINE

Greg Clarke Home Page, http://www. gregclarke.com (April 21, 2010).

Greg Clarke's artwork is featured in Allan Wolf's quirky **The Blood-hungry Spleen, and Other Poems about Our Parts.** (Illustration copyright © 2003 by Greg Clarke. Reproduced by permission of Candlewick Press.)

* * *

CLOVER, Peter 1952-

Personal

Born June 9, 1952, in London, England. *Education:* Studied in London, England. *Hobbies and other interests:* Painting, listening to music, reading, movies, gardening, exercise.

Addresses

Home—Mallorca, Spain. *Agent*—Pollinger Limited, 9 Staple Inn, Holborn, London WC1V 7QH, England.

Career

Writer, illustrator, and painter. Formerly worked as a freelance storyboard artist for advertising agencies in London, England. *Exhibitions:* Work exhibited at Collyer-Bristow Gallery, London, England. Work also appears in private collections.

Writings

Drawing Horses and Ponies, illustrated by James Field, Hamlyn Children's (London, England), 1994.

The Phantom Pony, illustrated by Robin Lawrie, Corgi (London, England), 1999.

The Storm Pony, illustrated by Robin Lawrie, Corgie (London, England), 2000.

Dead Cool, illustrated by Brann Garvey, Barrington Stoke (Edinburgh, Scotland), 2003, Stone Arch Books (Mankato, MN), 2007.

Dead Cooler, illustrated by Brann Garvey, Barrington Stoke (Edinburgh, Scotland), 2007.

"SHELTIE" SERIES; SELF-ILLUSTRATED

Sheltie the Shetland Pony, Puffin (London, England), 1996, Aladdin (New York, NY), 2000.

Sheltie Saves the Day!, Puffin (London, England), 1996, Aladdin (New York, NY), 2000.

Sheltie and the Runaway, Puffin (London, England), 1996, Aladdin (New York, NY), 2000.

Sheltie Finds a Friend, Puffin (London, England), 1996, Aladdin (New York, NY), 2000.

Sheltie in Danger, Puffin (London, England), 1997, Aladdin (New York, NY), 2001.

Sheltie to the Rescue, Puffin (London, England), 1997, Aladdin (New York, NY), 2000.

Sheltie Rides to Win, Puffin (London, England), 1998, Aladdin (New York, NY), 2001.

Sheltie in Trouble, Puffin (London, England), 1998, Scholastic, Inc. (New York, NY), 2005.

Sheltie and the Saddle Mystery, Puffin (London, England), 1998.

Sheltie Leads the Way, Puffin (London, England), 1998.

Sheltie the Hero, Puffin (London, England), 1998, Scholastic, Inc. (New York, NY), 2004.

Sheltie and the Stray, Puffin (London, England), 1998, Scholastic, Inc. (New York, NY), 2005.

Sheltie on Parade, Puffin (London, England), 1999.

Sheltie the Snow Pony, Puffin (London, England), 1999.

The Big Adventure, Puffin (London, England), 1999.

Sheltie on Patrol, Puffin (London, England), 1999.

Sheltie Goes to School, Puffin (London, England), 1999.

Sheltie Gallops Ahead, Puffin (London, England), 1999.

The Big Show, Puffin (London, England), 1999.

The Big Surprise, Puffin (London, England), 1999.

Sheltie in Double Trouble, Puffin (London, England), 1999, Scholastic, Inc. (New York, NY), 2004.

Sheltie Forever, Puffin (London, England), 1999.

The Big Present, Puffin (London, England), 1999.

Sheltie in Peril, Puffin (London, England), 2000.

Sheltie and the Foal, Puffin (London, England), 2000.

The Big Wish, Puffin (London, England), 2000, Scholastic, Inc. (New York, NY), 2005.

Sheltie by the Sea, Puffin (London, England), 2000.

Sheltie Races On, Puffin (London, England), 2000, Scholastic, Inc. (New York, NY), 2005.

Sheltie at the Funfair, Puffin (London, England), 2001.

"RESCUE RIDERS" SERIES

Race against Time, illustrated by Shelagh McNicholas, Hodder (London, England), 1998.

Fire Alert, illustrated by Shelagh McNicholas, Hodder (London, England), 1998.

Ghost Pony, illustrated by Shelagh McNicholas, Hodder (London, England), 1998.

"HERCULES" SERIES

New Pup on the Block, Hodder (London, England), 2000.

Operation Snowsearch, Hodder (London, England), 2000.

Treasure Hound, Hodder (London, England), 2000.

"DONKEY DIARIES" SERIES

Donkey Danger, illustrated by Carolyn Dinan, Oxford University Press (Oxford, England), 2001.

Donkey Disaster, illustrated by Carolyn Dinan, Oxford University Press (Oxford, England), 2001.

Donkey Drama, illustrated by Carolyn Dinan, Oxford University Press (Oxford, England), 2001.

Donkey in Distress, illustrated by Carolyn Dinan, Oxford University Press (Oxford, England), 2002.

"LITTLE BRIDGE FARM" SERIES

Dilly Saves the Day, illustrated by Angela Swan, Scholastic (London, England), 2007.

Oscar's New Friend, illustrated by Angela Swan, Scholastic (London, England), 2007.

Smudge Finds the Trail, illustrated by Angela Swan, Scholastic (London, England), 2007.

Socks Cleans Up, illustrated by Angela Swan, Scholastic (London, England), 2007.

Tiger's Great Adventure, illustrated by Angela Swan, Scholastic (London, England), 2007.

OTHER

(Illustrator) Christine Pullein-Thompson, *The Best Pony for Me!,* Macdonald (Hemel Hempsted, England), 1995.

Sidelights

British author and illustrator Peter Clover is the creator of the popular "Sheltie" series of chapter books which focus on the relationship between a young girl and her beloved Shetland pony. In addition, Clover has written

numerous other children's stories, including the works in the "Rescue Riders," "Hercules," "Donkey Diaries," and "Little Bridge Farm" series. A former storyboard artist, Clover decided to enter the world of children's literature after realizing that the two things he most enjoyed doing were penning tales and creating pictures. "Writing adventure stories for children seemed like the perfect combination," he noted on his home page. "I wasn't wrong. It's brilliant."

The works in Clover's "Sheltie the Shetland Pony" series were inspired by experiences in the West Country of England. On his home page the author recalled, "I was immediately impressed by the breathtaking countryside and the magic of the open moors. I was equally amazed at the number of young children who seemed to pop up everywhere on ponies." *Sheltie Rides to Win* and *Sheltie and the Runaway* are two of the many books that feature Clover's shaggy Shetland pony. In *Sheltie and the Runaway* Sheltie and Emma—Sheltie's young owner—wish they had other friends who understand the unique friendship between girls and ponies. Their wish is answered when they meet Sally and her pony, Minnow, and quickly become fast friends. Soon that friendship is tested when Sally and Minnow run away from home and Sally's overprotective father blames Emma for encouraging his daughter to flee. "Sheltie" fans join Emma and Sheltie as the pair attempts to find Sally and Minnow and bring them home safely. *Sheltie Rides to Win* finds Emma and her pony joining Sally and Minnow in a local pony show, where they hope to outrank some snobby neighbors. Other works include *Sheltie Leads the Way* and *Sheltie and the Snow Pony*. In the former, Emma and Sheltie help locate a rider lost on the foggy moors, and in the latter, Emma and Sheltie rescue an abandoned, malnourished pony.

The "Rescue Riders" stories center on three horse-loving girls who use their equestrian skills to avert disaster. Clover introduces an ungainly but lovable canine in his "Hercules" series, and his "Donkey Diaries" books recount the adventures at a donkey sanctuary. The stories in the "Little Bridge Farm" series focus on familiar childhood concerns. A duckling must overcome her fear of swimming in *Dilly Saves the Day,* and in *Oscar's New Friends,* a pony adjusts to life in his new surroundings.

Clover finds inspirations in his surroundings, never knowing when an idea will hit him. "I always take a pencil and paper away with me. I keep a notebook handy at all times and jot down anything which might trigger off a storyline," he explained on his home page. While he enjoys both writing and illustrating equally, Clover recognizes how lucky he is to have the ability to create stories in his mind, write them out, and then capture those same characters and events in his illustrations. "When a story starts to form in my head, it just grows and grows," he noted on the Oxford University Press Web site, but quickly added: "The story that is, not my head!"

Biographical and Critical Sources

ONLINE

Oxford University Press Web site, http://www.oup.co.uk/ (February 5, 2004), "Peter Clover."

Peter Clover Home Page, http://www.peterclover.com (March 1, 2010).

Pollinger Limited Web site, http://www.pollingerltd.com/ (March 1, 2010), "Peter Clover."

Puffin Books Web site, http://www.puffin.co.uk/ (March 1, 2010), "About Peter Clover."*

*   *   *

COCHRANE, Hamilton E.
See COCHRANE, Mick

*   *   *

COCHRANE, Mick 1956-
(Hamilton E. Cochrane)

Personal

Born Hamilton E. Cochrane, 1956, in St. Paul, MN; married; wife's name Mary; children: Henry, Sam. *Education:* University of St. Thomas, B.A. (English), 1979; University of Minnesota, Ph.D. (English literature), 1985. *Hobbies and other interests:* Reading, spending time with his children, listening to music.

Addresses

Home—Kenmore, NY. *Office*—Department of English, Canisius College, 2001 Main St., Buffalo, NY 14208-1098. *E-mail*—cochrane@canisius.edu.

Career

Writer and educator. Canisius College, Buffalo, NY, member of English department, 1985—, currently professor of English, Lowery writer-in-residence, and coordinator of Canisius Contemporary Writers series, 1999—.

Awards, Honors

Saltonstall Foundation grant; National Endowment for the Humanities grant; three Peter Canisius Distinguished Teaching Professor awards; Barnes and Noble's Discover Great New Writers Competition finalist, for *Flesh Wounds;* Books for the Teen Age selection, New York Public Library, for *Sport.*

Writings

NOVELS

Flesh Wounds, Nan A. Talese/Doubleday (New York, NY), 1997.

Sport, Thomas Dunne Books (New York, NY), 2001.

The Girl Who Threw Butterflies, Knopf (New York, NY), 2009.

OTHER

(Compiler; as Hamilton E. Cochrane) *Boswell's Literary Art: An Annotated Bibliography of Critical Studies, 1900-1985,* Garland (New York, NY), 1991.

Contributor to *Highway 61 Revisited: Bob Dylan's Road from Minnesota to the World,* edited by Thom Swiss and Colleen J. Sheehy, University of Minnesota Press (Minneapolis, MN), 2009. Contributor to periodicals, including *Cincinnati Review, Northwest Review, Kansas Quarterly, Water-stone, Biography, Eighteenth-Century Life, Studies in Eighteenth-Century Culture, Aethlon,* and *Dayton Review.*

Sidelights

Mick Cochrane, a professor of English at Canisius College, is the author of two critically acclaimed novels for young adults: *Sport* and *The Girl Who Threw Butterflies.* The works feature ordinary adolescents who must learn how to cope with painful and confusing circum-

Cover of Mick Cochrane's emotionally resonant middle-grade novel **The Girl Who Threw Butterflies.** (Jacket photographs copyright © Veer and Jupiter Images. Reproduced by permission of Alfred A. Knopf, a division of Random House, Inc.)

stances; in the words of *Buffalo News* contributor Jean Westmoore, Cochrane "writes beautifully crafted, heartfelt novels about people who endure what should be mortal blows and somehow survive with grace and spirit. That he manages to be very funny at the same time is somewhat of a miracle."

Set in the 1960s, *Sport* concerns Harlan Hawkins, a sensitive twelve year old whose life takes a dramatic turn after his mother is diagnosed with multiple sclerosis and his father abandons the family, and then refuses to pay child support. Harlan finds solace on the baseball field, where a sympathetic coach nurtures his talent and helps him earn a scholarship to a private school. In *Library Journal* Marylaine Block described *Sport* as a "believable, affecting coming-of-age story," and a *Publishers Weekly* contributor asserted that the novel should "attract readers who will then be seduced by the unassuming richness of Cochrane's prose and his gift for subdued yet potent storytelling."

An eighth grader mourns the death of her father, with whom she shared a love of baseball, in *The Girl Who Threw Butterflies,* "a compassionate, perceptive, pitch-perfect portrait of teenage grief," according to Tanya D. Auger in *Horn Book.* Following a tragic automobile accident that took her father's life, Molly Williams decides to try out for the boys' baseball team at her school by employing her skills as a knuckleballer, using a pitch taught to her by her dad. Writing in *Booklist,* Cindy Dobrez called *The Girl Who Threw Butterflies* "an honest, sometimes humorous, and emotionally moving account," and *School Library Journal* reviewer Marilyn Taniguchi stated that "Cochrane crafts an awkward yet engaging heroine whose perceptions and interactions with family, friends, and supporting characters ring true."

Biographical and Critical Sources

PERIODICALS

Booklist, March 15, 2009, Cindy Dobrez, review of *The Girl Who Threw Butterflies,* p. 54.
Buffalo News, February 25, 2009, Jean Westmoore, "Competitive Spirit Fires up Author."
Horn Book, May-June, 2009, Tanya D. Auger, review of *The Girl Who Threw Butterflies,* p. 293.
Kirkus Reviews, January 15, 2009, review of *The Girl Who Threw Butterflies.*
Library Journal, August, 1997, Judith Ann Akalaitis, review of *Flesh Wounds,* p. 125; November 1, 2000, Marylaine Block, review of *Sport,* p. 132.
Publishers Weekly, July 28, 1997, review of *Flesh Wounds,* p. 52; November 20, 2000, review of *Sport,* p. 46.
School Library Journal, March, 2009, Marilyn Taniguchi, review of *The Girl Who Threw Butterflies,* p. 142.
Star Tribune (Minneapolis, MN), October 14, 1997, Elaine Gale, interview with Cochrane, p. 1E.
USA Today, May 14, 2009, Bob Minzesheimer, review of *The Girl Who Threw Butterflies,* p. 3D.

ONLINE

Canisius College Web site, http://www.canisius.edu/
    (March 1, 2010), "Mick Cochrane."
Mick Cochrane Home Page, http://mickcochrane.com
    (March 1, 2010).*

*   *   *

COHEN, Santiago 1954-

Personal

Born 1954, in Mexico; married; children: two. *Education:* Universidad Autónoma Metropolitana, B.F.A., 1979; Pratt Institute, M.F.A., 1985.

Addresses

Office—820 Park Ave., Hoboken, NJ 07030. *E-mail*—elsan1@gmail.com.

Career

Designer, illustrator, and animator. Universidad Autónoma Metropolitana, Mexico City, Mexico, animation teacher, 1978-82; *High Times* magazine, associate art director, 1983-84; *Raw* magazine, assistant art director, 1985; *MBM* magazine, art director, 1985-86; *Spy* magazine, associate art director, 1986; Ink Tank (animation studio), New York, NY, associate art director, 1986-88; Santiago Cohen Studio, Hoboken, NJ, founder and director, 1988—. Designer for "Troubles the Cat" segment of *Big Bag* (television series), Children's Television Workshop, 1996-98; animation director for *'Twas the Night,* Home Box Office, 2002. *Exhibitions:* Work displayed at solo and group fine-art shows in New York, NY, and Mexico.

Member

Society of Children's Book Writers and Illustrators.

Awards, Honors

Bronze Award, Broadcast Designer Association, 1992, for Comedy Central brochure, 1997, for Tele-TV logo; Award of Merit, Art Directors Club of New York, 1993; Asifa-East Awards, second place for animation, 1997, for "Cutey Kitty," first place for animation, 1998, for "Surf's Up," Excellence in Design award, 1999, for "How Nehemiah Got Free"; Xeric Foundation grant, 2000, for *The Fifth Name.*

Writings

SELF-ILLUSTRATED

The Fifth Name (graphic novel; based on a story by Stefan Zweig), introduction by R.O. Blechman, Fantagraphics Books (Seattle, WA), 2001.

Santiago Cohen (Photograph by Ethel Cesarman. Reproduced by permission.)

Author and illustrator of *Uno más Uno* (comic strip), 1981-82.

ILLUSTRATOR

Richard Chevat, adapter, *Troubles, the Cat: It's Magic,* Golden Books (Racine, WI), 1997.
Harriet Ziefert, *Kitty Says Meow!,* Grosset & Dunlap (New York, NY), 2002.
Harriet Ziefert, *Home for Navidad,* Houghton Mifflin (Boston, MA), 2003.
Harriet Ziefert, *It's Hanukkah,* Blue Apple Books (Maplewood, NJ), 2003.
Harriet Ziefert, *Fiddle-I-Fee,* Blue Apple Books (Maplewood, NJ), 2003.
Harriet Ziefert, *This Is Passover,* Blue Apple Books (Maplewood, NJ), 2004.
Harriet Ziefert, *One Smart Skunk,* Blue Apple Books (Maplewood, NJ), 2004.
Harriet Ziefert, *Go Away, Crows!,* Sterling Publishing (New York, NY), 2005.
Adam Gamble, *Good Night, San Francisco,* Our World of Books (Dennis, MA), 2006.
Rhonda Gowler Greene, *One Lost Sheep,* Zonderkidz (Grand Rapids, MI), 2007.
Rhonda Gowler Greene, *Zacchaeus and the Happy Day,* Zonderkidz (Grand Rapids, MI), 2007.
Rhonda Gowler Greene, *Jonah and the Great Big Fish,* Zonderkidz (Grand Rapids, MI), 2007.
Rhonda Gowler Greene, *Noah and the Mighty Ark,* Zonderkidz (Grand Rapids, MI), 2007.
Phillis Gershator, *Zoo Day, ¡Olé!: A Counting Book,* Marshall Cavendish (New York, NY), 2008.
Play Ball!, Marshall Cavendish (New York, NY), 2008.
Samantha R. Vamos, *Before You Were Here, Mi Amor,* Viking (New York, NY), 2009.

Contributor to periodicals, including *New York Times, New Yorker, Boston Globe,* and *Washington Post.*

Sidelights

Santiago Cohen, an award-winning artist, animator, and designer, has provided the illustrations for more than a dozen children's books, including *One Smart Skunk* by Harriet Ziefert and *Before You Were Here, Mi Amor* by Samantha R. Vamos. A native of Mexico, Cohen has also worked as an art director for several magazines, exhibited his paintings at galleries in New York City and Mexico, and released the self-illustrated graphic novel *The Fifth Name.*

Cohen has illustrated a number of books with religious themes. *This Is Passover,* a cumulative tale reminiscent of "The House That Jack Built," explores the traditions of the important Jewish holiday. "Cohen's colorful cartoons lend an air of festivity" to Ziefert's tale, Sandra Kitain remarked in *School Library Journal.* In *Noah and the Mighty Ark,* Rhonda Gowler Greene recounts the famous Biblical tale of the great flood. According to *School Library Journal* reviewer Kathy Piehl, Cohen's "impressionistic style suggests shapes through use of shading and flowing lines." Cohen and Greene also team up to create *Jonah and the Great Big Fish,* another popular Bible story, as well as *Zacchaeus and the Happy Day,* a narrative from the New Testament.

Cohen has enjoyed a successful collaboration with Ziefert, a prolific children's author. *Home for Navidad* centers on Rosa, a ten-year-old girl who lives with her grandmother, uncle, and younger brother in a small, rural Mexican village. As the Christmas season approaches, Rosa longs for her mother, who has spent the past three years working in New York City to raise money for the family, and the youngster's dreams of a reunion are sparked by a special letter from the United States. Cohen's art for the book, which was compared by several critics to the work of *Madeline* creator Ludwig Bemelmans, earned strong critical praise. "His loosely drawn, fanciful illustrations burst off the pages like fireworks on Navidad," asserted *Horn Book* reviewer Kitty Flynn. A *Publishers Weekly* contributor wrote that in *Home for Navidad* Cohen "paints in satu-

Cohen creates artwork that brings to life Phillis Gershator's engaging Zoo Day Ole! A Counting Book. (Illustration copyright © 2009 by Santiago Cohen. All rights reserved. Reproduced by permission.)

rated fiesta-bright colors that have an instant appeal," and Susan Patron maintained in *School Library Journal* that the paintings "vibrate with feeling and intensity."

Ziefert's *One Smart Skunk* focuses on a wily critter that settles under a family's porch and cleverly evades a series of traps. Here "Cohen's illustrations are luminous," remarked Piper L. Nyman in her *School Library Journal* review of the work.

Told in verse, Phillis Gershator's *Zoo Day, ¡Olé!: A Counting Book* follows a preschooler's visit to the zoo with her grandmother and features a text that includes both English and Spanish terms. Cohen's digitally colored illustrations for Gershator's rhyming text, "featuring bright colors outlined in bold black strokes, create a fun-loving atmosphere for the story," wrote Mary Landrum in *School Library Journal.*

An expectant mother recounts her family's extensive preparations for the new addition to their family in yet another of Cohen's illustration projects: Vamos's bilingual picture book *Before You Were Here, Mi Amor.* The book's "easily interpreted story is matched by . . . black-outlined folk-art-style drawings in bright primary hues," as a *Kirkus Reviews* contributor observed, and Susan E. Murray noted in *School Library Journal* that the artist "uses the texture of the paper and his watercolor paints to create depth and movement" in his pictures.

Biographical and Critical Sources

PERIODICALS

Booklist, September 1, 2003, Hazel Rochman, review of *Home for Navidad,* p. 136; November 1, 2003, Hazel Rochman, review of *It's Hanukkah!,* p. 508; February 15, 2009, Linda Perkins, review of *Before You Were Here, Mi Amor,* p. 86; May 1, 2009, Hazel Rochman, review of *Zoo Day ¡Ole!: A Counting Book,* p. 84.

Horn Book, September-October, 2003, Kitty Flynn, review of *Home for Navidad,* p. 605.

Kirkus Reviews, November 1, 2003, review of *Home for Navidad,* p. 1321; November 15, 2004, review of *One Smart Skunk,* p. 1095; February 15, 2009, review of *Before You Were Here, Mi Amor;* February 15, 2009, review of *Zoo Day ¡Ole!*

Publishers Weekly, September 22, 2003, review of *Home for Navidad,* p. 70.

School Library Journal, October, 2003, Susan Patron, review of *Home for Navidad,* p. 69; January, 2004, Kathleen Simonetta, review of *Fiddle-I-Fee,* p. 114; January, 2005, Piper L. Nyman, review of *One Smart Skunk,* p. 100; February, 2005, Sandra Kitain, review of *This Is Passover,* p. 115; September, 2005, Elaine Lesh Morgan, review of *Go Away, Crows!,* p. 167; March, 2007, Kathy Piehl, review of *Noah and the Mighty Ark,* p. 163; March, 2009, Susan E. Murray, review of *Before You Were Here, Mi Amor,* p. 129; April, 2009, Mary Landrum, review of *Zoo Day ¡Ole!,* p. 104.

ONLINE

Santiago Cohen Home Page, http://www.santiagocohen. com (March 1, 2010).

Shannon Associates Web site, http://www.shannon associates.com/ (March 1, 2010), "Santiago Cohen."

D

DEAN, Claire

Personal

Married; husband's name Robert; children: one son, one daughter. *Education:* California State University, Northridge, B.A. (magna cum laude).

Addresses

Home—Boise, ID. *E-mail*—claire@clairedean.net.

Career

Writer of young-adult fiction. Member of writing staff of *Bop* (teen magazine).

Writings

Girlwood, Houghton-Mifflin (Boston, MA), 2008.

Sidelights

Claire Dean is a freelance writer and novelist who is best known for her young-adult novel *Girlwood*. The story follows Polly Greene, a thirteen year old with a profound sense of the natural world's spiritual richness. Under the guidance of her herbalist grandmother, Polly works to save her troubled older sister, who has disappeared and, Polly believes, is hiding in the forest near her home. She also hopes to save the forest itself, as outside developers threaten to raze the trees in order to build a gated community. Each chapter of *Girlwood* begins with a brief factual overview of the medicinal, culinary, or metaphysical properties of a given wild plant. In an interview on the *Embracing the Child* Web site, Dean explained: "In a way, writing *Girlwood* was like writing a lullaby for my teenager. My main goal was to write a hopeful story, something that would bring strength and solace not only to my daughter, but to all my readers."

A contributor to *Children's Bookwatch* called *Girlwood* "a fine story of magic and fantasy," while *Teenreads. com* reviewer Donna Volkenannt called *Girlwood* "a moving story about the fragile nature of family and the environment—and how a lot of love and a little attention can save them both." *Kliatt* contributor Lesley Farmer noted that Dean's "light-handed treatment of some serious issues" makes her novel a likely good fit for middle-school girls, while Jennifer Mattson, writing for *Booklist,* recommended *Girlwood* to teens with a flair for Wiccan spiritualism. A reviewer for *Publishers Weekly* concluded that, although the novel sometimes sags under the weight of an older teen's clichéd problems, Dean's "typically lush" writing "succeeds in creating a fast-paced story and sympathetic characters that eco-minded readers will appreciate."

Dean once commented: "Nature is my passion. There is nowhere on the planet that soothes me as much as the woods. I grew up in Los Angeles, so . . . I know what it's like to spend a childhood surrounded by buildings, freeways, and concrete, to go weeks, in fact, without walking on bare earth! But I was lucky. My grandfather was a true cowboy, growing up on an isolated ranch in Arizona, and my dad is still an avid outdoorsman. Through them, I learned that mountains are not only beautiful, they give you strength, inspiration, and inner peace. I don't care what your problems are; if you go into the woods and sit a bit, you'll feel better.

"Kids today are technology-rich and nature-poor. So many have never gone camping, never sat under the stars, never smelled the deliciousness of pine-scented air or pushed themselves to climb a mountain. It is my hope that *Girlwood* will inspire at least one child or teenager to go outside, to see how far she can walk, to find her unique gifts and strength in nature, to protect the last wild spaces that, in turn, will protect and nourish her. My generation has ruined much of this planet; I truly believe it's the young people who will save it."

Biographical and Critical Sources

PERIODICALS

Booklist, February 15, 2008, Jennifer Mattson, review of *Girlwood,* p. 88.
Bulletin of the Center for Children's Books, May 1, 2008, April Spisak, review of *Girlwood,* p. 380.
Children's Bookwatch, July 1, 2008, review of *Girlwood.*
Kirkus Reviews, April 1, 2008, review of *Girlwood.*
Kliatt, May 1, 2008, Lesley Farmer, review of *Girlwood,* p. 8.
Publishers Weekly, May 19, 2008, review of *Girlwood,* p. 55.
School Library Journal, June 1, 2008, Susan Hepler, review of *Girlwood,* p. 136.
Voice of Youth Advocates, June 1, 2008, Jamie S. Hansen, review of *Girlwood,* p. 158.

ONLINE

Claire Dean Home Page, http://www.clairedean.net (June 1, 2010).
Embracing the Child Web site, http://www.embracing thechild.org/ (April 1, 2008), interview with Dean.
Teenreads.com, http://www.teenreads.com/ (December 16, 2008), Donna Volkenannt, review of *Girlwood.*

* * *

Marfe Ferguson Delano (Photograph by Pam Knecht. Reproduced by permission.)

DELANO, Marfé Ferguson

Personal

First name pronounced mar-FAYE; born in Memphis, TN; married; children: two. *Education:* Duke University, B.A. *Hobbies and other interests:* Reading, singing with a choral society, cooking, walking and hiking.

Addresses

Home—Alexandria, VA. *Office*—c/o National Geographic Children's Books, 1145 17th St. NW, Washington, DC 20036. *E-mail*—marfe@marfebooks.com.

Career

Writer and editor. Charles Scribner's Sons, New York, NY, editorial assistant; *Working Mother* magazine, New York, NY, copyeditor; Time-Life Books, Alexandria, VA, copyeditor and staff writer; freelance writer.

Member

Authors Guild, Society of Children's Book Writers and Illustrators, Children's Book Guild of Washington, DC.

Awards, Honors

Outstanding Science Trade Book for Students designation, National Science Teachers Association/Children's Book Council (NSTA/CBC), for *Exploring Caves;* Notable Book for Children designation, American Library Association (ALA), James Madison Book Award Honor Book designation, Outstanding Science Trade Book for Children designation, NSTA/CBC, Notable Social Studies Trade Book for Young People designation, National Council for the Social Studies/CBC, and Silver Honor Award, National Parenting Publications, all for *Inventing the Future;* Outstanding Science Trade Book for Children designation, NSTA/CBC, Notable Book for Children designation, ALA, Notable Children's Book of Jewish Content designation, Association of Jewish Libraries, Orbis Pictus Honor Book designation, and Books for the Teen Age selection, New York Public Library, all for *Genius;* Best of the Best selection, Chicago Public Library, 2008, and Cooperative Children's Book Center Choices designation, and Jefferson Cup Honor Book designation, both 2009, all for *Helen's Eyes;* Green Earth Book Award for nonfiction, 2010, for *Earth in the Hot Seat.*

Writings

Wildflowers, National Geographic (Washington, DC), 1998.
Desert, National Geographic (Washington, DC), 1999.

Dogs and Wild Dogs, National Geographic (Washington, DC), 1999.

Sea Otters, National Geographic (Washington, DC), 1999.

Tigers, National Geographic (Washington, DC), 1999.

Wonder Bugs, National Geographic (Washington, DC), 2000.

Kangaroos, National Geographic (Washington, DC), 2000.

Tree Frogs, National Geographic (Washington, DC), 2000.

(With Nancy Holler Aulenbach and Hazel A. Barton) *Exploring Caves: Journeys into the Earth,* National Geographic (Washington, DC), 2001.

Inventing the Future: A Photobiography of Thomas Alva Edison, National Geographic (Washington, DC), 2002.

American Heroes, introduction by Robert D. Johnston, National Geographic (Washington, DC), 2005.

Genius: A Photobiography of Albert Einstein, National Geographic (Washington, DC), 2005.

Sea Monsters: A Prehistoric Adventure, National Geographic (Washington, DC), 2007.

Helen's Eyes: A Photobiography of Annie Sullivan, Helen Keller's Teacher, National Geographic (Washington, DC), 2008.

Earth in the Hot Seat: Bulletins from a Warming World, National Geographic (Washington, DC), 2009.

Contributor to periodicals.

Sidelights

Marfé Ferguson Delano is the author of several award-winning works of nonfiction, including *American He-*

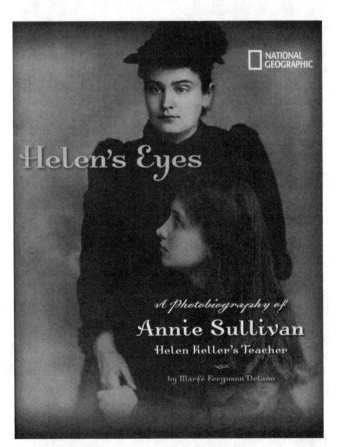

Cover of Delano's Helen's Eyes, *an illustrated biography of nineteenth-century teacher Annie Sullivan.* (Jacket copyright © 2008 by National Geographic Society. Front cover © American Foundation for the Blind; IStockPhoto (background). Reproduced by permission.)

roes, Inventing the Future: A Photobiography of Thomas Alva Edison, and *Helen's Eyes: A Photobiography of Annie Sullivan, Helen Keller's Teacher.* She also turns to natural history in *Exploring Caves: Journeys into the Earth,* and focuses on the subject of climate change in *Earth in the Hot Seat: Bulletins from a Warming World.* "The urgency of our global warming problem comes across very clearly" in *Earth in the Hot Seat,* according to *Horn Book* reviewer Danielle J. Ford.

In *American Heroes* Delano examines such well-known individuals as Benjamin Franklin, Martin Luther King, Jr., and Amelia Earhart, as well as George Mason, one of the founding fathers of the nation, and Queen Lili'oukalani, the last remaining monarch of the Hawaiian Islands. *School Library Journal* critic Delia Carruthers praised Delano's "clearly written, beautifully laid out profiles" in *American Heroes,* and Ilene Cooper observed in *Booklist* that the volume "invites kids to pick it up."

Inventing the Future centers on Thomas Edison, the man who invented the incandescent light bulb as well as several other staples of twentieth-century life. "The technological features of Edison's gizmos are cogently explained within the text," wrote a critic in a *Kirkus Reviews* appraisal of Delano's book. Another work of nonfiction, *Genius: A Photobiography of Albert Einstein,* explores the life of the groundbreaking physicist and offers straightforward explanations of Einstein's scientific discoveries. One strength of the work, noted a *Kirkus Reviews* contributor, "is in its humane exploration of Einstein's growth as a thinker," and Anne Chapman Callaghan asserted in *School Library Journal* that Delano's "entertaining effort displays clarity and intelligence."

In *Helen's Eyes* Delano profiles pioneering educator Anne Sullivan, a woman who was dubbed a "miracle worker" in honor of her efforts with her deaf-blind student, Helen Keller. The numerous quotations Delano cites in her biography of the noted teacher "convey not only the facts of Sullivan's life, but the everyday realities and emotions as well," Kathleen Felly MacMillan wrote in *School Library Journal.*

Biographical and Critical Sources

PERIODICALS

Booklist, April 1, 2005, Ilene Cooper, review of *Genius: A Photobiography of Albert Einstein,* p. 1358; December 1, 2005, Ilene Cooper, review of *American Heroes,* p. 39; June 1, 2008, Ilene Cooper, review of *Helen's Eyes: A Photobiography of Annie Sullivan, Helen Keller's Teacher,* p. 96.

Horn Book, September-October, 2005, Betty Carter, review of *Genius,* p. 600; July-August, 2009, Danielle J. Ford, review of *Earth in the Hot Seat: Bulletins from a Warming World,* p. 439.

Kirkus Reviews, September 1, 2002, review of *Inventing the Future,* p. 1307; March 15, 2005, review of *Genius,* p. 350.

School Library Journal, August, 2000, Michele Snyder, reviews of *Tree Frogs* and *Kangaroos,* both p. 153; May, 2005, Anne Chapman Callaghan, review of *Genius,* p. 148; February, 2006, Delia Carruthers, review of *American Heroes,* p. 143; September, 2008, Kathleen Kelly MacMillan, review of *Helen's Eyes,* p. 200; July, 2009, Eva Elisabeth VonAncken, review of *Earth in the Hot Seat,* p. 99.

ONLINE

Duke Magazine Online, http://www.dukemagazine.duke.edu/ (November-December, 2009), Bridget Booher, "Children's Book Author Marfé Ferguson Delano."

Marfé Ferguson Delano Home Page, http://www.marfebooks.com (March 1, 2010).

*   *   *

DeWIN, Howie
See HOWIE, Betsy

*   *   *

DUGGER, Elizabeth L.
See KANELL, Beth

*   *   *

DuPRAU, Jeanne 1944-

Personal

Born June, 1944, in San Francisco, CA; daughter of James B. (a steel company executive) and Dolly Allison (a homemaker and painter) DuPrau. *Ethnicity:* "White." *Education:* Scripps College, B.A. (English), 1966; University of California—Berkeley, secondary teaching credential, 1967. *Politics:* Democrat. *Hobbies and other interests:* Music, gardening.

Addresses

Home—Menlo Park, CA. *Agent*—Nancy Gallt, Nancy Gallt Literary Agency, 273 Charlton Ave., South Orange, NJ 07079. *E-mail*—jduprau@mac.com.

Career

Writer, editor, and educator. Formerly taught English; former editor for educational publishing companies; Apple Computer, former technical writer. Volunteer work includes teaching computer classes for seniors, community garden projects, and grief counseling.

Jeanne DuPrau (Reproduced by permission.)

Member

Society of Children's Book Writers and Illustrators.

Awards, Honors

Notable Book for Children designation, American Library Association, 100 Titles for Reading and Sharing inclusion, New York Public Library, and California Book Award, Commonwealth Club of California, all 2003, all for *The City of Ember;* several state readers' choice awards.

Writings

NONFICTION

Adoption: The Facts, Feelings, and Issues of a Double Heritage, Simon & Schuster (New York, NY), 1981.

(With Molly Tyson) *The Apple IIGS Book,* Bantam (New York, NY), 1986.

Cloning, Lucent Books (San Diego, CA), 2000.

Cells, Kidhaven Press (San Diego, CA), 2002.

The American Colonies, Kidhaven Press (San Diego, CA), 2002.

"BOOKS OF EMBER" NOVEL SERIES

The City of Ember (also see below), Random House (New York, NY), 2003.

The People of Sparks (also see below), Random House (New York, NY), 2004.

The Prophet of Yonwood (also see below), Random House (New York, NY), 2006.

The Books of Ember (contains *The City of Ember, The People of Sparks,* and *The Prophet of Yonwood*), Random House (New York, NY), 2008.

The Diamond of Darkhold, Random House (New York, NY), 2008.

OTHER

The Earth House (memoir), New Chapter Press (Pound Ridge, NY), 1992.

Car Trouble (young-adult novel), Greenwillow Books (New York, NY), 2005.

(Author of introduction) George MacDonald, *The Princess and the Goblin,* Random House (New York, NY), 2010.

Contributor to textbooks; contributor of essays and book reviews to periodicals.

Adaptations

The City of Ember was adapted for film as *City of Ember,* Twentieth Century-Fox, 2008.

Sidelights

A former teacher, editor, and technical writer, Jeanne DuPrau is the author of nonfiction titles, including *Cloning,* as well as several novels and the memoir *The Earth House.* She is best known for her popular and critically acclaimed "Books of Ember" fantasy series, which is set in a post-apocalyptic, subterranean city. Becoming a bestselling novelist was never one of DuPrau's goals, a she remarked in a Random House Web site interview. "I just wrote and kept on writing, because writing was what I liked to do," she explained. "What could be more interesting than thinking of mysterious happenings, finding the answers to intriguing questions, and making up new worlds? Writers have a great job. I'm glad to be one."

DuPrau began her authorial career penning nonfiction books such as *Adoption: The Facts, Feelings, and Issues of a Double Heritage,* which presents a portrayal of the psychological and emotional impact of adopting a child or being adopted. *The Earth House* describes the author's experience with Zen Buddhism and the task of building of a rammed-earth house with her partner, who died of cancer before the house could be completed. "DuPrau's clearly written prose is both poetic and lyrical," remarked Susanne Carter in a *Belles Lettres* review of *The Earth House.*

In *Cloning,* DuPrau introduces middle-and high-school students to many aspects of a controversial scientific issue. In a text praised for its clarity and straightforward approach to its subject, *Cloning* discusses the benefits of cloning in agriculture and medicine as well as the fears of cloning's opponents, who expect widespread

use of the technique to have a detrimental effect on biodiversity, with possible exploitation in pursuit of ethnic cleansing or eugenics schemes. Arguments both for and against are presented in a way that is "always well balanced and gives readers ample information to form their own opinions," according to Randy Meyer in *Booklist.*

The City of Ember, the first work in DuPrau's "Books of Ember" middle-grade novel series, centers on twelve year olds Lina and Doon, who live in a city where there is no natural light. Unless the electricity is on, the streets of Ember are engulfed in darkness. The city is old, and the generator that keeps its lights going is breaking down, so darkness descends more and more often. The storerooms that hold all of Ember's supplies are nearly empty, and the crops in the greenhouses that grow Ember's food are beginning to fail. Although the city's mayor assures residents that all is well, Lina and Doon know that the situation has become critical. When Lina finds an ancient document which seems to containe instructions for leaving the city, she and Doon embark on a desperate trip that leads them through Ember's dark streets and into the labyrinthine tunnels below on their

Cover of DuPrau's middle-grade fantasy **The City of Ember.** (Cover art © 2008 by Walden Media, LLC. Reproduced by permission of A Yearling Book, an imprint of Random House Children's Books, a division of Random House, Inc.)

way to a new world. Elizabeth Devereaux, writing in the *New York Times,* remarked of *The City of Ember* that DuPrau's "rapidly and solidly developed story lines keep such a tight focus on Lina and Doon's struggles that the sheer thrill of the climax almost sneaks up on the reader." *School Library Journal* critic John Peters predicted that the "quick pace and the uncomplicated characters and situations" in *The City of Ember* "will keep voracious fans of the [fantasy] genre engaged."

DuPrau continues the adventures of Lina and Doon in *The People of Sparks* and *The Diamond of Darkhold. The People of Sparks* finds the duo fleeing from the underground city and leading over 400 survivors to the rural community of Sparks, where they are fed and housed. Tensions soon arise between the refugees and the townspeople, however, when the Emberites have trouble adjusting to Sparks' agrarian way of life and the city's foodstores quickly become depleted. According to a *Publishers Weekly* contributor, in *The People of Sparks* DuPrau presents "a sprawling world on the surface of the planet, and . . . skillfully and confidently develops the idea of scarcity and how human beings react to a depletion of resources." Beth L. Meister observed in *School Library Journal* that the narrative "smoothly involves new readers and fans of the first story, creating a range of three-dimensional characters in both the Ember and Sparks groups."

With the publication of *The Diamond of Darkhold,* DuPrau concludes her "Books of Ember" series. As the citizens of Sparks and the refugees from Ember attempt to reconcile their differences, Doon and Lina return to the underground city to retrieve supplies, including an enigmatic device with mysterious powers. Once in Ember, they encounter members of the Trogg family, a hostile group that has moved into the preteens' former home. A contributor in *Kirkus Reviews* applauded the "fast-paced and clever final installment," and Roger Sutton, writing in *Booklist,* reported that *The Diamond of Darkhold* "is everything a series closer should be, satisfying but provocative."

The Prophet of Yonwood serves as a prequel to *The City of Ember* and focuses on Nickie Randolph, an eleven year old who travels with her aunt to Yonwood, North Carolina, to prepare her great-grandfather's house for sale. With the United States now on the brink of war, though, anxious Yonwood residents have interpreted the ramblings of an elderly woman as prophetic. In addition, a self-appointed watchdog group begins outlawing "sinful" behavior, which includes singing and keeping pets, to form a "shield of goodness" around the town. Sharon Rawlins, writing in *School Library Journal,* noted that *The Prophet of Yonwood* "sharply brings home the idea of people blindly following a belief without questioning it," and a *Kirkus Reviews* critic asserted that audiences "will find it a provocative read with an appealingly conflicted protagonist."

In DuPrau's contemporary young-adult novel *Car Trouble,* readers meet tech-savvy Duff Pringle, a recent

high-school graduate who is preparing to travel from his home in Virginia to Silicon Valley, where a job designing computer games awaits. When his car breaks down early in the journey, Duff agrees to transport a vintage Chevrolet to California, and before long, he picks up Stu, a charismatic hitchhiker, and Bonnie, the car owner's teenaged daughter. As the travelers begin their cross-country odyssey, it becomes apparent that they are being trailed by unsavory characters who want the stolen loot hidden in the automobile's trunk. Reviewing *Car Trouble* in *Kliatt,* Paula Rohrlick observed that DuPrau "crafts an intriguing road trip/coming-of-age tale with some interesting characters and plot twists." Tracy Karbel remarked in *School Library Journal* that the novel's plot "is kept moving by strong characters who steer the flow of the story."

Biographical and Critical Sources

BOOKS

DuPrau, Jeanne, *The Earth House* (memoir), New Chapter Press (Pound Ridge, NY), 1992.

PERIODICALS

Belles Lettres, winter, 1992, Susanne Carter, review of *The Earth House,* p. 57.
Booklist, March 15, 1990, Stephanie Zvirin, review of *Adoption: The Facts, Feelings, and Issues of a Double Heritage,* p. 1423; November 15, 1999, Randy Meyer, review of *Cloning,* p. 611; April 15, 2003, Sally Estes, review of *The City of Ember,* p. 1466; April 15, 2004, Sally Estes, review of *The People of Sparks,* p. 1453.
Book Report, September-October, 1990, Brooke Dillon, review of *Adoption,* p. 68.
Bulletin of the Center for Children's Books, May, 1990, Deborah Stevenson, review of *Adoption,* p. 212.
Horn Book, May-June, 2003, Roger Sutton, review of *The City of Ember,* p. 343; May-June, 2006, Roger Sutton, review of *The Prophet of Yonwood,* p. 313; September-October, 2008, Roger Sutton, review of *The Diamond of Darkhold,* p. 582.
Kirkus Reviews, July 1, 2005, review of *Car Trouble,* p. 733; April 1, 2006, review of *The Prophet of Yonwood,* p. 345; July 1, 2008, review of *The Diamond of Darkhold.*
Kliatt, September, 2005, Paula Rohrlick, review of *Car Trouble,* p. 7.
Library Journal, April 1, 1992, Harriet Gottfried, review of *The Earth House,* p. 126.
New York Times, June 22, 2003, Elizabeth Devereaux, review of *The City of Ember.*
Publishers Weekly, June 30, 2003, Jennifer M. Brown, "Flying Starts," p. 18; March 1, 2004, review of *The People of Sparks,* p. 69; April 3, 2006, review of *The Prophet of Yonwood,* p. 74.
School Library Journal, July, 1990, Anna Biagioni Hart, review of *Adoption,* p. 90; May, 2003, John Peters, review of *The City of Ember,* p. 150; May, 2004, Beth

L. Meister, review of *The People of Sparks,* p. 146; October, 2005, Tracy Karbel, review of *Car Trouble,* p. 158; June, 2006, Sharon Rawlins, review of *The Prophet of Yonwood,* p. 152; November, 2008, Mara Alpert, review of *The Diamond of Darkhold,* p. 118.

ONLINE

Jeanne DuPrau Home Page, http://www.jeanneduprau. com (March 1, 2010).

Random House Web site, http://www.randomhouse.com/ (March 1, 2010), "Jeanne DuPrau."

Suite 101 Web site, http://www.suite101.com/ (March 1, 2010) interview with DuPrau.

*   *   *

DURANGO, Julia 1967-

Personal

Born March 15, 1967, in Las Vegas, NV; married Santiago Durango (an attorney); children: Kyle, Ryan. *Education:* University of Illinois, B.A., M.A.

Addresses

Home—Ottawa, IL. *Agent*—Barry Goldblatt, PMB 266, 320 7th Ave., Brooklyn, NY 11215. *E-mail*—juliadurango@yahoo.com.

Career

Children's book author and librarian. McKinley Elementary School, Ottawa, IL, librarian.

Member

Society of Children's Book Writers and Illustrators (Illinois chapter), Illinois Reading Council.

Awards, Honors

Nick Jr. magazine Best Book designation, and American Library Association Notable Book for Younger Readers designation, both with Linda Sue Park, both 2005, both for *Yum! Yuck!;* Syndey Taylor Book Award Notable Book designation, 2009, and *Américas* Award Commended designation, both 2009, both for *The Walls of Cartagena;* Parents' Choice Award Silver Medal, 2009, and Golden Kite Award for fiction, Society of Children's Book Writers and Illustrators, and Best Books designation, Bank Street College, both 2010, all for *Sea of the Dead.*

Writings

Peter Claver, Patron Saint of Slaves, illustrated by Rebecca García-Franco, Paulist Press (New York, NY), 2002.

Dream Hop, illustrated by Jared Lee, Simon & Schuster Books for Young Readers (New York, NY), 2005.

(With Linda Sue Park) *Yum! Yuck!: A Foldout Book of People Sounds,* illustrated by Sue Ramá, Charlesbridge Publishing (Watertown, MA), 2005.

Cha-Cha Chimps, illustrated by Eleanor Taylor, Simon & Schuster Books for Young Readers (New York, NY), 2006.

Angels Watching over Me, illustrated by Elisa Kleven, Simon & Schuster Books for Young Readers (New York, NY), 2007.

Pest Fest, illustrated by Kurt Cyrus, Simon & Schuster Books for Young Readers (New York, NY), 2007.

The Walls of Cartagena, illustrated by Tom Pohrt, Simon & Schuster Books for Young Readers (New York, NY), 2008.

Sea of the Dead, Simon & Schuster Books for Young Readers (New York, NY), 2009.

Go-Go Gorillas, illustrated by Eleanor Taylor, Simon & Schuster Books for Young Readers (New York, NY), 2010.

Under the Mambo Moon, illustrated by Fabricio Vanden Broeck, Charlesbridge (Watertown, MA), 2011.

(With Katie Belle Trupiano) *Dream Away,* illustrated by Robert Goldstrom, Simon & Schuster Books for Young Readers (New York, NY), 2011.

Sidelights

Julia Durango has focused her career around books, both as a writer and as a school librarian. Although her first book for children was a biography, Durango quickly turned to fiction, and she has produced entertaining picture books such as *Cha-Cha Chimps,* quiet bedtime stories such as *Angels Watching over Me* and *Dream Away,* and the elementary-grade novels *Sea of the Dead* and *The Walls of Cartagena.*

After graduating from the University of Illinois, Durango spent time traveling around Latin America, working with impoverished families and homeless children. Drawing on her interest in Latin-American history, she made her publishing debut in 2002 with *Peter Claver, Patron Saint of Slaves.* The book takes readers back to the seventeenth century and introduces a young Jesuit who, while traveling from his native Spain to Colombia, encountered the horrors of slavery first hand. Father Claver made a vow to be the "slave of slaves forever" and kept true to this vow for the rest of his life by caring for and aiding enslaved peoples.

Set in the seventeenth century, and similar in theme to *Peter Claver, Patron Saint of Slaves, The Walls of Cartagena* introduces readers to Calepino. Born on a slave ship sailing from Africa to Colombia, Calepino was rescued by a Jesuit priest and provided with a good education. Now thirteen years old and evidencing a gift for languages, Calepino aids Father Pedro in his work ministering to slaves arriving on similar ships. He is inspired to activism by Father Pedro, as well as by the Jewish Doctor Lopez, who works with the lepers living

outside the walls of the city. In *Booklist* Hazel Rochman praised *The Walls of Cartagena* as a "gripping" story that is enriched by "the authentic history of people desperate and brave," while a *Kirkus Reviews* writer cited Durango's tale as full of "well-researched detail" and featuring "a clever young hero."

Durango's lighthearted *Yum! Yuck!: A Foldout Book of People Sounds,* coauthored with Linda Sue Park, features interactive illustrations and introduces children to the way humans of different cultures verbally express emotions. Praised as an introduction to the earth's kaleidoscopic array of languages—including Danish, Farsi, and Korean—the book was dubbed "entertaining" by a *Kirkus Reviews* critic. Watercolor illustrations by Sue Ramá depict children from around the world engaging in scenarios relevant to each emotion being discussed, while English translations hidden under page flaps make the book an effective learning tool. "This original offering is a delightful addition to the canon of multicultural picture books and a fun read-aloud guessing game," commented Rachel G. Payne in a review for *School Library Journal.*

Durango continues her lighthearted approach in *Cha-Cha Chimps, Go-Go Gorillas, Dream Hop,* and *Pest Fest.* In *Cha-Cha Chimps* Durango integrates a counting lesson into her story about ten young chimpanzees that dance the night away at the forest home of Mamba Jamba, until "a clever surprise ending . . . keeps them toe-tappin' happy," as Julie Cummins commented in *Booklist.* "Durango's dancing rhyme is infectious," noted a *Kirkus Reviews* contributor, while Susan E. Murray wrote in *School Library Journal* that the chimps' "cha-cha-cha chant" joins with Eleanor Taylor's "upbeat" illustrations to make *Cha-Cha Chimps* "a good storytime addition."

With its focus on a young boy trying to deal with a common childhood dilemma, *Dream Hop* "suggests a novel coping mechanism for dealing with bad dreams," according to *School Library Journal* critic Rosalyn Pierini. In *Pest Fest* Durango teams up with artist Kurt Cyrus to tell an entertaining story about the Best Pest of the Year contest and the housefly that wins it. Calling the story "clever and appealing," a *Kirkus Reviews* writer added that *Pest Fest* "begs to be read aloud."

More somber in tone, *Angels Watching over Me* was inspired by an African-American spiritual. Brought to life in mixed-media artwork by Elisa Kleven, Durango's story focuses on a young boy and the guardian angels that watch over him throughout the course of a day by taking the form of the sun, wind, a tree, and other natural objects. While a *Publishers Weekly* contributor remarked on Durango's use of sophisticated imagery, the critic added that "the melody of the [book's] language and its reverence for the natural world are sure to spark interest" in young children. Judith Constantinides noted in her *School Library Journal* review that Durango avoids religious terms in her narration, making *Angels Watching over Me* "a beautiful nondenominational paean to creation and the Earth's many blessings."

Biographical and Critical Sources

PERIODICALS

Booklist, December 1, 2005, Gillian Engberg, review of *Dream Hop,* p. 53; January 1, 2006, Julie Cummins, review of *Cha-Cha Chimps,* p. 110; July 1, 2008, Hazel Rochman, review of *The Walls of Cartagena,* p. 68; May 1, 2010, Ilene Cooper, review of *Go-Go Gorillas,* p. 94.

Kirkus Reviews, June 15, 2005, review of *Yum! Yuck!: A Foldout Book of People Sounds,* p. 688; September 15, 2005, review of *Dream Hop,* p. 1025; December 15, 2005, review of *Cha-Cha Chimps,* p. 1321; March 1, 2007, review of *Angels Watching over Me,* p. 211; May 15, 2007, review of *Pest Fest;* June 15, 2008, review of *The Walls of Cartagena;* March 1, 2010, review of *Go-Go Gorillas.*

Publishers Weekly, February 6, 2006, review of *Cha-Cha Chimps,* p. 68; May 14, 2007, review of *Angels Watching over Me,* p. 58.

School Library Journal, August, 2005, Rachel G. Payne, review of *Yum! Yuck!,* p. 104; October, 2005, Rosalyn Pierini, review of *Dream Hop,* p. 112; February, 2006, Susan E. Murray, review of *Cha-Cha Chimps,* p. 96; May, 2007, Judith Constantinides, review of *Angels Watching over Me,* p. 91; July, 2007, Linda Ludke, review of *Pest Fest,* p. 74; September, 2008, Diana Pierce, review of *The Walls of Cartagena,* p. 178; January, 2010, Alyson Low, review of *Sea of the Dead,* p. 100; March, 2010, Kathleen Kelly MacMillan, review of *Go-Go Gorillas,* p. 117.

ONLINE

Carus Publishing Web site, http://www.cricketmag.com/ (April 15, 2010), "Julia Durango."

Curled up with a Good Kid's Book Web site, http://www.curledupkids.com/ (September 10, 2006), Marie D. Jones, review of *Dream Hop.*

Julia Durango Home Page, http://www.juliadurango.com (April 15, 2010).

SCBWI-Illinois Web site, http://www.scbwi-illinois.org/ (April 15, 2010), "Julia Durango."

F-G

FORMAN, Mark L.
See FORMAN, M.L.

* * *

FORMAN, M.L. 1964-
(Mark L. Forman)

Personal

Born 1964, in UT. *Religion:* Church of Jesus Christ of Latter-day Saints (Mormon). *Hobbies and other interests:* Fishing, camping, hiking.

Career

Writer. Works as a computer systems administrator.

Writings

Slathbog's Gold ("Adventurers Wanted" series), Shadow Mountain Publishing (Salt Lake City, UT), 2009.

Adaptations

Slathbog's Gold was adapted as an audio book.

Sidelights

The inspiration for M.L. Forman's novel *Slathbog's Gold,* the first work in his "Adventurers Wanted" series, came to the author from an unusual source: the classified ads. After losing his job during the recession of the early 2000s, Forman turned to the classifieds each day, searching for employment opportunities. He soon conceived of an advertisement for an adventure agency seeking explorers to travel the world in search of treasure. Although he eventually found a new job, Forman worked on his fantasy tale for years, finally releasing it in 2009. The goal of the work, the author told *Deseret*

News online contributor Carma Wadley, "was to write a fun story, and although there are lessons to be learned, I didn't want a Big Moral that hits you over the head."

Slathbog's Gold centers on Alexander Taylor, a fifteen year old who is working unhappily in his stepfather's tavern when he spots a sign in a bookstore window pro-

Cover of M.L. Forman's middle-grade adventure novel Slathbog's Gold, *featuring artwork by Ben Sowards.* (Illustration © 2008 Ben Sowards. Reproduced by permission.)

claiming "Adventurer's Wanted." Acting on impulse, Alex meets with the store owner who immediately recruits the teen to join a team of seven other explorers tasked with slaying a fearsome dragon named Slathbog the Red and claiming his treasure. During his journey, Alex meets a host of magical creatures, including wizards, elves, and dwarves, and discovers that he possesses strange and wonderful powers. Reviewing *Slathbog's Gold* in *Booklist,* Krista Hutley offered praise for the work, noting that "the camaraderie among the group members is a strong draw."

Biographical and Critical Sources

PERIODICALS

Booklist, February 15, 2009, Krista Hutley, review of *Slathbog's Gold,* p. 84.
Kirkus Reviews, January 15, 2009, review of *Slathbog's Gold.*
Library Journal, February 15, 2009, Jackie Cassada, review of *Slathbog's Gold,* p. 98.

ONLINE

Adventurers Wanted Web site, http://www.adventurerswanted.com/ (March 1, 2010).
Deseret News Online, http://www.deseretnews.com/ (February 28, 2009), Carma Wadley, "Classified Ads Inspire Author's Fantasy Novel."
Fear Knocks Web site, http://fearknocks.com/ (October, 2008), interview with Forman.
Shadow Mountain Publishing Web site, http://www.shadowmountain.com/ (March 1, 2010), "M.L. Forman."*

*　　*　　*

FURLONGER, Patricia
See WRIGHTSON, Patricia

*　　*　　*

GENTRY, Marita

Personal
Born in MO.

Addresses
Home and office—P.O. Box 1053, Walker, LA 70785.

Career
Illustrator, artist, muralist, and educator. Studio Marita, Walker, LA, founder. Teacher of children; serves as artist in residence. *Exhibitions:* Work exhibited at Circa

1857 Gallery and Acadian Frame and Art, both Walker, LA. Murals installed in southern Louisiana public schools.

Member
Society of Children's Book Writers and Illustrators, Louisiana Watercolor Society.

Awards, Honors
Numerous awards from local and national art shows.

Illustrator
Dianne de la Casas, *Madame Poulet and Monsieur Roach,* Pelican Publishing (Gretna, LA), 2009.
Dianne de la Casas, *The Cajun Cornbread Boy: A Well-loved Tale Spiced Up,* Pelican Publishing (Gretna, LA), 2009.

Biographical and Critical Sources

PERIODICALS

Kirkus Reviews, January 15, 2009, review of *The Cajun Cornbread Boy: A Well-loved Tale Spiced Up.*
School Library Journal, March, 2009, Judith Constantinides, review of *The Cajun Cornbread Boy,* p. 108.

ONLINE

Marita Gentry Home Page, http://www.studiomarita.com (April 20, 2010).*

*　　*　　*

GIRAUDON, David 1975-

Personal
Born 1975, in Mâcon, France. *Education:* École Supérieure d'Arts Graphiques, degree.

Addresses
Home—Mâcon, France. *E-mail*—contact@davidgiraudon.fr.

Career
Graphic designer and illustrator.

Illustrator
Jean-Paul Nozière, *Retour à Ithaque,* Gallimard Jeunesse (Paris, France), 2000.

Terre vue du ciel, photographs by Yann Arthus-Bertrand, 2000, adapted by Robert Burleigh as *The Earth from Above for Young Readers*, Harry N. Abrams (New York, NY), 2002, published as *The Earth from the Air for Children*, Thames & Hudson (London, England), 2002.

Alexis de Rougè *Le secret de Djem Nefer*, Gallimard Jeunesse (Paris, France), 2001.

Michael Morpurgo, *Tempête sur Shangri-La*, translated from the English, Gallimard Jeunesse (Paris, France), 2001.

La terre racontée aux enfants, photographs by Yann Arthus-Bertrand, text by Hércúle Montardre, Martinière Jeunesse (Paris, France), 2002.

Volcans racontés aux enfants (board book), photographs by Philippe Bourseiller, text by Hércúle Montardre, Martinière Jeunesse (Paris, France), 2002, adapted by Robert Burleigh as *Volcanoes: Journey to the Crater's Edge*, H.N. Abrams (New York, NY), 2003.

David Almond, *Rêve de tigre*, translated from the English, Gallimard Jeunesse (Paris, France), 2003.

Jean-Pierre Verdet, *Cluny*, JPM Éditions (Mâcon, France), 2004.

Gérard Théllier, *Mâcon*, JPM Éditions (Mâcon, France), 2005.

Laurent Michele, *Le mont d'or lyonnais et son val de Saône*, photographs by Max Martin, JPM Éditions (Mâcon, France), 2005.

Corinne Albaut, *L'Abbaye de Cluny*, Éditions du Patrimoine (Paris, France), 2006.

Our Living Earth: A Story of People, Ecology, and Preservation, photographs by Yann Arthus-Bertrand, text by Isabelle Delannoy, translated by Gita Daneshjoo, H.N. Abrams Books for Young Readers (New York, NY), 2008.

Ma terre aux milles merveilles, photographs by Yann Arthus-Bertrand, Martinière Jeunesse (Paris, France), 2009.

Contributor to books, including *Invitation à la flânerie*, JPM Éditions.

Biographical and Critical Sources

PERIODICALS

Audubon, November-December 2008, Julie Leibach, review of *Our Living Earth: A Story of People, Ecology, and Preservation*, p. 99.

Publishers Weekly, September 30, 2002, review of *Earth from Above for Young Readers*, p. 75.

School Library Journal, December, 2003, Pam Spencer Holley, review of *Volcanoes: Journey to the Crater's Edge*, p. 164; January, 2009, Judith V. Lechner, review of *Our Living Earth: A Story of People, Ecology, and Preservation*, p. 126.

ONLINE

David Giraudon Home Page, http://www.davidgiraudon.fr (March 15, 2010).*

GOLD, August 1955-

Personal
Born February 26, 1955.

Addresses
Home—New York, NY; CT. *Office*—Sacred Center NY, 330 W. 38th St., Ste. 704, New York, NY 10018. *E-mail*—info@sacredcenterny.org.

Career
Writer, minister, administrator, educator, broadcaster, and public speaker. Sacred Center New York, New York, NY, cofounder with Joel Fotinos, senior minister, and spiritual director. Interfaith minister, 2001—. Guest on television programs, including *A New Day*, Hallmark Channel. Host of weekly radio program in metropolitan New York, NY. Speaker at corporations, churches, and other organizations.

Awards, Honors
Independent Publishers Book Award for Most Inspirational Book for Children, c. 2001, for *Where Does God Live?*

Writings

(With Joel Fotinos) *The Prayer Chest: A Novel about Receiving All of Life's Riches*, Doubleday (New York, NY), 2007.

(Adaptor, with Joel Fotinos) *The Think and Grow Rich Workbook*, based on the book by Napoleon Hill, Jeremy P. Tarcher/Penguin (New York, NY), 2009.

(With Joel Fotinos) *A Little Daily Wisdom: 365 Inspiring Bible Verses to Change Your Life*, Paraclete Press (Brewster, MA), 2010.

FOR YOUNGER READERS

(With Matthew J. Perlman) *Where Does God Live?*, SkyLight Paths (Woodstock, VT), 2001.

Does God Hear My Prayer?, photographs by Diane Hardy Waller, SkyLight Paths (Woodstock, VT), 2005.

Does God Forgive Me?, photographs by Diane Hardy Waller, SkyLight Paths (Woodstock, VT), 2006.

Thank You, God, for Everything, illustrated by Wendy Anderson Halperin, G.P. Putnam's Sons (New York, NY), 2009.

Sidelights
August Gold is a prolific writer, interfaith minister, spiritual leader, and public speaker. Ordained in 1989, she is a cofounder of the Sacred Center for Spiritual Living in New York City, where she also serves as senior minister and spiritual director. Gold's teaching

combines both Western religious practices and ancient Eastern spiritual ideas, such as those found in the Tao te Ching. She is a frequent speaker at corporate events, conventions, churches, spiritual centers, and other gatherings around the country, and she regularly appears on the television program *A New Day,* broadcast on the Hallmark Channel. Gold has also developed her own trademarked educational system, called Soul-Work, which allows her to extend her ministry and provide enriching spiritual teachings to her clients and listeners. As a teacher and spiritual counselor, Gold "weaves exciting ideas and concepts with practical tools to give audiences a fresh approach to life," according to the Sacred Center New York Web site.

In addition to her work as a minister, Gold has also written several religious books for younger audiences. Designed for readers between ages three and six, the books address basic questions about God, prayer, and spirituality in a multicultural and nondenominational context. In *Where Does God Live?,* written with Matthew J. Perlman, Gold addresses a child's reasonable curiosity about God's home place, and offers a lesson teaching that God and the divine can be found everywhere and in everything. Gold and Perlman address, in an accessible way, the seeming contradiction in not being able to view God directly, but to see Him and His works in all things through emotional feelings and spiritual acceptance. "Hats off to Gold and Perlman for this delightful and wonder-filled tribute to seeing with the heart that God lives in and all around us," commented

August Gold shares her gentle spirituality with young children in the picture book **Than You, God, for Everything,** *featuring artwork by Wendy Halperin.* (Illustration copyright © 2009 by Wendy Anderson Halperin. All rights reserved. Reproduced by permission of G.P. Putnam's Sons, a division of Penguin Putnam Books for Young Readers.)

reviewers Frederic Brussat and Mary Ann Brussat, for the Spirituality and Practice Web site. Ilene Cooper, writing in *Booklist,* called *Where Does God Live?* "a sweet, safe place to start a conversation about God."

Does God Hear My Prayer? contains Gold's explanation of prayer for children in a book that "manages to hit some issues that children think about when it comes to prayer," according to Cooper. Gold comments on the source of prayers, and whether they are made up by each person or read from books. Using a child's unfulfilled prayer for a new bicycle as a springboard for discussion, she comments on why some prayers are answered and some are not. She also offers wisdom and advice on what to do after praying, and how and when to start listening for God's answers. Another book for children, *Does God Forgive Me?,* finds Gold explaining "the essentials of forgiveness and mak[ing] . . . it relevant to those who are ages three through six years," explained the Brussats in another Spirituality and Practice Web site review.

In *Thank You, God, for Everything,* a book illustrated in pencil and oil paints by Wendy Anderson Halperin, Gold uses the story of a girl named Daisy to illustrate the value of thankfulness. Daisy watches her parents express appreciation for the many things in their life, and the girl models their example by listing the many wonderful things in her own world, from family members to God's presence. Although Lisa Egly Lehmuller wondered whether Daisy's appreciation focused on "abstract gifts" rather than the "tangible things" children commonly relate to, a *Kirkus Reviews* writer praised *Thank You, God, for Everything* as a "gentle, encouraging story of Christian faith." Citing Halperin's "signature softly colored" illustrations, Cooper concluded in *Booklist* that Gold's picture book will inspire "young readers . . . to find their own answers" to the question: What are you thankful for?"

Collaborating with author Joel Fotinos, Gold is also the author of the inspirational *The Prayer Chest: A Novel about Receiving All of Life's Riches.* Geared for adult readers, the story focuses on Joseph Hutchinson, a late nineteenth-century farmer who lives on Long Island. Hardworking, spiritually earnest, married, and the father of two young children, Joseph dreads the apparent family curse that kills the males of his lineage when they reach their twenties. He finds respite from his worries by retreating to the attic of his house, a comforting space that helps to soothe his concerns and where his prayers seem to find a receptive audience. When his wife, Miriam, dies of pneumonia, Joseph becomes bitter and turns away from the attic and his spirituality. Soon he finds himself saddled with debt, wracked with guilt over unresolved feelings for neighbor Grace, and concerned for his children's welfare. Joseph's future looks bleak until he discovers an unusual chest that, filled with slips of paper and a notebook, may help him reconnect with his religious life and learn the enduring

secrets of sincere prayer. A *Publishers Weekly* reviewer wrote of *The Prayer Chest* that Gold's "easy, inspirational read will warm the hearts of seekers everywhere."

Biographical and Critical Sources

PERIODICALS

Booklist, October 1, 2001, Ilene Cooper, review of *Where Does God Live?,* p. 334; April 1, 2005, Ilene Cooper, review of *Does God Hear My Prayer?,* p. 1362; December 15, 2008, Ilene Cooper, review of *Thank You, God, for Everything,* p. 50.

Kirkus Reviews, September 1, 2007, review of *The Prayer Chest: A Novel about Receiving All of Life's Riches;* January 15, 2009, review of *Thank You, God, for Everything.*

Publishers Weekly, July 9, 2007, review of *The Prayer Chest,* p. 27.

School Library Journal, July, 2005, Linda L. Walkins, review of *Does God Hear My Prayer?,* p. 89; January, 2009, Lisa Egly Lehmuller, review of *Thank You, God, for Everything,* p. 76.

ONLINE

Sacred Center New York Web site, http://www.sacred centerny.org/ (April 28, 2010), "August Gold."

Spirituality and Practice Web site, http://www.spirituality andpractice.com/ (May 7, 2008), Frederic Brussat and Mary Ann Brussat, reviews of *Where Does Got Live?* and *Does God Forgive Me?**

H

HAAS, Jessie 1959-

Personal

Born July 27, 1959, in Westminster, VT; daughter of Robert Joseph (a truck driver and freight manager) and Patricia Anne (a farmer and homemaker) Haas; married Michael Joseph Daley (a writer and educator), April 25, 1981. *Education:* Wellesley College, B.A. (English), 1981. *Politics:* "Progressive Democrat." *Hobbies and other interests:* Horseback riding, animals, cooking, knitting, drawing, reading, Scottish dancing, politics.

Addresses

Home—Putney, VT. *E-mail*—kjh@sover.net.

Career

Writer, 1981—. Worker at a vegetable stand, early 1980s; yarn mill laborer, mid-1980s-91. Trustee, Westminster West Library, 1984-87; member of board of directors, Vermont Public Interest Research Group. Volunteer for Westminster Cares (Meals-on-Wheels delivery).

Member

Society of Children's Book Writers and Illustrators, Vermont Citizens Campaign for Health (president of board).

Awards, Honors

Pick of the Lists selection, *American Bookseller,* 1993, for *Beware the Mare,* 1994, for *Busybody Brandy,* 1995, for *No Foal Yet,* and 1996, for *Clean House;* Children's Book of the Year, Child Study Association, 1996, for *Be Well, Beware* and for *Clean House,* and 1997, for *Sugaring;* Notable Children's Book in the Field of Social Studies designation, National Council for Social Studies (NCSS)/ Children's Book Council (CBC), 1997, for *Sugaring; Publishers Weekly* Best Book citation, and *School Library Journal* Best Book citation, both 1999, *Bulletin of the Center for Children's Books* Choice designation, 2000, and Notable Children's Trade Book in Social Studies designation, Parent's Choice Gold Award, and *Voice of Youth Advocates* Outstanding Book for Middle School Students designation, all for *Unbroken; Bulletin of the Center for Children's Books* Blue Ribbon designation, *Horn Book* Fanfare listee, and American Library Association Notable Book designation, all 2001, all for *Runaway Radish;* Golden Kite Honor Book selection, Society of Children's Book Writers and Illustrators, 2002, for *Shaper;* 100 Books to Read and Share selection, New York Public Library, Gryphon Award Honor Book, and Beverly Cleary Award nominee, all c. 2005, all for *Jigsaw Pony.*

Writings

Keeping Barney, Greenwillow (New York, NY), 1982.

Working Trot, Greenwillow (New York, NY), 1983.

The Sixth Sense and Other Stories, Greenwillow (New York, NY), 1988.

Skipping School, Greenwillow (New York, NY), 1992.

Beware the Mare, illustrated by Martha Haas, Greenwillow (New York, NY), 1993.

Chipmunk!, illustrated by Joseph A. Smith, Greenwillow (New York, NY), 1993.

A Horse like Barney, Greenwillow (New York, NY), 1993.

Mowing, illustrated by Joseph A. Smith, Greenwillow (New York, NY), 1994.

Uncle Daney's Way, Greenwillow (New York, NY), 1994.

Busybody Brandy, illustrated by Yossi Abolafia, Greenwillow (New York, NY), 1994.

Safe Horse, Safe Rider: A Young Rider's Guide to Responsible Horsekeeping, Storey Communications (Pownal, VT), 1994.

Getting Ready to Drive a Horse and Cart, illustrated by Christine Erickson, Storey Communications (Pownal, VT), 1995.

A Blue for Beware, illustrated by Joseph A. Smith, Greenwillow (New York, NY), 1995.

No Foal Yet, illustrated by Joseph A. Smith, Greenwillow (New York, NY), 1995.

Be Well, Beware, illustrated by Joseph A. Smith, Greenwillow (New York, NY), 1996.

Clean House, illustrated by Yossi Abolafia, Greenwillow (New York, NY), 1996.

Sugaring, illustrated by Joseph A. Smith, Greenwillow (New York, NY), 1996.

Westminster West, Greenwillow (New York, NY), 1997.

Fire!: My Parents' Story, Greenwillow (New York, NY), 1998.

(And illustrator) *Beware and Stogie,* Greenwillow (New York, NY), 1998.

Unbroken, Greenwillow (New York, NY), 1999.

Hay in the Barn, Greenwillow (New York, NY), 1999.

Hurry!, illustrated by Joseph A. Smith, Greenwillow (New York, NY), 2000.

Will You, Won't You?, Greenwillow (New York, NY), 2000.

Runaway Radish, illustrated by Margot Apple, Greenwillow (New York, NY), 2001.

Appaloosa Zebra: A Horse Lover's Alphabet, illustrated by Margot Apple, Greenwillow (New York, NY), 2002.

Shaper, Greenwillow (New York, NY), 2002.

Birthday Pony, illustrated by Margot Apple, Greenwillow (New York, NY), 2004.

Scamper and the Horse Show, illustrated by Margot Apple, Greenwillow (New York, NY), 2004.

Hoofprints: Horse Poems, Greenwillow (New York, NY), 2004.

Jigsaw Pony, illustrated by Ying-Hwa Hu, Greenwillow (New York, NY), 2005.

Chase, Greenwillow (New York, NY), 2007.

Haas's works have been translated into Swedish.

Adaptations

Sound recordings of *Unbroken* were produced by Recorded Books (Prince Frederick, MD), 1999, and by American Printing House for the Blind (Louisville, KY), 2000; sound recordings of *Uncle Daney's Way* and *No Foal Yet* were produced by American Printing House for the Blind in 1996 and 1997, respectively.

Sidelights

Jessie Haas is the author of novels and picture books for children, most of which deal with one of Haas's reigning passions—horses. In award-winning titles such as *Keeping Barney, Beware the Mare, Uncle Daney's Way, Shaper,* and *Jigsaw Pony,* Haas illuminates the life of farming and working with farm animals. The topic is a familiar one to Haas, who was raised on a Vermont farm that she still calls home.

"My childhood was full of haying, gardening, horseback riding, and animals," Haas once commented. "I trained my own horse. I was given a goat for my sixteenth birthday. My mother was the town pound-keeper, so we had an endless stream of stray cats and dogs coming through. Lots of them stayed." If animals were a vital part of Haas's growing up, so was reading, an activity that was not limited to the confines of an easy chair. "I read all the horse stories ever written, as first choice, and then anything else printed on a page," she recalled. This magpie curiosity stood Haas in good stead when she attended college, at Wellesley College and studied English literature and writing.

Influenced by English novelist Jane Austen and by her love of horse stories, Haas wrote her first novel while still a college student. One of her teachers recommended that she try to publish the book and gave her the name of a former student who had become editor-in-chief at Greenwillow Books. The novel, *Keeping Barney,* was initially rejected, but with helpful suggestions it was accepted by Greenwillow upon its second submission, a month before Haas graduated from college.

That same month, Haas married and settled on property near her parents' farm, building a simple cabin. "We had one room at first," she once explained, "with no insulation, no phone, no plumbing, and no electricity— but a very small mortgage. The little house gave us— still gives us—the freedom to pursue our interests without having to get 'real jobs.' I've worked at a vegetable stand, a village store, and a yarn mill, all part-time, while concentrating mainly on my writing."

Meanwhile, *Keeping Barney* was published to favorable reviews, earning several awards to boot. Barney is a cranky and stubborn horse who causes his young owner no end of trouble. Sarah Miles is thirteen and has long waited for the day she would have her own horse, imagining a lovely partnership between human and animal. Barney is a far cry from the sleek stallion of her imagination, however, and his feistiness is intimidating. Finally, Sarah learns that the "secret of success is frequently self-control," as Mary M. Burns wrote in *Horn Book,* and the realization that Barney "would never really be hers was not only the moment of demarcation between childhood and adolescence but is also the climax of the story." *Booklist* critic Denise M. Wilms noted that "there is much truth in the portrayal of Sarah's struggles with a real rather than a dream horse, and her girlish joy in horses and riding will surely be communicated to readers." Calling the story "satisfying and sustaining," a *Kirkus Reviews* contributor dubbed *Keeping Barney* a "nicely managed girl-gets-horse story—with individuated characters and some unexpected twists."

Working Trot again features horses, but this time Haas's protagonist is a young man. James graduates from high school with plans far different from those of his parents, who want him to attend college and pursue a business career. Instead James wants to train as a dressage rider, working with a somewhat dilapidated Lipizzan stallion at his uncle's riding establishment in Vermont. The demands of a professional riding career prove greater than James first imagined, however, and he struggles to balance his study with his social life, at-

tempting to fit in with a young equestrian who wants to ride on the Olympic team. Pat Harrington, writing in *School Library Journal,* observed that "Haas conveys an impressive knowledge of her subject" and "has written a novel that is realistic and satisfying."

In *A Horse like Barney,* a sequel to *Keeping Barney,* Sarah continues the search for a horse of her own. Again, the search is more difficult than Sarah imagined: Should she pick the lively Roy or the older and needier Thunder? Watson, writing in *Horn Book,* felt that the story has "depth and texture, provided by insights into the emotions Sarah feels," while Hazel Rochman noted in *Booklist* that Haas's short chapters make the book ideal "for young readers ready to go beyond illustrated fiction." *A Horse like Barney* stands as "a wholesome, introspective novel," according to Rochman, and "just right for horse enthusiasts."

In the novel *Uncle Daney's Way,* young Cole learns important lessons about life and managing a workhorse when his disabled uncle moves into the family's barn. Watson noted in *Horn Book* that the "middle-grade reader will identify with Cole's growing enthusiasm fueled by increasing accomplishment in this refreshing treatment of a loving family's successful attempt to cope with a challenge," while Deborah Stevenson observed in *Bulletin of the Center for Children's Books* that *Uncle Daney's Way* is "a good old story told with affection and subtlety."

In her novel *Shaper,* Haas introduces fourteen-year-old Chad Holloway, a frustrated, sullen youth who is grieving after the tragic death of his beloved dog, Shep. David Burton, a dog trainer who uses the clicker method to "shape" an animal's behavior, hires Chad as his research assistant, allowing the teen to come to terms with his loss. *Horn Book* critic Peter D. Sieruta complimented the novel's growth as a writer, observing that Haas "uses well-chosen details to create living, breathing characters with family traditions and personal histories that began before we ever met them." Kay Weisman, writing in *Booklist,* described *Shaper* as "a thoughtful piece featuring quirky characters with believable problems."

In *Skipping School* fifteen-year-old Phillip feels isolated and confused as he learns to cope with his father's terminal illness. Still reeling from the move from a farm to the suburbs, Phillip skips school and finds solace at a nearby abandoned farmhouse, where he spends afternoons chopping wood and caring for a pair of kittens while slowly coming to terms with his father's imminent death. A *Publishers Weekly* reviewer commended Haas, writing that her "eye for telling details give[s] this heartwarming novel its subtle power" and concluded that *Skipping School* "is a book to savor." *Horn Book* critic Watson observed that Haas has created "a provocative, satisfying novel that contrasts the value of life against the constant presence of death." "A wonder-

ful book to read and discuss," *Skipping School* marks "probably the only time skipping school resulted in an A+," Watson added.

Haas turns to the short-story format in *The Sixth Sense and Other Stories,* a collection of nine "wonderful stories," according to *Horn Book* reviewer Elizabeth Watson. Her two main characters, James and Kris, tie together many of these stories about cats, dogs, and horses, and which examine the relationship between humans and animals through themes of loyalty, death, responsibility, love, and understanding. Watson dubbed *The Sixth Sense and Other Stories* a "superb collection with deeply felt emotion for animal lovers," and Betsy Hearne noted in the *Bulletin of the Center for Children's Books* that Haas's tales "make a real contribution to the short story genre, being both resonant and readable."

Haas has also written historical fiction. In *Westminster West,* set in 1884, two sisters must deal with their roles as women, both in the family and in society, when an arsonist threatens their Vermont village. "*Westminster West* is based on real events which took place within three miles of my home, over a hundred years ago," Haas once explained. "I fictionalized the story, trying to understand and make convincing one version of why people might have behaved as they did. A story about arson and about taking to one's bed with the vapors, it was poised between melodrama and no drama at all, and required a complex understructure." In any event, Haas's technical efforts proved successful; *Horn Book* reviewer Mary M. Burns concluded that *Westminster West* "grapples effectively with the conflicting issues of personal freedom and family responsibilities," and Elizabeth Bush noted in *Bulletin of the Center for Children's Books* that "Haas builds a rich and sensitive portrait of a late nineteenth-century Vermont farm family."

Another work of historical fiction, *Fire!: My Parents' Story,* tells the story of the burning of Haas's mother's house when she was eight years old. Haas tried to write this book for years, "in various complex ways," as she once said. "It only worked when I found the way to tell it in the eight-year-old voice, as simply as possible." *New York Times Book Review* contributor Andrea Higbie described *Fire!* as "a plain, well-told tale" and noted that Haas "imaginatively captures the facts and fears of being in a fire."

In *Chase,* a work of historical fiction set in post-U.S. Civil War Pennsylvania, a stable boy goes on the run after he is accused of murder. When orphan Phin Chase witnesses the killing of a mine boss, he flees to the countryside, pursued by member of the Sleepers, a secret brotherhood of Irish coalminers, and a tireless Pinkerton detective aboard a black stallion. "There's not a lot of time for psychological study in this breathless plot," Ruth Conniff noted in the *New York Times Book Review.* "The book's strength is its intriguing setting, and Haas sprinkles the story with vivid historical de-

tails." "Haas writes gracefully and evocatively of boy, horse, and desperate men," wrote *Booklist* critic Francisca Goldsmith, and *Kliatt* reviewer Claire Rosser called *Chase* "fine historical fiction, with suspense on every page and a courageous young man who is quite a hero."

In addition to her novels for older children, Haas also creates picture books and beginning chapter readers. *Beware the Mare* was the first of her illustrated books for younger readers in a series that features a mare named Beware. In this story, Gramps gets a good bargain on a seemingly perfect mare for young Lily, although the horse's name does make him suspect that something might be wrong. Haas uses this mystery "to provide enough tension to hold this charming vignette together," according to a critic in *Kirkus Reviews*. "Horse lovers who like their fiction short and easy are frequently disappointed," noted Stevenson in *Bulletin of the Center for Children's Books*, "but here's a well-written offering that conveys a flavorful lot in a small space." Lily and her horse Beware continue their adventures in further titles in the "Beware" series. A horse show ribbon is won in *A Blue for Beware*, a book to be "greeted with unbridled enthusiasm," according to Stevenson in *Bulletin of the Center for Children's Books*. A case of colic has to be treated in *Be Well, Beware*, a book in which the "plot takes off from the first page and maintains intensity right until the end," according to Christina Linz in *School Library Journal*. The fourth work in the series is *Beware and Stogie*, for which Haas herself illustrated the chapter headers. She described illustration as "my newest adventure" and finds it "exciting to be learning something completely new, and to go beyond what I thought were limits."

In another early reader, *Clean House*, Tess and her mother have to tidy the house for the arrival of Tess's cousin, Kate. The more they clean, the messier things get, but finally the house is spotless. It is also very boring and antiseptic, but once the relatives arrive they help to mess things up nicely again. Roger Sutton noted in *Bulletin of the Center for Children's Books* that *Clean House* admits "the little-acknowledged truth about house work: why bother? . . . Cognizant of both parent and child demands, this easy chapter book would make a fine intergenerational read-together."

Haas's books aimed at preschool and first-grade readers include the companion volumes *Mowing, No Foal Yet, Sugaring,* and *Hurry!*, all featuring the winning duo of Gramp and Nora. Nora helps her grandfather in the first title with horse-drawn mowing, avoiding a fawn and a killdeer nest in the process. A *Kirkus Reviews* critic noted that "the warm interaction between Nora and Gramp grows naturally from their companionable dialogue, while art and text work beautifully together to bring out the story's quiet drama." In *No Foal Yet* Nora and Gramp are back on the farm waiting for Bonnie to give birth to her foal. Nora helps Gramp make maple syrup and sugar in *Sugaring*, a "satisfying story," according to Caroline Ward in *School Library Journal,* and one that "will be a welcome addition during any season." In *Hurry!* Nora and Gramp race to harvest the hay on their farm before the rain falls. "Readers cannot help but be pulled into the story," Lee Bock commented in *School Library Journal,* and Martha V. Parravano, writing in *Horn Book,* also complimented the narrative, stating that "Haas's language is simple but evocative."

In *Unbroken* Haas tells another story involving horses. When young Harriet, called Model T. Harry, has no way to get to school, a young colt must be trained or Harry will have to quit school. As a reviewer for *Publishers Weekly* noted, "Haas has a gift for description and graceful simile, and her characters are sharply observed, especially honest and wise 13-year-old Harry who can coax compassion from even her frozen Aunt Sarah."

Haas uses her interest in politics to tell the story of *Will You, Won't You?*, a contemporary novel that focuses on young Madison "Mad" Parker. Mad spends the summer with her grandmother, who happens to be chair of the Senate Finance Committee in Washington, DC,, and she ends up speaking out about a bill to ban clear-cut logging. "Haas creates a large cast of well-rounded characters to weave engaging details about political life, Scottish country dancing, horse training, and personal growth," wrote Laura Scott in her review of *Will You, Won't You?* in *School Library Journal*.

Haas has also enjoyed a successful collaboration with illustrator Margot Apple. Their first effort, *Runaway Radish,* concerns a pony that grows too big for the girls who own him. "The story is simply written, yet it has a truthful ring," stated Lisa Falk in *School Library Journal,* and *Horn Book* contributor Anita L. Burkam noted that the work gives readers "a vicarious thrill of horse ownership without disguising the fact that the responsibilities aren't always glamorous or pleasant." In a follow-up, *Birthday Pony,* a youngster who shares the same birthdate as a stubborn pony learns to tame the horse with the help of her grandmother. "Haas contributes another winning story that's just right for horse-smitten new readers," *Booklist* reviewer Gillian Engberg stated.

Haas and Apple also join forces on *Appaloosa Zebra: A Horse Lover's Alphabet,* in which a girl dreams about the horses she will have when she gets older. A critic in *Kirkus Reviews* applauded the work, describing it as a "fitting addition to the creator's equine oeuvre; a fine supplement to the ABC canon." In *Scamper and the Horse Show,* two sisters discover the difficulty of keeping their pony's white coat clean when a rainstorm dissolves Scamper's red, white, and blue ensemble. According to Carol Schene, writing in *School Library Journal,* "this charming story presents an accurate and appealing look at the ambience of a local horse show."

In a departure from her other works, Haas's *Hoofprints: Horse Poems* examines the history of her favorite ani-

mal in more than 100 poems, providing a look at the horse's prehistoric ancestors, the ways humans have used horses over the centuries, and the emotional bonds between horse and rider. "The language is precise, careful, and true," noted a *Kirkus Reviews* contributor in appraising *Hoofprints,* and *School Library Journal* critic Susan Scheps praised Haas's "deft use of rhymes and rhythms, descriptive narrative verse, occasional touches of humor, and subtle inferences."

For Haas, writing is similar to riding—both are processes that demand balance and profound concentration. "Each novel is different and requires a different process," she noted. "Some come inch by inch, arriving in polished sentences which remain the same from first draft to printed book. Others come scattershot; you catch the fragments and press them into shape like a meat loaf." Haas, who meets her reading public regularly, finds ample rewards in her literary pursuits. As she stated on her home page, "I love the act of writing, I've learned to love rewriting, and I adore getting that first copy of a new book in the mail. But what I love best is knowing that out there in the world, kids are finding my books and curling up in private with them, having their own experience of them, and making of it whatever they will."

Literary awards and a growing readership have not greatly changed Haas's lifestyle. She and her husband haul water by hand and heat their Vermont house with wood. However, they do have electricity (supplied primarily by solar power) for lighting and their writing work. "I still live the same kind of life I did growing up," she reported. "I ride a horse I trained myself. A cat sleeps on my desk as I work. I walk to my parents' farm every day and can pick out the exact spot in the pasture where my horse Josey gave me *Beware the Mare.* It's an immense privilege to live this way—to make up stories and people, to spend all day drawing pictures of cows, to find a way to tell a family story so it will reach a wider audience, move perfect strangers, and be preserved."

Biographical and Critical Sources

PERIODICALS

Booklist, June 1, 1982, Denise M. Wilms, review of *Keeping Barney,* p. 1312; September 15, 1993, Hazel Rochman, review of *A Horse like Barney,* p. 152; April 15, 1997, Ilene Cooper, review of *Westminster West,* p. 1422; May 1, 1998, Linda Perkins, review of *Fire!: My Parents' Story,* p. 1514; August, 1998, Shelle Rosenfeld, review of *Beware and Stogie,* p. 2004; March 15, 1999, Lauren Peterson, review of *Unbroken,* p. 1325; April 15, 2001, Gillian Engberg, review of *Runaway Radish,* p. 1552; September 15, 2001, Lolly Gepson, review of *Unbroken,* p. 240; February 1, 2001, Jean Franklin, review of *Will You, Won't You?,* p. 1053; January 1, 2002, Julie Cummins, review of *Appaloosa Zebra: A Horse Lover's Alphabet,* p. 864; July, 2002, Kay Weisman, review of *Shaper,* p. 1844; March 15, 2004, Gillian Engberg, review of *Hoofprints: Horse Poems,* p. 1297; June 1, 2004, John Peters, review of *Scamper and the Horse Show,* p. 1741; August, 2004, Gillian Engberg, review of *Birthday Pony,* p. 1934; September 1, 2005, Julie Cummins, review of *Jigsaw Pony,* p. 133; February 1, 2007, Francisca Goldsmith, review of *Chase,* p. 42.

Book Report, September-October, 1997, Jennifer Schwelik, review of *Westminster West,* p. 35; September-October, 1999, Catherine M. Andronik, review of *Unbroken,* p. 59.

Bulletin of the Center for Children's Books, January, 1989, Betsy Hearne, review of *The Sixth Sense and Other Stories,* p. 122; July-August, 1993, Deborah Stevenson, review of *Beware the Mare,* p. 345; April, 1994, Deborah Stevenson, review of *Uncle Daney's Way,* p. 259; March, 1995, Deborah Stevenson, review of *A Blue for Beware,* p. 236; March, 1996, Roger Sutton, review of *Clean House,* p. 227; April, 1997, Elizabeth Bush, review of *Westminster West,* p. 284.

Horn Book, August, 1982, Mary M. Burns, review of *Keeping Barney,* p. 403; March-April, 1989, Elizabeth Watson, review of *The Sixth Sense and Other Stories,* p. 216; January-February, 1993, Elizabeth Watson, review of *Skipping School,* p. 90; November-December, 1993, Elizabeth Watson, review of *A Horse like Barney,* p. 744; July-August, 1994, Elizabeth Watson, review of *Uncle Daney's Way,* p. 452; July-December, 1996, review of *Sugaring,* p. 30; May-June, 1997, Mary M. Burns, review of *Westminster West,* p. 321; September-October, 1998, Elizabeth S. Watson, review of *Beware and Stogie,* p. 608; July, 1999, Bridget T. McCaffrey, review of *Unbroken,* p. 464; July, 2000, Martha V. Parravano, review of *Hurry!,* p. 435; May, 2001, Anita L. Burkam, review of *Runaway Radish,* p. 324; May-June, 2002, Peter D. Sieruta, review of *Shaper,* p. 330; September-October, 2004, Betty Carter, review of *Birthday Pony,* p. 584; September-October, 2005, Betty Carter, review of *Jigsaw Pony,* p. 578.

Kliatt, July, 2002, Paula Rohrlick, review of *Shaper,* p. 10; March, 2007, Claire Rosser, review of *Chase,* p. 12.

Kirkus Reviews, April 1, 1982, review of *Keeping Barney,* p. 417; May 15, 1993, review of *Beware the Mare,* p. 661; May 14, 1994, review of *Mowing,* p. 698; February 1, 1997, review of *Westminster West,* p. 223; December 1, 2001, review of *Appaloosa Zebra,* p. 1685; May 1, 2002, review of *Shaper,* p. 655; January 15, 2004, review of *Hoofprints,* p. 83; April 1, 2004, review of *Scamper and the Horse Show,* p. 330; July 1, 2004, review of *Birthday Pony,* p. 630; July 15, 2005, review of *Jigsaw Pony,* p. 790; April 1, 2007, review of *Chase.*

New York Times Book Review, December 20, 1998, Andrea Higbie, review of *Fire!,* p. 25; May 16, 1999, Emily Arnold McCully, review of *Unbroken,* p. 25; April 15, 2007, Ruth Coniff, review of *Chase.*

Publishers Weekly, November 9, 1992, review of *Skipping School,* p. 87; May 11, 1998, review of *Fire!,* p. 69;

February 8, 1999, review of *Unbroken*, p. 215; October 2, 2000, review of *Will You, Won't You?*, p. 82; March 8, 2004, "Poetry in Motion," review of *Hoofprints*, p. 76.

School Library Journal, January, 1984, Pat Harrington, review of *Walking Trot*, p. 86; April, 1996, Christina Linz, review of *Be Well, Beware*, p. 132; October, 1996, Caroline Ward, review of *Sugaring*, p. 94; May, 1997, Wendy D. Caldiero, review of *Westminster West*, p. 133; May, 1998, Anne Chapman Callaghan, review of *Fire!*, p. 133; November 1, 1998, Lee Bock, review of *Beware and Stogie*, p. 85; April, 1999, Christy Norris Blanchette, review of *Unbroken*, p. 134; June, 2000, Lee Bock, review of *Hurry!*, p. 114; October, 2000, Laura Scott, review of *Will You, Won't You?*, p. 160; May, 2001, Lisa Falk, review of *Runaway Radish*, p. 122; February, 2002, Wanda Meyers-Hines, review of *Appaloosa Zebra*, p. 101; May, 2002, William McLoughlin, review of *Shaper*, p. 152; March, 2004, Susan Scheps, review of *Hoofprints*, p. 234; July, 2004, Carol Schene, review of *Scamper and the Horse Show*, p. 77; October, 2004, Kristina Aaronson, review of *Birthday Pony*, p. 114; December, 2005, Carol Schene, review of *Jigsaw Pony*, p. 113; April, 2007, Vicki Reutter, review of *Chase*, p. 136.

ONLINE

Jessie Haas Home Page, http://www.jessiehaas.com (June 1, 2010).*

*   *   *

HANDLER, Daniel
See SNICKET, Lemony

*   *   *

HAWORTH-ATTARD, Barbara 1953-

Personal

Born July 25, 1953, in Kitchener, Ontario, Canada; married; husband's name, Joe; children: Jason, Jesse. *Hobbies and other interests:* Cats, quilting, reading, writing.

Addresses

Home—London, Ontario, Canada. *Agent*—Scott Treimel, 434 Lafayette St., New York, NY 10003. *E-mail*—battard@rogers.com.

Career

Writer. Teaches creative writing courses for adults.

Member

Writers' Union of Canada, Canadian Children's Book Centre, Canadian Society of Children's Authors, Illustrators, and Performers.

Awards, Honors

Our Choice selection, Canadian Children's Book Centre (CCBC), 1995-96, and Manitoba Young Reader's Choice Award shortlist, 1997-98, both for *Dark of the Moon;* Mr. Christie Book Award shortlist, and Geoffrey Bilson Historical Fiction Award shortlist, both 1997, Silver Birch Award shortlist, and CCBC Our Choice selection, both 1997-98, and Manitoba Young Readers' Choice Award shortlist, and Red Cedar Award shortlist, both 1998, all for *Home Child;* CCBC Our Choice selection, 1997-98, for *Truth Singer;* CCBC Our Choice selection, 1999-2000, and Manitoba Young Reader's Choice Award shortlist, 2001, both for *Buried Treasure;* CCBC Our Choice selection, 2000-01, Geoffrey Bilson Historical Fiction Award shortlist, 2001, and Red Cedar Award shortlist, 2002, all for *Love-Lies-Bleeding;* CCBC Our Choice selection, 2002, Manitoba Young Reader's Choice Award shortlist, and Silver Birch Award shortlist, both 2003, and Red Cedar Award shortlist, 2004, all for *Flying Geese;* Red Maple Award Honor Book designation, and Geoffrey Bilson Historical Fiction Award Honor Book designation, both 2003, and Manitoba Young Readers' Choice Award shortlist, 2004, all for *Irish Chain;* Governor General's Award finalist, 2003, Young Adult Canadian Book Award shortlist, Canadian Library Association (CLA), 2004, and Stellar Book Award, 2006, all for *Theories of Relativity;* Book of the Year for Children shortlist, CLA, 2005, for *A Trail of Broken Dreams;* Geoffrey Bilson Award for Historical Fiction Honor Book designation, 2006, and Stellar Award shortlist, 2007, both for *Forget-Me-Not;* Young Adult Canadian Book Award shortlist, CLA, 2010, for *Haunted.*

Writings

NOVELS

The Three Wishbells, Roussan (Montreal, Quebec, Canada), 1995.

Dark of the Moon, Roussan (Montreal, Quebec, Canada), 1995.

Home Child, Roussan (Montreal, Quebec, Canada), 1996.

Truth Singer, Roussan (Montreal, Quebec, Canada), 1996.

Buried Treasure, Roussan (Montreal, Quebec, Canada), 1998.

WyndMagic, Roussan (Montreal, Quebec, Canada), 1999.

Love-Lies-Bleeding, Roussan (Montreal, Quebec, Canada), 1999.

Flying Geese, HarperCollins (Toronto, Ontario, Canada), 2001.

Irish Chain, HarperTrophy Canada (Toronto, Ontario, Canada), 2002.

Theories of Relativity, HarperTrophy Canada (Toronto, Ontario, Canada), 2003, Henry Holt (New York, NY), 2005.

A Trail of Broken Dreams: The Gold Rush Diary of Harriet Palmer: Overland to the Cariboo, 1862, Scholastic Canada (Markham, Ontario, Canada), 2004.

Forget-Me-Not (sequel to *Love-Lies-Bleeding*), HarperTrophy Canada (Toronto, Ontario, Canada), 2005.

A Is for Angst, HarperTrophy Canada (Toronto, Ontario, Canada), 2007.

Haunted, HarperTrophy Canada (Toronto, Ontario, Canada), 2009.

My Life from Air-bras to Zits, Flux (Woodbury, MN), 2009.

OTHER

Contributor to anthologies, including *Winds through Time,* Beach Holme Publishers, 1998, and *The Horrors,* Red Deer Press, 2005.

Sidelights

Canadian author Barbara Haworth-Attard has garnered numerous honors for her many novels, which include *Truth Singer,* a fantasy tale, *Irish Chain,* a work of historical fiction, and *Theories of Relativity,* a contemporary novel for young adults. Haworth-Attard published her first book for young readers, *The Three Wishbells,* in 1995, and in addition to producing a steady stream of popular novels she also inspires others through her work as a writing teacher.

Cover of Barbara Haworth-Attard's humorous girl-centered coming-of-age novel **My Life from Air-bras to Zits.** *(Flux, 2009. Cover image © 2008 by Image Source/Jupiter Images. Reproduced by permission.)*

In *Truth Singer* young Nathan learns that he possesses an unusual power and that he must it employ to save a kingdom in a parallel world. According to *Resource Links* critic Mary Duffy, Nathan's character "is superbly drawn and instantly recognizable," and the critic described *Truth Singer* as "an appealing novel about a young boy who finds his own voice."

In *Home Child,* one of Haworth-Attard's early efforts, the author explores a little-known chapter of Canada's past. Set in 1914, the work concerns thirteen-year-old Arthur, a British-born orphan who is sent to Canada to work on a rural Ontario farm. "Written in simple direct language," as Anne Letain reported in the *Canadian Review of Materials,* "*Home Child* fictionalizes and renders alive a compelling and underreported segment of Canadian history."

In *Irish Chain* Haworth-Attard looks at the Halifax Explosion—a man-made disaster that collapsed buildings, injured over 9,000, and killed more than 2,000 people in December of 1917—through the eyes of Rose Dunlea, a troubled but sensitive teenage girl. Still on record as the world's largest accidental man-made detonation, the Halifax Explosion was caused when a French cargo ship carrying explosives intended for use in World War I collided with a Norwegian liner in the harbor of the Nova Scotian city. "In telling detail, Haworth-Attard captures the daily drama and struggles of Rose and vividly establishes what life was like in the [city's] . . . close-knit Irish community," Sherie Posesorski stated in a review of Haworth-Attard's novel for *Quill & Quire.*

A coming-of-age story told via diary excerpts, *Love-Lies-Bleeding* focuses on Ontario teenager Roberta "Bobby" Harrison, whose father, brother, and uncle are serving with Canadian forces in Europe during World War II. "Haworth-Attard deftly captures the nuances of human behaviour and effectively brings the historical period alive, painting a portrait rich in details of everyday life," Darleen Golke noted in her review of the novel for *Canadian Review of Materials.* In a sequel, *Forget-Me-Not,* Bobby struggles to understand the devastation wrought by the bombings of Hiroshima and Nagasaki. The author "infuses the diary entries with humour and wit as Bobby sorts through her daily concerns and difficulties," Golke commented. Haworth-Attard "presents Bobby's outrage and horror at learning of man's inhumanity to man perceptively and sensitively," the critic added.

A sixteen year old learns to survive on the streets after his cruel, uncaring mother kicks him out of the house in *Theories of Relativity,* an "honest look at the desperation of teen homelessness," as Johanna Lewis remarked in *School Library Journal.* Haworth-Attard's story centers on Dylan Wallace, an intelligent young man who applies concepts developed by his hero, Albert Einstein, to make sense of his troubling situation. "This dark

novel takes a hard look at a pervasive urban problem," Susan Perren commented in the Toronto *Globe & Mail*, and in *Horn Book* Timothy Capehart maintained that "Dylan's snarky yet vulnerable voice is a particular strength" of *Theories of Relativity*.

Haworth-Attard tackles much lighter fare in *My Life from Air-bras to Zits,* a humorous novel about an angst-ridden tenth grader who worries about her flat chest, her ever-changing social status, and her manic, soon-to-be-wed older sister. The novel "does an excellent job of depicting the trials and tribulations of a typical teenage girl," wrote *School Library Journal* contributor Robyn Zaneski in a review of *My Life from Air-bras to Zits*.

Biographical and Critical Sources

PERIODICALS

Booklist, November 1, 2005, Jennifer Mattson, review of *Theories of Relativity,* p. 37.

Canadian Review of Materials, November 1, 2002, Betsy Fraser, review of *Irish Chain;* April 23, 2004, Anne Letain, review of *Home Child;* February 4, 2005, Darleen Golke, review of *Love-Lies-Bleeding;* October 14, 2005, Darleen Golke, review of *Forget-Me-Not.*

Globe & Mail (Toronto, Ontario, Canada), November 1, 2003, Susan Perren, review of *Theories of Relativity,* p. D22.

Horn Book, September-October, 2005, Timothy Capehart, review of *Theories of Relativity,* p. 578.

Kirkus Reviews, July 15, 2005, review of *Theories of Relativity,* p. 791; January 15, 2009, review of *My Life from Air-bras to Zits.*

Quill & Quire, September, 1996, Joanne Schott, review of *The Truthsinger;* August, 2002, Sherie Posesorski, review of *Irish Chain.*

Resource Links, June, 1997, Denise Parrott, review of *Home Child,* pp. 215, 218, and Mary Duffy, review of *Truthsinger,* p. 218; February, 2000, review of *Love-Lies-Bleeding,* p. 25; April, 2003, Victoria Pennell, review of *Irish Chain,* p. 13; December, 2004, Victoria Pennell, review of *A Trail of Broken Dreams: The Gold Rush Diary of Harriet Palmer: Overland to the Cariboo, 1862,* p. 14.

School Library Journal, November, 2005, Johanna Lewis, review of *Theories of Relativity,* p. 136; March, 2009, Robyn Zaneski, review of *My Life from Air-bras to Zits,* p. 145.

ONLINE

Barbara Haworth-Attard Home Page, http://www.barbara haworthattard.com (March 1, 2010).

Canadian Society of Children's Authors, Illustrators, and Performers Web site, http://www.canscaip.org/ (March 1, 2010), "Barbara Haworth-Attard."

Scholastic Canada Web site, http://www.scholastic.ca/ dearcanada/ (March 1, 2010), "Barbara Haworth-Attard."

HESSE, Karen 1952-

Personal

Born August 28, 1952, in Baltimore, MD; married Randy Hesse, November 27, 1971; children: Kate, Rachel. *Education:* Attended Towson State College; University of Maryland, B.A. (English, psychology, anthropology), 1975. *Religion:* Jewish.

Addresses

Home—VT.

Career

Writer and librarian. Writer, beginning 1969; University of Maryland, leave-benefit coordinator, 1975-76; worked variously as a teacher, librarian, advertising secretary, typesetter, and proofreader. Affiliated with Mental Health Care and Hospice, 1988—; Newfane, VT, Elementary School board chair, 1989; board member of Moore Free Library, Newfane, 1989-91.

Member

Society of Children's Book Writers and Illustrators (head of southern Vermont chapter, 1985-92).

Awards, Honors

Children's Book of Distinction designation, *Hungry Mind Review,* 1992, for *Wish on a Unicorn;* poetry awards from *Writer's Digest* and Poetry Society of Vermont; Best Books designation, *School Library Journal,* One Hundred Titles for Reading and Sharing selection, New York Public Library, International Reading Association (IRA) Children's Book of the Year designation, National Jewish Book Award, Sydney Taylor Award, Association of Jewish Libraries, and Best Books for Young Adults and Notable Books selections, American Library Association (ALA), all 1992, and Christopher Award, 1993, all for *Letters from Rifka;* Golden Kite award shortlist, Society of Children's Book Writers and Illustrators, and ALA Best Books for Young Adults designation, all 1996, all for *The Music of Dolphins;* IRA Young Adults' Choice designation, 1997, for *A Time of Angels;* Newbery Medal, Scott O'Dell Award for Historical Fiction, and Jefferson Cup Honor Book designation, Virginia Library Association, all 1998, all for *Out of the Dust;* Heartland Award for Excellence in Young-Adult Literature, 1998, for *Phoenix Rising;* Christopher Award, 2002, for *Witness;* MacArthur fellowship, 2002; Sydney Taylor Book Award, 2009, for *Brooklyn Bridge.*

Writings

Wish on a Unicorn, Holt (New York, NY), 1991.
Letters from Rifka, Holt (New York, NY), 1992.

Karen Hesse (Reproduced by permission.)

Poppy's Chair (picture book), illustrated by Kay Life, Macmillan (New York, NY), 1993.

Lester's Dog (early chapter book), illustrated by Nancy Carpenter, Crown (New York, NY), 1993.

Lavender (chapter book), illustrated by Andrew Glass, Holt (New York, NY), 1993.

Sable (early chapter book), illustrated by Marcia Sewall, Holt (New York, NY), 1994.

Phoenix Rising, Holt (New York, NY), 1994.

A Time of Angels, Hyperion (New York, NY), 1995.

The Music of Dolphins, Scholastic, Inc. (New York, NY), 1996.

Out of the Dust, Scholastic, Inc. (New York, NY), 1997.

Just Juice (early chapter book), illustrated by Robert Andrew Parker, Scholastic, Inc. (New York, NY), 1998.

Come on, Rain, illustrated by Jon J. Muth, Scholastic, Inc. (New York, NY), 1999.

A Light in the Storm: The Civil War Diary of Amelia Martin, Scholastic, Inc. (New York, NY), 1999.

Stowaway, illustrated by Robert Andrew Parker, Margaret K. McElderry Books (New York, NY), 2000.

Witness, Scholastic, Inc. (New York, NY), 2001.

The Stone Lamp: Eight Stories of Hannukkah through History, illustrated by Brian Pinkney, Hyperion (New York, NY), 2002.

Aleutian Sparrow, illustrated by Evon Zerbertz, Margaret K. McElderry Books (New York, NY), 2003.

The Cats in Krasinski Square, illustrated by Wendy Watson, Scholastic, Inc. (New York, NY), 2004.

The Young Hans Christian Andersen, illustrated by Erik Blegvad, Scholastic, Inc. (New York, NY), 2005.

Brooklyn Bridge (novel), Feiwel & Friends (New York, NY), 2008.

Spuds, illustrated by Wendy Watson, Scholastic, Inc. (New York, NY), 2008.

Contributor of short story to *When I Was Your Age, II,* Candlewick Press (Cambridge, MA), 1999.

Author's books have been translated into several languages, including Chinese and Spanish.

Adaptations

Many of Hesse's books have been adapted as audiobooks, including *The Music of Dolphins, Aleutian Sparrow, Stowaway, Out of Dust, A Time of Angels, Wish on a Unicorn, Just Juice, Light in the Storm, Come on, Rain!, Witness,* and *Brooklyn Bridge.*

Sidelights

"A profound and visceral sense of place is one of the qualities that is most memorable about Karen Hesse's writing," maintained Brenda Bowen in *Horn Book* on the occasion of Hesse's win of the 1998 Newbery Medal. This "sense of place" encompasses not only landscape—physical locations from Russia to Vermont to Oklahoma—but also spaces in the heart and mind. Whether taking on questions of death and hope in *Phoenix Rising,* of the meaning of being human and its relationship to language in *The Music of Dolphins,* the tenacity of the human spirit in the Newbery Medal-winning *Out of the Dust,* or the blessings of a strong family in *Brooklyn Bridge,* Hesse explores her chosen emotional terrain with a sure hand. History is also part of Hesse's sense of place. Her historical novels, including *Letters from Rifka, Out of the Dust,* and *Brooklyn Bridge,* have transported readers to Russia, Belgium, and the United States during the first decades of the 1900s.

Hesse has garnered an impressive list of awards for her work, including a prestigious Newbery award, the Scott O'Dell Award, and two Christopher awards. In 2002 she also became the second children's author ever to receive a MacArthur Foundation fellowship, which is granted to people who, as Debra Lau Whelan noted in *School Library Journal,* "lift our spirits, illuminate human potential, and shape our collective future." The grant could not have found a worthier recipient: as the Foundation noted in its presentation, Hesse is the author of books that "expand the possibilities of literature for children and young adults." Responding to the award, Hesse commented in *Children's Literature:* "I was stunned when I heard, and I continue to be stunned. I just hope that this brings recognition to the entire field of children's literature, where such extraordinary work is being done."

Hesse was born in Baltimore, Maryland, in 1952. She developed a love for reading at an early age, and often spent time at the Enoch Pratt Free Library near her

house, where, "beginning with Dr. Seuss, I read my way through the picture books, the shorter chapter books, and finally the novels," as she recalled in an essay for *Something about the Author Autobiography Series* (*SAAS*). As Hesse neared the teenage years, she began to read adult novels. One of these was John Hersey's *Hiroshima,* a book "that changed my life," she remembered. "The courage, the profound compassion, dignity, and humanity of the Japanese people in the face of such unfathomable destruction helped me see the world in a way I never had before. When I closed the covers of *Hiroshima,* I closed the door on my childhood." The impact of this book would later be echoed in her own novel, *Phoenix Rising.*

In high school Hesse became interested in acting. Although her grades at first were poor, they improved during her last two years, and with the help of an enthusiastic drama teacher she was admitted to Towson State College. However, Hesse's studies were cut short after just two years when she met her future husband. In 1971 the young couple eloped, and soon after that Hesse's husband was shipped out with the U.S. Navy to the Mediterranean.

Cover of Hesse's middle-grade novel The Music of Dolphins, *featuring cover art by Greg Harlin.* (Illustration copyright © 1996 by Greg Harlin. Reprinted by permission of Scholastic, Inc.)

Hesse lived in Norfolk, Virginia, while she waited for her husband's return. She also finished her undergraduate work, transferring to the University of Maryland, where she helped fund her studies by working in the university library. During this time she began writing and giving readings, gaining a reputation as a poet. Upon graduation, Hesse worked for a time as a leave-benefit coordinator for her alma mater, but mostly she took work that was close to books and words: as an advertising secretary, a typesetter, and a proofreader. Upon settling in Vermont, Hesse and her husband had two children, one born in 1979 and one in 1982. Her poetry was put on hold by motherhood, but soon she was experimenting with writing books. "It was typesetting that led me to believe I could succeed as a children's book writer," she noted in *SAAS*. "Some of the work I set struck me as very unsatisfying. I thought I could write at least as well if not better."

Sixth-grader Maggie, the protagonist of Hesse's first novel, *Wish on a Unicorn,* loves her younger brother, Mooch, and her slightly brain-damaged sister, Hannie. Even so, Maggie sometimes feels overwhelmed with the responsibility of looking after her siblings while her single-parent mom works nights. At school, all three are bullied, especially when Hannie wets herself. As a result, Maggie worries that she will never have friends. When Hannie finds a dirty stuffed unicorn, she believes that the toy animal has magical powers to grant wishes. In spite of herself, Maggie also begins to believe in the powers of the unicorn, and some wishes seem to come true, although not necessarily in the way she hoped. Eventually a family crisis—the disappearance of Hannie and her unicorn—crystallizes the importance of family for Maggie. Reviewing *Wish on a Unicorn* for *Horn Book,* Nancy Vasilakis noted that Hesse's debut is "a compassionate story of a family who have little in the way of worldly goods but who are rich in solidarity and spirit." Vasilakis also observed that the "use of the unicorn as a symbol of this family's essential strength is understated and effective."

Letters from Rifka drew its inspiration from Hesse's own family history. Based on the experiences of her great aunt, the book tells of the adventures of a young Jewish girl and her family. The letters referred to in the title, written in the margins of a book of verse by famed nineteenth-century Russian writer Aleksandr Pushkin, are penned by young Rifka to her cousin Tovah. Fleeing the harsh conditions endured by Jews living in Russia in the wake of the Bolshevik revolution, Rifka's family first crosses into Poland in 1919. Humiliatingly examined by a doctor and stricken with typhus, they nonetheless survive, make their way to Belgium, and then sail for America. Unfortunately, Rifka catches ringworm while trying to help a fellow passenger on the way to Warsaw, and she is denied passage on the ship. She lives with a Belgian family while she recovers, and when she finally leaves to join her family in America, she survives a storm at sea only to be detained by immigration officials at Ellis Island because of her

ringworm-induced baldness. During her weeks of detainment, Rifka befriends a young Russian boy who is in a similar predicament. At her hearing, Rifka makes an eloquent plea on behalf of both herself and her new friend.

Letters from Rifka was enthusiastically received by reviewers. Writing in *Horn Book,* Hanna B. Zeiger commented that this "moving account of a brave young girl's story brings to life the day-to-day trials and horrors experienced by many immigrants as well as the resourcefulness and strength they found within themselves." Writing in the *Bulletin of the Center for Children's Books,* Betsy Hearne observed that, while many novels focus on the immigration experiences of Russian Jews, *Letters from Rifka* "is vivid in detailing the physical and emotional toll exacted for passage."

In *Phoenix Rising* Hesse tells a futuristic tale of nuclear disaster and its aftereffects. After a nuclear power plant spreads radiation throughout New England, thirteen-year-old Nyle and her grandmother continue tending their sheep on their Vermont farm, wearing protective masks and hoping that the winds will keep the contamination away. Then two evacuees arrive from Boston: fifteen-year-old Ezra and his mother, who stay in the back bedroom on Grandma's farm. Nyle is afraid of intimacy and at first she keeps her distance from the deathly ill Ezra. However, her fears and self-protectiveness eventually erode and she comes to love the radiation-stricken youth. Nyle takes care of Ezra until his death, finally learning how to let go of a loved one. "Nyle's emotional growth allows her to face his death with newfound strength," explained Vasilakis in her review of *Phoenix Rising* for *Horn Book.* "The story is told in measured, laconic tones," Vasilakis continued, and "by focusing on the love story between the two main characters, Hesse has made this story essentially one of hope and determination."

Catastrophic events are also at the heart of *A Time of Angels.* Here, instead of the future, readers are transported to the past: to the influenza epidemic that spread throughout the world following World War I. Hannah and her sisters are living in Boston with Tanta Rose, waiting for their parents to return from Europe. Then Rose is killed by the flu, and Hanna's sisters become infected. Although she is evacuated from the city, Hanna also comes down with the flu and ends up in Brattleboro, Vermont, guided by an angel that has saved her life before. She is brought back to health by an old German farmer who is treated as an outcast because of his former nationality. A *Publishers Weekly* reviewer noted that "Hesse intensifies the apocalyptic mood of *A Time of Angels,* palpably recreating the terror in the streets as the influenza spreads," while Hearne commented in the *Bulletin of the Center for Children's Books* that the author "has taken on a lot here and managed to do justice to it all."

Hesse's novel *The Music of Dolphins* was described by a *Publishers Weekly* reviewer as being as "moving as a sonnet, as eloquently structured as a Bell Curve" and

Hesse transports readers to a tragic era in twentieth-century history in her novel **Out of the Dust.** (AP Images.)

one that "poignantly explores the most profound of themes—what it means to be human." The narrator of the tale, Mila, is a so-called feral child who was raised by dolphins. As a four year old, she survived a plane crash off the coast of Cuba and she was nurtured by dolphins for ten years, until her discovery by the U.S. Coast Guard. Dubbed "Mila"—"miracle" in Spanish—the girl now becomes the subject of a government study. She is taught language and music by a team of scientists, and learns with amazing speed. She also attempts to teach the scientists dolphin language. All the while, however, the call of the wild echoes in the girl's mind and she longs to return to her island. "Mila's rich inner voice makes her a lovely, lyrical character," noted Mary Arnold in a review of *The Music of Dolphins* for *Voice of Youth Advocates.* Arnold went on to call the book a "profound study of being human and the ways in which communication unites and separates human beings."

Hesse worked on her novel *Out of the Dust* for several years, drawing inspiration from a 1993 car trip to Colorado. She was awestruck by the country she saw and amazed by the subtle varieties of color and by the wind that never ceased. After several years she melded these memories in an historical look at the Dust-Bowl years

of the 1930s. She also saturated herself in research, reading her way through newspapers of the time, getting a feel for daily life in those days. Then came characters Billie Jo and her family, and the format: free verse. "I never attempted to write this book any other way than in free verse," Hesse noted in her Newbery acceptance speech for *Out of the Dust*. "The frugality of the life, the hypnotically hard work of farming, the grimness of conditions during the dust bowl demanded an economy of words."

In *Out of the Dust* readers glimpse a bygone way of life. The family barely scrapes together a living, and the father refuses to plant anything but wheat even though this crop is destroyed by the winds and dust season after season. Dust is everywhere: blowing through the sills, coating the piano keys, choking the body. Billie Jo takes solace in her piano playing, but when her mother and infant brother are killed in a kitchen fire, Billie Joe is scarred on her hands, as well as in her soul. Both she and her father are left to bottle up their grief for a time. The young girl becomes an outcast, but ultimately father and daughter build hope out of utter desolation and redefine what it means to be a family.

Reviewers enthusiastically praised *Out of the Dust*, *Booklist* contributor Susan Dove Lempke commenting that, although the story is bleak, "Hesse's writing transcends the gloom and transforms it into a powerfully compelling tale of a girl with enormous strength, courage, and love." Thomas S. Owens wrote in *Five Owls* that Hesse's novel is more than "vivid storytelling"; it "gives a face to history." Owens concluded that "*Out of the Dust* seems destined to become [Hesse's] signature work, a literary groundbreaker as stunning as Oklahoma's dust bowl recovery."

Another historical offering is served up in *Stowaway*, in which a butcher's apprentice flees eighteenth-century England as a stowaway on Captain James Cook's ship, bound for the South Pacific. Based on the actual story of eleven-year-old Nicholas Young, who was made an official member of the crew once Cook's ship reached Tahiti in 1769, Hesse's book is an "imaginative tale [that is] firmly anchored in fact," according to a reviewer for *Publishers Weekly*. During the course of the three-year voyage, Nick suffers hardships, experiences adventures and disappointments, and comes of age in the pressure-cooker environment created on a ship at sea. William McLoughlin, writing in *School Library Journal*, lauded the "author's subtle yet thorough attention to detail [that] creates a memorable tale . . . a virtual encyclopedia of life in the days when England ruled the seas."

Hesse turns readers' attention to the Ku Klux Klan of the 1920s in *Witness*. Written in free verse, the award-winning novel uses various people from a small Vermont town, including victims and victimizers, to tell its tale. Again basing her book on actual events, Hesse employs eleven different voices in five acts to tell this story. Including both Klan members and antiracists, these voices reflect the thoughts of nine adults and two children, all who describe what happened to their small town after the arrival of the Klan in 1924. Sides are drawn in this battle, and even those who oppose not only the Klan but also violence are slowly drawn into the cycle of hate. Then a twelve-year-old African-American girl and a six-year-old Jewish girl take a stand, hoping that the rest of the town will follow their lead. Writing in *School Library Journal*, Lauralyn Persson called *Witness* a "remarkable and powerful book" in which the "small details seem just right." Persson further commented that Hesse's story "is much more than a social tract. It's a thoughtful look at people and their capacity for love and hate."

In her young-adult novel *Brooklyn Bridge* Hesse takes readers back to 1903, introducing fourteen-year-old Joseph Michtom. The son of Russian Jews Morris and Rose Michtom, who have immigrated to a new home in Brooklyn, Joseph has mixed feelings about his parents' growing celebrity as the inventors of the Teddy bear. Either caring for his younger siblings or working in his family's toymaking business, the teen longs for the freedom to play with friends and make something of his own life. He also experiences the pangs of first love. As his family gains in affluence, the stories of the Old World ground Joe in the Michtoms' past, a heritage that has much in common with the impoverished homeless children he glimpses hiding in the city's shadowed corners. In *Publishers Weekly* a contributor called *Brooklyn Bridge* a "memorable story" that "explodes with dark drama before its eerie but moving resolution." In *Kliatt* Claire Rosser dubbed Hesse "a masterful writer" who "shows her enormous skill as the story unfolds." Hazel Rochman, writing in *Booklist*, cited the "intricate" connections in Hesse's novel, predicting that readers turning the final page of the "gripping" *Brooklyn Bridge* will start again at the beginning "and see everything in a new way."

Aleutian Sparrow, another of Hesse's historical free-verse novels, concerns the relocation of the inhabitants of the Aleutian Islands during World War II. After the Japanese attacked their homeland in 1942, the Aleuts were forced by the U.S. government to move to resettlement camps on the Alaskan mainland. Vera, the novel's teenage narrator, watches as many of her people die of disease under horrible, crowded conditions for which they are completely unprepared. "Contained in Vera's unrhymed verses are Aleutian traditions, small details of camp life, and hints of racism," observed a critic in *Kirkus Reviews*. Although some critics maintained that Hesse fails to fully develop the character of Vera, others offered praise for the author's work. As Rosser remarked in *Kliatt*, *Aleutian Sparrow* "does add to her impressive body of literature for YAs."

Hesse explores significant episodes in Jewish history in *The Stone Lamp: Eight Stories of Hannukkah through History*, employing an unusual dual narrative. She pro-

Hesse teams up with illustrator Wendy Watson in her picture book The Cats in Krasinski Square. (Illustration copyright © 2004 by Wendy Watson. Reproduced by permission of Scholastic, Inc.)

vides a brief description of each episode, accompanied by a first-person account told in verse by a young narrator. Among the events covered are the Crusades, the Inquisition, Kristallnacht, and the assassination of Israeli Prime Minister Yitzhak Rabin. Discussing her approach to the work, Hesse told *Booklist* contributor Ilene Cooper, "I couldn't write a poem conveying the unique experience of each child if the poem also had to encapsulate the historical event that had been the catalyst for the poem. The poetry would have been stilted, prosaic, and forced." Hesse continued, "The final structure, with its eight-century time line, gave me the greatest latitude to explore the themes of history, tragedy, and hope." According to *Horn Book* reviewer Susan P. Bloom, the work "echoes the hope embodied in the lights of Hanukkah." *School Library Journal* contributor Eva Mitnick called *The Stone Lamp* a "unique and moving book that should be shared year-round."

In addition to contemporary and historical novels, Hesse has also produced picture books such as *Poppy's Chair, The Cats in Krasinski Square,* and *Spuds,* as well as the chapter books *Lavender* and *Sable* and the picture-book biography *The Young Hans Christian Andersen.* Focusing on the early years of the noted nineteenth-century Danish writer, *The Young Hans Christian Andersen* features what a *Publishers Weekly* critic described as a "tightly constructed narrative [that] brims with . . . memorable images" of the creative but enigmatic writer, while in *Horn Book* Deirdre F. Baker noted that "Hesse's own figurative language help her underscore Andersen's tangled imagination."

In *The Cats in Krasinski Square* she focuses on an episode from World War II. "In her spare yet lyrical narrative, Newbery medalist Hesse relays a haunting story based on an actual incident involving Poland's Warsaw Ghetto," stated a contributor in *Publishers Weekly.* The book's narrator, a young Jewish girl who has escaped

from the ghetto and avoids being detected by the Nazis, plots to smuggle food to her friends through holes in the ghetto wall. The Gestapo learn of her scheme, however, and station dogs along the wall to sniff out contraband. With the help of her sister, the girl rounds up a number of the city's stray cats and uses them to distract the dogs, allowing the much-needed food to reach those in need. According to a critic in *Kirkus Reviews,* Hesse makes "a grave subject enormously accessible, gently humorous, and affectingly triumphant." *Booklist* reviewer Gillian Engberg called *The Cats in Krasinski Square* "an empowering story about the bravery and impact of young people" and noted that the author's "clear, spare poetry, from the girl's viewpoint, refers to the hardships suffered without didacticism."

Also featuring mixed-media artwork by Watson, the picture book *Spuds* tells a heartwarming story about a rural family who remains close-knit even during hard times. When their mother goes to work one frosty night, Jack and his siblings Maybelle and Eddie decide to sneak into the fields of neighbor Mr. Kenny and dig up a dinner of tasty potatoes. When they arrive back home with their crop, the three children realize that, instead of digging up potatoes in the dark, they have actually harvested a pot-full of round, potato-shaped rocks. Although their mother makes them confess their attempted theft, all resolves into smiles and a tasty dinner in what *School Library Journal* contributor Marilyn Taniguch dubbed a "beautifully crafted picture book" that features a "sweetly understated affirmation of hard work and honesty." The author's use of a folksy free-verse narration in her story "set[s] the mood of tender nostalgia" in *Spuds,* asserted a *Kirkus Reviews* writer, and Watson's warm-toned illustrations "perfectly complement the text." In *Booklist* Gillian Engberg praised *Spuds,* writing that "the subtlety in Hesse's spare, regional poetry is beautifully extended in Watson's uncluttered pictures."

According to Bowen, Hesse is extremely empathic and "makes everyone feel cherished—from the taxi drivers in New York who are startled by such unprovoked kindness; to her family, her publishers, her friends." However, Bowen also pointed out that the author "has a backbone of steel." As for Hesse, her goal in writing is clear. "Ultimately, the most important thing for me is to write the best book I am capable of writing," the author said in a *Publishers Weekly* article. "And get it into the readers' hands. Whatever I can do, to do that, I'll do."

Biographical and Critical Sources

BOOKS

Beacham's Guide to Literature for Young Adults, Volume 9, Beacham Publishing (Osprey, FL), 1999, pp. 4829-4844.
Children's Literature Review, Volume 54, Gale (Detroit, MI), 1999.
St. James Guide to Young-Adult Writers, 2nd edition, St. James Press (Detroit, MI), 1999.
Something about the Author Autobiography Series, Volume 25, Gale (Detroit, MI), 1998, pp. 117-137.

PERIODICALS

Book, March, 2001, Kathleen Odean, review of *Stowaway,* p. 86.
Booklinks, September, 1999, Judy O'Malley, "Talking with . . . Karen Hesse," pp. 54-61.
Booklist, March 15, 1991, Hazel Rochman, review of *Wish on a Unicorn,* p. 1493; July, 1992, Hazel Rochman, review of *Letters from Rifka,* p. 1931; October 1, 1993, Hazel Rochman, review of *Lavender,* p. 344; October 1, 1997, Susan Dove Lempke, review of *Out of the Dust,* p. 330; November 1, 1998, Hazel Rochman, review of *Just Juice,* p. 492; February 1, 1999, Stephanie Zvirin, review of *Come on, Rain!,* p. 982; October 15, 1999, Kay Weisman, review of *A Light in the Storm: The Civil War Diary of Amelia Martin,* p. 444; September 1, 2001, Hazel Rochman, review of *Witness,* p. 108; October 1, 2003, Ilene Cooper, *The Stone Lamp: Eight Stories of Hanukkah through History,* p. 334, and Ilene Cooper, "Tragedy and Hope," p. 335; October 15, 2003, Hazel Rochman, review of *Aleutian Sparrow,* p. 405; October 15, 2004, Gillian Engberg, review of *The Cats in Krasinski Square,* p. 404; August 1, 2008, Hazel Rochman, review of *Brooklyn Bridge,* p. 58; September 15, 2008, Gillian Engberg, review of *Spuds,* p. 55.
Bulletin of the Center for Children's Books, October, 1992, Betsy Hearne, review of *Letters from Rifka,* p. 44; June, 1994, Betsy Hearne, review of *Phoenix Rising,* pp. 321-322; January, 1996, Betsy Hearne, review of *A Time of Angels,* p. 161.
Childhood Education, spring, 2002, Jeanie Burnett, review of *Witness,* p. 171.
English Journal, Ken Donelson, review of *Out of the Dust,* pp. 120-121.

Five Owls, January-February, 1998, Thomas S. Owens, review of *Out of the Dust,* pp. 60-61; May, 1999, John Peters, review of *Come on, Rain,* p. 107.
Horn Book, July-August, 1991, Nancy Vasilakis, review of *Wish on a Unicorn,* pp. 457-458; September-October, 1992, Hanna B. Zeiger, review of *Letters from Rifka,* p. 585; March-April, 1994, Mary M. Burns, review of *Lester's Dog,* pp. 190-191; July-August, 1994, Elizabeth S. Watson, review of *Sable,* p. 452; September-October, 1994, Nancy Vasilakis, review of *Phoenix Rising,* p. 599; January-February, 1998, Peter D. Sieruta, review of *Out of the Dust,* p. 73; July-August, 1998, Karen Hesse, "Newbery Medal Acceptance," pp. 422-427; July-August, 1998, Brenda Bowen, "Karen Hesse," pp. 428-432; July, 1999, Leo Landry, review of *Come on, Rain!,* p. 454; January-February, 2001, review of *Stowaway,* p. 91; November-December, 2001, Christine M. Hepperman, review of *Witness,* p. 749; November-December, 2003, Susan P. Bloom, review of *The Stone Lamp,* p. 765; January-February, 2004, Jennifer M. Brabander, review of *Aleutian Sparrow,* p. 82; September-October, 2004, Susan Dove Lempke, review of *The Cats in Krasinski Square,* p. 569; November-December, 2005, Deirdre F. Baker, review of *The Young Hans Christian Andersen,* p. 735; September-October, 2008, Michael Santangelo, review of *Brooklyn Bridge,* p. 585.
Journal of Adolescent and Adult Literacy, April, 2002, Tasha Tropp Laman, review of *Witness,* pp. 659-660.
Kirkus Reviews, February 15, 1993, review of *Poppy's Chair,* p. 227; April 1, 1994, review of *Phoenix Rising,* p. 480; August 15, 1996, review of *The Music of Dolphins,* p. 1235; September 15, 2003, review of *Aleutian Sparrow,* p. 1175; November 1, 2003, review of *The Stone Lamp,* p. 1317; August 1, 2004, review of *The Cats in Krasinski Square,* p. 742; August 15, 2008, review of *Spuds.*
Kliatt, September, 1999, Claire Rosser, review of *A Light in the Storm,* p. 8; September, 2003, Claire Rosser, review of *Aleutian Sparrow,* p. 8; September, 2008, Claire Rosser, review of *Brooklyn Bridge,* p. 12.
Language-Arts, January, 1999, "Talking about Books: Karen Hesse," pp. 263-271.
Magpies, November, 1998, p. 36; November, 1999, Margaret Kedian, review of *Come on, Rain!,* p. 6.
New York Times, January 13, 1998, Eden Ross Lipson, "Girls' Stressful Tales Draw Newbery and Caldecott Awards," p. E8.
New York Times Book Review, June 19, 1994, review of *Phoenix Rising,* p. 28.
Publishers Weekly, June 29, 1992, review of *Letters from Rifka,* p. 64; August 30, 1993, review of *Lester's Dog,* p. 95; October 23, 1995, review of *A Time of Angels,* p. 70; September 2, 1996, review of *The Music of Dolphins,* p. 131; February 8, 1999, Elizabeth Devereaux, "Karen Hesse: A Poetics of Perfectionism," p. 190; October 23, 2000, review of *Stowaway,* p. 75; August 20, 2001, review of *Witness,* p. 80; September 22, 2003, review of *The Stone Lamp,* p. 66; September 22, 2003, review of *Aleutian Sparrow,* pp. 104-105; August 23, 2004, review of *The Cats in Krasinski Square,* p. 54; September 19, 2005, review of *The Young Hans Christian Andersen,* p. 68; August 25,

2008, review of *Spuds,* p. 73; September 1, 2008, review of *Brooklyn Bridge,* p. 54.

Reading Teacher, May, 1999, interview with Hesse, pp. 856-858.

Reading Today, February-March, 2002, Lynne T. Burke, review of *Witness,* p. 32.

School Library Journal, December, 1993, Rita Soltan, review of *Lavender,* p. 89; May, 1994, Maggie McEwen, review of *Sable,* p. 114; November, 1996, Kate McClelland, review of *The Music of Dolphins,* pp. 120, 123; November, 1999, Shawn Brommer, review of *A Light in the Storm,* pp. 158-159; November, 2000, William McLoughlin, review of *Stowaway,* p. 156; September, 2001, Lauralyn Persson, review of *Witness,* p. 225; November 2002, Debra Lay Whelan, "Karen Hesse Awarded MacArthur Fellowship," p. 23; October 2003, Eva Mitnick, review of *The Stone Lamp,* pp. 63-64, and Jennifer Ralston, review of *Witness,* p. 98; October, 2005, Kristen Cutler, review of *The Young Hans Christian Andersen,* p. 140; September, 2008, Marilyn Taniguchi, review of *Spuds,* p. 148.

Voice of Youth Advocates, February, 1997, Mary Arnold, review of *The Music of Dolphins,* p. 328; April, 1998, Sarah K. Hetz, review of *Out of the Dust,* p. 46; October, 1998, Faith Brautigam, review of *Just Juice,* pp. 100-101; March, 1999, Alicia Eames, review of *Come on, Rain!,* p. 190; November, 2000, William McLoughlin, review of *Stowaway,* p. 156; September, 2001, Lauralyn Persson, review of *Witness,* p. 225.

Voices from the Middle, April, 1997, Ellen Bryant, interview with Hesse, pp. 38-49.

Washington Post, January 13, 1998, David Streitfeld, "'Rapunzel' and Dust Bowl Tale Win Awards; Paul Zelinsky, Karen Hesse Take Newbery and Caldecott Medals," p. C1.

Writing, October 2001, "Dust Storm (Examining Karen Hesse Poem)," p. 12.

ONLINE

Audiofile Online, http://www.audiofilemagazine.com/ (December, 2008-January, 2009), Aurelia C. Scott, interview with Hesse.

Children's Literature, http://www. childrenslit.com/ (September 25, 2002), "Karen Hesse Awarded MacArthur Fellowship."

Scholastic Web site, http://www.scholastic.com/ (April 28, 2010), "Karen Hesse."

OTHER

Good Conversation! A Talk with Karen Hesse (video), Tim Podell Productions (Scarborough, NY), 1997.*

*   *   *

HOOSE, Phillip 1947-
(Phillip M. Hoose)

Personal

Surname pronounced "Hose"; born 1947, in South Bend, IN; son of Darwin Hoose and Patti Williams;

Phillip Hoose (Photograph by Gordon Chibroski. Reproduced by permission.)

married Sandi Ste. George; children: Hannah, Ruby. *Education:* Attended Indiana University and Yale University. *Hobbies and other interests:* Music, bird studies, baseball, bicycling.

Addresses

Home—Portland, ME.

Career

Author, musician, and conservationist. Nature Conservancy, Portland, ME, staff member, 1977—; songwriter and performing musician, 1984—. Cofounder, Children's Music Network, 1986—.

Awards, Honors

Christopher Award, and Notable Book citation, American Library Association (ALA), both 1993, and Books for the Teen Age selection, New York Public Library, all for *It's Our World, Too!;* Jane Addams Children's Book Award Honor Book citation, 1999, for *Hey, Little Ant;* National Book Award finalist, 2001, for *We Were There, Too!;* Boston Globe/Horn Book Award for Nonfiction, 2005, for *The Race to Save the Lord God Bird;* National Book Award for Young People's Literature, 2009, Best Book for Young Adults selection, and Award for Excellence in Nonfiction finalist, both ALA, and Robert F. Sibert Informational Book Medal Honor Book designation, Association for Library Service to Children, 2010, all for *Claudette Colvin.*

Writings

FOR CHILDREN

It's Our World, Too!: Stories of Young People Who Are Making a Difference, Joy Street Books (Boston, MA), 1993, revised as *It's Our World, Too!: Stories of Young*

People Who Are Making a Difference: How They Do It—How YOU Can, Too!, foreword by Pete Seeger, Farrar, Straus (New York, NY), 2002.

(With daughter, Hannah Hoose) *Hey, Little Ant,* illustrated by Debbie Tilley, Tricycle Press (Berkeley, CA), 1998.

We Were There, Too!: Young People in U.S. History, Farrar, Straus (New York, NY), 2001.

The Race to Save the Lord God Bird, Melanie Kroupa Books (New York, NY), 2004.

Claudette Colvin: Twice toward Justice, Melanie Kroupa Books (New York, NY), 2009.

OTHER

(As Phillip M. Hoose) *Building an Ark: Tools for the Preservation of Natural Diversity through Land Protection,* Island Press (Covelo, CA), 1981.

(As Phillip M. Hoose) *Hoosiers: The Fabulous Basketball Life of Indiana,* Vintage Books (New York, NY), 1986, revised edition, Guild Press of Indiana (Indianapolis, IN), 1995.

(As Phillip M. Hoose) *Necessities: Racial Barriers in American Sports,* Random House (New York, NY), 1989.

Perfect, Once Removed: When Baseball Was All the World to Me (memoir), Walker (New York, NY), 2006.

Author of songs, including "What If the Russians Don't Come?," published in *Sing Out* magazine, 1984, and anthologized in *Rise up Singing,* 1988.

Sidelights

Phillip Hoose, a conservationist, author, and musician by profession, has written a number of highly regarded works of nonfiction, including *The Race to Save the Lord God Bird,* which received the *Boston Globe/Horn Book* Award, and the biography *Claudette Colvin: Twice toward Justice,* winner of National Book Award for Young People's Literature. "I don't think it's possible for me to write about things that don't matter," Hoose remarked in an interview with Willie Perdomo for the National Book Foundation Web site. "Each of my . . . books has been connected with building and preserving community in one way or another. I try to inspire activism through stories. The same elements that make fiction powerful animate non-fiction too: strong characters with deep feelings, interesting relationships among them, obstacles, suspense, conflict, desire. I think people learn mainly through stories."

Hoose's first book for children, *It's Our World Too!: Stories of Young People Who Are Making a Difference,* was the recipient of a Christopher award. The book collects fourteen true stories that illustrate how children and teens have stood up and taken action on behalf of various causes, such as feeding the homeless, lobbying for a new community park, and opposing racism and gang violence. A *Publishers Weekly* reviewer called *It's Our World Too!* a "highly inspirational and engaging book," while *Horn Book* critic Margaret A. Bush noted that "Hoose's upbeat scenarios and practical advice should persuade many that they really can make a difference."

Originally created as a performance piece with music, *Hey, Little Ant* was written with Hoose's daughter, Hannah Hoose. The simple tale features an ant that begs for its life when a young child is about to step on it. Although the ant pleads with the child, noting that it has a family at home, the child has friends who are urging him on and he does not really believe that ants have feelings. Hoose never reveals if the ant lives or dies; instead, he asks the reader to decide. A *Publishers Weekly* reviewer called *Hey, Little Ant* a "parable about mercy and empathy," and Reed Mangels, writing in *Vegetarian Journal,* deemed it "a great resource for thinking and talking about respecting other beings." Translated into ten languages, *Hey, Little Ant* has also been used in classrooms as an aid in lessons on tolerance.

It took Hoose six years to research and write *We Were There, Too!: Young People in U.S. History,* which became a finalist for the National Book Award. The collection of seventy true stories demonstrates that children and teens have played an important part in the history of the United States. A reviewer for *Horn Book* commented that, whether the author's focus is on an individual or on young people within a group, "Hoose ties lively narratives to larger historical events through cogent chapter introductions." In *Children's Literature,* a reviewer observed of *We Were There, Too!* that, "written with great care and compassion, this is one of the finest children's books dealing with American history this writer has come across in recent years." "A treasure chest of history come to life," according to *School Library Journal* critic Herman Sutter, Hoose's book stands as "an inspired collection."

A staff member of the Nature Conservancy since 1977, Hoose combined his passions for the environment and literature to create *The Race to Save the Lord God Bird.* Described as "a compelling tale of a species' decline" by a *Publishers Weekly* critic, the book recounts the history of the Ivory-billed woodpecker, an ornithological wonder that faces extinction. "As a writer, naturally I think the best way to encourage readers to care about the planet's biological diversity is to tell them a story," the author stated in his *Boston Globe/Horn Book* Award acceptance speech, reprinted in *Horn Book.* "And most good stories, fiction or nonfiction, contain the same elements: characters you care about, intriguing relationships between and among them, suspense, difficult obstacles, and a good setting. So, because I have a special love for birds, and to write about the work that I do, I set out to find a Clark Gable of a bird and a *Gone with the Wind* of a story."

With its chiseled bill, prominent crest, and shiny black-and-white markings, the Ivory-billed woodpecker is—or was—found primarily in the hardwood swamps and

pine forests of the American South. After the U.S. Civil War, timber companies deforesting huge tracts of land devastated its habitat and endangered its survival. Unfortunately, concerted efforts by conservationists have not succeeded in reversing the bird's decline. _The Race to Save the Lord God Bird_ is "a gripping, unbearably sad tale of bad luck, public apathy, and corporate obduracy," noted Joanna Rudge Long in _Horn Book,_ while Eric Nagourney commented in the _New York Times Book Review_ that Hoose's "meticulously researched book . . . tells a good story meant to prompt questions about the loss of other species as well." "Researching and writing _The Race to Save the Lord God Bird_ was a great and satisfying adventure," the author remarked in his acceptance speech. "The experience deepened my sense of why I do what I do, both as a conservationist and a writer. It made me appreciate those who sought to save habitats before me. It deepened my love for the beauty and mystery of the Earth and the creatures that inhabit it."

In _Claudette Colvin_ Hoose examines the life of an important but seldom-discussed figure from the civil rights movement of the mid-twentieth century. In 1955, some nine months before African-American Rosa Parks refused to give up her seat to a white passenger on a Montgomery, Alabama, bus and threw a spotlight on racial issues in the United States, fifteen-year-old Colvin was arrested and jailed for doing the exact same thing. However, because she was so young, had a police record, and later became pregnant (though she was not

married), Colvin was not considered "respectable" enough to be promoted as the public face of a mass protest against the treatment of African Americans on public buses. Still, after fighting her arrest in court, she further agreed to be one of four plaintiffs in a landmark discrimination case, _Browder v. Gayle,_ which swept away the legal underpinnings for racially segregated seating in intrastate, public buses. Discussing his inspiration for the work, Hoose told _School Library Journal_ interview Jennifer M. Brown: "I think many people know there was a teen who refused to give up her seat before Rosa Parks did; in the good histories, she's mentioned, but always in contrast to Rosa Parks, and often followed by a string of adjectives [characterizing her as] profane and emotional, unqualified to lead the movement. How would that feel? People are ready for a fuller story of that episode in American history, one that gives Claudette her due and her rightful place within it, and presents her as a human being with nuance and feeling."

In addition to winning the National Book Award, _Claudette Colvin_ was named a Newberry Honor Book, and a Robert F. Sibert Informational Book Medal Honor Book. According to _New York Times Book Review_ critic Ruth Conniff, Hoose's biography "gives depth and context to the larger-than-life, sometimes mythologized history of the civil rights movement," and "describes her [Colvin's] personal struggle against the culture around her in terms young people of any era can readily understand." Mary Mueller, writing in _School Library Journal,_ observed that the book "puts Colvin back into the historical record, combining her reminiscences with narrative about her life and the tumultuous events of fire boycott," and in _Booklist_ Gillian Engberg asserted that the young woman's "frank, candid words about both her personal and political experiences will galvanize young readers."

Geared for adult readers, _Necessities: Racial Barriers in American Sports_ examines the attitudes of players, coaches, managers, owners, and the media toward members of minorities in sports. Hoose interviewed more than one hundred people, including coaches, athletes, and journalists, and found that minorities are largely kept out of positions that require complex decision making.

The memoir _Perfect, Once Removed: When Baseball Was All the World to Me_ describes the author's relationship with his cousin, New York Yankees pitcher Don Larsen, whose letters gave encouragement to the then-nine-year-old Hoose, a struggling ballplayer. Hoose also recalls the day in 1956 when Larsen tossed the only perfect game in World Series history. In the words of _Booklist_ critic Bill Ott, _Perfect, Once Removed_ "speaks to every baseball-loving kid whose talent on the field wasn't equal to his passion for the game."

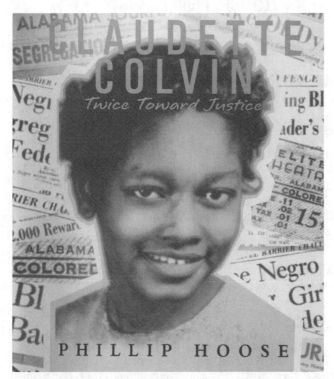

Cover of Hoose's picture-book biography **Claudette Colvin,** _featuring artwork by Jaclyn Sinquette._ (Illustration © by Jaclyn Sinquett. Jacket photograph of Claudette Colvin, courtesy of the Montgomery Advertiser. Reproduced by permission of Melanie Kroupa Books, a division of Farrar, Straus & Giroux, LLC.)

Biographical and Critical Sources

BOOKS

Hoose, Phillip, *Perfect, Once Removed: When Baseball Was All the World to Me,* Walker (New York, NY), 2006.

PERIODICALS

American Libraries, December, 1986, Bill Ott, review of *Hoosiers: The Fabulous Basketball Life of Indiana,* p. 824.

Booklist, August, 2001, Ilene Cooper, review of *We Were There, Too!: Young People in U.S. History,* p. 2117; June 1, 2004, Carolyn Phelan, review of *The Race to Save the Lord God Bird,* p. 1723; October 25, 2004, Nathalie Op De Beeck, review of *Championing a Cause,* p. 23; September 1, 2006, Bill Ott, review of *Perfect, Once Removed,* p. 46; February 1, 2009, Gillian Engberg, review of *Claudette Colvin: Twice toward Justice,* p. 49.

Business Week, June 19, 1989, Ron Stodghill II, review of *Necessities: Racial Barriers in American Sports,* p. 16.

Horn Book, September-October, 1993, Margaret A. Bush, review of *It's Our World Too!: Stories of Young People Who Are Making a Difference,* pp. 621-622; September, 2001, review of *We Were There, Too!,* p. 610; September-October, 2004, Joanna Rudge Long, review of *The Race to Save the Lord God Bird,* p. 605; January-February, 2006, Phillip Hoose, transcript of *Boston Globe/Horn Book* award acceptance speech, p. 29; March-April, 2009, Jonathan Hunt, review of *Claudette Colvin,* p. 212.

Kirkus Reviews, April 15, 1989, review of *Necessities,* p. 603; July 15, 2006, review of *Perfect, Once Removed,* p. 710.

Library Journal, March 15, 1981, Susan Beverly Kuklin, review of *Building an Ark: Tools for the Preservation of Natural Diversity through Land Protection,* p. 671; May 1, 1989, William A. Hoffman, review of *Necessities,* p. 82; September 1, 2006, Paul Kaplan, review of *Perfect, Once Removed,* p. 154.

Nation, May 8, 1989, Nicolaus Mills, review of *Necessities,* pp. 634-636.

New York Times, October 3, 2006, Clyde Haberman, "Immortalized by a Moment of Perfection," p. B1.

New York Times Book Review, August 8, 2004, Eric Nagourney, *The Race to Save the Lord God Bird,* p. 17; May 10, 2009, Ruth Conniff, review of *Claudette Colvin,* p. 14.

Peacework, May, 2000, Phillip Hoose, "How *Hey, Little Ant* Became a Book."

Publishers Weekly, June 7, 1993, review of *It's Our World Too!,* p. 72; September 14, 1998, review of *Hey, Little Ant,* p. 67; August 20, 2001, review of *We Were There, Too,* p. 81; August 23, 2004, review of *The Race to Save the Lord God Bird,* p. 56; June 19, 2006, review of *Perfect, Once Removed,* p. 49; February 2, 2009, review of *Claudette Colvin,* p. 51.

School Library Journal, December, 1998, Maryann H. Owen, review of *Hey, Little Ant,* p. 98; August, 2001, Herman Sutter, review of *We Were There, Too,* p. 198; September, 2004, Laurie von Mehren, review of *The Race to Save the Lord God Bird,* p. 227; November, 2006, Will Marston, review of *Perfect, Once Removed,* p. 173; February, 2009, Mary Mueller, review of *Claudette Colvin,* p. 120.

Time, November 20, 2006, Sean Gregory, review of *Perfect Once Removed,* p. 76.

Vegetarian Journal, May, 2001, Reed Mangels, review of *Hey, Little Ant,* p. 31.

Virginia Quarterly Review, spring, 1987, review of *Hoosiers,* p. 68.

Voice of Youth Advocates, April, 1987, Hilary King, review of *Hoosiers,* p. 45; October, 1993, Sari Feldman, review of *It's Our World Too!,* p. 242.

ONLINE

BookPage.com, http://www.bookpage.com/ (January 13, 2002), Ron Kaplan, review of *We Were There, Too!*

National Book Foundation Web site, http://www.nationalbook.org/ (March 1, 2010), Willie Perdomo, interview with Hoose.

Phillip Hoose Home Page, http://www.philliphoose.com (March 1, 2010).

*   *   *

HOOSE, Phillip M.
See HOOSE, Phillip

*   *   *

HOPKINS, Lee Bennett 1938-

Personal

Born April 13, 1938, in Scranton, PA; son of Leon Hall Hopkins (a police officer) and Gertrude Thomas. *Education:* Newark State Teachers College (now Kean College), B.A., 1960; Bank Street College of Education, M.Sc., 1964; Hunter College of the City University of New York, professional diploma in educational supervision and administration, 1967.

Addresses
Home—Cape Coral, FL.

Career
Writer, editor, and educator. Public school teacher in Fair Lawn, NJ, 1960-66; Bank Street College of Education, New York, NY, senior consultant, 1966-68; Scholastic Magazines, Inc., New York, NY, curriculum and editorial specialist, 1968-74; full-time writer, 1976—. Lecturer on children's literature; host and consultant to

Lee Bennett Hopkins (Photograph by Rocco Nunno. Reproduced by permission.)

children's television series *Zebra Wings,* Agency for Instructional Television, beginning 1976. Consultant to school systems and publishers. National trustee, National Center for Children's Illustrated Literature, beginning 1991. Namesake and founder of Lee Bennett Hopkins Poetry Award, established in 1993, in cooperation with Pennsylvania Center for the Book, and Lee Bennett Hopkins Promising Poet Award, established in 1995, in cooperation with International Reading Association.

Member

International Reading Association, American Library Association, National Council of Teachers of English (member of board of directors, 1975-78; chair of 1978 and 1991 poetry award committees; member of Commission on Literature, 1983-85; member of Children's Literature Assembly, 1985-88; honorary board member of Children's Literature Council of Pennsylvania, 1990—).

Awards, Honors

Notable Books selection, American Library Association, for *Don't You Turn Back, Rainbows Are Made, Surprises,* and *A Song in Stone;* Outstanding Alumnus in the Arts award, Kean College, 1972; Notable Book selection, National Council for the Social Studies (NCSS), for *Mama;* Choice designation, International Youth Library exhibition (Munich, Germany), 1978, for *To Look*

at Any Thing; Children's Choice Award, International Reading Association (IRA)/Children's Book Council (CBC), 1980, for *Wonder Wheels;* honorary doctor of laws, Kean College, 1980; Phi Delta Kappa Educational Leadership Award, 1980; IRA Broadcast Media Award for Radio, 1982; named ambassador extraordinary in the Order of the Long Leaf Pine (NC), 1982; IRA Manhattan Council Literacy Award, 1983; named National Children's Book Week Poet, 1985; Pick-of-the-List selection, American Booksellers Association (ABA), 1988, for both *Side by Side* and *Voyages;* University of Southern Mississippi Medallion, 1989, for lasting contributions to children's literature; Pennsylvania Author of the Year award, 1989; ABA Choice Award, 1991, for *Good Books, Good Times!;* Child Study Committee Children's Books of the Year award, both 1992, for *Ring out Wild Bells* and *Questions;* Pick of the List selection, ABA, and Southern California Council of Literature and Young People Excellence in Illustration award, both 1994, both for *Extra Innings;* Outstanding Children's Book designation, Westchester Library System, 1994, for *The Writing Bug;* New York Public Library Best Children's Books designation, Few Good Books selection, *Book Links,* and Notable Children's Trade Books in the Field of Social Studies designation, NCSS/CBC, all 1994, and ABC Choice Award, 1995, all for *Hand in Hand;* Best Books of the Year selection, *School Library Journal,* 1995, Christopher Award, and Golden Kite Honor Book designation, all for *Been to Yesterdays;* Pick of the List designation, ABA, 1995, for *Blast Off;* Best Books of the Year selection, *School Library Journal,* 2005, for *Oh, No! Where Are My Pants?, and Other Disasters;* Notable Children's Book in Social Studies designation, NCSS/CBC, for *America at War;* Award for Excellence in Poetry for Children, National Council of Teachers of English, 2009.

Writings

FOR CHILDREN

Important Dates in Afro-American History, F. Watts (New York, NY), 1969.
This Street's for Me (poetry), illustrated by Ann Grifalconi, Crown (New York, NY), 1970.
(With Misha Arenstein) *Faces and Places: Poems for You,* illustrated by Lisl Weil, Scholastic, Inc. (New York, NY), 1970.
Happy Birthday to Me!, Scholastic, Inc. (New York, NY), 1972.
When I Am All Alone: A Book of Poems, Scholastic, Inc. (New York, NY), 1972.
Charlie's World: A Book of Poems, Bobbs-Merrill (New York, NY), 1972.
Kim's Place and Other Poems, Holt (New York, NY), 1974.
I Loved Rose Ann, illustrated by Ingrid Fetz, Knopf (New York, NY), 1976.

A Haunting We Will Go: Ghostly Stories and Poems, illustrated by Vera Rosenberry, Albert Whitman (Chicago, IL), 1976.

Witching Time: Mischievous Stories and Poems, illustrated by Vera Rosenberry, Albert Whitman (Chicago, IL), 1976.

Kits, Cats, Lions, and Tigers: Stories, Poems, and Verse, illustrated by Vera Rosenberry, Albert Whitman (Chicago, IL), 1979.

Pups, Dogs, Foxes, and Wolves: Stories, Poems, and Verse, illustrated by Vera Rosenberry, Albert Whitman (Chicago, IL), 1979.

How Do You Make an Elephant Float?, and Other Delicious Food Riddles, illustrated by Rosekranz Hoffman, Albert Whitman (Morton Grove, IL), 1983.

Animals from Mother Goose, Harcourt (New York, NY), 1989.

People from Mother Goose, illustrated by Kathryn Hewitt, Harcourt (New York, NY), 1989.

Good Rhymes, Good Times!, illustrated by Frané Lessac, HarperCollins (New York, NY), 1995.

Mother Goose and Her Children, illustrated by JoAnn Adinolfi, Emilie Chollat, and Gerardo Suzan, Sadlier-Oxford, 1999.

Alphathoughts: Alphabet Poems, illustrated by Marla Baggetta, Wordsong (Honesdale, PA), 2003.

City I Love (poems), illustrated by Marcellus Hall, Abrams Books for Young Readers/Field Museum (New York, NY), 2009.

COMPILER; FOR CHILDREN

I Think I Saw a Snail: Young Poems for City Seasons, illustrated by Harold James, Crown (New York, NY), 1969.

Don't You Turn Back: Poems by Langston Hughes, illustrated by Ann Grifalconi, foreword by Arna Bontemps, Knopf (New York, NY), 1969.

City Talk, illustrated by Roy Arnella, Knopf (New York, NY), 1970.

The City Spreads Its Wings, illustrated by Moneta Barnett, Franklin Watts (New York, NY), 1970.

Me!: A Book of Poems, illustrated by Talavaldis Stubis, Seabury (New York, NY), 1970.

Zoo!: A Book of Poems, illustrated by Robert Frankenberg, Crown (New York, NY), 1971.

Girls Can Too!: A Book of Poems, illustrated by Emily McCully, Franklin Watts (New York, NY), 1972.

(With Misha Arenstein) *Time to Shout: Poems for You,* illustrated by Lisl Weil, Scholastic, Inc. (New York, NY), 1973.

(With Sunna Rasch) *I Really Want to Feel Good about Myself: Poems by Former Addicts,* Thomas Nelson (Nashville, TN), 1974.

On Our Way: Poems of Pride and Love, illustrated by David Parks, Knopf (New York, NY), 1974.

Hey-How for Halloween, illustrated by Janet McCaffery, Harcourt (New York, NY), 1974.

Take Hold!: An Anthology of Pulitzer Prize-winning Poems, Thomas Nelson (Nashville, TN), 1974.

Poetry on Wheels, illustrated by Frank Aloise, Garrard, 1974.

Sing Hey for Christmas Day, illustrated by Laura Jean Allen, Harcourt (New York, NY), 1975.

Good Morning to You, Valentine, illustrated by Tomie de Paola, Harcourt (New York, NY), 1976.

Merrily Comes Our Harvest In, illustrated by Ben Shecter, Harcourt (New York, NY), 1976.

(With Misha Arenstein) *Thread One to a Star,* Four Winds (New York, NY), 1976.

(With Misha Arenstein) *Potato Chips and a Slice of Moon: Poems You'll Like,* illustrated by Wayne Blickenstaff, Scholastic, Inc. (New York, NY), 1976.

Beat the Drum! Independence Day Has Come, illustrated by Tomie de Paola, Harcourt (New York, NY), 1977.

Monsters, Ghoulies, and Creepy Creatures: Fantastic Stories and Poems, illustrated by Vera Rosenberry, Albert Whitman (Morton Grove, IL), 1977.

To Look at Any Thing, illustrated by John Earl, Harcourt (New York, NY), 1978.

Easter Buds Are Springing: Poems for Easter, illustrated by Tomie de Paola, Harcourt (New York, NY), 1979.

Merely Players: An Anthology of Life Poems, Thomas Nelson (Nashville, TN), 1979.

My Mane Catches the Wind: Poems about Horses, illustrated by Sam Savitt, Harcourt (New York, NY), 1979.

By Myself, illustrated by Glo Coalson, Crowell (New York, NY), 1980.

Elves, Fairies, and Gnomes, illustrated by Rosekranz Hoffman, Knopf (New York, NY), 1980.

Moments: Poems about the Seasons, illustrated by Michael Hague, Harcourt (New York, NY), 1980.

Morning, Noon, and Nighttime, Too!, illustrated by Nancy Hannans, Harper (New York, NY), 1980.

I Am the Cat, illustrated by Linda Rochester Richards, Harcourt (New York, NY), 1981.

And God Bless Me: Prayers, Lullabies and Dream-Poems, illustrated by Patricia Henderson Lincoln, Knopf (New York, NY), 1982.

Circus! Circus!, illustrated by John O'Brien, Knopf (New York, NY), 1982.

Rainbows Are Made: Poems by Carl Sandburg, illustrated by Fritz Eichenberg, Harcourt (New York, NY), 1982.

A Dog's Life, illustrated by Linda Rochester Richards, Harcourt (New York, NY), 1983.

The Sky Is Full of Song, illustrated by Dirk Zimmer, Harper (New York, NY), 1983.

A Song in Stone: City Poems, illustrated by Anna Held Audette, Crowell (New York, NY), 1983.

Crickets and Bullfrogs and Whispers of Thunder: Poems and Pictures by Harry Behn, Harcourt (New York, NY), 1984.

Love and Kisses (poems), illustrated by Kris Boyd, Houghton (Burlington, MA), 1984.

Surprises: An I-Can-Read Book of Poems, illustrated by Meagan Lloyd, Harper (New York, NY), 1984.

Creatures, illustrated by Stella Ormai, Harcourt (New York, NY), 1985.

Munching: Poems about Eating, illustrated by Nelle Davis, Little, Brown (Boston, MA), 1985.

Best Friends, illustrated by James Watts, Harper (New York, NY), 1986.

The Sea Is Calling Me, illustrated by Walter Gaffney-Kessel, Harcourt (New York, NY), 1986.

Click, Rumble, Roar: Poems about Machines, illustrated by Anna Held Audette, Crowell (New York, NY), 1987.

Dinosaurs, illustrated by Murray Tinkelman, Harcourt (New York, NY), 1987.

More Surprises: An I-Can-Read Book, illustrated by Meagan Lloyd, Harper (New York, NY), 1987.

Voyages: Poems by Walt Whitman, illustrated by Charles Mikolaycak, Harcourt (New York, NY), 1988.

Side by Side: Poems to Read Together, illustrated by Hilary Knight, Simon & Schuster (New York, NY), 1988.

Still as a Star: Nighttime Poems, illustrated by Karen Malone, Little, Brown (Boston, MA), 1988.

Good Books, Good Times!, illustrated by Harvey Stevenson, Harper (New York, NY), 1990.

On the Farm, illustrated by Laurel Molk, Little, Brown (Boston, MA), 1991.

Happy Birthday, illustrated by Hilary Knight, Simon & Schuster (New York, NY), 1991.

Questions: An I-Can-Read Book, illustrated by Carolyn Croll, HarperCollins (New York, NY), 1992.

Through Our Eyes: Poems and Pictures about Growing Up, illustrated by Jeffrey Dunn, Little, Brown (Boston, MA), 1992.

To the Zoo: Animal Poems, illustrated by John Wallner, Little, Brown (Boston, MA), 1992.

Ring out, Wild Bells: Poems of Holidays and Seasons, illustrated by Karen Baumann, Harcourt (New York, NY), 1992.

Pterodactyls and Pizza: A Trumpet Club Book of Poetry, illustrated by Nadine Bernard Westcott, Trumpet Club, 1992.

Flit, Flutter, Fly!: Poems about Bugs and Other Crawly Creatures, illustrated by Peter Palagonia, Doubleday (New York, NY), 1992.

Ragged Shadows: Poems of Halloween Night, illustrated by Giles Laroche, Little, Brown (Boston, MA), 1993.

Extra Innings: Baseball Poems, illustrated by Scott Medlock, Harcourt (New York, NY), 1993.

It's about Time, illustrated by Matt Novak, Simon & Schuster (New York, NY), 1993.

Hand in Hand: An American History through Poetry, illustrated by Peter Fiore, Simon & Schuster (New York, NY), 1994.

April, Bubbles, Chocolate: An ABC of Poetry, illustrated by Barry Root, Simon & Schuster (New York, NY), 1994.

Weather: An I-Can-Read Book, illustrated by Melanie Hill, HarperCollins (New York, NY), 1994.

Blast Off: Poems about Space: An I-Can-Read Book, illustrated by Melissa Sweet, HarperCollins (New York, NY), 1995.

Small Talk: A Book of Short Poems, illustrated by Susan Gaber, Harcourt (New York, NY), 1995.

School Supplies, illustrated by Renee Flower, Simon & Schuster (New York, NY), 1996.

Opening Days: Sports Poems, illustrated by Scott Medlock, Harcourt (New York, NY), 1996.

Marvelous Math: A Book of Poems, illustrated by Karen Barbour, Simon & Schuster (New York, NY), 1997.

Song and Dance, illustrated by Cheryl Munro Taylor, Simon & Schuster (New York, NY), 1997.

All God's Children: A Book of Prayers, illustrated by Amanda Schaffer, Harcourt Brace (New York, NY), 1998.

(With Mary Perrotta Rich) *Book Poems: Poems from National Children's Book Week, 1959-1989,* Children's Book Council, 1998.

Climb into My Lap: First Poems to Read Together, illustrated by Kathryn Brown, Simon & Schuster (New York, NY), 1998.

Dino-Roars, illustrated by Cynthia Fisher, Golden Books (New York, NY), 1999.

Lives: Poems about Famous Americans, illustrated by Leslie Staub, HarperCollins (New York, NY), 1999.

Spectacular Science: A Book of Poems, illustrated by Virginia Halstead, Simon & Schuster (New York, NY), 1999.

Sports! Sports! Sports!: An I-Can-Read Book, illustrated by Brian Floca, HarperCollins (New York, NY), 1999.

My America, illustrated by Stephen Alcorn, Simon & Schuster (New York, NY), 2000.

Yummy!: Eating through a Day, illustrated by Renee Flower, Simon & Schuster (New York, NY), 2000.

Hoofbeats, Claws, and Rippled Fins: Creature Poems, illustrated by Stephen Alcorn, HarperCollins (New York, NY), 2002.

Home to Me: Poems across America, illustrated by Stephen Alcorn, Orchard (New York, NY), 2002.

A Pet for Me, illustrated by Jane Manning, HarperCollins (New York, NY), 2003.

Wonderful Words: Poems about Reading, Writing, Speaking, and Listening, illustrated by Karen Barbour, Simon & Schuster (New York, NY), 2004.

Hanukkah Lights: Holiday Poetry, illustrated by Melanie Hall, HarperCollins (New York, NY), 2004.

Christmas Presents: Holiday Poetry, illustrated by Melanie Hall, HarperCollins (New York, NY), 2004.

Days to Celebrate: A Full Year of Poetry, People, Holidays, History, Fascinating Facts, and More, illustrated by Stephen Alcorn, Greenwillow (New York, NY), 2005.

Valentine Hearts: Holiday Poetry, illustrated by JoAnn Adinolfi, HarperCollins (New York, NY), 2005.

Oh, No! Where Are My Pants?, and Other Disasters, illustrated by Wolf Erlbruch, HarperCollins (New York, NY), 2005.

Halloween Howls: Holiday Poetry, illustrated by Stacey Schuett, HarperCollins (New York, NY), 2005.

Got Geography!, illustrated by Philip Stanton, Greenwillow (New York, NY), 2006.

Behind the Museum Door: Poems to Celebrate the Wonders of Museums, illustrated by Stacey Dressen-McQueen, Abrams Books for Young Readers (New York, NY), 2007.

America at War, illustrated by Stephen Alcorn, Margaret K. McElderry Books (New York, NY), 2008.

Hamsters, Shells, and Spelling Bees: School Poems, illustrated by Sachiko Yoshikawa, HarperCollins (New York, NY), 2008.

Incredible Inventions, illustrated by Julia Sarcone-Roach, Greenwillow Books (New York, NY), 2009.

Sky Magic, illustrated by Mariusz Stawarski, Dutton Children's Books (New York, NY), 2009.

Amazing Faces, illustrated by Chris Soentpiet, Lee & Low Books (New York, NY), 2010.

Give Me Wings, illustrated by Ponder Goembel, Holiday House (New York, NY), 2010.

I Am the Book, illustrated by Diego "Yayo" Herrera, Holiday House (New York, NY), 2010.

Sharing the Seasons: A Book of Poems, illustrated by David Diaz, Margaret K. McElderry Books (New York, NY), 2010.

YOUNG-ADULT NOVELS

Mama, Dell (New York, NY), 1977, reprinted, Boyds Mills Press (Honesdale, PA), 2000.

Wonder Wheels, Dell (New York, NY), 1980.

Mama and Her Boys, Harper (New York, NY), 1981, reprinted, Boyds Mills Press (Honesdale, PA), 2000.

OTHER

(With Annette F. Shapiro) *Creative Activities for Gifted Children,* Fearon, 1968.

Books Are by People, Citation Press (New York, NY), 1969.

Let Them Be Themselves: Language Arts Enrichment for Disadvantaged Children in Elementary Schools, Citation Press (New York, NY), 1969, second edition published as *Let Them Be Themselves: Language Arts for Children in Elementary Schools,* 1974, third edition, Harper (New York, NY), 1992.

(With Misha Arenstein) *Partners in Learning: A Child-centered Approach to Teaching the Social Studies,* Citation Press (New York, NY), 1971.

Pass the Poetry, Please!: Bringing Poetry into the Minds and Hearts of Children, Citation Press (New York, NY), 1972, third revised edition, HarperCollins (New York, NY), 1998.

More Books by More People, Citation Press (New York, NY), 1974.

(With Misha Arenstein) *Do You Know What Day Tomorrow Is?: A Teacher's Almanac,* Citation Press (New York, NY), 1975.

The Best of Book Bonanza, Holt (New York, NY), 1980.

The Writing Bug: An Autobiography, Richard C. Owen (Katonah, NY), 1994.

Been to Yesterdays: Poems of a Life, Boyds Mills Press (Honesdale, PA), 1995.

Pauses: Autobiographical Reflections on 101 Creators of Children's Books, HarperCollins (New York, NY), 1995.

Also author of "Poetry Plus" column in *Creative Classroom* magazine, and column "A Poetry Workshop in Print," for *Teaching K-8.*

Sidelights

Lee Bennett Hopkins is a prolific and respected poet and anthologist who has garnered numerous honors for his work, including a Christopher award, an University of Southern Mississippi Medallion, and the Award for Excellence in Poetry for Children. Hopkins is best known for his work compiling thematic collections that include both classic and contemporary American poetry. Most critics consider Hopkins' anthologies to be both unusual and inviting, and they consistently praise the selection of material in them as well as the respect for the poets that his books reflect. "Poetry is magical, mystical," Hopkins remarked in a HarperCollins Web site interview. "I maintain that more can be said or felt in 8 or 10 or 12 lines than sometimes an entire novel can convey."

Born in Scranton, Pennsylvania, in 1938, Hopkins grew up in a poor but close-knit family. When he was ten years old, his family moved in with other relatives to make ends meet, and he spent most of his youth in Newark, New Jersey. The oldest child in the family, Hopkins had to help out with the family finances, often missing school so he could work a paying job. Although the family was able to get on its feet again and rent a basement apartment, relations soon deteriorated between Hopkins's parents, leading to a lifelong separation. The circumstances of his youth would later play a prominent part in his fiction writing for young adults.

Hopkins' early reading encompassed everything from comic books and movie magazines to the occasional adult novel, and in spite of frequent absences, he earned passing grades in school while excelling in English classes. Providentially, a schoolteacher reached out to the boy and helped to change his life. "Mrs. McLaughlin saved me," Hopkins wrote in *Something about the Author Autobiography Series (SAAS).* "She introduced me to two things that had given me direction and hope—the love of reading and theatre."

After graduating from high school, Hopkins determined that he would like to teach, and he worked several jobs to pay his way through teacher's training college. Working in a suburban, middle-class school district, he soon became the resource teacher, gathering and organizing materials for the other teachers. Hopkins began using poetry as an aid in teaching reading, and it quickly became apparent to him that poetry could be expanded to introduce all subject areas. In the 1960s, while working as a consultant at Bank Street College of Education, Hopkins again used poetry as a learning tool. In 1968 he became an editor at Scholastic, Inc., a post he held until 1976 when he became a full-time writer and anthologist.

During his years at Scholastic, Hopkins hit on his charmed formula for poetry anthologies, a pattern that can be seen in his early volume, the award-winning *Don't You Turn Back: Poems by Langston Hughes.* In *SAAS* he discussed the key elements in his compilations. "Balance is important in an anthology," he explained. "I want many voices within a book, so I rarely use more than one or two works by the same poet. I also envision each volume as a stage play or film, hav-

Hopkins' award-winning poetry compilations include Moment to Moment, *which features artwork by Michael Hague.* (Illustration copyright © 1980 by Michael Hague. Reproduced by permission of the illustrator.)

ing a definite beginning, middle, and end. The right flow is a necessity for me. Sometimes a word at the end of a work will lead into the title of the next selection. I want my collections to read like a short story or novel—not a hodgepodge of works thrown together aimlessly."

Since 1969, Hopkins has compiled scores of poetry anthologies, each employing this same successful formula. Anthologies centering on the works of individual poets include *Crickets and Bullfrogs and Whispers of Thunder: Poems and Pictures by Harry Behn, Rainbows Are Made: Poems by Carl Sandburg,* and the award-winning *Voyages: Poems by Walt Whitman.* Reviewing *Voyages, Booklist* contributor Hazel Rochman called it a "spacious, handsome edition that helps make accessible a poet of vigor and sensitivity." In *Horn Book,* Nancy Vasilakis deemed the same book a "well-conceived and elegantly produced anthology."

Hopkins often works with single themes for his anthologies, such as holidays. *Valentine Hearts: Holiday Poetry* collects twelve poems about the romantic holiday, forming a "delectable and accessible" selection, according to a *School Library Journal* contributor. "It's

easy to imagine these gems enlivening poem-a-day assignments," commented Jennifer Mattson in *Booklist.* The poems in *Halloween Howls: Holiday Poetry* are each "presented on a distinctive spread," noted a *School Library Journal* contributor, while the twelve short poems in *Christmas Presents: Holiday Poems* are designed so that the "poetry text [is] integrated within the illustration, giving the volume a lively flair," according to a critic for *Kirkus Reviews. Hanukkah Lights: Holiday Poetry* features poetry from Jane Yolen, Maria Fleming, and Lillian Fisher and provides readers with "good, basic, and simple holiday reading," noted a contributor to *Kirkus Reviews.*

Narrow subjects are presented in *Weather, It's about Time!* and *Blast Off!: Poems about Space.* Reviewing *Blast Off!* in *Horn Book,* Maeve Visser Knoth dubbed the beginning reader a "perfect match of subject, format, and interest level" and "a sure winner." Food poems are served up in *Yummy!: Eating through a Day,* a "book to be savored in many delicious bites," according to *School Library Journal* Kathleen Whalin. Bugs and insects take center stage in *Flit, Flutter, Fly!,* a "charming assortment of 20 easy-to-read creature features," ac-

cording to *Booklist* critic Quraysh Ali. Musical and dance themes come into play in *Song and Dance*, "an inspired and free-spirited arrangement of poems with musical themes," as a reviewer for *Publishers Weekly* described the collection.

Hopkins turns his editorial gaze to school days with the poetry collections *School Supplies, Marvelous Math, Got Geography!*, and *Spectacular Science*, the last two which deal with seemingly non-poetic subjects. Reviewing *Marvelous Math* in the *Bulletin of the Center for Children's Books*, Elizabeth Bush called the anthology a "delight for independent readers" and a "boon to teachers attempting to integrate math across the curriculum." Lee Bock Brown, writing in *School Library Journal*, called the same book a "delightful collection."

In *Spectacular Science* Hopkins deals with topics ranging from what happens to insects in winter to magnets. "Hopkins . . . has rounded up a satisfying variety of works," noted Stephanie Zvirin in a *Booklist* review, while *School Library Journal* contributor Carolyn Angus called the book a "delightful, thought-provoking anthology that is—in short—spectacular." The anthology *Hamsters, Shells, and Spelling Bees: School Poems* contains works by Alice Schertle, Jane Yolen, and J. Patrick Lewis, among others, and looks at such familiar classroom activities as storytime and caring for a class pet. Writing in *Booklist*, Gillian Engberg noted that "these reassuring poems will find an accepting audience among both young readers and listeners."

U.S. history, geography, and biography are presented in other anthologies by Hopkins. *Hand in Hand* includes over seventy poems that offer "a singular outlook on American history as viewed by some of America's foremost poets, past and present," according to Nancy Vasilakis in *Horn Book*. As Vasilakis concluded, Hopkins' "well-conceived anthology should be a welcome supplement to any study of American history." Noted Americans are celebrated in *Lives: Poems about Famous Americans*, an anthology in which specially commissioned verses focus on fourteen Americans that include Thomas Edison, Sacagawea, and Rosa Parks. "Teachers looking for poetry to enhance social-studies units will find several good choices here," noted Phelan in *Booklist*. *My America* is a geographical description of the country in verse form, while the poems in *America at War* explore the emotional impact of combat by focusing on major conflicts in U.S. history from the American Revolution to the War in Iraq. "The poems vary from elegiac to angry," a critic stated in *Kirkus Review*, while Nancy Palmer wrote in *School Library Journal* that several "poems are infused with the exultant rhetoric of war but many are small narratives or vignettes in which families ache and grieve, soldiers long for home."

Wonderful Words: Poems about Reading, Writing, Speaking, and Listening deals with the nuances of language. "Hopkins's selection of poems about words will

delight both readers and children," a *Publishers Weekly* contributor wrote of the collection. Corrina Austin commented in *School Library Journal* that "all of the selections are excellent," although in *Booklist* Rochman advised that the poems "will work best if an adult reads the poems aloud." Collaborating with illustrator Maria Baggetta, Hopkins explores the alphabet in *Alphathoughts: Alphabet Poems*, called "a clever and child-friendly book of pithy poetry" by Ilene Cooper in *Booklist*.

Hopkins turns his attention to athletics in several volumes, including *Extra Innings, Sports! Sports! Sports!*, and *Opening Days*. In *Sports!, Sports! Sports!* he gathers verse about SCUBA diving, baseball, and ice skating, among other activities, in an easy reader that is "a good way to attract new readers to poetry," according to *Booklist* reviewer Zvirin. Andrew Medlar, writing in *School Library Journal*, found the selections to be "short, entertaining, and energetic."

Animals are the focus of both *A Pet for Me* and *Hoofbeats, Claws, and Rippled Fins: Creature Poems*. The former title describes the love between the narrators of the poems and their pets, which come in all shapes, colors, and sizes and include such creatures as tarantulas, turtles, cats, and dogs. Jane Marino, writing in *School Library Journal*, noted that *A Pet for Me* will make "a charming addition to either poetry or easy reader shelves." The creatures addressed in *Hoofbeats, Claws, and Rippled Fins* are more wild and exotic than their domesticated counterparts. "Each selection centers around physical images of the animals' distinctive movement, body, and personality," noted Gillian Engberg in *Booklist*. Noting that there are other books of poetry about wild creatures, Nina Lindsay noted in *School Library Journal* that the collection "provides new material for the same audience."

Home to Me: Poems across America contains fifteen commissioned verses. Each poem is accompanied by text introducing the poet and describing the unique region where the poet lives. In *Booklist* Diane Foote considered the title "a welcome addition to the poetry shelves." Shawn Brommer commented in *School Library Journal* that "the poems celebrate simple, basic aspects of life," giving each a universal feel, despite the different locations. "What has emerged is a rather powerful sense of Americans who not only love their country, but their particular corner of it," wrote a *Kirkus Reviews* contributor. A volume of sixteen poems, *Got Geography!* extols the virtues of studying the planet and celebrates forests, mountains, and other natural wonders. "The gentle, often-moving verses cover a wide spectrum of ways to explore the Earth," commented Julie Roach in her review of the book for *School Library Journal*.

Excruciating embarrassment and other difficult emotions are the subject of the fourteen poems in *Oh No! Where Are My Pants?, and Other Disasters*. The poetry

in this collection deals with a host of familiar situations, including bad haircuts, fumbling a catch during a baseball game, stage fright, and the death of a pet. Martha V. Parravano noted in *Horn Book* that the first-person narration in each poem makes it easy for readers "to identify with the situations and emotions." In *Booklist* Rochman noted that "the scenarios in words and pictures show young children that books are about them." Lauralyn Persson in *School Library Journal* wrote that the poems in *Oh No! Where Are My Pants?, and Other Disasters* "all depict little moments of being human," while a *Kirkus Reviews* critic observed that while some of the topics covered in the collection are serious, most of "the contributors keep the mood light."

The anthology *Behind the Museum Door: Poems to Celebrate the Wonders of Museums* captures the excitement of a child's visit to a world of ancient artifacts, artistic masterpieces, and archeological treasures. For example, verses by Lilian Moore and Myra Cohn Livingston describe a patron's reaction to viewing such items as a dinosaur skeleton, a suit of armor, and a wondrous tapestry. Writing in *Booklist,* Engberg applauded *Behind the Museum Door* as a "bright, energetic poetry collection."

Carl Sandburg, Rebecca Kai Dotlich, and David McCord are among the contributors to *Sky Magic,* an anthology of fourteen poems that describes the majesty of celestial objects. "Each poem conveys the sense of wonder and awe people often feel when considering the cosmos," wrote according to Susan Dove Lempke in *Horn Book,* and Donna Cardon stated in *School Library Journal* that "almost all of the selections are short, wistful, free verse, and well crafted." The origins of such everyday items as popsicles, blue jeans, Velcro, jigsaw puzzles, and roller coasters are described in verse in *Incredible Inventions* Hopkins' collection of sixteen verses. Engberg observed that "the selections represent a wide range of styles, from reflective haikus to high-energy concrete poems," and *School Library Journal* reviewer Carolyn Janssen asserted that *Incredible Inventions* "does an excellent job of uniting the creativity of words, art, and innovation."

The multi-talented Hopkins has also penned his own works, including autobiographies, classroom materials, poetry, picture books, and novels for young adults. Two of his novels, *Mama* and *Mama and Her Boys,* tell about a resourceful single mother and her two sons. In *Mama* the reader is confronted with a chatty, shoplifting, and slightly obnoxious single mother who, while annoying to live with, is a loving and caring person nevertheless. Narrated by the woman's older son, the story finds the woman going from job to job while the family barely keeps its head above water. Reviewing *Mama,* a contributor to *Publishers Weekly* called the work a "not-to-be-missed first novel." "You'll remember Mama," wrote Zena Sutherland in a *Bulletin of the Center for Children's Books* review, noting that the mother is "tough, cheerfully vulgar in her tastes," but "passionately dedicated to see that her two sons whose father has decamped have everything they need." Mama takes a curtain call in *Mama and Her Boys,* in which the boys are now worried that their mother might marry her boss, Mr. Jacobs; a better match, as far as they are concerned, is the school custodian, Mr. Carlisle. Reviewing the sequel, another contributor for *Publishers Weekly* concluded that Hopkins "packs the ensuing incidents with merriment and an understated lesson about different kinds of love and companionship."

Hopkins's original poetry has won high praise. *Good Rhymes, Good Times!* is a "joyous collection of 21 original poems," according to a reviewer for *Publishers Weekly,* the critic also noting that "Hopkins brings freshness and immediacy to his subjects" and "deftly depicts a sense of delight and wonder in everyday experience." In *Been to Yesterdays: Poems of Life* Hopkins gathers poems that recall his thoughts and outlook at age thirteen, when his parents separated. "This autobiographical cycle of poems is a rare gift, a careful exploration of one life that illumines the lives of all who read it," wrote Kathleen Whalin in a *School Library Journal* review of *Been to Yesterdays.* In *City I Love* he presents a tribute to the glories of urban life. The eighteen poems explore the marvels of Paris, Cairo, London, New Orleans, and other celebrated metropolitan areas and "express deep affection for city life, sights, buildings, noises, subways, entertainments and seasons," as a critic in *Kirkus Reviews* observed. "This book is really special, a global tour de force," Teresa Pfeifer remarked in her *School Library Journal* review of *City I Love.*

With well over one hundred works to his credit, Hopkins shows no signs of slowing down. In *The Writing Bug,* a short autobiographical sketch, Hopkins confessed the secret of his amazing productivity: "There isn't a day that goes by that I'm not reading poetry or working on a poem of my own." Asked if he could change one thing about the publishing industry, Hopkins told *Cynsations* online interviewer Cynthia Leitich Smith: "It would be to have more editors who know the craft of poetry . . . who would be willing to take chances with new poets, to get away from the hang-up that exists that every book should be thematic. A book of poetry should be a book of poetry . . . about many different topics . . . about what the poet must say . . . feel . . . hear inside one's self."

Biographical and Critical Sources

BOOKS

Children's Books and Their Creators, edited by Anita Silvey, Houghton (Boston, MA), 1995.
Children's Literature Review, Volume 44, Gale (Detroit, MI), 1997.
Hopkins, Lee Bennett, *The Writing Bug,* Richard C. Owen (Katonah, NY), 1993.

Something about the Author Autobiography Series, Volume 4, Gale (Detroit, MI), 1987.

Strong, Amy, *Lee Bennett Hopkins: A Children's Poet,* Franklin Watts (New York, NY), 2004.

PERIODICALS

Booklist, November 15, 1988, Hazel Rochman, review of *Voyages: Poems by Walt Whitman,* p. 565; December 15, 1992, Quraysh Ali, review of *Flit, Flutter, Fly!* p. 739; March 15, 1999, Carolyn Phelan, review of *Lives: Poems about Famous Americans,* pp. 1340, 1343; April 1, 1999, Stephanie Zvirin, review of *Sports! Sports! Sports!,* pp. 1418-1419; July, 1999, Stephanie Zvirin, review of *Spectacular Science,* pp. 1948-1949; May 1, 2002, Gillian Engberg, review of *Hoofbeats, Claws, and Rippled Fins: Creature Poems,* p. 1520; October 15, 2002, Diane Foote, review of *Home to Me: Poems across America,* p. 403; June 1, 2003, Ilene Cooper, review of *A Pet for Me,* p. 899; April 1, 2003, Ilene Cooper, review of *Alphathoughts: Alphabet Poems,* p. 1408; February 1, 2004, Hazel Rochman, review of *Wonderful Words: Poems about Reading, Writing, Speaking, and Listening,* p. 973; January 1, 2005, Jennifer Mattson, review of *Valentine Hearts: Holiday Poetry,* p. 867; February 15, 2005, Hazel Rochman, review of *Oh, No! Where Are My Pants?, and Other Disasters,* p. 1082; April 1, 2007, Gillian Engberg, review of *Behind the Museum Door: Poems to Celebrate the Wonders of Museums,* p. 50; June 1, 2008, Gillian Engberg, review of *Hamsters, Shells, and Spelling Bees: School Poems,* p. 83; December 1, 2008, Gillian Engberg, review of *Incredible Inventions,* p. 64.

Bulletin of the Center for Children's Books, July-August, 1977, Zena Sutherland, review of *Mama,* p. 175; September, 1997, Elizabeth Bush, review of *Marvelous Math,* pp. 13-14.

Children's Literature Association Quarterly, summer, 1985, Anthony L. Manna, "In Pursuit of the Crystal Image: Lee Bennett Hopkins's Poetry Anthologies," pp. 80-82.

Christian Science Monitor, June 29, 1983, Steven Ratiner, review of *The Sky Is Full of Song.*

Horn Book, January-February, 1989, Nancy Vasilakis, review of *Voyages,* pp. 86-87; September-October, 1993, Nancy Vasilakis, review of *The Writing Bug,* p. 616; July-August, 1994, Nancy Vasilakis, review of *April Bubbles Chocolate: An ABC of Poetry,* p. 467; March-April, 1995, Nancy Vasilakis, review of *Hand in Hand,* p. 209; July-August, 1995, Maeve Visser Knoth, review of *Blast Off!: Poems about Space,* pp. 472-473; January-February, 1999, Roger Sutton, review of *Sports! Sports! Sports!: A Poetry Collection,* p. 77; March-April, 2002, Susan P. Bloom, review of *Hoofbeats, Claws, and Rippled Fins,* p. 222; November-December, 2004, review of *Christmas Presents: Holiday Poetry* and *Hanukkah Lights: Holiday Poetry,* p. 661; May-June, 2005, Martha V. Parravano, review of *Oh No! Where Are My Pants?, and Other Disasters,* p. 337; July-August, 2009, Susan Dove Lempke, review of *Sky Magic,* p. 437.

Instructor, March, 1982, interview with Hopkins.

Kirkus Reviews, August 1, 2002, review of *Home to Me,* p. 1132; February 13, 2003, review of *A Pet for Me,* p. 307; April 1, 2003, review of *Alphathoughts,* p. 535; January 15, 2004, review of *Wonderful Words,* p. 84; November 1, 2004, reviews of *Hanukkah Lights* and *Christmas Presents,* p. 1050; January 15, 2005, review of *Oh No! Where Are My Pants?, and Other Disasters,* p. 121; February 15, 2006, review of *Got Geography!,* p. 183; February 1, 2008, review of *America at War;* May 15, 2008, review of *Hamsters, Shells, and Spelling Bees;* March 1, 2009, review of *City I Love.*

Language Arts, September, 2009, Janet Wong and and Rebecca Kai Dotlich, "Mining with a Jeweler's Eye: The Work of Lee Bennett Hopkins," pp. 62-65.

Publishers Weekly, February 21, 1977, review of *Mama,* p. 79; December 11, 1981, review of *Mama and Her Boys,* p. 62; August 31, 1992, review of *Ring out, Wild Bells: Poems about Holidays and Seasons,* p. 80; July 3, 1995, review of *Good Rhymes, Good Times!,* pp. 60-61; August 12, 1996, review of *School Supplies,* p. 84; March 31, 1997, review of *Song and Dance,* p. 77; July 28, 1997, review of *Marvelous Math,* p. 76; June 21, 1999, review of *Lives,* p. 70; July 31, 2000, review of *Yummy!: Eating through a Day,* p. 95; March 17, 2003, review of *Alphathoughts,* p. 76; March 8, 2004, review of *Wonderful Words,* p. 74; March 17, 2008, review of *America at War,* p. 71; March 16, 2009, review of *City I Love,* p. 60.

School Library Journal, September, 1995, Kathleen Whalin, review of *Been to Yesterdays: Poems of a Life,* p. 209; September, 1997, Meg Stackpole, review of *Ragged Shadows,* p. 224; October, 1997, Lee Bock Brown, review of *Marvelous Math,* p. 118; September, 1999, Carolyn Angus, review of *Spectacular Science,* p. 213; August, 2000, Kathleen Whalin, review of *Yummy!,* p. 170; September, 2000, Barbara Chatton, review of *My America,* p. 248; April, 2002, Nina Lindsay, review of *Hoofbeats, Claws, and Rippled Fins,* p. 132; October, 2002, Shawn Brommer, review of *Home to Me,* p. 146; March, 2003, Jane Marino, review of *A Pet for Me,* p. 219; March, 2004, Andrew Medlar, review of *Sports! Sports! Sports!* p. 68, and Corrina Austin, review of *Wonderful Words,* p. 196; July, 2004, Lisa G. Kropp, review of *School Supplies,* p. 45; January, 2005, Lynda Ritterman, review of *Days to Celebrate: A Full Year of Poetry, People, Holidays, History, Fascinating Facts, and More,* p. 110; February, 2005, Lauralyn Persson, review of *Oh, No! Where Are My Pants?, and Other Disasters,* p. 122; April, 2005, Nina Lindsay, review of *Lives,* p. 56; October, 2005, reviews of *Days to Celebrate* and *Oh, No! Where Are My Pants?, and Other Disasters,* p. 38, review of *Valentine Hearts,* p. 40, and Laura Scott, review of *Halloween Howls: Holiday Poetry,* p. 140; May, 2006, Julie Roach, review of *Got Geography!,* p. 112; June, 2007, Susan Scheps, review of *Behind the Museum Door,* p. 134; March, 2008, Nancy Palmer, review of *America at War,* p. 220; February, 2009, Carolyn Janssen, review of *Incredible Inventions,* p. 92; March, 2009, Teresa Pfeifer, review of *City I Love,* p. 134; June, 2009, Donna Cardon, review of *Sky Magic,* p. 108.

ONLINE

Cynsations Web log, http://cynthialeitichsmith.blogspot. com/ (February 23, 2009), Cynthia Leitich Smith, interview with Hopkins.

HarperCollins Web site, http://www.harpercollins.com/ (March 1, 2010), "Q&A with Lee Bennett Hopkins."*

* * *

HOWIE, Betsy 1962-
(Howie Dewin)

Personal

Born June 6, 1962, in Ann Arbor, MI; daughter of Charles R. (a physician) and Mary Lou (an administrator) Howie; married Frederick J. Tetzeli (divorced); former partner of Lonnie Carter (a playwright); children: (with Carter) Callie. *Ethnicity:* "White." *Education:* New York State University, B.F.A. *Religion:* Lutheran.

Addresses

Home—Falls Village, CT. *E-mail*—tatiferous@comcast. net.

Career

Actress, novelist, producer, and playwright. Worked variously as a Santa's elf at Macy's, Department Store, a speech writer for U.S. President Ronald Reagan, a hot-dog street vendor, nanny, golf-cart-driver, administrative assistant, and publicist.

Member

Actors Equity, Screen Actors Guild, American Federation of Television and Radio Artists, Dramatists Guild.

Awards, Honors

Carbonell Award nomination; Emmy Award nomination for outstanding children's program, 1991, for *Earth to Kids: A Guide to Products for a Healthy Planet.*

Writings

FOR CHILDREN

The Block Mess Monster, illustrated by C.B. Decker, Henry Holt (New York, NY), 2008.

FOR CHILDREN; AS HOWIE DEWIN

(Adaptor) *Pokémon: The Four-star Challenge,* Scholastic, Inc. (New York, NY), 2001.
Sand Hassle, Scholastic, Inc. (New York, NY), 2001.

Mojo Jojo's Yo-yo Tricks, Scholastic, Inc. (New York, NY), 2001.
(Adaptor) *Mewtwo Returns* (based on a screenplay by Michael Haigney), Scholastic, Inc. (New York, NY), 2002.
Mojo Jojo: My Story, Scholastic, Inc. (New York, NY), 2002.
The Voice of the Forest, Scholastic, Inc. (New York, NY), 2002.
Scooby-Doo's Guide to School, Scholastic, Inc. (New York, NY), 2002.
Dexter's Ink, Scholastic, Inc. (New York, NY), 2002.
Little Miss Pokey Oaks, Scholastic, Inc. (New York, NY), 2002.
Habitat Is Where It's At!: A Sticker Book Experience, Scholastic, Inc. (New York, NY), 2003.
Sleeping Ugly, Scholastic, Inc. (New York, NY), 2004.
Dexter's Joke Book for Geniuses, Scholastic, Inc. (New York, NY), 2004.
Book of Monsters: The Official Movie Scrapbook, Scholastic, Inc. (New York, NY), 2004.
(With Sarah Fisch) *Shrek 2 Gag Book,* Scholastic, Inc. (New York, NY), 2004.
Why Are Dogs' Noses Wet? and Other True Facts, Scholastic, Inc. (New York, NY), 2006.
Happy Howliday Book, Scholastic, Inc. (New York, NY), 2006.
Do You Know Your Dog?: A Breed-by-Breed Guide, Scholastic, Inc. (New York, NY), 2006.
The Circus Comes to Town, Scholastic, Inc. (New York, NY), 2006.
Why Do Dogs Love to Sniff?: The Do's and Don'ts of the Dogs, Scholastic, Inc. (New York, NY), 2007.
Dogs Rule and Cats Drool!, Scholastic, Inc. (New York, NY), 2007.
Hats off, Wildcats!: A Graduation Guide from Your Favorite Seniors, Disney Press (New York, NY), 2008.
Lab to the Rescue!, Scholastic, Inc. (New York, NY), 2009.

Also author of other books, including *A Star Is Born, Water Dog Hero, Leader of the Pack, Firehouse Dog,* and *Hollywood Spaniel,* all published by Scholastic, Inc.

OTHER

Cowgirls (musical play; produced off-Broadway, 1996), music and lyrics by Mary Murfitt, Dramatists Play Service (New York, NY), 1999.
Snow (novel), Harcourt Brace (New York, NY), 1998.
Callie's Tally: An Accounting of Baby's First Year; or, What My Daughter Owes Me (memoir), Jeremy P. Tarcher/Penguin (New York, NY), 2002.

Author of other plays, including *Big Stella, Yours Truly, How I Didn't Get Famous,* and *The Bridal Fit.*

Sidelights

Betsy Howie, a stage actress, novelist, and playwright who sometimes writes under the name Howie Dewin, is also the author of a number of children's books, among

them *The Block Mess Monster,* a humorous tale about an imaginative child who has trouble cleaning her room. Howie's works for adults include *Cowgirls,* a musical play; *Snow* a fictional story about a woman's troubled life; and the memoir *Callie's Tally: An Accounting of Baby's First Year; or, What My Daughter Owes Me.*

Written in collaboration with musician and lyricist Mary Murfitt, *Cowgirls* concerns Jo, who has only twenty-four hours to find a way to save her father's country-western saloon from foreclosure. She needs a paying crowd—and she needs one fast. The saloon's wise-cracking waitress, Mickey, and cook/cashier, Mo offer to get up on stage and help, but Jo has a better plan: She has booked the Cowgirl Trio, convinced that they will attract a big audience. The catch is that there is no Cowgirl Trio; because of a telephone misunderstanding, she has booked the Coghill Trio, three classical musicians on a reunion tour. When the trio arrives, they have one day to transform themselves from classical longhairs to foot-stompin' honky-tonk country-and-western musicians.

In *Callie's Tally* Howie offers a tongue-in-cheek look at the financial price associated with the birth of her child. In addition to "billing" her daughter for amniocentesis, unattractive maternity outfits, a car seat, prenatal vitamins, and diapers, the author records a number of other, rather questionable, expenditures, including the price of stamps for thank-you notes and the cost of Weight Watchers meetings. A *Publishers Weekly* contributor described *Callie's Tally* as an "irreverent look at new motherhood," and a critic in *Kirkus Reviews* called the work a "good-humored bottom-line account of the changes wrought when a successful and independent woman becomes a mother."

The mother-daughter relationship is also at the heart of *The Block Mess Monster,* a picture book that centers on Calpurnia, a playful youngster who blames the state of her messy bedroom on the dreaded "Block Mess Monster." Making matters worse, Calpurnia's exasperated mother cannot see the troublesome creature, and her attempts to persuade her daughter to tidy up constantly fall flat. Just when her patience seems at an end, however, Calpurnia's mom discovers a solution that pleases everyone, including the monster. A critic in *Kirkus Reviews* applauded the humorous dialog in *The Block Mess Monster,* stating that the young heroine's "priceless quips will have both parents and children in stitches." Marianne Saccardi, writing in *School Library Journal,* praised the combination of Howie's narrative and C.B.

Betsy Howie teams up with artist C.B. Decker to entertain readers with the picture book **The Block Mess Monster.** (Illustration copyright © 2008 by C.B. Decker. All rights reserved. Reprinted by arrangement with Henry Holt & Company, LLC.)

Decker's artwork, commenting of the same book that the "perfect pairing of text and illustrations is irresistible."

Biographical and Critical Sources

PERIODICALS

Kirkus Reviews, August 15, 2002, review of *Callie's Tally: An Accounting of Baby's First Year; or, What My Daughter Owes Me,* p. 1196; May 1, 2008, review of *The Block Mess Monster.*
Library Journal, October 1, 1997, review of *Snow,* p. 122.
Publishers Weekly, October 6, 1997, review of *Snow,* p. 72; August 26, 2002, review of *Callie's Tally,* p. 56.
School Library Journal, June, 2008, Marianne Saccardi, review of *The Block Mess Monster,* p. 104.
Variety, April 8-14, 1996, review of *Cowgirls,* p. 68.

ONLINE

American Theatre Wing Web site, http://americantheatre wing.org/ (March 1, 2010), profile of Howie.

I-J

IVES, Penny 1956-

Personal

Born 1956, in England; children: one son. *Education:* Attended Bath Academy of Art and Brighton Art School.

Addresses

Home—Bath, England. *E-mail*—penny@pennyives.co. uk.

Career

Author and illustrator.

Writings

SELF-ILLUSTRATED

Mrs Christmas, Hamish Hamilton (London, England), 1990, published as *Mrs. Santa Claus,* Delacorte Press (New York, NY), 1991.

Goldilocks and the Three Bears: A Peek-through-the-Window Book, Putnam (New York, NY), 1992.

On Christmas Eve: A Three-dimensional Celebration, paper engineering by David Hawcock, G.P. Putnam's Sons (New York, NY), 1992.

Granny's Quilt, Hamish Hamilton (London, England), 1993.

Santa's Christmas Journey: A Scrolling Picture Book, paper engineering by David Hawcock, Tango (London, England), 1994.

The Snow Angel: A Pop-up Ornament Book, Tango (London, England), 1995.

Millie and the Mermaid, Hamish Hamilton (London, England), 1996.

Nina the Gobblegoat, Puffin (London, England), 1998.

Five Little Ducks (die-cut book), Child's Play (Swindon, England) 2002.

Rabbit Pie, Viking (New York, NY), 2006.

Celestine, Drama Queen, Templar (Dorking, England), 2008, Arthur A. Levine Books (New York, NY), 2009.

ILLUSTRATOR

Tom Tully, *The Space Waifs,* Wheaton (Exeter, England), 1980.

Teresa Verschoyle, reteller, *Jack and the Beanstalk,* Macmillan (London, England), 1984.

Sally Sheringham, *Clifford the Sheep,* 1986, Derrydale Books (New York, NY) 1987.

Ruth Thomson, *All about Shapes,* 1986, Gareth Stevens (Milwaukee, WI), 1987.

Shona McKellar, *Pop into My Party,* Hutchinson (London, England), 1988.

Clement C. Moore, *The Night before Christmas,* Putnam (New York, NY), 1988.

Chris Baines, *The Old Boot,* Frances Lincoln/Windward (London, England), 1989, Crocodile Books (New York, NY), 1990.

Chris Baines, *The Flower,* Frances Lincoln/Windward (London, England), 1989, Crocodile Books (New York, NY), 1990.

Chris Baines, *The Nest,* Frances Lincoln/Windward (London, England), 1989, Crocodile Books (New York, NY), 1990.

Chris Baines, *The Picnic,* Frances Lincoln/Windward (London, England), 1989, Crocodile Books (New York, NY), 1990.

Jenny Wood, selector, *The Nursery Book,* Blackie (London, England), 1991.

Anne-Marie Chapouton, *Downy, Pistachio, and Fanny: A Story,* Child's World (Mankato, MN), 1992.

Kathy Henderson, selector, *The Bedtime Book: Stories and Poems to Read Aloud,* Frances Lincoln (London, England), 1992, published as *The Bedtime Book: Stories and Poems from around the World to Read Aloud,* Barron's (Hauppauge, NY), 1992.

Paul Heiney, *Grumpers' Farm: Farmyard Stories to Read Aloud,* Collins (London, England), 1996.

Jonathan Emmett, *Fox's New Coat,* Viking (London, England), 2000.

Paeony Lewis, *I'll Always Love You,* Little Tiger (London, England), 2000, Tiger Tales (Wilton, CT), 2002.

David Bedford, *The Long Journey Home,* Little Tiger (London, England), 2001.

Sidelights

An author and illustrator, Penny Ives creates picture books that use animal characters to capture the fun and foibles of growing up. In *Rabbit Pie,* for instance, six little bunnies find a myriad ways to avoid getting tucked into bed by their loving mother, while a young duckling wants to be the center of attention in *Celestine, Drama Queen.* Dubbing *Rabbit Pie* a "cozy" story, Ilene Cooper added in *Booklist* that Ives' tale features "a sweetness" that is matched by her "soft-candy-colored artwork." A *Publishers Weekly* contributor described the author/illustrator's creation of "delicate watercolored scenes," adding that *Rabbit Pie* "will go down as satisfyingly as a warm glass of milk," and *School Library Journal* contributor Kristine M. Casper recommended the "delightful" picture book "for one-on-one sharing."

In *Celestine, Drama Queen* Ives introduces a pink-loving young duckling who also loves attention and hopes to find it as star of the school play. Although the teacher assures the class that everyone's part is important, Celestine is sure that she is the star of the show. However, when she confronts a real live audience on opening night the duckling is struck dumb with a case of stage fright. Fortunately, the quick thinking of a teacher turns Celestine's attention to dancing and helps the duckling steal the show anyway. Noting Ives' skill at capturing the personality of young children in her quirky animal characters and "funny, sunny watercolors," Cooper called the duckling character "adorable, annoying, and utterly childlike," while Kathleen Finn wrote in *School Library Journal* that the author/illustrator's "watercolors and pencil drawings" in *Celestine, Drama Queen* "whimsically depict the adorable Celestine."

One of Ives' early self-illustrated picture books, *Mrs. Santa Claus,* features a holiday theme. The story describes the concern of Santa's wife when she realizes that her husband and his reindeer are covered with spots on the eve of their big ride. A resourceful woman, Mrs. Claus creates her own flying transportation using a bicycle, an umbrella, and a vacuum cleaner, and manages to deliver all the Christmas gifts throughout the world in a story brought to life in pictures "merrily colored and crowded with delectable details," according to a *Publishers Weekly* contributor.

In addition to her original works, Ives has also illustrated books for other writers. Praising her work for Paeony Lewis's *I'll Always Love You,* the story of a accident-prone young bear who learns that a parent's love is unconditional, Shawn Brommer wrote in *School Library Journal,* that Ives' "colored-pencil illustrations reveal a cheery home."

Biographical and Critical Sources

PERIODICALS

Booklist, January 1, 2006, Ilene Cooper, review of *Rabbit Pie,* p. 116; February 1, 2009, Ilene Cooper, review of *Celestine, Drama Queen,* p. 40.

Kirkus Reviews, January 15, 2009, review of *Celestine, Drama Queen.*

Publishers Weekly, November 15, 1991, review of *Mrs. Santa Claus,* p. 71; September 7, 1992, Elizabeth Devereaux, review of *On Christmas Eve: A Three-dimensional Celebration,* p. 66; February 13, 2006, review of *Rabbit Pie,* p. 88.

School Library Journal, October, 1991, Dorothy Houlihan, review of *Mrs. Santa Claus,* p. 30; August, 2002, Shawn Brommer, review of *I'll Always Love You,* p. 160; May, 2006, Kristine M. Casper, review of *Rabbit Pie,* p. 90; February, 2009, Kathleen Finn, review of *Celestine, Drama Queen,* p. 76.

ONLINE

Penny Ives Home Page, http://www.pennyives.co.uk (April 20, 2010).*

*   *   *

JENNEWEIN, James (Jim Jennewein)

Personal

Son of James Sr. (a company treasurer), and Thelma Jennewein; married Allison Robbins, May 20, 1995; children: one son. *Education:* University of Notre Dame, B.A. (fine art).

Addresses

Home—Santa Monica, CA.

Career

Screenwriter and author of children's fiction. Worked variously as an assembly-line worker, house painter, and author of advertising copy. University of California—Los Angeles Extension, instructor.

Writings

FOR CHILDREN

(With Tom S. Parker) *RuneWarriors,* Laura Geringer Books (New York, NY), 2008.

(With Tom S. Parker) *Sword of Doom,* HarperCollins (New York, NY), 2010.

OTHER

(Under Jim Jennewein; with Tom S. Parker) *Stay Tuned* (screenplay), Warner Bros., 1992.
(With Tom S. Parker and Steven E. De Souza) *The Flintstones* (screenplay), 1993.

Author of additional screenplays, with Parker, including: *Getting Even with Dad,* 1994, *Richie Rich,* 1994, and *Major League II,* 1994.

Adaptations

The Flintstones was adapted into several books for children. *RuneWarriors* was adapted as an audiobook, Recorded Books, 2009.

Sidelights

James Jennewein has worked in collaboration with Tom S. Parker to create screenplays for films that include *The Flintstones* and *Major League II.* Inspired by their interest in history and their desire to tell an entertaining and adventure-filled story featuring heroic role models for middle graders, Jennewein and Parker have also created the boy-friendly novels *RuneWarriors* and *Sword of Doom.*

Jennewein and Parker met in 1980, while working for the same employer. Although both young men were interested in writing, they did not begin collaborating on their first screenplay until a decade later. When the script sold, the two friends immediately quit their job and began dedicating themselves to their new career. Since the early 1990s, Jennewein and Parker have authored over twenty family-centered film scripts for Hollywood producers.

Set during the time of the Vikings, their debut novel *RuneWarriors* focuses on a teenager known as Dane the Defiant and his growth toward manhood. Incorporating elements of Norse mythology—Jennewein also visited Norway to study the story's setting—the novel follows Dane as a reading of the runes sends him on a quest to avenge the death of his father at the hand of the berserker Thidrek the Terrifying. On his journey Dane is joined by loyal companion Klint the raven and encounters trolls, giants, amulets, magical weapons, and even a beautiful maiden named Astrid. Dane's story continues in *Sword of Doom,* as he seeks a way to save his village from starvation and illness. At the court of King Eldred, he acquires a written secret that will help Dane and his friends rescue his mother, if only he can conquer the evil forces holding her hostage.

"Improbable twists of fate and history juxtaposed with modern references keep the story light," observed Deirdre Root in her *Kliatt* review of *RuneWarrior,* while in *Kirkus Reviews* a writer noted that the tale's inclusion of factually detail is balanced by "pell-mell action, the wisenheimer narration and the belch-and-flatulence hu-

mor embedded in the adventurous tale." The coauthors' "rigorous, vigorous, modern telling of ancient adventure . . . barrels along with a salty grace that makes the reader glad to know it's only the first of a planned trilogy," wrote Victoria Thomas in the *Bloomsbury Revew.* Weaving factual information about Viking life into their high-energy tale, Jennewein and Parker "never let us forget that the Vikings were bona fide badasses, even by medieval standards." "*RuneWarriors'* ruggedly Nordic mythscape will send shivers of anticipation down even the most jaded middle-school spine," the critic added.

In their successful writing collaboration, Jennewein and Parker have a system that they use when creating both screenplays and novels. After sifting through various ideas, they work together to formulate a rough plot, and one of the writers uses that to construct a short synopsis that contains all the plot details they wish to incorporate in their tale. The synopsis is then divided into the scenes or chapters that will build drama and hold viewer or reader attention over the course of the work. Jennewein and Parker each tackle separate chapters, reviewing each other's work to smooth out inconsistencies and ensure thematic continuity. When the first draft is done, they repeat the review process, fleshing out characters, adding a salting of preteen-friendly humor, and making their separate texts read as the work of one writer.

"A passion for storytelling lies at the heart of why I am a writer," Jennewein noted in a statement on the University of California—Los Angeles Extension Web site. "Whether it's reading them, writing them, or helping others craft their own, stories just help me feel more alive, more attuned to the things that matter. The facts of life as illuminated in great fiction, the heightened moments in great films—nothing could be more exciting. I believe in the power of stories to change lives: the lives of those who read them and those who write them."

Biographical and Critical Sources

PERIODICALS

Bloomsbury Review, November-December, 2008, Victoria Thomas, interview with Jennewein and review of *RuneWarriors.*
Kirkus Reviews, September 15, 2008, review of *RuneWarriors.*
Kliatt, September, 2008, Deirdre Root, review of *RuneWarriors,* p. 13.
School Library Journal, December, 2008, Saleena L. Davidson, review of *RuneWarriors,* p. 126.
Voice of Youth Advocates, December, 2008, Domina Daughtrey, review of *RuneWarriors,* p. 452.

ONLINE

RuneWarriors Web site, http://www.runewarriors.net (April 30, 2010).*

JENNEWEIN, Jim
See JENNEWEIN, James

* * *

JOHNSON, Gillian 1963-

Personal

Born February 26, 1963, in Winnipeg, Manitoba, Canada; married Nicholas Shakespeare (a writer); children: two sons. *Education:* University of Manitoba, B.A. (English); McGill University, teacher certification, then M.A. (English); University of California—Irvine, M.F.A. (adult writing). *Hobbies and other interests:* Swimming.

Addresses

Home—Swansea, Tasmania; Wiltshire, England.

Career

Author and illustrator. Former teacher of swimming and canoeing; teacher of English in Czechoslovakia; A.Y. Jackson Secondary School, Kanata, Ontario, Canada, teacher for two years; former high-school teacher in Ottawa, Ontario, Canada.

Awards, Honors

Honorable mention, Bologna Children's Book Fair Graphics Prize, 1992, for *Saranohair;* Alcuin Design Award 2000, for *My Sister Gracie.*

Writings

SELF-ILLUSTRATED

Saranohair, Annick Press (Willowdale, Ontario, Canada), 1992.
My Sister Gracie, Tundra Books (Plattsburgh, NY), 2000.
Thora, Angus & Robertson (Sydney, New South Wales, Australia), 2003, Katherine Tegen Books (New York, NY), 2005.
Gracie's Baby Chub Chop, Tundra Books (Toronto, Ontario, Canada), 2004.
Thora and the Green Sea-unicorn: Another Half-mermaid Tale, HarperTrophyCanada, (Toronto, Ontario, Canada), 2005, Katherine Tegen Books (New York, NY), 2007.

Author's work has been translated into Dutch, French, Icelandic, Spanish, and Braille.

ILLUSTRATOR

Richard Scrimger, *A Nose for Adventure,* Tundra Books (Plattsburgh, NY), 2000.

Dennis Lee, *The Cat and the Wizard,* Key Porter Books (Toronto, Ontario, Canada), 2000.
Richard Scrimger, *Bun Bun's Birthday,* Tundra Books (Plattsburgh, NY), 2001.
Richard Scrimger, *Princess Bun Bun,* Tundra Books (Plattsburgh, NY), 2002.
Richard Scrimger, *Eugene's Story,* Tundra Books (Plattsburgh, NY), 2003.
Thomas Keneally, *Roos in Shoes,* Random House (Milsons Point, New South Wales, Australia), 2003.
Linda Maybarduk, *James the Dancing Dog,* Tundra Books (Toronto, Ontario, Canada), 2004.
Katy Kelly, *Melonhead,* Delacorte Press (New York, NY), 2009.
Katy Kelly, *Melonhead and the Big Stink,* Delacorte Press (New York, NY), 2010.

Sidelights

A former teacher, Gillian Johnson divides her time between the United Kingdom and Tasmania. She began her book illustration career with the original story *Saranohair,* a fanciful tale that earned her an honorable mention at the prestigious Bologna Children's Book Fair. In her self-illustrated chapter books *Thora: A Half-Mermaid Tale* its sequels, Johnson introduces an unusual aquatic heroine, while her popular picture book *My Sister Gracie* earned her several other awards for illustration while also being translated into several languages.

The youngest of six children, Johnson grew up in Winnipeg, Manitoba, Canada, where she enjoyed competitive sports and qualified as part of the national speed skating training team during her late teens. While completing her English degree at the University of Manitoba, she explored an interest in art by creating cartoons for the school newspaper. Continuing to create caricatures and other drawings for enthusiastic family and friends, she also completed college, then earned her teaching certification. While completing her M.A. in English at McGill University, she produced what became her first original picture book, *Saranohair.* Published in 1992, the book features pen-and-ink drawings and a nonsensical story about two sisters that gives a nod to the work of noted nineteenth-century author/illustrator Edward Lear. Describing Johnson's text as "the kind of story that preschool children tell themselves when they are alone," *Horn Book* critic Sarah Ellis cited Johnson's skill in incorporating "lots of repetition, silly jokes, funny words, a bit of naughtiness, . . . and a comforting ending." "To create the illusion of child-told tale without succumbing once to the pitfalls of cuteness or condescension is a rare accomplishment," Ellis added, concluding that, "with *Saranohair,* Johnson joins the uncrowded field of writers who really understand nonsense."

Fabio the dog and his oversized canine companion Gracie are the focus of *My Sister Gracie* and *Gracie's Baby Chub Chop,* two picture books that feature full-color

artwork by Johnson. In *My Sister Gracie* Fabio is lonely and longs for a playmate. When his family goes to the animal shelter to find him a companion, however, they return with cuddly, sleepy Gracie, a dog who is more interested in spending time with humans than with Fabio. Eventually, however, the two dogs become friends, and they team together against a new threat to family stability—a visiting toddler—in *Gracie's Baby Chub Chop*. Describing the artwork in *My Sister Gracie* as "humorous, but understated and appealing," Roxanne Burg added in *School Library Journal* that Johnson's "rhyming tale" serves as "an endearing addition to stories about family relationships and sibling rivalry." In *Resource Links* Zoe Johnstone dubbed *Gracie's Baby Chub Chop* "a wonderful book in every way," while Wanda Meyers-Hines wrote that Johnson's "rhyming text" pairs with her "humorous" depiction of the two dogs to "keep . . . the action moving quickly."

The elementary-grade novel *Thora* was inspired by Johnson's visit to Iceland, the home of her ancestors. Set in the seaside town of Grimli, the story introduces an unusual cast of characters that includes ten-year-old Thora, Thora's mermaid mother Halla, a friendly guardian named Mr. Walters, and Thora's pet peacock, Cosmo. Because Halla had little understanding of the needs of a human baby, the elderly Mr. Walters stepped in and taught the mermaid how to feed, clothe, and shelter her unusual offspring. The girl's human father has been missing her entire life, and Thora and her mother have sails from place to place on his boat, the *Loki* for the necessary ten years. Now returned to Grimli, Thora lives on the *Loki* while her mother makes her home on a nearby rock. Due to her mixed race (although she can pass as almost human, Thora has a blowhole on the top of her head and her hands and feet are covered with purple fish scales) the girl is destined to live for ten years in the sea, followed by a decade on land, and she feels like a misfit on both.

In *Thora* the half-mermaid meets several new friends while also becoming involved in some local intrigue involving a local business developer. In *Thora and the Green Sea-Unicorn* Thora and company visit London on the *Loki* and deal with the disappearance of a new pet, a sea-unicorn named Shirley. In *Canadian Review of Materials,* Stacie Edgar recommended *Thora* as "an entertaining and fun read about an irresistible, likeable character," while in *School Library Journal* Elizabeth Bird predicted of *Thora and the Green Sea-Unicorn* that "fans of mermaids will be gently amused by Johnson's sense of humor and evident love of her characters."

In addition to illustrating her original stories, Johnson's artwork has also appeared in a number of other books, among them Thomas Keneally's *Roos in Shoes,* Dennis Lee's *The Cat and the Wizard,* Linda Maybarduk's *James the Dancing Dog,* and Katy Kelly's elementary-grade novel *Melonhead.* Maybarduk's picture book is based on the dog who served as the mascot of the Na-

Gillian Johnson captures the antics of a misfit preteen in her humorous artwork for Katy Kelly's beginning chapter book **Melonhead.** (Illustration copyright © 2009 by Gillian Johnson. All rights reserved. Reproduced by permission.)

tional Ballet of Canada from 1961 to 1972: James the beagle participates in dance rehearsals along with his ballet-dancer owner, and also mooches treats from dancers during lunch time. When a high-strung wolfhound gets stage fright after being cast in *Giselle,* the doughty James is waiting in the wings to perform the crucial doggy role. Maybarduk's "gently wry text" in *James the Dancing Dog* is balanced by Johnson's "fluid" watercolor-and-ink illustrations," wrote a *Publishers Weekly* contributor, and in *Resource Links* Isobel Lang maintained that the artist's "drawings reflect the humour, movement and energy imbued in the story."

One of Johnson's most frequent collaborators has been Richard Scrimger, with whom she has created the picture books *Bun Bun's Birthday, Princess Bun Bun,* and *Eugene's Story.* The trio of tales follows the adventures of three siblings: Winnifred, Eugene, and little Brenda, called "Bun Bun." Readers meet them in *Bun Bun's Birthday,* as Brenda turns one and Winnifred has to deal with the pangs of jealousy that the party is not for her. A visit to a relative and a trip in an elevator inspires Winnifred's imagination as Uncle Dave's apartment building becomes a castle complete with a monster (a spotted puppy), a guard (the doorman), and neighbors that are imaginatively transformed into a witch and a princess. Caught between Winnifred and Brenda, middle child Eugene remains a minor personality until *Eugene's Story,* when he reveals his point of view and shares his dreams of being an only child.

Noting that "Scrimger paints a very realistic picture of family life" in *Bun Bun's Birthday,* Heather Farmer added in *Resource Links* that Johnson's "colorful cartoons" for the story reflect the author's "droll writing" and "are humorous . . . ; whimsical; and odd" due to the "tiny eyes and skinny arms and legs of the charac-

ters." In *School Library Journal* Sue Sherif noted of the same book that the "pen-and-watercolor illustrations . . . portray household objects and family in child's-eye proportions and perspective," while a *Kirkus Reviews* writer remarked that Johnson's "willowy ink and watercolor pictures" for *Princess Bun Bun* are "drawn with humor." Hazel Rochman compared Johnson's work in *Eugene's Story* to that of noted illustrator William Steig, writing that her "small, scribbly" drawings capture the boy's "fury and frustration in a world where big means control."

Biographical and Critical Sources

PERIODICALS

Booklist, December 1, 2003, Hazel Rochman, review of *Eugene's Story,* p. 684; November, 15, 2004, Carolyn Phelan, review of *James the Dancing Dog,* p. 590; August, 2005, Carolyn Phelan, review of *Thora: A Half-Mermaid Tale,* p. 2028; June 1, 2007, Francisca Goldsmith, review of *Thora and the Green Sea-Unicorn: Another Half-Mermaid Tale,* p. 75; February 15, 2009, Andrew Medlar, review of *Melonhead,* p. 83.

Canadian Review of Materials, March 17, 2006, Stacie Edgar, review of *Thora.*

Horn Book, January-February 1993, Sarah Ellis, review of *Saranohair,* p. 113.

Kirkus Reviews, April 15, 2002, review of *Princess Bun Bun,* p. 578; April 1, 2007, review of *Thora and the Green Sea-Unicorn.*

Publishers Weekly, November 20, 2000, review of *My Sister Gracie,* p. 67; December 13, 2004, review of *James the Dancing Dog,* p. 66; February 23, 2009, review of *Melonhead,* p. 51.

Resource Links, April, 2001, Isobel Lang, review of *My Sister Gracie,* p. 4, and Heather Farmer, review of *Bun Bun's Birthday,* p. 6; December, 2001, Zoe Johnstone Guha, review of *The Cat and the Wizard,* p. 6; April, 2002, Linda Berezowski, review of *Princess Bun Bun,* p. 9; December, 2003, Liz Abercrombie, review of *Eugene's Story,* p. 9; October, 2004, Zoe Johnstone, review of *Gracie's Baby Chub Chop,* p. 4 and Isobel Lang, review of *James the Dancing Dog,* p. 8.

School Library Journal, December, 2000, Roxanne Burg, review of *My Sister Gracie,* p. 111; June, 2001, Sue Sherif, review of *Bun Bun's Birthday,* p. 129; July, 2002, Adele Greenlee, review of *Princess Bun Bun,* p. 98; March, 2004, Catherine Threadgill, review of *Eugene's Story,* p. 181; November, 2004, Wanda Meyers-Hines, review of *Gracie's Baby Chub Chop,* p. 108; December, 2004, Mary Hazelton, review of *James the Dancing Dog,* p. 114; June, 2007, Elizabeth Bird, review of *Thora and the Green Sea-Unicorn,* p. 148; March, 2009, Caitlin Augusta, review of *Melonhead,* p. 118.

ONLINE

Canadian Review of Materials Online, http://www.umani toba.ca/cm/profiles/ (October 4, 2005), Dave Jenkinson, interview with Johnson.

Random House Web site, http://www.randomhouse.com/ (May 5, 2010), "Gillian Johnson."*

K

KANELL, Beth
(Elizabeth L. Dugger)

Personal

Married David Kanell (a bookseller); children: two sons. *Hobbies and other interests:* Walking, local history.

Addresses

Home—Waterford, VT. *E-mail*—bethkanellauthor@gmail.com.

Career

Journalist, storyteller, bookseller, poet, and historian. Kingdom Books, Waterford, VT, cofounder. Author of grants for historic preservation; presenter to schools and historical societies.

Member

National Book Critics Circle.

Writings

FICTION

The Darkness under the Water, Candlewick Press (Cambridge, MA), 2008.

OTHER

(As Elizabeth L. Dugger) *Adventure Guide to New Hampshire,* Hunter Publishing (Edison, NJ), 1998.
(As Elizabeth L. Dugger) *Adventure Guide to Massachusetts and Western Connecticut,* Hunter Publishing (Edison, NJ), 1999.
(As Elizabeth L. Dugger) *Adventure Guide to Vermont,* Hunter Publishing (Edison, NJ), 2000.

Also author of *Mud Season at the Castle* (poetry chapbook).

Cover of Beth Kanell's dramatic teen novel **The Darkness under the Water.** (Jacket photographs copyright © 2008 by SassyStock (young woman); Copyright © 2008 by Hans Strand/Stone/Getty Images (water); Copyright © 2008 by Stephen Alvarez/National Geographic/Getty Images (leaves). Reproduced by permission of Candlewick Press.)

Sidelights

In *The Darkness under the Water,* her first novel for teen readers, Beth Kanell takes readers back to the 1930s and rural New England. Molly Ballou, a sixteen year old of mixed Abenaki and French-Canadian ancestry, is haunted by the memory of her older sister's drowning, which occurred before Molly was born, when her sister Gratia was five years old. She is also affected by her mother's continuing sadness over the loss, and when the woman once again becomes pregnant a great deal of emotional family turmoil is the result. Molly wrestles with her feelings regarding abandoning her education to help her mother, as well as her growing feelings for an Abenaki boy named Henry. She also realizes that her desire to explore and embrace her Native-American roots makes her vulnerable to a state government promoting eugenics: purifying the genetic strength of Vermont's predominately Yankee population by weeding out the influence of other races through voluntary sterilization.

Calling *The Darkness under the Water* "a subtle, richly drawn historical novel," Kim Ventrella added in *School Library Journal* that Kanell's "beautiful use of language" enhances her focus on a rarely explored moment in U.S. history. In *Kliatt* Aimee Coile predicted that "readers will be drawn into this historical story," and a *Kirkus Reviews* contributor concluded that Molly's "gracefully composed" narrative combines with Kanell's author's note describing the Vermont Eugenics Project to "provide a personal perspective on a grim episode in American history."

Biographical and Critical Sources

PERIODICALS

Kirkus Reviews, October 15, 2008, review of *The Darkness under the Water.*
Kliatt, November, 2008, Aimee Coile, review of *The Darkness under the Water,* p. 13.
School Library Journal, January, 2009, Kim Ventrella, review of *The Darkness under the Water,* p. 106.
Voice of Youth Advocates, February, 2009, Jenny Ingram, review of *The Darkness under the Water,* p. 530.

ONLINE

Beth Kanell Home Page, http://www.bethkanell.com (March 15, 2010).
Beth Kanell Web log, http://bethkanell.blogspot.com/ (April 15, 2010).

*   *   *

KELLY, Katy 1955-

Personal

Born 1955, in Washington, DC; daughter of Tom (a journalist) and Marguerite (a columnist and writer) Kelly; married; husband's name Steve (an art director for television); children: Emily, Marguerite. *Education:* Attended Virginia Commonwealth University.

Addresses

Home—Washington, DC.

Career

Journalist and author. *People* magazine, reporter, 1984-90; *USA Today,* feature writer for Life section; *U.S. News & World Report,* Washington, DC, senior editor.

Writings

"LUCY ROSE" ELEMENTARY-GRADE NOVEL SERIES

Lucy Rose: Here's the Thing about Me, illustrated by Adam Rex, Delacorte Press (New York, NY), 2004.
Lucy Rose: Big on Plans, illustrated by Adam Rex, Delacorte Press (New York, NY), 2005.
Lucy Rose: Busy like You Can't Believe, illustrated by Adam Rex, Delacorte Press (New York, NY), 2006.
Lucy Rose: Working Myself to Pieces and Bits, illustrated by Peter Ferguson, Delacorte Press (New York, NY), 2007.

"MELONHEAD" ELEMENTARY-GRADE NOVEL SERIES

Melonhead, illustrated by Gillian Johnson, Delacorte Press (New York, NY), 2009.
Melonhead and the Big Stink, illustrated by Gillian Johnson, Delacorte Press (New York, NY), 2010.

Adaptations

The "Lucy Rose" novels were adapted as audio books, Listening Library, 2005; *Lucy Rose: Here's the Thing about Me* was adapted for the stage.

Sidelights

Growing up in Washington, DC, as the daughter of journalists, Katy Kelly knew exactly what to expect in pursuing a career as a reporter and writer. In addition to a successful career that has included stints at *People, USA Today,* and *U.S. News & World Report,* Kelly is the author of a series of books for younger readers that feature a vivacious eight-year-old named Lucy Rose. These novels, which include *Lucy Rose: Here's the Thing about Me* and *Lucy Rose: Working Myself to Pieces and Bits,* have been praised for their engaging fourth-grade heroine and use of the diary format. "I lifted a lot of Lucy Rose's life from my own," the author told *Publishers Weekly* interviewer Sally Lodge, "and then . . . stirred it around." Kelly's work as a journalist has benefited her career as a children's book author; as she stated in a Random House Web site interview, "I learned to listen to what people were (and

weren't) saying, to understand what they cherished and what they feared. I can't imagine that I could write good fiction without having reported on so many real lives."

Readers meet Kelly's spunky protagonist in *Lucy Rose: Here's the Thing about Me,* as the youngster moves from Michigan to Washington, DC, on the heels of her parents' separation. While living with her mother, Lucy Rose also forms a strong bond with her grandmother, an advice columnist who lives nearby and becomes the young girl's confidante. Dealing with the ups and downs of a new school in fine style, Lucy Rose "narrates in breathless run-on sentences" and "has a truly original perspective," according to a *Publishers Weekly* reviewer. In *School Library Journal,* Linda Zeilstra Sawyer noted that Lucy Rose confronts the problems shared by many children dealing with broken homes and "meets her challenges with humor and honesty," while a *Kirkus Reviews* critic remarked that Kelly's text successfully "delivers . . . mature and complex concepts simply enough for her young audience."

A busy summer vacation rolls out in *Lucy Rose: Big on Plans,* as the young diarist expresses her worries about

Katy Kelly features a spunky young heroine in Lucy Rose: Busy like You Can't Believe, *featuring artwork by Adam Rex.* (Illustration copyright © 2006 by Adam Rex. Reproduced by permission of Yearling, an imprint of Random House Children's Books, a division of Random House, Inc.)

everything from her parent's divorce and her grandparents' problem with hungry squirrels to a bully who seems determined to cause Lucy Rose grief. "The book's language is rich and the characters are likeable," Teresa Bateman noted in *School Library Journal,* while in *Booklist* Cindy Dobrez wrote that "Lucy Rose's exuberance is evident in her long, run-on sentences." "Lucy is energetic and positive, but her life is a realistic blend of fun and challenges," according to a *Kirkus Reviews* contributor.

Lucy Rose: Busy like You Can't Believe details the further exploits of the enthusiastic youngster, who has now entered the fourth grade. While voicing concerns about her role in the school play, her difficulties learning the multiplication tables, and her inability to quit eavesdropping, Lucy must also deal with the fact that that her mother has begun dating and her best friend is moving away. "Kelly writes with a dual sophistication that offers the voice of a child's innocently misconstrued perceptions about language," a critic in *Kirkus Reviews* stated, and Kay Weisman asserted in *Booklist* that Lucy's "authentic voice speaks directly to readers." "The book's conversational tone is ideal for reluctant readers," concluded *School Library Journal* reviewer Shawn Brommer.

In *Lucy Rose: Working Myself to Pieces and Bits,* the protagonist pitches in when her family friends decide to open a bakery in town, devising a host of money-making schemes to help them finance the cost of rehabbing an old building. Lucy must also confront a troublemaker at school who is spreading rumors about her relationship with Melonhead, a friend and classmate. The author "gives a more nuanced and realistic picture of bullies than one normally sees" in children's books, Adrienne Furness wrote in *School Library Journal.* A critic in *Kirkus Reviews* applauded the book's whimsical plot and witty dialog, observing that *Lucy Rose: Working Myself to Pieces and Bits* contains "enough wordplay and banter to keep kids and adults sympathetically nodding their heads for this young heroine."

Kelly has also produced a spin-off series featuring the misadventures of Adam Melon, a.k.a. Melonhead, a boy who is Lucy's entertaining pal. In *Melonhead,* Adam attempts to hide a pet snake and from his parents, garners honors for his essay about head lice, wreaks havoc at home while preparing a science project, and gets his foot stuck in a tree, prompting a call to the local firefighters. The work "is laugh-out-loud funny," Caitlin Augusta remarked in *School Library Journal,* and a contributor in *Kirkus Reviews* reported that Kelly's "breezily paced text flows with wit and loads of jocular dialogue."

Biographical and Critical Sources

PERIODICALS

Booklist, November 1, 2004, Ilene Cooper, review of *Lucy Rose: Here's the Thing about Me,* p. 485; April 15,

Captured in artwork by Peter Ferguson, Kelly's likeable character shares more of her adventures in Lucy Rose: Working Myself to Pieces and Bits. *(Illustration copyright © 2007 by Peter Ferguson. All rights reserved. Reproduced by permission of the illustrator.)*

2005, Patricia Austin, review of *Lucy Rose: Here's the Thing about Me,* p. 1476; August, 2005, Cindy Dobrez, review of *Lucy Rose: Big on Plans,* p. 2028; October 15, 2006, Kay Weisman, review of *Lucy Rose: Busy like You Can't Believe,* p. 44; February 15, 2009, Andrew Medlar, review of *Melonhead,* p. 83.

Bulletin of the Center for Children's Books, October, 2004, Timnah Card, review of *Lucy Rose: Here's the Thing about Me,* p. 83.

Kirkus Reviews, September 1, 2004, review of *Lucy Rose: Here's the Thing about Me,* p. 868; June 1, 2005, review of *Lucy Rose: Big on Plans,* p. 638; July 15, 2006, review of *Lucy Rose: Busy like You Can't Believe,* p. 724; August 15, 2007, review of *Lucy Rose: Working Myself to Pieces and Bits;* January 15, 2009, review of *Melonhead.*

Library Media Connection, January, 2005, Terry Day, review of *Lucy Rose: Here's the Thing about Me,* p. 75.

Publishers Weekly, September 20, 2004, review of *Lucy Rose: Here's the Thing about Me,* p. 63; December 20, 2004, Sally Lodge, "Flying Starts: Five Acclaimed Fall Children's Book Debut," p. 30; February 23, 2009, review of *Melonhead,* p. 51.

School Library Journal, September, 2004, Linda Zeilstra Sawyer, review of *Lucy Rose: Here's the Thing about*

Me, p. 170; June, 2005, Terrie Dorio, review of *Lucy Rose: Big on Plans,* p. 118; September, 2005, Teresa Bateman, review of *Lucy Rose: Big on Plans,* p. 78; October, 2006, Shawn Brommer, review of *Lucy Rose: Busy like You Can't Believe,* p. 114; September, 2007, Adrienne Furness, review of *Lucy Rose: Working Myself to Pieces and Bits,* p. 167; March, 2009, Caitlin Augusta, review of *Melonhead,* p. 118.

U.S. News & World Report, October 11, 2004, Vicky Hallett, "Born to Write a Kid's Book," p. 68.

ONLINE

Embracing the Child Web site, http://www.embracing thechild.org/ (March, 2009), interview with Kelly.
Random House Web site, http://www.randomhouse.com/ (March 1, 2010), "Author Spotlight: Katy Kelly."*

*   *   *

KENDALL, Gideon 1966-

Personal

Born December 12, 1966, in Austin, TX; father an actor/director, mother an artist/dancer mother; married Julie Peppito (a sculptor, painter, jewelry maker, and playground designer), 1998. *Education:* Cooper Union for Science and Art, B.F.A., 1989. *Hobbies and other interests:* Cooking, eating Korean and Mexican food, playing Ultimate Frisbee, exploring Brooklyn on bicycle.

Addresses

Home—Brooklyn, NY. *Agent*—Herman Agency, 350 Central Park W., New York, NY 10025. *E-mail*—Gideon@gideonkendall.com.

Career

Artist, illustrator, animation designer, and musician. J.J. Sedelmaier Productions, New York, NY, production designer, 1995-98; also production designer for television shows *Pepper Ann,* ABC-TV, and *The Kids Next Door,* Cartoon Network. Illustrator for companies such as Children's Television Workshop and Geffen Records. Musician in bands, including Fake Brain, The Organ Donors, and Cooling Pies. *Exhibitions:* Artwork has been displayed at galleries in New York, NY, including PS 122, HERE Gallery, and Ethan Cohen Fine Arts.

Illustrator

Diane Mayr, *Littlebat's Halloween Story,* Albert Whitman and Company (Morton Grove, IL), 2001.

David Port and John Ralston, *The Caveman's Pregnancy Companion: A Survival Guide for Expectant Fathers,* Sterling Publishing (New York, NY), 2006.

John Hulme and Michael Wexler, *The Seems: The Glitch in Sleep,* Bloomsbury (New York, NY), 2007.

Lynn Plourde, *Dino Pets,* Dutton Children's Books (New York, NY), 2007.

Ann McCallum, *Rabbits, Rabbits Everywhere: A Fibonacci Tale,* Charlesbridge (Watertown, MA), 2007.

John Hulme and Michael Wexler, *The Split Second,* Bloomsbury (New York, NY), 2008.

John Hulme and Michael Wexler, *The Lost Train of Thought,* Bloomsbury (New York, NY), 2010.

Contributor to periodicals, including *HEEB* magazine and *College Music Journal.*

Sidelights

Gideon Kendall is an artist and animator whose book illustrations for children, teens, and adults that display an energetic style. Kendall claims that his interest in art began at a very young age; he started drawing as an infant, with a ballpoint pen his mother placed in his crib. His work was later influenced by such artists as M.C. Escher, Robert Crumb, and Dr. Sesss. After graduating from the Cooper Union for Science and Art, Kendall worked as an artist and animation designer.

In 2001 Kendall illustrated his first picture book, Diane Mayr's *Littlebat's Halloween Story.* The work follows the adventure of a baby bat who lives in a library. Though Littlebat longs to join in at story time, his mother cautions him to remain unseen until the time is right—when the librarian reads a Halloween tale. John Peters, writing in *Booklist,* praised "Kendall's warm-toned illustrations," and Susan Marie Pitard stated in *School Library Journal* that his pictures "accurately depict the bats and the cheerful library they inhabit."

Dino Pets, a work by Lynn Plourde, follows the story of a youngster who wants to buy the largest creature he can find at the local store. Maryann H. Owen, writing in *School Library Journal,* remarked that the "highlight of the tale is the skillfully rendered and entertaining double-page artwork." A critic in *Kirkus Reviews* applauded *Dino Pets,* noting that Plourde's "rhyming text and Kendall's wonderfully creative illustrations will keep young readers riveted."

The Seems: The Glitch in Sleep, a science-fiction novel by John Hulme and Michael Wexler, centers on Becker Drane, a twelve-year-old who lands a job in the Department of Sleep and must find a way to fix insomnia across the world. A contributor in *Publishers Weekly* stated that the book's "high sense of adventure and an abundance of goofball humor should appeal especially to boys," while Eric Norton commented in *School Library Journal* that Kendall's "dynamic full-page illustrations appear throughout."

Biographical and Critical Sources

PERIODICALS

Booklist, September 1, 2001, John Peters, review of *Littlebat's Halloween Story,* p. 121.

Kirkus Reviews, April 15, 2007, review of *Dino Pets.*

Publishers Weekly, June 5, 2006, review of *The Caveman's Pregnancy Companion: A Survival Guide for Expectant Fathers,* p. 55; October 8, 2007, review of *The Seems: The Glitch in Sleep,* p. 53.

School Library Journal, September, 2001, Susan Marie Pitard, review of *Littlebat's Halloween Story,* p. 199; June, 2007, Maryann H. Owen, review of *Dino Pets,* p. 120; November, 2007, Eric Norton, review of *The Seems,* p. 125.

ONLINE

Gideon Kendall Home Page, http://www.gideonkendall.com (June 1, 2010).

The Seems Web site, http://www.theseems.com/ (June 1, 2010).*

*   *   *

KORALEK, Jenny 1934-

Personal

Born November 5, 1934, in Vryburg, South Africa; daughter of Vivian (a farmer and cattle breeder) and Audrey Chadwick; married Paul Koralek (an architect), December 13, 1958; children: Catherine K. Ricks, Lucy K. Williams, Benjamin (deceased). *Education:* Attended Talbot Heath School (Bournemouth, England), 1947-52; Sorbonne, University of Paris, diploma (language and literature; with distinction), 1956. *Religion:* Church of England (Anglican). *Hobbies and other interests:* Reading, music (and piano playing), art, travel.

Addresses

Home—North London, England. *E-mail*—jennypaul.koralek@virgin.net.

Career

Children's book author and translator. Worked variously as a secretary in Great Britain, Switzerland, and Canada and for UNESCO, Paris, France.

Member

Authors Society.

Awards, Honors

Children's Book of the Year designation, 1987, for *The Knights of Hawthorn Crescent,* and 1988, for *Message in a Bottle.*

Writings

FOR CHILDREN

John Logan's Rooster, Hamish Hamilton (London, England), 1980.

The Song of Roland Smith, illustrated by Peter Rush, Patrick Hardy Books (London, England), 1983.

Badgers Three, illustrated by Martin Usell, Kaye & Ward (London, England), 1983.

Mabel's Story, illustrated by John Lawrence, Patrick Hardy Books (London, England), 1984.

The Knights of Hawthorn Crescent, illustrated by John Lawrence, Methuen (London, England), 1986.

Message in a Bottle, illustrated by Kate Fitzsimon, Lutterworth (Cambridge, England), 1987.

Going out with Hatty, illustrated by John Lawrence, Methuen (London, England), 1988.

The Friendly Fox, illustrated by Beverley Gooding, Little, Brown (Boston, MA), 1988.

Hanukkah: The Festival of Lights, illustrated by Juan Wijngaard, Walker (London, England), 1989, Lothrop (New York, NY), 1990.

Stories for the Very Young: The Cletterkin, Kingfisher (London, England), 1989.

The Cobweb Curtain: A Christmas Story, illustrated by Pauline Baynes, Henry Holt (New York, NY), 1989.

A Moon, a Star, a Story: Marika's Favourite Story (anthology), Blackie (London, England), 1990.

Heartache: Sea Changes, Methuen (London, England), 1991.

The Boy and the Cloth of Dreams, illustrated by James Mayhew, Walker (London, England), 1992, Candlewick Press (Cambridge, MA), 1994.

Cat and Kit, illustrated by Patricia MacCarthy, Hyperion (New York, NY), 1994.

(Reteller) *A Treasury of Stories from Hans Christian Andersen,* illustrated by Robin Lawrie, Kingfisher (New York, NY), 1996.

(Reteller) *A Treasury of Stories from the Brothers Grimm,* illustrated by Robin Lawrie, Kingfisher (New York, NY), 1996.

Keeping Secrets, illustrated by Steve Cox, Heinemann (London, England), 1997.

Dad, Me, and the Dinosaurs, illustrated by Doffy Weir, Puffin (London, England), 1998.

Once upon Olympus, illustrated by John Holder, Cambridge University Press (Cambridge, England), 1998.

Night Ride to Nanna's, illustrated by Mandy Sutcliffe, Candlewick Press (Cambridge, MA), 2000.

War Games, Egmont (London, England), 2002.

(Adaptor) *The Moses Basket,* illustrated by Pauline Baynes, Eerdmans Books for Young Readers (Grand Rapids, MI), 2003.

(Adaptor) *The Coat of Many Colors,* illustrated by Pauline Baynes, Eerdmans Books for Young Readers (Grand Rapids, MI), 2004.

The Story of Queen Esther, illustrated by Grizelda Holderness, Eerdmans Books for Young Readers (Grand Rapids, MI), 2009.

OTHER

(Editor, with Ellen Dooling Draper) *A Lively Oracle: A Centennial Celebration of P.L. Travers, Creator of Mary Poppins,* Larson Publications (Lanham, MD), 1999.

Mother, Do Not Weep for Me: A Son's Life Remembered, Morning Light Press, 2010.

Sidelights

British children's author Jenny Koralek pens stories for beginning readers that reviewers praise for their combination of whimsy and sensitivity. From stories for novice readers such as *Keeping Secrets* to biblical stories such as *The Story of Queen Esther* to read-aloud favorites like *Going out with Hatty* and *Night Ride to Nanna's,* Koralek takes a gentle approach in her books, imbuing her tales with a comforting, old-fashioned quality. Noting that Koralek spins her stories for young children "with marvelous economy," *Junior Bookshelf* contributor Marcus Crouch dubbed the author "a real find."

Born in South Africa, in 1937, Koralek spent her early adult life working and traveling throughout Europe and North America, and her knowledge and love of diverse cultures is apparent in her fiction. An avid reader since childhood, she began writing after her children were grown. "I have always enjoyed children and young people and feel immensely sympathetic to them," Koralek once commented to *SATA.* "I am not a crusader in my writing. I just hope to write stories which are true to the experiences they describe, hoping that children may identify with them or yearn for adventures and experiences of the imagination. I am deeply interested in mythology and traditional tales, and hope something of their underlying truths and archetypeness, so to speak, is somewhere in what I write."

Many of Koralek's books have been praised for their believable protagonists. In her free-verse story *The Song of Roland Smith,* a twelve-year-old boy who gets into trouble during his father's extended absence redeems himself by helping a young blind girl in a story that a *Junior Bookshelf* reviewer characterized as "deftly written." "The happenings are everyday," the critic added: "the grownups credible and full of character." "Linked episodes build into an impressive, vigorous portrait of a small boy," explained a *Growing Point* contributor, adding that the rhythmic narrative in *The Song of Roland Smith* "really sounds like the fragmentary, ingenuous commentary" Koralek intends it to.

In *Mabel's Story* Koralek introduces a bright young character, producing a "picture-book of classic quality," according to *Junior Bookshelf* reviewer Crouch. The imaginative Mabel joins with her grandfather to spin a tale of wonder while the elderly gentleman sits in his garden. Calling the book "altogether . . . enchanting," Jill Bennett added in her *School Librarian* review of *Mabel's Story* that the exchange between grandfather and granddaughter provides a lesson for those parents "trying to help young children to develop their skills as storytellers."

Fear of the dark and of creatures wrought of nightmares serve as the subject of the reassuring *The Boy and the Cloth of Dreams,* which finds a child asking his grand-

Jenny Koralek retells a beloved biblical tale in **The Story of Queen Esther,** *a book featuring artwork by Grizelda Holderness.* (Illustration copyright © 2009 by Grizelda Holderness. All rights reserved. Reproduced by permission.)

mother to repair the holes in his tattered bed blanket in order to prevent bad dreams from getting through at night. Praising Koralek's collaboration with illustrator James Mayhew, *School Librarian* critic Trevor Dickinson called *The Boy and the Cloth of Dreams* a picture book "of fascinating substance" and described Koralek's text "assured" in its brevity.

Another book that joins grandchild with grandparent, *Night Ride to Nanna's* follows Amy on a trip to her grandmother's house. Here Koralek's quiet text conjures images of the city streets through which the young girl and her family pass. "Reading this gentle story is like snuggling under a cozy quilt," noted *School Library Journal* contributor Joy Fleishhacker of the picture book.

Koralek mines the rich well of biblical lore in her picture books *The Moses Basket* and *The Coat of Many Colors,* both featuring illustrations by Pauline Baynes. In *The Moses Basket* she tells the well-known Old Testament story about the baby Moses being hidden among the bullrushes to avoid Pharaoh's decree, while *The Coat of Many Colors* describes the life of the biblical Joseph. Koralek's creation of "believable dialogue" in *The Moses Basket* inspired a *Kirkus Reviews* writer to complement the book's "thoughtful retelling and striking illustrations," and in *Publishers Weekly* a critic called *The Moses Basket* "a streamlined, child-friendly adaptation" enhanced by "paintings that . . . evoke ancient Egyptian art." Shortening the history of Joseph, who was sold into slavery and eventually led the Jews out of Egypt, Koralek makes *The Coat of Many Colors* "child-friendly," according to a *Publishers Weekly* critic,

and in *School Library Journal* Linda L. Watkins praised the book as a "condensed, well-written retelling" of the Old Testament story that "is perfect for reading aloud."

Jewish tradition comes to the fore in *The Story of Queen Esther,* a story by Koralek that is illustrated by Grizelda Holderness. The story focuses on the Jewish princess who is now honored in the Purim holiday because she was tested and found to have the courage of her convictions after a marriage to Persian King Ahasuersus. The "nicely told" story is accompanied by stylized, pastel illustrations that Ilene Cooper praised in *Booklist* for "captur[ing] . . . the Persian sensibility of the original tale." A *Publishers Weekly* reviewer dubbed Koralek's creative retelling in *The Story of Queen Esther* "admirably brisk and dramatic," and in *Kirkus Reviews* a critic described her text as "a well-composed and aesthetic" adaptation of the traditional story that features "lucid intrigue."

Koralek gains much of her knowledge of young people from eavesdropping—"I listen for new slang, new interests," she admitted—and her experiences with her own children and grandchildren have provided her with a steady stream of ideas. "I do not put anything down until a long period of reflection and often research has taken place," she explained of her writing process.

"I read all the time in a very eclectic fashion," Koralek also revealed, "everything from everywhere . . . adult classics, modern classics, and of course children's books. I can't imagine how one can write if one doesn't also read! I think the Anglo-Saxon world has produced children's writers second to none, and long may it continue to do so."

Biographical and Critical Sources

PERIODICALS

Booklist, January 15, 1989, Ilene Cooper, review of *The Friendly Fox,* p. 873; October 1, 1989, Carolyn Phelan, review of *The Cobweb Curtain: A Christmas Story,* p. 352; May 1, 1990, Ilene Cooper, review of *Hanukkah: The Festival of Lights,* p. 1706; July, 1995, Annie Ayres, review of *Cat and Kit,* p. 1884; December 1, 2000, Martha Segal, review of *Night Ride to Nanna's,* p. 721; October 1, 2003, Stephanie Zvirin, review of *The Moses Basket,* p. 333; October 15, 2004, Gillian Engberg, review of *The Coat of Many Colors,* p. 410; February 15, 2009, Ilene Cooper, review of *The Story of Queen Esther,* p. 85.

Books for Keeps, November, 1988, review of *The Knights of Hawthorn Crescent,* p. 9; May, 1990, review of *Going out with Hatty,* p. 12; July, 1991, Alan Brine, review of *The Cobweb Curtain,* p. 32; January, 1992, review of *Hanukkah,* p. 9; November, 1994, Jill Burridge, review of *The Boy and the Cloth of Dreams,* p. 4; May, 1996, review of *A Treasury of Stories from Hans Christian Andersen,* p. 16; September, 1997, review of *Keeping Secrets,* p. 24.

Growing Point, November, 1983, review of *The Song of Roland Smith,* p. 4161; March, 1984, review of *Badgers Three,* p. 4220; January, 1985, review of *Mabel's Story,* p. 4377.

Junior Bookshelf, December, 1983, review of *The Song of Roland,* p. 259; April, 1985, Marcus Crouch, review of *Mabel's Story,* p. 74; October, 1986, review of *The Knights of Hawthorn Crescent,* p. 186; October, 1987, review of *Message in a Bottle,* p. 236; August, 1988, review of *Going out with Hatty,* p. 190.

Kirkus Reviews, December 15, 1988, review of *The Friendly Fox,* p. 1813; July 15, 1989, review of *The Cobweb Curtain,* p. 1077; May 1, 1995, review of *Cat and Kit,* p. 635; September 15, 2000, review of *Night Ride to Nanna's,* p. 1357; July 15, 2003, review of *The Moses Basket,* p. 965; August, 15, 2004, review of *The Coat of Many Colors,* p. 808; January 15, 2009, review of *The Story of Queen Esther.*

Parabola, spring, 1995, Martha Heyneman, review of *The Boy and the Cloth of Dreams,* p. 106; spring, 2000, Nor Hall, review of *A Lively Oracle: A Centennial Celebration of P.L. Travers,* p. 112.

Publishers Weekly, May 22, 1995, review of *Cat and Kit,* p. 58; November 22, 1999, review of *A Lively Oracle,* p. 52; September 29, 2003, review of *The Moses Basket,* p. 62; October 25, 2004, review of *The Coat of Many Colors,* p. 46; January 19, 2009, review of *The Story of Queen Esther,* p. 59.

School Librarian, September, 1981, Caroline Wynburne, review of *John Logan's Rooster,* p. 237; March, 1985, Jill Bennett, review of *Mabel's Story,* p. 29; February, 1987, Dorothy Nimmo, review of *The Knights of Hawthorn Crescent,* p. 44; November, 1994, Trevor Dickinson, review of *The Boy and the Cloth of Dreams,* p. 146; November, 1994, Audrey Laski, review of *Cat and Kit,* p. 146; August, 1997, Joyce Banks, review of *Keeping Secrets,* p. 146.

School Library Journal, June, 1989, Jane Gardner Connor, review of *The Friendly Fox,* p. 90; October, 1994, George Delalis, review of *The Boy and the Cloth of Dreams,* p. 92; September, 1995, Jan Shepherd Ross, review of *Cat and Kit,* p. 180; December, 2000, Joy Fleishhacker, review of *Night Ride to Nanna's,* p. 112; November, 2004, Linda L. Walkins, review of *The Coat of Many Colors,* p. 127; February, 2009, Heidi Estrin, review of *The Story of Queen Esther,* p. 93.

Times Educational Supplement, April 13, 1984, Gerald Haigh, review of *The Song of Roland Smith,* p. 30.

L

LABATT, Mary 1944-

Personal

Born February 16, 1944, in London, Ontario, Canada; married; husband's name Larry; children: three. *Education:* York University (Ontario, Canada), degree. *Hobbies and other interests:* Gardening.

Addresses

Home—Port Rowan, Ontario, Canada.

Career

Writer, editor, and educator. Has worked as a teacher in Canada. Breeds and raises champion rough collies and Welsh Springer Spaniels.

Awards, Honors

Ontario Teachers' Federation fellow; Greer Award, Ontario Teachers' Federation; SMART Book Award shortlist, 2005, for *Sam Gets Lost.*

Writings

Barn Owls, illustrated by Pat Gangnon, Curriculum Plus (Georgetown, Ontario, Canada), 2003.

A New Home for Chip, illustrated by Rebecca Buchanan, Curriculum Plus (Georgetown, Ontario, Canada), 2003.

Chipmunks, illustrated by Lam Quach, Curriculum Plus (Georgetown, Ontario, Canada), 2003.

Mrs. Barn Owl Helps, illustrated by Rebecca Buchanan, Curriculum Plus (Georgetown, Ontario, Canada), 2003.

Making a Book, Curriculum Plus (Georgetown, Ontario, Canada), 2004.

Mrs. Barn Owl Has to Move, illustrated by Rebecca Buchanan, Curriculum Plus (Georgetown, Ontario, Canada), 2004.

A Friend for Chip, illustrated by Rebecca Buchanan, Curriculum Plus (Georgetown, Ontario, Canada), 2004.

All about Fossils, illustrated by Pat Gangnon, Curriculum Plus (Georgetown, Ontario, Canada), 2004.

Dinosaurs, illustrated by Pat Gangnon, Curriculum Plus (Georgetown, Ontario, Canada), 2004.

A Puppy Is for Loving, illustrated by Renata Liwska, Orca Book Publishers (Victoria, British Columbia, Canada), 2007.

"SAM: DOG DETECTIVE" SERIES

The Ghost of Captain Briggs, Kids Can Press (Toronto, Ontario, Canada), 1999.

Spying on Dracula, Kids Can Press (Toronto, Ontario, Canada), 1999.

Strange Neighbors, Kids Can Press (Toronto, Ontario, Canada), 2000.

Aliens in Woodford, Kids Can Press (Toronto, Ontario, Canada), 2000.

A Weekend at the Grand Hotel, Kids Can Press (Toronto, Ontario, Canada), 2001.

The Secret of Sagawa Lake, Kids Can Press (Toronto, Ontario, Canada), 2001.

The Mummy Lives!, Kids Can Press (Toronto, Ontario, Canada), 2002.

One Terrible Halloween, Kids Can Press (Toronto, Ontario, Canada), 2002.

EASY READERS

Pizza for Sam, illustrated by Marisol Sarrazin, Scholastic, Inc. (New York, NY), 2003.

Sam Finds a Monster, illustrated by Marisol Sarrazin, Scholastic, Inc. (New York, NY), 2003.

Sam Goes to School, illustrated by Marisol Sarrazin, Kids Can Press (Toronto, Ontario, Canada), 2004.

Sam Gets Lost, illustrated by Marisol Sarrazin, Kids Can Press (Toronto, Ontario, Canada), 2004.

Sam's Snowy Day, illustrated by Marisol Sarrazin, Scholastic, Inc. (New York, NY), 2005.

Sam's First Halloween, illustrated by Marisol Sarrazin, Kids Can Press (Toronto, Ontario, Canada), 2005.

A Parade for Sam, illustrated by Marisol Sarrazin, Kids Can Press (Toronto, Ontario, Canada), 2005.

Sam at the Seaside, illustrated by Marisol Sarrazin, Kids Can Press (Toronto, Ontario, Canada), 2006.

Sam Goes Next Door, illustrated by Marisol Sarrazin, Kids Can Press (Toronto, Ontario, Canada), 2006.

"SAM AND FRIENDS MYSTERY" SERIES; GRAPHIC NOVELS

Dracula Madness, illustrated by Jo Rioux, Kids Can Press (Toronto, Ontario, Canada), 2009.

Lake Monster Mix-up, illustrated by Jo Rioux, Kids Can Press (Toronto, Ontario, Canada), 2009.

OTHER

Always a Journey: A History of the Women Who Teach in the Public Elementary Schools of Ontario, 1918-1993, Federation of Women Teachers' Associations of Ontario (Toronto, Ontario, Canada), 1993.

(Editor) *Firsts: From Aboriginal Peoples to Pioneers,* Elementary Teachers' Federation of Ontario (Toronto, Ontario, Canada), 2002.

Founding editor of *Federation of Women Teachers' Associations of Ontario Newsletter.*

Mary Labatt's graphic novel **Dracula Madness** *features cartoon artwork by Jo Rioux.* (Illustration © 2009 by Jo Rioux. Used by permission of Kids Can Press Ltd., Toronto.)

Sidelights

An award-winning author, editor, and educator, Canadian writer Mary Labatt is perhaps best known for her works about Sam, a lovable sheepdog with a nose for mystery and adventure. Discussing her inspiration, Labatt explained in a Kids Can Press Web site interview that ideas come "from my own childhood. I love to remember the things we thought were funny or scary or fascinating. I also get a lot of ideas from my sheepdog named Sam, who was a real character. I have based the Sam books on her."

Labatt introduces her lively canine heroine in her "Sam: Dog Detective" books. In series installment *Strange Neighbors,* Sam joins forces with Jennie, a youngster who can hear the dog's thoughts, as well as Jennie's best friend, Beth, to investigate the unusual goings-on in their neighborhood that occur after three rather odd women move in down the street. After witnessing the ladies' bizarre behavior and discovering their menagerie of creatures, Sam becomes convinced that they are actually witches. In *Aliens in Woodford* Sam, Jennie, and Beth explore an abandoned airfield after spotting a series of mysterious lights. *Booklist* critic Shelley Townsend-Hudson remarked that "children who love detective fiction will relish the absurd premise and the surprise ending" in *Strange Neighbors,* while *Aliens in Woodford* will appeal to "readers who like dog stories mixed with humor and light mystery," as Janie Schomberg predicted in *School Library Journal.*

Sam and Jennie's relaxing weekend trip turns into a hunt for an eerie aquatic creature in *The Secret of Sagawa Lake,* another title in the "Sam: Dog Detective" series. "Sam will be endearing to young readers who will enjoy the easy to read, easy vocabulary chapter books," Judy Cottrell observed in a *Resource Links* review of *The Secret of Sagawa Lake.* With the help of Jennie and Beth, the pup attempts to evade the curse of an ancient Egyptian pharaoh in *The Mummy Lives!,* and Sam spots ghoulish figures at a neighbor's home while Jennie and Beth go trick-or-treating in *One Terrible Halloween.* "The writing is simple and the mystery is safe—not too scary," commented Jeanette Larson of *The Mummy Lives!* in *School Library Journal.* According to Debbie Stewart in her review of *One Terrible Halloween* for *School Library Journal,* "the mystery is solved steadily and predictably."

Sam also appears in easy readers by Labatt that focus on the endearing sheepdog during her years as an energetic puppy. In *Pizza for Sam* the dog's new owners learn just how finicky a puppy's appetite can be. The work is "filled with action, noise, and enough suspense and silliness to engage new readers," Gillian Engberg asserted in *Booklist.* After spotting a scary creature on television, Sam is determined to drive it from the house in *Sam Finds a Monster.* "Sam captures a kid's thought process, tenacity, and pride of accomplishment—no matter what the outcome," noted a critic in reviewing Labatt's easy reader for *Kirkus Reviews.* Appraising the

same books in *School Library Journal,* Laura Scott wrote that "children demystifying life and language will surely identify with the pup's antics."

In addition to her "Sam the Sheepdog" series, Labatt is also the creator of the "Sam and Friends Mystery" graphic novels, which are illustrated by Jo Rioux. In *Dracula Madness* Sam, Jennie, and Beth begin poking around the spooky home of their reclusive neighbor, Mr. MacIver, who is a suspected vampire. "There's just enough creepiness and suspense for younger readers," reported *Booklist* contributor Kat Kan of the book. *Lake Monster Mix-up,* a graphic novel based on Labatt's *The Secret of Sagawa Lake,* centers on the discovery of an old diary. Writing in the *Canadian Review of Materials,* Keith McPherson observed that "younger readers with active imaginations will likely enjoy this episode."

Biographical and Critical Sources

PERIODICALS

Booklist, May 1, 2000, Shelley Townsend-Hudson, review of *Strange Neighbors,* p. 1668; March 1, 2003, Gillian Engberg, review of *Pizza for Sam,* p. 1202; July, 2004, Ilene Cooper, reviews of *Sam Gets Lost* and *Sam Goes to School,* both p. 1851; October 15, 2005, Hazel Rochman, review of *A Parade for Sam,* p. 57; March 1, 2009, Kat Kan, review of *Dracula Madness,* p. 62.

Canadian Review of Materials, June 12, 2009, Gregory Bryan, review of *Dracula Madness;* November 13, 2009, Keith McPherson, review of *Lake Monster Mix-Up.*

Kirkus Reviews, February 1, 2003, review of *Sam Finds a Monster,* p. 234; January 15, 2009, review of *Dracula Madness;* July 1, 2009, review of *Lake Monster Mix-Up.*

Resource Links, February, 2001, review of *Aliens in Woodford,* p. 14; October, 2001, Judy Cottrell, review of *The Secret of Sagawa Lake,* p. 14; April, 2002, Connie Forst, review of *The Mummy Lives!,* p. 22; December, 2002, Gillian Richardson, review of *One Terrible Halloween,* p. 23; February, 2008, Mavis Holder, review of *A Puppy Is for Loving,* p. 10.

School Library Journal, September, 2000, Mary M. Hopf, review of *Strange Neighbors,* p. 202; December, 2000, Janie Schomberg, review of *Aliens in Woodford,* p. 113; April, 2001, Amy Stultz, review of *A Weekend at the Grand Hotel,* p. 114; November, 2001, Debbie Whitbeck, review of *The Secret of Sagawa Lake,* p. 127; May, 2002, Jeanette Larson, review of *The Mummy Lives!,* p. 120; October, 2002, Debbie Stewart, review of *One Terrible Halloween,* p. 116; May, 2003, Laura Scott, reviews of *Pizza for Sam* and *Sam Finds a Monster,* both p. 122; November, 2006, Lynda Ritterman, reviews of *Sam at the Seaside* and *Sam Goes Next Door,* both p. 99; March, 2009, Travis Jonker, review of *Dracula Madness,* p. 172.

ONLINE

Kids Can Press Web site, http://www.kidscanpress.com/ (March 1, 2010), "Mary Labatt."*

LANE, Alison Hoffman

Personal

Born in New Orleans, LA; children: David, Maria, Catherine, Mary Frances. *Education:* William Carey College, B.S.N., 1995.

Addresses

Home—New Orleans, LA. *E-mail*—ajhlane@gmail.com.

Career

Registered nurse and author of stories for children. Touro Infirmary, New Orleans, LA, currently staff registered nurse. Presenter at schools, libraries, and summer camps.

Writings

FOR CHILDREN

Uncle Arnel and the Awful, Angry Alligator, illustrated by Egil Thompson, Pelican Publishing (Gretna, LA), 2009.

Uncle Arnel and the Swamp Witch, illustrated by Egil Thompson, Pelican Publishing (Gretna, LA), 2009.

Sidelights

"My inspiration for writing first came from my children," Alison Hoffman Lane told *SATA.* "They energized me and sparked my creativity. As they became adults, it was my son who first suggested that I might try to publish my stories.

"Also, growing up in New Orleans gave me ample opportunity to be in and around swamps and bayous that further gave way to my vivid imaginations. Picture this: You are standing in a Louisiana swamp as the filtered sunlight casts distorted shadows through the cypress trees dripping with grey-green moss. You become acutely aware that you cannot be sure what it is that moves in the distance. The chirping crickets and throaty frogs become silent as you hear a splash in the murky water. You feel the hot, humid air but yet sense a chill. You cannot be sure that you are there alone. But you hope that you are."

Biographical and Critical Sources

PERIODICALS

Kirkus Reviews, January 15, 2009, review of *Uncle Arnel and the Swamp Witch.*

ONLINE

Alison Hoffman Lane Home Page, http://www.unclearnel. com (April 20, 2010).*

NewOrleans.com, http://www.neworleans.com /(April 20, 2010), review of *Uncle Arnel and the Swamp Witch.*

*   *   *

LEE, Jared 1943-
(Jared D. Lee)

Personal

Born August 19, 1943, in Van Buren, IN; married; wife's name P.J.; children: Jennifer, Jana. *Education:* John Herron Art Institute, B.F.A., 1966. *Hobbies and other interests:* Basketball, raising horses.

Addresses

Home and office—Jared Lee Studio, 2942 Hamilton Rd., Lebanon, OH 45036. *E-mail*—jaredlee@go-concepts. com.

Career

Illustrator. Gibson Greetings, card designer for one year, freelance artist and cartoonist, beginning 1970. Creator of horse-related cartoons, coloring books, and stationary for Horse Hollow Press.

Member

Society of Illustrators, National Cartoonist Society, Illustrators' Partnership.

Awards, Honors

Society of Illustrators award; Martha Kinney Cooper Award, Ohioana Library Association, National Cartoonist Society award; other awards for advertising art.

Illustrator

FOR CHILDREN

Valjean McLenighan, *You Can Go Jump,* Follett (Chicago, IL), 1977.

Ida Luttrell, *One Day at School,* Harcourt Brace Jovanovich (San Diego, CA), 1984.

Elizabeth S. Wall, *The Computer Alphabet Book,* Avon Books (New York, NY), 1984.

Mike Thaler, *Cream of Creature from the School Cafeteria,* Avon Books (New York, NY), 1985.

Joanna Cole, *Monster Manners,* Scholastic, Inc. (New York, NY), 1985.

Steve Kroll, *Gobbledygook,* new edition, Avon Books (New York, NY), 1985.

Mike Thaler, *Upside Down Day,* Avon Books (New York, NY), 1986.

Mike Thaler, *The Teacher from the Black Lagoon,* Scholastic, Inc. (New York, NY), 1989.

Mike Thaler, *Cannon the Librarian,* Avon Books (New York, NY), 1993.

Mike Thaler, *The Bully Brothers Trick the Tooth Fairy,* Grosset & Dunlap (New York, NY), 1993.

Mike Thaler, *The Bully Brothers: Gobblin' Halloween,* Grosset & Dunlap (New York, NY), 1993.

Mike Thaler, *The Principal from the Black Lagoon,* Scholastic, Inc. (New York, NY), 1993.

Mike Thaler, *Camp Rotten Time,* Troll Associates (Mahwah, NJ), 1994.

Mike Thaler, *Fang the Dentist,* Troll Associates (Mahwah, NJ), 1994.

Mike Thaler, *Miss Yonkers Goes Bonkers,* Avon Books (New York, NY), 1994.

Mike Thaler, *My Cat Is Going to the Dogs,* Troll Associates (Mahwah, NJ), 1994.

Mike Thaler, *The Gym Teacher from the Black Lagoon,* Scholastic, Inc. (New York, NY), 1994.

Mike Thaler, *Bad Day at Monster Elementary,* Avon Books (New York, NY), 1995.

Mike Thaler, *The Bully Brothers: Making the Grade,* Scholastic, Inc. (New York, NY), 1995.

Mike Thaler, *The Schmo Must Go On,* Troll Associates (Mahwah, NJ), 1995.

Mike Thaler, *The School Nurse from the Black Lagoon,* Scholastic, Inc. (New York, NY), 1995.

Mike Thaler, *Make Your Beds, Bananaheads,* Troll Associates(Mahwah, NJ), 1997.

Mike Thaler, *Schmoe White and the Seven Dorfs,* Scholastic, Inc. (New York, NY), 1997.

Mike Thaler, *The Princess and the Pea-ano,* Scholastic, Inc. (New York, NY), 1997.

Mike Thaler, *The Cafeteria Lady from the Black Lagoon,* Scholastic, Inc. (New York, NY), 1998.

Mike Thaler, *The School Bus Driver from the Black Lagoon,* Scholastic, Inc. (New York, NY), 1999.

George Edward Stanley, *Snake Camp,* Golden Books (New York, NY), 2000.

Mike Thaler, *The Music Teacher from the Black Lagoon,* Scholastic, Inc. (New York, NY), 2000.

Mike Thaler, *The Custodian from the Black Lagoon,* Scholastic, Inc. (New York, NY), 2001.

Crystal Wirth, *At 1600 Pennsylvania Avenue,* Scholastic, Inc. (New York, NY), 2002.

Matt Jacobson and Lisa Jacobson, *The Amazing Beginning of You,* Zonderkids (Grand Rapids, MI), 2002.

Mike Thaler, *The Class from the Black Lagoon,* Scholastic, Inc. (New York, NY), 2002.

Mike Thaler, *The Class Trip from the Black Lagoon,* Scholastic, Inc. (New York, NY), 2002.

Lucille Colandro, *There Was an Old Lady Who Swallowed a Bat!,* Scholastic, Inc. (New York, NY), 2002.

Don Wulffson and Pam Wulffson, *Abracadabra to Zombie: More than 300 Wacky Word Origins,* Dutton Children's Books (New York, NY), 2003.

Steven James, *Believe It!: Bible Basics That Won't Break Your Brain: Incredible Readable Rhymes,* Standard Pub. (Cincinnati, OH), 2003.

Mike Thaler, *The Class Election from the Black Lagoon,* Scholastic, Inc. (New York, NY), 2003.

Mike Thaler, *The Class Pet from the Black Lagoon,* Scholastic, Inc. (New York, NY), 2003.

Mike Thaler, *The Talent Show from the Black Lagoon,* Scholastic, Inc. (New York, NY), 2003.

Lucille Colandro, *There Was a Cold Lady Who Swallowed Some Snow!,* Scholastic, Inc. (New York, NY), 2003.

Justine Fontes, *Jordan's Silly Sick Day,* Children's Press (New York, NY), 2004.

Mike Thaler, *The Bully from the Black Lagoon,* Scholastic, Inc. (New York, NY), 2004.

Mike Thaler, *The Halloween Party from the Black Lagoon,* Scholastic, Inc. (New York, NY), 2004.

Mike Thaler, *The Science Fair from the Black Lagoon,* Scholastic, Inc. (New York, NY), 2004.

Julia Durango, *Dream Hop,* Simon & Schuster Books for Young Readers (New York, NY), 2005.

Mike Thaler, *The Field Day from the Black Lagoon,* Scholastic, Inc. (New York, NY), 2005.

Mike Thaler, *The School Carnival from the Black Lagoon,* Scholastic, Inc. (New York, NY), 2005.

Carson Kressley, *You're Different and That's Super,* Simon & Schuster Books for Young Readers (New York, NY), 2005.

Mike Thaler, *The Book Fair from the Black Lagoon,* Scholastic, Inc. (New York, NY), 2006.

Mike Thaler, *The Christmas Party from the Black Lagoon,* Scholastic, Inc. (New York, NY), 2006.

Lucille Coladro, *There Was an Old Lady Who Swallowed a Shell!,* Scholastic, Inc. (New York, NY), 2006.

Mike Thaler, *School Riddles from the Black Lagoon,* Scholastic, Inc. (New York, NY), 2007.

Mike Thaler, *The Computer Teacher from the Black Lagoon,* Scholastic, Inc. (New York, NY), 2007.

Mike Thaler, *The Little League Team from the Black Lagoon,* Scholastic, Inc. (New York, NY), 2007.

Mike Thaler, *The Vice Principal from the Black Lagoon,* Scholastic, Inc. (New York, NY), 2007.

Mike Thaler, *April Fools' Day from the Black Lagoon,* Scholastic, Inc. (New York, NY), 2008.

Mike Thaler, *Church Summer Cramp,* Zonderkidz (Grand Rapids, MI), 2009.

Mike Thaler, *Easter Egg Haunt,* Zonderkidz (Grand Rapids, MI), 2009.

Mike Thaler, *I-scream Sunday,* Zonderkidz (Grand Rapids, MI), 2009.

Mike Thaler, *Mission Trip Impossible,* Zonderkidz (Grand Rapids, MI), 2009.

Mike Thaler, *Preacher Creature Strikes on Sunday,* Zonderkidz (Grand Rapids, MI), 2009.

Mike Thaler, *The Three Wise Guys,* Zonderkidz (Grand Rapids, MI), 2009.

Mike Thaler, *Walking the Plank to the Baptism Tank,* Zonderkidz (Grand Rapids, MI), 2009.

Mike Thaler, *Bible Knock-knocks from the Back Pew,* Zonderkidz (Grand Rapids, MI), 2010.

Mike Thaler, *Bible Riddles from the Back Pew,* Zonderkidz (Grand Rapids, MI), 2010.

Mike Thaler, *Church Harvest Mess-tival,* Zondervan (Grand Rapids, MI), 2010.

Mike Thaler, *Vacation Bible Snooze,* Zondervan (Grand Rapids, MI), 2010.

OTHER

Howart Tomb, *Wicked Irish for the Traveler,* Workman (New York, NY), 1999.

Adaptations

The Teacher from the Black Lagoon was adapted for video by Weston Woods, 2003.

Sidelights

Since becoming an illustrator in the early 1970s, Jared Lee has worked for clients ranging from major corporations to the U.S. Postal Service, and he was also one of the artists selected to create images for the first Happy Meal boxes produced by McDonalds. In his work for picture books, Lee has teamed up with a number of authors, among them Lucille Colandro, Justine Fontes, Don and Pam Wulffson, and Mike Thaler. Reviewing Colandro's *There Was a Cold Lady Who Swallowed Some Snow!,* Gillian Engberg noted in *Booklist* that Lee's comic cartoon drawings "extend . . . the absurd humor in delightful drawings" featuring the story's quirky heroine. His "squiggly lined cartoon style" is a feature of Julia Durango's *Dream Hop,* wrote a *Kirkus Reviews* critic, and in this humorous rhyming picture book Lee diminishes the story's scary aspects by "keep-

Jared Lee's amusing cartoon art pairs with humorous stories by George Edward Stanley that include **Snake Camp.** (Illustration copyright © 2000 by Jared D. Lee Studio, Inc. Used by permission of Golden Books, an imprint of Random House Children's Books, a division of Random House, Inc.)

[ing] . . . it all on a humorous plane." In reviewing the illustrator's contribution to Carson Cressley's feel-good picture book *You're Different and That's Super,* Kathleen Kelly MacMillan noted in *School Library Journal* that "the real treat . . . is the liveliness of Lee's whimsical black-line illustrations."

Thaler has been Lee's most frequent collaborator, and the two have worked together on the "Bully Brothers," "Tales from the Back Pew," and "Black Lagoon" series of easy readers. Designed to make vocabulary-building fun, *The Bully Brothers: Gobblin' Halloween* stars troublesome siblings Bumpo and Bubba in a story that demonstrates that crime does not pay. While noting that Lee and Thaler "aim low" in their humor in the book, a *Publishers Weekly* contributor added that "their sense of mischief is deal on." Regarding another book in the series, *The Bully Brothers Trick the Tooth Fairy,* another *Publishers Weekly* critic concluded that "the success of this inventively twisted tale . . . is due as much to Lee's hilarious cartoon as to Thaler's waggish story." In a *Kirkus Reviews* appraisal of *Preacher Creature Strikes on Sunday,* the first volume in Thaler's "Tales from the Back Pew" series, the critic noted that "Lee's loose, cartoon-style illustrations in watercolor and ink add considerable appeal" to the story.

Biographical and Critical Sources

PERIODICALS

Booklist, December 1, 2000, Hazel Rochman, review of *Snake Camp,* p. 727; November 1, 2003, Hazel Rochman, review of *Abracadabra to Zombie: More than 500 Wacky Word Origins,* p. 495; February 1, 2004, Gillian Engberg, review of *There Was a Cold Lady Who Swallowed Some Snow!,* p. 980.
Kirkus Reviews, September 15, 2005, review of *Dream Hop,* p. 1025; January 15, 2009, review of *Preacher Creature Strikes on Sunday.*
New York Times Book Review, November 13, 2005, John Schwartz, review of *You're Different and That's Super,* p. 35.
Publishers Weekly, March 8, 1993, review of *The Bully Brothers Trick the Tooth Fairy,* p. 77; September 20, 1993, Elizabeth Devereaux and Kit Alderdice, review of *The Bully Brothers: Gobblin' Halloween,* p. 30; October 10, 2005, review of *You're Different and That's Super,* p. 59.
School Library Journal, January, 2004, Linda Wadleigh, review of *Abracadabra to Zombie,* p. 162; October, 2005, Rosalyn Pierini, review of *Dream Hop,* p. 112; May, 2006, Kathleen Kelly MacMillan, review of *You're Different and That's Super,* p. 92.

ONLINE

Jared Lee Home Page, http://www.jaredlee.com (April 21, 2010).*

LEE, Jared D.
See LEE, Jared

*   *   *

LERMAN, Josh

Personal

Married Christina Frank (a freelance writer); children: Olivia, Lucy. *Education:* Vassar College, B.A., 1985.

Addresses

Home—Brooklyn, NY. *Office*—The Parenting Group, 2 Park Ave., New York, NY 10016.

Career

Writer and editor. N.W. Ayer (advertising agency), New York, NY, media planner; *Skiing* magazine, editor for six years; *Parenting* magazine, New York, NY, senior editor, beginning 1996. Guest on television programs, including *CBS Early Show, CNN Headline News, Today,* and *Inside Edition.*

Writings

How to Raise Mom and Dad: Instructions from Someone Who Figured It Out, illustrated by Greg Clarke, Dutton Children's Books (New York, NY), 2009.

Sidelights

A senior editor at *Parenting* magazine, Josh Lerman is the author of *How to Raise Mom and Dad: Instructions from Someone Who Figured It Out,* a humorous picture book about family life. A graduate of Vassar College, Lerman began his career as a media planner for N.W. Ayer, a New York City advertising agency, and then spent six years as an editor at *Skiing* magazine. Since 1996, Lerman has worked at *Parenting,* editing the monthly "Parenting Picks" column, among other duties, and he is a frequent guest on television shows such as *Today* and *CNN Headline News.*

How to Raise Mom and Dad focuses on the efforts of an older sister to counsel her little brother on the most effective methods to deal with their parents. The girl dispenses satirical advice on such challenging matters as asking for a pet, getting help with homework, and avoiding green vegetables at dinner. "The book's comedy has an easy flow," noted a *Kirkus Reviews* contributor, the critic citing Lerman's "resonant, jesting story." Hazel Rochman, writing in *Booklist,* complimented the tale's "exploration of sly power games that undermine authority and put the young ones in charge." In *School Library Journal,* Ieva Bates applauded the

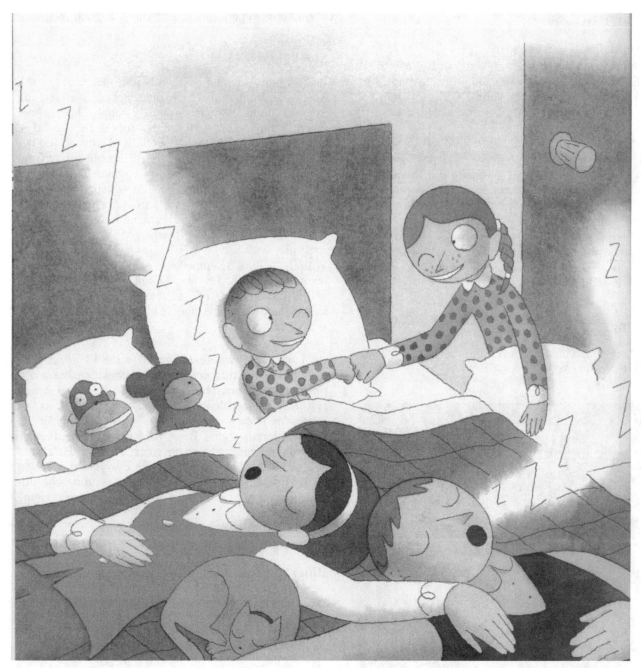

Josh Lerman's amusing picture book How to Raise Mom and Dad *gains an extra dose of humor from Greg Clarke's cartoon artwork.*

combination of Lerman's story and Greg Clarke's artwork, stating that the "gouache illustrations are as joyful as the text." According to Bates, *How to Raise Mom and Dad* "is a manual every child will want to read."

Biographical and Critical Sources

PERIODICALS

Booklist, March 1, 2009, Hazel Rochman, review of *How to Raise Mom and Dad: Instructions from Someone Who Figured It Out,* p. 50.

Bulletin of the Center for Children's Books, April, 2009, Deborah Stevenson, review of *How to Raise Mom and Dad,* p. 328.

Kirkus Reviews, January 15, 2009, review of *How to Raise Mom and Dad.*

School Library Journal, February, 2009, Ieva Bates, review of *How to Raise Mom and Dad,* p. 78.

ONLINE

Josh Lerman Home Page, http://joshlerman.com (March 1, 2010).

TLC Web site, http://tlc.discovery.com/ (March 1, 2010), "Josh Lerman."*

LEVCHUK, Lisa

Personal

Female. *Education:* Franklin & Marshall College, B.A. (English); University of Massachusetts at Amherst, M.F.A. (creative writing); St. John's College (Santa Fe, NM), M.A. (liberal arts), M.A. (Eastern classics).

Addresses

Home—Easthampton, MA. *Office*—Williston Northampton School, 19 Payson Ave., Easthampton, MA 01027. *E-mail*—llevchuk@williston.com.

Career

Writer and educator. Chase Manhattan Bank, New York, NY, administrative assistant, 1985; *Harper's* magazine, New York, NY, former intern; Williston Northampton School, Easthampton, MA, English teacher, 1998—.

Writings

Everything Beautiful in the World (novel), Farrar, Straus & Giroux (New York, NY), 2008.

Cover of Lisa Levchuk's young-adult novel Everything Beautiful in the World, *featuring artwork by Marc Yankus.* (Jacket photograph © 2008 by Marc Yankus. Reproduced by permission of Farrar, Straus & Giroux, a division of Farrar, Straus & Giroux, LLC.)

Contributor to periodicals, including *Crescent Review.*

Sidelights

In *Everything Beautiful in the World,* her debut novel, Massachusetts-based writer and teacher Lisa Levchuk explores the tumultuous world of a troubled high-school junior. Set in the early 1980s, the story centers on Edna, a seventeen year old whose world is shattered after her mother is diagnosed with cancer. Unable to confront her feelings, the teen refuses to communicate with or visit her mother after the woman is admitted to the hospital, and she distances herself from her father and her classmates. Distressed and vulnerable, Edna finds solace in the arms of her art teacher, Mr. Howland, a married man with whom she begins a clandestine affair. With the help of a sympathetic therapist, however, Edna learns to confront her fears about her mother's illness and absolve herself of her sense of responsibility for another family trauma, the death of her autistic brother years earlier.

Reviewing *Everything Beautiful in the World*, a *Publishers Weekly* critic noted that Levchuk "creates a distinctive and memorable voice for Edna" in her novel, and Ilene Cooper described the story in *Booklist* as "an interesting experiment in writing" that offers readers "a quite different sound from so many YA novels with their ubiquitous first-person voice." A *Kirkus Reviews* contributor also offered praise for *Everything Beautiful in the World*, calling it an "odd and unsettling but ultimately rewarding read by a debut author who is going places."

Biographical and Critical Sources

PERIODICALS

Booklist, November 15, 2008, Ilene Cooper, review of *Everything Beautiful in the World,* p. 54.

Bulletin of the Center for Children's Books, December, 2008, Deborah Stevenson, review of *Everything Beautiful in the World,* p. 161.

Kirkus Reviews, October 15, 2008, review of *Everything Beautiful in the World.*

Publishers Weekly, October 6, 2008, review of *Everything Beautiful in the World,* p. 55.

School Library Journal, January, 2009, Carolyn Lehman, review of *Everything Beautiful in the World,* p. 108.

Voice of Youth Advocates, August, 2008, Courtney Wika, review of *Everything Beautiful in the World,* p. 245.

ONLINE

Macmillan Web site, http://us.macmillan.com/ (March 1, 2010), autobiographical essay by Levchuk.*

LODGE, Bernard 1933-

Personal

Born October 19, 1933, in Chalfont, St. Peter, Buckinghamshire, England; son of William (an electrical engineer) and Olive (a nurse) Lodge; married Maureen Roffey (an illustrator), April 19, 1956; children: David, Josephine, Katherine. *Education:* Royal College of Art (London, England), degree, 1959. *Hobbies and other interests:* Making woodcut and linograph prints.

Addresses

Home—Surrey, England.

Career

Author, illustrator, and graphic designer. British Broadcasting Corporation, London, England, graphic designer, 1960-67, 1969-77; graphic designer for television advertising, 1977—. *Military service:* British Army, 1954-56; served in Royal Artillery.

Awards, Honors

Silver Award for television production design, Design and Art Direction (London, England), 1968, 1973, 1976; Kate Greenaway Medal Highly Commended designation, 1976, for *Tinker, Tailor, Soldier, Sailor.*

Writings

PICTURE BOOKS; FOR CHILDREN

(With wife, Maureen Roffey) *The Grand Old Duke of York,* illustrated by Roffey, Bodley Head (London, England), 1975, Merrimack Book Service (Salem, NH), 1978, reprinted, Whispering Coyote Press (Watertown, MA), 1993.

Tinker, Tailor, Soldier, Sailor: A Picture Book, illustrated by Maureen Roffey, Bodley Head (London, England), 1976, Merrimack Book Service (Salem, NH), 1978.

Rhyming Nell, illustrated by Maureen Roffey, Lothrop, Lee & Shepard (New York, NY), 1979.

Door to Door: A Picture Book, illustrated by Maureen Roffey, Lothrop, Lee & Shepard (New York, NY), 1980, published as *Door to Door: A Split-Page Picture Book,* Whispering Coyote Press (Watertown, MA), 1993.

Shoe Shoe Baby, illustrated by Katherine Lodge, Random House (New York, NY), 2000.

Custard Surprise, illustrated by Tim Bowers, HarperCollins (New York, NY), 2007.

SELF-ILLUSTRATED PICTURE BOOKS

There Was an Old Woman Who Lived in a Glove, Whispering Coyote Press (Watertown, MA), 1992.

(Reteller) *Prince Ivan and the Firebird: A Russian Folk Tale,* Whispering Coyote Press (Watertown, MA), 1993.

The Half-Mile Hat, Whispering Coyote Press (Watertown, MA), 1995.

Tanglebird, Houghton Mifflin (Boston, MA), 1997.

Mouldylocks, Houghton Mifflin (Boston, MA), 1998.

Cloud Cuckoo Land (and Other Odd Spots), Houghton Mifflin (Boston, MA), 1999.

How Scary!, Houghton Mifflin (Boston, MA), 2001.

ILLUSTRATOR

Maureen Roffey, *Let's Have a Party,* Bodley Head (London, England), 1974, Merrimack Book Service (Salem, NH), 1978.

Stella Blackstone, *My Granny Went to Market: A Round-the-World Counting Rhyme,* Barefoot Books (Bath, England), 1995, published as *Grandma Went to Market: A Round-the-World Counting Rhyme,* Houghton Mifflin (Boston, MA), 1996.

Nikki Siegen-Smith, compiler, *Songs for Survival: Songs and Chants from Tribal Peoples around the World,* Dutton (New York, NY), 1996.

Pippa Goodhart, *Noah Makes a Boat,* Houghton Mifflin (Boston, MA), 1997.

Grace Hallworth, *Mermaid and Monsters: Stories from the Sea,* Mammoth (London, England), 1997.

Paul Stewart, *Millie's Party,* Mammoth (London, England), 1999.

Adaptations

The Grand Old Duke of York has been adapted for audio cassette by Spoken Arts, 1994.

Sidelights

Bernard Lodge is a British author and illustrator of children's books who has blended his book writing with a successful career as a graphic designer in animation for television programming and advertising. Working with his wife, illustrator Maureen Roffey, he wrote texts for award-winning titles such as *Tinker, Tailor, Soldier, Sailor: A Picture Book.* In addition to illustrating for other authors, Lodge has also produced several self-illustrated titles, including *There Was an Old Woman Who Lived in a Glove, Mouldylocks,* and *How Scary!* After the publication of his first few titles, Lodge once told *SATA,* the "story of my career as an author could be engraved on the head of a pin except that it would need padding." Such understatement is a Lodge signature, both in his books and his life.

Lodge's first efforts as a writer of children's books were in collaboration with his wife, Roffey, and their literary debut, *The Grand Old Duke of York,* continues the title character's silly military escapades by adding ten new verses to the popular nursery rhyme. "The artwork—precisely delineated collages—catches the verve in bold fields of color, dynamic compositions and a hint

of mischief," wrote a contributor in *Publishers Weekly*. This initial title by Lodge and Roffey proved popular enough to encourage further joint efforts. A counting verse book, *Tinker, Tailor, Soldier, Sailor*, follows the four familiar characters of the title as they plan a party with various edible treats. A counting sequence from one to eight is blended into these preparations. *Growing Point* reviewer Margery Fisher called this book a "good joke, carried through most professionally," while a reviewer for *Junior Bookshelf* described *Tinker, Tailor, Soldier, Sailor* as a "cheerfully expanded nursery jingle, which develops into a cumulative counting story."

In a further collaborative effort, *Door to Door: A Picture Book*, a split-page layout reveals the happenings inside and outside twelve different houses located along the same road. "The verses are quite simple and pleasant for children to learn," noted a reviewer for *Junior Bookshelf*. A critic in *Publishers Weekly* called Lodge's verse "playful jingles." Everybody in the block is busy doing something or other; in *School Library Journal*, Carolyn Jenks noted that Roffey's pictures "are full of detail and activity" and that satisfying "the universal curiosity about what happens in other people's homes is a good theme." Ruth M. Stein, writing in *Language Arts*, called *Door to Door* a "clever picture book" and noted especially the "humorous verse and graphics" as well as the "brilliant use" of the double view design that allows the reader to see what is going on inside each house."

Lodge ended a lengthy hiatus from his involvement in the creation of children's picture books with publication of his self-illustrated *There Was an Old Woman Who Lived in a Glove*. In this story, a takeoff from the old nursery rhyme "There Was an Old Woman Who Lived in a Shoe," Lodge tells the story of a white-haired lady and her dove, Albert, as the pair sets off to see the world. Of course it takes a trip to make the old woman realize that her glove is actually the perfect place for her. *Booklist* contributor Ilene Cooper called Lodge's verse "clever though sometimes thin,." maintaining that "the attractive artwork . . . really makes the book a cut above." This artwork was also created by Lodge, who printed woodcuts on an antique handpress, and then assembled the prints into collages. The "expressive, boldly colored woodcuts give a sense of life, action and playfulness" to the story, observed Ronald Jobe in *School Library Journal*, and the text in rhyme is "fun."

Lodge turns to Eastern Europe for *Prince Ivan and the Firebird: A Russian Folk Tale*, using a mid-nineteenth-century version of the quest tale that is "enlivened by [his] exuberant folk-art-inspired illustrations," according to a writer for *Publishers Weekly*. Denise Anton Wright, writing in *School Library Journal*, praised Lodge's "natural integration of the white of the pages into his designs," which are full of onion domes and Cossack-inspired apparel. Wright concluded that although there are many versions of this tale available to children, "few are as imaginative."

A shepherd and a giant are at the center of Lodge's *The Half-Mile Hat*, a "fanciful story," according to a *Publishers Weekly* critic. In the work, a strong wind blows a shepherd's hat off his head, and during his search he comes upon a sleeping giant. The shepherd finds himself lost, however, as he attempts to crawl across the giant's body. The *Publishers Weekly* contributor praised the "mildly folkloric feel" of Lodge's illustrations.

For *Tanglebird*, Lodge once again chose woodcuts as his medium, this time tinting them in soft pastels. When the other birds ridicule Tanglebird, who has a difficult time making a tidy nest, he flies off to the city. There, unfortunately, he makes similar messes with yarn and kite string in an attempt to fashion a nest. Befriended by a little girl, he learns how to tie shoelaces and to weave, and back home in the woods again, he makes the most beautiful nests imaginable. A *Kirkus Reviews* commentator observed that although the lesson is a bit "manipulated," nevertheless "children will like Tanglebird's triumph over those who once mocked him." Cooper noted that Lodge's illustrations have their "own look that both kids and adults will respond to," and concluded that the book is a "great story-hour choice." A *Publishers Weekly* critic also praised the illustrations in *Tanglebird*, commenting that "Lodge's merry, rustic prints have moments of slapstick humor, and make wonderful use of pattern, subtly flattening foliage, clothing and freeways." Writing in *School Library Journal*, Lisa S. Murphy observed that Gina, the little girl who befriends Tanglebird, "subtly molds Tanglebird's weakness into strength, without compromising his free spirit." Murphy also noted that the woodcut/pastel artwork makes the visual "as appealing as its message."

With *Mouldylocks*, Lodge tells the story of the eponymous witch and her birthday. Mouldylocks receives a new broomstick first thing in the morning which whisks her away to a surprise party. There she receives all sorts of gifts, from a book of magic spells to a Snakes and Ladders game that uses *real* snakes. When things get out of hand, Mouldylocks uses magic to set everything right before the arrival of the birthday cake. "The most inventive aspect of the book is Lodge's stylized woodblock art," a critic in *Publishers Weekly* remarked. *Booklist* critic GraceAnne A. DeCandido described Mouldylock's hair as "acid-green vermicelli," going on to note that the woodcut illustrations "have a fiendish charm" and make "fine Halloween storytime fodder."

In *Cloud Cuckoo Land (and Other Odd Spots)* Lodge takes readers on a whimsical tour of imaginary destinations, including Ice Cone Island, where chocolate chips erupt from volcanoes, and the Sea of Socks, which features huge wooly waves. "Featuring a lustrous pastel palette, Lodge's woodcut art emanates a playfulness worthy of his appealing nonsensical verse," according to a reviewer in *Publishers Weekly*. In his self-illustrated counting book *How Scary!*, Lodge presents young readers with a host of wicked witches, skinny skeletons, an-

gry aliens, and other creatures. "The colorful cartoon illustrations are more amusing than frightening," McCoy stated of the child-friendly book.

Lodge has also illustrated several picture books for other authors, including Stella Blackstone's *Grandma Went to Market: A Round-the-World Counting Rhyme,* Nikki Siegen-Smith's *Songs for Survival: Songs and Chants from Tribal Peoples around the World,* and Pippa Goodhart's *Noah Makes a Boat.* The first title tells the story of a grandmother who travels the world to make a variety of interesting purchases, including a flying carpet from Istanbul and a pair of temple cats from Thailand. Reviewing *Grandma Went to Market,* Hazel Rochman noted in *Booklist* that "Lodge's line-and-color paintings show a nice English lady in a big hat with a shopping cart, surveying the sweet wonders of the world." A *Publishers Weekly* contributor called the illustrations "cheerful," while Marianne Saccardi noted in *School Library Journal* that "Lodge depicts characteristic landscapes or architecture in brightly colored gouache illustrations stretching across a page and a third."

Songs for Survival is an anthology of songs and chants from the tribal peoples of six continents. According to a *Publishers Weekly* commentator, Lodge's "lino-cuts" for this book 'seem generally primitivist but are specific to no one culture." *School Library Journal* contributor Renee Steinberg noted that Lodge's "vibrantly colored illustrations offer a celebration of life." The story of the Flood and of Noah's efforts to save two of each creature on his ark is retold by Pippa Goodhart in *Noah Makes a Boat.* Cooper, writing in *Booklist,* noted that there have been many versions of the old Bible story. "What makes this one a winner are Lodge's robust linocut illustrations," Cooper observed, and Lodge's illustrations "provide the perfect medium to convey the particulars of Noah's work." Reviewing *Noah Makes a Boat* in *Horn Book,* Martha V. Parravano stated that Lodge "combines strong lines with rounded shapes . . . to create pleasingly balanced, appropriately buoyant illustrations." A *Publishers Weekly* critic noted that the author's simple straightforward style "allows Lodge free reign for his full-bleed spreads of animals running rampant in pairs as they ready themselves for the ark-bound parade."

In 2000 Lodge teamed with his daughter, illustrator Katherine Lodge, to produce *Shoe Shoe Baby,* a humorous work about a devoted shoe-store owner. In the work, Shoe Shoe Baby helps her eccentric customers, including a ballerina named Popova and a cowboy named Tex from New Mex, find just the right footwear to match their needs. "The story is mildly amusing," noted *School Library Journal* reviewer Karen James, and a contributor in *Publishers Weekly* remarked that "the vividly hued, stylized art delivers some comical images."

In *Custard Surprise,* a work by Lodge that is illustrated by Tim Bowers, a pair of chickens, Dinah and Rufus, open their own diner. Dinah, who works the counter while Rufus does the cooking, soon notices that their customers have problems with the menu, a fact that forces Rufus to create some wildly inventive dishes. Erika Quails, writing in *School Library Journal,* described *Custard Surprise* as "a lively, action-packed easy reader."

Whether illustrating his own distinctive titles, or working in collaboration with other authors of children's books, Lodge has created his own style—a blend of whimsy and solid graphic skills—and has ultimately disproved his own self-effacing judgment of his work. The "head of the pin" upon which he once ironically commented that his career could be etched has grown significantly in both size and stature.

Biographical and Critical Sources

PERIODICALS

Booklist, October 15, 1992, Ilene Cooper, review of *There Was an Old Woman Who Lived in a Glove,* pp. 434-435; February 1, 1996, Hazel Rochman, review of *Grandma Went to Market: A Round-the-World Counting Rhyme,* p. 936; March 1, 1997, Ilene Cooper, review of *Tanglebird,* p. 1172; October 1, 1997, Ilene Cooper, review of *Noah Makes a Boat,* p. 323; September 1, 1998, GraceAnne A. DeCandido, review of *Mouldylocks,* p. 133; September 1, 2001, Hazel Rochman, review of *How Scary!,* p. 120.
Growing Point, January, 1977, Margery Fisher, review of *Tinker, Tailor, Soldier, Sailor: A Picture Book,* p. 3050.
Horn Book, September-October, 1997, Martha V. Parravano, review of *Noah Makes a Boat,* p. 557.
Junior Bookshelf, April, 1977, review of *Tinker, Tailor, Soldier, Sailor,* p. 80; December, 1980, review of *Door to Door,* p. 285.
Kirkus Reviews, March 1, 1997, review of *Tanglebird,* p. 384; June 15, 2007, review of *Custard Surprise.*
Language Arts, April, 1981, Ruth M. Stein, review of *Door to Door,* p. 474.
Publishers Weekly, November 21, 1980, review of *Door to Door,* p. 59; February 22, 1993, review of *The Grand Old Duke of York,* p. 95; August 9, 1993, review of *Prince Ivan and the Firebird,* p. 479; January 9, 1995, review of *The Half-Mile Hat,* p. 64; February 5, 1996, review of *Grandma Went to Market,* p. 881; June 3, 1996, review of *Songs for Survival: Songs and Chants from Tribal Peoples around the World,* p. 84; February 24, 1997, review of *Tanglebird,* p. 90; August 25, 1997, review of *Noah Makes a Boat,* p. 65; July 20, 1998, review of *Mouldylocks,* p. 218; September 13, 1999, review of *Cloud Cuckoo Land (and Other Odd Spots),* p. 83; September 25, 2000, review of *Shoe Shoe Baby,* p. 116.
School Library Journal, February, 1993, Ronald Jobe, review of *There Was an Old Lady Who Lived in a Glove,* pp. 84-85; November, 1993, Denise Anton Wright, review of *Prince Ivan and the Firebird,* p. 100; February, 1994, Carolyn Jenks, review of *Door to Door,* p. 89; April, 1996, Marianne Saccardi, review of *Grandma Went to Market,* p. 99; July, 1996, Renee

Steinberg, review of *Songs for Survival,* p. 96; April, 1997, Lisa S. Murphy, review of *Tanglebird,* p. 113; October, 2000, Karen James, review of *Shoe Shoe Baby,* p. 129; September, 2001, Jody McCoy, review of *How Scary!,* p. 193; August, 2007, Erika Qualls, review of *Custard Surprise,* p. 84.

ONLINE

British Broadcasting Corporation Web site, http://www.bbc.co.uk/ (December 27, 2002), "*Doctor Who:* Evolution of a Title Sequence."*

M

MARKEY, Kevin 1965-

Personal

Born May 5, 1965, in Kittery, ME; son of Martin James (a clinical psychologist) and Sarah Marie Markey; married; children: two. *Education:* Georgetown University, B.A., 1988. *Hobbies and other interests:* Conservation, sailing, jazz music.

Addresses

Home—Northampton, MA. *E-mail*—kevin@kevinmar key.com.

Career

Author and editor. *New England Monthly,* associate editor, 1988-90; freelance writer, 1990—. *Family Fun,* associate editor, 1992.

Member

Authors Guild, Mungo Park Full Brass Band and Whisky Society (member of board of trustees).

Writings

"SUPER SLUGGERS" MIDDLE-GRADE NOVEL SERIES

Slumpbuster, illustrated by Royce Fitzgerald, HarperCollins (New York, NY), 2009.
Wall Ball, HarperCollins (New York, NY), 2010.
Wing Ding, HarperCollins (New York, NY), 2011.

OTHER

(With Caroline Sutton) *More How Do They Do That?: Wonders of the Modern World Explained,* illustrated by Tom Vincent, Morrow (New York, NY), 1993.

100 Most Important Women of the Twentieth Century, Ladies' Home Journal Books (Des Moines, IA), 1998.
Around the World with Disney, Disney Editions (New York, NY), 2004.
Secrets of Disney's Glorious Gardens, Disney Editions (New York, NY), 2006.

Contributor to books, including *The Ultimate Baseball Book,* edited by Daniel Okrent and Harris Lewine, Houghton, 1992; *Our Times: The Illustrated History of the Twentieth Century,* Turner Publishing (New York, NY), 1995; and *Joel Kopp: Sculpture, Paintings, Carving,* Impress, Inc. (Northampton, MA), 2007.

Sidelights

Inspired by a lifelong love of baseball gained while growing up in Massachusetts, writer Kevin Markey created the "Super Sluggers" series of middle-grade novels. Set in a small town where little-league baseball draws numerous summertime fans, Markey's series follows the highs and lows of the hometown Rambletown Ramblers in a humorous narrative that features a kid-friendly mix of puns, exaggeration, and other silliness. Reviewing the first novel in the "Super Sluggers" series, Todd Morning predicted in *Booklist* that Markey's "straightforward, sunny, somewhat retro" baseball stories "will appeal to . . . fans looking for a simple, fun story."

Markey's novel *Slumpbuster* sets the stage for the "Super Sluggers" series. As the baseball season plays out, the Rambletown Rounders go head to head against longtime rivals the Hog City Haymakers. At eleven years of age, Banjo Hit Bishbash—alias The Great Walloper—keeps the competition keen, by batting in a steady stream of home runs. A young journalist from the hometown newspaper predicts that the Walloper will lead the Rounders to a series title, and suddenly Banjo finds himself in a slump. To make matters worse, a heat wave drains the energy from the entire team and the Rounders soon worry that their dreams of a winning season may be going up in smoke. New center-fielder Orlando

Ramirez is the focus of *Wall Ball,* and nature also threatens to foil a new season through a succession of unexpected snow storms. Unfortunately, Orlando's fielding skills do not translate well from grass to ice, and he takes so many falls while running for the ball that the Rounders fear he will seriously hurt himself, harming their chances for a win against the Haymakers in the process. In *School Library Journal* Blair Christolon cited *Slumpbuster* for its "interesting descriptive similes" and "clever metaphors," and a *Kirkus Review* writer concluded that Markey's "deadpan delivery" and "broad, punning prose [are] quite comical."

In addition to his novels, the author has also written or coauthored several nonfiction titles geared for general readers. Part of a question-and-answer series begun by coauthor Caroline Sutton that includes *How Do They Do That?* and *How Did They Do That?,* his work in *More How Do They Do That?: Wonders of the Modern World Explained* covers interesting subjects that range from science to the law and modern cultural phenomena. In *Publishers Weekly* a contributor dubbed *More How Do They Do That?* "a fine book for reading piecemeal." In *Booklist* Carolyn Mulac also recommended the book, noting that "what makes Sutton's works unique among trivia books is the practice of listing under each question the sources for its answer."

Biographical and Critical Sources

PERIODICALS

Booklist, October 15, 1994, Carolyn Mulac, review of *More How Do They Do That?: Wonders of the Modern World Explained,* p. 446; February 15, 2009, Todd Morning, review of *Slumpbuster,* p. 84.

Book Report, September-October, 1993, Carol Mann Simpson, review of *More How Do They Do That?,* p. 64.

Bulletin of the Center for Children's Books, March, 2009, Elizabeth Bush, review of *Slumpbuster,* p. 289.

Kirkus Reviews, January 15, 2009, review of *Slumpbuster.*

Library Journal, February 1, 1993, Scott Johnson, review of *More How Do They Do That?,* p. 108.

Publishers Weekly, January 25, 1993, review of *More How Do They Do That?,* p. 73.

School Library Journal, July, 1993, Pat Royal, review of *More How Do They Do That?,* p. 114; May, 2009, Blair Christolon, review of *Slumpbuster,* p. 84.

ONLINE

Kevin Markey Home Page, http://www.kevinmarkey.com (May 1, 2010).

* * *

MENDEZ, Simon 1975-

Personal

Born August 5, 1975, in York, England; father an illustrator and designer. *Education:* Attended York Technical College; attended Fyld College. *Hobbies and other interests:* Photography, golf, tennis, soccer.

Addresses

Home—England. *Agent*—Advocate Art, 39 Church Rd., Wimbledon Village, London SW19 5DQ, England.

Career

Artist and illustrator.

Illustrator

Sue Barraclough, *The Little Lost Duckling,* Templar (Dorking, Surrey, England), 1999.

(With Lisa Alderson) Linda Watters, *A Year on the Farm,* Brimax (London, England), 2002.

Katie Edwards, *Myths and Monsters: Secrets Revealed,* Charlesbridge (Watertown, MA), 2004.

Valerie Davies, *The Spectacular Spider Book,* School Specialty (Columbus, OH), 2006.

Norbert Landa, *Little Bear and the Wishing Tree,* Good Books (Intercourse, PA), 2007.

Claire Freedman, *I Love You, Sleepyhead,* Good Books (Intercourse, PA), 2008.

Illustrator of educational readers for British publishers, including Usborne.

"STARTING LIFE" SERIES

Claire Llewellyn, *Frog,* NorthWord Press (Chanhassen, MN), 2003.

Claire Llewellyn, *Butterfly,* NorthWord Press (Chanhassen, MN), 2003.

Claire Llewellyn, *Crocodile,* NorthWord Press (Chanhassen, MN), 2004.

Claire Llewellyn, *Duck,* NorthWord Press (Chanhassen, MN), 2004.

Claire Llewellyn, *Ladybug,* NorthWord Press (Chanhassen, MN), 2004.

Claire Llewellyn, *Tree,* NorthWord Press (Chanhassen, MN), 2004.

Biographical and Critical Sources

PERIODICALS

Kirkus Reviews, June 1, 2007, review of *Little Bear and the Wishing Tree.*

School Library Journal, November, 2004, Dona Ratterree, review of *Duck,* and Sandra Welzenbach, review of *Crocodile,* both p. 128; February, 2005, Linda M. Kenton, review of *Myths and Monsters: Secrets Revealed,* p. 116; August, 2007, Luiella Teuton, review of *Little Bear and the Wishing Tree,* p. 84.*

MICHAELIS, Antonia 1979-

Personal

Born 1979, in Kiel, Germany; married; children: one daughter. *Education:* Studied medicine at University of Greifswald.

Addresses

Home—Germany.

Career

Writer. Taught English, art, and theater classes in India.

Awards, Honors

Mildred L. Batchelder Award Honor Book designation, 2009, for *Tiger Moon.*

Writings

Leselöwen Internatsgeschichten, Loewe (Bindlach, Germany), 2002.

Dschungelgeschichten, Loewe (Bindlach, Germany), 2002.

So groß bin ich schon!, illustrated by Claudia Fries, Loewe (Bindlach, Germany), 2003.

Drei kleine Eisbären im Glitzerschnee, illustrated by Sigrid Leberer, Loewe (Bindlach, Germany), 2003.

Mike und ich und Max Ernst, Loewe (Bindlach, Germany), 2003.

Die wunderliche Reise von Oliver und Twist, Loewe (Bindlach, Germany), 2003.

Mäusejagd, Loewe (Bindlach, Germany), 2003.

Pizzakrise, Loewe (Bindlach, Germany), 2003.

Katzenfaxen, Loewe (Bindlach, Germany), 2004.

Hundeliebe, Loewe (Bindlach, Germany), 2004.

Das Adoptivzimmer, illustrated by Birgit Brandt, Loewe (Bindlach, Germany), 2004.

Der kleine Quengel-Engel, illustrated by Betina Gotzen-Beek, Loewe (Bindlach, Germany), 2004.

Morgenstern, Loewe (Bindlach, Germany), 2004.

Hier bei uns in Ammerlo, illustrated by Julia Ginsbach, Loewe (Bindlach, Germany), 2005.

Viel los bei uns in Ammerlo!, illustrated by Julia Ginsbach, Loewe (Bindlach, Germany), 2005.

Advent bei uns in Ammerlo, illustrated by Julia Ginsbach, Loewe (Bindlach, Germany), 2006.

Das Geheimnis der Geisterinsel, Loewe (Bindlach, Germany), 2006.

Tigermond, Loewe (Bindlach, Germany), 2006, translated by Anthea Bell as *Tiger Moon,* Amulet Books (New York, NY), 2008.

Laura und der Silberwolf, Herder (Freiburg, Germany), 2007.

Lampenfiebergeschichten, illustrated by Alexander Bux, Loewe (Bindlach, Germany), 2007.

Nikolausgeschichten, illustrated by Betina Gotzen-Beek, Loewe (Bindlach, Germany), 2007.

Das Geheimnis des 12. Kontinents, Loewe (Bindlach, Germany), 2007.

Nele und der Eiskristall, illustrated by Miriam Cordes, Herder (Freiburg, Germany), 2007.

Komm zurück, kleines Pony!, illustrated by Julia Ginsbach, Loewe (Bindlach, Germany), 2008.

Freundinnengeschichten, illustrated by Katharina Wieker, Loewe (Bindlach, Germany), 2008.

Die wilden Prinzessinnen, illustrated by Eva Czerwenka, Herder (Freiburg, Germany), 2008.

Ballerinageschichten, illustrated by Katharina Wieker, Loewe (Bindlach, Germany), 2008.

Drachen der Finsternis, Loewe (Bindlach, Germany), 2008, translated as *The Dragons of Darkness,* Amulet Books (New York, NY), 2010.

Zauberschlossgeschichten, illustrated by Heike Wiechmann, Loewe (Bindlach, Germany), 2008.

Die Nacht der gefangenen Träume, illustrated by Eva Schöffmann-Davidov, Oetinger (Hamburg, Germany), 2008.

Der kleine Dino und der 8-Uhr-Vulkan, illustrated by Leopé, Loewe (Bindlach, Germany), 2009.

Schokolade am Meer, illustrated by Eva Czerwenka, Herder (Freiburg, Germany), 2009.

Kreuzberg 007: Mission grünes Monster, illustrated by Annette Swoboda, Oetinger (Hamburg, Germany), 2009.

Drachengeschichten, illustrated by Betina Gotzen-Beek, Loewe (Bindlach, Germany), 2009.

Jenseits der Finsterbach-Brücke, illustrated by Almud Kunert, Oetinger (Hamburg, Germany), 2009.

Kleine Weihnachtsmann Geschichten zum Vorlesen, illustrated by Eva Czerwenka, Ellermann (Hamburg, Germany), 2009.

Der letzte Regen, Wißner (Augsburg, Germany), 2009.

Max und das Murks, illustrated by Betina Gotzen-Beek, Oetinger (Hamburg, Germany), 2010.

Kleine Lachgeschichten zum Vorlesen, illustrated by Annette Fienieg, Ellermann (Hamburg, Germany), 2010.

Schiffbruch auf der Pirateninsel, illustrated by Catharina Westphal, Oetinger (Hamburg, Germany), 2010.

Kreuzberg 007: Geheimnisvolle Graffiti, illustrated by Annette Swoboda, Oetinger (Hamburg, Germany), 2010.

Sidelights

A native of Germany, Antonia Michaelis is the author of more than forty works for children and young adults. Her books translated into English include the fantasy novels *Tiger Moon,* which was named a Mildred L. Batchelder Award honor book, and *The Dragons of Darkness.* Set in India at the turn of the twentieth century, *Tiger Moon* focuses on Safia, a young woman who fears for her life unless she can hide a secret from her husband-to-be, an evil and brutal merchant. While awaiting her fate, Safia spins a fanciful tale for Lalit, a palace servant. She describes the adventures of a young thief named Farhad and his companion, a sacred white tiger, after they are chosen to rescue the Hindu god Krishna's daughter. "As the stories of Safia and Farhad intertwine," Jennifer-Lynn Draper remarked in *School Library Journal,* "the lines between fantasy and reality are blurred."

Cover of Antonia Michaelis's young-adult novel Tiger Moon, *featuring artwork by Shane Rebenschied.* (Cover illustration copyright © 2009 by Shane Rebenschied. Reproduced by permission.)

Writing in *Kirkus Reviews,* a critic described *Tiger Moon* as a "superior fairy tale . . . down to the bittersweet but ultimately satisfying conclusion." "Deftly interweaving Indian history, culture, and mythology," as Shelle Rosenfeld observed in *Booklist,* Michaelis's "richly layered tale . . . beautifully illustrates the power of storytelling."

In *The Dragons of Darkness* a German teen, a Nepalese prince, and a Maoist rebel join forces to save the country from powerful, menacing dragons. When his brother disappears while traveling in Asia, Christopher finds himself mysteriously transported from Germany to Nepal, where he meets Jumar, a crown prince with powers of invisibility, and Niya, a young revolutionary. The trio begins an odyssey across a war-torn land, where guerrillas attempt to wrest control from ruling forces and dragons steal color and life from the kingdom. "Lush prose . . . weaves current events and fairy-tale archetypes into a dreamlike fable," a *Kirkus Reviews* contributor observed, and Rosenfeld noted that "the diverse characters' alternating stories build suspense and intimacy in scenes that are droll and poignant, sorrowful and inspiring."

Biographical and Critical Sources

PERIODICALS

Booklist, October 15, 2008, Shelle Rosenfeld, review of *Tiger Moon,* p. 41; March 1, 2010, Shelle Rosenfeld, review of *Dragons of Darkness,* p. 72.

Horn Book, November-December, 2008, Monika Schroder, review of *Tiger Moon,* p. 710.

Kirkus Reviews, October 15, 2008, review of *Tiger Moon;* December 15, 2009, review of *The Dragons of Darkness.*

Kliatt, November, 2008, Ashleigh Larsen, review of *Tiger Moon,* p. 15.

Publishers Weekly, October 20, 2008, review of *Tiger Moon,* p. 51; December 14, 2009, review of *Dragons of Darkness,* p. 61.

School Library Journal, November, 2008, Jennifer-Lynn Draper, review of *Tiger Moon,* p. 130; March, 2010, Jane Henriksen Baird, review of *Dragons of Darkness,* p. 164.

ONLINE

Loewe Publishing Web site, http://www.loewe-verlag.de/ (March 1, 2010), "Antonia Michaelis."*

*   *   *

MILLER, Christopher 1976-
(Miller Brothers, a joint pseudonym)

Personal

Born 1976; son of Christian booksellers. *Education:* Degree (computer animation).

Addresses

Home—Auburn, WA. *E-mail*—cmiller@luminationstudios.com.

Career

Author and illustrator. Lumination Studios, cofounder and computer animator; animator, with brother Allen Miller, for children's video series "Juniors Giants." Presenter at schools.

Awards, Honors

(With Allen Miller) Moonbeam Bronze Medal for Preteen Fiction, and Clive Staples Award for Christian Speculative Fiction short list, both 2009, both for *Hunter Brown and the Secret of the Shadow.*

Writings

"HEROES OF PROMISES" PICTURE-BOOK SERIES

(And illustrator, with Allen Miller, as The Miller Brothers) *The Legend of Gid the Kid and the Black Bean Bandits,* Warner Press (Anderson, IN), 2007.

(And illustrator, with Allen Miller, as The Miller Brothers) *Ten-Gallon Sam and the Perilous Mine,* Warner Press (Anderson, IN), 2008.

"CODEBREAKERS" ELEMENTARY-GRADE NOVEL SERIES

(With Allen Miller, as The Miller Brothers) *Hunter Brown and the Secret of the Shadow,* Warner Press (Anderson, IN), 2008.
(With Allen Miller, as The Miller Brothers) *Hunter Brown and the Consuming Fire,* Warner Press (Anderson, IN), 2009.

Biographical and Critical Sources

PERIODICALS

School Library Journal, March, 2009, Jake Pettit, review of *Hunter Brown and the Secret of the Shadow,* p. 148.
Voice of Youth Advocates, October, 2008, Laura Panter, review of *Hunter Brown and the Secret of the Shadow,* p. 354.

ONLINE

Christopher Miller Home Page, http://www.luminationstudios.com (March 15, 2010).
Codebearers Web site, http://www.codebearers.com/ (March 15, 2010).
Miller Brothers Web log, http://themillerbrothers.blogspot.com/ (April 15, 2010).*

* * *

MILLER BROTHERS
See MILLER, Christopher

* * *

MILWAY, Alex 1978-

Personal

Born 1978, in Hereford, England. *Education:* Cheltenham Art College, degree.

Addresses

Home—London, England. *Agent*—Laura Cecil, 17 Alwyne Villas, London N1 2HG, England.

Career

Author and illustrator of children's books. Formerly worked in magazine publishing. Presenter at schools and libraries.

Writings

SELF-ILLUSTRATED

The Mousehunter, Faber & Faber (London, England), 2008, Little, Brown (New York, NY), 2009.
The Curse of Mousebeard, Faber & Faber (London, England), 2008.
Mousebeard's Revenge, Faber & Faber (London, England), 2010.

Sidelights

British writer and illustrator Alex Milway grew up in Hereford, England, and at age sixteen he enrolled in art school. As a student at Cheltenham Art College, he earned the Royal Academy's David Murray Landscape Award. Although Milway first intended to become a fine-art painter, and then an animator, he opted for children's author with the publication of *The Mousehunter,* which grew out of the self-illustrated fantasy stories he wrote for his Web log, *Old Hokey's Whimsical Tales.*

The first volume in a trilogy, *The Mousehunter* introduces a quasi-fantasy world where mice of all sizes have a range of unusual powers and serve the human world as servants, friends, and sometimes the enemy of men. The action takes place in coastal Old Town, as wealthy local mouse collector Isiah Lovelock receives a grisly warning from a feared pirate called Mousebeard, a man so named because he allows mice to live in the tangles of his unkempt beard. When Emiline Orelia, the twelve year old who cares for Lovelock's many mice, is sent to track down the fearsome Mousebeard, she is threatened by other mouse creatures that are cast as spirits and ghosts that evoke familiar myths and legends. Emiline's story continues in *The Curse of Mousebeard,* as she fights a host of new enemies while searching the world for the mythic Lost World of mice and its cache of rare and exotic rodent species. In *Mousebeard's Revenge* the girl finally returns to Old Town, where she finds things on the brink of chaos.

In *School Library Journal,* Beth L. Meister called *The Mousehunter* an entertaining saga in which Milway treats readers to "an atmospheric and engaging world" rife with "action, chases, and plot twists." The author's "original narrative has a goofy charm enhanced by a vivid alternative-historical setting reminiscent of [noted children's author] Joan Aiken's work," observed a *Kirkus Reviews* writer of the same book. In *Booklist* Ian Chipman dubbed *The Mousehunter* "a quite different and just plain fun yarn" that benefits from "Milway's fanciful illustrations and his strong, persistent sense of quirkiness."

Biographical and Critical Sources

PERIODICALS

Booklist, December 15, 2008, Ian Chipman, review of *The Mousehunter,* p. 44.

Kirkus Reviews, January 15, 2009, review of *The Mouse-hunter.*

Publishers Weekly, January 12, 2009, review of *The Mouse-hunter,* p. 48.

School Library Journal, March, 2009, Beth L. Meister, review of *The Mousehunter,* p. 148.

ONLINE

Alex Milway Home Page, http://www.themousehunter.com (April 21, 2010).*

* * *

MOLSKI, Carol

Personal

Married; husband's name Kurt; children: Cassie, Courtney. *Education:* College degree. *Hobbies and other interests:* Taking walks, cooking, traveling.

Addresses

Home—Wisconsin Rapids, WI. *E-mail*—swimmingsal@ charter.net.

Career

Educator and author. Elementary-school teacher for over twenty years. Presenter at schools.

Writings

A Little Taste of God's Love: Bible Story Recipes and Activities, illustrated by Nate Evans, Concordia Publishing House (St. Louis, MO), 2001.

Bible Word Sudoku, Concordia Publishing House (St. Louis, MO), 2007.

Bible Puzzlers: 51 Mind Stretchers, Concordia Publishing House (St. Louis, MO), 2007.

Swimming Sal, illustrated by Mary Newell DePalma, Eerdmans Books for Young Readers (Grand Rapids, MI), 2009.

Also author of Christian teaching resources.

Biographical and Critical Sources

PERIODICALS

Booklist, April 15, 2009, Patricia Austin, review of *Swimming Sal,* p. 48.

Kirkus Reviews, January 15, 2009, review of *Swimming Sal.*

School Library Journal, March, 2009, Linda M. Kenton, review of *Swimming Sal,* p. 123.

ONLINE

Carol Molski Home Page, http://swimmingsal.books.office live.com (April 15, 2010).

Eerdmans Books Web site, http://eerdmans.com/ (April, 2009), interview with Molski.*

N

NAHOKO, Uehashi
See UEHASHI, Nahoko

*   *   *

NELSON, D.A. 1970-
(Dawn Ann Nelson)

Personal
Born November 39, 1970, in Glasgow, Scotland; married; children: one daughter, one son.

Addresses
Home—Cardross, Scotland. *E-mail*—d-a-nelson@tiscali.co.uk.

Career
Author and journalist. National Health Service, Glasgow, Scotland, currently member of staff. Glasgow University, part-time lecturer in creative writing.

Awards, Honors
Royal Mail Award for Scottish Children's Book, 2008, for *DarkIsle*.

Writings

DarkIsle, Strident Publishing (East Kilbride, Scotland), 2007, Delacorte Press (New York, NY), 2008.

Author's work has been translated into French, German, Italian, Japanese, Korean, Portuguese, and Spanish.

Sidelights
In *DarkIsle,* D.A. Nelson's first book for younger children, readers meet an orphaned ten year old named Morag. The girl lives with Jermy and Moira, evil foster parents who punish her by locking her in the basement. While confined in the dark, damp cellar, Morag meets a talking rat named Aldiss and a dodo named Bertie, both of which have been traveling via underground tunnels. The unhappy girl is so entranced by the story of their efforts to save Marnoch Mor, a magical kingdom lo-

Cover of D.A. Nelson's fantasy chapter book **DarkIsle,** *featuring cover art by Sharon Tancredi.* (Illustration © 2008 by Sharon Tancredi. Reproduced by permission of Dell Publishing, a division of Random House, Inc.)

cated in the Scottish highlands, that she escapes from her foster home and joins their crusade. The travelers eventually locate their ultimate guide, a small dragon named Shona, and their further adventures involve magic talismans, wizards and warlocks, and even threats to Morag's freedom.

The first volume in an eventual fantasy trilogy, Nelson's *DarkIsle* was "recommend[ed] to fans of Harry Potter" by *Booklist* critic Kay Weisman. According to a *Kirkus Reviews* writer, the novel is "a light fantasy" in which the menace is more unpleasant than truly malevolent. "Complete with kindly old wizards . . . , Morag's quest is derivative but sweet," the critic added, while in *School Library Journal* Saleena L. Davidson concluded that *DarkIsle* serves up "suspense, magic, and" humor in a story "that is quirky and fun to read."

Biographical and Critical Sources

PERIODICALS

Booklist, November 15, 2008, Kay Weisman, review of *DarkIsle*, p. 59.
Evening Times (Glasgow, Scotland), September 8, 2007, Catriona Stewart, review of *DarkIsle*, p. 8.
Kirkus Reviews, October 15, 2008, review of *DarkIsle*.
School Library Journal, January, 2009, Saleena L. Davidson, review of *DarkIsle*, p. 114.

ONLINE

D.A. Nelson Home Page, http://www.danelson.co.uk (March 15, 2010).
Scottish Book Trust Web site, http://www.scottishbooktrust. com/ (March 15, 2010), "D.A. Nelson."

*   *   *

NELSON, Dawn Ann
See NELSON, D.A.

*   *   *

NICHOLS, Michael 1952-
(Michael "Nick" Nichols)

Personal

Born 1952, in AL; married Reba Park (an artist); children: Eli, Ian. *Education:* Attended University of North Alabama.

Addresses

Home—Sugar Hollow, VA.

Career

Photographer and writer. *Geo* magazine, photographer, 1979-82; Magnum Photos, New York, NY, photographer, 1982-95; National Geographic Society, Washington, DC, staff photographer, 1996-2008, editor-at-large, 2008—. Founder of annual LOOK3 Festival of the Photograph, Charlottesville, VA, 2007. *Military service:* U.S. Army; member of photography unit, c. early 1970s.

Awards, Honors

Four-time winner of World Press Photo competition; named Wildlife Photographer of the Year, Natural History Museum/*BBC Wildlife* magazine; Pictures of the Year International Competition winner; Overseas Press Club of America award, 1982, for reporting "above and beyond the call of duty."

Writings

(With Jane Goodall, George B. Schaller, and Mary G. Smith; and photographer) *The Great Apes: Between Two Worlds,* National Geographic (Washington, DC), 1993.
(With Geoffrey C. Ward; and photographer) *The Year of the Tiger,* National Geographic (Washington, DC), 1998.
(With Jane Goodall; and photographer) *Brutal Kinship,* Aperture (New York, NY), 1999.
(And photographer) *The Last Place on Earth,* National Geographic (Washington, DC), 2005.
(As Michael "Nick" Nichols; with Elizabeth Carney; and photographer) *Face to Face with Gorillas,* National Geographic (Washington, DC), 2009.

PHOTOGRAPHER

George B. Schaller, *Gorilla: Struggle for Survival in the Virungas,* Aperture (New York, NY), 1989.
Virginia Harrison, *How Mountain Gorillas Live,* Gareth Stevens (Milwaukee, WI), 1991.
Virginia Harrison, *Mountain Gorillas and Their Young,* Gareth Stevens (Milwaukee, WI), 1991.
Rita Ritchie, *Mountain Gorillas in Danger,* Gareth Stevens (Milwaukee, WI), 1991.
John Charles Coe and others, *Keepers of the Kingdom: The New American Zoo,* Thomasson-Grant (New York, NY), 1996.
Mike Fay, *The Last Place on Earth* (two-volume boxed set), National Geographic (Washington, DC), 2005.

Contributor of photographs to periodicals, including *Rolling Stone, Life, Aperture,* and *American Photographer.*

Sidelights

During a career that has spanned more than three decades, award-winning photographer Michael Nichols has traveled the globe capturing dramatic, provocative

Michael Nichols' nature photography is a feature of **Face to Face with Gorillas,** *a book coauthored by Elizabeth Carney.*

images that cast a spotlight on pressing environmental issues. Since 1996, Nicholas has worked for the National Geographic Society, serving both as a photographer and, more recently, as an editor at large. His travels have taken him from the Pacific Northwest, where he documented the battle over the towering redwood forests, to Zakouma National Park in Chad, where he chronicled the plight of the African elephant. In an interview on the Canon Professional Network Web site, Nichols described his work as "a mission to give voice to those creatures, places and cultures on the planet that are gravely threatened."

A native of Alabama, Nichols entered the world of photography at the age of eighteen. "It started with my Photo 101 course in school, right before I got drafted in the Army," he remarked in an essay on his home page. "I had studied fine art, but the camera was more immediate, and I knew immediately that's what I wanted to do." After a stint in the U.S. Army's photography unit, Nichols studied at the University of North Alabama, then worked as a photographer for *Geo* magazine. He became a member of Magnum Photos, a cooperative founded by such celebrated individuals as Robert Capa and Henri Cartier-Bresson, before joining the staff of *National Geographic.* "There was a time when I took pictures just for the photograph, just to see if I could do it or if it was interesting," Nicholas stated on his home page. "But the *Geographic* has such a huge audience that I really started to see how much effect the work

can have. I think I'm addicted to it now. When the *Geographic* does a story, it reaches so many people that you can actually effect change."

In addition to his work for *National Geographic,* Nichols has provided the photographs for a number of well-received nonfiction titles. *Keepers of the Kingdom: The New American Zoo,* a collection of essays by leading conservationists and zoo officials, looks at the ways scientists, veterinarians, and animal behaviorists have worked to improve modern zoos by examining such topics as the breeding of endangered species. "The message is delivered in clear, understandable terms," noted *Library Journal* critic Edell Marie Schaefer, "and the photography is breathtaking." In *The Last Place on Earth* Nichols depicts his two-year, 2,000-mile trek though the African Congo with conservationist Mike Fay. According to *Booklist* contributor Brad Hooper, the book's "images are simply breathtaking on both subject matter and aesthetic levels."

Nichols joined forces with famed British primatologist Jane Goodall on *Brutal Kinship,* a work centering on the bond between humankind and chimpanzees. *Booklist* reviewer Nancy Bent remarked that the title includes "hard-to-view photographs documenting our less-than-humane treatment of our closest relatives," and Raymond Hamel asserted in *Library Journal* that Nichols and Goodall "serve as advocates for a species unable to speak for itself." In *Face to Face with Gorillas,* Nichols

and Elizabeth Carney provide young readers with a variety of information about the endangered creatures. Reviewing the work in *School Library Journal,* Nancy Call observed that "Nichols shares his brilliant photography and professional experiences in the world of the gorilla."

Biographical and Critical Sources

PERIODICALS

Booklist, February 15, 1997, Nancy Bent, review of *Keepers of the Kingdom: The New American Zoo,* p. 985; June 1, 1999, Nancy Bent, review of *Brutal Kinship,* p. 1757; September 15, 2005, Brad Hooper, review of *The Last Place on Earth,* p. 26; February 15, 2009, Randall Enos, review of *Face to Face with Gorillas,* p. 89.

Kirkus Reviews, January 15, 2009, review of *Face to Face with Gorillas.*

Library Journal, June 15, 1994, Beth Clewis, review of *The Great Apes: Between Two Worlds,* p. 90; January, 1997, Edell Marie Schaefer, review of *Keepers of the Kingdom,* p. 139; July, 1999, Raymond Hamel, review of *Brutal Kinship,* p. 125.

Natural History, January, 1989, Peter G. Veit, review of *Gorilla: The Struggle for Survival in the Virungas,* p. 28.

New York Times Book Review, April 9, 1989, Maggie Nichols, review of *Gorilla,* p. 32.

School Library Journal, June, 2009, Nancy Call, review of *Face to Face with Gorillas,* p. 145.

ONLINE

Canon Professional Network Web site, http://cpn.canon-europe.com/ (June, 2008), "Michael Nichols."

Michael Nichols Home Page, http://michaelnicknichols.com (March 1, 2010).

National Geographic Web site, http://www.nationalgeographic.com/ (March 1, 2010), "Michael Nichols."*

*   *   *

NICHOLS, Michael "Nick"
See NICHOLS, Michael

*   *   *

NOLAN, Lucy

Personal

Born in Columbia, SC; children: Angelina. *Education:* University of South Carolina, B.A. (journalism).

Addresses

Home—Columbia, SC. *E-mail*—lucynolanbooks@gmail.com.

Career

Marketing professional and author. Formerly worked in marketing for a broadcasting company and an advertising agency; CSC, Inc., member of marketing department.

Awards, Honors

Two-time winner of South Carolina Fiction Project, South Carolina Arts Commission; Pick of the Lists designation, American Booksellers Association, for *The Lizard Man of Crabtree County;* Best Children's Book of the Year selection, Bank Street College of Education, for *A Fairy in a Dairy;* Gryphon Award for Children's Literature Honor Book designation, 2005, for *Smarter than Squirrels;* Texas Bluebonnet Award, Texas Library Association, 2008, for *On the Road;* Best of the Best selection, Chicago Public Library, 2008, for *Bad to the Bone.*

Writings

Secret at Summerhaven, Atheneum (New York, NY), 1987.

The Lizard Man of Crabtree County, illustrated by Jill Kastner, Marshall Cavendish (New York, NY), 1999.

Jack Quack, illustrated by Andréa Wesson, Marshall Cavendish (New York, NY), 2001.

A Fairy in a Dairy, illustrated by Laura J. Bryant, Marshall Cavendish (New York, NY), 2003.

Mother Osprey: Nursery Rhymes for Buoys and Gulls, illustrated by Connie McLennan, Sylvan Dell (Mount Pleasant, SC), 2009.

"DOWN GIRL AND SIT" CHAPTER-BOOK SERIES

Smarter than Squirrels, illustrated by Mike Reed, Marshall Cavendish (New York, NY), 2004.

On the Road, illustrated by Mike Reed, Marshall Cavendish (New York, NY), 2005.

Bad to the Bone, illustrated by Mike Reed, Marshall Cavendish (New York, NY), 2008.

Home on the Range, illustrated by Mike Reed, Marshall Cavendish (New York, NY), 2010.

Adaptations

The Lizard Man of Crabtree County was adapted for video, Nutmeg Media, 2004.

Sidelights

Children's author Lucy Nolan is the creator of the well-received "Down Girl and Sit" series of chapter books, which are illustrated by Mike Reed and inspired by the antics of Nolan's Irish setter, Nutmeg. "I'm not sure I realized how smart dogs could be until she came along," the author remarked to *School Library Journal* interviewer Joan Oleck. "She's very alert and always trying to get your attention."

The humorous "Down Girl and Sit" books, which include *Smarter than Squirrels* and *Bad to the Bone,* are told from a canine's point of view and focus on typical doggy matters such as the excitement of barking at strangers and the rigors of obedience school. "As people we think their lives just aren't that exciting," Nolan stated to Oleck. "As dogs, they would beg to differ with us."

Series opener *Smarter than Squirrels* introduces a frisky pooch named "Down Girl" and her next-door neighbor, "Sit." Determined to assist their owners in any way possible, the misguided but well-meaning duo engages in all types of hijinks, including a run-in with their nemesis, Here Kitty Kitty. According to a *Kirkus Reviews* contributor, the work "is sure to tickle all lovers of man's best friend."

Down Girl's trips to the beach and the groomer are among the highlights of *On the Road,* a follow-up to *Smarter than Squirrels.* "Nolan's simple, peppy text is fun to read," observed Shelle Rosenfeld in reviewing this book for *Booklist.* The doggy adventures continue in *Bad to the Bone,* as Down Girl and Sit are sent to obedience school, with predictably comic results. A contributor in *Kirkus Reviews* asserted that "it's hard not to appreciate the funny miscommunications between loving pets and confused owners" in *Bad to the Bone,* and Carrie Rogers-Whitehead remarked in *School Library Journal* that Nolan's "hilarious story will delight classroom audiences and will also tempt reluctant readers."

Nolan's other books for children include the picture book *The Lizard Man of Crabtree County,* as well as *Jack Quack, A Fairy in a Dairy,* and *Mother Osprey: Nursery Rhymes for Buoys and Gulls,* the last which *School Library Journal,* critic Frances E. Millhouser described as "beach versions of Mother Goose rhymes [that] combine familiar rhythm and meter with new content."

The Lizard Man of Crabtree County centers on James Arthur, a bored youngster looking to stir up some excitement in his quiet neighborhood. To that end, he disguises himself as a shrub, a curious act that only serves to arouse the local insect population, and he must make a mad dash to a pond to rinse off. When a nearsighted neighbor begins spreading the news that she has spotted a "lizard man," James begins pursuing the elusive creature, oblivious to his own role in the commotion. According to a *Kirkus Reviews* critic, Nolan's "tongue-in-cheek tale . . . will have emerging readers predicting what happens next," and *Booklist* contributor Lauren Peterson noted that audiences will be "in on the joke from the start."

A duckling with a penchant for daydreaming is the focus of *Jack Quack.* Otis finds it difficult to concentrate on his swimming and flying lessons, so it is not surprising that he fails miserably when he tries to deliver a bouquet of flowers to the lovely Violet. Retreating into the woods, Otis reinvents himself as a heroic adventurer named Jack Quack and returns the next spring, determined to atone for his mistakes. "Nolan has a masterful pace, mixing the humorous with the adventurous," reported a contributor in *Kirkus Reviews,* and Be Astengo commented in *School Library Journal* that Nolan's "sweet, predictable tale takes a dreamy duck with a slight case of ADD and turns him into a hero."

A Fairy in a Dairy centers on the bizarre events occurring in Buttermilk Hollow, a rural community facing a severe shortage of farmers. After a toothpick-factory owner starts purchasing huge tracts of land, a variety of

Lucy Nolan's humorous picture book On the Road *features artwork by Mike Reed.* (Illustration copyright © 2005 by Mike Reed. All rights reserved. Reproduced by permission.)

dairy products begin appearing in the strangest places, as if by magic, and the town experiences a miraculous rebirth. "This fairy tale milks cow jokes for all they are worth," Connie Fletcher wrote in her *Booklist* review of *A Fairy in a Dairy.*

Biographical and Critical Sources

PERIODICALS

Booklist, November 15, 1999, Lauren Peterson, review of *The Lizard Man of Crabtree County,* p. 636; November 1, 2003, Connie Fletcher, review of *A Fairy in a Dairy,* p. 505; November 1, 2004, Ilene Cooper, review of *Smarter than Squirrels,* p. 493; November 15, 2005, Shelle Rosenfeld, review of *On the Road,* p. 52; November 15, 2008, Gillian Engberg, review of *Bad to the Bone,* p. 40.

Horn Book, November-December, 2005, Betty Carter, review of *On the Road,* p. 723.

Kirkus Reviews, September 1, 1999, review of *The Lizard Man of Crabtree County,* p. 1420; August 15, 2001, review of *Jack Quack,* p. 1219; September 15, 2003, review of *A Fairy in a Dairy,* p. 1179; August 1, 2004, review of *Smarter than Squirrels,* p. 747; September 15, 2005, review of *On the Road,* p. 1032; October 15, 2008, review of *Bad to the Bone.*

Publishers Weekly, December 15, 2003, review of *A Fairy in a Dairy,* p. 72; July 27, 2009, review of *Mother Osprey: Nursery Rhymes for Buoys and Gulls,* p. 61.

School Library Journal, October, 1999, Judith Constantinides, review of *The Lizard Man of Crabtree County,* p. 121; November, 2001, Be Astengo, review of *Jack Quack,* p. 132; November, 2003, Leslie Barban, review of *A Fairy in a Dairy,* p. 110; November, 2004, Debbie Whitbeck, review of *Smarter than Squirrels,* p. 113; March, 2006, Blair Christolon, review of *On the Road,* p. 199; January, 2009, Carrie Rogers-Whitehead, review of *Bad to the Bone,* p. 82; September, 2009, Frances E. Millhouser, review of *Mother Osprey,* p. 145.

ONLINE

Lucy Nolan Home Page, http://www.lucynolanbooks.com (March 1, 2010).

School Library Journal Online, http://www.schoollibrary journal.com/ (April 9, 2008), Joan Oleck, interview with Nolan.

TheState Online http://www.thestate.com/ (September 24, 2009), Carolyn Click, "A-rhyming We Will Go: Local Author Pens Eighth Children's Book."

* * *

NOVGORODOFF, Danica 1980-

Personal

Born 1980, in Chicago, IL. *Education:* Yale University, B.A. (art; with distinction, magna cum laude), 2002. *Hobbies and other interests:* Photography.

Addresses

Home—Brooklyn, NY. *E-mail*—danica.novgorodoff@ aya.yale.edu.

Career

Writer, designer, and creator of graphic novels. Teacher in art and English in schools in Ecuador, 2002; worked variously as a gallery associate and photographer's assistant; freelance writer, beginning 2004; First Second Books, New York, NY, book designer, 2005—. *Exhibitions:* Work included in exhibitions at Hite Gallery, University of Louisville, Louisville, KY, 2005; Nucleus Gallery, Los Angeles, CA, 2005; New York Institute of Technology, 2006; Doma Café and Gallery, New York, NY, 2008; and Charmingwall Gallery, New York, NY, 2009.

Member

Phi Beta Kappa.

Awards, Honors

Isotope Award for Excellence in Mini-Comics, 2006; Will Eisner Comic Industry Award for Best Single Issue nomination, 2007.

Writings

SELF-ILLUSTRATED GRAPHIC NOVELS

Circus Song, 2005.
A Late Freeze, 2006.
Slow Storm, First Second Books (New York, NY), 2008.
(With James Ponsoldt and Benjamin Percy) *Refresh, Refresh,* First Second Books (New York, NY), 2009.

Work included in *The Girl's Guide to Guy's Stuff,* 2007; and *Cabinet of Curiosities,* Candlewick Press (New York, NY), 2009.

Sidelights

Danica Novgorodoff is a designer, writer, and graphic novelist whose works include *Slow Storm* and *Refresh Refresh.* A graduate of Yale University, she spent the following year in Ecuador on a travel and research fellowship before returning to the United States to pursue her career in the arts. In 2005 Novgorodoff joined the staff of First Second Books, a New York City publisher of graphic novels and comics, as a book designer, and First Second has published her first two book-length works. Commenting that it is rare for an author to effectively illustrate his or her own works, Jesse Karp maintained in *Booklist* that "Novgorodoff has achieved a rare level of unification of story and art" in her work.

In the graphic novel *Slow Storm* Novgorodoff tells the story of Ursa Crain, a Kentucky firefighter who arrives at a burning stable and attempts to put out the fire with

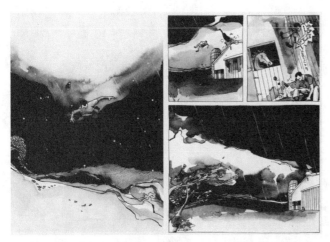

Danica Novgorodoff's spare story and evocative art pair dramatically in her graphic novel **Slow Storm.** (Copyright © 2008 by Danica Novgorodoff. All rights reserved. Reproduced by permission.)

the help of her hyper-critical brother, Grim. While fighting the fire, the distraught and unhappy Ursa becomes frustrated by the criticism of Grim and the other firefighters. She turns on Grim and attempts to trap him in the barn, but he manages to escape. In the fire's aftermath, blame for the incident is attributed to Rafi Sifuentes, a Mexican illegal immigrant who had been living in the barn's hayloft while working on the farm. Through the parallel stories of the two protagonists, *Slow Storm* crystallizes their conflicting perspectives.

In *Slow Storm* Novgorodoff uses what *School Library Journal* contributor Benjamin Russell described as "magical-realism" to evoke the emotions underlying these conflicts, producing "a curious, open-ended, and emotional reading experience." Her loosely drawn images, tinted with water color and pastels, reflect both "the turbulence of the characters' internal lives and the sweeping gray wall of the storm that bears down on them," according to *Newsarama.com* reviewer Michael C. Lorah. "*Slow Storm* has the feel of an atmospheric short film," wrote John Hogan in a *Bookreporter.com* review, the critic citing the artist's "ability to almost constantly convey motion and movement" and willingness to experiment with line of sight and perspective. Although Lorah found the interactions between Rafi and Ursa to be somewhat forced, he concluded his review of *Slow Storm* by noting that Novgorodoff's "excellent grasp of dialogue works to establish the characters' voices as believable, and her atmospheric artwork and attention to the story's setting make for an immersing reading experience."

Written with James Ponsoldt and Benjamin Percy, *Refresh, Refresh* also features Novgorodoff's effective visual images. In this graphic novel, readers meet Cody, Gordon, and Josh, three high-school seniors living in a small town in Oregon. The teens miss their fathers, who are fighting in Iraq, and they channel their fears and adolescent frustrations into fighting amongst themselves to prove their manhood. Three separate narratives weave through the story, capturing the worries of each teen as he attempts to fill the shoes of his missing father at home while also exposing the group dynamic that spirals into ever-increasing violence. Reviewing *Refresh, Refresh* in *Kirkus Reviews,* a critic deemed the "thoughtful" graphic novel both "disturbing and intense." "Novgorodoff's artfully misshapen lines and grotesque facial expressions capture the uneasy quality of her story," observed *Booklist* critic Ian Chipman, and Laura Amos concluded in *School Library Journal* that the author/artist's "striking" and "realistic" images in *Refresh, Refresh* "reflect the intense emotions that dominate this gripping and moving tale."

Biographical and Critical Sources

PERIODICALS

Booklist, August 1, 2008, Jesse Karp, review of *Slow Storm,* p. 62; September 15, 2009, Ian Chipman, review of *Refresh, Refresh,* p. 51.

Kirkus Reviews, September 15, 2009, review of *Refresh, Refresh.*

School Library Journal, September, 2008, Benjamin Russell, review of *Slow Storm,* p. 218; November, 2009, Laura Amos, review of *Refresh, Refresh.*

Voice of Youth Advocates, August, 2008, Steven Kral, review of *Slow Storm,* p. 248; April 1, 2009, review of *Refresh, Refresh.*

ONLINE

Bookreporter.com http://www.bookreporter.com/ (April 15, 2010), John Hogan, review of *Slow Storm.*

Danica Novgorodoff Home Page, http://www.danica novgorodoff.com (April 20, 2010).

Newsarama.com, http://www.newsarama.com/ (September 8, 2008), Michale C. Lorah, review of *Slow Storm.*

Oregonian Online, http://blog/oregonlive.com/ (September 3, 2008), Steve Duin, review of *Slow Storm.**

O-P

OSBORN, Jacob 1981(?)-

Personal

Born c. 1981, in NJ. *Education:* University of Wisconsin—Madison.

Addresses

Home—Los Angeles, CA.

Career

Writer. Formerly worked as a sales clerk, waiter, and caterer.

Awards, Honors

(With Amy Belason) Books for the Teen Age citation, New York Public Library, 2009, for *Jenny Green's Killer Junior Year.*

Writings

(With Amy Belasen) *Jenny Green's Killer Junior Year,* Simon Pulse (New York, NY), 2008.

Sidelights

When Jacob Osborn met Amy Belasen at a restaurant, little did he realize that the meeting would result in a writing collaboration and the ultimate publication of his first novel, *Jenny Green's Killer Junior Year.* During their initial conversation, Belasen recalled several miserable dating experiences and described her intention of writing a story in which the heroine kills off all her ex-boyfriends. Ultimately, the two teamed up to fulfill Belasen's goal, bringing her revenge fantasies to fictional life in an over-the-top story for teens that Robyn Zaneski dubbed "completely twisted" in her review of the novel for *School Library Journal.*

Going to boarding school in the French-speaking Canadian city of Montreal turns out to be less exciting than New Yorker Jenny Green thought it would be, especially after her hunky boyfriend Josh Beck turns into a creep. When she accidentally kills Josh and gets away with it, Jenny finds that there are plenty of other young men who deserve to be punished for their romantic crimes. With its certifiably crazy main character, graphic descriptions, and dark humor, *Jenny Green's Killer Junior Year* has "the potential to cross over beyond a young adult audience," according to *Maclean's* reviewer Jordan Timm, the critic comparing the book to the popular television programs *Gossip Girl* and *The Hills.* Readers with a taste for over-the-top stories "will find themselves laughing out loud at [Jenny's] crazy exploits," Zaneski added in her review of the novel, while Timm dubbed the title character in *Jenny Green's Killer Junior Year* "a proto-feminist anti-hero starring in a slasher novel for young adults."

Biographical and Critical Sources

PERIODICALS

Maclean's, Jordan Timm, review of *Jenny Green's Killer Junior Year,* p. 124.
School Library Journal, January, 2009, Robyn Zaneski, review of *Jenny Green's Killer Junior Year,* p. 99.

ONLINE

Slayground Web log, http://slayground.livejournal.com/ (October 19, 2008), interview with Amy Belasen and Osborn.*

*   *   *

OSBORNE, Linda Barrett 1949-

Personal

Born February 1, 1949, in New York, NY; daughter of James (in systems management) and Josephine Barrett;

married Robert Osborne (an architect), September 23, 1972. *Education:* Swarthmore College, B.A. (with honors), 1971. *Hobbies and other interests:* Dance, theatre, jogging, embroidery, travel (Europe and Mexico).

Addresses

Home—Houston, TX.

Career

Author, editor, and educator. Teacher in Navajo demonstration school in Chinle, AZ, 1971; Franklin Mint, Franklin Center, PA, and Franklin Mint International, London, England, researcher and writer, 1972-74; Museum of Fine Arts, Houston, TX, assistant librarian, 1975-76; R. Douglass Associates, editor and writer, beginning 1976; Library of Congress, senior writer and editor. Has conducted writing workshops. Member, Houston Rape Crisis Coalition, 1974-75.

Member

Associated Authors of Children's Literature (Houston, TX).

Awards, Honors

Writers-in-the-Schools grant from Texas Commission on the Arts and Humanities, 1976-77.

Writings

Song of the Harp: Old Welsh Folktales, Christopher Davies, 1975.

Wide Angle, Harcourt (New York, NY), 1983.

Oh, Freedom!: Kids Talk about the Civil Rights Movement with the People Who Made It Happen, Knopf (New York, NY), 1997.

(With Alan Bisbort) *The Nation's Library: The Library of Congress, Washington, DC*, Library of Congress (Washington, DC), 2000.

Women of the Civil Rights Movement, Pomegranate (San Francisco, CA), 2006.

The Library of Congress World War II Companion, Simon & Schuster (New York, NY), 2007.

Traveling the Freedom Road: From Slavery and the Civil War through Reconstruction, Abrams Books for Young Readers (New York, NY), 2009.

Contributor of articles and reviews to magazines and newspapers, including *New York Times* and *Washington Post*.

Sidelights

"I am interested in writing children's books which reflect my experiences in specific, unusual settings, such as a small Welsh town or the Navajo reservation in northeast Arizona, but which also focus on common feelings, perceptions and responses," noted Linda Barrett Osborne. "Background and research are important; I wrote *Song of the Harp: Old Welsh Folktales . . .* while living in Wales."

Biographical and Critical Sources

PERIODICALS

Booklist, April 1, 1997, Hazel Rochman, review of *Oh, Freedom!: Kids Talk about the Civil Rights Movement with the People Who Made It Happen*, p. 1328; February 1, 2009, Gillian Engberg, review of *Traveling the Freedom Road: From Slavery and the Civil War through Reconstruction*, p. 49.

Kirkus Reviews, January 15, 2009, review of *Traveling the Freedom Road*.

Library Journal, February 1, 2001, Thomas F. O'Connor, review of *The Nation's Library: The Library of Congress, Washington, DC*, p. 130.

School Library Journal, June, 1997, Marilyn Heath, review of *Oh, Freedom!*, p. 139; May, 2009, Margaret Auguste, review of *Traveling the Freedom Road*, p. 126.*

*   *   *

PARKER, Tom S.

Personal

Born in CA; children: one daughter. *Education:* California State University, Northridge, B.A. (communications), M.A. (communications). *Hobbies and other interests:* Golf, baseball, hiking, reader, going to the movies.

Addresses

Home—Topanga, CA.

Career

Screenwriter and novelist. Worked variously as a camp counselor, cannery worker, drugstore clerk, and copper miner; formerly worked in advertising.

Writings

FOR CHILDREN

(With James Jennewein) *RuneWarriors*, Laura Geringer Books (New York, NY), 2008.

(With James Jennewein) *Sword of Doom*, HarperCollins (New York, NY), 2010.

OTHER

(With Jim Jennewein) *Stay Tuned* (screenplay), Warner Bros., 1992.

(With James Jennewein and Steven E. De Souza) *The Flintstones* (screenplay), 1993.

Author of additional screenplays, with Jennewein, including: *Getting Even with Dad,* 1994, *Richie Rich,* 1994, and *Major League II,* 1994.

Adaptations

The Flintstones was adapted into several books for children. *RuneWarriors* was adapted as an audiobook, Recorded Books, 2009.

Sidelights

For SIDELIGHTS, see entry on James Jennewein, elsewhere in this volume.

Biographical and Critical Sources

PERIODICALS

Kirkus Reviews, September 15, 2008, review of *RuneWarriors.*
Kliatt, September, 2008, Deirdre Root, review of *RuneWarriors,* p. 13.
School Library Journal, December, 2008, Saleena L. Davidson, review of *RuneWarriors,* p. 126.
Voice of Youth Advocates, December, 2008, Domina Daughtrey, review of *RuneWarriors,* p. 452.

ONLINE

RuneWarriors Web site, http://www.runewarriors.net (April 30, 2010).*

* * *

PAVER, Michelle 1960-

Personal

Born 1960, in Nyasaland (now Malawi); daughter of a publisher and a teacher; immigrated to England, 1963. *Education:* Oxford University, degree (biochemistry; with first-class honors).

Addresses

Home—Wimbledon, England.

Career

Writer. Former attorney specializing in patent litigation, became partner; freelance writer, beginning c. 1997.

Member

U.K. Wolf Conservation Trust.

Awards, Honors

Fresh Talent award, W.H. Smith, for *Without Charity;* Parker Pen Romantic Novel of the Year shortlist, 2002, for *A Place in the Hills;* Gold Award, Parents' Choice List, 2005, for *Wolf Brother.*

Writings

NOVELS; FOR ADULTS

Without Charity, Corgi (London, England), 2000.
A Place in the Hills, Corgi (London, England), 2001.

"DAUGHTERS OF EDEN" NOVEL SERIES; FOR ADULTS

The Shadow Catcher, Corgi (London, England), 2002.
Fever Hill, Bantam (London, England), 2004.
The Serpent's Tooth, Bantam (London, England), 2005.

"CHRONICLES OF ANCIENT DARKNESS" NOVEL SERIES; FOR YOUNG READERS

Wolf Brother, illustrated by Geoff Taylor, HarperCollins (New York, NY), 2004.
Spirit Walker, illustrated by Geoff Taylor, Katherine Tegen Books (New York, NY), 2006.
Soul-Eater, illustrated by Geoff Taylor, Katherine Tegen Books (New York, NY), 2006.
Outcast, illustrated by Geoff Taylor, Orion Children's Books (London, England), 2007, Katherine Tegen Books (New York, NY), 2008.
Oath Breaker, illustrated by Geoff Taylor, Orion Children's Books (London, England), 2008, Katherine Tegen Books (New York, NY), 2009.
Ghost Hunter, illustrated by Geoff Taylor, Orion Children's Books (London, England), 2009, Katherine Tegen Books (New York, NY), 2010.

Author's books have been translated into several languages, including French, German, Japanese, and Russian.

Adaptations

The "Chronicles of Ancient Darkness" books were adapted for audio, narrated by Ian McKellan, HarperCollins, beginning 2005. Ridley Scott optioned the same series for film, c. 2007.

Sidelights

A former attorney, Michelle Paver writes evocative fiction that is inspired by her love of myth, folklore, and history. Jamaica is the setting of her "Daughters of Eden" novels for adults, while *A Place in the Hills* takes place in the Pyrenees Mountains. Geared for teen readers, Paver's six-volume "Chronicles of Ancient Darkness" series includes the novels *Wolf Brother, Spirit*

Walker, Soul-Eater, and *Ghost Hunter* and transports readers back to northeastern Europe after the end of the last Ice Age. "For parents and grandparents searching for something to replace Harry Potter, Michelle Paver's Chronicles of Ancient Darkness have been a godsend," exclaimed Amanda Craig in her review of *Ghost Hunter* in the London *Times.* In a series that Craig characterized as "thrilling, beautifully written, strongly characterised and featuring a magical prehistoric world," Paver presents young readers with a realistic view of an age that is usually portrayed as either simplistic or brutal, an age "as complex and sophisticated as our own," as the critic added.

Immigrating with her family from her birthplace—Nyasaland in southeast Africa—as a young child, Paver was raised in London, England, and eventually earned an honors degree in biochemistry at Oxford University. She knew by her senior year that she did not want to make science her career, however: she had discovered her passion for writing and wanted a job that allowed her the time to write. Casting about for a new career, Paver decided upon the law, and she worked for some time as a lawyer specializing in science-related patent litigation. Law gave her little time for writing, however, and the death of her father reminded Paver that life is too short to sacrifice the things you truly love. After taking a year off to write and travel, she completed her first novel, *Without Charity,* and when the novel found a publisher she gave up the law and focused on writing full time. Paver established herself as an author of adult fiction with her "Daughters of Eden" novels before turning to younger readers in the "Chronicles of Ancient Darkness" books.

"I got the inspiration for the 'Chronicles of Ancient Darkness' one afternoon at home," Paver recalled in a discussion about the series with Dirk Vander Ploeg for *PSI Talk* online. "I was sitting in my garden and the glimmer of an idea suddenly came to me and in a few hours I had mapped out the entire series of six books!" The six-volume saga is set in northeastern Europe some 6,000 years ago, following the last Ice Age. In the story's Stone-Age setting Man does not yet engage in agriculture: instead humans live as hunter-gatherers. To research her story, Paver traveled to remote areas in Finland, sometimes living outdoors in primitive conditions. Her dedication to researching the experiences of her characters makes her work vivid and compelling. "There's no message in these books at all," Paver explained to Stephen Moss in an interview for the London *Guardian,* "but regarding hunter-gatherers as the Flintstones is something I hope I will have changed a little bit. Dramatic reconstructions of the stone age on TV usually have them running around with awful, rough clothes flapping open in sub-zero temperatures, and they are all unshaven, with messy hair. I don't think it was like that because they wouldn't have survived—Eskimos and Inuit have very carefully engineered and highly sophisticated clothes. Indigenous people all over the world take quite a lot of trouble with their hair and their clothes."

Series opener *Wolf Brother* was inspired by Paver's encounter with a bear while she was visiting Southern California. In the novel a boy named Torak sees his father fatally attacked by a bear that is possessed by a mage. Torak's dying father commands him to journey to the Mountain of the World Spirit, the only force that will be able to defeat the demon bear and thus avenge the man's death. Joined on his quest by Wolf Brother, an orphaned wolf pup that is also his spirit guide, and a girl of the Raven clan named Renn, Torak comes to realize that he is the Listener, a person destined to hold back the evil Shadow from overrunning the land. He also learns that six evil mages, called Soul Eaters, are intent upon his demise.

Booklist reviewer Sally Estes described *Wolf Brother* as "fantasy adventure on a grand scale," and also praised Paver's characterizations and well-realized wilderness setting. In *Kliatt* Michele Winship observed that the author "has done her research and done it well," giving her tale a firm archaeological foundation with insights into the lives of hunter-gatherer societies such as the Inuits, many African tribes, and the Native Americans. Karen T. Bilton noted in *School Library Journal* that the novel presents spirituality and mysticism in an "intriguing and believable" way that is unusual in a children's book. In *Publishers Weekly* a critic described *Wolf Brother* as "part riveting nature story, part rite of passage saga," adding that the complex plot "remains involving thanks to Paver's unusual setting and eccentric characters."

Paver's "Chronicles of Ancient Darkness" series continues in *Spirit Walker.* Since Wolf Brother left to spend time with a pack of mountain wolves, Torak has joined the forest-dwelling Raven clan. When a fatal sickness soon begins to spread among all the forest clans, orak realizes that his unique and growing powers make him the only one able to discover a cure that will save the frightened clansmen. After several adventures, the boy is captured by three young members of the Seal clan and brought before the clan's mage, Tenris, on the mysterious Seal islands. There Torak is reunited with Renn and Wolf and the three follow Tenris's directions through the coastal region in search of a cure for the forest sickness. Along the way, Tenris learns to harness his shapeshifting skills and also gains understanding of why the Soul Eaters see him as a threat. Paver based *Spirit Walker* on "the traditions of the Sami and Inuit peoples," observed Winship, and her story gains contemporary relevance by "realistically depicting tensions between clans separated by time and geography." A *Kirkus Reviews* writer noted that Paver's "vivid descriptions" of clan culture "enrich her complex tale without impeding its quick pace." In *School Library Journal* Mara Alpert described the second "Chronicles of Ancient Darkness" novel as an "eerie, fast-paced '*Outbreak* meets *X-Files*' sequel" and predicted that series fans "will eagerly await the next installment."

Torak, Renn, and Wolf turn to the north in *Soul Eater,* accepting the young man's destiny to confront the pow-

erful Soul Eaters, who are marshaling disease and trans-forming lost children into a demon army in order to control the forests. Danger constantly threatens, and soon Wolf is captured by the evil mages. After trans-forming himself into a raven, Torak tracks Wolf and his captors, the Soul Eaters, who are heading to the frigid north for an evil purpose. Going in pursuit, the two teens fight both the harsh terrain and the terrible cold, in a "stirring and thrilling" novel that *School Library Journal* critic Walter Minkel predicted will keep "read-ers . . . on the edge of their chairs." "Paver's careful research and attention to detail [in *Soul Eater*] create the vivid ice-bound world of the tribes of the far north," noted Winship, and the underground lair that is home to the sinister mages "is a stunning contrast to the world above."

As readers reunite with Torak in *Outcast,* the teen is marked by the dreaded Soul Eaters, and when he re-turns to his clan he is feared and cast out into the for-est. Separated from loyal friends Wolf and Renn and wandering in the marshlands around Lake Axehead, Torak now must wrestle with intense loneliness, feel-ings of betrayal, and worries over the rightness of his quest. Members of the Otter Clan now hunt him, and while he evades his real-life pursuers Torak finds that his greatest threat is the tortures of his own soul and the sapping of his instinct for physical survival. "The viv-idly interwoven natural and spiritual settings that have distinguished this series emerge in long stretches seen from the point-of-view of Wolf," observed a *Kirkus Re-views* writer in discussing the fourth part of the "Chronicles of Ancient Darkness." Paver's "writing is immediately accessible and absorbing," noted S.F. Said in the London *Guardian,* reviewing *Outcast.* "She pulls off a tricky balancing act, providing plenty of back-story for newcomers, but adroitly anchoring it in drama."

Surviving the soul-sickness inflicted on him by an evil mage, Torak—now age fifteen—regains his internal compass and vows to avenge the death of a close friend of the Seal clan in *Oath Breaker.* The killer, the dreaded Oak mage, has also stolen the powerful fire opal, and when Torak and Renn follow the evil wizard to the Deep Forest they discover a place where humans have reverted to savages and a growing evil is about to be unleashed. Here, Torak finally learns why he is the Spirit Walker and discovers the true cost of revenge. In *Booklist* Ilene Cooper recommended *Oath Breaker* for mixing "heart-stopping action . . . with metaphysical moments," and Genevieve Gallagher predicted in *School Library Journal* that "fans of the series will not be dis-appointed." Noting that Paver's "writing is richly sen-sual," a London *Independent* contributor added that *Oath Breaker* "outclasses *Call of the Wild* and *The Jungle Book* in the pace of its plot, its sympathetically imagined characters, and its details of doings."

Paver concludes her "Chronicles of Ancient Darkness" series with *Ghost Hunter,* as Torak confronts the most powerful Soul Eater of all. The chill of Souls' Night has almost arrived, and on that night the last Soul Eater, the powerful Eagle Owl mage, plans to wrest control of all the forests. Hoping to stop this final evil, Torak trav-els to the Mountain of Ghosts, where a host of demons awaits. Noting the sensitivity of Paver's depiction of Wolf, a London *Independent* critic also commented on the novel's popularity among teens. "Coming of age en-tails learning," the critic added, "and Paver introduces thoroughly researched wilderness lore: making weapons and canoes; building shelters from storms and floods, using plants to heal wounds."

In an interview on her home page, Paver discussed the life of a writer. It is "marginalized, solitary, sometimes worryingly lonely, but above all, not in the slightest bit grown-up," she explained. "I spend my entire time day-dreaming, and getting paid for it. That's why I love it!"

Biographical and Critical Sources

PERIODICALS

Booklist, March 1, 2005, Sally Estes, review of *Wolf Brother,* p. 1185; April 1, 2009, Ilene Cooper, review of *Oath Breaker,* p. 32.

Guardian (London, England), September 6, 2007, Stephen Moss, interview with Paver, p. 14; October 27, 2007, S.F. Said, review of *Outcast,* p. 20.

Independent (London, England), September 15, 2008, re-view of *Oath Breaker,* p. 20; September 22, 2009, re-view of *Ghost Hunter,* p. 16.

Kirkus Reviews, January 15, 2005, review of *Wolf Brother,* p. 124; January 15, 2006, review of *Spirit Walker,* p. 88; January 15, 2007, review of *Soul Eater,* p. 79; May 1, 2008, review of *Outcast.*

Kliatt, March, 2005, Michele Winship, review of *Wolf Brother,* p. 15; January, 2006, Michele Winship, re-view of *Spirit Walker,* p. 10; March, 2007, Michele Winship, review of *Soul Eater,* p. 17.

MBR Bookwatch, May, 2005, Vicki Arkoff, review of *Wolf Brother.*

Publishers Weekly, January 10, 2005, review of *Wolf Brother,* p. 57.

School Library Journal, February, 2005, Karen T. Bilton, review of *Wolf Brother,* p. 140; June, 2006, Mara Alp-ert, review of *Spirit Walker,* p. 164; May, 2007, Walter Minkel, review of *Soul Eater,* p. 140; August, 2009, Genevieve Gallagher, review of *Oath Breaker,* p. 112.

Times (London, England), August 26, 2006, Amanda Craig, interview with Paver, p. 15; September 8, 2007, Amanda Craig, review of *Outcast,* p. 15; August 22, 2009, Amanda Craig, review of *Ghost Hunter,* p. 12.

ONLINE

Michelle Paver Home Page, http://www.michellepaver.com (April 25, 2010).

PSI Talk Web site, http://www.psitalk.com/ (September 1, 2005), Dirk Vander Ploeg, interview with Paver.*

*　　　*　　　*

PETERSON, Mary

Personal
Female.

Addresses
Agent—Jennifer Jaeger, Andrea Brown Literary Agency, jennifer@andreabrownlit.com. *E-mail*—mary@mary-peterson.com.

Career
Illustrator.

Awards, Honors
Early Childhood News Directors' Choice designation, 2007, for *Wiggle and Waggle* by Caroline Arnold.

Illustrator
Robert Zaugh, *Teddy Bear Goes to the Moon,* Dillingham (Los Angeles, CA), 1998.
Larry Dane Brimner, *Cat on Wheels,* Boyds Mills Press (Honesdale, PA), 2000.
Caroline Arnold, *Wiggle and Waggle,* Charlesbridge (Watertown, MA), 2007.
Mike Madison, *No Time to Nap,* Heyday Books (Berkeley, CA), 2007.

Biographical and Critical Sources

PERIODICALS

Booklist, December 1, 2000, Susan Dove Lempke, review of *Cat on Wheels,* p. 717; July 1, 2007, review of *Wiggle and Waggle,* p. 67.
Kirkus Reviews, June 1, 2007, review of *Wiggle and Waggle.*
Publishers Weekly, July 9, 2007, review of *Wiggle and Waggle,* p. 53.
School Library Journal, November, 2000, Olga R. Barnes, review of *Cat on Wheels,* p. 110; November, 2007, Elaine Lesh Morgan, review of *Wiggle and Waggle,* p. 184.

ONLINE

Mary Peterson Home Page, http://www.marypeterson.typepad.com (April 10, 2008).*

*　　　*　　　*

PHELAN, Matt 1970-

Personal
Born 1970, in PA. *Education:* Temple University, degree (film and theatre).

Addresses
Home—Philadelphia, PA. *Agent*—Rebecca Sherman, Writers House, 21 W. 26th St., New York, NY 10010. *E-mail*—matt@mattphelan.com.

Career
Children's book illustrator, beginning 2004.

Awards, Honors
Scott O'Dell Award, 2001, for *The Storm in the Barn.*

Writings

SELF-ILLUSTRATED

The Storm in the Barn, Candlewick Press (Somerville, MA), 2009.

ILLUSTRATOR

Betty G. Birney, *The Seven Wonders of Sassafras Springs,* Atheneum Books for Young Readers (New York, NY), 2005.
Jacqui Robbins, *The New Girl and Me,* Atheneum Books for Young Readers (New York, NY), 2006.
Liz Wu, *Rosa Farm: A Barnyard Tale,* Alfred A. Knopf (New York, NY), 2006.
Susan Patron, *The Higher Power of Lucky,* Atheneum Books for Young Readers (New York, NY), 2006.
Lorijo Metz, *Floridius Bloom and the Planet of Gloom,* Dial Books for Young Readers (New York, NY), 2007.
Sonia Manzano, *A Box Full of Kittens,* Atheneum Books for Young Readers (New York, NY), 2007.
Alice Schertle, *Very Hairy Bear,* Harcourt (Orlando, FL), 2007.
Eileen Spinelli, *Where I Live,* Dial Books for Young Readers (New York, NY), 2007.
Ann Stott, *Always,* Candlewick Press (Cambridge, MA), 2008.
Anne Rockwell, *Big George: How a Shy Boy Became President Washington,* Harcourt (Orlando, FL), 2009.
Susan Patron, *Lucky Breaks,* Atheneum Books for Young Readers (New York, NY), 2009.
Jacqui Robbins, *Two of a Kind,* Atheneum Books for Young Readers (New York, NY), 2009.
Jeanne Birdsall, *Flora's Very Windy Day,* Clarion Books (Boston, MA), 2010.
Ann Mazer and Ellen Potter, *Spilling Ink: A Young Writer's Handbook,* Roaring Brook Press (New York, NY), 2010.

Sidelights
Matt Phelan creates artwork that provides a colorful backdrop for stories by a number of well-known writers, among them Alice Shertle, Susan Patron, Eileen Spinelli, Ann Stott, and Sonia Manzano. His first illus-

tration project, Betty G. Birney's middle-grade novel *The Seven Wonders of Sassafras Springs,* prompted a *Publishers Weekly* critic to note Phelan's ability "to pique readers' interest," and in *Booklist* Ilene Cooper stated that "the most winning element" in Schertle's *Very Hairy Bear* is Phelan's depiction of the "big as a boulder" title character.

Reviewing Manzano's *A Box Full of Kittens,* a story about a 1950s Bronx neighborhood that is told by the actress familiar to children through her role as *Sesame Street*'s "Maria", a *Publishers Weekly* contributor noted that "Phelan's sunny and buoyant pencil-and-watercolor compositions capture the rhythms and period details of a bustling, friendly community."

Two of a Kind, one of two collaborations between Phelan and Jacqui Robbins, focuses on a young girl who must chose between her friendship with Julisa and the chance to join an exclusive clique of popular but sometimes bullying schoolmates. "Phelan's soft watercolor illustrations also add a gentle touch" to the tale, asserted *Horn Book* contributor Betty Carter, the critic adding that his creative use of perspective enhances the story's drama and "will strike readers most powerfully." The "straightforward and familiar situation" between long-time best friends "is made even clearer by Phelan's expressive watercolor illustrations," in the opinion of a *Kirkus Reviews* writer.

"Phelan's charming pencil drawings are a perfect complement to this heartfelt tale," concluded Marilyn Taniguchi in a *School Library Journal* review of Spinelli's engaging verse novel *Where I Live*. His watercolor-tinted pencil images for Stott's picture book *Always*

Matt Phelan teams up with author Ann Stott to create the toddler-themed picture book **Always.** (Illustration copyright © 2008 Matt Phelan. All rights reserved. Reproduced by permission of Candlewick Press.)

"bring this quiet text to exuberant life," noted Jane Marino in *School Library Journal*, while a *Kirkus Reviews* contributor maintained that Phelan's illustrations for the book "adeptly convey the gleeful mischief that is part and parcel of childhood."

Anne Rockwell's *Big George: How a Shy Boy Became President Washington* introduces young children to the first president of the United States, revealing General George Washington as a real person with both quirks and strengths. Phelan's pencil and gouache (opaque water color) illustrations for this picture-book biography "impart the sense of vivid memories being conjured up, of history being re-lived in all its urgency and telling details," according to a *Publishers Weekly* contributor. In *Booklist* Thom Barthelmess credited the artist's "bold, dynamic paintings" for "captur[ing] . . . the nuances" of Rockwell's profile of the first U.S. president.

In addition to his work as an illustrator, Phelan has also created artwork for his own story, the middle-grade graphic novel *The Storm in the Barn*, winner of the 2010 Scott O'Dell Award for Historical Fiction. The tale is set during the Dust Bowl of the 1930s, a time when many of the grain-growing regions of the central United States suffered from a terrible drought. Living on a Kansas farm and not remembering a time when the land was not parched and lifeless, and there was not widespread hunger and sickness, eleven-year-old Jack Clark senses his father's despair. Fortunately, the boy finds hope in the stories told by his mother, older sister, and family friends, stories that tell of "the time when the land was a fertile 'paradise,'" according to Lisa Goldstein in her *School Library Journal* review of the book. Noting Phelan's use of "simple, direct language," Goldstein praised *The Storm in the Barn* as "accessible and fascinating," and a *Kirkus Reviews* critic described Phelan's "pencil-[ink-]and-watercolor panels" as "cinematically framed." Also reviewing the work, Jesse Karp concluded in *Booklist* that *The Storm in the Barn* is a "superb graphic-novel evocation of childhood's yearning and triumphs."

"Illustrating books is an endlessly fascinating and rewarding vocation," Phelan told *SATA*. "Whether I am illustrating another author's story or creating pictures for a book of my own, I try serve the story to the best of my ability and hopefully add a dimension that will connect with readers. Illustration is a lifelong pursuit. . . there is always more to learn."

Biographical and Critical Sources

PERIODICALS

Booklist, September 1, 2005, Cindy Dobrez, review of *The Seven Wonders of Sassafras Springs*, p. 130; July 1, 2006, Jennifer Mattson, review of *The New Girl . . . and Me*, p. 57; May 1, 2007, Connie Fletcher, review

Phelan's illustration projects include creating the art for Anne Rockwell's **Big George: How a Shy Boy Became President Washington.** (Illustration copyright © 2009 by Matt Phelan. All rights reserved. Reproduced by permission of Harcourt.)

of *A Box Full of Kittens*, p. 99; October 1, 2007, Ilene Cooper, review of *Very Hairy Bear*, p. 67; January 1, 2009, Daniel Kraus, review of *Lucky Breaks*, p. 82, and Thom Barthelmess, review of *Big George: How a Shy Boy Became President Washington*, p. 86; August 1, 2009, Jesse Karp, review of *The Storm in the Barn*, p. 68.

Horn Book, March-April, 2009, Kathleen Isaacs, review of *Big George*, p. 214; September-October, 2009, Betty Carter, review of *Two of a Kind*, p. 545.

Kirkus Reviews, March 15, 2007, review of *Floridius Bloom and the Planet of Gloom;* May 15, 2007, reviews of *Where I Live* and *A Box Full of Kittens;* July 15, 2008, review of *Always;* June 1, 2009, review of *Two of a Kind;* July 15, 2009, review of *The Storm in the Barn*.

New York Times Book Review, November, 8, 2009, Jessica Bruder, review of *The Storm in the Barn*, p. 18.

Publishers Weekly, August 8, 2005, review of *The Seven Wonders of Sassafras Springs*, p. 234; June 25, 2007, review of *A Box Full of Kittens*, p. 58; January 5, 2009, review of *Big George*, p. 50; January 19, 2009, review of *Lucky Breaks*, p. 60.

School Library Journal, August, 2005, Connie Tyrrell Burns, review of *The Seven Wonders of Sassafras Springs*, p. 121; December, 2006, Adrienne Furness,

review of *The Higher Power of Lucky,* p. 152; January, 2007, Melissa Christy Buron, review of *Rosa Farm,* p. 111; April, 2007, Catherine Callegari, review of *Floridius Bloom and the Planet of Gloom,* p. 113; August, 2007, Shelley B. Sutherland, review of *A Box Full of Kittens,* p. 84; July, 2007, Marilyn Taniguchi, review of *Where I Live,* p. 85; December, 2007, Wendy Lukehart, review of *Very Hairy Bear,* p. 99; October, 2008, Jane Marino, review of *Always,* p. 125; August, 2009, Maryann H. Owen, review of *Two of a Kind,* p. 83; September, 2009, Lisa Goldstein, review of *The Storm in the Barn,* p. 190.

ONLINE

Matt Phelan Home Page, http://www.mattphelan.com (April 25, 2010).

R

REED, Lynn Rowe

Personal

Born in Garrett, IN. *Education:* Attended Creative Circus (a portfolio school). *Hobbies and other interests:* Running, yoga.

Addresses

Office—1301 Lafayette St., Ste. 207, Fort Wayne, IN 46802. *Agent*—Helen Ravenhill, Helen Ravenhill Represents; hravenhill@earthlink.net. *E-mail*—lynn@lynn rowereed.com.

Career

Painter, sculptor, designer, and author. *Exhibitions:* Works exhibited at National Museum of American Illustration, New York, NY; Kachmann Gallery, Fort Wayne, IN, 2009-10.

Writings

SELF-ILLUSTRATED

Rattlesnake Stew, Farrar, Straus & Giroux (New York, NY), 1990.
Pedro, His Perro, and the Alphabet Sombrero, Hyperion (New York, NY), 1995.
Julius Anteater, Misunderstood, Roaring Brook Press (Brookfield, CT), 2005.
Thelonius Turkey Lives! (on Felicia Ferguson's Farm), Alfred A. Knopf (New York, NY), 2005.
Please Don't Upset P.U. Zorilla!, Alfred A. Knopf (New York, NY), 2006.
Oliver, the Spaceship, and Me, Holiday House (New York, NY), 2009.
Basil's Birds, Marshall Cavendish (New York, NY), 2010.
Color Chaos, Holiday House (New York, NY), 2010.

ILLUSTRATOR

Eileen Ross, *The Halloween Showdown,* Holiday House (New York, NY), 1999.
Robin Pulver, *Punctuation Takes a Vacation,* Holiday House (New York, NY), 2003.
Robin Pulver, *Nouns and Verbs Have a Field Day,* Holiday House (New York, NY), 2006.
Debora Pearson, *Big City Song!,* Holiday House (New York, NY), 2006.
Barbara Kanninen, *A Story with Pictures,* Holiday House (New York, NY), 2007.
Robin Pulver, *Silent Letters Loud and Clear,* Holiday House (New York, NY), 2008.

Also illustrator of *Happy Endings,* Holiday House (New York, NY), 2011.

Sidelights

Lynn Rowe Reed, a painter, sculptor, and graphic designer, has provided the artwork for children's books that include *Punctuation Takes a Vacation* by Robin Pulver and *A Story with Pictures* by Barbara Kanninen. Reed has also garnered praise for creating original self-illustrated titles such as *Julius Anteater, Misunderstood* and *Oliver, the Spaceship, and Me,* which reflect her quirky humor. Praising her abstract art in the *New York Times,* Patricia T. O'Conner stated that "Reed's childlike acrylic paintings perfectly capture the mood of whimsical fantasy."

Reed's first original picture book, *Rattlesnake Stew,* features a Western theme as the stylized artwork and alliterative text finds singing cowboys dancing with grizzly bears in a young boy's day dreams. In *Pedro, His Perro, and the Alphabet Sombrero* another young boy receives an unusually talented dog for his birthday and together the two new friends decorate a giant sombrero with objects representing every letter of the Spanish alphabet. Noting the value of the latter book for both Spanish-speaking students and those starting to learn the lan-

guage, *Booklist* contributor Annie Ayres dubbed *Pedro, His Perro, and the Alphabet Sombrero* "exuberant," and cited the "cubist quality" of Reed's abstract illustrations.

Animal characters take center stage in a pair of the author/illustrator's creations: In *Julius Anteater, Misunderstood* Reed follows a misdirected anteater whose search for lunch leads to an act of heroism, while in *Thelonius Turkey Lives! (on Felicia Ferguson's Farm)* a farm's last remaining turkey resorts to desperate measures in order to avert an tragic fate as Thanksgiving's Day nears. "Anyone with a healthy appetite for nonsense . . . will relish this rhyming madcap adventure," predicted a *Kirkus Reviews* contributor in reviewing *Julius Anteater, Misunderstood,* while in *School Library Journal* Jane Barrer praised Reed's collage and acrylic illustrations for the same book as "bold and witty." The "lighthearted story" in *Thelonius Turkey Lives!* was praised by Roxanne Burg as "a nice holiday treat" in another *School Library Journal* review, while a *Kirkus Reviews* critic noted that Reed's "whimsical illustrations . . . suit this holiday tale perfectly."

A seemingly unemployable skunk lands the perfect job in *Please Don't Upset P.U. Zorilla!,* another of Reed's self-illustrated titles. After stints as a school-bus driver, popcorn seller, and pet-store employee, malodorous P.U. Zorilla finds his true calling while thwarting a rob-

Lynn Rowe Reed's colorful art is on display in the pages of Eileen Ross's picture book The Halloween Showdown. (Illustration copyright © 1999 by Lynn Rowe Reed. Reproduced by permission of Holiday House, Inc.)

bery. "Comical, stylized paint-and-collage illustrations accompany the clever text," observed a contributor in discussing the book in *Kirkus Reviews.*

In *Oliver, the Spaceship, and Me* young Carter is upset that his best friend has ignored him. The boy decides to get even by blasting off in a rocket that the two friends had planned to build and fly together. "Reed's razzmatazz mixed-media artwork [for *Oliver, the Spaceship, and Me*], with its juicy, funky acrylics and boldly incorporated photographs, floats the project," a *Kirkus Reviews* remarked.

In addition to original stories, Reed has enjoyed a successful collaboration as an illustrator working with award-winning author Pulver. In *School Library Journal* Grace Oliff noted of *Punctuation Takes a Vacation,* Pulver's fanciful tale about adventurous commas and apostrophes, that Reed's accompanying illustrations are "rich in color and texture, and add to the amusement" of the "lighthearted" story. A *Publishers Weekly* reviewer dubbed the same artwork "eye-popping" and "funky" due to the artist's use of "zippy oranges, teals, purples and cobalt blues."

In Pulver and Reed's companion book *Nouns and Verbs Have a Field Day* various parts of speech square off for a lively competition. Here "Reed's vividly colored cartoons capture the high-energy activity," asserted *Booklist* contributor Kay Weisman, and Gloria Koster, writing in *School Library Journal,* commented that the story's "animated words . . . are brightly colored, boldly labeled, and packed with personality." A group of frustrated students makes life miserable for some letters of the alphabet in a third collaboration, *Silent Letters Loud and Clear.* In *School Library Journal* Lynne Mattern described this work as a "grammar lesson with humorous examples and whimsical illustrations."

Debora Pearson offers an ode to the chaotic wonders of metropolitan life in *Big City Song!,* another book that features Reed's art. Complimenting the humorous portraits of city residents, who are pictured with oval-shaped heads and wearing bold, bright clothes, *School Library Journal* reviewer Linda Staskus wrote that Reed's "energetic artwork is filled with curving lines and contrasting colors." In Kanninen's *A Story with Pictures* an author realizes, too late, that she has forgotten to send her manuscript to the book's illustrator, resulting in a zany new creation that is an improvement over the original. "A combination of acrylic paints on canvas with cutout photos of various objects, Reed's colorful collages match the anything-can-happen tone" of Kanninen's imaginative tale, noted Joy Fleishhacker in *School Library Journal.* "Readers will enjoy the wild ride as Kanninen and Reed entertain various outlandish possibilities for the author's fate," concluded a reviewer in *Publishers Weekly.*

Reed once told *SATA:* "My picture-book career began . . . when I wrote and illustrated a book in its entirety, then naively took it to New York and walked it around

Reed's original, self-illustrated stories include the imaginative, galaxy-spanning **Oliver, the Spaceship, and Me.** (Illustration copyright © 2009 by Lynn Rowe Reed. All rights reserved. Reproduced by permission of Holiday House, Inc.)

the city. My last visit was with a young editor at Farrar, Straus & Giroux who miraculously fell in love with the project and offered me a contract on the spot.

"Since that initial success, the road has been challenging, frustrating and, ultimately, deeply rewarding," the artist added. The acceleration of Reed's career in children's literature, in her own opinion, "is directly due . . . to the huge success of the brilliantly written *Punctuation Takes a Vacation* by Pulver. I often say that the luckiest day of my career was the day I was offered the opportunity to illustrate that one!

"It has taken the entirety of this journey to begin to realize my genuine voice as an author as well an illustrator. It is a quirky, whimsical, crazy voice that I'm beginning to listen to more and more as it tries to penetrate the surface of my mundane, serious, adult self!"

Biographical and Critical Sources

PERIODICALS

Booklist, April 15, 1995, Annie Ayres, review of *Pedro, His Perro, and the Alphabet Sombrero,* p. 1507; April 1, 2006, Kay Weisman, review of *Nouns and Verbs Have a Field Day,* p. 49; May 1, 2009, John Peters, review of *Oliver, the Spaceship, and Me,* p. 89.

Horn Book, May-June, 2003, Peter D. Sieruta, review of *Punctuation Takes a Vacation,* p. 335; May-June, 2006, Vicky Smith, review of *Nouns and Verbs Have a Field Day,* p. 299.

New York Times, May 18, 2003, Patricia T. O'Conner, review of *Punctuation Takes a Vacation.*

Kirkus Reviews, May 15, 2005, review of *Julius Anteater, Misunderstood,* p. 594; August 15, 2005, review of *Thelonius Turkey Lives! (on Felicia Ferguson's Farm),* p. 921; August 1, 2006, review of *Big City Song,* p. 794; September 1, 2006, review of *Please Don't Upset P.U. Zorilla!,* p. 911; August 15, 2007, review of *A Story with Pictures;* January 15, 2009, review of *Oliver, the Spaceship, and Me.*

Publishers Weekly, November 2, 1990, review of *Rattlesnake Stew,* p. 73; September 27, 1999, review of *The Halloween Showdown,* p. 47; January 20, 2003, review of *Punctuation Takes a Vacation,* p. 82; September 26, 2005, review of *Thelonius Turkey Lives!,* p. 84; September 24, 2007, review of *A Story with Pictures,* p. 71.

School Library Journal, February, 1991, Carolyn Noah, review of *Rattlesnake Stew,* p. 73; April, 1995, Maria Redburn, review of *Pedro, His Perro, and the Alphabet Sombrero,* p. 114; September, 1999, Olga R. Barnes, review of *The Halloween Showdown,* p. 201; April, 2003, Grace Oliff, review of *Punctuation Takes a Vacation,* p. 136; July, 2005, Jane Barrer, review of *Julius Anteater, Misunderstood,* p. 81; August, 2005, Roxanne Burg, review of *Thelonius Turkey Lives!,* p. 104; March, 2006, Gloria Koster, review of *Nouns and Verbs Have a Field Day,* p. 200; September, 2006, Linda Staskus, review of *Big City Song,* p. 181; October, 2006, Marge Loch-Wouters, review of *Please Don't Upset P.U. Zorilla!,* p. 124; October, 2007, Joy Fleishhacker, review of *A Story with Pictures,* p. 118; June, 2008, Lynne Mattern, review of *Silent Letters Loud and Clear,* p. 113; April, 2009, Martha Simpson, review of *Oliver, the Spaceship, and Me,* p. 116.

Tribune Books (Chicago, IL), Elizabeth Ward, review of *Thelonius Turkey Lives!,* p. 11.

ONLINE

Fort Wayne Reader Web site, http://www.fortwaynereader.com/ (December 6, 2009), Dan Swartz, "Hidden in the Fort: Lynn Rowe Reed."

Lynn Rowe Reed Home Page, http://www.lynnrowereed.com (March 1, 2010).

*　　*　　*

RHUE, Morton
See STRASSER, Todd

*　　*　　*

RIPKEN, Cal, Jr. 1960-
(Calvin Edward Ripken, Jr.)

Personal

Born August 24, 1960, in Havre de Grace, MD; son of Cal Ripken, Sr. (a baseball player, manager, and coach); married; wife's name Kelly; children: Rachel, Ryan.

Addresses

Home—MD. *Office*—Ripken Baseball, 1427 Clarkview Rd., Ste. 100, Baltimore, MD 21209.

Career

Baltimore Orioles, professional baseball player, 1981-2001; Ripken Baseball, Inc., Baltimore, MD, president and chief executive officer, 2001—. Minor-league baseball player for Bluefield, Miami, Charlotte, and Rochester baseball teams, 1978-81. Studio analyst for *MLB on Deck,* TBS, 2007; American public diplomacy envoy, U.S. State Department, 2007—.

Awards, Honors

Named Rookie of the Year, International League, 1981; named Rookie of the Year, American League, Baseball Writers Association, 1982; named American League Rookie of the Year, *Sporting News,* 1982; named American League Player of the Year, *Sporting News,* 1983, 1991; named Major League Player of the Year, *Sporting News,* 1983; named American League Most Valuable Player, 1983, 1991; Silver Slugger awards, 1983-86, 1989, 1991, 1993-94; member of American League All-Star Team, 1983-2001; named All-Star Game Most Valuable Player, 1991, 2001; Gold Glove Awards, 1991-92; named Sportsman of the Year, *Sports Illustrated* and *Sporting News,* both 1995; Babe Ruth League changed the name of its largest division to Cal Ripken Baseball, 1999; member of Major League Baseball's All-Century Team; Ripken's 2,131st consecutive game voted Major League Baseball's "Most Memorable Moment" in history; inducted into Baseball Hall of Fame, 2007. Set major league records for most home runs by a shortstop, single-season fielding percentage, both 1990, most consecutive games played, 1995, and most errorless games by a shortstop, 1995.

Writings

Ripken: Cal on Cal (autobiography), edited by Mark Vancil, photographs by Walter Iooss, Jr., Summit (Arlington, TX), 1995.

(With Greg Brown) *Count Me In* (autobiography; for children), illustrations by Doug Keith, Taylor (Dallas, TX), 1995.

(With Mike Bryan) *The Only Way I Know* (autobiography; also see below), Viking (New York, NY), 1997.

(With Mike Bryan) *Cal Ripken, Jr.: My Story* (autobiography; for children), adapted by Dan Gutman from *The Only Way I Know*, Millbrook Press (Brookfield, CT), 1999.

(With Mike Bryan) *Cal Ripken, Jr.: Play Ball!* (autobiography; for children), adapted by Gail Herman from *The Only Way I Know*, illustrated by Stan Silver, Dial (New York, NY), 1999.

(With brother Bill Ripken and Larry Burke) *Play Baseball The Ripken Way: The Complete Illustrated Guide to the Fundamentals,* Random House (New York, NY), 2004.

(With Rick Wolff) *Parenting Young Athletes the Ripken Way: Ensuring the Best Experience for Your Kids in Any Sport,* Gotham Books (New York, NY), 2006.

(With Bill Ripken and Scott Lowe) *Coaching Youth Baseball the Ripken Way,* Human Kinetics (Champaign, IL), 2007.

(With Donald T. Phillips) *Get in the Game: Eight Elements of Perseverance That Make the Difference,* Gotham Books (New York, NY), 2007.

The Longest Season: The Story of the Orioles' 1988 Losing Streak, illustrated by Ron Mazellan, Philomel Books (New York, NY), 2007.

Adaptations

Get in the Game was adapted for audiobook.

Sidelights

Cal Ripken, Jr., played twenty-one seasons at shortstop for the Baltimore Orioles and was inducted into the National Baseball Hall of Fame in 2007. Ripkin became an American sports legend by quietly doing his job, day after day after day, and doing it exceptionally well. At a time when cynicism was rampant among sports fans, athletes, and journalists alike, his breaking of Lou Gehrig's longstanding record for consecutive games played seemed to signal a possible return to traditional values that honored the rewards of hard work. For many years, the record had been considered one of the few "unbreakables" in sports. In the words of Richard Hoffer, in an article crowning Ripken as *Sports Illustrated*'s Sportsman of the Year for 1995, Ripken "almost single-handedly restored the once loyal fan's faith in baseball, single-handedly turned attention to a pioneer work ethic."

The event, which had been widely anticipated for years, given the predictability of a season's 162-game schedule and the equal predictability of Ripken's attendance at the park, was "one of the great feel-good events in sports—ever," Hoffer avowed. "It released a pent-up emotion after two strike-shortened seasons, a missed World Series and a general surliness had destroyed a hundred-plus years' worth of fan loyalty."

Ripken himself is known as a stable, steady person who possesses superior self-discipline and who, in describing himself, declared: "The word *stubborn* does come to mind." His hair thinning and graying by the time of the consecutive-games record, he looked older than his thirty-five years, but played with the intensity and pleasure of a younger man. Ripken is also fiercely devoted to spending time with his family, which includes his wife Kelly and his children, Rachel and Ryan. Ripken himself had grown up in a baseball family as the son of Baltimore Orioles player, Cal Ripken, Sr., a man who later became a noted hitting coach for that team as well as its manager.

The advantages of being surrounded by knowledgeable, talented people within the baseball community as a youngster were surely instrumental in Ripken's development, yet as a minor-league prospect he was not highly touted: in 1978, he was the ninth shortstop selected in the baseball draft. Hard work made Ripken a player good enough to be selected Rookie of the Year in 1982 and Most Valuable Player in 1983 and 1991. Though not a flashy shortstop, he won Gold Gloves in 1991 and 1992 as the best at his position, achieving the highest fielding percentage in history and the longest errorless streak ever for a shortstop. This is not to say that there were no downturns in his career. In 1989 his batting average was only .257, and the following season his average sank below .220. Ripken worked through the slump, however, and went on to an outstanding season in 1991.

The response to Ripken's breaking of Gehrig's record in 1995 was warmly emotional on the part of teammates, opponents, and fans alike. The event, Hoffer surmised, came at a time when "there's hardly anything to root for anymore. . . . No home teams, few reliable citizens, and . . . not always a World Series . . . a sad time when neither virtue nor achievement can be taken for granted." Indeed, even the feat of remaining with one team throughout a long career seemed unusual, and Ripkin's habit of patiently remaining after games to sign autographs was sometimes looked upon by teammates as bizarre. Ripken's attachment to solid, old values, Hoffer suggested, might mark a subtle shift in the attitudes of an entire nation; hard work seemed to become fashionable again.

Ripken, who retired after the 2001 season, is one of only seven players to collect 3,000 hits and 400 homers during his career, and his career records for the Orioles included games, at-bats, runs, hits, doubles, homers and RBIs. "I had 13,000 at bats," he told *Baseball Digest* contributor Paul Post. "I know what it feels like to have some success in those moments, and a lot of failure.

But looking back on it, I played as much as I could for as long as I could. So I'm pretty fulfilled in that area." On July 29, 2007, he was inducted into the National Baseball Hall of Fame after being named on a record 537 ballots. "Looking back, I had many wonderful moments," he remarked to *Post.* "If they wanted me to play I performed and played. The Orioles were up and down in different rebuilding situations. There was a lot of change and a lot to deal with. But in the end I persevered through the tough times and maintained what I think is an honest and honorable approach to the game." Ripken now serves as the president and chief executive officer of Ripken Baseball, Inc., a youth baseball complex in Maryland, and in 2007 he was named an American public diplomacy envoy by the U.S. State Department.

Ripken's own words on his life and career are available in three autobiographies: two, for adults, are titled *Ripken: Cal on Cal* and *The Only Way I Know;* one for younger readers is *Count Me In.* In *Ripken,* published just after the author set his consecutive-games record, Ripken discusses his memories of the sport, his training methods, and his father's teachings, among other subjects. Ripken "has some interesting things to say," observed a contributor in the *Sporting News,* and Wes Lukowsky, reviewing the work in *Booklist,* stated that "Ripken's first-person text is self-effacing and modest yet revealing." *The Only Way I Know* follows Ripken's career from his days as a minor leaguer to his star run with the Orioles. *The Only Way I Know* "is an unusually good sports autobiography that captures the candor and generous spirit of a man," noted a contributor in *Publishers Weekly,* and Lukowsky described the book as "superior sports autobiography" and "excellent baseball fare."

The Only Way I Know has been adapted twice for children: *Cal Ripken, Jr.: My Story* is geared for middle graders and young adults and *Cal Ripken, Jr.: Play Ball!* is written for primary graders. The latter effort, a chapter book describing the ups and downs of Ripken's baseball career as well as his personal experiences, was a hit with beginning readers. Wendy Lukehart, writing in *School Library Journal,* praised the work as "a pro in a genre glutted with farm leaguers."

Ripken teamed with his brother, Bill Ripken, and writer Larry Burke on *Play Baseball the Ripken Way: The Complete Illustrated Guide to the Fundamentals,* an instructional book that covers all aspects of the game, including hitting, fielding, and base running. The book also offers advice for coaches and managers on dealing with their players. "This book is the next best thing to a personal lesson" with Ripken, a critic in *Publishers Weekly* stated, and *Library Journal* reviewer John Maxymuk commented that *Play Baseball the Ripken Way* "emphasizes the need to keep the experience fun and positive for the kids."

In *The Longest Season: The Story of the Orioles' 1988 Losing Streak,* a picture book illustrated by Ron Mazel-lan, Ripken chronicles his most frustrating period as a ballplayer. The Orioles opened the 1988 season with twenty-one consecutive losses, setting a dubious American League record. The horrific start resulted in the firing of Cal's father, who was managing the team at the time, and the team finished with only fifty-four wins that season. In the work, Ripken reflects on the lessons he learned during that tumultuous time. According to Marilyn Taniguchi, writing in *School Library Journal,* "Ripken's straightforward observations and heartfelt recollections make this a book that should connect with many young readers." "Though there's clearly a message here about perseverance and teamwork, Ripken doesn't preach," noted a *Publishers Weekly* critic, who called the work "a timeless palliative for any kid on the wrong side of a streak." In the opinion of a *Kirkus Reviews* contributor, *The Longest Season* "is a winner."

Biographical and Critical Sources

BOOKS

Gibbons, Jack, editor, *Cal Touches Home: The Biggest Sports Story of 1995 in Baltimore,* Baltimore Sun (Baltimore, MD), 1995.

Ripken, Cal, Jr., *Ripken: Cal on Cal,* edited by Mark Vancil, photographs by Walter Iooss, Jr., Summit (Arlington, TX), 1995.

Ripken, Cal, Jr., and Greg Brown, *Count Me In,* illustrations by Doug Keith, Taylor (Dallas, TX), 1995.

Ripken, Cal, Jr., and Mike Bryan, *The Only Way I Know,* Viking (New York, NY), 1997.

Ripken, Cal, Jr., and Mike Bryan, *Cal Ripken, Jr.: My Story,* adapted by Dan Gutman, Millbrook Press (Brookfield, CT), 1999.

Ripken, Cal, Jr., and Mike Bryan, *Cal Ripken, Jr.: Play Ball!,* adapted by Gail Herman, illustrated by Stan Silver, Dial (New York, NY), 1999.

Rosenfeld, Harvey, *Iron Man: The Cal Ripken, Jr. Story,* St. Martin's Press (New York, NY), 1995.

PERIODICALS

Baltimore Sun, August 14, 2007, "U.S. Drafts Ripken as Envoy of Good Will."

Baseball Digest, April, 2007, "Cal Ripken Packaged a Career of Greatness into His Cooperstown Resumé," p. 66.

Booklist, February 1, 1996, Wes Lukowsky, review of *Ripken: Cal on Cal,* p. 912; March 15, 1997, Wes Lukowsky, review of *The Only Way I Know,* p. 1203; September 1, 1999, Sally Estes, review of *Cal Ripken, Jr.: My Story,* p. 132.

Kirkus Reviews, March 15, 2007, review of *The Longest Season: The Story of the Orioles' 1988 Losing Streak.*

Library Journal, April 1, 2004, John Maxymuk, review of *Play Baseball the Ripken Way: The Complete Illustrated Guide to the Fundamentals,* p. 102.

People, September 18, 1995, William Plummer, "Man at Work: In an Age of Prima Donnas, Steady Cal Ripken Breaks Baseball's Ultimate Blue-Collar Record," p. 68.

Publishers Weekly, March 17, 1997, review of *The Only Way I Know,* p. 64; March 22, 1999, reviews of *Cal Ripken, Jr.: Play Ball!* and *Cal Ripken, Jr.: My Story,* both p. 94; March 1, 2004, review of *Play Baseball the Ripken Way,* p. 60; January 22, 2007, reviews of *Get in the Game: Eight Elements of Perseverance That Make the Difference,* p. 178, and *The Longest Season,* p. 184.

School Library Journal, June, 1999, Wendy Lukeheart, review of *Cal Ripken, Jr.: Play Ball!,* p. 120; May, 2007, Marilyn Taniguchi, review of *The Longest Season,* p. 123.

Sporting News, November 27, 1995, Steve Gietschier, review of *Ripken,* p. 8; Steve Gietschier, review of *The Only Way I Know,* p. 7; April 24, 2000, Arnie Stapleton, "Welcome to the Club," p. 62.

Sports Illustrated, December 18, 1995, Richard Hoffer, "Hand It to Cal," pp. 70-90; July 25, 2007, Tom Verducci, "Talking a Good Game," p. 46.

USA Today, August 8, 2007, Hal Bodley, "As Milestones Go, Ripken's Still Shine," p. C3.

ONLINE

Ripken Baseball Web site, http://www.ripkenbaseball.com (March 10, 2008).

Sporting News Online, http://www.sportingnews.com/ (March 10, 2008), "Scrapbook: Cal Ripken, Jr."

Washington Post Online, http://www.washingtonpost.com/ (March 10, 2008), "Cal Ripken Commemorative Section."*

*   *   *

RIPKEN, Calvin Edward, Jr.
See RIPKEN, Cal, Jr.

*   *   *

RITTER, John H. 1951-

Personal
Born October 31, 1951, in Dehesa, CA; son of Carl W. (a journalist) and Clara Mae Ritter; married, 1972; wife's name Cheryl (a teacher and curriculum developer); children: Jolie. *Education:* Attended University of California, San Diego. *Hobbies and other interests:* Growing fruit trees, raising chickens, playing guitar, composing music, snorkling, hiking, spending time with grandchildren.

Addresses
Home—Kaua'i Island, Hawai'i. *Agent*—Virginia Knowlton, Curtis Brown, Ltd., 10 Astor Pl., New York, NY 10003.

Career
Writer. Public speaker, beginning 1994; Oceanside Unified School District, Oceanside, CA, writer-in-residence, 1998-2000; leader of workshops, 2000-09. Custom painting contractor, 1973-98.

Member
American Civil Liberties Union, Amnesty International, Society of Children's Book Writers and Illustrators, National Council of Teachers of English (member, Assembly of Literature for Adolescents), Native Cultures Institute of Baja California.

Awards, Honors
Judy Blume Award, Society of Children's Book Writers and Illustrators, 1994; Children's Book Award, International Reading Association (IRA), Best Book for Young Adults designation, American Library Association (ALA), and Blue Ribbon designation, *Bulletin of the Center for Children's Books,* all 1999, and IRA Young-Adult Readers Choice designation, 2000, all for *Choosing up Sides;* Books for the Teen Age selection, New York Public Library, Parents' Guide to Children's Media Award, Shenandoah University, and Texas State Lone Star Book designation, all 2001, all for *Over the Wall;* Paterson Prize for Children's Literature, and Texas State Lone Star Book designation, both 2004, and Louisiana State Honor Book designation, 2006, all for *The Boy Who Saved Baseball.*

Writings
Choosing up Sides, Philomel (New York, NY), 1998.
Over the Wall, Philomel (New York, NY), 2000.
The Boy Who Saved Baseball, Philomel (New York, NY), 2003.
Under the Baseball Moon, Philomel (New York, NY), 2006.
The Desperado Who Stole Baseball, Philomel (New York, NY), 2009.

Contributor to periodicals, including *ALAN Review, California English Journal, Writer's Digest, Spitball: The Literary Baseball Magazine,* and *Christian Science Monitor.* Work included in books *Big City Cool,* Persea Books (New York, NY), 2002; *Making the Match: The Right Book for the Right Reader at the Right Time,* Stenhouse Books (Portland, ME), 2003; *Dreams and Visions: Fourteen Flights of Fantasy,* Starscape (New York, NY), 2006; and *This Family Is Driving Me Crazy,* Putnam (New York, NY), 2009.

Sidelights
Focusing on the mental, socio-political, and spiritual aspects of baseball, John H. Ritter is the author of several young-adult novels. According to Vicki Sherbert, writ-

Cover of John H. Ritter's middle-grade novel Over the Wall, *featuring artwork by Cliff Neilsen.* (Philomel Books, 2000. Jacket art © 2000 by Cliff Neilsen. Reproduced by permission of G.P. Putnam's Sons, a division of Penguin Putnam Books for Young Readers.)

ing in the *ALAN Review,* Ritter "uses the game of baseball, the glory of music, and the power of the written word to illustrate how young people can overcome everyday, and not-so-everyday, challenges. Each book goes beyond the story of the game, beyond the story of the problem, right to the heart of Ritter's message: What is really valuable in life?" As Ritter noted in his essay for *Making the Match: The Right Book for the Right Reader at the Right Time,* "The role of the storyteller . . . is to make the invisible visible. To tell the untold story, to shine a light on hidden truths. And one of a novelist's most sacred charges is to bring forward the marginalized souls among us and somehow, in a credible and fearless fashion, add definition, value, a spotlight, and a song to their lives. At least once in the story, we need to expose the innate sense of goodness that even the least among us is born with."

"I never intended [my books] to be play-by-play sports novels," Ritter told Chris Crowe in an *ALAN Review* interview. "I'm more interested in using baseball scenes as metaphor, or for challenges of character, or to advance the story." Success with his first novel, *Choosing up Sides,* meant Ritter could quit his day job and at-

tempt to write full time. Working for twenty-five years as a painting contractor, he was ready to give painting with words a larger place in his life.

"I grew up in a baseball family," Ritter noted on his home page. He and his brothers played one-on-one hardball in the dry hills of rural San Diego County, near the Mexican border. But there was more than simply sports in the family background. "We were also a family of musicians and mathematicians, house painters and poets," Ritter explained. He credits his father, a writer and one-time sports editor for the *Ashtabula (Ohio) Star Beacon*—as is Uncle Micah in *Choosing up Sides*—and the *San Diego Union,* with inspiring him with a love for writing as well as a love for the "holy game of baseball." Ritter's mother, of Irish and Blackfoot Indian descent, passed away when he was young, but he retains memories of how she "sang to us constantly, making up a special song for each of her four children. From her, I gained a sense of how to capture a person's spirit in a lyrical phrase."

Through his rural upbringing, Ritter gained the ability to depend on himself and his siblings for entertainment and friendship. However, he explained on his home page, for solitude and respite from an often abusive home life, he grew to depend upon nature: the vast mountains and ancient Indian camps just a few hundred yards from his back door where he would spend hours communing with envisioned spirits of the Kumeyaay people, rabbits, hawks, and rattlesnakes in the rugged chaparral, as depicted in nearly all of his novels. At school Ritter was, as he described himself to Crowe, a "wild student. . . . A rabble rouser and a contrarian." His questioning nature also made him a high achiever, but his school behavior was mixed. "I could be extremely focused one day, then get tossed out of class the next," he admitted to Crowe. "As proof, in high school I was voted both the Senior Class President and the Senior Class Clown." Nonetheless, his teachers discovered his way with words, and would read Ritter's work out loud to the class as an example of good writing.

Meanwhile, baseball continued to dominate Ritter's dreams until, as he wrote in *Making the Match,* "somewhere around my junior year in high school, somewhere between the time a Charlie Company 1st Battalion 20th Infantry unit slaughtered some 450 unarmed villagers in the hamlet of My Lai and my senior prom, I realized that whatever gift I'd had for hitting a baseball—and the dreams tied to it—were no longer important enough or relevant enough for me to pursue." At that point, roughly 1967, Ritter discovered song writing.

Graduating from high school, Ritter attended the University of California—San Diego, where he met his future wife. In the spring of his sophomore year, however, he knew that college was not the place he needed to be; "I knew I had to walk the streets, touch life, em-

brace life, gain experience," he told Crowe. "I wanted to learn from life. To hit the road like Kerouac, Dylan, and Twain. To have something real to write about." Withdrawing from school, he became a painter's apprentice. Working for three or four months per year, he could save enough to travel and write the rest of the year. After several years, he married and had a baby daughter; that upped the work year to nine months. However, Ritter always scheduled time for writing.

In the late 1980s Ritter joined a writing group led by YA novelist Joan Oppenheimer. He then took extension writing classes, started another writing group with Israeli novelist Anna Levine and biographer Beth Wagner Brust, and in 1994 won the Judy Blume Award for a novel in progress. The book was about girls' fastpitch softball and was later folded into *Under the Baseball Moon.* Although that novel remained unpublished for many years, it built his confidence and opened doors with editors. Beginning a second coming-of-age novel, Ritter opted for a baseball theme, a topic close to his heart and also one that carries a resonant metaphorical value in U.S. culture. Further influences for his first published novel came from the author's personal juvenile experiences growing up in the 1960s and watching news reports of civil-rights marches and racial violence. These influences coalesced in the novel *Choosing up Sides.*

Choosing up Sides is set in southern Ohio in the 1920s. The novel's protagonist is thirteen-year-old Luke Bledsoe, the oldest son of a preacher. Born left handed, Luke is, in the eyes of his Fundamentalist father, Ezekiel, a throwback, a potential follower of Satan, for the left hand is the hand of the devil. The authoritarian Ezekiel tries to "cure" Luke of his left-handedness, but with little luck. When Ezekiel becomes minister of the Baptist church in Crown Falls, Ohio, Luke looks forward to following the local baseball team, which won the county championship the previous year and seems poised to repeat their success. Unfortunately, Ezekiel views left-handedness as a conscious choice and views baseball as a temptation that needs to be resisted, so Luke must practice pitching in secret, by throwing apples. One day, while Luke is watching a forbidden game, a ball lands at his feet. Throwing it back with his left hand, he amazes the crowd with his distance and placement, and soon players join his uncle Micah, a sports editor for a northern Ohio newspaper, in trying to convince Luke that wasting a talent such as his is the real sin. When Luke decides to pitch for the team, a confrontation with his father ensues, leading to a violent beating and a subsequent tragedy.

Reviewing *Choosing up Sides,* Elizabeth Bush described it in the *Bulletin of the Center for Children's Books* as a novel that "pits fire and brimstone Fundamentalism against a rival religion—Baseball—and treats both with cathartic understanding." Patricia K. Ladd wrote in the *ALAN Review* that Ritter "addresses themes of autonomy and independence common to young adult read-

ers and portrays plot through authentic dialect and well-developed characters," and his use of dialogue, similes, metaphors, and imagery "add dimensions to the plot that leave readers pondering the book's messages long after turning the final page." "Unlike many sports novels, *Choosing up Sides* does more than offer a mere glimpse of the grand old game of baseball—it takes a deeper look at faith, truth, and individuality," maintained Stefani Koorey in her *Voice of Youth Advocates* review, the critic going on to call the tale a "well-designed study of personal choice."

In *Over the Wall,* which was inspired by the author's outrage at the circumstances surrounding the U.S. Gulf War in the early 1990s, Ritter once again adopts an historical setting in a story about a boy's attempt to reconnect with his father and discover who he is in the process. There are many "walls" in thirteen-year-old Tyler's life: the literal wall of the baseball field he wants to clear with a mighty slam; the Vietnam memorial wall bearing his grandfather's name; and the invisible wall Tyler's dad has built around himself ever since the death of Tyler's sister nine years earlier. When he is invited to spend the summer in New York City with his cousin,

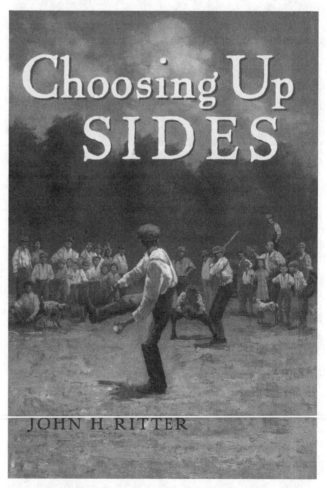

Ritter's sport-themed novels include Choosing up Sides, *featuring artwork by Ronald Himler.* (Jacket art © 1998 by Ronald Himler. Reproduced by permission of Philomel Books, an imprint of Penguin Putnam Books for Young Readers, a division of Penguin Putnam Inc.)

Tyler is determined to make it onto the roster of an all-star baseball team. However, his explosive temper gets in the way of his obvious talent. With the help of his pretty cousin and with the sage advice of his coach, a Vietnam vet who suffers from post-traumatic stress disorder and recognizes the same symptoms in Tyler, the young man manages to navigate the risky waters of this passage. "By the end," noted Todd Morning in a review of *Over the Wall* for *School Library Journal*, "Tyler has gained a level of self-awareness by unraveling some of the tangled stories in his family's past and understanding the intricacies lying beneath the surface of life." A *Publishers Weekly* reviewer described the novel as a "powerful lesson in compassion." Writing in the *ALAN Review*, Patty Ladd noted that "readers are left questioning societal mores and values, rules and politics, and their own moral development," and Roger Leslie commented in *Booklist* that *Over the Wall* is a "fully fleshed-out story about compassion and absolution."

Ritter uses a lighter and more humorous touch when taking on environmental issues in *The Boy Who Saved Baseball*. The work, based loosely on Gabriel García

Cover of Ritter's The Boy Who Saved Baseball, *a preteen novel geared for fans of America's Favorite Pastime.* (Cover photo courtesy of Jerry Koontz/ Index Stock. Reproduced by permission of Puffin Books, a division of Penguin Putnam Books for Young Readers.)

Márquez's *One Hundred Years of Solitude,* centers on Doc Altenheimer, the octogenarian owner of an apple orchard in Dillontown, California. Doc, who is preparing to sell his acres of land—including the town's centuries-old baseball field—to wealthy land developers. After talking with twelve-year-old Tom Gallagher, however, the man decides to let the fate of his land rest on the outcome of a single baseball game pitting a team of local ballplayers against an all-star squad from a neighboring community. With the help of a mysterious newcomer, Tom convinces disgraced former major leaguer and social recluse Dante Del Gato to whip the Dillontown team into shape. "Ritter delivers a baseball tale of legendary dimension, featuring several larger-than-life characters," according to *Booklist* critic John Peters, and Blair Christolon observed in *School Library Journal* that *The Boy Who Saved Baseball* "is peppered with both optimism and dilemmas; it has plenty of play-by-play action, lots of humor, and a triumphant ending."

Set in the wild west of the 1880s and written in the manner of a tall tale mixed with Mexican-style magical realism, *The Desperado Who Stole Baseball* is a prequel to *The Boy Who Saved Baseball* and serves as book one of Ritter's forthcoming "Dillontown Trilogy." On his way to Dillontown to find his long-lost uncle, the manager of a championship baseball team, twelve-year-old Jack Dillon meets Billy the Kid, who is looking for a fresh start in California. Upon his arrival, Jack learns that the Dillowntown Nine have scheduled a game against the powerful Chicago White Stockings, with the town's fortune hanging in the balance. "Ritter writes in an idiom-laden, mock-epic style full of bombast and bravado," Marilyn Taniguchi asserted in *School Library Journal,* and Ian Chipman, reviewing the work in *Booklist,* called *The Desperado Who Stole Baseball* a "wildly entertaining yarn." Noting that the work includes some unbelievable elements, a *Kirkus Reviews* contributor maintained that "fans of baseball will chortle all the way through every impossible moment."

A music-loving skateboarder is the focus of *Under the Baseball Moon,* "an unusual but engaging tale," according to Paula Rohrlick in *Kliatt.* Andy Ramos, a skilled trumpeter who hopes to revolutionize the music scene with his band's fusion of Latin jazz, rock, and hip-hop, finds himself strangely drawn to Glory Martinez, a childhood rival and talented softball pitcher who has returned to the neighborhood. Andy and Glory soon discover that their talents peak when they perform together, but when a mysterious benefactor promises to launch Andy's musical career, he agrees to walk away from his budding romance. "Ritter pulls out all the stops in his myth-heavy plot," wrote *Booklist* critic Bill Ott, who noted that the author incorporates "a splash of myth and a touch of otherworldliness." Jack Forman, writing in *School Library Journal,* praised the "descriptions of music improvisation and softball action," and a *Publishers Weekly* contributor noted that "Ritter's dia-

In The Desperado Who Stole Baseball *Ritter presents a prequel to* The Boy Who Saved Baseball. (Cover images courtesy of iStockphoto. Reproduced by permission of Philomel Books, a division of Penguin Putnam Books for Young Readers.)

logue crackles with the rhythms of the funky California setting, and Andy's passion and ambition give the novel its heartbeat."

Biographical and Critical Sources

BOOKS

Making the Match: The Right Book for the Right Reader at the Right Time, Stenhouse Books (Portland, ME), 2003, pp. 5-7.

PERIODICALS

ALAN Review, spring-summer, 2000, Chris Crowe, interview with Ritter, pp. 5-9; spring-summer, 2000, Patricia K. Ladd, "Covering the Bases with Young Adult Literature," pp. 10-17; fall, 2000, Connie Russell, review of *Over the Wall,* p. 33; winter, 2007, Vicky Sherbert, interview with Ritter.

Booklist, March 1, 1998, Candace Smith, review of *Choosing up Sides,* p. 1513; April 1, 2000, Roger Leslie, review of *Over the Wall,* p. 1451; May 1, 2003, John

Peters, review of *The Boy Who Saved Baseball,* p. 1595; August 1, 2006, Bill Ott, review of *Under the Baseball Moon,* p. 76; February 15, 2009, Ian Chipman, review of *The Desperado Who Stole Baseball,* p. 82.

Book Report, March-April, 1999, Kate Clarke, review of *Choosing up Sides,* p. 63.

Bulletin of the Center for Children's Books, June, 1998, Elizabeth Bush, "The Big Picture."

Kirkus Reviews, January 15, 1999, review of *The Desperado Who Stole Baseball.*

Kliatt, July, 2003, Claire Rosser, review of *The Boy Who Saved Baseball,* p. 17; May, 2006, Paula Rohrlick, review of *Under the Baseball Moon,* p. 14.

Publishers Weekly, April 13, 1998, review of *Choosing up Sides,* p. 76; May 29, 2000, review of *Over the Wall,* p. 83; May 19, 2003, review of *The Boy Who Saved Baseball,* p. 75; May 8, 2006, review of *Under the Baseball Moon,* p. 66.

School Library Journal, June, 1998, Joel Shoemaker, review of *Choosing up Sides,* p. 152; June, 2000, Todd Morning, review of *Over the Wall,* p. 152; June, 2003, Blair Christolon, review of *The Boy Who Saved Baseball,* p. 150; July, 2006, Jack Forman, review of *Under the Baseball Moon,* p. 111; April, 2009, Marilyn Taniguchi, review of *The Desperado Who Stole Baseball,* p. 141.

Teacher Librarian, March, 2001, Teri Lesesne, "Complexities, Choices, and Challenges," pp. 44-47.

Voice of Youth Advocates, December, 1998, Stefani Koorey, review of *Choosing up Sides.*

ONLINE

John H. Ritter Home Page, http://www.johnhritter.com (March 1, 2010).

Penguin Group Web Site, http://us.penguingroup.com/ (March 1, 2010), "John H. Ritter."

*   *   *

RUURS, Margriet 1952-

Personal

Born December 2, 1952, in the Netherlands; daughter of H. Bodbyl and W. Bodbyl-Schut; married Kees Ruurs (a parks and recreation manager), 1972; children: Alexander, Arnout. *Education:* Simon Fraser University, M.Ed., 1998. *Hobbies and other interests:* Gardening, traveling, hiking, camping.

Addresses

Home—Shedd, OR. *E-mail*—info@margrietruurs.com.

Career

Children's book author, educator, and poet. Teacher at creative writing workshops for schools and online; guest lecturer at University of Northern Iowa. Planned children's programming at Okanagan Regional Libraries for twelve years; former chair of local school board.

Member

International Board on Books for Young People, Society of Children's Book Writers and Illustrators, Canadian Society of Children's Authors, Illustrators, and Performers, Children's Writers and Illustrators, Writers Union of Canada, Children's Writers and Illustrators of British Columbia.

Awards, Honors

Storytelling World awards; International Reading Association (IRA) "Tellable" Stories honor title, 1997, for *Emma's Eggs;* Our Choice selection, Canadian Children's Book Centre, for both *A Mountain Alphabet* and *Emma's Eggs;* Mr. Christie's Book Award shortlist, for *Emma and the Coyote;* Patricia Gallagher Award shortlist, for *A Pacific Alphabet;* Silver Seal, Mr. Christie's Book Awards, Shining Willow Award shortlist, and Saskatchewan Young Reader's Choice Award shortlist, all c. 2001, all for *Emma's Cold Day;* Region West Presidential Award for Reading & Technology, IRA, 2005; Notable Book for Global Awareness designation, IRA, and Teacher's Choice Award, both for *My Librarian Is a Camel;* Blue Spruce Award shortlist, 2006, for *Wake Up, Henry Rooster!*

Writings

FOR CHILDREN

Apenkinderen (nonfiction), Leopold (the Netherlands), 1982.

Fireweed, illustrated by Roberta Mebs, Burns & Morton (Whitehorse, Yukon, Canada), 1986.

Big Little Dog, illustrated by Marc Houde, Penumbra (Waterloo, Ontario, Canada), 1992.

The R.C.M.P. (nonfiction), KGR Learning Aides, 1992.

Spectacular Spiders: Integrated Activities for Primary Classrooms, Pacific Edge Publishing (Gabriola, British Columbia, Canada), 1995.

A Mountain Alphabet, illustrated by Andrew Kiss, Tundra Books (Plattsburgh, NY), 1996.

Emma's Eggs, illustrated by Barbara Spurll, Stoddart Kids (Toronto, Ontario, Canada), 1996.

Emma and the Coyote, illustrated by Barbara Spurll, Stoddart Kids (New York, NY), 1999.

When We Go Camping, illustrated by Andrew Kiss, Tundra Books (Plattsburgh, NY), 2001.

Virtual Maniac: Silly and Serious Poems for Kids, illustrated by Eve Tanselle, Maupin House (Gainesville, FL), 2001.

A Pacific Alphabet, illustrated by Dianna Bonder, Whitecap Books (Vancouver, British Columbia, Canada), 2001.

Emma's Cold Day, illustrated by Barbara Spurll, Stoddart Kids (New York, NY), 2001.

Logan's Lake, Hodgepodge Books (Edmonton, Alberta, Canada), 2001.

Wild Babies, illustrated by Andrew Kiss, Tundra Books (Plattsburgh, NY), 2003.

Ms. Bee;s Magical Bookcase, illustrated by Andrew Gooderham, Chestnut Publishing (Toronto, Ontario, Canada), 2004.

My Librarian Is a Camel: How Books Are Brought to Children around the World, Boyds Mills Press (Honesdale, PA), 2005.

Animal Alphabed, Boyds Mills Press (Honesdale, PA), 2005.

Emma at the Fair, illustrated by Barbara Spurll, Fitzhenry & Whiteside (Markham, Ontario, Canada), 2005.

No Dogs Allowed, illustrated by Marc Houde, Chestnut Publishing (Toronto, Ontario, Canada), 2005.

Me and Martha Black, Penumbra Press (Manotick, Ontario, Canada), 2005.

Wake Up, Henry Rooster!, illustrated by Sean Cassidy, Fitzhenry & Whiteside (Markham, Ontario, Canada), 2006.

In My Backyard, illustrated by Ron Broda, Tundra Books (Toronto, Ontario, Canada), 2007.

OTHER

(Translator into Dutch) Judith Viorst, *Alexander and the Terrible, Horrible, No Good, Very Bad Day,* Leopold (the Netherlands), 1985.

On the Write Track! A Guide to Writing, Illustrating, and Publishing Stories (adult nonfiction), Pacific Educational Press (Vancouver, British Columbia, Canada), 1993.

The Power of Poems: Teaching the Joy of Writing Poetry, Maupin House (Gainesville, FL), 2001.

Also author of *Write On-line!: The Creation of an On-Line Magazine to Publish Children's Writing,* 1998. Editor of *Kidswwwrite* (online magazine). Contributor of articles and poems to periodicals.

Author's work has been published in Braille.

Sidelights

Born in the Netherlands, author and educator Margriet Ruurs draws inspiration for her books from the many places she has lived, among them California, Oregon, Northern Alberta, and the Yukon. Ruurs is known for penning picture books such as *When We Go Camping* and *Wild Babies,* which combine a lighthearted approach with a reverence for nature. *Canadian Review of Materials* reviewer Valerie Nielsen praised *Wild Babies* as "a perfect book for pre-school and primary children" because "of its simple prose and lush" illustrations. The author has also published *Emma at the Fair* and other works featuring a spirited chicken, as well as several well-received nonfiction titles, such as *In My Backyard.* "I love to use my imagination and to dream up stories," Ruurs stated on her home page.

Big Little Dog, one of Ruurs' first books for children, is an easy reader about a boy and his sled dog; according to *Quill & Quire* reviewer Fred Boer, the story is "told

simply and effectively, with both drama and suspense." Children and nature are also paired in *When We Go Camping,* in which a simple text draws listeners to a family's crackling campfire overlooking a mist-covered lake frequented by moose and surrounded by Canada's boreal forest. Enhanced by detailed paintings by Andrew Kiss, the "delightful picture book . . . will certainly help [children] . . . find a kinship with nature," noted Ian Stewart in *Canadian Review of Materials,* while *Booklist* reviewer Ilene Cooper cited *When We Go Camping* as "a good introduction for children who have never been camping" as well as "a nice remembrance" for young wilderness veterans.

Ruurs has also authored a number of alphabet books for beginning readers. *A Mountain Alphabet,* set in the Canadian Rockies, is organized around a hike through the mountain ranges, and *A Pacific Alphabet* presents what *Canadian Review of Materials* reviewer Cora Lee described as "an Alice-in-Wonderland consortium of creatures and objects, dropped together in the oddest of contexts." The texts and illustrations of both books present a wide range of plants and animals, and the volumes include both an introduction and an appendix that provide further information about the scenes depicted. Ruurs once told *SATA, A Mountain Alphabet* "took me almost two years to get the words just right, to say exactly what I wanted to say about life in the mountains." The author hopes that readers will "have as much fun as I did trying to find all the hidden objects and letters in the book's illustrations!" Praising *A Mountain Alphabet* in *School Library Journal,* Barbara Chatton commented that the "book will help young readers to explore this ecosystem," and in *Quill & Quire,* Janet McNaughton remarked that the book will also please "adults who have a special affinity with the subject matter."

A Pacific Alphabet also garnered strong reviews. According to Michael Jung in *Resource Links,* Ruurs' "poems are clever and often explain about certain phenomenon associated with the Pacific Ocean," and Alison Kastner, writing in *School Library Journal,* similarly noted that "many of the rhymes are funny and enjoyable to read out loud." Lee also applauded the work, complimenting the author's "unexpected" choice of words in *A Pacific Alphabet.* The critic concluded by claiming that "Ruurs' text well reflects the whimsy and wonder of the illustrations, and both are the enchanting result of sea-sharpened sense."

In *Animal Alphabed* a little girl preparing for bed notices that one of her stuffed animals is missing. As the youngster searches for the misplaced toy, she seeks the help of her other stuffed creatures as well as the animals displayed on her quilt, all of whom magically come to life. Though a contributor in *Kirkus Reviews* remarked of *Animal Alphabed* that Ruurs' "concept is creative," the critic also believed that readers might find the narrative difficult to follow, stating that the protagonist "repeatedly loses track of her mission." In *School*

Library Journal, Julie Roach also noted the "confusing" plot, but nonetheless predicted that young readers "may enjoy the rhyming words and alliteration."

Ruurs introduces Emma the chicken to picture book audiences in *Emma's Eggs.* The mixed-up hen notices what the humans on her farm are doing with her eggs—for example, scrambling them for eating, or decorating and hiding them for an Easter egg hunt—and tries to accommodate them by scrambling her eggs or hiding them herself. Not surprisingly, Emma's attempts at efficiency result in some confusion until the hen figures out what eggs are really for. Calling the book "well written," Bridget Donald added in her *Quill & Quire* review that *Emma's Eggs* "convey[s] the energy of Emma's human-like ambitions while preserving a strong sense of her chicken nature." Emma makes a return appearance in *Emma and the Coyote,* wherein the none-too-wary hen's efforts to turn the tables on a wily predator backfire. Praising Ruurs' "zippy dialogue," *Bulletin of the Center for Children's Books* reviewer Fern Kory called *Emma and the Coyote* "a natural readaloud from the story teller's poetic first line," and a *Resource Links* contributor added that the author "uses language effectively, and the story moves along quickly."

Emma's Cold Day finds the silly chicken in search of a warm way to pass the winter months. When her owners forget to turn on the heat lamps in the hen house, Emma leaves the shelter of her coop. She heads for the barnyard, where she slides off an icy fence; the cow barn, where the mess and smell are too much for her; and the pig shed, where she infuriates the boss hog. Finally, Emma tucks herself in the branches of a fir tree, much to the chagrin of the farmers. According to *Resource Links* contributor Heather Hamilton, *Emma's Cold Day* "is appealing because it entertains, and the story moves quickly enough to hold the attention of little people." Such praise was echoed by Mary St. Onge-Davidson, who noted of *Emma's Cold Day* in *Canadian Book Review Annual* that Ruurs tells her story with "humor and empathy," and that the text is "challenging and fast-paced enough" to entertain audiences of all ages.

In *Emma at the Fair,* the hen's family enters her in a variety of competitions, hoping she will receive a blue ribbon. Emma has no idea how to impress the judges, however, so she decides to imitate the other animals at the festival. Emma fails miserably at crowing like a rooster and strutting like a turkey, and only after she settles into her nest does she win a most unexpected reward. Writing in *Resource Links,* Anna S. Rinaldis called *Emma at the Fair* an "engaging, humorous story," adding that "Ruurs' use of alliteration such as 'cacophony of cackles,' 'gaggles of geese,' and 'dozens of ducks' are rich descriptions that make the text delightful to listen to."

A young bird with a penchant for staying up late has trouble performing his job in *Wake Up, Henry Rooster!* When Henry's father leaves town to attend a conven-

tion, the responsibility of crowing early in the morning falls to Henry. The youngster prefers playing cards and dancing till the wee hours, though, and as he sleeps through the sunrise, the ordered life on the farm suffers. When a wise old goat offers Henry some sound advice, the rooster begins to redeem himself. Ruurs "keeps her prose straightforward and uncluttered, dropping the odd, funny detail," noted *Quill & Quire* reviewer Nathan Whitlock, and Reesa Cohen, writing in *Canadian Review of Materials,* observed that Ruurs' tale "showcases her humour and storytelling abilities which result in the creation of quirky animal characters."

A teacher of creative writing who has worked with students in both Canada and the United States, Ruurs is also the author of *On the Write Track! A Guide to Writing, Illustrating, and Publishing Stories* and *The Power of Poems: Teaching the Joy of Writing Poetry,* the second of which was praised by an *Instructor* contributor as "a must have" book for those teaching "young writers in the craft of writing poetry."

In another informative title, *My Librarian Is a Camel: How Books Are Brought to Children around the World,* Ruurs describes the many ways literature reaches people in remote locales. To research her book, the author visited thirteen nations, including Azerbaijan and Zimbabwe, finding that librarians employ donkeys, bicycles, elephants, and wheelbarrows to serve their patrons. "The intriguing view of libraries and children around the world will appeal to many readers," Margaret A. Bush wrote in *Horn Book.*

Ruurs explores the variety of animals, birds, and insects that can be found around one's home and garden in her nonfiction work *In My Backyard.* The author's "informative text is short, poetic, and reminiscent of a haiku," observed Carlyn Zwarenstein in *Quill & Quire,* and *Canadian Review of Materials* reviewer Gregory Bryan remarked that Ruurs' book "reflects her admirable desire to help children learn to appreciate the majesty of their natural surrounds."

Ruurs once told *SATA:* "Nothing is more fun than playing with words! I started writing stories and poems when I was in grade 1. I wrote lots of stories and, thank goodness, my mom kept the scribblers with the poems I wrote when I was little." The Dutch-born Ruurs explained that, because English is her second language, "it was hard for me to write poetry for a while but now I write poetry in both Dutch and English and do some translating as well."

In addition to continuing her work as an author and editor of the Web magazine *Kidswwwrite,* Ruurs dedicates much of her time to working with young students, developing their love of words and of the craft of writing. "I love being home and creating stories—first in my head and eventually on the computer," she once told *SATA.* "But I also enjoy traveling to schools and libraries to meet the kids who read my books. A book sitting on the shelf is just cardboard and paper, but a book in the hands of a reader comes to life! I write the stories but you make the book a book by reading it!"

Biographical and Critical Sources

PERIODICALS

Booklist, December 15, 2001, Ilene Cooper, review of *When We Go Camping,* p. 741; May 15, 2006, Hazel Rochman, review of *Wake Up, Henry Rooster!,* p. 52; July, 2005, John Peters, review of *My Librarian Is a Camel: How Books Are Brought to Children around the World,* p. 1919.
Bulletin of the Center for Children's Books, December, 1999, Fern Kory, review of *Emma and the Coyote,* p. 148.
Canadian Book Review Annual, Volume 24, 1999, Steve Pitt, review of *Emma and the Coyotes,* p. 470; Volume 52, 2001, Mary St. Onge-Davidson, review of *Emma's Cold Day,* p. 465.
Canadian Review of Materials, September, 2001, Ian Stewart, review of *When We Go Camping;* March 1, 2002, Gail Hamilton, review of *Emma's Cold Day;* April 12, 2002, Cora Lee, review of *A Pacific Alphabet;* February 14, 2003, Valerie Nielsen, review of *Wild Babies;* March 31, 2006, Reesa Cohen, review of *Wake Up, Henry Rooster!;* January 14, 2007, Gregory Bryan, review of *In My Backyard.*
Chirp, May, 2003, "Waiting for a Friend," pp. 24-27.
Globe and Mail (Toronto, Ontario, Canada), May 26, 2001, review of *When We Go Camping,* p. D17.
Horn Book, September-October, 2005, Margaret A. Bush, review of *My Librarian Is a Camel,* p. 607.
Instructor, January-February, 2002, review of *The Power of Poems: Teaching the Joy of Writing Poetry,* p. 13.
Kirkus Reviews, August 1, 2005, review of *My Librarian Is a Camel,* p. 857; August 15, 2005, review of *Animal Alphabed,* p. 921; February 15, 2007, review of *In My Backyard.*
Publishers Weekly, July 17, 2000, review of *When We Go Camping,* p. 166.
Quill & Quire, May, 1993, Fred Boer, review of *Big Little Dog,* p. 34; August, 1996, Bridget Donald, review of *Emma's Eggs,* p. 42; December, 1996, Janet McNaughton, review of *A Mountain Alphabet,* pp. 36-37; July, 1999, review of *Emma and the Coyote,* p. 51; May, 2001, review of *When We Go Camping,* p. 33; April, 2006, Nathan Whitlock, review of *Wake Up, Henry Rooster!* April, 2007, Carlyn Zwarenstein, review of *In My Backyard.*
Resource Links, October, 1999, review of *Emma and the Coyote,* pp. 8-9; February, 2002, Heather Hamilton, review of *Emma's Cold Day,* p. 8; April, 2002, Michael Jung, review of *A Pacific Alphabet,* p. 9; April, 2003, Mavis Holder, review of *Wild Babies,* p. 27; February, 2006, Anna S. Rinaldis, review of *Emma at the Fair,* p. 12; June, 2006, Eva Wilson, review of *Wake Up, Henry Rooster!,* p. 4; April, 2007, Wendy Hogan, review of *In My Backyard,* p. 9.

School Library Journal, February, 1997, Barbara Chatton, review of *A Mountain Alphabet,* pp. 97-98; July, 2001, Susan Marie Pitard, review of *When We Go Camping,* p. 88; February, 2002, Alison Kastner, review of *A Pacific Alphabet,* p. 112; February, 2003, Patricia Manning, review of *Wild Babies,* p. 137; August, 2005, Anne L. Tormohlen, review of *My Librarian Is a Camel,* p. 116; September, 2005, Julie Roach, review of *Animal Alphabed,* p. 186; December, 2005, Maura Bresnahan, review of *Emma at the Fair,* p. 120; July, 2006, Linda Ludke, review of *Wake Up, Henry Rooster!,* p. 87; March, 2007, Kathy Piehl, review of *In My Backyard,* p. 200.

ONLINE

Canadian Society of Children's Authors, Illustrators, and Performers, http://www.canscaip.org/ (April 1, 2008), "Margriet Ruurs."
Children's Writers and Illustrators of British Columbia, http://www.cwill.bc.ca/ (April 1, 2008), "Margriet Ruurs."
Just One More Book Web site, http://www.justonemore book.com/ (August 20, 2007), podcast interview with Ruurs.
Margriet Ruurs Home Page, http://www.margrietruurs. com/ (June 1, 2010).*

S

SARCONE-ROACH, Julia

Personal

Born in Arlington, VA. *Education:* Rhode Island School of Design, degree, 2002.

Addresses

Home—Brooklyn, NY. *Agent*—Paul Rodeen, Rodeen Literary Management, 3501 N. Southport, No. 497, Chicago, IL 60657. *E-mail*—jsarconeroach@hotmail.com.

Career

Artist, animator, and author. Creator and director of *Call of the Wild* (short animated film), 2002. *Exhibitions:* Work included in Original Art Show, Society of Illustrators, New York, NY.

Awards, Honors

Gold Award, Oppenheim Toy Portfolio, and Best Picture Book designation, UBIE Award, both 2010, both for *The Secret Plan.*

Writings

(Illustrator) Lee Bennett Hopkins, compiler, *Incredible Inventions* (poems), Greenwillow Books (New York, NY), 2009.
(Self-illustrated) *The Secret Plan,* Knopf (New York, NY), 2009.

Sidelights

A Brooklyn-based artist, Julia Sarcone-Roach is the author and illustrator of *The Secret Plan,* her debut picture book. The work concerns a sprightly elephant named Milo and Milo's three feline friends, Hildy, Henry, and Harriet. The members of this energetic quartet love nothing more than spending the day playing together and they hate interrupting their games for such nuisances as meals and, especially, bedtime. One night, Milo concocts a clever method to fool their parents and avoid going to sleep. Though things do not go quite as planned, the four pals discover a new playroom filled with wonderful treasures. "Sarcone-Roach's brushy, full-bleed acrylics alternate warm and cool colors and provide plenty of humorous detail," a *Kirkus Reviews* critic noted, and in *School Library Journal* Kathleen

Julia Sarcone-Roach shares an amusing story in her quirky self-illustrated picture book The Secret Plan.

Kelly Macmillan applauded the "swirly acrylic paintings that evoke dreamy nighttime fantasy."

Sarcone-Roach has also provided the illustrations for *Incredible Inventions* a poetry collection by celebrated anthologist Lee Bennett Hopkins that examines the origins of blue jeans, jigsaw puzzles, popsicles, and other familiar items. "The mixed-media artwork's well-designed compositions add energy without overwhelming the words," Gillian Engberg observed in *Booklist*, and a contributor in *Kirkus Reviews* praised Sarcone-Roach for creating "active, splashy illustrations . . . that unify the book visually and contribute their own humorous touches."

Biographical and Critical Sources

PERIODICALS

Booklist, December 1, 2008, Gillian Engberg, review of *Incredible Inventions*, p. 64; December 1, 2009, Kara Dean, review of *The Secret Plan*, p. 53.
Kirkus Reviews, January 15, 2009, review of *Incredible Inventions*; September 15, 2009, review of *The Secret Plan*.
School Library Journal, February, 2009, Carolyn Janssen, review of *Incredible Inventions*, p. 92; November, 2009, Kathleen Kelly MacMillan, review of *The Secret Plan*, p. 88.

ONLINE

Julia Sarcone-Roach Web log, http://www.jsarconeroach.blogspot.com/ (March 1, 2010).
Rodeen Literary Management Web site, http://www.rodeenliterary.com/ (March 1, 2010), "Julia Sarcone-Roach."

*   *   *

SCALETTA, Kurtis 1968-

Personal

Born November 22, 1968, in LA; married. *Education:* M.A. (English). *Hobbies and other interests:* Sports, animals, music, literature.

Addresses

Home—Minneapolis, MN. *Office*—P.O. Box 22151, Minneapolis, MN 55422. *Agent*—Tina Dubois Wexler, International Creative Management, 825 8th Ave., New York, NY 10019; twexlericmtalent.com. *E-mail*—kurtis@kurtisscaletta.com.

Career

Writer.

Member

Society of Children's Book Writers and Illustrators, Children's Literature Network.

Writings

Mudville, Knopf (New York, NY), 2009.
Mamba Point, Knopf (New York, NY), 2010.

Contributor of stories to *Cicada*.

Sidelights

In *Mudville,* a novel for middle-grade readers, Kurtis Scaletta offers a fanciful tale about a baseball game that has been delayed by rain for more than two decades. "To be more honest," Scaletta remarked on his home page, "I write the stories I want to write and people who know the industry tell me it's perfect for ages nine to twelve. That has been since confirmed by nine to twelve year olds who seem to like it." The publication of his debut title was the culmination of decades of effort, what Scaletta termed "thirty years learning the craft of writing and the process for getting published, and a lot of hard work and patience."

Mudville focuses on Roy McGuire, a twelve-year-old baseball fan and resident of Moundville, a small town that has been deluged by a rainstorm for twenty-two years. After Ray's father agrees to take in a surly foster child named Sturgis, the sun miraculously appears, prompting Ray to assemble a baseball team featuring the hard-throwing Sturgis as its star pitcher. Fittingly, Ray's ragtag squad challenges Mudville's arch rival, Sinister Bend, the town team with which it was locked in a stirring, as-yet-unfinished contest when the storm began. "As the 'Mudville Nine' resurrect the soaked baseball field, they bring life to a whole town," Chelsey Philpot noted in *Horn Book*. According to *School Library Journal* reviewer John Peters, Scaletta "balances perceptive explorations of personal and domestic issues perfectly with fine baseball talk and (eventually) absorbing play-by-play." Daniel Kraus, writing in *Booklist*, compared Scaletta's novel to such classic baseball stories as *Field of Dreams*, noting that "that sort of larger-than-life magic realism lends his story the aura of a proper tall tale."

Biographical and Critical Sources

PERIODICALS

Booklist, March 1, 2009, Daniel Kraus, review of *Mudville*, p. 44.
Horn Book, July-August, 2009, Chelsey Philpot, review of *Mudville*, p. 430.

Kirkus Reviews, January 15, 2009, review of *Mudville.*
School Library Journal, March, 2009, John Peters, review of *Mudville,* p. 154.

ONLINE

Kurtis Scaletta Home Page, http://kurtisscaletta.com/home (March 1, 2010).*

* * *

SHIPTON, Jonathan 1948-

Personal

Born 1948, in United Kingdom; married; wife's name Vivien; children: Ceri (son), four other children. *Education:* Attended Leicester University, 1968. *Hobbies and other interests:* Gardening, riding bikes, cooking, attending films and the theatre, reading, drawing and sculpture.

Addresses

Home—Carmarthenshire, Wales.

Career

Author of books for children. Farmer, beginning 1974. Shippo Cards (recycled greeting cards), designer. Presenter at schools.

Awards, Honors

Austrian Children's Book Award, 1992, for *Busy! Busy! Busy!;* Stitching Nederlandske children's book award, 1996, for *Horrible Crocodile; Picture Book Quarterly* prize, 1999, for *What If?*

Writings

Busy! Busy! Busy!, illustrated by Michael Foreman, Andersen Press (London, England), 1991.
In the Night, illustrated by Gill Scriven, Collins (London, England), 1991, Little, Brown (Boston, MA), 1992.
Horrible Crocodile! illustrated by Claudio Muñoz, Heinemann (London, England), 1995, published as *No Biting, Horrible Crocodile!,* Golden Books (New York, NY), 1995.
The Cooking Pot (reader), Heinemann Educational (London, England), 1996.
How to Be a Happy Hippo, illustrated by Sally Percy, Little Tiger Press (Waukesha, WI), 1999.
What If?, illustrated by Barbara Nascimbeni, Dial Books for Young Readers (New York, NY), 1999.
Emily's Perfect Pet, illustrated by Garry Parsons, Gullane Children's (London, England), 2003.

Lucky Duck, illustrated by Suzanne Diederen, Macmillan Children's Books (London, England), 2005.
Baby Baby Blah Blah Blah!, illustrated by Francesca Chessa, Holiday House (New York, NY), 2009.

Poems featured in anthologies, including *Thoughts like an Ocean,* 1977, *Me,* edited by Wendy Cooling, Franklin Watts, 2000, *Second Thoughts,* 2003, and *Fire to a Cold World,* 2004.

Biographical and Critical Sources

PERIODICALS

Booklist, October 15, 1995, April Judge, review of *No Biting, Horrible Crocodile!,* p. 413.
Center for Children's Books, July, 1999, review of *What If?,* p. 400.
Canadian Review of Materials, November 17, 2000, review of *What If?*
Kirkus Reviews, January 15, 2009, review of *Baby Baby Blah Blah Blah.*
Publishers Weekly, August, 21, 1995, review of *No Biting, Horrible Crocodile!,* p. 64; June 28, 1999, review of *What If?,* p. 77; November 15, 1999, review of *How to Be a Happy Hippo,* p. 64.
School Library Journal, February, 1996, Kathy Mitchell, review of *No Biting, Horrible Crocodile!,* p. 89; August, 1999, Carol Ann Wilson, review of *What If?,* p. 142; March, 2009, Kathleen Kelly MacMillan, review of *Baby Baby Blah Blah Blah,* p. 128.

ONLINE

Jonathan Shipton Home Page, http://www.jonathanshipton.co.uk (April 21, 2010).*

* * *

SHORE, Diane Z.
(Diane ZuHone Shore)

Personal

Married; husband's name John; children: Jennifer, Sam.

Addresses

Home and office—Marietta, GA. *E-mail*—DZShore@bellsouth.net.

Career

Children's book author. Formerly worked as an accountant. Presenter at schools and libraries.

Awards, Honors

History Feature of the Year Award, *Highlights for Children* magazine, 2002, for article "Presidential Dreams"; Children's Choice Award, and Georgia Author of the

Year nomination, both 2004, both for *Bus-a-saurus Bop;* Georgia Author of the Year nomination, 2006, and Kansas Reads selection, 2007, both for *Look Both Ways;* Georgia Author of the Year nomination, and Simon Wiesenthal Center Children's Book Award, both 2007, both for *This Is the Dream;* named PEN Woman Author of the Year, 2010.

Writings

Bus-a-saurus Bop, illustrated by David Clark, Bloomsbury Children's Books (New York, NY), 2003.

Rosa Loves to Read, illustrated by Larry Day, Children's Press (New York, NY), 2004.

(With Jessica Alexander) *Look Both Ways: A Cautionary Tale,* illustrated by Teri Weidner, Bloomsbury Children's Books (New York, NY), 2005.

(With Jessica Alexander) *This Is the Dream,* illustrated by James Ransome, HarperCollins (New York, NY), 2006.

How to Drive Your Sister Crazy, illustrated by Laura Rankin, HarperCollins (New York, NY), 2008.

This Is the Feast, illustrated by Megan Lloyd, HarperCollins (New York, NY), 2008.

This Is the Game, illustrated by Owen Smith, HarperCollins (New York, NY), 2010.

Contributor to numerous periodicals, including *Highlights for Children, Humpty Dumpty, Jack & Jill, Turtle, Children's Playmate, Spider, Cricket,* and *Boys' Quest.*

Sidelights

Although she first worked as an accountant, Georgia-based writer Diane Z. Shore eventually found that creating imaginative stories for children was more to her liking. In addition to writing humorous picture-book texts, such as *Bus-a-saurus Bop* and *Look Both Ways: A Cautionary Tale,* and easy-reading stories such as *Rosa Loves to Read* and *How to Drive Your Sister Crazy,* Shore is also the coauthor of the award-winning nonfiction picture book *This Is the Dream.* Describing *Look Both Ways* as "an appealing tale with an important message about safety," Corrina Austin added in her *School Library Journal* review that Shore's story about an absent-minded young squirrel named Filbert benefits from a "fast pace and simple rhyme scheme." A *Kirkus Reviews* writer also had praise for the "humorous repetition" in the text of *How to Drive Your Sister Crazy,* adding that Laura Rankin's accompanying illustrations capture the sibling rivalry and "reinforce each chapter's action."

Together with fellow writer Jessica Alexander, Shore introduces young children to the civil-rights movement of the mid-twentieth century in *This Is the Dream.* In a rhyming text, the authors evoke the separate worlds of whites and blacks in the segregated South, and then follow the marches and boycotts that helped call attention to racial inequality and put an end to separate-but-equal public facilities. *This Is the Dream* features oil paintings by noted illustrator James Ransome, who mixes his original images with black-and-white photos and newspaper clippings dating from the 1960s. In *School Library Journal* Teresa Pfeifer praised the pairing of "lyrical verses and distinguished illustrations" in the book, recommending it as "a valuable addition to children's literature." A *Kirkus Reviews* writer hailed *This Is the Dream* as "a soaring tribute to the accomplishments of the Civil Rights Movement," and in *Booklist* Carolyn Phelan recommended the book's "rhythmic verse," which brings history to life "with simplicity and power."

Shore has followed *This Is the Dream* with *This Is the Feast* and *This Is the Game,* both of which focus on things that are unique to the United States of America and are geared for preschool as well as elementary-school audiences. *This Is the Game* focuses on the history of baseball, while in *This Is the Feast* readers witness the back story to the Pilgrims' celebration of their new home at a feast that is now commemorated as Thanksgiving Day. Brought to life in artwork by Megan Lloyd, Shore's rhyming text for *This Is the Feast* takes readers aboard the *Mayflower* and follows the Pilgrims as they land on Plymouth Rock and attempt to survive their first months in a harsh and unfamiliar new land. The author "packs a lot [of history] into the verse," wrote *School Library Journal* contributor Carol S. Surges, the critic also praising Lloyd's "primitive-inspired" acrylic paintings. In *Booklist* Hazel Rochman described *This Is the Feast* as a "simple, upbeat celebration of the first Thanksgiving" that benefits from "bouncy rhyme and sun-filled illustrations."

Biographical and Critical Sources

PERIODICALS

Black Issues Book Review, January-February, 2006, review of *This Is the Dream,* p. 37.

Booklinks, March, 2006, Carolyn Phelan, review of *This Is the Dream,* p. 8.

Booklist, February 1, 2006, Carolyn Phelan, review of *This Is the Dream,* p. 69; September 15, 2008, Hazel Rochman, review of *This Is the Feast,* p. 56.

Bulletin of the Center for Children's Books, February, 2006, Deborah Stevenson, review of *This Is the Dream,* p. 285.

Chicago Tribune, January 8, 2006, Mary Harris Russell, review of *This Is the Dream,* p. 2.

Children's Bookwatch, September, 2005, review of *Look Both Ways: A Cautionary Tale.*

Horn Book, March-April, 2006, Martha V. Parravano, review of *This Is the Dream,* p. 205.

Kirkus Reviews, June 15, 2003, review of *Bus-a-saurus Bop,* p. 864; July 1, 2005, review of *Look Both Ways,* p. 744; December 1, 2005, review of *This Is the Dream,* p. 1280; August 15, 2008, review of *This Is the Feast;* October 1, 2008, review of *How to Drive Your Sister Crazy.*

Publishers Weekly, July 21, 2003, review of *Bus-a-saurus Bop,* p. 194; November 21, 2005, review of *This Is the Dream,* p. 46.

School Library Journal, August, 2004, Bethany L.W. Hankinson, review of *Rosa Loves to Read,* p. 90; July, 2005, Corrina Austin, review of *Look Both Ways,* p. 82; January, 2006, Teresa Pfeifer, review of *This Is the Dream,* p. 124; October, 2008, Carol S. Surges, review of *Here Is the Feast,* p. 136.

ONLINE

Bloomsbury Press Web site, http://www.bloomsburyusa. com/ (April 25, 2010), "Diane Z. Shore."
Diane Z. Shore Home Page, http://www.dianezshore.com (April 25, 2010).

*   *   *

SHORE, Diane ZuHone
See SHORE, Diane Z.

*   *   *

SMITH, Cynthia Leitich 1967-

Personal

Born December 31, 1967, in Kansas City, MO; daughter of H.E. (a new-car sales manager) and Caroline Smith; married Greg Leitich Smith (a children's author and patent lawyer), September 4, 1994. *Education:* University of Kansas—Lawrence, B.S., 1990; University of Michigan Law School, J.D., 1994. *Hobbies and other interests:* Cats, historic restoration and preservation.

Addresses

Home—Austin, TX. *Office*—Children's and YA Literature Resources, P.O. Box 3255, Austin, TX 78764. *Agent*—Ginger Knowlton, Curtis Brown Ltd. 10 Astor Pl., New York, NY 10003. *E-mail*—cynthia@cynthialeitichsmith.com.

Career

Writer. Worked variously as a reporter for small-town and urban newspapers, in public relations for a non-profit agency, and for a greeting card company and an oil company; Department of Health and Human Services, law clerk, 1994-95; Vermont College of Fine Arts, faculty member of Writing for Children and Young Adults, 2005—.

Cynthia Leitich Smith (Photograph by Frances Hill Yansky. Reproduced by permission.)

Member

Society of Children's Book Writers and Illustrators, Writers' League of Texas.

Awards, Honors

Notable Children's Trade Book in the Field of Social Studies designation, National Council for the Social Studies/Children's Book Council (NCSS/CBC), Oklahoma Book Award finalist, Oklahoma Center for the Book, Storyteller Award runner-up, Western Writers Association, *Bulletin of the Center for Children's Books* Choice designation, and *Library Talk* Editor's Choice, all 2000, all for *Jingle Dancer;* Oklahoma Book Award finalist, and Writer of the Year award for Children's Prose, Wordcraft Circle of Native Writers and Storytellers, both 2001, both for *Rain Is Not My Indian Name;* Notable Children's Trade Book in the Field of Social Studies designation, NCSS/CBC, Texas Institute of Letters Award finalist, Native American Book List inclusion, National Education Association, Best Children's Books of the Year inclusion, Bank Street College of Education, and Cooperative Children's Book Center Choices selection, all 2003, all for *Indian Shoes;* Borders Original Voices nominee, 2007, and Best Books for Young Adults nominee, and Books for the Teen Age selection, New York Public Library, all for *Tantalize;* Teens Top Ten nominee, 2009, for *Eternal;* Great Site for Kids designation, American Library Association, for CynthiaLeitichSmith.com.

Writings

FOR CHILDREN

Jingle Dancer, illustrated by Cornelius Van Wright and Ying-Hwa Hu, Morrow (New York, NY), 2000.

Rain Is Not My Indian Name, HarperCollins (New York, NY), 2001.

Indian Shoes, illustrated by Jim Madsen, HarperCollins (New York, NY), 2002.

(With husband, Greg Leitich Smith) *Santa Knows,* illustrated by Steve Björkman, Dutton Children's Books (New York, NY), 2006.

Contributor to periodicals, including *Cicada, Horn Book, Library Talk,* and *Book Link.* Works collected in anthologies, including *In My Grandmother's House: Award-winning Authors Tell Stories about Their Grandmothers,* edited by Bonnie Christensen, HarperCollins (New York, NY), 2003; *Period Pieces: Stories for Girls* HarperCollins, 2003; *Over the River and through the Woods: Stories about Grandmothers,* HarperCollins, 2003; *Moccasin Thunder: American Indian Stories for Today,* edited by Lori M. Carlson, HarperCollins, 2005; *Immortal: Love Stories with Bite,* edited by P.C. Cast, BenBella Books (Dallas, TX), 2008; *Geetastic: Stories from the Nerd Herd,* edited by Holly Black and Cecil Castellucci, Little, Brown (New York, NY), 2009; and *Sideshow: Ten Original Dark Tales,* edited by Deborah Noyes, Candlewick Press (Somerville, MA), 2009.

YOUNG-ADULT NOVELS

Tantalize, Candlewick Press (Cambridge, MA), 2007.
Eternal, Candlewick Press (Somerville, MA), 2009.

Adaptations

Rain Is Not My Indian Name was adapted for audiocassette by Listening Library, 2001.

Sidelights

Cynthia Leitich Smith is the author of several picture books and young-adult novels that are noted for their sensitivity and humor, as well as their strong narratives and well-drawn characters. A mixed-blood member of the Muscogee (Creek) Nation, Smith often explores contemporary Native-American themes in her novels, picture books, and chapter books, while also focusing on loss, urban assimilation, and the importance of community. Smith's award-winning young-adult novel *Rain Is Not My Indian Name* focuses on a mixed-heritage teen who, in the midst of confronting a personal tragedy, gains understanding of her heritage, while the picture book *Jingle Dancer* finds a Creek-Chippewa girl honoring the women in her family while solving a personal difficulty. Additionally, Smith has penned two highly regarded teen horror novels, *Tantalize* and *Eternal.*

Smith was born on December 31, 1967, in Kansas City, Missouri. A shy child, she became a great fan of comic books, a hobby she took up when she accompanied her father for a weekly outing to buy his gun-enthusiast magazines. Although her parents did not read literary fiction, they did instill in their daughter the importance of reading. Smith dictated her first poem to her mother as a first grader, and by grade six she was writing the "Dear Gabby" column for her school newspaper. In junior high and high school she edited her school's newspapers, and at college at the University of Kansas she majored in journalism and English, intending to become a reporter. After graduating from the University of Kansas, Smith enrolled at the University of Michigan Law School, having shifted her career goals to legal reporter and media-law journalism professor. In addition to meeting the man who would become her husband, Smith also involved herself in Native American and feminist causes during law school.

While working as a law clerk after graduation, Smith began "scribbling stories after work and over my lunch hour," as she once told an *Authors and Artists for Young Adults* (*AAYA*) interviewer. She soon began to see that writing was what she wanted to do and decided to leave the law and begin a career as a children's author. Her first picture book, *Jingle Dancer,* tells of young Jenna, who determines to do the jingle dance for the next powwow. To get the cone-shaped jingles for her dress, Jenna visits several neighbors and relatives. A *Publishers Weekly* reviewer wrote that Smith "convincingly juxtaposes cherished Native American tradition and contemporary lifestyle in this smooth debut," and *Booklist* contributor Connie Fletcher had similar praise, noting that *Jingle Dancer* "highlights the importance of family and community."

Smith combines community, Native-American cultural traditions, and romantic elements in her first novel for young-adult readers, *Rain Is Not My Indian Name.* Cassidy Rain Berghoff is one of a handful of people of mixed Native-American heritage living in her small Kansas town. Cassidy experiences more than her share of tragedy: her mother died after being struck by lightning, and now, just after celebrating her fourteenth birthday with her best friend Galen, with whom she just shared a first kiss, Cassidy Rain learns that Galen too is dead, killed in a car accident. Torn by grief, she cannot deal with the loss until months later, when the death of a distant relative and participation in a community project inspires her to begin healing.

Rain Is Not My Indian Name was greeted with critical acclaim. Carol Edwards, writing in *School Library Journal,* called the book a "wonderful novel of a present-day teen and her 'patchwork tribe.'" A reviewer for *Publishers Weekly,* while noting that the various plot lines and non-chronological narrative "make it difficult to enter Smith's complex novel," added that readers will find an "ample reward" in the "warmth and texture of the writing."

Smith's chapter book *Indian Shoes* collects six humorous interconnected stories about Ray Halfmoon and his grandfather and their daily lives in urban Chicago and rural Oklahoma. While a *Publishers Weekly* contributor described the text as somewhat "flowery" in its depiction of the "strong bond" between generations, a *Kirkus Reviews* critic dubbed the volume a "very pleasing first-chapter book," and described Smith's story as both "funny" and "heartwarming." Similarly, Anne O'Malley, reviewing *Indian Shoes* for *Booklist,* described the lead characters as "charming" and the stories a "powerful, poignant evocation of a cross-generational bond."

Santa Knows, a humorous work that Smith coauthored with her husband, Greg Leitich Smith, centers on the adventures of Alfie F. Snorklepuss, a dour youngster who simply refuses to believe in Santa Claus. Thanks to a letter written by Alfie's lovable little sister, Noelle, jolly Saint Nick pays the doubting youngster a surprise visit on Christmas Eve, and together they head off to the North Pole to tour the workshop. When Noelle awakens on Christmas morning, she finds an unusual and unexpected gift beneath the tree. "Children will relate to Noelle's feelings when her brother tries to discourage her belief in Santa," Maureen Wade asserted in *School Library Journal,* while a *Kirkus Reviews* contributor dubbed *Santa Knows* "a newly minted winner."

Smith turns her attention to the Gothic fantasy genre in *Tantalize,* "a thinking reader's horror novel and an entertaining, empowering ride," as Elle Wolterbeek stated in her review for the *Journal of Adolescent & Adult Literacy.* Since the death of her parents years earlier, seventeen-year-old Quincie Morris has been living with her uncle Davidson, the owner of a vampire-themed restaurant, in Austin, Texas. Quincie's best friend and first love, Kieran, a hybrid werewolf, becomes a prime suspect when the head chef at the restaurant is brutally attacked. Meanwhile, the chef's replacement evidences an intense interest in Quincie and attempts to beguile her with exotic foods and wine. "The restaurant's heady mix of rich foods and supernatural sexuality sets the tone for the novel," Lauren Adams reported in her *Horn Book* review of *Tantalize,* and Donna Rosenblum predicted in *School Library Journal* that audiences will be captivated by the "disturbing fantasy of vampires, werewolves, and a strong no-nonsense heroine." Several critics applauded Smith's epistolary approach to the narrative, which incorporates menu pages, advertisements, and newspaper clippings to tell its tale. "Readers familiar with Bram Stoker's *Dracula* will be thrilled with this modern-day extension of the genre," Wolterbeek observed.

In *Eternal,* a dark love story with touches of humor, Smith revisits the alternate fantasy world she introduced in *Tantalize.* Told in alternating chapters from the perspective of the novel's protagonists, *Eternal* centers on the relationship between Miranda, a vampire princess, and Zachary, a disgraced guardian angel who failed in his attempt to save the young woman from her

Cover of Smith's young-adult horror novel Tantalize. (Copyright © 2007 Cynthia Leitich Smith. Front cover photograph copyright © 2007 by Photodisc Red/Getty Images. All rights reserved. Reproduced by permission of Candlewick Press.)

ghastly fate. To regain his honor, Zachary gains access to the house of Dracula, where he takes a job as Miranda's personal assistant and tries to revive her sense of humanity. "The suspenseful and entertaining story plays out in a parallel Chicago mingling mortal and immortal, damned and blessed," remarked Adams. A *Kirkus Reviews* contributor noted that "the pace of this entertaining romp is quick and the action plentiful," and a *Publishers Weekly* critic applauded "the action-packed finale."

In addition to her publications for young readers, Smith also maintains an award-winning Web site that serves as a resource through its interviews, links, and references. She described it to Wolterbeek as "my way of doing what I can to raise awareness and support my fellow book lovers, both the young and young at heart." Reflecting on her decision to pursue a literary life, she told Wolterbeek: "When I quit my day job in law, it was a heart decision—not a head decision, and certainly not a financial one. My commitment was not only to my own books but also to the body of fiction and nonfiction for young readers. I wanted to do my part to act as an ambassador for youth literacy, literature, and the grown-ups who champion both."

"I began, as we so often advise new voices, by writing what I knew," Smith told *SATA*. "For me, that meant stories of middle class, mixed-blood Native-American characters and communities from the mid-to-southwest.

"As I grew, I began diversifying my work to include more of the kinds of stories I loved to read: funny books for the youngest readers and more adventurous fantasies for teenagers. On the latter, it's a particular pleasure to offer strong girl characters and diverse casts to the Gothic fantasy tradition.

"Along the way, writing short stories has been a tremendous boon to my craft. I first tried humor, boy voice, and upper-level young-adult fiction through the short form, which is also a wonderful end unto itself."

Biographical and Critical Sources

BOOKS

Authors and Artists for Young Adults, Volume 51, Gale (Detroit, MI), 2003.

PERIODICALS

Better Homes & Gardens, July 11, 2000, Steve Cooper, "Raising a Reader."
Book, July, 2000, Kathleen Odean, "Debuts That Deliver."
Booklist, May 15, 2000, Connie Fletcher, review of *Jingle Dancer,* p. 1750; April 1, 2002, Judy Morrissey, "The Million Dollar Shot," p. 1348; June 1, 2002, Anne O'Malley, review of *Indian Shoes,* p. 1725.
Horn Book, March-April, 2007, Lauren Adams, review of *Tantalize,* p. 202; March-April, 2009, Lauren Adams, review of *Eternal,* p. 203.
Journal of Adolescent & Adult Literacy, October, 2005, James Blasingame, "People to Watch: Cynthia and Greg Leitich Smith," p. 163; September, 2007, Elle Wolterbeek, review of *Tantalize,* p. 74, and Elle Wolterbeek, interview with Smith, p. 81.
Kirkus Reviews, April 1, 2002, review of *Indian Shoes,* p. 499; November 1, 2006, review of *Santa Knows,* p. 1134; January 15, 2009, review of *Eternal.*
Kliatt, March, 2007, Cara Chancellor, review of *Tantalize,* p. 18.
Library Talk, March-April, 2002, Sharron L. McElmeel, "Author Profile: Cynthia Leitich Smith."
Publishers Weekly, May 15, 2000, review of *Jingle Dancer,* p. 117; July 9, 2001, review of *Rain Is Not My Indian Name,* p. 68; April 1, 2002, review of *Indian Shoes,* p. 83; March 5, 2007, review of *Tantalize,* p. 62; March 16, 2009, review of *Eternal,* p. 63.
School Library Journal, June, 2001, Carol Edwards, review of *Rain Is Not My Indian Name,* p. 156; October, 2006, Maureen Wade, review of *Santa Knows,* p. 101; May, 2007, Donna Rosenblum, review of *Tantalize,* p. 144; July, 2009, Leah J. Sparks, review of *Eternal,* p. 92.

Teacher Librarian, October, 2001, Teri Lesesne, interview with Smith, p. 51.
Writing for Kids, June, 2002, Alice Pope, "Sound off with Children's Writers."

ONLINE

Cynsations Web log, http://cynthialeitichsmith.blogspot. com/ (March 1, 2010).
Cynthia Leitich Smith Home Page, http://www.cynthia leitichsmith.com (March 1, 2010).
Vermont College of Fine Arts Web site, http://www.ver montcollege.edu/ (March 1, 2010), "Cynthia Leitich Smith."

*　　　*　　　*

SMITH, Emily Wing 1980-

Personal

Born 1980; married. *Education:* Brigham Young University, B.A. (English); Vermont College of Fine Arts, M.F.A. (writing for children and young adults). *Religion:* Church of Jesus Christ of Latter-day Saints (Mormon).

Emily Wing Smith (Photograph by Brittany Lissonbee. Reproduced by permission.)

Addresses

Home—Salt Lake City, UT. *Agent*—Michael Bourret, Dystel & Goderich Literary Management, 1 Union Square W., Ste. 904, New York, NY 10003; mbourret@ dystel.com. *E-mail*—emilywingsmith@gmail.com.

Career

Writer.

Awards, Honors

David O. McKay Essay Contest winner, Brigham Young University; Utah Book Award, Utah Center for the Book, 2008, for *The Way He Lived*.

Writings

The Way He Lived (novel), Flux (Woodbury, MN), 2008.

Contributor of stories to periodicals.

Sidelights

In her debut novel, *The Way He Lived*, Emily Wing Smith looks at the tragic death of a young man from the perspective of six vastly different individuals.

Cover of Smith's young-adult novel **The Way He Lived.** (Cover image © 2008 by Image Source/SuperStock. All rights reserved. Reproduced by permission.)

"People often ask me why I chose to write the book with multiple narrators and points of view," the author remarked in an *Interactive Reader* online interview with Jackie Parker. "I didn't really choose to write it that way—this story came to me as a collage of voices, each voice telling me how he or she was dealing with Joel's death. So having six different narrators wasn't as much of a challenge as each one needing to be told in a specific style."

The Way He Lived concerns Joel Espen, a sixteen-year-old Boy Scout who dies of thirst after sacrificing his supply of water during an ill-fated hiking expedition in the Grand Canyon. The news of Joel's death rocks his hometown of Haven, Utah, a small Mormon community, and prompts those who were closest to the boy, such as his sisters and classmates, to reconsider their own lives. In the words of a *Publishers Weekly* critic, Smith "preserves each narrator's complexity, investigating their defenses and revealing their core selves while dropping clues about the enigmatic Joel," and a *Kirkus Reviews* contributor observed that the voices of the six narrators "reveal introspection and doubt as the author skillfully shows how Joel influenced each life."

Biographical and Critical Sources

PERIODICALS

Kirkus Reviews, October 15, 2008, review of *The Way He Lived.*
Publishers Weekly, November 17, 2008, review of *The Way He Lived,* p. 58.
Voice of Youth Advocates, December, 2008, Amy S. Pattee, review of *The Way He Lived,* p. 441.

ONLINE

Emily Wing Smith Home Page, http://www.emilywing smith.com (March 1, 2010).
Interactive Reader Web log, http://interactivereader.blog spot.com/ (November 21, 2008), Jackie Parker, interview with Smith.

*   *   *

SNICKET, Lemony 1970-
(Daniel Handler)

Personal

Born Daniel Handler, February 28, 1970, in San Francisco, CA; married Lisa Brown (an art director); children: Otto. *Education:* Wesleyan University, graduated, 1992.

Lemony Snicket (Photograph by Jeff Geissler. AP Images. Reproduced by permission.)

Addresses

Home—San Francisco, CA. *E-mail*—lsnicket@harper collins.com.

Career

Author, poet, and "studied expert in rhetorical analysis." Comedy writer, *The House of Blues Radio Hour,* San Francisco, CA; freelance book and movie reviewer.

Awards, Honors

Academy of American Poets Prize, 1990; Olin fellowship, 1992; Quill Award, 2006, for *The Penultimate Peril.*

Writings

FOR CHILDREN; "A SERIES OF UNFORTUNATE EVENTS" SERIES

The Bad Beginning (also see below), illustrated by Bret Helquist, HarperCollins (New York, NY), 1999.
The Reptile Room (also see below), illustrated by Bret Helquist, HarperCollins (New York, NY), 1999.

The Wide Window (also see below), illustrated by Bret Helquist, HarperCollins (New York, NY), 2000.
The Miserable Mill (also see below), illustrated by Bret Helquist, HarperCollins (New York, NY), 2000.
The Austere Academy (also see below), illustrated by Bret Helquist, HarperCollins (New York, NY), 2000.
A Box of Unfortunate Events: The Trouble Begins (contains *The Bad Beginning, The Reptile Room,* and *The Wide Window*), HarperCollins (New York, NY), 2001.
The Ersatz Elevator (also see below), illustrated by Bret Helquist, HarperCollins (New York, NY), 2001.
The Vile Village (also see below), illustrated by Bret Helquist, HarperCollins (New York, NY), 2001.
The Hostile Hospital (also see below), illustrated by Bret Helquist, HarperCollins (New York, NY), 2001.
A Box of Unfortunate Events: The Situation Worsens (contains *The Miserable Mill, The Austere Academy,* and *The Ersatz Elevator*), HarperCollins (New York, NY), 2002.
The Carnivorous Carnival (also see below), illustrated by Bret Helquist, HarperCollins (New York, NY), 2002.
A Box of Unfortunate Events: The Dilemma Deepens (contains *The Vile Village, The Hostile Hospital,* and *The Carnivorous Carnival*), HarperCollins (New York, NY), 2003.
The Slippery Slope (also see below), illustrated by Bret Helquist, HarperCollins (New York, NY), 2003.
The Grim Grotto (also see below), illustrated by Bret Helquist, HarperCollins (New York, NY), 2004.
A Box of Unfortunate Events: The Ominous Omnibus (contains *The Bad Beginning, The Reptile Room,* and *The Wide Window*), HarperCollins (New York, NY), 2005.
The Penultimate Peril (also see below), illustrated by Bret Helquist, HarperCollins (New York, NY), 2005.
A Box of Unfortunate Events: The Loathsome Library (contains *The Bad Beginning, The Reptile Room, The Wide Window, The Miserable Mill, The Austere Academy,* and *The Ersatz Elevator*), HarperCollins (New York, NY), 2005.
A Box of Unfortunate Events: The Gloom Looms (contains *The Grim Grotto, The Slippery Slope,* and *The Penultimate Peril*), HarperCollins (New York, NY), 2005.
The End (also see below), illustrated by Bret Helquist, HarperCollins (New York, NY), 2006.
The Complete Wreck (omnibus), HarperCollins (New York, NY), 2006.
The Beatrice Letters, HarperCollins (New York, NY), 2006.

Author's work (under Snicket pseudonym) has been published in Germany, Italy, Norway, Israel, Japan, and Denmark.

FOR ADULTS; UNDER NAME DANIEL HANDLER

The Basic Eight, St. Martin's Press (New York, NY), 1999.
Watch Your Mouth, St. Martin's Press (New York, NY), 2000.
Adverbs, Ecco (New York, NY), 2006.

OTHER

Lemony Snicket: The Unauthorized Autobiography, HarperTrophy (New York, NY), 2002.
(Author of introduction) Dino Buzzati, *The Bears' Famous Invasion of Sicily,* HarperTrophy (New York, NY), 2005.
The Puzzling Puzzles: Bothersome Games Which Will Bother Some People (activity book), HarperTrophy (New York, NY), 2006.
The Notorious Notations (blank journal), HarperFestival (New York, NY), 2006.
Horseradish: Bitter Truths You Can't Avoid, HarperCollins (New York, NY), 2007.
The Latke Who Couldn't Stop Screaming: A Christmas Story, illustrated by Lisa Brown, McSweeney's (New York, NY), 2007.
The Composer Is Dead (with CD), illustrated by Carson Ellis, music by Nathaniel Stookey, HarperCollins (New York, NY), 2008.
The Lump of Coal, illustrated by Brett Helquist, HarperCollins (New York, NY), 2008.
Thirteen Words, illustrated by Maira Kalman, HarperCollins (New York, NY), 2010.

Contributor to *Little Lit: It Was a Dark and Silly Night,* edited by Art Spiegelman, HarperCollins, 2003. Contributor to periodicals, including *Voice Literary Supplement, Newsday, Salon,* and *New York Times.*

Adaptations

The Basic Eight was optioned for a film by New Regency; *A Series of Unfortunate Events* was adapted for film, Paramount Pictures, 2004. The "Series of Unfortunate Events" books were adapted for audiobook.

Sidelights

Writing under the pen name Lemony Snicket, Daniel Handler is the author of the wildly popular "A Series of Unfortunate Events" novels. The series, which features the grim misadventures of the orphaned Baudelaire children, has delighted youthful readers eager to deal with irony, intelligent silliness, and over-the-top melodrama in their fiction. "Stories like these aren't cheerful," Handler himself admitted in a *New York Times* essay, "but they offer a truth—that real trouble cannot be erased, only endured—that is more soothing to me than any determinedly cheerful grin." Other books by Handler/Snicket, including his arch, holiday-themed *The Latke Who Couldn't Stop Screaming: A Christmas Story* and *The Lump of Coal,* continue in the tradition established by Roald Dahl, a British writer that several critics have cited as being among the author's influences.

Handler was born and raised in San Francisco, the son of an accountant and a college dean. Growing up, he was "a bright and obvious person," as he later characterized himself to Sally Lodge in *Publishers Weekly.* However, the incipient novelist "always wanted to be a

dark, mysterious person": he preferred stories "in which mysterious and creepy things happen" and rejected stories "where everyone joined the softball team and had a grand time or found true love on a picnic." The youthful Handler sought out stories à la Dahl or Edward Gorey, the latter an author/illustrator who has also been cited as a major influence. In fact, the first book Handler bought with his own money was Gorey's *The Blue Aspic.*

A student of San Francisco's prestigious and demanding Lowell High School, Handler graduated in 1988, tying for Best Personality in his graduating class. Eleven years later, he would set his first novel at fictional Roewer High, a barely concealed stand-in for this school, wherein students "pushed to the limit academically, socially and athletically," as Handler wrote. Meanwhile, Handler attended Wesleyan University, winning a prize from the Academy of American Poets in 1990. His love for poetry eventually gave way to a passion for novels, and after graduation an Olin fellowship provided Handler with the financial support needed to focus on his writing. After the fellowship ended, Handler spent a couple of years in the mid-1990s writing comedy sketches for the nationally syndicated *The House of Blues Radio Hour,* based in San Francisco.

Things began looking up for Handler when he moved to New York City and established himself as a freelance movie and book critic. By 1999, his first novel, *The Basic Eight,* was finally published and earned respectful if not praiseworthy reviews. *The Basic Eight,* although written for adults, caused some reviewers and booksellers to label it "YA" because it focuses on a cast of high-school students in a clique called the Basic Eight.

The Basic Eight deals with a teenage murderer, and it hit bookstore shelves only weeks before the tragic shootings at Colorado's Columbine High School would focus national attention on teen violence. Handler's novel is narrated by Flannery Culp, who recounts the events of her senior year at Roewer High from a prison cell where she is serving time for the murder of a teacher and a fellow student. Flan is, as a reviewer for *Publishers Weekly* observed, "precocious" and "pretentious." Reviled by the media as a leader of a Satanic cult, she is determined to tell the real truth behind the tragicomic series of events that landed her in prison instead of in an Ivy League school.

Flan, editor of the student paper, has a group of good friends who form the Basic Eight: "Queen Bee" Kate, lovely Natasha, chef-in-the-making Gabriel, absinthe-fan Douglas, Jennifer Rose Milton, and "V," the last whose name is withheld to spare her wealthy family. Childhood games turn increasingly serious when the group begins experimenting with absinthe, and then Natasha comes to Flan's rescue by poisoning a biology teacher who has been plaguing her friend. There is also classmate Adam State, a love interest of Flan's, and her jealousy ultimately leads to Adam's murder—by cro-

quet mallet. The talk-show circuit quickly gins up the story, transforming the Basic Eight from a privileged clique to a Satanic cult.

In *Publishers Weekly* a critic observed of *The Basic Eight* that "Handler's confident satire is not only cheeky but packed with downright lovable characters whose youthful misadventures keep the novel neatly balanced between absurdity and poignancy." In *Booklist* Stephanie Zvirin called the book "part horror story, part black comedy," noting that *The Basic Eight* shows what can happen to "smart, privileged, cynical teens with too few rules, too much to drink, too little supervision, and boundless imagination."

In *Watch Your Mouth* Handler focuses on another coming-of-age crucible: the college years. Joseph is just finishing his junior year at prestigious Mather College. There he has met luscious and lascivious Cynthia Glass, whom he delights in calling Cyn with its intended double meaning. A surfeit of sex has caused Joseph to fall behind in his studies and earn an Incomplete in one class. When Cyn suggests that Joseph spend the summer with her and her family in Pittsburgh, he leaps at the chance to stay close to his lover. There the two will work days as Jewish day-camp counselors, Joseph will finish his Incomplete, and nights will be their own. Once settled in the Glass's home, however, Joseph senses that all is not right: father Ben pines too much for daughter Cyn, mother Mimi yearns too much for son Stephen, and Stephen seems to return his mother's feelings.

Written in the form of an opera and weaving realism with surrealism, *Watch Your Mouth* almost crosses the bounds of good taste, according to some reviewers. A *Publishers Weekly* reviewer called the novel so "twisted that even its protagonist can't keep up with the perverse turns of plot." The critic further observed that Handler's "melodramatic satire of family life trembles between virtuosity and utter collapse," while in *Library Journal* Rebecca Kelm dubbed *Watch Your Mouth* "quirky" and "offbeat."

The birth of Lemony Snicket came about when Handler was offered the chance to pen books he might have enjoyed reading when he was ten. Taking up the Snicket moniker—which he had once devised to avoid getting on unwanted mail lists—he set about to revamp the notion of what constitutes an appropriate novel for juveniles. The result was *The Bad Beginning,* the first of over a dozen volumes chronicling the adventures of the Baudelaire orphans. As the "A Series of Unfortunate Events" books unfold, siblings Violet, Klaus, and Sunny Baudelaire not only lose their parents, but are then set upon by the vile Count Olaf, whose one goal in life, it seems, is to bilk the children out of their fortune. The Baudelaire brood is led by inventive fourteen-year-old Violet, while her rather bookish brother, twelve-year-old Klaus, follows her lead. Then there is baby Sunny, who has incredibly sharp teeth for an infant and em-

ploys a baby argot that speaks volumes. Eschewing magic, Handler imbues these children with survival skills of a practical nature, enabling them to defend themselves from a cornucopia of hurled knives, falling lamps, storms, snakes, leeches, and just plain rotten folks. Their saga is related in a deadpan, sophisticated text that has its tongue firmly planted in cheek.

As readers join them in *The Bad Beginning,* the three Baudelaire children have lost their parents in a fire. Through the oversight of the ineffectual banker, Mr. Poe, they become the wards of Count Olaf, a distant cousin. Olaf sets the siblings to labor in his house, meanwhile devising schemes with his theatrical troupe to deprive the orphans of their inheritance. The three survive the count's attacks with spunk, initiative, and, in the case of Sunny, sharp teeth. Handler/Snicket "uses formal, Latinate language and intrusive commentary to hilarious effect," noted a reviewer in *Publishers Weekly,* the critic adding of *The Bad Beginning* that the author "paints the satire with such broad strokes that most readers will view it from a safe distance."

In *The Reptile Room,* it seems the orphans have a chance for happiness when they go to live with Dr. Montgomery Montgomery, a "very fun, but fatally naïve herpetologist," according to Ron Charles in the *Christian Science Monitor.* Unfortunately, their safe haven is short lived, spoiled by the arrival of the oafish Olaf. Susan Dove Lempke, reviewing the first two titles in *Booklist,* noted that the "droll humor, reminiscent of Edward Gorey's, will be lost on some children; others may not enjoy the old-fashioned storytelling style that frequently addresses the reader directly and includes definitions of terms." Lempke went on, however, to conclude that "plenty of children will laugh at the over-the-top satire; hiss at the creepy nefarious villains; and root for the intelligent, courageous, unfortunate Baudelaire orphans." Linda Bindner, writing in *School Library Journal,* maintained that "while the misfortunes hover on the edge of being ridiculous, Snicket's energetic blend of humor, dramatic irony, and literary flair makes it all perfectly believable."

The Wide Window finds the orphans with elderly Aunt Josephine, who lives on a house on stilts that overlooks Lake Lachrymose. Josephine is a widow as well as a frightful grammarian, and when Olaf finally tracks down the Baudelaires, he fools the woman into believing he is a sailboat captain. When Josephine finally stumbles onto his true identity, Olaf gets rid of her by pushing the good woman into leech-infested waters and leaving the peripatetic children to find a new protector. Lempke noted that in this installment Snicket adopts "an old-fashioned tone," offering "plenty advice to readers in asides." "The effect is often hilarious as well as edifying," the critic observed, adding that "readers never truly worry that [the Baudelaire orphans] will be defeated in this or their next adventure."

The orphans undertake a trip to Paltryville and yet another guardian in *The Miserable Mill.* Under the care of

the owner of the Lucky Smells Lumbermill, the children work in the mill and survive on gum for lunch and casserole for dinner. Count Olaf, is of course, lurking just offstage and preparing to pounce. "The story is deliciously mock-Victorian and self-mockingly melodramatic," noted *Booklist* reviewer Carolyn Phelan, the critic also citing Brett Helquist's amusing artwork and Handler's "many asides to the reader." As Sharon R. Pearce observed in *School Library Journal,* the humor in *The Miserable Mill* "exaggerates the sour and makes anyone's real life seem sweet in comparison."

The Baudelaires' saga continues in *The Austere Academy* and *The Ersatz Elevator.* In the former title, the Baudelaire children are consigned to a shack at the Prufrock Preparatory School where they face snapping crabs, strict punishments, dripping fungus, and the evils of the metric system, while the latter finds them contending with new guardians Jerome and Esme Squalor while trying to save two friends from the clutches of Count Olaf. "Series fans will enjoy the quick pace, entertaining authorial asides, and over-the-top characterizations, and . . . Helquist's droll pencil drawings will add to their reading pleasure," Phelan noted of *The Ersatz Elevator.*

In *The Vile Village* the Baudelaires are adopted by the residents of V.F.D., a town run by a strict council of elders whose myriad rules regulate every aspect of villagers' lives. When the children are falsely accused of murder, they must escape from jail to avoid being burned at the stake. "Arch literary allusions enhance the stories for readers on different levels," noted *School Library Journal* contributor Farida S. Dowler. The Baudelaires volunteer their services at Heimlich Hospital in *The Hostile Hospital,* "another darkly amusing, nightmarish adventure," as Phelan stated. The trio is once again pursued by Count Olaf and his cohorts, who this time threaten Violet with a cranioectomy. Writing in *Entertainment Weekly,* Daniel Fierman praised the author's "devilish carnivals of wit, wordplay, and adventure."

The Carnivorous Carnival finds the children disguised as circus freaks in order to investigate Madame Lulu, a fortune teller who uses her crystal ball to fuel Olaf's evil plans. "The humor is as sharp as ever," Heather Dieffenbach commented in *School Library Journal.* In *The Slippery Slope,* Violet and Klaus must rescue young Sunny, who has been kidnaped by the count and taken to the Mortmain Mountains. According to *Entertainment Weekly* reviewer Alynda Wheat, the tenth entry in the series "is as delightfully dark as ever."

While searching for a vitally important sugar bowl in *The Grim Grotto,* the Baudelaire children make a new ally in submarine captain Widdershins, who helps them battle Olaf and his nefarious colleagues, Esme Squalor and Carmelita Spats. Snicket/Handler's "villains remain deliciously villainous, and the long-suffering Baudelaires still accept struggle without complaint," Zvirin

stated of the series installment. In the aptly titled *The Penultimate Peril* the Baudelaires gather at the Hotel Denouement, a venue organized according to the Dewey decimal classification and whose guests include several characters from earlier series installments. As Zvirin noted, "this inventive go-round seems more dizzying . . . than usual."

Adrift in the open seas with Count Olaf, *The End* finds the Baudelaires washed ashore and welcomed by friendly islanders. Unfortunately, though, their haven does not remain safe for long in a novel that some critics have described as a fitting although somewhat ambiguous ending to the series. In the words of *Horn Book* reviewer Claire E. Gross, "where Snicket excels . . . is in balancing the expectation of happy ending against his own repeated declarations that none exists." Henry Alford, writing in the *New York Times Book Review,* offered a different assessment, remarking that *The End* offer an unconventional reading experience: "Where, in the end . . . does the 'Unfortunate Events' series leave us? It leaves us reminded of what an interesting and offbeat educator Handler is." According to Alford, "the books seem at times like a covert mission to turn their readers into slightly dark-hued sophisticates. . . . amply prepared for the rocky narrative landscapes of Borges and Eco."

"The Snicket novels are morality tales, albeit twisted ones," observed Amy Benfer in her *Salon.com* review. "Among other things, Snicket tells children that one should never stay up late on a school night, except to finish a very good book; he insists that there is nothing worse than someone who can't play the violin but insists upon doing so anyway." Through his use of continual authorial intrusions, interjection of definitions, and insertion of stage directions, Handler "was mostly just knocking the heavy-handedness that I remembered from kid's books that I didn't like as a child," as he reported to Benfer. "That sort of mockery seems to really appeal to kids."

Asked by Zvirin if he viewed the end of his series with nostalgia, Handler responded: "A little. It's like watching your baby learn to walk or your child graduate from college . . . but that doesn't mean I'd want to do it again." Admitting to *Publishers Weekly* contributor Sue Corbett that he misses the Baudelaire orphans, he added: "Every so often I instinctively jot down notes about more bad things happening to them before I remember, 'Oh, that series is over.' It's disorienting."

In the wake of the "A Series of Unfortunate Events," Handler has expanded his focus to adult fiction, but also gives his younger fans a welcome gift in the offbeat holiday stories *The Latke Who Couldn't Stop Screaming* and *The Lump of Coal,* the last which features "the particular brand of Snicket humor, characterized by intentionally oblique plotting, tenuous logic, and snappy wordplay," according to *Horn Book* contributor Elissa Gershowitz. In addition, he produced an

unsettling guide to orchestral music titled *The Composer Is Dead*. Inspired by Handler's ambivalence toward Sergei Prokofiev's classi 1936 composition *Peter and the Wolf*, *The Composer Is Dead* premiered as a production of the San Francisco Symphony in the summer of 2006, with narration by Snicket and music by Handler's high-school friend, Nathaniel Stookey. Narrated by the Inspector, the storyline of the picture-book version follows the investigation of a composer's death, and each section of the orchestra responds to the police interrogation in turn, providing their musical alibi. In *Kirkus Reviews* a critic dubbed *The Composer Is Dead* "more a send-up than an informational visit to the pit," while in *Booklist* Ian Chipman praised the "charmingly snide wit" that emanates from Handler/Snicket's "irreverent picture book."

Discussing his writing career, Handler told *Bookseller* interviewer Caroline Horn: "My problem isn't the search for ideas but how to whittle the ideas down."

Biographical and Critical Sources

BOOKS

Haugen, Hayley Mitchell, *Daniel Handler: The Real Lemony Snicket,* Gale (Detroit, MI), 2005.

PERIODICALS

ALAN Review, winter, 2001, Linda Broughton, review of *The Miserable Mill,* p. 35.
Book, July, 2001, *Kathleen Odean,* review of *The Ersatz Elevator,* p. 81.
Booklist, March 15, 1999, Stephanie Zvirin, review of *The Basic Eight,* p. 1289; December 1, 1999, Susan Dove Lempke, review of *The Bad Beginning,* p. 707; February 1, 2000, Susan Dove Lempke, review of *The Wide Window,* p. 1024; May 1, 2000, Carolyn Phelan, review of *The Miserable Mill,* p. 1670; June 1, 2000, Ted Leventhal, review of *Watch Your Mouth,* p. 1857; October 15, 2000, Susan Dove Lempke, review of *The Austere Academy,* p. 439; August, 2001, Carolyn Phelan, reviews of *The Ersatz Elevator* and *The Vile Village,* p. 2122; October 15, 2001, Carolyn Phelan, review of *The Hostile Hospital,* p. 392; June 1, 2002, review of *Lemony Snicket: The Unauthorized Autobiography,* p. 1725; December 15, 2002, Susan Dove Lempke, review of *The Carnivorous Carnival,* p. 761; November 15, 2004, Stephanie Zvirin, review of *The Grim Grotto,* p. 586; December 1, 2005, Stephanie Zvirin, review of *The Penultimate Peril,* p. 47; February 15, 2006, Allison Block, review of *Adverbs,* p. 5; October 15, 2006, Stephanie Zvirin, review of *The End,* p. 48; November 1, 2008, Ian Chipman, review of *The Composer Is Dead,* p. 56.
Bookseller, May 19, 2006, Caroline Horn, "Lemony Snicket—A Happy Ending?," p. 32.
Christian Science Monitor, August 12, 1999, Ron Charles, reviews of *The Bad Beginning* and *The Reptile Room,* both p. 21.

Entertainment Weekly, November 2, 2001, Daniel Fierman, review of *The Hostile Hospital,* p. 70; October 3, 2003, Alynda Wheat, review of *The Slippery Slope,* p. 79; September 24, 2004, Alynda Wheat, review of *The Grim Grotto,* p. 112; October 20, 2006, Alynda Wheat, review of *The End,* p. 86.
Guardian (London, England), June 7, 2006, Tim De Lisle, interview with Handler.
Horn Book, March, 2001, Christine Heppermann, "Angel Wings and Hard Knocks," p. 239; January-February, 2007, Claire E. Gross, review of *The End,* p. 73; November-December, 2008, Elissa Gershowitz, review of *The Lump of Coal,* p. 653.
Kirkus Reviews, November 1, 2008, review of *The Lump of Coal;* January 15, 2009, review of *The Composer Is Dead.*
Library Journal, March 15, 1999, Rebecca Kelm, review of *The Basic Eight,* p. 108; June 1, 2000, Rebecca Kelm, review of *Watch Your Mouth,* p. 196.
Newsweek, September 27, 2004, Malcolm Jones, interview with Snicket, p. 84.
New Yorker, June 21, 1999, review of *The Basic Eight.*
New York Times, October 20, 2001, Daniel Handler, "Frightening News: The Importance of Scary Stories," p. A17.
New York Times Book Review, October 22, 2006, Henry Alford, reviews of *The End* and *The Beatrice Letters,* both p. 18; December 21, 2008, Julie Just, review of *The Lump of Coal,* p. 13.
New York Times Magazine, April 29, 2001, Daphne Merkin, "Lemony Snicket Says, 'Don't Read My Books!'"
Publishers Weekly, March 1, 1999, review of *The Basic Eight,* p. 59; September 6, 1999, review of *The Bad Beginning,* p. 104; May 29, 2000, Sally Lodge, "Oh, Sweet Misery," p. 42; June 19, 2000, review of *Watch Your Mouth,* p. 60; October 6, 2003, review of *The Slippery Slope,* p. 86; October 18, 2004, review of *The Grim Grotto,* p. 66; January 30, 2006, review of *Adverbs,* p. 36; October 29, 2007, review of *The Latke Who Couldn't Stop Screaming: A Christmas Story,* p. 56; October 27, 2008, Sue Corbett, "Snicket Redux," p. 21; December 22, 2008, review of *The Composer Is Dead,* p. 51.
School Library Journal, November, 1999, Linda Bindner, review of *The Bad Beginning,* p. 165; July, 2000, Sharon R. Pearce, review of *The Miserable Mill,* p. 110; October, 2000, Ann Cook, review of *The Austere Academy,* p. 171; August, 2001, Farida S. Dowler, reviews of *The Ersatz Elevator* and *The Vile Village,* both pp. 188-189; November, 2001, Jean Gaffney, review of *The Hostile Hospital,* p. 164; January, 2003, Heather Dieffenbach, review of *The Carnivorous Carnival,* p. 144; January, 2004, Krista Tokarz, review of *The Slippery Slope,* p. 134; October, 2008, Linda Israelson, review of *The Lump of Coal,* p. 98; February, 2009, Wendy Lukehart, review of *The Composer Is Dead,* p. 86.

ONLINE

A Series of Unfortunate Events Web site, http://www.lemonysnicket.com (May 1, 2010).

BookBrowser.com, http://www.bookbrowser.com/ (July 15, 2000), Jonathan Shipley, review of *Watch Your Mouth.*

Lowell Online, http://www.thelowell.org/ (February 15, 1999), Philana Woo, "Author Reflects on High School Life."

Salon.com, http://www.salonmag.com/ (August 17, 2000), Amy Benfer, "The Mysterious Mr. Snicket."*

* * *

SPIRES, Elizabeth 1952-

Personal

Born May 28, 1952, in Lancaster, OH; daughter of Richard C. (in grounds maintenance) and Sue Spires; married Madison Smartt Bell (a novelist), June 15, 1985; children: Celia Dovell Bell. *Education:* Vassar College, B.A., 1974; Johns Hopkins University, M.A., 1979. *Hobbies and other interests:* Reading, playing the hammer dulcimer, snorkeling.

Addresses

Home—Baltimore, MD. *Office*—Department of English, Goucher College, Towson, MD 21204. *Agent*—Jane Gelfman, Gelfman Scheider Literary Agents, 250 W. 57th St., New York, NY 10107.

Career

Author, editor, and educator. Charles E. Merrill Publishing Co., Columbus, OH, assistant editor, 1976-77; freelance writer, beginning 1977; Washington College, Chestertown, MD, visiting assistant professor of English, 1981; Loyola College, Baltimore, MD, adjunct assistant professor of English and poet in residence, 1981-82; Johns Hopkins University, Baltimore, visiting associate professor in writing seminars, 1984-85, 1988-92; Goucher College, Towson, MD, professor of English and chair for distinguished achievement, 1996-99, writer in residence, 1982-86, 1988-95.

Member

Poetry Society of America.

Awards, Honors

Academy of American Poets' Prize, 1974; *Mademoiselle* magazine College Poetry Prize, 1974; W.K. Rose fellowship, Vassar College, 1976; Ohio Arts Council individual artist's grant, 1978; Pushcart Prize, 1981, 1995; Ingram Merrill Foundation award, 1981; Maryland State Arts Council artist's fellowship, 1982, 1989; National Endowment for the Arts fellowship, 1981, 1992; Amy Lowell traveling poetry scholarship, Harvard University, 1986-87; Sara Teasdale Poetry Award, 1990; Towson State University Prize for Literature, 1992; Guggenheim fellowship in poetry, 1992; Whiting Writers Award, 1996; Witter Bynner Prize for Poetry, American Academy of Arts & Letters, 1998.

Elizabeth Spires (Photograph by Jerry Bauer. Reproduced by permission.)

Writings

FOR CHILDREN

The Falling Star, illustrated by Carlo A. Michelini, C.E. Merrill (Columbus, OH), 1981.

Count with Me, C.E. Merrill (Columbus, OH), 1981.

The Wheels Go Round, C.E. Merrill (Columbus, OH), 1981.

Simon's Adventure, illustrated by Judy Hand, Antioch Publishing, 1982.

Top Bananas, Antioch Publishing, 1982.

Things That Go Fast, illustrated by Jean Rudegeair, Antioch Publishing, 1982.

With One White Wing: Puzzles in Poems and Pictures, illustrated by Erik Blegvad, Margaret K. McElderry Books (New York, NY), 1995.

Riddle Road: Puzzles in Poems and Pictures, illustrated by Erik Blegvad, Margaret K. McElderry Books (New York, NY), 1999.

The Mouse of Amherst: A Tale of Young Readers, illustrated by Claire A. Nivola, Farrar Straus & Giroux (New York, NY), 1999.

I Am Arachne: Fifteen Greek and Roman Myths, illustrated by Mordicai Gerstein, Frances Foster Books (New York, NY), 2001.

The Big Meow, illustrated by Cynthia Jabar, Candlewick Press (Cambridge, MA), 2002.

POETRY COLLECTIONS; FOR ADULTS

Boardwalk, Bits Press (Cleveland, OH), 1980.

Globe, Wesleyan University Press/University Press of New England (Hanover, NH), 1981.

Swan's Island, Holt, Rinehart & Winston (New York, NY), 1985.

Annonciade, Viking Penguin (New York, NY), 1989.

Worldling, W.W. Norton (New York, NY), 1995.

Now the Green Blade Rises, W.W. Norton (New York, NY), 2002.

The Wave-maker, W.W. Norton (New York, NY), 2008.

OTHER

W.D. Snodgrass, an Interview, Northouse & Northouse, 1988.

(Editor) Josephine Jacobsen, *The Instant of Knowing: Lectures, Criticism, and Occasional Prose,* University of Michigan Press (Ann Arbor, MI), 1998.

(Author of libretto, with Madison Smartt Bell and Elena Ruehr, *Toussaint before the Spirits: A Chamber Opera in One Act,* music by Elena Ruehr, Ione Press (Boston, MA), 2005.

(Editor) Josephine Jacobsen, *Contents of a Minute: Last Poems,* Sarabande Books (Louisville, KY), 2008.

I Heard God Talking to Me: William Edmondson and His Stone Carvings, Frances Foster Books (New York, NY), 2009.

Contributor of poems to anthologies, including *The Best American Poetry,* 1989, 1990, 1991, 1992; and to periodicals, including *Antaeus, New Yorker, New Republic, Mademoiselle, Poetry, American Poetry Review, Yale Review, Partisan Review, New Criterion,* and *Paris Review.*

Sidelights

A published poet and college professor, Elizabeth Spires has also written several stories for young children that pair her rhyming texts with illustrations by artists that range from Mordicai Gerstein and Erik Blegvad to Claire A. Nivola and Cynthia Jabar. Spires "makes ancient tales unusually vivid and immediate by recasting them as first-person accounts," noted *Booklist* contributor John Peters, the reviewer citing the author's picture books *The Mouse of Amherst: A Tale of Young Readers* and *I Am Arachne: Fifteen Greek and Roman Myths.* Praising her work crafting the unusual illustrated biography *I Heard God Talking to Me: William Edmondson and His Stone Carvings.* Set in the 1930s, the book focuses on a middle-aged Tennessee janitor who, illiterate and the son of slaves, was inspired to become an artist

when he heard the voice of God. Although a *Publishers Weekly* critic predicted that the photographs of Edmonson's primitive-styled limestone sculptures will best be appreciated by a sophisticated readership, "the immediacy in Spires's poems will speak to young readers."

"As a child, I was a classic 'bookworm,' haunting my small-town library on a daily basis and reading a book a day during summer vacations," Spires once told *SATA.* "By the time I was twelve, I had decided to be a writer. My original plan, influenced by my admiration for Flannery O'Connor, was to become a short-story writer. Instead, in college at Vassar, I began writing poetry seriously. This has led to my publishing several collections of poetry for adult readers. My daughter, Celia, . . . defined poetry one day (very appropriately, I thought) as 'playing with words.' I have 'played with words' in my writing for children in two picture books of riddles.

"I'm an Anglophile by nature, particularly interested in English literature and literary landmarks. Living in England in 1986-87 gave me a different perspective on the United States and allowed me to see it in a fresher

Spires joins artist Mordicai Gerstein to share fifteen classic myths in the picture book **I Am Arachne.** (Illustration copyright © 2001 by Mordicai Gerstein. All rights reserved. Reproduced by permission of Square Fish, a division of Farrar, Straus & Giroux, LLC.)

way. Being outside my native country pushed me toward thinking more about global problems, such as the ever-present threat of war, and about cultural differences and idiosyncrasies. I've also been thinking a lot about the future, what life ten or twenty or thirty years from now will be like, both for myself as an individual, and for society as a whole."

Characteristic of Spires' introspective nature, her poetry collection *Worldling* deals with motherhood, mortality, and questions about the soul's physical existence. Poems chronicle the poet's pregnancy, along with her daughter's birth and early life. Reviewer Donna Seaman described Spires' experience of motherhood in *Booklist* as "a vivifying series of poems about conception, expectancy, and birth" that contains "something . . . quietly spiritual." In *Library Journal*, Christine Stenstrom characterized Spires's work as having "a gossamer touch that draws the reader into the compelling rhythm of her struggle to come to terms with her own life."

Spires has teamed with veteran illustrator Blegvad to produce two children's books of riddles. The first, *With One White Wing: Puzzles in Poems and Pictures,* is a verbal/visual collaboration that offers the reader clues to solve the twenty-six puzzles contained therein. Deborah Stevenson, writing for the *Bulletin of the Center for Children's Books,* described the collection as "inventive," generally agreeing with Carolyn Phelan's assessment in *Booklist* that the material provides "a relief from the puns and groaners that fill most riddle books." Campbell Geeslin also noted in the *New York Times* that the musical quality of Spires's free-form verses make the riddles "fun to read out loud."

Spires and Blegvad again join forces on *Riddle Road: Puzzles in Poems and Pictures.* Also lively and entertaining, the book inspired a *Kirkus Reviews* contributor to note that "the game-like quality of the book demands attention to meaning . . . and helps children have fun actively reading not only words but pictures."

Inspired by a fondness for the poetry of nineteenth-century writer Emily Dickinson, Spires invented a mouse named Emmaline to help introduce Dickinson's work to young readers. *The Mouse of Amherst,* illustrated by Nivola, intersperses Emmaline's poems with those of Dickinson, adding facts about that poet's life and describing close-call encounters with cats and other mouse predators. In *Booklist* Susan Dove Lempke described *The Mouse of Amherst* as a "charmer" that conveys the "idea of the relationship formed between a poet and a reader."

In *I Am Arachne* Spires teams with artist Gerstein to introduce a pantheon of gods and demigods as well as the humans—Midas, Narcissus, Orpheus, and Eurydice among them—who play pivotal parts in Greek and Roman mythology. According to Angela J. Reynolds, "the softest version is presented" in Spires' story, so that the harshest consequences meted out by gods to errant humans are avoided. Remarking on Spires' inventive, first-person journalistic approach, a *Horn Book* critic dubbed the tales "breezy retellings" that feature a "playful manipulation of point of view [that] is entertainingly provocative."

Spires turns to an original story in *The Big Meow,* a picture book featuring colorful acrylic paintings by Jabar. Little Cat has a great big meow, and the fluffy orange tabby suffers relentless taunting from neighborhood cats as a result. However, when Bruno the bulldog decides that kitties would make a tasty snack, Little Cat's shrill mewling saves the day. In *School Library Journal* Marianne Saccardi praised the "large and brightly colored" cartoons in *The Big Meow* and added that Spires' "appropriately repetitive" text tells a story that "will likely resonate with young readers."

Biographical and Critical Sources

BOOKS

Contemporary Women Poets, St. James Press (Detroit, MI), 1998.
Dictionary of Literary Biography, Volume 120: *American Poets since World War II, Third Series,* Gale (Detroit, MI), 1992.

PERIODICALS

Antioch Review, fall, 2003, Ned Balbo, review of *Now the Green Blade Rises,* p. 786.
Booklist, October 1, 1995, Carolyn Phelan, review of *With One White Wing: Puzzles in Poems and Pictures,* p. 325; November 15, 1995, Donna Seaman, review of *Worldling,* p. 533; March 15, 1999, Susan Dove Lempke, review of *The Mouse of Amherst: A Tale of Young Readers,* p. 1330; June 1, 2001, John Peters, review of *I Am Arachne: Fifteen Greek and Roman Myths,* p. 1874; July 1, 2008, Donna Seaman, review of *The Wave-Maker,* p. 28; February 1, 2009, Gillian Engberg, review of *I Heard God Talking to Me: William Edmondson and His Stone Carvings,* p. 49; September 1, 2002, Donna Seaman, review of *Now the Green Blade Rises,* p. 49.
Bulletin of the Center for Children's Books, February, 1996, Deborah Stevenson, review of *With One White Wing,* p. 205.
Hollins Critic, April, 2002, Henry Taylor, "In the Everlasting Present: The Poetry of Elizabeth Spires," pp. 1-19.
Horn Book, September, 2001, review of *I Am Arachne,* p. 604.
Kirkus Reviews, May 15, 1999, review of *Riddle Road: Puzzles in Poems and Pictures,* p. 806; January 15, 2009, review of *I Heard God Talking to Me.*
Library Journal, November 15, 1995, Christine Stenstrom, review of *Worldling,* p. 79; June 1, 2008, Chris Pusateri, review of *The Wave-Maker,* p. 100.

New York Times, April 7, 1996, Campbell Geeslin, review of *With One White Wing.*

Publishers Weekly, February 18, 2002, review of *The Big Meow,* p. 94; August 19, 2002, review of *Now the Green Blade Rises,* p. 82; December 1, 2008, review of *I Heard God Talking to Me,* p. 45.

School Library Journal, May, 2001, Angela J. Reynolds, review of *I Am Arachne,* p. 171; May, 2002, Marianne Saccardi, review of *The Big Meow,* p. 128; March, 2009, Jill Heritage Maza, review of *I Heard God Talking to Me,* p. 169.

ONLINE

Goucher College Web site, http://www.goucher.edu/ (November 5, 2008), "Elizabeth Spires."*

* * *

SQUIRES, Janet

Personal

Married; children: two daughters. *Education: Hobbies and other interests:* Horseback riding.

Addresses

Home—CA. *E-mail*—jsquiresbooks@ca.rr.com.

Career

Librarian and author. Part-time library media specialist in Valencia, CA.

Member

Society of Children's Book Writers and Illustrators, Women Writing the West.

Awards, Honors

Fifth Annual Writers' Conference Award for outstanding magazine article, Pierce College.

Writings

The Gingerbread Cowboy, illustrated by Holly Berry, Laura Geringer Books (New York, NY), 2006.

Also author of screenplays, with Kat Fandino. Contributor of articles to magazines.

Sidelights

Janet Squires, a librarian and author, published her debut children's book, *The Gingerbread Cowboy,* in 2006. "I'm a writer because . . . I have to write," Squires remarked on her home page. "I've done many different things in my life, but writing was always a part of anything I did."

In *The Gingerbread Cowboy,* described as a "universal trickster tale with a cowboy slant" by *Booklist* critic Hazel Rochman, a rancher's wife tires of making biscuits and decides to create a cowpoke from gingerbread, complete with a big hat, a fringed vest, a belt buckle, and boots. When the rancher decides to sneak a peek at the tasty treat, the Gingerbread Cowboy hops out of the oven and scampers away, teasingly adding, "Giddyup, giddyup as fast as you can. You can't catch me, I'm the Gingerbread Man." As he traverses the desert landscape, the Gingerbread Cowboy meets a horned lizard, a roadrunner, javelinas, long-horned cattle, and cowboys before a sly coyote offers to help him cross a river. "This Wild West version of the traditional tale is sure to delight youngsters," noted a contributor in *Kirkus Reviews,* and Kirsten Cutler, reviewing *The Gingerbread Cowboy* in *School Library Journal,* called the work "a delightful, infectiously cheerful, Southwestern rendition of a familiar story" and "a fresh version of an old favorite."

Biographical and Critical Sources

PERIODICALS

Booklist, April 15, 2006, Hazel Rochman, review of *The Gingerbread Cowboy,* p. 50.

Kirkus Reviews, July 1, 2006, review of *The Gingerbread Cowboy,* p. 682.

School Library Journal, August, 2006, Kirsten Cutler, review of *The Gingerbread Cowboy,* p. 122.

ONLINE

Janet Squires Home Page, http://www.janetsquires.com (April 1, 2008).

Women Writing the West, www.womenwritingthewest.org/ (April 1, 2008), "Janet Squires."*

* * *

STRASSER, Todd 1950-
(Morton Rhue)

Personal

Born May 5, 1950, in New York, NY; son of Chester S. (a manufacturer of dresses) and Sheila (a copy editor) Strasser; married Pamela Older (a businesswoman), July 2, 1981; children: Lia, Geoff. *Education:* Attended New York University; Beloit College, B.A., 1974. *Hobbies and other interests:* Fishing, skiing, tennis, surfing.

Addresses

Office—Larchmont, NY. *E-mail*—todd@toddstrasser. com.

Todd Strasser (Reproduced by permission.)

Career

Freelance writer, 1975—. Beloit College, Beloit, WI, worked in public relations, 1973-74; *Times Herald Record,* Middletown, NY, reporter, 1974-76; Compton Advertising, New York, NY, copywriter, 1976-77; *Esquire,* New York, NY, researcher, 1977-78; Toggle, Inc. (fortune cookie company), New York, NY, owner, 1978-89. Speaker at schools and conferences; lectures and presenter at writing workshops for adults and teenagers.

Member

International Reading Association, Writers Guild of America, Authors Guild, Freedom to Read Foundation, PEN.

Awards, Honors

Best Books for Young Adults citations, American Library Association (ALA), 1981, for *Friends till the End,* and 1982, for *Rock 'n' Roll Nights;* Books for the Teen Age selection, New York Public Library, 1981, for *Angel Dust Blues,* 1982, for *The Wave* and *Friends till the End,* 1983, for *Rock 'n' Roll Nights,* and 1984, for *Workin' for Peanuts;* Notable Children's Trade Book in the Field of Social Studies designation, National Coun-

cil for Social Studies/Children's Book Council, 1982, and Young Reader Medal nomination, California Reading Association, 1983, both for *Friends till the End;* Book Award, Federation of Children's Books (Great Britain), 1983, for *The Wave,* and 1984, for *Turn It Up!;* Outstanding Book Award, Iowa Books for Young Adult Program, 1985, for *Turn It Up!;* Colorado Blue Spruce Award nomination, 1987, for *Angel Dust Blues;* Books for the Teen Age selection, New York Public Library, and Best Book for Young Adults selection, ALA, both for *How I Changed My Life;* Edgar Award nomination, Mystery Writers of America, 1998, for *The Accident;* Washington Irving Children's Choice Book Award, 1998, for *Abe Lincoln for Class President;* Volunteer State Book Award, 1998; New York State Charlotte Award, Rhode Island Teen Book Award, and Washington Irving Children's Choice Book Award, all 2002, all for *Give a Boy a Gun;* Best Book for Young Adults selection and Quick Pick for Reluctant Readers selection, both ALA, both 2005, and Young Adult Choice Award, International Reading Association, all for *Can't Get There from Here;* Books for the Teen Age selection, New York Public Library, and Quick Pick for Reluctant Readers selection, ALA, both 2007, both for *Boot Camp.*

Writings

Angel Dust Blues, Coward (New York, NY), 1979.

Friends till the End, Delacorte (New York, NY), 1981.

Rock 'n' Roll Nights, Delacorte (New York, NY), 1982.

Workin' for Peanuts, Delacorte (New York, NY), 1983.

Turn It Up! (sequel to *Rock 'n' Roll Nights*), Delacorte (New York, NY), 1984.

The Complete Computer Popularity Program, Delacorte (New York, NY), 1984.

A Very Touchy Subject, Delacorte (New York, NY), 1985.

Wildlife (sequel to *Turn It Up!*), Delacorte (New York, NY), 1987.

The Mall from Outer Space, Scholastic, Inc. (New York, NY), 1987.

The Family Man (adult novel), St. Martin's (New York, NY), 1988.

The Accident (also see below), Delacorte (New York, NY), 1988.

(With Dennis Freeland) *Moving Target,* Fawcett (New York, NY), 1989.

Beyond the Reef, illustrations by Debbie Heller, Delacorte (New York, NY), 1989.

Over the Limit (teleplay; based on Strasser's *The Accident*), *ABC Afterschool Special,* American Broadcasting Company (New York, NY), 1990.

The Diving Bell, illustrations by Debbie Heller, Scholastic, Inc. (New York, NY), 1992.

Summer's End, Scholastic, Inc. (New York, NY), 1993.

Summer's Promise, Scholastic, Inc. (New York, NY), 1993.

Please Don't Be Mine, Julie Valentine, Scholastic, Inc. (New York, NY), 1995.

How I Changed My Life, Simon & Schuster (New York, NY), 1995.

Howl-a-Ween, Scholastic, Inc. (New York, NY), 1995.

Abe Lincoln for Class President, Scholastic, Inc. (New York, NY), 1996.

Girl Gives Birth to Own Prom Date, Simon & Schuster (New York, NY), 1996, published as *How I Created My Perfect Prom Date,* Simon Pulse (New York, NY), 2008.

Playing for Love, HarperCollins (New York, NY), 1996.

The Boys in the Band, HarperCollins (New York, NY), 1996.

Hey Dad, Get a Life!, Holiday House (New York, NY), 1996.

How I Spent My Last Night on Earth, Simon & Schuster (New York, NY), 1998.

Kidnap Kids, Putnam (New York, NY), 1998.

Kids' Book of Gross Facts and Feats, Watermill Press (Mahwah, NJ), 1998.

Close Call, Putnam (New York, NY), 1999.

Here Comes Heavenly, Pocket Books (New York, NY), 1999.

Dance Magic, Pocket Books (New York, NY), 1999.

Pastabilities, Pocket Books (New York, NY), 2000.

Spell Danger, Pocket Books (New York, NY), 2000.

Give a Boy a Gun, Simon & Schuster (New York, NY), 2000.

CON-Fidence, Holiday House (New York, NY), 2002.

Thief of Dreams, Putnam (New York, NY), 2003.

Can't Get There from Here, Simon & Schuster (New York, NY), 2004.

Boot Camp, Simon & Schuster (New York, NY), 2007.

If I Grow Up, Simon & Schuster (New York, NY), 2009.

Wish You Were Dead, Egmont USA (New York, NY), 2009.

Contributor to periodicals, including *New Yorker, Esquire, New York Times,* and *Village Voice.*

NOVELIZATIONS

(Under pseudonym Morton Rhue) *The Wave* (based on the teleplay by Johnny Dawkins), Delacorte (New York, NY), 1981.

Ferris Bueller's Day Off, New American Library (New York, NY), 1986.

Cookie, New American Library (New York, NY), 1989.

Home Alone, Scholastic, Inc. (New York, NY), 1991.

Home Alone 2: Lost in New York, Scholastic, Inc. (New York, NY), 1991.

Honey, I Blew up the Kids, Disney Press (New York, NY), 1992.

The Good Son, Pocket Books (New York, NY), 1993.

The Addams Family Values, Pocket Books (New York, NY), 1993.

The Beverly Hillbillies, HarperCollins (New York, NY), 1993.

Hocus Pocus, Disney Press (New York, NY), 1993.

The Rookie of the Year, Dell (New York, NY), 1993.

Super Mario Bros., Hyperion (New York, NY), 1993.

Disney's "The Villains" Collection, poems by Mark Rifkin, illustrated by Gil DiCicco, Disney Press (New York, NY), 1993.

The Three Musketeers, Disney Press (New York, NY), 1993.

Free Willy, Scholastic, Inc. (New York, NY), 1993.

Disney's "It's Magic": Stories from the Films, poems by Richard Duke, illustrated by Philippe Harchy, Disney Press (New York, NY), 1994.

Walt Disney's Lady and the Tramp, illustrated by Franc Mateu, Disney Press (New York, NY), 1994.

Walt Disney's Peter Pan, illustrated by Jose Cardona and Fred Marvin, Disney Press (New York, NY), 1994.

Tall Tale: The Unbelievable Adventures of Pecos Bill, Disney Press (New York, NY), 1994.

Street Fighter, Newmarket Press (New York, NY), 1994.

Richie Rich, Scholastic, Inc. (New York, NY), 1994.

Pagemaster, Scholastic, Inc. (New York, NY), 1994.

The Miracle on 34th Street, Scholastic, Inc. (New York, NY), 1994.

Ninjas Kick Back, Scholastic, Inc. (New York, NY), 1994.

Little Panda, Scholastic, Inc. (New York, NY), 1995.

Man of the House, Disney Press (New York, NY), 1995.

(With others) *Free Willy 2,* Scholastic, Inc. (New York, NY), 1995.

Home Alone 3, Scholastic, Inc. (New York, NY), 1997.

Star Wars Episode One, Journal, Anakin Skywalker, Scholastic, Inc. (New York, NY), 1999.

"HELP! I'M TRAPPED" SERIES

Help! I'm Trapped in the First Day of School, Scholastic, Inc. (New York, NY), 1994.

Help! I'm Trapped in My Teacher's Body, Scholastic, Inc. (New York, NY), 1994.

Help! I'm Trapped in Obedience School, Scholastic, Inc. (New York, NY), 1995.

Help! I'm Trapped in Santa's Body, Scholastic, Inc. (New York, NY), 1997.

Help! I'm Trapped in My Sister's Body, Scholastic, Inc. (New York, NY), 1997.

Help! I'm Trapped in My Gym Teacher's Body, Scholastic, Inc. (New York, NY), 1997.

Help! I'm Trapped in the President's Body, Scholastic, Inc. (New York, NY), 1997.

Help! I'm Trapped in Obedience School Again, Scholastic, Inc. (New York, NY), 1997.

Help! I'm Trapped in the First Day of Summer Camp, Scholastic, Inc. (New York, NY), 1998.

Help! I'm Trapped in an Alien's Body, Scholastic, Inc. (New York, NY), 1998.

Help! I'm Trapped in a Movie Star's Body, Scholastic, Inc. (New York, NY), 1999.

Help! I'm Trapped in the Principal's Body, Scholastic, Inc. (New York, NY), 1999.

Help! I'm Trapped in My Lunch Lady's Body, Scholastic, Inc. (New York, NY), 1999.

Help! I'm Trapped in the Camp Counselor's Body, Scholastic, Inc. (New York, NY), 1999.

Help! I'm Trapped in a Professional Wrestler's Body, Scholastic, Inc. (New York, NY), 2000.

Help! I'm Trapped in a Vampire's Body, Scholastic, Inc. (New York, NY), 2000.

Help! I'm Trapped in a Supermodel's Body, Scholastic, Inc. (New York, NY), 2001.

"WORDSWORTH" SERIES

Wordsworth and the Cold Cut Catastrophe, illustrated by Leif Peng, HarperCollins (New York, NY), 1995.

Wordsworth and the Kibble Kidnapping, HarperCollins (New York, NY), 1995.

Wordsworth and the Roast Beef Romance, HarperCollins (New York, NY), 1995.

Wordsworth and the Mail-Order Meatloaf Mess, Harper-Collins (New York, NY), 1995.

Wordsworth and the Tasty Treat Trick, HarperCollins (New York, NY), 1995.

Wordsworth and the Lip-Smacking Licorice Love Affair, HarperCollins (New York, NY), 1996.

"CAMP RUN-A-MUCK" SERIES

Greasy Grimy Gopher Guts, Scholastic, Inc. (New York, NY), 1997.

Mutilated Monkey Meat, Scholastic, Inc. (New York, NY), 1997.

Chopped-Up Birdy's Feet, Scholastic, Inc. (New York, NY), 1997.

"AGAINST THE ODDS" SERIES

Shark Bite, Pocket Books (New York, NY), 1998.

Grizzly Attack, Pocket Books (New York, NY), 1998.

Buzzards' Feast, Pocket Books (New York, NY), 1999.

Gator Prey, Pocket Books (New York, NY), 1999.

"DON'T GET CAUGHT" SERIES

Don't Get Caught Driving the School Bus, Scholastic, Inc. (New York, NY), 2000.

Don't Get Caught in the Girls' Locker Room, Scholastic, Inc. (New York, NY), 2001.

Don't Get Caught Wearing the Lunch Lady's Hairnet, Scholastic, Inc. (New York, NY), 2001.

Don't Get Caught in the Teachers' Lounge, Scholastic, Inc. (New York, NY), 2002.

"IMPACT ZONE" SERIES

Close Out, Simon Pulse (New York, NY), 2004.

Cut Back, Simon Pulse (New York, NY), 2004.

Take Off, Simon Pulse (New York, NY), 2004.

"DRIFT X" SERIES

Battle Drift, illustrated by Craig Phillips, Simon Pulse (New York, NY), 2006.

Sidewayz Glory, illustrated by Craig Phillips, Simon Pulse (New York, NY), 2006.

Slide or Die, illustrated by Craig Phillips, Simon Pulse (New York, NY), 2006.

"MOB PRINCESS" SERIES

Count Your Blessings, Simon Pulse (New York, NY), 2007.

For Money and Love, Simon Pulse (New York, NY), 2007.

Stolen Kisses, Secrets, and Lies, Simon Pulse (New York, NY), 2007.

"TARDY BOYS" SERIES

Is That a Dead Dog in Your Locker?, Scholastic, Inc. (New York, NY), 2006.

Is That a Sick Cat in Your Backpack?, Scholastic, Inc. (New York, NY), 2007.

Is That a Glow-in-the-Dark Bunny in Your Pillowcase?, Scholastic, Inc. (New York, NY), 2007.

Is That an Angry Penguin in Your Gym Bag?, Scholastic, Inc. (New York, NY), 2008.

Is That an Unlucky Leprechaun in Your Lunch?, Scholastic, Inc. (New York, NY), 2009.

Adaptations

Workin' for Peanuts was adapted as a Home Box Office "Family Showcase" presentation, 1985; *A Very Touchy Subject* was adapted for television as an "ABC Afterschool Special" titled *Can a Guy Say No?,* 1986; *Help! I'm Trapped in the First Day of School* was adapted for television by the Disney Channel, 1999; *Girl Gives Birth to Own Prom Date* was adapted as a major motion picture by Rob Thomas for Twentieth Century-Fox, 1999.

Cover of Strasser's amusing middle-grade novel Hey, Dad, Get a Life!
(Copyright © 1996 by Todd Strasser. By permission of Todd Strasser.)

Sidelights

An award-winning author of critically recognized realistic fiction for young adults, Todd Strasser blends humor and romance with timely subjects to address various concerns of teens, including drugs, sex, illness, popularity, and music. In works ranging from *Friends till the End,* the story of a young man stricken with leukemia, to *Give a Boy a Gun,* a study of school violence, to *Wish You Were Dead,* a psychological thriller, Strasser captures the attention of his readers by focusing on their concerns, fears, and goals in works that reflect his familiarity with adolescent home and school life.

Lacing his work for younger audiences with a vein of humor, he has also tantalized even the most reluctant reader to open books with titles like *Hey Dad, Get a Life!; Help! I'm Trapped in My Gym Teacher's Body;* and *Is That a Dead Dog in Your Locker?* In addition to his many original works of fiction, Strasser has also written novelizations of several popular motion pictures, including some from Disney Studios. The release of works like *Home Alone* and *Free Willy* "help me establish a rapport with young people," the author noted in an interview on the Scholastic Web site. "It seems to make them eager to read my other books." Strasser's comic tales have also found a ready audience; he remarked in his Scholastic interview that "most kids today want books with characters they can identify with. They want to be entertained, not preached to. I try to make my books funny, but not frivolous."

Strasser was born in New York City, but he grew up on Long Island. While having the same insecurities common to young people, he was blessed with a stable family life, went to a decent summer camp, and credits his sense of humor in the face of trouble to his grandfather, with whom he had a close relationship. Regarding schoolwork, Strasser was an admitted underachiever and, surprisingly, had trouble with reading and spelling. While his efforts in the homework department were often just enough to get by, he would study in depth a subject he found interesting. Some of those favorite subjects included dinosaurs, seashells, and James Bond novels.

During his teen years, Strasser held to the "anti-establishment" philosophy that characterized adolescents of the 1960s. He grew long hair, listened to heavy metal music, and even attended the Woodstock festival. After high school, Strasser enrolled at New York University. He began to write poetry and some short fiction, but regarded it only as a hobby and did not expect his work to be published. A few years later he dropped out of school and spent two years hitchhiking around most of Europe and the United States, taking odd jobs whenever money ran low. He performed as a street musician in France and Germany, worked on a ship in Denmark, lived on a commune in Virginia, worked in a health-food store in New York, and was even kidnapped briefly by religious fanatics in South Bend, Indiana.

Cover of Strasser's young-adult novel **How I Changed My Life,** *featuring artwork by Tom Garrett.* (Cover illustration © 1996 by Tom Garrett. Reproduced by permission of the illustrator.)

During his wandering years, Strasser continued to write, documenting his travels in journals and letters. "Finally it occurred to me that perhaps I should give writing a try as a student and, possibly, some sort of profession," he recalled. Strasser enrolled at Beloit College and began taking courses in literature and writing. The author told Jim Roginski in *Behind the Covers:* "I guess my becoming a writer was really a process of elimination. I tried a variety of things in college. Medicine, law. Nothing worked. My family felt I had to be a business person, or if I was lucky, a doctor or a lawyer. I never really thought I would be a writer."

After graduation, Strasser worked temporarily for the public relations department at Beloit, wrote for two years for the *Times Herald-Record,* a Middletown, New York, newspaper, and then became an advertising copywriter for Compton Advertising in New York City as well as a researcher for *Esquire* magazine. "When I sold my first novel I quit my advertising job," Strasser

told Roginski. "And then I went the route of the poor struggling novelist. I used to do things like cut my own hair." After *Angel Dust Blues,* Strasser's first novel, was accepted for publication, the author used the $3,000 advance to start a business of his own, a fortune-cookie company called Toggle, Inc. Strasser found the cookie business more successful than he expected, and he operated the company until 1989.

Meanwhile, *Angel Dust Blues* appeared in 1979 and won Strasser critical acclaim. As Strasser told Nina Piwoz in *Media and Methods,* the story is about "a group of fairly well-to-do, suburban teenagers who get into trouble with drugs." It was based on actual events Strasser had witnessed when he was growing up. Two years later, he published another young-adult novel, again based on his own experiences. "My second book, *Friends till the End,* is about a healthy teenager who has a friend who becomes extremely ill with leukemia," he explained to Piwoz. "When I moved to New York, I had a roommate . . . an old friend of mine. Within a few weeks, he became very ill. I spent a year visiting him in the hospital, not knowing whether he was going to live or die."

Rock 'n' Roll Nights, Strasser's third novel under his own name, was a change of pace from the serious themes of his first two works. "It's about a teenage rock and roll band—something with which I had absolutely no direct experience," he told Piwoz. "However, I grew up in the 1960s when rock and roll was really our 'national anthem.' I relate much better to rock stars than to politicians. I always wanted to be in a rock band, as did just about everybody I knew." "I think the kind of music teens listen to may change, or what they wear may change," Strasser continued, "but dealing with being popular, friends or the opposite sex, or questions of morality and decency . . . [I don't think] those things really ever change. I hate to say this, but I think authors tell the same stories—just in today's language and in today's settings." Strasser continues the story of the band "Coming Attractions" in two sequels: *Turn It Up!* and *Wildlife.*

Strasser also writes hard-hitting, realistic stories about teenagers and their problems. For example, *The Accident* deals with a drunken-driving incident in which three high-school swimming stars are killed. The surviving teen commits himself to understanding what actually happened the night of the accident in a novel that, in the opinion of *Horn Book* reviewer Margaret A. Bush, "reads well and competently uses the troublesome occurrence of drunk driving and teenage death to provoke thought and discussion on multifaceted issues."

In *Give a Boy a Gun* Strasser "takes a ripped-from-the-headlines approach to the issues surrounding school violence," observed *Journal of Adolescent & Adult Literacy* contributor Devon Clancy Sanner. The novel focuses on Gary and Brendan, a pair of outsiders who are tormented by their peers at Middletown High School.

When a football player abuses Brendan at a party, the boys determine to seek revenge; armed with pipe bombs and semiautomatic weapons, they break into a school dance and hold their classmates hostage. "This is a disturbing and provocative novel for anyone who wonders how the events at Columbine could have happened, and how such horrors could be avoided," noted *Kliatt* reviewer Paula Rohrlick. "Both haunting and harrowing, the book deserves a wide readership, discussion, and debate," Michael Cart wrote in *Booklist.*

Thief of Dreams concerns thirteen-year-old Martin Hunter, whose workaholic parents decide to spend the Christmas holiday in China on a business trip and leave their son with his mysterious Uncle Lawrence. When his uncle disappears each night and returns each morning carrying a black bag, Martin becomes suspicious and soon discovers Lawrence's cache of sophisticated equipment, including a wetsuit and night-vision goggles. When Martin comes to the realization that Lawrence is a professional thief he is torn between his sense of morality and his love for his uncle. According to a *Publishers Weekly* reviewer, "Strasser shapes a briskly paced tale with some interesting contortions," and a contributor in *Kirkus Reviews* described the novel as "richly layered and exciting."

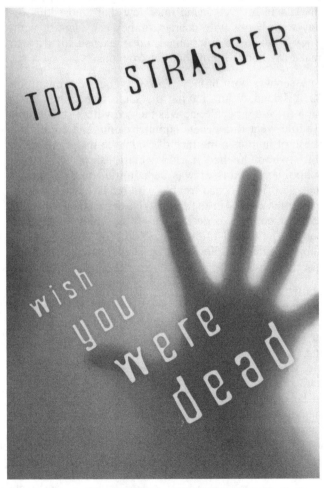

Cover of Strasser's young-adult novel Wish You Were Dead. (Cover photo copyright © iStock/TommL, 2009. Reproduced by permission.)

Set in New York City, *Can't Get There from Here* examines the problem of teen homelessness. Fifteen-year-old Maybe, tossed from her home by an abusive mother, struggles to survive on the streets during a brutal winter. Maybe and her friends, a ragtag group of runaways and throwaways, spend their days begging or foraging for food, using drugs, and running street scams. "The grimness of these generally short lives is rendered in unsparing detail—many characters die, and Strasser opens several chapters with staccato, police report-like profiles listing names, ages, backgrounds and cause of death," noted *Kliatt* reviewer Kathryn Kulpa. Joel Shoemaker, reviewing the novel in *School Library Journal*, called *Can't Get There from Here* "a powerful and disturbing look at the downward spiral of despair that remains too common for too many teens."

Boot Camp centers on Garrett Durrell, a rebellious, misunderstood youth whose parents disapprove of his relationship with a former teacher. At his parents' request, Garrett is abducted in the middle of the night and shipped to Lake Harmony, a disciplinary facility designed primarily for drug abusers and violent offenders. He rebels against the authoritarian nature of the camp and is subject to physical and psychological abuse by the staff. "Writing in the teen's mature and perceptive voice, Strasser creates characters who will provoke strong reactions from readers," commented *School Library Journal* reviewer Lynn Rashid, and a critic in *Publishers Weekly* remarked, "Strasser offers no easy answers, and nimbly navigates a host of moral gray areas." "The novel is a real eye-opener, and the helplessness of teens incarcerated in these boot camps, as exemplified by Garrett, is truly shocking," Rohrlick stated.

An inner-city youth living in an impoverished housing project rises to a position of power in his street gang in *If I Grow Up*. "Strasser's fans will recognize and appreciate his mastery at creating a dangerously isolated atmosphere and setting," remarked a *Kirkus Reviews* contributor, and Daniel Kraus, writing in *Booklist*, applauded the story's "hopeful and heartbreaking" conclusion. In *Wish You Were Dead*, the village of Soundview is shaken to its core when a number of high school girls mysteriously disappear shortly after a cyberstalker mentions their names in his blog posts. "Carefully plotted, this suspenseful novel blends the traditional with new tech details to successful end," asserted a critic in *Kirkus Reviews*. Brandy Danner, critiquing the work in *School Library Journal*, similarly noted that "the social-networking technologies are blended seamlessly into the narrative."

Strasser has also produced a large number of light-hearted books for middle-graders. *The Mall from Outer Space* is about aliens who have chosen, for mysterious reasons of their own, to construct shopping centers on Earth. *Hey Dad, Get a Life!* finds twelve-year-old Kelly and younger sister Sasha haunted by their deceased father. Ghostly Dad proves to be a great help around the house—he makes the girls' beds, tidies their room, does

Cover of Strasser's middle-grade novel Help! I'm Trapped in My Teacher's Body. (Illustration copyright © 2003 by Scholastic, Inc. Reproduced by permission of Scholastic, Inc.)

their homework, and even helps out on the soccer field. *Booklist* contributor Debbie Carton called the work a "light-hearted and occasionally poignant ghost story" that features "appealing, believable characters and a satisfying plot." Equally laudatory in *Bulletin of the Center for Children's Books,* Deborah Stevenson described *Hey, Dad, Get a Life!* as "touchingly yet surprisingly cheerful," calling it "a compassionate and accessible tale of a family's adjustment to loss."

Several novels reveal Strasser's more quirky, humorous side. *Girl Gives Birth to Own Prom Date* finds ardent environmentalist Nicole taking time off from saving the world to transform her grungy next-door neighbor Chase into the perfect prom date. Praising the novel's "goofy plot twists" and "effervescent dialogue," a *Kirkus Reviews* critic noted that Strasser's "high humor doesn't detract" from his "understated message about nonconformity and self-acceptance." The author's "Help! I'm Trapped" books position their young protagonists in everything from the unwieldy body of Santa Claus to the summer camp from hell. In *Help! I'm Trapped in Obedience School,* for example, Jake's dog Lance switches bodies with Jake's friend Andy, and while Andy excels at most things doggy—although he never quite acquires

a taste for dog food—Jake spends his time in human form chasing squirrels and barking during school. Calling Strasser's tale "briskly paced," *Booklist* contributor Chris Sherman predicted that the "easy, breezy" story will appeal to reluctant readers. *School Library Journal* contributor Cheryl Cufari wrote that readers will relate to the "predicaments in which Strasser's energetic boys find themselves and enjoy this light, entertaining read."

Strasser's "Impact Zone" books reflect the author's love of surfing. In *Take Off,* Strasser introduces Kai, a transplanted Hawaiian who moves with his con-artist father to Sun Haven, a coastal town near New York City. When Kai takes to the beaches, he finds that a group of wealthy surfers, headed by Lucas Frank, claim the beach as their own. In *Cut Back,* Kai helps a friend with Tourette's syndrome prepare for a surfing competition. "The combination of extreme sport, romance, and teenage melodrama should keep readers, particularly boys, engaged," noted *Booklist* contributor Ed Sullivan.

Despite his success as a young-adult novelist, Strasser sees no reason to limit his talents. As the author once remarked, "I guess I originally wrote books for teens because that was where I had my first success and felt the most confident. But as I grow older, I find my interests widening not only towards writing books for older people, but for younger ones as well. I'd like to think that the day will come when I will write books for people of all ages, from three to eighty-three."

Biographical and Critical Sources

BOOKS

Children's Literature Review, Volume 11, Gale (Detroit, MI), 1986.
Nilsen, Alleen Pace, and Kenneth L. Donelson, *Literature for Today's Young Adults,* second edition, Scott, Foresman (Glenview, IL), 1985.
Roginski, Jim, *Behind the Covers: Interviews with Authors and Illustrators of Books for Children and Young Adults,* Libraries Unlimited (Littleton, CO), 1985.
St. James Guide to Young-Adult Writers, 2nd edition, St. James Press (Detroit, MI), 1999.

PERIODICALS

Best Sellers, May, 1983, review of *Workin' for Peanuts,* p. 75; June, 1984, review of *Turn It Up!,* p. 18.
Booklist, April 15, 1987, Stephanie Zvirin, review of *Wildlife,* p. 1276; January 15, 1992, review of *A Very Touchy Subject,* p. 933; March 15, 1994, Ilene Cooper, review of *Walt Disney's Lady and the Tramp,* p. 1366; May 1, 1995, Anne O'Malley, review of *How I Changed My Life,* p. 1564; February 1, 1996, Chris Sherman, review of *Help! I'm Trapped in Obedience School,* p. 932; March 15, 1996, review of *How I Changed My Life,* p. 1296; February 15, 1997, Debbie Carton, review of *Hey Dad, Get a Life!,* p. 1024; November 1, 1998, Anne O'Malley, review of *How I Spent My Last Night on Earth,* p. 485; February 15, 1999, Chris Sherman, review of *Shark Bite,* p. 1072; March 1, 1999, Shelle Rosenfeld, review of *Against the Odds: Gator Prey,* p. 1214; January 1, 2000, Shelle Rosenfeld, review of *Here Comes Heavenly,* p. 906; October 1, 2000, Michael Cart, review of *Give a Boy a Gun,* p. 337; April 15, 2003, Ed Sullivan, review of *CON-fidence,* p. 1472; March 15, 2004, Hazel Rochman, review of *Can't Get There from Here,* p. 1299; July, 2004, Ed Sullivan, reviews of *Cut Back* and *Take Off,* p. 1835; January 1, 2009, Daniel Kraus, review of *If I Grow Up,* p. 70; October 1, 2009, Michael Cart, review of *Wish You Were Dead,* p. 39.
Book Report, November-December, 1989, Barbara Wendland, review of *Beyond the Reef,* p. 47; November-December, 1993, Annette Thorson, "Author Profile: Todd Strasser," p. 30; November-December, 1995, Marilyn Makowski, review of *How I Changed My Life,* p. 44.
Bulletin of the Center for Children's Books, May, 1983, review of *Workin' for Peanuts,* p. 180; April, 1984, review of *Turn It Up!,* p. 156; February, 1985, review of *The Complete Computer Popularity Program,* p. 117; June, 1985, review of *A Very Touchy Subject,* p. 196; June, 1995, review of *How I Changed My Life,* p. 361; March, 1997, Deborah Stevenson, review of *Hey Dad, Get a Life!,* p. 259.
Emergency Librarian, September, 1987, review of *A Very Touchy Subject,* p. 29; September, 1996, review of *How I Changed My Life,* p. 27.
English Journal, April, 1982, Dick Abrahamson, review of *The Wave,* p. 80; October, 1983, review of *Workin' for Peanuts,* p. 86; December, 1986, John W. Conner, review of *A Very Touchy Subject,* p. 60; March, 1988, Terry C. Ley, review of *A Very Touchy Subject,* p. 85; October, 1991, W. David LeNoir, review of *Beyond the Reef,* p. 94.
Horn Book, April, 1983, review of *Workin' for Peanuts,* p. 175; June, 1984, Kate F. Flanagan, review of *Turn It Up!,* p. 344; May-June, 1985, Ann A. Flowers, review of *A Very Touchy Subject,* p. 321; March-April, 1986, Todd Strasser, "Stalking the Teen," pp. 236-239; January-February, 1989, Margaret A. Bush, review of *The Accident,* p. 82; January-February, 1990, Ethel R. Twichell, review of *Beyond the Reef,* p. 90.
Journal of Adolescent & Adult Literacy, November, 1997, review of *How I Changed My Life,* p. 211; March, 2002, Devon Clancy Sanner and Beth M. Lehman, reviews of *Give a Boy a Gun,* p. 547.
Kirkus Reviews, August 1, 1996, review of *Girl Gives Birth to Own Prom Date,* p. 1158; December 1, 2002, review of *CON-fidence,* p. 1775; March 1, 2003, review of *Thief of Dreams,* p. 399; February 15, 2004, review of *Can't Get There from Here,* p. 186; January 15, 2009, review of *If I Grow Up;* September 15, 2009, review of *Wish You Were Dead.*
Kliatt, May, 2002, Paula Rohrlick, review of *Give a Boy a Gun,* p. 22; March, 2003, Paula Rohrlick, review of *Thief of Dreams,* p. 16; March, 2005, Sarah Apple-

gate, review of *Cut Back,* p. 23; March, 2006, Kathryn Kulpa, review of *Can't Get There from Here,* p. 25; May, 2007, Paula Rohrlick, review of *Boot Camp,* p. 21; July, 2007, Olivia Durant, reviews of *For Money and Love,* p. 28.

Library Journal, January 1, 1988, Joyce Smothers, review of *The Family Man,* p. 100.

Media and Methods, February, 1983, Nina Piwoz, interview with Strasser.

New York Times, November 8, 2009, Tammy La Gorce, "After 96 Novels, Still Waiting for a Best Seller," 15L.

Publishers Weekly, November 27, 1981, Jean F. Mercier, review of *The Wave,* p. 88; December 4, 1987, Sybil Steinberg, review of *The Family Man,* p. 63; June 14, 1991, review of *Beyond the Reef,* p. 59; June 5, 1995, review of *How I Changed My Life,* p. 64; February 15, 1999, review of *Close Call,* p. 108; November 15, 1999, review of *Here Comes Heavenly,* p. 67; November 25, 2002, review of *CON-fidence,* p. 69; February 24, 2003, review of *Thief of Dreams,* p. 73; April 26, 2004, review of *Can't Get There from Here,* p. 66; January 2, 2006, review of *Slide or Die,* p. 64; May 14, 2007, review of *Boot Camp,* p. 55; June 25, 2007, review of *For Money and Love,* p. 62; January 19, 2009, review of *If I Grow Up,* p. 61.

Reading Teacher, October, 1993, review of *Honey, I Blew up the Kid,* p. 138; November, 1993, review of *The Diving Bell,* p. 249; October, 1995, review of *Help! I'm Trapped in the First Day of School,* p. 145.

School Library Journal, March 1, 1982, review of *The Wave,* p. 160; August 1, 1983, review of *Workin' for Peanuts,* p. 80; August 1, 1984, review of *Turn It Up!,* p. 87; November 1, 1984, Maureen S. Dugan, review of *The Complete Computer Popularity Program,* p. 138; April 1, 1985, Gerry Larson, review of *A Very Touchy Subject,* p. 100; September 1, 1989, Susan H. Williamson, review of *Beyond the Reef,* p. 278; June 1, 1992, Gail Richmond, review of *The Diving Bell,* p. 126; May 1, 1995, Cindy Darling Codell, review of *How I Changed My Life,* p. 123; February, 1996, Cheryl Cufari, review of *Help! I'm Trapped in Obedience School,* p. 104; January 1, 2000, Shelle Rosenfeld, review of *Here Comes Heavenly,* p. 906; August, 2000, Jane Halsall, review of *Pastabilities,* p. 190; September, 2000, Vicki Reutter, review of *Give a Boy a Gun,* p. 237; February, 2002, Francisca Goldsmith, review of *Give a Boy a Gun,* p. 75; March, 2003, Todd Morning, review of *Thief of Dreams,* p. 241; March, 2004, Joel Shoemaker, review of *Can't Get There from Here,* p. 220; August, 2004, Ashley Larsen, review of *Take Off,* p. 130; February, 2006, Michele Capozzella, review of *Slide or Die,* p. 138; April, 2007, Lynn Rashid, review of *Boot Camp,* p. 148; September, 2007, Jennifer Barnes, review of *For Money and Love,* p. 208; October, 2009, Brandy Danner, reviews of *Wish You Were Dead,* p. 138.

Teacher Librarian, December, 2000, review of *Give a Boy a Gun,* p. 44; February, 2003, interview with Strasser, p. 48.

Times Educational Supplement, May 24, 1991, review of *The Wave,* p. 24.

Voice of Youth Advocates, October, 1983, review of *Workin' for Peanuts,* p. 209; June, 1984, review of *Turn It Up!,* p. 98; February, 1985, review of *The Complete Computer Popularity Program,* p. 333; June, 1985, review of *A Very Touchy Subject,* p. 136; October, 1989, review of *Beyond the Reef,* p. 217; February, 1990, review of *Cookie,* p. 348, and review of *Moving Target,* p. 348; June, 1992, review of *The Diving Bell,* p. 102; October, 1995, review of *How I Changed My Life,* p. 224; April, 2003, review of *CON-fidence,* p. 60.

Wilson Library Bulletin, April 1, 1983, Patty Campbell, review of *Workin' for Peanuts,* p. 693; March 1, 1985, Patty Campbell, review of *A Very Touchy Subject,* p. 485; January 1, 1990, review of *Beyond the Reef,* p. 4.

ONLINE

International Thriller Writers Web site, http://www.thrillerwriters.org/ (November, 2009), Dan Levy, interview with Strasser.

Scholastic Web site, http://www2.scholastic.com/ (March 1, 2010), biography of Strasser.

Simon & Schuster Web site, http://www.simonandschuster.com/ (March 1, 2010), "Todd Strasser."

Todd Strasser Home Page, http://www.toddstrasser.com (March 1, 2010).

OTHER

Good Conversation! A Talk with Todd Strasser (video), Tim Podell Productions, 2003.

*   *   *

SWARNER, Kristina 1965-

Personal

Born 1965. *Education:* Rhode Island School of Design, B.F.A. (illustration).

Addresses

Home—Chicago, IL. *E-mail*—swarner.kristina@gmail.com.

Career

Illustrator and artist. *Exhibitions:* Work exhibited at Robert's Show Benefit Show, Dana-Farber Cancer Institute, 2005, 2007; Loeb Gallery, Washington, DC, 2007; Chemers Gallery, Los Angeles, CA, 2009, and Skirball Cultural Center and Eric Carle Picture Book Museum, both 2010. Work included in private collections.

Awards, Honors

Koret International Book Award, 2005, for *Before You Were Born* by Howard Schwartz; Sydney Taylor Book Award for Younger Readers, Association of Jewish Libraries, 2008, for *The Bedtime Sh'ma* by Sarah Gershman; awards from *Print, How,* and other periodicals.

Illustrator

Yiddish Wisdom: Yiddishe Chochma, Chronicle Books (San Francisco, CA), 1996.

Yiddish Wisdom for Parents: Yiddishe khokhme far eltern, translated and introduced by Rae Meltzer, Chronicle Books (San Francisco, CA), 2001.

Yiddish Wisdom for Marriage, translated and introduced by Rae Meltzer, Chronicle Books (San Francisco, CA), 2002.

Vanessa Ochs and Elizabeth Ochs, *The Jewish Dream Book: The Key to Opening the Inner Meaning of Your Dreams,* Jewish Lights Publishing, 2003.

***Illustrator Kristina Swarner captures the magic in David T. Greenberg's picture book* Enchanted Lions.** (Illustration copyright © 2009 by Kristina Swarner. All rights reserved. Reproduced by permission of Dutton Children's Books, a division of Penguin Putnam Books for Young Readers.)

Howard Schwartz, reteller, *Before You Were Born,* Roaring Brook Press (Brookfield, CT), 2005.

Doris K. Gayzagian, *One White Wishing Stone: A Beach Day Counting Book,* National Geographic (Washington, DC), 2006.

Sarah Gershman, adaptor, *The Bedtime Sh'ma: A Good Night Book,* EKS Publishing (Oakland, CA), 2007.

David T. Greenberg, *Enchanted Lions,* Dutton Children's Books (New York, NY), 2007.

Dotti Enderle, *Man in the Moon,* Delacorte (New York, NY), 2008.

Howard Schwartz, editor, *Leaves from the Garden of Eden: One Hundred Classic Jewish Tales,* Oxford University Press (New York, NY), 2008.

Howard Schwartz, *Gathering Sparks,* Roaring Brook Press (New York, NY), 2010.

Contributor of artwork to periodicals, including *Cricket, Sassy* and *Utne Reader.*

Sidelights

Chicago-based artist and illustrator Kristina Swarner creates evocative artwork for books by authors that include Howard Schwartz, Doris K. Gayzagian, Sarah Gershman, and David T. Greenberg. Praising Gayzagian's summer-themed *One White Wishing Stone: A Beach Day Counting Book,* Kathy Piehl wrote in *School Library Journal* that Swarner's sophisticated water-color illustrations for the book "recall the world of French impressionists" due to their colorful, light-filled quality. Greenberg's picture-book introduction to the night sky in *Enchanted Lions* also benefits from Swarner's creative approach; in describing her textured art for this book, Randall Enos commented in *Booklist* that the "softly colored scratchboardlike illustrations . . . convey a quiet, calm tone" and a *Publishers Weekly* critic cited the artist's use of "fantastical shapes and . . . textural, surreal landscapes" in evoking the magic in Greenberg's rhyming tale. Another collaboration, Gershman's *The Bedtime Sh'ma,* earned both author and illustrator the Sydney Taylor Book Award for Younger Readers in 2008.

In her work for *Before You Were Born,* Schwartz's adaptation of a Jewish story dating from the fourteenth century, Swarner uses "gauzy textures and curvilinear stylings" rendered using linoleum print, gouache, water color, and colored pencil to evoke artwork by painters such as Marc Chagall, according to a *Publishers Weekly* contributor. In *School Library Journal* Martha Topol wrote of the same book that the "textured, mixed-media art has a nice mixture of unpolished innocence . . . and calm serenity." Praising *Before You Were Born* in *Booklist,* Julie Cummins asserted that "Swarner's ethe-

real . . . illustrations illuminate the spirituality of the telling" and create a bedtime read-aloud that "will comfort many young listeners."

"I've wanted to be an artist since I was a baby, I think," Swarner explained in an online interview for *Embracing the Child.* "When I was about three years old, my grandmother made me a little book. Each page had a nature stamp on it, and she wrote a caption under each one that sounded almost like a fortune cookie; for example, 'Before long you will see a little frog in your yard.' I owned picture books, but that was when I realized that you could actually make one.

"When I was old enough to read, I found that my other grandmother had a cellar full of musty old children's books up through the 1950s. The cellar became the most enchanting place on earth to me. My grandmother would hunt me down on sunny days and make me go outside, but I just wanted to stay downstairs and look at books. I still love the smell of mildewed paper!"

Biographical and Critical Sources

PERIODICALS

Booklist, May 15, 2005, Julie Cummins, review of *Before You Were Born,* p. 1662; September 15, 2008, Hazel Rochman, review of *Leaves from the Garden of Eden: One Hundred Classic Jewish Tales,* p. 7; May 15, 2009, Randall Enos, review of *Enchanted Lions,* p. 44.

Kirkus Reviews, April 1, 2005, Howard Schwartz, review of *Before You Were Born,* p. 424; April 15, 2009, review of *Enchanted Lions.*

Publishers Weekly, August 25, 2003, review of *The Jewish Dream Book: The Key to Opening the Inner Meaning of Your Dreams,* p. 58; April 18, 2005, review of *Before You Were Born,* p. 61; May 18, 2009, review of *Enchanted Lions,* p. 52.

School Library Journal, April, 2005, Martha Topol, review of *Before You Were Born,* p. 126; November, 2006, Kathy Piehl, review of *One White Wishing Stone: A Beach Day Counting Book,* p. 94; September, 2008, Teri Markson, review of *Man in the Moon,* p. 178; June, 2009, Kirsten Cutler, review of *Enchanted Lions,* p. 88.

ONLINE

Embracing the Child Web site, http://www.embracingthe child.org/ (March 1, 2005), interview with Swarner.

Kristina Swarner Home Page, http://www.kristinaswarner. com (March 15, 2010).

T

TANAKA, Yoko 1947-

Personal

Born 1947, in Japan. *Education:* Kwansei Gakuin University (Japan), B.A. (law); Art Center College of Design, B.F.A. (illustration).

Addresses

Home—Los Angeles, CA/Bangkok, Thailand. *E-mail*—yoko@yokotanaka.com.

Career

Painter and illustrator. *Exhibitions:* Works exhibited at Ann Nathan Gallery, Chicago, IL, 2003, 2005, 2008; Society of Illustrators 46th Annual Exhibition, New York, NY, 2004; Motel Gallery, Portland, OR, 2004; Bologna Book Fair, Bologna, Italy, 2004, 2007; Art Chicago, 2004; SYM-BOOK-SIS Project Show, Tokyo, Japan, 2005; The Drawing Club, Los Angeles, CA, 2005; Froden Gallery, Los Angeles, 2005; Bradley University, Peoria, IL, 2005; Santa Ana College Retrospective Show, Santa Ana, CA, 2005; Alyce de Roulet Williamson Gallery, Art Center College of Design, Pasadena, CA, 2006; Renowned Gallery, Portland, 2006; Billy Shire Fine Arts, Los Angeles, 2006, 2008, 2010; Hemphill Fine Arts, Washington, DC, 2007; Limited Addiction Gallery, Denver, CO, 2008; David B. Smith Gallery, Denver, 2009; and Mondo Bizzarro, Rome, Italy, 2009, 2011.

Member

Society of Children's Book Writers and Illustrators,

Awards, Honors

Fred and Barbara Meiers Memorial Award, 2001; Orange County, CA, fine-arts scholarship, 2001; Sequential category winner, New York Society of Illustrators, 2003; Gold Award, Society of Illustrators of Los Angeles, 2004; Portfolio Award, Society of Children's Book Writers and Illustrators, 2005; Bologna Book Fair award, 2004, 2007; Society of Illustrators of New York Student Show Best of Show award, 2006.

Illustrator

R.L. LaFevers, *Theodosia and the Serpents of Chaos,* Houghton Mifflin (Boston, MA), 2007.

R.L. LaFevers, *Theodosia and the Staff of Osiris,* Houghton Mifflin (Boston, MA), 2008.

Sara Pennypacker, *Sparrow Girl,* Disney/Hyperion Books (New York, NY), 2009.

Kate DiCamillo, *The Magician's Elephant,* Candlewick Press (Somerville, MA), 2009.

Keith McGowan, *The Witch's Guide to Cooking with Children,* Henry Holt (New York, NY), 2009.

Contributor to periodicals, including *Los Angeles Times, Wine & Spirits, Wall Street Journal Asia,* and *Yen.*

Sidelights

Yoko Tanaka, a gallery painter and illustrator who lives in Bangkok and Los Angeles, has provided the artwork for a number of critically acclaimed children's books, including *Sparrow Girl* by Sara Pennypacker and *The Magician's Elephant* by Kate DiCamillo. Describing Tanaka's art on the Tor Books Web site, Keith McGowan stated that, "When one looks at Yoko's paintings, one sees a masterful mind at work—a mind with intense focus and a singular vision."

Tanaka made her first contributions to the world of children's literature in 2007 with her illustrations for *Theodosia and the Serpents of Chaos,* a rousing adventure tale by R.L. LaFevers. Set at the turn of the twentieth century, the novel centers on Theodosia Throckmorton, a feisty eleven year old whose parents run the Museum of Legends and Antiquities in London, England. When Theodosia's mother returns from an archaeological expedition in Egypt, the youngster realizes that some of the artifacts, including a sacred amulet, bear a dark curse, and she soon finds herself battling a secret soci-

ety bent on world domination. "It's the delicious, precise, and atmospheric details (nicely extended in Tanaka's few, stylized illustrations) that will capture and hold readers," Gillian Engberg noted in *Booklist*. Tanaka also illustrated a sequel, *Theodosia and the Staff of Osiris*.

Set in 1958, Pennypacker's *Sparrow Girl* presents a fictional account of Mao Zedong's disastrous three-day war on China's sparrow population. Concerned that the birds were devouring too much grain, thus decimating the nation's wheat crop, Chairman Mao ordered every able-bodied citizen to help drive sparrows away by creating a cacophony using firecrackers, pots and pans, and drums and gongs. The frightened birds, which became too frightened to land, died of exhaustion; once they were gone, however, China's insect population multiplied, causing even greater damage to the wheat. Pennypacker's tale focuses on young Ming-Li, a girl who rescues several of the downed sparrows and nurses them back to health. "Tanaka's quiet, simple illustrations in subdued tones match the somber mood" of *Sparrow Girl*, according to a critic in *Kirkus Reviews*, and Thom Barthelmess similarly noted in *Booklist* that

Yoko Tanaka's magical paintings bring to life Kate Di Camillo's picture book The Magician's Elephant. (Illustration copyright © 2009 by Yoko Tanaka. All rights reserved. Reproduced by permission of Candlewick Press.)

the illustrator "matches the somber elegance of the text with opaque, folk-inspired paintings in a subdued palette."

DiCamillo's surreal fantasy tale *The Magician's Elephant* concerns Peter Augustus Duchene, an orphan who begins searching for his sister—who is believed to be dead—after a fortuneteller's pronouncement that an elephant will lead to her discovery. Amazingly, that very night a magician conjures an elephant from thin air at the local opera house and this event has far-reaching consequences. "Tanaka's acrylic artwork is meticulous in detail and aptly matches the tone of the narrative," Tim Wadham commented in his review of the book for *School Library Journal,* and *Booklist* reviewer Kristen McKulski asserted that the "charming black-and-white acrylic illustrations" in *The Magician's Elephant* "have a soft, period feel that perfectly matches the tone of this spellbinding story."

A modern version of "Hansel and Gretel," McGowan's *The Witch's Guide to Cooking with Children* pits Sol, an eleven-year-old technology expert, and Connie, Sol's spunky eight-year-old sister, against Fay Holaderry, a witch who loves nothing more than feasting on the children of Schoneberg. "Tanaka's occasional full-page views of grim, heavy-lidded figures add a suitably gothic tone" to McGowan's story, wrote a critic in *Kirkus Reviews,* and Shelle Rosenfeld observed in *Booklist* that the "shadowy illustrations add unsettling eeriness" to *The Witch's Guide to Cooking with Children.*

Biographical and Critical Sources

PERIODICALS

Booklist, May 1, 2007, Gillian Engberg, review of *Theodosia and the Serpents of Chaos,* p. 48; November 15, 2008, Ilene Cooper, review of *Theodosia and the Staff of Osiris,* p. 40; January 1, 2009, Thom Barthelmess, review of *Sparrow Girl,* p. 94; July 1, 2009, Shelle Rosenfeld, review of *The Witch's Guide to Cooking with Children,* p. 57, and Kristen McKulski, review of *The Magician's Elephant,* p. 63.

Horn Book, September-October, 2009, Martha V. Parravano, review of *The Magician's Elephant,* p. 557.

Kirkus Reviews, April 1, 2007, review of *Theodosia and the Serpents of Chaos;* January 15, 2009, review of *Sparrow Girl;* July 15, 2009, review of *The Witch's Guide to Cooking with Children;* August 1, 2009, review of *The Magician's Elephant.*

Publishers Weekly, April 9, 2007, review of *Theodosia and the Serpents of Chaos,* p. 54; January 26, 2009, review of *Sparrow Girl,* p. 119.

School Library Journal, April, 2007, Margaret A. Chang, review of *Theodosia and the Serpents of Chaos,* p. 140; December, 2008, Samantha Larsen Hastings, review of *Theodosia and the Staff of Osiris,* p. 130; March, 2009, Miriam Lang Budin, review of *Sparrow Girl,* p. 124; August, 2009, Tim Wadham, review of *The Magician's Elephant,* p. 102; October, 2009, Kathleen Meulen Ellison, review of *The Witch's Guide to Cooking with Children,* p. 132.

USA Today, October 29, 2009, Bob Minzesheimer, review of *The Witch's Guide to Cooking with Children,* p. D3.

ONLINE

Candlewick Press Web site, http://www.candlewick.com/ (March 1, 2010), "*The Magician's Elephant:* Q&A with Yoko Tanaka."

Tor Books Web site, http://www.tor.com/ (October 9, 2009), Keith McGowan, "Letters from Abroad: Illustrator Yoko Tanaka."

Yoko Tanaka Home Page, http://www.yokotanaka.com (March 1, 2010).

* * *

THALER, Michael C.
See THALER, Mike

* * *

THALER, Mike 1936-
(Michael C. Thaler)

Personal

Born 1936, in Los Angeles, CA; son of Ben (in sales; a poet and sculptor) and Jean Thaler; married Laurel Lee (a professor and writer), March 3, 1995. *Education:* Attended University of California, Los Angeles. *Hobbies and other interests:* Collecting art, netsuke, model and toy race cars, T-shirts, and laughter.

Addresses

Home and office—1305 Heater Ct., West Linn, OR 97068-2736. *Agent*—(literary) Andrea Brown, P.O. Box 429, El Granada, CA 94018-0429; (multimedia) Creative Artists Agency, 9830 Wilshire Blvd., Beverly Hills, CA 90212; (school visits) Riddle King Tours—Kay Meekins, 1318 Pisgah Church Rd., Greensboro, NC 27455. *E-mail*—mikethaler@yahoo.com.

Career

Author, illustrator, songwriter, and educator. Public Broadcasting Service (PBS), creator of "Letterman" character for television series *The Electric Company.* Teacher, lecturer, and presenter at workshops. Co-designer of software and computer games, including *The Riddle King's Riddle Magic* (software), and board games, including *Scrambled Legs* and *The Riddle King's Riddle Race.*

Member

PEN International, American Society of Composers, Authors, and Publishers (ASCAP).

Mike Thaler (Reproduced by permission.)

Awards, Honors

Children's Choice designation, International Reading Association/Children's Book Council, 1982, for *Moonkey.*

Writings

FOR CHILDREN; SELF-ILLUSTRATED

The Magic Boy, Harper (New York, NY), 1961.

The Clown's Smile, Harper (New York, NY), 1962, new edition, illustrated by Tracey Cameron, 1986.

The King's Flower, Orion Press (New York, NY), 1963.

Penny Pencil: The Story of a Pencil, Harper (New York, NY), 1963.

Moonboy, Harper (New York, NY), 1964.

(Editor with William Cole) *The Classic Cartoons: A Definitive Gallery of the Cartoon as Art and as Humor,* World Publishing, 1966.

Magic Letter Riddles, Scholastic, Inc. (New York, NY), 1974.

Wuzzles, Scholastic, Inc. (New York, NY), 1976.

Soup with Quackers! Funny Cartoon Riddles, F. Watts (Danbury, CT), 1976.

Riddle Riot, Scholastic, Inc. (New York, NY), 1976.

(With William Cole) *Knock Knocks: The Most Ever,* F. Watts (New York, NY), 1976.

Funny Bones: Cartoon Monster Riddles, F. Watts (New York, NY), 1976.

Silly Puzzles, Xerox Publications, 1976.

Dazzles, Grosset (New York, NY), 1977.

(With William Cole) *Knock Knocks You've Never Heard Before,* F. Watts (New York, NY), 1977.

(With William Cole) *The Square Bear and Other Riddle Rhymes,* Scholastic, Inc. (New York, NY), 1977.

Never Tickle a Turtle: Cartoons, Riddles, and Funny Stories, F. Watts (New York, NY), 1977.

What's Up, Duck? Cartoons, Riddles, and Jokes, F. Watts (New York, NY), 1978.

The Chocolate Marshmelephant Sundae, F. Watts (New York, NY), 1978.

The Yellow Brick Toad: Funny Frog Cartoons, Riddles, and Silly Stories, Doubleday (New York, NY), 1978.

(With William Cole) *Give Up? Cartoon Riddle Rhymes,* F. Watts (New York, NY), 1978.

(With William Cole) *Backwords,* Random House (Garden City, NJ), 1979.

Picture Riddles, Random House (Garden City, NJ), 1979.

Unicorns on the Cob, Grosset (New York, NY), 1979.

Screamers, Grosset (New York, NY), 1979.

Steer Wars, Grosset (New York, NY), 1979.

The Nose Knows, Grosset (New York, NY), 1979.

Grin and Bear It, Grosset (New York, NY), 1979.

Toucans on Two Cans, Grosset (New York, NY), 1979.

The Complete Cootie Book, Avon (New York, NY), 1980.

Oinkers Away: Pig Riddles, Cartoons, and Jokes, Archway, 1981.

Scared Silly: A Monster Riddle and Joke Scare-a-Thon Featuring Bugs Mummy and Count Quackula, Avon (New York, NY), 1982.

Story Puzzles, Scholastic, Inc. (New York, NY), 1982.

The Pac-Man Riddle and Joke Book, Archway, 1982.

Paws: Cat Riddles, Cat Jokes, and Catoons, Archway, 1982.

(With Cole) *Monster Knock Knocks,* Archway, 1982.

Stuffed Feet, Avon (New York, NY), 1983.

Riddle Rainbow, Hastings House, 1984.

Funny Side Up! How to Create Your Own Riddles, Scholastic, Inc. (New York, NY), 1985.

King Kong's Underwear, Avon (New York, NY), 1986.

Mr. Bananahead at Home, Scholastic, Inc. (New York, NY), 1987.

Godzilla's Pantyhose, Avon (New York, NY), 1989.

Frankenstein's Pantyhose, Avon (New York, NY), 1989.

Catzilla, Simon & Schuster (New York, NY), 1991.

Bad Day at Monster Elementary, Avon (New York, NY), 1995.

Thaler's books have been published in England, Canada, France, and Japan. Contributor of cartoons to magazines, including *Harper's Bazaar, Horizon, Humpty Dumpty,* and *Saturday Evening Post.*

FOR CHILDREN

The Prince and the Seven Moons, illustrated by Ursula Arndt, Macmillan (New York, NY), 1966.

The Rainbow, illustrated by Donald Leake, H. Quist, 1967.

The Smiling Book, illustrated by Arnie Levin, Lothrop (New York, NY), 1971.

My Little Friend, illustrated by Arnie Levin, Lothrop (New York, NY), 1971.

The Staff, illustrated by Joseph Schindelman, Random House (Garden City, NJ), 1971.

How Far Will a Rubberband Stretch?, illustrated by Jerry Joyner, Parents Magazine Press (New York, NY), 1974.

What Can a Hippopotamus Be?, illustrated by Robert Grossman, Parents Magazine Press (New York, NY), 1975.

There's a Hippopotamus under My Bed, illustrated by Ray Cruz, F. Watts (New York, NY), 1977.

Madge's Magic Show, illustrated by Carol Nicklaus, F. Watts (New York, NY), 1978.

My Puppy, illustrated by Madeleine Fishman, Harper (New York, NY), 1980.

Moonkey, illustrated by Giulio Maestro, Harper (New York, NY), 1981.

The Moose Is Loose, illustrated by Tony Gaffr, Scholastic, Inc. (New York, NY), 1981.

A Hippopotamus Ate the Teacher, illustrated by Jared Lee, Avon (New York, NY), 1981.

The Moon and the Balloon, illustrated by Madeleine Fishman, Hastings House, 1982.

Owly, illustrated by David Wiesner, Harper (New York, NY), 1982, reprinted, Walker (New York, NY), 1998.

It's Me, Hippo!, illustrated by Maxie Chambliss, Harper (New York, NY), 1983.

Montgomery Moose's Favorite Riddles, illustrated by Neal McPheeters, Scholastic, Inc. (New York, NY), 1985.

Cream of Creature from the School Cafeteria, illustrated by Jared Lee, Avon (New York, NY), 1985.

Upside Down Day, illustrated by Jared Lee, Avon (New York, NY), 1986.

Hippo Lemonade, illustrated by Maxie Chambliss, Harper (New York, NY), 1986.

Hink Pink Monsters, illustrated by Fred Winkowski, Scholastic, Inc. (New York, NY), 1987.

In the Middle of the Puddle, illustrated by Bruce Degen, Harper (New York, NY), 1988.

Pack 109, illustrated by Normand Chartier, Dutton (New York, NY), 1988.

Come and Play, Hippo, illustrated by Maxie Chambliss, Harper (New York, NY), 1989.

The Riddle King's Camp Riddles, illustrated by Paul Harvey, Random House (Garden City, NJ), 1989.

The Riddle King's Food Riddles, illustrated by Paul Harvey, Random House (Garden City, NJ), 1989.

The Riddle King's Pet Riddles, illustrated by Paul Harvey, Random House (Garden City, NJ), 1989.

The Riddle King's School Riddles, illustrated by Paul Harvey, Random House (Garden City, NJ), 1989.

Seven Little Hippos, illustrated by Jerry Smath, Simon & Schuster (New York, NY), 1991.

Cannon the Librarian, illustrated by Jared Lee, Avon (New York, NY), 1993.

Colossal Fossil, illustrated by Rick Brown, W.H. Freeman, 1994.

Miss Yonkers Goes Bonkers, illustrated by Jared Lee, Avon (New York, NY), 1994.

Earth Mirth: The Ecology Riddle Book, illustrated by Rick Brown, Scientific American Books for Young Readers, 1994.

Little Dinosaur, illustrated by Paige Miglio, Henry Holt (New York, NY), 2001.

Heroines of the Bible: God's Fair Ladies, illustrated by Dennis Adler, Faith Kids (Colorado Springs, CO), 2002.

Prophets of the Bible: God's Anchormen, illustrated by Dennis Adler, Faith Kids (Colorado Springs, CO), 2002.

Pig Little, illustrated by Paige Miglio, Henry Holt (New York, NY), 2006.

"LAGOON ELEMENTARY" SERIES

The Teacher from the Black Lagoon, illustrated by Jared Lee, Scholastic, Inc. (New York, NY), 1989.

The Principal from the Black Lagoon, illustrated by Jared Lee, Scholastic, Inc. (New York, NY), 1993.

The Gym Teacher from the Black Lagoon, illustrated by Jared Lee, Scholastic, Inc. (New York, NY), 1994.

The School Nurse from the Black Lagoon, illustrated by Jared Lee, Scholastic, Inc. (New York, NY), 1995.

The Librarian from the Black Lagoon, illustrated by Jared Lee, Scholastic, Inc. (New York, NY), 1997.

The Cafeteria Lady from the Black Lagoon, illustrated by Jared Lee, Scholastic, Inc. (New York, NY), 1998.

The School Bus Driver from the Black Lagoon, illustrated by Jared Lee, Scholastic, Inc. (New York, NY), 1999.

The Music Teacher from the Black Lagoon, illustrated by Jared Lee, Scholastic, Inc. (New York, NY), 2000.

The Custodian from the Black Lagoon, illustrated by Jared Lee, Scholastic, Inc. (New York, NY), 2001.

The Class Trip from the Black Lagoon, illustrated by Jared Lee, Scholastic, Inc. (New York, NY), 2002.

The Class from the Black Lagoon, Scholastic, Inc. (New York, NY), 2002.

The Class Election from the Black Lagoon, illustrated by Jared Lee, Scholastic, Inc. (New York, NY), 2003.

The Class Pet from the Black Lagoon, illustrated by Jared Lee, Scholastic, Inc. (New York, NY), 2003.

The Talent Show from the Black Lagoon, illustrated by Jared Lee, Scholastic, Inc. (New York, NY), 2003.

The Bully from the Black Lagoon, illustrated by Jared Lee, Scholastic, Inc. (New York, NY), 2004.

The Halloween Party from the Black Lagoon, illustrated by Jared Lee, Scholastic, Inc. (New York, NY), 2004.

The Science Fair from the Black Lagoon, illustrated by Jared Lee, Scholastic, Inc. (New York, NY), 2004.

The Field Day from the Black Lagoon, illustrated by Jared Lee, Scholastic, Inc. (New York, NY), 2005.

The School Carnival from the Black Lagoon, illustrated by Jared Lee, Scholastic, Inc. (New York, NY), 2005.

The Book Fair from the Black Lagoon, illustrated by Jared Lee, Scholastic, Inc. (New York, NY), 2006.

The Christmas Party from the Black Lagoon, illustrated by Jared Lee, Scholastic, Inc. (New York, NY), 2006.

School Riddles from the Black Lagoon, illustrated by Jared Lee, Scholastic, Inc. (New York, NY), 2007.

The Computer Teacher from the Black Lagoon, illustrated by Jared Lee, Scholastic, Inc. (New York, NY), 2007.

The Little League Team from the Black Lagoon, illustrated by Jared Lee, Scholastic, Inc. (New York, NY), 2007.

The Vice Principal from the Black Lagoon, illustrated by Jared Lee, Scholastic, Inc. (New York, NY), 2007.

April Fools' Day from the Black Lagoon, illustrated by Jared Lee, Scholastic, Inc. (New York, NY), 2008.

"BULLY BROTHERS" SERIES

The Bully Brothers Trick the Tooth Fairy, illustrated by Jared Lee, Grosset (New York, NY), 1993.

The Bully Brothers: Gobblin' Halloween, illustrated by Jared Lee, Grosset (New York, NY), 1993.

The Bully Brothers: Making the Grade, illustrated by Jared Lee, Scholastic, Inc. (New York, NY), 1995.

The Bully Brothers at the Beach, illustrated by Jared Lee, Scholastic, Inc. (New York, NY), 1996.

"FUNNY FIRSTS" SERIES

Camp Rotten Time, illustrated by Jared Lee, Troll Communications (Mahwah, NJ), 1994.

Fang the Dentist, illustrated by Jared Lee, Troll Communications (Mahwah, NJ), 1994.

My Cat Is Going to the Dogs, illustrated by Jared Lee, Troll Communications (Mahwah, NJ), 1994.

The Schmo Must Go On, illustrated by Jared Lee, Troll Communications (Mahwah, NJ), 1995.

I'm Dracula, Who Are You?, illustrated by Jared Lee, Troll Communications (Mahwah, NJ), 1996.

Love Stinks, illustrated by Jared Lee, Troll Communications (Mahwah, NJ), 1996.

Moving to Mars, illustrated by Jared Lee, Troll Communications (Mahwah, NJ), 1996.

Make Your Beds, Bananaheads, illustrated by Jared Lee, Troll Communications (Mahwah, NJ), 1997.

Schmoe White and the Seven Dorfs, illustrated by Jared Lee, Scholastic, Inc. (New York, NY), 1997.

"LAFFALONG" SERIES

Never Mail an Elephant, illustrated by Jerry Smath, Troll Communications (Mahwah, NJ), 1993.

Uses for Mooses and Other Popular Pets, illustrated by Jerry Smath, Troll Communications (Mahwah, NJ), 1993.

Never Give a Fish an Umbrella, illustrated by Jerry Smath, Troll Communications (Mahwah, NJ), 1996.

"HAPPILY EVER AFTER" SERIES

Cinderella Bigfoot, illustrated by Jared Lee, Scholastic, Inc. (New York, NY), 1997.

Hanzel and Pretzel, illustrated by Jared Lee, Scholastic, Inc. (New York, NY), 1997.

Schmoe White and the Seven Dorfs, illustrated by Jared Lee, Scholastic, Inc. (New York, NY), 1997.

The Princess and the Pea-ano, illustrated by Jared Lee, Scholastic, Inc. (New York, NY), 1997.

"HEAVEN AND MIRTH" SERIES

Adam and the Apple Turnover, and Other Bible Stories to Tickle Your Soul, illustrated by Dennis Adler, Faith Kids (Colorado Springs, CO), 2000.

Daniel, Nice Kitty!, and Other Bible Stories to Tickle Your Soul, illustrated by Dennis Adler, Faith Kids (Colorado Springs, CO), 2000.

David, God's Rock Star, and Other Bible Stories to Tickle Your Soul, illustrated by Dennis Adler, Faith Kids (Colorado Springs, CO), 2000.

Elijah, Prophet Sharing, and Other Bible Stories to Tickle Your Soul, illustrated by Dennis Adler, Faith Kids (Colorado Springs, CO), 2000.

Moses, Take Two Tablets and Call Me in the Morning, and Other Bible Stories to Tickle Your Soul, illustrated by Dennis Adler, Faith Kids (Colorado Springs, CO), 2000.

Paul, God's Message Sent Apostle Post, and Other Bible Stories to Tickle Your Soul, illustrated by Dennis Adler, Faith Kids (Colorado Springs, CO), 2000.

The Prodigal Son, Oh Brother!, and Other Bible Stories to Tickle Your Soul, illustrated by Dennis Adler, Chariot Victor Pub. (Colorado Springs, CO), 2000.

David and Bubblebath-Sheba, and Other Bible Stories to Tickle Your Soul, illustrated by Dennis Adler, Faith Kids (Colorado Springs, CO), 2001.

John the Baptist: Wet and Wild, and Other Bible Stories to Tickle Your Soul, illustrated by Dennis Adler, Faith Kids (Colorado Springs, CO), 2001.

"TALES FROM THE BACK PEW" SERIES

Church Summer Cramp, illustrated by Jared Lee, Zonderkidz (Grand Rapids, MI), 2009.

Easter Egg Haunt, illustrated by Jared Lee, Zonderkidz (Grand Rapids, MI), 2009.

I-Scream Sunday, illustrated by Jared Lee, Zonderkidz (Grand Rapids, MI), 2009.

Mission Trip Impossible, illustrated by Jared Lee, Zonderkidz (Grand Rapids, MI), 2009.

Preacher Creature Strikes on Sunday, illustrated by Jared Lee, Zonderkidz (Grand Rapids, MI), 2009.

The Three Wise Guys, illustrated by Jared Lee, Zonderkidz (Grand Rapids, MI), 2009.

Walking the Plank to the Baptism Tank, illustrated by Jared Lee, Zonderkidz (Grand Rapids, MI), 2009.

Bible Knock-knocks from the Back Pew, illustrated by Jared Lee, Zonderkidz (Grand Rapids, MI), 2010.

Bible Riddles from the Back Pew, illustrated by Jared Lee, Zonderkidz (Grand Rapids, MI), 2010.

Church Harvest Mess-tival, illustrated by Jared Lee, Zondervan (Grand Rapids, MI), 2010.

Vacation Bible Snooze, Zondervan (Grand Rapids, MI), 2010.

ACTIVITY BOOKS

(With Janet Pullen) *The Riddle King's Giant Book of Jokes, Riddles, and Activities,* Modern, 1987.

(With Janet Pullen) *The Riddle King's Jumbo Book of Jokes, Riddles, and Activities,* Modern, 1987.

The Riddle King's Super Book of Jokes, Riddles, and Activities, Modern, 1987.

The Riddle King's Book of Jokes, Riddles, and Activities, Modern, 1988.

OTHER

The Riddle King Tells His Favorite Riddles, Jokes, Stories, and Songs with Steve Charney (sound recording), Caedmon, 1985.

The Riddle King's Riddle Song: Scholastic Songs with Steve Charney (sound recording), Scholastic, Inc. (New York, NY), 1987.

Imagination, R.C. Owen Publishers (Katonah, NY), 2002.

Works included in cassette recordings *These Are the Questions, My Blanket Is the Sky,* and *Sing Me a Rainbow.*

Adaptations

The "Bully Brothers" series was optioned by ABC-TV and CBS-TV for a television series.

Sidelights

An author and illustrator of numerous picture books, beginning readers, and original joke and riddle books for children, Mike Thaler collaborates with illustrator Jared Lee to produce many of his entertaining and well-received works for children. In a review of their "Happily Ever After" books, which include *Hanzel and Pretzel* and *Schmoe White and the Seven Dorfs,* Cincinnati *Enquirer* commentator Sara Pearce dubbed Thaler and Lee "the court jesters of children's literature." Thaler shares his lighthearted vision of life and encourages young people to indulge in their natural sense of wonder in numerous other stories, including those in the "Black Lagoon" and "Tales from the Back Pew" books, the latter which introduce Christian themes.

***Thaler teams up with illustrator Jared Lee to produce numerous books, among them* Cannon the Librarian.** (Illustration copyright © 1993 by Jared D. Lee Studio, Inc. All rights reserved. Used by permission of the illustrator.)

Thaler's long-running collaboration with Lee includes the "Black Lagoon" installment **The Class from the Black Lagoon.** (Illustration copyright © 2002 by Jared Lee. Reproduced by permission of Scholastic, Inc.)

Born in Los Angeles, California, in 1936, Thaler attended classes at the University of California, Los Angeles before breaking away to follow his dreams. "What I really hoped to earn a living at was doing cartoons for adults," Thaler once told *SATA.* "Actually, they weren't even funny cartoons, they were the 'save-the-world' kind. Then one day Ursula Nordstrom, an editor at Harper & Row, saw a picture story I had done for *Harper's Bazaar* . . . and asked if I had ever thought of doing children's books." Thaler completed his first book for children, *The Magic Boy,* in 1961. The story of a young boy who could juggle rainbows that never dropped, *The Magic Boy* marked the start of a long career for the prolific writer/illustrator.

"Writing a story is like painting a picture," Thaler once explained to *SATA.* "You put down one color, and then you put down a second color next to it, and it changes the first color. You put down words next to words and

they change, too. So when you put two or three words together, there's an interaction." During the writing process, Thaler tries to tap the feelings of his inner child: "I sort of feel like I am more of a receiver than an originator, that I am merely the radio the music plays through. It's like the stories are already there. I am simply putting them down on paper."

Among the many picture books Thaler has written—and often illustrated—are *What Can a Hippopotamus Be?, Madge's Magic Show,* the award-winning *Moonkey, Pig Little,* and *Owly,* the last a story of a young owl full of curiosity about the world around him. The beginning reader *It's Me, Hippo!* contains four stories that find the portly title character involved in a range of activities alongside a group of his African animal friends in what a *Publishers Weekly* reviewer called a "buoyant collection." Animals are also featured in *Hippo Lemonade, Moonkey,* and *In the Middle of the Puddle,* the last

which finds Fred the frog and Ted the turtle watching their comfortably sized puddle stretch into a sea after a long rainstorm. "Paced by the phrase repetition that small children relish . . . this charmer will delight youngsters on rainy and sunny days," asserted Beth Ames Herbert in her review of *In the Middle of the Puddle* for *Booklist*.

In *Owly* readers meet an owlet that has a never-ending list of questions for his busy mother. Instead of answering them herself, Mother Owl sends her young son out into the world to discover the answers for himself. Reviewing the book for the *Bulletin of the Center for Children's Books*, Zena Sutherland noted that *Owly* "has a loving relationship and an interesting concept as appeals." *Pig Little*, which pairs Thaler's text with illustrations by Paige Miglio, follows a little pig as it spends a day at the seaside. Thaler's rhythmic text captures "Pig Little's childlike interpretation of an experience," asserted Marge Loch-Wouters in her *School Library Journal* review of the book, the critic predicting that young children "will recognize themselves in the warm verse" and Miglio's "lush watercolor-and-pencil" art. Giving the book equal praise, a *Kirkus Reviews* writer noted that the "deceptively simple poems" and *Pig Little* allows children "to delight in the day at the beach it renders so artfully."

"When you do children's [picture] books, there can be no waste, no fat," Thaler explained. "It has to be all muscle and bone. There has to be character development, plot and depth, all in thirty-two pages. And it has to be beauty and energy." According to the author, the words under the illustration are what fuel the story. "Words give an emotional feeling. They give you energy." While Thaler once believed children's books should also contain a message, he has since changed his mind. "Just the laughter of children is the message," he noted. "Laughter is a message in itself."

Thaler claims to have a poor reputation for understanding other people's jokes, so in his books he finds it simpler just to make up his own. He tries to extend that same originality to every part of each of his riddle books—from jokes and riddles to the stories and drawings that he includes alongside them. While many riddle books contain lists of riddles, Thaler's books are unusual in that he uses his ability as an artist to play up the visual humor through comic illustrations. In *Never Tickle a Turtle: Cartoons, Riddles, and Funny Stories*, which is illustrated with black-and-white cartoons, Thaler appeals to a variety of ages by featuring visual puns alongside his jokes and riddles. *The Yellow Brick Toad* contains an entire collection of jokes, riddles, stories, and cartoons featuring the high-hopping amphibians. Similarly, *Oinkers Away!* is full of swine humor, complete with illustrations by Thaler that add to the fun.

In addition to working on new books, Thaler travels to schools across the country, reading from his books and encouraging the children he meets to develop their own creativity. "I find riddles to be a valuable educational tool," he noted. "They get kids into all sorts of things—synonyms, rhythm, spelling syntax, syllables and, more importantly, into the dictionary, a marvelous source of riddles." During his visits to schools Thaler encourages students to make up their own stories, draw their own cartoons, and write their own "books" in order to help them build on their personal creativity and developing sense of humor. "There is pure creativity when you are around kids," he exclaimed. "The energy of children is the most amazing, important source of energy in this whole country. It should be protected and helped to develop. Teachers to me are the most important people in the world because they are shaping the future. The possibilities of kids are the possibilities of the future."

"There was a time in my life when everything had to be serious," Thaler once admitted to *SATA*. "Now I have

Thaler and Lee mine Sunday school for humor in their chapter-book series that includes **Preacher Creature Strikes on Sunday.** (Illustration © 2009 by Jared Lee. Reproduced by permission.)

learned that laughter is important, and I feel it is important for children to have a good body of humor, an intelligent body of humor." Thaler weaves his belief in the power of humor into each of his many books, joining it with another principle. "Love and creativity are the two basic elements of life to me," he explained. "If you put love and creativity into everything you do, you've got it made. This is the philosophy I live by, and the philosophy I teach."

Biographical and Critical Sources

PERIODICALS

Booklist, June 1, 1988, Beth Ames Herbert, review of *In the Middle of the Puddle,* pp. 1679-1680.
Bulletin of the Center for Children's Books, July-August, 1982, Zena Sutherland, review of *Owly,* p. 216.
Cincinnati Enquirer, March 18, 1997, Sara Pearce, "Authors Add Wackiness to Traditional Fairy Tales," p. C5.
Kirkus Reviews, June 1, 2006, review of *Pig Little,* p. 581; January 15, 2009, review of *Preacher Creatures Strikes on Sunday.*
Publishers Weekly, December 2, 1983, review of *It's Me, Hippo!,* p. 86.
School Library Journal, December, 2001, Ann Cook, review of *Little Dinosaur,* p. 113; July, 2006, Marge Loch-Wouters, review of *Pig Little,* p. 95.

ONLINE

Mike Thaler Home Page, http://www.mikethaler.com (April 15, 2010).*

*   *   *

THOMASON, Mark

Personal

Born in CA; immigrated to Australia; married. *Education:* Oklahoma State University, degree (structural engineering).

Addresses

Home—North Sydney, New South Wales, Australia.

Career

Author. Worked as a structural engineer. *Military service:* U.S. Navy.

Writings

Moonrunner, Scholastic Press (Gosford, New South Wales, Australia), 2008, Kane/Miller (La Jolla, CA), 2009.

Sidelights

An Australian transplant who was born and raised in the Sierra Nevada Mountains of California, Mark Thomason based his middle-grade novel, *Moonrunner,* on the stories his father shared about encountering wild mustangs in the range lands of Montana. A structural engineer who has lived throughout the world during the course of his career, Thomason now makes his home in Sydney, New South Wales, and it is here that he sets his novel.

In *Moonrunner* readers are transported to the last decade of the nineteenth century, a time when Australia was still mostly wilderness. The novel's narrator, twelve-year-old Casey, has come to Australia from Montana, his parents determined to make a new home amid the harsh, scrublands near the town of Omeo. They work a farm belonging to Casey's grandfather, a crotchety man who arrived in Australia during the gold rush. Missing the wide open spaces of Montana, Casey also misses his horse, and he feels humiliated when he must ride his parents' mule to school and back. Soon he must escape a gang of local bullies by running into the overgrowth, and there he discovers a wild and high-spirited black stallion that he adopts and names Moonrunner. As the relationship between horse and boy develops, Casey

Cover of Mark Thomason's middle-grade historical novel **Moonrunner,** *featuring artwork by Anja Hild.* (Kane/Miller, 2009. Reproduced by permission.)

also comes to terms with his new surroundings, wins over his schoolmates by teaching them the game of baseball, and earns respect for his knowledge of horses.

Noting the coming-of-age elements in *Moonrunner,* Claire Saxby wrote in *AussieReviews.com* that Thomason's book is "full of rich historical and geographical detail, including goldrushes, the High Plains cattlemen and much more." "Casey's homesickness and trouble fitting in will resonate with young readers, as will his love for animals," predicted Krista Hutley in her review of the novel for *Booklist,* and in *School Library Journal* Carol Schene praised Casey as "a strong, engaging protagonist" with a "determination" that will inspire readers. Although a *Kirkus Reviews* writer questioned the boy's ability to negotiate profitable bargains with local ranchers, the critic added that Thomson's "portrait of Down Under pioneer life [in *Moonrunner*] is built around a love of horses."

Biographical and Critical Sources

PERIODICALS

Booklist, April 15, 2009, Krista Hutley, review of *Moonrunner,* p. 51.

Kirkus Reviews, January 15, 2009, review of *Moonrunner.*

School Library Journal, June, 2009, Carol Schene, review of *Moonrunner,* p. 139.

ONLINE

AussieReviews.com, http://www.aussiereviews.com/ (May 1, 2010), Claire Saxby, review of *Moonrunner,*

Scholastic Australia Web site, http://www.scholastic.com/au/ (May 1, 2010), "Mark Thomason."*

U-V

UEHASHI, Nahoko 1962-
(Uehashi Nahoko)

Personal

Born July 15, 1962, in Tokyo, Japan. *Education:* Ph.D. (cultural anthropology).

Addresses

Home—Tokyo, Japan.

Career

Educator and author. Kawamura Gakuen Women's University, Tokyo, Japan, assistant then associate professor of anthropology.

Awards, Honors

Japanese Association of Writers for Children award, for *Tsuki no Mori ni Kamiyo Nemure,* and 1999, for *Seirei no Moribito;* Noma Children's Literature award, and Sankei Children's Culture and Publishment award, both 1996, both for *Seirei no Moribito;* Iwaya Sazanami literature award, 2002, for "Guardian" series; Noma Children's Literature Award, 2003, for *Koteki no Kanata;* Mildred L. Batchelder Award, American Library Association Notable Book designation, and U.S. Board on Books for Young People Outstanding International Book designation, all 2009, all for *Moribito,* all 2010, all for *Moribito II.*

Writings

FANTASY FICTION

Seirei no Ki, [Japan], 1989.
Tsuki no Mori ni Kamiyo Nemure, Kaisei-sha (Tokyo, Japan), 1991.

Seirei no Moribito ("Guardian" series), illustrated by Yuko Shimizu, Kaisei-sha (Tokyo, Japan), 1996, translated by Cathy Hirano as *Moribito: Guardian of the Spirit,* Arthur A. Levine Books (New York, NY), 2008.
Yami no Moribito ("Guardian" series), illustrated by Yuko Shimizu, Kaisei-sha (Tokyo, Japan), 1999, translated by Cathy Hirano as *Moribito II: Guardian of the Darkness,* Arthur A. Levine Books (New York, NY), 2009.
Yume no Moribito ("Guardian" series), illustrated by Yuko Shimizu, Kaisei-sha (Tokyo, Japan), 2000.
Koku no Tabibito ("Guardian" series), Kaisei-sha (Tokyo, Japan), 2001.
Kami no Moribito ("Guardian" series), two volumes, Kaisei-sha (Tokyo, Japan), 2003.
Koteki no Kanata ("Guardian" series), Kaisei-sha (Tokyo, Japan), 2003.
SŌro no Tabibito ("Guardian" series), Kaisei-sha (Tokyo, Japan), 2005.
Rota Ōkoku hen ("Guardian" series), Kaisei-sha (Tokyo, Japan), 2006.
Kemono no Souja Ichi Touja hen ("Beast Player" series), Kaisei-sha (Tokyo, Japan), 2006.
Kemono no Souja no Oujuu hen ("Beast Player" series), Kaisei-sha (Tokyo, Japan), 2006.
Kanbaru Ōkoku hen ("Guardian" series), Kaisei-sha (Tokyo, Japan), 2007.
Shin Yogo Ōkoku hen ("Guardian" series), Kaisei-sha (Tokyo, Japan), 2007.
Nagare yuku mono ("Guardian" series), Kaisei-sha (Tokyo, Japan), 2008.
Kemono no SŌja Tankyū hen ("Beast Player" series), Kaisei-sha (Tokyo, Japan), 2009.
Kemono no SŌja Kanketsu hen ("Beast Player" series), Kaisei-sha (Tokyo, Japan), 2009.

Author's work has been translated into French, German, Korean, Swedish, and Thai.

OTHER

Tonari no Aborijini (title means "Backyard Aborigines"), [Japan], 2000.

Adaptations

Seirei no Moribito was adapted as a manga comic, an anime television series, and a radio play.

Sidelights

Born and still living in Tokyo, Japan, Nahoko Uehashi earned her Ph.D. in cultural anthropology before beginning her career as an educator. She teaches at Kawamura Gakuen Women's University, where she is an associate professor of anthropology. Uehashi's popular "Guardian" fantasy novels, which have been adapted as an animated film and a manga (comic-book) series, are inspired by her interest in anthropology and have been praised for their detailed description of diverse cultures. Although most of the "Guardian" novels are published in Japanese, two—*Moribito: Guardian of the Spirit* and its sequel, *Moribito II: Guardian of the Darkness*—have been translated into English.

Set in the mythic kingdom of New Yogo, *Moribito* introduces the fearless warrior Balsa. Although Mikado Rogsam plotted her death years ago, at age six, she was rescued and trained in the spear and the martial arts by

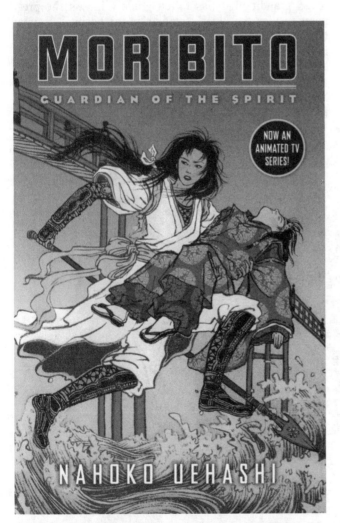

Nahoko Uehashi's "Guardian" series begins with Moribito, *a teen novel featuring artwork by Yuko Shimizu.* (Cover art © 2008 by Yuko Shimizu. All rights reserved. Reproduced by permission of Scholastic, Inc.)

royal bodyguard Jiguro, who was forced to kill eight bodyguards sent by the mikado. Now, twenty-four years later, Balsa dedicates herself to guarding the life of eleven-year-old Prince Chagum. Chagum is compelled by a water demon to secure a great egg and return it to the sea in order to avert a great drought, and his mother has asked the warrior to break the spirit's hold on her son and keep him safe. As Balsa and Chagum travel, they begin to more fully understand the influence of bad spirits, and Chagum learn to become independent. Meanwhile, they must avoid those who would stop them, including an egg-eating monster called Rarunga and the prince's own father, the evil Rogsam. Noting that the novel features "many familiar martial-arts fantasy elements," Chris Sherman added in *Booklist* that "Balsa is a smart, crotchety, fully realized heroine." In *Kirkus Reviews* a critic described *Moribito* as a compelling story that is "jam-packed with monstrous combat, ethnic conflicts and complex mythologies."

Balsa returns to her native kingdom, the mountainous Kanbal, in the sequel, *Moribito II,* determined to clear Jiguro's name by proving that he did not murder the eight royal bodyguards years before. Helped by two Kanbalese children whom she rescues from a cave as she pursues her goal, Balsa uncovers a conspiracy that draws her into a confrontation with the fearsome underground Guardians of the Dark. Writing in *Booklist,* Francisca Goldsmith praised Uehashi's "large but well differentiated cast . . . and constant plot twists," and predicted that the story would inspire new readers to seek out the prequel. Praising the "rich prose and compelling characters" in *Moribito II,* a *Publishers Weekly* contributor also noted that the fiercely loyal "Balsa is the core draw." Joanna K. Fabicon dubbed the novel "an engrossing story of redemption" and recommended Uehashi's "Guardian" novels as "a smooth transition between manga and straight narrative."

Biographical and Critical Sources

PERIODICALS

Booklist, August 1, 2008, Chris Sherman, review of *Moribito: Guardian of the Spirit,* p. 60; August 1, 2009, Francisca Goldsmith, review of *Guardian of the Darkness,* p. 60.

Kirkus Reviews, May 15, 2008, review of *Moribito.*

Kliatt, July, 2008, Claire Rosser, review of *Moribito,* p. 21.

Publishers Weekly, April 27, 2009, review of *Moribito II: Guardian of the Darkness,* p. 131.

School Library Journal, September, 2008, Eric Norton, review of *Moribito,* p. 194; August, 2009, Joanna K. Fabicon, review of *Moribito II,* p. 116.

ONLINE

Arthur A. Levine Web site, http://www.arthuralevinebooks. com/ (May 1, 2010), "Nahoko Uehashi."

Kaishi-sha Publisher Web site, http://www.kaisheisha.co.
jp/ (May 1, 2010), "Nahoko Uehashi."*

* * *

URDAHL, Catherine

Personal

Married; husband's name Mark; children: Anna, Leah.
Education: St. Olaf College, degree, 1984. *Hobbies and
other interests:* Walking, playing tennis, going to the
beach, spending time with her children.

Addresses

Home—Shorewood, MN. *E-mail*—cu@catherineurdahl.
com.

Career

Writer. Formerly worked in corporate communications;
teacher at The Loft Literary Center, Minneapolis, MN.

Member

Society of Children's Book Writers and Illustrators,
Children's Literature Network

Awards, Honors

Gold Book Award, Oppenheim Toy Portfolio, 2009, for
Emma's Question.

Writings

Emma's Question, illustrated by Janine Dawson, Charlesbridge (Watertown, MA), 2009.

Sidelights

Emma's Question, the debut picture book by Catherine
Urdahl, focuses on a young girl who struggles to understand the nature of her grandmother's serious illness.
The idea for the work stemmed from an episode from
Urdahl's own life: her mother's battle with ovarian cancer. Despite its weighty subject matter, the story in *Emma's Question* is a necessary one to tell, Urdahl maintains. In an essay on the *Unabridged* Web log, she
remarked that, "as a writer I believe that sometimes our
best stories come from the experiences we'd least like
to write about—our sharpest pain, our deepest fear, our
most humiliating moment." Urdahl further noted that
"as a mom and someone who loves children, I believe
that stories about difficult topics prepare children emotionally for life's inevitable challenges."

In *Emma's Question* a five year old learns that her beloved grandmother has fallen gravely ill. As she pre-
pares to visit the elderly woman in the hospital, Emma
becomes increasingly frightened at the prospect of losing her special friend. When Emma summons the courage to ask the elderly woman if she will die, Grandmother responds honestly and compassionately.
According to *Booklist* critic Hazel Rochman, *Emma's
Question* "will help kids cope with loss and celebrate

Catherine Urdahl helps children deal with a difficult life passage in her picture book Emma's Question, *featuring artwork by Janine Dawson.*

the lasting bond with someone they love," and Maryann H. Owen concluded in *School Library Journal*, Urdahl's "open-ended story offers a child-centric vehicle for discussion and is just right for one-on-one sharing."

Biographical and Critical Sources

PERIODICALS

Booklist, February 1, 2009, Hazel Rochman, review of *Emma's Question*, p. 46.

Kirkus Reviews, January 15, 2009, review of *Emma's Question*.

Publishers Weekly, December 8, 2008, review of *Emma's Question*, p. 58.

School Library Journal, May, 2009, Maryann H. Owen, review of *Emma's Question*, p. 91.

ONLINE

Catherine Urdahl Home Page, http://www.catherineurdahl.com (March 1, 2010).

Unabridged Web log, http://charlesbridge.blogspot.com/ (July 30, 2009), Catherine Urdahl, "Books Help Us Deal with the Tough Times."*

* * *

VAMOS, Samantha R.

Personal

Born in Madison, WI; married; children: one son. *Education:* Georgetown University Law Center, J.D., 1989. *Hobbies and other interests:* Movies, dogs, reading, traveling, music, hiking, skiing, running, reading, children's literature, crime fiction, mysteries.

Addresses

Home—Seattle, WA. *Agent*—Jennifer Rofé, Andrea Brown Literary Agency, 1076 Eagle Dr., Salinas, CA 93905; jennifer@andreabrownlit.com. *E-mail*—sam@samanthavamos.com.

Career

Attorney and author. Arent, Fox, Kintner, Plotkin & Kahn, Washington, DC, attorney, 1989-95; Kirkland & Ellis, LLP, Chicago, IL, attorney development manager, 2002-05; freelance writer, 2007—.

Member

Society of Children's Book Writers and Illustrators.

Writings

Before You Were Here, Mi Amor, illustrated by Santiago Cohen, Viking (New York, NY), 2009.

The Cazuela That the Farm Maiden Stirred, illustrated by Rafael López, Charlesbridge (New York, NY), 2011.

Sidelights

A former practicing attorney, Samantha R. Vamos was inspired to write her debut children's book, *Before You Were Here, Mi Amor*, after learning that her younger sister was pregnant with her first child. The news "generated memories of my mom telling me about my anticipation over the birth of my younger sister," Vamos told *Examiner.com* interviewer Lori Calabrese. "With those memories, I began writing. My book is an outgrowth of that experience. Of course, my nephew took a mere nine months to birth, and my book took almost eleven years, but I'm not bitter! *Before You Were Here, Mi Amor* is finally here and I'm thrilled."

Featuring an English-language text with Spanish terms sprinkled throughout the narrative, *Before You Were Here, Mi Amor* describes a family's extensive preparations to welcome a new baby. As Santiago Cohen shows in his accompanying illustrations, the child's grandfather (abuelo) plants a tree in the yard to commemorate the birth, and the big sister (hermana) draws a picture depicting the entire family, new baby included. Vamos's "Spanish-flavored introduction . . . will become a favorite among growing bilingual families," a *Kirkus Reviews* critic predicted, and Linda Perkins similarly noted in *Booklist* that *Before You Were Here, Mi Amor* "adds a distinctly Latino flavor to the familiar theme." According to Susan E. Murray, writing in *School Library*

Samantha R. Vamos teams with artist Santiago Cohen to create the family-affirming picture book **Before You Were Here, Mi Amor**. (Illustration copyright © by Santiago Cohen, 2009. All rights reserved. Reproduced by permission of Viking, a division of Penguin Putnam Books for Young Readers.)

Journal, the book's "lovely story may encourage discussions of individual birth preparations in readers' own families."

The Cazuela That the Farm Maiden Stirred is a children's picture book based on the familiar nursery rhyme, "The House That Jack Built." Like the nursery rhyme, Vamos's story is a cumulative tale: the action builds as the Spanish words woven throughout the English text repeat. Five different farm animals—a goat, cow, duck, donkey, and chicken—along with their farmer each contribute ingredients to a pot (cazuela) that is stirred by the farm maiden. A surprise recipe is created and at the book's end, Vamos provides the actual recipe, along with a glossary with a pronunciation guide.

"Writing has always been a passion," Vamos told *SATA.* "I've been writing stories for over twenty years and publishing my writing has been one of my greatest dreams. My first children's book took eleven years to become published. It was a long road and I received many rejections during that time, but I persisted because writing was my dream. To give myself hope, I wrote additional and different stories (all fiction, but they concerned a variety of topics) during those years and kept sending the stories out for review by publishers until I finally succeeded.

"I was most influenced to write by my mother, but both my parents, as well as my paternal grandfather and maternal grandmother, are and were excellent writers. As a young child, my mom encouraged me to write stories. Some of my stories were just a few lines long and others, when I grew older, were several hundred pages. All of my stories require a lot of rewriting. I revise over and over, and often a story of mine is not its best until it has 'sat' for a while. With time, I am able to look at the words I've written in a different light and later, improve the story."

Biographical and Critical Sources

PERIODICALS

Booklist, February 15, 2009, Linda Perkins, review of *Before You Were Here, Mi Amor,* p. 86.

Chicago Tribune, May 9, 2009, Mary Harris Russell, review of *Before You Were Here, Mi Amor.*

Kirkus Reviews, January 15, 2009, review of *Before You Were Here, Mi Amor.*

School Library Journal, March, 2009, Susan E. Murray, review of *Before You Were Here, Mi Amor,* p. 129.

Seattle Times, March 24, 2009, Michael Upchurch, review of *Before You Were Here, Mi Amor.*

ONLINE

Cynsations Web log, http://cynthialeitichsmith.blogspot.com/ (November 30, 2009), Cynthia Leitich Smith, interview with Vamos.

Examiner.com, http://www.examiner.com/ (September 10, 2009), Lori Calabrese, interview with Vamos.

Samantha R. Vamos Home Page, http://www.samanthavamos.com (March 1, 2010).

*   *   *

VESS, Charles 1951-

Personal

Born June 10, 1951, in Lynchburg, VA. *Education:* Virginia Commonwealth University, B.F.A., 1974.

Addresses

Office—Green Man Press, 152 E. Main St., Abingdon, VA 24210. *E-mail*—charles@greenmanpress.com.

Career

Illustrator and educator. Candy Apple Productions, Richmond, VA, commercial animator, 1974-76; freelance illustrator, 1976—; Parsons School of Design, New York, NY, instructor, 1980-82; William King Regional Arts Center, Abingdon, VA, artist-in-residence, 1992-96. Founder of Green Man Press, Abingdon. *Exhibitions:* Illustrations exhibited in the United States and England, including at Museum of American Art, New Britain, CT, 1980; Delaware Art Museum, Wilmington, 1989; Frameworks Gallery, Bristol, VA, 1992; Open Air Birch Garden, Devon, England, 1993; William King Regional Arts Center, Abingdon, VA, 1994-95; Repartee Gallery, Park City, UT, 1993; Four Color Images Gallery, New York, NY, 1996; and San Francisco Comic Art Museum, San Francisco, CA, 1998.

Member

Arthur Rackham Society.

Awards, Honors

Inkpot Award, 1990; (with Neil Gaiman) World Fantasy Award for best short story, 1991, for *Sandman,* number 19; Comic Creators Award for best cover, 1993; Silver Award, 1995; Eisner Award for best penciler/inker, 1996, for *The Book of Ballads and Sagas,* 1997, for *Sandman,* number 75; World Fantasy Award for best artist, 1999, for *Stardust;* Eisner Award for best painter, 2002, for *Rose;* Best Books for Young Adults selections, American Library Association, 2003, for both *Seven Wild Sisters* and *The Green Man;* Gold Award for Best Book Art, *Spectrum* magazine, for *A Circle of Cats.*

Writings

SELF-ILLUSTRATED

The Book of Night, (three-issue series), Dark Horse Comics (Milwaukie, OR), 1987, published in graphic-novel format, 1991.

(With others) *Concrete Celebrates Earth Day 1990,* Dark Horse Comics (Milwaukie, OR), 1990.

The Amazing Spider-Man: Spirits of the Earth, Marvel Comics (New York, NY), 1990.

(With Christopher Irving and Eric Nolen-Weathington) *Modern Masters, Volume Eleven: Charles Vess,* Two-Morrows (Raleigh, NC), 2007.

Drawing down the Moon: The Art of Charles Vess, foreword by Susanna Clarke, Dark Horse Comics (Milwaukie, OR), 2009.

ILLUSTRATOR

Alan Zelenetz, *The Raven Banner,* Marvel Comics (New York, NY), 1985.

William Shakespeare, *A Midsummer Night's Dream,* Donning Company (Norfolk, VA), 1988.

(With others) *Hook: The Official Movie Adaptation,* Marvel Comics (New York, NY), 1991.

(With others) Neil Gaiman, *Sandman: The Wake* (originally published in comic-book form as *Sandman,* volumes 70-75), DC Comics (New York, NY), 1997.

Neil Gaiman, *Stardust: Being a Romance within the Realms of Faerie* (a comic-book series), DC Comics (New York, NY), 1997–1998.

Ellen Datlow and Terri Windling, editors, *The Green Man: Tales from the Mythical Forest,* Viking (New York, NY), 2001.

Charles de Lint, *Seven Wild Sisters,* Subterranean Press (Burton, MI), 2002.

Jeff Smith, *Rose,* Cartoon Books, 2002.

Jeff Smith, *Bone Special,* Carlsen, 2002.

Jeff Smith, *Le Monde de Bone: Rose,* Delcourt, 2003.

Charles de Lint, *A Circle of Cats,* Viking (New York, NY), 2003.

J.M. Barrie, *Peter Pan,* Tor (New York, NY), 2003.

(Compiler, and contributor) *The Book of Ballads,* Tor (New York, NY), 2004.

Ellen Datlow and Terry Windling, editors, *The Faery Reel: Tales from the Twilight Realm,* Viking (New York, NY), 2004.

Charles de Lint, *Medicine Road,* Subterranean Press (Burton, MI), 2004.

Charles de Lint, *Moonheart,* 20th anniversary edition, Subterranean Press (Burton, MI), 2005.

Susanna Clarke, *The Ladies of Grace Adieu and Other Stories,* Bloomsbury (New York, NY), 2006.

Ellen Datlow and Terri Windling, editors, *The Coyote Road: Trickster Tales,* Viking (New York, NY), 2007.

Neil Gaiman, *Blueberry Girl,* HarperCollins (New York, NY), 2009.

Neil Gaiman, *Instructions,* Harper (New York, NY), 2010.

Contributor of illustrations to periodicals, including *National Lampoon, Reader's Digest,* and *Heavy Metal.* Contributor to comic-book series published by Marvel Comics, DC Comics, and Dark Horse Comics.

Sidelights

Charles Vess is an award-winning illustrator of science-fiction and fantasy art whose work has graced the pages of numerous comic books, graphic novels, and other literary works. Among his many honors, Vess has received an Inkpot award, two World Fantasy awards, and three Eisner awards. Influenced by such artists as Hal Foster, Aubrey Beardsley, Arthur Rackham, and Howard Pyle, Vess has provided the illustrations for titles by such celebrated authors as Neil Gaiman, Charles de Lint, and Susanna Clarke. In addition, he is the founder of Green Man Press, a small publishing company located in Abingdon, Virginia. Discussing the artist's work, *Roanoke Times* contributor Tom Angleberger stated that "Vess' talent is to illustrate impossible ideas in such a way that they don't seem impossible at all."

Vess has won numerous honors for his work on Gaiman's "Sandman" and "Stardust" comic-book series, the latter collected in four volumes as *Stardust: Being a Romance within the Realms of Faerie.* The story in "Stardust" takes place in the border village of Wall, where faeries and mortals can come together every nine years. During one such celebration, a mortal man crosses over, beginning a saga that includes both mortals and faeries and spans two lands and across two generations. Describing one of Vess's images for *Stardust,* Angleberger wrote that "his painting of the fantastical place is crafted in such detail that one might believe he has been there."

Charles Vess breathes new life into a children's classic in his artwork for J.M. Barrie's **Peter Pan.** (Illustration copyright © 2003 by Charles Vess. All rights reserved. Reproduced with permission of the artist.)

In *The Amazing Spider-Man: Spirits of the Earth* Vess takes Spider-Man to the Scottish Highlands, where the super hero discovers that local legend is being used to control the population. Mythology drives much of the story, as Spidey encounters ghosts and other creatures. The book includes sketches made by Vess during his visits to Scotland and maps of his travels as he worked on this project, which a *Booklist* reviewer called "an outstanding, beautiful piece of work." The writer noted that Vess has painted the green hills and the dark places below them "with lush colors and an awesome sense of lighting."

Among his many working relationships, Vess has enjoyed a successful collaboration with anthologists Ellen Datlow and Terri Windling, contributing illustrations to their coedited *The Green Man: Tales from the Mythical Forest,* which collects magical stories by such writers as Gaiman, de Lint, Emma Bull, Jane Yolen, Michael Cadnum, Patricia A. McKillip, and others. In addition, he has illustrated *The Faery Reel: Tales from the Twilight Realm* and *The Coyote Road: Trickster Tales,* two other collections edited by Datlow and Windling.

De Lint's novella *Seven Wild Sisters* was commissioned by Subterranean Press as a result of a feminist science-fiction convention held in 2000. The black-and-white drawings illustrate the story of the seven Dillard sisters, that story told mainly through Sarah Jane, the middle sister, whose forays into the woods seeking ginseng lead to the sisters' involvement in a faerie war. *Resource Links* contributor Gail de Vos called *Seven Wild Sisters* "a treat for both the eyes and the ears," adding that "Vess's fey black-and-white drawings, vignettes and full-page illustrations, complement de Lint's tight pacing and poetic prose."

De Lint and Vess have also teamed up to create *A Circle of Cats,* in which a girl named Lillian who lives with her aunt spends her time in the forest looking for faeries. Lillian cares for the many stray cats that live there, leaving them bowls of milk. She also brings a biscuit to the gnarled old Apple Tree Man every morning. While sleeping under a tree, Lillian is bitten by a poisonous snake, and the cats save her life by changing her into a kitten, a transformation that can only be reversed if she makes a bargain with the Father of Cats. A *Kirkus Reviews* contributor wrote that de Lint's language in *A Circle of Cats,* "is complemented beautifully by Vess's full-color line-and-watercolor illustrations." Vess and de Lint also joined forces on *Medicine Road,* a work that incorporates Native American mythology and features two characters first introduced in *Seven Wild Sisters.* According to *Booklist* critic Sally Estes, de Lint's story is "nicely complemented by . . . Vess's black-and-white illustrations."

A labor of love that was nearly two decades in the making, *The Book of Ballads* contains interpretations of traditional songs from England, Scotland, and Ireland by such authors as Jane Yolen, Emma Bull, and Jeff Smith.

In *Booklist,* Ray Olson complimented Vess's art for the book, most notably "its swirling lines, atmospheric shading, and heavy foliage and drapery." Jennifer Feigelman, writing in *Kliatt,* asserted that "Vess's line-driven art acts as a cohesive element for the volume." while a *Publishers Weekly* critic maintained that "Vess reaches the peak of his art" in *The Book of Ballads,* "standing proudly with the 19th-and early 20th-century illustrators who influence him."

Vess once again teamed with Gaiman on *Blueberry Girl,* a children's book that was described as "a secular prayer for an unborn baby" by Susan Perren in the Toronto *Globe & Mail.* The artist's "line-and-color illustrations fill each spread with velvet colors and the iconography of myths and fairy tales," asserted a critic in *Kirkus Reviews,* and a *Publishers Weekly* contributor also praised Vess's work for Gaiman's story, describing his fanciful subjects in *Blueberry Girl* as "potent mixtures of the charms of Arthur Rackham, Maxfield Parrish and Cecily Barker's flower fairies."

Biographical and Critical Sources

BOOKS

Vess, Charles, Christopher Irving, and Eric Nolen-Weathington, *Modern Masters Volume Eleven: Charles Vess,* TwoMorrows (Raleigh, NC), 2007.
Vess, Charles, *Drawing down the Moon: The Art of Charles Vess,* foreword by Susanna Clarke, Dark Horse Comics (Milwaukie, OR), 2009.

PERIODICALS

Booklist, January 1, 1991, review of *The Amazing Spider-Man: Spirits of the Earth,* p. 916; December 1, 2004, Ray Olson, review of *The Book of Ballads,* p. 644; April 15, 2004, Sally Estes, review of *Medicine Road,* p. 1431; May 1, 2007, Gordon Flagg, review of *Modern Masters Volume Eleven: Charles Vess,* p. 61; September 15, 2007, Carolyn Phelan, review of *The Coyote Road: Trickster Tales,* p. 61; January 1, 2010, Ray Olson, review of *Drawing down the Moon: The Art of Charles Vess.*
Globe and Mail (Toronto, Ontario, Canada), January 1, 2005, Robert Wiersema, "Ballads of Constant Sorrow Bring Frequent Joy," review of *The Book Of Ballads,* p. D7; May 9, 2009, Susan Perren, review of *Blueberry Girl,* p. F13.
Kirkus Reviews, June 1, 2003, review of *A Circle of Cats,* p. 802; January 15, 2009, Susan Perren, review of *Blueberry Girl.*
Kliatt, July, 2006, Jennifer Feigelman, review of *The Book of Ballads,* p. 29.
Publishers Weekly, March 29, 2004, review of *Medicine Road,* p. 43; November 29, 2004, review of *The Book of Ballads,* p. 25; December 15, 2008, review of *Blueberry Girl,* p. 52.

Roanoke Times, October 14, 2003, Tom Angleberger, "Dream Weaver," p. 1.

Resource Links, October, 2002, Gail de Vos, review of *Seven Wild Sisters,* p. 55.

School Library Journal, July, 2004, Sharon Rawlins, review of *The Faery Reel: Tales from the Twilight Realm,* p. 104; September, 2007, Susan Hepler, review of *The Coyote Road,* p. 215; January, 2009, Wendy Lukehart, review of *Blueberry Girl,* p. 74; September, 2009, Lisa Goldstein, review of *Rose,* p. 191.

ONLINE

Comics Journal Online, http://www.tcj.com/ (February 19, 2004), Chris Brayshaw, interview with Vess.

Graphic Novel Reporter.com, http://www.graphicnovel reporter.com/ (March 1, 2010), John Hogan, "Looking Back with Charles Vess."

Green Man Press Web site, http://www.greenmanpress. com/ (March 1, 2010).*

*   *   *

VIVIAN, Siobhan 1979(?)-

Personal

Born c. 1979. *Education:* Philadelphia University of the Arts, B.F.A. (writing for film and television), 2001; New School University, M.F.A. (writing for children), 2006. *Hobbies and other interests:* Sewing, music, writing letters.

Addresses

Home—Pittsburgh, PA. *E-mail*—siobhan@siobhanviv ian.com.

Career

Writer.

Awards, Honors

American Library Association Best Books for Young Adults listee, 2010, for *Same Difference.*

Writings

FOR CHILDREN AND YOUNG ADULTS

(With J. Otto Seibold) *Vunce upon a Time,* Chronicle Books (San Francisco, CA), 2008.

A Little Friendly Advice, Push/Scholastic (New York, NY), 2008.

Same Difference, Push (New York, NY), 2009.

Not That Kind of Girl, Push (New York, NY), 2010.

Sidelights

Siobhan Vivian is the author of books for both children and teens, all of which feature her sometimes humorous, sometimes quirky viewpoint. In *Vunce upon a Time* she introduces young children to a vampire whose sweet tooth prompts him to join human children in their Halloween festivities, while *A Little Friendly Advice* and *Same Difference* are written for teen readers and focus on young women learning to navigate friendships and family dramas while being true to themselves.

Vivian earned her bachelor's degree at the Philadelphia University of the Arts in 2001 before going on to receive her master's degree in fine arts from the New School University in 2006. Her first published work, a collaboration with J. Otto Siebold titled *Vunce upon a Time,* introduces readers to Dagmar, a vampire who loves to eat vegetables. In addition to his love of healthy foods, Dagmar loves sweets, and he is despondent when he runs out of candy. The vampire learns about the human holiday of Halloween from a skeleton friend, and he is excited to find out that, as long as he wears a costume, he will be given vast amounts of candy. Dagmar's vampire parents, however, are skeptical; they worry that their son is too young to celebrate Halloween. Dagmar proves them wrong by making his own costume, but it is promptly eaten by zombie moths. Reviewing *Vunce upon a Time,* a *Publishers Weekly* critic described Dagmar as a compelling protagonist who "has a charming habit of turning into a bat when startled." Although a *Kirkus Reviews* writer found Vivian's plot to be perhaps too complicated for younger readers, there is "humor inherent in the premise" of a vegetarian vampire.

In *A Little Friendly Advice* Vivian addresses a slightly older audience than *Vunce upon a Time.* As the author told a *Teen Book Review* online interviewer, she started the novel "during my last semester at school. . . . David Levithan was my thesis advisor, and he helped me massage a very rough idea into a full-fledged novel. He was vital in helping me tell Ruby's story in the best, most engaging way." When Levithan expressed the possiblity that Vivian could publish her story, she "got an agent and sold the book, unfinished, to Scholastic a few weeks later," as she recalled to the interviewer.

A Little Friendly Advice focuses on four high-school friends. The protagonist, sixteen-year-old Ruby, was abandoned by her father at the age of six, and Ruby's mother has never addressed the abandonment. Close friends Beth, Katherine, and Charlie are there for Ruby whenever the teen needs support. Beth is caring and kind, but she can often be bossy when dispensing her advice, wanted or not. When Ruby's father suddenly reappears to make amends with his daughter, her friends help her through the ordeal. Soon, however, Ruby learns that Beth has intercepted a letter to her from her father, and Ruby is unsure how to handle the situation. Critics applauded *A Little Friendly Advice,* finding it a mature and riveting read. As Francisca Goldsmith noted in

Siobhan Vivian's collaborations with author/artist J. Otto Seibold includes the Halloween-themed Vunce upon a Time. (Illustration © 2008 by J. Otto Seibold.

Booklist, the protagonist is "a compelling, evolving character who eventually comes to terms with her friends' shortcomings." *Kliatt* critic Myrna Marler recommended Vess's novel for middle-grade readers, adding that "the contents are of particular interest to young adolescents and their teachers."

In *Same Difference* Vivian follows the experience of Emily, a suburban New Jersey high schooler who dreams of a career in the arts and enrolls at a summer art school located in Philadelphia. Despite her affluent existence, Emily feels like an outsider compared to her city-sophisticated yet artsy classmates. Then Fiona takes the suburban teen under her wing and helps Emily define her unique identity. In *Booklist* Heather Booth recommended Vivian's novel for "teens longing to break free from predefined roles," and a *Publishers Weekly*

contributor wrote that "the author's talent for scene-setting and evocative imagery" in *Same Difference* "is especially effective." According to a *Kirkus Reviews* writer, *Same Difference* taps the interest of many readers through its "focus . . . on teenage girls' quests for identity and the consequences for their friendships."

Biographical and Critical Sources

PERIODICALS

Booklist, June 1, 2008, Francisca Goldsmith, review of *A Little Friendly Advice,* p. 67; May 1, 2009, Heather Booth, review of *Same Difference,* p. 74.
Bulletin of the Center for Children's Books, April 1, 2008, Karen Coats, review of *A Little Friendly Advice,* p. 357.
Kirkus Reviews, January 1, 2008, review of *A Little Friendly Advice;* July 15, 2008, review of *Vunce upon a Time;* January 15, 2009, review of *Same Difference.*

Kliatt, March 1, 2008, Myrna Marler, review of *A Little Friendly Advice,* p. 21.
Publishers Weekly, September 8, 2008, review of *Vunce upon a Time,* p. 50; March 2, 2009, review of *Same Difference,* p. 62.
School Library Journal, February 1, 2008, Julianna M. Helt, review of *A Little Friendly Advice,* p. 130; May, 2009, Alison Follos, review of *Same Difference,* p. 118.

ONLINE

Siobhan Vivian Home Page, http://www.siobhanvivian.com (May 1, 2010).
Siobhan Vivian Web log, http://www.siobhanvivian.blogspot.com (May 1, 2010).
Teen Book Review Web site, http://teenbookreview.wordpress.com/ (February 28, 2008), interview with Vivian.
Teenreads.com, http://www.teenreads.com/ (October 24, 2008), interview with Vivian.*

W-Y

WATKINS, Lis
See WATKINS, Liselotte

*   *   *

WATKINS, Liselotte 1971-
(Lis Watkins)

Personal
Born 1971, in Nyköping, Sweden. *Education:* Art Institute (Dallas, TX), graduated, c. 1998.

Addresses
Home—Stockholm, Sweden. *Agent*—LundLund, St. Paulsgatan 1, 118 46 Stockholm, Sweden.

Career
Illustrator and designer. Fashion illustrator; textile, set, and packaging designer; graphic artist.

Writings

ILLUSTRATOR

(Under name Lis Watkins) Clare Gogerty, *Stories in Art,* Marshall Cavendish (New York, NY), 1995.

Stefania Malmsten, *Watkins' Heroine,* Gestalten (Berlin, Germany), 2004.

Mariah Fredericks, *Love,* Atheneum (New York, NY), 2007.

Mariah Fredericks, *Fame,* Atheneum (New York, NY), 2008.

Contributor of illustrations to periodicals, including international editions of *Vogue, Elle, Glamour, Mademoiselle,* and *Übersee.*

Biographical and Critical Sources

PERIODICALS

Booklist, January 15, 1995, Mary Harris Veeder, review of *Stories in Art,* p. 916.

ONLINE

LundLund Web site, http://www.lundlund.com/ (April 10, 2008), "Liselotte Watkins."*

*   *   *

WEINSTEIN, Muriel Harris

Personal
Female.

Addresses
Home—Great Neck, NY. *E-mail*—miryom@optonline.net.

Career
Poet, author, and educator. Taught elementary school for twenty-three years; has also taught children's poetry, prose, and playwriting at United Nations International School and Lincoln Center Library for the Performing Arts.

Writings

When Louis Armstrong Taught Me Scat, illustrated by R. Gregory Christie, Chronicle Books (San Francisco, CA), 2008.

Contributor of poems to anthologies and periodicals, including *Comstock Review, Nassau Review, Kent State Review, Cape Rock, Ethereal Dances, Freshet, Listening Eye,* and *Nexus.*

Sidelights

An accomplished poet and former elementary-school teacher, Muriel Harris Weinstein is the author of *When Louis Armstrong Taught Me Scat,* a tribute to the celebrated American jazz trumpeter and singer fondly known as "Satchmo." Discussing the inspiration for her work on the Chronicle Books Web site, Weinstein remarked: "I've always loved Louis Armstrong's music and his wonderful gravelly voice." "I love his musical sense," she added: "how he adds scat, how that scat enhances the music, and lastly, his marvelous horn. Louis is the horn and the horn is Louis. He also never loses the integrity of a song or the music. His sense of what is 'good' in music is unerring. His musical intuition, his spirit, his ear, and his intelligence make his music."

When Louis Armstrong Taught Me Scat centers on a young girl's love of jazz. After an evening spent dancing to Armstrong's energetic, improvisational singing on the radio, the girl heads off to bed, where she dreams that the legendary musician teaches her to scat about a favorite treat: bubble gum! In Weinstein's upbeat picture book "freewheeling verbal and visual riffs elevate the simple plot," according to a *Publishers Weekly* contributor. Other critics praised the combination of Weinstein's text and R. Gregory Christie's illustrations. According to a *Kirkus Reviews* contributor, "Three typefaces, alternating upper-and lower-case, match the verve of the agreeably frenetic text" of *When Louis Armstrong Taught Me Scat* and Ian Chipman asserted in *Booklist* that "it's the bop-happy nonsense words themselves that highlight the art."

Biographical and Critical Sources

PERIODICALS

Booklist, February 1, 2009, Ian Chipman, review of *When Louis Armstrong Taught Me Scat,* p. 58.

Muriel Harris Weinstein's biographical picture book When Louis Armstrong Taught Me Scat *features paintings by noted illustrator R. Gregory Christie.* (Illustration © 2008 by R. Gregory Christie. Used with permission of Chronicle Books, LLC, San Francisco. Visit ChronicleBooks.com.)

Kirkus Reviews, January 15, 2009, review of *When Louis Armstrong Taught Me Scat.*
Publishers Weekly, March 2, 2009, review of *When Louis Armstrong Taught Me Scat,* p. 62.

ONLINE

Chronicle Books Web site, http://www.chroniclebooks. com/ (March 1, 2010), interview with Weinstein and R. Gregory Christie.
Poets & Writers Web site, http://www.pw.org/ (March 1, 2010), "Muriel Harris Weinstein."*

*   *   *

WILLIAMSON, Kate T. 1979-

Personal

Born 1979, in Washington, DC. *Education:* Harvard University, B.A. (visual arts), 2001.

Addresses

Home—New York, NY. *E-mail*—hello@katewilliamson.com.

Career

Author and artist. Worked variously as a dogwalker, S.A.T. tutor, flower-shop clerk, restaurant hostess, personal assistant, and proofreader.

Writings

Hello Kitty Everywhere!, photographs by Jennifer Butefish and Maria Fernanda Soares, Harry N. Abrams (New York, NY), 2004.
(Self-illustrated) *A Year in Japan,* Princeton Architectural Press (New York, NY), 2006.
Hello Kitty through the Seasons, photographs by Jennifer Butefish and Maria Fernanda Soares, Harry N. Abrams (New York, NY), 2006.
(Self-illustrated) *At a Crossroads: Between a Rock and My Parents' Place,* Princeton Architectural Press (New York, NY), 2008.

Sidelights

After graduating from Harvard University with a degree in film and visual arts, Kate T. Williamson won the school's George Peabody Gardner traveling fellowship. This funding allowed her to spend a year in Japan studying the visual elements of Japanese culture, such as its textile design, architecture, and graphic art. Williamson chronicles her experiences as a first-time traveler to that country in her illustrated travelogue simply titled *A Year in Japan.*

Featuring a hand-written text paired with pen-and-ink drawings painted with bright watercolors, *A Year in Japan* takes readers on a trip into another culture, acknowledging the beauties of cities such as Kyoto and the region's natural wonders. However, Williamson also shines light on the subtle textures of everyday Japanese life that distinguish it from life in the United States, such as interesting dining traditions, electric carpets, geisha culture, cell-phone straps, and Shinto shrines. Williamson's "delicately crafted artist's journal offers colorful impressions" of Japan as seen by a thoughtful and observant young woman, noted a *Publishers Weekly* critic, and Ravi Sheony commented in *Library Journal* that *A Year in Japan* "captures . . . the everyday aspects of Japanese culture that visitors notice but citizens take for granted."

Returning to her parents' home following her trip to Japan required a cultural readjustment and also prompted Williamson to contemplate her life plan as an adult. She chronicles the two years she spent living in her family home in Pennsylvania, sleeping in the room where she had grown up, in *At a Crossroads: Between a Rock and My Parents' Place*. In addition to addressing the questions of neighbors and family friends, who wonder what she is doing back at home, Williamson also works diligently to complete her first book and locate a publisher, chronicling her self-confessed "holding pattern" in an autobiographical graphic-novel format. Reviewing *At a Crossroads*, Matthew L. Moffett characterized the work in *School Library Journal* as a "touching story" and "a perfect picture of someone lost at age 20-something." In Pennsylvania's *Reading Eagle* Elizabeth Giorgi described Williamson's book as "a mix of quietly poignant and humorous vignettes about returning home and being unsure where your life is headed next." Williamson assured Giorgi in discussing *At a Crossroads* that it was not an "unhappy 23 months," adding: "'I hope people find it sort of hopeful.'"

Biographical and Critical Sources

BOOKS

Williamson, Kate T., *A Year in Japan* (travelogue), Princeton Architectural Press (New York, NY), 2006.
Williamson, Kate T., *At a Crossroads: Between a Rock and My Parents' Place* (memoir), Princeton Architectural Press (New York, NY), 2006.

PERIODICALS

Library Journal, February 1, 2006, Ravi Schenoy, review of *A Year in Japan*, p. 97.
Publishers Weekly, December 12, 2005, review of *A Year in Japan*, p. 50.
Reading Eagle (Reading, PA), March 24, 2006, Elizabeth Giorgi, review of *A Year in Japan;* May 25, 2008, Elizabeth Giorgi, review of *At a Crossroads.*

School Library Journal, September, 2008, Matthew L. Moffett, review of *At a Crossroads*, p. 219.

ONLINE

Kate T. Williamson Home Page, http://www.katewilliamson.com (March 15, 2010).

* * *

WILLIS, Cynthia Chapman

Personal

Born in Mount Vernon, NY. *Education:* Attended Lynchburg College.

Addresses

Home—Branchburg, NJ. *E-mail*—mailbox@cynthiawillis.com.

Career

Writer.

Writings

Dog Gone, Feiwel & Friends (New York, NY), 2008.
Buck Fever, Feiwel & Friends (New York, NY), 2009.

Sidelights

Cynthia Chapman Willis's middle-grade novel *Dog Gone* which features a twelve-year-old protagonist named Dylan who lives in a rural Virginia farming community. Dylan first observes that her dog, Dead End, has intermittent and lengthy absences from their home, and then she hears about a series of livestock killings, which local farmers blame on a pack of rogue canines. Dylan begins to wonder if her beloved pet may have joined the murderous pack, and her curiosity turns to alarm when she finds out that the town sheriff has issued an order for the pack to be destroyed. Fearing that her dog is on the death list, Dylan enlists her friend Cub in the investigation. Meanwhile, at home, Dylan is dealing with a volatile family life. Her mother has passed away, her mourning father has withdrawn, and her beloved grandfather has now taken ill. Amid the emotional conflict, Dylan must sort through her own feelings in order to find the truth.

Noting the novel's themes of self-reliance, responsibility, familial loyalty, and friendship, a *Booklist* contributor remarked that Willis's "lengthy first novel" appears "rooted in the daily sounds, sights, and smells of farm life." In her review of *Dog Gone* for *School Library Journal*, Nancy P. Reeder noted that Willis "keeps read-

ers in suspense about Dead End's fate until the very end, which drives the novel." Another recurring theme in the story is loss. After the loss of her mother, Dylan loses her dog, which offers young readers an insight into grief, dealing with the absence of a parent, and the problems inherent in refusing to manage complex life situations. A *Kirkus Reviews* contributor concluded that Willis's "well-told story, spiced with humor and facts on animal care, has a satisfying, appealing conclusion."

Willis once commented: "I've always been interested in writing, but reading great books further fueled my interest in writing novels.

"In the past, animals have influenced my writing, but anything I am passionate about influences me.

"I write my story idea on the first page of a blank notebook. This is almost a kind of ritual. I then fill the notebook with an outline, character sketches, research, notes—almost anything relevant to the story. From this notebook I write my first draft. And then I will revise, revise, and revise some more.

"My greatest hope is that readers will become lost in the worlds of my books and find the stories deeply satisfying and thought provoking."

Biographical and Critical Sources

PERIODICALS

Booklist, April 1, 2008, Hazel Rochman, review of *Dog Gone,* p. 44.
Kirkus Reviews, April 1, 2008, review of *Dog Gone.*
School Library Journal, July 1, 2008, Nancy P. Reeder, review of *Dog Gone,* p. 109.
Voice of Youth Advocates, April 1, 2008, Leah J. Sparks, review of *Dog Gone,* p. 57.

ONLINE

Cynthia Chapman Willis Home Page, http://www.cynthia willis.com (January 3, 2009).

*   *   *

WRIGHTSON, Alice Patricia
See WRIGHTSON, Patricia

*   *   *

WRIGHTSON, Patricia 1921-2010
(Patricia Furlonger, Alice Patricia Wrightson)

OBITUARY NOTICE—

See index for *SATA* sketch: Born June 19, 1921 in Lismore, New South Wales, Australia; died of natural causes, March 15, 2010, in New South Wales, Austra-

lia. Secretary, hospital administrator, editor, and author. Drawing upon her isolated, pastoral childhood and unique sense of Australian identity, Wrightson became Australia's foremost children's author garnering numerous prestigious awards over her four-decade long career. Raised on a farm in rural New South Wales, Wrightson was an avid reader from an early age, exchanging books with her neighbors. After a stint working in a Sydney munitions factory during World War II, Wrightson married and had two children. She returned to live with her parents in the country after her marriage ended, providing the perfect opportunity and setting to write about what she considered the real Australia for her own children. Her first series of adventure novels recall the early history of Australia and feature the elements of Aboriginal spirituality that would later become her hallmark. Her first novel, *The Crooked Snake* (1955), received a Book of the Year award from the Children's Book Council of Australia. With the publication of *A Racecourse for Andy* (1968), Wrightson earned international recognition as a leading children's author. She made her first forays into fantasy with *An Older Kind of Magic* (1972) and *The Nargun and the Stars* (1973), where she drew upon the oral histories of Aboriginal Australians. This interest in Aboriginal spirituality culminated with her "Book of Wirrun" trilogy. *The Ice is Coming* (1977) introduces the aboriginal boy Wirrun whose quest to save his people ties the three novels together. Sequels *The Dark Bright Water* (1978) and *Behind the Wind* (1981) provide fresh challenges for Wirrun as he tackles water-spirits and even Death itself. Critics praised the vivid imagery in the series, as well as Wrightson's descriptions of her native land. She rounded out her fantasy offerings with more-realistic fiction, but continued to incorporate elements of Aborginial spirituality. One of her final works, *Shadows of Time* (1994), relates the history of Australia through the eyes of two magical youngsters, one Aboriginal and one not, who never grow old. Patricia Wrightson received the biennial Hans Christian Andersen Award in 1986 for her lasting contribution to children's literature.

OBITUARIES AND OTHER SOURCES:

PERIODICALS

Guardian (London, England), May 10, 2010, p. 35.

*   *   *

YEATTS, Tabatha 1970-

Personal
Born 1970, in VA; married: children: three. *Education:* University of Mary Washington, B.A.; University of Iowa, M.A.

Addresses
Home—Rockville, MD. *E-mail*—tabatha@tabathayeatts. com.

Tabatha Yeatts (Caricature by Ami R. Somers. Reproduced by permission.)

Career

Writer. *Eye on Women* (magazine), Atlanta, GA, founder.

Member

Society of Children's Book Writers and Illustrators.

Awards, Honors

Notable Social Studies Trade Book for Young People designation, National Council for Social Studies (NCSS)/Children's Book Council (CBC), 1999, for *The Holocaust Survivors;* Best Books designation, Center for Children's Books, 2001, for *Forensics;* Do Something (nonprofit organization) grant.

Writings

The Holocaust Survivors, Enslow Publishers (Springfield, NJ), 1998.
Forensics: Solving the Crime, Oliver Press (Minneapolis, MN), 2001.
The Legendary Mae West, privately published, 2007.
Albert Einstein: The Miracle Mind, Sterling (New York, NY), 2007.
Joan of Arc: Heavenly Warrior, Sterling (New York, NY), 2009.

Contributor of articles to periodicals, including *Blue Jean, Christian Science Monitor, Cricket, Élan, Internet Writing Journal, Murderous Intent Mystery Magazine, Music for the Love of It, Women's International Net,* and *Logic Puzzles.*

Sidelights

Tabatha Yeatts told *SATA:* "I wrote a lot when I was a child—my first publication was a poem in *Jack and Jill* when I was about seven—and I filled many notebooks when I was a teenager. Being able to put my feelings down on paper helped me get through the ups and downs of high school. When I began writing nonfiction pieces, my main motivation was to share information with others. I started a periodical because there were things I wanted to know, and I figured other people would want to know, too. Write about what interests you and what moves you.

"I would also encourage anyone, but especially people who like to write, to feed your mind (and your spirit) with the good stuff: read wonderful writers and poets, seek out art you like, listen to great music. I started keeping an online journal called *Poetry Friday* (and later also *Art Thursday*) because it was invigorating to regularly spend time with beautiful imagery, surprising ideas, humorous twists—you know, the good stuff. Don't neglect yourself! It will make you a better writer and could help you be a more content, peaceful person."

Biographical and Critical Sources

ONLINE

Tabatha Yeatts Home Page, http://www.tabathayeatts.com (March 15, 2010).

Illustrations Index

(In the following index, the number of the *volume* in which an illustrator's work appears is given *before* the colon, and the *page number* on which it appears is given *after* the colon. For example, a drawing by Adams, Adrienne appears in Volume 2 on page 6, another drawing by her appears in Volume 3 on page 80, another drawing in Volume 8 on page 1, and so on and so on. . . .)

YABC

Index references to *YABC* refer to listings appearing in the two-volume *Yesterday's Authors of Books for Children,* also published by Gale, Cengage Learning. *YABC* covers prominent authors and illustrators who died prior to 1960.

A

Aas, Ulf 5: 174
Abbe, S. van
  See van Abbe, S.
Abel, Raymond 6: 122; 7: 195; 12: 3; 21: 86; 25: 119
Abelliera, Aldo 71: 120
Abolafia, Yossi 60: 2; 93: 163; 152: 202
Abrahams, Hilary 26: 205; 29: 24, 25; 53: 61
Abrams, Kathie 36: 170
Abrams, Lester 49: 26
Abulafia, Yossi 154: 67; 177: 3
Accardo, Anthony 191: 3, 8
Accornero, Franco 184: 8
Accorsi, William 11: 198
Acs, Laszlo 14: 156; 42: 22
Acuna, Ed 198: 79
Adams, Adrienne 2: 6; 3: 80; 8: 1; 15: 107; 16: 180; 20: 65; 22: 134, 135; 33: 75; 36: 103, 112; 39: 74; 86: 54; 90: 2, 3
Adams, Connie J. 129: 68
Adams, John Wolcott 17: 162
Adams, Lynn 96: 44
Adams, Norman 55: 82
Adams, Pam 112: 1, 2
Adams, Sarah 98: 126; 164: 180
Adams, Steve 209: 64
Adamson, George 30: 23, 24; 69: 64
Addams, Charles 55: 5
Addison, Kenneth 192: 173
Addy, Sean 180: 8
Ade, Rene 76: 198; 195: 162
Adinolfi, JoAnn 115: 42; 176: 2
Adkins, Alta 22: 250
Adkins, Jan 8: 3; 69: 4; 144: 2, 3, 4; 210: 11, 17, 18, 19
Adler, Kelynn 195: 47
Adler, Peggy 22: 6; 29: 31
Adler, Ruth 29: 29
Adlerman, Daniel 163: 2
Adragna, Robert 47: 145
Agard, Nadema 18: 1
Agee, Jon 116: 8, 9, 10; 157: 4; 196: 3, 4, 5, 6, 7, 8
Agre, Patricia 47: 195
Aguirre, Alfredo 152: 218
Ahjar, Brian 207: 126
Ahl, Anna Maria 32: 24
Ahlberg, Allan 68: 6, 7, 9; 165: 5; 214: 9

Ahlberg, Janet 68: 6, 7, 9; 214: 9
Aicher-Scholl, Inge 63: 127
Aichinger, Helga 4: 5, 45
Aitken, Amy 31: 34
Akaba, Suekichi 46: 23; 53: 127
Akasaka, Miyoshi YABC 2: 261
Akib, Jamel 181: 13; 182: 99
Akino, Fuku 6: 144
Alain 40: 41
Alajalov 2: 226
Albert, Chris 200: 64
Alborough, Jez 86: 1, 2, 3; 149: 3
Albrecht, Jan 37: 176
Albright, Donn 1: 91
Alcala, Alfredo 91: 128
Alcantará, Felipe Ugalde 171: 186
Alcorn, John 3: 159; 7: 165; 31: 22; 44: 127; 46: 23, 170
Alcorn, Stephen 110: 4; 125: 106; 128: 172; 150: 97; 160: 188; 165: 48; 201: 113; 203: 39; 207: 3
Alcott, May 100: 3
Alda, Arlene 44: 24; 158: 2
Alden, Albert 11: 103
Aldridge, Andy 27: 131
Aldridge, George 105: 125
Aldridge, Sheila 192: 4
Alejandro, Cliff 176: 75
Alex, Ben 45: 25, 26
Alexander, Ellen 91: 3
Alexander, Lloyd 49: 34
Alexander, Martha 3: 206; 11: 103; 13: 109; 25: 100; 36: 131; 70: 6, 7; 136: 3, 4, 5; 169: 120
Alexander, Paul 85: 57; 90: 9
Alexeieff, Alexander 14: 6; 26: 199
Alfano, Wayne 80: 69
Aliki
  See Brandenberg, Aliki
Allamand, Pascale 12: 9
Allan, Judith 38: 166
Alland, Alexandra 16: 255
Allen, Gertrude 9: 6
Allen, Graham 31: 145
Allen, Jonathan 131: 3, 4; 177: 8, 9, 10
Allen, Joy 168: 185
Allen, Pamela 50: 25, 26, 27, 28; 81: 9, 10; 123: 4, 5
Allen, Raul 207: 94
Allen, Rowena 47: 75

Allen, Thomas B. 81: 101; 82: 248; 89: 37; 104: 9
Allen, Tom 85: 176
Allender, David 73: 223
Alley, R.W. 80: 183; 95: 187; 156: 100, 153; 169: 4, 5; 179: 17
Allison, Linda 43: 27
Allon, Jeffrey 119: 174
Allport, Mike 71: 55
Almquist, Don 11: 8; 12: 128; 17: 46; 22: 110
Aloise, Frank 5: 38; 10: 133; 30: 92
Alsenas, Linas 186: 2
Alter, Ann 206: 4, 5
Althea
  See Braithwaite, Althea
Altschuler, Franz 11: 185; 23: 141; 40: 48; 45: 29; 57: 181
Alvin, John 117: 5
Ambrus, Victor G. 1: 6, 7, 194; 3: 69; 5: 15; 6: 44; 7: 36; 8: 210; 12: 227; 14: 213; 15: 213; 22: 209; 24: 36; 28: 179; 30: 178; 32: 44, 46; 38: 143; 41: 25, 26, 27, 28, 29, 30, 31, 32; 42: 87; 44: 190; 55: 172; 62: 30, 144, 145, 148; 86: 99, 100, 101; 87: 66, 137; 89: 162; 134: 160
Ames, Lee J. 3: 12; 9: 130; 10: 69; 17: 214; 22: 124; 151: 13
Amini, Mehrdokht 211: 119
Amon, Aline 9: 9
Amoss, Berthe 5: 5
Amstutz, André 152: 102; 214: 11, 16
Amundsen, Dick 7: 77
Amundsen, Richard E. 5: 10; 24: 122
Ancona, George 12: 11; 55: 144; 145: 7; 208: 13
Anderson, Alasdair 18: 122
Andersen, Bethanne 116: 167; 162: 189; 175: 17; 191: 4, 5
Anderson, Bob 139: 16
Anderson, Brad 33: 28
Anderson, Brian 211: 8
Anderson, C.W. 11: 10
Anderson, Carl 7: 4
Anderson, Catherine Corley 72: 2
Anderson, Cecil 127: 152
Anderson, David Lee 118: 176
Anderson, Derek 169: 9; 174: 180
Anderson, Doug 40: 111
Anderson, Erica 23: 65
Anderson, Laurie 12: 153, 155
Anderson, Lena 99: 26

Anderson, Peggy Perry *179:* 2
Anderson, Sara *173:* 3
Anderson, Scoular *138:* 13; *201:* 6
Anderson, Susan *90:* 12
Anderson, Tara *188:* 132; *211:* 115
Anderson, Wayne *23:* 119; *41:* 239; *56:* 7; *62:* 26; *147:* 6; *202:* 4, 5
Andreasen, Daniel *86:* 157; *87:* 104; *103:* 201, 202; *159:* 75; *167:* 106, 107; *168:* 184; *180:* 247; *186:* 9; *212:* 101
Andrew, Ian *111:* 37; *116:* 12; *166:* 2
Andrew, John *22:* 4
Andrews, Benny *14:* 251; *31:* 24; *57:* 6, 7; *183:* 8
Andrews, Vaughn *166:* 28
Anelay, Henry *57:* 173
Angel, Marie *47:* 22
Angelo, Valenti *14:* 8; *18:* 100; *20:* 232; *32:* 70
Anglund, Joan Walsh *2:* 7, 250, 251; *37:* 198, 199, 200
Anholt, Catherine *74:* 8; *131:* 7; *141:* 5
Anholt, Laurence *141:* 4
Anno, Mitsumasa *5:* 7; *38:* 25, 26, 27, 28, 29, 30, 31, 32; *77:* 3, 4; *157:* 10, 11
Antal, Andrew *1:* 124; *30:* 145
Antram, David *152:* 133
Apostolou, Christy Hale
    See Hale, Christy
Apple, Margot *33:* 25; *35:* 206; *46:* 81; *53:* 8; *61:* 109; *64:* 21, 22, 24, 25, 27; *71:* 176; *77:* 53; *82:* 245; *92:* 39; *94:* 180; *96:* 107; *152:* 4, 5; *162:* 192, 194; *173:* 44; *214:* 21, 22, 23, 24
Appleyard, Dev *2:* 192
Aragones, Sergio *48:* 23, 24, 25, 26, 27
Araneus *40:* 29
Arbo, Cris *103:* 4
Archambault, Matt *85:* 173; *138:* 19, 20; *143:* 33; *145:* 144; *179:* 103; *187:* 7
Archer, Janet *16:* 69; *178:* 156
Ardizzone, Edward *1:* 11, 12; *2:* 105; *3:* 258; *4:* 78; *7:* 79; *10:* 100; *15:* 232; *20:* 69,178; *23:* 223; *24:* 125; *28:* 25, 26, 27, 28, 29, 30, 31,33, 34, 35, 36, 37; *31:* 192, 193; *34:* 215, 217; *60:* 173; *64:* 145; *87:* 176; *YABC 2:* 25
Arena, Jill *176:* 49
Arenella, Roy *14:* 9
Argemi, David *197:* 2
Argent, Kerry *103:* 56; *138:* 17; *158:* 134
Arihara, Shino *201:* 98
Arisman, Marshall *162:* 50
Armer, Austin *13:* 3
Armer, Laura Adams *13:* 3
Armer, Sidney *13:* 3
Armitage, David *47:* 23; *99:* 5; *155:* 4
Armitage, Eileen *4:* 16
Armstrong, George *10:* 6; *21:* 72
Armstrong, Shelagh *102:* 114
Armstrong-Ellis, Carey *185:* 196
Arno, Enrico *1:* 217; *2:* 22, 210; *4:* 9; *5:* 43; *6:* 52; *29:* 217, 219; *33:* 152; *35:* 99; *43:* 31, 32, 33; *45:* 212, 213, 214; *72:* 72; *74:* 166; *100:* 169
Arnold, Alli *187:* 40, 41
Arnold, Caroline *174:* 5
Arnold, Emily *76:* 7, 9, 10
Arnold, Katya *115:* 11; *168:* 2, 3
Arnold, Tedd *116:* 14; *133:* 152; *160:* 5; *208:* 24, 25, 26, 176
Arnosky, Jim *22:* 20; *70:* 9, 10, 11; *118:* 3, 5; *160:* 8, 10; *189:* 5, 7, 8, 9, 10
Arnsteen, Katy Keck *105:* 97; *116:* 145
Arsenault, Isabelle *207:* 7
Arrowood, Clinton *12:* 193; *19:* 11; *65:* 210
Artell, Mike *89:* 8
Arting, Fred J. *41:* 63
Artzybasheff, Boris *13:* 143; *14:* 15; *40:* 152, 155
Aruego, Ariane *6:* 4

Aruego, José *4:* 140; *6:* 4; *7:* 64; *33:* 195; *35:* 208; *68:* 16, 17; *75:* 46; *93:* 91, 92; *94:* 197; *109:* 65, 67; *125:* 2, 3, 4, 5; *127:* 188; *143:* 25; *178:* 17, 19, 74; *188:* 166; *202:* 164
Arzoumanian, Alik *177:* 12; *194:* 115
Asare, Meshack *86:* 9; *139:* 19
Ascensios, Natalie *105:* 139
Asch, Frank *5:* 9; *66:* 2, 4, 6, 7, 9, 10; *102:* 18, 19,21; *154:* 12
Ashby, Gail *11:* 135
Ashby, Gil *146:* 4
Ashby, Gwynneth *44:* 26
Ashley, C.W. *19:* 197
Ashmead, Hal *8:* 70
Ashton, Tim *211:* 204
Aska, Warabe *56:* 10
Assel, Steven *44:* 153; *77:* 22, 97
Astrop, John *32:* 56
Atene, Ann *12:* 18
Atherton, Lisa *38:* 198
Atkinson, Allen *60:* 5
Atkinson, J. Priestman *17:* 275
Atkinson, Janet *86:* 147; *103:* 138
Atkinson, Mike *127:* 74
Atkinson, Wayne *40:* 46
Attard, Karl *196:* 22, 23
Attebery, Charles *38:* 170
Atwell, Debby *150:* 6
Atwood, Ann *7:* 9
Aubrey, Meg Kelleher *77:* 159
Auch, Herm *173:* 7, 8
Auch, Mary Jane *173:* 7
Augarde, Steve *25:* 22; *159:* 7; *210:* 43, 44
Austerman, Miriam *23:* 107
Austin, Margot *11:* 16
Austin, Robert *3:* 44
Austin, Virginia *81:* 205; *127:* 221
Auth, Tony *51:* 5; *192:* 18
Avendano, Dolores *158:* 74
Avedon, Richard *57:* 140
Averill, Esther *1:* 17; *28:* 39, 40, 41
Axeman, Lois *2:* 32; *11:* 84; *13:* 165; *22:* 8; *23:* 49; *61:* 116; *101:* 124
Axtel, David *155:* 110
Ayer, Jacqueline *13:* 7
Ayer, Margaret *15:* 12; *50:* 120
Ayers, Alan *91:* 58; *107:* 169
Ayliffe, Alex *95:* 164
Ayto, Russell *111:* 5; *112:* 54; *206:* 7, 8; *213:* 56
Azarian, Mary *112:* 9, 10; *114:* 129; *117:* 171; *137:* 163; *171:* 4, 5; *181:* 161; *188:* 128

B

B.T.B.
    See Blackwell, Basil T.
Babbitt, Bradford *33:* 158
Babbitt, Natalie *6:* 6; *8:* 220; *68:* 20; *70:* 242, 243; *194:* 8, 9
Baca, Maria *104:* 5
Bacchus, Andy *94:* 87
Bacha, Andy *109:* 169
Bachelet, Gilles *196:* 18
Bachem, Paul *48:* 180; *67:* 65; *144:* 206
Back, Adam *63:* 125
Back, George *31:* 161
Backes, Nick *190:* 72
Backhouse, Colin *78:* 142
Bacon, Bruce *4:* 74
Bacon, Paul *7:* 155; *8:* 121; *31:* 55; *50:* 42; *56:* 175; *62:* 82, 84
Bacon, Peggy *2:* 11, 228; *46:* 44
Baek, Matthew J. *169:* 95; *202:* 8
Baer, Julie *161:* 2
Baicker-McKee, Carol *177:* 15; *180:* 215
Bailey, Peter *58:* 174; *87:* 221; *194:* 12
Bailey, Sheila *155:* 11

Baker, Alan *22:* 22; *61:* 134; *93:* 11, 12; *146:* 6, 7, 10
Baker, Charlotte *2:* 12
Baker, Garin *89:* 65
Baker, Jeannie *23:* 4; *88:* 18, 19, 20
Baker, Jim *22:* 24
Baker, Joe *82:* 188; *111:* 55; *124:* 70; *197:* 73
Baker, Keith *179:* 6, 7
Baker, Leslie *112:* 214; *132:* 103, 246; *180:* 74, 246
Baldacci, Rudy *184:* 9
Baldridge, Cyrus LeRoy *19:* 69; *44:* 50
Baldus, Zachary *152:* 231; *187:* 60
Balet, Jan *11:* 22
Balian, Lorna *9:* 16; *91:* 16
Balit, Christina *102:* 24; *159:* 9; *162:* 118, 119; *212:* 2, 3
Ballantyne, R.M. *24:* 34
Ballis, George *14:* 199
Balouch, Kristen *176:* 11
Baltzer, Hans *40:* 30
Banbery, Fred *58:* 15
Banfill, A. Scott *98:* 7; *112:* 59
Bang, Molly *24:* 37, 38; *69:* 8, 9, 10; *111:* 7,9, 10, 11; *140:* 11; *158:* 37, 38, 39; *195:* 3; *215:* 11, 12, 13, 14
Banik, Yvette Santiago *21:* 136
Banks, Erin Bennett *211:* 12
Banner, Angela
    See Maddison, Angela Mary
Bannerman, Helen *19:* 13, 14
Banning, Greg *202:* 98
Bannon, Laura *6:* 10; *23:* 8
Bantock, Nick *74:* 229; *95:* 6
Banyai, Istvan *185:* 209; *193:* 14, 16; *209:* 155
Baptist, Michael *37:* 208
Baracca, Sal *135:* 206
Baranaski, Marcin *182:* 113
Barasch, Lynne *126:* 16; *186:* 15
Barbarin, Lucien C., Jr. *89:* 88
Barbour, Karen *96:* 5; *74:* 209; *170:* 16
Bare, Arnold Edwin *16:* 31
Bare, Colleen Stanley *32:* 33
Barger, Jan *147:* 11
Bargery, Geoffrey *14:* 258
Barkat, Jonathan *149:* 177; *164:* 254; *181:* 106; *184:* 186; *196:* 11; *198:* 148
Barker, Carol *31:* 27
Barker, Cicely Mary *49:* 50, 51
Barkley, James *4:* 13; *6:* 11; *13:* 112
Barks, Carl *37:* 27, 28, 29, 30, 31, 32, 33, 34
Barling, Joy *62:* 148
Barling, Tom *9:* 23
Barlow, Gillian *62:* 20
Barlow, Perry *35:* 28
Barlowe, Dot *30:* 223
Barlowe, Wayne *37:* 72; *84:* 43; *105:* 5
Barnard, Bryn *88:* 53; *13:* 55; *169:* 13; *193:* 194
Barneda, David *206:* 11
Barner, Bob *29:* 37; *128:* 33; *136:* 19, 20; *177:* 27
Barnes, Hiram P. *20:* 28
Barnes, Tim *137:* 28
Barnes-Murphy, Rowan *88:* 22
Barnett, Charles II *175:* 150
Barnett, Ivan *70:* 14
Barnett, Moneta *16:* 89; *19:* 142; *31:* 102; *33:* 30, 31, 32; *41:* 153; *61:* 94, 97
Barney, Maginel Wright *39:* 32, 33, 34; *YABC 2:* 306
Barnum, Jay Hyde *11:* 224; *20:* 5; *37:* 189, 190
Baron, Alan *80:* 3; *89:* 123
Barr, George *60:* 74; *69:* 64
Barragan, Paula S. *134:* 116; *186:* 158
Barrall, Tim *115:* 152
Barraud, Martin *189:* 38
Barrauds *33:* 114
Barrer-Russell, Gertrude *9:* 65; *27:* 31
Barret, Robert *85:* 134

Barrett, Angela *40:* 136, 137; *62:* 74; *75:* 10; *76:* 142; *144:* 137; *145:* 14
Barrett, Jennifer *58:* 149
Barrett, John E. *43:* 119
Barrett, Moneta *74:* 10
Barrett, Peter *55:* 169; *86:* 111
Barrett, Robert *62:* 145; *77:* 146; *82:* 35
Barrett, Ron *14:* 24; *26:* 35
Barron, John N. *3:* 261; *5:* 101; *14:* 220
Barrow, Ann *136:* 27
Barrows, Walter *14:* 268
Barry, Ethelred B. *37:* 79; *YABC 1:* 229
Barry, James *14:* 25
Barry, Katharina *2:* 159; *4:* 22
Barry, Robert E. *6:* 12
Barry, Scott *32:* 35
Barshaw, Ruth McNally *203:* 9
Bartenbach, Jean *40:* 31
Barth, Ernest Kurt *2:* 172; *3:* 160; *8:* 26; *10:* 31
Bartholomew, Caty *208:* 153
Bartholomew, Marie *200:* 66
Bartlett, Alison *101:* 88; *165:* 93; *209:* 51
Barton, Byron *8:* 207; *9:* 18; *23:* 66; *80:* 181; *90:* 18, 19, 20, 21; *126:* 29, 30
Barton, Harriett *30:* 71
Barton, Jill *129:* 108; *135:* 120; *145:* 185, 189; *184:* 177
Bartram, Robert *10:* 42
Bartsch, Jochen *8:* 105; *39:* 38
Bascove, Barbara *45:* 73
Base, Graeme *101:* 15, 16, 17, 18; *162:* 8, 10, 12
Baseman, Gary *174:* 12
Bash, Barbara *132:* 9
Baskin, Leonard *30:* 42, 43, 46, 47; *49:* 125, 126, 128, 129,133; *173:* 120
Bass, Saul *49:* 192
Bassett, Jeni *40:* 99; *64:* 30
Basso, Bill *99:* 139; *189:* 134
Batchelor, Joy *29:* 41, 47, 48
Bate, Norman *5:* 16
Bates, Amy June *188:* 170; *189:* 27, 28
Bates, Leo *24:* 35
Batet, Carmen *39:* 134
Batherman, Muriel *31:* 79; *45:* 185
Battaglia, Aurelius *50:* 44
Batten, John D. *25:* 161, 162
Batten, Mary *162:* 14, 15
Battles, Asa *32:* 94, 95
Bauer, Carla *193:* 6
Bauer, Jutta *150:* 32
Bauernschmidt, Marjorie *15:* 15
Baum, Allyn *20:* 10
Baum, Willi *4:* 24, 25; *7:* 173
Bauman, Leslie *61:* 121
Baumann, Jill *34:* 170
Baumhauer, Hans *11:* 218; *15:* 163, 165, 167
Baxter, Glen *57:* 100
Baxter, Leon *59:* 102
Baxter, Robert *87:* 129
Bayer, Herbert *181:* 16
Bayley, Dorothy *37:* 195
Bayley, Nicola *40:* 104; *41:* 34, 35; *69:* 15; *129:* 33, 34, 35
Baylin, Mark *158:* 233
Baynes, Pauline *2:* 244; *3:* 149; *13:* 133, 135,137, 141; *19:* 18, 19, 20; *32:* 208, 213, 214; *36:* 105, 108; *59:* 12, 13, 14, 16, 17, 18, 20; *100:* 158, 159, 243; *133:* 3, 4
Beach, Lou *150:* 150; *207:* 117, 118
Beame, Rona *12:* 40
Bean, Jonathan *196:* 102
Bear's Heart *73:* 215
Beard, Dan *22:* 31, 32
Beard, J.H. *YABC 1:* 158
Bearden, Romare *9:* 7; *22:* 35
Beardshaw, Rosalind *169:* 22; *190:* 22
Beardsley, Aubrey *17:* 14; *23:* 181; *59:* 130, 131
Bearman, Jane *29:* 38

Beaton, Cecil *24:* 208
Beaton, Clare *125:* 28; *208:* 67
Beauce, J.A. *18:* 103
Beaujard, Sophie *81:* 54
Beccia, Carlyn *189:* 29
Bechtold, Lisze *208:* 29
Beck, Charles *11:* 169; *51:* 173
Beck, Ian *138:* 27; *182:* 150; *190:* 25
Beck, Melinda *203:* 112
Beck, Ruth *13:* 11
Becker, Harriet *12:* 211
Beckerman, Jonathan *208:* 194
Beckett, Sheilah *25:* 5; *33:* 37, 38
Beckhoff, Harry *1:* 78; *5:* 163
Beckhorn, Susan Williams *189:* 32
Beckman, Kaj *45:* 38, 39, 40, 41
Beckman, Per *45:* 42, 43
Beddows, Eric *72:* 70
Bedford, F.D. *20:* 118, 122; *33:* 170; *41:* 220, 221,230, 233
Bee, Joyce *19:* 62
Bee, William *188:* 6
Beeby, Betty *25:* 36
Beech, Carol *9:* 149
Beech, Mark *192:* 122
Beek *25:* 51, 55, 59
Beeke, Tiphanie *177:* 127; *204:* 140; *212:* 178
Beekman, Doug *125:* 146, 148
Beerbohm, Max *24:* 208
Beeson, Bob *108:* 57
Begin, Mary Jane *82:* 13; *206:* 13
Beha, Philippe *172:* 85
Behr, Joyce *15:* 15; *21:* 132; *23:* 161
Behrens, Hans *5:* 97
Beier, Ellen *135:* 170; *139:* 47; *183:* 164
Beinicke, Steve *69:* 18
Beisner, Monika *46:* 128, 131; *112:* 127
Belden, Charles J. *12:* 182
Belina, Renate *39:* 132
Bell, Corydon *3:* 20
Bell, Graham *54:* 48
Bell, Julia *151:* 214
Bell, Julie *159:* 172; *165:* 18
Bell, Thomas P. *76:* 182
Bellamy, Glen *127:* 15
Beltran, Alberto *43:* 37
Bemelmans, Ludwig *15:* 19, 21; *100:* 27
Ben-Ami, Doron *75:* 96; *84:* 107; *108:* 132; *110:* 63; *159:* 157; *197:* 142
Bendall-Brunello, John *150:* 4; *157:* 163; *185:* 3, 4; *203:* 5
Benda, Wladyslaw T. *15:* 256; *30:* 76, 77; *44:* 182
Bender, Robert *77:* 162; *79:* 13; *160:* 23
Bendick, Jeanne *2:* 24; *68:* 27, 28
Benioff, Carol *121:* 42; *175:* 23
Benner, Cheryl *80:* 11
Bennett, Charles H. *64:* 6
Bennett, Erin Susanne *165:* 216
Bennett, F.I. *YABC 1:* 134
Bennett, James *146:* 240
Bennett, Jill *26:* 61; *41:* 38, 39; *45:* 54
Bennett, Rainey *15:* 26; *23:* 53
Bennett, Richard *15:* 45; *21:* 11, 12, 13; *25:* 175
Bennett, Susan *5:* 55
Benny, Mike *142:* 78; *203:* 13, 14; *207:* 85
Benoit, Elise *77:* 74
Benson, Linda *60:* 130; *62:* 91; *75:* 101; *79:* 156; *134:* 129
Benson, Patrick *68:* 162; *147:* 17, 18, 19, 20
Bentley, Carolyn *46:* 153
Bentley, James *149:* 30
Bentley, Roy *30:* 162
Benton, Jim *172:* 22
Benton, Thomas Hart *2:* 99
Berelson, Howard *5:* 20; *16:* 58; *31:* 50
Berenstain, Jan *12:* 47; *64:* 33, 34, 36, 37, 38, 40, 42, 44; *135:* 25, 28, 31, 35
Berenstain, Stan *12:* 47; *64:* 33, 34, 36, 37, 38, 40, 42, 44; *135:* 25, 28, 31, 35

Berenzy, Alix *65:* 13; *73:* 6; *78:* 115
Berg, Joan *1:* 115; *3:* 156; *6:* 26, 58
Berg, Ron *36:* 48, 49; *48:* 37, 38; *67:* 72
Bergen, David *115:* 44; *207:* 34
Berger, Barbara *77:* 14
Berger, Carin *185:* 6
Berger, William M. *14:* 143; *YABC 1:* 204
Bergherr, Mary *74:* 170; *151:* 123
Bergin, Mark *114:* 8, 9; *143:* 95; *160:* 26, 27
Bergstreser, Douglas *69:* 76
Bergum, Constance R. *121:* 14, 15; *208:* 31, 32, 33; *209:* 176
Bering, Claus *13:* 14
Berkeley, Jon *139:* 218
Berkowitz, Jeanette *3:* 249
Berman, Paul *66:* 14
Bernal, Richard *154:* 176
Bernadette
　See Watts, Bernadette
Bernardin, James *112:* 24; *167:* 94
Bernasconi, Pablo *183:* 10, 11
Bernath, Stefen *32:* 76
Berner, Rotraut Susanne *214:* 32
Bernhard, Durga *80:* 13
Bernstein, Michel J. *51:* 71
Bernstein, Ted *38:* 183; *50:* 131
Bernstein, Zena *23:* 46
Berridge, Celia *86:* 63
Berrill, Jacquelyn *12:* 50
Berry, Erick
　See Best, Allena
Berry, Holly *205:* 116; *210:* 49, 50
Berry, William D. *14:* 29; *19:* 48
Berry, William A. *6:* 219
Berson, Harold *2:* 17, 18; *4:* 28, 29, 220; *9:* 10; *12:* 19; *17:* 45; *18:* 193; *22:* 85; *34:* 172; *44:* 120; *46:* 42; *80:* 240
Bertholf, Bret *187:* 9; *189:* 32, 33
Berton, Patsy *99:* 16
Bertschmann, Harry *16:* 1
Besco, Don *70:* 99
Beskow, Elsa *20:* 13, 14, 15
Bess, Clayton *63:* 94
Best, Allena *2:* 26; *34:* 76
Betera, Carol *74:* 68
Bethell, Thomas N. *61:* 169
Bethers, Ray *6:* 22
Betteridge, Deirdre *214:* 34
Bettina
　See Ehrlich, Bettina
Betts, Ethel Franklin *17:* 161, 164, 165; *YABC 2:* 47
Betz, Rudolf *59:* 161
Bewick, Thomas *16:* 40, 41, 43, 44, 45, 47; *54:* 150; *YABC 1:* 107
Beyer, Paul J. III *74:* 24
Bezencon, Jacqueline *48:* 40
Biamonte, Daniel *40:* 90
Bianchi, John *91:* 19
Bianco, Pamela *15:* 31; *28:* 44, 45, 46
Bible, Charles *13:* 15
Bice, Clare *22:* 40
Biedrzycki, David *186:* 170
Bierman, Don *57:* 184
Biggers, John *2:* 123
Biggs, Brian *192:* 38; *196:* 15; *207:* 170
Bikadoroff, Roxanna *201:* 74
Bileck, Marvin *3:* 102; *40:* 36, 37
Bilibin, Ivan *61:* 8, 9, 12, 13, 14, 15, 151, 152, 154, 162
Billington, Patrick *98:* 71
Billout, Guy *144:* 38, 39
Bimen, Levent *5:* 179
Binch, Caroline *81:* 18; *140:* 15, 16; *144:* 115; *211:* 82
Binder, Hannes *169:* 163
Bing, Christopher *126:* 34
Binger, Bill *121:* 46
Binks, Robert *25:* 150
Binzen, Bill *24:* 47

Birch, Reginald *15:* 150; *19:* 33, 34, 35, 36; *37:* 196,197; *44:* 182; *46:* 176; *YABC 1:* 84; *2:* 34, 39
Birchall, Mark *123:* 188
Bird, Esther Brock *1:* 36; *25:* 66
Birdsong, Keith *167:* 85
Birkett, Georgie *204:* 121
Birkett, Rachel *78:* 206
Birling, Paul *109:* 30
Birmingham, Christian *132:* 243; *143:* 114; *209:* 58
Birmingham, Lloyd P. *12:* 51; *83:* 13
Biro, Val *1:* 26; *41:* 42; *60:* 178; *67:* 23, 24; *84:* 242, 243
Bischoff, Ilse *44:* 51
Bishop, Don *199:* 133
Bishop, Gavin *97:* 17, 18; *144:* 42, 44
Bishop, Kathleen Wong *115:* 67
Bishop, Rich *56:* 43
Bite, I. *60:* 14
Bittinger, Ned *93:* 117; *205:* 115
Bjorklund, Lorence *3:* 188, 252; *7:* 100; *9:* 113; *10:* 66; *19:* 178; *33:* 122, 123; *35:* 36, 37, 38, 39,41, 42, 43; *36:* 185; *38:* 93; *47:* 106; *66:* 194; *YABC 1:* 242
Bjorkman, Steve *91:* 199; *160:* 110; *198:* 18
Blabey, Aaron *214:* 35
Black Sheep *164:* 100
Blackburn, Loren H. *63:* 10
Blackall, Sophie *194:* 140; *209:* 157
Blackford, John *137:* 105; *180:* 36
Blackwell, Basil T. *YABC 1:* 68, 69
Blackwood, Freya *199:* 9
Blackwood, Gary L. *118:* 17
Blades, Ann *16:* 52; *37:* 213; *50:* 41; *69:* 21; *99:* 215
Blair, Jay *45:* 46; *46:* 155
Blaisdell, Elinore *1:* 121; *3:* 134; *35:* 63
Blake, Anne Catharine *189:* 71
Blake, Francis *198:* 4
Blake, Quentin *3:* 170; *10:* 48; *13:* 38; *21:* 180; *26:* 60; *28:* 228; *30:* 29, 31; *40:* 108; *45:* 219; *46:* 165, 168; *48:* 196; *52:* 10, 11, 12,13, 14, 15, 16, 17; *73:* 41, 43; *78:* 84, 86; *80:* 250, 251; *84:* 210, 211, 212; *87:* 177; *96:* 24, 26, 28; *124:* 79; *125:* 32, 34; *181:* 139; *211:* 26, 27
Blake, Robert J. *37:* 90; *53:* 67; *54:* 23; *160:* 28, 29
Blake, William *30:* 54, 56, 57, 58, 59, 60
Blanchard, N. Taylor *82:* 140
Blass, Jacqueline *8:* 215
Blazek, Scott R. *91:* 71
Bleck, Cathie *118:* 116
Bleck, Linda *204:* 124
Blegvad, Erik *2:* 59; *3:* 98; *5:* 117; *7:* 131; *11:* 149; *14:* 34, 35; *18:* 237; *32:* 219; *60:* 106; *66:* 16, 17, 18, 19; *70:* 233; *76:* 18; *82:* 106; *87:* 45; *100:* 188; *129:* 125; *132:* 17, 18, 19, 20; *176:* 14; *200:* 100; *YABC 1:* 201
Blessen, Karen *93:* 126
Bliss, Corinne Demas *37:* 38
Bliss, Harry *196:* 27, 28, 29
Blitt, Barry *179:* 199; *187:* 13
Bloch, Lucienne *10:* 12
Blondon, Herve *129:* 48; *183:* 22
Bloom, Lloyd *35:* 180; *36:* 149; *47:* 99; *62:* 117; *68:* 231; *72:* 136; *75:* 185; *83:* 99; *108:* 19
Bloom, Suzanne *172:* 23, 24
Blossom, Dave *34:* 29
Blumenschein, E.L. *YABC 1:* 113, 115
Blumer, Patt *29:* 214
Blundell, Kim *29:* 36
Bluthenthal, Diana Cain *93:* 32; *104:* 106; *177:* 26
Blythe, Benjamin *128:* 7
Blythe, Gary *112:* 52; *181:* 166; *182:* 64; *185:* 7; *186:* 116, 117
Boake, Kathy *176:* 185
Board, Perry *171:* 99

Boardman, Gwenn *12:* 60
Boatwright, Phil *211:* 195
Bober, Richard *125:* 145; *132:* 40
Bock, Vera *1:* 187; *21:* 41
Bock, William Sauts *8:* 7; *14:* 37; *16:* 120; *21:* 141; *36:* 177; *62:* 203
Bodecker, N(iels) M(ogens) *8:* 13; *14:* 2; *17:* 55, 56, 57; *73:* 22, 23, 24
Boehm, Linda *40:* 31
Bogacki, Tomek *138:* 31, 32; *144:* 123; *202:* 13
Bogan, Paulette *197:* 152; *201:* 17
Bogdan, Florentina *107:* 43
Bohdal, Susi *22:* 44; *101:* 20
Bohlen, Nina *58:* 13
Boies, Alex *96:* 53
Bok, Chip *205:* 16
Bolam, Emily *101:* 216; *159:* 12; *205:* 59
Bolian, Polly *3:* 270; *4:* 30; *13:* 77; *29:* 197
Bolle, Frank *87:* 100; *208:* 101
Bollen, Roger *79:* 186; *83:* 16
Bolling, Vickey *114:* 44
Bollinger, Peter *101:* 7; *128:* 198; *172:* 26
Bolognese, Don *2:* 147, 231; *4:* 176; *7:* 146; *17:* 43; *23:* 192; *24:* 50; *34:* 108; *36:* 133; *71:* 24, 25; *103:* 131; *129:* 39, 40
Bolster, Rob *186:* 169
Bolton, A.T. *57:* 158
Bond, Arnold *18:* 116
Bond, Barbara Higgins *21:* 102
Bond, Bruce *52:* 97
Bond, Felicia *38:* 197; *49:* 55, 56; *89:* 170; *90:* 171; *126:* 37
Bond, Higgins *177:* 22, 23; *209:* 175
Bonn, Pat *43:* 40
Bonner, Hannah *197:* 13, 14
Bonners, Susan *41:* 40; *85:* 36; *94:* 99, 100; *151:* 105, 106
Bono, Mary *184:* 73
Bonsall, Crosby *23:* 6
Boon, Debbie *103:* 6; *144:* 188
Boon, Emilie *86:* 23, 24
Boone, Debbie *165:* 77
Boore, Sara *60:* 73
Bootman, Colin *155:* 13; *159:* 35; *174:* 192
Booth, Franklin *YABC 2:* 76
Booth, George *191:* 13
Booth, Graham *32:* 193; *37:* 41, 42
Borda, Juliette *102:* 188
Bordier, Georgette *16:* 54
Boren, Tinka *27:* 128
Borges, Jose Francisco *119:* 62
Borja, Robert *22:* 48
Born, Adolf *49:* 63
Bornstein, Ruth *14:* 44; *88:* 45, 46; *107:* 30
Borten, Helen *3:* 54; *5:* 24
Bosin, Blackbear *69:* 104
Bossom, Naomi *35:* 48
Bostock, Mike *83:* 221; *114:* 14; *188:* 205
Boston, Peter *19:* 42
Bosustow, Stephen *34:* 202
Boszko, Ron *75:* 47
Bottner, Barbara *14:* 46
Boucher, Joelle *41:* 138
Boulat, Pierre *44:* 40
Boulet, Susan Seddon *50:* 47
Bouma, Paddy *118:* 25; *128:* 16
Bour, Daniele *66:* 145
Bourke-White, Margaret *15:* 286, 287; *57:* 102
Boutavant, Marc *200:* 136
Boutet de Monvel, M. *30:* 61, 62, 63, 65
Bowen, Betsy *105:* 222
Bowen, Richard *42:* 134
Bowen, Ruth *31:* 188
Bower, Ron *29:* 33
Bowers, David *95:* 38; *115:* 20; *127:* 169, 170; *165:* 57; *207:* 11
Bowers, Tim *185:* 35; *201:* 41
Bowman, Claire *174:* 177
Bowman, Eric *151:* 23

Bowman, Leslie *85:* 203; *105:* 108; *116:* 76; *128:* 234; *182:* 24, 25
Bowman, Peter *146:* 214, 215; *150:* 115
Bowser, Carolyn Ewing *22:* 253
Boxall, Ed *178:* 28
Boyd, Aaron *158:* 242
Boyd, Patti *45:* 31
Boyle, Eleanor Vere *28:* 50, 51
Boynton, Sandra *57:* 13, 14, 15; *107:* 36, 37; *152:* 12, 13, 14
Bozzo, Frank *4:* 154
Brabbs, Derry *55:* 170
Brace, Eric *132:* 193, 194; *152:* 71; *184:* 195; *197:* 6; *201:* 54
Brackers de Hugo, Pierre *115:* 21
Bradford, June *158:* 138
Bradford, Ron *7:* 157
Bradley, David P. *69:* 105
Bradley, Richard D. *26:* 182
Bradley, William *5:* 164
Brady, Irene *4:* 31; *42:* 37; *68:* 191
Bragg, Michael *32:* 78; *46:* 31
Bragg, Ruth Gembicki *77:* 18
Brainerd, John W. *65:* 19
Braithwaite, Althea *23:* 12, 13; *119:* 16
Brak, Syd *146:* 187
Bralds, Braldt *90:* 28; *91:* 151
Bram, Elizabeth *30:* 67
Bramley, Peter *4:* 3
Brandenberg, Aliki *2:* 36, 37; *24:* 222; *35:* 49, 50, 51,52, 53, 54, 56, 57; *75:* 15, 17; *92:* 205; *113:* 18, 19, 20; *157:* 28; *156:* 111
Brandenburg, Alexa *75:* 19
Brandenburg, Jim *38:* 149; *150:* 212
Brandi, Lillian *31:* 158
Brandon, Brumsic, Jr. *9:* 25
Brannen, Sarah S. *202:* 15
Bransom, Paul *17:* 121; *43:* 44
Braren, Loretta Trezzo *87:* 193
Brassard, France *186:* 22
Braun, Wendy *80:* 17, 18; *213:* 14
Brautigam, Don *115:* 175, 176
Brazell, Derek *75:* 105; *79:* 9
Breathed, Berkeley *86:* 27, 28, 29; *161:* 13, 14
Breckenreid, Julia *192:* 209
Breen, Steve *186:* 23
Brennan, Steve *83:* 230; *101:* 184
Brenner, Fred *22:* 85; *36:* 34; *42:* 34
Brett, Bernard *22:* 54
Brett, Harold M. *26:* 98, 99, 100
Brett, Jan *30:* 135; *42:* 39; *71:* 31, 32; *130:* 23, 24, 25, 26, 27; *171:* 15, 16
Brewer, Paul *106:* 115; *145:* 202
Brewer, Sally King *33:* 44
Brewster, Patience *40:* 68; *45:* 22, 183; *51:* 20; *66:* 144; *89:* 4; *97:* 30, 31; *212:* 99
Brick, John *10:* 15
Brickman, Robin D. *131:* 88; *142:* 150; *155:* 18; *178:* 109; *184:* 32
Bridge, David R. *45:* 28
Bridgman, L.J. *37:* 77
Bridwell, Norman *4:* 37; *138:* 36, 37, 40
Brierley, Louise *91:* 22; *96:* 165; *183:* 51
Briggs, Harry *172:* 187
Briggs, Raymond *10:* 168; *23:* 20, 21; *66:* 29, 31, 32; *131:* 28, 29; *184:* 15, 16
Brigham, Grace A. *37:* 148
Bright, Robert *24:* 55
Brighton, Catherine *107:* 39; *206:* 23
Brinckloe, Julie *13:* 18; *24:* 79, 115; *29:* 35; *63:* 140; *81:* 131
Brion *47:* 116
Brisley, Joyce L. *22:* 57
Brisson, James F. *110:* 60
Brittingham, Geoffrey *88:* 37
Brix-Henker, Silke *81:* 194
Broadway, Hannah *208:* 104
Brock, Charles E. *15:* 97; *19:* 247, 249; *23:* 224, 225; *36:* 88; *42:* 41, 42, 43, 44, 45; *100:* 189; *YABC 1:* 194, 196, 203
Brock, Emma *7:* 21

Brock, Henry Matthew *15:* 81; *16:* 141; *19:* 71; *34:* 115; *40:* 164; *42:* 47, 48, 49; *49:* 66
Brocksopp, Arthur *57:* 157
Broda, Ron *136:* 180; *174:* 123
Brodkin, Gwen *34:* 135
Brodovitch, Alexi *52:* 22
Bromhall, Winifred *5:* 11; *26:* 38
Bromley, Lizzy *159:* 179
Bronson, Linda *150:* 210; *174:* 133; *203:* 16, 17
Brooke, L. Leslie *16:* 181, 182, 183, 186; *17:* 15, 16, 17; *18:* 194
Brooker, Christopher *15:* 251
Brooker, Kyrsten *111:* 94; *140:* 28; *162:* 111; *175:* 108; *186:* 42, 225; *199:* 12; *201:* 30
Brooks, Erik *166:* 52; *182:* 30
Brooks, Karen Stormer *186:* 110
Brooks, Maya Itzna *92:* 153
Brooks, Ron *94:* 15; *197:* 188; *212:* 6, 7, 8, 9
Brooks, S.G. *178:* 127
Broomfield, Maurice *40:* 141
Brotman, Adolph E. *5:* 21
Brown, Buck *45:* 48
Brown, Calef *179:* 18; *210:* 206
Brown, Christopher *62:* 124, 125, 127, 128
Brown, Craig McFarland *73:* 28; *84:* 65
Brown, Dan *61:* 167; *115:* 183, 184; *116:* 28, 29; *193:* 190; *200:* 21, 23
Brown, David *7:* 47; *48:* 52
Brown, Denise *11:* 213
Brown, Don *172:* 29
Brown, Elbrite *195:* 39; *198:* 5
Brown, Ford Madox *48:* 74
Brown, Hunter *191:* 111, 112
Brown, Judith Gwyn *1:* 45; *7:* 5; *8:* 167; *9:* 182, 190; *20:* 16, 17, 18; *23:* 142; *29:* 117; *33:* 97; *36:* 23, 26; *43:* 184; *48:* 201, 223; *49:* 69; *86:* 227; *110:* 188; *153:* 7
Brown, Kathryn *98:* 26
Brown, Lisa *187:* 175
Brown, Laurie Krasny *99:* 30
Brown, Marc (Tolon) *10:* 17, 197; *14:* 263; *51:* 18; *53:* 11, 12, 13, 15, 16, 17; *75:* 58; *80:* 24, 25, 26; *82:* 261; *99:* 29; *145:* 22, 23, 25, 27; *162:* 198
Brown, Marcia *7:* 30; *25:* 203; *47:* 31, 32, 33, 34, 35,36, 37, 38, 39, 40, 42, 43, 44; *YABC 1:* 27
Brown, Margery W. *5:* 32, 33; *10:* 3
Brown, Martin *101:* 43
Brown, Mary Barrett *97:* 74
Brown, Palmer *36:* 40
Brown, Paul *25:* 26; *26:* 107
Brown, Richard *61:* 18; *67:* 30
Brown, Rick *78:* 71; *150:* 154
Brown, Robert S. *85:* 33
Brown, Rod *157:* 142
Brown, Ruth *55:* 165; *86:* 112, 113; *105:* 16, 17, 18; *171:* 178
Brown, Trevor *99:* 160; *139:* 247; *189:* 206
Browne, Anthony *45:* 50, 51, 52; *61:* 21, 22, 23, 24, 25; *105:* 21, 22, 23, 25
Browne, Dik *8:* 212; *67:* 32, 33, 35, 37, 39
Browne, Gordon *16:* 97; *64:* 114, 116, 117, 119, 121
Browne, Hablot K. *15:* 65, 80; *21:* 14, 15, 16, 17, 18, 19,20; *24:* 25
Browne, Jane *165:* 222
Browning, Coleen *4:* 132
Browning, Mary Eleanor *24:* 84
Bruce, Robert *23:* 23
Brude, Dick *48:* 215
Bruel, Nick *166:* 41; *205:* 17, 18
Brule, Al *3:* 135
Brumbeau, Jeff *157:* 29
Bruna, Dick *43:* 48, 49, 50; *76:* 27, 28
Brundage, Frances *19:* 244
Brunhoff, Jean de *24:* 57, 58
Brunhoff, Laurent de *24:* 60; *71:* 35, 36, 37
Brunkus, Denise *84:* 50; *123:* 117; *178:* 209; *193:* 99; *204:* 10, 11, 12; *209:* 202

Brunson, Bob *43:* 135
Bryan, Ashley *31:* 44; *72:* 27, 28, 29; *107:* 92; *116:* 192; *132:* 24; *178:* 33, 34, 35; *208:* 83
Bryant, Laura J. *176:* 36; *183:* 168; *214:* 141
Bryant, Michael *93:* 74
Brychta, Alex *21:* 21
Bryer, Diana *107:* 121
Bryson, Bernarda *3:* 88, 146; *39:* 26; *44:* 185; *131:* 40
Buba, Joy *12:* 83; *30:* 226; *44:* 56
Buchanan, George *166:* 198
Buchanan, Lilian *13:* 16
Buchanan, Rachel *171:* 71
Bucholtz-Ross, Linda *44:* 137
Buchs, Thomas *40:* 38
Buck, Margaret Waring *3:* 30
Buckhardt, Marc *172:* 59
Buckley, Mike *166:* 180
Budwine, Greg *175:* 172
Buehner, Mark *104:* 12, 15; *105:* 160; *119:* 98; *157:* 188; *159:* 39, 40, 43; *192:* 111
Buehr, Walter *3:* 31
Buff, Conrad *19:* 52, 53, 54
Buff, Mary *19:* 52, 53
Bull, Charles Livingston *18:* 207; *88:* 175, 176
Bullen, Anne *3:* 166, 167
Buller, Jon *205:* 21
Bullock, Kathleen *77:* 24
Bumgarner-Kirby, Claudia *77:* 194
Burbank, Addison *37:* 43
Burchard, Peter Duncan *3:* 197; *5:* 35; *6:* 158, 218; *143:* 17
Burckhardt, Marc *94:* 48; *110:* 89; *196:* 41; *199:* 116
Burger, Carl *3:* 33; *45:* 160, 162
Burgeson, Marjorie *19:* 31
Burgess, Anne *76:* 252
Burgess, Gelett *32:* 39, 42
Burgess, Mark *157:* 31
Burke, Jim *179:* 19; *185:* 63
Burke, Phillip *95:* 117
Burkert, Nancy Ekholm *18:* 186; *22:* 140; *24:* 62, 63,64, 65; *26:* 53; *29:* 60, 61; *46:* 171; *YABC 1:* 46
Burkhardt, Bruce *142:* 86
Burkhardt, Melissa A. *142:* 86
Burleson, Joe *104:* 35; *172:* 139
Burn, Doris *6:* 172
Burn, Jeffrey *89:* 125; *152:* 132
Burn, Ted
    See Burn, Thomas E.
Burn, Thomas E. *151:* 41
Burnard, Damon *115:* 23
Burnett, Lindy *210:* 59
Burnett, Virgil *44:* 42
Burningham, John *9:* 68; *16:* 60, 61; *59:* 28, 29, 30,31, 32, 33, 35; *111:* 18, 19, 21; *160:* 37
Burns, Howard M. *12:* 173
Burns, Jim *47:* 70; *86:* 32; *91:* 197; *123:* 16
Burns, M.F. *26:* 69
Burns, Raymond *9:* 29
Burns, Robert *24:* 106
Burr, Dan *65:* 28; *108:* 134; *164:* 203; *182:* 68
Burr, Dane *12:* 2
Burra, Edward *YABC 2:* 68
Burrell, Galen *56:* 76
Burri, Rene *41:* 143; *54:* 166
Burridge, Marge Opitz *14:* 42
Burris, Burmah *4:* 81
Burroughs, John Coleman *41:* 64
Burroughs, Studley O. *41:* 65
Burton, Marilee Robin *46:* 33
Burton, Virginia Lee *2:* 43; *44:* 49, 51; *100:* 46, 47; *YABC 1:* 24; *147:* 56
Busoni, Rafaello *1:* 186; *3:* 224; *6:* 126; *14:* 5; *16:* 62, 63
Butchkes, Sidney *50:* 58
Butler, Geoff *94:* 20
Butler, Ralph *116:* 212
Butterfield, Ned *1:* 153; *27:* 128; *79:* 63

Butterworth, Ian *184:* 48, 49
Butterworth, Nick *106:* 43, 44; *149:* 34
Buxton, John *123:* 12
Buzelli, Christopher *105:* 149
Buzonas, Gail *29:* 88
Buzzell, Russ W. *12:* 177
Byard, Carole *39:* 44; *57:* 18, 19, 20; *60:* 60; *61:* 93, 96; *69:* 210; *78:* 246; *79:* 227
Byars, Betsy *46:* 35
Byfield, Barbara Ninde *8:* 18
Byfield, Graham *32:* 29
Bynum, Janie *176:* 50
Byrd, Robert *13:* 218; *33:* 46; *158:* 70; *212:* 100
Byrd, Samuel *123:* 104

C

Cabat, Erni *74:* 38
Cabban, Vanessa *138:* 73; *176:* 39; *185:* 65
Cabrera, Jane *103:* 24; *152:* 27; *182:* 33, 34
Caceres, Ana Palmero *198:* 106
Caddy, Alice *6:* 41
Cady, Harrison *17:* 21, 23; *19:* 57, 58
Caffrey, Aileen *72:* 223; *141:* 154
Cairns, Julia *177:* 37
Caldecott, Randolph *16:* 98, 103; *17:* 32, 33, 36, 38, 39; *26:* 90; *100:* 49, 50; *YABC 2:* 172
Calder, Alexander *18:* 168
Calderón, Gloria *179:* 5
Calderon, W. Frank *25:* 160
Caldwell, Ben *105:* 75; *149:* 60; *195:* 61
Caldwell, Clyde *98:* 100; *116:* 39; *208:* 145
Caldwell, Doreen *23:* 77; *71:* 41
Caldwell, John *46:* 225
Call, Greg *126:* 135; *165:* 49; *182:* 105, 163; *197:* 18, 19; *200:* 159; *209:* 166; *212:* 161
Callahan, Kevin *22:* 42
Callahan, Philip S. *25:* 77
Callan, Jamie *59:* 37
Calvin, James *61:* 92
Camburn-Bracalente, Carol A. *118:* 22
Cameron, Chad *190:* 144
Cameron, Julia Margaret *19:* 203
Cameron, Scott *99:* 18
Camm, Martin *140:* 208, 209, 210
Campbell, Ann *11:* 43; *123:* 182; *183:* 68
Campbell, Bill *89:* 39
Campbell, Ken *126:* 143; *205:* 162
Campbell, Robert *55:* 120
Campbell, Rod *51:* 27; *98:* 34
Campbell, Walter M. *YABC 2:* 158
Camps, Luis *28:* 120, 121; *66:* 35
Canga, C.B. *187:* 165
Caniglia, Jeremy *201:* 89
Cann, Helen *124:* 50; *141:* 78; *170:* 138; *179:* 22, 23
Cannell, Jon *196:* 43
Cannon, Janell *78:* 25; *128:* 40
Canright, David *36:* 162
Cantone, AnnaLaura *182:* 146; *196:* 80
Canty, Thomas *85:* 161; *92:* 47; *113:* 192; *134:* 60; *185:* 117
Canyon, Christopher *150:* 44; *151:* 112
Caparo, Antonio Javier *204:* 128
Caporale, Wende *70:* 42
Capp, Al *61:* 28, 30, 31, 40, 41, 43, 44
Cappon, Manuela *154:* 64
Caras, Peter *36:* 64
Caraway, Caren *57:* 22
Caraway, James *3:* 200, 201
Carbe, Nino *29:* 183
Cares, Linda *67:* 176
Carigiet, Alois *24:* 67
Carle, Eric *4:* 42; *11:* 121; *12:* 29; *65:* 32,33, 34, 36; *73:* 63, 65; *163:* 55, 56
Carling, Amelia Lau *164:* 46
Carlino, Angela *168:* 43; *188:* 20

Carlson, Nancy L. *41:* 116; *56:* 25; *90:* 45; *144:* 48, 50; *213:* 24, 25, 26
Carlluccio, Maria *175:* 129
Carmi, Giora *79:* 35; *149:* 40; *208:* 126
Carpenter, Nancy *76:* 128; *86:* 173; *89:* 171; *131:* 186; *134:* 8; *138:* 215; *153:* 204; *159:* 93; *165:* 232; *211:* 134
Carr, Archie *37:* 225
Carrick, Donald *5:* 194; *39:* 97; *49:* 70; *53:* 156; *63:* 15, 16, 17, 18, 19, 21; *80:* 131; *86:* 151; *118:* 24
Carrick, Malcolm *28:* 59, 60
Carrick, Paul *118:* 26; *194:* 28
Carrick, Valery *21:* 47
Carrier, Lark *71:* 43
Carroll, Jim *88:* 211; *140:* 177; *153:* 99; *195:* 75
Carroll, Lewis
  See Dodgson, Charles L.
Carroll, Michael *72:* 5
Carroll, Pamela *84:* 68; *128:* 214; *199:* 130
Carroll, Ruth *7:* 41; *10:* 68
Carter, Abby *81:* 32; *97:* 121; *102:* 61; *163:* 139; *164:* 125; *184:* 22, 23; *191:* 85
Carter, Barbara *47:* 167, 169
Carter, David A. *114:* 24, 25; *170:* 42, 43
Carter, Don *124:* 54; *184:* 100; *192:* 43, 44, 45
Carter, Harry *22:* 179
Carter, Helene *15:* 38; *22:* 202, 203; *YABC 2:* 220, 221
Carter, Penny *173:* 91
Cartlidge, Michelle *49:* 65; *96:* 50, 51
Cartwright, Reg *63:* 61, 62; *78:* 26; *143:* 4
Cartwright, Shannon *176:* 81
Carty, Leo *4:* 196; *7:* 163; *58:* 131
Cary *4:* 133; *9:* 32; *20:* 2; *21:* 143
Cary, Page *12:* 41
Casale, Paul *71:* 63; *109:* 122; *136:* 28
Case, Chris *209:* 23
Case, Sandra E. *16:* 2
Caseley, Judith *87:* 36; *159:* 47, 48, 49
Casilla, Robert *78:* 7; *167:* 124; *211:* 41; *212:* 165
Casino, Steve *85:* 193
Cassel, Lili
  See Wronker, Lili Cassel
Cassel-Wronker, Lili
  See Wronker, Lili Cassel
Cassels, Jean *8:* 50; *150:* 119; *173:* 37; *186:* 182
Cassen, Melody *140:* 51
Cassity, Don *104:* 24
Cassler, Carl *75:* 137, 138; *82:* 162
Casson, Hugh *65:* 38, 40, 42, 43
Castellon, Federico *48:* 45, 46, 47, 48
Castle, Jane *4:* 80
Castro, Antonio *84:* 71
Casu, Danny "casroc" *201:* 10
Catalano, Dominic *94:* 79; *163:* 60, 61; *162:* 54
Catalanotto, Peter *63:* 170; *70:* 23; *71:* 182; *72:* 96; *74:* 114; *76:* 194, 195; *77:* 7; *79:* 157; *80:* 28, 67; *83:* 157; *85:* 27; *108:* 11; *113:* 30, 31, 33, 34, 36; *114:* 27, 28, 29; *117:* 53; *124:* 168; *159:* 54, 55; *195:* 19, 20, 21, 22, 24, 174; *200:* 156; *207:* 103; *209:* 184
Catania, Tom *68:* 82
Cather, Carolyn *3:* 83; *15:* 203; *34:* 216
Catlin, George *214:* 172
Catrow, David *117:* 179; *152:* 31, 33; *173:* 24; *206:* 29
Cauley, Lorinda Bryan *44:* 135; *46:* 49
Cayard, Bruce *38:* 67
Cazet, Denys *52:* 27; *99:* 39, 40; *163:* 65, 66; *191:* 25, 27, 28
Ceccoli, Nicoletta *181:* 39; *188:* 99; *199:* 118; *209:* 6
Cecil, Randy *127:* 132, 133; *187:* 16, 17; *191:* 168; *209:* 5
Cellini, Joseph *2:* 73; *3:* 35; *16:* 116; *47:* 103

Cepeda, Joe *90:* 62; *109:* 91; *134:* 172; *159:* 57, 58, 164; *197:* 157; *203:* 69, 95; *215:* 38, 39, 40
Chabrian, Debbi *45:* 55
Chabrian, Deborah *51:* 182; *53:* 124; *63:* 107; *75:* 84; *79:* 85; *82:* 247; *89:* 93; *101:* 197; *212:* 13
Chagnon, Mary *37:* 158
Chalmers, Mary *3:* 145; *13:* 148; *33:* 125; *66:* 214
Chamberlain, Christopher *45:* 57
Chamberlain, Margaret *46:* 51; *106:* 89; *188:* 193; *212:* 16, 17
Chamberlain, Nigel *78:* 140
Chambers, C.E. *17:* 230
Chambers, Dave *12:* 151
Chambers, Jill *134:* 110
Chambers, Mary *4:* 188
Chambliss, Maxie *42:* 186; *56:* 159; *93:* 163, 164; *103:* 178; *186:* 33, 34; *196:* 39
Champlin, Dale *136:* 124
Chan, Harvey *96:* 236; *99:* 153; *143:* 218; *179:* 144; *211:* 219
Chan, Peter *207:* 21
Chandler, David P. *28:* 62
Chaney, Howard *139:* 27
Chang, Warren *101:* 209
Chapel, Jody *68:* 20
Chapman, C.H. *13:* 83, 85, 87
Chapman, Frederick T. *6:* 27; *44:* 28
Chapman, Gaye *203:* 133
Chapman, Gaynor *32:* 52, 53
Chapman, Jane *145:* 186; *150:* 56; *166:* 220; *174:* 202; *176:* 43, 44; *179:* 131; *202:* 189; *212:* 20, 21, 22
Chapman, Lynne *175:* 31; *197:* 25; *208:* 44
Chappell, Warren *3:* 172; *21:* 56; *27:* 125
Charles, Donald *30:* 154, 155
Charlip, Remy *4:* 48; *34:* 138; *68:* 53, 54; *119:* 29, 30; *210:* 63, 64
Charlot, Jean *1:* 137, 138; *8:* 23; *14:* 31; *48:* 151; *56:* 21
Charlot, Martin *64:* 72
Charlton, Michael *34:* 50; *37:* 39
Charmatz, Bill *7:* 45
Chartier, Normand *9:* 36; *52:* 49; *66:* 40; *74:* 220; *145:* 169; *168:* 91; *177:* 108
Chase, Lynwood M. *14:* 4
Chast, Roz *97:* 39, 40; *212:* 25
Chastain, Madye Lee *4:* 50
Chateron, Ann *152:* 19
Chatterton, Martin *68:* 102; *152:* 19
Chau, Tungwai *140:* 35
Chauncy, Francis *24:* 158
Chayka, Doug *145:* 97; *177:* 150; *196:* 46; *212:* 58
Chee, Cheng-Khee *79:* 42; *81:* 224; *180:* 245
Chen, Chih-sien *90:* 226
Chen, Tony *6:* 45; *19:* 131; *29:* 126; *34:* 160
Chen, Yong *183:* 34
Cheney, T.A. *11:* 47
Cheng, Andrea *205:* 28
Cheng, Judith *36:* 45; *51:* 16
Chermayeff, Ivan *47:* 53
Cherry, David *93:* 40
Cherry, Lynne *34:* 52; *65:* 184; *87:* 111; *99:* 46, 47
Chesak, Lina *135:* 118
Chess, Victoria *12:* 6; *33:* 42, 48, 49; *40:* 194; *41:* 145; *69:* 80; *72:* 100; *92:* 33, 34; *104:* 167
Chessare, Michele *41:* 50; *56:* 48; *69:* 145
Chesterton, G.K. *27:* 43, 44, 45, 47
Chestnutt, David *47:* 217
Chesworth, Michael *75:* 24, 152; *88:* 136; *94:* 25; *98:* 155; *160:* 42; *207:* 23, 24, 25; *214:* 145
Chetham, Celia *134:* 34
Chetwin, Grace *86:* 40
Cheung, Irving *158:* 96
Chevalier, Christa *35:* 66

Chew, Ruth *7:* 46; *132:* 147
Chewning, Randy *92:* 206
Chichester Clark, Emma *72:* 121; *77:* 212; *78:* 209; *87:* 143; *117:* 37, 39, 40; *144:* 138; *156:* 24, 25; *209:* 26
Chifflart *47:* 113, 127
Child, Lauren *119:* 32; *183:* 30, 31
Chin, Alex *28:* 54
Chitwood, Susan Tanner *163:* 16
Cho, Shinta *8:* 126
Chodos-Irvine, Margaret *52:* 102, 103, 107; *152:* 44
Choi, Yangsook *171:* 134; *173:* 135; *178:* 38, 39, 40
Chollat, Emilie *170:* 203
Chollick, Jay *25:* 175
Choma, Christina *99:* 169
Chomey, Steve *188:* 53
Chorao, Kay *7:* 200, 201; *8:* 25; *11:* 234; *33:* 187; *35:* 239; *69:* 35; *70:* 235; *123:* 174; *193:* 179; *215:* 43, 44, 45, 46
Chow, Frances J. Soo Ping *206:* 36
Chowdhury, Subrata *62:* 130; *162:* 22, 23
Christelow, Eileen *38:* 44; *83:* 198, 199; *90:* 57, 58; *184:* 26
Christensen, Bonnie *93:* 100; *153:* 67; *213:* 29, 30
Christensen, Gardell Dano *1:* 57
Christensen, James C. *140:* 226
Christiana, David *90:* 64; *135:* 13; *171:* 7; *195:* 26, 27
Christiansen, Per *40:* 24
Christie, R. Gregory *116:* 107; *127:* 20, 21; *162:* 179; *164:* 114; *165:* 137; *174:* 157; *179:* 172; *185:* 17, 18, 19; *200:* 2; *204:* 85; *215:* 207
Christy, Howard Chandler *17:* 163, 164, 165, 168, 169; *19:* 186, 187; *21:* 22, 23, 24, 25
Christy, Jana *194:* 21
Chronister, Robert *23:* 138; *63:* 27; *69:* 167
Church, Caroline Jayne *179:* 27
Church, Frederick *YABC 1:* 155
Chute, Marchette *1:* 59
Chwast, Jacqueline *1:* 63; *2:* 275; *6:* 46, 47; *11:* 125; *12:* 202; *14:* 235
Chwast, Seymour *3:* 128, 129; *18:* 43; *27:* 152; *92:* 79; *96:* 56, 57, 58; *146:* 32, 33; *197:* 99
Cieslawksi, Steve *101:* 142; *127:* 116; *158:* 169, 171; *190:* 174; *212:* 85
Cinelli, Lisa *146:* 253
Cirlin, Edgard *2:* 168
Clairin, Georges *53:* 109
Clapp, John *105:* 66; *109:* 58; *126:* 7; *129:* 148; *130:* 165; *195:* 48
Clark, Brenda *119:* 85; *153:* 55
Clark, David *77:* 164; *134:* 144, 145
Clark, Emma Chichester
  See Chichester Clark, Emma
Clark, Victoria *35:* 159
Clarke, Greg *169:* 134; *215:* 47, 115
Clarke, Gus *72:* 226; *134:* 31
Clarke, Harry *23:* 172, 173
Clarke, Peter *75:* 102
Claverie, Jean *38:* 46; *88:* 29
Clavis, Philippe Goossens *182:* 167
Clay, Wil *203:* 29
Clayton, Elaine *159:* 60; *209:* 32
Clayton, Robert *9:* 181
Cleary, Brian P. *186:* 37
Cleaver, Elizabeth *8:* 204; *23:* 36
Cleland, T.M. *26:* 92
Clemens, Peter *61:* 125
Clement, Charles *20:* 38
Clement, Gary *186:* 79; *191:* 32
Clement, Janet *182:* 50
Clement, Nathan *200:* 30
Clement, Rod *97:* 42
Clement, Stephen *88:* 3
Clementson, John *84:* 213
Clemesha, David *192:* 49, 50

Clevin, Jorgen *7:* 50
Clifford, Judy *34:* 163; *45:* 198
Clokey, Art *59:* 44
Clouse, Dennis *187:* 158
Clouse, James *84:* 15
Clouse, Nancy L. *78:* 31; *114:* 90
Clover, Peter *152:* 45
Cneut, Carll *156:* 166; *165:* 67; *197:* 26
Coalson, Glo *9:* 72, 85; *25:* 155; *26:* 42; *35:* 212; *53:* 31; *56:* 154; *94:* 37, 38, 193
Cober, Alan E. *17:* 158; *32:* 77; *49:* 127
Cober-Gentry, Leslie *92:* 111
Cocca-Leffler, Maryann *80:* 46; *136:* 60; *139:* 193; *194:* 31, 33, 34
Cochran, Bobbye *11:* 52
CoConis, Ted *4:* 41; *46:* 41; *51:* 104
Cocozza, Chris *87:* 18; *110:* 173; *111:* 149
Cockroft, Jason *152:* 20
Coerr, Eleanor *1:* 64; *67:* 52
Coes, Peter *35:* 172
Cogancherry, Helen *52:* 143; *69:* 131; *77:* 93; *78:* 220; *109:* 204; *110:* 129; *203:* 92
Coggins, Jack *2:* 69
Cohen, Alix *7:* 53
Cohen, Miriam *155:* 23, 24
Cohen, Nancy R. *165:* 35
Cohen, Santiago *164:* 26; *215:* 52, 199
Cohen, Sheldon *105:* 33, 34; *166:* 46, 47
Cohen, Vincent O. *19:* 243
Cohen, Vivien *11:* 112
Coker, Paul *51:* 172
Colbert, Anthony *15:* 41; *20:* 193
Colby, C.B. *3:* 47
Cole, Babette *58:* 172; *96:* 63, 64; *155:* 29
Cole, Brock *68:* 223; *72:* 36, 37, 38, 192; *127:* 23; *136:* 64, 65; *197:*
Cole, Gwen *87:* 185
Cole, Henry *178:* 120; *181:* 42, 43; *189:* 60; *213:* 35, 36
Cole, Herbert *28:* 104
Cole, Michael *59:* 46
Cole, Olivia H.H. *1:* 134; *3:* 223; *9:* 111; *38:* 104
Cole, Rachael *209:* 39
Colin, Paul *102:* 59; *123:* 118; *126:* 152; *192:* 129
Colley, Jacqui *202:* 20
Collicott, Sharleen *98:* 39; *143:* 29, 30
Collier, Bryan *126:* 54; *151:* 166; *174:* 16, 17, 18; *204:* 18, 19; *208:* 84; *211:* 143
Collier, David *13:* 127
Collier, John *27:* 179; *208:* 154
Collier, Steven *50:* 52
Collier-Morales, Roberta *168:* 61
Collins, Heather *66:* 84; *67:* 68; *81:* 40; *98:* 192, 193; *129:* 95, 96, 98
Collins, Matt *167:* 90
Collins, Ross *140:* 23, 24; *200:* 36, 37; *209:* 54
Colman, Audrey *146:* 161
Colón, Raul *108:* 112; *113:* 5; *117:* 167; *134:* 112; *146:* 23; *159:* 92; *166:* 73; *180:* 107; *186:* 156; *190:* 6; *193:* 24, 205; *202:* 21, 22, 23
Colonna, Bernard *21:* 50; *28:* 103; *34:* 140; *43:* 180; *78:* 150
Comport, Sally Wern *117:* 169; *169:* 104; *190:* 42; *207:* 50
Conahan, Carolyn *215:* 17
Conde, J.M. *100:* 120
Condon, Grattan *54:* 85 Condon, Ken *161:* 44; *195:* 28, 29
Cone, Ferne Geller *39:* 49
Cone, J. Morton *39:* 49
Conklin, Paul *43:* 62
Connelly, Gwen *212:* 30
Connelly, James *198:* 12
Connolly, Howard *67:* 88
Connolly, Jerome P. *4:* 128; *28:* 52
Connolly, Peter *47:* 60
Conoly, Walle *110:* 224

Conover, Chris *31:* 52; *40:* 184; *41:* 51; *44:* 79; *213:* 39
Constantin, Pascale *207:* 159
Contreras, Gerry *72:* 9
Converse, James *38:* 70
Conway *62:* 62
Conway, Michael *69:* 12; *81:* 3; *92:* 108
Cook, Ande *188:* 135
Cook, G.R. *29:* 165
Cook, Joel *108:* 160
Cookburn, W.V. *29:* 204
Cooke, Donald E. *2:* 77
Cooke, Tom *52:* 118
Coomaraswamy, A.K. *50:* 100
Coombs, Charles *43:* 65
Coombs, Deborah *139:* 175
Coombs, Patricia *2:* 82; *3:* 52; *22:* 119; *51:* 32, 33, 34, 35, 36, 37, 38, 39, 40, 42, 43
Cooney, Barbara *6:* 16, 17, 50; *12:* 42; *13:* 92; *15:* 145; *16:* 74, 111; *18:* 189; *23:* 38, 89, 93; *32:* 138; *38:* 105; *59:* 48, 49, 51, 52, 53; *74:* 222; *81:* 100; *91:* 25; *96:* 71, 72, 74; *100:* 149; *YABC2:* 10
Cooper, Elisha *157:* 38, 39
Cooper, Floyd *79:* 95; *81:* 45; *84:* 82; *85:* 74; *91:* 118; *96:* 77, 78; *103:* 149; *144:* 54; *145:* 151; *159:* 198; *176:* 133, 134; *187:* 26, 27, 28, 29; *188:* 22; *199:* 175
Cooper, Heather *50:* 39
Cooper, Helen *102:* 42, 43, 44
Cooper, Mario *24:* 107
Cooper, Marjorie *7:* 112
Cope, Jane *61:* 201; *108* 52
Copeland, Mark *180:* 12
Copelman, Evelyn *8:* 61; *18:* 25
Copley, Heather *30:* 86; *45:* 57
Corace, Jen *208:* 48
Corbett, Grahame *30:* 114; *43:* 67
Corbino, John *19:* 248
Corcos, Lucille *2:* 223; *10:* 27; *34:* 66
Cordell, Matthew *197:* 93; *199:* 20, 21
Corey, Robert *9:* 34
Corlass, Heather *10:* 7
Cornell, James *27:* 60
Cornell, Jeff *11:* 58
Cornell, Laura *94:* 179; *95:* 25
Corr, Christopher *204:* 98
Corral, Ridrigs *212:* 87
Corrigan, Barbara *8:* 37
Corrigan, Patrick *145:* 149
Corwin, Judith Hoffman *10:* 28
Corwin, Oliver *191:* 119
Cory, Fanny Y. *20:* 113; *48:* 29
Cosentino, Ralph *169:* 32
Cosgrove, Margaret *3:* 100; *47:* 63; *82:* 133
Costabel, Eva Deutsch *45:* 66, 67
Costanza, John *58:* 7, 8, 9
Costello, Chris *86:* 78
Costello, David F. *23:* 55
Côté, Geneviéve *184:* 37, 39; *210:* 256; *211:* 151
Cote, Nancy *126:* 139; *156:* 101; *174:* 101; *182:* 53, 54, 55
Cottenden, Jeff *190:* 45
Couch, Greg *94:* 124; *110:* 13; *162:* 31; *168:* 149; *199:* 22
Councell, Ruth Tietjen *79:* 29
Courtney, Cathy *58:* 69, 144; *59:* 15; *61:* 20, 87
Courtney, R. *35:* 110
Counihan, Claire *133:* 106
Cousineau, Normand *89:* 180; *112:* 76
Cousins, Lucy *172:* 53, 54; *205:* 34, 35
Couture, Christin *41:* 209
Covarrubias, Miguel *35:* 118, 119, 123, 124, 125
Coville, Katherine *32:* 57; *36:* 167; *92:* 38
Covington, Neverne *113:* 87
Cowdrey, Richard *169:* 170; *178:* 205; *204:* 22, 23; *215:* 31
Cowell, Cressida *140:* 39

Cowell, Lucinda *77:* 54
Cowles, Rose *203:* 164, 167
Cox *43:* 93
Cox, Charles *8:* 20
Cox, David *56:* 37; *90:* 63; *119:* 38
Cox, Palmer *24:* 76, 77
Cox, Steve *140:* 96
Coxe, Molly *69:* 44
Coxon, Michele *158:* 80
Crabb, Gordon *70:* 39
Crabtree, Judith *98:* 42
Craft, Kinuko *22:* 182; *36:* 220; *53:* 122, 123, 148,149; *74:* 12; *81:* 129; *86:* 31; *89:* 139; *127:* 27, 28, 29; *132:* 142; *139:* 38
Craig, Daniel *177:* 67; *180:* 11; *185:* 203; *211:* 212
Craig, David *136:* 198; *205:* 37
Craig, Helen *49:* 76; *62:* 70, 71, 72; *69:* 141; *94:* 42, 43, 44; *112:* 53; *135:* 101, 102; *213:* 45, 46, 47, 55, 81, 82
Crane, Alan H. *1:* 217
Crane, H.M. *13:* 111
Crane, Jack *43:* 183
Crane, Jordan *174:* 21
Crane, Walter *18:* 46, 47, 48, 49, 53, 54, 56, 57, 59, 60, 61; *22:* 128; *24:* 210, 217; *100:* 70, 71
Cravath, Lynne W. *98:* 45; *182:* 58, 59
Crawford, Allen *212:* 181
Crawford, Denise *137:* 213
Crawford, Will *43:* 77
Credle, Ellis *1:* 69
Czernecki, Stefan *154:* 104; *178:* 68, 69
Crespi, Francesca *87:* 90
Cressy, Michael *124:* 55; *203:* 132
Crews, Donald *32:* 59, 60; *76:* 42, 43, 44
Crews, Nina *97:* 49
Crichlow, Ernest *74:* 88; *83:* 203
Crilley, Mark *210:* 71
Croft, James *150:* 57
Crofut, Bob *80:* 87; *81:* 47
Crofut, Susan *23:* 61
Croll, Carolyn *80:* 137; *102:* 52
Cross, Peter *56:* 78; *63:* 60, 65
Crowe, Elizabeth *88:* 144
Crowell, Pers *3:* 125
Cruikshank, George *15:* 76, 83; *22:* 74, 75, 76, 77, 78, 79,80, 81, 82, 84, 137; *24:* 22, 23
Crump, Fred H. *11:* 62
Cruz, Ray *6:* 55; *70:* 234; *123:* 173; *172:* 192
Csatari, Joe *44:* 82; *55:* 152; *63:* 25, 28; *102:* 58
Cuetara, Mittie *158:* 85
Cuffari, Richard *4:* 75; *5:* 98; *6:* 56; *7:* 13,84, 153; *8:* 148, 155; *9:* 89; *11:* 12, 55, 96,114; *15:* 51, 202; *18:* 5; *20:* 139; *21:* 197; *22:* 14, 192; *23:* 15, 106; *25:* 97; *27:* 133; *28:* 196; *29:* 54; *30:* 85; *31:* 35; *36:* 101; *38:* 171; *42:* 97; *44:* 92, 192; *45:* 212, 213; *46:* 36, 198; *50:* 164; *54:* 80, 136, 137, 145; *56:* 17; *60:* 63; *66:* 49, 50; *70:* 41; *71:* 132; *77:* 157; *78:* 58, 149; *79:* 120; *85:* 2, 152
Cugat, Xavier *19:* 120
Cumings, Art *35:* 160
Cummings, Chris *29:* 167
Cummings, Michael *159:* 142
Cummings, Pat *42:* 61; *61:* 99; *69:* 205; *71:* 57,58; *78:* 24, 25; *93:* 75; *107:* 49, 50; *164:* 259; *203:* 45, 46
Cummings, Richard *24:* 119
Cunette, Lou *20:* 93; *22:* 125
Cunningham, Aline *25:* 180
Cunningham, David *11:* 13
Cunningham, Imogene *16:* 122, 127
Cunningham, Kelley *176:* 159
Cupples, Pat *107:* 12; *126:* 109; *182:* 13; *198:* 68
Curlee, Lynn *98:* 48; *141:* 39; *190:* 48
Currey, Anna *190:* 145; *202:* 130, 132
Curry, John Steuart *2:* 5; *19:* 84; *34:* 36; *144:* 126

Curry, Tom *127:* 131; *185:* 25, 26
Curtis, Bruce *23:* 96; *30:* 88; *36:* 22
Curtis, Neil *167:* 30
Curtis, Stacy *205:* 38
Cusack, Margaret *58:* 49, 50, 51
Cushman, Doug *65:* 57; *101:* 39, 40; *133:* 179; *157:* 45; *186:* 157; *210:* 76, 77
Cutting, Ann *196:* 194
Cyrus, Kurt *132:* 39; *179:* 36, 37
Czechowski, Alicia *95:* 21; *171:* 37
Czernecki, Stefan *117:* 173

D

Dabcovich, Lydia *25:* 105; *40:* 114; *99:* 75, 76
Dacey, Bob *82:* 175; *152:* 65
d'Achille, Gino *127:* 175, 176
Dailey, Don *78:* 197
Dain, Martin J. *35:* 75
Dale, Penny *127:* 224; *151:* 57; *160:* 89; *197:* 75
Dale, Rae *72:* 197
Daley, Joann *50:* 22
Dalton, Anne *40:* 62; *63:* 119
Daly, Deborah M. *74:* 213
Daly, Jim *103:* 60; *150:* 48
Daly, Jude *138:* 118, 119; *213:* 41
Daly, Nicholas *37:* 53; *76:* 48, 49
Daly, Niki *107:* 15; *114:* 38, 39, 40; *164:* 86; *192:* 53; *198:* 26, 27
Daly, Paul *97:* 205
Dalziel, Brothers *33:* 113
D'Amato, Alex *9:* 48; *20:* 25
D'Amato, Janet *9:* 48; *20:* 25; *26:* 118
D'Amico, Steve *170:* 52
Danalis, Johnny *167:* 27
D'Andrea, Domenick *183:* 108
Daniel, Alan *23:* 59; *29:* 110; *76:* 50, 53, 55, 56; *153:* 76 *115:* 74; *134:* 70
Daniel, Lea *76:* 53, 55; *153:* 76
Daniel, Lewis C. *20:* 216
Daniels, Beau *73:* 4
Daniels, Steve *22:* 16
Daniels, Stewart *56:* 12
Dann, Bonnie *31:* 83
Dann, Penny *82:* 128
Danska, Herbert *24:* 219
Dardik, Helen *208:* 200
Danyell, Alice *20:* 27
Darley, F.O.C. *16:* 145; *19:* 79, 86, 88, 185; *21:* 28,36; *35:* 76, 77, 78, 79, 80, 81; *YABC 2:* 175
Darling, Lois *3:* 59; *23:* 30, 31
Darling, Louis *1:* 40, 41; *2:* 63; *3:* 59; *23:* 30,31; *43:* 54, 57, 59; *121:* 53
Darnell, K.L. *210:* 247
Darrow, David R. *84:* 101
Darrow, Whitney, Jr. *13:* 25; *38:* 220, 221
Darwin, Beatrice *43:* 54
Darwin, Len *24:* 82
Dastolfo, Frank *33:* 179
Dauber, Liz *1:* 22; *3:* 266; *30:* 49
Daugherty, James *3:* 66; *8:* 178; *13:* 27, 28, 161; *18:* 101; *19:* 72; *29:* 108; *32:* 156; *42:* 84; *YABC 1:* 256; *2:* 174
d'Aulaire, Edgar Parin *5:* 51; *66:* 53
d'Aulaire, Ingri Parin *5:* 51; *66:* 53
Davalos, Felipe *99:* 197; *159:* 66; *174:* 163
Davenier, Christine *125:* 88; *127:* 32; *128:* 152; *179:* 39, 40
Davick, Linda *151:* 124; *208:* 187
David, Jacques-Louis *193:* 22
David, Jonathan *19:* 37
Davidson, Kevin *28:* 154
Davidson, Raymond *32:* 61
Davie, Helen K. *77:* 48, 49
Davies, Andy Robert *205:* 169
Davies, Lottie *214:* 69

Davis, Allen *20:* 11; *22:* 45; *27:* 222; *29:* 157; *41:* 99; *47:* 99; *50:* 84; *52:* 105
Davis, Bette J. *15:* 53; *23:* 95
Davis, Dimitris *45:* 95
Davis, Eleanor *209:* 33
Davis, Hendon *151:* 122
Davis, Jack E. *145:* 139; *175:* 84, 85; *208:* 102; *210:* 81, 82; *213:* 151
Davis, Jim *32:* 63, 64
Davis, Katie *152:* 52, 53, 54; *208:* 52
Davis, Lambert *110:* 23, 24; *176:* 58
Davis, Marguerite *31:* 38; *34:* 69, 70; *100:* 34; *YABC 1:* 126, 230
Davis, Nelle *69:* 191
Davis, Paul *78:* 214
Davis, Rich *206:* 38
Davis, Stuart *211:* 69
Davis, Yvonne LeBrun *94:* 144
Davisson, Virginia H. *44:* 178
DaVolls, Andy *85:* 53
Dawson, Diane *24:* 127; *42:* 126; *52:* 130; *68:* 104
Dawson, Janine *215:* 198
Dawson, Willow *208:* 54
Day, Alexandra *67:* 59; *97:* 54; *166:* 65; *169:* 40; *197:* 50, 51, 52, 54
Day, Larry *169:* 88; *185:* 59
Day, Rob *94:* 110; *127:* 24; *197:* 32
Dean, Bob *19:* 211
Dean, David *192:* 55
de Angeli, Marguerite *1:* 77; *27:* 62, 65, 66, 67, 69, 70, 72; *100:* 75, 76; *YABC 1:* 166
DeArmond, Dale *70:* 47
Deas, Michael *27:* 219, 221; *30:* 156; *67:* 134; *72:* 24; *75:* 155; *84:* 206; *88:* 124
Deas, Rich *191:* 87; *193:* 10; *212:* 79
deBarros, Jim *196:* 60
Debon, Nicolas *151:* 60; *177:* 46
de Bosschere, Jean *19:* 252; *21:* 4; *186:* 44, 45
De Bruyn, M(onica) G. *13:* 30, 31
Decker, C.B. *172:* 120; *215:* 94
De Cuir, John F. *1:* 28, 29
Deeter, Catherine *74:* 110; *103:* 150; *137:* 50
Degen, Bruce *40:* 227, 229; *57:* 28, 29; *56:* 156; *75:* 229; *76:* 19; *81:* 36, 37; *92:* 26; *93:* 199; *97:* 56, 58, 59; *124:* 40; *147:* 39, 40, 41; *168:* 23; *205:* 45, 46
De Grazia *14:* 59; *39:* 56, 57
DeGrazio, George *88:* 40
deGroat, Diane *9:* 39; *18:* 7; *23:* 123; *28:* 200, 201; *31:* 58, 59; *34:* 151; *41:* 152; *43:* 88; *46:* 40, 200; *49:* 163; *50:* 89; *52:* 30, 34; *54:* 43; *63:* 5; *70:* 136; *71:* 99; *73:* 117,156; *77:* 34; *85:* 48; *86:* 201; *87:* 142; *90:* 72, 73, 143; *95:* 182; *111:* 123; *118:* 160; *126:* 8; *130:* 130; *138:* 93, 94; *169:* 46, 47
de Groot, Lee *6:* 21
Deines, Brian *110:* 139
DeJohn, Marie *89:* 78
Dekhteryov, B. *61:* 158
de Kiefte, Kees *94:* 107
Delacre, Lulu *36:* 66; *156:* 35; *202:* 10, 53; *209:* 36
Delaney, A. *21:* 78
Delaney, Michael *180:* 16
Delaney, Molly *80:* 43
Delaney, Ned *28:* 68; *56:* 80; *102:* 11
DeLapine, Jim *79:* 21
De La Roche Saint Andre, Anne *75:* 37
de Larrea, Victoria *6:* 119, 204; *29:* 103; *72:* 203; *87:* 199
DeLeon, Melanie *210:* 43
Delessert, Étienne *7:* 140; *46:* 61, 62, 63, 65, 67, 68; *130:* 38, 39, 40, 41, 42; *179:* 46, 47, 48, 49; *YABC 2:* 209
Delezenne, Christine *186:* 126
Del Negro, Janice *196:* 161
DeLorenzo, Christopher *154:* 149
Delulio, John *15:* 54
DeLuna, Tony *88:* 95

Demarest, Chris L. *45:* 68, 69, 70; *73:* 172, 173, 176; *78:* 106; *82:* 48, 49; *89:* 212; *92:* 86; *128:* 57, 58; *175:* 46, 48
De Mejo, Oscar *40:* 67
De Muth, Roger *205:* 184
Demi *11:* 135; *15:* 245; *66:* 129, 130; *89:* 216; *102:* 66, 67, 68; *210:* 86, 87, 89
Denetsosie, Hoke *13:* 126; *82:* 34
Denise, Christopher *147:* 43, 44; *176:* 101; *193:* 35, 36, 37; *201:* 37
Dennis, Morgan *18:* 68, 69; *64:* 89
Dennis, Wesley *2:* 87; *3:* 111; *11:* 132; *18:* 71, 72, 73, 74; *22:* 9; *24:* 196, 200; *46:* 178; *69:* 94, 96; *129:* 62
Denos, Julia *202:* 26
Denslow, W.W. *16:* 84, 85, 86, 87; *18:* 19, 20, 24; *29:* 211; *100:* 21
Denton, Kady MacDonald *110:* 82; *130:* 70; *181:* 54, 55, 56; *192:* 75
Denton, Terry *72:* 163; *174:* 26; *186:* 52; *196:* 83, 84
DePalma, Mary Newell *132:* 114; *139:* 75; *185:* 30, 31; *186:* 121; *213:* 62
dePaola, Tomie *8:* 95; *9:* 93; *11:* 69; *25:* 103; *28:* 157; *29:* 80; *39:* 52, 53; *40:* 226; *46:* 187; *59:* 61, 62, 63, 64, 65, 66, 67, 68, 69, 71, 72, 74; *62:* 19; *108:* 63, 67, 68, 70; *155:* 62, 64, 66; *180:* 105; *200:* 47, 48, 49, 50
Deraney, Michael J. *77:* 35; *78:* 148
deRosa, Dee *70:* 48; *71:* 210; *91:* 78
Dervaux, Isabelle *111:* 117
DeSaix, Deborah Durland *180:* 15; *188:* 24
De Saulles, Tony *119:* 39
de Seve, Peter *146:* 261; *207:* 78
Deshaprabhu, Meera Dayal *86:* 192
Desimini, Lisa *86:* 68; *94:* 47; *96:* 7; *104:* 107; *125:* 194; *131:* 180; *172:* 56
de St. Menin, Charles *70:* 17
Detmold, Edward J. *22:* 104, 105, 106, 107; *35:* 120; *64:* 5; *YABC 2:* 203
Detrich, Susan *20:* 133
Deutermann, Diana *77:* 175
DeVelasco, Joseph E. *21:* 51
de Veyrac, Robert *YABC 2:* 19
DeVille, Edward A. *4:* 235
de Visser, John *55:* 119
Devito, Bert *12:* 164
Devlin, Harry *11:* 74; *74:* 63, 65; *136:* 77, 78
Dewan, Ted *108:* 73; *157:* 55; *165:* 129
Dewar, Nick *133:* 122
Dewdney, Anna *184:* 43, 44
Dewey, Ariane *7:* 64; *33:* 195; *35:* 208; *68:* 16,17; *75:* 46; *93:* 91; *94:* 197; *109:* 65, 66, 67; *125:* 2, 3, 4, 5; *127:* 188; *143:* 25; *178:* 17, 19, 74; *188:* 166; *202:* 164
Dewey, Jennifer (Owings) *58:* 54; *64:* 214; *65:* 207; *88:* 169; *103:* 45
Dewey, Kenneth *39:* 62; *51:* 23; *56:* 163
de Zanger, Arie *30:* 40
Diakité, Baba Wagué *174:* 28
Diamond, Donna *21:* 200; *23:* 63; *26:* 142; *35:* 83, 84, 85, 86, 87, 88, 89; *38:* 78; *40:* 147; *44:* 152; *50:* 144; *53:* 126; *69:* 46, 47, 48, 201; *71:* 133; *123:* 19
Dias, Ron *71:* 67
Diaz, David *80:* 213; *96:* 83, 84; *108:* 228; *110:* 29; *149:* 106; *150:* 63; *179:* 160; *184:* 95, 97; *189:* 51, 52, 53
Dibley, Glin *138:* 83; *141:* 128; *211:* 162
DiCesare, Joe *70:* 38; *71:* 63, 106; *79:* 214; *93:* 147; *116:* 217; *143:* 111; *166:* 57
Dick, John Henry *8:* 181
Dickens, Frank *34:* 131
Dickey, Robert L. *15:* 279
Dickson, Mora *84:* 21
Didier, Sam *166:* 114
Dietz, James *128:* 223; *193:* 136
di Fate, Vincent *37:* 70; *90:* 11; *93:* 60; *109:* 219, 220
Di Fiori, Lawrence *10:* 51; *12:* 190; *27:* 97; *40:* 219; *93:* 57; *130:* 45

Digby, Desmond *97:* 180
Dignan, James *196:* 143
Di Grazia, Thomas *32:* 66; *35:* 241
Dillard, Annie *10:* 32
Dillard, Sarah *136:* 186
Dillon, Corinne B. *1:* 139
Dillon, Diane *4:* 104, 167; *6:* 23; *13:* 29; *15:* 99; *26:* 148; *27:* 136, 201; *51:* 29, 48, 51, 52, 53, 54,55, 56, 57, 58, 59, 60, 61, 62; *54:* 155; *56:* 69; *58:* 127,128; *61:* 95; *62:* 27; *64:* 46; *68:* 3; *69:* 209; *74:* 89; *79:* 92; *86:* 89; *92:* 28, 177; *93:* 7, 210; *94:* 239, 240; *97:* 167; *106:* 58, 59,61, 64; *107:* 3; *139:* 246; *167:* 77; *189:* 202; *191:* 191; *194:* 45, 46, 48, 49
Dillon, Leo *4:* 104, 167; *6:* 23; *13:* 29; *15:* 99; *26:* 148; *27:* 136, 201; *51:* 29, 48, 51, 52, 53, 54,55, 56, 57, 58, 59, 60, 61, 62; *54:* 155; *56:* 69; *58:* 127,128; *61:* 95; *62:* 27; *64:* 46; *68:* 3; *69:* 209; *74:* 89; *79:* 92; *86:* 89; *92:* 28, 177; *93:* 7, 210; *94:* 239, 240; *97:* 167; *106:* 58, 59,61, 64; *107:* 3; *139:* 246; *167:* 77; *189:* 202; *191:* 191; *194:* 45, 46, 48, 49
Dillon, Sharon Saseen *59:* 179, 188
DiMaccio, Gerald *121:* 80
DiMaggio, Joe *36:* 22
DiMassi, Gina *169:* 17
Dinan, Carol *25:* 169; *59:* 75
Dines, Glen *7:* 66, 67
Dinesen, Thomas *44:* 37
Dinh, Pham Viet *167:* 184
Dinnerstein, Harvey *42:* 63, 64, 65, 66, 67, 68; *50:* 146
Dinsdale, Mary *10:* 65; *11:* 171
Dinyer, Eric *86:* 148; *109:* 163; *110:* 239; *124:* 11; *150:* 69; *170:* 4; *171:* 30
Dion, Nathalie *170:* 124; *213:* 52
DiRocco, Carl *181:* 23
DiSalvo-Ryan, DyAnne *59:* 77; *62:* 185; *117:* 46; *144:* 64; *150:* 153; *186:* 162
Disney, Walt *28:* 71, 72, 73, 76, 77, 78, 79, 80, 81, 87, 88, 89,90, 91, 94
DiTerlizzi, Tony *105:* 7; *147:* 22; *154:* 31, 32, 33; *214:* 74
Divito, Anna *83:* 159
Dixon, Don *74:* 17; *109:* 196
Dixon, Larry *127:* 125
Dixon, Maynard *20:* 165
Doares, Robert G. *20:* 39
Dob, Bob *205:* 14
Dobias, Frank *22:* 162
Dobrin, Arnold *4:* 68
Dobson, Steven Gaston *102:* 103
Dockray, Tracy *139:* 77
Docktor, Irv *43:* 70
Dodd, Ed *4:* 69
Dodd, Emma *203:* 57
Dodd, Julie *74:* 73
Dodd, Lynley *35:* 92; *86:* 71; *132:* 45, 46, 47
Dodge, Bill *96:* 736; *118:* 7, 8, 9; *133:* 135
Dodgson, Charles L. *20:* 148; *33:* 146; *YABC 2:* 98
Dodson, Bert *9:* 138; *14:* 195; *42:* 55; *54:* 8; *60:* 49; *101:* 125
Dodson, Liz Brenner *105:* 117; *111:* 15
Dohanos, Stevan *16:* 10
Dolce, J. Ellen *74:* 147; *75:* 41
Dolch, Marguerite P. *50:* 64
Dolesch, Susanne *34:* 49
Dollar, Diane *57:* 32
Dolobowsky, Mena *81:* 54
Dolson, Hildegarde *5:* 57
Domanska, Janina *6:* 66, 67; *YABC 1:* 166
Domi *134:* 113
Dominguez, El *53:* 94
Domjan, Joseph *25:* 93
Domm, Jeffrey C. *84:* 69; *135:* 70
Donahey, William *68:* 209
Donahue, Dorothy *76:* 170
Donahue, Vic *2:* 93; *3:* 190; *9:* 44

Donald, Elizabeth *4:* 18
Donalty, Alison *149:* 195, 196, 197
Donato *85:* 59; *149:* 204; *191:* 19
Donato, Michael A. *200:* 143
Doner, Kim *208:* 57
Doney, Todd L.W. *87:* 12; *93:* 112; *98:* 135; *101:* 57; *104:* 40; *118:* 163; *135:* 162, 163; *151:* 18
Donna, Natalie *9:* 52
Donohue, Dorothy *95:* 2; *132:* 30; *176:* 54, 55; *178:* 77, 78, 79
Dooling, Michael *82:* 19; *105:* 55; *106:* 224; *125:* 135; *171:* 46; *172:* 12; *176:* 120; *197:* 89
Doran, Ben-Ami *128:* 189
Doran, Colleen *211:* 48
Dore, Gustave *18:* 169, 172, 175; *19:* 93, 94, 95, 96, 97, 98,99, 100, 101, 102, 103, 104, 105; *23:* 188; *25:* 197, 199
Doremus, Robert *6:* 62; *13:* 90; *30:* 95, 96, 97; *38:* 97
Dorfman, Ronald *11:* 128
Doriau *86:* 59; *91:* 152
Dorman, Brandon *197:* 35; *204:* 6; *210:* 104; *212:* 95
Dormer, Frank W. *200:* 55
Dorros, Arthur *78:* 42, 43; *91:* 28
Doruyter, Karel *165:* 105
dos Santos, Joyce Audy *57:* 187, 189
Doty, Roy *28:* 98; *31:* 32; *32:* 224; *46:* 157; *82:* 71; *142:* 7
Doucet, Bob *132:* 238; *169:* 159
Dougherty, Charles *16:* 204; *18:* 74
Doughty, Rebecca *177:* 174
Doughty, Thomas *118:* 31; *140:* 60
Douglas, Aaron *31:* 103
Douglas, Carole Nelson *73:* 48
Douglas, Goray *13:* 151
Dow, Brian *150:* 92
Dowd, Jason *132:* 51, 52; *164:* 244
Dowd, Vic *3:* 244; *10:* 97
Dowden, Anne Ophelia *7:* 70, 71; *13:* 120
Dowdy, Mrs. Regera *29:* 100
Downard, Barry *202:* 32
Downes, Belinda *180:* 29
Downing, Julie *60:* 140; *81:* 50; *86:* 200; *99:* 129
Doyle, Janet *56:* 31
Doyle, Richard *21:* 31, 32, 33; *23:* 231; *24:* 177; *31:* 87
Draper, Angie *43:* 84
Drath, Bill *26:* 34
Drawson, Blair *17:* 53; *126:* 65
Dray, Matt *177:* 47
Drescher, Henrik *105:* 60, 62, 63; *172:* 72
Drescher, Joan *30:* 100, 101; *35:* 245; *52:* 168; *137:* 52
Dressell, Peggy *186:* 41
Drew, Janet *201:* 177
Drew, Patricia *15:* 100
Dronzek, Laura *199:* 28, 29; *207:* 69
Drummond, Allan *209:* 41
Drummond, V.H. *6:* 70
Drury, Christian Potter *105:* 97; *186:* 224
Dubanevich, Arlene *56:* 44
Dubin, Jill *205:* 56
Dubois, Claude K. *196:* 2
Dubois, Gerard *182:* 9
DuBurke, Randy *187:* 89
Ducak, Danilo *99:* 130; *108:* 214
Duchesne, Janet *6:* 162; *79:* 8
Duda, Jana *102:* 155; *209:* 134
Dudash, C. Michael *32:* 122; *77:* 134; *82:* 149; *212:* 93, 94
Duer, Douglas *34:* 177
Duewell, Kristina *195:* 76
Duffy, Daniel Mark *76:* 37; *101:* 196; *108:* 147, 148
Duffy, Joseph *38:* 203
Duffy, Pat *28:* 153
Dugan, Karen *181:* 26; *202:* 35

Dugin, Andrej *77:* 60
Dugina, Olga *77:* 60
Duke, Chris *8:* 195; *139:* 164
Duke, Kate *87:* 186; *90:* 78, 79, 80, 81; *192:* 21, 59, 60, 61, 63
Duke, Marion *165:* 87
Dulac, Edmund *19:* 108, 109, 110, 111, 112, 113, 114, 115, 117; *23:* 187; *25:* 152; *YABC 1:* 37; *2:* 147
Dulac, Jean *13:* 64
Dumas, Philippe *52:* 36, 37, 38, 39, 40, 41, 42, 43, 45; *119:* 40, 41, 42
Dunaway, Nancy *108:* 161
Dunbar, James *76:* 63
Dunbar, Polly *181:* 60, 61; *211:* 51, 52, 53; *212:* 42
Duncan, Beverly *72:* 92
Duncan, John *116:* 94
Dunn, H.T. *62:* 196
Dunn, Harvey *34:* 78, 79, 80, 81
Dunn, Iris *5:* 175
Dunn, Phoebe *5:* 175
Dunne, Jeanette *72:* 57, 173, 222
Dunnick, Regan *176:* 51; *178:* 83, 84
Dunnington, Tom *3:* 36; *18:* 281; *25:* 61; *31:* 159; *35:* 168; *48:* 195; *79:* 144; *82:* 230
Dunn-Ramsey, Marcy *117:* 131
Dunrea, Olivier *59:* 81; *118:* 53, 54; *124:* 43
Duntze, Dorothee *88:* 28; *160:* 76
Dupasquier, Philippe *86:* 75; *104:* 76; *151:* 63
duPont, Lindsay Harper *207:* 39
DuQuette, Keith *90:* 83; *155:* 73, 74
Durand, Delphine *200:* 56
Durham, Sarah *192:* 248
Durney, Ryan *208:* 122
Duroussy, Nathalie *146:* 150
Durrell, Julie *82:* 62; *94:* 62
Dutz *6:* 59
Duvoisin, Roger *2:* 95; *6:* 76, 77; *7:* 197; *28:* 125; *30:* 101, 102, 103, 104, 105, 107; *47:* 205; *84:* 254
Dyer, Dale *141:* 71
Dyer, Jane *75:* 219; *129:* 28; *147:* 49, 50, 51; *168:* 121; *190:* 4; *191:* 57, 59, 60; *203:* 4
Dyer, Sarah *212:* 40
Dypold, Pat *15:* 37

E

E.V.B.
　See Boyle, Eleanor Vere (Gordon)
Eachus, Jennifer *29:* 74; *82:* 201; *164:* 153
Eadie, Bob *63:* 36
Eagle, Bruce *95:* 119
Eagle, Ellen *82:* 121; *89:* 3
Eagle, Jeremy *141:* 71
Eagle, Michael *11:* 86; *20:* 9; *23:* 18; *27:* 122; *28:* 57; *34:* 201; *44:* 189; *73:* 9; *78:* 235; *85:* 43
Earl-Bridges, Michele *159:* 128
Earle, Edwin *56:* 27
Earle, Olive L. *7:* 75
Earle, Vana *27:* 99
Earley, Lori *132:* 2; *186:* 4; *195:* 8
Early, Margaret *72:* 59
East, Stella *131:* 223
Eastman, P.D. *33:* 57
Easton, Reginald *29:* 181
Eaton, Tom *4:* 62; *6:* 64; *22:* 99; *24:* 124
Ebbeler, Jeffrey *193:* 62; *206:* 45
Ebel, Alex *11:* 89
Eberbach, Andrea *192:* 115
Ebert, Len *9:* 191; *44:* 47
Echevarria, Abe *37:* 69
Echo Hawk, Bunky *187:* 192
Eckersley, Maureen *48:* 62
Eckert, Horst *72:* 62
Ede, Janina *33:* 59
Edens, Cooper *49:* 81, 82, 83, 84, 85; *112:* 58

Edens, John *109:* 115
Edgar, Sarah E. *41:* 97
Edgerton, Perky *195:* 144
Edliq, Emily S. *131:* 107
Edrien *11:* 53
Edwards, Freya *45:* 102
Edwards, George Wharton *31:* 155
Edwards, Gunvor *2:* 71; *25:* 47; *32:* 71; *54:* 106
Edwards, Jeanne *29:* 257
Edwards, Linda Strauss *21:* 134; *39:* 123; *49:* 88, 89
Edwards, Michelle *152:* 62, 63
Edwards, Wallace *170:* 55
Egan, Tim *155:* 76, 77, 78
Egge, David *102:* 71
Eggenhofer, Nicholas *2:* 81
Eggleton, Bob *74:* 40; *81:* 190, 191; *105:* 6; *121:* 183; *149:* 203; *166:* 215
Egielski, Richard *11:* 90; *16:* 208; *33:* 236; *38:* 35; *49:* 91, 92, 93, 95, 212, 213, 214, 216; *79:* 122; *106:* 67, 68, 69; *134:* 135; *144:* 244; *163:* 82, 84; *207:* 125
Ehlert, Lois *35:* 97; *69:* 51; *112:* 7; *113:* 208; *128:* 63, 64, 65; *172:* 77, 79, 80
Ehrlich, Bettina *1:* 83
Eitan, Ora *160:* 165
Eichenberg, Fritz *1:* 79; *9:* 54; *19:* 248; *23:* 170; *24:* 200; *26:* 208; *50:* 67, 68, 69, 70, 71, 72, 73,74, 75, 77, 79, 80, 81; *60:* 165; *100:* 137; *YABC 1:* 104, 105; *2:* 213
Einsel, Naiad *10:* 35; *29:* 136
Einsel, Walter *10:* 37
Einzig, Susan *3:* 77; *43:* 78; *67:* 155; *129:* 154
Eisner, Will *165:* 82, 83
Eitzen, Allan *9:* 56; *12:* 212; *14:* 226; *21:* 194; *38:* 162; *76:* 218
Eldridge, H. *54:* 109
Eldridge, Harold *43:* 83
Elgaard, Greta *19:* 241
Elgin, Kathleen *9:* 188; *39:* 69
Ellacott, S.E. *19:* 118
Elliot, David *192:* 26; *208:* 62, 63
Elliott, Mark *93:* 69; *105:* 108; *107:* 123; *140:* 53; *165:* 189; *173:* 67; *195:* 95; *203:* 67; *210:* 99
Elliott, Sarah M. *14:* 58
Ellis, Dianne *130:* 208
Ellis, Jan Davey *88:* 50; *115:* 80
Ellis, Richard *130:* 47, 48
Ellison, Chris *196:* 66; *199:* 131; *207:* 193
Ellison, Pauline *55:* 21
Ellwand, David *213:* 60
Elmer, Richard *78:* 5
Elmore, Larry *90:* 8
Elschner, Géraldine *183:* 38
Elwell, Peter *195:* 150
Elwell, Tristan *110:* 39; *121:* 182; *127:* 46; *137:* 144; *141:* 173; *151:* 236; *158:* 264; *167:* 119, 120, 121; *169:* 20; *190:* 12; *202:* 16
Elzbieta *88:* 80, 81
Ember, Kathi *214:* 147
Emberley, Ed *8:* 53; *70:* 53, 54; *146:* 65, 69, 70
Emberley, Michael *34:* 83; *80:* 72; *119:* 47, 48; *147:* 100; *158:* 115; *189:* 62, 64; *203:* 87, 89
Emerling, Dorothy *104:* 27
Emery, Leslie *49:* 187
Emmett, Bruce *49:* 147; *80:* 175; *101:* 206
Emry-Perrott, Jennifer *61:* 57
Emshwiller, Ed *174:* 45
Endle, Kate *191:* 167; *207:* 41
Engel, Diana *70:* 57
Engle, Mort *38:* 64
Englebert, Victor *8:* 54
English, Mark *101:* 207
Enik, Ted *142:* 39
Enos, Randall *20:* 183

Enright, Maginel Wright *19:* 240, 243; *39:* 31, 35, 36
Enrique, Romeo *34:* 135
Ensor, Barbara *180:* 30
Epstein, Stephen *50:* 142, 148
Erdogan, Buket *174:* 179
Erdrich, Louise *141:* 62
Erhard, Walter *1:* 152
Erickson, Jim *196:* 190
Erickson, Phoebe *11:* 83; *59:* 85
Erikson, Mel *31:* 69
Eriksson, Eva *63:* 88, 90, 92, 93; *203:* 99; *207:* 44
Ering, Timothy Basil *131:* 100; *176:* 63, 64; *202:* 29; *204:* 8
Erlbruch, Wolf *181:* 66
Ernst, Lisa Campbell *47:* 147; *95:* 47; *154:* 46, 47, 48; *164:* 88; *212:* 45
Esco, Jo *61:* 103
Escourido, Joseph *4:* 81
Escrivá, Viví *119:* 51; *181:* 36
Essakalli, Julie Klear *200:* 58
Este, Kirk *33:* 111
Estep, David *73:* 57
Estes, Eleanor *91:* 66
Estoril, Jean *32:* 27
Estrada, Pau *74:* 76
Estrada, Ric *5:* 52, 146; *13:* 174
Etchemendy, Teje *38:* 68
Etheredges, the *73:* 12
Etienne, Kirk-Albert *145:* 184
Ets, Marie Hall *2:* 102
Ettlinger, Doris *171:* 98; *186:* 106; *197:* 126; *214:* 125
Eulalie *YABC 2:* 315
Evangelista, Theresa M. *213:* 67
Evans, Greg *73:* 54, 55, 56; *143:* 40, 41
Evans, Katherine *5:* 64
Evans, Leslie *144:* 227; *207:* 57; *214:* 88
Evans, Shane W. *159:* 142; *160:* 190; *168:* 39; *188:* 88; *189:* 66, 67, 68
Everitt, Betsy *151:* 110
Ewart, Claire *76:* 69; *145:* 59, 60
Ewing, Carolyn *66:* 143; *79:* 52
Ewing, Juliana Horatia *16:* 92
Eyolfson, Norman *98:* 154

F

Fabian, Limbert *136:* 114
Facklam, Paul *132:* 62
Falconer, Ian *125:* 66; *179:* 59
Falconer, Pearl *34:* 23
Falkenstern, Lisa *70:* 34; *76:* 133; *78:* 171; *127:* 16; *191:* 151
Falls, C.B. *1:* 19; *38:* 71, 72, 73, 74
Falter, John *40:* 169, 170
Falwell, Cathryn *118:* 77; *137:* 185; *196:* 71, 72
Fancher, Lou *138:* 219; *141:* 64; *144:* 199; *177:* 51; *214:* 95
Fanelli, Sara *89:* 63; *126:* 69
Faria, Rosana *150:* 143
Faricy, Patrick *185:* 182; *212:* 61
Farooqi, Musharraf Ali *207:* 46
Farmer, Andrew *49:* 102
Farmer, Peter *24:* 108; *38:* 75
Farnsworth, Bill *93:* 189; *116:* 147; *124:* 8; *135:* 52; *146:* 242, 243, 244; *182:* 176; *186:* 31, 83, 84, 85; *191:* 197
Farquharson, Alexander *46:* 75
Farrell, David *40:* 135
Farrell, Russell *196:* 38
Farris, David *74:* 42
Fasolino, Teresa *118:* 145
Fatigati, Evelyn *24:* 112
Fatus, Sophie *182:* 74; *190:* 218
Faul-Jansen, Regina *22:* 117
Faulkner, Jack *6:* 169

Faulkner, Matt *161:* 174; *167:* 75
Fava, Rita *2:* 29
Fax, Elton C. *1:* 101; *4:* 2; *12:* 77; *25:* 107
Fay *43:* 93
Fearnley, Jan *153:* 82, 83; *205:* 63, 64, 65
Fearrington, Ann *146:* 80
Federspiel, Marian *33:* 51
Fedorov, Nickolai Ivanovich *110:* 102
Feelings, Tom *5:* 22; *8:* 56; *12:* 153; *16:* 105; *30:* 196; *49:* 37; *61:* 101; *69:* 56, 57; *93:* 74; *105:* 88
Fehr, Terrence *21:* 87
Feiffer, Jules *3:* 91; *8:* 58; *61:* 66, 67, 70, 74, 76,77, 78; *111:* 47, 48, 49, 50; *132:* 122; *157:* 62; *201:* 48, 49, 50
Feigeles, Neil *41:* 242
Feldman, Elyse *86:* 7
Feller, Gene *33:* 130
Fellows, Muriel H. *10:* 42
Felstead, Cathie *116:* 85
Felts, Shirley *33:* 71; *48:* 59
Fennell, Tracy *171:* 69
Fennelli, Maureen *38:* 181
Fenton, Carroll Lane *5:* 66; *21:* 39
Fenton, Mildred Adams *5:* 66; *21:* 39
Ferguson, Peter *177:* 30, 31; *181:* 154; *197:* 4; *199:* 40; *215:* 104
Ferguson, Walter W. *34:* 86
Fernandes, Eugenie *77:* 67; *205:* 68
Fernandes, Stanislaw *70:* 28
Fernandez, Fernando *77:* 57
Fernandez, Laura *77:* 153; *101:* 117; *131:* 222; *170:* 119; *175:* 182
Ferrari, Alex *188:* 121
Ferrington, Susan *172:* 22
Fetz, Ingrid *11:* 67; *12:* 52; *16:* 205; *17:* 59; *29:* 105; *30:* 108, 109; *32:* 149; *43:* 142; *56:* 29; *60:* 34; *85:* 48; *87:* 146
Fiammenghi, Gioia *9:* 66; *11:* 44; *12:* 206; *13:* 57, 59; *52:* 126, 129; *66:* 64; *85:* 83; *91:* 161; *166:* 169
Fiedler, Joseph Daniel *96:* 42; *113:* 173; *129:* 164; *146:* 17; *159:* 68; *162:* 104
Field, Rachel *15:* 113
Fielding, David *70:* 124
Fieser, Stephen *152:* 36
Fine, Howard *145:* 159; *159:* 64; *165:* 134; *174:* 129; *181:* 68
Fine, Peter K. *43:* 210
Finger, Helen *42:* 81
Fink, Sam *18:* 119
Finlay, Winifred *23:* 72
Finney, Pat *79:* 215
Fiore, Peter *99:* 196; *125:* 139; *144:* 225; *160:* 169; *180:* 72; *212:* 103
Fiorentino, Al *3:* 240
Firehammer, Karla *174:* 202
Firmin, Charlotte *29:* 75; *48:* 70
Firmin, Peter *58:* 63, 64, 65, 67, 68, 70, 71
Firth, Barbara *81:* 208; *127:* 218; *179:* 62
Fischel, Lillian *40:* 204
Fischer, Hans *25:* 202
Fischer, Scott *207:* 37
Fischer-Nagel, Andreas *56:* 50
Fischer-Nagel, Heiderose *56:* 50
Fisher, Carolyn *154:* 50
Fisher, Chris *79:* 62; *158:* 248; *188:* 195
Fisher, Cynthia *117:* 45; *137:* 118; *195:* 40
Fisher, Jeffrey *142:* 80
Fisher, Leonard Everett *3:* 6; *4:* 72, 86; *6:* 197; *9:* 59; *16:* 151, 153; *23:* 44; *27:* 134; *29:* 26; *34:* 87, 89, 90, 91, 93, 94, 95, 96; *40:* 206; *50:* 150; *60:* 158; *73:* 68, 70, 71, 72, 73; *176:* 71, 72, 73; *208:* 131; *YABC 2:* 169
Fisher, Lois *20:* 62; *21:* 7
Fisher, Valorie *177:* 55; *214:* 92
Fisk, Nicholas *25:* 112
Fitschen, Marilyn *2:* 20, 21; *20:* 48
Fitz-Maurice, Jeff *175:* 2
Fitzgerald, F.A. *15:* 116; *25:* 86, 87

Fitzgerald, Joanne *157:* 153, 154; *198:* 34, 35
Fitzgerald, Royce *205:* 5
Fitzhugh, Louise *1:* 94; *9:* 163; *45:* 75, 78
Fitzhugh, Susie *11:* 117
Fitzpatrick, Jim *109:* 130
Fitzpatrick, Marie-Louise *125:* 69, 70; *189:* 72, 73
Fitzsimmons, Arthur *14:* 128
Fix, Philippe *26:* 102
Flack, Marjorie *21:* 67; *100:* 93; *YABC 2:* 122
Flagg, James Montgomery *17:* 227
Flavin, Teresa *132:* 115; *186:* 119
Flax, Zeona *2:* 245
Fleetwood, Tony *171:* 51
Fleishman, Seymour *14:* 232; *24:* 87
Fleming, Denise *71:* 179; *81:* 58; *126:* 71, 72, 73; *173:* 52, 53
Fleming, Guy *18:* 41
Flesher, Vivienne *85:* 55
Fletcher, Claire *80:* 106; *157:* 159
Flint, Russ *74:* 80
Floate, Helen *111:* 163
Floca, Brian *155:* 88, 89; *190:* 10, 66, 67
Floethe, Richard *3:* 131; *4:* 90
Floherty, John J., Jr. *5:* 68
Flook, Helen *160:* 81
Flora, James *1:* 96; *30:* 111, 112
Florczak, Robert *166:* 51
Florian, Douglas *19:* 122; *83:* 64, 65; *125:* 71, 72, 74, 76; *128:* 130; *177:* 58, 60
Flory, Jane *22:* 111
Flower, Renee *125:* 109
Floyd, Gareth *1:* 74; *17:* 245; *48:* 63; *62:* 35,36, 37, 39, 40, 41; *74:* 245; *79:* 56
Fluchere, Henri A. *40:* 79
Flynn, Alice *183:* 2
Flynn, Barbara *7:* 31; *9:* 70
Fogarty, Thomas *15:* 89
Foley, Greg *190:* 69
Folger, Joseph *9:* 100
Folkard, Charles *22:* 132; *29:* 128, 257, 258
Foott, Jeff *42:* 202
Forberg, Ati *12:* 71, 205; *14:* 1; *22:* 113; *26:* 22; *48:* 64, 65
Ford, George *24:* 120; *31:* 70, 177; *58:* 126; *81:* 103; *107:* 91; *136:* 100; *194:* 47; *208:* 81
Ford, Gilbert *199:* 10
Ford, H.J. *16:* 185, 186
Ford, Jason *174:* 119
Ford, Pamela Baldwin *27:* 104
Fordham, John *168:* 160, 161
Foreman, Michael *2:* 110, 111; *67:* 99; *73:* 78, 79, 80,81, 82; *93:* 146; *135:* 55, 56, 57; *184:* 58, 59
Forrester, Victoria *40:* 83
Forsey, Chris *140:* 210
Fortnum, Peggy *6:* 29; *20:* 179; *24:* 211; *26:* 76, 77, 78; *39:* 78; *58:* 19, 21, 23, 27; *YABC 1:* 148
Fortune, Eric *191:* 52
Foster, Brad W. *34:* 99
Foster, Genevieve *2:* 112
Foster, Gerald L. *7:* 78; *198:* 40
Foster, Jon *146:* 18; *198:* 7
Foster, Laura Louise *6:* 79
Foster, Marian Curtis *23:* 74; *40:* 42
Foster, Sally *58:* 73, 74
Foucher, Adele *47:* 118
Foust, Mitch *168:* 50
Fowler, Jim *184:* 190
Fowler, Mel *36:* 127
Fowler, Richard *87:* 219
Fowles, Shelley *165:* 127; *205:* 72
Fox, Charles Phillip *12:* 84
Fox, Christyan *188:* 36
Fox, Jim *6:* 187
Fox, Nathan *208:* 64
Fox-Davies, Sarah *76:* 150; *182:* 63; *199:* 42, 43
Frace, Charles *15:* 118

Frailey, Joy *72:* 108
Frame, Paul *2:* 45, 145; *9:* 153; *10:* 124; *21:* 71; *23:* 62; *24:* 123; *27:* 106; *31:* 48; *32:* 159; *34:* 195; *38:* 136; *42:* 55; *44:* 139; *60:* 39, 40, 41, 42, 43, 44, 46; *73:* 183
Frampton, David *85:* 72; *102:* 33; *139:* 182; *152:* 37; *189:* 171
Francis, Guy *198:* 164
Francois, Andre *25:* 117
Francoise
    See Seignobosc, Francoise
Frank, Lola Edick *2:* 199
Frank, Mary *4:* 54; *34:* 100
Franke, Phil *45:* 91
Frankel, Alona *66:* 70
Frankel, Julie *40:* 84, 85, 202
Frankenberg, Robert *22:* 116; *30:* 50; *38:* 92, 94, 95; *68:* 111
Frankfeldt, Gwen *84:* 223; *110:* 92
Frankland, David *169:* 137; *182:* 164; *201:* 159
Franklin, Ashton *165:* 144
Franklin, John *24:* 22
Franson, Leanne R. *111:* 57, 58; *151:* 7
Frascino, Edward *9:* 133; *29:* 229; *33:* 190; *48:* 80, 81, 82, 83, 84, 85, 86
Frasconi, Antonio *6:* 80; *27:* 208; *53:* 41, 43, 45, 47,48; *68:* 145; *73:* 226; *131:* 68
Fraser, Betty *2:* 212; *6:* 185; *8:* 103; *31:* 72,73; *43:* 136; *111:* 76
Fraser, Eric *38:* 78; *41:* 149, 151
Fraser, F.A. *22:* 234
Fraser, James *171:* 68
Fraser, Mary Ann *137:* 63; *214:* 98
Frasier, Debra *69:* 60; *112:* 67; *182:* 81, 82, 83
Fraustino, Lisa Rowe *146:* 87
Frazee, Marla *72:* 98; *105:* 79, 80; *151:* 67, 68; *164:* 165; *171:* 190, 191; *187:* 53, 54,55, 56, 143
Frazetta, Frank *41:* 72; *58:* 77, 78, 79, 80, 81, 82, 83
Frazier, Craig *177:* 63
Freas, John *25:* 207
Fredrickson, Mark *103:* 33
Freeland, Michael J. *118:* 115
Freeman, Don *2:* 15; *13:* 249; *17:* 62, 63, 65, 67, 68; *18:* 243; *20:* 195; *23:* 213, 217; *32:* 155; *55:* 129
Freeman, Irving *67:* 150
Freeman, Laura *144:* 111; *200:* 62, 63
Freeman, Pietri *140:* 223
Freeman, Tom *167:* 118
Freeman, Tor *164:* 93
Fregosi, Claudia *24:* 117
Fremaux, Charlotte Murray *138:* 29; *141:* 95
French, Fiona *6:* 82, 83; *75:* 61; *109:* 170; *132:* 79, 80, 81, 82
French, Martin *163:* 4
Frendak, Rodney *126:* 97, 98
Freschet, Gina *175:* 73
Freynet, Gilbert *72:* 221
Fried, Janice *202:* 121
Frieden, Sarajo *213:* 119
Friedman, Judith *43:* 197; *131:* 221
Friedman, Marvin *19:* 59; *42:* 86
Frinta, Dagmar *36:* 42
Frith, Michael K. *15:* 138; *18:* 120
Fritz, Ronald *46:* 73; *82:* 124
Fromm, Lilo *29:* 85; *40:* 197
Frost, A.B. *17:* 6, 7; *19:* 123, 124, 125, 126, 127, 128, 129,130; *100:* 119; *YABC 1:* 156, 157, 160; *2:* 107
Frost, Helen *183:* 51
Frost, Kristi *118:* 113
Frost, Michael *151:* 209; *209:* 44; *212:* 70
Froud, Brian *150:* 82, 83
Froud, Wendy *151:* 237
Fry, Guy *2:* 224
Fry, Rosalie *3:* 72; *YABC 2:* 180, 181
Fry, Rosalind *21:* 153, 168
Fryer, Elmer *34:* 115

Fuchs, Bernie *110:* 10; *162:* 46
Fuchs, Erich *6:* 84
Fuchshuber, Annegert *43:* 96
Fufuka, Mahiri *32:* 146
Fuge, Charles *144:* 91, 93
Fujikawa, Gyo *39:* 75, 76; *76:* 72, 73, 74
Fulford, Deborah *23:* 159
Fuller, Margaret *25:* 189
Fulweiler, John *93:* 99
Funai, Mamoru *38:* 105
Funfhausen, Christian *196:* 30
Funk, Tom *7:* 17, 99
Furchgott, Terry *29:* 86
Furness, William Henry, Jr. *94:* 18
Furukawa, Mel *25:* 42
Fusari, Erika *164:* 227

G

Gaadt, David *78:* 212; *121:* 166; *201:* 171
Gaadt, George *71:* 9
Gaber, Susan *99:* 33; *115:* 57, 58; *164:* 195; *169:* 61, 62, 63; *185:* 50, 51; *188:* 124
Gaberell, J. *19:* 236
Gable, Brian *195:* 68, 69
Gabler, Mirko *99:* 71; *195:* 32
Gackenbach, Dick *19:* 168; *41:* 81; *48:* 89, 90, 91, 92,93, 94; *54:* 105; *79:* 75, 76, 77
Gad, Victor *87:* 161
Gaetano, Nicholas *23:* 209
Gaffney-Kessell, Walter *94:* 219; *174:* 188
Gag, Flavia *17:* 49, 52
Gag, Wanda *100:* 101, 102; *YABC 1:* 135, 137, 138, 141, 143
Gagnon, Cecile *11:* 77; *58:* 87
Gaillard, Jason *200:* 69; *204:* 74
Gal, Laszlo *14:* 127; *52:* 54, 55, 56; *65:* 142; *68:* 150; *81:* 185; *96:* 104, 105
Galazinski, Tom *55:* 13
Galbraith, Ben *200:* 70
Galdone, Paul *1:* 156, 181, 206; *2:* 40, 241; *3:* 42,144; *4:* 141; *10:* 109, 158; *11:* 21; *12:* 118, 210; *14:* 12; *16:* 36, 37; *17:* 70, 71, 72, 73, 74; *18:* 111, 230; *19:* 183; *21:* 154; *22:* 150, 245; *33:* 126; *39:* 136, 137; *42:* 57; *51:* 169; *55:* 110; *66:* 80, 82, 139; *72:* 73; *100:* 84
Gale, Cathy *140:* 22; *143:* 52; *213:* 166
Gall, Chris *176:* 79, 80
Gallagher, Jack *187:* 100
Gallagher, S. Saelig *105:* 154; *198:* 91
Gallagher, Sears *20:* 112Gallagher-Cole, Mernie *206:* 56
Galloway, Ewing *51:* 154
Galouchka, Annouchka Gravel *95:* 55; *182:* 40
Galster, Robert *1:* 66
Galsworthy, Gay John *35:* 232
Galvez, Daniel *125:* 182
Gamble, Kim *112:* 64, 65; *124:* 77; *183:* 40, 42, 43, 56, 57; *187:* 170
Gammell, Stephen *7:* 48; *13:* 149; *29:* 82; *33:* 209; *41:* 88; *50:* 185, 186, 187; *53:* 51, 52, 53, 54, 55, 56,57, 58; *54:* 24, 25; *56:* 147, 148, 150; *57:* 27, 66; *81:* 62, 63; *87:* 88; *89:* 10; *106:* 223; *126:* 2; *128:* 71, 73, 74, 77; *154:* 34; *211:* 210
Gamper, Ruth *84:* 198
Gampert, John *58:* 94
Ganly, Helen *56:* 56
Gannett, Ruth Chrisman *3:* 74; *18:* 254; *33:* 77, 78
Gannon, Ned *205:* 6
Gantschev, Ivan *45:* 32
Garafano, Marie *73:* 33
Garbot, Dave *131:* 106
Garbutt, Bernard *23:* 68
Garcia *37:* 71
Garcia, Manuel *74:* 145
Garcia-Franco, Rebecca *173:* 46

Gardiner, Lindsey *178:* 128; *186:* 137
Gardner, Earle *45:* 167
Gardner, Joan *40:* 87
Gardner, Joel *40:* 87, 92
Gardner, John *40:* 87
Gardner, Lucy *40:* 87
Gardner, Richard
    See Cummings, Richard
Gardner, Sally *171:* 177; *177:* 66, 68
Gargiulo, Frank *84:* 158
Garland, Michael *36:* 29; *38:* 83; *44:* 168; *48:* 78, 221, 222; *49:* 161; *60:* 139; *71:* 6, 11; *72:* 229; *74:* 142; *89:* 187; *93:* 183; *104:* 110; *131:* 55; *139:* 209; *168:* 56; *208:* 72, 73, 75
Garland, Peggy *60:* 139
Garland, Sarah *62:* 45; *135:* 67, 68; *171:* 118
Garn, Aimee *75:* 47
Garner, Joan *128:* 170
Garneray, Ambroise Louis *59:* 140
Garnett, Eve *3:* 75
Garnett, Gary *39:* 184
Garns, Allen *80:* 125; *84:* 39; *165:* 231; *209:* 44
Garófoli, Viviana *186:* 123
Garraty, Gail *4:* 142; *52:* 106
Garrett, Agnes *46:* 110; *47:* 157
Garrett, Edmund H. *20:* 29
Garrett, Tom *107:* 194; *215:* 179
Garrick, Jacqueline *67:* 42, 43; *77:* 94
Garrison, Barbara *19:* 133; *104:* 146; *109:* 87
Garro, Mark *108:* 131; *128:* 210
Garvey, Robert *98:* 222
Garza, Carmen Lomas *80:* 211; *182:* 86
Garza, Xavier *184:* 64
Gates, Frieda *26:* 80
Gaughan, Jack *26:* 79; *43:* 185
Gaver, Becky *20:* 61
Gavril, David *211:* 196
Gawing, Toby *72:* 52
Gay, Marie-Louise *68:* 76, 77, 78; *102:* 136; *126:* 76, 78, 81, 83; *127:* 55, 56; *179:* 70, 72, 73, 74
Gay, Zhenya *19:* 135, 136
Gaydos, Tim *62:* 201
Gazsi, Ed *80:* 48
Gazso, Gabriel *73:* 85
Geary, Clifford N. *1:* 122; *9:* 104; *51:* 74
Geary, Rick *142:* 44, 46
Gee, Frank *33:* 26
Geehan, Wayne *157:* 181
Geer, Charles *1:* 91; *3:* 179; *4:* 201; *6:* 168; *7:* 96; *9:* 58; *10:* 72; *12:* 127; *39:* 156,157, 158, 159, 160; *42:* 88, 89, 90, 91; *55:* 111, 116
Geerinck, Manuel *173:* 128
Gehm, Charlie *36:* 65; *57:* 117; *62:* 60, 138
Geis, Alissa Imre *189:* 77
Geisel, Theodor Seuss *1:* 104, 105, 106; *28:* 108, 109, 110,111, 112, 113; *75:* 67, 68, 69, 70, 71; *89:* 127, 128; *100:* 106, 107, 108
Geisert, Arthur *92:* 67, 68; *133:* 72, 73, 74; *165:* 97, 98; *171:* 64, 65
Geldart, William *15:* 121; *21:* 202
Genia *4:* 84
Gentry, Cyrille R. *12:* 66
Genzo, John Paul *136:* 74
George, Jean *2:* 113
George, Lindsay Barrett *95:* 57; *155:* 97, 98
Geraghty, Paul *130:* 60, 61
Gerard, Jean Ignace *45:* 80
Gerard, Rolf *27:* 147, 150
Gerber, Mark *61:* 105
Gerber, Mary Jane *112:* 124; *171:* 56
Gerber, Stephanie *71:* 195
Gerdstein, Mordecai *169:* 105
Gergely, Tibor *54:* 15, 16
Geritz, Franz *17:* 135
Gerlach, Geff *42:* 58
Gerrard, Roy *47:* 78; *90:* 96, 97, 98, 99
Gerritsen, Paula *177:* 69
Gershinowitz, George *36:* 27

Gerstein, Mordicai *31:* 117; *47:* 80, 81, 82, 83, 84, 85, 86; *51:* 173; *69:* 134; *107:* 122; *142:* 49, 52; *165:* 209; *176:* 119; *178:* 95, 97, 99; *215:* 173
Gervase *12:* 27
Geter, Tyrone *146:* 249; *150:* 86
Getz, Arthur *32:* 148
Gévry, Claudine *188:* 47
Gewirtz, Bina *61:* 81
Giancola, Donato *95:* 146; *164:* 226
Gibala-Broxholm, Scott *205:* 76
Gibbons, Gail *23:* 78; *72:* 77, 78, 79; *82:* 182; *104:* 65; *160:* 99, 100; *201:* 59, 60, 62
Gibbs, Tony *40:* 95
Gibran, Kahlil *32:* 116
Gibson, Barbara Leonard *205:* 77; *212:* 151
Gider, Iskender *81:* 193
Giebfried, Rosemary *170:* 135
Giesen, Rosemary *34:* 192, 193
Giffard, Hannah *83:* 70
Giguere, George *20:* 111
Gilbert, John *19:* 184; *54:* 115; *YABC 2:* 287
Gilbert, W.S. *36:* 83, 85, 96
Gilbert, Yvonne *116:* 70; *128:* 84; *149:* 119; *185:* 69; *192:* 25; *195:* 81
Gilchrist, Jan Spivey *72:* 82, 83, 84, 85, 87; *77:* 90; *105:* 89, 91; *130:* 63, 64; *155:* 105, 107; *182:* 67
Giles, Will *41:* 218
Gili, Phillida *70:* 73
Gill, Margery *4:* 57; *7:* 7; *22:* 122; *25:* 166; *26:* 146, 147
Gillen, Denver *28:* 216
Gillette, Henry J. *23:* 237
Gilliam, Stan *39:* 64, 81
Gillies, Chuck *62:* 31
Gilliland, Jillian *87:* 58
Gillman, Alec *98:* 105
Gilman, Esther *15:* 124
Gilman, Phoebe *104:* 70, 71
Gilpin, Stephen *213:* 68
Ginsberg, Sari *111:* 184
Ginsburg, Max *62:* 59; *68:* 194 Girard, Roge *161:* 30
Girouard, Patrick *155:* 100
Giovanopoulos, Paul *7:* 104; *60:* 36
Giovine, Sergio *79:* 12; *93:* 118; *139:* 118; *205:* 114
Gist, E.M. *206:* 60
Githens, Elizabeth M. *5:* 47
Gladden, Scott *99:* 108; *103:* 160; *193:* 46, 47
Gladstone, Gary *12:* 89; *13:* 190
Gladstone, Lise *15:* 273
Glanzman, Louis S. *2:* 177; *3:* 182; *36:* 97, 98; *38:* 120, 122; *52:* 141, 144; *71:* 191; *91:* 54, 56
Glaser, Byron *154:* 59, 60
Glaser, Milton *3:* 5; *5:* 156; *11:* 107; *30:* 26; *36:* 112; *54:* 141; *151:* 70
Glass, Andrew *36:* 38; *44:* 133; *48:* 205; *65:* 3; *68:* 43, 45; *90:* 104, 105; *150:* 89
Glass, Marvin *9:* 174
Glasser, Judy *41:* 156; *56:* 140; *69:* 79; *72:* 101
Glattauer, Ned *5:* 84; *13:* 224; *14:* 26
Glauber, Uta *17:* 76
Gleeson, J.M. *YABC 2:* 207
Glegg, Creina *36:* 100
Glienke, Amelie *63:* 150
Gleewe, Unada *3:* 78, 79; *21:* 73; *30:* 220
Gliori, Debi *72:* 91; *138:* 82; *162:* 37; *189:* 79, 81, 82
Glovach, Linda *7:* 105
Gobbato, Imero *3:* 180, 181; *6:* 213; *7:* 58; *9:* 150; *18:* 39; *21:* 167; *39:* 82, 83; *41:* 137, 251; *59:* 177
Goble, Paul *25:* 121; *26:* 86; *33:* 65; *69:* 68, 69; *131:* 79, 80
Goble, Warwick *46:* 78, 79; *194:* 143
Godal, Eric *36:* 93
Godkin, Celia *145:* 84, 86

Godfrey, Michael *17:* 279
Godon, Ingrid *166:* 163; *186:* 99
Goede, Irene *208:* 87
Goembel, Ponder *42:* 124
Goffe, Toni *61:* 83, 84, 85; *89:* 11; *90:* 124; *178:* 118
Goffstein, M.B. *8:* 71; *70:* 75, 76, 77
Golbin, Andre *15:* 125
Gold, Robert *166:* 151, 152
Goldfeder, Cheryl *11:* 191
Goldfinger, Jennifer P. *185:* 71
Goldsborough, June *5:* 154, 155; *8:* 92, *14:* 226; *19:* 139; *54:* 165
Goldsmith, Robert *110:* 77
Goldstein, Barry *198:* 147
Goldstein, Leslie *5:* 8; *6:* 60; *10:* 106
Goldstein, Nathan *1:* 175; *2:* 79; *11:* 41, 232; *16:* 55
Goldstrom, Robert *98:* 36; *145:* 51, 52
Golembe, Carla *79:* 80, 81; *136:* 91; *144:* 113; *193:* 53
Golin, Carlo *74:* 112
Gomez, Elena *188:* 122; *191:* 72
Gomez, Elizabeth *127:* 70; *133:* 76
Gomi, Taro *64:* 102; *103:* 74, 76
Gon, Adriano *101:* 112
Gonsalves, Ron *178:* 213; *212:* 196
Gonzalez, Maya Christina *104:* 3; *136:* 92; *215:* 4, 5
Gonzalez, Yolanda *212:* 65
Good, Karen Hillard *212:* 143; *214:* 103
Goodall, John S. *4:* 92, 93; *10:* 132; *66:* 92, 93; *YABC 1:* 198
Goode, Diane *15:* 126; *50:* 183; *52:* 114, 115; *76:* 195; *84:* 94; *99:* 141; *114:* 76, 77, 78; *170:* 99, 101
Goodelman, Aaron *40:* 203
Goodenow, Earle *40:* 97
Goodfellow, Peter *62:* 95; *94:* 202
Goodman, Joan Elizabeth *50:* 86
Goodman, Vivienne *82:* 251; *146:* 181, 182
Goodnow, Patti *117:* 33
Goodwin, Harold *13:* 74
Goodwin, Philip R. *18:* 206
Goor, Nancy *39:* 85, 86
Goor, Ron *39:* 85, 86
Goossens, Philippe *195:* 71
Gorbachev, Valeri *89:* 96; *112:* 97; *143:* 63, 64; *184:* 66, 67, 68, 101
Gordon, Gwen *12:* 151
Gordon, Margaret *4:* 147; *5:* 48, 49; *9:* 79
Gordon, Mike *101:* 62, 63, 64
Gordon, Russell *136:* 204; *137:* 214
Gordon, Walter *138:* 9
Gore, Leonid *89:* 51; *94:* 74; *136:* 8; *158:* 117; *166:* 136; *168:* 36; *170:* 107; *181:* 94; *185:* 73
Gorecka-Egan, Erica *18:* 35
Gorey, Edward *1:* 60, 61; *13:* 169; *18:* 192; *20:* 201; *29:* 90, 91, 92, 93, 94, 95, 96, 97, 98, 99, 100; *30:* 129; *32:* 90; *34:* 200; *65:* 48; *68:* 24, 25; *69:* 79; *70:* 80, 82, 83, 84; *85:* 136; *127:* 62
Gorsline, Douglas *1:* 98; *6:* 13; *11:* 113; *13:* 104; *15:* 14; *28:* 117, 118; *YABC 1:* 15
Gorton, Julia *108:* 94; *178:* 81, 82
Gosfield, Josh *118:* 165, 166; *149:* 67
Gosner, Kenneth *5:* 135
Gosney, Joy *167:* 142
Gotlieb, Jules *6:* 127
Goto, Scott *115:* 86; *136:* 69; *203:* 77, 78
Gott, Barry *197:* 95; *212:* 102
Gottlieb, Dale *67:* 162; *107:* 16; *149:* 6
Goudey, Ray *97:* 86
Gough, Alan *91:* 57
Gough, Philip *23:* 47; *45:* 90
Gould, Chester *49:* 112, 113, 114, 116, 117, 118
Gould, Jason *151:* 232
Gourbault, Martine *177:* 159
Govern, Elaine R. *26:* 94

Gower, Teri *102:* 184
Gowing, Toby *60:* 25; *63:* 33; *78:* 70, 252; *83:* 228; *86:* 187; *93:* 145; *108:* 133; *110:* 217; *184:* 125
Grabianski *20:* 144
Grabianski, Janusz *39:* 92, 93, 94, 95
Graboff, Abner *35:* 103, 104
Graef, Renée *61:* 188; *72:* 207; *204:* 45; *210:* 249
Grafe, Max *156:* 173; *178:* 237; *192:* 240; *198:* 51
Graham, A.B. *11:* 61
Graham, Bob *101:* 66, 67, 68; *151:* 74, 75; *187:* 65, 67, 68, 70
Graham, Georgia *188:* 3; *190:* 75
Graham, L. *7:* 108
Graham, Margaret Bloy *11:* 120; *18:* 305, 307
Graham, Mark *88:* 208; *159:* 153; *182:* 3
Grahame-Johnstone, Janet *13:* 61
Grahame-Johnstone, Anne *13:* 61
Grainger, Sam *42:* 95
Gralley, Jean *166:* 86
Gramatky, Hardie *1:* 107; *30:* 116, 119, 120, 122, 123
Gran, Julie *168:* 118
Granahan, Julie *84:* 84
GrandPré, Mary *84:* 131; *109:* 199; *118:* 76; *180:* 65; *184:* 70, 71, 180; *192:* 87; *215:* 24
Grandström, Brita *176:* 139
Grandville, J.J. *45:* 81, 82, 83, 84, 85, 86, 87, 88; *47:* 125; *64:* 10
Granger, Paul *39:* 153
Granström, Brita *162:* 35; *167:* 46
Grant, (Alice) Leigh *10:* 52; *15:* 131; *20:* 20; *26:* 119; *48:* 202
Grant, Gordon *17:* 230, 234; *25:* 123, 124, 125, 126; *52:* 69; *YABC 1:* 164
Grant, Melvyn *159:* 186, 187; *170:* 48, 49; *213:* 168, 169
Grant, Michelle *210:* 95
Grant, Renee *77:* 40
Grant, Shirley *109:* 45
Graves, Elizabeth *45:* 101
Graves, Keith *167:* 89; *191:* 74
Gray, Harold *33:* 87, 88
Gray, Les *82:* 76; *83:* 232
Gray, Reginald *6:* 69
Greco, Tony *184:* 6
Greder, Armin *76:* 235
Green, Ann Canevari *62:* 48
Green, Eileen *6:* 97
Green, Elizabeth Shippen *139:* 109
Green, Jonathan *86:* 135; *105:* 109
Green, Ken *111:* 68
Green, Michael *32:* 216
Green, Robina *87:* 138
Green, Jonathan *157:* 105
Greene, Jeffrey *117:* 93
Greenaway, Kate *17:* 275; *24:* 180; *26:* 107; *41:* 222, 232; *100:* 115, 116; *YABC 1:* 88, 89; *2:* 131, 133, 136,138, 139, 141
Greenberg, Melanie Hope *72:* 93; *80:* 125; *101:* 174; *133:* 180; *186:* 189; *214:* 105
Greenseid, Diane *178:* 106, 107
Greenstein, Elaine *150:* 100
Greenwald, Sheila *1:* 34; *3:* 99; *8:* 72
Greger, Carol *76:* 86
Gregorian, Joyce Ballou *30:* 125
Gregory, Emilian *177:* 146; *187:* 10
Gregory, Fran *130:* 4; *140:* 93
Gregory, Frank M. *29:* 107
Greiffenhagen, Maurice *16:* 137; *27:* 57; *YABC 2:* 288
Greiner, Robert *6:* 86
Gretter, J. Clemens *31:* 134
Gretz, Susanna *7:* 114
Gretzer, John *1:* 54; *3:* 26; *4:* 162; *7:* 125; *16:* 247; *18:* 117; *28:* 66; *30:* 85, 211; *33:* 235; *56:* 16
Grey, Mini *166:* 90; *192:* 71
Grey Owl *24:* 41

Gri *25:* 90
Grieder, Walter *9:* 84
Griesbach/Martucci *59:* 3
Grifalconi, Ann *2:* 126; *3:* 248; *11:* 18; *13:* 182; *46:* 38; *50:* 145; *66:* 99, 100, 101, 104, 106; *69:* 38; *70:* 64; *87:* 128; *90:* 53; *93:* 49; *128:* 48; *133:* 79, 81; *210:* 111
Griffin, Gillett Good *26:* 96
Griffin, James *30:* 166
Griffin, John Howard *59:* 186
Griffin, Rachel *131:* 23
Griffith, Gershom *94:* 214
Griffiths, Dave *29:* 76
Griffiths, Dean *168:* 180; *169:* 182
Grimly, Gris *186:* 102; *192:* 112; *197:* 86
Grimsdell, Jeremy *83:* 75
Grimwood, Brian *82:* 89
Gringhuis, Dirk *6:* 98; *9:* 196
Gripe, Harald *2:* 127; *74:* 98
Grisha *3:* 71
Grobler, Piet *201:* 100
Grohmann, Susan *84:* 97
Gropper, William *27:* 93; *37:* 193
Gros *60:* 199
Grose, Helen Mason *YABC 1:* 260; *2:* 150
Grossman, Nancy *24:* 130; *29:* 101
Grossman, Robert *11:* 124; *46:* 39
Groth, John *15:* 79; *21:* 53, 54; *83:* 230
Grover, Lorie Ann *168:* 59
Grubb, Lisa *160:* 116
Grue, Lisa *187:* 193
Gruelle, Johnny *35:* 107
Gschwind, William *11:* 72
Guarnaccia, Steven *201:* 170, 173
Guay-Mitchell, Rebecca *110:* 95, 96; *135:* 240; *180:* 76; *181:* 71, 73
Guback, Georgia *88:* 102
Gudeon, Karla *212:* 67
Guerguerion, Claudine *105:* 73
Guevara, Susan *97:* 87; *167:* 49; *194:* 54
Guggenheim, Hans *2:* 10; *3:* 37; *8:* 136
Guhathaakurta, Ajanta *183:* 199
Guida, Lisa Chauncy *172:* 188
Guilbeau, Honore *22:* 69
Guillette, Joseph *137:* 37
Guisewite, Cathy *57:* 52, 53, 54, 56, 57
Gukova, Julia *95:* 104; *154:* 103; *168:* 195
Gundersheimer, Karen *35:* 240; *82:* 100
Gunderson, Nick *57:* 120
Gunnella *192:* 144
Gurney, James *76:* 97; *86:* 32
Gurney, John Steven *75:* 39, 82; *110:* 175; *143:* 67, 68; *169:* 172
Gusman, Annie *38:* 62
Gustafson, Scott *34:* 111; *43:* 40
Gustavson, Adam *104:* 10; *171:* 183; *176:* 87; *197:* 94; *204:* 35
Guthridge, Bettina *108:* 79; *186:* 92
Guthrie, R. Dale *64:* 143
Guthrie, Robin *20:* 122
Gutierrez, Akemi *172:* 87; *205:* 135
Gutierrez, Alan *136:* 31, 32
Gutierrez, Rudy *97:* 162; *203:* 79
Gutmann, Bessie Pease *73:* 93, 94
Gwynne, Fred *41:* 94, 95
Gyberg, Bo-Erik *38:* 131

H

Haas, Irene *17:* 77; *87:* 46; *96:* 117
Hack, Konrad *51:* 127
Hader, Berta H. *16:* 126
Hader, Elmer S. *16:* 126
Haeffele, Deborah *76:* 99
Haemer, Alan *62:* 109
Hafner, Marylin *22:* 196, 216; *24:* 44; *30:* 51; *35:* 95; *51:* 25, 160, 164; *86:* 16; *105:* 196; *121:* 93, 94; *149:* 208, 209; *179:* 82, 83, 84, 115; *190:* 200; *201:* 29

Hagerty, Sean *62:* 181
Hague, Michael *32:* 128; *48:* 98, 99, 100, 101, 103, 105,106, 107, 108, 109, 110; *49:* 121; *51:* 105; *64:* 14, 15; *79:* 134; *80:* 91, 92; *83:* 135; *100:* 241; *102:* 29; *129:* 101, 103, 104; *185:* 80, 81, 82; *215:* 89
Hair, Jonathan *115:* 135
Halas, John *29:* 41, 47, 48
Haldane, Roger *13:* 76; *14:* 202
Hale, Bruce *203:* 83
Hale, Christy *79:* 124; *84:* 200; *114:* 201; *128:* 2, 3; *146:* 203; *158:* 243; *167:* 99; *179:* 87
Hale, Irina *26:* 97
Hale, James Graham *88:* 207
Hale, Kathleen *17:* 79; *66:* 114, 116, 118
Hale, Nathan *210:* 115, 116; *214:* 179
Haley, Amanda *205:* 82, 83
Haley, Gail E. *43:* 102, 103, 104, 105; *78:* 65, 67; *136:* 106, 107
Hall, Amanda *96:* 110
Hall, Chuck *30:* 189
Hall, Douglas *15:* 184; *43:* 106, 107; *86:* 100; *87:* 82; *129:* 72
Hall, H. Tom *1:* 227; *30:* 210
Hall, Melanie *116:* 48, 49; *169:* 77, 78
Hall, Sydney P. *31:* 89
Hall, Tim *164:* 196; *202:* 41
Hall, Vicki *20:* 24
Hallinan, P.K. *39:* 98
Hallman, Tom *98:* 166
Hally, Greg *101:* 200; *151:* 224
Halperin, Wendy Anderson *96:* 151; *125:* 96, 97, 98, 99; *139:* 22; *140:* 84; *200:* 77, 78; *210:* 157; *215:* 65
Halpern, Joan *10:* 25
Halpern, Shari *174:* 172
Halsey, Megan *96:* 172; *114:* 185; *180:* 8; *185:* 85
Halstead, Virginia *125:* 105
Halverson, Janet *49:* 38, 42, 44
Hallensleben, Georg *134:* 5, 6; *172:* 17
Hamanaka, Sheila *71:* 100
Hamann, Brad *78:* 151
Hamann, Sigune *104:* 115
Hamberger, John *6:* 8; *8:* 32; *14:* 79; *34:* 136; *88:* 78
Hamil, Tom *14:* 80; *43:* 163
Hamilton, Bill and Associates *26:* 215
Hamilton, Helen S. *2:* 238
Hamilton, J. *19:* 83, 85, 87
Hamilton, Laurie *116:* 210
Hamilton, Todd Cameron *84:* 15
Hamlin, Janet *97:* 136; *124:* 90; *137:* 157; *182:* 117
Hamlin, Louise *71:* 135
Hammill, Matt *206:* 65
Hammond, Chris *21:* 37
Hammond, Elizabeth *5:* 36, 203
Hampshire, Michael *5:* 187; *7:* 110, 111; *48:* 150; *51:* 129
Hampson, Denman *10:* 155; *15:* 130
Hampton, Blake *41:* 244
Handford, Martin *64:* 105, 106, 107, 109
Handforth, Thomas *42:* 100, 101, 102, 103, 104, 105, 109
Handville, Robert *1:* 89; *38:* 76; *45:* 108, 109
Hane, Roger *17:* 239; *44:* 54
Haney, Elizabeth Mathieu *34:* 84
Hanke, Ted *71:* 10
Hankinson, Phil *181:* 164
Hanley, Catherine *8:* 161
Hann, Jacquie *19:* 144
Hanna, Cheryl *91:* 133
Hanna, Wayne A. *67:* 145
Hannon, Mark *38:* 37
Hanrahan, Kelly-Anne *203:* 142
Hansen, Gaby *159:* 11; *186:* 25
Hansen, Mia *149:* 76
Hanson, Joan *8:* 76; *11:* 139
Hanson, Peter E. *52:* 47; *54:* 99, 100; *73:* 21; *84:* 79; *116:* 144

Hansson, Gunilla *64:* 111, 112
Hardcastle, Nick *121:* 82; *175:* 185
Hardy, David A. *9:* 96; *119:* 74
Hardy, Paul *YABC 2:* 245 *Haring, Keith 145:* 65
Harlan, Jerry *3:* 96
Harlin, Greg *89:* 194; *103:* 82; *118:* 161; *121:* 167; *182:* 76; *201:* 172; *215:* 76
Harman, Dominic *206:* 48
Harness, Cheryl *106:* 80; *131:* 87; *178:* 111; *200:* 39
Harnischfeger *18:* 121
Harper, Arthur *YABC 2:* 121
Harper, Betty *126:* 90
Harper, Jamie *174:* 71; *214:* 212
Harper, Piers *79:* 27; *105:* 102; *161:* 67
Harrington, Glenn *82:* 18; *94:* 66, 68; *185:* 118
Harrington, Jack *83:* 162
Harrington, Richard *5:* 81
Harris, Andrew N. *191:* 78
Harris, Jim *127:* 130; *183:* 4
Harris, John *83:* 25
Harris, Nick *86:* 177
Harris, Susan Yard *42:* 121
Harrison, Florence *20:* 150, 152
Harrison, Harry *4:* 103
Harrison, Jack *28:* 149
Harrison, Mark *105:* 157; *165:* 190
Harrison, Ted *56:* 73
Harsh, Fred *72:* 107
Harston, Jerry *105:* 143
Hart, Lewis *98:* 115
Hart, Thomas *181:* 165
Hart, William *13:* 72
Hartland, Jessie *171:* 80, 81; *186:* 165
Hartung, Susan Kathleen *150:* 107, 108; *173:* 106; *175:* 106; *192:* 78; *211:* 19
Hartelius, Margaret *10:* 24
Hartshorn, Ruth *5:* 115; *11:* 129
Harvey, Amanda *145:* 44
Harvey, Bob *48:* 219
Harvey, Gerry *7:* 180
Harvey, Lisa *97:* 21
Harvey, Paul *88:* 74
Harvey, Roland *71:* 88; *123:* 63; *179:* 94
Haskamp, Steve *195:* 36
Hassall, Joan *43:* 108, 109
Hassell, Hilton *YABC 1:* 187
Hassett, John *162:* 59
Hasselriis, Else *18:* 87; *YABC 1:* 96
Hastings, Glenn *89:* 183
Hastings, Ian *62:* 67
Hauman, Doris *2:* 184; *29:* 58, 59; *32:* 85, 86, 87
Hauman, George *2:* 184; *29:* 58, 59; *32:* 85, 86, 87
Hausherr, Rosmarie *15:* 29
Hawkes, Kevin *78:* 72; *104:* 198; *105:* 197; *112:* 109; *126:* 87; *144:* 88; *149:* 210; *150:* 110, 135; *156:* 94; *164:* 35; *186:* 18; *190:* 197; *198:* 152; *201:* 70, 71, 72
Hawkins, Jacqui *112:* 86; *162:* 64
Hawkinson, John *4:* 109; *7:* 83; *21:* 64
Hawkinson, Lucy *21:* 64
Hawthorne, Mike *140:* 228
Haxton, Elaine *28:* 131
Haydock, Robert *4:* 95
Hayes, Geoffrey *26:* 111; *44:* 133; *91:* 85; *207:* 63
Hayes, Karel *207:* 65
Haynes, Max *72:* 107
Hays, Michael *73:* 207; *83:* 93; *139:* 197; *146:* 202, 250; *202:* 47
Haywood, Carolyn *1:* 112; *29:* 104
Heale, Jonathan *104:* 117
Healy, Daty *12:* 143
Healy, Deborah *58:* 181, 182; *101:* 111
Heap, Sue *102:* 207; *150:* 113, 114; *187:* 84, 85, 87

Hearn, Diane Dawson *79:* 99; *113:* 13; *209:* 71, 72; *211:* 106
Hearon, Dorothy *34:* 69
Heaslip, William *57:* 24, 25
Hechtkopf, H. *11:* 110
Heck, Ed *173:* 81
Hector, Julian *205:* 85
Hedderwick, Mairi *30:* 127; *32:* 47; *36:* 104; *77:* 86; *145:* 91, 93, 95
Heffernan, Phil *146:* 197; *195:* 172
Hefter, Richard *28:* 170; *31:* 81, 82; *33:* 183
Hehenberger, Shelly *126:* 91
Heigh, James *22:* 98
Heighway, Richard *25:* 160; *64:* 4
Heighway-Bury, Robin *159:* 89
Heine, Helme *67:* 86; *135:* 91, 92
Heinly, John *45:* 113
Hellard, Susan *81:* 21; *204:* 82; *209:* 92
Hellebrand, Nancy *26:* 57
Heller, Linda *46:* 86
Heller, Ruth M. *66:* 125; *77:* 30, 32
Hellmuth, Jim *38:* 164
Helms, Georgeann *33:* 62
Helquist, Brett *142:* 203; *146:* 133, 134; *156:* 10; *173:* 25; *180:* 106; *187:* 90, 91; *193:* 12
Helweg, Hans *41:* 118; *50:* 93; *58:* 22, 26
Hemingway, Edward *212:* 71
Hemphill, Helen *179:* 95
Henba, Bobbie *90:* 195
Henderling, Lisa *214:* 65
Henderson, Dave *73:* 76; *75:* 191, 192, 193, 194; *82:* 4
Henderson, Douglas *103:* 68
Henderson, Kathy *55:* 32; *155:* 118
Henderson, Keith *35:* 122
Henderson, Meryl *127:* 58, 60; *169:* 81
Hendrix, John *187:* 133; *208:* 106, 107, 108
Hendry, Linda *80:* 104; *83:* 83; *164:* 216
Hengeveld, Dennis *142:* 86
Henkes, Kevin *43:* 111; *108:* 106, 107, 108
Henneberger, Robert *1:* 42; *2:* 237; *25:* 83
Henriksen, Harold *35:* 26; *48:* 68
Henriquez, Celeste *103:* 137
Henriquez, Elsa *82:* 260
Henriquez, Emile F. *89:* 88; *211:* 56
Henry, Everett *29:* 191
Henry, Matthew *117:* 58
Henry, Paul *93:* 121; *194:* 125
Henry, Thomas *5:* 102
Hensel,27: 119
Henshaw, Jacqui *141:* 127
Henstra, Friso *8:* 80; *36:* 70; *40:* 222; *41:* 250; *73:* 100, 101
Henterly, Jamichael *93:* 4
Heo, Yumi *89:* 85, 86; *94:* 89, 90; *146:* 40, 137, 138; *163:* 227; *201:* 192
Hepple, Norman *28:* 198
Herbert, Helen *57:* 70
Herbert, Jennifer *189:* 47
Herbert, Wally *23:* 101
Herbster, Mary Lee *9:* 33
Herder, Edwin *182:* 104
Herge
   See Remi, Georges
Hermansen, Pal *133:* 113
Hermanson, Dennis *10:* 55
Hermes, Gertrude *54:* 161
Herr, Margo *57:* 191
Herr, Susan *83:* 163
Herriman, George *140:* 74, 75, 76, 77, 78
Herriman, Lisa *87:* 190
Herring, Michael *121:* 76; *182:* 103
Herrington, Roger *3:* 161
Herscovici, C. *165:* 240
Hescox, Richard *85:* 86; *90:* 30; *139:* 35
Heslop, Mike *38:* 60; *40:* 130
Hess, Lydia J. *85:* 17
Hess, Mark *111:* 146; *113:* 207
Hess, Paul *134:* 47; *166:* 133; *193:* 13
Hess, Richard *42:* 31
Hester, Ronnie *37:* 85

Heuser, Olga J. *121:* 116
Heusser, Sibylle *168:* 195
Heustis, Louise L. *20:* 28
Hewgill, Jodi *201:* 90
Hewitson, Jennifer *74:* 119; *124:* 167
Hewitt, Kathryn *80:* 126; *149:* 105; *184:* 93; *196:* 36
Hewitt, Margaret *84:* 112
Heyduck-Huth, Hilde *8:* 82
Heyer, Carol *74:* 122; *130:* 72, 73; *192:* 35; *203:* 78
Heyer, Hermann *20:* 114, 115
Heyer, Marilee *102:* 108
Heyman, Ken *8:* 33; *34:* 113
Heyne, Ulrike *146:* 151
Heywood, Karen *48:* 114
Hickling, P.B. *40:* 165
Hickman, Stephen *85:* 58; *136:* 33; *171:* 128
Hierstein, Judith *56:* 40; *162:* 168; *212:* 72
Higashi, Sandra *154:* 59, 60
Higginbottom, J. Winslow *8:* 170; *29:* 105, 106
Higgins, Chester *101:* 79
Higham, David *50:* 104
Hilb, Nora *176:* 8
Hild, Anja *215:* 194
Hildebrandt, Greg *8:* 191; *55:* 35, 36, 38, 39, 40, 42, 46; *172:* 110
Hildebrandt, Tim *8:* 191; *55:* 44, 45, 46
Hilder, Rowland *19:* 207
Hill, Eric *66:* 127, 128; *133:* 91
Hill, Gregory *35:* 190
Hill, Pat *49:* 120
Hillenbrand, Will *84:* 115; *92:* 76, 80; *93:* 131; *104:* 168; *128:* 137; *145:* 187; *146:* 184; *147:* 105, 106, 107; *152:* 59; *184:* 179; *195:* 34, 180; *196:* 125; *210:* 122, 123, 124
Hilliard, Richard *183:* 74
Hillier, Matthew *45:* 205
Hillman, Priscilla *48:* 115
Hills, Tad *113:* 4; *137:* 147; *173:* 83; *208:* 199
Himler, Ronald *6:* 114; *7:* 162; *8:* 17, 84, 125; *14:* 76; *19:* 145; *26:* 160; *31:* 43; *38:* 116; *41:* 44, 79; *43:* 52; *45:* 120; *46:* 43; *54:* 44, 83; *58:* 180; *59:* 38; *68:* 146; *69:* 231; *70:* 98; *71:* 177, 178; *77:* 219; *79:* 212; *83:* 62; *89:* 5; *91:* 160; *92:* 91, 92, 93; *94:* 93; *95:* 69, 174, 194; *99:* 99, 112; *113:* 92; *118:* 114; *137:* 73, 74, 77, 167; *163:* 99; *165:* 138; *178:* 9, 220; *183:* 77, 79, 80, 81; *184:* 80, 83; *215:* 151
Himmelman, John *47:* 109; *65:* 87; *94:* 96, 97; *159:* 85
Hinds, Bill *37:* 127, 130
Hines, Anna Grossnickle *51:* 90; *74:* 124; *95:* 78, 79, 80, 81
Hines, Bob *135:* 149, 150
Hirao, Amiko *203:* 98
Hiroko *99:* 61
Hiroshige *25:* 71
Hirsh, Marilyn *7:* 126
Hiscock, Bruce *137:* 80, 81; *204:* 51, 53
Hissey, Jane *103:* 90; *130:* 81
Hitch, Jeff *99:* 206; *128:* 86
Hitz, Demi *11:* 135; *15:* 245; *66:* 129, 130; *152:* 94, 95
Hnizdovsky, Jacques *32:* 96; *76:* 187
Ho, Kwoncjan *15:* 132
Hoban, Lillian *1:* 114; *22:* 157; *26:* 72; *29:* 53; *40:* 105, 107, 195; *41:* 80; *69:* 107, 108; *71:* 98; *77:* 168; *106:* 50; *113:* 86; *136:* 118
Hoban, Tana *22:* 159; *104:* 82, 83, 85
Hobbie, Jocelyn *190:* 78; *196:* 92
Hobbie, Nathaniel *196:* 92
Hobbs, Leigh *166:* 95
Hoberman, Norman *5:* 82
Hobson, Sally *77:* 185
Hockerman, Dennis *39:* 22; *56:* 23
Hodgell, P.C. *42:* 114

Hodges, C. Walter 2: 139; 11: 15; 12: 25; 23: 34; 25: 96; 38: 165; 44: 197; 45: 95; 100: 57; YABC 2: 62, 63
Hodges, David 9: 98
Hodgetts, Victoria 43: 132
Hofbauer, Imre 2: 162
Hoff, Syd 9: 107; 10: 128; 33: 94; 72: 115,116, 117, 118; 138: 114, 115
Hoffman, Rosekrans 15: 133; 50: 219; 63: 97
Hoffman, Sanford 38: 208; 76: 174; 88: 160, 161; 151: 156
Hoffmann, Felix 9: 109
Hoffnung, Gerard 66: 76, 77
Hofsinde, Robert 21: 70
Hogan, Inez 2: 141
Hogan, Jamie 192: 94; 198: 177
Hogarth, Burne 41: 58; 63: 46, 48, 49, 50, 52, 53, 54, 55,56
Hogarth, Paul 41: 102, 103, 104; YABC 1: 16
Hogarth, William 42: 33
Hogenbyl, Jan 1: 35
Hogner, Nils 4: 122; 25: 144
Hogrogian, Nonny 3: 221; 4: 106, 107; 5: 166; 7: 129; 15: 2; 16: 176; 20: 154; 22: 146; 25: 217; 27: 206; 74: 127, 128, 129, 149, 152; 127: 99; YABC 2: 84, 94
Hokanson, Lars 93: 111; 172: 137; 212: 88
Hokusai 25: 71
Hol, Colby 126: 96
Holberg, Richard 2: 51
Holbrook, Kathy 107: 114
Holdcroft, Tina 38: 109
Holden, Caroline 55: 159
Holder, Heidi 36: 99; 64: 9
Holder, Jim 204: 163
Holder, Jimmy 151: 224
Holderness, Grizelda 215: 107
Hole, Stian 204: 55
Holiday, Henry YABC 2: 107
Holl, F. 36: 91
Holland, Brad 45: 59, 159
Holland, Gay W. 128: 105
Holland, Janice 18: 118
Holland, Marion 6: 116
Holldobler, Turid 26: 120
Holliday, Keaf 144: 236
Holling, Holling C. 15: 136, 137
Hollinger, Deanne 12: 116
Holm, Sharon Lane 114: 84; 115: 52
Holmes, B. 3: 82
Holmes, Bea 7: 74; 24: 156; 31: 93
Holmes, Dave 54: 22
Holmes, Lesley 135: 96
Holmgren, George Ellen 45: 112
Holmlund, Heather D. 150: 140
Holt, Norma 44: 106
Holt, Pater 151: 188
Holtan, Gene 32: 192
Holub, Joan 149: 72
Holyfield, John 149: 231
Holz, Loretta 17: 81
Hom, Nancy 79: 195
Homar, Lorenzo 6: 2
Homer, Winslow 128: 8; YABC 2: 87
Honey, Elizabeth 112: 95, 96; 137: 93, 94
Honeywood, Varnette P. 110: 68, 70
Hong, Lily Toy 76: 104
Honigman, Marian 3: 2
Honore, Paul 42: 77, 79, 81, 82
Hood, Alun 69: 145, 218; 72: 41; 80: 226; 87: 4; 95: 139
Hood, Susan 12: 43
Hook, Christian 104: 103
Hook, Frances 26: 188; 27: 127
Hook, Jeff 14: 137; 103: 105
Hook, Richard 26: 188
Hooks 63: 30
Hooper, Hadley 177: 145
Hoover, Carol A. 21: 77
Hoover, Russell 12: 95; 17: 2; 34: 156
Hope, James 141: 116

Hopkins, Chris 99: 127
Hopkinson, Leigh 202: 70
Hopman, Philip 178: 184
Hoppe, Paul 209: 85
Hoppin, Augustus 34: 66
Horacek, Judy 211: 86
Horacek, Petr 163: 117; 214: 113
Horder, Margaret 2: 108; 73: 75
Horen, Michael 45: 121
Horne, Daniel 73: 106; 91: 153; 109: 127; 110: 232; 164: 176
Horne, Richard 111: 80
Horowitz, Dave 204: 58
Horse, Harry 128: 195; 169: 86
Horton, Anthony 211: 98
Horvat, Laurel 12: 201
Horvath, David 192: 95
Horvath, Ferdinand Kusati 24: 176
Horvath, Maria 57: 171
Horwitz, Richard 57: 174
Hotchkiss, De Wolfe 20: 49
Hough, Charlotte 9: 112; 13: 98; 17: 83; 24: 195
Houlihan, Ray 11: 214
House, Caroline 183: 121
Housman, Laurence 25: 146, 147
Houston, James 13: 107; 74: 132, 134, 135
Hovland, Gary 88: 172; 171: 148
Hoyt, Eleanor 158: 231
How, W.E. 20: 47
Howard, Alan 16: 80; 34: 58; 45: 114
Howard, Arthur 165: 111, 112; 190: 5
Howard, J.N. 15: 234
Howard, John 33: 179
Howard, Kim 116: 71
Howard, Paul 142: 126, 129; 144: 187
Howard, Rob 40: 161
Howarth, Daniel 170: 34
Howe, John 79: 101; 80: 150; 115: 47; 176: 106; 207: 32, 35
Howe, Phillip 79: 117; 175: 115
Howe, Stephen 1: 232
Howell, Karen 119: 123
Howell, Pat 15: 139
Howell, Troy 23: 24; 31: 61; 36: 158; 37: 184; 41: 76, 235; 48: 112; 56: 13; 57: 3; 59: 174; 63: 5; 74: 46; 89: 188; 90: 231; 95: 97; 98: 130; 99: 189; 153: 156, 157, 158; 176: 104; 199: 96, 98
Howes, Charles 22: 17
Hoyt, Ard 145: 141; 190: 82; 207: 148
Hranilovich, Barbara 127: 51
Hu, Ying-Hwa 116: 107; 152: 236; 173: 171
Huang, Benrei 137: 55
Huang, Zhong-Yang 117: 30, 32; 213: 18
Hubbard, Woodleigh Marx 98: 67; 115: 79; 160: 138; 214: 120
Hubley, Faith 48: 120, 121, 125, 130, 131, 132, 134
Hubley, John 48: 125, 130, 131, 132, 134
Hudak, Michal 143: 74
Hudnut, Robin 14: 62
Huerta, Catherine 76: 178; 77: 44, 45; 90: 182; 210: 202
Huffaker, Sandy 10: 56
Huffman, Joan 13: 33
Huffman, Tom 13: 180; 17: 212; 21: 116; 24: 132; 33: 154; 38: 59; 42: 147
Hughes, Arthur 20: 148, 149, 150; 33: 114, 148, 149
Hughes, Darren 95: 44
Hughes, David 36: 197
Hughes, Shirley 1: 20, 21; 7: 3; 12: 217; 16: 163; 29: 154; 63: 118; 70: 102, 103, 104; 73: 169; 88: 70; 110: 118, 119, 159: 103
Hugo, Victor 47: 112
Huliska-Beith, Laura 204: 108
Hull, Cathy 78: 29
Hull, Richard 95: 120; 123: 175; 172: 195
Hulsmann, Eva 16: 166
Hume, Lachie 189: 93

Hummel, Berta 43: 137, 138, 139
Hummel, Lisl 29: 109; YABC 2: 333, 334
Humphrey, Henry 16: 167
Humphreys, Graham 25: 168
Humphries, Tudor 76: 66; 80: 4; 124: 4, 5
Huneck, Stephen 183: 88, 89
Hunt, James 2: 143
Hunt, Jonathan 84: 120
Hunt, Paul 119: 104; 129: 135; 139: 160; 173: 112
Hunt, Robert 110: 206, 235; 147: 136, 137; 170: 3; 211: 76
Hunt, Scott 190: 143
Hunter, Anne 133: 190; 178: 150
Huntington, Amy 180: 99
Hurd, Clement 2: 148, 149; 64: 127, 128, 129, 131, 133, 134,135, 136; 100: 37, 38
Hurd, Peter 24: 30, 31,; YABC 2: 56
Hurd, Thacher 46: 88, 89; 94: 114, 115, 116; 123: 81, 82, 84
Hurlimann, Ruth 32: 99
Hurst, Carol Otis 185: 92
Hurst, Philip 196: 79
Hurst, Tracey 192: 238
Hussar, Michael 114: 113; 117: 159
Hustler, Tom 6: 105
Hutchins, Laurence 55: 22
Hutchins, Pat 15: 142; 70: 106, 107, 108; 178: 131, 132
Hutchinson, Sascha 95: 211
Hutchinson, William M. 6: 3, 138; 46: 70
Hutchison, Paula 23: 10
Hutton, Clarke YABC 2: 335
Hutton, Kathryn 35: 155; 89: 91
Hutton, Warwick 20: 91
Huyette, Marcia 29: 188
Hyatt, John 54: 7
Hyatt, Mitch 178: 162
Hyde, Maureen 82: 17; 121: 145, 146
Hyman, David 117: 64
Hyman, Miles 210: 132
Hyman, Trina Schart 1: 204; 2: 194; 5: 153; 6: 106; 7: 138, 145; 8: 22; 10: 196; 13: 96; 14: 114; 15: 204; 16: 234; 20: 82; 22: 133; 24: 151; 25: 79, 82; 26: 82; 29: 83; 31: 37, 39; 34: 104; 38: 84, 100, 128; 41: 49; 43: 146; 46: 91, 92, 93, 95, 96, 97, 98, 99, 100, 101, 102, 103, 104, 105,108, 109, 111, 197; 48: 60, 61; 52: 32; 60: 168; 66: 38; 67: 214; 72: 74; 75: 92; 79: 57; 82: 95, 238; 89: 46; 95: 91, 92, 93; 100: 33, 199; 132: 12; 147: 33, 35, 36; 167: 58, 60; 177: 189, 190; 211: 188

I

Ibarra, Rosa 147: 91
Ibatoulline, Bagram 156: 48; 174: 33, 82; 202: 30; 211: 213
Ichikawa, Satomi 29: 152; 41: 52; 47: 133, 134,135, 136; 78: 93, 94; 80: 81; 146: 143, 145, 146; 208: 117, 118, 119
Ide, Jacqueline YABC 1: 39
Ilsley, Velma 3: 1; 7: 55; 12: 109; 37: 62; 38: 184
Imai, Ayano 190: 85, 86
in den Bosch, Nicole 150: 204
Inga 1: 142
Ingman, Bruce 134: 50; 182: 91, 92; 214: 10
Ingpen, Robert 109: 103, 104; 132: 138; 137: 177; 166: 103; 181: 140
Ingraham, Erick 21: 177; 84: 256; 103: 66
Inkpen, Mick 99: 104, 105; 106: 44
Innerst, Stacy 149: 104
Innocenti, Roberto 21: 123; 96: 122; 159: 111, 197; 199: 176
Inoue, Yosuke 24: 118
Iofin, Michael 97: 157
Iosa, Ann 63: 189

Ipcar, Dahlov *1:* 124, 125; *49:* 137, 138, 139, 140, 141, 142,143, 144, 145; *147:* 122, 124, 126
Irvin, Fred *13:* 166; *15:* 143, 144; *27:* 175
Irving, Jay *45:* 72
Irving, Laurence *27:* 50
Isaac, Joanne *21:* 76
Isaacs, Gary *170:* 188
Isadora, Rachel *43:* 159, 160; *54:* 31; *79:* 106, 107,108; *121:* 100, 102; *165:* 116, 117; *204:* 61, 63, 64
Ishmael, Woodi *24:* 111; *31:* 99
Ives, Ruth *15:* 257
Iwai, Melissa *149:* 233; *183:* 92; *199:* 115
Iwamura, Kazuo *213:* 87

J

Jabar, Cynthia *101:* 201; *210:* 134, 135
Jackness, Andrew *94:* 237
Jackson, Julian *91:* 104, 106
Jackson, Michael *43:* 42
Jackson, Shelley *79:* 71; *99:* 109; *187:* 82
Jacob, Murv *89:* 30
Jacobi, Kathy *62:* 118
Jacobs, Barbara *9:* 136
Jacobs, Lou, Jr. *9:* 136; *15:* 128
Jacobsen, Laura *176:* 98; *177:* 85, 86
Jacobson, Rick *131:* 222; *170:* 119
Jacobus, Tim *79:* 140; *109:* 126; *129:* 180
Jacques, Robin *1:* 70; *2:* 1; *8:* 46; *9:* 20; *15:* 187; *19:* 253; *32:* 102, 103, 104; *43:* 184; *73:* 135; *YABC 1:* 42
Jaeggi, Yoshiko *186:* 184
Jaffee, Al *66:* 131, 132
Jagr, Miloslav *13:* 197
Jahn-Clough, Lisa *88:* 114; *152:* 104; *193:* 70, 71
Jahnke, Robert *84:* 24
Jainschigg, Nicholas *80:* 64; *91:* 138; *95:* 63; *99:* 25; *108:* 50; *171:* 41
Jakesavic, Nenad *85:* 102
Jakobsen, Kathy *116:* 83
Jakubowski, Charles *14:* 192
Jambor, Louis *YABC 1:* 11
James, Ann *73:* 50; *82:* 113; *158:* 61; *183:* 44
James, Brian *140:* 91
James, Curtis E. *182:* 93
James, Derek *35:* 187; *44:* 91; *61:* 133; *74:* 2; *80:* 57; *86:* 88; *130:* 30; *179:* 29
James, Gilbert *YABC 1:* 43
James, Gordon C. *195:* 89
James, Harold *2:* 151; *3:* 62; *8:* 79; *29:* 113; *51:* 195; *74:* 90
James, Kennon *126:* 211
James, Robin *50:* 106; *53:* 32, 34, 35
James, Simon *202:* 73, 74
James, Will *19:* 150, 152, 153, 155, 163
Janosch
    See Eckert, Horst
Janovitch, Marilyn *68:* 168
Janovitz, Marilyn *87:* 187; *130:* 198; *194:* 91
Jansons, Inese *48:* 117
Jansson, Tove *3:* 90; *41:* 106, 108, 109, 110, 111, 113, 114
Jaques, Faith *7:* 11, 132, 133; *21:* 83, 84; *69:* 114,116; *73:* 170
Jaques, Frances Lee *29:* 224
Jarrett, Clare *201:* 77
Jauss, Anne Marie *1:* 139; *3:* 34; *10:* 57, 119; *11:* 205; *23:* 194
Jay, Alison *158:* 97, 98; *183:* 126, 127; *196:* 95, 96, 97, 98; *200:* 72, 73, 74; *212:* 39
Jeffers, Oliver *175:* 111; *213:* 89
Jeffers, Susan *17:* 86, 87; *25:* 164, 165; *26:* 112; *50:* 132, 134, 135; *70:* 111, 112, 113; *137:* 107, 108, 109, 110, 111; *202:* 77, 78
Jefferson, Louise E. *4:* 160
Jenkin-Pearce, Susie *78:* 16

Jenkins, Debra Reid *85:* 202; *114:* 89; *173:* 134
Jenkins, Jean *98:* 79, 102
Jenkins, Leonard *157:* 169; *167:* 128; *189:* 96, 97; *190:* 89
Jenkins, Patrick *72:* 126
Jenkins, Steve *124:* 177; *154:* 90, 91, 92, 93; *185:* 194; *188:* 81, 82, 83, 84, 85, 86
Jenks, Aleta *73:* 117; *124:* 225
Jenkyns, Chris *51:* 97
Jensen, Bruce *95:* 39
Jensinius, Kirsten *56:* 58
Jeram, Anita *89:* 135; *102:* 122, 123; *129:* 112; *154:* 96, 97, 98; *164:* 154; *203:* 123, 124
Jernigan, E. Wesley *85:* 92
Jerome, Karen A. *72:* 194
Jeruchim, Simon *6:* 173; *15:* 250; *41:* 84; *42:* 120
Jeschke, Susan *20:* 89; *39:* 161; *41:* 84; *42:* 120
Jessel, Camilla *29:* 115
Jessell, Tim *159:* 3; *177:* 87; *181:* 95; *205:* 4; *213:* 74
Jeyaveeran, Ruth *182:* 100
Jiang, Cheng An *109:* 108
Jiang, Wei *109:* 108
Jimenez, Maria *77:* 158; *93:* 127
Jobling, Curtis *138:* 74
Jocelyn, Marthe *118:* 83; *137:* 219; *163:* 119, 120; *198:* 62
Joerns, Consuelo *38:* 36; *44:* 94
John, Diana *12:* 209
John, Helen *1:* 215; *28:* 204
Johns, Elizabeth *127:* 33
Johns, Jasper *61:* 172
Johns, Jeanne *24:* 114
Johnson, Adrian *143:* 50
Johnson, Bruce *9:* 47
Johnson, Cathy *92:* 136
Johnson, Crockett
    See Leisk, David
Johnson, D. William *23:* 104
Johnson, D.B. *183:* 98, 139
Johnson, David *175:* 18; *191:* 91
Johnson, Gillian *119:* 175; *164:* 217; *215:* 99
Johnson, Harper *1:* 27; *2:* 33; *18:* 302; *19:* 61; *31:* 181; *44:* 46, 50, 95
Johnson, Ingrid *37:* 118
Johnson, James Ralph *1:* 23, 127
Johnson, James David *12:* 195
Johnson, Jane *48:* 136
Johnson, Joel Peter *98:* 18; *128:* 111; *201:* 13; *213:* 189
Johnson, John E. *34:* 133
Johnson, Kevin *72:* 44
Johnson, Kevin Eugene *109:* 215
Johnson, Larry *47:* 56; *123:* 107; *159:* 203
Johnson, Layne *187:* 94; *209:* 63
Johnson, Margaret S. *35:* 131
Johnson, Meredith Merrell *71:* 181; *83:* 158; *89:* 103; *104:* 88
Johnson, Milton *1:* 67; *2:* 71; *26:* 45; *31:* 107; *60:* 112; *68:* 96
Johnson, Pamela *16:* 174; *52:* 145; *62:* 140; *73:* 116; *85:* 64
Johnson, Paul Brett *83:* 95; *132:* 119
Johnson, Stephen T. *80:* 15; *131:* 35; *141:* 96; *145:* 40; *164:* 187; *175:* 32; *189:* 99, 100; *208:* 43
Johnson, Steve *138:* 219; *141:* 64; *144:* 199; *177:* 51; *214:* 95
Johnson, William R. *38:* 91
Johnson-Petrov, Arden *115:* 206
Johnston, David McCall *50:* 131, 133
Johnston, Lynne *118:* 85, 87, 89
Johnstone, Anne *8:* 120; *36:* 89
Johnstone, Janet Grahame *8:* 120; *36:* 89
Jonas, Ann *50:* 107, 108, 109; *135:* 113
Jones, Bob *71:* 5; *77:* 199
Jones, Carol *5:* 131; *72:* 185, 186; *153:* 111, 112

Jones, Chuck *53:* 70, 71
Jones, Curtis *211:* 144
Jones, Davy *89:* 176
Jones, Douglas B. *185:* 192; *202:* 82
Jones, Elizabeth Orton *18:* 124, 126, 128, 129
Jones, Harold *14:* 88; *52:* 50
Jones, Holly *127:* 3
Jones, Jeff *41:* 64
Jones, Laurian *25:* 24, 27
Jones, Margaret *74:* 57
Jones, Noah Z. *182:* 37; *203:* 159
Jones, Randy *131:* 104
Jones, Richard *127:* 222
Jones, Robert *25:* 67
Jones, Wilfred *35:* 115; *YABC 1:* 163
Jordan, Charles *89:* 58
Jordan, Jess *158:* 136; *203:* 111
Jordan, Martin George *84:* 127
Jordan, Richard *84:* 36
Jorgenson, Andrea *91:* 111
Jorisch, Stéphane *153:* 56, 193; *177:* 29; *178:* 138, 139; *187:* 23; *211:* 182
Joseph, James *53:* 88
Joudrey, Ken *64:* 145; *78:* 6
Joyce, William *72:* 131, 132, 133, 134; *73:* 227; *145:* 37
Joyner, Jerry *34:* 138
Joyner, Loraine M. *209:* 17
Joysmith, Brenda *210:* 237
Juan, Ana *175:* 38; *179:* 111, 112; *213:* 9
Jucker, Sita *5:* 93
Judge, Lita *192:* 99
Judkis, Jim *37:* 38
Juhasz, Victor *31:* 67
Jullian, Philippe *24:* 206; *25:* 203
Jung, Tom *91:* 217
Junge, Alexandra *183:* 37
Junge, Walter *67:* 150
Jupo, Frank *7:* 148, 149
Jurisch, Stephane *154:* 105
Justice, Martin *34:* 72

K

Kabatova-Taborska, Zdenka *107:* 153
Kachik, John *165:* 230
Kaczman, James *156:* 98
Kadair, Deborah Ousley *184:* 45, 89
Kahl, David *74:* 95; *97:* 35; *109:* 174; *110:* 213; *198:* 15
Kahl, M.P. *37:* 83
Kahl, Virginia *48:* 138
Kahn, Katherine Janus *90:* 135; *211:* 155
Kakimoo, Kozo *11:* 148
Kalett, Jim *48:* 159, 160, 161
Kalin, Victor *39:* 186
Kalis, Jennifer *207:* 82
Kalman, Maira *96:* 131, 132; *137:* 115
Kalmenoff, Matthew *22:* 191
Kalow, Gisela *32:* 105
Kamen, Gloria *1:* 41; *9:* 119; *10:* 178; *35:* 157; *78:* 236; *98:* 82
Kaminsky, Jef *102:* 153
Kandell, Alice *35:* 133
Kane, Henry B. *14:* 90; *18:* 219, 220
Kane, Robert *18:* 131
Kanfer, Larry *66:* 141
Kangas, Juli *200:* 88
Kappes, Alfred *28:* 104
Karalus, Bob *41:* 157
Karas, G. Brian *80:* 60; *99:* 179; *115:* 41; *118:* 50; *136:* 168; *145:* 166; *149:* 245; *159:* 65; *171:* 192; *178:* 142, 143; *202:* 38; *209:* 142
Karasz, Ilonka *128:* 163
Karlin, Eugene *10:* 63; *20:* 131
Karlin, Nurit *63:* 78; *103:* 110
Karpinski, Tony *134:* 160
Kasamatsu, Shiro *139:* 155
Kasparavicius, Kestutis *139:* 210

Kassian, Olena *64:* 94
Kastner, Jill *79:* 135; *117:* 84, 85
Kasuya, Masahiro *41:* 206, 207; *51:* 100
Kasza, Keiko *191:* 99, 100, 101, 102, 103
Katona, Robert *21:* 85; *24:* 126
Katz, Avi *199:* 55
Katz, Karen *158:* 123
Kauffer, E. McKnight *33:* 103; *35:* 127; *63:* 67
Kaufman, Angelika *15:* 156
Kaufman, Joe *33:* 119
Kaufman, John *13:* 158
Kaufman, Stuart *62:* 64; *68:* 226; *137:* 44
Kaufmann, John *1:* 174; *4:* 159; *8:* 43, 1; *10:* 102; *18:* 133, 134; *22:* 251
Kaye, Graham *1:* 9; *67:* 7, 8
Kaye, M.M. *62:* 95
Kazalovski, Nata *40:* 205
Keane, Bil *4:* 135
Kearney, David *72:* 47; *121:* 83
Keating, Pamel T. *77:* 37
Keats, Ezra Jack *3:* 18, 105, 257; *14:* 101, 102; *33:* 129; *57:* 79, 80, 82, 83, 84, 87
Keegan, Charles *166:* 211
Keegan, Marcia *9:* 122; *32:* 93
Keeler, Patricia A. *81:* 56; *183:* 102, 103
Keely, Jack *119:* 95
Keely, John *26:* 104; *48:* 214
Keen, Eliot *25:* 213
Keep, Richard C. *170:* 122
Keeping, Charles *9:* 124, 185; *15:* 28, 134; *18:* 115; *44:* 194, 196; *47:* 25; *52:* 3; *54:* 156; *69:* 123, 124; *74:* 56; *155:* 9
Keeter, Susan *168:* 46; *183:* 192
Keith, Eros *4:* 98; *5:* 138; *31:* 29; *43:* 220; *52:* 91, 92, 93, 94; *56:* 64, 66; *60:* 37; *79:* 93
Keleinikov, Andrei *65:* 101, 102
Kelen, Emery *13:* 115
Keller, A.J. *62:* 198
Keller, Arthur I. *26:* 106
Keller, Dick *36:* 123, 125
Keller, Holly *45:* 79; *76:* 118, 119, 120, 121; *108:* 137, 138, 140; *157:* 117, 118, 119
Keller, Katie *79:* 222; *93:* 108
Keller, Laurie *196:* 105, 106
Keller, Ronald *45:* 208
Kelley, Gary *183:* 105
Kelley, Marty *211:* 91
Kelley, True *41:* 114, 115; *42:* 137; *75:* 35; *92:* 104, 105; *124:* 62; *130:* 100, 101; *179:* 120, 121, 122; *192:* 251
Kellogg, Steven *8:* 96; *11:* 207; *14:* 130; *20:* ; *201:* 38 58; *29:* 140, 141; *30:* 35; *41:* 141; *57:* 89, 90, 92,93, 94, 96; *59:* 182; *73:* 141; *77:* 129; *130:* 105, 106; *177:* 94, 95, 96, 97; *199:* 57; *YABC 1:* 65, 73
Kelly, Billy *158:* 143
Kelly, Geoff *97:* 196; *112:* 25
Kelly, Irene *147:* 134; *210:* 144, 145
Kelly, John *194:* 186
Kelly, Joseph *174:* 94
Kelly, Kathleen M. *71:* 109
Kelly, Laura *89:* 217
Kelly, True *163:* 87
Kelly, Walt *18:* 136, 137, 138, 139, 140, 141, 144, 145, 146, 148, 149
Kemble, E.W. *34:* 75; *44:* 178; *YABC 2:* 54, 59
Kemly, Kathleen *209:* 165
Kemp-Welsh, Lucy *24:* 197; *100:* 214
Kendall, Jane *150:* 105; *186:* 109
Kendall, Peter *152:* 85
Kendrick, Dennis *79:* 213
Kennaway, Adrienne *60:* 55, 56; *171:* 88, 89
Kennedy, Anne *212:* 34
Kennedy, Doug *189:* 104
Kennedy, Paul Edward *6:* 190; *8:* 132; *33:* 120
Kennedy, Richard *3:* 93; *12:* 179; *44:* 193; *100:* 15; *YABC 1:* 57
Kent, Jack *24:* 136; *37:* 37; *40:* 81; *84:* 89; *86:* 150; *88:* 77

Kent, Rockwell *5:* 166; *6:* 129; *20:* 225, 226, 227,229; *59:* 144
Kenyon, Tony *81:* 201; *127:* 74
Kepes, Juliet *13:* 119
Kerins, Anthony *76:* 84
Kerr, Judity *24:* 137
Kerr, Phyllis Forbes *72:* 141
Kessler, Leonard *1:* 108; *7:* 139; *14:* 107, 227; *22:* 101; *44:* 96; *67:* 79; *82:* 123
Kest, Kristin *168:* 99; *173:* 23
Kesteven, Peter *35:* 189
Ketcham, Hank *28:* 140, 141, 142
Kettelkamp, Larry *2:* 164
Key, Alexander *8:* 99
Khalsa, Dayal Kaur *62:* 99
Kiakshuk *8:* 59
Kid, Tom *207:* 54
Kidd, Chip *94:* 23
Kidd, Richard *152:* 110
Kidd, Tom *64:* 199; *81:* 189; *185:* 173
Kiddell-Monroe, Joan *19:* 201; *55:* 59, 60; *87:* 174; *121:* 112
Kidder, Harvey *9:* 105; *80:* 41
Kidwell, Carl *43:* 145
Kieffer, Christa *41:* 89
Kiesler, Kate *110:* 105; *136:* 142
Kiff, Ken *40:* 45
Kilbride, Robert *37:* 100
Kilby, Don *141:* 144
Kim, David *201:* 79; *202:* 97
Kim, Glenn *99:* 82
Kimball, Anton *78:* 114; *119:* 105
Kimball, Yeffe *23:* 116; *37:* 88
Kimber, Murray *171:* 91
Kimmel, Warren *176:* 112
Kincade, Orin *34:* 116
Kindersley, Barnabas *96:* 110
Kindred, Wendy *7:* 151
King, Colin *53:* 3
King, Robin *10:* 164, 165
King, Stephen Michael *141:* 31; *197:* 191
King, Tara Calahan *139:* 172
King, Tony *39:* 121
Kingman, Dong *16:* 287; *44:* 100, 102, 104
Kingsley, Charles *YABC 2:* 182
Kingston, Julie *147:* 14
Kingston, Maxine Hong *53:* 92
Kinney, Jeff *187:* 97
Kipling, John Lockwood *YABC 2:* 198
Kipling, Rudyard *YABC 2:* 196
Kipniss, Robert *29:* 59
Kirchherr, Astrid *55:* 23
Kirchhoff, Art *28:* 136
Kirk, Daniel *153:* 115, 116, 117; *173:* 101; *196:* 113, 114, 115, 116
Kirk, David *117:* 88, 89; *161:* 97, 98
Kirk, Ruth *5:* 96
Kirk, Steve *170:* 37
Kirk, Tim *32:* 209, 211; *72:* 89; *83:* 49
Kirmse, Marguerite *15:* 283; *18:* 153
Kirsch, Vincent X. *124:* 207
Kirschner, Ruth *22:* 154
Kirwan, Wednesday *198:* 73
Kish, Ely *73:* 119; *79:* 2
Kitamura, Satoshi *62:* 102; *98:* 91; *101:* 147; *138:* 2; *143:* 83, 85, 86; *201:* 83
Kiss, Andrew *168:* 115
Kitchel, JoAnn E. *133:* 32
Kitchen, Bert *70:* 126; *193:* 49
Kittelsen, Theodor *62:* 14
Kiuchi, Tatsuro *114:* 71
Kiwak, Barbara *172:* 135
Klahr, Susan *176:* 196
Klapholz, Mel *13:* 35
Klee, Jutte *209:* 136
Klein, Bill *89:* 105
Klein, Robert *55:* 77
Klein, Suzanna *63:* 104
Kleinman, Zalman *28:* 143
Kleven, Elisa *173:* 96, 97
Kliban, B. *35:* 137, 138

Kline, Michael *127:* 66
Klise, M. Sarah *180:* 117, 118; *181:* 97
Knabel, Lonnie *73:* 103; *75:* 187, 228; *194:* 216
Kneen, Maggie *140:* 139
Knight, Ann *34:* 143
Knight, Christopher *13:* 125
Knight, Hilary *1:* 233; *3:* 21; *15:* 92, 158, 159; *16:* 258, 259, 260; *18:* 235; *19:* 169; *35:* 242; *46:* 167; *52:* 116; *69:* 126, 127; *132:* 129; *YABC 1:* 168, 169, 172
Knorr, Laura *200:* 91
Knorr, Peter *126:* 92, 93
Knotts, Howard *20:* 4; *25:* 170; *36:* 163
Knutson, Barbara *112:* 134; *202:* 108
Knutson, Kimberley *115:* 90
Kobayashi, Ann *39:* 58
Kochalka, James *196:* 120, 121, 122
Kocsis, J.C.
　See Paul, James
Kodman, Stanislawa *201:* 85
Koehler, Hanne Lore *176:* 203
Koehn, Ilse *34:* 198; *79:* 123
Koelsch, Michael *99:* 182; *107:* 164; *109:* 239; *138:* 142; *150:* 94; *176:* 105; *187:* 63; *198:* 63
Koering, Ursula *3:* 28; *4:* 14; *44:* 5; *64:* 140,141; *85:* 46
Koerner, Henry
　See Koerner, W.H.D.
Koerner, W.H.D. *14:* 216; *21:* 88, 89, 90, 91; *23:* 211
Koetsch, Mike *166:* 68
Koffler, Camilla *36:* 113
Kogan, Deborah Ray *161:* 101, 102
Koide, Yasuko *50:* 114
Kolado, Karen *102:* 228
Komoda, Kiyo *9:* 128; *13:* 214
Kompaneyets, Marc *169:* 92
Konashevich, Vladimir *61:* 160
Konashevicha, V. *YABC 1:* 26
Konigsburg, E.L. *4:* 138; *48:* 141, 142, 144, 145; *94:* 129, 130; *126:* 129, 130, 131; *194:* 95, 98
Kono, Erin Eitter *177:* 99
Kooiker, Leonie *48:* 148
Koonook, Simon *65:* 157
Koontz, Robin Michal *136:* 155
Koopmans, Loek *101:* 121
Kopelke, Lisa *154:* 107
Kopper, Lisa *72:* 152, 153; *105:* 135, 136
Korach, Mimi *1:* 128, 129; *2:* 52; *4:* 39; *5:* 159; *9:* 129; *10:* 21; *24:* 69
Koren, Edward *5:* 100; *65:* 65, 67
Kosaka, Fumi *164:* 130
Koscielniak, Bruce *99:* 122; *153:* 120, 121, 122
Koshkin, Alexander *92:* 180
Kossin, Sandy *10:* 71; *23:* 105
Kostin, Andrej *26:* 204
Kosturko, Bob *164:* 56
Kotzky, Brian *68:* 184
Kovacevic, Zivojin *13:* 247
Kovalski, Maryann *58:* 120; *84:* 88; *97:* 124, 125, 126; *158:* 3; *186:* 80
Kozjan, Drazen *209:* 99
Krahn, Fernando *2:* 257; *34:* 206; *49:* 152
Kramer, Anthony *33:* 81
Kramer, David *96:* 162; *109:* 132; *150:* 220
Kramer, Frank *6:* 121
Krantz, Kathy *35:* 83
Kratter, Paul *139:* 65
Kraus, Robert *13:* 217; *65:* 113; *93:* 93, 94
Krause, Jon *176:* 62
Krauss, Trisha *174:* 10
Kredel, Fritz *6:* 35; *17:* 93, 94, 95, 96; *22:* 147; *24:* 175; *29:* 130; *35:* 77; *YABC 2:* 166, 300
Kreloff, Eliot *189:* 107, 108; *205:* 182
Krementz, Jill *17:* 98; *49:* 41
Krenina, Katya *117:* 106; *125:* 133; *176:* 117

Kresin, Robert *23:* 19
Krieger, Salem *54:* 164
Kriegler, Lyn *73:* 29
Krinitz, Esther Nisenthal *193:* 196
Krommes, Beth *128:* 141; *149:* 136; *181:* 100, 101; *184:* 105; *188:* 125; *208:* 135; *209:* 185
Krone, Mike *101:* 71
Kronheimer, Ann *135:* 119
Krosoczka, Jarrett J. *155:* 142; *200:* 93, 94
Kruck, Gerald *88:* 181
Krudop, Walter Lyon *199:* 19
Krupinski, Loretta *67:* 104; *102:* 131; *161:* 105, 106
Krupp, Robin Rector *53:* 96, 98
Krush, Beth *1:* 51, 85; *2:* 233; *4:* 115; *9:* 61; *10:* 191; *11:* 196; *18:* 164, 165; *32:* 72; *37:* 203; *43:* 57; *60:* 102, 103, 107, 108, 109
Krush, Joe *2:* 233; *4:* 115; *9:* 61; *10:* 191; *11:* 196; *18:* 164, 165; *32:* 72, 91; *37:* 203; *43:* 57; *60:* 102, 103, 107, 108, 109
Krych, Duane *91:* 43
Krykorka, Vladyana *96:* 147; *143:* 90, 91; *168:* 14
Kubick, Dana *165:* 91; *212:* 104, 105, 212
Kubinyi, Laszlo *4:* 116; *6:* 113; *16:* 118; *17:* 100; *28:* 227; *30:* 172; *49:* 24, 28; *54:* 23; *167:* 149
Kubricht, Mary *73:* 118
Kucharik, Elena *139:* 31
Kuchera, Kathleen *84:* 5
Kuhn, Bob *17:* 91; *35:* 235
Kulikov, Boris *163:* 185; *185:* 23; *205:* 99, 100
Kulka, Joe *188:* 110
Kukalis, Romas *90:* 27; *139:* 37
Kuklin, Susan *63:* 82, 83, 84
Kunhardt, Dorothy *53:* 101
Kunhardt, Edith *67:* 105, 106
Kunstler, Mort *10:* 73; *32:* 143
Kurchevsky, V. *34:* 61
Kurczok, Belinda *121:* 118
Kurelek, William *8:* 107
Kuriloff, Ron *13:* 19
Kurisu, Jane *160:* 120
Kuskin, Karla *2:* 170; *68:* 115, 116; *111:* 116
Kutzer, Ernst *19:* 249
Kuzma, Steve *57:* 8; *62:* 93
Kuznetsova, Berta *74:* 45
Kvasnosky, Laura McGee *93:* 103; *142:* 83; *182:* 108
Kwas, Susan Estelle *179:* 116
Kyong, Yunmee *165:* 139

L

LaBlanc, Andre *24:* 146
Laboccetta, Mario *27:* 120
LaBrose, Darcie *157:* 134
Labrosse, Darcia *58:* 88; *108:* 77; *178:* 89
LaCava, Vince *95:* 118
Laceky, Adam *32:* 121
Lacis, Astra *85:* 117
Lacome, Julie *174:* 96, 97
La Croix *YABC 2:* 4
Ladd, London *206:* 50
Ladwig, Tim *98:* 212; *117:* 76; *215:* 32
La Farge, Margaret *47:* 141
LaFave, Kim *64:* 177; *72:* 39; *97:* 146; *99:* 172; *106:* 123; *149:* 126; *196:* 128, 129
Lafontaine, Roger *167:* 158
Lafrance, Marie *197:* 109
Lagarrigue, Jerome *136:* 102; *187:* 81
Laimgruber, Monika *11:* 153
Laio, Jimmy *213:* 57
Laite, Gordon *1:* 130, 131; *8:* 209; *31:* 113; *40:* 63; *46:* 117
Laliberté, Louise-Andrée *169:* 98
LaMarche, Jim *46:* 204; *61:* 56; *94:* 69; *114:* 22; *129:* 163; *162:* 78, 80

Lamb, Jim *10:* 117
Lambase, Barbara *101:* 185; *150:* 221; *166:* 234
Lambert, J.K. *38:* 129; *39:* 24
Lambert, Sally Anne *133:* 191
Lambert, Saul *23:* 112; *33:* 107; *54:* 136
Lambert, Stephen *109:* 33; *174:* 99
Lambo, Don *6:* 156; *35:* 115; *36:* 146
Lamontagne, Jacques *166:* 227
Lamut, Sonja *57:* 193
Lamut, Sonya *85:* 102
Landa, Peter *11:* 95; *13:* 177; *53:* 119
Landau, Jacob *38:* 111
Landis, Joan *104:* 23; *203:* 32
Landon, Lucinda *79:* 31
Landshoff, Ursula *13:* 124
Landström, Lena *146:* 165, 166
Landström, Olof *146:* 166, 168; *170:* 22
Lane, Daniel *112:* 60
Lane, John R. *8:* 145
Lane, John *15:* 176, 177; *30:* 146
Lane, Nancy *166:* 74
Lang, G.D. *48:* 56
Lang, Gary *73:* 75
Lang, Jerry *18:* 295
Langdo, Bryan *186:* 187; *191:* 113, 114, 115
Lange, Dorothea *50:* 141
Langley, Jonathan *162:* 128
Langner, Nola *8:* 110; *42:* 36
Lanino, Deborah *105:* 148
Lantz, Paul *1:* 82, 102; *27:* 88; *34:* 102; *45:* 123
Larkin, Bob *84:* 225
Laroche, Giles *126:* 140; *146:* 81
LaRochelle, David *171:* 97
Larrecq, John *44:* 108; *68:* 56
Larsen, Suzanne *1:* 13
Larson, Gary *57:* 121, 122, 123, 124, 125, 126, 127
Larsson, Carl *35:* 144, 145, 146, 147, 148, 149, 150, 152, 153, 154
Larsson, Karl *19:* 177
Lartitegui, Ana G. *105:* 167
LaRue, Michael D. *13:* 215
La Rue, Michael D. *13:* 215
Lasker, Joe *7:* 186, 187; *14:* 55; *38:* 115; *39:* 47; *83:* 113, 114, 115
Latham, Barbara *16:* 188, 189; *43:* 71
Lathrop, Dorothy *14:* 117, 118, 119; *15:* 109; *16:* 78, 79, 81; *32:* 201, 203; *33:* 112; *YABC 2:* 301
Lattimore, Eleanor Frances *7:* 156
Lauden, Claire *16:* 173
Lauden, George, Jr. *16:* 173
Laune, Paul *2:* 235; *34:* 31
Laure, Jason *49:* 53; *50:* 122
Lauter, Richard *63:* 29; *67:* 111; *77:* 198
Lavallee, Barbara *74:* 157; *92:* 154; *96:* 126; *145:* 193; *166:* 125, 126; *186:* 155; *192:* 172
Lave, Fitz Hugh *59:* 139
Lavis, Stephen *43:* 143; *87:* 137, 164, 165
Layton, Neal *152:* 120, 121; *182:* 65; *187:* 103, 105, 106
Law, Jenny *201:* 31
Lawrason, June *168:* 30
Lawrence, John *25:* 131; *30:* 141; *44:* 198, 200; *214:* 7
Lawrence, Stephen *20:* 195
Lawson, Carol *6:* 38; *42:* 93, 131; *174:* 56; *189:* 89; *209:* 59
Lawson, George *17:* 280
Lawson, Robert *5:* 26; *6:* 94; *13:* 39; *16:* 11; *20:* 100, 102, 103; *54:* 3; *66:* 12; *100:* 144, 145; *YABC 2:* 222, 224, 225, 227, 228, 229, 230, 231, 232, 233, 234, 235, 237, 238, 239, 240, 241
Layfield, Kathie *60:* 194
Lazare, Jerry *44:* 109; *74:* 28
Lazarevich, Mila *17:* 118
Lazarus, Claire *103:* 30
Lazarus, Keo Felker *21:* 94

Lazzaro, Victor *11:* 126
Lea, Bob *166:* 208; *203:* 108
Lea, Tom *43:* 72, 74
Leacroft, Richard *6:* 140
Leaf, Munro *20:* 99
Leake, Donald *70:* 41
Leander, Patricia *23:* 27
Lear, Edward *18:* 183, 184, 185
Lear, Rebecca *149:* 46
Lebenson, Richard *6:* 209; *7:* 76; *23:* 145; *44:* 191; *87:* 153
Le Cain, Errol *6:* 141; *9:* 3; *22:* 142; *25:* 198; *28:* 173; *68:* 128, 129; *86:* 49
Lechon, Daniel *113:* 211
Leder, Dora *129:* 172
Ledger, Bill *181:* 58
Leduc, Bernard *102:* 36
Lee, Alan *62:* 25, 28
Lee, Bryce *99:* 60; *101:* 195; *196:* 53
Lee, Chinlun *181:* 138; *182:* 112
Lee, Declan *191:* 20
Lee, Dom *83:* 118, 120; *93:* 123; *121:* 121, 126; *146:* 174, 175, 206, 207; *174:* 204
Lee, Doris *13:* 246; *32:* 183; *44:* 111
Lee, Hector Viveros *115:* 96
Lee, Ho Baek *200:* 160
Lee, Jeanne M. *158:* 56
Lee, Jared *93:* 200; *157:* 229; *215:* 113, 191, 192, 193
Lee, Jody *81:* 121; *82:* 225; *91:* 155; *100:* 182
Lee, Jody A. *127:* 124, 126, 127
   See also Lee, Jody
Lee, Manning de V. *2:* 200; *17:* 12; *27:* 87; *37:* 102, 103, 104; *YABC 2:* 304
Lee, Margaret *213:* 179
Lee, Marie G. *138:* 157
Lee, Paul *97:* 100; *105:* 72, 209; *109:* 177; *128:* 113; *202:* 45
Lee, Robert J. *3:* 97; *67:* 124
Lee, Victor *96:* 228; *105:* 182; *140:* 196; *208:* 191
Lee, Virginia *208:* 139, 140
Leech, Dorothy *98:* 76
Leech, John *15:* 59
Leedy, Loreen *84:* 142; *128:* 144, 145, 146; *175:* 125, 126, 127
Leeman, Michael *44:* 157
Leeming, Catherine *87:* 39
Lees, Harry *6:* 112
LeFever, Bill *88:* 220, 221
Legenisel *47:* 111
Legrand, Edy *18:* 89, 93
Lehman, Barbara *73:* 123; *170:* 130
Lehrman, Rosalie *2:* 180
Leichman, Seymour *5:* 107
Leick, Bonnie *205:* 104
Leighton, Clare *25:* 130; *33:* 168; *37:* 105, 106, 108,109
Leisk, David *1:* 140, 141; *11:* 54; *30:* 137, 142, 143,144
Leister, Brian *89:* 45; *106:* 37; *114:* 67; *149:* 236
Leloir, Maurice *18:* 77, 80, 83, 99
Lemaître, Pascal *144:* 175; *176:* 130; *189:* 135
Lemieux, Michele *100:* 148; *139:* 153
Lemke, Horst *14:* 98; *38:* 117, 118, 119
Lemke, R.W. *42:* 162
Lemon, David Gwynne *9:* 1
LeMoult, Adolph *82:* 116
Lenn, Michael *136:* 89
Lennon, John *114:* 100
Lennox, Elsie *95:* 163; *143:* 160
Lenski, Lois *1:* 144; *26:* 135, 137, 139, 141; *100:* 153, 154
Lent, Blair *1:* 116, 117; *2:* 174; *3:* 206, 207; *7:* 168, 169; *34:* 62; *68:* 217; *133:* 101; *183:* 60
Leonard, David *212:* 149
Leonard, Richard *91:* 128
Leonard, Tom *207:* 95
Leone, Leonard *49:* 190

Lerner, Carol *86:* 140, 141, 142
Lerner, Judith *116:* 138
Lerner, Sharon *11:* 157; *22:* 56
Leroux-Hugon, Helene *132:* 139
Leslie, Cecil *19:* 244
Lessac, Frané *80:* 182, 207; *96:* 182; *202:* 58; *209:* 104
Lessing, Erich *167:* 52; *173:* 60
Lester, Alison *50:* 124; *90:* 147, 148; *129:* 130
Lester, Mike *208:* 50
Lethcoe, Jason *191:* 116, 117
Le Tord, Bijou *49:* 156; *95:* 112
Leutz, Emanuel *165:* 27
Levai, Blaise *39:* 130
Levert, Mireille *211:* 101
Levin, Ted *12:* 148
Levine, David *43:* 147, 149, 150, 151, 152; *64:* 11
Levine, Joe *71:* 88
Levine, Marge *81:* 127
Levinson, David *178:* 232
Levit, Herschel *24:* 223
Levstek, Ljuba *131:* 192; *134:* 216; *149:* 65; *168:* 180
Levy, Jessica Ann *19:* 225; *39:* 191
Levy, Lina *117:* 126
Lewin, Betsy *32:* 114; *48:* 177; *90:* 151; *91:* 125; *92:* 85; *115:* 105; *169:* 110, 111; *178:* 47; *186:* 188; *194:* 201
Lewin, Ted *4:* 77; *8:* 168; *20:* 110; *21:* 99,100; *27:* 110; *28:* 96, 97; *31:* 49; *45:* 55; *48:* 223; *60:* 20, 119, 120; *62:* 139; *66:* 108; *71:* 12; *72:* 21; *74:* 226; *76:* 139, 140; *77:* 82; *79:* 87; *85:* 49, 177; *86:* 55; *88:* 182; *93:* 28, 29; *94:* 34, 182, 194; *99:* 156; *104:* 8; *115:* 123; *118:* 74; *119:* 114, 116; *131:* 54; *145:* 99; *165:* 151; *177:* 75; *178:* 42; *190:* 30; *192:* 86; *195:* 101, 102; *203:* 52
Lewis, Allen *15:* 112
Lewis, E.B. *88:* 143; *93:* 109; *119:* 79; *124:* 113; *128:* 49; *151:* 167; *168:* 110; *173:* 121; *174:* 66; *176:* 7; *184:* 150; *185:* 191; *211:* 108, 109, 110, 111
Lewis, H.B. *170:* 124
Lewis, J. Patrick *162:* 83
Lewis, Jan *81:* 22
Lewis, Kim *136:* 165
Lewis, Richard W. *52:* 25
Lewis, Robin Baird *98:* 193
Leydon, Rita Floden *21:* 101
Li, Xiojun *187:* 172
Liao, Jimmy *202:* 100
Lichtenheld, Tom *152:* 125, 126
Lieblich, Irene *22:* 173; *27:* 209, 214
Lieder, Rick *108:* 197; *199:* 58, 59, 60
Lies, Brian *92:* 40; *141:* 101; *150:* 138; *190:* 97, 98, 99,
Liese, Charles *4:* 222
Life, Kay *79:* 49
Lifton, Robert Jay *66:* 154
Lightburn, Ron *86:* 153; *91:* 122
Lightfoot, Norman R. *45:* 47
Lignell, Lois *37:* 114
Lill, Debra *121:* 70
Lilly, Charles *8:* 73; *20:* 127; *48:* 53; *72:* 9,16; *77:* 98; *102:* 94
Lilly, Ken *37:* 224
Lim, John *43:* 153
Limona, Mercedes *51:* 183
Lin, Grace *143:* 217; *162:* 86, 87; *174:* 185
Lincoln, Patricia Henderson *27:* 27; *78:* 127
Lindahn, Ron *84:* 17
Lindahn, Val *84:* 17
Lindberg, Howard *10:* 123; *16:* 190
Lindberg, Jeffrey *64:* 77; *77:* 71; *79:* 54; *80:* 149; *174:* 109; *179:* 52
Linden, Seymour *18:* 200, 201; *43:* 140
Lindenbaum, Pija *144:* 143; *183:* 113
Linder, Richard *27:* 119
Lindman, Maj *43:* 154
Lindsay, Norman *67:* 114

Lindsay, Vachel *40:* 118
Lindstrom, Jack *145:* 118
Line, Les *27:* 143
Linell
　　See Smith, Linell
Lionni, Leo *8:* 115; *72:* 159, 160, 161
Lipinsky, Lino *2:* 156; *22:* 175
Lippincott, Gary A. *70:* 35; *119:* 118
Lippman, Peter *8:* 31; *31:* 119, 120, 160
Lisi, Victoria *89:* 145
Lisker, Emily *169:* 114
Lisker, Sonia O. *16:* 274; *31:* 31; *44:* 113, 114
Lisowski, Gabriel *47:* 144; *49:* 157
Lissim, Simon *17:* 138
Little, Ed *89:* 145; *151:* 53
Little, Harold *16:* 72
Little, Mary E. *28:* 146
Littlewood, Karen *165:* 126; *211:* 112
Litty, Julie *111:* 63
Litzinger, Rosanne *151:* 101; *176:* 118; *196:* 133, 134, 135; *208:* 129; *209:* 147
Liu, Lesley *143:* 72
Lively, Lorna *19:* 216
Livingston, Susan *95:* 22
Liwska, Renata *164:* 113; *199:* 25, 69
Ljungkvist, Laura *180:* 120
Llerena, Carlos Antonio *19:* 181
Lloyd, Errol *11:* 39; *22:* 178
Lloyd, Megan *77:* 118; *80:* 113; *97:* 75; *117:* 94, 95; *189:* 121, 122; *208:* 128; *211:* 72
Lloyd, Sam *183:* 116, 117
Lo, Beth *165:* 154
Lo, Koon-chiu *7:* 134
Loates, Glen *63:* 76
Lobel, Anita *6:* 87; *9:* 141; *18:* 248; *55:* 85,86, 87, 88, 93, 104; *60:* 67; *78:* 263; *82:* 110; *96:* 157, 159; *101:* 84; *132:* 35; *162:* 93, 94
Lobel, Arnold *1:* 188, 189; *5:* 12; *6:* 147; *7:* 167, 209; *18:* 190, 191; *25:* 39, 43; *27:* 40; *29:* 174; *52:* 127; *55:* 89, 91, 94, 95, 97, 98, 99, 100, 101, 102,103, 105, 106; *60:* 18, 31; *66:* 181, 183; *75:* 57; *82:* 246; *136:* 146
Lobel, Gillian *190:* 21
Locker, Thomas *109:* 134
Lodge, Bernard *107:* 125, 126; *153:* 93
Loeb, Jeph *153:* 177
Lodge, Jo *112:* 119
Loefgren, Ulf *3:* 108
Loescher, Ann *20:* 108
Loescher, Gil *20:* 108
Loew, David *93:* 184; *171:* 120; *211:* 187
Lofting, Hugh *15:* 182, 183; *100:* 161, 162
Lofts, Pamela *60:* 188
Loh, George *38:* 88
Lomberg, Jon *58:* 160
Lonette, Reisie *11:* 211; *12:* 168; *13:* 56; *36:* 122; *43:* 155
Long, Ethan *168:* 146; *178:* 12; *182:* 120, 121; *196:* 124
Long, Laurel *162:* 135; *190:* 11; *203:* 113, 114
Long, Loren *99:* 176; *172:* 65; *182:* 78; *188:* 114, 115
Long, Melinda *152:* 128
Long, Miles *115:* 174
Long, Sally *42:* 184
Long, Sylvia *74:* 168; *132:* 63; *179:* 134
Longoni, Eduardo *73:* 85
Longtemps, Ken *17:* 123; *29:* 221; *69:* 82
Looser, Heinz *YABC 2:* 208
Lopez, Loretta *190:* 100
López, Rafael *197:* 160; *198:* 85
Lopshire, Robert *6:* 149; *21:* 117; *34:* 166; *73:* 13
Lord, John Vernon *21:* 104; *23:* 25; *51:* 22
Lorenz, Albert *40:* 146; *115:* 127
Loretta, Sister Mary *33:* 73
Lorraine, Walter H. *3:* 110; *4:* 123; *16:* 192; *103:* 119
Los, Marek *146:* 22; *193:* 23
Loss, Joan *11:* 163
Louderback, Walt *YABC 1:* 164

Loughridge, Stuart *214:* 131
Louis, Catherine *212:* 186
Lousada, Sandra *40:* 138
Louth, Jack *149:* 252; *151:* 191, 192
Love, Judy *173:* 43; *196:* 40
Lovelock, Brian *214:* 132, 197
Low, Joseph *14:* 124, 125; *18:* 68; *19:* 194; *31:* 166; *80:* 239
Low, William *62:* 175; *80:* 147; *112:* 194; *150:* 202; *169:* 175; *177:* 110; *192:* 27
Lowe, Vicky *177:* 130
Lowenheim, Alfred *13:* 65, 66
Lowenstein, Sallie *116:* 90, 91
Lowitz, Anson *17:* 124; *18:* 215
Lowrey, Jo *8:* 133
Lubach, Vanessa *142:* 152
Lubell, Winifred *1:* 207; *3:* 15; *6:* 151
Lubin, Leonard B. *19:* 224; *36:* 79, 80; *45:* 128, 129,131, 132, 133, 134, 135, 136, 137, 139, 140, 141; *70:* 95; *YABC2:* 96
Lucas, David *208:* 148
Lucht, Irmgard *82:* 145
Ludwig, Helen *33:* 144, 145
Luebs, Robin *212:* 109
Lufkin, Raymond *38:* 138; *44:* 48
Luhrs, Henry *7:* 123; *11:* 120
Lujan, Tonita *82:* 33
Lupo, Dom *4:* 204
Lustig, Loretta *30:* 186; *46:* 134, 135, 136, 137
Lutes, Jason *210:* 163
Luthardt, Kevin *172:* 125, 126
Luxbacher, Irene *153:* 145
Luzak, Dennis *52:* 121; *99:* 142
Lydbury, Jane *82:* 98
Lydecker, Laura *21:* 113; *42:* 53
Lynch, Charles *16:* 33
Lynch, Marietta *29:* 137; *30:* 171
Lynch, P.J. *126:* 228; *129:* 110; *132:* 247; *183:* 64; *207:* 184; *213:* 100, 101, 102
Lyne, Alison Davis *188:* 118, 198
Lyon, Carol *102:* 26
Lyon, Elinor *6:* 154
Lyon, Fred *14:* 16
Lyon, Lea *212:* 110
Lyon, Tammie *175:* 170
Lyons, Oren *8:* 193
Lyster, Michael *26:* 41

M

Maas, Dorothy *6:* 175
Maas, Julie *47:* 61
Macaulay, David *46:* 139, 140, 141, 142, 143, 144, 145, 147, 149, 150; *72:* 167, 168, 169; *137:* 129, 130, 131, 132
MacCarthy, Patricia *69:* 141
Macdonald, Alister *21:* 55
Macdonald, Roberta *19:* 237; *52:* 164
MacDonald, Norman *13:* 99
MacDonald, Ross *201:* 103
MacDonald, Suse *54:* 41; *109:* 138; *130:* 156; *193:* 106, 107, 109, 110
Mace, Varian *49:* 159
MacEachern, Stephen *206:* 2
Macguire, Robert Reid *18:* 67
Machetanz, Fredrick *34:* 147, 148
MacInnes, Ian *35:* 59
MacIntyre, Elisabeth *17:* 127, 128
Mack, Jeff *161:* 128; *194:* 119, 120
Mack, Stan *17:* 129; *96:* 33
Mackay, Donald *17:* 60
MacKaye, Arvia *32:* 119
Mackenzie, Robert *204:* 78
Mackenzie, Stuart *73:* 213
MacKenzie, Garry *33:* 159
Mackie, Clare *87:* 134
Mackinlay, Miguel *27:* 22

MacKinstry, Elizabeth *15:* 110; *42:* 139, 140, 141, 142, 143,144, 145
MacLeod, Lee *91:* 167
Maclise, Daniel *YABC 2:* 257
Macnaughton, Tina *182:* 145
MacRae, Tom *181:* 112
Madden, Don *3:* 112, 113; *4:* 33, 108, 155; *7:* 193; *78:* 12; *YABC 2:* 211
Maddison, Angela Mary *10:* 83
Madsen, Jim *146:* 259; *152:* 237; *184:* 106; *197:* 21; *202:* 103, 104
Maestro, Giulio *8:* 124; *12:* 17; *13:* 108; *25:* 182; *54:* 147; *59:* 114, 115, 116, 117, 118, 121, 123, 124, 125,126, 127; *68:* 37, 38; *106:* 129, 130, 131, 136, 137, 138
Maffia, Daniel *60:* 200
Maggio, Viqui *58:* 136, 181; *74:* 150; *75:* 90; *85:* 159; *90:* 158; *109:* 184; *193:* 113
Magnus, Erica *77:* 123
Magnuson, Diana *28:* 102; *34:* 190; *41:* 175
Magoon, Scott *181:* 104
Magovern, Peg *103:* 123
Maguire, Sheila *41:* 100
Magurn, Susan *91:* 30
Mahony, Will *37:* 120
Mahony, Will *85:* 116
Mahood, Kenneth *24:* 141
Mahurin, Matt *164:* 225; *175:* 95; *189:* 37; *196:* 14; *209:* 163
Maik, Henri *9:* 102
Maione, Heather *106:* 5; *178:* 8; *189:* 126, 127; *193:* 58
Maisto, Carol *29:* 87
Maitland, Antony *1:* 100, 176; *8:* 41; *17:* 246; *24:* 46; *25:* 177, 178; *32:* 74; *60:* 65, 195; *67:* 156; *87:* 131; *101:* 110
Majewski, Dawn W. *169:* 95
Mak, Kam *72:* 25; *75:* 43; *87:* 186; *97:* 24; *102:* 154; *149:* 195; *186:* 28; *209:* 132
Makie, Pam *37:* 117
Maktima, Joe *116:* 191
Maland, Nick *99:* 77
Male, Alan *132:* 64
Malone, James Hiram *84:* 161
Malone, Nola Langner *82:* 239
Malone, Peter *191:* 121, 122, 123
Malsberg, Edward *51:* 175
Malvern, Corinne *2:* 13; *34:* 148, 149
Manchess, Gregory *165:* 241; *203:* 119
Mancusi, Stephen *63:* 198, 199
Mandelbaum, Ira *31:* 115
Manders, John *138:* 152, 155; *188:* 171; *190:* 92; *199:* 5
Manet, Edouard *23:* 170
Mangiat, Jeff *173:* 127
Mangurian, David *14:* 133
Manham, Allan *42:* 109; *77:* 180; *80:* 227
Manley, Matt *103:* 167; *117:* 98; *172:* 49; *212:* 207
Manna, Giovanni *178:* 44
Manniche, Lise *31:* 121
Manning, Jane *96:* 203
Manning, Jo *63:* 154
Manning, Lawrence *191:* 153
Manning, Maurie J. *211:* 116
Manning, Mick *176:* 139
Manning, Samuel F. *5:* 75
Mantel, Richard *57:* 73; *63:* 106; *82:* 255
Mantha, John *205:* 164
Maraja *15:* 86; *YABC 1:* 28; *2:* 115
Marcellino, Fred *20:* 125; *34:* 222; *53:* 125; *58:* 205; *61:* 64, 121, 122; *68:* 154, 156, 157, 158, 159; *72:* 25; *86:* 184; *98:* 181; *118:* 129, 130, 131; *149:* 218; *194:* 7
Marchesi, Stephen *34:* 140; *46:* 72; *50:* 147; *66:* 239; *70:* 33; *73:* 18, 114, 163; *77:* 47, 76,147; *78:* 79; *80:* 30; *81:* 6; *89:* 66; *93:* 21,130; *94:* 94; *97:* 66; *98:* 96; *114:* 115, 116
Marchiori, Carlos *14:* 60

Marciano, John Bemelmans *118:* 133; *167:* 110, 111, 112
Marcus, Barry David *139:* 248; *145:* 18
Maren, Julie *199:* 73
Margules, Gabriele *21:* 120
Mariana
  See Foster, Marian Curtis
Mariano, Michael *52:* 108
Marino, Dorothy *6:* 37; *14:* 135
Mario, Heide Stetson *101:* 202
Maris, Ron *71:* 123
Maritz, Nicolaas *85:* 123
Mark, Mona *65:* 105; *68:* 205; *116:* 213
Markham, R.L. *17:* 240
Marklew, Gilly *211:* 118
Marks, Alan *104:* 104; *109:* 182; *164:* 92; *185:* 134; *187:* 120, 121, 122
Marks, Cara *54:* 9
Marks, Colin *203:* 129
Marokvia, Artur *31:* 122
Marquez, Susan *108:* 121
Marrella, Maria Pia *62:* 116
Marriott, Pat *30:* 30; *34:* 39; *35:* 164, 165, 166; *44:* 170; *48:* 186, 187, 188, 189, 191, 192, 193; *91:* 92
Mars, W.T. *1:* 161; *3:* 115; *4:* 208, 225; *5:* 92, 105, 186; *8:* 214; *9:* 12; *13:* 121; *27:* 151; *31:* 180; *38:* 102; *48:* 66; *62:* 164, 165; *64:* 62; *68:* 229; *79:* 55
Marschall, Ken *85:* 29
Marsh, Christine *3:* 164
Marsh, James *73:* 137
Marsh, Reginald *17:* 5; *19:* 89; *22:* 90, 96
Marshall, Anthony D. *18:* 216
Marshall, Felicia *170:* 190
Marshall, James *6:* 160; *40:* 221; *42:* 24, 25, 29; *51:* 111, 112, 113, 114, 115, 116, 117, 118, 119, 120, 121; *64:* 13; *75:* 126, 127, 128, 129; *102:* 10, 12
Marshall, Janet *97:* 154
Marstall, Bob *55:* 145; *84:* 153, 170; *104:* 145; *154:* 166, 167, 168
Martchenko, Michael *50:* 129, 153, 155, 156, 157; *83:* 144,145; *154:* 137, 138, 139
Marten, Ruth *129:* 52
Martin, Brad *199:* 186
Martin, Charles E. *70:* 144
Martin, Courtney A. *214:* 28
Martin, David Stone *24:* 232; *62:* 4
Martin, Fletcher *23:* 151
Martin, Rene *7:* 144; *42:* 148, 149, 150
Martin, Richard E. *51:* 157; *131:* 203
Martin, Ron *32:* 81
Martin, Stefan *8:* 68; *32:* 124, 126; *56:* 33
Martin, Whitney *166:* 137
Martinez, Ed *58:* 192; *72:* 231; *77:* 33; *80:* 214; *167:* 123
Martinez, John *6:* 113; *118:* 13; *139:* 143
Martinez, Sergio *158:* 190
Martini, Angela *183:* 161
Martiniere, Stephan *171:* 130
Marton, Jirina *95:* 127, 128; *144:* 145
Martorell, Antonio *84:* 6; *97:* 161
Martucci, Griesbach *52:* 106
Marvin, Frederic *83:* 86
Marx, Robert F. *24:* 143
Marzollo, Jean *190:* 127
Masefield, Judith *19:* 208, 209
Masheris, Robert *78:* 51
Masiello, Ralph *186:* 171; *214:* 134
Mason, George F. *14:* 139
Mason, Robert *84:* 96
Masse, Josée *208:* 45
Massey, Barbara *68:* 142
Massie, Diane Redfield *16:* 194
Massie, Kim *31:* 43
Massini, Sarah *213:* 79
Mataya, David *121:* 66
Mathers, Petra *119:* 135; *163:* 104; *176:* 143, 144; *187:* 142; *196:* 101
Mathewuse, James *51:* 143

Mathieu, Joseph *14:* 33; *39:* 206; *43:* 167; *56:* 180; *79:* 126; *94:* 147; *185:* 140
Matje, Martin *169:* 177, 178; *172:* 180
Matsubara, Naoko *12:* 121
Matsuda, Shizu *13:* 167
Matsuoka, Mei *192:* 135; *214:* 84
Matte, L'Enc *22:* 183
Mattelson, Marvin *36:* 50, 51
Mattheson, Jenny *180:* 132
Matthews, Elizabeth *194:* 128
Matthews, F. Leslie *4:* 216
Matthews, Tina *190:* 130
Mattingly, David *71:* 76, 77; *82:* 64; *91:* 216, 217; *109:* 25
Matulay, Laszlo *5:* 18; *43:* 168
Matus, Greta *12:* 142
Maughan, Bill *181:* 31; *211:* 211
Mauldin, Bill *27:* 23
Mauterer, Erin Marie *119:* 5
Mawicke, Tran *9:* 137; *15:* 191; *47:* 100
Mawson, Matt *74:* 115
Max, Peter *45:* 146, 147, 148, 149, 150
Maxie, Betty *40:* 135
Maxwell, John Alan *1:* 148
May, Steve *204:* 30
Mayan, Earl *7:* 193
Mayer, Bill *200:* 138
Mayer, Danuta *117:* 103
Mayer, Marianna *32:* 132
Mayer, Mercer *11:* 192; *16:* 195, 196; *20:* 55, 57; *32:* 129, 130, 132, 133, 134; *41:* 144, 248, 252; *58:* 186; *73:* 140, 142, 143; *137:* 137, 138
Mayforth, Hal *166:* 77
Mayhew, James *85:* 121; *138:* 187; *149:* 140; *204:* 81
Mayhew, Richard *3:* 106
Mayo, Gretchen Will *38:* 81; *84:* 166
Mays, Victor *5:* 127; *8:* 45, 153; *14:* 245; *23:* 50; *34:* 155; *40:* 79; *45:* 158; *54:* 91; *66:* 240
Mazal, Chanan *49:* 104
Maze, Deborah *71:* 83
Mazellan, Ron *75:* 97, 98; *210:* 169
Mazetti, Alan *112:* 72
Mazille, Capucine *96:* 168
Mazza, Adriana Saviozzi *19:* 215
Mazzella, Mary Jo *82:* 165
Mazzetti, Alan *45:* 210
McAfee, Steve *135:* 146; *167:* 176; *191:* 84; *210:* 117
McAlinden, Paul *112:* 128
McBride, Angus *28:* 49; *103:* 40
McBride, Will *30:* 110
McCaffery, Janet *38:* 145
McCall, Bruce *209:* 119
McCallum, Graham *78:* 78
McCallum, Stephen *141:* 143; *156:* 5; *166:* 228
McCann, Gerald *3:* 50; *4:* 94; *7:* 54; *41:* 121
McCarthy, Dan *174:* 74
McCarthy, Linda *177:* 128
McCarthy, Meghan *168:* 134; *199:* 74
McCauley, Adam *157:* 36; *184:* 199; *193:* 100; *209:* 122
McCay, Winsor *41:* 124, 126, 128, 129, 130, 131; *134:* 77, 79
McClary, Nelson *1:* 111
McClements, George *196:* 146
McClennan, Connie *210:* 181
McClintock, Barbara *57:* 135; *95:* 130; *146:* 190; *213:* 3, 5, 107, 108
McClintock, Theodore *14:* 141
McCloskey, Robert *1:* 184, 185; *2:* 186, 187; *17:* 209; *39:* 139, 140, 141, 142, 143, 146, 147, 148; *85:* 150, 151; *100:* 172, 173, 174
McClung, Robert *2:* 189; *68:* 166, 167
McClure, Gillian *31:* 132; *150:* 53
McConnel, Jerry *31:* 75, 187
McConnell, Mary *102:* 49
McCord, Kathleen Garry *78:* 236

McCormack, John *66:* 193
McCormick, A.D. *35:* 119
McCormick, Dell J. *19:* 216
McCoy, Glenn *212:* 132
McCrady, Lady *16:* 198; *39:* 127
McCrea, James *3:* 122; *33:* 216
McCrea, Ruth *3:* 122; *27:* 102; *33:* 216
McCue, Lisa *65:* 148, 149; *77:* 54; *80:* 132; *175:* 33; *177:* 133, 135; *212:* 136, 137, 138
McCully, Emily Arnold *2:* 89; *4:* 120, 121, 146, 197; *5:* 2, 129; *7:* 191; *11:* 122; *15:* 210; *33:* 23; *35:* 244; *37:* 122; *39:* 88; *40:* 103; *50:* 30,31, 32, 33, 34, 35, 36, 37; *52:* 89, 90; *57:* 6; *62:* 3; *70:* 195; *86:* 82; *96:* 192; *97:* 93; *110:* 143,144; *117:* 47; *167:* 96; *210:* 175, 176
McCurdy, Michael *13:* 153; *24:* 85; *81:* 160; *82:* 157, 158; *86:* 125; *97:* 92; *117:* 178; *132:* 6; *147:* 159, 160
McCusker, Paul *99:* 19
McDaniel, Jerry *132:* 135
McDaniel, Preston *160:* 206; *170:* 139
McDermott, Beverly Brodsky *11:* 180
McDermott, Gerald *16:* 201; *74:* 174, 175; *163:* 150, 151
McDermott, Mike *96:* 187
McDonald, Jill *13:* 155; *26:* 128
McDonald, Mercedes *169:* 118
McDonald, Ralph J. *5:* 123, 195
McDonnell, Flora *146:* 199, 200
McDonnell, Patrick *179:* 153, 154
McDonough, Don *10:* 163
McElligott, Matt *196:* 147
McElmurry, Jill *137:* 148; *163:* 141; *202:* 186
McElrath-Eslick, Lori *129:* 145; *142:* 21; *173:* 123; *202:* 194; *204:* 88, 89
McEntee, Dorothy *37:* 124
McEwan, Keith *88:* 116; *165:* 122, 123
McEwen, Katharine *169:* 34
McFall, Christie *12:* 144
McFeely, Daniel *160:* 213
McGaw, Laurie *109:* 243; *143:* 216; *211:* 218
McGee, Barbara *6:* 165
McGee, Marni *163:* 153
McGillvray, Kim *158:* 171; *165:* 213; *186:* 183; *190:* 175
McGinley-Nally, Sharon *131:* 19
McGinnis, Robert *110:* 113; *177:* 80
McGovern, Tara *98:* 171
McGraw, Sheila *83:* 146
McGregor, Barbara *200:* 155
McGregor, Malcolm *23:* 27
McGrory, Anik *193:* 120
McGuire, Robert *204:* 57; *209:* 86
McGuirk, Leslie *152:* 159
McHale, John *138:* 190
McHenry, E.B. *193:* 122
McHugh, Tom *23:* 64
McIntosh, Jon *42:* 56
McKay, Donald *2:* 118; *32:* 157; *45:* 151, 152
McKean, Dave *150:* 71; *174:* 156; *197:* 83, 118
McKeating, Eileen *44:* 58
McKee, David *10:* 48; *21:* 9; *70:* 154, 155; *107:* 139, 140, 141; *134:* 218; *158:* 148, 149, 150, 151
McKee, Diana *109:* 185
McKelvey, Patrick *164:* 141
McKendry, Joe *170:* 136
McKeveny, Tom *164:* 60; *173:* 79
McKie, Roy *7:* 44
McKie, Todd *205:* 181
McKillip, Kathy *30:* 153
McKinney, Ena *26:* 39
McKinnon, James *136:* 75
McKowen, Scott *172:* 63; *202:* 49
McLachlan, Edward *5:* 89
McLaren, Chesley *133:* 53; *213:* 112
McLaren, Kirsty *123:* 99; *124:* 226
Mclean, Andrew *113:* 117, 118, 120, 121; *172:* 130, 131

Mclean, Janet *172:* 130
McLean, Meg *94:* 196
McLean, Sammis *32:* 197
McLean, Wilson *90:* 29; *113:* 195
McLoughlin, John C. *47:* 149
McLoughlin, Wayne *102:* 230; *134:* 178
McMahon, Robert *36:* 155; *69:* 169
McManus, Shawn *85:* 71
McMenemy, Sarah *156:* 139 ; *211:* 93
McMillan, Bruce *22:* 184
McMullan, James *40:* 33; *67:* 172; *87:* 142; *99:* 63, 64; *189:* 133; *196:* 51
McMullen, Nigel *146:* 177
McNeely, Tom *162:* 55
McNaught, Harry *12:* 80; *32:* 136
McNaughton, Colin *39:* 149; *40:* 108; *92:* 144, 145, 146; *134:* 104, 106; *211:* 122, 123, 124
McNicholas, Maureen *38:* 148
McNicholas, Shelagh *173:* 61; *191:* 125, 126
McPhail, David *14:* 105; *23:* 135; *37:* 217, 218, 220,221; *47:* 151, 152, 153, 154, 155, 156, 158, 159, 160, 162, 163, 164; *71:* 211; *81:* 139, 140, 142; *86:* 123; *132:* 150; *140:* 129, 131, 132; *183:* 134, 135, 137; *189:* 132
McPhee, Richard B. *41:* 133
McPheeters, Neal *78:* 132; *86:* 90; *99:* 162; *111:* 141; *142:* 162
McQuade, Jacqueline *124:* 223
McQueen, Lucinda *28:* 149; *41:* 249; *46:* 206; *53:* 103
McQuillan, Mary *153:* 97; *200:* 140
McVay, Tracy *11:* 68
McVicker, Charles *39:* 150
Mead, Ben Carlton *43:* 75
Meade, Holly *90:* 102; *94:* 101; *149:* 8; *151:* 107
Mecray, John *33:* 62
Meddaugh, Susan *20:* 42; *29:* 143; *41:* 241; *77:* 50; *84:* 173, 174, 175, 176, 177, 178; *125:* 160, 161, 162; *176:* 148, 149, 150, 151
Meehan, Dennis B. *56:* 144
Meents, Len W. *73:* 147, 150
Meers, Tony *99:* 113
Meisel, Paul *98:* 137; *124:* 18; *162:* 180; *179:* 16; *181:* 62; *194:* 154
Melanson, Luc *149:* 229; *198:* 97, 98
Melendez, Francisco *72:* 180
Melling, David *202:* 199
Melnychuk, Monika *153:* 65
Melo, Esperança *196:* 90
Melo, John *16:* 285; *58:* 203
Meloni, Maria Teresa *98:* 62
Meltzer, Ericka
   See O'Rourke, Ericka
Menasco, Milton *43:* 85
Menchin, Scott *188:* 129
Mendelson, Steven T. *86:* 154
Mendelssohn, Felix *19:* 170
Mendola, Christopher *88:* 223
Meng, Heinz *13:* 158
Merian, Maria Sibylla *140:* 88
Mero, Lee *34:* 68
Merrell, David *205:* 3
Merrill, Frank T. *16:* 147; *19:* 71; *YABC 1:* 226, 229,273
Merriman, Rachel *98:* 108; *114:* 122; *149:* 142
Merveille, David *200:* 142
Meryman, Hope *27:* 41
Meryweather, Jack *10:* 179
Meseldzija, Petar *168:* 97
Meserve, Jessica *184:* 137; *211:* 127
Messick, Dale *64:* 150, 151, 152
Meth, Harold *24:* 203
Meyer, Herbert *19:* 189
Meyer, Renate *6:* 170
Meyers, Bob *11:* 136
Meyers, Nancy *172:* 124
Meynell, Louis *37:* 76
Micale, Albert *2:* 65; *22:* 185
Miccuci, Charles *82:* 163; *144:* 150
Micich, Paul *164:* 163

Middleton, Jeffrey *177:* 173
Middleton, Joshua *208:* 146
Middleton-Sandford, Betty *2:* 125
Mieke, Anne *45:* 74
Mighell, Patricia *43:* 134
Miglio, Paige *101:* 203; *151:* 223; *201:* 118, 119; *204:* 162
Mikec, Larry *204:* 125
Mikolaycak, Charles *9:* 144; *12:* 101; *13:* 212; *21:* 121; *22:* 168; *30:* 187; *34:* 103, 150; *37:* 183; *43:* 179; *44:* 90; *46:* 115, 118, 119; *49:* 25; *78:* 121, 122, 205, 207; *81:* 4
Milelli, Pascal *129:* 66; *135:* 153; *187:* 45
Miles, Elizabeth *117:* 77
Miles, Jennifer *17:* 278
Milgrim, David *158:* 157; *187:* 125, 126, 128
Milhous, Katherine *15:* 193; *17:* 51
Millais, John E. *22:* 230, 231
Millar, H.R. *YABC 1:* 194, 195, 203
Millard, C.E. *28:* 186
Millard, Kerry *105:* 124; *204:* 93, 94
Miller, Don *15:* 195; *16:* 71; *20:* 106; *31:* 178
Miller, Edna *29:* 148
Miller, Edward *115:* 64; *183:* 140, 141
Miller, Frank J. *25:* 94
Miller, Grambs *18:* 38; *23:* 16
Miller, Ian *99:* 128
Miller, Jane *15:* 196
Miller, Marcia *13:* 233
Miller, Marilyn *1:* 87; *31:* 69; *33:* 157
Miller, Mitchell *28:* 183; *34:* 207
Miller, Phil *175:* 150
Miller, Shane *5:* 140
Miller, Virginia *81:* 206
Millman, Isaac *172:* 18
Mills, Elaine *72:* 181
Mills, Judith Christine *130:* 168, 169
Mills, Lauren *92:* 170
Mills, Yaroslava Surmach *35:* 169, 170; *46:* 114
Millsap, Darrel *51:* 102
Milone, Karen *89:* 169
Milord, Susan *147:* 163, 164; *200:* 144
Milton, Debbie *162:* 161
Mims, Ashley *170:* 51
Miner, Julia *98:* 69
Minor, Wendell *39:* 188; *52:* 87; *56:* 171; *58:* 116; *62:* 56; *66:* 109; *74:* 93; *78:* 129; *94:* 67; *117:* 12, 13; *124:* 84, 86; *136:* 121; *164:* 168, 169; *170:* 71; *199:* 79, 80, 81, 82
Minter, Daniel *176:* 154; *179:* 177
Mirocha, Paul *81:* 133; *192:* 148; *194:* 36
Misako Rocks! *192:* 149, 150
Mitchell, Judith *109:* 117
Mitchell, Mark *91:* 208
Mitchell, Tracy *190:* 15
Mitgutsch, Ali *76:* 161
Mitsuhashi, Yoko *45:* 153
Miyake, Yoshi *38:* 141
Mizumura, Kazue *10:* 143; *18:* 223; *36:* 159
Mochi, Ugo *8:* 122; *38:* 150
Mock, Paul *55:* 83; *123:* 32
Modarressi, Mitra *90:* 236; *126:* 168; *173:* 165, 166; *200:* 147, 148
Modell, Frank *39:* 152
Mogenson, Jan *74:* 183
Mohn, Susan *89:* 224
Mohr, Mark *133:* 201
Mohr, Nicholasa *8:* 139; *113:* 127
Molan, Christine *60:* 177; *84:* 183
Moldon, Peter L. *49:* 168
Molk, Laurel *92:* 150
Mollica, Gene *197:* 11
Momaday, N. Scott *48:* 159
Mombourquette, Paul *112:* 91; *126:* 142
Monk, Julie *165:* 231; *191:* 96
Monks, Lydia *189:* 136, 137
Monroy, Manuel *199:* 192
Montgomery, Lucy *150:* 126
Montgomery, Michael G. *208:* 159
Montgomery-Higham, Amanda *169:* 131

Monteiel, David *201:* 95
Montiel, David *69:* 106; *84:* 145
Montijo, Rhode *193:* 164
Montresor, Beni *2:* 91; *3:* 138; *38:* 152, 153, 154,155, 156, 157, 158, 159, 160; *68:* 63
Montserrat, Pep *128:* 135; *181:* 119; *184:* 53
Moon, Carl *25:* 183, 184, 185
Moon, Eliza *14:* 40
Moon, Ivan *22:* 39; *38:* 140
Moore, Adrienne *67:* 147
Moore, Agnes Kay Randall *43:* 187
Moore, Cyd *117:* 107, 108; *159:* 137, 138; *186:* 148, 149, 151; *203:* 15; *214:* 138, 139
Moore, Gustav *127:* 181, 182; *170:* 162, 163
Moore, Jackie *128:* 79
Moore, Janet *63:* 153
Moore, Margie *176:* 156
Moore, Mary *29:* 160
Moore, Patrick *184:* 121
Moore, Yvette *101:* 11, 12; *154:* 141
Mora, Giovanni *179:* 127; *184:* 11
Mora, Raul Mina *20:* 41
Moraes, Odilon *102:* 144
Morales, Yuyi *154:* 144
Moran, Rosslyn *111:* 26
Moran, Tom *60:* 100
Mordan, C.B. *193:* 115
Mordvinoff, Nicolas *15:* 179
Moreno, René King *169:* 59; *190:* 133, 209; *212:* 52
Morgan, Barbara *169:* 116
Morgan, Jacqui *58:* 57
Morgan, Mary *114:* 133, 134, 135; *123:* 11; *213:* 115, 116, 117
Morgan, Tom *42:* 157
Morgan, Pierr *173:* 148
Morgenstern, Michael *158:* 7, 57; *171:* 103; *174:* 60
Morice, Dave *93:* 142
Morin, Paul *73:* 132; *79:* 130; *88:* 140; *137:* 143
Moriuchi, Mique *177:* 203
Morning, Tuesday *205:* 25
Morozumi, Atsuko *110:* 155
Morrill, Leslie *18:* 218; *29:* 177; *33:* 84; *38:* 147; *42:* 127; *44:* 93; *48:* 164, 165, 167, 168, 169, 170,171; *49:* 162; *63:* 136, 180; *70:* 72; *71:* 70, 91,92; *72:* 228; *80:* 163, 164, 165; *90:* 121; *121:* 88; *178:* 117
Morrill, Rowena A. *84:* 16; *98:* 163
Morris *47:* 91
Morris, Frank *55:* 133; *60:* 28; *76:* 2
Morris, Harry O. *119:* 138
Morris, Jackie *128:* 194; *144:* 119; *151:* 146; *202:* 126, 127; *204:* 83; *211:* 80; *214:* 163
Morris, Jennifer E. *179:* 157
Morris, Oradel Nolen *128:* 180
Morris, Tony *62:* 146; *70:* 97
Morrison, Bill *42:* 116; *66:* 170; *69:* 40
Morrison, Gordon *87:* 150; *113:* 93; *128:* 181, 182; *183:* 144, 145, 146
Morrison, Frank *169:* 162; *205:* 156
Morrison, Taylor *159:* 144, 145; *187:* 131
Morrow, Gray *2:* 64; *5:* 200; *10:* 103, 114; *14:* 175
Morse, Scott *200:* 149, 150
Morton, Lee Jack *32:* 140
Morton, Marian *3:* 185
Mosberg, Hilary *117:* 195; *118:* 164; *149:* 55
Moser, Barry *56:* 68, 117, 118, 119, 120, 121, 122, 123, 124; *59:* 141; *60:* 160; *79:* 91, 147, 149, 151, 152; *82:* 81; *90:* 118; *91:* 35; *95:* 210; *97:* 91, 93; *102:* 152; *126:* 4; *128:* 175; *133:* 141; *138:* 167, 171, 174; *153:* 205; *174:* 130; *185:* 152, 154; *195:* 163; *204:* 115; *209:* 201
Moser, Cara *90:* 118; *138:* 167
Moses, Grandma *18:* 228
Moses, Will *178:* 170, 171
Moskof, Martin Stephen *27:* 152
Mosley, Francis *57:* 144

Moss, Donald *11:* 184
Moss, Geoffrey *32:* 198
Moss, Marissa *71:* 130; *104:* 127; *163:* 156
Most, Bernard *48:* 173; *91:* 142, 143; *134:* 120
Mowll, Joshua *188:* 133
Mowry, Carmen *50:* 62
Moxley, Sheila *96:* 174; *169:* 26; *206:* 16
Moyers, William *21:* 65
Moyler, Alan *36:* 142
Mozley, Charles *9:* 87; *20:* 176, 192, 193; *22:* 228; *25:* 205; *33:* 150; *43:* 170, 171, 172, 173, 174; *YABC2:* 89
Mueller, Hans Alexander *26:* 64; *27:* 52, 53
Mugnaini, Joseph *11:* 35; *27:* 52, 53; *35:* 62
Mujica, Rick *72:* 67; *88:* 95; *111:* 53; *180:* 185; *197:* 70
Mullen, Douglas *180:* 178
Muller, Robin *86:* 161
Muller, Steven *32:* 167
Muller, Jorg *35:* 215; *67:* 138, 139
Mulock, Julie *163:* 112
Mullins, Edward S. *10:* 101
Mullins, Patricia *51:* 68
Multer, Scott *80:* 108
Munari, Bruno *15:* 200
Munch, Edvard *140:* 143
Munowitz, Ken *14:* 148; *72:* 178, 179
Muñoz, Claudio *208:* 161
Munoz, William *42:* 160
Munro, Roxie *58:* 134; *136:* 177; *137:* 218; *184:* 133, 134
Munsinger, Lynn *33:* 161; *46:* 126; *71:* 92; *82:* 80; *89:* 218; *92:* 125; *94:* 157, 158, 159, 160; *98:* 196; *103:* 198; *142:* 143; *145:* 133, 134, 136; *153:* 203; *176:* 162; *177:* 140, 141, 142; *189:* 113, 114, 116, 117; *201:* 42
Munson, Russell *13:* 9
Munster, Sebastian *166:* 107
Munzar, Barbara *149:* 75
Murdocca, Salvatore *73:* 212; *98:* 132; *111:* 168; *157:* 228; *164:* 257
Murphy, Bill *5:* 138; *130:* 170
Murphy, Jill *37:* 142; *70:* 166; *142:* 132, 134
Murphy, Kelly *130:* 212; *143:* 119; *176:* 158; *190:* 135
Murphy, Liz *210:* 183; *212:* 157
Murphy, Mary *196:* 158
Murphy, Tom *192:* 40
Murr, Karl *20:* 62
Murray, Joe *175:* 37
Murray, Ossie *43:* 176
Mussino, Attilio *29:* 131; *100:* 164
Mutchler, Dwight *1:* 25
Myers, Bernice *9:* 147; *36:* 75; *81:* 146, 147, 148
Muth, Jon J. *165:* 169; *167:* 109; *190:* 227; *193:* 59
Myers, Christopher *183:* 150; *193:* 139
Myers, Duane O. *99:* 145
Myers, Tim *147:* 168
Myers, V.G. *142:* 41
Myers, Lou *11:* 2

N

Nachreiner, Tom *29:* 182
Nacht, Merle *65:* 49
Nadler, Ellis *88:* 91
Nagle, Shane *180:* 223
Nagy, Ian *195:* 64
Najaka, Marlies *62:* 101
Nakai, Michael *30:* 217; *54:* 29
Nakata, Hiroe *157:* 156; *162:* 30; *205:* 124, 125
Nakatani, Chiyoko *12:* 124
Narahashi, Keiko *77:* 188; *82:* 213; *115:* 142, 143, 144
Nascimbene, Yan *133:* 128; *173:* 132, 133
Nash, Lesa *87:* 135

Nash, Linell *46:* 175
Nash, Scott *130:* 36; *188:* 196
Naso, John *33:* 183
Nason, Thomas W. *14:* 68
Nasser, Muriel *48:* 74
Nast, Thomas *21:* 29; *28:* 23; *51:* 132, 133, 134, 135,136, 137, 138, 139, 141
Nasta, Vincent *78:* 185
Natale, Vincent *76:* 3; *78:* 125; *112:* 47; *166:* 81; *174:* 189; *185:* 212; *197:* 59
Natchev, Alexi *96:* 177
Nathan, Charlott *125:* 151
Nathan, Cheryl *150:* 104; *186:* 112
Natti, Susanna *20:* 146; *32:* 141, 142; *35:* 178; *37:* 141; *71:* 49; *93:* 98; *125:* 166, 168; *126:* 228; *151:* 6; *178:* 8; *188:* 106
Navarra, Celeste Scala *8:* 142
Naylor, Penelope *10:* 104
Nazz, James *72:* 8
Nebel, M. *45:* 154
Neebe, William *7:* 93
Needham, Dave *196:* 85
Needler, Jerry *12:* 93
Neel, Alice *31:* 23
Neely, Beth *119:* 184
Neely, Keith R. *46:* 124
Neff, Leland *78:* 74
Negri, Rocco *3:* 213; *5:* 67; *6:* 91, 108; *12:* 159
Negrin, Fabian *174:* 125; *175:* 15
Neidigh, Sherry *128:* 53; *204:* 101, 102, 103
Neilan, Eujin Kim *180:* 241; *200:* 151, 152
Neill, John R. *18:* 8, 10, 11, 21, 30; *100:* 22
Neilsen, Cliff *158:* 131; *177:* 112, 121; *209:* 8; *215:* 150
Neilsen, Terese *116:* 74
Nelson, Craig *62:* 151; *153:* *183:* 86
Nelson, Gail White *68:* 140
Nelson, Jennifer *129:* 152; *199:* 132
Nelson, Kadir *151:* 185; *154:* 146, 147; *157:* 189, 222; *181:* 122, 124; *197:* 155; *213:* 122, 123, 124
Nelson, S.D. *131:* 34; *181:* 126, 127
Ness, Evaline *1:* 164, 165; *2:* 39; *3:* 8; *10:* 147; *12:* 53; *26:* 150, 151, 152, 153; *49:* 30, 31, 32; *56:* 30; *60:* 113
Neubecker, Robert *170:* 143; *214:* 157
Neville, Vera *2:* 182
Nevins, Daniel *191:* 173
Nevwirth, Allan *79:* 168
Newberry, Clare Turlay *1:* 170
Newbold, Greg *108:* 125; *145:* 199; *151:* 23; *193:* 178; *197:* 10; *199:* 92, 93
Newfeld, Frank *14:* 121; *26:* 154
Newman, Andy *61:* 61; *195:* 63
Newman, Ann *43:* 90
Newman, Barbara Johansen *191:* 137, 138
Newsham, Ian *143:* 162
Newsom, Carol *40:* 159; *44:* 60; *47:* 189; *65:* 29; *70:* 192; *80:* 36; *85:* 137, 138; *92:* 167; *191:* 82
Newsom, Tom *49:* 149; *71:* 13, 62; *75:* 156; *91:* 113
Newton, Jill *83:* 105; *200:* 154
Ng, Michael *29:* 171
Ng, Simon *167:* 7
Nguyen, Vincent *189:* 49
Nicholson, William *15:* 33, 34; *16:* 48
Nickens, Bessie *104:* 153
Nicklaus, Carol *45:* 194; *62:* 132, 133
Nickle, John *181:* 128
Nickless, Will *16:* 139
Nicholas, Corasue *154:* 20
Nicolas *17:* 130, 132, 133; *YABC 2:* 215
Niebrugge, Jane *6:* 118
Nielsen, Cliff *95:* 207, 208; *105:* 58; *114:* 112; *124:* 12; *125:* 91, 92; *132:* 224; *135:* 187; *136:* 40; *137:* 168; *145:* 54; *149:* 28; *158:* 129; *165:* 64, 158; *168:* 169; *170:* 6; *175:* 114, 116; *187:* 75, 76; *194:* 107; *197:* 172; *201:* 14; *208:* 192; *211:* 186

Nielsen, Jon 6: 100; 24: 202
Nielsen, Kay 15: 7; 16: 211, 212, 213, 215, 217; 22: 143; YABC 1: 32, 33
Niemann, Christoph 191: 141
Nikola-Lisa, W. 180: 180
Niland, Deborah 25: 191; 27: 156; 135: 50; 172: 143
Niland, Kilmeny 25: 191; 75: 143
Nino, Alex 59: 145
Ninon 1: 5; 38: 101, 103, 108
Nissen, Rie 44: 35
Nithael, Mark 158: 237
Nivola, Claire A. 78: 126; 140: 147; 208: 164
Nixon, K. 14: 152
Nobati, Eugenia 194: 118
Noble, Louise 61: 170
Noble, Marty 97: 168; 125: 171
Noble, Trinka Hakes 39: 162; 84: 157
Noda, Takayo 168: 143
Noguchi, Yoshie 30: 99
Nolan, Dennis 42: 163; 67: 163; 78: 189; 82: 225; 83: 26; 92: 169, 170; 103: 166; 111: 35; 112: 213; 127: 171; 166: 161; 194: 218
Noll, Sally 82: 171
Nolte, Larry 121: 63, 65
Nones, Eric Jon 61: 111; 76: 38; 77: 177
Noonan, Daniel 100: 224
Noonan, Julia 4: 163; 7: 207; 25: 151; 91: 29; 95: 149
Norcia, Ernie 108: 155; 140: 47
Nordenskjold, Birgitta 2: 208
Noreika, Robert 173: 20
Norling, Beth 149: 153, 154; 209: 77
Norman, Elaine 77: 72, 176; 94: 35; 136: 63; 178: 42
Norman, Mary 36: 138, 147
Norman, Michael 12: 117; 27: 168
Northway, Jennifer 85: 96
Nostlinger, Christiana 162: 131
Novak, Linda 166: 205
Novak, Matt 104: 132, 133; 165: 173, 174; 204: 104, 106
Novelli, Luca 61: 137
Novgorodoff, Danica 215: 133
Nugent, Cynthia 106: 189; 205: 126, 127; 209: 180
Numeroff, Laura Joffe 28: 161; 30: 177
Nurse, Chris 164: 91
Nussbaumer, Paul 16: 219; 39: 117
Nutt, Ken 72: 69; 97: 170
Nyce, Helene 19: 219
Nygren, Tord 30: 148; 127: 164

O

Oakley, Graham 8: 112; 30: 164, 165; 84: 188,189, 190, 191, 192
Oakley, Thornton YABC 2: 189
Oberheide, Heide 118: 37
Obligado, Lilian 2: 28, 66, 67; 6: 30; 14: 179; 15: 103; 25: 84; 61: 138, 139, 140, 141, 143
Oblinski, Rafael 190: 139
Obrant, Susan 11: 186
O'Brien, Anne Sibley 53: 116, 117; 155: 115; 213: 127
O'Brien, John 41: 253; 72: 12; 89: 59, 60; 98: 16; 161: 185; 169: 16; 180: 196
O'Brien, Patrick 193: 142, 143, 144
O'Brien, Teresa 87: 89
O'Brien, Tim 93: 25; 136: 94; 164: 57; 169: 57; 173: 55; 175: 86; 184: 192; 191: 134; 193: 137; 210: 159
O'Clair, Dennis 127: 25
O'Connor, George 183: 153
Odell, Carole 35: 47
Odem, Mel 99: 164; 167: 84, 87
O'Donohue, Thomas 40: 89
Oechsli, Kelly 5: 144, 145; 7: 115; 8: 83, 183; 13: 117; 20: 94; 81: 199

Ofer, Avi 208: 143
Offen, Hilda 42: 207
Ogden, Bill 42: 59; 47: 55
Ogg, Oscar 33: 34
Ogle, Nancy Gray 163: 144
Ohi, Ruth 90: 175, 177; 131: 63; 135: 106; 175: 107; 179: 55
Ohlsson, Ib 4: 152; 7: 57; 10: 20; 11: 90; 19: 217; 41: 246; 82: 106; 92: 213
Ohtomo, Yasuo 37: 146; 39: 212, 213
O'Keefe, Jennifer 136: 184
O'Kelley, Mattie Lou 36: 150
Olbinski, Rafal 149: 27; 158: 77; 203: 36
O'Leary, Chris 208: 166
Oleynikov, Igor 202: 134
Oliver, Isaac 171: 182
Oliver, Jenni 23: 121; 35: 112
Oliver, Narelle 152: 192; 197: 129, 130
Oller, Erika 128: 186; 134: 126
Olschewski, Alfred 7: 172
Olsen, Ib Spang 6: 178, 179; 81: 164
Olson, Alan 77: 229
Olson-Brown, Ellen 183: 154
Olugebefola, Ademola 15: 205
O'Malley, Kevin 94: 180; 106: 8; 113: 108; 136: 70; 157: 193; 191: 146; 203: 78
O'Neil, Dan IV 7: 176
O'Neill, Catharine 72: 113; 84: 78; 134: 153
O'Neill, Jean 22: 146
O'Neill, Martin 187: 39; 203: 118
O'Neill, Michael J. 54: 172
O'Neill, Rose 48: 30, 31
O'Neill, Steve 21: 118
Ono, Chiyo 7: 97
Orbaan, Albert 2: 31; 5: 65, 171; 9: 8; 14: 241; 20: 109
Orbach, Ruth 21: 112
Orback, Craig 197: 132
Orfe, Joan 20: 81
Org, Ed 119: 93
Ormai, Stella 72: 129
Ormerod, Jan 55: 124; 70: 170, 171; 90: 39; 132: 172, 173, 174; 147: 98
Ormsby, Virginia H. 11: 187
O'Rourke, Ericka 108: 216; 117: 194; 111: 142; 119: 194; 137: 152; 150: 134; 167: 64; 172: 164; 188: 163; 191: 172; 201: 15; 203: 75; 209: 130
O'Rourke, Ericka Meltzer
    See O'Rourke, Ericka
Orozco, Jose Clemente 9: 177
Orr, Forrest W. 23: 9
Orr, N. 19: 70
Ortiz, Vilma 88: 158
Osborn, Kathy 152: 232; 199: 101, 102; 206: 67
Osborn, Robert 65: 49
Osborne, Billie Jean 35: 209
Osmond, Edward 10: 111
O'Sullivan, Tom 3: 176; 4: 55; 78: 195
Otani, June 124: 42; 156: 53
Otis, Rebecca 185: 92
Ottley, Matt 147: 221; 171: 133
Otto, Svend 22: 130, 141; 67: 188, 189
Oudry, J.B. 18: 167
Oughton, Taylor 5: 23; 104: 136
Overeng, Johannes 44: 36
Overlie, George 11: 156
Owens, Carl 2: 35; 23: 521
Owens, Gail 10: 170; 12: 157; 19: 16; 22: 70; 25: 81; 28: 203, 205; 32: 221, 222; 36: 132; 46: 40; 47: 57; 54: 66, 67, 68, 69, 70, 71, 72, 73; 71: 100; 73: 64; 77: 157; 80: 32; 82: 3; 99: 226
Owens, Mary Beth 113: 202, 203; 191: 148, 149
Owens, Nubia 84: 74
Oxenbury, Helen 3: 150, 151; 24: 81; 68: 174, 175,176; 81: 209; 84: 213, 245; 129: 56; 149: 159; 184: 181
Oz, Robin 88: 167; 185: 181

P

Padgett, Jim 12: 165
Page, Gail 205: 128
Page, Homer 14: 145
Page, Mark 162: 70
Paget, Sidney 24: 90, 91, 93, 95, 97
Paget, Walter 64: 122
Paillot, Jim 173: 89
Pajouhesh, Noushin 160: 121
Pak 12: 76
Pak, Yu Cha 86: 174
Paladino, Lance 134: 30
Palazzo, Tony 3: 152, 153
Palecek, Josef 56: 136; 89: 158
Palen, Debbie 135: 88; 195: 148, 149
Palencar, John Jude 84: 12, 45; 85: 87; 92: 187; 99: 128; 110: 204; 150: 122; 171: 86; 207: 36
Palin, Nicki 81: 201; 89: 161
Palladini, David 4: 113; 40: 176, 177, 178, 179, 181,224, 225; 50: 138; 78: 186
Pallarito, Don 43: 36
Palmer, Carol 158: 230; 195: 187
Palmer, Heidi 15: 207; 29: 102
Palmer, Jan 42: 153; 82: 161
Palmer, Judd 153: 160, 161
Palmer, Juliette 6: 89; 15: 208
Palmer, Kate Salley 104: 143; 154: 169
Palmer, Lemuel 17: 25, 29
Palmisciano, Diane 110: 62; 162: 26; 202: 138, 139
Palmquist, Eric 38: 133
Pamintuan, Macky 214: 160
Panesis, Nicholas 3: 127
Panter, Gary 182: 191
Panton, Doug 52: 99
Paparone, Pamela 129: 174
Papas, William 11: 223; 50: 160
Papin, Joseph 26: 113
Papish, Robin Lloyd 10: 80
Papp, Robert 198: 41; 205: 130
Paradis, Susan 40: 216
Paraquin, Charles H. 18: 166
Pardo DeLange, Alex 179: 128; 211: 135, 136
Paris, Peter 31: 127
Parisi, Elizabeth B. 141: 82; 164: 57
Park, Nick 113: 143
Park, Seho 39: 110
Park, W.B. 22: 189
Parker, Ant 82: 87, 88; 104: 121
Parker, Lewis 2: 179
Parker, Nancy Winslow 10: 113; 22: 164; 28: 47, 144; 52: 7; 69: 153; 91: 171, 174; 132: 175
Parker, Robert 4: 161; 5: 74; 9: 136; 29: 39
Parker, Robert Andrew 11: 81; 29: 186; 39: 165; 40: 25; 41: 78; 42: 123; 43: 144; 48: 182; 54: 140; 74: 141; 91: 24; 111: 115; 151: 201; 154: 156; 200: 163, 164; 211: 67
Parker-Rees, Guy 149: 145; 193: 149, 150
Parkin, Trevor 140: 151
Parkins, David 114: 123; 146: 176; 176: 168; 192: 107
Parkinson, Kathy 71: 143; 144: 234
Parkinson, Keith 70: 66
Parks, Gordon, Jr. 33: 228
Parnall, Peter 5: 137; 16: 221; 24: 70; 40: 78; 51: 130; 69: 17, 155; 136: 22, 23, 24
Parnall, Virginia 40: 78
Paros, Jennifer 210: 197
Parow, Lorraine 158: 127
Parr, Todd 134: 139, 140; 179: 163, 164, 165
Parrish, Anne 27: 159, 160
Parrish, Dillwyn 27: 159
Parrish, Maxfield 14: 160, 161, 164, 165; 16: 109; 18: 12, 13; YABC 1: 149, 152, 267; 2: 146, 149
Parry, David 26: 156
Parry, Marian 13: 176; 19: 179

Parsons, Garry *197:* 135
Partch, Virgil *45:* 163, 165
Pascal, David *14:* 174
Paschkis, Julie *177:* 153, 154
Pasquier, J.A. *16:* 91
Pastel, Elyse *201:* 123
Pasternak, Robert *119:* 53
Paterson, Diane *13:* 116; *39:* 163; *59:* 164, 165, 166,167; *72:* 51, 53; *129:* 175; *177:* 156, 157
Paterson, Helen *16:* 93
Patkau, Karen *112:* 123
Paton, Jane *15:* 271; *35:* 176
Patricelli, Leslie *207:* 129
Patrick, John *139:* 190
Patrick, Pamela *90:* 160; *93:* 211; *105:* 12
Patrick, Tom *190:* 103
Patterson, Geoffrey *54:* 75
Patterson, Robert *25:* 118
Patti, Joyce *187:* 145, 146
Patz, Nancy *111:* 40; *154:* 161; *214:* 80
Paul, James *4:* 130; *23:* 161
Paul, Korky *102:* 85
Paull, Grace *24:* 157; *87:* 127
Paulsen, Ruth Wright *79:* 160, 164; *189:* 146
Pavlov, Elena *80:* 49
Payne, Adam S. *135:* 166
Payne, C.F. *145:* 138, 140; *179:* 168
Payne, Joan Balfour *1:* 118
Payne, Tom *170:* 27
Payson, Dale *7:* 34; *9:* 151; *20:* 140; *37:* 22
Payzant, Charles *21:* 147
Peacock, Ralph *64:* 118
Peake, Mervyn *22:* 136, 149; *23:* 162, 163, 164; *YABC2:* 307
Pearson, Larry *38:* 225
Pearson, Tracey Campbell *64:* 163, 164, 167, 168, 169; *118:* 51; *156:* 169, 171, 172; *163:* 140
Peat, Fern B. *16:* 115
Peck, Anne Merriman *18:* 241; *24:* 155
Peck, Beth *66:* 242; *79:* 166; *80:* 136; *91:* 34; *95:* 9; *101:* 77; *164:* 197; *190:* 170
Peddicord, Jane Ann *199:* 106
Pedersen, Janet *193:* 152
Pedersen, Judy *66:* 217; *121:* 36; *172:* 67
Pedersen, Vilhelm *YABC 1:* 40
Pederson, Sharleen *12:* 92
Pedlar, Elaine *161:* 45
Peek, Merle *39:* 168
Peet, Bill *2:* 203; *41:* 159, 160, 161, 162, 163; *78:* 158, 159, 160, 161
Peguero, Adrian *116:* 133
Peguero, Gerard *116:* 133
Pels, Winslow Pinney *55:* 126
Peltier, Leslie C. *13:* 178
Peltzer, Marc *202:* 92
Penberthy, Mark *171:* 78
Pendle, Alexy *7:* 159; *13:* 34; *29:* 161; *33:* 215; *86:* 62
Pendola, Joanne *76:* 203; *81:* 125; *105:* 181; *178:* 152, 153
Pene du Bois, William *4:* 70; *10:* 122; *26:* 61; *27:* 145, 211; *35:* 243; *41:* 216; *68:* 180, 181; *73:* 45
Penfound, David *102:* 185
Pennington, Eunice *27:* 162
Peppe, Mark *28:* 142
Peppe, Rodney *4:* 164, 165; *74:* 187, 188, 189
Pepper, Hubert *64:* 143
Percy, Graham *63:* 2
Pericoli, Matteo *178:* 177
Perini, Ben *173:* 77
Perkins, David *60:* 68
Perkins, Lucy Fitch *72:* 199
Perkins, Lynne Rae *172:* 146; *212:* 153
Perl, Susan *2:* 98; *4:* 231; *5:* 44, 45, 118; *6:* 199; *8:* 137; *12:* 88; *22:* 193; *34:* 54, 55; *52:* 128; *YABC 1:* 176
Perrone, Donna *78:* 166
Perry, Marie Fritz *165:* 180

Perry, Patricia *29:* 137; *30:* 171
Perry, Roger *27:* 163
Perske, Martha *46:* 83; *51:* 108, 147
Persson, Stina *175:* 166
Pesek, Ludek *15:* 237
Petach, Heidi *149:* 166; *200:* 207
Peters, David *72:* 205; *182:* 116
Petersen, Jeff *181:* 95
Petersham, Maud *17:* 108, 147, 148, 149, 150, 151, 152, 153
Petersham, Miska *17:* 108, 147, 148, 149, 150, 151, 152, 153
Peterson, Eric *109:* 125
Peterson, Nisse *99:* 27
Peterson, R.F. *7:* 101
Peterson, Russell *7:* 130
Petie, Haris *2:* 3; *10:* 41, 118; *11:* 227; *12:* 70
Petricic, Dusan *153:* 75, 76, 77; *170:* 12; *172:* 13; *176:* 170; *179:* 56
Petrides, Heidrun *19:* 223
Petrone, Valeria *159:* 160; *171:* 92; *186:* 173; *204:* 49
Petrosino, Tamara *177:* 40; *193:* 154, 155
Petruccio, Steven James *67:* 159; *127:* 5
Pettingill, Ondre *64:* 181; *70:* 64
Peyo *40:* 56, 57
Peyton, K.M. *15:* 212
Pfeifer, Herman *15:* 262
Pfister, Marcus *83:* 165, 166, 167; *146:* 152; *150:* 160; *207:* 132, 134, 135, 136
Pfloog, Jan *124:* 60
Pham, LeUyen *160:* 48; *175:* 154, 156; *179:* 149; *201:* 124, 125, 126, 127; *204:* 28; *208:* 206
Phelan, Matt *182:* 160; *184:* 222; *215:* 140, 141
Phillips, Craig *70:* 151; *207:* 74
Phillips, Douglas *1:* 19
Phillips, F.D. *6:* 202
Phillips, Louise *133:* 67
Phillips, Matt *184:* 173
Phillips, Thomas *30:* 55
Philpot, Glyn *54:* 46
Phiz
  See Browne, Hablot K.
Piatti, Celestino *16:* 223
Pica, Steve *115:* 181
Picarella, Joseph *13:* 147
Picart, Gabriel *121:* 165; *201:* 169
Pichon, Liz *174:* 168
Pickard, Charles *12:* 38; *18:* 203; *36:* 152
Picken, George A. *23:* 150
Pickens, David *22:* 156
Pickering, Jimmy *195:* 152; *197:* 163
Pienkowski, Jan *6:* 183; *30:* 32; *58:* 140, 141, 142,143, 146, 147; *73:* 3; *87:* 156, 157; *131:* 189
Pieper, Christiane *200:* 168
Pignataro, Anna *163:* 220 Pileggi, Steve *145:* 122
Pilkey, Dav *68:* 186; *115:* 164, 166; *166:* 173, 174, 175
Pimlott, John *10:* 205
Pincus, Harriet *4:* 186; *8:* 179; *22:* 148; *27:* 164, 165; *66:* 202
Pini, Wendy *89:* 166
Pinkett, Neil *60:* 8
Pinkney, Brian *81:* 184, 185; *94:* 107; *113:* 146, 147; *117:* 121, 166; *132:* 145; *158:* 108, 191; *160:* 189; *200:* 8
Pinkney, Jerry *8:* 218; *10:* 40; *15:* 276; *20:* 66; *24:* 121; *33:* 109; *36:* 222; *38:* 200; *41:* 165, 166, 167, 168, 169, 170, 171, 173, 174; *44:* 198; *48:* 51; *53:* 20; *56:* 61, 68; *58:* 184; *60:* 59; *61:* 91; *71:* 146, 148, 149; *72:* 17; *73:* 149; *74:* 159,192; *75:* 45; *80:* 206; *81:* 44; *85:* 144; *95:* 50; *107:* 158, 159, 160; *108:* 164; *112:* 114, 115; *133:* 58; *195:* 140
Pinkwater, Daniel Manus *8:* 156; *46:* 180, 181, 182, 185, 188, 189, 190; *151:* 161 *76:* 178, 179, 180; *210:* 203

Pinkwater, Manus
  See Pinkwater, Daniel Manus
Pinkwater, Jill *114:* 160, 161; *158:* 179; *188:* 143, 145, 146
Pinto, Ralph *10:* 131; *45:* 93
Pinto, Sara *200:* 165
Pinon, Mark *74:* 22
Piven, Hanoch *173:* 142
Pistolesi *73:* 211
Pitcairn, Ansel *188:* 10
Pittman, Helena Clare *71:* 151
Pitz, Henry C. *4:* 168; *19:* 165; *35:* 128; *42:* 80; *YABC 2:* 95, 176
Pitzenberger, Lawrence J. *26:* 94
Pitzer, Susanna *181:* 131
Plant, Andrew *214:* 166
Player, Stephen *82:* 190
Plecas, Jennifer *84:* 201; *106:* 124; *149:* 168; *205:* 180
Ploog, Mike *180:* 19
Plume, Ilse *170:* 149
Plummer, William *32:* 31
Podevin, Jean François *184:* 185
Podwal, Mark *56:* 170, 173; *101:* 154, 155, 157; *149:* 176; *160:* 194
Pogany, Willy *15:* 46, 49; *19:* 222, 256; *25:* 214; *44:* 142, 143, 144, 145, 146, 147, 148
Pohrt, Tom *67:* 116; *104:* 80; *152:* 199; *195:* 154; *199:* 85
Poirson, V.A. *26:* 89
Polacco, Patricia *74:* 195, 196, 197, 198; *123:* 121, 122, 123; *180:* 189, 190, 191, 193, 194; *212:* 168, 170, 171
Polgreen, John *21:* 44
Polhemus, Coleman *210:* 209
Politi, Leo *1:* 178; *4:* 53; *21:* 48; *47:* 173,174, 176, 178, 179, 180, 181
Pollema-Cahill, Phyllis *123:* 126
Pollen, Samson *64:* 80
Polonsky, Arthur *34:* 168
Polseno, Jo *1:* 53; *3:* 117; *5:* 114; *17:* 154; *20:* 87; *32:* 49; *41:* 245
Pomaska, Anna *117:* 148
Pons, Bernadette *184:* 100
Ponter, James *5:* 204
Poole, Colin *111:* 27
Poortvliet, Rien *6:* 212; *65:* 165, 166, 167
Pope, Kevin *183:* 158
Popp, Wendy *72:* 122; *158:* 68
Poppel, Hans *71:* 154, 155
Porfirio, Guy *76:* 134
Portal, Colette *6:* 186; *11:* 203
Porter, George *7:* 181
Porter, Janice Lee *136:* 175; *164:* 37
Porter, John *113:* 47
Porter, Pat Grant *84:* 112; *125:* 101
Porter, Sue *146:* 246, 247; *213:* 139, 140, 141
Porter, Walter *124:* 175
Posada, Mia *187:* 151
Posen, Michael *175:* 82
Posthuma, Sieb *150:* 163
Postier, Jim *202:* 140; *204:* 25
Postma, Lidia *79:* 17
Potter, Beatrix *100:* 194, 195; *132:* 179, 180, 181, 182; *YABC 1:* 208, 209, 210, 212, 213
Potter, Giselle *117:* 123; *143:* 44; *144:* 170, 197; *149:* 7; *150:* 165; *187:* 152, 153; *190:* 198; *196:* 152; *200:* 12
Potter, Katherine *104:* 147; *171:* 135; *173:* 136
Potter, Miriam Clark *3:* 162
Poulin, Stephane *98:* 140, 141
Poullis, Nick *146:* 210
Powell, Constance Buffington *174:* 141
Powell, Gary *151:* 208
Powell, Ivan *67:* 219
Power, Margaret *105:* 122
Powers, Daniel *161:* 173
Powers, Richard M. *1:* 230; *3:* 218; *7:* 194; *26:* 186
Powledge, Fred *37:* 154

Powzyk, Joyce *74:* 214
Poydar, Nancy *96:* 149; *190:* 180, 181, 182
Pracher, Richard *91:* 166
Prachaticka, Marketa *126:* 126
Prange, Beckie *181:* 169
Prap, Lila *177:* 165
Prater, John *103:* 142, 143, 144; *149:* 172
Pratt, Charles *23:* 29
Pratt, Christine Joy *214:* 167
Pratt, George *116:* 208; *212:* 37
Pratt, Pierre *150:* 73; *166:* 183; *168:* 172; *201:* 27; *208:* 171, 172, 173
Prebenna, David *73:* 174
Preiss-Glasser, Robin *123:* 176; *152* 40; *172:* 194
Press, Jenny *116:* 95
Preston, Mark *152:* 162
Pretro, Korinna *91:* 126
Prevost, Mikela *209:* 111
Price, Christine *2:* 247; *3:* 163, 253; *8:* 166
Price, Cynthia *118:* 156
Price, Edward *33:* 34
Price, Garrett *1:* 76; *2:* 42
Price, Hattie Longstreet *17:* 13
Price, Norman *YABC 1:* 129
Price, Willard *48:* 184
Priceman, Marjorie *81:* 171; *136:* 169; *156:* 200; *168:* 153, 154; *188:* 45
Priestley, Alice *168:* 33
Priestley, Chris *198:* 144
Primavera, Elise *26:* 95; *58:* 151; *73:* 37; *80:* 79; *86:* 156; *105:* 161; *213:* 157
Primrose, Jean *36:* 109
Prince, Alison *86:* 188, 189
Prince, Leonora E. *7:* 170
Pritchett, Shelley *116:* 148
Prittie, Edwin J. *YABC 1:* 120
Proimos, James *176:* 4
Proimos, John *173:* 144
Prosmitsky, Jenya *132:* 33
Provensen, Alice *37:* 204, 215, 222; *70:* 176, 177, 178, 180; *71:* 213; *147:* 184; *191:* 190
Provensen, Martin *37:* 204, 215, 222; *70:* 176, 177, 178, 180; *71:* 213; *191:* 190
Pucci, Albert John *44:* 154
Pudlo *8:* 59
Puggaard, Ulla *196:* 25
Pullen, Zachary *211:* 161
Pulver, Harry, Jr. *129:* 159
Pulver, Robin *160:* 4
Punchatz, Don *99:* 57
Purdy, Susan *8:* 162
Pursell, Weimer *55:* 18
Purtscher, Alfons *97:* 6
Puskas, James *5:* 141
Pyk, Jan *7:* 26; *38:* 123
Pyle, Chuck *99:* 149; *191:* 83
Pyle, Howard *16:* 225, 226, 227, 228, 230, 231, 232, 235; *24:* 27; *34:* 124, 125, 127, 128; *59:* 132; *100:* 198

Q

Quackenbush, Robert *4:* 190; *6:* 166; *7:* 175, 178; *9:* 86; *11:* 65, 221; *41:* 154; *43:* 157; *70:* 185, 186; *71:* 137; *85:* 47; *92:* 148; *133:* 154, 164, 169
Qualls, Sean *177:* 167, 168; *193:* 43
Quennell, Marjorie (Courtney) *29:* 163, 164
Quidor, John *19:* 82
Quirk, John *62:* 170
Quirk, Thomas *12:* 81

R

Rackham, Arthur *15:* 32, 78, 214-227; *17:* 105, 115; *18:* 233; *19:* 254; *20:* 151; *22:* 129, 131, 132, 133; *23:* 175; *24:* 161, 181; *26:* 91; *32:* 118; *64:* 18; *100:* 9, 16, 203, 204; *YABC 1:* 25, 45, 55, 147; *2:* 103, 142, 173, 210

Racz, Michael *56:* 134
Raczka, Bob *191:* 155, 156
Radcliffe, Andrew *82:* 215
Rader, Laura *101:* 219; *197:* 147; *203:* 53
Radunsky, Vladimir *177:* 170; *192:* 30
Radzinski, Kandy *212:* 174
Rafilson, Sidney *11:* 172
Raglin, Tim *125:* 24
Raible, Alton *1:* 202, 203; *28:* 193; *35:* 181; *110:* 207
Raine, Patricia *82:* 74; *88:* 154
Ramá, Sue *173:* 45; *185:* 186; *190:* 184
Ramhorst, John *117:* 11
Ramirez, Gladys *177:* 19
Ramirez, Jose *207:* 27
Ramsey, James *16:* 41
Ramsey, Marcy Dunn *82:* 11; *180:* 186
Ramus, Michael *51:* 171
Rand, Paul *6:* 188
Rand, Ted *67:* 9, 10, 121, 123; *74:* 190; *84:* 170; *103:* 170; *112:* 6; *114:* 73; *139:* 168; *143:* 194; *156:* 154; *161:* 9, 10; *200:* 38; *204:* 7
Randazzo, Tony *81:* 98
Randell, William *55:* 54
Rane, Walter *93:* 144; *143:* 109; *184:* 126
Rankin, Joan *163:* 40; *212:* 176
Rankin, Laura *176:* 173, 174; *179:* 150
Ransome, Arthur *22:* 201
Ransome, James E. *74:* 137; *75:* 80; *84:* 181; *94:* 108; *117:* 115; *123:* 128, 129, 130; *158:* 101, 102; *159:* 205; *178:* 188, 189, 190
Rantz, Don *119:* 184
Rao, Anthony *28:* 126
Raphael, Elaine *23:* 192; *71:* 24, 25
Rappaport, Eva *6:* 190
Raschka, Chris *80:* 187, 189, 190; *97:* 211; *115:* 210; *117:* 151, 152, 153, 154; *143:* 195; *145:* 153; *166:* 190, 191; *170:* 114; *207:* 140, 143, 144, 145; *208:* 82
Rash, Andy *158:* 178; *162:* 172; *210:* 204
Raskin, Ellen *2:* 208, 209; *4:* 142; *13:* 183; *22:* 68; *29:* 139; *36:* 134; *38:* 173, 174, 175, 176, 177, 178,179, 180, 181; *60:* 163; *86:* 81
Rathmann, Peggy *93:* 32; *94:* 168; *157:* 212, 214
Ratkus, Tony *77:* 133
Ratzkin, Lawrence *40:* 143
Rau, Margaret *9:* 157
Raverat, Gwen *YABC 1:* 152
Ravid, Joyce *61:* 73
Ravielli, Anthony *1:* 198; *3:* 168; *11:* 143
Ravilious, Robin *77:* 169
Rawlins, Donna *72:* 198; *73:* 15, 129
Rawlins, Janet *76:* 79
Rawlings, Steve *143:* 139; *151:* 54; *208:* 150
Rawlinson, Debbie *75:* 132
Ray, Deborah Kogan *8:* 164; *29:* 238; *50:* 112, 113; *62:* 119; *78:* 191; *203:* 149, 150, 151
Ray, Jane *96:* 166; *97:* 104; *152:* 208; *190:* 221; *196:* 165
Ray, Ralph *2:* 239; *5:* 73
Rayann, Omar *162:* 205; *186:* 29, 30
Rayevsky, Robert *64:* 17; *70:* 173; *80:* 204; *117:* 79; *190:* 187, 188
Raymond, Larry *31:* 108; *97:* 109
Rayner, Hugh *151:* 170
Rayner, Mary *22:* 207; *47:* 140; *72:* 191; *87:* 171, 172; *192:* 104
Rayner, Shoo
　See Rayner, Hugh
Raynes, John *71:* 19
Raynor, Dorka *28:* 168
Raynor, Paul *24:* 73
Rayyan, Omar *110:* 222; *112:* 17; *125:* 131
Razzi, James *10:* 127
Read, Alexander D. *20:* 45
Reader, Dennis *71:* 157
Reasoner, Charles *53:* 33, 36, 37
Rebenschied, Shane *203:* 76; *215:* 124
Reczuch, Karen *115:* 132; *145:* 131

Redlich, Ben *163:* 221; *198:* 193
Reddy, Mike *203:* 67
Reed, Joseph *116:* 139
Reed, Lynn Rowe *115:* 173; *171:* 146; *208:* 177; *215:* 144, 145
Reed, Mike *211:* 147; *215:* 131
Reed, Tom *34:* 171
Reeder, Colin *74:* 202; *77:* 113
Rees, Mary *134:* 219
Reese, Bob *60:* 135
Reeve, Philip *171:* 50
Reeves, Eira B. *130:* 173, 174; *141:* 151
Reeves, Rick *181:* 179
Reeves, Rosie *202:* 200
Regan, Dana *117:* 116
Regan, Laura *103:* 198; *153:* 206
Reichert, Renée *169:* 127
Reid, Barbara *82:* 178; *92:* 17; *93:* 169, 170
Reid, Stephen *19:* 213; *22:* 89
Reim, Melanie *104:* 151; *150:* 98
Reinert, Kirk *89:* 138; *195:* 129
Reinertson, Barbara *44:* 150; *62:* 103
Reiniger, Lotte *40:* 185
Reisberg, Mira *119:* 2
Reisch, Jesse *158:* 130
Reiser, Lynn *81:* 175; *138:* 184; *180:* 200
Reiss, John J. *23:* 193
Relf, Douglas *3:* 63
Relyea, C.M. *16:* 29; *31:* 153
Remi, Georges *13:* 184
Remington, Frederic *19:* 188; *41:* 178, 179, 180, 181, 183,184, 185, 186, 187, 188; *62:* 197
Remkiewicz, Frank *67:* 102; *77:* 171; *80:* 130; *113:* 107; *152:* 116; *152:* 211, 212; *157:* 148
Rendon, Maria *116:* 141; *192:* 134; *134:* 152
Renfro, Ed *79:* 176
Renier, Aaron *202:* 141; *207:* 119
Renlie, Frank *11:* 200
Reschofsky, Jean *7:* 118
Rethi *60:* 181
Rethi, Lili *2:* 153; *36:* 156
Reusswig, William *3:* 267
Revell, Cindy *195:* 93
Rex, Adam *156:* 172; *169:* 91; *186:* 178, 179; *215:* 103
Rex, Michael *157:* 147; *191:* 159, 160
Rey, H.A. *1:* 182; *26:* 163, 164, 166, 167, 169; *69:* 172, 173, 174, 175; *86:* 195, 196, 197; *100:* 211; *YABC 2:* 17
Rey, Luis V. *201:* 162
Reynolds, Adrian *192:* 159, 160
Reynolds, Doris *5:* 71; *31:* 77
Reynolds, Peter H. *142:* 12; *179:* 175, 176; *202:* 113, 114
Rhead, Louis *31:* 91; *100:* 228
Rhodes, Andrew *38:* 204; *50:* 163; *54:* 76; *61:* 123, 124; *87:* 200
Ribbons, Ian *3:* 10; *37:* 161; *40:* 76
Ricci, Regolo *93:* 22; *164:* 148
Rice, Elizabeth *2:* 53, 214
Rice, Eve *34:* 174, 175; *91:* 172
Rice, James *22:* 210; *93:* 173
Rich, Anna *212:* 180
Rich, Martha *195:* 16
Richards, Chuck *170:* 154
Richards, George *40:* 116, 119, 121; *44:* 179
Richards, Henry *YABC 1:* 228, 231
Richardson, Ernest *2:* 144
Richardson, Frederick *18:* 27, 31
Richardson, John *110:* 88
Richman, Hilda *26:* 132
Richmond, George *24:* 179
Riddell, Chris *114:* 170, 195; *166:* 179; *199:* 164, 166, 167
Riddle, Tohby *74:* 204; *151:* 179
Riding, Peter *63:* 195
Rieniets, Judy King *14:* 28
Riger, Bob *2:* 166
Riggio, Anita *73:* 191; *85:* 63; *137:* 184; *172:* 165

Riley, Jon *74:* 70
Riley, Kenneth *22:* 230
Riley, Terry *203:* 100
Riley-Webb, Charlotte *153:* 143
Rinaldi, Angelo *165:* 60, 69
Ringgold, Faith *71:* 162; *114:* 173, 174, 176;
    187: 160, 161, 163
Ringi, Kjell *12:* 171
Rios, Tere
    See Versace, Marie
Rioux, Jo *215:* 110
Ripper, Charles L. *3:* 175
Ripplinger, Henry *117:* 31
Ritchie, William *74:* 183
Ritter, John *175:* 14
Ritz, Karen *41:* 117; *72:* 239; *87:* 125; *102:* 7;
    106: 6
Rivas, Victor *209:* 193
Rivers, Ruth *178:* 193
Rivkin, Jay *15:* 230
Rivoche, Paul *45:* 125
Roach, Marilynne *9:* 158
Robbin, Jodi *44:* 156, 159
Robbins, Frank *42:* 167
Robbins, Ken *147:* 191, 192
Robbins, Ruth *52:* 102
Roberts, Cliff *4:* 126
Roberts, David *154:* 4, 6; *191:* 162; *196:* 184;
    197: 105; *210:* 257
Roberts, Doreen *4:* 230; *28:* 105
Roberts, Jim *22:* 166; *23:* 69; *31:* 110
Roberts, Tony *109:* 195, 214
Roberts, W. *22:* 2, 3
Robertson, M.P. *197:* 153
Robins, Arthur *137:* 172; *151:* 225; *204:* 161
Robinson, Aminah Brenda Lynn *86:* 205; *103:*
    55; *159:* 175
Robinson, Charles [1870-1937] *17:* 157, 171,
    172, 173, 175, 176; *24:* 207; *25:* 204; *YABC*
    2: 308, 309, 310, 331
Robinson, Charles *3:* 53; *5:* 14; *6:* 193; *7:*
    150; *7:* 183; *8:* 38; *9:* 81; *13:* 188; *14:* 248,
    249; *23:* 149; *26:* 115; *27:* 48; *28:* 191; *32:*
    28; *35:* 210; *36:* 37; *48:* 96; *52:* 33; *53:* 157;
    56: 15; *62:* 142; *77:* 41; *111:* 148
Robinson, Jerry *3:* 262
Robinson, Joan G. *7:* 184
Robinson, Lolly *90:* 227
Robinson, T.H. *17:* 179, 181, 182, 183; *29:*
    254
Robinson, W. Heath *17:* 185, 187, 189, 191,
    193, 195, 197, 199, 202; *23:* 167; *25:* 194;
    29: 150; *YABC 1:* 44; *2:* 183
Rocco, John *187:* 4; *188:* 151; *208:* 180, 181,
    182; *213:* 94
Roche, Christine *41:* 98
Roche, Denis *99:* 184; *180:* 32; *196:* 168
Roche, P.K. *57:* 151, 152
Rocker, Fermin *7:* 34; *13:* 21; *31:* 40; *40:*
    190,191
Rocklen, Margot *101:* 181
Rockwell, Anne *5:* 147; *33:* 171, 173; *71:* 166,
    167,168; *114:* 183, 184; *194:* 152, 155
Rockwell, Gail *7:* 186
Rockwell, Harlow *33:* 171, 173, 175
Rockwell, Lizzy *114:* 182; *162:* 182; *185:* 189
Rockwell, Norman *23:* 39, 196, 197, 199, 200,
    203, 204, 207; *41:* 140, 143; *123:* 47; *YABC*
    2: 60
Rockwood, Richard *119:* 75
Rodanas, Kristina *156:* 183, 184
Rodegast, Roland *43:* 100
Rodgers, Frank *69:* 177
Rodriguez, Albert G. *182:* 50
Rodriguez, Christina *184:* 12
Rodriguez, Edel *204:* 86
Rodriguez, Joel *16:* 65
Rodriguez, Robert *145:* 145; *212:* 33
Rodriguez-Howard, Pauline *177:* 18
Roe, Monika *210:* 94
Roeckelein, Katrina *134:* 223

Roennfeldt, Robert *66:* 243
Roever, J.M. *4:* 119; *26:* 170
Roffey, Maureen *33:* 142, 176, 177
Rogasky, Barbara *46:* 90
Rogé *173:* 160
Rogers, Carol *2:* 262; *6:* 164; *26:* 129
Rogers, Chris M. *150:* 59; *196:* 61
Rogers, Forest *87:* 160; *101:* 76
Rogers, Frances *10:* 130
Rogers, Gregory *104:* 76; *126:* 57; *171:* 26
Rogers, Jacqueline *78:* 249; *80:* 34; *86:* 54
    103: 70; *115:* 72; *129:* 173; *131:* 57, 225;
    143: 211; *153:* 100; *193:* 186; *203:* 51; *213:*
    144, 145, 146; *214:* 142
Rogers, Sherry *191:* 66
Rogers, Walter S. *31:* 135, 138; *67:* 65, 168;
    100: 81
Rogers, William A. *15:* 151, 153, 154; *33:* 35
Rogoff, Barbara *95:* 20
Rohmann, Eric *103:* 152; *198:* 151
Rojankovsky, Feodor *6:* 134, 136; *10:* 183; *21:*
    128,129, 130; *25:* 110; *28:* 42; *68:* 120
Rolfsen, Alf *62:* 15
Rolston, Steve *209:* 154
Romain, Trevor *134:* 157
Roman, Barbara J. *103:* 171
Romas *114:* 111; *165:* 63
Romano, Robert *64:* 68
Romero, Alejandro *187:* 185
Roos, Maryn *168:* 198
Root, Barry *80:* 212; *90:* 196; *146:* 78; *156:*
    165; *159:* 161; *182:* 18, 172
Root, Kimberly Bulcken *86:* 72; *98:* 21; *108:*
    111; *127:* 114; *159:* 162; *176:* 134; *192:* 163
Roper, Bob *65:* 153
Roraback, Robin *111:* 156
Rorer, Abigail *43:* 222; *85:* 155
Rosales, Melodye *80:* 35
Rosamilia, Patricia *36:* 120
Rose, Carl *5:* 62
Rose, David S. *29:* 109; *70:* 120
Rose, Gerald *68:* 200, 201; *86:* 48
Rose, Ted *93:* 178
Rosen, Elizabeth *205:* 137
Rosenbaum, Jonathan *50:* 46
Rosenberg, Amye *74:* 207, 208
Rosenberry, Vera *87:* 22, 26; *144:* 212, 213;
    158: 120
Rosenblum, Richard *11:* 202; *18:* 18
Rosenstiehl, Agnès *203:* 153
Rosier, Lydia *16:* 236; *20:* 104; *21:* 109; *22:*
    125; *30:* 151, 158; *42:* 128; *45:* 214; *77:*
    227, 228
Rosing, Jens *85:* 142
Ross
    See Thomson, Ross
Ross, Christine *83:* 172, 173
Ross, Clare Romano *3:* 123; *21:* 45; *48:* 199
Ross, Dave *32:* 152; *57:* 108
Ross, Graham *199:* 4
Ross, Herbert *37:* 78
Ross, John *3:* 123; *21:* 45
Ross, Johnny *32:* 190
Ross, Larry *47:* 168; *60:* 62
Ross, Ruth *109:* 233
Ross, Tony *17:* 204; *56:* 132; *65:* 176, 177,
    179; *90:* 123; *123:* 186, 187, 190; *130:* 188,
    190, 191, 192; *132:* 242; *174:* 159; *176:* 181,
    182, 183; *202:* 198
Rossetti, Dante Gabriel *20:* 151, 153
Rostant, Larry *180:* 221; *194:* 108; *195:* 96;
    197: 12; *207:* 53; *210:* 189
Roth, Arnold *4:* 238; *21:* 133
Roth, Julie Jersild *180:* 206
Roth, Marci *135:* 223
Roth, R.G. *184:* 50
Roth, Rob *105:* 98; *146:* 41
Roth, Robert *176:* 159
Roth, Roger *61:* 128; *190:* 192
Roth, Stephanie *136:* 171, 172

Roth, Susan L. *80:* 38; *93:* 78; *134:* 165, 166;
    181: 145, 146
Rothenberg, Joani Keller *162:* 190, 191
Rothman, Michael *139:* 62; *184:* 34 Rotman,
    Jeffrey L. 145: 30
Rotondo, Pat *32:* 158
Roughsey, Dick *35:* 186
Rouille, M. *11:* 96
Rounds, Glen *8:* 173; *9:* 171; *12:* 56; *32:* 194;
    40: 230; *51:* 161, 162, 166; *56:* 149; *70:*
    198, 199; *YABC 1:* 1, 2, 3; *112:* 163
Roundtree, Katherine *114:* 88; *168:* 102
Rovetch, Lissa *201:* 164
Rowan, Evadne *52:* 51
Rowe, Eric *111:* 161
Rowe, Gavin *27:* 144; *72:* 47; *88:* 201
Rowe, John *132:* 70, 71; *180:* 126
Rowell, Kenneth *40:* 72
Rowen, Amy *52:* 143
Rowena *116:* 101
Rowland, Andrew *164:* 136
Rowland, Jada *83:* 73
Rowles, Daphne *58:* 24
Roy, Jeroo *27:* 229; *36:* 110
Royo *118:* 32; *144:* 105, 106, 108; *165:* 19;
    166: 166
Rubel, Nicole *18:* 255; *20:* 59; *81:* 66, 67; *95:*
    169, 170; *119:* 60; *135:* 177, 179, 180; *169:*
    68; *181:* 150
Rubel, Reina *33:* 217
Rud, Borghild *6:* 15
Ruddell, Gary *110:* 238; *116:* 207
Rudolph, Norman Guthrie *17:* 13
Rue, Leonard Lee III *37:* 164
Rueda, Claudia *183:* 170, 171
Ruelle, Karen Gray *126:* 193
Ruff, Donna *50:* 173; *72:* 203; *78:* 49; *80:*
    120,121; *93:* 162; *164:* 121
Ruffins, Reynold *10:* 134, 135; *41:* 191, 192,
    193, 194, 195, 196; *125:* 187, 188, 189; *162:*
    197
Ruhlin, Roger *34:* 44
Ruiz, Art *95:* 154; *110:* 91
Rumford, James *193:* 167
Runnerstroem, Bengt Arne *75:* 161
Ruse, Margaret *24:* 155
Rush, Ken *98:* 74
Rush, Peter *42:* 75
Russell, Charles M. *167:* 171
Russell, E.B. *18:* 177, 182
Russell, Jim *53:* 134
Russell, P. Craig *80:* 196; *146:* 102; *162:* 186
Russo, Marisabina *84:* 51; *106:* 164; *151:* 183;
    188: 153, 154, 155, 156
Russo, Susan *30:* 182; *36:* 144
Russon, Mary *87:* 145
Ruth, Greg *183:* 125
Ruth, Rod *9:* 161
Rutherford, Alexa *110:* 108
Rutherford, Jenny *78:* 5
Rutherford, Meg *25:* 174; *34:* 178, 179; *69:*
    73; *72:* 31
Rutland, Jonathan *31:* 126
Ruurs, Margriet *147:* 195
Ruzzier, Sergio *159:* 176, 177; *163:* 184; *210:*
    214, 216
Ryan, Amy *188:* 50
Ryan, Will *86:* 134
Ryden, Hope *8:* 176
Rylant, Cynthia *112:* 170, 172
Rymer, Alta M. *34:* 181
Ryniak, Christopher *178:* 11
Rystedt, Rex *49:* 80

S

Saaf, Chuck *49:* 179
Saaf, Donald *101:* 220; *124:* 180
Sabaka, Donna R. *21:* 172

Sabin, Robert *45:* 35; *60:* 30; *99:* 161
Sabuda, Robert *170:* 166, 167, 168
Sacker, Amy *16:* 100
Saelig, S.M. *129:* 73; *173:* 59
Saffioti, Lino *36:* 176; *48:* 60
Saflund, Birgitta *94:* 2
Sagsoorian, Paul *12:* 183; *22:* 154; *33:* 106; *87:* 152
Sahara, Tony *168:* 106; *177:* 181; *178:* 228; *186:* 132; *207:* 89
Sahlberg, Myron *57:* 165
Saidens, Amy *145:* 162; *191:* 131; *210:* 129
Saint Exupery, Antoine de *20:* 157
Saint James, Synthia *152:* 220; *188:* 90; *200:* 7
Sakai, Komako *213:* 148
Saldutti, Denise *39:* 186; *57:* 178
Sale, Morton *YABC 2:* 31
Sale, Tim *153:* 177
Salerno, Steven *150:* 79; *176:* 188; *202:* 39
Salter, George *72:* 128, 130
Saltzberg, Barney *135:* 184, 185; *194:* 160
Saltzman, David *86:* 209
Salwowski, Mark *71:* 54
Salzman, Yuri *86:* 12
Sambourne, Linley *YABC 2:* 181
Sampson, Katherine *9:* 197
Samson, Anne S. *2:* 216
San Souci, Daniel *40:* 200; *96:* 199, 200; *113:* 171; *157:* 149; *170:* 69; *192:* 167, 168
Sancha, Sheila *38:* 185
Sanchez, Enrique O. *155:* 84
Sand, George X. *45:* 182
Sandberg, Lasse *15:* 239, 241
Sanders, Beryl *39:* 173
Sanderson, Ruth *21:* 126; *24:* 53; *28:* 63; *33:* 67; *41:* 48, 198, 199, 200, 201, 202, 203; *43:* 79; *46:* 36,44; *47:* 102; *49:* 58; *62:* 121, 122; *85:* 3; *109:* 207, 208, 209, 210; *172:* 157, 158
Sandia *119:* 74
Sandin, Joan *4:* 36; *6:* 194; *7:* 177; *12:* 145,185; *20:* 43; *21:* 74; *26:* 144; *27:* 142; *28:* 224, 225; *38:* 86; *41:* 46; *42:* 35; *59:* 6; *80:* 136; *94:* 188; *140:* 116; *153:* 179, 180; *197:* 168
Sandland, Reg *39:* 215
Sandoz, Edouard *26:* 45, 47
Sanford, John *66:* 96, 97
Sanger, Amy Wilson *205:* 140
Sankey, Tom *72:* 103
Sano, Kazuhiko *153:* 208; *195:* 171; *203:* 21
Santat, Dan *188:* 160
Santiago, Wilfred *210:* 48
Santore, Charles *54:* 139; *200:* 171, 172
Santoro, Christopher *74:* 215
Santos, Jesse J. *99:* 24
Sapieha, Christine *1:* 180
Saport, Linda *123:* 137, 138; *215:* 29
Sara
    See De La Roche Saint Andre, Anne
Sarcone-Roach, Julia *215:* 158
Sardinha, Rick *175:* 151
Sarg, Tony *YABC 2:* 236
Sargent, Claudia *64:* 181
Sargent, Robert *2:* 217
Saris *1:* 33
Sarony *YABC 2:* 170
Saroff, Phyllis V. *202:* 160
Sasaki, Goro *170:* 46
Sasek, Miroslav *16:* 239, 240, 241, 242
Sassman, David *9:* 79
Satty *29:* 203, 205
Sauber, Robert *40:* 183; *76:* 256; *78:* 154; *87:* 92
Saunders, Dave *85:* 163, 164, 165
Savadier, Elivia *84:* 50; *145:* 45; *164:* 206
Savage, Naomi *56:* 172
Savage, Steele *10:* 203; *20:* 77; *35:* 28
Savage, Stephen *174:* 182
Savio *76:* 4

Savitt, Sam *8:* 66, 182; *15:* 278; *20:* 96; *24:* 192; *28:* 98
Sawyer, Kem Knapp *84:* 228, 229
Say, Allen *28:* 178; *69:* 182, 183, 232; *110:* 194, 195,196; *161:* 154, 155
Sayles, Elizabeth *82:* 93; *105:* 155; *109:* 116; *180:* 64
Scabrini, Janet *13:* 191; *44:* 128
Scanlan, Peter *83:* 27; *153:* 165; *187:* 149
Scanlon, Paul *83:* 87
Scannell, Reece *105:* 105
Scarry, Huck *35:* 204, 205
Scarry, Richard *2:* 220, 221; *18:* 20; *35:* 193, 194, 195,196, 197, 198, 199, 200, 201, 202; *75:* 165, 167, 168
Schachner, Judith Byron *88:* 180; *92:* 163; *93:* 102; *142:* 82; *178:* 199, 200; *190:* 140
Schade, Susan *205:* 21
Schaeffer, Mead *18:* 81, 94; *21:* 137, 138, 139; *47:* 128
Schaffer, Amanda *90:* 206
Schanzer, Rosalyn *138:* 192, 193
Scharl, Josef *20:* 132; *22:* 128
Scheel, Lita *11:* 230
Scheffler, Axel *180:* 23, 24
Scheib, Ida *29:* 28
Schermer, Judith *30:* 184
Schick, Eleanor *82:* 210, 211; *144:* 222
Schick, Joel *16:* 160; *17:* 167; *22:* 12; *27:* 176; *31:* 147, 148; *36:* 23; *38:* 64; *45:* 116, 117; *52:* 5, 85; *104:* 159
Schields, Gretchen *75:* 171, 203
Schindelman, Joseph *1:* 74; *4:* 101; *12:* 49; *26:* 51; *40:* 146; *56:* 158; *73:* 40
Schindler, Edith *7:* 22
Schindler, S.D. *38:* 107; *46:* 196; *74:* 162; *75:* 172, 173; *99:* 133; *112:* 177; *118:* 185, 186; *121:* 71; *136:* 159; *143:* 45; *149:* 120; *156:* 30; *169:* 135; *171:* 161, 162, 163; *172:* 9; *186:* 163; *194:* 109; *195:* 35; *198:* 170, 171, 172
Schlesinger, Bret *7:* 77
Schmid, Eleanore *12:* 188; *126:* 196, 197
Schmiderer, Dorothy *19:* 224
Schmidt, Bill *73:* 34; *76:* 220, 222, 224
Schmidt, Elizabeth *15:* 242
Schmidt, George Paul *132:* 122
Schmidt, Karen Lee *54:* 12; *71:* 174; *92:* 56; *94:* 190, 191; *127:* 103
Schmidt, Lynette *76:* 205
Schmitz, Tamara *207:* 147
Schneider, Christine M. *171:* 165
Schneider, Howie *181:* 159
Schneider, Rex *29:* 64; *44:* 171
Schnurr, Edward *170:* 62
Schoberle, Cecile *80:* 200; *92:* 134
Schoenherr, Ian *32:* 83; *173:* 41
Schoenherr, John *1:* 146, 147, 173; *3:* 39, 139; *17:* 75; *29:* 72; *32:* 83; *37:* 168, 169, 170; *43:* 164, 165; *45:* 160, 162; *51:* 127; *66:* 196, 197, 198; *68:* 83; *72:* 240; *75:* 225; *88:* 176
Scholder, Fritz *69:* 103
Schomburg, Alex *13:* 23
Schongut, Emanuel *4:* 102; *15:* 186; *47:* 218, 219; *52:* 147, 148, 149, 150; *185:* 27
Schoonover, Frank *17:* 107; *19:* 81, 190, 233; *22:* 88,129; *24:* 189; *31:* 88; *41:* 69; *YABC 2:* 282, 316
Schories, Pat *164:* 210
Schottland, Miriam *22:* 172
Schramm, Ulrik *2:* 16; *14:* 112
Schreiber, Elizabeth Anne *13:* 193
Schreiber, Ralph W. *13:* 193
Schreiter, Rick *14:* 97; *23:* 171; *41:* 247; *49:* 131
Schroades, John *214:* 129
Schroeder, Binette *56:* 128, 129
Schroeder, E. Peter *12:* 112
Schroeder, Ted *11:* 160; *15:* 189; *30:* 91; *34:* 43

Schrotter, Gustav *22:* 212; *30:* 225
Schubert, Dieter *101:* 167, 168
Schubert-Gabrys, Ingrid *101:* 167, 168
Schucker, James *31:* 163
Schuett, Stacey *72:* 137; *208:* 204
Schulder, Lili *146:* 29
Schulke, Debra *57:* 167
Schulke, Flip *57:* 167
Schulz, Barbara *167:* 24
Schulz, Charles M. *10:* 137, 138, 139, 140, 141, 142; *118:* 192, 193, 194, 196, 199
Schutzer, Dena *109:* 32
Schwark, Mary Beth *51:* 155; *72:* 175
Schwartz, Amy *47:* 191; *82:* 100; *83:* 178, 179, 180,181; *129:* 107; *131:* 197, 198; *189:* 166, 168
Schwartz, Carol *124:* 41; *130:* 199
Schwartz, Charles *8:* 184
Schwartz, Daniel *46:* 37
Schwartz, Joanie *124:* 170
Schwartzberg, Joan *3:* 208
Schwarz, Viviane *204:* 132
Schweitzer, Iris *2:* 137; *6:* 207
Schweninger, Ann *29:* 172; *82:* 246; *159:* 202; *168:* 166; *211:* 193
Schwinger, Laurence *84:* 44; *91:* 61
Scofield, Penrod *61:* 107; *62:* 160
Scott, Anita Walker *7:* 38
Scott, Art *39:* 41
Scott, Frances Gruse *38:* 43
Scott, Julian *34:* 126
Scott, Roszel *33:* 238
Scott, Sally *87:* 27
Scott, Steve *166:* 230, 231; *171:* 93
Scott, Trudy *27:* 172
Scotton, Rob *214:* 183
Scrace, Carolyn *143:* 95, 96
Scrambly, Crab *198:* 196
Scribner, Joanne *14:* 236; *29:* 78; *33:* 185; *34:* 208; *78:* 75; *164:* 237; *203:* 73
Scrofani, Joseph *31:* 65; *74:* 225
Scroggs, Kirk *187:* 169
Seaman, Mary Lott *34:* 64
Searle, Ronald *24:* 98; *42:* 172, 173, 174, 176, 177, 179; *66:* 73, 74; *70:* 205, 206, 207
Searle, Townley *36:* 85
Sebree, Charles *18:* 65
Sedacca, Joseph M. *11:* 25; *22:* 36
Seder, Jason *108:* 102
Seeger, Laura Vaccaro *172:* 162
Seegmiller, Don *174:* 57
Seely, David *164:* 173
Seeley, Laura L. *97:* 105
Segal, John *178:* 202
Segar, E.C. *61:* 179, 181
Segur, Adrienne *27:* 121
Seibold, J. Otto *83:* 188, 190, 191; *149:* 212, 214, 215, 216; *196:* 177, 179; *215:* 204
Seignobosc, Francoise *21:* 145, 146
Sejima, Yoshimasa *8:* 187
Selig, Sylvie *13:* 199
Seltzer, Isadore *6:* 18; *133:* 59
Seltzer, Meyer *17:* 214
Selven, Maniam *144:* 133
Selway, Martina *169:* 157
Selznick, Brian *79:* 192; *104:* 25; *117:* 175; *126:* 156; *134:* 171; *158:* 76, 78; *169:* 70; *171:* 172, 173; *191:* 106; *192:* 130; *197:* 158; *203:* 35; *205:* 92; *210:* 219, 220, 221, 222
Sempe, Jean-Jacques *47:* 92; *YABC 2:* 109
Sendak, Maurice *1:* 135, 190; *3:* 204; *7:* 142; *15:* 199; *17:* 210; *27:* 181, 182, 183, 185, 186, 187, 189,190, 191, 192, 193, 194, 195, 197, 198, 199, 203; *28:* 181, 182; *32:* 108; *33:* 148, 149; *35:* 238; *44:* 180, 181; *45:* 97, 99; *46:* 174; *73:* 225; *91:* 10, 11 *YABC1:* 167; *113:* 163, 165, 167, 168; *118:* 153; *127:* 161
Senders, Marci *180:* 79
Sengler, Johanna *18:* 256

Senn, Steve *60:* 145
Seredy, Kate *1:* 192; *14:* 20, 21; *17:* 210
Sergeant, John *6:* 74
Serra, Sebastía *212:* 215
Servello, Joe *10:* 144; *24:* 139; *40:* 91; *70:* 130, 131; *146:* 159
Seton, Ernest Thompson *18:* 260-269, 271
Seuss, Dr.
    See Geisel, Theodor
Severin, John Powers *7:* 62
Sewall, Marcia *15:* 8; *22:* 170; *37:* 171, 172, 173; *39:* 73; *45:* 209; *62:* 117; *69:* 185, 186; *71:* 212; *90:* 232; *96:* 127; *102:* 101; *107:* 129; *119:* 176, 177, 178, 180
Seward, James *70:* 35
Seward, Prudence *16:* 243
Sewell, Helen *3:* 186; *15:* 308; *33:* 102; *38:* 189, 190, 191, 192
Seymour, Stephen *54:* 21
Sfar, Joann *182:* 183
Shachat, Andrew *82:* 179
Shadbolt, Robert *203:* 68
Shahn, Ben *39:* 178; *46:* 193
Shalansky, Len *38:* 167
Shanks, Anne Zane *10:* 149
Shannon, David *57:* 137; *107:* 184; *112:* 216; *135:* 12; *152:* 223, 224, 225; *158:* 192; *212:* 159, 160, 163
Sharkey, Niamh *213:* 152
Sharp, Paul *52:* 60
Sharp, William *6:* 131; *19:* 241; *20:* 112; *25:* 141
Sharratt, Nick *102:* 207, 208; *104:* 163; *153:* 198; *175:* 176; *192:* 208; *199:* 141, 142, 143, 184, 187, 188
Shaw, Barclay *74:* 14, 16; *118:* 138
Shaw, Charles *21:* 135; *38:* 187; *47:* 124; *126:* 219
Shaw, Charles G. *13:* 200
Shaw-Smith, Emma *144:* 117
Shea, Edmund *56:* 19
Shearer, Ted *43:* 193, 194, 195, 196
Sheban, Chris *182:* 185; *190:* 102, 104; *202:* 28; *204:* 112, 114; *209:* 150; *210:* 107
Shecter, Ben *16:* 244; *25:* 109; *33:* 188, 191; *41:* 77
Shed, Greg *74:* 94; *84:* 204; *129:* 149, *167:* 91; *179:* 192
Sheeban, Chris *144:* 190; *158:* 163
Shefcik, James *48:* 221, 222; *60:* 141
Shefelman, Karl *58:* 168
Shefelman, Tom *204:* 137
Shefts, Joelle *48:* 210
Shein, Bob *139:* 189
Sheinkin, Stephen *204:* 139
Shekerjian, Haig *16:* 245
Shekerjian, Regina *16:* 245; *25:* 73
Sheldon, David *184:* 174; *185:* 204; *211:* 189
Shelley, John *186:* 223
Shemie, Bonnie *96:* 207
Shenton, Edward *45:* 187, 188, 189; *YABC 1:* 218, 219, 221
Shepard, Ernest H. *3:* 193; *4:* 74; *16:* 101; *17:* 109; *25:* 148; *33:* 152, 199, 200, 201, 202, 203, 204, 205, 206,207; *46:* 194; *98:* 114; *100:* 111, 178, 179, 217, 219, 220,221; *YABC 1:* 148, 153, 174, 176, 180, 181
Shepard, Mary *4:* 210; *22:* 205; *30:* 132, 133; *54:* 150, 152, 153, 157, 158; *59:* 108, 109, 111; *100:* 246
Shepherd, Amanda *198:* 14
Shepherd, Irana *171:* 112
Sheppard, Kate *195:* 176
Shepperson, Rob *96:* 153; *177:* 163; *178:* 204; *197:* 34; *205:* 108
Sheridan, Brian *196:* 193
Sherman, Theresa *27:* 167
Sherwan, Earl *3:* 196
Shields, Charles *10:* 150; *36:* 63
Shields, Leonard *13:* 83, 85, 87
Shiffman, Lena *139:* 167; *168:* 136

Shigley, Neil K. *66:* 219
Shillabeer, Mary *35:* 74
Shilston, Arthur *49:* 61; *62:* 58
Shimin, Symeon *1:* 93; *2:* 128, 129; *3:* 202; *7:* 85; *11:* 177; *12:* 139; *13:* 202, 203; *27:* 138; *28:* 65; *35:* 129; *36:* 130; *48:* 151; *49:* 59; *56:* 63, 65, 153
Shimizu, Yuko *215:* 197
Shine, Andrea *104:* 165; *128:* 34
Shinn, Everett *16:* 148; *18:* 229; *21:* 149, 150, 151; *24:* 218
Shinn, Florence Scovel *63:* 133, 135
Shore, Robert *27:* 54; *39:* 192, 193; *YABC 2:* 200
Shortall, Leonard *4:* 144; *8:* 196; *10:* 166; *19:* 227, 228, 229, 230; *25:* 78; *28:* 66, 167; *33:* 127; *52:* 125; *73:* 12, 212
Shortt, T.M. *27:* 36
Shpitalnik, Vladimir *83:* 194
Shropshire, Sandy *170:* 191
Shtainments, Leon *32:* 161
Shulevitz, Uri *3:* 198, 199; *17:* 85; *22:* 204; *27:* 212; *28:* 184; *50:* 190, 191, 192, 193, 194, 195, 196,197, 198, 199, 201; *106:* 181, 182, 183; *165:* 203, 205; *166:* 138
Shulman, Dee *180:* 140
Shupe, Bobbi *139:* 80, 81
Shute, A.B. *67:* 196
Shute, Linda *46:* 59; *74:* 118
Siberell, Anne *29:* 193
Sibley, Don *1:* 39; *12:* 196; *31:* 47
Sibthorp, Fletcher *94:* 111, 112
Sidjakov, Nicolas *18:* 274
Siebel, Fritz *3:* 120; *17:* 145
Siebold, J. Otto *158:* 227
Siegel, Hal *74:* 246
Sieger, Ted *189:* 172
Siegl, Helen *12:* 166; *23:* 216; *34:* 185, 186
Silin-Palmer, Pamela *184:* 102
Sill, John *140:* 194; *141:* 157
Sills, Joyce *5:* 199
Silva, Simon *108:* 122
Silver, Maggie *85:* 210
Silveria, Gordon *96:* 44
Silverstein, Alvin *8:* 189
Silverstein, Shel *33:* 211; *92:* 209, 210
Silverstein, Virginia *8:* 189
Silvey, Joe *135:* 203
Simard, Remy *95:* 156
Simmons, Elly *110:* 2; *127:* 69; *134:* 181
Simon, Eric M. *7:* 82
Simon, Hilda *28:* 189
Simon, Howard *2:* 175; *5:* 132; *19:* 199; *32:* 163, 164, 165
Simont, Marc *2:* 119; *4:* 213; *9:* 168; *13:* 238,240; *14:* 262; *16:* 179; *18:* 221; *26:* 210; *33:* 189, 194; *44:* 132; *58:* 122; *68:* 117; *73:* 204, 205, 206; *74:* 221; *126:* 199, 200; *133:* 195; *164:* 128
Sims, Agnes *54:* 152
Sims, Blanche *44:* 116; *57:* 129; *75:* 179, 180; *77:* 92; *104:* 192; *152:* 117; *156:* 160; *160:* 70; *168:* 174, 175; *198:* 17
Singer, Edith G. *2:* 30
Singer, Gloria *34:* 56; *36:* 43
Singer, Julia *28:* 190
Singh, Jen *178:* 146
Sinquette, Jaclyn *215:* 83
Siomades, Lorianne *134:* 45; *204:* 48
Simont, Marc *163:* 40
Siracusa, Catherine *68:* 135; *82:* 218
Sís, Peter *67:* 179, 181, 183, 184, 185; *96:* 96, 98; *106:* 193, 194, 195; *149:* 224, 226; *180:* 177; *192:* 180, 182
Sivard, Robert *26:* 124
Sivertson, Liz *116:* 84
Skardinski, Stanley *23:* 144; *32:* 84; *66:* 122; *84:* 108
Slack, Michael *185:* 108; *189:* 173, 174
Slackman, Charles B. *12:* 201
Slade, Christian *193:* 187; *204:* 134

Slade, Paul *61:* 170
Slark, Albert *99:* 212; *205:* 161
Slater, Rod *25:* 167
Slavin, Bill *182:* 14, 15; *196:* 90; *199:* 148, 149, 150
Sloan, Joseph *16:* 68
Sloane, Eric *21:* 3; *52:* 153, 154, 155, 156, 157, 158, 160
Sloat, Teri *164:* 231
Slobodkin, Louis *1:* 200; *3:* 232; *5:* 168; *13:* 251; *15:* 13, 88; *26:* 173, 174, 175, 176, 178, 179; *60:* 180
Slobodkina, Esphyr *1:* 201
Slonim, David *166:* 167, 168
Small, David *50:* 204, 205; *79:* 44; *95:* 189, 190, 191; *126:* 203, 204; *136:* 119; *143:* 201, 202, 203; *144:* 246; *150:* 5; *161:* 176; *183:* 181, 182, 183, 184; *200:* 211; *212:* 86
Small, W. *33:* 113
Smalley, Janet *1:* 154
Smath, Jerry *198:* 179, 180
Smedley, William T. *34:* 129
Smee, David *14:* 78; *62:* 30
Smee, Nicola *167:* 156
Smith, A.G., Jr. *35:* 182
Smith, Ali *204:* 68
Smith, Alvin *1:* 31, 229; *13:* 187; *27:* 216; *28:* 226; *48:* 149; *49:* 60
Smith, Andy *188:* 20; *207:* 151
Smith, Anne *194:* 147
Smith, Anne Warren *41:* 212
Smith, Barry *75:* 183
Smith, Brian *200:* 183
Smith, Carl *36:* 41
Smith, Cat Bowman *146:* 39; *164:* 219; *201:* 55, 184
Smith, Craig *97:* 197; *172:* 175; *206:* 40; *215:* 19
Smith, Donald A. *178:* 7
Smith, Doris Susan *41:* 139
Smith, Douglas *189:* 159; *213:* 170
Smith, Duane *171:* 152; *208:* 97
Smith, E. Boyd *19:* 70; *22:* 89; *26:* 63; *YABC 1:* 4, 5, 240, 248, 249
Smith, Edward J. *4:* 224
Smith, Elwood H. *157:* 231; *181:* 79; *203:* 160, 161, 162
Smith, Eunice Young *5:* 170
Smith, Gary *113:* 216
Smith, George *102:* 169
Smith, Howard *19:* 196
Smith, J. Gerard *95:* 42
Smith, Jacqueline Bardner *27:* 108; *39:* 197
Smith, Jay J. *61:* 119
Smith, Jeff *93:* 191
Smith, Jessie Willcox *15:* 91; *16:* 95; *18:* 231; *19:* 57, 242; *21:* 29, 156, 157, 158, 159, 160, 161; *34:* 65; *100:* 223; *YABC 1:* 6; *2:* 180, 185, 191, 311, 325
Smith, Jos. A. *52:* 131; *72:* 120; *74:* 151; *84:* 147, 148; *85:* 146; *87:* 96; *94:* 219; *96:* 97; *104:* 33; *108:* 126, 127, 128; *111:* 140; *136:* 145; *181:* 173; *200:* 213; *201:* 94
Smith, Kenneth R. *47:* 182
Smith, Kevin Warren *89:* 112
Smith, Kristin *209:* 197
Smith, L.H. *35:* 174
Smith, Lane *76:* 211, 213; *88:* 115; *105:* 202, 203,204, 205; *131:* 207; *160:* 217, 221; *179:* 183, 184, 185, 186; *199:* 122, 123, 124, 126
Smith, Lee *29:* 32
Smith, Linell Nash *2:* 195
Smith, Maggie Kaufman *13:* 205; *35:* 191; *110:* 158; *178:* 226; *190:* 204; *209:* 145
Smith, Mavis *101:* 219
Smith, Moishe *33:* 155
Smith, Philip *44:* 134; *46:* 203
Smith, Ralph Crosby *2:* 267; *49:* 203
Smith, Robert D. *5:* 63
Smith, Sally J. *84:* 55
Smith, Susan Carlton *12:* 208

Smith, Terry *12:* 106; *33:* 158
Smith, Virginia *3:* 157; *33:* 72
Smith, William A. *1:* 36; *10:* 154; *25:* 65
Smith-Moore, J.J. *98:* 147
Smolinski, Dick *84:* 217
Smoljan, Joe *112:* 201
Smollin, Mike *39:* 203
Smyth, Iain *105:* 207
Smyth, M. Jane *12:* 15
Smythe, Fiona *151:* 213
Smythe, Theresa *141:* 37
Snair, Andy *176:* 4
Sneed, Brad *125:* 25; *191:* 175, 176; *211:* 194
Snyder, Andrew A. *30:* 212
Snyder, Jerome *13:* 207; *30:* 173
Snyder, Joel *28:* 163
So, Meilo *162:* 201; *208:* 188
Soentpiet, Chris K. *97:* 208; *110:* 33; *159:* 184; *161:* 10; *163:* 130
Sofia *1:* 62; *5:* 90; *32:* 166; *86:* 43
Sofilas, Mark *93:* 157
Sogabe, Aki *207:* 153
Sohn, Jiho *182:* 78
Sokol, Bill *37:* 178; *49:* 23
Sokolov, Kirill *34:* 188
Solbert, Ronni *1:* 159; *2:* 232; *5:* 121; *6:* 34; *17:* 249
Solomon, Michael *174:* 115
Solonevich, George *15:* 246; *17:* 47
Soma, Liana *81:* 118
Soman, David *90:* 122; *102:* 126; *140:* 120; 93; *188:* 43, 89; *200:* 180, 181
Sommer, Robert *12:* 211
Song, Jae *203:* 27
Soo, Kean *201:* 185
Sorel, Edward *4:* 61; *36:* 82; *65:* 191, 193; *126:* 214
Sorensen, Henri *196:* 58
Sorensen, Henrik *62:* 16
Sorensen, Svend Otto *22:* 130, 141; *67:* 188, 189
Sorra, Kristin *155:* 80
Sosa, Hernan *198:* 66
Sostre, Maria *187:* 36
Sotomayor, Antonio *11:* 215
Souhami, Jessica *112:* 128; *176:* 193
Sousa, Natalie C. *209:* 89
Souza, Diana *71:* 139
Sovak, Jan *115:* 190
Sowards, Ben *215:* 62
Soyer, Moses *20:* 177
Spaenkuch, August *16:* 28
Spafford, Suzy *160:* 228
Spain, Valerie *105:* 76
Spain, Sunday Sahara *133:* 204
Spalenka, Greg *149:* 69; *151:* 228; *184:* 195; *191:* 21; *196:* 12; *198:* 181, 182, 201; *208:* 92
Spanfeller, James *1:* 72, 149; *2:* 183; *19:* 230, 231,232; *22:* 66; *36:* 160, 161; *40:* 75; *52:* 166; *76:* 37
Spangler, Brie *212:* 188
Sparks, Mary Walker *15:* 247
Spears, Rick *182:* 187
Speidel, Sandra *78:* 233; *94:* 178; *134:* 180; *210:* 67
Speirs, John *67:* 178
Spence, Geraldine *21:* 163; *47:* 196
Spence, Jim *38:* 89; *50:* 102
Spencer, Laurie *113:* 12
Spencer, Mark *57:* 170
Spengler, Kenneth J. *146:* 256
Sperling, Andrea *133:* 182
Spiegel, Beth *184:* 203
Spiegel, Doris *29:* 111
Spiegelman, Art *109:* 227
Spier, Jo *10:* 30
Spier, Peter *3:* 155; *4:* 200; *7:* 61; *11:* 78; *38:* 106; *54:* 120, 121, 122, 123, 124, 125, 126, 127, 128, 129, 130,131, 132, 133, 134
Spilka, Arnold *5:* 120; *6:* 204; *8:* 131

Spirin, Gennady *95:* 196, 197; *113:* 172; *128:* 9; *129:* 49; *134:* 210; *153:* 9; *204:* 143, 144, 145
Spiro, Ruth *208:* 197
Spivak, I. Howard *8:* 10; *13:* 172
Spohn, David *72:* 233
Spohn, Kate *87:* 195; *147:* 201, 202
Spollen, Christopher J. *12:* 214
Spooner, Malcolm *40:* 142
Spowart, Robin *82:* 228; *92:* 149; *133:* 131; *176:* 163; *177:* 183, 184
Sprague, Kevin *150:* 60; *196:* 62
Spranger, Nina *201:* 199
Sprattler, Rob *12:* 176
Spring, Bob *5:* 60
Spring, Ira *5:* 60
Springer, Harriet *31:* 92
Spudvilas, Anne *110:* 74; *197:* 192; *199:* 154
Spurll, Barbara *78:* 199; *88:* 141, 142; *99:* 215
Spurrier, Steven *28:* 198
Spuvilas, Anne *85:* 114
Spy
    See Ward, Leslie
Squires, Stuart *127:* 74
St. Aubin, Bruno *179:* 54
St. John, J. Allen *41:* 62
Staake, Bob *209:* 168, 169
Stabin, Victor *101:* 131; *164:* 158
Stadler, John *62:* 33; *204:* 149
Stadnyk, Greg *212:* 55
Staffan, Alvin E. *11:* 56; *12:* 187
Stahl, Ben *5:* 181; *12:* 91; *49:* 122; *71:* 128; *87:* 206; *112:* 107
Stair, Gobin *35:* 214
Stallwood, Karen *73:* 126
Stamaty, Mark Alan *12:* 215
Stammen, JoEllen McAllister *113:* 14
Stampnick, Ken *51:* 142
Stanbridge, Joanne *150:* 91
Stanley, Diane *3:* 45; *37:* 180; *80:* 217, 219
Stanley, Sanna *145:* 228
Starcke, Helmut *86:* 217
Stark, Ken *197:* 102
Starr, Branka *73:* 25
Stasiak, Krystyna *49:* 181; *64:* 194
Staub, Leslie *103:* 54
Staunton, Ted *112:* 192
Stawicki, Matt *164:* 250
Stead, L. *55:* 51, 56
Steadman, Broeck *97:* 185, 186; *99:* 56; *121:* 48; *208:* 190
Steadman, Henry *211:* 130
Steadman, Ralph *32:* 180; *123:* 143, 145
Stearn, Nick *183:* 26
Steckler, June *90:* 178
Steele, Robert Gantt *169:* 174
Steichen, Edward *30:* 79
Steig, William *18:* 275, 276; *70:* 215, 216, 217, 218; *111:* 173, 174, 175, 176, 177
Stein, David Ezra *211:* 168
Stein, Harve *1:* 109
Steinberg, Saul *47:* 193
Steinel, William *23:* 146
Steiner, Charlotte *45:* 196
Steiner, Joan *110:* 219; *199:* 160, 161
Steirnagel, Michael *80:* 56
Stemp, Eric *60:* 184
Stephens, Alice Barber *66:* 208, 209
Stephens, Charles H. *YABC 2:* 279
Stephens, Pam *198:* 69
Stephens, Pat *126:* 110; *128:* 101
Stephens, William M. *21:* 165
Steptoe, Javaka *151:* 203, 204; *190:* 169; *213:* 163, 164
Steptoe, John *8:* 197; *57:* 9; *63:* 158, 159, 160, 161,163, 164, 165, 166, 167; *96:* 4; *105:* 87
Stern, Simon *15:* 249, 250; *17:* 58; *34:* 192, 193
Sterret, Jane *53:* 27
Stetsios, Debbie *165:* 108, 109
Steven, Kat *158:* 237

Stevens, David *62:* 44
Stevens, Helen *189:* 31; *207:* 83
Stevens, Janet *40:* 126; *57:* 10, 11; *80:* 112; *90:* 221, 222; *109:* 156; *130:* 34; *166:* 202; *176:* 53, 116; *193:* 199, 200, 202; *208:* 127; *212:* 182
Stevens, Mary *11:* 193; *13:* 129; *43:* 95
Stevenson, Harvey *66:* 143; *80:* 201, 221; *153:* 60; *191:* 166
Stevenson, James *42:* 182, 183; *51:* 163; *66:* 184; *71:* 185, 187, 188; *78:* 262; *87:* 97; *113:* 182, 183,184, 185; *161:* 182, 183
Stevenson, Sucie *92:* 27; *104:* 194, 195; *112:* 168; *160:* 202; *194:* 172, 173; *195:* 166
Stewart, April Blair *75:* 210
Stewart, Arvis *33:* 98; *36:* 69; *60:* 118; *75:* 91; *127:* 4
Stewart, Charles *2:* 205
Stewart, Joel *151:* 205; *211:* 170, 171
Stieg, William *172:* 58
Stiles, Fran *26:* 85; *78:* 56; *82:* 150
Stillman, Susan *44:* 130; *76:* 83
Stimpson, Tom *49:* 171
Stimson, James *208:* 46
Stinemetz, Morgan *40:* 151
Stinson, Paul *110:* 86
Stirnweis, Shannon *10:* 164
Stites, Joe *86:* 96
Stobbs, William *1:* 48, 49; *3:* 68; *6:* 20; *17:* 117, 217; *24:* 150; *29:* 250; *60:* 179; *87:* 204, 205,206
Stock, Catherine *37:* 55; *65:* 198; *72:* 7; *99:* 225; *114:* 197, 198, 199; *126:* 3; *145:* 161; *161:* 82; *173:* 149; *208:* 210; *214:* 192,194
Stockman, Jack *113:* 24
Stoeke, Janet Morgan *90:* 225; *136:* 196; *202:* 182, 183
Stoerrle, Tom *55:* 147
Stolp, Jaap *49:* 98
Stolp, Todd *89:* 195
Stone, David L. *87:* 154
Stone, David *9:* 173
Stone, David K. *4:* 38; *6:* 124; *9:* 180; *43:* 182; *60:* 70
Stone, Helen V. *6:* 209
Stone, Helen *44:* 121, 122, 126
Stone, Kazuko G. *134:* 43
Stone, Kyle M. *202:* 185
Stone, Phoebe *86:* 212; *134:* 213; *162:* 188; *205:* 145
Stone, Steve *166:* 213; *208:* 185
Stone, Tony *150:* 34, 35
Storrings, Michael *191:* 108
Stoud, Virginia A. *89:* 31
Stover, Jill *82:* 234
Strachan, Bruce *205:* 146
Stratton, Helen *33:* 151
Stratton-Porter, Gene *15:* 254, 259, 263, 264, 268, 269
Straub, Matt *192:* 176
Straub, Phillip *197:* 22
Streano, Vince *20:* 173
Street, Janet Travell *84:* 235
Streeter, Clive *121:* 2
Strickland, Shadra *209:* 179
Stringer, Lauren *129:* 187; *154:* 172, 173; *161:* 127; *183:* 187, 188
Strodl, Daniel *47:* 95
Strogart, Alexander *63:* 139
Stromoski, Rick *111:* 179; *124:* 161, 190
Strong, Joseph D., Jr. *YABC 2:* 330
Stroyer, Poul *13:* 221
Strugnell, Ann *27:* 38
Struzan, Drew *117:* 6
Stubbs, William *73:* 196
Stubis, Talivaldis *5:* 182, 183; *10:* 45; *11:* 9; *18:* 304; *20:* 127
Stubley, Trevor *14:* 43; *22:* 219; *23:* 37; *28:* 61; *87:* 26
Stuck, Marion *104:* 44
Stuecklen, Karl W. *8:* 34, 65; *23:* 103

Stull, Betty *11:* 46
Stutzman, Mark *119:* 99
Stutzmann, Laura *73:* 185
Suarez, Maribel *162:* 208; *200:* 202
Suave, Gordon *209:* 66
Suba, Susanne *4:* 202, 203; *14:* 261; *23:* 134; *29:* 222; *32:* 30
Sue, Majella Lue *209:* 182; *212:* 146
Sueling, Barbara *98:* 185
Sueling, Gwenn *98:* 186
Sugarman, Tracy *3:* 76; *8:* 199; *37:* 181, 182
Sugimoto, Yugo *170:* 144
Sugita, Yutaka *36:* 180, 181
Suh, John *80:* 157
Sullivan, Dorothy *89:* 113
Sullivan, Edmund J. *31:* 86
Sullivan, James F. *19:* 280; *20:* 192
Sully, Tom *104:* 199, 200; *182:* 77
Sumichrast, Jozef *14:* 253; *29:* 168, 213
Sumiko *46:* 57
Summers, Leo *1:* 177; *2:* 273; *13:* 22
Summers, Mark *118:* 144
Summers, Mike *190:* 176
Sutton, Judith *94:* 164
Svarez, Juan *56:* 113
Svendsen, Mark *181:* 176
Svolinsky, Karel *17:* 104
Swain, Carol *172:* 182
Swain, Su Zan Noguchi *21:* 170
Swan, Susan *22:* 220, 221; *37:* 66; *60:* 146; *145:* 205; *181:* 168
Swann, Susan *86:* 55
Swanson, Karl *79:* 65; *89:* 186
Swarner, Kristina *203:* 62; *215:* 184
Swayne, Sam *53:* 143, 145
Swayne, Zoa *53:* 143, 145
Swearingen, Greg *152:* 56; *165:* 135; *173:* 2
Sweat, Lynn *25:* 206; *57:* 176; *73:* 184; *168:* 178
Sweet, Darrell K. *60:* 9; *69:* 86; *74:* 15; *75:* 215; *76:* 130, 131; *81:* 96, 122; *82:* 253; *83:* 11; *84:* 14; *85:* 37; *89:* 140; *90:* 6; *91:* 137,139; *95:* 160, 161; *126:* 25; *185:* 175; *195:* 132
Sweet, Darrell K. *1:* 163; *4:* 136; *164:* 175
Sweet, Melissa *71:* 94; *72:* 172; *111:* 82; *139:* 53, 58; *141:* 88; *142:* 231; *155:* 121; *159:* 121, 122; *172:* 185; *188:* 127; *209:* 81; *211:* 174, 175
Sweet, Ozzie *31:* 149, 151, 152
Sweetland, Robert *12:* 194
Swiatkowska, Gabi *132:* 43; *175:* 139; *180:* 218; *183:* 176
Swope, Martha *43:* 160; *56:* 86, 87, 89
Sylvada, Peter *154:* 174
Sylvester, Natalie G. *22:* 222
Szafran, Gene *24:* 144
Szasz, Susanne *13:* 55, 226; *14:* 48
Szekeres, Cyndy *2:* 218; *5:* 185; *8:* 85; *11:* 166; *14:* 19; *16:* 57, 159; *26:* 49, 214; *34:* 205; *60:* 150, 151, 152, 153, 154; *73:* 224; *74:* 218; *131:* 213, 215
Szpura, Beata *81:* 68; *119:* 65; *168:* 201

T

Taback, Simms *40:* 207; *52:* 120; *57:* 34; *80:* 241; *104:* 202, 203; *170:* 176, 177; *205:* 183
Taber, Patricia *75:* 124
Tabor, Nancy Maria Grande *89:* 210; *161:* 188
Taddei, Richard *112:* 13, 14
Tadgell, Nicole *150:* 77; *161:* 20; *177:* 186; *209:* 16
Tadiello, Ed *133:* 200
Tafuri, Nancy *39:* 210; *75:* 199, 200; *92:* 75; *130:* 215, 216, 217
Tailfeathers, Gerald *86:* 85
Tait, Douglas *12:* 220; *74:* 105, 106
Takabayashi, Mari *113:* 112; *130:* 22; *156:* 169

Takahashi, Hideko *136:* 160; *187:* 6; *209:* 152, 187
Takakjian, Portia *15:* 274
Takashima, Shizuye *13:* 228
Talarczyk, June *4:* 173
Talbott, Hudson *84:* 240; *163:* 100; *212:* 191, 192, 193
Tallarico, Tony *116:* 197
Tallon, Robert *2:* 228; *43:* 200, 201, 202, 203, 204, 205,206, 207, 209
Tamaki, Jillian *201:* 188
Tamas, Szecsko *29:* 135
Tamburine, Jean *12:* 222
Tanaka, Yoko *215:* 187
Tancredi, Sharon *215:* 127
Tandy, H.R. *13:* 69
Tandy, Russell H. *65:* 9; *100:* 30, 131
Tang, Charles *81:* 202; *90:* 192
Tang, Susan *80:* 174; *108:* 158
Tang, You-shan *63:* 100
Tankersley, Paul *69:* 206; *133:* 219
Tannenbaum, Robert *48:* 181
Tanner, Jane *87:* 13; *97:* 37
Tanner, Tim *72:* 192; *84:* 35
Tanobe, Miyuki *23:* 221
Tarabay, Sharif *110:* 149; *113:* 123; *169:* 83
Tarkington, Booth *17:* 224, 225
Tarlow, Phyllis *61:* 198
Tate, Don *159:* 141, 191; *183:* 69; *186:* 120
Tauss, Herbert *95:* 179
Tauss, Marc *117:* 160; *126:* 155; *178:* 221; *197:* 7
Tavares, Matt *159:* 192, 193; *198:* 188, 189, 190; *199:* 86
Taylor, Ann *41:* 226
Taylor, Dahl *129:* 157
Taylor, Geoff *93:* 156; *197:* 173, 175; *204:* 151, 152
Taylor, Isaac *41:* 228
Taylor, Mike *143:* 99, 100
Teague, Mark *83:* 6; *139:* 241; *170:* 180, 181; *205:* 150, 151
Teale, Edwin Way *7:* 196
Teason, James *1:* 14
Teckentrup, Britta *200:* 191, 192
Teeple, Lyn *33:* 147
Tee-Van, Helen Damrosch *10:* 176; *11:* 182
Teicher, Dick *50:* 211
Teichman, Mary *77:* 220; *124:* 208; *127:* 22; *197:* 33
Temertey, Ludmilla *96:* 232; *104:* 43, 45; *109:* 244
Tempest, Margaret *3:* 237, 238; *88:* 200
Temple, Frances *85:* 185, 186, 187
Temple, Herbert *45:* 187
Templeton, Owen *11:* 77
ten Cate, Marijke *183:* 193
Tenggren, Gustaf *18:* 277, 278, 279; *19:* 15; *28:* 86; *YABC2:* 145
Tennent, Julie *81:* 105
Tenneson, Joyce *153:* 166
Tenney, Gordon *24:* 204
Tenniel, John *74:* 234, 235; *100:* 89; *YABC 2:* 99; *153:* 63
Tepper, Matt *116:* 80
Terkel, Ari *103:* 162
Terry, Michael *180:* 209
Terry, Will *131:* 73; *205:* 155
Teskey, Donald *71:* 51
Tessler, Manya *200:* 193
Thacher, Mary M. *30:* 72
Thackeray, William Makepeace *23:* 224, 228
Thamer, Katie *42:* 187
Tharlet, Eve *146:* 149
Thelwell, Norman *14:* 201
Theobalds, Prue *40:* 23
Theurer, Marilyn Churchill *39:* 195
Thiesing, Lisa *89:* 134; *95:* 202; *156:* 190; *159:* 195
Thiewes, Sam *133:* 114
Thistlethwaite, Miles *12:* 224

Thollander, Earl *11:* 47; *18:* 112; *22:* 224
Thomas, Allan *22:* 13
Thomas, Art *48:* 217
Thomas, Eric *28:* 49
Thomas, Harold *20:* 98
Thomas, Jacqui *125:* 95
Thomas, Jan *197:* 180
Thomas, Mark *42:* 136
Thomas, Martin *14:* 255
Thomas, Middy *177:* 114
Thompson, Arthur *34:* 107
Thompson, Carol *85:* 189; *95:* 75; *102:* 86; *147:* 166; *189:* 179, 180, 181; *190:* 84; *207:* 18
Thompson, Colin *95:* 204
Thompson, Ellen *51:* 88, 151; *60:* 33; *67:* 42; *77:* 148; *78:* 75, 219; *79:* 122, 170; *84:* 219; *85:* 97; *87:* 37; *88:* 192, 194; *89:* 80; *93:* 37; *98:* 59; *132:* 14
Thompson, George W. *22:* 18; *28:* 150; *33:* 135
Thompson, John *58:* 201; *102:* 226; *124:* 154; *128:* 228; *129:* 157; *150:* 49; *185:* 160; *191:* 192
Thompson, Julie *44:* 158
Thompson, Katherine *132:* 146
Thompson, K. Dyble *84:* 6
Thompson, Miles *152:* 77
Thompson, Sharon *74:* 113; *158:* 60; *165:* 87
Thomson, Arline K. *3:* 264
Thomson, Bill *186:* 160
Thomson, Hugh *26:* 88
Thomson, Ross *36:* 179
Thorkelson, Gregg *95:* 183, 184; *98:* 58; *165:* 30, 31
Thorn, Lori *189:* 119
Thornberg, Dan *104:* 125
Thornburgh, Rebecca McKillip *143:* 37
Thorne, Diana *25:* 212
Thornhill, Jan *77:* 213
Thorpe, Peter *58:* 109
Thorvall, Kerstin *13:* 235
Threadgall, Colin *77:* 215
Thurber, James *13:* 239, 242, 243, 245, 248, 249
Thurman, Mark *63:* 173; *168:* 116
Tibbles, Jean-Paul *115:* 200
Tibbles, Paul *45:* 23
Tibo, Gilles *67:* 207; *107:* 199, 201
Tichenor, Tom *14:* 207
Tichnor, Richard *90:* 218
Tiegreen, Alan *36:* 143; *43:* 55, 56, 58; *77:* 200; *94:* 216, 217; *121:* 54, 59
Tierney, Tom *113:* 198, 200, 201
Tildes, Phyllis Limbacher *210:* 240
Tilley, Debbie *102:* 134; *133:* 226; *137:* 101; *159:* 96; *190:* 211, 212; *213:* 51
Tillman, Nancy *211:* 129, 178
Tilney, F.C. *22:* 231
Timbs, Gloria *36:* 90
Timmins, Harry *2:* 171
Timmons, Bonnie *194:* 189
Tinkelman, Murray *12:* 225; *35:* 44
Titherington, Jeanne *39:* 90; *58:* 138; *75:* 79; *135:* 161
Tjader, Ella *209:* 14
Tobin, Nancy *145:* 197
Toddy, Irving *172:* 144
Tokunbo, Dimitrea *181:* 183; *187:* 182, 183
Tolbert, Jeff *128:* 69
Toledo, Francisco *197:* 182; *198:* 199
Toledo, Natalia *197:* 182
Tolford, Joshua *1:* 221
Tolkien, J.R.R. *2:* 243; *32:* 215
Tolman, Marije *195:* 43
Tolmie, Ken *15:* 292
Tomei, Lorna *47:* 168, 171
Tomes, Jacqueline *2:* 117; *12:* 139

Tomes, Margot *1:* 224; *2:* 120, 121; *16:* 207; *18:* 250; *20:* 7; *25:* 62; *27:* 78, 79; *29:* 81, 199; *33:* 82; *36:* 186, 187, 188, 189, 190; *46:* 129; *56:* 71; *58:* 183; *70:* 228; *75:* 73, 75; *80:* 80; *83:* 97; *90:* 205
Tommaso, Rich *200:* 198
Toner, Raymond John *10:* 179
Tong, Gary *66:* 215
Tongier, Stephen *82:* 32
Tooke, Susan *173:* 162
Toothill, Harry *6:* 54; *7:* 49; *25:* 219; *42:* 192
Toothill, Ilse *6:* 54
Topolski, Feliks *44:* 48
Torbert, Floyd James *22:* 226
Torgersen, Don *55:* 157
Torline, Kevin *169:* 171
Tormey, Bertram M. *75:* 3, 4
Torrecilla, Pablo *176:* 207
Torres, Leyla *156:* 199, 201
Torrey, Helen *87:* 41
Torrey, Marjorie *34:* 105
Torrey, Richard *189:* 182; *205:* 24
Toschik, Larry *6:* 102
Totten, Bob *13:* 93
Toy, Julie *128:* 112
Trachok, Cathy *131:* 16
Tracy, Libba *82:* 24
Trago, Keith *158:* 253
Trail, Lee *55:* 157
Trang, To Ngoc *167:* 180
Trang, Winson *89:* 151
Trapani, Iza *116:* 202; *214:* 203
Travers, Bob *49:* 100; *63:* 145
Treatner, Meryl *95:* 180
Tremain, Ruthven *17:* 238
Tresilian, Stuart *25:* 53; *40:* 212
Trez, Alain *17:* 236
Trezzo, Loretta *86:* 45
Trier, Walter *14:* 96
Trimby, Elisa *47:* 199
Trinkle, Sally *53:* 27
Triplett, Gina *182:* 193; *188:* 100; *198:* 38
Tripp, F.J. *24:* 167
Tripp, Wallace *2:* 48; *7:* 28; *8:* 94; *10:* 54,76; *11:* 92; *31:* 170, 171; *34:* 203; *42:* 57; *60:* 157; *73:* 182
Trivas, Irene *53:* 4; *54:* 168; *82:* 46, 101
Trnka, Jiri *22:* 151; *43:* 212, 213, 214, 215; *YABC 1:* 30, 31
Trondheim, Lewis *182:* 183
Troughton, Joanna *37:* 186; *48:* 72
Troyer, Johannes *3:* 16; *7:* 18
Trudeau, G.B. *35:* 220, 221, 222; *48:* 119, 123, 126, 127,128, 129, 133; *168:* 189
Trueman, Matthew *165:* 208; *183:* 191
Truesdell, Sue *55:* 142; *108:* 219, 220; *212:* 202
Tryon, Leslie *84:* 7; *139:* 214; *143:* 10; *181:* 10
Tseng, Jean *72:* 195; *94:* 102; *119:* 126; *151:* 106; *173:* 138, 139; *200:* 158
Tseng, Mou-sien *72:* 195; *94:* 102; *119:* 126; *151:* 106; *173:* 138, 139; *200:* 158
Tsinajinie, Andy *2:* 62
Tsinganos, Jim *180:* 142
Tsugami, Kyuzo *18:* 198, 199
Tucker, Ezra *156:* 31
Tuckwell, Jennifer *17:* 205
Tudor, Bethany *7:* 103
Tudor, Tasha *18:* 227; *20:* 185, 186, 187; *36:* 111; *69:* 196, 198; *100:* 44; *YABC 2:* 46, 314; *160:* 234
Tuerk, Hanne *71:* 201
Tugeau, Jeremy *199:* 170; *203:* 96
Tulloch, Maurice *24:* 79
Tunis, Edwin *1:* 218, 219; *28:* 209, 210, 211, 212
Tunnicliffe, C.F. *62:* 176, 177, 178, 179; 181
Turkle, Brinton *1:* 211, 213; *2:* 249; *3:* 226; *11:* 3; *16:* 209; *20:* 22; *50:* 23; *67:* 50; *68:* 65; *79:* 205, 206, 207; *128:* 47; *YABC 1:* 79

Turnbull, Christopher J. *143:* 99, 100
Turner, Gwenda *59:* 195
Turner, Helen *203:* 154
Turska, Krystyna *12:* 103; *31:* 173, 174, 175; *56:* 32,34; *100:* 66
Tusa, Tricia *72:* 242; *111:* 180, 181; *157:* 165; *164:* 186; *189:* 40; *201:* 9; *207:* 163, 164
Tusan, Stan *6:* 58; *22:* 236, 237
Tworkov, Jack *47:* 207
Tyers, Jenny *89:* 220
Tylden-Wright, Jenny *114:* 119
Tyrol, Adelaide Murphy *103:* 27
Tyrrell, Frances *107:* 204
Tzimoulis, Paul *12:* 104

U

Uchida, Yoshiko *1:* 220
Uderzo *47:* 88
Udovic, David *189:* 185; *195:* 201
Ueno, Noriko *59:* 155
Ugliano, Natascia *196:* 186
Ulm, Robert *17:* 238
Ulrich, George *73:* 15; *75:* 136, 139; *99:* 150
Ulriksen, Mark *101:* 58; *182:* 43; *210:* 243
Unada *84:* 67
    See Gliewe, Unada
Underhill, Liz *53:* 159
Underwood, Beck *192:* 36
Underwood, Clarence *40:* 166
Unger, Jim *67:* 208
Ungerer, Tomi *5:* 188; *9:* 40; *18:* 188; *29:* 175; *33:* 221, 222, 223, 225; *71:* 48; *106:* 209, 210, 211, 212
Unwin, Nora S. *3:* 65, 234, 235; *4:* 237; *44:* 173, 174; *YABC 1:* 59; *2:* 301
Upitis, Alvis *145:* 179
Urban, Helle *149:* 243
Urbanovic, Jackie *86:* 86; *189:* 186, 187
U'ren, Andrea *213:* 177
Uris, Jill *49:* 188, 197
Ursell, Martin *50:* 51
Utpatel, Frank *18:* 114
Utz, Lois *5:* 190

V

Vagin, Vladimir *66:* 10; *142:* 215
Vaillancourt, Francois *107:* 199
Vainio, Pirkko *123:* 157, 158
Valério, Geraldo *180:* 225; *194:* 116
Vallejo, Boris *62:* 130; *72:* 212; *91:* 38; *93:* 61
Van Abbe, S. *16:* 142; *18:* 282; *31:* 90; *YABC 2:* 157, 161
Van Allsburg, Chris *37:* 205, 206; *53:* 161, 162, 163, 165,166, 167, 168, 169, 170, 171; *105:* 215, 216, 217, 218; *156:* 176, 177, 178
Vance, James *65:* 28
Van Der Linde, Henry *99:* 17
van der Meer, Ron *98:* 204, 205
van der Meer, Atie *98:* 204, 205
Vandivert, William *21:* 175
Van Dongen, H.R. *81:* 97
Van Dusen, Chris W. *173:* 169
Vane, Mitch *210:* 160
Van Everen, Jay *13:* 160; *YABC 1:* 121
Van Fleet, John *165:* 12, 13
Van Frankenhuyzen, Gijsbert *145:* 230; *149:* 164; *184:* 151; *210:* 248
van Genechten, Guido *165:* 226
van Haeringen, Annemarie *193:* 206
Van Horn, William *43:* 218
van Hout, Mies *195:* 191; *207:* 58
van Kampen, Vlasta *194:* 217
van Lawick, Hugo *62:* 76, 79
Van Lieshout, Maria *201:* 196

Van Loon, Hendrik Willem *18:* 285, 289, 291
Van Munching, Paul *83:* 85
van Ommen, Sylvia *186:* 192
Van Patter, Bruce *183:* 195
Van Rynbach, Iris *102:* 192
Van Sciver, Ruth *37:* 162
VanSeveren, Joe *63:* 182
Van Stockum, Hilda *5:* 193
Van Vleet, John *213:* 180
Van Wassenhove, Sue *202:* 193
Van Wely, Babs *16:* 50; *79:* 16
Van Wright, Cornelius *72:* 18; *102:* 208; *116:* 107; *152:* 236; *173:* 170, 171; *199:* 185
Van Zyle, Jon *103:* 125; *160:* 181, 182; *176:* 199, 200
Vardzigulyants, Ruben *90:* 54
Varga, Judy *29:* 196
Vargo, Kurt *79:* 224
Varley, Susan *61:* 199; *63:* 176, 177; *101:* 148; *134:* 220
Varon, Sara *195:* 208
Vasconcellos, Daniel *80:* 42
Vasiliu, Mircea *2:* 166, 253; *9:* 166; *13:* 58; *68:* 42
Vaughn, Frank *34:* 157
Vavra, Robert *8:* 206
Vawter, Will *17:* 163
Vayas, Diana *71:* 61
Vazquez, Carlos *125:* 184
Veeder, Larry *18:* 4
Velasquez, Eric *45:* 217; *61:* 45; *63:* 110, 111; *88:* 162; *90:* 34, 144; *94:* 213; *107:* 147; *132:* 192; *138:* 213; *159:* 126; *181:* 184; *184:* 96; *191:* 16; *192:* 234; *208:* 37; *214:* 81
Velasquez, Jose A. *63:* 73
Velez, Walter *71:* 75; *91:* 154; *121:* 181; *168:* 49; *207:* 52
Velthuijs, Max *110:* 228, 229
Vendrell, Carme Sole *42:* 205
Venezia, Mike *54:* 17
Venti, Anthony Bacon *124:* 103; *126:* 26
Venturo, Piero *61:* 194, 195
Ver Beck, Frank *18:* 16, 17
Verkaaik, Ben *110:* 209
Verling, John *71:* 27
Verney, John *14:* 225; *75:* 8
Vernon, Ursula *204:* 157
Verrier, Suzanne *5:* 20; *23:* 212
Versace, Marie *2:* 255
Verstraete, Randy *108:* 193
Vess, Charles *215:* 201
Vestal, H.B. *9:* 134; *11:* 101; *27:* 25; *34:* 158
Vestergaard, Hope *190:* 203
Vicatan *59:* 146
Vickrey, Robert *45:* 59, 64
Victor, Joan Berg *30:* 193
Vieceli, Emma *210:* 245
Viereck, Ellen *3:* 242; *14:* 229
Vigna, Judith *15:* 293; *102:* 194, 195, 196, 197
Vila, Laura *207:* 172
Vilato, Gaspar E. *5:* 41
Villiard, Paul *51:* 178
Vimnera, A. *23:* 154
Vincent, Eric *34:* 98
Vincent, Felix *41:* 237
Vincent, Gabrielle *121:* 175
Vip *45:* 164
Viskupic, Gary *83:* 48
Vitale, Stefano *109:* 71; *107:* 114:* 219, 220; *123:* 106; *138:* 232; *180:* 228, 229; *212:* 38
Vivas, Julie *51:* 67, 69; *96:* 225; *197:* 190; *199:* 71
Voake, Charlotte *114:* 221, 222; *180:* 232
Vo-Dinh, Mai *16:* 272; *60:* 191
Vogel, Ilse-Margret *14:* 230
Voigt, Erna *35:* 228
Vojnar, Kamil *95:* 31; *114:* 4; *115:* 62; *121:* 90; *124:* 72; *130:* 31; *141:* 81; *146:* 196; *150:* 123; *158:* 5, 6; *158:* 154; *171:* 119, 188; *179:* 15; *180:* 112; *203:* 74

Vojtech, Anna *42:* 190; *108:* 222, 223; *150:* 203; *174:* 173
von Buhler, Cynthia *149:* 237; *162:* 177; *177:* 205; *180:* 77; *185:* 214, 215, 216
von Roehl, Angela *126:* 191
von Schmidt, Eric *8:* 62; *50:* 209, 210
von Schmidt, Harold *30:* 80
Vosburgh, Leonard *1:* 161; *7:* 32; *15:* 295, 296; *23:* 110; *30:* 214; *43:* 181
Voss, Tom *127:* 104
Voter, Thomas W. *19:* 3, 9
Vroman, Tom *10:* 29
Vulliamy, Clara *72:* 65

W

Waber, Bernard *47:* 209, 210, 211, 212, 213, 214; *95:* 215, 216, 217; *156:* 203, 205, 206, 207
Wachenje, Benjamin *194:* 170
Wack, Jeff *95:* 140; *110:* 90
Wagner, John *8:* 200; *52:* 104
Wagner, Ken *2:* 59
Wagner, Michael *211:* 159
Waide, Jan *29:* 225; *36:* 139
Wainwright, Jerry *14:* 85
Waites, Joan C. *171:* 2
Wakeen, Sandra *47:* 97
Wakiyama, Hanako *171:* 96; *192:* 236; *200:* 16
Waldherr, Kris *81:* 186
Waldman, Bruce *15:* 297; *43:* 178
Waldman, Neil *35:* 141; *50:* 163; *51:* 180; *54:* 78; *77:* 112; *79:* 162; *82:* 174; *84:* 5, 56, 106; *94:* 232, 233, 234; *96:* 41; *111:* 139; *113:* 9; *118:* 30; *142:* 220, 223; *203:* 173, 174
Waldrep, Richard *111:* 147; *198:* 202
Walker, Brian *144:* 128
Walker, Charles *1:* 46; *4:* 59; *5:* 177; *11:* 115; *19:* 45; *34:* 74; *62:* 168; *72:* 218
Walker, Dugald Stewart *15:* 47; *32:* 202; *33:* 112
Walker, Gil *8:* 49; *23:* 132; *34:* 42
Walker, Jeff *55:* 154; *123:* 116
Walker, Jim *10:* 94
Walker, Mort *8:* 213
Walker, Norman *41:* 37; *45:* 58
Walker, Stephen *12:* 229; *21:* 174
Wallace, Beverly Dobrin *19:* 259
Wallace, Cly *87:* 93
Wallace, Ian *53:* 176, 177; *56:* 165, 166; *58:* 4; *98:* 4; *101:* 191; *112:* 124; *141:* 197, 198, 199, 200; *151:* 212
Wallace, John *105:* 228
Wallace, Nancy Elizabeth *141:* 204; *186:* 195, 197, 199
Wallenta, Adam *123:* 180
Waller, S.E. *24:* 36
Wallner, Alexandra *15:* 120; *156:* 183
Wallner, John C. *9:* 77; *10:* 188; *11:* 28; *14:* 209; *31:* 56, 118; *37:* 64; *51:* 186, 187, 188, 189, 190, 191,192, 193, 194, 195; *52:* 96; *53:* 23, 26; *71:* 99; *73:* 158; *89:* 215; *141:* 9
Wallner, John *162:* 17
Wallower, Lucille *11:* 226
Walotsky, Ron *93:* 87
Walsh, Ellen Stoll *99:* 209; *147:* 219; *194:* 194, 195, 196
Walsh, Rebecca *158:* 193
Walsh, Vivian *149:* 215; *158:* 227
Walters, Anita *205:* 163
Walters, Audrey *18:* 294
Walther, Tom *31:* 179
Walton, Garry *69:* 149
Walton, Tony *11:* 164; *24:* 209; *153:* 8; *177:* 73
Waltrip, Lela *9:* 195
Waltrip, Mildred *3:* 209; *37:* 211
Waltrip, Rufus *9:* 195

Wan *12:* 76
Wan, Shelly *212:* 131
Wang, Suling *191:* 183; *213:* 194
Warburton, Sarah *154:* 187
Wappers, G. *121:* 40
Ward, Fred *52:* 19
Ward, Helen *72:* 244; *144:* 240, 242
Ward, John *42:* 191; *96:* 54; *97:* 110; *123:* 105; *124:* 71; *173:* 66
Ward, Keith *2:* 107; *132:* 69
Ward, Leslie *34:* 126; *36:* 87
Ward, Lynd *1:* 99, 132, 133, 150; *2:* 108, 158, 196, 259; *18:* 86; *27:* 56; *29:* 79, 187, 253, 255; *36:* 199,200, 201, 202, 203, 204, 205, 206, 207, 209; *43:* 34; *56:* 28; *60:* 116; *100:* 65
Ward, Peter *37:* 116
Waring, Geoff *172:* 84
Warhola, James *92:* 5; *115:* 85, 87; *118:* 174, 175, 177; *176:* 84; *187:* 189, 190
Warner, Ben *159:* 171
Warner, Peter *14:* 87
Warner, Sally *214:* 210
Warnes, Tim *175:* 159; *202:* 188
Warnick, Elsa *113:* 223
Warren, Betsy *2:* 101
Warren, Jim *85:* 81
Warren, Marion Cray *14:* 215
Warshaw, Jerry *30:* 197, 198; *42:* 165
Wasden, Kevin *102:* 162
Washington, Nevin *20:* 123
Washington, Phyllis *20:* 123
Wasserman, Amy L. *92:* 110; *209:* 95
Waterman, Stan *11:* 76
Watkins-Pitchford, D.J. *6:* 215, 217
Watling, James *67:* 210; *78:* 112; *101:* 81; *117:* 189, 190; *127:* 119, 120
Watson, Aldren A. *2:* 267; *5:* 94; *13:* 71; *19:* 253; *32:* 220; *42:* 193, 194, 195, 196, 197, 198, 199, 200, 201; *YABC 2:* 202
Watson, G. *83:* 162
Watson, Gary *19:* 147; *36:* 68; *41:* 122; *47:* 139
Watson, J.D. *22:* 86
Watson, Jesse Joshua *197:* 124; *199:* 181; *202:* 136
Watson, Karen *11:* 26
Watson, Mary *117:* 193
Watson, Richard Jesse *62:* 188, 189; *211:* 201
Watson, Wendy *5:* 197; *13:* 101; *33:* 116; *46:* 163; *64:* 12; *74:* 242, 243; *91:* 21; *142:* 228; *215:* 79
Watt, Mélanie *136:* 206; *193:* 211
Wattenberg, Jane *174:* 200; *185:* 46; *187:* 108
Watterson, Bill *66:* 223, 225, 226
Watts, Bernadette *4:* 227; *103:* 182, 183
Watts, James *59:* 197; *74:* 145; *86:* 124
Watts, John *37:* 149
Watts, Leslie Elizabeth *150:* 207; *165:* 106; *209:* 67
Watts, Stan *116:* 205
Weatherby, Mark Alan *77:* 141
Webb, Jennifer *110:* 79
Webb, Lanny *142:* 175
Webb, Sophie *135:* 214
Webber, Helen *3:* 141
Webber, Irma E. *14:* 238
Weber, Erik *56:* 19, 20
Weber, Florence *40:* 153
Weber, Jill *127:* 227, 228; *189:* 163; *208:* 157; *209:* 190, 191
Weber, Roland *61:* 204
Weber, Sam *190:* 227
Weber, William J. *14:* 239
Webster, Jean *17:* 241
Weeks, Sarah *162:* 39
Wegman, William *78:* 243
Wegner, Fritz *14:* 250; *20:* 189; *44:* 165; *86:* 62
Weidenear, Reynold H. *21:* 122
Weigel, Jeff *170:* 193

Weihs, Erika *4:* 21; *15:* 299; *72:* 201; *107:* 207, 208
Weil, Lisl *7:* 203; *10:* 58; *21:* 95; *22:* 188,217; *33:* 193
Weiman, Jon *50:* 162, 165; *52:* 103; *54:* 78, 79, 81; *78:* 80; *82:* 107; *93:* 82; *97:* 69; *105:* 179; *193:* 65
Weiner, Greg *215:* 21
Weiner, Sandra *14:* 240
Weiner, Scott *55:* 27
Weinhaus, Karen Ann *53:* 90; *71:* 50; *86:* 124
Weinman, Brad *197:* 20
Weinstock, Robert *204:* 165, 166
Weisgard, Leonard *1:* 65; *2:* 191, 197, 204, 264, 265; *5:* 108; *21:* 42; *30:* 200, 201, 203, 204; *41:* 47; *44:* 125; *53:* 25; *85:* 196, 198, 200, 201; *100:* 139,207; *YABC 2:* 13
Weisman, David *173:* 47
Weiss, Ellen *44:* 202
Weiss, Emil *1:* 168; *7:* 60
Weiss, Harvey *1:* 145, 223; *27:* 224, 227; *68:* 214; *76:* 245, 246, 247
Weiss, Nicki *33:* 229
Weissman, Bari *49:* 72; *90:* 125; *139:* 142
Weitzman, David L. *172:* 199
Welch, Sheila Kelly *130:* 221
Welkes, Allen *68:* 218
Wellington, Monica *99:* 223; *157:* 259, 260, 261
Welliver, Norma *76:* 94
Wellner, Fred *127:* 53
Wells, Frances *1:* 183
Wells, H.G. *20:* 194, 200
Wells, Haru *53:* 120, 121
Wells, Robert E. *184:* 208
Wells, Rosemary *6:* 49; *18:* 297; *60:* 32; *66:* 203; *69:* 215, 216; *114:* 227; *118:* 149, 150; *156:* 188, 189, 190, 191; *207:* 180, 181, 182, 183
Wells, Rufus III *56:* 111, 113
Wells, Susan *22:* 43
Wendelin, Rudolph *23:* 234
Wengenroth, Stow *37:* 47
Weninger, Brigitte *189:* 192, 194
Werenskiold, Erik *15:* 6; *62:* 17
Werner, Honi *24:* 110; *33:* 41; *88:* 122
Werth, Kurt *7:* 122; *14:* 157; *20:* 214; *39:* 128
Wesson,
West, Harry A. *124:* 38
Westcott, Nadine Bernard *68:* 46; *84:* 49; *86:* 133; *106:* 199; *111:* 78; *113:* 111; *130:* 224; *139:* 54; *158:* 256; *194:* 199
Westerberg, Christine *29:* 226
Westerduin, Anne *105:* 229
Westerman, Johanna *162:* 206
Weston, Martha *29:* 116; *30:* 213; *33:* 85, 100; *53:* 181, 182, 183, 184; *77:* 95; *80:* 152; *119:* 196,197, 198, 199; *127:* 189; *133:* 196; *209:* 199
Wetherbee, Margaret *5:* 3
Wexler, Jerome *49:* 73; *150:* 129
Whalley, Peter *50:* 49
Whatley, Bruce *186:* 93, 95; *207:* 127; *213:* 183, 184
Wheatley, Arabelle *11:* 231; *16:* 276
Wheeler, Cindy *49:* 205
Wheeler, Dora *44:* 179
Wheelright, Rowland *15:* 81; *YABC 2:* 286
Whelan, Michael *56:* 108; *70:* 27, 29, 67, 68, 148; *74:* 18; *84:* 14; *91:* 195, 196; *95:* 147; *98:* 150, 151; *106:* 157; *113:* 218, 220; *116:* 99, 100
Whelan, Patrick *135:* 145
Whistler, Rex *16:* 75; *30:* 207, 208
White, Craig *110:* 130; *119:* 193; *130:* 33; *179:* 31
White, David Omar *5:* 56; *18:* 6
White, Joan *83:* 225
White, Martin *51:* 197; *85:* 127
Whitear *32:* 26
Whitehead, Beck *86:* 171

Whitehead, S.B. *154:* 132
Whithorne, H.S. *7:* 49
Whitman, Candace *208:* 208
Whitney, George Gillett *3:* 24
Whitney, Jean *99:* 53
Whitson, Paul *102:* 161
Whittam, Geoffrey *30:* 191
Whyte, Mary *96:* 127
Wiberg, Harald *38:* 127; *93:* 215
Wick, Walter *77:* 128
Wickstrom, Sylvie *106:* 87; *169:* 180; *214:* 110
Wickstrom, Thor *200:* 205
Widener, Terry *105:* 230; *106:* 7; *163:* 23; *200:* 17; *209:* 195
Wiese, Kurt *3:* 255; *4:* 206; *14:* 17; *17:* 18, 19; *19:* 47; *24:* 152; *25:* 212; *32:* 184; *36:* 211,213, 214, 215, 216, 217, 218; *45:* 161; *100:* 92
Wiesner, David *33:* 47; *51:* 106; *57:* 67; *58:* 55; *64:* 78, 79, 81; *69:* 233; *72:* 247, 248, 249, 251,252, 253, 254; *83:* 134; *104:* 31; *117:* 197, 199, 200, 202; *139:* 223, 224; *151:* 51; *181:* 189, 190
Wiesner, William *4:* 100; *5:* 200, 201; *14:* 262
Wiggins, George *6:* 133
Wijngaard, Juan *111:* 36; *114:* 124
Wikkelsoe, Otto *45:* 25, 26
Wikland, Ilon *5:* 113; *8:* 150; *38:* 124, 125, 130; *127:* 162
Wikler, Madeline *114:* 233
Wilbur, C. Keith, M.D. *27:* 228
Wilburn, Kathy *53:* 102; *68:* 234
Wilcox, Cathy *105:* 123
Wilcox, J.A.J. *34:* 122
Wilcox, Lydia *207:* 187
Wilcox, R. Turner *36:* 219
Wild, Jocelyn *46:* 220, 221, 222; *80:* 117
Wilde, George *7:* 139
Wildsmith, Brian *16:* 281, 282; *18:* 170, 171; *66:* 25; *69:* 224, 225, 227; *77:* 103; *83:* 218; *124:* 214,217, 219
Wildsmith, Mike *140:* 229
Wilhelm, Hans *58:* 189, 191; *73:* 157; *77:* 127; *135:* 229, 230, 233, 234; *196:* 209
Wilkin, Eloise *36:* 173; *49:* 208, 209, 210
Wilkinson, Barry *50:* 213
Wilkinson, Gerald *3:* 40
Wilkon, Jozef *31:* 183, 184; *71:* 206, 207, 209; *133:* 222
Wilks, Mike *34:* 24; *44:* 203
Willems, Mo *154:* 245, 246, 247; *180:* 236, 237, 239
Willey, Bee *103:* 129; *139:* 159; *173:* 115
Willhoite, Michael A. *71:* 214
William, Maria *168:* 51
Williams, Berkeley, Jr. *64:* 75
Williams, Ferelith Eccles *22:* 238
Williams, Garth *1:* 197; *2:* 49, 270; *4:* 205; *15:* 198, 302, 304, 307; *16:* 34; *18:* 283, 298, 299, 300, 301; *29:* 177, 178, 179, 232, 233, 241, 242, 243, 244, 245, 248; *40:* 106; *66:* 229, 230, 231, 233, 234; *71:* 192; *73:* 218, 219, 220; *78:* 261; *100:* 251, 252, 255; *136:* 117; *YABC 2:* 15, 16, 19
Williams, J. Scott *48:* 28
Williams, Jennifer *102:* 201
Williams, Jenny *60:* 202; *81:* 21; *88:* 71
Williams, Kent *180:* 18
Williams, Kit *44:* 206, 207, 208, 209, 211, 212
Williams, Marcia *97:* 214; *159:* 208, 209
Williams, Maureen *12:* 238
Williams, Patrick *14:* 218
Williams, Richard *44:* 93; *72:* 229; *74:* 133; *78:* 155, 237; *91:* 178; *110:* 212; *136:* 201, 202, 203; *152:* 115
Williams, Sam *124:* 222; *153:* 11; *177:* 201, 202; *180:* 34; *212:* 49
Williams, Sophy *135:* 236
Williams, Vera B. *53:* 186, 187, 188, 189; *102:* 201, 202, 203; *210:* 65

Williamson, Alex *177:* 180; *205:* 50
Williamson, Mel *60:* 9
Willingham, Fred *104:* 206; *154:* 157
Willis, Adam *181:* 75; *209:* 11
Willmore, J.T. *54:* 113, 114
Wilsdorf, Anne *180:* 122; *189:* 124; *191:* 195
Wilson, Anne *160:* 114
Wilson, Charles Banks *17:* 92; *43:* 73
Wilson, Connie *113:* 179
Wilson, Dagmar *10:* 47
Wilson, Dawn *67:* 161; *81:* 120; *113:* 158
Wilson, Edward A. *6:* 24; *16:* 149; *20:* 220, 221; *22:* 87; *26:* 67; *38:* 212, 214, 215, 216, 217
Wilson, Forrest *27:* 231
Wilson, Gahan *35:* 234; *41:* 136
Wilson, George *76:* 87
Wilson, Helen Miranda *140:* 61
Wilson, Jack *17:* 139
Wilson, Janet *77:* 154; *96:* 114; *99:* 219, 220; *153:* 64 *106:* 122; *130:* 210; *145:* 178; *173:* 64
Wilson, John *22:* 240
Wilson, Maurice *46:* 224
Wilson, Patten *35:* 61
Wilson, Peggy *15:* 4; *84:* 20
Wilson, Phil *181:* 29
Wilson, Rowland B. *30:* 170
Wilson, Sarah *50:* 215
Wilson, Tom *33:* 232
Wilson, W.N. *22:* 26
Wilson-Max, Ken *170:* 196; *180:* 181
Wilton, Nicholas *103:* 52; *183:* 111
Wilwerding, Walter J. *9:* 202
Wimmer, Mike *63:* 6; *70:* 121; *75:* 186; *76:* 21,22, 23; *91:* 114; *97:* 45, 68; *98:* 28; *107:* 130; *146:* 21; *149:* 47; *173:* 126; *193:* 21, 25; *194:* 204, 205
Winborn, Marsha *78:* 34; *99:* 70; *192:* 20
Winch, John *165:* 233
Winchester, Linda *13:* 231
Wind, Betty *28:* 158
Windham, Kathryn Tucker *14:* 260
Windham, Sophie *184:* 212
Winfield, Alison *115:* 78; *214:* 121
Winfield, Wayne *72:* 23
Wing, Gary *64:* 147
Wing, Ron *50:* 85
Wingerter, Linda S. *132:* 199; *174:* 181; *200:* 196
Winick, Judd *124:* 227, 228, 229
Winn-Lederer, Ilene *202:* 91
Winnick, Karen B. *211:* 207
Winslow, Will *21:* 124
Winstead, Rosie *180:* 243
Winsten, Melanie Willa *41:* 41
Winter, Jeanette *151:* 240, 241, 242; *184:* 215, 217, 218, 219
Winter, Milo *15:* 97; *19:* 221; *21:* 181, 203, 204, 205; *64:* 19; *YABC 2:* 144
Winter, Paula *48:* 227
Winter, Susan *163:* 177; *182:* 201
Winters, Greg *70:* 117
Winters, Nina *62:* 194
Wise, Louis *13:* 68
Wiseman, Ann *31:* 187
Wiseman, B. *4:* 233
Wishnefsky, Phillip *3:* 14
Wiskur, Darrell *5:* 72; *10:* 50; *18:* 246
Wisniewski, David *95:* 220, 221
Wisniewski, Robert *95:* 10; *119:* 192
Witschonke, Alan *153:* 149, 150
Witt, Dick *80:* 244
Wittmann, Patrick *162:* 204
Wittman, Sally *30:* 219
Wittner, Dale *99:* 43
Wittwer, Hala *158:* 267; *195:* 80
Woehr, Lois *12:* 5
Wohlberg, Meg *12:* 100; *14:* 197; *41:* 255
Wohnoutka, Mike *137:* 68; *190:* 199; *195:* 218; *205:* 132

Wojtowycz, David *167:* 168
Woldin, Beth Weiner *34:* 211
Wolf, Elizabeth *133:* 151; *208:* 175
Wolf, J. *16:* 91
Wolf, Janet *78:* 254
Wolf, Linda *33:* 163
Wolfe, Corey *72:* 213
Wolfe, Gillian *199:* 193
Wolff, Ashley *50:* 217; *81:* 216; *156:* 216, 217; *170:* 57; *174:* 174; *184:* 72; *203:* 181, 182, 183, 184
Wolff, Glenn *178:* 230
Wolff, Jason *213:* 186
Wolfsgruber, Linda *166:* 61
Wondriska, William *6:* 220
Wong, Janet S. *98:* 225; *152:* 43
Wong, Nicole *174:* 13; *214:* 216; *215:* 25
Wonsetler, John C. *5:* 168
Wood, Audrey *50:* 221, 222, 223; *81:* 219, 221; *198:* 206
Wood, Don *50:* 220, 225, 226, 228, 229; *81:* 218, 220; *139:* 239, 240
Wood, Grant *19:* 198
Wood, Heather *133:* 108
Wood, Ivor *58:* 17
Wood, Jakki *211:* 209
Wood, Muriel *36:* 119; *77:* 167; *171:* 55; *187:* 46
Wood, Myron *6:* 220
Wood, Owen *18:* 187; *64:* 202, 204, 205, 206, 208, 210
Wood, Rob *193:* 48
Wood, Ruth *8:* 11
Woodbridge, Curtis *133:* 138; *204:* 113
Wooding, Sharon L. *66:* 237
Woodruff, Liza *132:* 239; *182:* 46, 204
Woodruff, Thomas *171:* 73
Woods, John, Jr. *109:* 142
Woodson, Jack *10:* 201
Woodson, Jacqueline *94:* 242
Woodward, Alice *26:* 89; *36:* 81
Wool, David *26:* 27
Woolley, Janet *112:* 75
Woolman, Steven *106:* 47; *163:* 73
Wooten, Vernon *23:* 70; *51:* 170
Worboys, Evelyn *1:* 166, 167
Word, Reagan *103:* 204
Wormell, Christopher *154:* 251; *202:* 206
Worth, Jo *34:* 143
Worth, Wendy *4:* 133
Wosmek, Frances *29:* 251
Wrenn, Charles L. *38:* 96; *YABC 1:* 20, 21
Wright, Barbara Mullarney *98:* 161
Wright, Cliff *168:* 203
Wright, Dare *21:* 206
Wright-Frierson, Virginia *58:* 194; *110:* 246
Wright, George *YABC 1:* 268
Wright, Joseph *30:* 160
Wronker, Lili Cassel *3:* 247; *10:* 204; *21:* 10
Wu, Donald *200:* 18
Wummer, Amy *154:* 181; *168:* 150; *176:* 85; *201:* 202, 203
Wyant, Alexander Helwig *110:* 19
Wyatt, David *97:* 9; *101:* 44; *114:* 194; *140:* 20; *167:* 13; *188:* 48
Wyatt, Stanley *46:* 210
Wyeth, Andrew *13:* 40; *YABC 1:* 133, 134
Wyeth, Jamie *41:* 257
Wyeth, N.C. *13:* 41; *17:* 252, 253, 254, 255, 256, 257, 258, 259, 264, 265, 266, 267, 268; *18:* 181; *19:* 80, 191, 200; *21:* 57, 183; *22:* 91; *23:* 152; *24:* 28, 99; *35:* 61; *41:* 65; *100:* 206; *YABC1:* 133, 223; *2:* 53, 75, 171, 187, 317
Wyman, Cherie R. *91:* 42
Wynne, Patricia J. *210:* 260

X

Xuan, YongSheng *119:* 202, 207, 208; *140:* 36; *187:* 21

Y

Yaccarino, Dan *141:* 208, 209; *147:* 171; *192:* 244, 245; *207:* 168
Yakovetic, Joe *59:* 202; *75:* 85
Yalowitz, Paul *93:* 33; *211:* 92
Yamaguchi, Marianne *85:* 118
Yamasaki, James *167:* 93
Yang, Belle *170:* 198
Yang, Jay *1:* 8; *12:* 239
Yap, Weda *6:* 176
Yaroslava
    See Mills, Yaroslava Surmach
Yashima, Taro *14:* 84
Yates, John *74:* 249, 250
Yates, Kelly *208:* 214
Yayo *178:* 88
Yeatts, Tabatha *215:* 210
Yee, Cora *166:* 233
Yee, Wong Herbert *115:* 216, 217; *172:* 204, 205; *194:* 59
Yelchin, Eugene *204:* 4
Yeo, Brad *135:* 121; *192:* 106
Yerxa, Leo *181:* 195
Yezerski, Thomas F. *162:* 29
Ylla
    See Koffler, Camilla
Yohn, F.C. *23:* 128; *YABC 1:* 269
Yoo, Taeeun *191:* 198
Yorinks, Adrienne *144:* 248; *200:* 214
Yorke, David *80:* 178
Yoshida, Toshi *77:* 231
Yoshikawa, Sachiko *168:* 104; *177:* 28; *181:* 196, 197
Youll, Paul *91:* 218

Youll, Stephen *92:* 227; *118:* 136, 137; *164:* 248; *202:* 92
Young, Amy L. *185:* 218; *190:* 46
Young, Cybéle *167:* 9
Young, Ed *7:* 205; *10:* 206; *40:* 124; *63:* 142; *74:* 250, 251, 252, 253; *75:* 227; *81:* 159; *83:* 98; *94:* 154; *115:* 160; *137:* 162; *YABC 2:* 242; *173:* 174, 175, 176; *205:* 29; *212:* 82
Young, Mary O'Keefe *77:* 95; *80:* 247; *134:* 214; *140:* 213; *211:* 223, 225
Young, Noela *8:* 221; *89:* 231; *97:* 195
Young, Paul *190:* 222
Young, Selina *153:* 12; *201:* 204, 205
Yum, Hyewon *211:* 228
Yun, Cheng Mung *60:* 143

Z

Zacharow, Christopher *88:* 98
Zacks, Lewis *10:* 161
Zadig *50:* 58
Zaffo, George *42:* 208
Zagwyn, Deborah Turney *138:* 227
Zahares, Wade *193:* 219
Zaid, Barry *50:* 127; *51:* 201
Zaidenberg, Arthur *34:* 218, 219, 220
Zalben, Jane Breskin *7:* 211; *79:* 230, 231, 233; *170:* 202
Zallinger, Jean *4:* 192; *8:* 8, 129; *14:* 273; *68:* 36; *80:* 254; *115:* 219, 220, 222
Zallinger, Rudolph F. *3:* 245
Zakrajsek, Molly *177:* 146
Zappa, Ahmet *180:* 250
Zebot, George *83:* 214
Zecca, Katherine *207:* 195
Zeck, Gerry *40:* 232
Zeff, Joe *181:* 98
Zeifert, Harriet *154:* 265, 267
Zeiring, Bob *42:* 130
Zeldich, Arieh *49:* 124; *62:* 120
Zeldis, Malcah *86:* 239; *94:* 198; *146:* 265, 266

Zelinsky, Paul O. *14:* 269; *43:* 56; *49:* 218-223; *53:* 111; *68:* 195; *102:* 219, 222, 221, 222; *154:* 255, 256, 257; *171:* 141; *185:* 96
Zelvin, Diana *72:* 190; *76:* 101; *93:* 207
Zemach, Kaethe *149:* 250
Zemach, Margot *3:* 270; *8:* 201; *21:* 210, 211; *27:* 204, 205, 210; *28:* 185; *49:* 22, 183, 224; *53:* 151; *56:* 146; *70:* 245, 246; *92:* 74
Zeman, Ludmila *153* 212
Zemsky, Jessica *10:* 62
Zepelinsky, Paul *35:* 93
Zerbetz, Evon *127:* 34; *158:* 109
Zezejl, Daniel *197:* 74
Zhang, Ange *101:* 190; *172:* 41
Zhang, Son Nang *163:* 113; *170:* 206
Ziegler, Jack *84:* 134
Zimdars, Berta *129:* 155
Zimet, Jay *147:* 94; *152:* 74; *196:* 75
Zimic, Tricia *72:* 95
Zimmer, Dirk *38:* 195; *49:* 71; *56:* 151; *65:* 214; *84:* 159; *89:* 26; *147:* 224
Zimmer, Tracie Vaughn *169:* 183
Zimmerman, Andrea *192:* 49, 50
Zimmermann, H. Werner *101:* 223; *112:* 197
Zimnik, Reiner *36:* 224
Zingone, Robin *180:* 134
Zinkeisen, Anna *13:* 106
Zinn, David *97:* 97
Zoellick, Scott *33:* 231
Zollars, Jaime *190:* 190
Zonia, Dhimitri *20:* 234, 235
Zorn, Peter A., Jr. *142:* 157
Zudeck, Darryl *58:* 129; *63:* 98; *80:* 52
Zug, Mark *88:* 131; *204:* 169
Zulewski, Tim *164:* 95
Zuma *99:* 36
Zvorykin, Boris *61:* 155
Zweifel, Francis *14:* 274; *28:* 187
Zwerger, Lisbeth *54:* 176, 178; *66:* 246, 247, 248; *130:* 230, 231, 232, 233; *181:* 92; *194:* 224, 225, 226
Zwinger, Herman H. *46:* 227
Zwolak, Paul *67:* 69, 71, 73, 74

Author Index

The following index gives the number of the volume in which an author's biographical sketch, Autobiography Feature, Brief Entry, or Obituary appears.

This index includes references to all entries in the following series, which are also published by The Gale Group.

YABC—*Yesterday's Authors of Books for Children: Facts and Pictures about Authors and Illustrators of Books for Young People from Early Times to 1960*

CLR—*Children's Literature Review: Excerpts from Reviews, Criticism, and Commentary on Books for Children*

SAAS—*Something about the Author Autobiography Series*

A

Aardema, Verna 1911-2000 .... *107*
  Obituary *119*
  Earlier sketches in SATA *:4, 68*
  See also CLR *17*
  See also SAAS *8*
Aaron, Chester 1923- *74*
  Earlier sketch in SATA *9*
  See also SAAS *12*
Aaseng, Nate
  See Aaseng, Nathan
Aaseng, Nathan 1953- *172*
  Brief entry *38*
  Earlier sketches in SATA *51, 88*
  See also CLR *54*
  See also SAAS *12*
Abadzis, Nick 1965- *193*
Abalos, Rafael 1956-
  See Abalos, Rafael
Abalos, Rafael 1956- *197*
Abbas, Jailan 1952- *91*
Abbey, Lynn
  See Abbey, Marilyn Lorraine
Abbey, Marilyn Lorraine 1948- *156*
Abbott, Alice
  See Borland, Kathryn Kilby
  and Speicher, Helen Ross S(mith)
Abbott, Jacob 1803-1879 .... *22*
Abbott, Manager Henry
  See Stratemeyer, Edward L.
Abbott, R(obert) Tucker 1919-1995 .... *61*
  Obituary *87*
Abbott, Sarah
  See Zolotow, Charlotte
Abbott, Tony 1952- *205*
  Earlier sketch in SATA *159*
Abdelsayed, Cindy 1962- *123*
Abdul, Raoul 1929- *12*
Abeele, Veronique van den *196*
Abel, Raymond 1911- *12*
Abell, Kathleen 1938- *9*
Abelove, Joan *110*
Abels, Harriette S(heffer) 1926- *50*
Abercrombie, Barbara 1939- *182*
  Earlier sketch in SATA *16*
Abercrombie, Barbara Mattes
  See Abercrombie, Barbara

Abercrombie, Lynn
  See Sorrells, Walter
Abernethy, Robert G(ordon) 1927- *5*
Abisch, Roslyn Kroop 1927- *9*
Abisch, Roz
  See Abisch, Roslyn Kroop
Ablow, Gail 1962- *198*
Abodaher, David J. (Naiph) 1919- *17*
Abolafia, Yossi 1944-
  See Abulafia, Yossi
Abouzeid, Chris *175*
Abrahall, Clare Hoskyns
  See Hoskyns-Abrahall, Clare (Constance Drury)
Abrahams, Hilary (Ruth) 1938- *29*
Abrahams, Peter 1947- *194*
Abrahams, Robert David 1905-1998 .... *4*
Abramovitz, Anita (Zeltner Brooks) 1914- *5*
Abrams, Joy 1941- *16*
Abrams, Lawrence F. *58*
  Brief entry *47*
Abrashkin, Raymond 1911-1960 .... *50*
Abulafia, Yossi 1944- *177*
  Brief entry *46*
  Earlier sketch in SATA *60*
Acampora, Paul *175*
Accardo, Anthony *191*
Acer, David *206*
Achebe, Albert Chinualumogu
  See Achebe, Chinua
Achebe, Chinua 1930- *40*
  Brief entry *38*
  Earlier sketch in SATA *38*
  See also CLR *20*
Ackerman, Diane 1948- *102*
Ackerman, Eugene (Francis) 1888-1974 ...... *10*
Ackerman, Karen 1951- *126*
Ackerman, Susan Yoder 1945- *92*
Ackison, Wendy Wassink 1956- *103*
Ackley, Peggy Jo 1955- *58*
Ackroyd, Peter 1949- *153*
Acorn, John (Harrison) 1958- *79*
Acredolo, Linda (Potter) 1947- *159*
Acs, Laszlo (Bela) 1931- *42*
  Brief entry *32*
Acuff, Selma Boyd 1924- *45*
Ada, Alma Flor 1938- *181*
  Earlier sketches in SATA *43, 84, 143*
  See also CLR *62*

Adair, Gilbert 1944- *98*
Adair, Ian 1942- *53*
Adair, Margaret Weeks (?)-1971 .... *10*
Adam, Cornel
  See Lengyel, Cornel Adam
Adam, Mark
  See Alexander, Marc
Adam, Robert 1948- *93*
Adams, Adrienne 1906- *90*
  Earlier sketch in SATA *8*
  See also CLR *73*
Adams, Andy 1859-1935
  See YABC *1*
Adams, Barbara Johnston 1943- *60*
Adams, Bruin
  See Ellis, Edward S.
Adams, Captain Bruin
  See Ellis, Edward S.
Adams, Captain J. F. C.
  See Ellis, Edward S.
Adams, Dale
  See Quinn, Elisabeth
Adams, Daniel
  See Nicole, Christopher (Robin)
Adams, Debra
  See Speregen, Devra Newberger
Adams, Douglas 1952-2001 .... *116*
  Obituary *128*
Adams, Douglas Noel
  See Adams, Douglas
Adams, Edith
  See Shine, Deborah
Adams, Florence 1932- *61*
Adams, Harriet S(tratemeyer) 1892(?)-1982 .. *1*
  Obituary *29*
Adams, Harrison
  See Rathborne, St. George (Henry)
  and Stratemeyer, Edward L.
Adams, Hazard 1926- *6*
Adams, Hazard Simeon
  See Adams, Hazard
Adams, John Anthony 1944- *67*
Adams, Laurie 1941- *33*
Adams, Lowell
  See Joseph, James (Herz)
Adams, Nicholas
  See Pine, Nicholas
Adams, Nicholas
  See Smith, Sherwood

Adams, Nicholas
   See Doyle, Debra
   and Macdonald, James D.
Adams, Pam 1919- 112
Adams, Pamela
   See Adams, Pam
Adams, Richard 1920- 69
   Earlier sketch in SATA 7
   See also CLR 121
Adams, Richard George
   See Adams, Richard
Adams, Ruth Joyce 14
Adams, Tricia
   See Kite, Pat
Adams, William Taylor 1822-1897 28
Adam Smith, Janet (Buchanan) 1905-1999 .. 63
Adamson, Gareth 1925-1982(?) 46
   Obituary 30
Adamson, George 1906-1989
   Obituary 63
Adamson, George (Worsley) 1913-2005 30
Adamson, Graham
   See Groom, Arthur William
Adamson, Joy(-Friederike Victoria)
   1910-1980 11
   Obituary 22
Adamson, Wendy Writson 1942- 22
Addasi, Maha 1968- 205
Addison, Kenneth 1949(?)-2005 187
Addison, Kenneth L.
   See Addison, Kenneth
Addona, Angelo F. 1925- 14
Addy, Sharon Hart 1943- 192
   Earlier sketch in SATA 108
Addy, Ted
   See Winterbotham, R(ussell) R(obert)
Adelberg, Doris
   See Orgel, Doris
Adelson, Leone 1908- 11
Adinolfi, JoAnn 176
Adkins, Jan 1944- 210
   Autobiography Feature 210
   Earlier sketches in SATA 8, 69, 144
   See also CLR 77
   See also SAAS 19
Adler, C. S. 1932- 126
   Earlier sketches in SATA 26, 63, 102
   See also CLR 78
   See also SAAS 15
Adler, Carole Schwerdtfeger
   See Adler, C. S.
Adler, David A. 1947- 178
   Earlier sketches in SATA 14, 70, 106, 151
   See also CLR 108
Adler, Irene
   See Penzler, Otto
   and Storr, Catherine (Cole)
Adler, Irving 1913- 29
   Autobiography Feature 164
   Earlier sketch in SATA 1
   See also CLR 27
   See also SAAS 15
Adler, Larry 1939- 36
Adler, Peggy 22
Adler, Ruth 1915-1968 1
Adlerman, Daniel (Ezra) 1963- 163
   Earlier sketch in SATA 96
Adlerman, Kim
   See Adlerman, Kimberly M(arie)
Adlerman, Kimberly M(arie) 1964- 163
   Earlier sketch in SATA 96
Adoff, Arnold 1935- 96
   Earlier sketches in SATA 5, 57
   See also CLR 7
   See also SAAS 15
Adoff, Jaime 163
Adoff, Jaime Levi
   See Adoff, Jaime
Adorjan, Carol (Madden) 1934- 71
   Earlier sketch in SATA 10

Adrian, Frances
   See Polland, Madeleine A(ngela Cahill)
Adrian, Mary
   See Jorgensen, Mary Venn
Adshead, Gladys L(ucy) 1896-1985 3
Aesop 620(?)B.C.-560(?)B.C. 64
   See also CLR 14
Aesop, Abraham
   See Newbery, John
Affabee, Eric
   See Stine, R.L.
Agapida, Fray Antonio
   See Irving, Washington
Agard, John 1949- 138
Agard, Nadema 1948- 18
Agarwal, Deepa 1947- 141
Agee, Jon 1960- 196
   Earlier sketches in SATA 116, 157
Agell, Charlotte 1959- 214
   Earlier sketches in SATA 99, 150
Agent Orange
   See Moseley, James W(illett)
Aghill, Gordon
   See Garrett, Randall
   and Silverberg, Robert
Agle, Nan Hayden 1905- 3
   See also SAAS 10
Agnew, Edith J(osephine) 1897-1988 11
Agonito, Joseph 177
Agonito, Rosemary 1937- 177
Aguilar, David 214
Aguilar, David A.
   See Aguilar, David
Ahern, Margaret McCrohan 1921- 10
Ahl, Anna Maria 1926- 32
Ahlberg, Allan 1938- 214
   Brief entry 35
   Earlier sketches in SATA 68, 120, 165
   See also CLR 18
Ahlberg, Janet 1944-1994 120
   Brief entry 32
   Obituary 83
   Earlier sketch in SATA 68
   See also CLR 18
Aho, Julia Kay
   See Kay, Julia
Aichinger, Helga 1937- 4
Aiken, Clarissa (M.) Lorenz 1899-1992 12
   Obituary 109
Aiken, Conrad 1889-1973 30
   Earlier sketch in SATA 3
Aiken, Conrad Potter
   See Aiken, Conrad
Aiken, Joan (Delano) 1924-2004 73
   Autobiography Feature 109
   Obituary 152
   Earlier sketches in SATA 2, 30
   See also CLR 90
   See also SAAS 1
Aillaud, Cindy Lou 1955- 184
Ainsley, Alix
   See Steiner, Barbara A(nnette)
Ainsworth, Catherine Harris 1910- 56
Ainsworth, Norma 1911-1987 9
Ainsworth, Ruth (Gallard) 1908- 73
   Earlier sketch in SATA 7
Ainsworth, William Harrison 1805-1882 24
Aistrop, Jack 1916- 14
Aitken, Amy 1952- 54
   Brief entry 40
Aitken, Dorothy 1916- 10
Aitmatov, Chingiz 1928-2008 56
Aitmatov, Chingiz Torekulovich
   See Aitmatov, Chingiz
Akaba, Suekichi 1910- 46
Akers, Floyd
   See Baum, L. Frank
Akib, Jamel 181
Aks, Patricia 1926-1994 68
Alagoa, Ebiegberi Joe 1933- 108

Alain
   See Brustlein, Daniel
Alajalov, Constantin 1900-1987
   Obituary 53
Alalou, Ali 203
Alalou, Elizabeth 203
Alan, David
   See Horsfield, Alan
Alan, Robert
   See Silverstein, Robert Alan
Alarcon, Francisco X. 1954- 215
   Earlier sketch in SATA 104
Alarcon, Francisco Xavier
   See Alarcon, Francisco X.
Alarcon, Karen Beaumont
   See Beaumont, Karen
Albert, Burton 1936- 22
Albert, Louise 1928- 157
Albert, Michael 1966- 202
Albert, Richard E. 1909-1999 82
Albert, Susan Wittig 1940- 107
Alberts, Frances Jacobs 1907-1989 14
Albertson, Susan
   See Wojciechowski, Susan
Albion, Lee Smith 29
Alborough, Jez 1959- 149
   Earlier sketch in SATA 86
Albrecht, Lillie (Vanderveer H.)
   1894-1985 12
Albyn, Carole Lisa 1955- 83
Alchemy, Jack
   See Gershator, David
Alcock, Gudrun 1908- 56
   Brief entry 33
Alcock, Vivien (Dolores) 1924-2003 76
   Brief entry 38
   Obituary 148
   Earlier sketch in SATA 45
   See also CLR 26
Alcorn, John 1935- 31
   Brief entry 30
Alcorn, Stephen 1958- 207
   Earlier sketch in SATA 110
Alcott, Louisa May 1832-1888 100
   See also YABC 1
   See also CLR 109
Alda, Arlene 1933- 205
   Brief entry 36
   Earlier sketches in SATA 44, 106, 158
   See also CLR 93
Alden, Isabella (Macdonald) 1841-1930 115
   See also YABC 2
Alden, Sue
   See Francis, Dorothy
Alderman, Clifford Lindsey 1902-1988 3
Alderson, Sue Ann 1940- 59
   Brief entry 48
Alding, Peter
   See Jeffries, Roderic
Aldis, Dorothy (Keeley) 1896-1966 2
Aldiss, Brian W. 1925- 34
Aldiss, Brian Wilson
   See Aldiss, Brian W.
Aldon, Adair
   See Meigs, Cornelia Lynde
Aldous, Allan (Charles) 1911- 27
Aldrich, Ann
   See Meaker, Marijane
Aldrich, Bess Streeter 1881-1954
   See CLR 70
Aldrich, Thomas (Bailey) 1836-1907 114
   Earlier sketch in SATA 17
Aldridge, (Harold Edward) James 1918- 87
Aldridge, Josephine Haskell 14
Aldridge, Sheila 1974- 192
Aleas, Richard
   See Appelt, Kathi
Alegria, Malin 1974(?)- 190
Alegria, Ricardo E(nrique) 1921- 6
Aleksin, Anatolii Georgievich 1924- 36
Alenov, Lydia 1948- 61

Alex, Ben (a pseudonym) 1946- 45
Alex, Marlee (a pseudonym) 1948- 45
Alexander, Anna B(arbara Cooke) 1913- 1
Alexander, Anne
  See Alexander, Anna B(arbara Cooke)
Alexander, Ellen 1938- 91
Alexander, Frances (Laura) 1888-1979 4
Alexander, Janet 1907-1994 97
  Earlier sketch in SATA 1
Alexander, Jocelyn Anne Arundel 1930- 22
Alexander, Linda 1935- 2
Alexander, Lloyd 1924-2007 135
  Obituary 182
  Earlier sketches in SATA 3, 49, 81, 129
  See also CLR 48
  See also SAAS 19
Alexander, Lloyd Chudley
  See Alexander, Lloyd
Alexander, Marc 1929- 117
Alexander, Martha 1920- 136
  Earlier sketches in SATA 11, 70
Alexander, Rae Pace
  See Alexander, Raymond Pace
Alexander, Raymond Pace 1898-1974 22
Alexander, Robert 200
Alexander, Rod
  See Pellowski, Michael (Joseph)
Alexander, Sally Hobart 1943- 84
Alexander, Sue 1933-2008 136
  Obituary 195
  Earlier sketches in SATA 12, 89
  See also SAAS 15
Alexander, Vincent Arthur 1925-1980
  Obituary 23
Alexeieff, Alexandre A. 1901-1979 14
Alger, Horatio, Jr.
  See Stratemeyer, Edward L.
Alger, Horatio, Jr. 1832-1899 16
  See also CLR 87
Alger, Leclaire (Gowans) 1898-1969 15
Aliki
  See Brandenberg, Aliki
Alkema, Chester Jay 1932- 12
Al-Khalili, Jim 1962- 124
Alkiviades, Alkis 1953- 105
Alkouatli, Claire 186
Allaby, John Michael
  See Allaby, Michael
Allaby, Michael 1933- 167
Allamand, Pascale 1942- 12
Allan, Mabel Esther 1915-1998 75
  Earlier sketches in SATA 5, 32
  See also CLR 43
  See also SAAS 11
Allan, Nicholas 1956- 123
  Earlier sketch in SATA 79
Allan-Meyer, Kathleen 1918- 51
  Brief entry 46
Allard, Harry
  See Allard, Harry G(rover), Jr.
Allard, Harry G(rover), Jr. 1928- 102
  Earlier sketch in SATA 42
  See also CLR 85
Allee, Marjorie Hill 1890-1945 17
Allen, Adam
  See Epstein, Beryl
  and Epstein, Samuel
Allen, Alex B.
  See Heide, Florence Parry
Allen, Allyn
  See Eberle, Irmengarde
Allen, Betsy
  See Harrison, Elizabeth (Allen) Cavanna
Allen, Bob 1961- 76
Allen, Gertrude E(lizabeth) 1888-1984 9
Allen, Grace
  See Hogarth, Grace (Weston Allen)
Allen, Jeffrey (Yale) 1948- 42
Allen, John
  See Perry, Ritchie (John Allen)

Allen, Jonathan 1957- 177
  Earlier sketch in SATA 131
Allen, Jonathan Dean
  See Allen, Jonathan
Allen, Judy (Christina) 1941- 124
  Earlier sketch in SATA 80
Allen, Kenneth S. 1913-1981 56
Allen, Leroy 1912- 11
Allen, Linda 1925- 33
Allen, Marjorie 1931- 22
Allen, Maury 1932- 26
Allen, Merritt Parmelee 1892-1954 22
Allen, Nancy Kelly 1949- 171
  Earlier sketch in SATA 127
Allen, Nina (Stroemgren) 1935- 22
Allen, Pamela (Kay) 1934- 123
  Earlier sketches in SATA 50, 81
  See also CLR 44
Allen, Raul 205
Allen, Rodney F. 1938-1999 27
Allen, Roger MacBride 1957- 105
Allen, Ruth
  See Peterson, Esther (Allen)
Allen, Samuel W(ashington) 1917- 9
Allen, T. D.
  See Allen, Terril Diener
Allen, Terril Diener 1908- 35
Allen, Terry D.
  See Allen, Terril Diener
Allen, Thomas B. 1929- 193
  Earlier sketches in SATA 45, 140
Allen, Thomas Benton
  See Allen, Thomas B.
Allen, Tom
  See Allen, Thomas B.
Allende, Isabel 1942- 163
  See also CLR 99
Allerton, Mary
  See Govan, (Mary) Christine Noble
Alley, Robert W.
  See Alley, R.W.
Alley, R.W. 211
  Earlier sketch in SATA 169
Alley, Zoe B. 214
Alleyn, Ellen
  See Rossetti, Christina
Allington, Richard L(loyd) 1947- 39
  Brief entry 35
Allison, Amy 1956- 138
Allison, Bob 14
Allison, Diane Worfolk 78
Allison, Jennifer 173
Allison, Linda 1948- 43
Allison, Margaret
  See Klam, Cheryl
Allman, Barbara 1950- 137
Allmendinger, David F(rederick), Jr. 1938- . 35
Allred, Alexandra Powe 1965- 144
Allred, Gordon T(hatcher) 1930- 10
Allsop, Kenneth 1920-1973 17
Allsopp, Sophie 188
Alma, Ann 1946- 201
Almedingen, E. M.
  See Almedingen, Martha Edith von
Almedingen, Martha Edith von 1898-1971 3
Almon, Russell
  See Clevenger, William R.
  and Downing, David A(lmon)
Almond, David 1951- 158
  Earlier sketch in SATA 114
  See also CLR 85
Almond, Linda Stevens 1881(?)-1987
  Obituary 50
Almquist, Don 1929- 11
Alonzo, Sandra 199
Alphin, Elaine Marie 1955- 139
  Autobiography Feature 139
  Earlier sketches in SATA 80, 130
Alsenas, Linas 1979- 186

Alsop, Mary O'Hara 1885-1980 34
  Obituary 24
  Earlier sketch in SATA 2
Alter, Anna 1974- 206
  Earlier sketch in SATA 135
Alter, Judith 1938- 101
  Earlier sketch in SATA 52
Alter, Judith MacBain
  See Alter, Judith
Alter, Judy
  See Alter, Judith
Alter, Robert Edmond 1925-1965 9
Alter, Stephen 1956- 187
Althea
  See Braithwaite, Althea
Altman, Linda Jacobs 1943- 21
Altman, Suzanne
  See Orgel, Doris
  and Schecter, Ellen
Alton, Steve 169
Altschuler, Franz 1923- 45
Altsheler, Joseph A(lexander) 1862-1919
  See YABC 1
Alvarez, John
  See del Rey, Lester
Alvarez, Joseph A. 1930- 18
Alvarez, Julia 1950- 129
al-Windawi, Thura
  See Windawi, Thura al-
Alyer, Philip A.
  See Stratemeyer, Edward L.
Amado, Elisa 193
Amann, Janet 1951- 79
Amato, Carol A. 1942- 92
Amato, Mary 1961- 178
  Earlier sketch in SATA 140
Ambrose, Stephen E. 1936-2002 138
  Earlier sketch in SATA 40
Ambrose, Stephen Edward
  See Ambrose, Stephen E.
Ambrus, Gyozo Laszlo 1935- 1
  See also SAAS 4
Ambrus, Victor G.
  See Ambrus, Gyozo Laszlo
Amend, Bill 1962- 147
Amerman, Lockhart 1911-1969 3
Ames, Evelyn 1908-1990 13
  Obituary 64
Ames, Gerald 1906-1993 11
  Obituary 74
Ames, Lee J(udah) 1921- 151
  Earlier sketch in SATA 3
Ames, Mildred 1919-1994 85
  Earlier sketches in SATA 22, 81
Amico, Tom 1960(?)- 176
Amit, Ofra 1966- 205
Ammon, Richard 1942- 124
Amon, Aline 1928- 9
Amoss, Berthe 1925- 112
  Earlier sketch in SATA 5
Amstutz, Andre 1925- 214
Anastasio, Dina 1941- 94
  Brief entry 30
  Earlier sketch in SATA 37
Anaya, Rudolfo 1937-
  See CLR 129
Anaya, Rudolfo A.
  See Anaya, Rudolfo
Anaya, Rudolpho Alfonso
  See Anaya, Rudolfo
Anckarsvard, Karin Inez Maria 1915-1969 6
Ancona, George 1929- 208
  Autobiography Feature 208
  Earlier sketches in SATA 12, 85, 145, 192
  See also SAAS 18
Anders, C. J.
  See Bennett, Cherie
Anders, Isabel 1946- 101
Anders, Lou 176
Andersdatter, Karla M(argaret) 1938- 34
Andersen, Bethanne 1954- 191

Andersen, Hans Christian 1805-1875 .... *100*
  See also YABC *1*
  See also CLR *113*
Andersen, Ted
  See Boyd, Waldo T.
Andersen, Yvonne 1932- *27*
Anderson, Bernice G(oudy) 1894-1997 .... *33*
Anderson, Bob 1944- *139*
  Earlier sketch in SATA *136*
Anderson, Brad 1924- *33*
  Brief entry *31*
Anderson, Bradley Jay
  See Anderson, Brad
Anderson, Brian 1974- *211*
Anderson, C. C.
  See Anderson, Catherine Corley
Anderson, C(larence) W(illiam) 1891-1971 . *11*
Anderson, Carolyn Dunn
  See Dunn, Carolyn
Anderson, Catherine C.
  See Anderson, Catherine Corley
Anderson, Catherine Corley 1909-2001 .... *72*
Anderson, Clifford
  See Gardner, Richard (M.)
Anderson, Daryl Shon 1963- *93*
Anderson, Dave
  See Anderson, David
Anderson, David 1929- *60*
Anderson, Derek 1969- *169*
Anderson, Eloise Adell 1927- *9*
Anderson, George
  See Groom, Arthur William
Anderson, Grace Fox 1932- *43*
Anderson, J(ohn) R(ichard) L(ane)
  1911-1981 .... *15*
  Obituary *27*
Anderson, Jodi Lynn *182*
Anderson, John David *197*
Anderson, John L. 1905- *2*
Anderson, Joy 1928- *1*
Anderson, Kevin J. 1962- *117*
  Earlier sketch in SATA *74*
Anderson, Kevin James
  See Anderson, Kevin J.
Anderson, Kirsty 1978- *108*
Anderson, K.J.
  See Moesta, Rebecca
Anderson, Laurie Halse 1961- *186*
  Earlier sketches in SATA *95, 132*
  See also CLR *138*
Anderson, LaVere Francis Shoenfelt
  1907-1998 .... *27*
Anderson, Leone Castell 1923- *53*
  Brief entry *49*
Anderson, Lisa G. 1963- *108*
Anderson, Lonzo
  See Anderson, John L.
Anderson, Lucia (Lewis) 1922- *10*
Anderson, Madelyn Klein 1926-2005 .... *28*
Anderson, Margaret J(ean) 1931- *27*
  See also SAAS *8*
Anderson, Marilyn D. 1943- *144*
Anderson, Mary 1939- *82*
  Earlier sketch in SATA *7*
  See also SAAS *23*
Anderson, Matthew Tobin
  See Anderson, M.T.
Anderson, Mona 1910-2004 .... *40*
Anderson, Mrs. Melvin
  See Anderson, Catherine Corley
Anderson, M.T. 1968- *182*
  Earlier sketches in SATA *97, 146*
Anderson, Norman Dean 1928- *22*
Anderson, Peggy Perry 1953- *179*
  Earlier sketch in SATA *84*
Anderson, Poul 1926-2001 .... *90*
  Autobiography Feature *106*
  Brief entry *39*
  See also CLR *58*
Anderson, Poul William
  See Anderson, Poul

Anderson, Rachel 1943- *86*
  Earlier sketch in SATA *34*
  See also SAAS *18*
Anderson, Rebecca M.
  See Moesta, Rebecca
Anderson, Rebecca Moesta
  See Moesta, Rebecca
Anderson, Richard
  See Anderson, J(ohn) R(ichard) L(ane)
Anderson, Sara *173*
Anderson, Scoular *201*
Anderson, (Tom) Scoular *138*
Anderson, Susan 1952- *90*
Anderson, Thomas Scoular
  See Anderson, Scoular
Anderson, W. B.
  See Schultz, James Willard
Anderson, Wayne 1946- *202*
  Earlier sketches in SATA *56, 147*
Andersson, Kenneth 1970- *200*
Andre, Evelyn M. 1924- *27*
Andre, Evelyn Marie
  See Andre, Evelyn M.
Andreasen, Dan *186*
Andreassen, Karl
  See Boyd, Waldo T.
Andreassi, K. Robert
  See DeCandido, Keith R.A.
Andree, Louise
  See Coury, Louise Andree
Andrew, Ian 1962- *166*
  Earlier sketch in SATA *116*
Andrew, Ian Peter
  See Andrew, Ian
Andrew, Prudence (Hastings) 1924- *87*
Andrews, Benny 1930-2006 .... *31*
  Obituary *178*
Andrews, Eleanor Lattimore
  See Lattimore, Eleanor Frances
Andrews, Elton V.
  See Pohl, Frederik
Andrews, F(rank) Emerson 1902-1978 .... *22*
Andrews, J(ames) S(ydney) 1934- *4*
Andrews, Jan 1942- *167*
  Brief entry *49*
  Earlier sketches in SATA *58, 98*
Andrews, Julie 1935- *153*
  Earlier sketch in SATA *7*
  See also CLR *85*
Andrews, Laura
  See Coury, Louise Andree
Andrews, Roy Chapman 1884-1960 .... *19*
Andrews, Tamra 1959- *129*
Andrews, V(irginia) C(leo) 1924(?)-1986
  Obituary *50*
Andrews, Wendy
  See Sharmat, Marjorie Weinman
Andrews, William G. 1930- *74*
Andrews, William George
  See Andrews, William G.
Andrezel, Pierre
  See Blixen, Karen
Andriani, Renee
  See Williams-Andriani, Renee
Andriola, Alfred J. 1912-1983
  Obituary *34*
Andrist, Ralph K. 1914-2004 .... *45*
Andronik, Catherine M. *189*
Andryszewski, Tricia 1956- *148*
  Earlier sketch in SATA *88*
Anelli, Melissa 1979- *215*
Angel, Ann 1952- *192*
Angel, Carl *178*
Angel, Marie 1923- *47*
Angeles, Peter A. 1931- *40*
Angeletti, Roberta 1964- *124*
Angeli, Marguerite (Lofft) de
  See de Angeli, Marguerite (Lofft)
Angell, Judie 1937- *78*
  Earlier sketch in SATA *22*
  See also CLR *33*

Angell, Madeline 1919- *18*
Angelo, Valenti 1897- *14*
Angelou, Maya 1928- *136*
  Earlier sketch in SATA *49*
  See also CLR *53*
Angier, Bradford -1997 .... *12*
Angle, Kimberly Greene *203*
Angle, Paul M(cClelland) 1900-1975
  Obituary *20*
Anglund, Joan Walsh 1926- *2*
  See also CLR *94*
Ango, Fan D.
  See Longyear, Barry B(rookes)
Angrist, Stanley W(olff) 1933- *4*
Anholt, Catherine 1958- *131*
  Earlier sketch in SATA *74*
Anholt, Laurence 1959- *141*
  Earlier sketch in SATA *74*
Anita
  See Daniel, Anita
Anmar, Frank
  See Nolan, William F.
Annett, Cora
  See Scott, Cora Annett (Pipitone)
Annie-Jo
  See Blanchard, Patricia
  and Suhr, Joanne
Annixter, Jane
  See Sturtzel, Jane Levington
Annixter, Paul
  See Sturtzel, Howard A(llison)
Anno, Mitsumasa 1926- *157*
  Earlier sketches in SATA *5, 38, 77*
  See also CLR *122*
Anrooy, Francine Van
  See Van Anrooy, Francine
Ansary, Mir Tamim 1948- *140*
Anstey, Caroline 1958- *81*
Antell, Will D. 1935- *31*
Anthony, Barbara
  See Barber, Antonia
Anthony, C. L.
  See Smith, Dorothy Gladys
Anthony, Edward 1895-1971 .... *21*
Anthony, John
  See Beckett, Ronald Brymer
  and Ciardi, John (Anthony)
  and Sabini, John Anthony
Anthony, Joseph Patrick 1964- *103*
Anthony, Patricia 1947- *109*
Anthony, Piers 1934- *129*
  Autobiography Feature *129*
  Earlier sketch in SATA *84*
  See also CLR *118*
  See also SAAS *22*
Anthony, Susan C(arol) 1953- *87*
Anticaglia, Elizabeth 1939- *12*
Antieau, Kim *214*
Antilles, Kem
  See Moesta, Rebecca
Antle, Nancy 1955- *102*
Antolini, Margaret Fishback 1904-1985
  Obituary *45*
Anton, Michael J(ames) 1940- *12*
Antonacci, Robert J(oseph) 1916- *45*
  Brief entry *37*
Anvil, Christopher 1925-2009 .... *102*
Anzaldua, Gloria (Evanjelina) 1942-2004
  Obituary *154*
Aoki, Hisako 1942- *45*
Apfel, Necia H(alpern) 1930- *51*
  Brief entry *41*
Aphrodite, J.
  See Livingston, Carole
Apikuni
  See Schultz, James Willard
Apostolina, M. *184*
Apostolina, Michael
  See Apostolina, M.
Apostolou, Christine Hale 1955- *179*
  Earlier sketches in SATA *82, 128*

Appel, Allen (R.) 1945- *115*
Appel, Benjamin 1907-1977 .... *39*
  Obituary *21*
Appel, Martin 1948- *45*
Appel, Martin Eliot
  See Appel, Martin
Appel, Marty
  See Appel, Martin
Appelbaum, Diana Muir Karter 1953- *132*
Appelt, Kathi 1954- *190*
  Earlier sketches in SATA *83, 129*
Apperley, Dawn 1969- *135*
Appiah, Peggy 1921-2006 .... *84*
  Earlier sketch in SATA *15*
  See also SAAS *19*
Apple, Margot *214*
  Brief entry *42*
  Earlier sketches in SATA *64, 152*
Applebaum, Stan 1922- *45*
Applegate, K.A.
  See Applegate, Katherine
Applegate, Katherine 1956- *196*
  Earlier sketches in SATA *109, 162*
  See also CLR *90*
Applegate, Katherine Alice
  See Applegate, Katherine
Appleton, Victor
  See Barrett, Neal, Jr.
  and Doyle, Debra
  and Macdonald, James D.
  and Stratemeyer, Edward L.
  and Vardeman, Robert E(dward)
Appleton, Victor II
  See Goulart, Ron
Appollo 1969- *214*
Appollodorus, Olivier
  See Apple, Margot
Apsler, Alfred 1907-1982 .... *10*
Aragones, Sergio 1937- *48*
  Brief entry *39*
Araujo, Frank P. 1937- *86*
Arbo, Cris 1950- *103*
Arbuckle, Dorothy Fry 1910-1982
  Obituary *33*
Arbuthnot, May Hill 1884-1969 .... *2*
Archambault, John *163*
  Earlier sketches in SATA *67, 112*
Archbold, Rick 1950- *97*
Archer, Colleen Rutherford 1949- *164*
Archer, Frank
  See O'Connor, Richard
Archer, Jules 1915- *85*
  Earlier sketch in SATA *4*
  See also SAAS *5*
Archer, Lily 1981- *193*
Archer, Marion Fuller 1917- *11*
Archer, Nathan
  See Watt-Evans, Lawrence
Archer, Peggy 1947- *199*
Archibald, Joe
  See Archibald, Joseph S(topford)
Archibald, Joseph S(topford) 1898-1986 .... *3*
  Obituary *47*
Ard, William
  See Jakes, John
Ardagh, Philip 1961- *154*
Ardai, Charles 1969- *85*
Arden, Barbi
  See Stoutenburg, Adrien (Pearl)
Arden, William
  See Lynds, Dennis
Ardizzone, Edward (Jeffrey Irving)
  1900-1979 .... *28*
  Obituary *21*
  Earlier sketch in SATA *1*
  See also CLR *3*
Ardley, Neil 1937- *121*
  Earlier sketch in SATA *43*
Ardley, Neil Richard
  See Ardley, Neil
Arehart-Treichel, Joan 1942- *22*

Arena, Felice 1968- *151*
Arenella, Roy 1939- *14*
Argent, Kerry 1960- *138*
Arguelles, Francisco Xavier
  See Stork, Francisco X.
Argueta, Jorge *179*
Arihara, Shino 1973- *201*
Arkin, Alan 1934- *59*
  Brief entry *32*
Arkin, Alan Wolf
  See Arkin, Alan
Arksey, Neil *158*
Arlen, Leslie
  See Nicole, Christopher (Robin)
Arley, Robert
  See Jackson, Mike
Armer, Alberta (Roller) 1904-1986 .... *9*
Armer, Laura Adams 1874-1963 .... *13*
Armistead, John 1941- *130*
Armitage, David 1943- *155*
  Brief entry *38*
  Earlier sketch in SATA *99*
Armitage, Frank
  See Carpenter, John
Armitage, Ronda (Jacqueline) 1943- *155*
  Brief entry *38*
  Earlier sketches in SATA *47, 99*
Armour, Richard (Willard) 1906-1989 .... *14*
  Obituary *61*
Armstrong, Alan 1939- *172*
Armstrong, Alan W.
  See Armstrong, Alan
Armstrong, George D. 1927- *10*
Armstrong, Gerry (Breen) 1929- *10*
Armstrong, Jeannette (C.) 1948- *102*
Armstrong, Jennifer 1961- *165*
  Autobiography Feature *120*
  Earlier sketches in SATA *77, 111*
  See also CLR *66*
  See also SAAS *24*
Armstrong, Louise *43*
  Brief entry *33*
Armstrong, Martin Donisthorpe
  1882-1974 .... *115*
Armstrong, Matthew 1975- *188*
Armstrong, Matthew S.
  See Armstrong, Matthew
Armstrong, Ralph Richard
  See Armstrong, Richard
Armstrong, Richard 1903-1986 .... *11*
Armstrong, William H(oward) 1914-1999 ...... *4*
  Obituary *111*
  See also CLR *117*
Armstrong-Ellis, Carey (Fraser) 1956- *145*
Arndt, Ursula (Martha H.) *56*
  Brief entry *39*
Arneson, D(on) J(on) 1935- *37*
Arnett, Caroline
  See Cole, Lois Dwight
Arnett, Jack
  See Goulart, Ron
Arnette, Robert
  See Silverberg, Robert
Arno, Enrico 1913-1981 .... *43*
  Obituary *28*
Arnold, Ann 1953(?)- *207*
Arnold, Caroline 1944- *174*
  Brief entry *34*
  Earlier sketches in SATA *36, 85, 131*
  See also CLR *61*
  See also SAAS *23*
Arnold, Elizabeth 1944- *164*
Arnold, Elliott 1912-1980 .... *5*
  Obituary *22*
Arnold, Emily 1939- *134*
  Autobiography Feature *134*
  Earlier sketches in SATA *5, 50, 76, 110*
  See also CLR *46*
  See also SAAS *7*
  See McCully, Emily Arnold

Arnold, Gillian Clare
  See Cross, Gillian
Arnold, Katya 1947- *168*
  Earlier sketches in SATA *82, 115*
Arnold, Louise *175*
Arnold, Marsha Diane 1948- *147*
  Earlier sketch in SATA *93*
Arnold, Nick 1961- *113*
Arnold, Oren 1900-1980 .... *4*
Arnold, Susan (Riser) 1951- *58*
Arnold, Tedd 1949- *208*
  Earlier sketches in SATA *69, 116, 160*
Arnoldy, Julie
  See Bischoff, Julia Bristol
Arnosky, James Edward 1946- *189*
  Earlier sketches in SATA *70, 118*
  See also CLR *93*
Arnosky, Jim
  See Arnosky, James Edward
Arnott, Kathleen 1914- *20*
Arnov, Boris, Jr. 1926- *12*
Arnow, Harriette (Louisa) Simpson
  1908-1986 .... *42*
  Obituary *47*
Arnsteen, Katy Keck 1934- *68*
Arnstein, Helene S(olomon) 1915- *12*
Arntson, Herbert E(dward) 1911-1982 .... *12*
Aroner, Miriam *82*
Aronin, Ben 1904-1980
  Obituary *25*
Aronson, Marc 1950- *189*
  Autobiography Feature *189*
  Earlier sketches in SATA *126, 175*
Aronson, Marc Henry
  See Aronson, Marc
Aronson, Sarah *196*
Aronson, Virginia 1954- *122*
Arora, Shirley (Lease) 1930- *2*
Arrasmith, Patrick *176*
Arrick, Fran
  See Angell, Judie
Arrigan, Mary 1943- *142*
Arrington, Aileen *183*
Arrington, Stephen L. 1948- *97*
Arrington, Stephen Lee
  See Arrington, Stephen L.
Arrley, Richmond
  See Delany, Samuel R., Jr.
Arrowood, (McKendrick Lee) Clinton
  1939- *19*
Arrowsmith, Pat 1930- *59*
Arsenault, Isabelle 1978- *207*
Artell, Mike 1948- *183*
  Earlier sketches in SATA *89, 134*
Arthur, Robert (Andrew) 1909-1969
  See Arthur, Robert, (Jr.)
Arthur, Robert, (Jr.) 1909-1969 .... *118*
Arthur, Ruth M(abel) 1905-1979 .... *26*
  Earlier sketch in SATA *7*
Artis, Vicki Kimmel 1945- *12*
Artzybasheff, Boris (Miklailovich)
  1899-1965 .... *14*
Aruego, Ariane
  See Dewey, Ariane
Aruego, Jose 1932- *178*
  Earlier sketches in SATA *6, 68, 125*
  See also CLR *5*
Aruego, Jose Espiritu
  See Aruego, Jose
Arundel, Honor (Morfydd) 1919-1973 .... *4*
  Obituary *24*
  See also CLR *35*
Arundel, Jocelyn
  See Alexander, Jocelyn Anne Arundel
Arvey, Michael 1948- *79*
Arzoumanian, Alik *177*
Asare, Meshack (Yaw) 1945- *139*
  Earlier sketch in SATA *86*
Asaro, Catherine 1955- *165*
  Earlier sketch in SATA *101*

Asaro, Catherine Ann 1955-
  See Asaro, Catherine
Asay, Donna Day 1945- 127
Asbjornsen, Peter Christen 1812-1885 15
  See also CLR 104
Asch, Frank 1946- 154
  Earlier sketches in SATA 5, 66, 102
Ash, Jutta 1942- 38
Ashabranner, Brent 1921- 166
  Earlier sketches in SATA 1, 67, 130
  See also CLR 28
  See also SAAS 14
Ashabranner, Brent Kenneth
  See Ashabranner, Brent
Ashbless, William
  See Blaylock, James P.
  and Powers, Tim
Ashby, Gil 1958- 146
Ashby, Gwynneth 1922- 44
Ashby, Ruth 170
Ashby, Yvonne 1955- 121
Ashe, Arthur (Robert, Jr.) 1943-1993 65
  Obituary 87
Ashe, Geoffrey (Thomas) 1923- 17
  Autobiography Feature 125
Ashe, Mary Ann
  See Lewis, Mary
Asher, Bridget
  See Baggott, Julianna
Asher, Sandra Fenichel
  See Asher, Sandy
Asher, Sandy 1942- 71
  Autobiography Feature 158
  Brief entry 34
  Earlier sketch in SATA 36
  See also SAAS 13
Asheron, Sara
  See Moore, Lilian
Ashey, Bella
  See Breinburg, Petronella
Ashford, Daisy
  See Ashford, Margaret Mary
Ashford, Jeffrey
  See Jeffries, Roderic
Ashford, Margaret Mary 1881-1972 10
Ashland, Monk 1972- 207
Ashley, Bernard (John) 1935- 155
  Brief entry 39
  Earlier sketches in SATA 47, 79
  See also CLR 4
Ashley, Elizabeth
  See Salmon, Annie Elizabeth
Ashley, Ray
  See Abrashkin, Raymond
Ashman, Linda 1960- 203
  Earlier sketch in SATA 150
Ashton, Lorayne
  See Gottfried, Theodore Mark
Ashton, Warren T.
  See Adams, William Taylor
Asimov, Isaac 1920-1992 74
  Earlier sketches in SATA 1, 26
  See also CLR 79
Asinof, Eliot 1919-2008 6
Asinof, Eliot Tager
  See Asinof, Eliot
Aska, Warabe
  See Masuda, Takeshi
Asprin, Robert 1946-2008 92
Asprin, Robert L.
  See Asprin, Robert
Asprin, Robert Lynn
  See Asprin, Robert
Asquith, Cynthia Mary Evelyn (Charteris)
  1887-1960 107
Asquith, Ros 153
Astley, Juliet
  See Lofts, Norah (Robinson)
Aston, Dianna Hutts 1964- 176
Aston, James
  See White, T(erence) H(anbury)

Ata, Te 1895-1995 119
Atene, Ann
  See Atene, (Rita) Anna
Atene, (Rita) Anna 1922- 12
Atheling, William, Jr.
  See Blish, James
Atkins, Catherine 160
Atkins, Jeannine 1953- 172
  Earlier sketch in SATA 113
Atkinson, Allen G. 1953(?)-1987 60
  Brief entry 46
  Obituary 55
Atkinson, Elizabeth 215
Atkinson, M. E.
  See Frankau, Mary Evelyn Atkinson
Atkinson, Margaret Fleming 14
Atteberry, Kevan J. 186
Attema, Martha 1949- 156
  Earlier sketch in SATA 94
Atticus
  See Davies, Hunter
  and Fleming, Ian
  and Pawle, Gerald Strachan
  and Wilson, (Thomas) Woodrow
Atwater, Florence (Hasseltine Carroll)
  1896-1979 66
  Earlier sketch in SATA 16
  See also CLR 19
Atwater, Montgomery Meigs 1904-1976 15
Atwater, Richard (Tupper) 1892-1948 66
  Brief entry 27
  Earlier sketch in SATA 54
  See also CLR 19
Atwater-Rhodes, Amelia 1984- 170
  Earlier sketch in SATA 124
Atwell, Debby 1953- 150
  Earlier sketch in SATA 87
Atwood, Ann (Margaret) 1913-1992 7
Atwood, Margaret 1939- 170
  Earlier sketch in SATA 50
Atwood, Margaret Eleanor
  See Atwood, Margaret
Aubrey, Meg Kelleher 1963- 83
Aubry, Claude B. 1914-1984 29
  Obituary 40
Auch, Herm 173
Auch, Mary Jane 173
  Earlier sketch in SATA 138
Auch, M.J.
  See Auch, Mary Jane
Auclair, Joan 1960- 68
Auel, Jean 1936- 91
Auel, Jean M.
  See Auel, Jean
Auel, Jean Marie
  See Auel, Jean
Auer, Martin 1951- 77
Augarde, Steve 1950- 210
  Earlier sketches in SATA 25, 159
Augelli, John P(at) 1921- 46
Augustine, Mildred
  See Benson, Mildred
Ault, Phil
  See Ault, Phillip H(alliday)
Ault, Phillip H(alliday) 1914- 23
Ault, Rosalie Sain 1942- 38
Ault, Roz
  See Ault, Rosalie Sain
Aung, (Maung) Htin 1909- 21
Auntie Deb
  See Coury, Louise Andree
Auntie Louise
  See Coury, Louise Andree
Aunt Weedy
  See Alcott, Louisa May
Auseon, Andrew 1976- 166
Austen, Carrie
  See Bennett, Cherie
Austin, Carrie
  See Seuling, Barbara
Austin, Elizabeth S. 1907-1977 5

Austin, Harry
  See McInerny, Ralph
Austin, Margot 1909(?)-1990 11
  Obituary 66
Austin, Michael 178
Austin, Oliver L(uther), Jr. 1903-1988 7
  Obituary 59
Austin, Patricia 1950- 137
Austin, R. G.
  See Gelman, Rita Golden
  and Lamb, Nancy
Austin, Virginia 1951- 152
  Earlier sketch in SATA 80
Auteur, Hillary
  See Gottfried, Theodore Mark
Auth, Tony
  See Auth, William Anthony, Jr.
Auth, William Anthony, Jr. 1942- 192
Autry, Gloria Diener
  See Allen, Terril Diener
Auvil, Peggy A 1954- 122
Auvil, Peggy Appleby
  See Auvil, Peggy A
Aveni, Anthony F. 1938- 181
Aveni, Anthony Francis
  See Aveni, Anthony F.
Averbeck, Jim 1963- 201
Averill, Esther (Holden) 1902-1992 28
  Obituary 72
  Earlier sketch in SATA 1
Avery, A. A.
  See Montgomery, Rutherford George
Avery, Al
  See Montgomery, Rutherford George
Avery, Gillian 1926- 137
  Autobiography Feature 137
  Earlier sketches in SATA 7, 75
  See also SAAS 6
Avery, Gillian Elise
  See Avery, Gillian
Avery, Kay 1908- 5
Avery, Lorraine
  See Older, Effin
  and Older, Jules
Avery, Lynn
  See Cole, Lois Dwight
Avi 1937- 190
  Earlier sketches in SATA 14, 71, 108, 156
  See also CLR 68
Avishai, Susan 1949- 82
Avril, Francois 1961- 191
Avril, Lynne
  See Cravath, Lynne W.
Awdry, Christopher Vere 1940- 67
Awdry, Wilbert Vere 1911-1997 94
  See also CLR 23
Axelrod, Amy 131
Axelsen, Stephen 1953- 165
Axton, David
  See Koontz, Dean
Ayars, James S(terling) 1898-1986 4
Aye, A. K.
  See Edwards, Hazel (Eileen)
Ayer, Eleanor H. 1947-1998 121
  Earlier sketch in SATA 78
Ayer, Jacqueline 1930- 13
Ayer, Margaret (?)-1981 15
Aylesworth, Jim 1943- 213
  Earlier sketches in SATA 38, 89, 139
  See also CLR 89
Aylesworth, Thomas G(ibbons) 1927-1995 .. 88
  Earlier sketch in SATA 4
  See also CLR 6
  See also SAAS 17
Ayliffe, Alex 190
Aylward, Marcus
  See Alexander, Marc
Aymar, Brandt 1911- 22
Ayme, Marcel (Andre) 1902-1967 91
  See also CLR 25

Ayres, Becky
  See Hickox, Rebecca (Ayres)
Ayres, Katherine 1947- 187
Ayres, Pam 1947- 90
Ayres, Patricia Miller 1923-1985
  Obituary 46
Aytmatov, Chingiz
  See Aitmatov, Chingiz
Ayto, Russell 1960- 206
  Earlier sketches in SATA 111, 166
Azaid
  See Zaidenberg, Arthur
Azar, Penny 1952- 121
Azarian, Mary 1940- 171
  Earlier sketch in SATA 112
Azore, Barbara 1934- 188

B

Baastad, Babbis Friis
  See Friis-Baastad, Babbis Ellinor
Bab
  See Gilbert, W(illiam) S(chwenck)
Babbis, Eleanor
  See Friis-Baastad, Babbis Ellinor
Babbitt, Lucy Cullyford 1960- 85
Babbitt, Natalie 1932- 194
  Earlier sketches in SATA 6, 68, 106
  See also CLR 141
  See also SAAS 5
Babbitt, Natalie Zane Moore
  See Babbitt, Natalie
Babcock, Chris 1963- 83
Babcock, Dennis 1948- 22
Babcock, Dennis Arthur
  See Babcock, Dennis
Baber, Carolyn Stonnell 1936- 96
Baboni, Elena 198
Baca, Ana 1967- 191
Baca, Maria 1951- 104
Bach, Alice (Hendricks) 1942- 93
  Brief entry 27
  Earlier sketch in SATA 30
Bach, Bellamy
  See Windling, Terri
Bach, Mary 1960- 125
Bach, Richard 1936- 13
Bach, Richard David
  See Bach, Richard
Bache, Ellyn 1942- 124
Bachel, Beverly K. 1957- 142
Bachelet, Gilles 1952- 196
Bachman, Fred 1949- 12
Bachman, Richard
  See King, Stephen
Bachrach, Deborah 80
Backus, James Gilmore 1913-1989
  Obituary 63
Backus, Jim
  See Backus, James Gilmore
Bacmeister, Rhoda W(arner) 1893-1991 11
Bacon, Betty
  See Bacon, Elizabeth
Bacon, Elizabeth 1914-2001 3
  Obituary 131
Bacon, Joan Chase
  See Bowden, Joan Chase
Bacon, Josephine Dodge (Daskam)
  1876-1961 48
Bacon, Margaret Frances
  See Bacon, Peggy
Bacon, Margaret Hope 1921- 6
Bacon, Martha Sherman 1917-1981 18
  Obituary 27
  See also CLR 3
Bacon, Melvin 1950- 93
Bacon, Melvin L.
  See Bacon, Melvin
Bacon, Peggy 1895-1987 50

Bacon, R(onald) L(eonard) 1924- 84
  Earlier sketch in SATA 26
Baddiel, Ivor 1963- 210
Baden, Robert 1936- 70
Baden-Powell, Robert (Stephenson Smyth)
  1857-1941 16
Badt, Karin L(uisa) 1963- 91
Bae, Hyun-Joo 186
Baehr, Kingsley M. 1937- 89
Baehr, Patricia 1952- 65
Baehr, Patricia Goehner
  See Baehr, Patricia
Baek, Matthew J. 1971- 202
Baer, Jill
  See Gilbert, (Agnes) Joan (Sewell)
Baer, Judy 1951- 71
Baer, Julie 1960- 161
Baer-Block, Roxanna 172
Baerg, Harry J(ohn) 1909-1996 12
Baeten, Lieve 1954- 83
Bagert, Brod 1947- 191
  Earlier sketch in SATA 80
Baggette, Susan K. 1942- 126
Baggott, Julianna 1969- 197
Bagnold, Enid 1889-1981 25
  Earlier sketch in SATA 1
Baguley, Elizabeth 1959- 199
Bahlke, Valerie Worth -1994
  See Worth, Valerie
Bahous, Sally 1939- 86
Bahr, Mary (Madelyn) 1946- 95
Bahr, Robert 1940- 38
Bahti, Tom 1926-1972 57
  Brief entry 31
Bai, Durga 211
Baicker-McKee, Carol 1958- 177
Bailey, Alice Cooper 1890-1978 12
Bailey, Anne 1958- 71
Bailey, Bernadine (Freeman) 1901-1995 14
Bailey, Carolyn Sherwin 1875-1961 14
Bailey, Debbie 1954- 123
Bailey, Donna (Veronica Anne) 1938- 68
Bailey, Jane H(orton) 1916- 12
Bailey, John (Robert) 1940- 52
Bailey, Len 193
Bailey, Linda 1948- 182
  Earlier sketch in SATA 107
Bailey, Maralyn Collins (Harrison) 1941- 12
Bailey, Matilda
  See Radford, Ruby L(orraine)
Bailey, Maurice Charles 1932- 12
Bailey, Pearl (Mae) 1918-1990 81
Bailey, Peter 1946- 194
Bailey, Ralph Edgar 1893-1982 11
Bailey, Sheila (Lucas) 1960- 155
Baillie, Allan 1943- 151
  Earlier sketch in SATA 87
  See also CLR 49
  See also SAAS 21
Baillie, Allan Stuart
  See Baillie, Allan
Baines, John (David) 1943- 71
Bains, Larry
  See Sabin, Louis
Baird, Alison 1963- 138
Baird, Bil 1904-1987 30
  Obituary 52
Baird, Thomas (P.) 1923-1990 45
  Brief entry 39
  Obituary 64
Baird, William Britton
  See Baird, Bil
Baity, Elizabeth Chesley 1907-1989 1
Baiul, Oksana 1977- 108
Bajoria, Paul 1964- 187
Bakeless, John (Edwin) 1894-1978 9
Bakeless, Katherine Little 1895-1992 9
Baker, Alan 1951- 146
  Earlier sketches in SATA 22, 93
Baker, Augusta 1911-1998 3
Baker, Barbara 1947- 192

Baker, Betty Lou 1928-1987 73
  Obituary 54
  Earlier sketch in SATA 5
Baker, Carin Greenberg 1959- 79
Baker, Charlotte 1910- 2
Baker, Christina
  See Kline, Christina Baker
Baker, Christopher W. 1952- 144
Baker, Deirdre 1955- 195
Baker, E.D. 190
Baker, (Mary) Elizabeth (Gillette) 1923- 7
Baker, Gayle Cunningham 1950- 39
Baker, James W. 1924- 65
  Earlier sketch in SATA 22
Baker, James W. 1926- 122
Baker, Janice E(dla) 1941- 22
Baker, Jeanette 178
Baker, Jeannie 1950- 156
  Earlier sketches in SATA 23, 88
  See also CLR 28
Baker, Jeffrey J(ohn) W(heeler) 1931- 5
Baker, Jim
  See Baker, James W.
Baker, Keith 1953- 179
Baker, Ken 1962- 133
Baker, Laura Nelson 1911- 3
Baker, Margaret 1890-1965 4
Baker, Margaret J(oyce) 1918- 12
  See also SAAS 8
Baker, Mary Gladys Steel 1892-1974 12
Baker, (Robert) Michael (Graham) 1938- 4
Baker, Nina (Brown) 1888-1957 15
Baker, Pamela J. 1947- 66
Baker, Rachel 1904-1978 2
  Obituary 26
Baker, Roberta 206
Baker, Rosalie F. 1945- 166
Baker, Samm Sinclair 1909-1997 12
  Obituary 96
Baker, Sharon Reiss 1962- 207
Baker, Susan (Catherine) 1942-1991 29
Balaam
  See Lamb, G(eoffrey) F(rederick)
Balan, Bruce 1959- 113
Balcavage, Dynise 1965- 137
Balch, Glenn 1902-1989 3
  Obituary 83
  See also SAAS 11
Baldacci, David 1960- 184
Baldacci, David G.
  See Baldacci, David
  and Baldacci, David
Balderose, Nancy Ward 1952- 93
Balderson, Margaret 1935- 151
Baldini, Michelle 205
Baldry, Cherith 1947- 167
  Earlier sketch in SATA 72
Balducci, Carolyn 1946- 5
Balducci, Carolyn Feleppa
  See Balducci, Carolyn
Baldwin, Alex
  See Griffin, W.E.B.
Baldwin, Anne Norris 1938- 5
Baldwin, Clara 11
Baldwin, Gordo
  See Baldwin, Gordon C(ortis)
Baldwin, Gordon C(ortis) 1908-1983 12
Baldwin, James 1841-1925 24
Baldwin, James 1924-1987 9
  Obituary 54
Baldwin, Louis 1919- 110
Baldwin, Margaret
  See Weis, Margaret
Baldwin, Stan(ley C.) 1929- 62
  Brief entry 28
Bales, Carol Ann 1940- 57
  Brief entry 29
Balet, Jan (Bernard) 1913- 11
Balgassi, Haemi 1971- 131
Balian, Lorna 1929- 91
  Earlier sketch in SATA 9

Balit, Christina 1961- 212
　Earlier sketches in SATA *102, 159*
Ball, Duncan 1941- 73
Ball, Zachary
　See Janas, Frankie-Lee
　and Masters, Kelly R(ay)
Ballantine, Lesley Frost
　See Frost, Lesley
Ballantyne, R(obert) M(ichael) 1825-1894 ... 24
　See also CLR *137*
Ballard, James G.
　See Ballard, J.G.
Ballard, James Graham
　See Ballard, J.G.
Ballard, Jane
　See Gorman, Carol
Ballard, J.G. 1930-2009 93
　Obituary 203
Ballard, Jim G.
　See Ballard, J.G.
Ballard, John 1945- 110
Ballard, Lowell C(lyne) 1904-1986 12
　Obituary 49
Ballard, (Charles) Martin 1929- 1
Ballard, Mignon F. 1934- 64
　Brief entry 49
Ballard, Mignon Franklin
　See Ballard, Mignon F.
Ballard, Robert D(uane) 1942- 85
　See also CLR *60*
Ballard, Robin 1965- 126
Balliett, Blue 1955- 156
Ballinger, Bryan 1968- 161
Ballouhey, Pierre 1944- 90
Balogh, Penelope 1916-1975 1
　Obituary 34
Balouch, Kristen 176
Balow, Tom 1931- 12
Baltazzi, Evan S(erge) 1921- 90
Balterman, Marcia Ridlon 1942- 22
Baltimore, J.
　See Catherall, Arthur
Baltzer, Hans (Adolf) 1900- 40
Balzano, Jeanne (Koppel) 1912- 7
Bambara, Toni Cade 1939-1995 112
Bamfylde, Walter
　See Bevan, Tom
Bamman, Henry A. 1918- 12
Banat, D. R.
　See Bradbury, Ray
Bancroft, Griffing 1907-1999 6
Bancroft, Laura
　See Baum, L. Frank
Bandel, Betty 1912- 47
Baner, Skulda Vanadis 1897-1964 10
Banfill, A. Scott 1956- 98
Bang, Betsy 1912- 48
　Brief entry 37
Bang, Garrett
　See Bang, Molly
Bang, Molly 1943- 215
　Earlier sketches in SATA *24, 69, 111, 158*
　See also CLR *8*
Bang, Molly Garrett
　See Bang, Molly
Bang-Campbell, Monika 1975(?)- 195
　Earlier sketch in SATA *140*
Banjo, The
　See Paterson, A(ndrew) B(arton)
Banke, Cecile de
　See de Banke, Cecile
Banks, Erin Bennett 1978- 211
Banks, Kate 1960- 200
　Earlier sketches in SATA *134, 172*
Banks, Laura Stockton Voorhees 1908(?)-1980
　Obituary 23
Banks, Lynne Reid
　See Reid Banks, Lynne
Banks, Merry 197
Banks, Michael A. 1951- 101

Banks, Paul 1952- 174
Banks, Sara (Jeanne Gordon Harrell) 26
　See Harrell, Sara (Jeanne) Gordon
Bannatyne-Cugnet, Elizabeth Jo-Anne
　See Bannatyne-Cugnet, Jo
Bannatyne-Cugnet, Jo 1951- 101
Banner, Angela
　See Maddison, Angela Mary
Bannerman, Helen (Brodie Cowan Watson)
　1862(?)-1946 19
　See also CLR *144*
Banning, Evelyn I. 1903-1993 36
Bannon, Laura (?)-1963 6
Bannor, Brett 1959- 143
Banta, Susan 181
Bantock, Nick 1950(?)- 95
Banyai, Istvan 193
Barakat, Ibtisam 1963- 186
Barasch, Lynne 1939- 186
　Earlier sketches in SATA *74, 126*
Barbalet, Margaret 1949- 77
Barbary, James
　See Baumann, Amy Beeching
　and Beeching, Jack
Barbash, Shepard 1957- 84
Barbe, Walter Burke 1926- 45
Barber, Antonia 1932- 163
　Earlier sketch in SATA *29*
Barber, Atiim Kiambu
　See Barber, Tiki
Barber, Lynda
　See Graham-Barber, Lynda
Barber, Lynda Graham
　See Graham-Barber, Lynda
Barber, Richard (William) 1941- 35
Barber, Ronde 1975- 182
Barber, Tiki 1975- 182
Barbera, Joe 1911-2006 51
　Obituary 179
Barbera, Joseph
　See Barbera, Joe
Barbera, Joseph Roland
　See Barbera, Joe
Barberis, Juan C(arlos) 1920- 61
Barbour, Karen 1956- 170
　Earlier sketches in SATA *63, 121*
Barbour, Ralph Henry 1870-1944 16
Barclay, Bill
　See Moorcock, Michael
Barclay, Isabel
　See Dobell, I(sabel) M(arian) B(arclay)
Barclay, William Ewert
　See Moorcock, Michael
Barclay, William Ewert
　See Moorcock, Michael
Bardhan-Quallen, Sudipta 1977- 214
　Earlier sketch in SATA *168*
Bardoe, Cheryl 181
Bare, Arnold Edwin 1920- 16
Bare, Colleen Stanley 32
Bar-el, Dan 199
Barenholtz, Bernard 1914-1989
　Obituary 64
Bargar, Gary W. 1947-1985 63
Barger, Jan 1948- 147
Barish, Matthew 1907-2000 12
Barkan, Joanne 127
　Earlier sketch in SATA *77*
Barker, Albert W. 1900- 8
Barker, Carol (Minturn) 1938- 31
Barker, Cicely Mary 1895-1973 49
　Brief entry 39
　See also CLR *88*
Barker, Melvern 1907-1989 11
Barker, S. Omar 1894-1985 10
Barker, Squire Omar
　See Barker, S. Omar
Barker, Will 1913-1983 8
Barkin, Carol 1944- 52
　Earlier sketch in SATA *42*

Barklem, Jill 1951- 96
　See also CLR *31*
Barkley, Brad 178
Barkley, James Edward 1941- 6
Barks, Carl 1901-2000 37
Barley, Janet Crane 1934- 95
Barlow, Steve 1952- 211
Barnaby, Ralph S(tanton) 1893-1986 9
Barnard, A. M.
　See Alcott, Louisa May
Barnard, Bryn 1956- 169
　Earlier sketch in SATA *115*
Barne, Kitty
　See Barne, Marion Catherine
Barne, Marion Catherine 1883-1957 97
Barneda, David 206
Barner, Bob 1947- 136
　Earlier sketch in SATA *29*
Barnes, Dawn 1957- 175
Barnes, Derrick 191
Barnes, Derrick D.
　See Barnes, Derrick
Barnes, (Frank) Eric Wollencott 1907-1962 . 22
Barnes, Joyce Annette 1958- 85
Barnes, Laura T. 1958- 119
Barnes, Loutricia
　See Barnes-Svarney, Patricia L(ou)
Barnes, Malcolm 1909(?)-1984
　Obituary 41
Barnes, Michael 1934- 55
Barnes-Murphy, Frances 1951- 88
Barnes-Murphy, Rowan 1952- 88
Barnes-Svarney, Patricia L(ou) 1953- 67
Barnet, Nancy 1954- 84
Barnett, Ivan 1947- 70
Barnett, Lincoln (Kinnear) 1909-1979 36
Barnett, Moneta 1922-1976 33
Barnett, Naomi 1927- 40
Barney, Maginel Wright 1881(?)-1966 39
　Brief entry 32
Barnhart, Clarence L(ewis) 1900-1993 48
　Obituary 78
Barnouw, Adriaan Jacob 1877-1968
　Obituary 27
Barnouw, Victor 1915-1989 43
　Brief entry 28
Barnstone, Willis 1927- 20
Barnum, Jay Hyde 1888(?)-1962 20
Barnum, P. T., Jr.
　See Stratemeyer, Edward L.
Barnum, Richard 67
　Earlier sketch in SATA *1*
Barnum, Theodore
　See Stratemeyer, Edward L.
Barnwell, Ysaye M. 1946- 200
Baron, Kathy 1954- 90
Baron, Virginia Olsen 1931- 46
　Brief entry 28
Barr, Donald 1921-2004 20
　Obituary 152
Barr, George 1907-1992 2
Barr, Jene 1922-1985 16
　Obituary 42
Barr, Nevada 1952- 126
　Earlier sketch in SATA *115*
Barrer, Gertrude
　See Barrer-Russell, Gertrude
Barrer-Russell, Gertrude 1921- 27
Barrett, Angela (Jane) 1955- 145
　Earlier sketch in SATA *75*
Barrett, Ethel 87
　Brief entry 44
Barrett, Joyce Durham 1943- 138
Barrett, Judi 204
　See Barrett, Judith
Barrett, Judith 1941- 26
　See also CLR *98*
　See Barrett, Judi
Barrett, Robert T(heodore) 1949- 92
Barrett, Ron 1937- 14
Barrett, Susan (Mary) 1938- 113

Barrett, Tracy 1955- 207
  Earlier sketches in SATA *84, 115, 156*
Barrett, William E(dmund) 1900-1986
  Obituary 49
Barretta, Gene 214
  Earlier sketch in SATA *176*
Barretton, Grandall
  See Garrett, Randall
Barrie, Baronet
  See Barrie, J. M.
Barrie, J. M. 1860-1937 100
  See also YABC *1*
  See also CLR *124*
Barrie, James Matthew
  See Barrie, J. M.
Barringer, William 1940-1996 153
Barrington, Michael
  See Moorcock, Michael
Barris, George 1925- 47
Barrol, Grady
  See Bograd, Larry
Barron, Rex 1951- 84
Barron, T.A. 1952- 192
  Earlier sketches in SATA *83, 126*
  See also CLR *86*
Barron, Thomas Archibald
  See Barron, T.A.
Barron, Tom
  See Barron, T.A.
Barrow, Lloyd H. 1942- 73
Barrows, Annie 1962- 180
Barry, Dan 1958- 177
Barry, Dana (Marie Malloy) 1949- 139
Barry, James P(otvin) 1918- 14
Barry, Katharina Watjen 1936- 4
Barry, Robert 1931- 6
Barry, Robert Everett
  See Barry, Robert
Barry, Scott 1952- 32
Barry, Sheila Anne -2003 91
Barshaw, Ruth McNally 203
Bartell, Susan S. 175
Bartenbach, Jean 1918- 40
Barth, Edna 1914-1980 7
  Obituary 24
Barth, Kelly L. 1964- 152
Barthelme, Donald 1931-1989 7
  Obituary 62
Barth-Grozinger, Inge 1950- 185
Bartholomew, Barbara 1941- 86
  Brief entry 42
Bartholomew, Jean
  See Beatty, Patricia (Robbins)
Bartlett, Alison 153
Bartlett, Philip A. 1
Bartlett, Robert Merrill 1899-1995 12
Bartoletti, Susan Campbell 1958- 173
  Earlier sketches in SATA *88, 129, 135*
Barton, Byron 1930- 126
  Earlier sketches in SATA *9, 90*
Barton, Jill(ian) 1940- 75
Barton, May Hollis 67
  Earlier sketch in SATA *1*
Barton, Pat
  See Arrowsmith, Pat
Bartos-Hoeppner, Barbara 1923- 5
Bartram, Simon 156
Bartsch, Jochen 1906- 39
Baruch, Dorothy W(alter) 1899-1962 21
Barunga, Albert 1912(?)-1977 120
Baryshnikov, Mikhail 1948- 192
Bas, Rutger
  See Rutgers van der Loeff-Basenau, An(na)
  Maria Margaretha
Base, Graeme 1958- 162
  Earlier sketches in SATA *67, 101*
  See also CLR *22*
Base, Graeme Rowland
  See Base, Graeme
Baseman, Gary 1960- 174
Bash, Barbara 1948- 132

Bashevis, Isaac
  See Singer, Isaac Bashevis
Bashevis, Yitskhok
  See Singer, Isaac Bashevis
Bashista, Adrienne Ehlert 203
Basile, Gloria Vitanza 1929- 180
Baskin, Leonard 1922-2000 120
  Brief entry 27
  Earlier sketch in SATA *30*
Baskin, Nora Raleigh 1961- 189
  Earlier sketch in SATA *129*
Bason, Lillian 1913- 20
Bass, L. G.
  See Geringer, Laura
Bassett, Jeni 1959- 64
  Brief entry 43
Bassett, John Keith
  See Keating, Lawrence A.
Bassett, Lisa 1958- 61
Bassil, Andrea
  See Nilsen, Anna
Bastyra, Judy 108
Basye, Dale E. 205
Bataille, Marion 1963- 209
Bat-Ami, Miriam 1950- 150
  Autobiography Feature 150
  Earlier sketches in SATA *82, 122*
Bate, Lucy 1939-1993 18
Bate, Norman (Arthur) 1916- 5
Bateman, Colin 1962- 172
Bateman, Donna M. 190
Bateman, Teresa 1957- 168
  Earlier sketch in SATA *112*
Bates, Amy June 189
Bates, Barbara S(nedeker) 1919- 12
Bates, Betty
  See Bates, Elizabeth
Bates, Dianne 1948- 147
Bates, Elizabeth 1921- 19
Bates, Ivan 175
Bates, Katharine Lee 1859-1929 113
Bates, Martine
  See Leavitt, Martine
Bateson, Catherine 1960- 197
  Earlier sketch in SATA *157*
Batey, Tom 1946- 52
  Brief entry 41
Bath, Kevin P.
  See Bath, K.P.
Bath, K.P. 1959- 171
Batherman, Muriel
  See Sheldon, Muriel
Batson, Larry 1930- 35
Batt, Tanya Robyn 1970- 131
Battaglia, Aurelius 1910- 50
  Brief entry 33
Batten, H(arry) Mortimer 1888-1958 25
Batten, Mary 1937- 162
  Earlier sketches in SATA *5, 102*
Batterberry, Ariane Ruskin 1935- 13
Batterberry, Michael Carver 1932- 32
Battle-Lavert, Gwendolyn 1951- 155
  Earlier sketches in SATA *85, 131*
Battles, (Roxy) Edith 1921- 7
Baudouy, Michel-Aime 1909- 7
Bauer, A.C.E. 201
Bauer, Caroline Feller 1935- 98
  Brief entry 46
  Earlier sketch in SATA *52*
  See also SAAS *24*
Bauer, Fred 1934- 36
Bauer, Helen 1900-1988 2
Bauer, Joan 1951- 160
  Earlier sketch in SATA *117*
Bauer, Jutta 1955- 150
Bauer, Marion Dane 1938- 192
  Autobiography Feature 144
  Earlier sketches in SATA *20, 69, 113, 144*
  See also SAAS *9*
Bauer, Michael Gerard 1955(?)- 167
Bauer, Steven 1948- 125

Bauerschmidt, Marjorie 1926- 15
Baughman, Dorothy 1940- 61
Baum, Allyn Z(elton) 1924-1997 98
  Earlier sketch in SATA *20*
Baum, L. Frank
  See Thompson, Ruth Plumly
Baum, L. Frank 1856-1919 100
  Earlier sketch in SATA *18*
  See also CLR *107*
Baum, Louis 1948- 182
  Brief entry 52
  Earlier sketch in SATA *64*
Baum, Louis F.
  See Baum, L. Frank
Baum, Lyman Frank
  See Baum, L. Frank
Baum, Maxie 188
Baum, Willi 1931- 4
Baumann, Amy Beeching 1922- 10
Baumann, Amy Brown Beeching
  See Baumann, Amy Beeching
Baumann, Hans 1914- 2
  See also CLR *35*
Baumann, Kurt 1935- 21
Baumgartner, Barbara 1939- 86
Baurys, Flo 1938- 122
Baurys, Florence
  See Baurys, Flo
Bausum, Ann 173
Bawden, Nina 1925- 132
  Earlier sketches in SATA *4, 72*
  See also CLR *51*
  See also SAAS *16*
Bawden, Nina Mary Mabey
  See Bawden, Nina
Baxter, Valerie
  See Meynell, Laurence Walter
Bay, Jeanette Graham 1928- 88
Bayer, Harold
  See Gregg, Andrew K.
Bayer, Jane E. (?)-1985
  Obituary 44
Bayley, Nicola 1949- 129
  Earlier sketches in SATA *41, 69*
Baylor, Byrd 1924- 136
  Earlier sketches in SATA *16, 69*
  See also CLR *3*
Baynes, Pauline 1922-2008 133
  Obituary 196
  Earlier sketches in SATA *19, 59*
Baynes, Pauline Diana
  See Baynes, Pauline
Bayoc, Cbabi 186
Bayrock, Fiona 215
BB
  See Watkins-Pitchford, Denys James
Beach, Charles
  See Reid, (Thomas) Mayne
Beach, Charles Amory 1
Beach, Edward L. 1918-2002 12
  Obituary 140
Beach, Edward Latimer
  See Beach, Edward L.
Beach, Lisa 1957- 111
Beach, Lynn
  See Lance, Kathryn
Beach, Stewart T(aft) 1899-1979 23
Beachcroft, Nina 1931- 18
Beagle, Peter S. 1939- 130
  Earlier sketch in SATA *60*
Beagle, Peter Soyer
  See Beagle, Peter S.
Beaglehole, Helen 1946- 117
Beake, Lesley 1949- 209
Beale, Fleur 107
Bealer, Alex W(inkler III) 1921-1980 8
  Obituary 22
Beales, Valerie 1915- 74
Beals, Carleton 1893-1979 12
Beals, Frank Lee 1881-1972
  Obituary 26

Beam, Matt 1970- *187*
Beame, Rona 1934- *12*
Beamer, Charles 1942- *43*
Beamer, George Charles, Jr.
    See Beamer, Charles
Bean, Jonathan 1979- *194*
Bean, Normal
    See Burroughs, Edgar Rice
Beaney, Jan
    See Udall, Jan Beaney
Beaney, Jane
    See Udall, Jan Beaney
Bear, Carolyn
    See Rayban, Chloe
Bear, Greg 1951- *105*
    Earlier sketch in SATA *65*
Bear, Gregory Dale
    See Bear, Greg
Bearanger, Marie
    See Messier, Claire
Beard, Charles A(ustin) 1874-1948 .... *18*
Beard, Dan(iel Carter) 1850-1941 .... *22*
Beard, Darleen Bailey 1961- *96*
Bearden, Romare (Howard) 1914(?)-1988 ... *22*
    Obituary *56*
Beardmore, Cedric
    See Beardmore, George
Beardmore, George 1908-1979 .... *20*
Beardshaw, Rosalind 1969- *190*
Beardsley, Martyn R. 1957- *150*
Bearman, Jane (Ruth) 1917- *29*
Beaton, Clare 1947- *125*
Beatty, Elizabeth
    See Holloway, Teresa (Bragunier)
Beatty, Hetty Burlingame 1907-1971 .... *5*
Beatty, Jerome, Jr. 1918- *5*
Beatty, John (Louis) 1922-1975 .... *6*
    Obituary *25*
Beatty, Patricia (Robbins) 1922-1991 .... *73*
    Obituary *68*
    Earlier sketches in SATA *1, 30*
    See also SAAS *4*
Beaty, Andrea *186*
Beaty, Mary (T.) 1947- *146*
Beaudoin, Sean *210*
Beaumont, Karen 1954- *204*
Beccia, Carlyn *189*
Bechard, Margaret 1953- *164*
    Earlier sketch in SATA *85*
Bechtel, Louise Seaman 1894-1985 .... *4*
    Obituary *43*
Bechtold, Lisze *208*
Beck, Barbara L. 1927- *12*
Beck, Ian 1947- *190*
    Earlier sketch in SATA *138*
    See Beck, Ian Archibald
Beck, Peggy 1949- *171*
Beck, Scott *197*
Becker, Beril 1901-1999 .... *11*
Becker, Bonny *184*
Becker, Deborah Zimmett 1955- *138*
Becker, Helaine 1961- *142*
Becker, John (Leonard) 1901- *12*
Becker, John E(mil) 1942- *148*
Becker, Joyce 1936- *39*
Becker, May Lamberton 1873-1958 .... *33*
Becker, Neesa 1951- *123*
Becker, Shari *174*
Beckerman, Chad W. *198*
Beckett, Sheilah 1913- *33*
Beckhorn, Susan Williams 1953- *189*
Beckles Willson, Robina 1930- *27*
Beckman, Delores 1914-1994 .... *51*
Beckman, Gunnel 1910- *6*
    See also CLR *25*
    See also SAAS *9*
Beckman, Kaj
    See Beckman, Karin
Beckman, Karin 1913- *45*
Beckman, Per (Frithiof) 1913- *45*

Bedard, Michael 1949- *154*
    Earlier sketch in SATA *93*
    See also CLR *35*
Beddor, Frank *194*
Beddows, Eric
    See Nutt, Ken
Bedford, A. N.
    See Watson, Jane Werner
Bedford, Annie North
    See Watson, Jane Werner
Bedford, David *159*
Bedoukian, Kerop 1907-1981 .... *53*
Bee, Jay
    See Brainerd, John W(hiting)
Bee, William *188*
Beebe, B. F.
    See Johnson, B. F.
Beebe, (Charles) William 1877-1962 .... *19*
Beeby, Betty 1923- *25*
Beech, Mark 1971- *191*
Beech, Webb
    See Griffin, W.E.B.
Beecham, Jahnna *161*
Beechcroft, William
    See Hallstead, William F(inn III)
Beeching, Jack 1922- *14*
Beeke, Tiphanie *163*
Beeler, Janet
    See Shaw, Janet
Beeler, Nelson F(rederick) 1910-1978 .... *13*
Beere, Peter 1951- *97*
Beers, Dorothy Sands 1917- *9*
Beers, Lorna 1897-1989 .... *14*
Beers, V(ictor) Gilbert 1928- *130*
    Earlier sketch in SATA *9*
Beeton, Max
    See Redding, Robert Hull
Begay, Shonto 1954- *137*
Begaye, Lisa Shook
    See Beach, Lisa
Begin, Mary Jane 1963- *82*
Begin-Callanan, Mary Jane
    See Begin, Mary Jane
Begley, Kathleen A. 1948- *21*
Begley, Kathleen Anne
    See Begley, Kathleen A.
Beha, Philippe *211*
Behan, Leslie
    See Gottfried, Theodore Mark
Behler, Deborah A. 1947- *145*
Behler, John L. 1943-2006 .... *145*
    Obituary *173*
Behler, John Luther
    See Behler, John L.
Behn, Harry 1898-1973 .... *2*
    Obituary *34*
Behnke, Frances L. *8*
Behr, Joyce 1929- *15*
Behrens, June York 1925- *19*
Behrman, Carol H(elen) 1925- *144*
    Earlier sketch in SATA *14*
Beifuss, John, (Jr.) 1959- *92*
Beil, Karen Magnuson 1950- *124*
Beiler, Edna 1923- *61*
Beinicke, Steve 1956- *69*
Beirne, Barbara 1933- *71*
Beiser, Arthur 1931- *22*
Beiser, Germaine 1931- *11*
Belair, Richard L. 1934- *45*
Belaney, Archibald Stansfeld 1888-1938 ...... *24*
    See also CLR *32*
Belasen, Amy 1983- *213*
Belbin, David 1958- *164*
    Earlier sketch in SATA *106*
Belden, Wilanne Schneider 1925- *56*
Belfrage, Sally 1936-1994 .... *65*
    Obituary *79*
Belknap, B. H.
    See Ellis, Edward S.
Belknap, Boynton
    See Ellis, Edward S.

Belknap, Boynton M.D.
    See Ellis, Edward S.
Bell, Anthea 1936- *148*
    Earlier sketch in SATA *88*
Bell, Cathleen Davitt 1971- *203*
Bell, Cece *202*
Bell, Clare (Louise) 1952- *99*
Bell, Corydon Whitten 1894-1980 .... *3*
Bell, David Owen 1949- *99*
Bell, Emerson
    See Stratemeyer, Edward L.
Bell, Emily Mary
    See Cason, Mabel Earp
Bell, Frank
    See Benson, Mildred
Bell, Gertrude (Wood) 1911-1987 .... *12*
Bell, Gina
    See Balzano, Jeanne (Koppel)
Bell, Hilari 1958- *197*
    Earlier sketch in SATA *151*
Bell, Jadrien
    See Golden, Christie
Bell, Janet
    See Clymer, Eleanor
Bell, Janet Cheatham 1937- *127*
Bell, Krista 1950- *215*
    Earlier sketch in SATA *126*
Bell, Krista Anne Blakeney
    See Bell, Krista
Bell, Margaret E(lizabeth) 1898-1990 .... *2*
Bell, Mary Reeves 1946- *88*
Bell, Norman (Edward) 1899- *11*
Bell, Raymond Martin 1907-1999 .... *13*
Bell, Siobhan *177*
Bell, Thelma Harrington 1896-1985 .... *3*
Bell, William 1945- *90*
    See also CLR *91*
Bellairs, John (Anthony) 1938-1991 .... *160*
    Obituary *66*
    Earlier sketches in SATA *2, 68*
    See also CLR *37*
Beller, Susan Provost 1949- *128*
    Earlier sketch in SATA *84*
    See also CLR *106*
Bellingham, Brenda 1931- *99*
    Brief entry *51*
Bello, Rosario de
    See De Bello, Rosario
Belloc, Hilaire 1870-1953 .... *112*
    See also YABC *1*
    See also CLR *102*
Belloc, Joseph Hilaire Pierre Sebastien Rene
    Swanton
    See Belloc, Hilaire
Belloc, Joseph Peter Rene Hilaire
    See Belloc, Hilaire
Belloc, Joseph Pierre Hilaire
    See Belloc, Hilaire
Belloli, Andrea P. A. 1947- *86*
Bell-Rehwoldt, Sheri 1962- *199*
Bellville, Cheryl Walsh 1944- *54*
    Brief entry *49*
Bell-Zano, Gina
    See Balzano, Jeanne (Koppel)
Belpre, Pura 1899-1982 .... *16*
    Obituary *30*
Belting, Natalia Maree 1915-1997 .... *6*
Belton, John Raynor 1931- *22*
Belton, Sandra 1939- *186*
    Earlier sketches in SATA *85, 134*
Belton, Sandra Yvonne
    See Belton, Sandra
Beltran, Alberto 1923- *43*
Beltran-Hernandez, Irene 1945- *74*
Belvedere, Lee
    See Grayland, Valerie (Merle Spanner)
Bemelmans, Ludwig 1898-1962 .... *100*
    Earlier sketch in SATA *15*
    See also CLR *93*
Benander, Carl D. 1941- *74*

Benary, Margot
    See Benary-Isbert, Margot
Benary-Isbert, Margot 1889-1979 2
    Obituary 21
    See also CLR 12
Benasutti, Marion 1908-1992 6
Benatar, Raquel 1955- 167
Benchley, Nathaniel (Goddard) 1915-1981 .. 25
    Obituary 28
    Earlier sketch in SATA 3
Benchley, Peter 1940-2006 164
    Earlier sketches in SATA 3, 89
Benchley, Peter Bradford
    See Benchley, Peter
Bendall-Brunello, John 185
Bender, Edna 1941- 92
Bender, Esther 1942- 88
Bender, Lucy Ellen 1942- 22
Bender, Robert 1962- 160
    Earlier sketch in SATA 79
Bendick, Jeanne 1919- 135
    Earlier sketches in SATA 2, 68
    See also CLR 5
    See also SAAS 4
Bendick, Robert L(ouis) 1917- 11
Benedetto, William R. 1928- 180
Benedetto, William Ralph
    See Benedetto, William R.
Benedict, Andrew
    See Arthur, Robert, (Jr.)
Benedict, Dorothy Potter 1889-1979 11
    Obituary 23
Benedict, Lois Trimble 1902-1967 12
Benedict, Rex 1920-1995 8
Benedict, Stewart H(urd) 1924- 26
Beneduce, Ann Keay 128
Benet, Laura 1884-1979 3
    Obituary 23
Benet, Stephen Vincent 1898-1943
    See YABC 1
Benet, Sula 1906-1982 21
    Obituary 33
Ben-Ezer, Ehud 1936- 122
Benezra, Barbara (Beardsley) 1921- 10
Benham, Leslie 1922- 48
Benham, Lois (Dakin) 1924- 48
Benham, Mary Lile 1914-1991 55
Benjamin, E. M. J.
    See Bache, Ellyn
Benjamin, Floella 1949- 206
Benjamin, Nora
    See Kubie, Nora Gottheil Benjamin
Benjamin, Saragail Katzman 1953- 86
Benner, Cheryl 1962- 80
Benner, Judith Ann 1942- 94
Bennett, Alice
    See Ziner, Florence
Bennett, Cherie 1960- 158
    Earlier sketch in SATA 97
Bennett, Dorothea
    See Young, Dorothea Bennett
Bennett, Erin Susanne
    See Banks, Erin Bennett
Bennett, Holly 1957- 181
Bennett, James (W.) 1942- 153
    Autobiography Feature 153
    Earlier sketches in SATA 93, 148
Bennett, Jay 1912- 87
    Brief entry 27
    Earlier sketch in SATA 41
    See also SAAS 4
Bennett, Jill (Crawford) 1934- 41
Bennett, John 1865-1956
    See YABC 1
Bennett, Penelope (Agnes) 1938- 94
Bennett, Rachel
    See Hill, Margaret (Ohler)
Bennett, Rainey 1907-1998 15
    Obituary 111
Bennett, Richard 1899- 21
Bennett, Russell H(oradley) 1896- 25

Bennett, Veronica 1953- 178
Bennett, William (John) 1943- 102
Benning, Elizabeth
    See Rice, Bebe Faas
Benny, Mike 1964- 203
Benson, Elizabeth P(olk) 1924- 65
Benson, Kathleen 1947- 183
    Earlier sketches in SATA 62, 111
Benson, Linda M(aria) 1959- 84
Benson, Mildred 1905-2002 100
    Obituary 135
    Earlier sketches in SATA 1, 65, 67
Benson, Mildred Augustine Wirt
    See Benson, Mildred
Benson, Mildred Wirt
    See Benson, Mildred
Benson, Millie
    See Benson, Mildred
Benson, Patrick 1956- 147
Benson, Sally 1900-1972 35
    Obituary 27
    Earlier sketch in SATA 1
Bentley, Judith (McBride) 1945- 89
    Earlier sketch in SATA 40
Bentley, Karen
    See Taschek, Karen
Bentley, Nancy (L.) 1946- 78
Bentley, Nicolas Clerihew 1907-1978
    Obituary 24
Bentley, Phyllis Eleanor 1894-1977 6
    Obituary 25
Bentley, Roy 1947- 46
Bentley, William (George) 1916- 84
Benton, Jim 1963- 172
ben Uzair, Salem
    See Horne, Richard Henry Hengist
Ben-Zvi, Rebeccca Tova
    See O'Connell, Rebecca
Bercaw, Edna Coe 1961- 124
Berck, Judith 1960- 75
Berelson, Howard 1940- 5
Berends, Polly Berrien 1939- 50
    Brief entry 38
Berenstain, Jan 1923- 135
    Earlier sketches in SATA 12, 64, 129
    See also CLR 150
    See also SAAS 20
Berenstain, Janice
    See Berenstain, Jan
Berenstain, Michael 1951- 45
Berenstain, Mike
    See Berenstain, Michael
Berenstain, Stan 1923-2005 135
    Obituary 169
    Earlier sketches in SATA 12, 64, 129
    See also CLR 150
    See also SAAS 20
Berenstain, Stanley
    See Berenstain, Stan
Berenzy, Alix 1957- 168
    Earlier sketch in SATA 65
Beresford, Elisabeth 1928- 141
    Earlier sketches in SATA 25, 86
    See also SAAS 20
Berg, Adriane G(ilda) 1948- 152
Berg, Dave
    See Berg, David
Berg, David 1920-2002 27
    Obituary 137
Berg, Elizabeth 1948- 104
Berg, Jean Horton 1913-1995 6
Berg, Joan
    See Victor, Joan Berg
Berg, Ron 1952- 48
Bergaust, Erik 1925-1978 20
Bergel, Colin J. 1963- 137
Bergen, Joyce 1949- 95
Berger, Barbara (Helen) 1945- 77
Berger, Carin 185
Berger, Gilda 1935- 88
    Brief entry 42

Berger, Josef 1903-1971 36
Berger, Lou 1950- 213
Berger, Melvin H. 1927- 158
    Autobiography Feature 124
    Earlier sketches in SATA 5, 88
    See also CLR 32
    See also SAAS 2
Berger, Phil 1942-2001 62
Berger, Samantha (Allison) 1969- 140
Berger, Terry 1933- 8
Bergey, Alyce 1934- 45
Bergey, Alyce Mae
    See Bergey, Alyce
Bergin, Mark 1961- 160
    Earlier sketch in SATA 114
Berglin, Ruth Marie 1970- 181
Bergman, Donna 1934- 73
Bergman, Mara 1956- 196
Bergman, Tamar 1939- 95
Bergren, Lisa T.
    See Bergren, Lisa Tawn
Bergren, Lisa Tawn 200
Bergsma, Jody Lynn 163
Bergstein, Rita M. 211
Bergum, Constance R. 1952- 208
    Earlier sketch in SATA 121
Berk, Ari 208
Berkebile, Fred D(onovan) 1900-1978
    Obituary 26
Berkeley, Jon 1962- 204
Berkes, Marianne 173
Berkey, Barry Robert 1935- 24
Berkowitz, Freda Pastor 1908-1994 12
Berkus, Clara Widess 1909- 78
Berlan, Kathryn Hook 1946- 78
Berlfein, Judy Reiss 1958- 79
Berlin, Eric 1968- 195
Berliner, Don 1930- 33
Berliner, Franz 1930- 13
Berlitz, Charles (L. Frambach) 1914-2003 ... 32
    Obituary 151
Berman, Linda 1948- 38
Berman, Paul (Lawrence) 1949- 66
Berna, Paul 1910-1994 15
    Obituary 78
    See also CLR 19
Bernadette
    See Watts, (Anna) Bernadette
Bernard, Bruce 1928-2000 78
    Obituary 124
Bernard, George I. 1949- 39
Bernard, Jacqueline (de Sieyes) 1921-1983 ... 8
    Obituary 45
Bernard, Patricia 1942- 181
    Earlier sketch in SATA 106
Bernard, Trish
    See Bernard, Patricia
Bernardin, James (B.) 1966- 112
Bernardo, Anilu 184
Bernards, Neal 1963- 71
Bernasconi, Pablo 1973- 183
Bernays, Anne 1930- 32
Berner, Rotraut Susanne 1948- 214
Bernhard, Durga T. 1961- 80
Bernhard, Emery 1950- 80
Bernheimer, Kate 201
Bernier-Grand, Carmen T. 1947- 202
Bernstein, Daryl (Evan) 1976- 81
Bernstein, Joanne E(ckstein) 1943- 15
Bernstein, Margery 1933- 114
Bernstein, Nina 1949- 180
Bernstein, Theodore M(enline) 1904-1979 ... 12
    Obituary 27
Berrien, Edith Heal
    See Heal, Edith
Berrill, Jacquelyn (Batsel) 1905- 12
Berrington, John
    See Brownjohn, Alan
Berry, B. J.
    See Berry, Barbara J.
Berry, Barbara J. 1937- 7

Berry, Erick
  See Best, (Evangel) Allena Champlin
Berry, Holly 1957- 210
Berry, James 1924- 110
  Earlier sketch in SATA 67
  See also CLR 143
Berry, Jane Cobb 1915(?)-1979
  Obituary 22
Berry, Joy 1944- 58
  Brief entry 46
Berry, Joy Wilt
  See Berry, Joy
Berry, Lynne 190
Berry, William D(avid) 1926- 14
Bersani, Shennen 1961- 164
Berson, Harold 1926- 4
Bertagna, Julie 1962- 151
Bertholf, Bret 189
Bertin, Charles-Francois
  See Berlitz, Charles (L. Frambach)
Bertolet, Paul
  See McLaughlin, Frank
Berton, Pierre (Francis de Marigny)
  1920-2004 99
  Obituary 158
Bertrand, Cecile 1953- 76
Bertrand, Diane Gonzales 1956- 177
  Earlier sketch in SATA 106
Bertrand, Lynne 1963- 164
  Earlier sketch in SATA 81
Beskow, Elsa (Maartman) 1874-1953 20
  See also CLR 17
Bess, Clayton
  See Locke, Robert
Besson, Luc 1959- 199
Best, (Evangel) Allena Champlin 1892-1974 . 2
  Obituary 25
Best, Cari 1951- 200
  Earlier sketches in SATA 107, 149
Best, (Oswald) Herbert 1894-1980 2
Bestall, A(lfred) E(dmeades) 1892-1986 97
  Obituary 48
Betancourt, Jeanne 1941- 148
  Brief entry 43
  Earlier sketches in SATA 55, 96
Beth, Mary
  See Miller, Mary Beth
Bethancourt, T. Ernesto
  See Paisley, Tom
Bethel, Dell 1929- 52
Bethell, Jean (Frankenberry) 1922- 8
Bethers, Ray 1902-1973 6
Bethke, Bruce Raymond 1955- 114
Bethlen, T.D.
  See Silverberg, Robert
Bethune, J. G.
  See Ellis, Edward S.
Bethune, J. H.
  See Ellis, Edward S.
Betteridge, Anne
  See Potter, Margaret
Betteridge, Deirdre 214
Bettina
  See Ehrlich, Bettina Bauer
Bettmann, Otto Ludwig 1903-1998 46
Bettoli, Delana 187
Betts, James
  See Haynes, Betsy
Betz, Eva Kelly 1897-1968 10
Bevan, Tom 1868-1930(?)
  See YABC 2
Bevis, Mary 1939- 202
Bewick, Thomas 1753-1828 16
Beyer, Audrey White 1916- 9
Beyer, Paul J. III 1950- 74
Beynon, John
  See Harris, John (Wyndham Parkes Lucas)
  Beynon
Bezencon, Jacqueline (Buxcel) 1924- 48
Bhatia, Jamunadevi 1919- 48

Bhatia, June
  See Bhatia, Jamunadevi
Bial, Morrison David 1917- 62
Bial, Raymond 1948- 165
  Earlier sketches in SATA 76, 116
Biala
  See Brustlein, Janice Tworkov
Biale, Rachel 1952- 99
Bialk, Elisa
  See Krautter, Elisa (Bialk)
Bianchi, John 1947- 91
Bianchi, Robert S(teven) 1943- 92
Bianco, Margery
  See Bianco, Margery Williams
Bianco, Margery Williams 1881-1944 15
  See also CLR 146
Bianco, Pamela 1906- 28
Bibby, Violet 1908-1996 24
Bible, Charles 1937- 13
Bibo, Bobette
  See Gugliotta, Bobette
Bice, Clare 1909-1976 22
Bickerstaff, Isaac
  See Swift, Jonathan
Bidner, Jenni 1963- 193
Biegel, Paul 1925- 79
  Earlier sketch in SATA 16
  See also CLR 27
  See also SAAS 18
Biemiller, Carl L(udwig), Jr.) 1912-1979 40
  Obituary 21
Bienenfeld, Florence L(ucille) 1929- 39
Bierhorst, John (William) 1936- 149
  Autobiography Feature 149
  Earlier sketches in SATA 6, 91
  See also SAAS 10
Biggar, Joan R. 1936- 120
Biggar, Joan Rawlins
  See Biggar, Joan R.
Biggle, Lloyd, Jr. 1923-2002 65
Biggs, Brian 1968- 192
Bilal, Abdel W(ahab) 1970- 92
Bilbrough, Norman 1941- 111
Bildner, Phil 173
Bileck, Marvin 1920- 40
Bilibin, Ivan (Iakolevich) 1876-1942 61
Bill, Alfred Hoyt 1879-1964 44
Billam, Rosemary 1952- 61
Billings, Charlene W(interer) 1941- 41
Billingsley, Franny 1954- 132
Billington, Elizabeth T(hain) 50
  Brief entry 43
Billout, Guy (Rene) 1941- 144
  Earlier sketch in SATA 10
  See also CLR 33
Bilson, Geoffrey 1938-1987 99
Binch, Caroline (Lesley) 1947- 140
  Earlier sketch in SATA 81
Bing, Christopher (H.) 126
Bingham, Caroline 1962- 158
Bingham, Jane M. 1941- 163
Bingham, Jane Marie
  See Bingham, Jane M.
Bingham, Janet 1959- 200
Bingham, Kelly 1967- 207
Bingham, Sam(uel A.) 1944- 96
Bingley, Margaret (Jane Kirby) 1947- 72
Binkley, Anne
  See Rand, Ann (Binkley)
Binzen, Bill
  See Binzen, William
Binzen, William 24
Birch, David (W.) 1913-1996 89
Birch, Reginald B(athurst) 1856-1943 19
Birchman, David 1949- 72
Birchmore, Daniel A. 1951- 92
Bird, Carmel 1940- 124
Bird, E(lzy) J(ay) 1911- 58
Birdsall, Jeanne 1952(?)- 170
Birdseye, Tom 1951- 148
  Earlier sketches in SATA 66, 98

Birenbaum, Barbara 1941- 65
Birmingham, Lloyd P(aul) 1924- 83
  Earlier sketch in SATA 12
Birmingham, Ruth
  See Sorrells, Walter
Birney, Betty G. 1947- 169
  Earlier sketch in SATA 98
Biro, B.
  See Biro, B. S.
Biro, B. S. 1921- 1
  See also CLR 28
  See also SAAS 13
Biro, Val
  See Biro, B. S.
Bischoff, Julia Bristol 1899-1970 12
Bishop, Bonnie 1943- 37
Bishop, Claire Huchet 1899(?)-1993 14
  Obituary 74
  See also CLR 80
Bishop, Courtney
  See Ruemmler, John D(avid)
Bishop, Curtis (Kent) 1912-1967 6
Bishop, Elizabeth 1911-1979
  Obituary 24
Bishop, Gavin 1946- 144
  Earlier sketch in SATA 97
Bishop, Kathleen Wong 1954- 120
Bishop, Kathy
  See Bishop, Kathleen Wong
Bishop, Nic 1955- 161
  Earlier sketch in SATA 107
Bisset, Donald 1910-1995 86
  Earlier sketch in SATA 7
Bisson, Terry 1942- 99
Bisson, Terry Ballantine
  See Bisson, Terry
Bitter, Gary G(len) 1940- 22
Bixby, William (Courtney) 1920-1986 6
  Obituary 47
Bjoerk, Christina 1938- 99
  Earlier sketch in SATA 67
  See also CLR 22
Bjork, Christina
  See Bjoerk, Christina
Bjorklund, Lorence F. 1913-1978 35
  Brief entry 32
Bjorkman, Steve 163
Blabey, Aaron 1975(?)- 214
Black, Algernon David 1900-1993 12
  Obituary 76
Black, Holly 1971- 210
  Earlier sketch in SATA 147
Black, Irma Simonton 1906-1972 2
  Obituary 25
Black, Mansell
  See Trevor, Elleston
Black, MaryAnn
  See Easley, MaryAnn
Black, Susan Adams 1953- 40
Blackall, Bernie 1956- 126
Blackall, Sophie 182
Blackburn, Claire
  See Altman, Linda Jacobs
Blackburn, John(ny) Brewton 1952- 15
Blackburn, Joyce Knight 1920- 29
Blacker, Terence 1948- 194
Blacker, Tina
  See Louise, Tina
Blackett, Veronica Heath 1927- 12
Blackie, Jean Cutler 1943- 79
Blacklin, Malcolm
  See Chambers, Aidan
Blacklock, Dyan 1951- 112
Blackman, Malorie 1962- 196
  Earlier sketches in SATA 83, 128
Blackton, Peter
  See Wilson, Lionel
Blackwood, Alan 1932- 70
Blackwood, Freya 199
Blackwood, Gary
  See Blackwood, Gary L.

Blackwood, Gary L. 1945- 169
  Earlier sketches in SATA 72, 118
Blade, Alexander
  See Garrett, Randall
  and Hamilton, Edmond
  and Silverberg, Robert
Blades, Ann (Sager) 1947- 69
  Earlier sketch in SATA 16
  See also CLR 15
Bladow, Suzanne Wilson 1937- 14
Blaine, Chris
  See Gardner, Craig Shaw
Blaine, John
  See Goodwin, Harold L(eland)
Blaine, Marge
  See Blaine, Margery Kay
Blaine, Margery Kay 1937- 11
Blair, Alison
  See Lerangis, Peter
Blair, Anne Denton 1914-1993 46
Blair, David Nelson 1954- 80
Blair, Eric
  See Orwell, George
Blair, Jay 1953- 45
Blair, Lucile
  See Yeakley, Marjory Hall
Blair, Margaret Whitman 1951- 124
Blair, Mary 1911-1978 195
Blair, Pauline Hunter
  See Clarke, Pauline
Blair, Ruth Van Ness 1912-1999 12
Blair, Shannon
  See Kaye, Marilyn
Blair, Walter 1900-1992 12
  Obituary 72
Blaisdell, Bob
  See Blaisdell, Robert
Blaisdell, Robert 1959- 105
Blake, Bronwyn 1940- 149
Blake, Francis 198
Blake, Jon 1954- 171
  Earlier sketch in SATA 78
Blake, Olive
  See Supraner, Robyn
Blake, Quentin 1932- 211
  Earlier sketches in SATA 9, 52, 96, 125
  See also CLR 31
Blake, Robert 1949- 42
Blake, Robert J. 160
Blake, Walker E.
  See Griffin, W.E.B.
Blake, William 1757-1827 30
  See also CLR 52
Blakely, Gloria 1950- 139
Blakely, Roger K. 1922- 82
Blakeney, Jay D.
  See Chester, Deborah
Blakey, Nancy 1955- 94
Blanc, Esther S. 1913-1997 66
Blanc, Mel 1908-1989
  Obituary 64
Blanchard, Patricia 125
Blanchet, M(uriel) Wylie 1891-1961 106
Blanco, Richard L(idio) 1926- 63
Bland, E.
  See Nesbit, E.
Bland, Edith Nesbit
  See Nesbit, E.
Bland, Fabian
  See Nesbit, E.
Blane, Gertrude
  See Blumenthal, Gertrude
Blank, Clarissa Mabel 1915-1965 62
Blankenship, LeeAnn 1944- 181
Blassingame, Wyatt Rainey 1909-1985 34
  Obituary 41
  Earlier sketch in SATA 1
Blatchford, Claire H. 1944- 94
Blauer, Ettagale 1940- 49
Bleck, Linda 207
Bledsoe, Glen L. 1951- 108

Bledsoe, Glen Leonard
  See Bledsoe, Glen L.
Bledsoe, Karen E. 1962- 167
  Earlier sketch in SATA 108
Bledsoe, Karen Elizabeth
  See Bledsoe, Karen E.
Bledsoe, Lucy Jane 1957- 162
  Earlier sketch in SATA 97
Bleeker, Sonia
  See Zim, Sonia Bleeker
Blegen, Daniel M. 1950- 92
Blegvad, Erik 1923- 132
  Earlier sketches in SATA 14, 66
Blegvad, Lenore 1926- 176
  Earlier sketches in SATA 14, 66
Bley, Anette 1967- 188
Blish, James 1921-1975 66
Blish, James Benjamin
  See Blish, James
Blishen, Edward (William) 1920-1996 66
  Obituary 93
  Earlier sketch in SATA 8
Bliss, Corinne Demas 1947- 131
  Earlier sketch in SATA 37
  See Demas, Corinne
Bliss, Frederick
  See Card, Orson Scott
Bliss, Gillian
  See Paton Walsh, Jill
Bliss, Harry 1964- 196
  Earlier sketch in SATA 156
Bliss, Reginald
  See Wells, H. G.
Bliss, Ronald G(ene) 1942- 12
Blitt, Barry 187
Bliven, Bruce, Jr. 1916-2002 2
Blixen, Karen 1885-1962 44
Blizzard, Gladys S. (?)-1992 79
Blobaum, Cindy 1966- 123
Bloch, Lucienne 1909-1999 10
Bloch, Marie Halun 1910-1998 6
  See also SAAS 9
Bloch, Robert (Albert) 1917-1994 12
  Obituary 82
Bloch, Serge 1956- 213
Blochman, Lawrence G(oldtree)
  1900-1975 22
Block, Francesca Lia 1962- 213
  Earlier sketches in SATA 80, 116, 158
  See also CLR 116
  See also SAAS 21
Block, Irvin 1917- 12
Blomgren, Jennifer (Alice) 1954- 136
Blonder, Terry Joyce
  See Golson, Terry
Blood, Charles Lewis 1929- 28
Bloom, Barbara Lee 1943- 146
Bloom, Freddy 1914-2000 37
  Obituary 121
Bloom, Lloyd 1947- 108
  Brief entry 43
Bloom, Suzanne 1950- 172
Bloomfield, Michaela 1966- 70
Bloor, Edward 1950- 201
  Earlier sketches in SATA 98, 155
Bloor, Edward William
  See Bloor, Edward
Blos, Joan W. 1928- 153
  Autobiography Feature 153
  Brief entry 27
  Earlier sketches in SATA 33, 69, 109
  See also CLR 18
  See also SAAS 11
Blos, Joan Winsor
  See Blos, Joan W.
Blough, Glenn O(rlando) 1907-1995 1
Blue, Rose 1931- 166
  Autobiography Feature 117
  Earlier sketches in SATA 5, 91, 93
  See also SAAS 24

Blue, Zachary
  See Stine, R.L.
Bluemle, Elizabeth 209
Bluggage, Oranthy
  See Alcott, Louisa May
Blumberg, Leda 1956- 59
Blumberg, Rhoda 1917- 123
  Earlier sketches in SATA 35, 70
  See also CLR 21
Blume, Judy 1938- 195
  Earlier sketches in SATA 2, 31, 79, 142
  See also CLR 69
Blume, Judy Sussman
  See Blume, Judy
Blume, Lesley M.M. 1975- 180
Blumenthal, Deborah 204
  Earlier sketch in SATA 161
Blumenthal, Gertrude 1907-1971
  Obituary 27
Blumenthal, Shirley 1943- 46
Blutig, Eduard
  See Gorey, Edward (St. John)
Bly, Janet 1945- 43
Bly, Janet Chester
  See Bly, Janet
Bly, Stephen A(rthur) 1944- 116
  Earlier sketch in SATA 43
Blyler, Allison Lee 1966- 74
Blythe, Gary 1959- 185
Blyton, Carey 1932-2002 9
  Obituary 138
Blyton, Enid 1897-1968 25
  See also CLR 31
Blyton, Enid Mary
  See Blyton, Enid
Bo, Ben
  See Richardson, V.A.
Boardman, Fon Wyman, Jr. 1911-2000 6
Boardman, Gwenn R.
  See Petersen, Gwenn Boardman
Boase, Wendy 1944-1999 28
  Obituary 110
Boatner, Mark Mayo III 1921- 29
Bobbe, Dorothie de Bear 1905-1975 1
  Obituary 25
Bober, Natalie S. 1930- 134
  Earlier sketch in SATA 87
  See also SAAS 23
Bobette, Bibo
  See Gugliotta, Bobette
Bobri, Vladimir V. 1898-1986 47
  Brief entry 32
Bobritsky, Vladimir
  See Bobri, Vladimir V.
Bochak, Grayce 1956- 76
Bock, Hal
  See Bock, Harold I.
Bock, Harold I. 1939- 10
Bock, William Sauts Netamux'we 1939- 14
Bodanis, David 179
Bode, Janet 1943-1999 96
  Obituary 118
  Earlier sketch in SATA 60
Bode, N.E.
  See Baggott, Julianna
Bodecker, N(iels) M(ogens) 1922-1988 73
  Obituary 54
  Earlier sketch in SATA 8
Bodeen, S. A. 1965- 158
  Earlier sketch in SATA 114
Boden, Hilda
  See Bodenham, Hilda Morris
Bodenham, Hilda Morris 1901- 13
Bodett, Thomas Edward 1955- 70
Bodett, Tom
  See Bodett, Thomas Edward
Bodie, Idella F(allaw) 1925- 89
  Earlier sketch in SATA 12
Bodker, Cecil
  See Bodker, Cecil

Bodker, Cecil 1927- *133*
  Earlier sketch in SATA *14*
  See also CLR *23*
Bodsworth, (Charles) Fred(erick) 1918- *27*
Boeckman, Charles 1920- *12*
Boegehold, Betty (Doyle) 1913-1985
  Obituary *42*
Boelts, Maribeth 1964- *200*
  Earlier sketches in SATA *78, 163*
Boerst, William J. 1939- *170*
  Earlier sketch in SATA *121*
Boesch, Mark J(oseph) 1917- *12*
Boesen, Victor 1908- *16*
Bogacki, Tomek 1950- *214*
  Earlier sketch in SATA *138*
Bogaerts, Gert 1965- *80*
Bogan, Paulette 1960- *201*
  Earlier sketch in SATA *129*
Bogart, Jo Ellen 1945- *92*
  See also CLR *59*
Boggs, Ralph Steele 1901-1994 .... *7*
Bograd, Larry 1953- *89*
  Earlier sketch in SATA *33*
  See also SAAS *21*
Bogue, Gary 1938- *195*
Bogue, Gary L.
  See Bogue, Gary
Bohdal, Susi 1951- *101*
  Earlier sketch in SATA *22*
Bohlen, Nina 1931- *58*
Bohlmeijer, Arno 1956- *94*
Bohner, Charles (Henry) 1927- *62*
Bohnhoff, Maya Kaathryn 1954- *88*
Boiger, Alexandra *178*
Boissard, Janine 1932- *59*
Bojunga, Lygia
  See Nunes, Lygia Bojunga
Bojunga-Nunes, Lygia
  See Nunes, Lygia Bojunga
Bok, Arthur
  See Bok, Chip
Bok, Chip 1952- *205*
Bolam, Emily 1969- *206*
Boland, Janice *98*
Bolden, Tonya 1959- *188*
  Earlier sketches in SATA *79, 138*
Bolden, Tonya Wilyce
  See Bolden, Tonya
Boles, Paul Darcy 1916-1984 .... *9*
  Obituary *38*
Bolian, Polly 1925- *4*
Bollen, Roger 1941(?)- *83*
  Brief entry *29*
Bolliger, Max 1929- *7*
Bollinger, Max 1929- *167*
Bollinger, Peter *172*
Bolognese, Don(ald Alan) 1934- *129*
  Earlier sketches in SATA *24, 71*
Bolognese, Elaine 1933- *23*
Bolotin, Norman (Phillip) 1951- *93*
Bolton, Carole 1926- *6*
Bolton, Elizabeth
  See St. John, Nicole
Bolton, Evelyn
  See Bunting, Eve
Bonar, Veronica
  See Bailey, Donna (Veronica Anne)
Bond, B. J.
  See Heneghan, James
Bond, Bruce 1939- *61*
Bond, Felicia 1954- *126*
  Earlier sketch in SATA *49*
Bond, Gladys Baker 1912- *14*
Bond, Higgins 1951- *177*
  Earlier sketch in SATA *83*
Bond, J. Harvey
  See Winterbotham, R(ussell) R(obert)
Bond, (Thomas) Michael 1926- *157*
  Earlier sketches in SATA *6, 58*
  See also CLR *95*
  See also SAAS *3*

Bond, Nancy 1945- *159*
  Autobiography Feature *159*
  Earlier sketches in SATA *22, 82*
  See also CLR *11*
  See also SAAS *13*
Bond, Nancy Barbara
  See Bond, Nancy
Bond, Rebecca 1972- *214*
  Earlier sketch in SATA *130*
Bond, Ruskin 1934- *87*
  Earlier sketch in SATA *14*
Bondie, J. D.
  See Cunningham, Chet
Bondoux, Anne-Laure 1971- *175*
Bone, Ian 1956- *158*
  Earlier sketch in SATA *117*
Bonehill, Captain Ralph
  See Stratemeyer, Edward L.
Bonestell, Chesley 1888-1986
  Obituary *48*
Bonham, Barbara Thomas 1926- *7*
Bonham, Frank 1914-1989 .... *49*
  Obituary *62*
  Earlier sketch in SATA *1*
  See also SAAS *3*
Boniface, William 1963- *182*
  Earlier sketch in SATA *102*
Bonino, Louise
  See Williams, Louise Bonino
Bonk, John J. *189*
Bonn, Pat
  See Bonn, Patricia Carolyn
Bonn, Patricia Carolyn 1948- *43*
Bonner, Hannah *197*
Bonner, Mary Graham 1890-1974 .... *19*
Bonner, Mike 1951- *121*
Bonners, Susan 1947- *85*
  Brief entry *48*
Bonnett-Rampersaud, Louise *173*
Bonning, Tony 1948- *169*
Bonsall, Crosby Barbara (Newell)
  1921-1995 .... *23*
  Obituary *84*
Bonsall, Joseph S. 1948- *119*
Bonsignore, Joan 1959- *140*
Bontemps, Arna 1902-1973 .... *44*
  Obituary *24*
  Earlier sketch in SATA *2*
  See also CLR *6*
Bontemps, Arnaud Wendell
  See Bontemps, Arna
Bonzon, Paul-Jacques 1908-1978 .... *22*
Boock, Paula 1964- *134*
Booher, Dianna Daniels 1948- *33*
Book, Rick 1949- *119*
Book, Rita
  See Holub, Joan
Bookman, Charlotte
  See Zolotow, Charlotte
Boon, Debbie 1960- *103*
Boon, Emilie (Laetitia) 1958- *86*
Boone, Charles Eugene
  See Boone, Pat
Boone, Pat 1934- *7*
Booraem, Ellen *211*
Boorman, Linda 1940- *46*
Boorman, Linda Kay
  See Boorman, Linda
Boorstin, Daniel J(oseph) 1914-2004 .... *52*
Boos, Ben 1971- *206*
Booth, Coe *187*
Booth, Ernest Sheldon 1915-1984 .... *43*
Booth, George 1926- *191*
Booth, Graham (Charles) 1935- *37*
Bootman, Colin *159*
Borden, Louise 1949- *190*
  Autobiography Feature *141*
  Earlier sketches in SATA *68, 104, 141*
Bordier, Georgette 1924- *16*
Borgman, James
  See Borgman, Jim

Borgman, James Mark
  See Borgman, Jim
Borgman, Jim 1954- *122*
Borgo, Lacy Finn 1972- *194*
Boring, Mel 1939- *168*
  Earlier sketch in SATA *35*
Borja, Corinne 1929- *22*
Borja, Robert 1923- *22*
Borland, Hal
  See Borland, Harold Glen
Borland, Harold Glen 1900-1978 .... *5*
  Obituary *24*
Borland, Kathryn Kilby 1916- *16*
Borlenghi, Patricia 1951- *79*
Born, Adolf 1930- *49*
Bornstein, Ruth Lercher
  See Bornstein-Lercher, Ruth
Bornstein-Lercher, Ruth 1927- *88*
  Autobiography Feature *107*
  Earlier sketch in SATA *14*
Borski, Lucia Merecka *18*
Borten, Helen Jacobson 1930- *5*
Bortolotti, Dan 1969- *157*
Borton, Elizabeth
  See Trevino, Elizabeth B(orton) de
Borton, Lady 1942- *98*
Borton de Trevino, Elizabeth
  See Trevino, Elizabeth B(orton) de
Bortstein, Larry 1942-2010 .... *16*
Bortz, Alfred B(enjamin) 1944- *139*
  Earlier sketch in SATA *74*
Bortz, Fred
  See Bortz, Alfred B(enjamin)
Bosch, Pseudonymous *199*
Bosco, Jack
  See Holliday, Joseph
Boshell, Gordon 1908-1991 .... *15*
Boshinski, Blanche 1922- *10*
Bosman, Paul 1929- *107*
Bosse, Malcolm (Joseph, Jr.) 1926-2002 .... *136*
  Earlier sketch in SATA *35*
Bosserman, (Charles) Phillip 1931- *84*
Bossom, Naomi 1933- *35*
Bostock, Mike 1962- *114*
Boston, L(ucy) M(aria Wood) 1892-1990 .... *19*
  Obituary *64*
  See also CLR *3*
Bostrom, Kathleen (Susan) Long 1954- *139*
Bostrom, Kathy
  See Bostrom, Kathleen (Susan) Long
Boswell, Addie *208*
Boswell, Addie Kay
  See Boswell, Addie
Bosworth, J. Allan 1925- *19*
Bothwell, Jean (?)-1977 .... *2*
Botkin, B(enjamin) A(lbert) 1901-1975 .... *40*
Botsford, Ward 1927-2004 .... *66*
Botting, Douglas (Scott) 1934- *43*
Bottner, Barbara 1943- *170*
  Autobiography Feature *121*
  Earlier sketches in SATA *14, 93*
  See also SAAS *26*
Bottone, Frank G., Jr. 1969- *141*
Bouchard, David 1952- *213*
  Earlier sketch in SATA *117*
Boucher, (Clarence) Carter 1954- *129*
Boudelang, Bob
  See Pell, Ed(ward)
Boughton, Richard 1954- *75*
Boulet, Susan Seddon 1941- *50*
Boulle, Pierre (Francois Marie-Louis)
  1912-1994 .... *22*
  Obituary *78*
Boulton, Jane 1921- *91*
Bouma, Paddy 1947- *128*
Bour, Daniele 1939- *62*
Bourbonniere, Sylvie 1966- *182*
Bourdon, David 1934-1998 .... *46*
Bourgeois, Paulette 1951- *153*
Bourne, Lesley
  See Marshall, Evelyn

Bourne, Miriam Anne 1931-1989 .... *16*
   Obituary *63*
Boutavant, Marc 1970- *200*
Boutet de Monvel, (Louis) M(aurice)
   1850(?)-1913 .... *30*
   See also CLR *32*
Bouwman, Heather M.
   See Bouwman, H.M.
Bouwman, H.M. *209*
Bova, Ben 1932- *133*
   Earlier sketches in SATA *6, 68*
   See also CLR *96*
Bova, Benjamin William
   See Bova, Ben
Bovaird, Anne E(lizabeth) 1960- *90*
Bow, Patricia 1946- *168*
Bowden, Joan Chase 1925- *51*
   Brief entry *38*
Bowe, Julie 1962- *194*
Bowen, Alexandria Russell *97*
Bowen, Andy Russell
   See Bowen, Alexandria Russell
Bowen, Anne 1952- *202*
   Earlier sketch in SATA *170*
Bowen, Betty Morgan
   See West, Betty
Bowen, Catherine (Shober) Drinker
   1897-1973 .... *7*
Bowen, David
   See Bowen, Joshua David
Bowen, Fred 1953- *136*
Bowen, Joshua David 1930- *22*
Bowen, Rhys
   See Quin-Harkin, Janet
Bowen, Robert Sydney 1900-1977 .... *52*
   Obituary *21*
Bowermaster, Jon 1954- *135*
   Earlier sketch in SATA *77*
Bowers, Terrell L. 1945- *101*
Bowers, Terry
   See Bowers, Terrell L.
Bowers, Tim *185*
Bowie, C. W.
   See Old, Wendie C(orbin)
   and Wirths, Claudine (Turner) G(ibson)
Bowie, Jim
   See Norwood, Victor G(eorge) C(harles)
   and Stratemeyer, Edward L.
Bowkett, Stephen 1953- *67*
Bowler, Jan Brett
   See Brett, Jan
Bowler, Tim 1953- *209*
   Earlier sketch in SATA *149*
Bowman, Catherine
   See Smith, Cat Bowman
Bowman, Crystal 1951- *105*
Bowman, James Cloyd 1880-1961 .... *23*
Bowman, John S(tewart) 1931- *16*
Bowman, Kathleen (Gill) 1942- *52*
   Brief entry *40*
Bowman, Leslie
   See Bowman, Leslie W.
Bowman, Leslie W. *182*
Bowsher, Melodie *195*
Boxall, Ed *178*
Boyce, Frank Cottrell *182*
Boyce, George A(rthur) 1898- *19*
Boyd, Candy Dawson 1946- *72*
   See also CLR *50*
Boyd, Pauline
   See Schock, Pauline
Boyd, Selma
   See Acuff, Selma Boyd
Boyd, Waldo T. 1918- *18*
Boyden, Linda 1948- *143*
Boyer, Allen B. 1963- *153*
Boyer, Robert E(rnst) 1929- *22*
Boyes, Vivien 1952- *106*
Boyes, Vivien Elizabeth
   See Boyes, Vivien
Boyle, Ann (Peters) 1916- *10*

Boyle, Eleanor Vere (Gordon) 1825-1916 .... *28*
Boyle, Robert H. 1928- *65*
Boylston, Helen Dore 1895-1984 .... *23*
   Obituary *39*
Boyne, John 1971- *181*
Boynton, Sandra (Keith) 1953- *152*
   Brief entry *38*
   Earlier sketches in SATA *57, 107*
   See also CLR *105*
Boz
   See Dickens, Charles
Braasch, Gary *201*
Bracken, Charles
   See Pellowski, Michael (Joseph)
Brackers de Hugo, Pierre 1960- *115*
Brackett, Dolli Tingle 1911-1993 .... *137*
Brackett, Virginia 1950- *166*
   Earlier sketch in SATA *121*
Brackett, Virginia Roberts Meredith
   See Brackett, Virginia
Bradbury, Bianca (Ryley) 1908-1982 .... *56*
   Earlier sketch in SATA *3*
Bradbury, Edward P.
   See Moorcock, Michael
Bradbury, Ray 1920- *123*
   Earlier sketches in SATA *11, 64*
Bradbury, Ray Douglas
   See Bradbury, Ray
Bradby, Marie *161*
Bradfield, Carl 1942- *91*
Bradford, Ann (Liddell) 1917- *56*
   Brief entry *38*
Bradford, Barbara Taylor 1933- *66*
Bradford, Chris 1974- *215*
Bradford, Karleen 1936- *96*
   Earlier sketch in SATA *48*
Bradford, Lois J(ean) 1936- *36*
Bradford, Richard (Roark) 1932-2002 .... *59*
   Obituary *135*
Bradley, Duane
   See Sanborn, Duane
Bradley, Kimberly Brubaker 1967- *179*
Bradley, Marion Zimmer 1930-1999 .... *139*
   Obituary *116*
   Earlier sketch in SATA *90*
Bradley, Timothy J. *193*
Bradley, Virginia 1912- *23*
Bradley, Will
   See Strickland, Brad
Bradman, Tony 1954- *152*
   Earlier sketch in SATA *81*
Bradshaw, Gillian (Joan) 1949- *118*
Bradshaw, Gillian 1956- *127*
Bradshaw, Gillian Marucha
   See Bradshaw, Gillian
Bradstreet, T. J.
   See Thesman, Jean
Brady, Esther Wood 1905-1987 .... *31*
   Obituary *53*
Brady, Irene 1943- *4*
Brady, Kimberley S. 1953- *101*
Brady, Kimberley Smith
   See Brady, Kimberley S.
Brady, Lillian 1902- *28*
Bragdon, Elspeth MacDuffie 1897-1980 ...... *6*
Bragdon, Lillian Jacot *24*
Brager, Bruce L. 1949- *146*
Bragg, Mabel Caroline 1870-1945 .... *24*
Bragg, Michael 1948- *46*
Bragg, Ruth Gembicki 1943- *77*
Brahm, Sumishta 1954- *58*
Brailsford, Frances
   See Wosmek, Frances
Brainerd, John W(hiting) 1918- *65*
Braithwaite, Althea 1940- *23*
   Autobiography Feature *119*
   See also SAAS *24*
Bram, Elizabeth 1948- *30*
Brancato, Robin F. 1936- *97*
   See also CLR *32*
   See also SAAS *9*

Brancato, Robin Fidler
   See Brancato, Robin F.
Branch, Muriel Miller 1943- *152*
   Earlier sketch in SATA *94*
Brand, Christianna
   See Lewis, Mary
Brand, Rebecca
   See Charnas, Suzy McKee
Brande, Robin *194*
Brandel, Marc 1919- *71*
Brandenberg, Alexa (Demetria) 1966- *97*
Brandenberg, Aliki 1929- *157*
   Earlier sketches in SATA *2, 35, 75, 113*
   See also CLR *71*
Brandenberg, Franz 1932- *75*
   Earlier sketches in SATA *8, 35*
Brandenburg, Jim 1945- *87*
Brandhorst, Carl T(heodore) 1898-1988 ...... *23*
Brandis, Marianne 1938- *149*
   Earlier sketches in SATA *59, 96*
Brandon, Brumsic, Jr. 1927- *9*
Brandon, Curt
   See Bishop, Curtis (Kent)
Brandreth, Gyles 1948- *28*
Brandreth, Gyles Daubeney
   See Brandreth, Gyles
Brandt, Catharine 1905-1997 .... *40*
Brandt, Keith
   See Sabin, Louis
Brandt, Sue R(eading) 1916- *59*
Branfield, John (Charles) 1931- *11*
Branford, Henrietta 1946-1999 .... *106*
Branley, Franklyn M(ansfield) 1915-2002 .. *136*
   Earlier sketch in SATA *4, 68*
   See also CLR *13*
   See also SAAS *16*
Brannen, Sarah S. *202*
Branscum, Robbie (Tilley) 1937-1997 .... *72*
   Obituary *96*
   Earlier sketch in SATA *23*
   See also SAAS *17*
Bransom, (John) Paul 1885-1979 .... *43*
Brashares, Ann 1967- *188*
   Earlier sketch in SATA *145*
   See also CLR *113*
Brassard, France 1963- *186*
Braswell, E.J.
   See Lynn, Tracy
Braswell, Elizabeth J.
   See Lynn, Tracy
Braswell, Liz
   See Lynn, Tracy
Bratton, Helen 1899-1986 .... *4*
Bratun, Katy 1950- *160*
   Earlier sketch in SATA *83*
Braude, Michael 1936- *23*
Braun, Lilian Jackson 1916(?)- *109*
Brautigan, Richard 1935-1984 .... *56*
Brautigan, Richard Gary
   See Brautigan, Richard
Bray, Libba *203*
   Earlier sketch in SATA *159*
Bray, Martha E.
   See Bray, Libba
Braymer, Marjorie Elizabeth 1911-1988 ...... *6*
Breathed, Berke 1957- *161*
   Earlier sketch in SATA *86*
Breathed, Berkeley
   See Breathed, Berke
Breathed, Guy Berkeley
   See Breathed, Berke
Brecht, Edith 1895-1975 .... *6*
   Obituary *25*
Breck, Vivian
   See Breckenfeld, Vivian Gurney
Breckenfeld, Vivian Gurney 1895-1992 .... *1*
Breda, Tjalmar
   See DeJong, David C(ornel)
Bredeson, Carmen 1944- *163*
   Earlier sketch in SATA *98*
Breen, Steve 1970- *186*

Breinburg, Petronella 1927- *11*
  See also CLR *31*
Breisky, William J(ohn) 1928- 22
Brenaman, Miriam *172*
Brennan, Caitlin
  See Tarr, Judith
Brennan, Gale (Patrick) 1927- *64*
  Brief entry *53*
Brennan, Herbie 1940- *214*
  Autobiography Feature *214*
  Earlier sketches in SATA *140, 183*
Brennan, James Herbert
  See Brennan, Herbie
Brennan, Jan
  See Brennan, Herbie
Brennan, J.H.
  See Brennan, Herbie
Brennan, Joseph Lomas 1903-2000 .... *6*
Brennan, Linda Crotta 1952- *130*
Brennan, Tim
  See Conroy, John Wesley
Brennan-Nelson, Denise *203*
Brenner, Anita 1905-1974 .... *56*
Brenner, Barbara (Johnes) 1925- *124*
  Earlier sketches in SATA *4, 42, 76*
  See also SAAS *14*
Brenner, Fred 1920- *36*
  Brief entry *34*
Brent, Hope 1935(?)-1984
  Obituary *39*
Brent, Stuart *14*
Breskin, Jane
  See Zalben, Jane Breskin
Breslin, Theresa *128*
  Autobiography Feature *128*
  Earlier sketch in SATA *70*
Breslow, Maurice 1935- *72*
Breslow, Maurice A
  See Breslow, Maurice
Breslow, Susan 1951- *69*
Brett, Bernard 1925- *22*
Brett, Grace N(eff) 1900-1975 .... *23*
Brett, Jan 1949- *171*
  Earlier sketches in SATA *42, 71, 130*
  See also CLR *27*
Brett, Jan Churchill
  See Brett, Jan
Brett Bowler, Jan
  See Brett, Jan
Brewer, Heather 1973- *196*
Brewer, James D. 1951- *108*
Brewer, Sally King 1947- *33*
Brewster, Benjamin
  See Folsom, Franklin (Brewster)
Brewster, Hugh 1950- *191*
  Earlier sketch in SATA *95*
Brewster, Patience 1952- *97*
Brewton, John E(dmund) 1898-1982 .... *5*
Brian, Janeen (Paulette) 1948- *141*
Briant, Ed *180*
Brick, John 1922-1973 .... *10*
Brickman, Robin D. 1954- *155*
Bride, Nadja
  See Nobisso, Josephine
Bridgers, Sue Ellen 1942- *90*
  Autobiography Feature *109*
  Earlier sketch in SATA *22*
  See also CLR *18*
  See also SAAS *1*
Bridges, Laurie
  See Bruck, Lorraine
Bridges, Ruby (Nell) 1954- *131*
Bridges, William (Andrew) 1901-1984 .... *5*
Bridwell, Norman (Ray) 1928- *138*
  Earlier sketches in SATA *4, 68*
  See also CLR *96*
Brier, Howard M(axwell) 1903-1969 .... *8*
Brierley, (Louise) 1958- *59*
Briggs, Katharine Mary 1898-1980 .... *101*
  Obituary *25*

Briggs, Peter 1921-1975 .... *39*
  Obituary *31*
Briggs, Raymond 1934- *184*
  Earlier sketches in SATA *23, 66, 131*
  See also CLR *10*
Briggs, Raymond Redvers
  See Briggs, Raymond
Bright, Paul 1949- *182*
Bright, Robert Sr.) 1902-1988 .... *63*
  Obituary *60*
  Earlier sketch in SATA *24*
Bright, Robert Douglas
  See Bright, Robert Sr.)
Bright, Sarah
  See Shine, Deborah
Brightfield, Richard 1927- *65*
  Brief entry *53*
Brightfield, Rick
  See Brightfield, Richard
Brighton, Catherine 1943- *206*
  Earlier sketches in SATA *65, 107*
Brignall, Richard 1977(?)- *213*
Brill, Marlene Targ 1945- *124*
  Earlier sketch in SATA *77*
Brimberg, Stanlee 1947- *9*
Brimner, Larry Dane 1949- *170*
  Autobiography Feature *112*
  Earlier sketch in SATA *79*
Brin, David 1950- *65*
Brin, Ruth Firestone 1921- *22*
Brinckloe, Julie 1950- *13*
Brinckloe, Julie Lorraine
  See Brinckloe, Julie
Brindel, June (Rachuy) 1919- *7*
Brindle, Max
  See Fleischman, Sid
Brindze, Ruth 1903-1984 .... *23*
Brink, Carol Ryrie 1895-1981 .... *100*
  Obituary *27*
  Earlier sketches in SATA *1, 31*
  See also CLR *149*
Brinsmead, H. F(ay)
  See Brinsmead, H(esba) F(ay)
Brinsmead, H. F.
  See Brinsmead, H(esba) F(ay)
Brinsmead, H(esba) F(ay) 1922- *78*
  Earlier sketch in SATA *18*
  See also CLR *47*
  See also SAAS *5*
Briquebec, John
  See Rowland-Entwistle, (Arthur) Theodore
  (Henry)
Brisbane, Henry R.
  See Ellis, Edward S.
Brisco, P. A.
  See Matthews, Patricia
Brisco, Patty
  See Matthews, Patricia
  and Matthews, Clayton (Hartley)
Briscoe, Jill (Pauline) 1935- *56*
  Brief entry *47*
Brisley, Joyce Lankester 1896-1978 .... *22*
  Obituary *84*
Brissenden, Connie
  See Brissenden, Constance
Brissenden, Constance 1947- *150*
Brisson, Pat 1951- *177*
  Autobiography Feature *133*
  Earlier sketches in SATA *67, 128, 133*
Britt, Albert 1874-1969
  Obituary *28*
Britt, Dell 1934- *1*
Brittain, Bill
  See Brittain, William
Brittain, C. Dale 1948- *82*
Brittain, William 1930- *76*
  Earlier sketch in SATA *36*
  See also SAAS *7*
Brittingham, Geoffrey (Hugh) 1959- *76*
Brittney, L. *209*

Britton, Kate
  See Stegeman, Janet Allais
Britton, Louisa
  See McGuire, Leslie (Sarah)
Britton, Rick 1952- *82*
Bro, Margueritte (Harmon) 1894-1977 .... *19*
  Obituary *27*
Broach, Elise 1963- *173*
Broadhead, Helen Cross 1913- *25*
Broadway, Hannah *208*
Brochmann, Elizabeth 1938- *41*
Brock, Betty (Carter) 1923-2003 .... *4*
  Obituary *150*
Brock, C(harles) E(dmund) 1870-1938 .... *42*
  Brief entry *32*
Brock, Delia
  See Ephron, Delia
Brock, Emma L(illian) 1886-1974 .... *8*
Brock, H(enry) M(atthew) 1875-1960 .... *42*
Brockett, Eleanor Hall 1913-1967 .... *10*
Brockman, C(hristian) Frank 1902-1985 ...... *26*
Brockmeier, Kevin 1972- *176*
Broda, Ron 1954- *209*
Broderick, Dorothy M. 1929- *5*
Brodeur, Ruth Wallace
  See Wallace-Brodeur, Ruth
Brodie, Sally
  See Cavin, Ruth (Brodie)
Brodsky, Beverly
  See McDermott, Beverly Brodsky
Brody, Wendy
  See Staub, Wendy Corsi
Broekel, Rainer Lothar
  See Broekel, Ray
Broekel, Ray 1923- *38*
Broekstra, Lorette 1964- *189*
  Earlier sketch in SATA *124*
Brogden, Sherryl
  See Jordan, Sherryl
Broger, Achim
  See Broger, Achim
Broger, Achim 1944- *31*
Broida, Marian *154*
Brokamp, Marilyn 1920- *10*
Broman, Fred
  See Moseley, James W(illett)
Bromhall, Winifred *26*
Brommer, Gerald F(rederick) 1927- *28*
Brondfield, Jerome 1913-1998 .... *22*
Brondfield, Jerry
  See Brondfield, Jerome
Bronner, Stephen Eric 1949- *101*
Bronowski, Jacob 1908-1974 .... *55*
Bronson, Alice
  See Watkins, Dawn L.
Bronson, Linda *203*
Bronson, Lynn
  See Lampman, Evelyn Sibley
Bronson, Wilfrid Swancourt 1894-1985
  Obituary *43*
Brook, Judith (Penelope) 1926- *59*
  Brief entry *51*
Brook, Judy
  See Brook, Judith (Penelope)
Brooke, L(eonard) Leslie 1862-1940 .... *17*
  See also CLR *20*
Brooke, William J. 1946- *139*
Brooke-Haven, P.
  See Wodehouse, P. G.
Brooker, Kyrsten *199*
Brookins, Dana 1931- *28*
Brooks, Anita
  See Abramovitz, Anita (Zeltner Brooks)
Brooks, Bill 1939- *59*
Brooks, Bruce 1950- *112*
  Brief entry *53*
  Earlier sketch in SATA *72*
  See also CLR *25*
Brooks, Caryl 1924- *84*
Brooks, Charlotte K(endrick) 1918-1998 ..... *24*
  Obituary *112*

Brooks, Erik 1972- *182*
   Earlier sketch in SATA *152*
Brooks, George
   See Baum, L. Frank
Brooks, Gwendolyn 1917-2000 .... *6*
   Obituary *123*
   See also CLR 27
Brooks, Gwendolyn Elizabeth
   See Brooks, Gwendolyn
Brooks, Jerome 1931- *23*
Brooks, Kevin 1959- *197*
   Earlier sketch in SATA *150*
Brooks, Kevin M.
   See Brooks, Kevin
Brooks, Laurie *209*
Brooks, Lester 1924- *7*
Brooks, Martha 1944- *134*
   Autobiography Feature *134*
   Earlier sketches in SATA *68, 121*
Brooks, Maurice (Graham) 1900- *45*
Brooks, Polly Schoyer 1912- *12*
Brooks, Ron 1948- *212*
   Brief entry *33*
   Earlier sketch in SATA *94*
Brooks, Ronald George
   See Brooks, Ron
Brooks, Terry 1944- *60*
Brooks, Walter R(ollin) 1886-1958 .... *17*
Brooks-Hill, Helen (Mason) 1908-1994 .... *59*
Broome, Errol 1937- *158*
   Earlier sketch in SATA *105*
Brophy, Nannette 1963- *73*
Brosnan, James Patrick 1929- *14*
Brosnan, Jim
   See Brosnan, James Patrick
Brostoff, Anita 1931- *132*
Brothers Grimm
   See Grimm, Jacob Ludwig Karl
   and Grimm, Wilhelm Karl
Brothers Hildebrandt, The
   See Hildebrandt, Greg
   and Hildebrandt, Tim
Broun, Emily
   See Sterne, Emma Gelders
Brouwer, S. W.
   See Brouwer, Sigmund (W.)
Brouwer, Sigmund (W.) 1959- *109*
Brow, Thea 1934- *60*
Brower, Millicent *8*
Brower, Pauline 1929- *22*
Browin, Frances Williams 1898-1986 .... *5*
Brown, Alexis
   See Baumann, Amy Beeching
Brown, Anne Ensign 1937- *61*
Brown, Beverly Swerdlow *97*
Brown, Bill
   See Brown, William L(ouis)
Brown, Billye Walker
   See Cutchen, Billye Walker
Brown, Bob
   See Brown, Robert Joseph
Brown, Buck 1936- *45*
Brown, Calef *179*
Brown, Cassie 1919-1986 .... *55*
Brown, Charlotte Lewis *181*
Brown, Conrad 1922- *31*
Brown, Craig McFarland 1947- *73*
Brown, David
   See Brown, David A(lan)
   and Myller, Rolf
Brown, Dee 1908-2002 .... *110*
   Obituary *141*
   Earlier sketch in SATA *5*
Brown, Dee Alexander
   See Brown, Dee
Brown, Don 1949- *200*
   Earlier sketch in SATA *172*
Brown, Drew T. III 1955- *83*
Brown, Drollene P. 1939- *53*
Brown, Elbrite *198*
Brown, Eleanor Frances 1908-1987 .... *3*

Brown, Elizabeth Ferguson 1937- *153*
Brown, Elizabeth M(yers) 1915- *43*
Brown, Fern G. 1918- *34*
Brown, (Robert) Fletch 1923- *42*
Brown, Fornan 1901-1996 .... *71*
   Obituary *88*
Brown, George Earl 1883-1964 .... *11*
Brown, George Mackay 1921-1996 .... *35*
Brown, Irene Bennett 1932- *3*
Brown, Irving
   See Adams, William Taylor
Brown, Ivor (John Carnegie) 1891-1974 .... *5*
   Obituary *26*
Brown, Jane Clark 1930- *81*
Brown, Janet Mitsui *87*
Brown, Jo 1964- *170*
Brown, Joanne 1933- *147*
Brown, Joe David 1915-1976 .... *44*
Brown, Joseph E(dward) 1929- *59*
   Brief entry *51*
Brown, Judith Gwyn 1933- *20*
Brown, Kathryn 1955- *168*
   Earlier sketch in SATA *98*
Brown, Kathy
   See Brown, Kathryn
Brown, Ken (James) *129*
Brown, Kevin 1960- *101*
Brown, Laurene Krasny 1945- *99*
   Earlier sketch in SATA *54*
Brown, Laurie Krasny
   See Brown, Laurene Krasny
Brown, Lloyd Arnold 1907-1966 .... *36*
Brown, Mahlon A.
   See Ellis, Edward S.
Brown, Marc (Tolon) 1946- *145*
   Earlier sketches in SATA *10, 53, 80*
   See also CLR 29
Brown, Marcia (Joan) 1918- *47*
   Earlier sketch in SATA *7*
   See also CLR 12
Brown, Margaret Wise 1910-1952 .... *100*
   See also YABC 2
   See also CLR 107
Brown, Margery (Wheeler) *78*
   Earlier sketch in SATA *5*
Brown, Marion Marsh 1908-2001 .... *6*
Brown, Myra Berry 1918- *6*
Brown, Palmer 1919- *36*
Brown, Pamela (Beatrice) 1924-1989 .... *5*
   Obituary *61*
Brown, Peter 1979- *178*
Brown, Rachel W.N. 1947- *203*
Brown, Reeve Lindbergh
   See Lindbergh, Reeve
Brown, Richard E. 1946- *61*
Brown, Robert Joseph 1907-1989 .... *14*
Brown, Roderick (Langmere) Haig-
   See Haig-Brown, Roderick (Langmere)
Brown, Rosalie
   See Moore, Rosalie (Gertrude)
Brown, Roswell
   See Webb, Jean Francis (III)
Brown, Roy (Frederick) 1921-1982 .... *51*
   Obituary *39*
Brown, Ruth 1941- *170*
   Earlier sketch in SATA *105*
Brown, Scott 1971- *134*
Brown, Sue Ellen 1954- *81*
Brown, Tricia 1954- *114*
Brown, Vinson 1912-1991 .... *19*
Brown, Walter R(eed) 1929- *19*
Brown, Will
   See Ainsworth, William Harrison
Brown, William L(ouis) 1910-1964 .... *5*
Browne, Anthony 1946- *163*
   Brief entry *44*
   Earlier sketches in SATA *45, 61, 105*
   See also CLR 19
Browne, Anthony Edward Tudor
   See Browne, Anthony

Browne, Dik
   See Browne, Richard Arthur Allen
Browne, Hablot Knight 1815-1882 .... *21*
Browne, Matthew
   See Rands, William Brighty
Browne, Nicki M.
   See Browne, N.M.
Browne, Nicky Matthews
   See Browne, N.M.
Browne, N.M. 1960- *167*
Browne, Richard Arthur Allen 1917-1989 ... *67*
   Brief entry *38*
Browne, Vee F. 1956- *214*
   Earlier sketch in SATA *90*
Browning, Robert 1812-1889
   See YABC 1
   See also CLR 97
Brownjohn, Alan 1931- *6*
Brownlee, Walter 1930- *62*
Brownlie, Betty 1946- *159*
Brownlow, Kevin 1938- *65*
Brownlow, Mike *183*
Brownridge, William R(oy) 1932- *94*
Broyles, Anne 1953- *201*
Bruce, Dorita Fairlie 1885-1970
   Obituary *27*
Bruce, (William) Harry 1934- *77*
Bruce, Mary 1927- *1*
Bruchac, Joseph III
   See Bruchac, Joseph
Bruchac, Joseph 1942- *176*
   Autobiography Feature *176*
   Earlier sketches in SATA *42, 89, 131*
   See also CLR 46
Bruchac, Margaret M.
   See Bruchac, Marge
Bruchac, Marge *181*
Bruck, Lorraine 1921- *55*
   Brief entry *46*
Bruel, Nick *205*
   Earlier sketch in SATA *166*
Bruel, Robert O. 1929-2002 .... *189*
Bruemmer, Fred 1929- *47*
Brugman, Alyssa (F.) 1974- *152*
Brumbeau, Jeff 1955- *157*
Bruna, Dick 1927- *76*
   Brief entry *30*
   Earlier sketch in SATA *43*
   See also CLR 7
Brunhoff, Jean de 1899-1937 .... *24*
   See also CLR 116
Brunhoff, Laurent de 1925- *150*
   Earlier sketches in SATA *24, 71*
   See also CLR 116
Brunkus, Denise *204*
Brunskill, Elizabeth Ann Flatt
   See Flatt, Lizann
Brush, Karen A(lexandra) 1960- *85*
Brussel-Smith, Bernard 1914- *58*
Brust, Steven 1955- *121*
   Earlier sketch in SATA *86*
Brust, Steven K. Zoltan
   See Brust, Steven
Brustlein, Daniel 1904- *40*
Brustlein, Janice Tworkov -2000 .... *40*
   Obituary *126*
Brutschy, Jennifer 1960- *84*
Bryan, Ashley 1923- *178*
   Earlier sketches in SATA *31, 72, 132*
   See also CLR 66
Bryan, Ashley F.
   See Bryan, Ashley
Bryan, Dorothy M. 1896(?)-1984
   Obituary *39*
Bryan, Jennifer *190*
Bryan, Sean *192*
Bryant, Bernice (Morgan) 1908-1976 .... *11*
Bryant, Jen 1960- *175*
   Earlier sketch in SATA *94*
Bryant, Jennifer
   See Bryant, Jen

Bryant, Jennifer Fisher
  See Bryant, Jen
Bryant, Laura J. 176
Brychta, Alex 1956- 21
Brynie, Faith H. 1946- 113
Brynie, Faith Hickman
  See Brynie, Faith H.
Bryson, Bernarda 1903-2004 9
Buba, Joy Flinsch 1904- 44
Buchan, Bryan 1945- 36
Buchan, John 1875-1940
  See YABC 2
Buchan, Stuart 1942-1987
  Obituary 54
Buchanan, Debby 1952- 82
Buchanan, Deborah Leevonne
  See Buchanan, Debby
Buchanan, Jane 1956- 160
Buchanan, Paul 1959- 116
Buchanan, Sue 1939- 139
Buchheimer, Naomi Barnett
  See Barnett, Naomi
Buchignani, Walter 1965- 84
Buchmann, Stephen L. 194
Buchwald, Art 1925-2007 10
Buchwald, Arthur
  See Buchwald, Art
Buchwald, Emilie 1935- 7
Buck, Gisela 1941- 101
Buck, Lewis 1925- 18
Buck, Margaret Waring 1905-1997 3
Buck, Nola
  See Godwin, Laura
Buck, Pearl S. 1892-1973 25
  Earlier sketch in SATA *1*
Buck, Pearl Sydenstricker
  See Buck, Pearl S.
Buck, Siegfried 1941- 101
Buckalew, Clare B.
  See Dunkle, Clare B.
Buckeridge, Anthony (Malcolm)
  1912-2004 85
  Earlier sketch in SATA *6*
Buckholtz, Eileen (Garber) 1949- 54
  Brief entry 47
Buckingham, Royce 1966- 210
Buckingham, Royce Scott
  See Buckingham, Royce
Buckler, Ernest 1908-1984 47
Buckless, Andrea K. 1968- 117
Buckley, Helen E(lizabeth) 1918- 90
  Earlier sketch in SATA *2*
Buckley, James, Jr. 1963- 166
  Earlier sketch in SATA *114*
Buckley, Michael 177
Buckley, Susan 184
Buckley, Susan Washburn
  See Buckley, Susan
Buckley-Archer, Linda 185
Buckmaster, Henrietta
  See Stephens, Henrietta Henkle
Bucks, Brad
  See Holub, Joan
Budd, E. S.
  See Sirimarco, Elizabeth
Budd, Lillian (Peterson) 1897-1989 7
Budhos, Marina 173
Buehler, Stephanie Jona 1956- 83
Buehner, Caralyn (M.) 1963- 159
  Earlier sketch in SATA *104*
Buehner, Mark 1959- 159
  Earlier sketch in SATA *104*
Buehr, Walter Franklin 1897-1971 3
Buell, Ellen Lewis
  See Cash, Ellen Lewis Buell
Buell, Janet 1952- 185
  Earlier sketch in SATA *106*
Buergel, Paul-Hermann H. 1949- 83
Buettner, Dan 1960- 95
Buff, Conrad 1886-1975 19
Buff, Mary (E. Marsh) 1890-1970 19

Buffett, Jimmy 1946- 110
  Earlier sketch in SATA *76*
Buffie, Margaret 1945- 161
  Earlier sketches in SATA *71, 107*
  See also CLR 39
Bugbee, Emma 1888(?)-1981
  Obituary 29
Bugni, Alice 1951- 122
Buhhos, Marina Tamar
  See Budhos, Marina
Bujold, Lois McMaster 1949- 136
Bulfinch, Thomas 1796-1867 35
Bulion, Leslie 1958- 209
  Earlier sketch in SATA *161*
Bull, Angela (Mary) 1936- 45
Bull, Emma 1954- 190
  Autobiography Feature 103
  Earlier sketch in SATA *99*
Bull, Norman John 1916- 41
Bull, Peter (Cecil) 1912-1984
  Obituary 39
Bull, Schuyler M. 1974- 138
Bulla, Clyde R. 1914-2007 139
  Obituary 182
  Earlier sketches in SATA *2, 41, 91*
  See also SAAS 6
Bullard, Lisa 1961- 142
Buller, Jon 205
Bullock, Kathleen (Mary) 1946- 77
Bullock, Robert (D.) 1947- 92
Bulpin, (Barbara) Vicki 92
Bulwer-Lytton, Edward 1803-1873 23
Bulwer-Lytton, Edward George Earle Lytton
  See Bulwer-Lytton, Edward
Bumstead, Kathleen Mary 1918-1987 53
Bundles, A'Lelia Perry 1952- 76
Bunge, Daniela 1973- 207
Bunin, Catherine 1967- 30
Bunin, Sherry 1925- 30
Bunkers, Suzanne L. 1950- 136
Bunting, A.E.
  See Bunting, Eve
Bunting, Anne Evelyn
  See Bunting, Eve
Bunting, Eve 1928- 196
  Earlier sketches in SATA *18, 64, 110, 158*
  See also CLR 82
Bunting, Glenn (Davison) 1957- 22
Bunyan, John 1628-1688
  See CLR 124
Bupp, Walter
  See Garrett, Randall
Burack, Sylvia K. 1916-2003 35
  Obituary 143
Burbank, Addison (Buswell) 1895-1961 37
Burch, Joann J(ohansen) 75
Burch, Robert J(oseph) 1925- 74
  Earlier sketch in SATA *1*
  See also CLR 63
Burchard, Peter Duncan 1921- 143
  Earlier sketches in SATA *5, 74*
  See also SAAS 13
Burchard, S. H.
  See Burchard, Sue
Burchard, Sue 1937- 22
Burchardt, Nellie 1921- 7
Burckhardt, Marc 1962- 196
Burdett, Lois 117
Burdick, Eugene (Leonard) 1918-1965 22
Burford, Eleanor
  See Hibbert, Eleanor Alice Burford
Burg, Shana 1968- 204
Burgan, Michael 1960- 167
  Earlier sketch in SATA *118*
Burger, Carl 1888-1967 9
Burgess, Ann Marie
  See Gerson, Noel Bertram
Burgess, Barbara Hood 1926- 69
Burgess, Em
  See Burgess, Mary Wyche

Burgess, (Frank) Gelett 1866-1951 32
  Brief entry 30
Burgess, Mark 157
Burgess, Mary Wyche 1916- 18
Burgess, Melvin 1954- 198
  Earlier sketches in SATA *96, 146*
Burgess, Michael
  See Gerson, Noel Bertram
Burgess, Robert F(orrest) 1927- 4
Burgess, Starling
  See Tudor, Tasha
Burgess, Thornton Waldo 1874-1965 17
Burgess, Trevor
  See Trevor, Elleston
Burgwyn, Mebane Holoman 1914-1992 7
Burke, David 1927- 46
Burke, Diana G.
  See Gallagher, Diana G.
Burke, Diana Gallagher
  See Gallagher, Diana G.
Burke, Dianne O'Quinn 1940- 89
Burke, Janine 1952- 139
Burke, Jim 1973- 179
Burke, John
  See O'Connor, Richard
Burke, Katie 1953- 168
Burke, Patrick 1958- 114
Burke, Ralph
  See Garrett, Randall
  and Silverberg, Robert
Burkert, Nancy Ekholm 1933- 24
  See also SAAS 14
Burkett, D. Brent 194
Burke-Weiner, Kimberly 1962- 95
Burks, Brian 1955- 95
Burland, Brian (Berkeley) 1931- 34
Burland, C. A.
  See Burland, Cottie (Arthur)
Burland, Cottie (Arthur) 1905-1983 5
Burleigh, Robert 1936- 193
  Earlier sketches in SATA *55, 98, 146*
Burlingame, (William) Roger 1889-1967 2
Burman, Alice Caddy 1896(?)-1977
  Obituary 24
Burman, Ben Lucien 1896-1984 6
  Obituary 40
Burn, Doris 1923- 1
Burn, Ted
  See Burn, Thomas E.
Burn, Thomas E. 1940- 150
Burnard, Damon 1963- 115
Burnett, Constance Buel 1893-1975 36
Burnett, Frances Eliza Hodgson
  See Burnett, Frances Hodgson
Burnett, Frances Hodgson 1849-1924 100
  See also YABC 2
  See also CLR 122
Burnett, Lindy 210
Burnett Bossi, Lisa 193
Burney, Anton
  See Hopkins, (Hector) Kenneth
Burnford, Sheila (Philip Cochrane Every)
  1918-1984 3
  Obituary 38
  See also CLR 2
Burnham, Gretchen
  See Sprague, Gretchen
Burnham, Nicole 1970- 161
Burnham, Niki
  See Burnham, Nicole
Burnham, Sophy 1936- 65
Burningham, John 1936- 160
  Earlier sketches in SATA *16, 59, 111*
  See also CLR 9
Burningham, Robin Yoko
  See Racoma, Robin Yoko
Burns, Diane L. 1950- 81
  See also SAAS 24
Burns, Eloise Wilkin
  See Wilkin, Eloise
Burns, Florence M. 1905-1988 61

Burns, Khephra 1950- 92
Burns, Loree Griffin 193
Burns, Marilyn 1941- 96
  Brief entry 33
Burns, Olive Ann 1924-1990 65
Burns, Paul C. 5
Burns, Ray
  See Burns, Raymond (Howard)
Burns, Raymond (Howard) 1924- 9
Burns, Theresa 1961- 84
Burns, William A. 1909-1999 5
Burr, Dan 1951- 65
Burr, Lonnie 1943- 47
Burrell, Roy E(ric) C(harles) 1923- 72
Burroughs, Edgar Rice 1875-1950 41
Burroughs, Jean Mitchell 1908- 28
Burroughs, Polly 1925- 2
Burroway, Janet (Gay) 1936- 23
Burstein, Chaya M(alamud) 1923- 64
Burstein, Fred 1950- 83
Burstein, John 1949- 54
  Brief entry 40
Burstein, Stanley M.
  See Burstein, Stanley Mayer
Burstein, Stanley Mayer 1941- 175
Bursztynski, Sue 1953- 114
Burt, Jesse Clifton 1921-1976 46
  Obituary 20
Burt, Olive Woolley 1894-1981 4
Burtinshaw, Julie 185
Burton, Gennett 1945- 95
Burton, Hester (Wood-Hill) 1913-2000 74
  Earlier sketch in SATA 7
  See also CLR 1
  See also SAAS 8
Burton, Leslie
  See McGuire, Leslie (Sarah)
Burton, Marilee Robin 1950- 82
  Earlier sketch in SATA 46
Burton, Maurice 1898-1992 23
Burton, Rebecca 1970- 183
Burton, Robert (Wellesley) 1941- 22
Burton, Virginia Lee 1909-1968 100
  Earlier sketch in SATA 2
  See also CLR 11
Burton, William H(enry) 1890-1964 11
Busby, Ailie 192
Busby, Cylin 1970- 118
Busby, Edith (A. Lake) (?)-1964
  Obituary 29
Busby, John 1942- 209
Buscaglia, (Felice) Leo(nardo) 1924-1998 ... 65
Buscaglia, Leo F.
  See Buscaglia, (Felice) Leo(nardo)
Busch, Phyllis S. 1909- 30
Bush, Anne Kelleher
  See Kelleher, Anne
Bush, Catherine 1961- 128
Bush, Jenna 1981- 208
Bush, Laura 1946- 208
Bushmiller, Ernest Paul 1905-1982 31
Bushmiller, Ernie
  See Bushmiller, Ernest Paul
Bushnell, Jack 1952- 86
Busoni, Rafaello 1900-1962 16
Buss, Helen M.
  See Clarke, Margaret
Busse, Sarah Martin 194
Busselle, Rebecca 1941- 80
Bustard, Anne 1951- 173
Butcher, Kristin 1951- 140
Butenko, Bohdan 1931- 90
Butler, Beverly Kathleen 1932- 7
Butler, Bill
  See Butler, William Vivian
  and Butler, Ernest Alton
  and Butler, William Huxford
Butler, Charles 1963- 175
  Earlier sketch in SATA 121
Butler, Charles Cadman
  See Butler, Charles

Butler, Dori Hillestad 1965- 207
  Earlier sketch in SATA 164
Butler, Dorothy 1925- 73
Butler, Geoff 1945- 94
Butler, M. Christina 1934- 170
  Earlier sketch in SATA 72
Butler, Octavia 1947-2006 84
  See also CLR 65
Butler, Octavia E.
  See Butler, Octavia
Butler, Octavia Estelle
  See Butler, Octavia
Butler, Vivian
  See Butler, William Vivian
Butler, William
  See Butler, William Vivian
Butler, William Vivian 1927-1987 79
Butters, Dorothy Gilman
  See Gilman, Dorothy
Butterworth, Emma Macalik 1928- 43
Butterworth, Nick 1946- 149
  Earlier sketch in SATA 106
Butterworth, Oliver 1915-1990 1
  Obituary 66
Butterworth, W.E.
  See Griffin, W.E.B.
Butterworth, William E.
  See Griffin, W.E.B.
Butterworth, William Edmund III
  See Griffin, W.E.B.
Butts, Ed 1951- 177
Butts, Edward P.
  See Butts, Ed
Butts, Ellen R(ubinstein) 1942- 93
Butzer, C.M. 1974- 212
Buxton, Ralph
  See Silverstein, Alvin
  and Silverstein, Virginia B.
Buzzeo, Toni 1951- 215
  Earlier sketch in SATA 135
Byalick, Marcia 1947- 141
  Earlier sketch in SATA 97
Byard, Carole (Marie) 1941- 57
Byars, Betsy 1928- 163
  Autobiography Feature 108
  Earlier sketches in SATA 4, 46, 80
  See also CLR 72
  See also SAAS 1
Byars, Betsy Cromer
  See Byars, Betsy
Byfield, Barbara Ninde 1930- 8
Byman, Jeremy 1944- 129
Bynum, Janie 133
Byrd, Elizabeth 1912-1989 34
Byrd, Nicole
  See Zach, Cheryl (Byrd)
Byrd, Robert (John) 1942- 158
  Earlier sketches in SATA 33, 112
Byrne, Mary Gregg 1951- 162

C

C. 3. 3.
  See Wilde, Oscar
C. E. M.
  See Mastrangelo, Charles E(lmer)
Cabaniss, J(ames) Allen 1911-1997 5
Cabat, Erni 1914- 74
Cabban, Vanessa 1971- 176
Cable, Mary 1920- 9
Cabot, Meg 1967- 175
  Earlier sketch in SATA 127
  See also CLR 85
Cabot, Meggin
  See Cabot, Meg
Cabot, Meggin Patricia
  See Cabot, Meg
Cabot, Patricia
  See Cabot, Meg

Cabral, O. M.
  See Cabral, Olga
Cabral, Olga 1909- 46
Cabrera, Cozbi A. 1963- 177
Cabrera, Jane 1968- 182
  Earlier sketches in SATA 103, 152
Cabrera, Marcela 1966- 90
Caddy, Alice
  See Burman, Alice Caddy
Cade, Toni
  See Bambara, Toni Cade
Cadmus and Harmonia
  See Buchan, John
Cadnum, Michael 1949- 165
  Earlier sketches in SATA 87, 121
  See also CLR 78
Caduto, Michael J. 1955- 103
Cadwallader, Sharon 1936- 7
Cady, (Walter) Harrison 1877(?)-1970 19
Caffey, Donna (J.) 1954- 110
Cagle, Malcolm W(infield) 1918- 32
Cahn, Rhoda 1922- 37
Cahn, William 1912-1976 37
Cain, Arthur H(omer) 1913-1981 3
Cain, Christopher
  See Fleming, Thomas
Cain, Sheridan 1952- 186
Caine, Geoffrey
  See Walker, Robert W.
Caines, Jeannette (Franklin) 1938- 78
  Brief entry 43
  See also CLR 24
Cairns, Trevor 1922- 14
Calabro, Marian 1954- 79
Caldecott, Moyra 1927- 22
Caldecott, Randolph (J.) 1846-1886 100
  Earlier sketch in SATA 17
  See also CLR 110
Calder, Charlotte 1952- 125
Calder, David 1932-1997 105
Calder, Lyn
  See Calmenson, Stephanie
Calder, Marie D(onais) 1948- 96
Calderone-Stewart, Lisa
  See Calderone-Stewart, Lisa-Marie
Calderone-Stewart, Lisa-Marie 1958- 123
Caldwell, Doreen (Mary) 1942- 71
Caldwell, John C(ope) 1913-1984 7
Caletti, Deb 1963- 171
Calhoun, B. B. 1961- 98
Calhoun, Chad
  See Barrett, Neal, Jr.
  and Cunningham, Chet
  and Goulart, Ron
Calhoun, Dia 1959- 183
  Earlier sketch in SATA 129
Calhoun, Mary
  See Wilkins, Mary Huiskamp
Calhoun, T.B.
  See Bisson, Terry
Cali, Davide 1972- 190
Calif, Ruth 1922- 67
Calkins, Franklin
  See Stratemeyer, Edward L.
Call, Greg 197
Call, Hughie Florence 1890-1969 1
Callahan, Dorothy M. 1934- 39
  Brief entry 35
Callahan, Dorothy Monahan
  See Callahan, Dorothy M.
Callahan, Philip Serna 1923- 25
Callan, Jamie 1954- 59
Callan, Jim 1951- 181
Callaway, Bernice (Anne) 1923- 48
Callaway, Kathy 1943- 36
Callen, Larry
  See Callen, Lawrence Willard, Jr.
Callen, Lawrence Willard, Jr. 1927- 19
Calley, Karin 1965- 92

Calmenson, Stephanie 1952- *211*
    Brief entry *37*
    Earlier sketches in SATA *51, 84, 139*
Calvert, Elinor H.
    See Lasell, Elinor H.
Calvert, John
    See Leaf, (Wilbur) Munro
Calvert, Pam 1966- *205*
Calvert, Patricia 1931- *132*
    Earlier sketches in SATA *45, 69*
    See also SAAS *17*
Camburn, Carol A.
    See Camburn-Bracalente, Carol A.
Camburn-Bracalente, Carol A. 1962- *118*
Cameron, Ann 1943- *129*
    Earlier sketches in SATA *27, 89*
    See also SAAS *20*
Cameron, Edna M. 1905-1999 .... *3*
Cameron, Eleanor (Frances) 1912-1996 .... *25*
    Obituary *93*
    Earlier sketch in SATA *1*
    See also CLR *72*
    See also SAAS *10*
Cameron, Elizabeth
    See Nowell, Elizabeth Cameron
Cameron, Elizabeth Jane 1910-1976 .... *32*
    Obituary *30*
Cameron, Ian
    See Payne, Donald Gordon
Cameron, M(alcolm) G(ordon) Graham
    See Graham-Cameron, M(alcolm) G(ordon)
Cameron, M. Graham
    See Graham-Cameron, M(alcolm) G(ordon)
Cameron, Mike Graham
    See Graham-Cameron, M(alcolm) G(ordon)
Cameron, Polly 1928- *2*
Cameron, Scott 1962- *84*
Camp, Charles L. 1893-1975
    Obituary *31*
Camp, Lindsay 1957- *133*
Camp, Madeleine L'Engle
    See L'Engle, Madeleine
Camp, Walter (Chauncey) 1859-1925
    See YABC *1*
Campbell, (Elizabeth) Andrea 1963- *50*
Campbell, Ann R. 1925- *11*
Campbell, Bill 1960- *89*
Campbell, Bruce
    See Epstein, Samuel
Campbell, Camilla 1905-1992 .... *26*
Campbell, Carole R. 1939- *125*
Campbell, Hope 1925- *20*
Campbell, Hugh 1930- *90*
Campbell, Jane
    See Edwards, Jane Campbell
Campbell, Julie
    See Tatham, Julie Campbell
Campbell, Patricia J(ean) 1930- *45*
Campbell, Patty
    See Campbell, Patricia J(ean)
Campbell, Peter A. 1948- *99*
Campbell, R. W.
    See Campbell, Rosemae Wells
Campbell, Robin
    See Strachan, Ian
Campbell, Rod 1945- *98*
    Brief entry *44*
    Earlier sketch in SATA *51*
Campbell, Rosemae Wells 1909- *1*
Campbell, Sarah C. 1966- *207*
Camper, Cathy 1956- *170*
Campion, Nardi Reeder 1917-2007 .... *22*
Campling, Elizabeth 1948- *53*
Campoy, F. Isabel 1946- *181*
    Earlier sketch in SATA *143*
Camps, Luis 1928- *66*
Canales, Viola 1957- *141*
Candell, Victor 1903-1977
    Obituary *24*
Canfield, Dorothea F.
    See Fisher, Dorothy (Frances) Canfield

Canfield, Dorothea Frances
    See Fisher, Dorothy (Frances) Canfield
Canfield, Dorothy
    See Fisher, Dorothy (Frances) Canfield
Canfield, Jack 1944- *164*
Canfield, Jane White 1897-1984 .... *32*
    Obituary *38*
Canfield, Muriel 1935- *94*
Caniff, Milton 1907-1988
    Obituary *58*
Caniff, Milton Arthur Paul
    See Caniff, Milton
Cann, Helen 1969- *179*
    Earlier sketch in SATA *124*
Cann, Kate 1954- *152*
    Earlier sketch in SATA *103*
Cannan, Joanna
    See Pullein-Thompson, Joanna Maxwell
Cannell, Jon *196*
Cannell, Jonathan C.
    See Cannell, Jon
Cannon, A.E. *202*
    Earlier sketches in SATA *93, 163*
Cannon, Ann Edwards
    See Cannon, A.E.
Cannon, Bettie (Waddell) 1922- *59*
Cannon, Curt
    See Hunter, Evan
Cannon, Eileen E(mily) 1948- *119*
Cannon, Frank
    See Mayhar, Ardath
Cannon, Janell 1957- *128*
    Earlier sketch in SATA *78*
    See also CLR *120*
Cannon, Marian G. 1923- *85*
Cannon, Taffy
    See Cannon, Eileen E(mily)
Cantone, AnnaLaura *182*
Canusi, Jose
    See Barker, S. Omar
Canyon, Christopher 1966- *150*
    Earlier sketch in SATA *104*
Caparo, Antonio
    See Caparo, Antonio Javier
Caparo, Antonio Javier *205*
Capek, Michael 1947- *142*
    Earlier sketch in SATA *96*
Capes, Bernard (Edward Joseph)
    1854-1918 .... *116*
Caple, Kathy *193*
Caple, Laurie 1958- *201*
Caplin, Alfred Gerald 1909-1979 .... *61*
    Obituary *21*
Caponigro, John Paul 1965- *84*
Capote, Truman 1924-1984 .... *91*
Capp, Al
    See Caplin, Alfred Gerald
Cappel, Constance 1936- *22*
Cappetta, Cynthia 1949- *125*
Cappo, Nan Willard 1955- *143*
Capps, Benjamin (Franklin) 1922- *9*
Cappy Dick
    See Cleveland, George
Captain Kangaroo
    See Keeshan, Robert J.
Captain Wheeler
    See Ellis, Edward S.
Captain Young of Yale
    See Stratemeyer, Edward L.
Capucilli, Alyssa Satin 1957- *203*
    Earlier sketches in SATA *115, 163*
Capucine
    See Mazille, Capucine
Caraher, Kim(berley Elizabeth) 1961- *105*
Caraker, Mary 1929- *74*
Caras, Roger A(ndrew) 1928-2001 .... *12*
    Obituary *127*
Caravantes, Peggy 1935- *140*
Caraway, Caren 1939- *57*
Carbone, Elisa 1954- *173*
    Earlier sketches in SATA *81, 137*

Carbone, Elisa Lynn
    See Carbone, Elisa
Carbonnier, Jeanne 1894-1974 .... *3*
    Obituary *34*
Card, Orson Scott 1951- *127*
    Earlier sketch in SATA *83*
    See also CLR *116*
Care, Felicity
    See Coury, Louise Andree
Carew, Jan 1925- *51*
    Brief entry *40*
Carew, Jan Rynveld
    See Carew, Jan
Carey, Bonnie
    See Marshall, Bonnie C.
Carey, Charles W., Jr. 1951- *170*
Carey, Ernestine Gilbreth 1908-2006 .... *2*
    Obituary *177*
Carey, Janet Lee 1954(?)- *185*
Carey, Lisa *110*
Carey, M. V.
    See Carey, Mary V(irginia)
Carey, Mary V(irginia) 1925-1994 .... *44*
    Brief entry *39*
Carey, Peter 1943- *94*
Carey, Peter Philip
    See Carey, Peter
Carey, Valerie Scho 1949- *60*
Carheden, Goorel Kristina
    See Naaslund, Goorel Kristina
Carigiet, Alois 1902-1985 .... *24*
    Obituary *47*
    See also CLR *38*
Carini, Edward 1923- *9*
Carkeet, David 1946- *75*
Carle, Eric 1929- *163*
    Earlier sketches in SATA *4, 65, 120*
    See also CLR *72*
    See also SAAS *6*
Carleton, Captain L. C.
    See Ellis, Edward S.
Carleton, Captain Latham C.
    See Ellis, Edward S.
Carleton, Latham C.
    See Ellis, Edward S.
Carley, V(an Ness) Royal 1906-1976
    Obituary *20*
Carling, Amelia Lau 1949- *164*
    Earlier sketch in SATA *119*
Carlisle, Carolyn
    See Hawes, Louise
Carlisle, Clark
    See Holding, James (Clark Carlisle, Jr.)
Carlisle, Olga Andreyev 1930- *35*
Carlock, Miriam
    See Eyerly, Jeannette
Carls, Claudia 1978- *198*
Carlsen, G(eorge) Robert 1917- *30*
Carlsen, Ruth C(hristoffer) 1918- *2*
Carlson, Bernice Wells 1910- *8*
Carlson, Christopher C. *202*
Carlson, Dale (Bick) 1935- *1*
Carlson, Daniel (Bick) 1960- *27*
Carlson, Kirsten 1968- *192*
Carlson, Kirsten M.
    See Carlson, Kirsten
Carlson, Laurie 1952- *173*
    Earlier sketch in SATA *101*
Carlson, Laurie Winn
    See Carlson, Laurie
Carlson, Melody 1956- *171*
    Earlier sketch in SATA *113*
Carlson, Nancy 1953- *213*
    Brief entry *45*
    Earlier sketches in SATA *56, 90, 144*
Carlson, Nancy L.
    See Carlson, Nancy
Carlson, Natalie Savage 1906-1997 .... *68*
    Earlier sketch in SATA *2*
    See also SAAS *4*
Carlson, Susan Johnston 1953- *88*

Carlson, Vada F. 1897- 16
Carlstrom, Nancy White 1948- 215
    Brief entry 48
    Earlier sketches in SATA 53, 92, 156
Carlton, Keith
    See Robertson, Keith (Carlton)
Carlton, Susan 1960- 195
Carlyon, Richard 55
Carman, Patrick 1966- 197
    Earlier sketch in SATA 161
Carmer, Carl (Lamson) 1893-1976 37
    Obituary 30
Carmer, Elizabeth Black 1904- 24
Carmi, Giora 1944- 149
    Earlier sketch in SATA 79
Carmichael, Carrie
    See Carmichael, Harriet
Carmichael, Harriet 40
Carmody, Isobelle 1958- 191
    Earlier sketch in SATA 161
Carmody, Isobelle Jane
    See Carmody, Isobelle
Carney, Elizabeth 1981- 199
Carney, Jeff 1962- 196
Carney, Mary Lou 1949- 170
Carol, Bill J.
    See Knott, William C(ecil, Jr.)
Caron, Romi
    See Caron-Kyselkova', Romana
Caron-Kyselkova', Romana 1967- 94
Caroselli, Remus F(rancis) 1916- 36
Carpelan, Bo 1926- 8
Carpelan, Bo Gustaf Bertelsson
    See Carpelan, Bo
Carpenter, (John) Allan 1917- 81
    Earlier sketch in SATA 3
Carpenter, Angelica Shirley 1945- 153
    Earlier sketch in SATA 71
Carpenter, Frances 1890-1972 3
    Obituary 27
Carpenter, John 1948- 58
Carpenter, John Howard
    See Carpenter, John
Carpenter, Johnny
    See Carpenter, John
Carpenter, Nancy 215
Carpenter, Nancy Sippel
    See Carpenter, Nancy
Carpenter, Patricia (Healy Evans) 1920- 11
Carr, Glyn
    See Styles, (Frank) Showell
Carr, Harriett H(elen) 1899-1977 3
Carr, Jan 1953- 132
    Earlier sketch in SATA 89
Carr, M. J.
    See Carr, Jan
Carr, Mary Jane 1899-1988 2
    Obituary 55
Carr, Philippa
    See Hibbert, Eleanor Alice Burford
Carr, Roger Vaughan 1937- 95
Carrel, Annette Felder 1929- 90
Carrick, Carol (Hatfield) 1935- 118
    Earlier sketches in SATA 7, 63
    See also SAAS 18
Carrick, Donald (F.) 1929-1989 63
    Earlier sketch in SATA 7
Carrick, Malcolm 1945- 28
Carrick, Paul 1972- 194
Carrier, Lark 1947- 71
    Brief entry 50
Carrier, Roch 1937- 166
    Earlier sketch in SATA 105
Carrighar, Sally 1898-1985 24
Carrillo, Patricia S.
    See Carrillo, P.S.
Carrillo, P.S. 209
Carrington, G. A.
    See Cunningham, Chet
Carrington, Marsha Gray 1954- 168
    Earlier sketch in SATA 111

Carris, Joan 1938- 182
    Brief entry 42
    Earlier sketch in SATA 44
Carris, Joan Davenport
    See Carris, Joan
Carroll, Curt
    See Bishop, Curtis (Kent)
Carroll, Elizabeth
    See Barkin, Carol
    and James, Elizabeth
Carroll, Jaye
    See Carroll, Michael
Carroll, Jenny
    See Cabot, Meg
Carroll, (Archer) Latrobe 1894-1996 7
Carroll, Laura
    See Parr, Lucy
Carroll, Lewis 1832-1898 100
    See also YABC 2
    See also CLR 108
Carroll, Michael 1966- 203
Carroll, Raymond 1924- 86
    Brief entry 47
Carruth, Hayden 1921-2008 47
    Obituary 197
Carryl, Charles E. 1841-1920 114
Carryl, Charles Edward
    See Carryl, Charles E.
Carse, Robert 1902-1971 5
Carson, J(ohn) Franklin 1920-1981 1
    Obituary 107
Carson, Mary Kay 1964- 200
    Earlier sketch in SATA 150
Carson, Rachel 1907-1964 23
Carson, Rachel Louise
    See Carson, Rachel
Carson, Rosalind
    See Chittenden, Margaret
Carson, S. M.
    See Gorsline, (Sally) Marie
Carson, William C. 1928- 154
Carter, Abby 184
Carter, Alden R 1947- 137
    Earlier sketch in SATA 67
    See also CLR 22
    See also SAAS 18
Carter, Alden Richardson
    See Carter, Alden R
Carter, Andy 1948- 134
Carter, Angela 1940-1992 66
    Obituary 70
Carter, Angela Olive
    See Carter, Angela
Carter, Anne Laurel 1953- 209
    Earlier sketch in SATA 135
Carter, Asa Earl
    See Carter, Forrest
Carter, Avis Murton
    See Allen, Kenneth S.
Carter, Bruce
    See Hough, Richard (Alexander)
Carter, Carol S(hadis) 1948- 124
Carter, David A. 1957- 170
    Earlier sketch in SATA 114
Carter, Don 1958- 192
    Earlier sketch in SATA 124
Carter, Dorothy Sharp 1921- 8
Carter, Forrest 1927(?)-1979 32
Carter, Helene 1887-1960 15
Carter, (William) Hodding, Jr. 1907-1972 2
    Obituary 27
Carter, James Earl, Jr.
    See Carter, Jimmy
Carter, Jimmy 1924- 79
Carter, Katharine J(ones) 1905-1984 2
Carter, Lin(wood Vrooman) 1930-1988 91
Carter, Mike 1936- 138

Carter, Nick
    See Avallone, Michael (Angelo, Jr.)
    and Ballard, (Willis) Todhunter
    and Crider, Bill
    and Cassiday, Bruce (Bingham)
    and Chastain, Thomas
    and Dey, Frederic (Merrill) Van Rensselaer
    and Garside, Jack
    and Hayes, Ralph E(ugene)
    and Henderson, M(arilyn) R(uth)
    and Lynds, Dennis
    and Lynds, Gayle (Hallenbeck)
    and Randisi, Robert J.
    and Rasof, Henry
    and Stratemeyer, Edward L.
    and Smith, Martin Cruz
    and Swain, Dwight V(reeland)
    and Vardeman, Robert E(dward)
    and Wallmann, Jeffrey M(iner)
    and White, Lionel
Carter, Peter 1929- 57
Carter, Phyllis Ann
    See Eberle, Irmengarde
Carter, Samuel (Thomson) III 1904-1988 37
    Obituary 60
Carter, William E. 1926-1983 1
    Obituary 35
Cartlidge, Michelle 1950- 96
    Brief entry 37
    Earlier sketch in SATA 49
Cartner, William Carruthers 1910- 11
Cartwright, Ann 1940- 78
Cartwright, Reg(inald Ainsley) 1938- 64
Cartwright, Sally 1923- 9
Carusone, Al 1949- 89
Carvell, Marlene 172
Carver, John
    See Gardner, Richard (M.)
Carwell, L'Ann
    See McKissack, Patricia C.
Cary
    See Cary, Louis F(avreau)
Cary, Barbara Knapp 1912(?)-1975
    Obituary 31
Cary, Kate 1967(?)- 174
Cary, Louis F(avreau) 1915- 9
Caryl, Jean
    See Kaplan, Jean Caryl Korn
Casanova, Mary 1957- 186
    Earlier sketches in SATA 94, 136
Cascone, A.G.
    See Cascone, Annette
    and Cascone, Gina
Cascone, Annette 1960- 103
Cascone, Gina 1955- 103
Case, Chris 1976- 209
Case, Marshal T(aylor) 1941- 9
Case, Michael
    See Howard, Robert West
Caseley, Judith 1951- 159
    Brief entry 53
    Earlier sketch in SATA 87
Casewit, Curtis W(erner) 1922-2002 4
Casey, Barbara (Louise) 1944- 147
    Earlier sketch in SATA 79
Casey, Brigid 1950- 9
Casey, Tina 1959- 141
Cash, Ellen Lewis Buell 1905-1989
    Obituary 64
Cash, Megan Montague 160
Cashore, Kristin 1976(?)- 206
Casilla, Robert 1959- 211
    Earlier sketches in SATA 75, 146
Cason, Mabel Earp 1892-1965 10
Cass, Joan E(velyn) 1
Cass-Beggs, Barbara 1904- 62
Cassedy, Patrice (Rinaldo) 1953- 149
Cassedy, Sylvia 1930-1989 77
    Obituary 61
    Earlier sketch in SATA 27
    See also CLR 26

Cassel, Lili
See Wronker, Lili Cassel
Cassels, Jean 173
Cassidy, Anne 1952- 166
Cassidy, Anne Josephine
See Cassidy, Anne
Cassidy, Cathy 1962- 183
Casson, Hugh Maxwell 1910-1999 65
Obituary 115
Cassutt, Michael 1954- 78
Cassutt, Michael Joseph
See Cassutt, Michael
Castaldi, Elicia 194
Castaldo, Nancy Fusco 1962- 151
Earlier sketch in SATA 93
Castaneda, Omar S. 1954- 71
Castell, Megan
See Williams, Jeanne
Castellanos, Jane Mollie Robinson
1913-2001 9
Castellon, Federico 1914-1971 48
Castellucci, Cecil 1969- 176
Castillo, Edmund L. 1924-2005 1
Obituary 167
Castillo, Lauren 195
Castle, Lee
See Ogan, George F.
and Ogan, Margaret E. (Nettles)
Castle, Paul
See Howard, Vernon (Linwood)
Castle, Robert
See Hamilton, Edmond
Castrovilla, Selene 1966- 186
Caswell, Brian 1954- 171
Earlier sketch in SATA 97
Caswell, Helen (Rayburn) 1923- 12
Catalano, Dominic 1956- 163
Earlier sketch in SATA 76
Catalano, Grace (A.) 1961- 99
Catalanotto, Peter 1959- 195
Autobiography Feature 113
Earlier sketches in SATA 70, 114, 159
See also CLR 68
See also SAAS 25
Catanese, P.W. 1961- 179
Cate, Annette LeBlanc 196
Cate, Dick
See Cate, Richard Edward Nelson
Cate, Richard Edward Nelson 1932- 28
Cather, Willa 1873-1947 30
See also CLR 98
Catherall, Arthur 1906-1980 74
Earlier sketches in SATA 3, 4
Cathon, Laura E(lizabeth) 1908-1991 27
Catlett, Elizabeth 1919(?)- 82
Catlin, Wynelle 1930- 13
Catlow, Nikalas
See Catlow, Niki
Catlow, Niki 1975- 193
Cato, Heather 105
Cato, Sheila 114
Catran, Ken 1944- 190
Catrow, David 206
See Catrow, David J. III
Catrow, David J. III 152
See Catrow, David
Catt, Louis
See French, Vivian
Cattell, James 1954- 123
Catton, (Charles) Bruce 1899-1978 2
Obituary 24
Catz, Max
See Glaser, Milton
Caudell, Marian 1930- 52
Caudill, Rebecca 1899-1985 1
Obituary 44
Cauley, Lorinda Bryan 1951- 46
Brief entry 43
Caulfield, Peggy F. 1926-1987
Obituary 53
Cauman, Samuel 1910-1971 48

Causley, Charles (Stanley) 1917-2003 66
Obituary 149
Earlier sketch in SATA 3
See also CLR 30
Cavallaro, Ann (Abelson) 1918- 62
Cavallo, Diana 1931- 7
Cavanagh, Helen (Carol) 1939- 98
Brief entry 37
Earlier sketch in SATA 48
Cavanah, Frances 1899-1982 31
Earlier sketch in SATA 1
Cavanna, Betty
See Harrison, Elizabeth (Allen) Cavanna
Cavanna, Elizabeth
See Harrison, Elizabeth (Allen) Cavanna
Cave, Kathryn 1948- 123
Earlier sketch in SATA 76
Cavendish, Peter
See Horler, Sydney
Cavin, Ruth (Brodie) 1918- 38
Cavoukian, Raffi 1948- 68
Cawley, Winifred 1915- 13
Cazeau, Charles J(ay) 1931- 65
Cazet, Denys 1938- 191
Brief entry 41
Earlier sketches in SATA 52, 99, 163
Cazzola, Gus 1934- 73
Cebulash, Mel 1937- 91
Earlier sketch in SATA 10
Ceccoli, Nicoletta 181
Cecil, Randy 1968- 187
Cecka, Melanie 199
Ceder, Georgiana Dorcas -1985 10
Celenza, Anna Harwell 133
Celestino, Martha Laing
See Laing, Martha
Cepeda, Joe 215
Earlier sketch in SATA 159
Cerf, Bennett (Alfred) 1898-1971 7
Cerf, Christopher (Bennett) 1941- 2
Cermak, Martin
See Duchacek, Ivo D(uka)
Cerullo, Mary M. 1949- 145
Earlier sketch in SATA 86
Cervon, Jacqueline
See Moussard, Jacqueline
Cetin, Frank Stanley 1921- 2
Chabon, Michael 1963- 145
Chabrian, Deborah
See Chabrian, Deborah L.
Chabrian, Deborah L. 212
Chaconas, D.J.
See Chaconas, Dori
Chaconas, Dori 1938- 208
Earlier sketches in SATA 145, 175
Chaconas, Doris J.
See Chaconas, Dori
Chadwick, Lester 67
Earlier sketch in SATA 1
Chaffee, Allen 3
Chaffin, Lillie D(orton) 1925- 4
Chaikin, Miriam 1924- 152
Earlier sketches in SATA 24, 102
Chall, Marsha Wilson 150
Challand, Helen J(ean) 1921- 64
Challans, Mary
See Renault, Mary
Chalmers, Mary (Eileen) 1927- 6
See also SAAS 14
Chamberlain, Barbara A.
See Azore, Barbara
Chamberlain, Margaret 1954- 212
Earlier sketch in SATA 46
Chamberlin, Kate 1945- 105
Chamberlin, Mary 1960- 177
Chamberlin, Rich 177
Chamberlin, Richard
See Chamberlin, Rich

Chambers, Aidan 1934- 171
Earlier sketches in SATA 1, 69, 108
See also CLR 151
See also SAAS 12
Chambers, Bradford 1922-1984
Obituary 39
Chambers, Catherine E.
See St. John, Nicole
Chambers, John W. 1933- 57
Brief entry 46
Chambers, Kate
See St. John, Nicole
Chambers, Margaret Ada Eastwood 1911- 2
Chambers, Peggy
See Chambers, Margaret Ada Eastwood
Chambers, Robert W(illiam) 1865-1933 107
Chambliss, Maxie 186
Chan, Gillian 1954- 147
Earlier sketch in SATA 102
Chan, Peter 1980(?)- 207
Chance, James T.
See Carpenter, John
Chance, John T.
See Carpenter, John
Chance, Stephen
See Turner, Philip (William)
Chandler, Caroline A(ugusta) 1906-1979 22
Obituary 24
Chandler, David P. 1933- 28
Chandler, David Porter
See Chandler, David P.
Chandler, Edna Walker 1908-1982 11
Obituary 31
Chandler, Jennifer
See Westwood, Jennifer
Chandler, Karen 1959- 122
Chandler, Linda S(mith) 1929- 39
Chandler, Pauline 175
Chandler, Robert 1953- 40
Chandler, Ruth Forbes 1894-1978 2
Obituary 26
Chandonnet, Ann F. 1943- 92
Chaney, Jill 1932- 87
Chang, Chih-Wei 1966- 111
Chang, Cindy 1968- 90
Chang, Margaret 1941- 71
Chang, Margaret Scrogin
See Chang, Margaret
Chang, Raymond 1939- 142
Earlier sketches in SATA 71, 142 PEN
Chanin, Michael 1952- 84
Channel, A. R.
See Catherall, Arthur
Chapian, Marie 1938- 29
Chapin, Alene Olsen Dalton 1915(?)-1986
Obituary 47
Chapin, Tom 1945- 83
Chapman, Allen 67
Earlier sketch in SATA 1
Chapman, Cheryl O(rth) 1948- 80
Chapman, (Constance) Elizabeth (Mann)
1919- 10
Chapman, Gaye 1970- 200
Chapman, Gaye Coralie
See Chapman, Gaye
Chapman, Gaynor 1935- 32
Chapman, Gillian 1955- 120
Chapman, Jane 1970- 212
Earlier sketches in SATA 122, 176
Chapman, Jean 104
Earlier sketch in SATA 34
See also CLR 65
Chapman, John Stanton Higham 1891-1972
Obituary 27
Chapman, Lee
See Bradley, Marion Zimmer
Chapman, Lynne 1960- 197
Chapman, Lynne F(erguson) 1963- 150
Earlier sketch in SATA 94
Chapman, Maristan
See Chapman, John Stanton Higham

Chapman, Vera (Ivy May) 1898-1996 .... *33*
Chapman, Walker
  See Silverberg, Robert
Chappell, Audrey 1954- *72*
Chappell, Crissa-Jean *198*
Chappell, Warren 1904-1991 .... *68*
  Obituary *67*
  Earlier sketch in SATA *6*
  See also SAAS *10*
Chapra, Mimi *182*
Charbonneau, Eileen 1951- *118*
  Earlier sketch in SATA *84*
Charbonnet, Gabrielle 1961- *81*
Chardiet, Bernice 1927(?)- *27*
Chardiet, Bernice Kroll
  See Chardiet, Bernice
Charest, Emily MacLachlan *198*
Charles, Donald
  See Meighan, Donald Charles
Charles, Louis
  See Stratemeyer, Edward L.
Charles, Nicholas
  See Kuskin, Karla
Charles, Nicholas J.
  See Kuskin, Karla
Charles, Norma *153*
Charles, Veronika Martenova *182*
Charlip, Remy 1929- *119*
  Earlier sketches in SATA *4, 68*
  See also CLR *8*
Charlot, Jean 1898-1979 .... *8*
  Obituary *31*
Charlot, Martin 1944- *64*
Charlot, Martin Day
  See Charlot, Martin
Charlton, Michael (Alan) 1923- *34*
Charlton-Trujillo, e.E. *189*
Charmatz, Bill 1925-2005 .... *7*
Charnas, Suzy McKee 1939- *110*
  Earlier sketch in SATA *61*
Charosh, Mannis 1906- *5*
Chartier, Normand L. 1945- *66*
Chase, Alice
  See McHargue, Georgess
Chase, Alyssa 1965- *92*
Chase, Andra 1942- *91*
Chase, Emily
  See Aks, Patricia
  and Garwood, Julie
  and Sachs, Judith
  and White, Carol
Chase, Mary (Coyle) 1907-1981 .... *17*
  Obituary *29*
Chase, Mary Ellen 1887-1973 .... *10*
Chase, Paula *214*
Chase, Richard 1904-1988 .... *64*
  Obituary *56*
Chase, Samantha
  See Glick, Ruth (Burtnick)
Chast, Roz 1954- *212*
  Earlier sketch in SATA *97*
Chastain, Madye Lee 1908-1989 .... *4*
Chataway, Carol 1955- *140*
Chatterjee, Debjani 1952- *83*
Chauncy, Nan(cen Beryl Masterman)
  1900-1970 .... *6*
  See also CLR *6*
Chaundler, Christine 1887-1972 .... *1*
  Obituary *25*
Chayka, Doug *196*
Chbosky, Stephen 1972- *164*
Cheaney, Janie B.
  See Cheaney, J.B.
Cheaney, J.B. 1950- *188*
Chee, Cheng-Khee 1934- *79*
Cheese, Chloe 1952- *118*
Chekhonte, Antosha
  See Chekhov, Anton
Chekhov, Anton 1860-1904 .... *90*
Chekhov, Anton Pavlovich
  See Chekhov, Anton

Chelushkin, Kirill 1968- *186*
Chen, Anthony 1929- *6*
Chen, Chih-Yuan 1975- *155*
Chen, Ju-Hong 1941- *78*
Chen, Pauline 1966- *202*
Chen, Sara
  See Odgers, Sally Farrell
Chen, Tony
  See Chen, Anthony
Chen, Yong 1963- *183*
Chen, Yuan-tsung 1932- *65*
Chenault, Nell
  See Smith, Linell Nash
Chenery, Janet (Dai) 1923- *25*
Cheney, Cora 1916-1999 .... *3*
  Obituary *110*
Cheney, Glenn (Alan) 1951- *99*
Cheney, Lynne V. 1941- *152*
Cheney, Lynne Vincent
  See Cheney, Lynne V.
Cheney, Ted
  See Cheney, Theodore Albert
Cheney, Theodore A. Rees
  See Cheney, Theodore Albert
Cheney, Theodore Albert 1928- *11*
Cheng, Andrea 1957- *205*
  Earlier sketches in SATA *128, 172*
Cheng, Christopher 1959- *173*
  Earlier sketch in SATA *106*
Cheng, Judith 1955- *36*
Cheng, Shan
  See Jiang, Cheng An
Cheripko, Jan 1951- *155*
  Earlier sketch in SATA *83*
Chermayeff, Ivan 1932- *47*
Chernenko, Dan
  See Chernenko, Dan
Chernoff, Dorothy A.
  See Ernst, (Lyman) John
Chernoff, Goldie Taub 1909- *10*
Cherry, Carolyn Janice
  See Cherryh, C.J.
Cherry, Lynne 1952- *99*
  Earlier sketch in SATA *34*
Cherryh, C.J. 1942- *172*
  Earlier sketch in SATA *93*
Cherryholmes, Anne
  See Price, Olive
Cheshire, Simon *172*
Chesler, Bernice 1932-2002 .... *59*
Chess, Victoria (Dickerson) 1939- *92*
  Earlier sketch in SATA *33*
Chessa, Francesca *191*
Chester, Deborah 1957- *85*
Chester, Kate
  See Guccione, Leslie Davis
Chesterton, G. K. 1874-1936 .... *27*
Chesterton, Gilbert Keith
  See Chesterton, G. K.
Chesworth, Michael *207*
  Earlier sketch in SATA *160*
Chetin, Helen 1922- *6*
Chetwin, Grace *86*
  Brief entry *50*
Chevalier, Christa 1937- *35*
Chevalier, Tracy 1962- *128*
Chew, Ruth 1920-2010 .... *7*
Chichester Clark, Emma 1955- *209*
  Earlier sketches in SATA *117, 156, 69*
Chidsey, Donald Barr 1902-1981 .... *3*
  Obituary *27*
Chiefari, Janet D. 1942- *58*
Chien, Catia *193*
Chien-min, Lin
  See Rumford, James
Child, L. Maria
  See Child, Lydia Maria
Child, Lauren 1965- *183*
  Earlier sketches in SATA *119, 160*
Child, Lincoln 1957- *113*

Child, Lincoln B.
  See Child, Lincoln
Child, Lydia Maria 1802-1880 .... *67*
Child, Mrs.
  See Child, Lydia Maria
Child, Philip 1898-1978 .... *47*
Children's Shepherd, The
  See Westphal, Arnold Carl
Childress, Alice 1920-1994 .... *81*
  Earlier sketches in SATA *7, 48*
  See also CLR *14*
Childs, H(alla) Fay (Cochrane) 1890-1971 .... *1*
  Obituary *25*
Chilton, Charles (Frederick William)
  1917- *102*
Chima, Cinda Williams *192*
Chimaera
  See Farjeon, Eleanor
Chin, Richard (M.) 1946- *52*
Chinery, Michael 1938- *26*
Chin-Lee, Cynthia 1958- *102*
Chin-Lee D., Cynthia
  See Chin-Lee, Cynthia
Chippendale, Lisa A. *158*
Chipperfield, Joseph Eugene 1912-1980(?) .. *87*
  Earlier sketch in SATA *2*
Chisholm, P. F.
  See Finney, Patricia
Chislett, Gail (Elaine) 1948- *58*
Chittenden, Elizabeth F. 1903-1999 .... *9*
Chittenden, Margaret 1935- *28*
Chittum, Ida 1918- *7*
Chitwood, Suzanne Tanner 1958- *160*
Chmielarz, Sharon Lee 1940- *72*
Choate, Judith (Newkirk) 1940- *30*
Chocolate, Debbi 1954- *96*
Chocolate, Deborah M. Newton
  See Chocolate, Debbi
Chodos-Irvine, Margaret *211*
  Earlier sketch in SATA *152*
Choi, Sook Nyul 1937- *73*
  Autobiography Feature *126*
  See also CLR *53*
Choi, Yangsook *178*
Choldenko, Gennifer 1957- *182*
  Earlier sketch in SATA *135*
Chorao, Kay 1936- *215*
Chorao, (Ann Mc)Kay (Sproat) 1936- *162*
  Earlier sketches in SATA *8, 69*
Choron, Sandra (Zena Samelson) 1950- *146*
Choung, Eun-hee *199*
Chown, Marcus 1959- *137*
Choyce, Lesley 1951- *165*
  Earlier sketch in SATA *94*
Choyce, Lesley Willis
  See Choyce, Lesley
Chrisman, Arthur Bowie 1889-1953 .... *124*
  See also YABC *1*
Christelow, Eileen 1943- *184*
  Autobiography Feature *120*
  Brief entry *35*
  Earlier sketches in SATA *38, 90*
Christensen, Bonnie 1951- *213*
  Earlier sketches in SATA *110, 157*
Christensen, Gardell Dano 1907-1991 .... *1*
Christensen, Laurie
  See Steding, Laurie
Christesen, Barbara 1940- *40*
Christgau, Alice Erickson 1902-1977 .... *13*
Christian, Mary Blount 1933- *9*
Christiana, David *195*
Christie, Agatha 1890-1976 .... *36*
Christie, Agatha Mary Clarissa
  See Christie, Agatha
Christie, Ann Philippa
  See Pearce, Philippa
Christie, Gregory
  See Christie, R. Gregory
Christie, Philippa
  See Pearce, Philippa

Christie, R. Gregory 1971- 185
  Earlier sketch in SATA 127
Christopher, John
  See Youd, Samuel
Christopher, Louise
  See Hale, Arlene
Christopher, Matt(hew Frederick)
  1917-1997 80
  Obituary 99
  Earlier sketches in SATA 2, 47
  See also CLR 119
  See also SAAS 9
Christopher, Milbourne 1914(?)-1984 46
Christy, Howard Chandler 1873-1952 21
Chrustowski, Rick 176
Chrystie, Frances N(icholson) 1904-1986 60
Chu, Daniel 1933- 11
Chukovsky, Kornei (Ivanovich) 1882-1969 . 34
  Earlier sketch in SATA 5
Church, Caroline Jayne 179
Church, Richard 1893-1972 3
Churchill, E(lmer) Richard 1937- 11
Churchill, Elizabeth
  See Hough, Richard (Alexander)
Chute, B(eatrice) J(oy) 1913-1987 2
  Obituary 53
Chute, Marchette (Gaylord) 1909-1994 1
Chwast, Jacqueline 1932- 6
Chwast, Seymour 1931- 146
  Earlier sketches in SATA 18, 96
Ciardi, John (Anthony) 1916-1986 65
  Obituary 46
  Earlier sketch in SATA 1
  See also CLR 19
  See also SAAS 26
Ciccone, Madonna Louise Veronica
  See Madonna
Ciddor, Anna 1957- 213
Ciment, James D. 1958- 140
Cirrone, Dorian 182
Cisneros, Sandra 1954-
  See CLR 123
Citra, Becky 1954- 137
Citrin, Michael 1965(?)- 183
Claflin, Willy 1944- 208
Clair, Andree 19
Clampett, Bob 1914(?)-1985 44
  Obituary 38
Clampett, Robert
  See Clampett, Bob
Clapp, John 1968- 109
Clapp, Patricia 1912- 74
  Earlier sketch in SATA 4
  See also SAAS 4
Clare, Ellen
  See Sinclair, Olga
Clare, Helen
  See Clarke, Pauline
Claremont, Chris 1950- 87
Claremont, Christopher Simon
  See Claremont, Chris
Clark, Ann Nolan 1896-1995 82
  Obituary 87
  Earlier sketch in SATA 4
  See also CLR 16
  See also SAAS 16
Clark, Champ 1923-2002 47
Clark, Christopher (Anthony) Stuart
  See Stuart-Clark, Christopher (Anthony)
Clark, Clara Gillow 1951- 154
  Earlier sketch in SATA 84
Clark, David
  See Hardcastle, Michael
Clark, David Allen
  See Ernst, (Lyman) John
Clark, Emma Chichester
  See Chichester Clark, Emma
Clark, Frank J(ames) 1922- 18
Clark, Garel
  See Garelick, May

Clark, Halsey
  See Deming, Richard
Clark, Joan
  See Benson, Mildred
Clark, Joan 1934- 182
  Earlier sketches in SATA 59, 96
Clark, Leonard 1905-1981 30
  Obituary 29
Clark, M. R.
  See Clark, Mavis Thorpe
Clark, Margaret (D.) 1943- 126
Clark, Margaret Goff 1913- 82
  Earlier sketch in SATA 8
Clark, Mary Higgins 1929- 46
Clark, Mavis Thorpe 1909-1999 74
  Earlier sketch in SATA 8
  See also CLR 30
  See also SAAS 5
Clark, Merle
  See Gessner, Lynne
Clark, Patricia Denise 1921- 117
Clark, Patricia Finrow 1929- 11
Clark, Ronald Harry 1904-1999 193
Clark, Ronald William 1916-1987 2
  Obituary 52
Clark, Sherryl 1956- 149
Clark, Van D(eusen) 1909-1974 2
Clark, Virginia
  See Gray, Patricia (Clark)
Clark, Walter Van Tilburg 1909-1971 8
Clarke, Arthur
  See Clarke, Arthur C.
Clarke, Arthur C. 1917-2008 115
  Obituary 191
  Earlier sketches in SATA 13, 70
  See also CLR 119
Clarke, Arthur Charles
  See Clarke, Arthur C.
Clarke, Clorinda 1917- 7
Clarke, Elizabeth L. 1934- 103
Clarke, Greg 1959- 215
Clarke, Gus 1948- 134
Clarke, J.
  See Clarke, Judith
Clarke, James Hall
  See Rowland-Entwistle, (Arthur) Theodore
  (Henry)
Clarke, Joan B. 1921- 42
  Brief entry 27
Clarke, John
  See Laklan, Carli
  and Sontup, Dan(iel)
Clarke, Judith 1943- 164
  Earlier sketches in SATA 75, 110
  See also CLR 61
Clarke, Julia 1950- 138
Clarke, Kenneth 1957- 107
Clarke, Lea
  See Rowland-Entwistle, (Arthur) Theodore
  (Henry)
Clarke, Margaret 1941-
  See CLR 99
Clarke, Mary Stetson 1911-1994 5
Clarke, Michael
  See Newlon, (Frank) Clarke
Clarke, Pauline 1921- 131
  Earlier sketch in SATA 3
  See also CLR 28
Clarkson, E(dith) Margaret 1915- 37
Clarkson, Ewan 1929- 9
Claudia, Susan
  See Goulart, Ron
  and Johnston, William
Claverie, Jean 1946- 38
Clay, Patrice 1947- 47
Clay, Wil 203
Clayman, Deborah Paula
  See Da Costa, Deborah
Claypool, Jane
  See Miner, Jane Claypool

Clayton, Elaine 1961- 209
  Earlier sketches in SATA 94, 159
Clayton, Lawrence (Otto, Jr.) 1945- 75
Clayton, Sandra 1951- 110
Cle, Troy 202
Clea, Super
  See Hantman, Clea
Cleary, Beverly 1916- 121
  Earlier sketches in SATA 2, 43, 79
  See also CLR 72
  See also SAAS 20
Cleary, Beverly Atlee Bunn
  See Cleary, Beverly
Cleary, Brian P. 1959- 186
  Earlier sketches in SATA 93, 132
Cleaver, Bill
  See Cleaver, William J.
Cleaver, Carole 1934- 6
Cleaver, Elizabeth (Ann Mrazik)
  1939-1985 23
  Obituary 43
  See also CLR 13
Cleaver, Hylton Reginald 1891-1961 49
Cleaver, Vera 1919-1993 76
  Earlier sketch in SATA 22
  See also CLR 6
Cleaver, Vera Allen
  See Cleaver, Vera
Cleaver, William J. 1920-1981 22
  Obituary 27
  See also CLR 6
Cleishbotham, Jebediah
  See Scott, Sir Walter
Cleland, Mabel
  See Widdemer, Mabel Cleland
Clem, Margaret H(ollingsworth) 1923- 90
Clemens, Samuel
  See Twain, Mark
Clemens, Samuel Langhorne
  See Twain, Mark
Clemens, Virginia Phelps 1941- 35
Clement, Gary 191
Clement, Janet 182
Clement, Nathan 1966- 200
Clement, Priscilla Ferguson 1942- 171
Clement, Rod 97
Clement-Moore, Rosemary 188
Clements, Andrew 1949- 203
  Earlier sketches in SATA 104, 158
Clements, Bruce 1931- 178
  Earlier sketches in SATA 27, 94
Clemesha, David 192
Clemons, Elizabeth
  See Nowell, Elizabeth Cameron
Clerk, N. W.
  See Lewis, C. S.
Cleveland, Bob
  See Cleveland, George
Cleveland, George 1903(?)-1985
  Obituary 43
Cleveland-Peck, Patricia 80
Cleven, Cathrine
  See Cleven, Kathryn Seward
Cleven, Kathryn Seward 2
Clevenger, William R. 1954- 84
Clevenger, William Russell
  See Clevenger, William R.
Clevin, Joergen 1920- 7
Clevin, Jorgen
  See Clevin, Joergen
Clewes, Dorothy (Mary) 1907-2003 86
  Obituary 138
  Earlier sketch in SATA 1
Clifford, David
  See Rosenberg, Eth Clifford
Clifford, Eth
  See Rosenberg, Eth Clifford
Clifford, Harold B(urton) 1893-1988 10
Clifford, Margaret Cort 1929- 1
Clifford, Martin
  See Hamilton, Charles (Harold St. John)

Clifford, Mary Louise Beneway 1926- 23
Clifford, Peggy
    See Clifford, Margaret Cort
Clifford, Rachel Mark
    See Lewis, Brenda Ralph
Clifton, Lucille 1936-2010 128
    Earlier sketches in SATA *20, 69*
    See also CLR *5*
Clifton, Thelma Lucille
    See Clifton, Lucille
Climo, Shirley 1928- 166
    Autobiography Feature 110
    Brief entry 35
    Earlier sketches in SATA *39, 77*
    See also CLR *69*
Cline-Ransome, Lesa 201
Clinton, Catherine 1952- 203
Clinton, Cathryn 1957- 136
Clinton, Dirk
    See Silverberg, Robert
Clinton, Jon
    See Prince, J(ack) H(arvey)
Clippinger, Carol 193
Clish, (Lee) Marian 1946- 43
Clive, Clifford
    See Hamilton, Charles (Harold St. John)
Clokey, Art 1921- 59
Cloudsley-Thompson, J(ohn) L(eonard)
    1921- 19
Clouse, Nancy L. 1938- 78
Clover, Peter 1952- 215
    Earlier sketch in SATA *152*
Clutha, Janet Paterson Frame
    See Frame, Janet
Clymer, Eleanor 1906-2001 85
    Obituary 126
    Earlier sketch in SATA *9*
    See also SAAS *17*
Clyne, Patricia (Edwards) 31
Cneut, Carll 1969- 197
Coalson, Glo 1946- 94
    Earlier sketch in SATA *26*
Coates, Anna 1958- 73
Coates, Belle 1896-1986 2
Coates, Ruth Allison 1915- 11
Coats, Alice M(argaret) 1905-1976 11
Coatsworth, Elizabeth (Jane) 1893-1986 100
    Obituary 49
    Earlier sketches in SATA *2, 56*
    See also CLR *2*
Cobalt, Martin
    See Mayne, William
Cobb, Jane
    See Berry, Jane Cobb
Cobb, Mary 1931- 88
Cobb, Vicki 1938- 136
    Autobiography Feature 136
    Earlier sketches in SATA *8, 69, 131*
    See also CLR *2*
    See also SAAS *6*
Cobbett, Richard
    See Pluckrose, Henry (Arthur)
Cober, Alan E(dwin) 1935-1998 7
    Obituary 101
Cobham, Sir Alan
    See Hamilton, Charles (Harold St. John)
Coburn, Jake 1978- 155
Cocagnac, Augustin Maurice(-Jean) 1924- 7
Cocca-Leffler, Maryann 1958- 194
    Earlier sketches in SATA *80, 136*
Cochran, Bill 187
Cochran, Bobbye A. 1949- 11
Cochran, Thomas 1955- 198
Cochrane, Hamilton E.
    See Cochrane, Mick
Cochrane, Mick 1956- 215
Cockett, Mary 3
Cocks, Peter 204
Cocovini, Abby 202
Coddell, Esme Raji
    See Codell, Esme Raji

Codell, Esme Raji 1968- 160
Cody, C. S.
    See Waller, Leslie
Cody, Jess
    See Cunningham, Chet
Coe, Anne (E.) 1949- 95
Coe, Douglas
    See Epstein, Beryl
    and Epstein, Samuel
Coe, Lloyd 1899(?)-1976
    Obituary 30
Coen, Rena Neumann 1925- 20
Coerr, Eleanor (Beatrice) 1922- 67
    Earlier sketch in SATA *1*
Cofer, Judith Ortiz 1952- 164
    Earlier sketch in SATA *110*
Coffelt, Nancy 1961- 189
Coffey, Brian
    See Koontz, Dean
Coffin, Geoffrey
    See Mason, F(rancis) van Wyck
Coffin, M. T.
    See Stanley, George Edward
Coffman, Ramon Peyton 1896-1989 4
Cogan, Karen 1954- 125
Coggins, Jack (Banham) 1911-2006 2
Cohen, Barbara 1932-1992 77
    Obituary 74
    Earlier sketch in SATA *10*
    See also SAAS *7*
Cohen, Daniel (E.) 1936- 70
    Earlier sketch in SATA *8*
    See also CLR *43*
    See also SAAS *4*
Cohen, Deborah Bodin 1968- 180
Cohen, Jan Barger
    See Barger, Jan
Cohen, Jene Barr
    See Barr, Jene
Cohen, Joan Lebold 1932- 4
Cohen, Judith Love 1933- 78
Cohen, Miriam 1926-1955 155
    Earlier sketches in SATA *29, 106*
    See also SAAS *11*
Cohen, Nora 75
Cohen, Paul 1945- 58
Cohen, Paul S.
    See Cohen, Paul
Cohen, Peter Zachary 1931- 150
    Earlier sketch in SATA *4*
Cohen, Robert Carl 1930- 8
Cohen, Santiago 1954- 215
Cohen, Sholom 1951- 94
Cohn, Angelo 1914-1997 19
Cohn, Diana 194
Cohn, Rachel 1968- 161
Coit, Margaret Louise 1922-2003 2
    Obituary 142
Colasanti, Susane 1973- 214
Colato Lainez, Rene 1970- 176
Colbert, Anthony 1934-2007 15
Colbert, Nancy A. 1936- 139
Colby, C(arroll) B(urleigh) 1904-1977 35
    Earlier sketch in SATA *3*
Colby, Jean Poindexter 1909-1993 23
Cole, Annette
    See Steiner, Barbara A(nnette)
Cole, Babette 1949- 155
    Earlier sketches in SATA *61, 96*
Cole, Betsy 1940- 83
Cole, Brock 1938- 200
    Earlier sketches in SATA *72, 136*
    See also CLR *18*
Cole, Davis
    See Elting, Mary
Cole, Hannah 1954- 74
Cole, Henry 1955- 213
    Earlier sketch in SATA *181*
Cole, Jack -1974
    See Stewart, John

Cole, Jackson
    See Curry, Thomas Albert
    and Germano, Peter B.
    and Heckelmann, Charles N(ewman)
    and Newton, D(wight) B(ennett)
    and Schisgall, Oscar
Cole, Jennifer
    See Zach, Cheryl (Byrd)
Cole, Joanna 1944- 168
    Brief entry 37
    Earlier sketches in SATA *49, 81, 120*
    See also CLR *40*
Cole, Lois Dwight 1903-1979 10
    Obituary 26
Cole, Michael 1947- 59
Cole, Samantha
    See Cole, Stephen
Cole, Sheila 1939- 171
    Earlier sketches in SATA *24, 95*
Cole, Sheila R.
    See Cole, Sheila
Cole, Sheila Rotenberg
    See Cole, Sheila
Cole, Stephen 1971- 161
Cole, William (Rossa) 1919-2000 71
    Earlier sketch in SATA *9*
    See also SAAS *9*
Coleman, Andrew
    See Pine, Nicholas
Coleman, Clare
    See Bell, Clare (Louise)
    and Easton, M(alcolm) Coleman
Coleman, Janet Wyman 184
Coleman, Loren 1947- 164
Coleman, Loren Elwood, Jr.
    See Coleman, Loren
Coleman, Mary Ann 1928- 83
Coleman, Michael
    See Jones, Allan Frewin
Coleman, Michael 1946- 199
    Autobiography Feature 133
    Earlier sketches in SATA *108, 133*
Coleman, Rowan 187
Coleman, William L(eRoy) 1938- 49
    Brief entry 34
Coleman, Wim 1926- 212
Coles, Robert (Martin) 1929- 23
Colfer, Eoin 1965- 197
    Earlier sketch in SATA *148*
    See also CLR *112*
Colin, Ann
    See Ure, Jean
Collard, Sneed B. III 1959- 184
    Earlier sketches in SATA *84, 139*
Colledge, Anne 1939- 142
Colley, Jacqui 1965- 202
Collicott, Sharleen 1937- 143
    Earlier sketch in SATA *98*
Collier, Bryan 204
    Earlier sketches in SATA *126, 174*
Collier, Christopher 1930- 70
    Earlier sketch in SATA *16*
    See also CLR *126*
Collier, Ethel 1903-1999 22
Collier, James Lincoln 1928- 166
    Earlier sketches in SATA *8, 70*
    See also CLR *126*
    See also SAAS *21*
Collier, Jane
    See Collier, Zena
Collier, Kristi 182
Collier, Steven 1942- 61
Collier, Zena 1926- 23
Collings, Gillian 1939- 102
Collington, Peter 1948- 99
    Earlier sketch in SATA *59*
Collins, Ace 1953- 82
Collins, Andrew J.
    See Collins, Ace
Collins, B.R. 1981- 214

Collins, David R(aymond) 1940-2001 .... *121*
  Earlier sketch in SATA *7*
Collins, Heather 1946- *81*
Collins, Hunt
  See Hunter, Evan
Collins, Michael
  See Lynds, Dennis
Collins, Michael 1930- *58*
Collins, Pat(ricia) Lowery 1932- *151*
  Earlier sketch in SATA *31*
Collins, Paul 1954- *126*
Collins, Ross 1972- *200*
Collins, Ruth Philpott 1890-1975
  Obituary *30*
Collins, Suzanne *180*
Collins, Yvonne *194*
Collinson, A. S.
  See Collinson, Alan S.
Collinson, Alan S. 1934- *80*
Collinson, Roger (Alfred) 1936- *133*
Collison, Linda 1953- *185*
Collodi, Carlo 1826-1890 .... *100*
  Earlier sketch in SATA *29*
  See also CLR *120*
Colloms, Brenda 1919- *40*
Colman, Hila *53*
  Earlier sketch in SATA *1*
  See also SAAS *14*
Colman, Morris 1899(?)-1981
  Obituary *25*
Colman, Penny (Morgan) 1944- *160*
  Autobiography Feature *160*
  Earlier sketches in SATA *77, 114*
Colman, Warren (David) 1944- *67*
Colombo, John Robert 1936- *50*
Colon, Raul *156*
Colon, Raul 1952- *202*
Colonius, Lillian 1911-1992 .... *3*
Colorado, Antonio J.
  See Colorado (Capella), Antonio J(ulio)
Colorado (Capella), Antonio J(ulio)
  1903-1994 .... *23*
  Obituary *79*
Colquhoun, Glenn 1964- *165*
Colston, Fifi E. 1960- *150*
Colt, Martin
  See Epstein, Beryl
  and Epstein, Samuel
Colum, Padraic 1881-1972 .... *15*
  See also CLR *36*
Columbus, Chris 1959- *97*
Columbus, Christopher
  See Columbus, Chris
Columella
  See Moore, Clement Clarke
Colver, Anne 1908- *7*
Colvin, James
  See Moorcock, Michael
Colwell, Eileen (Hilda) 1904-2002 .... *2*
Colwyn, Stewart
  See Pepper, Frank S.
Coman, Carolyn 1951- *197*
  Earlier sketch in SATA *127*
Combs, Lisa M.
  See McCourt, Lisa
Combs, Robert
  See Murray, John
Comfort, Jane Levington
  See Sturtzel, Jane Levington
Comfort, Mildred Houghton 1886-1976 .... *3*
Comins, Ethel M(ae) *11*
Comins, Jeremy 1933- *28*
Commager, Henry Steele 1902-1998 .... *23*
  Obituary *102*
Comora, Madeleine *190*
Compere, Mickie
  See Davidson, Margaret
Compestine, Ying Chang 1963- *187*
  Earlier sketch in SATA *140*
Comport, Sally Wern *190*
Compton, Patricia A. 1936- *75*

Comte, The Great
  See Hawkesworth, Eric
Comus
  See Ballantyne, R(obert) M(ichael)
Comyns, Nance
  See Comyns-Toohey, Nantz
Comyns-Toohey, Nantz 1956- *86*
Conan Doyle, Arthur
  See Doyle, Sir Arthur Conan
Condie, Ally *204*
Condie, Allyson B.
  See Condie, Ally
Condit, Martha Olson 1913- *28*
Condon, Bill 1949- *142*
Condon, Judith *83*
Condon, Ken *195*
Condy, Roy 1942- *96*
Cone, Ferne Geller 1921- *39*
Cone, Molly (Lamken) 1918- *151*
  Autobiography Feature *151*
  Earlier sketches in SATA *1, 28, 115*
  See also SAAS *11*
Cone, Patrick 1954- *89*
Coney, Michael G. 1932-2005 .... *61*
  Obituary *170*
Coney, Michael Greatrex
  See Coney, Michael G.
Coney, Mike
  See Coney, Michael G.
Conford, Ellen 1942- *162*
  Earlier sketches in SATA *6, 68, 110*
  See also CLR *71*
Conger, Lesley
  See Suttles, Shirley (Smith)
Conklin, Gladys Plemon 1903- *2*
Conklin, Paul S. 1929(?)-2003 .... *43*
  Brief entry *33*
  Obituary *147*
Conkling, Hilda 1910-1986 .... *23*
Conlan, Kathleen Elizabeth 1950- *145*
Conlan, Kathy
  See Conlan, Kathleen Elizabeth
Conley, Robyn 1963- *125*
Conley-Weaver, Robyn
  See Conley, Robyn
Conlon-McKenna, Marita 1956- *71*
Conly, Jane Leslie 1948- *164*
  Earlier sketches in SATA *80, 112*
Conly, Robert Leslie 1918(?)-1973 .... *23*
  See also CLR *2*
Connell, Kirk
  See Chapman, John Stanton Higham
Connell, Tom *206*
Connelly, Gwen 1952- *212*
Connelly, Marc(us Cook) 1890-1980
  Obituary *25*
Connolly, Jerome P(atrick) 1931- *8*
Connolly, Pat 1943- *74*
Connolly, Peter 1935- *105*
  Earlier sketch in SATA *47*
Conover, Chris 1950- *213*
  Earlier sketch in SATA *31*
Conquest, Owen
  See Hamilton, Charles (Harold St. John)
Conrad, Joseph 1857-1924 .... *27*
Conrad, Pam 1947-1996 .... *133*
  Brief entry *49*
  Obituary *90*
  Earlier sketches in SATA *52, 80*
  See also CLR *18*
  See also SAAS *19*
Conroy, Jack
  See Conroy, John Wesley
Conroy, John Wesley 1899-1990 .... *19*
  Obituary *65*
Conroy, Robert
  See Goldston, Robert (Conroy)
Constable, Kate 1966- *172*
Constant, Alberta Wilson 1908-1981 .... *22*
  Obituary *28*
Constantin, Pascale *185*

Conway, Celeste *210*
Conway, David 1970- *213*
Conway, Diana C(ohen) 1943- *91*
Conway, Gordon
  See Hamilton, Charles (Harold St. John)
Cook, Ande *192*
Cook, Bernadine 1924- *11*
Cook, Fred J(ames) 1911-2003 .... *2*
  Obituary *145*
Cook, Glen 1944- *171*
  Earlier sketch in SATA *108*
Cook, Glen Charles
  See Cook, Glen
Cook, Hugh 1956- *85*
Cook, Hugh, Walter Gilbert
  See Cook, Hugh
Cook, Jean Thor 1930- *94*
Cook, Joel 1934- *79*
Cook, Joseph Jay 1924- *8*
Cook, Lisa Broadie *157*
Cook, Lyn
  See Waddell, Evelyn Margaret
Cook, Roy
  See Silverberg, Robert
Cook, Sally *207*
Cook, Trish *175*
Cooke, Ann
  See Cole, Joanna
Cooke, Arthur
  See Lowndes, Robert A(ugustine) W(ard)
Cooke, Barbara
  See Alexander, Anna B(arbara Cooke)
Cooke, David Coxe 1917- *2*
Cooke, Donald Ewin 1916-1985 .... *2*
  Obituary *45*
Cooke, Frank E. 1920- *87*
Cooke, Jean (Isobel Esther) 1929- *74*
Cooke, John Estes
  See Baum, L. Frank
Cooke, Trish 1962- *129*
Cookson, Catherine (McMullen) 1906-1998 .. *9*
  Obituary *116*
Cooley, Beth *210*
Cooley, Elizabeth
  See Cooley, Beth
Cooley, Regina Francoise 1940- *177*
Coolidge, Olivia E(nsor) 1908- *26*
  Earlier sketch in SATA *1*
Cooling, Wendy *169*
  Earlier sketch in SATA *111*
Coombs, Charles I(ra) 1914-1994 .... *43*
  Earlier sketch in SATA *3*
  See also SAAS *15*
Coombs, Chick
  See Coombs, Charles I(ra)
Coombs, Jonathan *204*
Coombs, Kate *190*
Coombs, Patricia 1926- *51*
  Earlier sketch in SATA *3*
  See also SAAS *22*
Cooney, Barbara 1917-2000 .... *96*
  Obituary *123*
  Earlier sketches in SATA *6, 59*
  See also CLR *23*
Cooney, Caroline B. 1947- *179*
  Brief entry *41*
  Earlier sketches in SATA *48, 80, 113, 130*
Cooney, Doug *181*
Cooney, Nancy Evans 1932- *42*
Coontz, Otto 1946- *33*
Cooper, Ann (Catharine) 1939- *104*
Cooper, Dutch
  See Kuyper, Sjoerd
Cooper, Elisha 1971- *157*
  Earlier sketch in SATA *99*
Cooper, Elizabeth Keyser -1992 .... *47*
Cooper, Floyd *187*
  Earlier sketches in SATA *96, 144*
  See also CLR *60*
Cooper, Gordon 1932- *23*

Cooper, Helen 1963- *169*
    Earlier sketch in SATA *102*
Cooper, Henry S. F., Jr. 1933- *65*
Cooper, Henry Spotswood Fenimore, Jr.
    See Cooper, Henry S. F., Jr.
Cooper, Ilene 1948- *145*
    Earlier sketches in SATA *66, 97*
Cooper, James Fenimore 1789-1851 .... *19*
    See also CLR *105*
Cooper, John R. *1*
Cooper, Kay 1941- *11*
Cooper, Lee Pelham 1926- *5*
Cooper, Lester (Irving) 1919-1985 .... *32*
    Obituary *43*
Cooper, Lettice (Ulpha) 1897-1994 .... *35*
    Obituary *82*
Cooper, Louise 1952-2009 .... *152*
Cooper, M.E.
    See Davis, Maggie S.
Cooper, M.E.
    See Lerangis, Peter
Cooper, Melrose
    See Kroll, Virginia L.
Cooper, Michael L. 1950- *181*
    Earlier sketches in SATA *79, 117*
Cooper, Patrick 1949- *134*
Cooper, Susan 1935- *151*
    Earlier sketches in SATA *4, 64, 104*
    See also CLR *67*
    See also SAAS *6*
Cooper, Susan Mary
    See Cooper, Susan
Cope, Jane U(rsula) 1949- *108*
Copeland, Helen 1920- *4*
Copeland, Mark 1956- *180*
Copeland, Paul W. *23*
Coplans, Peta 1951- *84*
Copley (Diana) Heather Pickering 1918- *45*
Coppard, A(lfred) E(dgar) 1878-1957
    See YABC *1*
Copper, Melinda 1952- *172*
Copper, Melinda McConnaughey
    See Copper, Melinda
Corace, Jen *208*
Coralie
    See Anderson, Catherine Corley
Corbett, Grahame *43*
    Brief entry *36*
Corbett, Scott 1913- *42*
    Earlier sketch in SATA *2*
    See also CLR *1*
    See also SAAS *2*
Corbett, Sue *174*
Corbett, W(illiam) J(esse) 1938- *102*
    Brief entry *44*
    Earlier sketch in SATA *50*
    See also CLR *19*
Corbin, Sabra Lee
    See Malvern, Gladys
Corbin, William
    See McGraw, William Corbin
Corbman, Marjorie 1987- *179*
Corby, Dan
    See Catherall, Arthur
Corcoran, Barbara (Asenath) 1911-2003 ...... *77*
    Autobiography Feature *125*
    Earlier sketch in SATA *3*
    See also CLR *50*
    See also SAAS *20*
Corcos, Lucille 1908-1973 .... *10*
Cordell, Alexander
    See Graber, Alexander
Cordell, Matthew 1975- *199*
Corder, Zizou
    See Young, Louisa
Corella, Joseph
    See Odgers, Sally Farrell
Coren, Alan 1938-2007 .... *32*
    Obituary *187*
Corey, Dorothy *23*
Corey, Shana 1974- *133*

Corfe, Thomas Howell 1928- *27*
Corfe, Tom
    See Corfe, Thomas Howell
Corfield, Robin Bell 1952- *74*
Corlett, William 1938-2005 .... *46*
    Brief entry *39*
Cormack, M(argaret) Grant 1913- *11*
Cormack, Maribelle B. 1902-1984 .... *39*
Cormier, Robert 1925-2000 .... *83*
    Obituary *122*
    Earlier sketches in SATA *10, 45*
    See also CLR *55*
Cormier, Robert Edmund
    See Cormier, Robert
Cornelius, Carol 1942- *40*
Cornelius, Kay 1933- *157*
Cornell, J.
    See Cornell, Jeffrey
Cornell, James (Clayton, Jr.) 1938- *27*
Cornell, Jean Gay 1920- *23*
Cornell, Jeffrey 1945- *11*
Cornell, Laura *189*
Cornish, D.M. 1972- *185*
Cornish, Sam(uel James) 1935- *23*
Cornwall, Nellie
    See Sloggett, Nellie
Cornwell, Autumn *195*
Corr, Christopher 1955- *189*
Correy, Lee
    See Stine, G(eorge) Harry
Corrick, James A. 1945- *76*
Corrigan, (Helen) Adeline 1909- *23*
Corrigan, Barbara 1922- *8*
Corrigan, Eireann 1977- *163*
Corrin, Sara 1918- *86*
    Brief entry *48*
Corrin, Stephen *86*
    Brief entry *48*
Corsi, Wendy
    See Staub, Wendy Corsi
Cort, M. C.
    See Clifford, Margaret Cort
Cort, Margaret
    See Clifford, Margaret Cort
Corwin, Judith H(offman) 1946- *10*
Corwin, Oliver
    See Corwin, Oliver J.
Corwin, Oliver J. *206*
Cory, Rowena
    See Lindquist, Rowena Cory
Cosby, Bill 1937- *110*
    Earlier sketch in SATA *66*
Cosby, William Henry, Jr.
    See Cosby, Bill
    and Cosby, Bill
Cosentino, Ralph *169*
Cosgrave, John O'Hara II 1908-1968
    Obituary *21*
Cosgrove, Margaret (Leota) 1926- *47*
Cosgrove, Stephen E(dward) 1945- *53*
    Brief entry *40*
Coskey, Evelyn 1932- *7*
Cosner, Shaaron 1940- *43*
Cossi, Olga 1921- *102*
    Earlier sketch in SATA *67*
Costabel, Eva Deutsch 1924- *45*
Costabel-Deutsch, Eva
    See Costabel, Eva Deutsch
Coste, Marion 1938- *183*
Costello, David *174*
Costello, David F(rancis) 1904-1990 .... *23*
Cte, Genevieve 1964- *184*
Cote, Nancy 1952- *182*
Cott, Jonathan 1942- *23*
Cottam, Clarence 1899-1974 .... *25*
Cotten, Cynthia *188*
Cottin, Menena 1950- *213*
Cottle, Joan 1960- *135*
Cottler, Joseph 1899-1996 .... *22*
Cottonwood, Joe 1947- *92*
Cottrell, Leonard 1913-1974 .... *24*

Cottringer, Anne 1952- *150*
    Earlier sketch in SATA *97*
Couch, Greg *199*
Coulman, Valerie 1969- *161*
Couloumbis, Audrey *173*
Counsel, June 1926- *70*
Countryman, The
    See Whitlock, Ralph
Courlander, Harold 1908-1996 .... *6*
    Obituary *88*
Coursen, Valerie 1965(?)- *102*
Courtis, Stuart Appleton 1874-1969
    Obituary *29*
Courtland, Tyler
    See Stevens, Serita
Courtney, Dayle
    See Goldsmith, Howard
Coury, Louise Andree 1895(?)-1983
    Obituary *34*
Cousins, Linda 1946- *90*
Cousins, Lucy 1964- *205*
    Earlier sketch in SATA *172*
Cousins, Margaret 1905-1996 .... *2*
    Obituary *92*
Cousteau, Jacques 1910-1997 .... *98*
    Earlier sketch in SATA *38*
Cousteau, Jacques-Yves
    See Cousteau, Jacques
Couture, Christin 1951- *73*
Couvillon, Jacques *195*
Covert, Ralph 1968- *197*
Coville, Bruce 1950- *155*
    Autobiography Feature *155*
    Earlier sketches in SATA *32, 77, 118*
Covington, Dennis *109*
Covington, Linda
    See Windsor, Linda
Cowan, Catherine *121*
Cowan, Rebecca M.
    See Moesta, Rebecca
Cowan, Rebecca Moesta
    See Moesta, Rebecca
Coward, Fiona 1963- *178*
Cowdrey, Richard 1959- *204*
Cowell, Cressida 1966- *140*
Cowen, Eve
    See Werner, Herma
Cowen, Ida 1898-1993 .... *64*
Cowie, Leonard W(allace) 1919- *4*
Cowles, Kathleen
    See Krull, Kathleen
Cowley, Cassia Joy
    See Cowley, Joy
Cowley, Joy 1936- *164*
    Autobiography Feature *118*
    Earlier sketches in SATA *4, 90*
    See also CLR *55*
    See also SAAS *26*
Cowley, Marjorie 1925- *111*
Cox, (Christopher) Barry 1931- *62*
Cox, Clinton 1934- *108*
    Earlier sketch in SATA *74*
Cox, David 1933- *56*
Cox, David Dundas
    See Cox, David
Cox, Donald William 1921- *23*
Cox, Jack
    See Cox, John Roberts
Cox, John Roberts 1915-1981 .... *9*
Cox, Judy 1954- *198*
    Earlier sketches in SATA *117, 160*
Cox, Marion Monroe 1898-1983
    Obituary *34*
Cox, Palmer 1840-1924 .... *24*
    See also CLR *24*
Cox, Vic 1942- *88*
Cox, Vicki 1945- *158*
Cox, Victoria
    See Garretson, Victoria Diane
Cox, Wallace 1924-1973 .... *25*

Cox, Wally
  See Cox, Wallace
Cox, William R(obert) 1901-1988 46
  Brief entry 31
  Obituary 57
Coxe, Molly 1959- 101
  Earlier sketch in SATA 69
Coxon, Michele 1950- 158
  Earlier sketch in SATA 76
Coy, Harold 1902-1986 3
Coy, John 1958- 171
  Earlier sketch in SATA 120
Craats, Rennay 1973- 131
Crabtree, Judith 1928- 98
  Earlier sketch in SATA 63
Crabtree, Julie 1970- 214
Cracker, Edward E.B.
  See Odgers, Sally Farrell
Craft, Elizabeth 1971(?)- 204
Craft, K. Y.
  See Craft, Kinuko Y(amabe)
Craft, Kinuko
  See Craft, Kinuko Y(amabe)
Craft, Kinuko Y(amabe) 1940- 127
  Earlier sketch in SATA 65
Craft, Ruth 1935- 87
  Brief entry 31
Craig, A. A.
  See Anderson, Poul
Craig, Alisa
  See MacLeod, Charlotte (Matilda)
Craig, David 205
  See James, Bill
Craig, Helen 1934- 213
  Earlier sketches in SATA 46, 49, 94
Craig, Joe 1979- 198
Craig, Joe Alexander
  See Craig, Joe
Craig, John Eland
  See Chipperfield, Joseph Eugene
Craig, John Ernest 1921- 23
Craig, Kit
  See Reed, Kit
Craig, M. F.
  See Craig, Mary (Francis) Shura
Craig, M. Jean 17
Craig, M. S.
  See Craig, Mary (Francis) Shura
Craig, Margaret (Maze) 1911-1964 9
Craig, Mary
  See Craig, Mary (Francis) Shura
Craig, Mary Shura
  See Craig, Mary (Francis) Shura
Craig, Mary (Francis) Shura 1923-1991 86
  Obituary 65
  Earlier sketch in SATA 6
  See also SAAS 7
Craig, Ruth 1922- 95
Craik, Mrs.
  See Craik, Dinah Maria (Mulock)
Craik, Dinah Maria (Mulock) 1826-1887 34
Crandall, Court 1965- 175
Crandell, Rachel 1943- 152
Crane, Barbara (Joyce) 1934- 31
Crane, Caroline 1930- 11
Crane, Jordan 1973- 174
Crane, M. A.
  See Wartski, Maureen (Ann Crane)
Crane, Royston Campbell 1901-1977
  Obituary 22
Crane, Stephen 1871-1900
  See YABC 2
  See also CLR 132
Crane, Stephen Townley
  See Crane, Stephen
Crane, Walter 1845-1915 100
  Earlier sketch in SATA 18
  See also CLR 56
Crane, William D(wight) 1892-1976 1
Cranfield, Ingrid 1945- 74

Cranshaw, Stanley
  See Fisher, Dorothy (Frances) Canfield
Crary, Elizabeth (Ann) 1942- 99
  Brief entry 43
Crary, Margaret (Coleman) 1906-1986 9
Craste, Marc 201
Cravath, Lynne Avril
  See Cravath, Lynne W.
Cravath, Lynne W. 1951- 182
  Earlier sketches in SATA 98, 148
Craven, Thomas 1889-1969 22
Crawford, Charles P. 1945- 28
Crawford, Deborah 1922- 6
Crawford, John E(dmund) 1904-1971 3
Crawford, K(aren) Michael 1959- 155
Crawford, Mel 1925- 44
  Brief entry 33
Crawford, Phyllis 1899- 3
Crawley, Dave 177
Cray, Roberta
  See Emerson, Ru
Crayder, Dorothy 7
Crayder, Teresa
  See Colman, Hila
Crayon, Geoffrey
  See Irving, Washington
Craz, Albert G. 1926- 24
Crebbin, June 1938- 169
  Earlier sketch in SATA 80
Crecy, Jeanne
  See Williams, Jeanne
Credle, Ellis 1902-1998 1
Creech, Sharon 1945- 172
  Earlier sketches in SATA 94, 139
  See also CLR 89
Creeden, Sharon 1938- 91
Creel, Ann Howard 1953- 187
Creighton, (Mary) Helen 1899-1989
  Obituary 64
Creighton, Jill 1949- 96
Crenson, Victoria 1952- 159
  Earlier sketch in SATA 88
Cresp, Gael 1954- 119
Crespo, George 1962- 82
Cresswell, Helen 1934-2005 79
  Obituary 168
  Earlier sketches in SATA 1, 48
  See also CLR 18
  See also SAAS 20
Cressy, Michael 1955- 124
Cressy, Mike
  See Cressy, Michael
Cretan, Gladys (Yessayan) 1921- 2
Cretzmeyer, Stacy (Megan) 1959- 124
Crew, Gary 1947- 163
  Earlier sketches in SATA 75, 110
  See also CLR 42
Crew, Helen (Cecilia) Coale 1866-1941
  See YABC 2
Crew, Linda (Jean) 1951- 137
  Earlier sketch in SATA 71
Crews, Donald 1938- 76
  Brief entry 30
  Earlier sketch in SATA 32
  See also CLR 7
Crews, Nina 1963- 158
  Earlier sketch in SATA 97
Crichton, John Michael
  See Crichton, Michael
Crichton, Michael 1942-2008 88
  Obituary 199
  Earlier sketch in SATA 9
Crider, Allen Billy
  See Crider, Bill
Crider, Bill 1941- 99
Crilley, Mark 1966- 210
  Autobiography Feature 148
  Earlier sketches in SATA 120, 148
Crimi, Carolyn 1959- 176
Cripps, Enid Margaret
  See Appiah, Peggy

Crisler, Curtis L. 188
Crisman, Ruth 1914- 73
Crisp, Marta Marie
  See Crisp, Marty
Crisp, Marty 1947- 128
Crispin, A(nn) C(arol) 1950- 86
Crist, James J. 1961- 168
Cristall, Barbara 79
Crist-Evans, Craig 1954- 153
Crocker, Carter 193
Crocker, Nancy 1956- 185
Crofford, Emily (Ardell) 1927- 61
Crofut, William E. III 1934- 23
Croggon, Alison 1962- 194
Croll, Carolyn 1945- 102
  Brief entry 52
  Earlier sketch in SATA 56
Croman, Dorothy Young
  See Rosenberg, Dorothy
Cromie, Alice Hamilton 1914-2000 24
Cromie, William J(oseph) 1930- 4
Crompton, Anne Eliot 1930- 73
  Earlier sketch in SATA 23
Crompton, Richmal
  See Lamburn, Richmal Crompton
Cronbach, Abraham 1882-1965 11
Crone, Ruth 1919-2003 4
Cronin, A(rchibald) J(oseph) 1896-1981 47
  Obituary 25
Cronin, Doreen (A.) 125
Cronin, Doreen 1966(?)- 178
  See also CLR 136
Cronin, Doreen A.
  See Cronin, Doreen
Crook, Beverly Courtney 38
  Brief entry 35
Crook, Connie Brummel 1930- 168
  Earlier sketch in SATA 98
Crook, Constance
  See Crook, Connie Brummel
Crosby, Alexander L. 1906-1980 2
  Obituary 23
Crosby, Harry C.
  See Anvil, Christopher
Crosby, Margaret
  See Rathmann, Peggy
Crosher, G. R. 14
Cross, Gilbert B. 1939- 60
  Brief entry 51
Cross, Gillian 1945- 178
  Autobiography Feature 178
  Earlier sketches in SATA 38, 71, 110, 165
  See also CLR 28
Cross, Gillian Clare
  See Cross, Gillian
Cross, Helen Reeder
  See Broadhead, Helen Cross
Cross, Peter 1951- 95
Cross, Shauna 1976(?)- 196
Cross, Tom 1954- 146
Cross, Verda 1914- 75
Cross, Wilbur Lucius III 1918- 2
Crossland, Caroline 1964- 83
Crossley-Holland, Kevin 1941- 165
  Earlier sketches in SATA 5, 74, 120
  See also CLR 84
  See also SAAS 20
Crossley-Holland, Kevin John William
  See Crossley-Holland, Kevin
Crouch, Karen Hillard
  See Good, Karen Hillard
Crouch, Marcus 1913-1996 4
Crout, George C(lement) 1917- 11
Crow, Donna Fletcher 1941- 40
Crow, Francis Luther
  See Luther, Frank
Crow, Kristyn 208
Crowe, Andrew 111
Crowe, Carole 1943- 204
Crowe, Chris 206
Crowe, Ellie 203

Crowe, John
  See Lynds, Dennis
Crowe, (Bettina) Peter Lum 1911- 6
Crowell, Grace Noll 1877-1969 34
Crowell, Pers 1910-1990 2
Crowell, Robert Leland 1909-2001 63
Crowfield, Christopher
  See Stowe, Harriet Beecher
Crowley, Arthur 1945- 38
Crowley, Arthur McBlair
  See Crowley, Arthur
Crowley, John 1942- 140
  Earlier sketch in SATA 65
Crowley, Suzanne 1963- 196
Crowley, Suzanne Carlisle
  See Crowley, Suzanne
Crownfield, Gertrude 1867-1945
  See YABC 1
Crowther, James Gerald 1899-1983 14
Crowther, Robert 1948- 163
Cruikshank, George 1792-1878 22
  See also CLR 63
Cruise, Robin 1951- 179
Crum, Shutta 192
  Earlier sketch in SATA 134
Crummel, Susan Stevens 1949- 176
  Earlier sketch in SATA 130
Crump, Fred H., Jr. 1931- 76
  Earlier sketch in SATA 11
Crump, J(ames) Irving 1887-1979 57
  Obituary 21
Crump, William D(rake) 1949- 138
Crunden, Reginald
  See Cleaver, Hylton Reginald
Crunk, T.
  See Crunk, Tony
Crunk, Tony 1956- 130
Crutcher, Chris 1946- 196
  Earlier sketches in SATA 52, 99, 153
  See also CLR 28
Crutcher, Christopher C.
  See Crutcher, Chris
Cruz, Ray(mond) 1933- 6
Cruz Martinez, Alejandro (?)-1987 74
Crystal, Billy 1947- 154
Crystal, William
  See Crystal, Billy
Ctvrtek, Vaclav 1911-1976
  Obituary 27
Cuetara, Mittie 1957- 158
  Earlier sketch in SATA 106
Cuffari, Richard 1925-1978 66
  Obituary 25
  Earlier sketch in SATA 6
Cuffe-Perez, Mary 1946- 199
Cullen, Countee 1903-1946 18
Cullen, Lynn 190
Culliford, Pierre 1928-1992 40
  Obituary 74
Cullinan, Bernice E(llinger) 1926- 135
Culp, Louanna McNary 1901-1965 2
Culper, Felix
  See McCaughrean, Geraldine
Cumbaa, Stephen 1947- 72
Cumming, Peter 1951- 168
Cumming, Primrose Amy 1915- 24
Cumming, Robert 1945- 65
Cummings, Betty Sue 1918- 15
  See also SAAS 9
Cummings, Mary 1951- 185
Cummings, Parke 1902-1987 2
  Obituary 53
Cummings, Pat 1950- 203
  Earlier sketches in SATA 42, 71, 107
  See also CLR 48
  See also SAAS 13
Cummings, Phil 1957- 123
  Earlier sketch in SATA 74
Cummings, Priscilla 1951- 170
  Earlier sketch in SATA 129

Cummings, Richard
  See Gardner, Richard (M.)
Cummins, Julie 200
Cummins, Maria Susanna 1827-1866
  See YABC 1
Cumpiano, Ina 207
Cuneo, Mary Louise -2001 85
Cunliffe, John Arthur 1933- 86
  Earlier sketch in SATA 11
Cunliffe, Marcus (Falkner) 1922-1990 37
  Obituary 66
Cunnane, Kelly 175
Cunningham, Bob
  See May, Julian
Cunningham, Captain Frank
  See Glick, Carl (Cannon)
Cunningham, Cathy
  See Cunningham, Chet
Cunningham, Chet 1928- 23
Cunningham, Dale S(peers) 1932- 11
Cunningham, Dru 91
Cunningham, E. V.
  See Fast, Howard
Cunningham, Julia (Woolfolk) 1916- 132
  Earlier sketches in SATA 1, 26
  See also SAAS 2
Cunningham, Lawrence J. 1943- 125
Cunningham, Virginia
  See Holmgren, Virginia C(unningham)
Curiae, Amicus
  See Fuller, Edmund (Maybank)
Curie, Eve 1904-2007 1
  Obituary 188
Curlee, Lynn 1947- 190
  Earlier sketches in SATA 98, 141
Curley, Daniel 1918-1988 23
  Obituary 61
Curley, Marianne 1959- 175
  Earlier sketch in SATA 131
Currey, Anna 194
Currie, Robin 1948- 120
Currie, Stephen 1960- 132
  Earlier sketch in SATA 82
Curry, Ann (Gabrielle) 1934- 72
Curry, Jane L(ouise) 1932- 138
  Autobiography Feature 138
  Earlier sketches in SATA 1, 52, 90
  See also CLR 31
  See also SAAS 6
Curry, Peggy Simson 1911-1987 8
  Obituary 50
Curry, Tom 185
Curtis, Bruce (Richard) 1944- 30
Curtis, Chara M(ahar) 1950- 78
Curtis, Christopher Paul 1954(?)- 187
  Earlier sketches in SATA 93, 140
  See also CLR 68
Curtis, Gavin 1965- 107
Curtis, Jamie Lee 1958- 144
  Earlier sketch in SATA 95
  See also CLR 88
Curtis, Jennifer Keats 185
Curtis, Marci 160
Curtis, Munzee
  See Caseley, Judith
Curtis, Neil 1950-2006 202
Curtis, Patricia 1921- 101
  Earlier sketch in SATA 23
Curtis, Peter
  See Lofts, Norah (Robinson)
Curtis, Philip (Delacourt) 1920- 62
Curtis, Richard 1937- 29
Curtis, Richard Alan
  See Curtis, Richard
Curtis, Richard Hale
  See Deming, Richard
  and Levinson, Leonard
  and Rothweiler, Paul Roger
Curtis, Stacy 205
Curtis, Wade
  See Pournelle, Jerry (Eugene)

Curtiss, A(rlene) B. 1934- 90
Cusack, Margaret 1945- 58
Cushman, Doug 1953- 210
  Earlier sketches in SATA 65, 101, 157
Cushman, Jerome 2
Cushman, Karen 1941- 147
  Earlier sketch in SATA 89
  See also CLR 55
Cusick, Richie Tankersley 1952- 140
  Earlier sketch in SATA 67
Cutbill, Andy 1972- 201
Cutchen, Billye Walker 1930- 15
Cutchins, Judy 1947- 59
Cutler, Daniel S. 1951- 78
Cutler, Daniel Solomon
  See Cutler, Daniel S.
Cutler, Ebbitt 1923- 9
Cutler, Ivor 1923-2006 24
  Obituary 174
Cutler, Jane 1936- 162
  Earlier sketches in SATA 75, 118
Cutler, May Ebbitt
  See Cutler, Ebbitt
Cutler, Samuel
  See Folsom, Franklin (Brewster)
Cutlip, Kimbra L(eigh-Ann) 1964- 128
Cutrate, Joe
  See Spiegelman, Art
Cutt, W(illiam) Towrie 1898-1981 16
  Obituary 85
Cuyler, Margery 1948- 195
  Earlier sketches in SATA 39, 99, 156
Cuyler, Margery Stuyvesant
  See Cuyler, Margery
Cuyler, Stephen
  See Bates, Barbara S(nedeker)
Cyrus, Kurt 1954- 179
  Earlier sketch in SATA 132
Czernecki, Stefan 1946- 178

                    D

Dabba Smith, Frank 174
Dabcovich, Lydia 99
  Brief entry 47
  Earlier sketch in SATA 58
Dace, Dolores B(oelens) 1929- 89
Da Costa, Deborah 193
Daddo, Andrew 1967- 198
Dadey, Debbie 1959- 136
  Earlier sketch in SATA 73
Dahl, Borghild (Margarethe) 1890-1984 7
  Obituary 37
Dahl, Roald 1916-1990 73
  Obituary 65
  Earlier sketches in SATA 1, 26
  See also CLR 111
Dahlberg, Maurine F. 1951- 171
Dahlstedt, Marden (Stewart) 1921-1983 8
  Obituary 110
Dahme, Joanne 206
Dain, Martin J. 1924-2000 35
Dakos, Kalli 1950- 115
  Earlier sketch in SATA 80
Dale, Anna 1971- 170
Dale, Gary
  See Reece, Colleen L.
Dale, George E.
  See Asimov, Isaac
Dale, Jack
  See Holliday, Joseph
Dale, Kim 1957- 123
Dale, Margaret J(essy) Miller 1911- 39
Dale, Mitzi
  See Hemstock, Gillian
Dale, Norman
  See Denny, Norman (George)
Dale, Penny 1954- 151
  Earlier sketch in SATA 70

Daley, Michael J. *170*
Dalgliesh, Alice 1893-1979 .... *17*
  Obituary *21*
  See also CLR 62
Dalkey, Kara 1953- *132*
Dalkey, Kara Mia
  See Dalkey, Kara
Dallas, Ruth 1919- *86*
Dalmas, John
  See Jones, John R(obert)
Dalton, Alene
  See Chapin, Alene Olsen Dalton
Dalton, Annie 1948- *140*
  Earlier sketch in SATA 40
Dalton, Kit
  See Cunningham, Chet
Dalton, Pamela
  See Johnson, Pamela
Dalton, Sean
  See Chester, Deborah
Dalton, Sheila 1949- *108*
D'Aluisio, Faith 1957- *205*
Daly, Jim
  See Stratemeyer, Edward L.
Daly, Jude 1951- *177*
Daly, Kathleen N(orah) *124*
  Brief entry *37*
Daly, Maureen 1921-2006 .... *129*
  Obituary *176*
  Earlier sketch in SATA 2
  See also CLR 96
  See also SAAS 1
Daly, Nicholas 1946- *164*
  Earlier sketches in SATA 37, 76, 114
  See also CLR 41
  See also SAAS 21
  See Daly, Niki
Daly, Niki *198*
  See Daly, Nicholas
D'Amato, Alex 1919- *20*
D'Amato, Janet (Potter) 1925- *9*
Damerow, Gail 1944- *83*
Damerow, Gail Jane
  See Damerow, Gail
D'Amico, Carmela *170*
D'Amico, Steve *170*
Damrell, Liz 1956- *77*
Damrosch, Helen
  See Tee-Van, Helen Damrosch
Dana, Barbara 1940- *22*
Dana, Richard Henry, Jr. 1815-1882 .... *26*
Danachair, Caoimhin O
  See Danaher, Kevin
Danaher, Kevin 1913-2002 .... *22*
Danakas, John 1963- *94*
Dandi
  See Mackall, Dandi Daley
D'Andrea, Kate
  See Steiner, Barbara A(nnette)
Dangerfield, Balfour
  See McCloskey, (John) Robert
Daniel, Alan 1939- *76*
  Brief entry *53*
Daniel, Anita 1893(?)-1978 .... *23*
  Obituary *24*
Daniel, Anne
  See Steiner, Barbara A(nnette)
Daniel, Becky 1947- *56*
Daniel, Claire 1949- *164*
Daniel, Colin
  See Windsor, Patricia
Daniel, Hawthorne 1890- *8*
Daniel, (Donna) Lee 1944- *76*
Daniel, Rebecca
  See Daniel, Becky
Daniels, Guy 1919-1989 .... *11*
  Obituary *62*
Daniels, Lucy
  See Oldfield, Jenny
Daniels, Max
  See Gellis, Roberta

Daniels, Olga
  See Sinclair, Olga
Daniels, Patricia 1955- *93*
Daniels, Zoe
  See Laux, Constance
Dank, Gloria Rand 1955- *56*
  Brief entry *46*
Dank, Leonard D(ewey) 1929- *44*
Dank, Milton 1920- *31*
Dann, Max 1955- *62*
Danneberg, Julie 1958- *173*
Dantz, William R.
  See Philbrick, Rodman
Danzig, Dianne *213*
Danziger, Paula 1944-2004 .... *149*
  Brief entry *30*
  Obituary *155*
  Earlier sketches in SATA 36, 63, 102
  See also CLR 20
Darby, Gene Kegley
  See Darby, Jean (Kegley)
Darby, J. N.
  See Govan, (Mary) Christine Noble
Darby, Jean (Kegley) 1921- *68*
Darby, Patricia (Paulsen) *14*
Darby, Ray(mond) 1912-1982 .... *7*
d'Arcy, Willard
  See Cox, William R(obert)
Dare, Geena
  See McNicoll, Sylvia (Marilyn)
Darian, Shea 1959- *97*
Daringer, Helen Fern 1892-1986 .... *1*
Darke, Marjorie 1929- *87*
  Earlier sketch in SATA 16
Darley, F(elix) O(ctavius) C(arr)
  1822-1888 .... *35*
Darling, David J. 1953- *60*
  Brief entry *44*
Darling, Kathy
  See Darling, Mary Kathleen
Darling, Lois (MacIntyre) 1917-1989 .... *3*
  Obituary *64*
Darling, Louis, (Jr.) 1916-1970 .... *3*
  Obituary *23*
Darling, Mary Kathleen 1943- *124*
  Earlier sketches in SATA 9, 79
Darling, Sandra Louise Woodward
  See Day, Alexandra
Darnell, K(athryn) L(ynne) 1955- *150*
Darroll, Sally
  See Odgers, Sally Farrell
Darrow, Sharon *181*
Darrow, Whitney, (Jr.) 1909-1999 .... *13*
  Obituary *115*
Darwin, Len
  See Darwin, Leonard
Darwin, Leonard 1916- *24*
Dasent, Sir George Webbe 1817-1896 .... *62*
  Brief entry *29*
Dash, Joan 1925- *142*
Daskam, Josephine Dodge
  See Bacon, Josephine Dodge (Daskam)
D'ath, Justin 1953- *174*
  Earlier sketch in SATA 106
Dauer, Rosamond 1934- *23*
Daugherty, Charles Michael 1914- *16*
Daugherty, James (Henry) 1889-1974 .... *13*
  See also CLR 78
Daugherty, Richard D(eo) 1922- *35*
Daugherty, Sonia Medwedeff (?)-1971
  Obituary *27*
d'Aulaire, Edgar Parin 1898-1986 .... *66*
  Obituary *47*
  Earlier sketch in SATA 5
  See also CLR 21
d'Aulaire, Ingri 1904-1980 .... *66*
  Obituary *24*
  Earlier sketch in SATA 5
  See also CLR 21
d'Aulaire, Ingri Mortenson Parin
  See d'Aulaire, Ingri

Dave, Dave
  See Berg, David
Daveluy, Paule Cloutier 1919- *11*
Davenier, Christine 1961- *179*
  Earlier sketch in SATA 127
Davenport, John 1960- *156*
Daves, Michael 1938- *40*
David, A. R.
  See David, A(nn) Rosalie
David, A(nn) Rosalie 1946- *103*
David, Jonathan
  See Ames, Lee J(udah)
David, Lawrence 1963- *165*
  Earlier sketch in SATA 111
David, Peter 1956- *72*
David, Peter Allen
  See David, Peter
David, Rosalie
  See David, A(nn) Rosalie
Davidson, Alice Joyce 1932- *54*
  Brief entry *45*
Davidson, Basil 1914- *13*
Davidson, (Marie) Diane 1924- *91*
Davidson, Hugh
  See Hamilton, Edmond
Davidson, Jessica 1915-1986 .... *5*
Davidson, Judith 1953- *40*
Davidson, Lionel 1922-2009 .... *87*
Davidson, Margaret 1936- *5*
Davidson, Marion
  See Garis, Howard R.
Davidson, Mary R. 1885-1973 .... *9*
Davidson, Mary S. 1940- *61*
Davidson, Mickie
  See Davidson, Margaret
Davidson, Nicole
  See Jensen, Kathryn
Davidson, R.
  See Davidson, Raymond
Davidson, Raymond 1926- *32*
Davidson, Rosalie 1921- *23*
Davie, Helen K(ay) 1952- *148*
  Earlier sketch in SATA 77
Davies, Andrew (Wynford) 1936- *27*
Davies, Andy Robert *200*
Davies, Bettilu D(onna) 1942- *33*
Davies, Hunter 1936- *55*
  Brief entry *45*
Davies, Jacqueline 1962- *186*
  Earlier sketch in SATA 155
Davies, Joan 1934- *50*
  Brief entry *47*
Davies, Nicola 1958- *182*
  Earlier sketches in SATA 99, 150
Davies, Peter J(oseph) 1937- *52*
Davies, Sumiko 1942- *46*
Davis, (A.) Aubrey 1949- *153*
Davis, Barbara Steincrohn
  See Davis, Maggie S.
Davis, Bette J. 1923- *15*
Davis, Burke 1913- *4*
Davis, Christopher 1928- *6*
Davis, D(elbert) Dwight 1908-1965 .... *33*
Davis, Daniel S(heldon) 1936- *12*
Davis, David R. 1948- *106*
Davis, Donald 1944- *169*
  Earlier sketch in SATA 93
Davis, Donald D.
  See Davis, Donald
Davis, Eleanor 1983(?)- *209*
Davis, Emma
  See Davis, Maggie S.
Davis, Gibbs 1953- *102*
  Brief entry *41*
  Earlier sketch in SATA 46
Davis, Grania 1943- *88*
  Brief entry *50*
Davis, H(arold) L(enoir) 1896-1960 .... *114*
Davis, Hubert J(ackson) 1904-1997 .... *31*
Davis, Jack E. *210*
Davis, Jacky *204*

Davis, James Robert 1945- 32
Davis, Jenny 1953- 74
Davis, Jim
  See Davis, James Robert
Davis, Julia 1900(?)-1993 6
  Obituary 75
Davis, Karen (Elizabeth) 1944- 109
Davis, Katie 1959(?)- 208
  Earlier sketch in SATA 152
Davis, Lambert 176
Davis, Leslie
  See Guccione, Leslie Davis
Davis, Louise Littleton 1921- 25
Davis, Maggie S. 1943- 57
Davis, Marguerite 1889- 34
Davis, Mary L(ee) 1935- 9
Davis, Mary Octavia 1901-1976 6
Davis, Nelle 1958- 73
Davis, Ossie 1917-2005 81
  See also CLR 56
Davis, Paxton 1925-1994 16
Davis, Rich 1958- 206
Davis, Robert 1881-1949
  See YABC 1
Davis, Robin W(orks) 1962- 87
Davis, Russell Gerard 1922- 3
Davis, Tanita S. 212
Davis, Tim(othy N.) 1957- 94
Davis, Verne Theodore 1889-1973 6
Davis, Yvonne 1927- 115
Davol, Marguerite W. 1928- 146
  Earlier sketch in SATA 82
DaVolls, Andy (P.) 1967- 85
DaVolls, Linda 1966- 85
Davys, Sarah
  See Manning, Rosemary
Dawes, Claiborne 1935- 111
Dawson, Arthur L. 207
Dawson, Elmer A. 67
  Earlier sketch in SATA 1
Dawson, Imogen (Zoe) 1948- 126
  Earlier sketch in SATA 90
Dawson, Janine 1957- 196
Dawson, Mary 1919- 11
Dawson, Willow 1975- 208
Day, A(rthur) Grove 1904-1994 59
Day, Alexandra 1941- 197
  Autobiography Feature 197
  Earlier sketches in SATA 67, 97, 169
  See also CLR 22
  See also SAAS 19
Day, Beth (Feagles) 1924- 33
Day, Donna
  See Asay, Donna Day
Day, Edward C. 1932- 72
Day, Jon 1936(?)- 79
Day, Karen 187
Day, Larry 1956- 181
Day, Nancy 1953- 140
Day, Nancy Raines 1951- 148
  Earlier sketch in SATA 93
Day, Shirley 1962- 94
Day, Thomas 1748-1789
  See YABC 1
Day, Trevor 1955- 124
Dazey, Agnes J(ohnston) 2
Dazey, Frank M. 2
Deacon, Alexis 1978- 139
Deacon, Eileen
  See Geipel, Eileen
Deacon, Richard
  See McCormick, (George) Donald (King)
Deadman, Ronald 1919-1988(?)
  Obituary 56
Deak, Erzsi 1959- 152
Dean, Anabel 1915- 12
Dean, Carolee 1962- 148
Dean, Claire 215
Dean, David 1976- 192
Dean, Karen Strickler 1923- 49
Dean, Ruth (Brigham) 1947- 145

Dean, Zoey
  See Bennett, Cherie
de Angeli, Marguerite (Lofft) 1889-1987 ... 100
  Obituary 51
  Earlier sketches in SATA 1, 27
  See also CLR 1
Deans, Karen 195
Deans, Sis Boulos 1955- 136
  Earlier sketch in SATA 78
DeArmand, Frances Ullmann 1904(?)-1984 . 10
  Obituary 38
DeArmond, Dale 1914- 70
DeArmond, Dale Burlison
  See DeArmond, Dale
Deary, Terry 1946- 171
  Brief entry 41
  Earlier sketches in SATA 51, 101
Deaver, Julie Reece 1953- 68
de Banke, Cecile 1889-1965 11
De Bello, Rosario 1923- 89
Debon, Nicolas 186
  Earlier sketch in SATA 151
de Bono, Edward 1933- 66
de Brissac, Malcolm
  See Dickinson, Peter
de Brunhoff, Jean
  See Brunhoff, Jean de
De Brunhoff, Laurent
  See Brunhoff, Laurent de
De Bruyn, Monica G. 1952- 13
De Bruyn, Monica Jean Grembowicz
  See De Bruyn, Monica G.
DeBry, Roger K. 1942- 91
de Camp, Catherine Crook 1907-2000 83
  Earlier sketch in SATA 12
de Camp, L. Sprague 1907-2000 83
  Earlier sketch in SATA 9
de Camp, Lyon Sprague
  See de Camp, L. Sprague
DeCandido, Keith R.A. 112
Dechausay, Sonia E. 94
Decker, C.B. 172
Decker, Cynthia B.
  See Decker, C.B.
Decker, Duane 1910-1964 5
Decker, Timothy 1974- 197
DeClements, Barthe 1920- 131
  Earlier sketches in SATA 35, 71
  See also CLR 23
DeClements, Barthe Faith
  See DeClements, Barthe
de Clercq Zubli, Rita la Fontaine 1929- 199
de Conte, Sieur Louis
  See Twain, Mark
Dedman, Stephen 108
Dee, Catherine 1964- 138
Dee, Ruby
  See Wallace, Ruby Ann
Deedy, Carmen Agra 1960- 196
Deedy, John 1923- 24
Deegan, Paul Joseph 1937- 48
  Brief entry 38
Deem, James M. 1950- 191
  Autobiography Feature 191
  Earlier sketches in SATA 75, 134
Deem, James Morgan
  See Deem, James M.
Deeter, Catherine 1947- 137
DeFelice, Cynthia 1951- 165
  Earlier sketches in SATA 79, 121
DeFelice, Cynthia C.
  See DeFelice, Cynthia
Defoe, Daniel 1660(?)-1731 22
  See also CLR 61
DeFord, Deborah H. 123
deFrance, Anthony
  See DiFranco, Anthony (Mario)
Degen, Bruce 1945- 205
  Brief entry 47
  Earlier sketches in SATA 57, 97, 147
DeGering, Etta (Belle) Fowler 1898-1996 7

De Goldi, Kate 1959- 123
De Goldi, Kathleen Domenica
  See De Goldi, Kate
de Goursac, Olivier 1959- 184
De Grazia, Ettore 1909-1982 39
De Grazia, Ted
  See De Grazia, Ettore
deGroat, Diane 1947- 169
  Earlier sketches in SATA 31, 90
deGros, J. H.
  See Villiard, Paul
de Grummond, Lena Young 62
  Earlier sketch in SATA 6
de Hamel, Joan Littledale 1924- 86
De Haven, Tom 1949- 72
de Hugo, Pierre
  See Brackers de Hugo, Pierre
Deiss, Joseph Jay 1915- 12
de Jenkins, Lyll Becerra 1925-1997 102
DeJong, David C(ornel) 1905-1967 10
de Jong, Dola
  See de Jong, Dorothea Rosalie
de Jong, Dorothea Rosalie 1911-2003 7
  Obituary 149
DeJong, Meindert 1906-1991 2
  Obituary 68
  See also CLR 73
DeJonge, Joanne E. 1943- 56
Deka, Connie
  See Laux, Constance
de Kay, Ormonde (Jr.) 1923-1998 7
  Obituary 106
DeKeyser, Stacy 1959- 214
de Kiriline, Louise
  See Lawrence, Louise de Kiriline
Dekker, Carl
  See Laffin, John (Alfred Charles)
  and Lynds, Dennis
deKruif, Paul (Henry) 1890-1971 50
  Earlier sketch in SATA 5
Delacre, Lulu 1957- 209
  Earlier sketches in SATA 36, 156
DeLaCroix, Alice 1940- 195
  Earlier sketch in SATA 75
de la Cruz, Melissa 1971- 179
De la Garza, Phyllis 1942- 169
De Lage, Ida 1918- 11
de la Mare, Walter (John) 1873-1956 16
  See also CLR 148
Delaney, Harry 1932- 3
Delaney, Joseph 1945- 172
Delaney, M.C.
  See Delaney, Michael
Delaney, Michael 1955- 180
  Earlier sketch in SATA 96
Delaney, Michael Clark
  See Delaney, Michael
Delaney, Ned 1951- 28
Delaney, Thomas Nicholas III
  See Delaney, Ned
DeLange, Alex Pardo
  See Pardo DeLange, Alex
Delano, Hugh 1933- 20
Delano, Marfe Ferguson 215
Delany, Samuel R., Jr. 1942- 92
Delany, Samuel Ray
  See Delany, Samuel R., Jr.
de la Pena, Matt 205
De La Ramee, Marie Louise 1839-1908 20
de la Roche, Mazo 1879-1961 64
De La Roche Saint Andre, Anne 1950- 75
Delaune, (Jewel) Lynn (de Grummond) 7
DeLaurentis, Louise Budde 1920- 12
del Barco, Lucy Salamanca 1900(?)-1989
  Obituary 64
Delderfield, Eric R(aymond) 1909-1995 14
Delderfield, Ronald Frederick 1912-1972 20
DeLeeuw, Adele (Louise) 1899-1988 30
  Obituary 56
  Earlier sketch in SATA 1
De Leon, Nephtali 1945- 97

Delessert, Etienne 1941- *179*
   Brief entry 27
   Earlier sketches in SATA *46, 130*
   See also CLR *81*
Delgado, James P. 1958- *122*
de Lint, Charles 1951- *207*
   Earlier sketches in SATA *115, 157*
de Lint, Charles Henri Diederick Hofsmit
   See de Lint, Charles
Delmar, Roy
   See Wexler, Jerome (LeRoy)
Del Negro, Janice M. *197*
Deloria, Vine, Jr. 1933-2005 .... *21*
   Obituary *171*
Deloria, Vine Victor, Jr.
   See Deloria, Vine, Jr.
del Rey, Lester 1915-1993 .... *22*
   Obituary *76*
Delrio, Martin
   See Doyle, Debra
   and Macdonald, James D.
Delton, Judy 1931-2001 .... *77*
   Obituary *130*
   Earlier sketch in SATA *14*
   See also SAAS *9*
Delulio, John 1938- *15*
Delving, Michael
   See Williams, Jay
de Marcken, Gail *186*
Demarest, Chris L. 1951- *175*
   Brief entry 44
   Earlier sketches in SATA *45, 82, 128*
Demarest, Christopher Lynn
   See Demarest, Chris L.
Demarest, Doug
   See Barker, Will
De Mari, Silvana 1953- *193*
Demas, Corinne *203*
   See Bliss, Corinne Demas
Demas, Vida 1927- *9*
Dematons, Charlotte 1957- *203*
DeMatteis, J.M. 1953- *180*
DeMatteis, John Marc
   See DeMatteis, J.M.
De Mejo, Oscar 1911-1992 .... *40*
Demers, Dominique 1956- *177*
de Messieres, Nicole 1930- *39*
Demi 1942- *210*
   Earlier sketches in SATA *11, 66, 102, 152*
   See also CLR *58*
Demijohn, Thom
   See Disch, Thomas M.
   and Sladek, John
Deming, Richard 1915-1983 .... *24*
Deming, Sarah *191*
de Monfreid, Dorothee 1973- *189*
Demuth, Patricia Brennan 1948- *84*
   Brief entry *51*
Dendinger, Roger E. 1952- *158*
Denenberg, Barry 1940- *175*
Dengler, Marianna (Herron) 1935- *103*
Dengler, Sandy 1939- *54*
   Brief entry *40*
Denim, Sue
   See Pilkey, Dav
Denise, Anika *210*
Denise, Christopher 1968- *193*
   Earlier sketch in SATA *147*
Denman, K.L. 1957- *186*
Denmark, Harrison
   See Zelazny, Roger
Dennard, Deborah 1953- *136*
   Earlier sketch in SATA *78*
Denney, Diana 1910-2000 .... *25*
   Obituary *120*
Dennis, Morgan 1891(?)-1960 .... *18*
Dennis, Wesley 1903-1966 .... *18*
Denniston, Elinore 1900-1978
   Obituary *24*
Denny, Norman (George) 1901-1982 .... *43*
Denos, Julia *202*

Denslow, Sharon Phillips 1947- *142*
   Earlier sketch in SATA *68*
Denslow, W(illiam) W(allace) 1856-1915 .... *16*
   See also CLR *15*
Dent, Grace 1973- *187*
Denton, Kady MacDonald *181*
   Earlier sketches in SATA *66, 110*
   See also CLR *71*
Denton, Terry 1950- *186*
Denver, Walt
   See Redding, Robert Hull
   and Sherman, Jory (Tecumseh)
Denzel, Justin F(rancis) 1917-1999 .... *46*
   Brief entry *38*
Denzer, Ann Wiseman
   See Wiseman, Ann (Sayre)
DePalma, Mary Newell 1961- *185*
   Earlier sketch in SATA *139*
De Palma, Toni *199*
dePaola, Thomas Anthony 1934- *155*
   Earlier sketches in SATA *11, 59, 108*
   See also CLR *81*
   See also SAAS *15*
   See dePaola, Tomie
dePaola, Tomie *200*
   See dePaola, Thomas Anthony
deParrie, Paul 1949- *74*
DePauw, Linda Grant 1940- *24*
DeRan, David 1946- *76*
Derby, Ken 1956- *181*
Derby, Kenneth R.
   See Derby, Ken
Derby, Pat 1942- *172*
Derby, Sally 1934- *189*
   Earlier sketches in SATA *89, 132*
de Regniers, Beatrice Schenk (Freedman)
   1914-2000 .... *68*
   Obituary *123*
   Earlier sketch in SATA *2*
   See also SAAS *6*
Dereske, Jo 1947- *72*
Deriso, Christine Hurley 1961- *210*
Derleth, August (William) 1909-1971 .... *5*
Derman, Martha (Winn) *74*
Derman, Sarah Audrey 1915- *11*
DeRoberts, Lyndon
   See Silverstein, Robert Alan
de Roo, Anne Louise 1931-1997 .... *84*
   Earlier sketch in SATA *25*
   See also CLR *63*
deRosa, Dee *70*
Derrick, Lionel
   See Cunningham, Chet
Derrickson, Jim 1959- *141*
Derry Down Derry
   See Lear, Edward
Dervaux, Isabelle 1961- *106*
Derwent, Lavinia *14*
Desai, Anita 1937- *126*
   Earlier sketch in SATA *63*
DeSaix, Deborah Durland *188*
De Saulles, Tony 1958- *119*
Desbarats, Peter 1933- *39*
de Selincourt, Aubrey 1894-1962 .... *14*
de Seve, Randall *198*
Deshpande, Chris 1950- *69*
Desimini, Lisa 1964- *148*
   Earlier sketch in SATA *86*
Desjarlais, John 1953- *71*
Desjarlais, John J.
   See Desjarlais, John
Desmoinaux, Christel 1967- *149*
   Earlier sketch in SATA *103*
Desmond, Adrian 1947- *51*
Desmond, Adrian J.
   See Desmond, Adrian
Desmond, Adrian John
   See Desmond, Adrian
Desmond, Alice Curtis 1897-1990 .... *8*
Desnoettes, Caroline *183*
DeSpain, Pleasant 1943- *87*

Desputeaux, Helene 1959- *95*
Dessen, Sarah 1970- *172*
   Earlier sketch in SATA *120*
Detine, Padre
   See Olsen, Ib Spang
de Trevino, Elizabeth B.
   See Trevino, Elizabeth B(orton) de
de Trevino, Elizabeth Borton
   See Trevino, Elizabeth B(orton) de
Detwiler, Susan Dill 1956- *58*
Deuker, Carl 1950- *196*
   Earlier sketches in SATA *82, 150*
Deutsch, Babette 1895-1982 .... *1*
   Obituary *33*
Deutsch, Eva Costabel
   See Costabel, Eva Deutsch
Deutsch, Helen 1906-1992 .... *76*
Deutsch, Kurt
   See Singer, Kurt D.
De Valera, Sinead 1879(?)-1975
   Obituary *30*
Devaney, John 1926-1994 .... *12*
de Varennes, Monique 1947- *168*
de Varona, Frank J. 1943- *83*
Devereux, Frederick L(eonard), Jr.
   1914-1993 .... *9*
Devi, Nila
   See Woody, Regina Jones
deVinck, Christopher 1951- *85*
DeVita, James *195*
DeVito, Cara 1956- *80*
Devlin, Dorothy Wende
   See Devlin, Wende
Devlin, Harry 1918-2001 .... *136*
   Earlier sketches in SATA *11, 74*
Devlin, Wende 1918-2002 .... *74*
   Earlier sketch in SATA *11*
Devon, Paddie 1953- *92*
Devons, Sonia 1974- *72*
Devorah-Leah *111*
de Vos, Gail 1949- *122*
DeVries, Douglas 1933- *122*
De Waard, E(lliott) John 1935- *7*
Dewan, Ted 1961- *157*
   Earlier sketch in SATA *108*
Dewdney, Anna *184*
Dewdney, Selwyn (Hanington) 1909-1979 ... *64*
DeWeese, Gene
   See DeWeese, Thomas Eugene
DeWeese, Jean
   See DeWeese, Thomas Eugene
DeWeese, Thomas Eugene 1934- *46*
   Brief entry *45*
Dewey, Ariane 1937- *178*
   Earlier sketches in SATA *7, 109*
Dewey, Jennifer (Owings) 1941- *103*
   Brief entry *48*
   Earlier sketch in SATA *58*
Dewey, Kenneth Francis 1940- *39*
Dewin, Howie
   See Howie, Betsy
De Wire, Elinor 1953- *180*
deWit, Dorothy (May Knowles) 1916-1980 . *39*
   Obituary *28*
Dexter, Alison 1966- *125*
Dexter, John
   See Bradley, Marion Zimmer
Deyneka, Anita 1943- *24*
Deyrup, Astrith Johnson 1923- *24*
Dezern, Chad *201*
Dhami, Narinder 1958- *152*
Dhondy, Farrukh 1944- *152*
   Earlier sketch in SATA *65*
   See also CLR *41*
Diakite, Baba Wague 1961- *174*
Diakite, Penda 1993(?)- *174*
Diamond, Arthur 1957- *76*
Diamond, Donna 1950- *69*
   Brief entry *30*
   Earlier sketch in SATA *35*

Diamond, Petra
  See Sachs, Judith
Diamond, Rebecca
  See Sachs, Judith
Dias, Earl Joseph 1916- 41
Dias, Ron 1937- 71
Diaz, David 1959(?)- 189
  Earlier sketches in SATA *96, 150*
  See also CLR *65*
Dibley, Glin 188
DiCamillo, Kate 1964- 202
  Earlier sketches in SATA *121, 163*
  See also CLR *117*
Di Certo, J(oseph) J(ohn) 1933- 60
DiCianni, Ron 1952- 107
Dick, Trella Lamson 1889-1974 9
Dickens, Charles 1812-1870 15
  See also CLR *95*
Dickens, Charles John Huffam
  See Dickens, Charles
Dickens, Frank
  See Huline-Dickens, Frank William
Dickens, Monica (Enid) 1915-1992 4
  Obituary 74
Dickerson, Roy Ernest 1886-1965
  Obituary 26
Dickinson, Emily 1830-1886 29
Dickinson, Emily Elizabeth
  See Dickinson, Emily
Dickinson, Mary 1949- 48
  Brief entry 41
Dickinson, Mary-Anne
  See Rodda, Emily
Dickinson, Peter 1927- 150
  Earlier sketches in SATA *5, 62, 95*
  See also CLR *125*
Dickinson, Peter Malcolm de Brissac
  See Dickinson, Peter
Dickinson, Susan 1931- 8
Dickinson, Terence 1943- 102
Dickinson, W(illiam) Croft 1897-1963 13
Dickson, Gordon R. 1923-2001 77
Dickson, Gordon Rupert
  See Dickson, Gordon R.
Dickson, Helen
  See Reynolds, Helen Mary Greenwood Campbell
Dickson, Naida 1916- 8
Diehn, Gwen 1943- 80
Dierssen, Andreas 1962- 190
Diesen, Deborah 1967- 200
Dieterich, Michele M. 1962- 78
Dietz, David H(enry) 1897-1984 10
  Obituary 41
Dietz, Lew 1907-1997 11
  Obituary 95
Diffily, Deborah 159
Di Fiori, Larry
  See Di Fiori, Lawrence
Di Fiori, Lawrence 1934- 130
DiFranco, Anthony (Mario) 1945- 42
Digby, Anne 1935- 72
Digges, Jeremiah
  See Berger, Josef
Digman, Kristina 1959- 176
D'Ignazio, Fred(erick) 1949- 39
  Brief entry 35
Di Grazia, Thomas (?)-1983 32
Dijkstra, Lida 1961- 195
Dikty, Julian May
  See May, Julian
Dillard, Annie 1945- 140
  Earlier sketch in SATA *10*
Dillard, Kristine 1964- 113
Dillard, Polly Hargis 1916- 24
Diller, Harriett 1953- 78
Dillon, Anna
  See Scott, Michael
Dillon, Barbara 1927- 44
  Brief entry 39

Dillon, Diane 1933- 194
  Earlier sketches in SATA *15, 51, 106*
  See also CLR *44*
Dillon, Diane Claire
  See Dillon, Diane
Dillon, Eilis 1920-1994 74
  Autobiography Feature 105
  Obituary 83
  Earlier sketch in SATA *2*
  See also CLR *26*
Dillon, Jana (a pseudonym) 1952- 117
Dillon, Leo 1933- 194
  Earlier sketches in SATA *15, 51, 106*
  See also CLR *44*
Dillon, Sharon Saseen
  See Saseen, Sharon (Dillon)
Dils, Tracey E. 1958- 83
Dilson, Jesse 1914-1988 24
Dinan, Carolyn 59
  Brief entry 47
Dines, Carol 1956- 175
Dines, (Harry) Glen 1925-1996 7
Dinesen, Isak
  See Blixen, Karen
Dinessi, Alex
  See Schembri, Jim
Dinneen, Betty 1929- 61
Dinnerstein, Harvey 1928- 42
Dinsdale, Tim(othy Kay) 1924-1987 11
Dion, Nathalie 1964- 213
Diop, Birago (Ismael) 1906-1989
  Obituary 64
Diouf, Sylviane A. 168
Diouf, Sylviane Anna
  See Diouf, Sylviane A.
DiPucchio, Kelly 204
  Earlier sketch in SATA *159*
Dirk
  See Gringhuis, Richard H.
Dirks, Wilhelmina 1916- 59
Dirks, Willy
  See Dirks, Wilhelmina
Dirtmeister
  See Tomecek, Steve
DiSalvo, DyAnne 1960- 144
  Earlier sketch in SATA *59*
DiSalvo-Ryan, DyAnne
  See DiSalvo, DyAnne
Disch, Thomas M. 1940-2008 92
  Obituary 195
  See also CLR *18*
  See also SAAS *15*
Disch, Thomas Michael
  See Disch, Thomas M.
Disch, Tom
  See Disch, Thomas M.
Disher, Garry 1949- 125
  Earlier sketch in SATA *81*
Disney, Walt(er Elias) 1901-1966 28
  Brief entry 27
Ditchfield, Christin 1973- 189
DiTerlizzi, Tony 1969- 214
  Earlier sketch in SATA *154*
DiTerlooney, Tiny
  See DiTerlizzi, Tony
Divakaruni, Chitra Banerjee 1956- 160
Di Valentin, Maria (Amelia) Messuri
  1911-1985 7
Divine, Arthur Durham 1904-1987
  Obituary 52
Divine, David
  See Divine, Arthur Durham
Dixon, Ann 1954- 212
  Earlier sketches in SATA *77, 127*
Dixon, Ann Renee
  See Dixon, Ann
Dixon, Dougal 1947- 190
  Earlier sketches in SATA *45, 127*

Dixon, Franklin W.
  See Barrett, Neal, Jr.
  and Goulart, Ron
  and Lantz, Francess L(in)
  and Lerangis, Peter
  and McFarlane, Leslie
  and Stanley, George Edward
  and Stratemeyer, Edward L.
Dixon, Jeanne 1936- 31
Dixon, Paige
  See Corcoran, Barbara (Asenath)
Dixon, Peter L(ee) 1931- 6
Dixon, Rachel 1952- 74
Djoleto, (Solomon Alexander) Amu 1929- ... 80
d'lacey, Chris 1949- 165
Doak, Annie
  See Dillard, Annie
Doane, Pelagie 1906-1966 7
Dob, Bob 207
Dobell, I(sabel) M(arian) B(arclay)
  1909-1998 11
Dobie, J(ames) Frank 1888-1964 43
Dobkin, Alexander 1908-1975
  Obituary 30
Dobler, Lavinia G. 1910- 6
Dobrin, Arnold 1928- 4
Dobson, Jill 1969- 140
Dobson, Julia 1941- 48
Dobson, Mary 1954- 117
Docherty, James
  See Docherty, Jimmy
Docherty, Jimmy 1976- 204
Dockery, Wallene T. 1941- 27
Dockray, Tracy 1962- 139
Dockrey, Karen 1955- 103
Doctor, Bernard
  See Doctor, Bernard Aquina
Doctor, Bernard Aquina 1950- 81
Doctor X
  See Nourse, Alan E(dward)
Dodd, Ed(ward Benton) 1902-1991 4
  Obituary 68
Dodd, Emma 1969- 203
Dodd, Lynley (Stuart) 1941- 132
  Earlier sketches in SATA *35, 86*
  See also CLR *62*
Dodd, Marty 1921- 142
Dodd, Quentin 1972- 137
Dodds, Bill 1952- 78
Dodds, Dayle Ann 1952- 201
  Earlier sketches in SATA *75, 150*
Doder, Josh 1968- 187
Dodge, Bertha S(anford) 1902-1995 8
Dodge, Fremont
  See Grimes, Lee
Dodge, Gil
  See Hano, Arnold
Dodge, Mary (Elizabeth) Mapes
  1831(?)-1905 100
  Earlier sketch in SATA *21*
  See also CLR *62*
Dodgson, Charles Lutwidge
  See Carroll, Lewis
Dodson, Kenneth MacKenzie 1907-1999 11
Dodson, Susan 1941- 50
  Brief entry 40
Doerrfeld, Cori 1964- 214
Dogar, Sharon 1962- 211
Dogyear, Drew
  See Gorey, Edward (St. John)
Doherty, Berlie 1943- 111
  Earlier sketch in SATA *72*
  See also CLR *21*
  See also SAAS *16*
Doherty, Charles Hugh 1913- 6
Doherty, Craig A. 1951- 169
  Earlier sketch in SATA *83*
Doherty, Katherine M(ann) 1951- 83
Doherty, Kieran 1945- 164
Dokey, Cameron 1956- 97

Dolan, Edward F(rancis), Jr. 1924- *94*
   Brief entry *31*
   Earlier sketch in SATA *45*
Dolan, Ellen M(eara) 1929-1998 .... *88*
Dolan, Sean J. 1958- *74*
Dolce, J. Ellen 1948- *75*
Dolch, Edward William 1889-1961 .... *50*
Dolch, Marguerite Pierce 1891-1978 .... *50*
Dollar, Diane (Hills) 1933- *57*
Dolson, Hildegarde
   See Lockridge, Hildegarde (Dolson)
Domanska, Janina 1913(?)-1995 .... *68*
   Obituary *84*
   Earlier sketch in SATA *6*
   See also CLR *40*
   See also SAAS *18*
Dominguez, Angel 1953- *76*
Domino, John
   See Averill, Esther (Holden)
Domjan, Joseph (Spiri) 1907-1992 .... *25*
Domm, Jeffrey C. 1958- *84*
Donahue, Dorothy *178*
Donald, Rhonda Lucas 1962- *147*
Donalds, Gordon
   See Shirreffs, Gordon D(onald)
Donaldson, Bryna
   See Stevens, Bryna
Donaldson, Gordon 1913-1993 .... *64*
   Obituary *76*
Donaldson, Joan 1953- *78*
Donaldson, Julia 1948- *180*
   Earlier sketches in SATA *82, 132*
Donaldson, Stephen R. 1947- *121*
Donaldson, Stephen Reeder
   See Donaldson, Stephen R.
Doner, Kim 1955- *208*
   Earlier sketch in SATA *91*
Doney, Todd L. W. 1959- *104*
Dong-Sung, Kim 1970- *195*
Dong-Sung Kim
   See Dong-Sung, Kim
Donkin, Nance (Clare) 1915- *95*
Donna, Natalie 1934-1979 .... *9*
Donnelly, Elfie 1950-
   See CLR *104*
Donnelly, Jennifer 1963- *154*
Donnelly, Matt 1972- *148*
Donnio, Sylviane *188*
Donofrio, Beverly 1950- *209*
Donoghue, Emma 1969- *101*
Donohue, Moira Rose 1954- *201*
Donoughue, Carol 1935- *139*
Donovan, Frank (Robert) 1906-1975
   Obituary *30*
Donovan, John 1928-1992 .... *72*
   Brief entry *29*
   See also CLR *3*
Donovan, Mary Lee 1961- *86*
Donovan, William
   See Berkebile, Fred D(onovan)
Donze, Mary Terese 1911- *89*
Doob, Leonard W(illiam) 1909-2000 .... *8*
Dooley, Norah 1953- *74*
Dooling, Michael 1958- *105*
Dor, Ana
   See Ceder, Georgiana Dorcas
Doran, Colleen 1963- *211*
Dore, (Louis Christophe Paul) Gustave
   1832-1883 .... *19*
Doremus, Robert 1913- *30*
Doren, Marion (Walker) 1928- *57*
Dorenkamp, Michelle 1957- *89*
Dorflinger, Carolyn 1953- *91*
Dorfman, Joaquin 1979- *180*
Dorfman, Joaquin Emiliano
   See Dorfman, Joaquin
Dorian, Edith M(cEwen) 1900-1983 .... *5*
Dorian, Harry
   See Hamilton, Charles (Harold St. John)
Dorian, Marguerite *7*

Dorin, Patrick C(arberry) 1939- *59*
   Brief entry *52*
Dorman, Brandon *194*
Dorman, Michael 1932- *7*
Dorman, N. B. 1927- *39*
Dormer, Frank W. *200*
Dorris, Michael 1945-1997 .... *75*
   Obituary *94*
   See also CLR *58*
Dorris, Michael A.
   See Dorris, Michael
Dorris, Michael Anthony
   See Dorris, Michael
Dorritt, Susan
   See Schlein, Miriam
Dorros, Alex 1991- *194*
Dorros, Arthur 1950- *168*
   Earlier sketches in SATA *78, 122*
   See also CLR *42*
   See also SAAS *20*
Dorros, Arthur M.
   See Dorros, Arthur
Dorson, Richard M(ercer) 1916-1981 .... *30*
Doss, Helen (Grigsby) 1918- *20*
Doss, Margot Patterson *6*
dos Santos, Joyce Audy 1949- *57*
   Brief entry *42*
Dothers, Anne
   See Chess, Victoria (Dickerson)
Dotlich, Rebecca Kai 1951- *182*
Dottig
   See Grider, Dorothy
Dotts, Maryann J. 1933- *35*
Doty, Jean Slaughter 1929- *28*
Doty, Roy 1922- *28*
Doubtfire, Dianne (Abrams) 1918- *29*
Doucet, Sharon Arms 1951- *144*
   Autobiography Feature *144*
   Earlier sketch in SATA *125*
Dougherty, Charles 1922- *18*
Dougherty, Terri (L.) 1964- *146*
Doughty, Rebecca 1955- *174*
Douglas, Blaise 1960- *101*
Douglas, Carole Nelson 1944- *73*
Douglas, Garry
   See Kilworth, Garry
Douglas, James McM.
   See Griffin, W.E.B.
Douglas, Kathryn
   See Ewing, Kathryn
Douglas, Leonard
   See Bradbury, Ray
Douglas, Lola
   See Zeises, Lara M.
Douglas, Marjory Stoneman 1890-1998 .... *10*
Douglas, Michael
   See Bright, Robert Sr.)
Douglas, Michael
   See Crichton, Michael
Douglas, Shirley Stewart
   See Tepper, Sheri S.
Douglass, Barbara 1930- *40*
Douglass, Frederick 1817(?)-1895 .... *29*
Douglass, Keith
   See Cunningham, Chet
Douty, Esther M(orris) 1909-1978 .... *8*
   Obituary *23*
Dow, Emily R. 1904-1987 .... *10*
Dow, Vicki
   See McVey, Vicki
Dowd, John David 1945- *78*
Dowd, Siobhan 1960-2007 .... *204*
Dowdell, Dorothy (Florence) Karns 1910- ... *12*
Dowden, Anne Ophelia Todd 1907-2007 .... *7*
   Obituary *180*
   See also SAAS *10*
Dowdey, Landon Gerald 1923- *11*
Dowdy, Mrs. Regera
   See Gorey, Edward (St. John)
Dowell, Frances O'Roark *205*
   Earlier sketch in SATA *157*

Dower, Laura 1967- *185*
Dowling, Terry 1947- *101*
Downard, Barry 1956- *202*
Downer, Ann 1960- *155*
Downer, Marion 1892(?)-1971 .... *25*
Downes, Belinda 1962- *180*
Downey, Fairfax D(avis) 1893-1990 .... *3*
   Obituary *66*
Downey, Lisa *214*
Downey, Lynn 1961- *185*
Downham, Jenny 1964- *192*
Downie, John 1931- *87*
Downie, Mary Alice 1934- *171*
   Earlier sketches in SATA *13, 87*
Downie, Mary Alice Dawe
   See Downie, Mary Alice
Downing, David A(lmon) 1958- *84*
Downing, Johnette *184*
Downing, Julie 1956- *148*
   Earlier sketch in SATA *81*
Downing, Paula E. 1951- *80*
Downing, Warwick
   See Downing, Wick
Downing, Wick 1931- *138*
Dowswell, Paul 1957- *184*
Doyle, A. Conan
   See Doyle, Sir Arthur Conan
Doyle, Sir Arthur Conan 1859-1930 .... *24*
   See also CLR *106*
Doyle, Brian 1935- *156*
   Earlier sketches in SATA *67, 104*
   See also CLR *22*
   See also SAAS *16*
Doyle, Charlotte 1937- *178*
   Earlier sketch in SATA *94*
Doyle, Charlotte Lackner
   See Doyle, Charlotte
Doyle, Conan
   See Doyle, Sir Arthur Conan
Doyle, Debra 1952- *165*
   Earlier sketch in SATA *105*
Doyle, Donovan
   See Boegehold, Betty (Doyle)
Doyle, John
   See Graves, Robert
Doyle, Malachy 1954- *165*
   Earlier sketch in SATA *120*
   See also CLR *83*
Doyle, Richard 1824-1883 .... *21*
Doyle, Sir A. Conan
   See Doyle, Sir Arthur Conan
Dr. A
   See Asimov, Isaac
   and Silverstein, Alvin
   and Silverstein, Virginia B.
Dr. Alphabet
   See Morice, Dave
Dr. Fred
   See Bortz, Alfred B(enjamin)
Dr. Laura
   See Schlessinger, Laura (Catherine)
Dr. Seuss 1904-1991 .... *100*
   Obituary *67*
   Earlier sketches in SATA *1, 28, 75*
   See also CLR *100*
Dr. Zed
   See Penrose, Gordon
Drabble, Margaret 1939- *48*
Drackett, Phil(ip Arthur) 1922- *53*
Draco, F.
   See Davis, Julia
Dracup, Angela 1943- *74*
Dragisic, Patricia *116*
Dragonwagon, Crescent 1952- *186*
   Autobiography Feature *186*
   Earlier sketches in SATA *11, 41, 75, 133*
   See also SAAS *14*
Drake, David 1945- *85*
Drake, David Allen
   See Drake, David

Drake, Frank
　See Hamilton, Charles (Harold St. John)
Drake, Jane 1954- 82
Drake, Salamanda
　See Barlow, Steve
Drakeford, Dale B 1952- 113
Drakeford, Dale Benjamin
　See Drakeford, Dale B
Draper, Hastings
　See Jeffries, Roderic
Draper, Sharon
　See Draper, Sharon M.
Draper, Sharon M. 1948- 195
　Autobiography Feature 146
　Earlier sketches in SATA 98, 146
　See also CLR 57
Draper, Sharon Mills
　See Draper, Sharon M.
Drapier, M. B.
　See Swift, Jonathan
Drawson, Blair 1943- 126
　Earlier sketch in SATA 17
Dray, Matt 1967- 177
Dray, Matthew Frederick
　See Dray, Matt
Dresang, Eliza (Carolyn Timberlake) 1941- . 19
Drescher, Henrik 1955- 172
　Earlier sketches in SATA 67, 105
　See also CLR 20
Drescher, Joan E(lizabeth) 1939- 137
　Earlier sketch in SATA 30
Dressen-McQueen, Stacey 191
Dreves, Veronica R. 1927-1986
　Obituary 50
Drew, Patricia (Mary) 1938- 15
Drewery, Mary 1918- 6
Drewery, Melanie 1970- 165
Drewry, Henry N(athaniel) 1924- 138
Dreyer, Ellen 177
Drial, J. E.
　See Laird, Jean E(louise)
Drimmer, Frederick 1916-2000 60
　Obituary 124
Driskill, J. Lawrence 1920- 90
Driskill, Larry
　See Driskill, J. Lawrence
Driving Hawk, Virginia
　See Sneve, Virginia Driving Hawk
Dron, Laura
　See Matthews, L.S.
Dronzek, Laura 199
Drucker, Malka 1945- 214
　Brief entry 29
　Earlier sketches in SATA 39, 111
Drucker, Olga Levy 1927- 79
Druitt, Tobias
　See Purkiss, Diane
Drummond, Allan 1957- 209
Drummond, V(iolet) H(ilda) 1911-2000 6
Drummond, Walter
　See Silverberg, Robert
Drury, Clare Marie
　See Hoskyns-Abrahall, Clare (Constance
　Drury)
Drury, Roger W(olcott) 1914-1996 15
Druse, Eleanor
　See King, Stephen
Dryden, Pamela
　See St. John, Nicole
D.T., Hughes
　See Hughes, Dean
Duane, Diane (Elizabeth) 1952- 145
　Brief entry 46
　Earlier sketches in SATA 58, 95
Dubanevich, Arlene 1950- 56
Dubelaar, Thea 1947- 60
Dubin, Jill 205
du Blane, Daphne
　See Groom, Arthur William
Duble, Kathleen Benner 1958- 164
Dubois, Claude K. 1960- 196

DuBois, Rochelle Holt 1946- 41
Du Bois, Shirley Graham 1907(?)-1977 24
　See Graham, Shirley
Du Bois, W. E. B. 1868-1963 42
Du Bois, William Edward Burghardt
　See Du Bois, W. E. B.
du Bois, William Pene
　See Pene du Bois, William (Sherman)
Duboise, Novella 1911-1999 88
Dubosarsky, Ursula 1961- 193
　Earlier sketches in SATA 107, 147
DuBose, LaRocque (Russ) 1926- 2
Dubrovin, Vivian 1931- 139
　Earlier sketch in SATA 65
DuBurke, Randy 172
Ducey, Jean Sparks 1915- 93
Duchacek, Ivo D(uka) 1913-1988
　Obituary 55
Du Chaillu, Paul (Belloni) 1835(?)-1903 26
Ducharme, Dede Fox
　See Ducharme, Lilian Fox
Ducharme, Lilian Fox 1950- 122
Ducornet, Erica 1943- 7
Ducornet, Rikki
　See Ducornet, Erica
Duden, Jane 1947- 136
Duder, Tessa 1940- 117
　Earlier sketch in SATA 80
　See also CLR 43
　See also SAAS 23
Dudley, Helen
　See Hope Simpson, Jacynth
Dudley, Martha Ward 1909(?)-1985
　Obituary 45
Dudley, Nancy
　See Cole, Lois Dwight
Dudley, Robert
　See Baldwin, James
Dudley, Ruth H(ubbell) 1905-2001 11
Dudley-Smith, T.
　See Trevor, Elleston
Due, Linnea A. 1948- 64
Dueck, Adele 1955- 97
Dueland, Joy V(ivian) 27
Duerr, Gisela 1968- 89
Duey, Kathleen 1950- 199
　Earlier sketch in SATA 132
Dufault, Joseph Ernest Nephtali
　See James, Will(iam Roderick)
Duff, Annis (James) 1904(?)-1986
　Obituary 49
Duff, Maggie
　See Duff, Margaret K(app)
Duff, Margaret K(app) 1916-2003 37
　Obituary 144
Duffey, Betsy (Byars) 1953- 131
　Earlier sketch in SATA 80
Duffie, Charles 1960- 144
Duffield, Katy S. 1961- 147
Duffy, Carol Ann 1955- 165
　Earlier sketch in SATA 95
Dugan, Jack
　See Griffin, W.E.B.
Dugan, John Kevin
　See Griffin, W.E.B.
Dugan, Karen 202
Dugan, Karen M.
　See Dugan, Karen
Dugan, Michael (Gray) 1947- 15
Duggan, Alfred Leo 1903-1964 25
Duggan, Maurice 1922-1974 40
　Obituary 30
Duggan, Maurice Noel
　See Duggan, Maurice
Dugger, Elizabeth L.
　See Kanell, Beth
Duggleby, John 1952- 94
Dugin, Andrej 1955- 77
Dugina, Olga 1964- 77
du Jardin, Rosamond Neal 1902-1963 2

Duka, Ivo
　See Duchacek, Ivo D(uka)
Duke, Kate 1956- 192
　Earlier sketches in SATA 90, 148
　See also CLR 51
Duke, Will
　See Gault, William Campbell
Dulac, Edmund 1882-1953 19
Dumas, Alexandre (pere) 1802-1870 18
　See also CLR 134
Dumas, Jacqueline 1946- 55
Dumas, Philippe 1940- 119
　Earlier sketch in SATA 52
du Maurier, Daphne 1907-1989 27
　Obituary 60
Dumbleton, Mike 1948- 206
　Earlier sketches in SATA 73, 124
Dunbar, Fiona 1961- 167
Dunbar, Joyce 1944- 213
　Earlier sketches in SATA 76, 112, 162
Dunbar, Paul Laurence 1872-1906 34
Dunbar, Polly 1980(?)- 211
　Earlier sketch in SATA 181
Dunbar, Robert E(verett) 1926- 32
Duncan, Alexandra
　See Moore, Ishbel (Lindsay)
Duncan, Alice Faye 1967- 168
　Earlier sketch in SATA 95
Duncan, Gregory
　See McClintock, Marshall
Duncan, Jane
　See Cameron, Elizabeth Jane
Duncan, Julia K.
　See Benson, Mildred
Duncan, Lois 1934- 141
　Autobiography Feature 141
　Earlier sketches in SATA 1, 36, 75, 133
　See also CLR 129
　See also SAAS 2
Duncan, Norman 1871-1916
　See YABC 1
Duncan, Terence
　See Nolan, William F.
Duncombe, Frances (Riker) 1900-1994 25
　Obituary 82
Dungy, Anthony
　See Dungy, Tony
Dungy, Tony 1955- 206
Dunham, Montrew 1919- 162
Dunham, Montrew Goetz
　See Dunham, Montrew
Dunkle, Clare B. 1964- 155
Dunlap, Julie 1958- 84
Dunleavy, Deborah 1951- 133
Dunlop, Agnes M. R. (?)-1982 87
Dunlop, Eileen (Rhona) 1938- 76
　Earlier sketch in SATA 24
　See also SAAS 12
Dunmore, Helen 1952- 201
Dunn, Anne M. 1940- 107
Dunn, Carolyn 1965- 208
Dunn, Harvey T(homas) 1884-1952 34
Dunn, Herb
　See Gutman, Dan
Dunn, John M. (III) 1949- 93
Dunn, Judy
　See Spangenberg, Judith Dunn
Dunn, Mary Lois 1930- 6
Dunnahoo, Terry Janson 1927- 7
Dunne, Jeanette 1952- 72
Dunne, Kathleen 1933- 126
Dunne, Marie
　See Clark, Ann Nolan
Dunne, Mary Collins 1914- 11
Dunne, Mary Jo
　See Dunne, Mary Collins
Dunnett, Kaitlyn
　See Emerson, Kathy Lynn
Dunnett, Margaret (Rosalind) 1909-1977 42
Dunnick, Regan 178

Dunrea, Olivier 1953- *160*
  Brief entry *46*
  Earlier sketches in SATA *59, 118*
Dunrea, Olivier Jean-Paul Dominique
  See Dunrea, Olivier
Dunton, Dorothy 1912- *92*
Dupasquier, Philippe 1955- *151*
  Earlier sketch in SATA *86*
duPont, Lindsay *207*
duPont, Lindsay Harper
  See duPont, Lindsay
DuPrau, Jeanne 1944- *215*
  Earlier sketch in SATA *144*
Dupuy, T(revor) N(evitt) 1916-1995 .... *4*
  Obituary *86*
DuQuette, Keith 1960- *155*
  Earlier sketch in SATA *90*
Duran, Gloria 1924- *171*
Duran, Gloria Bradley
  See Duran, Gloria
Duranceau, Suzanne 1952- *162*
Durand, Delphine 1971- *200*
Durango, Julia 1967- *215*
  Earlier sketch in SATA *173*
Durant, Alan 1958- *214*
  Earlier sketches in SATA *121, 165*
Durant, John 1902- *27*
Durbin, William 1951- *174*
  Earlier sketch in SATA *143*
Durell, Ann 1930- *66*
Durkee, Sarah *173*
Durney, Ryan *205*
Durrant, Lynda 1954- *212*
  Earlier sketches in SATA *96, 148*
Durrant, Sabine *210*
Durrell, Gerald (Malcolm) 1925-1995 .... *8*
  Obituary *84*
Durrell, Julie 1955- *94*
Durrett, Deanne 1940- *144*
  Earlier sketch in SATA *92*
Durst, Sarah Beth 1974- *203*
Du Soe, Robert C. 1892-1958
  See YABC 2
Dussling, Jennifer 1970- *143*
  Earlier sketch in SATA *96*
DuTemple, Lesley A. 1952- *113*
Dutton, Sandra *191*
Dutz
  See Davis, Mary Octavia
Duval, Katherine
  See James, Elizabeth
Duval, Kathy 1946- *181*
Duvall, Aimee
  See Thurlo, Aimee
  and Thurlo, David
Duvall, Evelyn Millis 1906- *9*
Duvall, Jill D. 1932- *102*
Duvall, Jill Donovan
  See Duvall, Jill D.
Duvoisin, Roger (Antoine) 1904-1980 .... *30*
  Obituary *23*
  Earlier sketch in SATA *2*
  See also CLR 23
Dwiggins, Don(ald J.) 1913-1988 .... *4*
  Obituary *60*
Dwight, Allan
  See Cole, Lois Dwight
Dwyer, Deanna
  See Koontz, Dean
Dwyer, K.R.
  See Koontz, Dean
Dyck, Peter J. 1914- *75*
Dyer, James (Frederick) 1934- *37*
Dyer, Jane *191*
  Earlier sketch in SATA *147*
Dyer, Sarah 1978- *212*
Dyer, Sarah L.
  See Dyer, Sarah
Dyess, John (Foster) 1939- *76*

Dygard, Thomas J. 1931-1996 .... *97*
  Obituary *92*
  Earlier sketch in SATA *24*
  See also SAAS 15
Dyke, John 1935- *35*

E

E. V. L.
  See Lucas, E(dward) V(errall)
Eagar, Frances (Elisabeth Stuart)
  1940-1978 .... *11*
  Obituary *55*
Eager, Edward (McMaken) 1911-1964 .... *17*
  See also CLR 43
Eager, George 1921- *56*
Eager, George B.
  See Eager, George
Eagle, Ellen 1953- *61*
Eagle, Kin
  See Adlerman, Daniel (Ezra)
  and Adlerman, Kimberly M(arie)
Eagle, Mike 1942- *11*
Earle, Olive L(ydia) 1888-1982 .... *7*
Earle, William
  See Johns, W(illiam) E(arle)
Earls, Nick 1963- *156*
  Earlier sketch in SATA *95*
Early, Jack
  See Scoppettone, Sandra
Early, Jon
  See Johns, W(illiam) E(arle)
Early, Margaret 1951- *72*
Earnshaw, Brian 1929- *17*
Earnshaw, Micky
  See Earnshaw, Spencer Wright
Earnshaw, Spencer Wright 1939- *88*
Easley, MaryAnn *94*
Eason, Alethea 1957- *197*
Eastman, Charles A(lexander) 1858-1939
  See YABC 1
Eastman, P(hilip) D(ey) 1909-1986 .... *33*
  Obituary *46*
Easton, Kelly 1960- *192*
  Earlier sketch in SATA *141*
Eastwick, Ivy (Ethel) O(live) *3*
Eaton, Anne T(haxter) 1881-1971 .... *32*
Eaton, Anthony 1971- *167*
Eaton, George L.
  See Verral, Charles Spain
Eaton, Janet
  See Givens, Janet E(aton)
Eaton, Jeanette 1886-1968 .... *24*
Eaton, Maxwell III 1981- *199*
Eaton, Tom 1940- *22*
Ebbeler, Jeff
  See Ebbeler, Jeffrey
Ebbeler, Jeffrey 1974- *206*
Ebel, Alex 1927- *11*
Eber, Dorothy (Margaret) Harley 1930- *27*
Eberhart, Sheri S.
  See Tepper, Sheri S.
Eberle, Irmengarde 1898-1979 .... *2*
  Obituary *23*
Eble, Diane 1956- *74*
Eboch, Chris *113*
Eccles Williams, Ferelith 1920- *22*
Echlin, Kim 1955- *166*
Eckblad, Edith Berven 1923- *23*
Ecke, Wolfgang 1927-1983
  Obituary *37*
Eckert, Allan W. 1931- *91*
  Brief entry *27*
  Earlier sketch in SATA *29*
  See also SAAS 21
Eckert, Horst 1931- *72*
  Earlier sketch in SATA *8*
  See also CLR 26
Ecklar, Julia (Marie) 1964- *112*

Eddings, David 1931-2009 .... *91*
Eddings, David Carroll
  See Eddings, David
Ede, Janina 1937- *33*
Edell, Celeste *12*
Edelman, Lily (Judith) 1915-1981 .... *22*
Edelson, Edward 1932- *51*
Edens, Cooper 1945- *166*
  Earlier sketches in SATA *49, 112*
Edens, (Bishop) David 1926- *39*
Edey, Maitland A(rmstrong) 1910-1992 .... *25*
  Obituary *71*
Edgerton, Perky *196*
Edgeworth, Maria 1768-1849 .... *21*
  See also CLR 153
Edgson, Alison *211*
Edgy, Wardore
  See Gorey, Edward (St. John)
Edison, Theodore
  See Stratemeyer, Edward L.
Edler, Tim(othy) 1948- *56*
Edmiston, Jim 1948- *80*
Edmonds, I(vy) G(ordon) 1917- *8*
Edmonds, Walter D(umaux) 1903-1998 .... *27*
  Obituary *99*
  Earlier sketch in SATA *1*
  See also SAAS 4
Edmund, Sean
  See Pringle, Laurence
Edsall, Marian (Stickney) 1920- *8*
Edwards, Al
  See Nourse, Alan E(dward)
Edwards, Anne 1927- *35*
Edwards, Audrey 1947- *52*
  Brief entry *31*
Edwards, Becky (Jane) 1966- *125*
Edwards, Bertram
  See Edwards, Herbert Charles
Edwards, Bronwen Elizabeth
  See Rose, Wendy
Edwards, Cecile Pepin 1916- *25*
Edwards, David 1962- *198*
Edwards, Dorothy 1914-1982 .... *88*
  Obituary *31*
  Earlier sketch in SATA *4*
Edwards, F. E.
  See Nolan, William F.
Edwards, Frank B. 1952- *93*
Edwards, Gunvor *32*
Edwards, Harvey 1929- *5*
Edwards, Hazel (Eileen) 1945- *135*
Edwards, Herbert Charles 1912- *12*
Edwards, Jane Campbell 1932- *10*
Edwards, Julia
  See Stratemeyer, Edward L.
Edwards, Julie
  See Andrews, Julie
Edwards, Julie Andrews
  See Andrews, Julie
Edwards, June
  See Bhatia, Jamunadevi
Edwards, Linda Strauss 1948- *49*
  Brief entry *42*
Edwards, Margaret (Alexander) 1902-1988
  Obituary *56*
Edwards, Michelle 1955- *152*
  Earlier sketch in SATA *70*
Edwards, Monica le Doux Newton
  1912-1998 .... *12*
Edwards, Olwen
  See Gater, Dilys
Edwards, Page (Lawrence, Jr.) 1941-1999 ... *59*
Edwards, Pamela Duncan *189*
Edwards, R. T.
  See Goulart, Ron
Edwards, Sally (Cary) 1929- *7*
Edwards, Samuel
  See Gerson, Noel Bertram
Edwards, Wallace 1957(?)- *170*
Eeckhout, Emmanuelle 1976- *208*
Egan, E(dward) W(elstead) 1922- *35*

Author Index

Egan, Kerry 175
Egan, Lorraine Hopping 1960- 134
Earlier sketch in SATA 91
Egan, Tim 1957- 191
Earlier sketches in SATA 89, 155
Egermeier, Elsie E(milie) 1890-1986 65
Eggenberger, David 1918- 6
Eggleston, Edward 1837-1902 27
Egielski, Richard 1952- 163
Earlier sketches in SATA 11, 49, 106
Egypt, Ophelia Settle 1903-1984 16
Obituary 38
Ehlert, Lois 1934- 172
Earlier sketches in SATA 35, 69, 128
See also CLR 28
Ehlert, Lois Jane
See Ehlert, Lois
Ehling, Katalin Olah 1941- 93
Ehrenfreund, Norbert 1921- 86
Ehrenhaft, Daniel 1970- 185
Ehrhardt, Karen 1963- 184
Ehrlich, Amy 1942- 132
Earlier sketches in SATA 25, 65, 96
Ehrlich, Bettina Bauer 1903-1985 1
Ehrlich, Fred 205
Ehrlich, Fred M.D.
See Ehrlich, Fred
Ehrlich, H. M.
See Ziefert, Harriet
Eichenberg, Fritz 1901-1990 50
Earlier sketch in SATA 9
Eichler, Margrit 1942- 35
Eichner, James A. 1927- 4
Eidson, Thomas 1944- 112
Eifert, Virginia (Louise) S(nider) 1911-1966 . 2
Eige, (Elizabeth) Lillian 1915- 65
Eiken, J. Melia 1967- 125
Einhorn, Edward 1970- 204
Einsel, Naiad 10
Einsel, Walter 1926- 10
Einzig, Susan 1922- 43
Eiseman, Alberta 1925- 15
Eisenberg, Azriel (Louis) 1903-1985 12
Eisenberg, Lisa 1949- 155
Brief entry 50
Earlier sketch in SATA 57
Eisenberg, Phyllis Rose 1924- 41
Eisner, Vivienne
See Margolis, Vivienne
Eisner, Will 1917-2005 165
Earlier sketch in SATA 31
Eisner, William Erwin
See Eisner, Will
Eitzen, Allan 1928- 9
Eitzen, Ruth (Carper) 1924- 9
Ekwensi, C. O. D.
See Ekwensi, Cyprian
Ekwensi, Cyprian 1921-2007 66
Ekwensi, Cyprian Odiatu Duaka
See Ekwensi, Cyprian
Elam, Richard M(ace, Jr.) 1920- 9
Elborn, Andrew
See Clements, Andrew
and Clements, Andrew
Elboz, Stephen 1956- 152
Eldin, Peter 1939- 154
Eldon, Kathy 1946- 107
Eldridge, Marion 199
Elfman, Blossom 1925- 8
Elgin, Kathleen 1923- 39
Elia
See Lamb, Charles
Eliot, A. D.
See Jewett, Sarah Orne
Eliot, Alice
See Jewett, Sarah Orne
Eliot, Anne
See Cole, Lois Dwight
Eliot, Dan
See Silverberg, Robert

Elish, Dan 1960- 204
Earlier sketches in SATA 68, 129
Elisha, Ron 1951- 104
Elisofon, Eliot 1911-1973
Obituary 21
Elkeles, Simone 1970- 187
Elkin, Benjamin 1911-1995 3
Elkins, Dov Peretz 1937- 5
Ellacott, S(amuel) E(rnest) 1911- 19
Elleman, Barbara 1934- 147
Ellen, Jaye
See Nixon, Joan Lowery
Eller, Scott
See Holinger, William (Jacques)
and Shepard, Jim
Ellestad, Myrvin
See Ellestad, Myrvin H.
Ellestad, Myrvin H. 1921- 120
Elliot, Bruce
See Field, Edward
Elliot, David 1952- 208
Earlier sketch in SATA 122
Elliott, Bruce
See Field, Edward
Elliott, David 1947- 201
Earlier sketch in SATA 163
Elliott, Don
See Silverberg, Robert
Elliott, Elizabeth Shippen Green
See Green, Elizabeth Shippen
Elliott, Janice 1931-1995 119
Elliott, Joey
See Houk, Randy
Elliott, Laura Malone 1957- 197
Elliott, L.M.
See Elliott, Laura Malone
Elliott, Louise 111
Elliott, Mark 1949- 210
Elliott, Odette 1939- 75
Elliott, Patricia 1946- 176
Elliott, Sarah M(cCarn) 1930- 14
Elliott, (Robert) Scott 1970- 153
Elliott, William
See Bradbury, Ray
Elliott, Zetta 206
Ellis, (Mary) Amabel (Nassau Strachey)
Williams
See Williams-Ellis, (Mary) Amabel (Nassau
Strachey)
Ellis, Ann Dee 210
Ellis, Anyon
See Rowland-Entwistle, (Arthur) Theodore
(Henry)
Ellis, Carson 1975- 190
Ellis, Carson Friedman
See Ellis, Carson
Ellis, Deborah 1960- 187
Earlier sketch in SATA 129
Ellis, E. S.
See Ellis, Edward S.
Ellis, Edward S. 1840-1916
See YABC 1
Ellis, Edward Sylvester
See Ellis, Edward S.
Ellis, Ella Thorp 1928- 127
Earlier sketch in SATA 7
See also SAAS 9
Ellis, Harry Bearse 1921-2004 9
Ellis, Herbert
See Wilson, Lionel
Ellis, Mel(vin Richard) 1912-1984 7
Obituary 39
Ellis, Richard 1938- 130
Ellis, Sarah 1952- 179
Earlier sketches in SATA 68, 131
See also CLR 42
Ellison, Chris 196
Ellison, Elizabeth Stow 1970- 209
Ellison, Emily 114
Ellison, Lucile Watkins 1907(?)-1979 50
Obituary 22

Ellison, Virginia H(owell) 1910- 4
Ellsberg, Edward 1891-1983 7
Ellsworth, Loretta 1954- 199
Ellsworth, Mary Ellen (Tressel) 1940- 146
Ellwand, David 1965(?)- 213
Elmer, Robert 1958- 154
Earlier sketch in SATA 99
Elmore, (Carolyn) Patricia 1933- 38
Brief entry 35
El-Moslimany, Ann P(axton) 1937- 90
Elschner, Geraldine 1954- 183
Elspeth
See Bragdon, Elspeth MacDuffie
Elster, Jean Alicia 1953- 150
Elting, Mary 1906- 88
Earlier sketch in SATA 2
See also SAAS 20
Elvgren, Jennifer Riesmeyer 179
Elwart, Joan Potter 1927- 2
Elwood, Ann 1931- 55
Brief entry 52
Elwood, Roger 1943-2007 58
Ely, Lesley 212
Elya, Susan Middleton 1955- 202
Earlier sketches in SATA 106, 159
Elzbieta 88
Ember, Kathi 190
Emberley, Barbara A. 1932- 146
Earlier sketches in SATA 8, 70
See also CLR 5
Emberley, Barbara Anne
See Emberley, Barbara A.
Emberley, Ed 1931- 146
Earlier sketches in SATA 8, 70
See also CLR 81
Emberley, Edward Randolph
See Emberley, Ed
Emberley, Michael 1960- 189
Earlier sketches in SATA 34, 80, 119
Embry, Margaret Jacob 1919-1975 5
Emecheta, Buchi 1944- 66
Emecheta, Florence Onye Buchi
See Emecheta, Buchi
Emerson, Alice B.
See Benson, Mildred
Emerson, Kathy Lynn 1947- 63
Emerson, Kevin 209
Emerson, Ru 1944- 107
Earlier sketch in SATA 70
Emerson, Sally 1952- 111
Emerson, William K(eith) 1925- 25
Emert, Phyllis R(aybin) 1947- 93
Emery, Anne (McGuigan) 1907- 33
Earlier sketch in SATA 1
Emmens, Carol Ann 1944- 39
Emmett, Jonathan 1965- 188
Earlier sketch in SATA 138
Emmons, Della (Florence) Gould 1890-1983
Obituary 39
Emory, Jerry 1957- 96
Emrich, Duncan (Black Macdonald)
1908-1970(?) 11
Emshwiller, Carol 1921- 174
Autobiography Feature 174
Emshwiller, Carol Fries
See Emshwiller, Carol
Emslie, M. L.
See Simpson, Myrtle L(illias)
Ende, Michael (Andreas Helmuth)
1929-1995 130
Brief entry 42
Obituary 86
Earlier sketch in SATA 61
See also CLR 138
Enderle, Dotti 1954- 203
Earlier sketch in SATA 145
Enderle, Judith (Ann) Ross 1941- 89
Autobiography Feature 114
Earlier sketch in SATA 38
See also SAAS 26
Endle, Kate 207

Enell, Trinka (Gochenour) 1951- *79*
Enfield, Carrie
  See Smith, Susan Vernon
Engdahl, Sylvia Louise 1933- *4*
  Autobiography Feature *122*
  See also CLR 2
  See also SAAS 5
Engel, Diana 1947- *70*
Engelbreit, Mary 1952- *169*
Engelhart, Margaret S. 1924- *59*
Engelmann, Kim (V.) 1959- *87*
England, George Allan 1877-1936 .... *102*
Englart, Mindi Rose 1965- *146*
Engle, Eloise
  See Paananen, Eloise (Katherine)
Engle, Margarita 1951- *193*
Englebert, Victor 1933- *8*
English, James W(ilson) 1915- *37*
English, Karen *202*
Engstrom, Elizabeth 1951- *110*
Enright, D(ennis) J(oseph) 1920-2002 .... *25*
  Obituary *140*
Enright, Dominique *194*
Enright, Elizabeth (Wright) 1909-1968 .... *9*
  See also CLR 4
Ensor, Barbara *180*
Ensor, Robert (T.) 1922- *93*
Enthoven, Sam 1974- *187*
Entwistle, (Arthur) Theodore (Henry) Rowland
  See Rowland-Entwistle, (Arthur) Theodore
    (Henry)
Enys, Sarah L.
  See Sloggett, Nellie
Epanya, Christian A(rthur Kingue) 1956- *91*
Ephraim, Shelly S(chonebaum) 1952- *97*
Ephron, Delia 1944- *197*
  Brief entry *50*
  Earlier sketch in SATA *65*
Epler, Doris M. 1928- *73*
Epp, Margaret A(gnes) 1913- *20*
Eppenstein, Louise (Kohn) 1892-1987
  Obituary *54*
Epple, Anne Orth 1927- *20*
Epstein, Anne Merrick 1931- *20*
Epstein, Beryl 1910- *31*
  Earlier sketch in SATA *1*
  See also CLR 26
  See also SAAS 17
Epstein, Beryl M. Williams
  See Epstein, Beryl
Epstein, Perle S(herry) 1938- *27*
Epstein, Rachel S. 1941- *102*
Epstein, Samuel 1909-2000 .... *31*
  Earlier sketch in SATA *1*
  See also CLR 26
  See also SAAS 17
Erdman, Loula Grace 1905(?)-1976 .... *1*
Erdoes, Richard 1912- *33*
  Brief entry *28*
Erdogan, Buket *187*
Erdrich, Karen Louise
  See Erdrich, Louise
Erdrich, Louise 1954- *141*
  Earlier sketch in SATA *94*
Erickson, Betty J. 1923- *97*
Erickson, Betty Jean
  See Erickson, Betty J.
Erickson, John R. 1943- *136*
  Earlier sketch in SATA *70*
Erickson, Jon 1948- *141*
Erickson, Phoebe *59*
Erickson, Russell E(verett) 1932- *27*
Erickson, Sabra Rollins 1912-1995 .... *35*
Erickson, Walter
  See Fast, Howard
Ericson, Walter
  See Fast, Howard
Ericsson, Jennifer A. *170*
Erikson, Mel 1937- *31*
Eriksson, Eva 1949- *207*
Ering, Timothy Basil *176*

Erlanger, Baba
  See Trahey, Jane
Erlbach, Arlene 1948- *160*
  Earlier sketches in SATA *78, 115*
Erlbruch, Wolf 1948- *181*
Erlich, Lillian (Feldman) 1910-1983 .... *10*
Erlings, Fridrik 1962- *196*
Erlingsson, Fri****rik
  See Erlings, Fridrik
Ermatinger, James W. 1959- *170*
Ernest, William
  See Berkebile, Fred D(onovan)
Ernst, (Lyman) John 1940- *39*
Ernst, Kathleen
  See Ernst, Kathleen A.
Ernst, Kathleen A. 1959- *162*
Ernst, Kathryn (Fitzgerald) 1942- *25*
Ernst, Lisa Campbell 1957- *212*
  Brief entry *44*
  Earlier sketches in SATA *55, 95, 154*
Erskine, Kathryn *193*
Ervin, Janet Halliday 1923- *4*
Erwin, Will
  See Eisner, Will
Esbaum, Jill *213*
  Earlier sketch in SATA *174*
Esbensen, Barbara J(uster) 1925-1996 .... *97*
  Brief entry *53*
  Earlier sketch in SATA *62*
Eschbacher, Roger *160*
Eschmeyer, R. E. 1898-1989 .... *29*
Escriva, Vivi *182*
Eseki, Bruno
  See Mphahlele, Es'kia
Esekie, Bruno
  See Mphahlele, Es'kia
Eshmeyer, Reinhart Ernst
  See Eschmeyer, R. E.
Eskridge, Ann E. 1949- *84*
Espeland, Pamela (Lee) 1951- *128*
  Brief entry *38*
  Earlier sketch in SATA *52*
Espinosa, Laura *203*
Espinosa, Leo *203*
Espriella, Don Manuel Alvarez
  See Southey, Robert
Espy, Willard R(ichardson) 1910-1999 .... *38*
  Obituary *113*
Essakalli, Julie Klear *200*
Essrig, Harry 1912- *66*
Estep, Irene Compton *5*
Esterl, Arnica 1933- *77*
Estes, Eleanor (Ruth) 1906-1988 .... *91*
  Obituary *56*
  Earlier sketch in SATA *7*
  See also CLR 70
Estoril, Jean
  See Allan, Mabel Esther
Estrada, Pau 1961- *200*
  Earlier sketch in SATA *74*
Etchemendy, Nancy 1952- *166*
  Earlier sketch in SATA *38*
Etchemendy, Nancy Elise Howell
  See Etchemendy, Nancy
Etchison, Birdie L(ee) 1937- *38*
Etchison, Craig 1945- *133*
Etherington, Frank 1945- *58*
Eton, Robert
  See Meynell, Laurence Walter
Ets, Marie Hall 1893-1984 .... *2*
  See also CLR 33
Ettlinger, Doris 1950- *173*
Eunson, (John) Dale 1904-2002 .... *5*
  Obituary *132*
Evan, Frances Y. 1951- *167*
Evanoff, Vlad 1916- *59*
Evans, Cambria 1981- *178*
Evans, Douglas 1953- *144*
  Earlier sketch in SATA *93*
Evans, Eva (Knox) 1905-1998 .... *27*

Evans, Freddi Williams 1957- *211*
  Earlier sketch in SATA *134*
Evans, Greg 1947- *143*
  Earlier sketch in SATA *73*
Evans, Hubert Reginald 1892-1986 .... *118*
  Obituary *48*
Evans, Katherine (Floyd) 1901-1964 .... *5*
Evans, Larry
  See Evans, Laurence Chubb
Evans, Laurence Chubb 1939- *88*
Evans, Lawrence Watt
  See Watt-Evans, Lawrence
Evans, Leslie 1953- *214*
Evans, Lezlie *180*
Evans, Mari 1923- *10*
Evans, Mark *19*
Evans, Nancy 1950- *65*
Evans, Nate *201*
Evans, Patricia Healy
  See Carpenter, Patricia (Healy Evans)
Evans, (Alice) Pearl 1927- *83*
Evans, Shane W. *189*
Evans, Shirlee 1931- *58*
Evans, Tabor
  See Cameron, Lou
  and Knott, William C(ecil, Jr.)
  and Wallmann, Jeffrey M(iner)
  and Whittington, Harry (Benjamin)
Evarts, Esther
  See Benson, Sally
Evarts, Hal G., (Jr.) 1915-1989 .... *6*
Everett, Gail
  See Hale, Arlene
Evernden, Margery 1916- *5*
Eversole, Robyn 1971- *74*
Eversole, Robyn H.
  See Eversole, Robyn
Eversole, Robyn Harbert
  See Eversole, Robyn
Evslin, Bernard 1922-1993 .... *83*
  Brief entry *28*
  Obituary *77*
  Earlier sketch in SATA *45*
Ewart, Claire 1958- *145*
  Earlier sketch in SATA *76*
Ewart, Franzeska G. 1950- *205*
Ewen, David 1907-1985 .... *4*
  Obituary *47*
Ewing, Juliana (Horatia Gatty) 1841-1885 ... *16*
  See also CLR 78
Ewing, Kathryn 1921- *20*
Eyerly, Jeannette 1908-2008 .... *86*
  Obituary *196*
  Earlier sketch in SATA *4*
  See also SAAS 10
Eyerly, Jeannette Hyde
  See Eyerly, Jeannette
Eyre, Dorothy
  See McGuire, Leslie (Sarah)
Eyre, Frank 1910-1988
  Obituary *62*
Eyre, Katherine Wigmore 1901-1970 .... *26*
Ezzell, Marilyn 1937- *42*
  Brief entry *38*

F

Fabe, Maxene 1943- *15*
Faber, Doris (Greenberg) 1924- *78*
  Earlier sketch in SATA *3*
Faber, Harold 1919-2010 .... *5*
Fabre, Jean Henri (Casimir) 1823-1915 .... *22*
Fabry, Glenn 1961- *205*
Facklam, Margaret
  See Thomas, Peggy
Facklam, Margery (Metz) 1927- *132*
  Earlier sketches in SATA *20, 85*
Fadden, David Kanietakeron *196*

Fadiman, Clifton (Paul) 1904-1999 .... *11*
  Obituary *115*
Fagan, Cary 1957- *186*
Fahs, Sophia Blanche Lyon 1876-1978 ...... *102*
Failing, Barbara Larmon *182*
Fain, Sarah 1971- *204*
Fair, David 1952- *96*
Fair, Sylvia 1933- *13*
Fairfax-Lucy, Brian (Fulke Cameron-Ramsay)
  1898-1974 .... *6*
  Obituary *26*
Fairfield, Flora
  See Alcott, Louisa May
Fairlie, Gerard 1899-1983
  Obituary *34*
Fairman, Joan A(lexandra) 1935- *10*
Faithfull, Gail 1936- *8*
Falcone, L(ucy) M. 1951- *155*
Falconer, Ian 1959- *179*
  Earlier sketch in SATA *125*
  See also CLR *146*
Falconer, James
  See Kirkup, James
Falconer, Lee N.
  See May, Julian
Falkner, Brian 1962- *206*
Falkner, Leonard 1900-1977 .... *12*
Fall, Andrew
  See Arthur, Robert, (Jr.)
Fall, Thomas
  See Snow, Donald Clifford
Faller, Regis 1968- *187*
Falls, C(harles) B(uckles) 1874-1960 .... *38*
  Brief entry *27*
Falstein, Louis 1909-1995 .... *37*
Falwell, Cathryn 1952- *196*
Fancher, Lou 1960- *177*
Fanelli, Sara 1969- *126*
  Earlier sketch in SATA *89*
Fanning, Leonard M(ulliken) 1888-1967 .... *5*
Faralla, Dana 1909- *9*
Faralla, Dorothy W.
  See Faralla, Dana
Farb, Peter 1929-1980 .... *12*
  Obituary *22*
Farber, Norma 1909-1984 .... *75*
  Obituary *38*
  Earlier sketch in SATA *25*
Fardell, John 1967- *195*
Fardell, John William
  See Fardell, John
Faria, Rosana *213*
Farish, Terry 1947- *146*
  Earlier sketch in SATA *82*
Farjeon, (Eve) Annabel 1919-2004 .... *11*
  Obituary *153*
Farjeon, Eleanor 1881-1965 .... *2*
  See also CLR *34*
Farley, Carol (J.) 1936- *137*
  Earlier sketch in SATA *4*
Farley, Terri *165*
Farley, Walter (Lorimer) 1915-1989 .... *132*
  Earlier sketches in SATA *2, 43*
Farlow, James O(rville, Jr.) 1951- *75*
Farmer, Jacqueline *210*
Farmer, Nancy 1941- *161*
  Earlier sketches in SATA *79, 117*
Farmer, Patti 1948- *79*
Farmer, Penelope (Jane) 1939- *105*
  Brief entry *39*
  Earlier sketch in SATA *40*
  See also CLR *8*
  See also SAAS *22*
Farmer, Peter 1950- *38*
Farmer, Philip Jose
  See Farmer, Philip Jose
Farmer, Philip Jose 1918-2009 .... *93*
  Obituary *201*
Farmer, Philipe Jos
  See Farmer, Philip Jose

Farnham, Burt
  See Clifford, Harold B(urton)
Farnsworth, Bill 1958- *186*
  Earlier sketches in SATA *84, 135*
Farooqi, Musharraf Ali 1968- *207*
Farquhar, Margaret C(utting) 1905-1988 ...... *13*
Farquharson, Alexander 1944- *46*
Farquharson, Martha
  See Finley, Martha
Farr, Diana *82*
  Earlier sketch in SATA *3*
Farr, Finis (King) 1904-1982 .... *10*
Farr, Richard 1960- *209*
Farrar, Jill
  See Morris, Jill
Farrar, Susan Clement 1917- *33*
Farrell, Ben
  See Cebulash, Mel
Farrell, John 1951- *204*
Farrell, Patrick
  See Odgers, Sally Farrell
Farrell, Sally
  See Odgers, Sally Farrell
Farrer, Vashti *167*
Farrington, Benjamin 1891-1974
  Obituary *20*
Farrington, S(elwyn) Kip, Jr. 1904-1983 ...... *20*
Farris, Christine King 1927- *206*
Farshtey, Greg(ory T.) 1965- *148*
Farthing, Alison 1936- *45*
  Brief entry *36*
Farthing-Knight, Catherine 1933- *92*
Fassler, Joan (Grace) 1931- *11*
Fast, Howard 1914-2003 .... *7*
  Autobiography Feature *107*
Fast, Howard Melvin
  See Fast, Howard
Fasulo, Michael 1963- *83*
Fatchen, Max 1920- *84*
  Earlier sketch in SATA *20*
  See also SAAS *20*
Fate, Marilyn
  See Collins, Paul
Father Goose
  See Ghigna, Charles
Fatigati, (Frances) Evelyn 1948- *24*
Fatio, Louise 1904-1993 .... *6*
Fatus, Sophie 1957- *182*
Faulhaber, Martha 1926- *7*
Faulkner, Anne Irvin 1906- *23*
Faulkner, Frank
  See Ellis, Edward S.
Faulkner, Nancy
  See Faulkner, Anne Irvin
Faulknor, Cliff(ord Vernon) 1913- *86*
Favole, Robert J(ames) 1950- *125*
Fax, Elton Clay 1909-1993 .... *25*
Faxon, Lavinia
  See Russ, Lavinia (Faxon)
Feagles, Anita M(acRae) 1927- *9*
Feagles, Elizabeth
  See Day, Beth (Feagles)
Feague, Mildred H. 1915- *14*
Fearnley, Jan 1965- *205*
  Earlier sketch in SATA *153*
Fearrington, Ann (Peyton) 1945- *146*
Fecher, Constance
  See Heaven, Constance (Christina)
Feder, Chris Welles 1938- *81*
Feder, Harriet K. 1928- *73*
Feder, Paula (Kurzband) 1935- *26*
Federici, Debbie 1965- *175*
Federici, Debbie Tanner
  See Federici, Debbie
Feelings, Muriel 1938- *16*
  See also CLR *5*
  See also SAAS *8*
Feelings, Muriel Lavita Grey
  See Feelings, Muriel

Feelings, Thomas 1933-2003 .... *69*
  Obituary *148*
  Earlier sketch in SATA *8*
  See also CLR *58*
  See also SAAS *19*
Feelings, Tom
  See Feelings, Thomas
Fehler, Gene 1940- *201*
  Earlier sketch in SATA *74*
Fehrenbach, T(heodore) R(eed, Jr.) 1925- *33*
Feiffer, Jules 1929- *201*
  Earlier sketches in SATA *8, 61, 111, 157*
Feiffer, Jules Ralph
  See Feiffer, Jules
Feiffer, Kate 1964- *206*
  Earlier sketch in SATA *170*
Feig, Barbara Krane 1937- *34*
Feikema, Feike
  See Manfred, Frederick (Feikema)
Feil, Hila 1942- *12*
Feilen, John
  See May, Julian
Feinberg, Barbara Jane 1938- *123*
  Earlier sketch in SATA *58*
Feinberg, Barbara Silberdick
  See Feinberg, Barbara Jane
Feinstein, John 1956- *195*
  Earlier sketch in SATA *163*
Feldman, Anne (Rodgers) 1939- *19*
Feldman, Elane *79*
Feldman, Jody *200*
Felin, M. Sindy *194*
Felix
  See Vincent, Felix
Fell, Derek 1939- *167*
Fell, Derek John
  See Fell, Derek
Fellowes, Julian 1950- *198*
Fellows, Muriel H. *10*
Fellows, Stan 1957- *177*
Fellows, Stanley
  See Fellows, Stan
Felsen, Henry Gregor 1916-1995 .... *1*
  See also SAAS *2*
Felstead, Cathie 1954- *192*
Feltenstein, Arlene 1934- *119*
Feltenstine, Arlene H.
  See Feltenstein, Arlene
Felton, Harold William 1902-1991 .... *1*
Felton, Ronald Oliver 1909- *3*
Felts, Shirley 1934- *33*
Felts, Susannah 1973- *214*
Fenderson, Lewis H., Jr. 1907-1983 .... *47*
  Obituary *37*
Fenner, Carol (Elizabeth) 1929-2002 .... *89*
  Obituary *132*
  Earlier sketch in SATA *7*
  See also SAAS *24*
Fenner, Phyllis R(eid) 1899-1982 .... *1*
  Obituary *29*
Fensham, Elizabeth *169*
Fenten, Barbara D(oris) 1935- *26*
Fenten, D(onald) X. 1932- *4*
Fenton, Carroll Lane 1900-1969 .... *5*
Fenton, Edward 1917-1995 .... *7*
  Obituary *89*
Fenton, Joe *213*
Fenton, Mildred Adams 1899-1995 .... *21*
Fenwick, Patti
  See Grider, Dorothy
Feravolo, Rocco Vincent 1922- *10*
Ferber, Brenda A. 1967- *184*
Ferber, Edna 1887-1968 .... *7*
Fergus, Charles *114*
Ferguson, Alane 1957- *182*
  Earlier sketch in SATA *85*
Ferguson, Bob
  See Ferguson, Robert Bruce
Ferguson, Cecil 1931- *45*
Ferguson, Peter 1968- *199*
Ferguson, Robert Bruce 1927-2001 .... *13*

Ferguson, Sarah 1959- *180*
  Earlier sketches in SATA *66, 110*
Ferguson, Sarah Margaret
  See Ferguson, Sarah
Ferguson, Walter (W.) 1930- *34*
Fergusson, Erna 1888-1964 .... *5*
Fermi, Laura 1907-1977 .... *6*
  Obituary *28*
Fern, Eugene A. 1919-1987 .... *10*
  Obituary *54*
Fern, Tracey E. *202*
Fernandes, Eugenie 1943- *205*
  Earlier sketches in SATA *77, 139*
Fernandez, Laura 1960- *171*
Ferraiolo, Jack D. *208*
Ferrari, Maria *123*
Ferreiro, Carmen 1958- *158*
Ferrell, Nancy Warren 1932- *70*
Ferri, Giuliano 1965- *197*
Ferrier, Lucy
  See Penzler, Otto
Ferris, Helen Josephine 1890-1969 .... *21*
Ferris, James Cody
  See McFarlane, Leslie
Ferris, Jean 1939- *202*
  Brief entry *50*
  Earlier sketches in SATA *56, 105, 149*
Ferris, Jeri Chase 1937- *84*
Ferry, Charles 1927- *92*
  Earlier sketch in SATA *43*
  See also CLR *34*
  See also SAAS *20*
Fetz, Ingrid 1915- *30*
Feydy, Anne Lindbergh
  See Sapieyevski, Anne Lindbergh
Fiammenghi, Gioia 1929- *66*
  Earlier sketch in SATA *9*
Fiarotta, Noel
  See Ficarotta, Noel
Fiarotta, Phyllis
  See Ficarotta, Phyllis
Ficarotta, Noel 1944- *15*
Ficarotta, Phyllis 1942- *15*
Fichter, George S. 1922-1993 .... *7*
Ficocelli, Elizabeth *189*
Fidler, Kathleen (Annie) 1899-1980 .... *87*
  Obituary *45*
  Earlier sketch in SATA *3*
Fiedler, Jean(nette Feldman) *4*
Fiedler, Joseph Daniel *159*
Fiedler, Lisa *185*
Field, Dorothy 1944- *97*
Field, Edward 1924- *109*
  Earlier sketch in SATA *8*
Field, Elinor Whitney 1889-1980
  Obituary *28*
Field, Eugene 1850-1895 .... *16*
Field, Gans T.
  See Wellman, Manly Wade
Field, James 1959- *113*
Field, Peter
  See Drago, Harry Sinclair
  and Dresser, Davis
  and Mann, E(dward) B(everly)
Field, Rachel (Lyman) 1894-1942 .... *15*
  See also CLR *21*
Fielding, Kate
  See Oldfield, Jenny
Fields, Bryan W. 1958(?)- *188*
Fields, Terri 1948- *191*
Fields, T.S.
  See Fields, Terri
Fienberg, Anna 1956- *183*
  Earlier sketch in SATA *112*
Fiery, Ann
  See Barrows, Annie
Fife, Dale (Odile Hollerbach) 1901- *18*
Fighter Pilot, A
  See Johnston, H(ugh) A(nthony) S(tephen)
Figler, Jeanie 1949- *123*

Figley, Marty Rhodes 1948- *158*
  Earlier sketch in SATA *88*
Figueredo, D(anilo) H. 1951- *155*
Figueroa, Pablo 1938- *9*
Fijan, Carol 1918- *12*
Filderman, Diane E(lizabeth) 1959- *87*
Files, Meg 1946- *107*
Fillmore, Parker H(oysted) 1878-1944
  See YABC *1*
Filstrup, Chris
  See Filstrup, E(dward) Christian
Filstrup, E(dward) Christian 1942- *43*
Filstrup, Janie
  See Merrill, Jane
Finchler, Judy 1943- *93*
Finder, Martin
  See Salzmann, Siegmund
Findlay, Jamieson 1958- *169*
Findon, Joanne 1957- *161*
Fine, Anne 1947- *197*
  Earlier sketches in SATA *29, 72, 111, 160*
  See also CLR *25*
  See also SAAS *15*
Fine, Edith Hope *169*
Fine, Howard 1961- *181*
Fine, Jane
  See Ziefert, Harriet
Finger, Charles J(oseph) 1869(?)-1941 .... *42*
Fink, William B(ertrand) 1916- *22*
Finke, Blythe Foote 1922- *26*
Finkel, George (Irvine) 1909-1975 .... *8*
Finkelstein, Norman H. 1941- *137*
  Earlier sketch in SATA *73*
Finkelstein, Norman Henry
  See Finkelstein, Norman H.
Finlay, Alice Sullivan 1946- *82*
Finlay, Winifred Lindsay Crawford
  (McKissack) 1910-1989 .... *23*
Finlayson, Ann 1925- *8*
Finley, Martha 1828-1909 .... *43*
  See also CLR *148*
Finley, Mary Peace 1942- *83*
Finn, Mary *208*
Finney, Jack 1911-1995 .... *109*
Finney, Patricia 1958- *163*
Finney, Shan 1944- *65*
Finney, Walter Braden
  See Finney, Jack
Firer, Ben Zion
  See Firer, Benzion
Firer, Benzion 1914- *64*
Fireside, Bryna J. 1932- *73*
Firmin, Charlotte 1954- *29*
Firmin, Peter 1928- *58*
  Earlier sketch in SATA *15*
Firth, Barbara *179*
Fischbach, Julius 1894-1988 .... *10*
Fischer, John
  See Fluke, Joanne
Fischer, R.J.
  See Fluke, Joanne
Fischer, Scott M. 1971- *195*
Fischer-Nagel, Andreas 1951- *56*
Fischer-Nagel, Heiderose 1956- *56*
Fischler, Shirley (Walton) *66*
Fischler, Stan(ley I.) *66*
  Brief entry *36*
Fischtrom, Harvey 1933-1974 .... *3*
Fishback, Margaret
  See Antolini, Margaret Fishback
Fishbone, Greg R. *195*
Fisher, Aileen (Lucia) 1906-2002 .... *73*
  Obituary *143*
  Earlier sketches in SATA *1, 25*
  See also CLR *49*
Fisher, Barbara 1940- *44*
  Brief entry *34*
Fisher, Carolyn 1968- *154*
Fisher, Catherine 1957- *155*
Fisher, Chris 1958- *80*
Fisher, Clavin C(argill) 1912- *24*

Fisher, Cynthia *195*
Fisher, Dorothy (Frances) Canfield 1879-1958
  See YABC *1*
  See also CLR *71*
Fisher, Gary L. 1949- *86*
Fisher, John 1909-1996 .... *15*
Fisher, John Oswald Hamilton
  See Fisher, John
Fisher, Laura Harrison 1934- *5*
Fisher, Leonard Everett 1924- *176*
  Autobiography Feature *122*
  Earlier sketches in SATA *4, 34, 73, 120*
  See also CLR *18*
  See also SAAS *1*
Fisher, Lois I. 1948- *38*
  Brief entry *35*
Fisher, Margery (Turner) 1913-1992 .... *20*
  Obituary *74*
Fisher, Marshall Jon 1963- *113*
Fisher, Nikki
  See Strachan, Ian
Fisher, Robert (Tempest) 1943- *47*
Fisher, Suzanne
  See Staples, Suzanne Fisher
Fisher, Valorie *214*
  Earlier sketch in SATA *177*
Fishman, Cathy Goldberg 1951- *106*
Fisk, Nicholas
  See Higginbottom, David
Fisk, Pauline 1948- *160*
  Earlier sketch in SATA *66*
Fiske, Tarleton
  See Bloch, Robert (Albert)
Fisscher, Catharina G. M. 1958- *142*
Fisscher, Tiny
  See Fisscher, Catharina G. M.
Fitch, Clarke
  See Sinclair, Upton
Fitch, John IV
  See Cormier, Robert
Fitch, Sheree 1956- *178*
  Earlier sketch in SATA *108*
Fitschen, Dale 1937- *20*
Fitzalan, Roger
  See Trevor, Elleston
Fitzgerald, Captain Hugh
  See Baum, L. Frank
FitzGerald, Cathleen 1932-1987
  Obituary *50*
Fitzgerald, Dawn *175*
Fitzgerald, Edward Earl 1919-2001 .... *20*
Fitzgerald, F(rancis) A(nthony) 1940- *15*
Fitzgerald, Joanne 1956- *198*
Fitzgerald, John D(ennis) 1907(?)-1988 ...... *20*
  Obituary *56*
  See also CLR *1*
Fitzgerald, Merni Ingrassia 1955- *53*
Fitzgibbon, Terry 1948- *121*
Fitzhardinge, Joan Margaret 1912- *73*
  Earlier sketch in SATA *2*
  See also CLR *5*
  See also SAAS *3*
Fitzhugh, Louise (Perkins) 1928-1974 .... *45*
  Obituary *24*
  Earlier sketch in SATA *1*
  See also CLR *72*
Fitzhugh, Percy Keese 1876-1950 .... *65*
Fitzpatrick, Marie-Louise 1962- *189*
  Earlier sketch in SATA *125*
FitzRalph, Matthew
  See McInerny, Ralph
Fitz-Randolph, Jane (Currens) 1915- *51*
Fitzsimons, Cecilia 1952- *97*
Fitzsimons, Cecilia A.L.
  See Fitzsimons, Cecilia
Flack, Marjorie 1897-1958 .... *100*
  See also YABC *2*
  See also CLR *28*
Flack, Naomi John White -1999 .... *40*
  Brief entry *35*
Flake, Sharon G. *166*

Flanagan, John 1944- *180*
Flanagan, John Anthony
  See Flanagan, John
Flannery, Kate
  See De Goldi, Kate
Flatt, Lizann 1966- *88*
Fleagle, Gail S(hatto) 1940- *117*
Fleetwood, Jenni 1947- *80*
Fleischer, Jane
  See Oppenheim, Joanne
Fleischhauer-Hardt, Helga 1936- *30*
Fleischman, Albert Sidney
  See Fleischman, Sid
Fleischman, John 1948- *145*
Fleischman, Paul 1952- *156*
  Brief entry *32*
  Earlier sketches in SATA *39, 72, 110*
  See also CLR *66*
  See also SAAS *20*
Fleischman, Sid 1920-2010 .... *185*
  Earlier sketches in SATA *8, 59, 96, 148*
  See also CLR *15*
Fleischner, Jennifer 1956- *188*
  Earlier sketch in SATA *93*
Fleisher, Paul 1948- *132*
  Earlier sketch in SATA *81*
Fleisher, Robbin 1951-1977 .... *52*
  Brief entry *49*
Fleishman, Seymour 1918- *66*
  Brief entry *32*
Fleming, A. A.
  See Arthur, Robert, (Jr.)
Fleming, Alice Mulcahey 1928- *9*
Fleming, Candace 1962- *190*
  Earlier sketches in SATA *94, 143*
Fleming, Denise 1950- *173*
  Earlier sketches in SATA *81, 126*
Fleming, Elizabeth P. 1888-1985
  Obituary *48*
Fleming, Ian 1908-1964 .... *9*
Fleming, Ian Lancaster
  See Fleming, Ian
Fleming, Ronald Lee 1941- *56*
Fleming, Sally
  See Walker, Sally M(acArt)
Fleming, Stuart
  See Knight, Damon (Francis)
Fleming, Susan 1932- *32*
Fleming, Thomas 1927- *8*
Fleming, Thomas James
  See Fleming, Thomas
Fleming, Virginia (Edwards) 1923- *84*
Flesch, Y.
  See Flesch, Yolande (Catarina)
Flesch, Yolande (Catarina) 1950- *55*
Fletcher, Charlie May Hogue 1897-1977 .... *3*
Fletcher, Colin 1922-2007 .... *28*
Fletcher, Dirk
  See Cunningham, Chet
Fletcher, George U.
  See Pratt, (Murray) Fletcher
Fletcher, Helen Jill 1910- *13*
Fletcher, Ralph 1953- *195*
  Earlier sketches in SATA *105, 149*
  See also CLR *104*
Fletcher, Ralph J.
  See Fletcher, Ralph
Fletcher, Richard E. 1917(?)-1983
  Obituary *34*
Fletcher, Rick
  See Fletcher, Richard E.
Fletcher, Susan 1951- *181*
  Earlier sketches in SATA *70, 110*
Fletcher, Susan Clemens
  See Fletcher, Susan
Fleur, Paul
  See Pohl, Frederik
Flexner, James Thomas 1908-2003 .... *9*
Flinn, Alex 1966- *198*
  Earlier sketch in SATA *159*
Flint, Helen 1952- *102*

Flint, Russ 1944- *74*
Flitner, David P(erkins), Jr. 1949- *7*
Floca, Brian *190*
  Earlier sketch in SATA *155*
Floethe, Louise Lee 1913-1988 .... *4*
Floethe, Richard 1901-1998 .... *4*
Floherty, John Joseph 1882-1964 .... *25*
Flood, Bo
  See Flood, Nancy Bo
Flood, Nancy Bo 1945- *130*
Flood, Pansie Hart 1964- *140*
Flood, William 1942- *129*
Flooglebuckle, Al
  See Spiegelman, Art
Flora, James (Royer) 1914-1998 .... *30*
  Obituary *103*
  Earlier sketch in SATA *1*
  See also SAAS *6*
Flores-Galbis, Enrique 1952- *186*
Florian, Douglas 1950- *177*
  Earlier sketches in SATA *19, 83, 125*
Flory, Jane Trescott 1917- *22*
Flournoy, Valerie 1952- *95*
Flournoy, Valerie Rose
  See Flournoy, Valerie
Flowerdew, Phyllis -1994 .... *33*
Flowers, Pam 1946- *136*
Flowers, Sarah 1952- *98*
Floyd, Gareth 1940- *62*
  Brief entry *31*
Fluchere, Henri 1914-1991 .... *40*
Fluke, Joanne 1943- *88*
Flutsztejn-Gruda, Ilona 1930- *170*
Flynn, Barbara 1928- *9*
Flynn, Jackson
  See Bensen, Donald R.
  and Shirreffs, Gordon D(onald)
Flynn, Nicholas
  See Odgers, Sally Farrell
Flynn, Pat 1968- *214*
Flynn, Patrick
  See Flynn, Pat
Flynn, Rachel 1953- *171*
  Earlier sketch in SATA *109*
Flynn, Warren (G.) 1950- *154*
Fodor, R(onald) V(ictor) 1944- *25*
Fogelin, Adrian 1951- *175*
  Earlier sketch in SATA *129*
Foley, (Anna) Bernice Williams 1902-1987 . *28*
Foley, Greg E. 1969- *190*
Foley, June 1944- *44*
Foley, (Mary) Louise Munro 1933- *106*
  Brief entry *40*
  Earlier sketch in SATA *54*
Foley, Rae
  See Denniston, Elinore
Folke, Will
  See Bloch, Robert (Albert)
Follett, Helen Thomas 1884(?)-1970
  Obituary *27*
Folsom, Franklin (Brewster) 1907-1995 .... *5*
  Obituary *88*
Folsom, Michael (Brewster) 1938-1990 .... *40*
  Obituary *88*
Fontenot, Mary Alice 1910-2003 .... *91*
  Obituary *209*
  Earlier sketch in SATA *34*
Fontes, Justine *172*
Fontes, Ron 1952- *183*
Foon, Dennis 1951- *119*
Fooner, Michael *22*
Foote, Timothy (Gilson) 1926- *52*
Forberg, Ati
  See Forberg, Beate Gropius
Forberg, Beate Gropius 1925- *22*
Forbes, Anna 1954- *101*
Forbes, Bryan 1926- *37*
Forbes, Cabot L.
  See Hoyt, Edwin P(almer), Jr.

Forbes, Esther 1891-1967 .... *100*
  Earlier sketch in SATA *2*
  See also CLR *147*
Forbes, Graham B. *1*
Forbes, Kathryn
  See McLean, Kathryn (Anderson)
Forbes, Robert
  See Arthur, Robert, (Jr.)
Ford, Albert Lee
  See Stratemeyer, Edward L.
Ford, Barbara *56*
  Brief entry *34*
Ford, Bernette *212*
Ford, Bernette G.
  See Ford, Bernette
Ford, B.G.
  See Ford, Bernette
Ford, Brian J(ohn) 1939- *49*
Ford, Carolyn (Mott) 1938- *98*
Ford, Christine 1953- *176*
Ford, David
  See Baldacci, David
  and Baldacci, David
Ford, David B.
  See Baldacci, David
Ford, David Baldacci
  See Baldacci, David
Ford, Elbur
  See Hibbert, Eleanor Alice Burford
Ford, Ellen 1949- *89*
Ford, George (Jr.) *31*
Ford, Hilary
  See Youd, Samuel
Ford, Hildegarde
  See Morrison, Velma Ford
Ford, Jerome W. 1949- *78*
Ford, Jerry
  See Ford, Jerome W.
Ford, Juwanda G(ertrude) 1967- *102*
Ford, Marcia
  See Radford, Ruby L(orraine)
Ford, Nancy K(effer) 1906-1961
  Obituary *29*
Ford, Peter 1936- *59*
Ford, S. M.
  See Uhlig, Susan
Forde, Catherine 1961- *170*
Foreman, Mark *199*
Foreman, Michael 1938- *184*
  Earlier sketches in SATA *2, 73, 129, 135*
  See also CLR *32*
  See also SAAS *21*
Foreman, Wilmoth 1939- *153*
Forest, Antonia 1915-2003 .... *29*
  Obituary *149*
Forest, Dial
  See Gault, William Campbell
Forest, Heather 1948- *185*
  Earlier sketch in SATA *120*
Forester, C. S. 1899-1966 .... *13*
Forester, Cecil Scott
  See Forester, C. S.
Forester, Victoria *214*
Forman, Brenda 1936- *4*
Forman, James
  See Forman, James D.
Forman, James D. 1932- *70*
  Earlier sketch in SATA *8*
Forman, James Douglas
  See Forman, James D.
Forman, Mark L.
  See Forman, M.L.
Forman, M.L. 1964- *215*
Forman, Ruth 1970- *186*
Forrest, Elizabeth
  See Salsitz, Rhondi Vilott
Forrest, Mary
  See Pausacker, Jenny
Forrest, Sybil
  See Markun, Patricia Maloney

Forrestal, Elaine 1941- 165
  Earlier sketch in SATA *117*
Forrester, Frank H. 1919(?)-1986
  Obituary 52
Forrester, Helen
  See Bhatia, Jamunadevi
Forrester, Jade
  See Pausacker, Jenny
Forrester, Marian
  See Schachtel, Roger
Forrester, Sandra 1949- 166
  Earlier sketch in SATA *90*
Forrester, Victoria 1940- 40
  Brief entry 35
Forsee, (Frances) Aylesa -1986 .... *1*
Forsey, Chris 1950- 59
Forshay-Lunsford, Cin 1965- 60
Forster, E. M. 1879-1970 57
Forster, Edward Morgan
  See Forster, E. M.
Forsyth, Kate 1966- 154
Fort, Paul
  See Stockton, Francis Richard
Forte, Maurizio 1961- 110
Fortey, Richard 1946- 109
Fortey, Richard A.
  See Fortey, Richard
Fortey, Richard Alan
  See Fortey, Richard
Forth, Melissa D(eal) 96
Fortnum, Peggy
  See Nuttall-Smith, Margaret Emily Noel
Fortune, Eric 182
Forward, Robert L(ull) 1932-2002 82
Foster, Alan Dean 1946- 70
Foster, Brad W. 1955- 34
Foster, Doris Van Liew 1899-1993 10
Foster, E(lizabeth) C(onnell) 1902- 9
Foster, Elizabeth 1902- 12
Foster, Elizabeth 1905-1963 10
Foster, F. Blanche 1919- 11
Foster, G(eorge) Allen 1907-1969 26
Foster, Genevieve (Stump) 1893-1979 2
  Obituary 23
  See also CLR *7*
Foster, Gerald L. 198
Foster, Hal
  See Foster, Harold
Foster, Harold 1892-1982 31
Foster, Jeanne
  See Williams, Jeanne
Foster, John
  See Foster, John L(ouis)
  and Furcolo, Foster
Foster, John (Thomas) 1925- 8
Foster, John L(ouis) 1941- 102
Foster, Juliana 196
Foster, Laura Louise (James) 1918- 6
Foster, Leila Merrell 1929- 73
Foster, Lynne 1937- 74
Foster, Margaret Lesser 1899(?)-1979
  Obituary 21
Foster, Marian Curtis 1909-1978 23
Foster, Mark 1961- 197
Foster, Sally 58
Fotheringham, Edwin 201
Foulds, E. V.
  See Foulds, Elfrida Vipont
Foulds, Elfrida Vipont 1902-1992 52
Fountas, Angela Jane 180
Fourie, Corlia 1944- 91
Fourth Brother, The
  See Aung, (Maung) Htin
Fowke, Edith (Margaret) 1913-1996 14
Fowles, John 1926-2005 22
  Obituary 171
Fowles, John Robert
  See Fowles, John
Fowles, Shelley 1956- 205
Fox, Aileen 1907-2005 58
  Obituary 170

Fox, Aileen Mary
  See Fox, Aileen
Fox, Annie 1950- 175
Fox, Charles Philip 1913-2003 12
  Obituary 150
Fox, Christyan 188
Fox, Diane 188
Fox, Eleanor
  See St. John, Wylly Folk
Fox, Fontaine Talbot, Jr. 1884-1964
  Obituary 23
Fox, Fred 1903(?)-1981
  Obituary 27
Fox, Freeman
  See Hamilton, Charles (Harold St. John)
Fox, Geoffrey 1941- 73
Fox, Grace
  See Anderson, Grace Fox
Fox, Helen 1962- 181
Fox, Larry 30
Fox, Lorraine 1922-1976 27
  Earlier sketch in SATA *11*
Fox, Louisa
  See Kroll, Virginia L.
Fox, Mary Virginia 1919- 152
  Brief entry 39
  Earlier sketches in SATA *44, 88*
Fox, Mem 211
  See Fox, Merrion Frances
Fox, Merrion Frances 1946- 155
  Earlier sketches in SATA *51, 103*
  See also CLR *80*
  See Fox, Mem
Fox, Michael W(ilson) 1937- 15
Fox, Norma Diane
  See Mazer, Norma Fox
Fox, Paula 1923- 167
  Earlier sketches in SATA *17, 60, 120*
  See also CLR *96*
Fox, Robert J. 1927- 33
Fox-Davies, Sarah 1956- 199
Foyt, Victoria .... 187.
Fradin, Dennis
  See Fradin, Dennis Brindell
Fradin, Dennis Brindell 1945- 185
  Earlier sketches in SATA *29, 90, 135*
Fradin, Judith Bloom 1945- 185
  Earlier sketches in SATA *90, 152*
Frailey, Paige (Menefee) 1965- 82
Frame, Janet 1924-2004 119
Frame, Paul 1913-1994 60
  Brief entry 33
  Obituary 83
Frances, Miss
  See Horwich, Frances R(appaport)
Franchere, Ruth 18
Francis, Charles
  See Holme, Bryan
Francis, Dee
  See Haas, Dorothy F.
Francis, Dorothy 1926- 127
  Earlier sketch in SATA *10*
Francis, Dorothy B.
  See Francis, Dorothy
Francis, Dorothy Brenner
  See Francis, Dorothy
Francis, Jaye
  See Pausacker, Jenny
Francis, Pamela (Mary) 1926- 11
Franck, Eddie
  See Cooke, Frank E.
Franco, Betsy 188
  Earlier sketch in SATA *150*
Franco, Eloise (Bauder) 1910- 62
Franco, Johan (Henri Gustave) 1908-1988 ... 62
Franco, Marjorie 38
Francois, Andre 1915-2005 25
Francoise
  See Seignobosc, Francoise

Frank, Anne 1929-1945 87
  Brief entry 42
  See also CLR *101*
Frank, Annelies Marie
  See Frank, Anne
Frank, Daniel B. 1956- 55
Frank, E.R. 1967- 157
Frank, Emily R.
  See Frank, E.R.
Frank, Helene
  See Vautier, Ghislaine
Frank, Hillary 1976- 148
Frank, John 199
Frank, Josette 1893-1989 10
  Obituary 63
Frank, Lucy 1947- 166
  Earlier sketch in SATA *94*
Frank, Mary 1933- 34
Frank, R., Jr.
  See Ross, Frank (Xavier), Jr.
Frankau, Mary Evelyn Atkinson 1899-1974 .. *4*
Frankel, Alona 1937- 66
Frankel, Bernice 9
Frankel, Edward 1910- 44
Frankel, Ellen 1951- 78
Frankel, Julie 1947- 40
  Brief entry 34
Frankenberg, Robert 1911- 22
Frankland, David 207
Franklin, Cheryl J. 1955- 70
Franklin, Harold 1926- 13
Franklin, Kristine L. 1958- 124
  Earlier sketch in SATA *80*
Franklin, Lance
  See Lantz, Francess L(in)
Franklin, Madeleine
  See L'Engle, Madeleine
Franklin, Madeleine L'Engle
  See L'Engle, Madeleine
Franklin, Madeleine L'Engle Camp
  See L'Engle, Madeleine
Franklin, Max
  See Deming, Richard
Franklin, Steve
  See Stevens, Franklin
Franson, Leanne R. 1963- 111
Franson, Scott E. 1966- 192
Franzen, Nils-Olof 1916- 10
Frascino, Edward 48
  Brief entry 33
  See also SAAS *9*
Frasconi, Antonio 1919- 131
  Earlier sketches in SATA *6, 53*
  See also SAAS *11*
Fraser, Betty
  See Fraser, Elizabeth Marr
Fraser, Elizabeth Marr 1928- 31
Fraser, Eric (George) 1902-1983 38
Fraser, Mary Ann 1959- 214
  Earlier sketches in SATA *76, 137*
  See also SAAS *23*
Fraser, Wynnette (McFaddin) 1925- 90
Frasier, Debra 1953- 182
  Earlier sketches in SATA *69, 112*
Fraustino, Lisa Rowe 1961- 146
  Autobiography Feature 146
  Earlier sketch in SATA *84*
Frazee, Marla 1958- 187
  Earlier sketches in SATA *105, 151*
Frazetta, Frank 1928-2010 58
Frazier, Craig 1955- 177
Frazier, Neta (Osborn) Lohnes 1890-1990 7
Frazier, Sundee T. 1968- 198
Frazier, Sundee Tucker
  See Frazier, Sundee T.
Frederic, Mike
  See Cox, William R(obert)
Frederick, Heather Vogel 207
Fredericks, Anthony D. 1947- 113
Freed, Alvyn M. 1913-1993 22
Freedman, Benedict 1919- 27

Freedman, Claire 185
Freedman, Deborah 1960- 191
Freedman, Jeff 1953- 90
Freedman, Nancy 1920- 27
Freedman, Russell 1929- 175
  Earlier sketches in SATA 16, 71, 123
  See also CLR 71
Freedman, Russell Bruce
  See Freedman, Russell
Freeman, Barbara C. 1906-1999 28
Freeman, Barbara Constance
  See Freeman, Barbara C.
Freeman, Bill
  See Freeman, William Bradford
Freeman, Don 1908-1978 17
  See also CLR 90
Freeman, Ira Maximilian 1905-1987 21
Freeman, Kimberley
  See Wilkins, Kim
Freeman, Laura 200
Freeman, Lucy (Greenbaum) 1916-2004 24
Freeman, Mae 1907-1985 25
Freeman, Mae Blacker
  See Freeman, Mae
Freeman, Marcia S. 1937- 102
Freeman, Marcia Sheehan
  See Freeman, Marcia S.
Freeman, Martha 1956- 201
  Earlier sketches in SATA 101, 152
Freeman, Nancy 1932- 61
Freeman, Peter J.
  See Calvert, Patricia
Freeman, Sarah (Caroline) 1940- 66
Freeman, Tor 1977- 164
Freeman, VicToria
  See Freeman, Tor
Freeman, William Bradford 1938- 58
  Brief entry 48
Fregosi, Claudia (Anne Marie) 1946- 24
Freitas, Donna 1972- 205
French, Allen 1870-1946
  See YABC 1
French, Dorothy Kayser 1926- 5
French, Fiona 1944- 132
  Earlier sketches in SATA 6, 75
  See also CLR 37
  See also SAAS 21
French, Jackie 186
  Autobiography Feature 139
  Earlier sketches in SATA 108, 139
  See French, Jackie Anne
  and French, Jacqueline Anne
French, Kathryn
  See Mosesson, Gloria R(ubin)
French, Michael 1944- 176
  Brief entry 49
French, Paul 38
  See Asimov, Isaac
French, Simon 1957- 147
  Earlier sketch in SATA 86
French, Vivian 209
  Earlier sketch in SATA 165
Frenette, Liza 126
Freschet, Gina 1960- 175
  Earlier sketch in SATA 139
Frewer, Glyn (M.) 1931- 11
Frey, Darcy 98
Freymann, Saxton 1958(?)- 178
Freymann-Weyr, (Rhoda) Garret (Michaela)
  1965- 145
Frick, C. H.
  See Irwin, Constance (H.) Frick
Frick, Constance
  See Irwin, Constance (H.) Frick
Fricke, Aaron 1962- 89
Fridell, Ron 1943- 124
Fried, Janice 197
Friedlander, Joanne K(ohn) 1930- 9
Friedman, Aimee 1979- 189
Friedman, D. Dina 1957- 180

Friedman, Debra 1955- 150
Friedman, Estelle (Ehrenwald) 1920- 7
Friedman, Frieda 1905- 43
Friedman, Ina R(osen) 1926- 136
  Brief entry 41
  Earlier sketch in SATA 49
Friedman, Jerrold David
  See Gerrold, David
Friedman, Judi 1935- 59
Friedman, Laurie 1964- 179
  Earlier sketch in SATA 138
Friedman, Marvin 1930- 42
  Brief entry 33
Friedman, Robin 1968- 162
Friedmann, Stan 1953- 80
Friedrich, Otto (Alva) 1929-1995 33
Friedrich, Priscilla 1927- 39
Friend, Catherine 1957(?)- 194
Friend, David Michael 1975- 195
Friend, Natasha 1972- 184
Friendlich, Dick
  See Friendlich, Richard J.
Friendlich, Richard J. 1909- 11
Friermood, Elisabeth Hamilton 1903-1992 5
Friesen, Bernice (Sarah Anne) 1966- 105
Friesen, Gayle 1960- 200
  Earlier sketch in SATA 109
Friesen, Jonathan 1967(?)- 206
Friesner, Esther 1951- 207
  Earlier sketches in SATA 71, 168
Friesner, Esther M.
  See Friesner, Esther
Friis-Baastad, Babbis Ellinor 1921-1970 7
Frimmer, Steven 1928- 31
Frischmuth, Barbara 1941- 114
Friskey, Margaret (Richards) 1901-1995 5
Fritts, Mary Bahr
  See Bahr, Mary (Madelyn)
Fritz, Jean (Guttery) 1915- 163
  Autobiography Feature 122
  Earlier sketches in SATA 1, 29, 72, 119
  See also CLR 96
  See also SAAS 2
Froehlich, Margaret W(alden) 1930- 56
Frois, Jeanne 1953- 73
Froissart, Jean 1338(?)-1410(?) 28
Froman, Elizabeth Hull 1920-1975 10
Froman, Robert (Winslow) 1917- 8
Fromm, Lilo 1928- 29
Frommer, Harvey 1937- 41
Frost, A(rthur) B(urdett) 1851-1928 19
Frost, Elizabeth
  See Frost-Knappman, Elizabeth
Frost, Erica
  See Supraner, Robyn
Frost, Helen 1949- 194
  Autobiography Feature 194
  Earlier sketches in SATA 157, 183
Frost, Helen Marie
  See Frost, Helen
Frost, Lesley 1899-1983 14
  Obituary 34
Frost, Robert 1874-1963 14
  See also CLR 67
Frost, Robert Lee
  See Frost, Robert
Frost, Shelley 1960- 138
Frost-Knappman, Elizabeth 1943- 179
Froud, Brian 1947- 150
Fry, Annette R(iley) 89
Fry, Christopher 1907-2005 66
Fry, Edward Bernard 1925- 35
Fry, Rosalie Kingsmill 1911-1992 3
  See also SAAS 11
Fry, Virginia Lynn 1952- 95
Frye, Sally
  See Moore, Elaine
Fuchs, Bernie 1932- 162
  Earlier sketch in SATA 95
Fuchs, Erich 1916- 6
Fuchshuber, Annegert 1940- 43

Fuerst, Jeffrey B. 1956- 143
Fuertes, Gloria 1918-1998 115
Fuge, Charles 1966- 144
  Earlier sketch in SATA 74
Fujikawa, Gyo 1908-1998 76
  Brief entry 30
  Obituary 110
  Earlier sketch in SATA 39
  See also CLR 25
  See also SAAS 16
Fujita, Tamao 1905-1999 7
Fujiwara, Kim 1957- 81
Fujiwara, Michiko 1946- 15
Fuka, Vladimir 1926-1977
  Obituary 27
Fulcher, Jennifer
  See Westwood, Jennifer
Fuller, Catherine Leuthold 1916- 9
Fuller, Edmund (Maybank) 1914- 21
Fuller, Iola
  See McCoy, Iola Fuller
Fuller, John G(rant, Jr.) 1913-1990 65
Fuller, Kathleen
  See Gottfried, Theodore Mark
Fuller, Lois Hamilton 1915- 11
Fuller, Margaret 1810-1850 25
Fuller, Maud
  See Petersham, Maud
Fuller, Roy (Broadbent) 1912-1991 87
Fuller, Sarah Margaret
  See Fuller, Margaret
Fults, John Lee 1932- 33
Funk, Thompson 1911- 7
  See Funk, Tom
Funk, Tom
  See Funk, Thompson
Funke, Cornelia 1958- 209
  Earlier sketches in SATA 154, 174
  See also CLR 145
Funke, Cornelia Caroline
  See Funke, Cornelia
Funke, Lewis 1912-1992 11
Fuqua, Jonathon Scott 1966- 141
Furbee, Mary R.
  See Furbee, Mary Rodd
Furbee, Mary Rodd 1954- 138
Furchgott, Terry 1948- 29
Furlong, Monica (Mavis) 1930-2003 86
  Obituary 142
Furlonger, Patricia
  See Wrightson, Patricia
Furman, Gertrude Lerner Kerman 1909- 21
Furniss, Tim 1948- 49
Furrow, Robert 1985- 172
Furukawa, Toshi 1924- 24
Fusillo, Archimede 1962- 137
Futcher, Jane P. 1947- 76
Futehali, Zahida
  See Whitaker, Zai
Fyleman, Rose (Amy) 1877-1957 21
Fyson, Jenny Grace
  See Fyson, J.G.
Fyson, J.G. 1904-1998 42

G

Gaan, Margaret 1914- 65
Gaber, Susan 1956- 169
  Earlier sketch in SATA 115
Gaberman, Judie Angell
  See Angell, Judie
Gabhart, Ann
  See Gabhart, Ann H.
Gabhart, Ann H. 1947- 75
Gable, Brian 1949- 195
Gabler, Mirko 1951- 77
Gabriel, Adriana
  See Rojany, Lisa

Gabrys, Ingrid Schubert
    See Schubert-Gabrys, Ingrid
Gackenbach, Dick 1927- 79
    Brief entry 30
    Earlier sketch in SATA 48
Gadd, Jeremy 1949- 116
Gaddis, Vincent H. 1913-1997 35
Gadler, Steve J. 1905-1985 36
Gaeddert, Lou Ann (Bigge) 1931- 103
    Earlier sketch in SATA 20
Gaeddert, Louann
    See Gaeddert, Lou Ann (Bigge)
Gaer, Joseph 1897-1969 118
Gaer, Yossef
    See Gaer, Joseph
Gaetz, Dayle Campbell 1947- 138
Gaffney, Timothy R. 1951- 170
    Earlier sketch in SATA 69
Gaffron, Norma (Bondeson) 1931- 97
Gag, Flavia 1907-1979
    Obituary 24
Gag, Wanda (Hazel) 1893-1946 100
    See also YABC 1
    See also CLR 150
Gage, Brian 162
Gage, Wilson
    See Steele, Mary Q(uintard Govan)
Gagliano, Eugene M. 1946- 150
Gagliardo, Ruth Garver 1895(?)-1980
    Obituary 22
Gagnon, Cecile 1936- 58
Gaillard, Jason 1965- 200
Gaiman, Neil 1960- 197
    Earlier sketches in SATA 85, 146
    See also CLR 109
Gaiman, Neil Richard
    See Gaiman, Neil
Gainer, Cindy 1962- 74
Gaines, Ernest J. 1933- 86
    See also CLR 62
Gaines, Ernest James
    See Gaines, Ernest J.
Gaither, Gloria 1942- 127
Gal, Laszlo 1933- 96
    Brief entry 32
    Earlier sketch in SATA 52
    See also CLR 61
Galbraith, Ben 1980- 200
Galbraith, Kathryn O(sebold) 1945- 85
Galdone, Paul 1907(?)-1986 66
    Obituary 49
    Earlier sketch in SATA 17
    See also CLR 16
Galindo, Claudia 1979- 203
Galinsky, Ellen 1942- 23
Gall, Chris 1961- 176
Gallagher, Diana G. 1946- 153
Gallagher, Lurlene Nora
    See McDaniel, Lurlene
Gallagher-Cole, Mernie 1958- 206
Gallant, Roy A(rthur) 1924- 110
    Earlier sketches in SATA 4, 68
    See also CLR 30
Gallardo, Evelyn 1948- 78
Gallaz, Christophe 1948- 162
    See also CLR 126
Gallego Garcia, Laura 1977- 173
Gallico, Paul (William) 1897-1976 13
Gallo, Donald R. 1938- 112
    Autobiography Feature 104
Gallo, Donald Robert
    See Gallo, Donald R.
Galloway, Owateka (S.) 1981- 121
Galloway, Priscilla 1930- 112
    Earlier sketch in SATA 66
Gallup, Joan 1957- 128
Galouchko, Annouchka Gravel 1960- 95
Galt, Thomas Franklin, Jr. 1908-1989 5
Galt, Tom
    See Galt, Thomas Franklin, Jr.
Galvin, Matthew R. 1950- 93

Galvin, Matthew Reppert
    See Galvin, Matthew R.
Gamble, Kim 1952- 183
    Earlier sketches in SATA 81, 124
Gambrell, Jamey 82
Gamerman, Martha 1941- 15
Gammell, Stephen 1943- 128
    Earlier sketches in SATA 53, 81
    See also CLR 83
Ganly, Helen (Mary) 1940- 56
Gannett, Ruth Chrisman (Arens)
    1896-1979 33
Gannett, Ruth Stiles 1923- 3
Gannij, Joan 208
Gannij, Joan Levine
    See Gannij, Joan
Gannon, Ned 1974- 205
Gannon, Robert Haines 1931- 8
Gano, Lila 1949- 76
Gans, Roma 1894-1996 45
    Obituary 93
Gant, Matthew
    See Hano, Arnold
Gantner, Susan (Verble) 1939- 63
Gantos, Jack 1951- 169
    Earlier sketches in SATA 20, 81, 119
    See also CLR 85
Gantos, John Bryan, Jr.
    See Gantos, Jack
Ganz, Yaffa 1938- 61
    Brief entry 52
Garafano, Marie 1942- 84
Garant, Andre J. 1968- 123
Garbe, Ruth Moore
    See Moore, Ruth (Ellen)
Garber, Esther
    See Lee, Tanith
Garcia, Cristina 1958- 208
Garcia, Emma 1969- 198
Garcia, Yolanda P. 1952- 113
Garcia, Yolanda Pacheco
    See Garcia, Yolanda P.
Gard, Janice
    See Latham, Jean Lee
Gard, Joyce
    See Reeves, Joyce
Gard, Robert Edward 1910-1992 18
    Obituary 74
Gard, (Sanford) Wayne 1899-1986
    Obituary 49
Gardam, Jane 1928- 130
    Brief entry 28
    Earlier sketches in SATA 39, 76
    See also CLR 12
    See also SAAS 9
Gardam, Jane Mary
    See Gardam, Jane
Gardella, Tricia 1944- 96
Garden, Nancy 1938- 147
    Autobiography Feature 147
    Earlier sketches in SATA 12, 77, 114
    See also CLR 51
    See also SAAS 8
Gardiner, John Reynolds 1944-2006 64
    Obituary 174
Gardiner, Lindsey 1971- 144
Gardner, Craig Shaw 1949- 99
Gardner, Dic
    See Gardner, Richard (M.)
Gardner, Graham 159
Gardner, Hugh 1910-1986
    Obituary 49
Gardner, Jane Mylum 1946- 83
Gardner, Jeanne LeMonnier 1925- 5
Gardner, John, Jr. 1933-1982 40
    Obituary 31
Gardner, John Champlin, Jr.
    See Gardner, John, Jr.
Gardner, John E(dward) 1917- 192
Gardner, Lyn 192

Gardner, Martin 1914-2010 142
    Earlier sketch in SATA 16
Gardner, Miriam
    See Bradley, Marion Zimmer
Gardner, Richard (M.) 1931- 24
Gardner, Richard A(lan) 1931-2003 13
    Obituary 144
Gardner, Sally 177
Gardner, Sandra 1940- 70
Gardner, Scot 1968- 143
Gardner, Sheldon 1934- 33
Gardner, Ted
    See Gardner, Theodore Roosevelt II
Gardner, Theodore Roosevelt
    See Gardner, Theodore Roosevelt II
Gardner, Theodore Roosevelt II 1934- 84
Garelick, May 1910-1989 19
Garfield, James B. 1881-1984 6
    Obituary 38
Garfield, Leon 1921-1996 76
    Obituary 90
    Earlier sketches in SATA 1, 32
    See also CLR 21
Garfinkle, Debra L.
    See Garfinkle, D.L.
Garfinkle, D.L. 187
Garis, Howard R. 1873-1962 13
Garis, Howard Roger
    See Garis, Howard R.
Garland, Mark 1953- 79
Garland, Mark A.
    See Garland, Mark
Garland, Michael 1952- 208
    Earlier sketch in SATA 168
Garland, Sarah 1944- 135
    Earlier sketch in SATA 62
Garland, Sherry 1948- 145
    Autobiography Feature 145
    Earlier sketches in SATA 73, 114
Garner, Alan 1934- 69
    Autobiography Feature 108
    Earlier sketch in SATA 18
    See also CLR 130
Garner, David 1958- 78
Garner, Eleanor Ramrath 1930- 122
Garner, James Finn 1960(?)- 92
Garnet, A. H.
    See Slote, Alfred
Garnett, Eve C. R. 1900-1991 3
    Obituary 70
Garofoli, Viviana 1970- 186
Garou, Louis P.
    See Bowkett, Stephen
Garraty, John A. 1920-2007 23
    Obituary 189
Garraty, John Arthur
    See Garraty, John A.
Garren, Devorah-Leah
    See Devorah-Leah
Garret, Maxwell R. 1917- 39
Garretson, Victoria Diane 1945- 44
Garrett, Helen 1895- 21
Garrett, Randall 1927-1987 180
Garrett, Richard 1920- 82
Garrigue, Sheila 1931- 21
Garrison, Barbara 1931- 163
    Earlier sketch in SATA 19
Garrison, Frederick
    See Sinclair, Upton
Garrison, Mary 1952- 146
Garrison, Peter
    See Gardner, Craig Shaw
Garrison, Webb B(lack) 1919-2000 25
Garrity, Jennifer Johnson 1961- 124
Garrity, Linda K. 1947- 128
Garsee, Jeannine 199
Garst, Doris Shannon 1894-1981 1
Garst, Shannon
    See Garst, Doris Shannon

Garth, Will
  See Hamilton, Edmond
  and Kuttner, Henry
Garthwaite, Marion H(ook) 1893-1981 7
Garton, Malinda D(ean) (?)-1976
  Obituary 26
Garvie, Maureen 1944- 175
Garvie, Maureen McCallum
  See Garvie, Maureen
Garza, Carmen Lomas 1948- 182
Garza, Xavier 184
Gascoigne, Bamber 1935- 62
Gaskins, Pearl Fuyo 1957- 134
Gasperini, Jim 1952- 54
  Brief entry 49
Gater, Dilys 1944- 41
Gates, Doris 1901-1987 34
  Obituary 54
  Earlier sketch in SATA *1*
  See also SAAS *1*
Gates, Frieda 1933- 26
Gates, Susan 1950- 153
Gates, Viola R. 1931- 101
Gathorne-Hardy, Jonathan G. 1933- 124
  Earlier sketch in SATA *26*
Gatti, Anne 1952- 103
Gatty, Juliana Horatia
  See Ewing, Juliana (Horatia Gatty)
Gauch, Patricia Lee 1934- 80
  Earlier sketch in SATA *26*
  See also CLR *56*
  See also SAAS *21*
Gaudasinska, Elzbieta 1943- 190
Gaul, Randy 1959- 63
Gault, Clare 1925- 36
Gault, Frank 1926-1982 36
  Brief entry 30
Gault, William Campbell 1910-1995 8
Gauthier, Gail 1953- 203
  Earlier sketches in SATA *118, 160*
Gaver, Becky
  See Gaver, Rebecca
Gaver, Rebecca 1952- 20
Gavin, Jamila 1941- 125
  Earlier sketch in SATA *96*
Gay, Amelia
  See Hogarth, Grace (Weston Allen)
Gay, Francis
  See Gee, H(erbert) L(eslie)
Gay, Kathlyn 1930- 144
  Earlier sketch in SATA *9*
Gay, Marie-Louise 1952- 179
  Earlier sketches in SATA *68, 126*
  See also CLR *27*
  See also SAAS *21*
Gay, Michel 1947- 162
Gay, Zhenya 1906-1978 19
Gaze, Gillian
  See Barklem, Jill
Gear, Kathleen M. O'Neal
  See Gear, Kathleen O'Neal
Gear, Kathleen O'Neal 1954- 166
  Earlier sketch in SATA *71*
Gear, W. Michael 1955- 166
  Earlier sketch in SATA *71*
Geary, Rick 1946- 142
Geason, Susan 1946- 122
Gedalof, Robin
  See McGrath, Robin
Gedge, Pauline (Alice) 1945- 101
Gee, H(erbert) L(eslie) 1901-1977
  Obituary 26
Gee, Maurice 1931- 101
  Earlier sketch in SATA *46*
  See also CLR *56*
Gee, Maurice Gough
  See Gee, Maurice
Geehan, Wayne (E.) 1947- 107
Geer, Charles 1922- 42
  Brief entry 32

Geeslin, Campbell 1925- 163
  Earlier sketch in SATA *107*
Gehman, Mary W. 1923- 86
Gehr, Mary 1910(?)-1997 32
  Obituary 99
Geipel, Eileen 1932- 30
Geis, Alissa Imre 1976- 189
Geis, Darlene Stern 1918(?)-1999 7
  Obituary 111
Geisel, Helen 1898-1967 26
Geisel, Theodor Seuss
  See Dr. Seuss
Geisert, Arthur 1941- 171
  Brief entry 52
  Earlier sketches in SATA *56, 92, 133*
  See also CLR *87*
  See also SAAS *23*
Geisert, Arthur Frederick
  See Geisert, Arthur
Geisert, Bonnie 1942- 165
  Earlier sketch in SATA *92*
Geist, Ken 191
Gelber, Lisa 210
Geldart, William 1936- 15
Gelinas, Paul J. 1904-1996 10
Gellis, Roberta 1927- 128
Gellis, Roberta Leah Jacobs
  See Gellis, Roberta
Gellman, Marc 112
Gelman, Amy 1961- 72
Gelman, Jan 1963- 58
Gelman, Rita Golden 1937- 131
  Brief entry 51
  Earlier sketch in SATA *84*
Gelman, Steve 1934- 3
Gemming, Elizabeth 1932- 11
Gendel, Evelyn W. 1916(?)-1977
  Obituary 27
Gennaro, Joseph F(rancis), Jr. 1924- 53
Gentieu, Penny 204
Gentile, Petrina 1969- 91
Gentle, Mary 1956- 48
Gentleman, David (William) 1930- 7
Gentry, Marita 215
Geoghegan, Adrienne 1962- 143
George, Barbara
  See Katz, Bobbi
George, Emily
  See Katz, Bobbi
George, Gail
  See Katz, Bobbi
George, Jean
  See George, Jean Craighead
George, Jean C.
  See George, Jean Craighead
George, Jean Craighead 1919- 170
  Earlier sketches in SATA *2, 68, 124*
  See also CLR *136*
George, Jessica Day 1976- 210
George, John L(othar) 1916- 2
George, Kristine O'Connell 1954- 156
  Earlier sketch in SATA *110*
George, Lindsay Barrett 1952- 206
  Earlier sketches in SATA *95, 155*
George, S(idney) C(harles) 1898- 11
George, Sally
  See Orr, Wendy
George, Twig C. 1950- 114
George, W(illiam) Lloyd 1900(?)-1975
  Obituary 30
Georgiou, Constantine 1927- 7
Georgiou, Theo
  See Odgers, Sally Farrell
Geraghty, Paul 1959- 130
Gerard, Jean Ignace Isidore 1803-1847 45
Geras, Adele 1944- 180
  Autobiography Feature 180
  Earlier sketches in SATA *23, 87, 129, 173*
  See also SAAS *21*
Geras, Adele Daphne Weston
  See Geras, Adele

Gerber, Carole 1947- 207
Gerber, Linda 213
Gerber, Merrill Joan 1938- 170
  Autobiography Feature 170
  Earlier sketches in SATA *64, 127*
Gerber, Perren 1933- 104
Gerberg, Mort 1931- 64
Gergely, Tibor 1900-1978 54
  Obituary 20
Geringer, Laura 1948- 164
  Earlier sketches in SATA *29, 94*
Gerler, William R(obert) 1917-1996 47
Gerrard, Jean 1933- 51
Gerrard, Roy 1935-1997 90
  Brief entry 45
  Obituary 99
  Earlier sketch in SATA *47*
  See also CLR *23*
Gerritsen, Paula 1956- 177
Gerrold, David 1944- 144
  Earlier sketch in SATA *66*
Gershator, David 1937- 180
Gershator, Phillis 1942- 188
  Earlier sketches in SATA *90, 158*
Gershon, Dann 1955- 187
Gershon, Gina 1962- 187
Gerson, Corinne 1927- 37
Gerson, Mary-Joan 136
  Earlier sketch in SATA *79*
Gerson, Noel Bertram 1914-1988 22
  Obituary 60
Gerstein, Mordicai 1935- 178
  Brief entry 36
  Earlier sketches in SATA *47, 81, 142*
  See also CLR *102*
Gertridge, Allison 1967- 132
Gervais, Bernadette 1959- 80
Gervay, Susanne 183
Gesner, Clark 1938-2002 40
  Obituary 143
Gessner, Lynne 1919- 16
Geter, Tyrone 150
Getz, David 1957- 91
Getzinger, Donna 1968- 128
Geus, Mireille 1964- 207
Gevirtz, Eliezer 1950- 49
Gevry, Claudine 188
Gewe, Raddory
  See Gorey, Edward (St. John)
Ghan, Linda (R.) 1947- 77
Ghent, Natale 1962- 148
Gherman, Beverly 1934- 123
  Earlier sketch in SATA *68*
Ghigna, Charles 1946- 153
  Earlier sketch in SATA *108*
Giacobbe, Beppe 1953- 174
Giambastiani, Kurt R. A. 1958- 141
Giannini, Enzo 1946- 68
Gibala-Broxholm, Scott 1959(?)- 205
Gibbons, Alan 1953- 198
  Earlier sketch in SATA *124*
Gibbons, Faye 1938- 103
  Earlier sketch in SATA *65*
Gibbons, Gail 1944- 201
  Earlier sketches in SATA *23, 72, 104, 160*
  See also CLR *8*
  See also SAAS *12*
Gibbons, Gail Gretchen
  See Gibbons, Gail
Gibbons, Kaye 1960- 117
Gibbs, Adrea 1960- 126
Gibbs, Alonzo (Lawrence) 1915-1992 5
Gibbs, (Cecilia) May 1877-1969
  Obituary 27
Gibbs, Tony
  See Gibbs, Wolcott, Jr.
Gibbs, Wolcott, Jr. 1935- 40
Giblin, James Cross 1933- 197
  Earlier sketches in SATA *33, 75, 122*
  See also CLR *29*
  See also SAAS *12*

Gibson, Andrew (William) 1949- 72
Gibson, Barbara L. 205
Gibson, Barbara Leonard
    See Gibson, Barbara L.
Gibson, Betty 1911- 75
Gibson, Jo
    See Fluke, Joanne
Gibson, Josephine
    See Hine, Sesyle Joslin
    and Hine, Al(fred Blakelee)
Gibson, Sarah P. 1962- 211
Gibson, William 1914-2008 66
    Obituary 199
Gibson, William Ford
    See Gibson, William
Gidal, Nachum
    See Gidal, Tim Nachum
Gidal, Sonia (Epstein) 1922- 2
Gidal, Tim Nachum 1909-1996 2
Gidalewitsch, Nachum
    See Gidal, Tim Nachum
Gideon, Melanie 1963- 175
Giegling, John A(llan) 1935- 17
Gifaldi, David 1950- 209
    Earlier sketch in SATA 76
Giff, Patricia Reilly 1935- 203
    Earlier sketches in SATA 33, 70, 121, 160
Giffard, Hannah 1962- 83
Gifford, Clive 1966- 198
Gifford, Griselda 1931- 171
    Earlier sketch in SATA 42
Gifford, Kerri 1961- 91
Gifford, Peggy 1952- 191
Gilbert, Ann
    See Taylor, Ann
Gilbert, Anne Yvonne 1951- 185
Gilbert, Barbara Snow 1954- 97
Gilbert, Catherine
    See Murdock, Catherine Gilbert
Gilbert, Frances
    See Collings, Gillian
Gilbert, Harriett 1948- 30
Gilbert, (Agnes) Joan (Sewell) 1931- 10
Gilbert, John (Raphael) 1926- 36
Gilbert, Nan
    See Gilbertson, Mildred Geiger
Gilbert, Roby Goodale 1966- 90
Gilbert, Ruth Gallard Ainsworth
    See Ainsworth, Ruth (Gallard)
Gilbert, Sara (Dulaney) 1943- 82
    Earlier sketch in SATA 11
Gilbert, Sheri L. 157
Gilbert, Suzie 1956- 97
Gilbert, W(illiam) S(chwenck) 1836-1911 ... 36
Gilbert, Yvonne
    See Gilbert, Anne Yvonne
Gilbertson, Mildred Geiger 1908-1988 2
Gilbreath, Alice 1921- 12
Gilbreth, Frank B., Jr. 1911-2001 2
Gilbreth, Frank Bunker
    See Gilbreth, Frank B., Jr.
Gilchrist, Jan Spivey 1949- 130
    Earlier sketch in SATA 72
Gilden, Mel 1947- 97
Giles, Gail 196
    Earlier sketch in SATA 152
Gilfond, Henry 2
Gilge, Jeanette 1924- 22
Gili, Phillida 1944- 70
Gill, Derek (Lewis Theodore) 1919-1997 9
Gill, Margery Jean 1925- 22
Gill, Shelley 176
Gill, Stephen 1932- 63
Gillespie, Carol Ann 1951- 158
Gillett, Mary (Bledsoe) 7
Gillette, Henry Sampson 1915- 14
Gillette, J. Lynett 1946- 103
Gillette, Jan Lynett
    See Gillette, J. Lynett
Gilley, Jeremy 1969- 174

Gillham, Bill
    See Gillham, W(illiam) E(dwin) C(harles)
Gillham, W(illiam) E(dwin) C(harles)
    1936- 42
Gilliam, Stan 1946- 39
    Brief entry 35
Gilliland, Alexis A(rnaldus) 1931- 72
Gilliland, (Cleburne) Hap 1918- 92
Gilliland, Judith Heide 180
Gillmor, Don 1954- 127
Gilman, Dorothy 1923- 5
Gilman, Esther 1925- 15
Gilman, Laura Anne 178
Gilman, Phoebe 1940-2002 104
    Obituary 141
    Earlier sketch in SATA 58
Gilmore, Iris 1900-1982 22
Gilmore, Kate 1931- 87
Gilmore, Mary (Jean Cameron) 1865-1962 . 49
Gilmore, Rachna 1953- 209
Gilmore, Susan 1954- 59
Gilpin, Stephen 213
    Earlier sketch in SATA 177
Gilroy, Beryl (Agatha) 1924- 80
Gilson, Barbara
    See Gilson, Charles James Louis
Gilson, Charles James Louis 1878-1943
    See YABC 2
Gilson, Jamie 1933- 176
    Brief entry 34
    Earlier sketches in SATA 37, 91
Gimpel, Carolyn
    See Hart, Carolyn
Ginsburg, Mirra 1909-2000 92
    Earlier sketch in SATA 6
    See also CLR 45
Giovanni, Nikki 1943- 208
    Earlier sketches in SATA 24, 107
    See also CLR 73
Giovanni, Yolanda Cornelia
    See Giovanni, Nikki
Giovanni, Yolande Cornelia
    See Giovanni, Nikki
Giovanni, Yolande Cornelia, Jr.
    See Giovanni, Nikki
Giovanopoulos, Paul (Arthur) 1939- 7
Gipson, Billie
    See Letts, Billie
Gipson, Fred(erick Benjamin) 1908-1973 2
    Obituary 24
Girard, Linda (Walvoord) 1942- 41
Giraudon, David 1975- 215
Girion, Barbara 1937- 78
    Earlier sketch in SATA 26
    See also SAAS 14
Girl, Nerdy
    See Castellucci, Cecil
Girouard, Patrick 1957- 155
Girzone, Joseph F. 1930- 76
Girzone, Joseph Francis
    See Girzone, Joseph F.
Gise, Joanne
    See Mattern, Joanne
Gist, E.M. 206
Gittings, Jo (Grenville) Manton 1919- 3
Gittings, Robert (William Victor) 1911-1992 . 6
    Obituary 70
Givens, Janet E(aton) 1932- 60
Givner, Joan 1936- 171
Givner, Joan Mary
    See Givner, Joan
Gladstone, Eve
    See Werner, Herma
Gladstone, Gary 1935- 12
Gladstone, M(yron) J. 1923- 37
Glanville, Brian (Lester) 1931- 42
Glanzman, Louis S. 1922- 36
Glaser, Byron 1954- 154
Glaser, Dianne E(lizabeth) 1937- 50
    Brief entry 31
Glaser, Isabel Joslin 1929- 94

Glaser, Milton 1929- 151
    Earlier sketch in SATA 11
Glaser, Shirley 151
Glaspell, Susan 1882(?)-1948
    See YABC 2
Glass, Andrew 1949- 150
    Brief entry 46
    Earlier sketch in SATA 90
Glass, Linzi 175
Glass, Linzi Alex
    See Glass, Linzi
Glasscock, Amnesia
    See Steinbeck, John
Glassman, Bruce 1961- 76
Glauber, Uta (Heil) 1936- 17
Glazer, Thomas (Zachariah) 1914-2003 9
Glazer, Tom
    See Glazer, Thomas (Zachariah)
Gleasner, Diana (Cottle) 1936- 29
Gleason, Judith 1929- 24
Gleason, Katherine (A.) 1960- 104
Gleeson, Libby 1950- 142
    Autobiography Feature 142
    Earlier sketches in SATA 82, 118
Gleiter, Jan 1947- 111
Gleitzman, Morris 1953- 156
    Earlier sketch in SATA 88
    See also CLR 88
Glen, Maggie 1944- 88
Glendinning, Richard 1917-1988 24
Glendinning, Sally
    See Glendinning, Sara W(ilson)
Glendinning, Sara W(ilson) 1913-1993 24
Glenn, John W. 195
Glenn, Mel 1943- 93
    Brief entry 45
    Earlier sketch in SATA 51
    See also CLR 51
Glenn, Patricia Brown 1953- 86
Glenn, Sharlee 159
Glenn, Sharlee Mullins
    See Glenn, Sharlee
Glennon, Karen M. 1946- 85
Gles, Margaret Breitmaier 1940- 22
Glick, Carl (Cannon) 1890-1971 14
Glick, Ruth (Burtnick) 1942- 125
Glick, Virginia Kirkus 1893-1980
    Obituary 23
Gliewe, Unada (Grace) 1927- 3
Glimmerveen, Ulco 1958- 85
Glines, Carroll V(ane), Jr. 1920- 19
Gliori, Debi 1959- 189
    Earlier sketches in SATA 72, 138
Globe, Leah Ain 1900- 41
Glori Ann
    See Blakely, Gloria
Glovach, Linda 1947- 105
    Earlier sketch in SATA 7
Glover, Denis (James Matthews) 1912-1980 . 7
Glubok, Shirley (Astor) 146
    Autobiography Feature 146
    Earlier sketches in SATA 6, 68
    See also CLR 1
    See also SAAS 7
Gluck, Felix 1923-1981
    Obituary 25
Glyman, Caroline A. 1967- 103
Glynne-Jones, William 1907-1977 11
Gobbato, Imero 1923- 39
Gobbletree, Richard
    See Quackenbush, Robert M(ead)
Goble, Dorothy 26
Goble, Paul 1933- 131
    Earlier sketches in SATA 25, 69
    See also CLR 21
Goble, Warwick (?)-1943 46
Godden, (Margaret) Rumer 1907-1998 36
    Obituary 109
    Earlier sketch in SATA 3
    See also CLR 20
    See also SAAS 12

Gode, Alexander
  See Gode von Aesch, Alexander (Gottfried Friedrich)
Gode von Aesch, Alexander (Gottfried Friedrich) 1906-1970 14
Godfrey, Jane
  See Bowden, Joan Chase
Godfrey, Martyn
  See Godfrey, Martyn N.
  and Godfrey, Martyn N.
Godfrey, Martyn N. 1949-2000 95
  See also CLR 57
Godfrey, William
  See Youd, Samuel
Godkin, Celia (Marilyn) 1948- 145
  Earlier sketch in SATA 66
Godon, Ingrid 1958- 186
Godwin, Laura 1956- 179
Godwin, Sam
  See Pirotta, Saviour
Godwin, Sarah Massini
  See Massini, Sarah
Goede, Irene 1966- 208
Goedecke, Christopher (John) 1951- 81
Goekler, Susan
  See Wooley, Susan Frelick
Goembel, Ponder 204
Goertzen, Glenda 172
Goettel, Elinor 1930- 12
Goetz, Delia 1898-1996 22
  Obituary 91
Goffe, Toni 1936- 61
Goffstein, Brooke
  See Goffstein, M(arilyn) B(rooke)
Goffstein, M(arilyn) B(rooke) 1940- 70
  Earlier sketch in SATA 8
  See also CLR 3
Goforth, Ellen
  See Francis, Dorothy
Gogol, Sara 1948-2004 80
Goh, Chan Hon 1969- 145
Going, Kelly L.
  See Going, K.L.
Going, Kelly Louise
  See Going, K.L.
Going, K.L. 199
  Earlier sketch in SATA 156
Golann, Cecil Paige 1921-1995 11
Golbin, Andree 1923- 15
Gold, Alison Leslie 1945- 104
Gold, August 1955- 215
Gold, Bernice 150
Gold, Phyllis
  See Goldberg, Phyllis
Gold, Robert S(tanley) 1924- 63
Gold, Sharlya 9
Gold, Susan
  See Gold, Susan Dudley
Gold, Susan Dudley 1949- 147
Goldberg, Grace 1956- 78
Goldberg, Herbert S. 1926- 25
Goldberg, Jacob 1943- 94
Goldberg, Jake
  See Goldberg, Jacob
Goldberg, Myla 1972(?)- 210
Goldberg, Phyllis 1941- 21
Goldberg, Stan J. 1939- 26
Goldberg, Susan 1948- 71
Goldberg, Whoopi 1955- 119
Goldberger, Judith M. 1948- 80
Goldblatt, Stacey 1969(?)- 191
Golden, Christie 1963- 167
  Earlier sketch in SATA 116
Goldentyer, Debra 1960- 84
Goldfeder, Cheryl
  See Pahz, Cheryl Suzanne
Goldfeder, James
  See Pahz, James Alon
Goldfeder, Jim
  See Pahz, James Alon
Goldfinger, Jennifer P. 1963- 185

Goldfrank, Helen Colodny 1912- 6
Goldin, Augusta 1906-1999 13
Goldin, Barbara Diamond 1946- 129
  Autobiography Feature 129
  Earlier sketch in SATA 92
  See also SAAS 26
Goldin, David 1963- 101
Golding, Julia 1969- 188
Golding, Theresa Martin 1960- 150
Golding, William 1911-1993
  See CLR 130
Golding, William Gerald
  See Golding, William
Goldman, Alex J. 1917- 65
Goldman, E. M. 1943- 103
Goldman, Eleanor Maureen
  See Goldman, E. M.
Goldman, Elizabeth 1949- 90
Goldman, Judy 1955- 212
Goldman, Steven 1964- 207
Goldring, Ann 1937- 149
Goldsborough, June 1923- 19
Goldschmidt, Judy 202
Goldsmith, Connie 1945- 147
Goldsmith, Howard 1943- 108
  Earlier sketch in SATA 24
Goldsmith, John Herman Thorburn 1903-1987
  Obituary 52
Goldsmith, Oliver 1730(?)-1774 26
Goldsmith, Ruth M. 1919- 62
Goldstein, Nathan 1927- 47
Goldstein, Philip 1910-1997 23
Goldston, Robert (Conroy) 1927- 6
Goldstone, Bruce 183
Goldstone, Lawrence A.
  See Treat, Lawrence
Goldszmit, Henryk 1878-1942 65
  See also CLR 152
Golembe, Carla 1951- 79
Golenbock, Peter 1946- 99
Goll, Reinhold W(eimar) 1897-1993 26
Gollub, Matthew 1960- 134
  Earlier sketch in SATA 83
Golson, Terry 213
Golson, Terry Blonder
  See Golson, Terry
Gomes, Filomena 1965- 183
Gomez, Elena 191
Gomez, Elizabeth 133
Gomez-Freer, Elizabeth
  See Gomez, Elizabeth
Gomi, Taro 1945- 103
  Earlier sketch in SATA 64
  See also CLR 57
Gondosch, Linda 1944- 58
Gonsalves, Rob 1959- 209
Gonyea, Mark 194
Gonzalez, Catherine Troxell 1917-2000 87
Gonzalez, Christina
  See Gonzalez, Maya Christina
Gonzalez, Gloria 1940- 23
Gonzalez, Julie 1958- 174
Gonzalez, Julie Sehers
  See Gonzalez, Julie
Gonzalez, Lucia M. 1957- 202
Gonzalez, Maya
  See Gonzalez, Maya Christina
Gonzalez, Maya Christina 1964- 175
  Earlier sketch in SATA 115
Gonzalez, Rigoberto 1970- 147
Goobie, Beth 1959- 128
Good, Alice 1950- 73
Good, Clare
  See Romano, Clare
Good, Karen Hillard 214
Goodall, Daphne Machin
  See Machin Goodall, Daphne (Edith)
Goodall, Jane 1934- 111

Goodall, John S(trickland) 1908-1996 66
  Obituary 91
  Earlier sketch in SATA 4
  See also CLR 25
Goodbody, Slim
  See Burstein, John
Goode, Diane 1949- 170
  Earlier sketches in SATA 15, 84, 114
Goode, Diane Capuozzo
  See Goode, Diane
Goode, Stephen Ray 1943- 55
  Brief entry 40
Goodenow, Earle 1913- 40
Goodhart, Pippa 1958- 196
  Earlier sketch in SATA 153
Goodhue, Thomas W. 1949- 143
Goodin, Sallie (Brown) 1953- 74
Goodman, Alison 1966- 111
Goodman, Deborah Lerme 1956- 50
  Brief entry 49
Goodman, Elaine 1930- 9
Goodman, Joan Elizabeth 1950- 162
  Earlier sketches in SATA 50, 94
Goodman, Susan E. 1952- 181
Goodman, Walter 1927-2002 9
Goodman Koz, Paula 211
Goodrich, Samuel Griswold 1793-1860 23
Goodsell, Jane Neuberger 1921(?)-1988
  Obituary 56
Goodweather, Hartley
  See King, Thomas
GoodWeather, Hartley
  See King, Thomas
Goodwin, Hal
  See Goodwin, Harold L(eland)
Goodwin, Harold L(eland) 1914-1990 51
  Obituary 65
  Earlier sketch in SATA 13
Goodwin, William 1943- 117
Goor, Nancy (Ruth Miller) 1944- 39
  Brief entry 34
Goor, Ron(ald Stephen) 1940- 39
  Brief entry 34
Goossen, Agnes
  See Epp, Margaret A(gnes)
Goossens, Philippe 1963- 195
Gootman, Marilyn E. 1944- 179
Gopnik, Adam 1956- 171
Gorbachev, Valeri 1944- 184
  Autobiography Feature 143
  Earlier sketches in SATA 98, 143
Gordion, Mark
  See Turtledove, Harry
Gordon, Ad
  See Hano, Arnold
Gordon, Amy 1949- 197
  Earlier sketches in SATA 115, 156
Gordon, Bernard Ludwig 1931-2010 27
Gordon, Colonel H. R.
  See Ellis, Edward S.
Gordon, David
  See Garrett, Randall
Gordon, Donald
  See Payne, Donald Gordon
Gordon, Dorothy 1893-1970 20
Gordon, Esther S(aranga) 1935- 10
Gordon, Frederick 1
Gordon, Gaelyn 1939-1997
  See CLR 75
Gordon, Garrett
  See Garrett, Randall
Gordon, Gary
  See Edmonds, I(vy) G(ordon)
Gordon, Hal
  See Goodwin, Harold L(eland)
Gordon, Jeffie Ross
  See Enderle, Judith (Ann) Ross
  and Gordon, Stephanie Jacob
Gordon, John
  See Gesner, Clark
Gordon, John (William) 1925- 84

Gordon, Lew
See Baldwin, Gordon C(ortis)
Gordon, Margaret (Anna) 1939- 9
Gordon, Mike 1948- 101
Gordon, Mildred 1912-1979
Obituary 24
Gordon, Selma
See Lanes, Selma Gordon
Gordon, Sheila 1927- 88
See also CLR 27
Gordon, Shirley 1921- 48
Brief entry 41
Gordon, Sol 1923- 11
Gordon, Stephanie Jacob 1940- 89
Autobiography Feature 114
Earlier sketch in SATA 64
See also SAAS 26
Gordon, Stewart
See Shirreffs, Gordon D(onald)
Gordons, The
See Gordon, Mildred
and Gordon, Gordon
Gore, Leonid 185
Gorelick, Molly C(hernow) 1920-2003 9
Obituary 153
Gorey, Edward (St. John) 1925-2000 70
Brief entry 27
Obituary 118
Earlier sketch in SATA 29
See also CLR 36
Gorham, Charles Orson 1868-1936 36
Gorham, Michael
See Folsom, Franklin (Brewster)
Gorman, Carol 187
Earlier sketch in SATA 150
Gorman, Jacqueline Laks 1955- 148
Gorman, Mike 206
Gormley, Beatrice 1942- 202
Brief entry 35
Earlier sketches in SATA 39, 127
Gorog, Judith (Katharine Allen) 1938- 75
Earlier sketch in SATA 39
Gorrell, Gena K. 1946- 170
Gorsline, Douglas (Warner) 1913-1985 11
Obituary 43
Gorsline, (Sally) Marie 1928- 28
Gorsline, S. M.
See Gorsline, (Sally) Marie
Gorton, Kaitlyn
See Emerson, Kathy Lynn
Gorton, Kathy Lynn
See Emerson, Kathy Lynn
Goryan, Sirak
See Saroyan, William
Goschke, Julia 1973- 208
Goscinny, Rene 1926-1977 47
Brief entry 39
See also CLR 37
Goss, Clay(ton E.) 1946- 82
Goss, Gary 1947- 124
Goss, Mini 1963- 186
Goto, Scott 203
Gott, Barry 197
Gottesman, S. D.
See Kornbluth, C(yril) M.
and Lowndes, Robert A(ugustine) W(ard)
and Pohl, Frederik
Gottfried, Ted
See Gottfried, Theodore Mark
Gottfried, Theodore Mark 1928- 150
Earlier sketch in SATA 85
Gottlieb, Gerald 1923- 7
Gottlieb, William P. 1917-2006 24
Gottlieb, William Paul
See Gottlieb, William P.
Goudey, Alice E(dwards) 1898-1993 20
Goudge, Eileen 1950- 88
Goudge, Elizabeth (de Beauchamp)
1900-1984 2
Obituary 38
See also CLR 94

Gough, Catherine
See Mulgan, Catherine
Gough, Philip 1908-1986 45
Gough, Sue 1940- 106
Goulart, Ron 1933- 67
Earlier sketch in SATA 1
Goulart, Ronald Joseph
See Goulart, Ron
Gould, Alberta 1945- 96
Gould, Chester 1900-1985 49
Obituary 43
Gould, Jean R(osalind) 1909-1993 11
Obituary 77
Gould, Lilian 6
Gould, Marilyn 1928- 76
Earlier sketch in SATA 15
Gould, Robert 154
Gould, Steven 1955- 95
Gould, Steven Charles
See Gould, Steven
Gourley, Catherine 1950- 190
Earlier sketch in SATA 95
Gourse, Leslie 1939-2004 89
Govan, (Mary) Christine Noble 1898-1985 ... 9
Gove, Doris 1944- 72
Govenar, Alan 1952- 189
Govenar, Alan Bruce
See Govenar, Alan
Govern, Elaine 1939- 26
Gowen, L. Kris 1968- 156
Graaf, Peter
See Youd, Samuel
Graber, Alexander 1914-1997 98
Earlier sketch in SATA 7
Graber, George Alexander
See Graber, Alexander
Graber, Janet 1942- 170
Graber, Richard (Fredrick) 1927- 26
Grabianski, Janusz 1928-1976 39
Obituary 30
Graboff, Abner 1919-1986 35
Grace, Fran(ces Jane) 45
Grace, N.B.
See Harper, Suzanne
Grace, Theresa
See Mattern, Joanne
Gracza, Margaret Young 1928- 56
Graduate of Oxford, A
See Ruskin, John
Grady, Denise 1952- 189
Graeber, Charlotte Towner 106
Brief entry 44
Earlier sketch in SATA 56
Graef, Renee 1956- 204
Graeme, Roderic
See Jeffries, Roderic
Graf, Michael
See Graf, Mike
Graf, Mike 1960- 164
Grafe, Max 198
Graff, Lisa 1981- 188
Graff, Polly Anne Colver
See Colver, Anne
Graff, (S.) Stewart 1908- 9
Graham, Ada 1931- 11
Graham, Alastair 1945- 74
Graham, Arthur Kennon
See Harrison, David L.
Graham, Bob 1942- 187
Earlier sketches in SATA 63, 101, 151
See also CLR 31
Graham, Brenda Knight 1942- 32
Graham, Charlotte
See Bowden, Joan Chase
Graham, Eleanor 1896-1984 18
Obituary 38
Graham, Ennis
See Molesworth, Mary Louisa
Graham, Frank, Jr. 1925- 11
Graham, Georgia 1959- 190
Graham, Ian 1953- 112

Graham, John 1926-2007 11
Graham, Kennon
See Harrison, David L.
Graham, Larry
See Graham, Lawrence
Graham, Lawrence 1962- 63
Graham, Lawrence Otis
See Graham, Lawrence
Graham, Linda
See Graham-Barber, Lynda
Graham, Lorenz (Bell) 1902-1989 74
Obituary 63
Earlier sketch in SATA 2
See also CLR 10
See also SAAS 5
Graham, Margaret Bloy 1920- 11
Graham, Robin Lee 1949- 7
Graham, Shirley 1896(?)-1977
See Du Bois, Shirley Graham
Graham-Barber, Lynda 1944- 159
Earlier sketch in SATA 42
Graham-Cameron, M.
See Graham-Cameron, M(alcolm) G(ordon)
Graham-Cameron, M(alcolm) G(ordon)
1931- 53
Brief entry 45
Graham-Cameron, Mike
See Graham-Cameron, M(alcolm) G(ordon)
Grahame, Kenneth 1859-1932 100
See also YABC 1
See also CLR 135
Gralley, Jean 166
Gramatky, Hardie 1907-1979 30
Obituary 23
Earlier sketch in SATA 1
See also CLR 22
Grambling, Lois G. 1927- 206
Earlier sketches in SATA 71, 148
Grambo, Rebecca L(ynn) 1963- 109
Grammer, June Amos 1927- 58
Grand, Samuel 1912-1988 42
Grandits, John 1949- 192
GrandPre, Mary 1954- 184
Grandville, J. J.
See Gerard, Jean Ignace Isidore
Grandville, Jean Ignace Isidore Gerard
See Gerard, Jean Ignace Isidore
Granfield, Linda 1950- 160
Earlier sketch in SATA 96
Grange, Peter
See Nicole, Christopher (Robin)
Granger, Margaret Jane 1925(?)-1977
Obituary 27
Granger, Michele 1949- 88
Granger, Peggy
See Granger, Margaret Jane
Granowsky, Alvin 1936- 101
Granstaff, Bill 1925- 10
Granstrom, Brita 1969- 167
Earlier sketch in SATA 111
Grant, Bruce 1893-1977 5
Obituary 25
Grant, Cynthia D. 1950- 147
Earlier sketches in SATA 33, 77
Grant, Eva 1907-1996 7
Grant, Evva H. 1913-1977
Obituary 27
Grant, Gordon 1875-1962 25
Grant, Gwen(doline Ellen) 1940- 47
Grant, Judyann Ackerman 211
Grant, Katie M.
See Grant, K.M.
Grant, K.M. 175
Grant, (Alice) Leigh 1947- 10
Grant, Matthew G.
See May, Julian
Grant, Maxwell
See Gibson, Walter B(rown)
and Lynds, Dennis
Grant, Melvyn 183
Grant, Myrna (Lois) 1934- 21

Grant, Neil 1938- *154*
   Earlier sketch in SATA *14*
Grant, Nicholas
   See Nicole, Christopher (Robin)
Grant, Richard 1948- *80*
Grant, Skeeter
   See Spiegelman, Art
Grater, Michael 1923- *57*
Gratz, Alan 1972- *212*
Gravel, Fern
   See Hall, James Norman
Gravelle, Karen 1942- *166*
   Earlier sketch in SATA *78*
Graves, Charles Parlin 1911-1972 .... *4*
Graves, Keith *191*
   Earlier sketch in SATA *156*
Graves, Robert 1895-1985 .... *45*
Graves, Robert von Ranke
   See Graves, Robert
Graves, Valerie
   See Bradley, Marion Zimmer
Gravett, Emily 1972(?)- *189*
Gray, Betsy
   See Poole, Gray Johnson
Gray, Caroline
   See Nicole, Christopher (Robin)
Gray, Claudia *213*
Gray, Dianne E. *183*
Gray, Elizabeth Janet
   See Vining, Elizabeth Gray
Gray, Genevieve S(tuck) 1920-1995 ...... *4*
Gray, Harold (Lincoln) 1894-1968 .... *33*
   Brief entry *32*
Gray, Jenny
   See Gray, Genevieve S(tuck)
Gray, John Lee
   See Jakes, John
Gray, Judith A. 1949- *93*
Gray, Judith Anne
   See Gray, Judith A.
Gray, Keith *151*
Gray, Kes 1960- *153*
Gray, Les 1929- *82*
Gray, Libba Moore 1937- *83*
Gray, Luli 1945- *149*
   Earlier sketch in SATA *90*
Gray, Marian
   See Pierce, Edith Gray
Gray, Nicholas Stuart 1922-1981 .... *4*
   Obituary *27*
Gray, Nigel 1941- *104*
   Earlier sketch in SATA *33*
Gray, (Lucy) Noel (Clervaux) 1898-1983 .... *47*
Gray, Patricia (Clark) *7*
Gray, Patsey
   See Gray, Patricia (Clark)
Gray, Rita *184*
Graydon, Shari 1958- *158*
Grayland, V. Merle
   See Grayland, Valerie (Merle Spanner)
Grayland, Valerie (Merle Spanner) *7*
Grayson, Devin (Kalile) 1970- *119*
Grayson, Kristine
   See Rusch, Kristine Kathryn
Grayson, Paul 1946- *79*
Graystone, Lynn
   See Brennan, Joseph Lomas
Great Comte, The
   See Hawkesworth, Eric
Greaves, Margaret 1914-1995 .... *87*
   Earlier sketch in SATA *7*
Greaves, Nick 1955- *77*
Gree, Alain 1936- *28*
Green, Adam
   See Weisgard, Leonard (Joseph)
Green, Anne Canevari 1943- *62*
Green, Brian
   See Card, Orson Scott
Green, Cliff(ord) 1934- *126*
Green, Connie Jordan 1938- *80*

Green, D.
   See Casewit, Curtis W(erner)
Green, Elizabeth Shippen 1871-1954 ...... *139*
Green, Hannah
   See Greenberg, Joanne (Goldenberg)
Green, Jane 1937- *9*
Green, Jessica *211*
Green, John 1977(?)- *170*
Green, Mary Moore 1906- *11*
Green, Morton 1937- *8*
Green, Norma B(erger) 1925- *11*
Green, Phyllis 1932- *20*
Green, Roger (Gilbert) Lancelyn 1918-1987 . *2*
   Obituary *53*
Green, (James Le)Roy 1948- *89*
Green, Sheila Ellen 1934- *148*
   Earlier sketches in SATA *8, 87*
Green, Timothy 1953- *91*
Greenaway, Kate 1846-1901 .... *100*
   See also YABC *2*
   See also CLR *111*
Greenbank, Anthony Hunt 1933- *39*
Greenberg, David 1954- *171*
Greenberg, David T.
   See Greenberg, David
Greenberg, Harvey R. 1935- *5*
Greenberg, Jan 1942- *211*
   Earlier sketches in SATA *61, 125*
Greenberg, Joanne (Goldenberg) 1932- *25*
Greenberg, Melanie Hope 1954- *214*
   Earlier sketch in SATA *72*
Greenberg, Polly 1932- *52*
   Brief entry *43*
Greenblat, Rodney Alan 1960- *106*
Greenburg, Dan 1936- *175*
   Earlier sketch in SATA *102*
Greene, Bette 1934- *161*
   Earlier sketches in SATA *8, 102*
   See also CLR *140*
   See also SAAS *16*
Greene, Carla 1916- *67*
   Earlier sketch in SATA *1*
Greene, Carol *102*
   Brief entry *44*
   Earlier sketch in SATA *66*
Greene, Constance C(larke) 1924- *72*
   Earlier sketch in SATA *11*
   See also CLR *62*
   See also SAAS *11*
Greene, Edgar
   See Papademetriou, Lisa
Greene, Ellin 1927- *23*
Greene, Graham 1904-1991 .... *20*
Greene, Graham Henry
   See Greene, Graham
Greene, Jacqueline Dembar 1946- *212*
   Earlier sketches in SATA *76, 131*
Greene, Laura Offenhartz 1935- *38*
Greene, Meg
   See Malvasi, Meg Greene
Greene, Michele 1962- *178*
Greene, Michele Dominguez
   See Greene, Michele
Greene, Rhonda Gowler 1955- *160*
   Earlier sketch in SATA *101*
Greene, Stephanie 1950- *173*
   Earlier sketch in SATA *127*
Greene, Wade 1933- *11*
Greene, Yvonne
   See Flesch, Yolande (Catarina)
Greenfeld, Howard (Scheinman) 1928- ... *140*
   Earlier sketch in SATA *19*
Greenfeld, Josh(ua Joseph) 1928- *62*
Greenfield, Eloise 1929- *155*
   Earlier sketches in SATA *19, 61, 105*
   See also CLR *38*
   See also SAAS *16*
Greenhaus, Thelma Nurenberg 1903-1984
   Obituary *45*
Greenhut, Josh
   See Mercer, Sienna

Greening, Hamilton
   See Hamilton, Charles (Harold St. John)
Greenlaw, M. Jean 1941- *107*
Greenleaf, Barbara Kaye 1942- *6*
Greenleaf, Peter 1910-1997 .... *33*
Greenlee, Sharon 1935- *77*
Greeno, Gayle 1949- *81*
Greenseid, Diane 1948- *178*
   Earlier sketch in SATA *93*
Greenspun, Adele Aron 1938- *142*
   Earlier sketch in SATA *76*
Greenstein, Elaine 1959- *150*
   Earlier sketch in SATA *82*
Greenwald, Sheila
   See Green, Sheila Ellen
Greenwood, Barbara 1940- *129*
   Earlier sketch in SATA *90*
Greenwood, Mark 1958- *202*
Greenwood, Pamela D. 1944- *115*
Greer, Richard
   See Garrett, Randall
   and Silverberg, Robert
Gregg, Andrew K. 1929- *81*
Gregg, Charles T(hornton) 1927- *65*
Gregg, Walter H(arold) 1919- *20*
Gregor, Arthur 1923- *36*
Gregor, Lee
   See Pohl, Frederik
Gregori, Leon 1919- *15*
Gregorian, Joyce Ballou 1946-1991 .... *30*
   Obituary *83*
Gregorich, Barbara 1943- *184*
   Earlier sketch in SATA *66*
Gregorowski, Christopher 1940- *30*
Gregory, Diana (Jean) 1933- *49*
   Brief entry *42*
Gregory, Harry
   See Gottfried, Theodore Mark
Gregory, Jean
   See Ure, Jean
Gregory, Kristiana 1951- *212*
   Earlier sketches in SATA *74, 136*
Gregory, Nan 1944- *192*
   Earlier sketch in SATA *148*
Gregory, Philippa 1954- *122*
Gregory, Stephen
   See Penzler, Otto
Gregory, Valiska 1940- *82*
Greif, Jean-Jacques 1944- *195*
Greisman, Joan Ruth 1937- *31*
Grendon, Stephen
   See Derleth, August (William)
Grenville, Pelham
   See Wodehouse, P. G.
Gretz, Susanna 1937- *7*
Gretzer, John *18*
Grewdead, Roy
   See Gorey, Edward (St. John)
Grey, Carol
   See Lowndes, Robert A(ugustine) W(ard)
Grey, Christopher *191*
Grey, Christopher Peter
   See Grey, Christopher
Grey, Jerry 1926- *11*
Grey, Mini *205*
   Earlier sketch in SATA *166*
Greybeard the Pirate
   See Macintosh, Brownie
Grey Owl
   See Belaney, Archibald Stansfeld
Gri
   See Denney, Diana
Gribbin, John 1946- *159*
Gribbin, John R.
   See Gribbin, John
Grice, Frederick 1910-1983 .... *6*
Grider, Dorothy 1915- *31*
Gridley, Marion E(leanor) 1906-1974 ..... *35*
   Obituary *26*
Grieco-Tiso, Pina 1954- *108*
Grieder, Walter 1924- *9*

Griego, Tony A. 1955- 77
Griese, Arnold A(lfred) 1921- 9
Griessman, Annette 1962- 170
  Earlier sketch in SATA *116*
Grieve, James 1934- 146
Grifalconi, Ann 1929- 210
  Earlier sketches in SATA *2, 66, 133*
  See also CLR *35*
  See also SAAS *16*
Griffin, Adele 1970- 195
  Earlier sketches in SATA *105, 153*
Griffin, Elizabeth May 1985- 89
Griffin, Gillett Good 1928- 26
Griffin, Judith Berry 34
Griffin, Kitty 1951- 137
Griffin, Peni R. 1961- 193
  Earlier sketches in SATA *67, 99*
Griffin, Steven A. 1953- 89
Griffin, Steven Arthur
  See Griffin, Steven A.
Griffin, W.E.B. 1929- 5
Griffith, Connie 1946- 89
Griffith, Gershom 1960- 85
Griffith, Helen V(irginia) 1934- 87
  Autobiography Feature 107
  Earlier sketch in SATA *39*
Griffith, Jeannette
  See Eyerly, Jeannette
Griffith, Saul 1974- 200
Griffiths, Andy 1961- 196
  Earlier sketch in SATA *152*
Griffiths, G(ordon) D(ouglas) 1910-1973
  Obituary 20
Griffiths, Helen 1939- 86
  Earlier sketch in SATA *5*
  See also CLR *75*
  See also SAAS *5*
Grigson, Jane (McIntire) 1928-1990 63
Grimes, Lee 1920- 68
Grimes, Nikki 1950- 174
  Earlier sketches in SATA *93, 136*
  See also CLR *42*
Grimly, Gris 186
Grimm, Jacob Ludwig Karl 1785-1863 22
  See also CLR *112*
Grimm, Wilhelm Karl 1786-1859 22
  See also CLR *112*
Grimm, William C(arey) 1907-1992 14
Grimm and Grim
  See Grimm, Jacob Ludwig Karl
  and Grimm, Wilhelm Karl
Grimm Brothers
  See Grimm, Jacob Ludwig Karl
  and Grimm, Wilhelm Karl
Grimsdell, Jeremy 1942- 83
Grimshaw, Nigel (Gilroy) 1925- 23
Grimsley, Gordon
  See Groom, Arthur William
Grindley, Jane Sally
  See Grindley, Sally
Grindley, Sally 1953- 148
Gringhuis, Dirk
  See Gringhuis, Richard H.
Gringhuis, Richard H. 1918-1974 6
  Obituary 25
Grinnell, David
  See Wollheim, Donald A(llen)
Grinnell, George Bird 1849-1938 16
Grinspoon, David
  See Grinspoon, David H.
Grinspoon, David H. 1959- 156
Grinspoon, David Harry
  See Grinspoon, David H.
Gripe, Maria 1923- 74
  Earlier sketch in SATA *2*
  See also CLR *5*
Gripe, Maria Kristina
  See Gripe, Maria
Grobler, Piet 1959- 201
Groch, Judith (Goldstein) 1929- 25

Grode, Redway
  See Gorey, Edward (St. John)
Groener, Carl
  See Lowndes, Robert A(ugustine) W(ard)
Groening, Matt 1954- 116
  Earlier sketch in SATA *81*
Grohmann, Susan 1948- 84
Grohskopf, Bernice 7
Grol, Lini R(icharda) 1913- 9
Grollman, Earl A. 1925- 22
Groom, Arthur William 1898-1964 10
Grooms, Duffy 1964- 169
Gross, Alan 1947- 54
  Brief entry 43
Gross, Ernie 1913- 67
Gross, Philip 1952- 164
  Earlier sketch in SATA *84*
Gross, Philip John
  See Gross, Philip
Gross, Ruth Belov 1929- 33
Gross, Sarah Chokla 1906-1976 9
  Obituary 26
Grosser, Morton 1931- 74
Grosser, Vicky 1958- 83
Grossman, Bill 1948- 126
  Earlier sketch in SATA *72*
Grossman, Nancy 1940- 29
Grossman, Patricia 1951- 73
Grossman, Robert 1940- 11
Grote, JoAnn A. 1951- 113
Groten, Dallas 1951- 64
Groth, John (August) 1908-1988 21
  Obituary 56
Groth-Fleming, Candace
  See Fleming, Candace
Grove, Vicki 1948- 151
  Autobiography Feature 151
  Earlier sketch in SATA *122*
Grover, Lorie Ann 1964- 168
Grover, Wayne 1934- 69
Groves, Georgina
  See Symons, (Dorothy) Geraldine
Groves, Maketa 1950- 107
Groves, Seli 77
Grubb, Lisa 160
Gruber, Michael 1940- 173
Gruber, Terry (deRoy) 1953- 66
Gruelle, John 1880-1938 35
  Brief entry 32
  See also CLR *34*
Gruelle, Johnny
  See Gruelle, John
Gruenberg, Sidonie Matsner 1881-1974 2
  Obituary 27
Gruhzit-Hoyt, Olga (Margaret) 1922- 127
  Earlier sketch in SATA *16*
Grummer, Arnold E(dward) 1923- 49
Grunewalt, Pine
  See Kunhardt, Edith
Grunwell, Jeanne Marie 1971- 147
Grupper, Jonathan 137
Gryski, Camilla 1948- 72
Guarino, Dagmar
  See Guarino, Deborah
Guarino, Deborah 1954- 68
Guay, Georgette (Marie Jeanne) 1952- 54
Guay, Rebecca 209
Guay-Mitchell, Rebecca
  See Guay, Rebecca
Guback, Georgia 88
Guccione, Leslie Davis 1946- 111
  Earlier sketch in SATA *72*
Guck, Dorothy 1913-2002 27
Gudeon, Karla 212
Guerny, Gene
  See Gurney, Gene
Guest, Elissa Haden 1953- 125
Guest, Jacqueline 1952- 135
Guevara, Susan 167
  Earlier sketch in SATA *97*
Gugler, Laurel Dee 95

Gugliotta, Bobette 1918-1994 7
Guianan, Eve 1965- 102
Guiberson, Brenda Z. 1946- 211
  Earlier sketches in SATA *71, 124*
Guibert, Emmanuel 1964- 181
Guile, Melanie 1949- 152
  Earlier sketch in SATA *104*
Guillaume, Jeanette G. Flierl 1899-1990 8
Guillot, Rene 1900-1969 7
  See also CLR *22*
Guisewite, Cathy (Lee) 1950- 57
Gulbis, Stephen 1959- 142
Gulley, Judie 1942- 58
Gump, P. Q.
  See Card, Orson Scott
Gundrey, Elizabeth 1924- 23
Gunn, James E. 1923- 35
Gunn, James Edwin
  See Gunn, James E.
Gunn, Robin Jones 1955- 84
Gunnella 1956- 197
Gunning, Monica Olwen 1930- 161
Gunston, Bill
  See Gunston, William Tudor
Gunston, William Tudor 1927- 9
Gunterman, Bertha Lisette 1886(?)-1975
  Obituary 27
Gunther, John 1901-1970
Guravich, Dan 1918- 74
Gurko, Leo 1914- 9
Gurko, Miriam 1910(?)-1988 9
  Obituary 58
Gurney, Gene 1924- 65
Gurney, James 1958- 120
  Earlier sketch in SATA *76*
Gurney, John Steven 1962- 143
  Earlier sketch in SATA *75*
Gustafson, Sarah R.
  See Riedman, Sarah R(egal)
Gustafson, Scott 1956- 34
Gustavson, Adam 1974- 214
  Earlier sketch in SATA *176*
Guthrie, A(lfred) B(ertram), Jr. 1901-1991 .. 62
  Obituary 67
Guthrie, Anne 1890-1979 28
Guthrie, Donna W. 1946- 105
  Earlier sketch in SATA *63*
Gutierrez, Akemi 172
Gutierrez, Rudy 203
Gutman, Bill 128
  Brief entry 43
  Earlier sketch in SATA *67*
Gutman, Dan 1955- 188
  Earlier sketches in SATA *77, 139*
Gutman, Naham 1899(?)-1981
  Obituary 25
Gutmann, Bessie Pease 1876-1960 73
Guy, Geoffrey 1942- 153
Guy, Ginger Foglesong 1954- 171
Guy, Rosa 1925- 122
  Earlier sketches in SATA *14, 62*
  See also CLR *137*
Guy, Rosa Cuthbert
  See Guy, Rosa
Guy, Susan 1948- 149
Guymer, (Wilhelmina) Mary 1909- 50
Guzman, Lila 1952- 168
Guzman, Rick 1957- 168
Gwaltney, Doris 1932- 181
Gwynne, Fred(erick Hubbard) 1926-1993 41
  Brief entry 27
  Obituary 75
Gwynne, Oscar A.
  See Ellis, Edward S.
Gwynne, Oswald A.
  See Ellis, Edward S.

Author Index

H

Haab, Sherri 1964- *169*
  Earlier sketch in SATA *91*
Haar, Jaap ter
  See ter Haar, Jaap
Haarsma, P.J. *183*
Haas, Carolyn Buhai 1926- *43*
Haas, Dan 1957- *105*
Haas, Dorothy F. *46*
  Brief entry *43*
  See also SAAS *17*
Haas, Irene 1929- *96*
  Earlier sketch in SATA *17*
Haas, James E(dward) 1943- *40*
Haas, (Katherine) Jessie 1959- *135*
  Autobiography Feature *135*
  Earlier sketch in SATA *98*
Haas, Jessie 1959- *215*
Haas, Merle S. 1896(?)-1985
  Obituary *41*
Habenstreit, Barbara 1937- *5*
Haber, Karen 1955- *78*
Haber, Louis 1910-1988 .... *12*
Hacker, Randi 1951- *185*
Hacker, Randi Dawn
  See Hacker, Randi
Hackett, John Winthrop 1910-1997 .... *65*
Hacks, Peter 1928-2003
  Obituary *151*
Haddix, Margaret Peterson 1964- *187*
  Earlier sketches in SATA *94, 125*
Haddon, Mark 1962- *155*
Hader, Berta (Hoerner) 1891(?)-1976 .... *16*
Hader, Elmer (Stanley) 1889-1973 .... *16*
Hadithi, Mwenye
  See Hobson, Bruce
Hadley, Franklin
  See Winterbotham, R(ussell) R(obert)
Hadley, Lee 1934-1995 .... *89*
  Brief entry *38*
  Obituary *86*
  Earlier sketch in SATA *47*
  See also CLR *40*
  See also SAAS *14*
Haeffele, Deborah 1954- *76*
Haenel, Wolfram 1956- *89*
  See also CLR *64*
Hafner, Marylin 1925- *179*
  Earlier sketches in SATA *7, 121*
Haft, Erin
  See Ehrenhaft, Daniel
Hager, Alan 1940- *176*
Hager, Alice Rogers 1894-1969
  Obituary *26*
Hager, Betty 1923- *89*
Hager, Jenna Bush
  See Bush, Jenna
Hager, Sarah *171*
Hager, Thomas 1953- *119*
Hager, Tom
  See Hager, Thomas
Hagerup, Klaus 1946- *186*
Haggard, H(enry) Rider 1856-1925 .... *16*
Haggerty, James J(oseph) 1920- *5*
Hagon, Priscilla
  See Allan, Mabel Esther
Hague, (Susan) Kathleen 1949- *49*
  Brief entry *45*
Hague, Michael 1948- *185*
  Brief entry *32*
  Earlier sketches in SATA *48, 80, 129*
Hague, Michael R.
  See Hague, Michael
Hahn, Emily 1905-1997 .... *3*
  Obituary *96*
Hahn, Hannelore *8*
Hahn, James (Sage) 1947- *9*
Hahn, (Mona) Lynn 1949- *9*

Hahn, Mary Downing 1937- *208*
  Autobiography Feature *157*
  Brief entry *44*
  Earlier sketches in SATA *50, 81, 138, 157*
  See also SAAS *12*
Hahn, Michael T. 1953- *92*
Haig-Brown, Roderick (Langmere)
  1908-1976 .... *12*
  See also CLR *31*
Haight, Anne Lyon 1895-1977
  Obituary *30*
Haight, Rip
  See Carpenter, John
Haight, Sandy 1949- *79*
Haij, Vera
  See Jansson, Tove (Marika)
Haines, Gail Kay 1943- *11*
Haines, Margaret Ann Beck
  See Beck, Peggy
Haining, Peter 1940-2007 .... *14*
  Obituary *188*
Haining, Peter Alexander
  See Haining, Peter
Hains, Harriet
  See Watson, Carol
Hajdusiewicz, Babs Bell *163*
Hakim, Joy 1931- *173*
  Earlier sketch in SATA *83*
Halacy, D. S., Jr. 1919-2002 .... *36*
  See also SAAS *8*
Halacy, Dan
  See Halacy, D. S., Jr.
Halam, Ann
  See Jones, Gwyneth A(nn)
Haldane, Roger John 1945- *13*
Hale, Arlene 1924-1982 .... *49*
Hale, Bruce 1957- *203*
  Earlier sketch in SATA *123*
Hale, Christy
  See Apostolou, Christine Hale
Hale, Edward Everett 1822-1909 .... *16*
Hale, Glenn
  See Walker, Robert W.
Hale, Helen
  See Mulcahy, Lucille Burnett
Hale, Irina 1932- *26*
Hale, Kathleen 1898-2000 .... *66*
  Obituary *121*
  Earlier sketch in SATA *17*
Hale, Linda (Howe) 1929- *6*
Hale, Lucretia P.
  See Hale, Lucretia Peabody
Hale, Lucretia Peabody 1820-1900 .... *26*
  See also CLR *105*
Hale, Marian *194*
Hale, Nancy 1908-1988 .... *31*
  Obituary *57*
Hale, Nathan 1976- *210*
Hale, Shannon *200*
  Earlier sketch in SATA *158*
Haley, Amanda *205*
Haley, Gail E(inhart) 1939- *161*
  Autobiography Feature *161*
  Brief entry *28*
  Earlier sketches in SATA *43, 78, 136*
  See also CLR *21*
  See also SAAS *13*
Haley, Neale *52*
Halfmann, Janet 1944- *208*
Hall, Adam
  See Trevor, Elleston
Hall, Adele 1910- *7*
Hall, Anna Gertrude 1882-1967 .... *8*
Hall, August *207*
Hall, Barbara 1961- *68*
Hall, Becky 1950- *186*
Hall, Beverly B. 1918- *95*
Hall, Borden
  See Yates, Raymond F(rancis)
Hall, Brian P(atrick) 1935- *31*

Hall, Cameron
  See del Rey, Lester
Hall, Caryl
  See Hansen, Caryl (Hall)
Hall, Donald 1928- *97*
  Earlier sketch in SATA *23*
Hall, Donald Andrew, Jr.
  See Hall, Donald
Hall, Douglas 1931- *43*
Hall, Elizabeth 1929- *77*
Hall, Elvajean 1910-1984 .... *6*
Hall, Francie 1940- *166*
Hall, James Norman 1887-1951 .... *21*
Hall, Jesse
  See Boesen, Victor
Hall, Katy
  See McMullan, Kate
Hall, Kirsten Marie 1974- *67*
Hall, Lynn 1937- *79*
  Earlier sketches in SATA *2, 47*
  See also SAAS *4*
Hall, Malcolm 1945- *7*
Hall, Marcellus *203*
Hall, Marjory
  See Yeakley, Marjory Hall
Hall, Melanie W. 1949- *169*
  Earlier sketches in SATA *78, 116*
Hall, Patricia 1940- *136*
Hall, Rosalys Haskell 1914- *7*
Hall, Willis 1929-2005 .... *66*
Hallard, Peter
  See Catherall, Arthur
Hallas, Richard
  See Knight, Eric
Hall-Clarke, James
  See Rowland-Entwistle, (Arthur) Theodore
  (Henry)
Hallensleben, Georg 1958- *173*
Haller, Dorcas Woodbury 1946- *46*
Hallett, Mark 1947- *83*
Halliburton, Richard 1900-1939(?) *81*
Halliburton, Warren J. 1924- *19*
Halliday, Brett
  See Dresser, Davis
  and Johnson, (Walter) Ryerson
  and Terrall, Robert
Halliday, William R(oss) 1926- *52*
Hallin, Emily Watson 1916-1995 .... *6*
Hallinan, P(atrick) K(enneth) 1944- *39*
  Brief entry *37*
Hallman, Ruth 1929- *43*
  Brief entry *28*
Hallowell, Tommy
  See Hill, Thomas
Hall-Quest, (Edna) Olga W(ilbourne)
  1899-1986 .... *11*
  Obituary *47*
Halls, Kelly Milner 1957- *131*
Hallstead, William F(inn III) 1924- *11*
Hallward, Michael 1889-1982 .... *12*
Halperin, Michael *156*
Halperin, Wendy Anderson 1952- *200*
  Earlier sketches in SATA *80, 125*
Halpern, Julie 1975- *198*
Halpin, Brendan 1968- *193*
Halpin, Marlene 1927- *88*
Halsell, Grace (Eleanor) 1923-2000 .... *13*
Halsey, Megan *185*
Halsted, Anna Roosevelt 1906-1975
  Obituary *30*
Halter, Jon C(harles) 1941- *22*
Halverson, Deborah *202*
Halvorson, Marilyn 1948- *123*
Hamalian, Leo 1920- *41*
Hamberger, John 1934- *14*
Hamblin, Dora Jane 1920- *36*
Hambly, Barbara 1951- *108*
Hambly, Barbara Joan
  See Hambly, Barbara
Hamer, Martyn
  See Eldin, Peter

Hamerstrom, Frances 1907-1998 .... *24*
Hamil, Thomas Arthur 1928- *14*
Hamill, Ethel
  See Webb, Jean Francis (III)
Hamilton, (John) Alan 1943- *66*
Hamilton, Alice
  See Cromie, Alice Hamilton
Hamilton, Anita 1919- *92*
Hamilton, Buzz
  See Hemming, Roy G.
Hamilton, Carol (Jean Barber) 1935- *94*
Hamilton, Charles (Harold St. John)
  1876-1961 .... *13*
Hamilton, Charles 1913-1996 .... *65*
  Obituary *93*
Hamilton, Clive
  See Lewis, C. S.
Hamilton, Dorothy (Drumm) 1906-1983 ...... *12*
  Obituary *35*
Hamilton, Edith 1867-1963 .... *20*
Hamilton, Edmond 1904-1977 .... *118*
Hamilton, (Muriel) Elizabeth (Mollie)
  1906- *23*
Hamilton, Emma Walton 1962- *177*
Hamilton, Franklin
  See Silverberg, Robert
Hamilton, Gail
  See Corcoran, Barbara (Asenath)
  and Dodge, Mary Abigail
Hamilton, Kersten 1958- *204*
  Earlier sketch in SATA *134*
Hamilton, K.R.
  See Hamilton, Kersten
Hamilton, Martha 1953- *183*
  Earlier sketch in SATA *123*
Hamilton, Mary (E.) 1927- *55*
Hamilton, Mollie
  See Kaye, M.M.
Hamilton, Morse 1943-1998 .... *101*
  Earlier sketch in SATA *35*
Hamilton, Peter F. 1960- *109*
Hamilton, Priscilla
  See Gellis, Roberta
Hamilton, Ralph
  See Stratemeyer, Edward L.
Hamilton, Virginia 1936-2002 .... *123*
  Obituary *132*
  Earlier sketches in SATA *4, 56, 79*
  See also CLR *127*
Hamilton, Virginia Esther
  See Hamilton, Virginia
Hamilton-Paterson, James 1941- *82*
Hamlet, Ova
  See Lupoff, Richard A(llen)
Hamley, D. C.
  See Hamley, Dennis
Hamley, Dennis 1935- *69*
  Earlier sketch in SATA *39*
  See also CLR *47*
  See also SAAS *22*
Hamley, Dennis C.
  See Hamley, Dennis
Hamlin, Peter J. 1970- *84*
Hamm, Diane Johnston 1949- *78*
Hammer, Charles 1934- *58*
Hammer, Richard 1928- *6*
Hammerman, Gay M(orenus) 1926- *9*
Hammill, Matt 1982- *206*
Hammond, Andrew 1970- *181*
Hammond, Ralph
  See Hammond Innes, Ralph
Hammond, Winifred G(raham) 1899-1992 ... *29*
  Obituary *107*
Hammond Innes, Ralph 1913-1998 .... *116*
Hammontree, Marie (Gertrude) 1913- *13*
Hample, Zack 1977- *161*
Hampshire, Joyce Gregorian
  See Gregorian, Joyce Ballou
Hampshire, Susan 1942- *98*
Hampson, (Richard) Denman 1929- *15*

Hampson, Frank 1918(?)-1985
  Obituary *46*
Hampton, Wilborn 1940- *196*
  Earlier sketch in SATA *156*
Hamre, Leif 1914- *5*
Hamsa, Bobbie 1944- *52*
  Brief entry *38*
Han, Jenny 1981- *175*
Han, Lu
  See Stickler, Soma Han
Han, Soma
  See Stickler, Soma Han
Han, Suzanne Crowder 1953- *89*
Hancock, Mary A. 1923- *31*
Hancock, Sibyl 1940- *9*
Hand, Elizabeth 1957- *167*
  Earlier sketch in SATA *118*
Handford, Martin (John) 1956- *64*
  See also CLR *22*
Handforth, Thomas (Schofield) 1897-1948 .. *42*
Handler, Daniel
  See Snicket, Lemony
Handville, Robert (Tompkins) 1924- *45*
Hane, Roger 1940-1974
  Obituary *20*
Hanel, Wolfram
  See Haenel, Wolfram
Haney, Lynn 1941- *23*
Hanff, Helene 1916-1997 .... *97*
  Earlier sketch in SATA *11*
Hanft, Josh 1956- *197*
Hanft, Joshua E.
  See Hanft, Josh
Hanley, Boniface Francis 1924- *65*
Hanlon, Emily 1945- *15*
Hann, Jacquie 1951- *19*
Hann, Judith 1942- *77*
Hanna, Bill
  See Hanna, William (Denby)
Hanna, Cheryl 1951- *84*
Hanna, Dan *200*
Hanna, Jack (Bushnell) 1947- *74*
Hanna, Nell(ie L.) 1908- *55*
Hanna, Paul R(obert) 1902-1988 .... *9*
Hanna, William (Denby) 1910-2001 .... *51*
  Obituary *126*
Hannam, Charles 1925- *50*
Hannan, Peter 1954- *187*
Hannigan, Katherine *170*
Hannon, Ezra
  See Hunter, Evan
Hann-Syme, Marguerite *127*
Hano, Arnold 1922- *12*
Hano, Renee Roth
  See Roth-Hano, Renee
Hanover, Terri
  See Huff, Tanya
Hansen, Ann Larkin 1958- *96*
Hansen, Brooks 1965- *104*
Hansen, Caryl (Hall) 1929- *39*
Hansen, Ian V. 1929- *113*
Hansen, Jennifer 1972- *156*
Hansen, Joyce 1942- *172*
  Autobiography Feature *172*
  Brief entry *39*
  Earlier sketches in SATA *46, 101*
  See also CLR *21*
  See also SAAS *15*
Hansen, Joyce Viola
  See Hansen, Joyce
Hansen, Mark Victor *112*
Hansen, Ron 1947- *56*
Hansen, Ronald Thomas
  See Hansen, Ron
Hanser, Richard (Frederick) 1909-1981 .... *13*
Hanson, Joan 1938- *8*
Hanson, Joseph E. 1894(?)-1971
  Obituary *27*
Hanson, Mary Elizabeth *188*
Hanson, Warren 1949- *155*
Hansson, Gunilla 1939- *64*

Hantman, Clea *200*
Harald, Eric
  See Boesen, Victor
Harazin, S. A. *210*
Harcourt, Ellen Knowles 1890(?)-1984
  Obituary *36*
Hard, Charlotte (Ann) 1969- *98*
Hardcastle, Michael 1933- *47*
  Brief entry *38*
Harding, Lee 1937- *32*
  Brief entry *31*
Hardinge, Frances 1973- *210*
Hardt, Helga Fleischhauer
  See Fleischhauer-Hardt, Helga
Hardwick, Richard Holmes, Jr. 1923- *12*
Hardy, Alice Dale *67*
  Earlier sketch in SATA *1*
Hardy, David A(ndrews) 1936- *9*
Hardy, Jon 1958- *53*
Hardy, LeAnne 1951- *154*
Hardy, Stuart
  See Schisgall, Oscar
Hare, Norma Q(uarles) 1924- *46*
  Brief entry *41*
Harel, Nira 1936- *154*
Harford, Henry
  See Hudson, W(illiam) H(enry)
Hargrave, Leonie
  See Disch, Thomas M.
Hargreaves, (Charles) Roger 1935-1988
  Obituary *56*
Hargrove, James 1947- *57*
  Brief entry *50*
Hargrove, Jim
  See Hargrove, James
Harik, Elsa
  See Marston, Elsa
Harik, Elsa M.
  See Marston, Elsa
Harik, Elsa Marston
  See Marston, Elsa
Hariton, Anca I. 1955- *79*
Hark, Mildred
  See McQueen, Mildred Hark
Harkaway, Hal
  See Stratemeyer, Edward L.
Harkins, Philip 1912-1997 .... *6*
  Obituary *129*
Harlan, Elizabeth 1945- *41*
  Brief entry *35*
Harlan, Glen
  See Cebulash, Mel
Harlan, Judith 1949- *135*
  Earlier sketch in SATA *74*
  See also CLR *81*
Harland, Richard 1947- *152*
Harlee, J. V.
  See Leese, Jennifer L.B.
Harler, Ann
  See Van Steenwyk, Elizabeth (Ann)
Harley, Avis *183*
Harley, Bill 1954- *208*
  Earlier sketch in SATA *87*
Harlow, Joan Hiatt 1932- *157*
Harman, Fred 1902(?)-1982
  Obituary *30*
Harman, Hugh 1903-1982
  Obituary *33*
Harmelink, Barbara (Mary) *9*
Harmer, Mabel 1894-1992 .... *45*
Harmon, Dan
  See Harmon, Daniel E(lton)
Harmon, Daniel E(lton) 1949- *157*
Harmon, Margaret 1906- *20*
Harmon, Michael 1969- *189*
Harmon, Michael B.
  See Harmon, Michael
Harmon, William (Ruth) 1938- *65*
Harnan, Terry 1920- *12*
Harness, Cheryl 1951- *178*
  Earlier sketch in SATA *131*

Harnett, Cynthia (Mary) 1893-1981 5
  Obituary 32
Harper, Anita 1943- 41
Harper, Betty 1946- 126
Harper, Charise
  See Harper, Charise Mericle
Harper, Charise Mericle 179
Harper, Elaine
  See Hallin, Emily Watson
Harper, Ellen
  See Noble, Marty
Harper, Jamie 174
Harper, Jessica 1949- 148
Harper, Jo 1932- 169
  Earlier sketch in SATA 97
Harper, Lee 201
Harper, Mary Wood
  See Dixon, Jeanne
Harper, Piers 1966- 161
  Earlier sketch in SATA 105
Harper, Suzanne 194
Harper, Wilhelmina 1884-1973 4
  Obituary 26
Harrah, Madge 1931- 154
Harrah, Michael 1940- 41
Harrah, Monique
  See Harrah, Madge
Harrar, George E. 1949- 124
Harrell, Beatrice Orcutt 1943- 93
Harrell, Janice 1945- 70
Harries, Joan 1922- 39
Harrill, Ronald 1950- 90
Harrington, Denis J(ames) 1932- 88
Harrington, Evelyn Davis 1911- 5
Harrington, Janice N. 1956- 187
Harrington, Lyn
  See Harrington, Evelyn Davis
Harris, Alan 1944- 71
Harris, Aurand 1915-1996 37
  Obituary 91
Harris, Bob
  See Harris, Robert J.
Harris, Carol Flynn 1933- 135
Harris, Catherine
  See Ainsworth, Catherine Harris
Harris, Christie
  See Harris, Christie (Lucy) Irwin
Harris, Christie (Lucy) Irwin 1907-2002 74
  Autobiography Feature 116
  Earlier sketch in SATA 6
  See also CLR 47
  See also SAAS 10
Harris, Christine 1955- 105
Harris, Colver
  See Colver, Anne
Harris, David 1942- 118
Harris, David William
  See Harris, David
Harris, Dorothy Joan 1931- 153
  Earlier sketch in SATA 13
Harris, Geraldine (Rachel) 1951- 54
Harris, Jacqueline L. 1929- 62
Harris, Janet 1932-1979 4
  Obituary 23
Harris, Jesse
  See Standiford, Natalie
Harris, Joan 1946- 146
Harris, Joe 1928- 201
Harris, Joel Chandler 1848-1908 100
  See also YABC 1
  See also CLR 128
Harris, John (Wyndham Parkes Lucas) Beynon
  1903-1969 118
Harris, Johnson
  See Harris, John (Wyndham Parkes Lucas)
  Beynon
Harris, Jonathan 1921-1997 52
Harris, Larry Vincent 1939- 59
Harris, Lavinia
  See St. John, Nicole
Harris, Leon A., Jr. 1926-2000 4

Harris, Lois V. 199
Harris, Lorle K(empe) 1912-2001 22
Harris, Marilyn
  See Springer, Marilyn Harris
Harris, Mark Jonathan 1941- 84
  Earlier sketch in SATA 32
Harris, Mary K(athleen) 1905-1966 119
Harris, Robert J. 1955- 195
Harris, Robie H. 1940- 203
  Brief entry 53
  Earlier sketches in SATA 90, 147
Harris, Robin
  See Shine, Deborah
Harris, Rosemary (Jeanne) 82
  Earlier sketch in SATA 4
  See also CLR 30
  See also SAAS 7
Harris, Ruth Elwin 1935- 164
Harris, Sherwood 1932-2009 25
Harris, Steven Michael 1957- 55
Harris, Trudy 1949- 191
  Earlier sketch in SATA 128
Harris-Filderman, Diane
  See Filderman, Diane E(lizabeth)
Harrison, C(hester) William 1913-1994 35
Harrison, Carol
  See Harrison, Carol Thompson
Harrison, Carol Thompson 113
Harrison, David L. 1937- 186
  Earlier sketches in SATA 26, 92, 150
Harrison, Deloris 1938- 9
Harrison, Edward Hardy 1926- 56
Harrison, Elizabeth (Allen) Cavanna
  1909-2001 30
  Earlier sketch in SATA 1
  See also SAAS 4
Harrison, Harry 1925- 4
Harrison, Harry Max
  See Harrison, Harry
Harrison, Mette Ivie 1970- 202
  Earlier sketch in SATA 149
Harrison, Michael 1939- 106
Harrison, Molly (Hodgett) 1909-2002 41
Harrison, Sarah 1946- 63
Harrison, Ted
  See Harrison, Edward Hardy
Harsh, Fred (T.) 1925- 72
Harshaw, Ruth H(etzel) 1890-1968 27
Harshman, Marc 1950- 109
  Earlier sketch in SATA 71
Hart, Alexandra 1939- 14
Hart, Alison
  See Leonhardt, Alice
Hart, Bruce 1938-2006 57
  Brief entry 39
Hart, Carole 1943- 57
  Brief entry 39
Hart, Carolyn 1936- 74
Hart, Carolyn G.
  See Hart, Carolyn
Hart, Carolyn Gimpel
  See Hart, Carolyn
Hart, Jan Siegel 1940- 79
Hart, Joyce 1954- 148
Hart, Karen 185
Hart, Lenore 171
Hart, Philip S. 1944- 180
Hart, Virginia 1949- 83
Harte, Bret 1836(?)-1902 26
Harte, Francis Brett
  See Harte, Bret
Harter, Debbie 1963- 107
Hartfield, Claire 1957- 147
Hartinger, Brent 1964- 174
  Earlier sketch in SATA 145
Hartland, Jessie 171
Hartley, Ellen (Raphael) 1915-1980 23
Hartley, Fred Allan III 1953- 41
Hartley, William B(rown) 1913-1980 23
Hartling, Peter
  See Hartling, Peter

Hartling, Peter 1933- 66
  See also CLR 29
Hartman, Cassie 202
Hartman, Dan 1955- 202
Hartman, Evert 1937- 38
  Brief entry 35
Hartman, Jane E(vangeline) 1928- 47
Hartman, Louis F(rancis) 1901-1970 22
Hartman, Rachel 174
Hartman, Victoria 1942- 91
Hartnett, Sonya 1968- 176
  Earlier sketches in SATA 93, 130
Hartshorn, Ruth M. 1928- 11
Hartung, Susan Kathleen 192
  Earlier sketch in SATA 150
Hartwig, Manfred 1950- 81
Harvey, Brett 1936- 61
Harvey, Edith 1908(?)-1972
  Obituary 27
Harvey, Gill 189
Harvey, Karen D. 1935- 88
Harvey, Roland 1945- 179
  Earlier sketches in SATA 71, 123
Harvey-Fitzhenry, Alyxandra 1974- 189
Harwick, B. L.
  See Keller, Beverly L(ou)
Harwin, Brian
  See Henderson, LeGrand
Harwood, Pearl Augusta (Bragdon)
  1903-1998 9
Haseley, Dennis 1950- 157
  Brief entry 44
  Earlier sketches in SATA 57, 105
Hashmi, Kerri 1955- 108
Haskell, Arnold L(ionel) 1903-1981(?) 6
Haskins, James
  See Haskins, James S.
Haskins, James S. 1941-2005 132
  Autobiography Feature 132
  Earlier sketches in SATA 9, 69, 105
  See also CLR 39
  See also SAAS 4
Haskins, Jim
  See Haskins, James S.
Hasler, Eveline 1933- 181
Hasler, Joan 1931- 28
Hass, Robert 1941- 94
Hassall, Joan 1906-1988 43
  Obituary 56
Hassett, Ann 1958- 162
Hassett, John 162
Hassler, Jon 1933-2008 19
  Obituary 191
Hassler, Jon Francis
  See Hassler, Jon
Hastings, Beverly
  See Barkin, Carol
  and James, Elizabeth
Hastings, Graham
  See Jeffries, Roderic
Hastings, Ian 1912- 62
Hastings, Victor
  See Disch, Thomas M.
Haszard, Patricia Moyes 1923-2000 63
Hatch, Lynda S. 1950- 90
Hathaway, Barbara 164
Hathorn, Elizabeth
  See Hathorn, Elizabeth Helen
Hathorn, Elizabeth Helen 1943- 156
  Autobiography Feature 156
  Earlier sketches in SATA 74, 120
Hathorn, Libby 1943-
  See Hathorn, Elizabeth Helen
Hatkoff, Craig 1954- 192
Hatlo, Jimmy 1898-1963
  Obituary 23
Hatton, Caroline 1957- 205
Haugaard, Erik Christian 1923- 68
  Earlier sketch in SATA 4
  See also CLR 11
  See also SAAS 12

Haugaard, Kay 117
Haugen, Hayley Mitchell 1968- 172
Haugen, Tormod 1945- 66
Hauman, Doris 1898-1984 32
Hauman, George 1890-1961 32
Hauptly, Denis J(ames) 1945- 57
Hauser, Jill Frankel 1950- 127
Hauser, Margaret L(ouise) 1909- 10
Hausherr, Rosmarie 1943- 86
Hausman, Gerald 1945- 180
    Earlier sketches in SATA *13, 90, 132*
    See also CLR *89*
Hausman, Gerry
    See Hausman, Gerald
Hauth, Katherine B. 1940- 99
Hautman, Pete 1952- 173
    Earlier sketches in SATA *82, 128*
Hautman, Peter Murray
    See Hautman, Pete
Hautzig, Deborah 1956- 106
    Earlier sketch in SATA *31*
Hautzig, Esther Rudomin 1930-2009 148
    Earlier sketches in SATA *4, 68*
    See also CLR *22*
    See also SAAS *15*
Havel, Geoff 1955- 152
Havel, Jennifer
    See Havill, Juanita
Havelin, Kate 1961- 143
Haven, Paul 1971(?)- 213
Havighurst, Walter (Edwin) 1901-1994 1
    Obituary 79
Haviland, Virginia 1911-1988 6
    Obituary 54
Havill, Juanita 1949- 155
    Earlier sketch in SATA *74*
Hawes, Judy 1913- 4
Hawes, Louise 1943- 180
    Earlier sketch in SATA *60*
Hawke, Rosanne 1953- 165
    Earlier sketch in SATA *124*
Hawke, Rosanne Joy
    See Hawke, Rosanne
Hawkes, Kevin 1959- 201
    Earlier sketches in SATA *78, 150*
Hawkes, Nigel 1943- 119
Hawkesworth, Eric 1921- 13
Hawking, Lucy 1969- 197
Hawkins, Arthur 1903-1985 19
Hawkins, Colin 1945- 162
    Earlier sketch in SATA *112*
Hawkins, Jacqui 162
    Earlier sketch in SATA *112*
Hawkins, Jimmy 1941- 188
Hawkins, Laura 1951- 74
Hawkins, (Helena Ann) Quail 1905-2002 6
    Obituary 141
Hawkinson, John (Samuel) 1912-1994 4
Hawkinson, Lucy (Ozone) 1924-1971 21
Hawks, Robert 1961- 85
Hawley, Mabel C. 67
    Earlier sketch in SATA *1*
Haworth, Danette 207
Haworth-Attard, Barbara 1953- 215
Hawthorne, Captain R. M.
    See Ellis, Edward S.
Hawthorne, Nathaniel 1804-1864
    See YABC *2*
    See also CLR *103*
Hay, Jeff T. 154
Hay, John 1915- 13
Hay, Samantha 213
Hay, Timothy
    See Brown, Margaret Wise
Hayashi, Leslie Ann 1954- 115
Hayashi, Nancy 1939- 186
    Earlier sketch in SATA *80*
Haycak, Cara 1961- 180
Haycock, Kate 1962- 77
Haycraft, Howard 1905-1991 6
    Obituary 70

Haycraft, Molly Costain 1911- 6
Hayden, Gwendolen Lampshire 1904- 35
Hayden, Robert
    See Hayden, Robert Earl
Hayden, Robert C(arter), Jr. 1937- 47
    Brief entry 28
Hayden, Robert E.
    See Hayden, Robert Earl
Hayden, Robert Earl 1913-1980 19
    Obituary 26
Hayden, Torey L. 1951- 163
    Earlier sketch in SATA *65*
Hayden, Torey Lynn
    See Hayden, Torey L.
Hayes, Carlton J(oseph) H(untley)
    1882-1964 11
Hayes, Daniel 1952- 109
    Earlier sketch in SATA *73*
Hayes, Geoffrey 1947- 207
    Earlier sketches in SATA *26, 91*
Hayes, Joe 1945- 131
    Earlier sketch in SATA *88*
Hayes, John F. 1904-1980 11
Hayes, Karel 1949- 207
Hayes, Rosemary 158
Hayes, Sarah 1945- 208
Hayes, Sheila 1937- 51
    Brief entry 50
Hayes, Will 7
Hayes, William D(imitt) 1913-1976 8
Haynes, Betsy 1937- 94
    Brief entry 37
    Earlier sketch in SATA *48*
    See also CLR *90*
Haynes, David 1955- 97
Haynes, Linda
    See Swinford, Betty (June Wells)
Haynes, Mary 1938- 65
Haynes, Max 1956- 72
Hays, Anna Jane 214
Hays, H(offmann) R(eynolds) 1904-1980 26
Hays, Thomas Anthony 1957- 84
Hays, Tony
    See Hays, Thomas Anthony
Hays, Wilma Pitchford 1909- 28
    Earlier sketch in SATA *1*
    See also CLR *59*
    See also SAAS *3*
Hayward, Linda 1943- 185
    Brief entry 39
    Earlier sketch in SATA *101*
Haywood, Carolyn 1898-1990 75
    Obituary 64
    Earlier sketches in SATA *1, 29*
    See also CLR *22*
Hazell, Rebecca (Eileen) 1947- 141
Hazen, Barbara Shook 1930- 178
    Earlier sketches in SATA *27, 90*
Hazen, Lynn E. 202
Head, Gay
    See Hauser, Margaret L(ouise)
Head, Tom 1978- 167
Headley, Elizabeth
    See Harrison, Elizabeth (Allen) Cavanna
Headley, Justina Chen 1968- 176
Headstrom, (Birger) Richard 1902-1985 8
Heady, Eleanor B(utler) 1917-1979 8
Heagy, William D. 1964- 76
Heal, Edith 1903-1995 7
Heal, Gillian 1934- 89
Heale, Jay (Jeremy Peter Wingfield) 1937- .. 84
Healey, Brooks
    See Albert, Burton
Healey, Larry 1927- 44
    Brief entry 42
Heap, Sue 1954- 187
    Earlier sketch in SATA *150*
Heaps, Willard A(llison) 1908-1987 26
Hearn, Diane Dawson 1952- 209
    Earlier sketch in SATA *79*

Hearn, Emily
    See Valleau, Emily
Hearn, Julie 1958- 212
    Earlier sketch in SATA *152*
Hearn, Lian
    See Rubinstein, Gillian
Hearn, Sneed
    See Gregg, Andrew K.
Hearne, Betsy 1942- 146
    Earlier sketches in SATA *38, 95*
Heath, Charles D(ickinson) 1941- 46
Heath, Veronica
    See Blackett, Veronica Heath
Heaven, Constance (Christina) 1911- 7
Hebert-Collins, Sheila 1948- 111
Hecht, George J(oseph) 1895-1980
    Obituary 22
Hecht, Henri Joseph 1922- 9
Hechtkopf, Henryk 1910- 17
Heck, Bessie (Mildred) Holland 1911-1995 . 26
Heck, Ed 1963- 173
Heckert, Connie K(aye Delp) 1948- 82
Hector, Julian 205
Hedderwick, Mairi 1939- 145
    Earlier sketches in SATA *30, 77*
Hedges, Sid(ney) G(eorge) 1897-1974 28
Hedrick, Irene Hope 1920- 175
Heelan, Jamee Riggio 1965- 146
Heerboth, Sharon
    See Leon, Sharon
Heffernan, John 1949- 168
    Earlier sketch in SATA *121*
Heffron, Dorris 1944- 68
Hefter, Richard 1942- 31
Hegamin, Tonya C. 1975- 209
Hegarty, Reginald Beaton 1906-1973 10
Hehenberger, Shelly 1968- 126
Heidbreder, Robert 1947- 196
    Earlier sketch in SATA *130*
Heidbreder, Robert K.
    See Heidbreder, Robert
Heide, Florence Parry 1919- 192
    Earlier sketches in SATA *32, 69, 118*
    See also CLR *60*
    See also SAAS *6*
Heiderstadt, Dorothy 1907-2001 6
Heidi Louise
    See Erdrich, Louise
Heidler, David S(tephen) 1955- 132
Heidler, Jeanne T. 1956- 132
Heilbroner, Joan Knapp 1922- 63
Heilbrun, Lois Hussey 1922(?)-1987
    Obituary 54
Heiligman, Deborah 1958- 193
    Earlier sketches in SATA *90, 144*
Heilman, Joan Rattner 50
Heimann, Rolf 1940- 164
    Earlier sketch in SATA *120*
Hein, Lucille Eleanor 1915-1994 20
Heine, Helme 1941- 135
    Earlier sketch in SATA *67*
    See also CLR *18*
Heinlein, Robert A. 1907-1988 69
    Obituary 56
    Earlier sketch in SATA *9*
    See also CLR *75*
Heinlein, Robert Anson
    See Heinlein, Robert A.
Heins, Ethel L(eah) 1918-1997 101
Heins, Paul 1909- 13
Heintze, Carl 1922- 26
Heinz, Bill
    See Heinz, W. C.
Heinz, Brian J. 1946- 181
    Earlier sketch in SATA *95*
Heinz, Brian James
    See Heinz, Brian J.
Heinz, W. C. 1915-2008 26
Heinz, Wilfred Charles
    See Heinz, W. C.

Author Index

Heinzen, Mildred
  See Masters, Mildred
Heisel, Sharon E(laine) 1941- *125*
  Earlier sketch in SATA *84*
Heitzmann, William Ray 1948- *73*
Heitzmann, Wm. Ray
  See Heitzmann, William Ray
Helakoski, Leslie *178*
Helberg, Shirley Adelaide Holden 1919- ... *138*
Helfer, Andrew *187*
Helfer, Ralph 1937- *177*
Helfman, Elizabeth S(eaver) 1911-2001 .... *3*
Helfman, Harry Carmozin 1910-1995 .... *3*
Helgerson, Joseph 1950- *181*
Hellard, Susan *182*
Hellberg, Hans-Eric 1927- *38*
Heller, Linda 1944- *46*
  Brief entry *40*
Heller, Mike
  See Hano, Arnold
Heller, Ruth M. 1924- *112*
  Earlier sketch in SATA *66*
Hellman, Hal
  See Hellman, Harold
Hellman, Harold 1927- *4*
Helman, Andrea (Jean) 1946- *160*
  Earlier sketch in SATA *107*
Helmer, Diana Star 1962- *86*
Helmer, Marilyn *160*
  Earlier sketch in SATA *112*
Helps, Racey 1913-1971 .... *2*
  Obituary *25*
Helquist, Brett *187*
  Earlier sketch in SATA *146*
Helweg, Hans H. 1917- *50*
  Brief entry *33*
Helyar, Jane Penelope Josephine 1933- *5*
  Autobiography Feature *138*
  See also SAAS *2*
Hemingway, Edward 1969(?)- *212*
Hemmant, Lynette 1938- *69*
Hemming, Roy G. 1928-1995 .... *11*
  Obituary *86*
Hemphill, Helen 1955- *179*
Hemphill, Kris (Harrison) 1963- *118*
Hemphill, Martha Locke 1904-1973 .... *37*
Hemphill, Stephanie *190*
Hemstock, Gillian 1956- *173*
Henba, Bobbie 1926- *87*
Henbest, Nigel 1951- *55*
  Brief entry *52*
Henderley, Brooks *1*
Henderson, Aileen Kilgore 1921- *178*
Henderson, Aileen Mary
  See Fox, Aileen
Henderson, Gordon 1950- *53*
Henderson, Kathy 1949- *155*
  Brief entry *53*
  Earlier sketches in SATA *55, 95*
Henderson, Lauren 1966- *201*
Henderson, LeGrand 1901-1965 .... *9*
Henderson, Nancy Wallace 1916- *22*
Henderson, Zenna (Chlarson) 1917-1983 .... *5*
Hendrickson, Walter Brookfield, Jr. 1936- *9*
Hendrix, John 1976- *208*
Hendry, Diana 1941- *213*
  Earlier sketches in SATA *68, 106*
Hendry, Frances Mary 1941- *171*
  Earlier sketch in SATA *110*
Hendry, Linda (Gail) 1961- *83*
Heneghan, James 1930- *160*
  Earlier sketches in SATA *53, 97*
Henkes, Kevin 1960- *207*
  Earlier sketches in SATA *43, 76, 108, 154*
  See also CLR *108*
Henn, Astrid *214*
Hennessy, Barbara G.
  See Hennessy, B.G.
Hennessy, Barbara Gulbrandsen
  See Hennessy, B.G.
Hennessy, B.G. 1951- *175*

Henney, Carolee Wells 1928- *102*
Henriod, Lorraine 1925- *26*
Henriquez, Emile F. 1937- *170*
  Earlier sketch in SATA *89*
Henry, April 1959- *174*
Henry, Ernest 1948- *107*
Henry, Joanne Landers 1927- *6*
Henry, Maeve 1960- *75*
Henry, Marguerite 1902-1997 .... *100*
  Obituary *99*
  See also CLR *4*
  See also SAAS *7*
Henry, Marie H. 1935- *65*
Henry, Marilyn 1939- *117*
Henry, Marion
  See del Rey, Lester
Henry, O. 1862-1910
  See YABC *2*
Henry, Oliver
  See Henry, O.
Henry, T. E.
  See Rowland-Entwistle, (Arthur) Theodore
  (Henry)
Henschel, Elizabeth Georgie *56*
Henson, Heather *206*
Henson, James Maury
  See Henson, Jim
Henson, Jim 1936-1990 .... *43*
  Obituary *65*
Henstra, Friso 1928- *73*
  Earlier sketch in SATA *8*
  See also SAAS *14*
Hentoff, Nat(han Irving) 1925- *133*
  Brief entry *27*
  Earlier sketches in SATA *42, 69*
  See also CLR *52*
Henty, G(eorge) A(lfred) 1832-1902 .... *64*
  See also CLR *76*
Heo, Yumi 1964- *206*
  Earlier sketches in SATA *94, 146*
Hepler, Heather *177*
Herald, Kathleen
  See Peyton, Kathleen Wendy
Herb, Angela M. 1970- *92*
Herbert, Cecil
  See Hamilton, Charles (Harold St. John)
Herbert, Don 1917-2007 .... *2*
  Obituary *184*
Herbert, Donald Jeffrey
  See Herbert, Don
Herbert, Frank 1920-1986 .... *37*
  Obituary *47*
  Earlier sketch in SATA *9*
Herbert, Frank Patrick
  See Herbert, Frank
Herbert, Helen (Jean) 1947- *57*
Herbert, Janis 1956- *139*
Herbert, Wally 1934-2007 .... *23*
Herbert, Walter William
  See Herbert, Wally
Herbst, Judith 1947- *74*
Herda, D.J. 1948- *80*
Herge
  See Remi, Georges
Heritage, Martin
  See Horler, Sydney
Herkimer, L(awrence) R(ussell) 1925(?)- *42*
Herlihy, Dirlie Anne 1935- *73*
Herlong, Madaline
  See Herlong, M.H.
Herlong, M.H. *211*
Herman, Charlotte 1937- *203*
  Earlier sketches in SATA *20, 99*
Hermanson, Dennis (Everett) 1947- *10*
Hermes, Jules 1962- *92*
Hermes, Patricia 1936- *191*
  Earlier sketches in SATA *31, 78, 141*
Hermes, Patricia Mary
  See Hermes, Patricia
Hernandez, Natalie Nelson 1929- *123*
Herndon, Ernest *91*

Herold, Ann Bixby 1937- *72*
Herrera, Juan Felipe 1948- *127*
Herrick, Steven 1958- *209*
  Earlier sketches in SATA *103, 156*
Herriman, George (Joseph) 1880-1944 .... *140*
Herriot, James 1916-1995 .... *135*
  Brief entry *44*
  Earlier sketch in SATA *86*
  See also CLR *80*
Herrmanns, Ralph 1933- *11*
Herrold, Tracey
  See Dils, Tracey E.
Herron, Carolivia 1947- *203*
Herron, Edward A(lbert) 1912- *4*
Herschler, Mildred Barger *130*
Hersey, John 1914-1993 .... *25*
  Obituary *76*
Hersey, John Richard
  See Hersey, John
Hershberger, Priscilla (Gorman) 1951- *81*
Hershenhorn, Esther 1945- *151*
Hershey, Kathleen M. 1934- *80*
Hershey, Mary *173*
Hersom, Kathleen 1911- *73*
Hertz, Grete Janus 1915- *23*
Herzig, Alison Cragin 1935- *87*
Herzog, Brad 1968- *131*
Heslewood, Juliet 1951- *82*
Hess, Lilo 1916- *4*
Hess, Paul 1961- *134*
Hesse, Hermann 1877-1962 .... *50*
Hesse, Karen 1952- *215*
  Autobiography Feature *113*
  Earlier sketches in SATA *74, 103, 158*
  See also CLR *141*
  See also SAAS *25*
Hest, Amy 1950- *193*
  Earlier sketches in SATA *55, 82, 129*
Heuer, Karsten 1968(?)- *202*
Heuer, Kenneth John 1927- *44*
Heuman, William 1912-1971 .... *21*
Heuston, Kimberley 1960- *167*
Heuston, Kimberley Burton
  See Heuston, Kimberley
Hewes, Agnes Danforth 1874-1963 .... *35*
Hewett, Anita 1918-1989 .... *13*
Hewett, Joan 1930- *140*
  Earlier sketch in SATA *81*
Hewett, Richard 1929- *81*
Hewitson, Jennifer 1961- *97*
Hewitt, Margaret 1961- *84*
Hewitt, Sally 1949- *127*
Hext, Harrington
  See Phillpotts, Eden
Hey, Nigel S(tewart) 1936- *20*
Heyduck-Huth, Hilde 1929- *8*
Heyer, Carol 1950- *130*
  Earlier sketch in SATA *74*
Heyer, Marilee 1942- *102*
  Earlier sketch in SATA *64*
Heyerdahl, Thor 1914-2002 .... *52*
  Earlier sketch in SATA *2*
Heyes, (Nancy) Eileen 1956- *150*
  Earlier sketch in SATA *80*
Heyliger, William 1884-1955
  See YABC *1*
Heyman, Ken(neth Louis) 1930- *114*
  Earlier sketch in SATA *34*
Heyward, (Edwin) DuBose 1885-1940 .... *21*
Heywood, Karen 1946- *48*
Hezlep, William (Earl) 1936- *88*
Hiaasen, Carl 1953- *208*
Hibbert, Arthur Raymond
  See Hibbert, Christopher
Hibbert, Christopher 1924-2008 .... *4*
  Obituary *201*
Hibbert, Eleanor Alice Burford 1906-1993 .... *2*
  Obituary *74*
Hickman, Estella (Lee) 1942- *111*
Hickman, Janet 1940- *127*
  Earlier sketch in SATA *12*

Hickman, Martha Whitmore 1925- 26
Hickman, Pamela 1958- 186
  Earlier sketch in SATA 128
Hickock, Will
  See Harrison, C(hester) William
Hickok, Lorena A. 1893-1968 20
Hickox, Rebecca (Ayres) 116
Hicks, Barbara Jean 1953- 165
Hicks, Betty 191
Hicks, Clifford B. 1920- 50
Hicks, Eleanor B.
  See Coerr, Eleanor (Beatrice)
Hicks, Harvey
  See Stratemeyer, Edward L.
Hicks, Peter 1952- 111
Hicyilmaz, Gaye 1947- 157
  Earlier sketch in SATA 77
Hieatt, Constance B(artlett) 1928- 4
Hiebert, Ray Eldon 1932- 13
Hierstein, Judith 212
Hierstein, Judy
  See Hierstein, Judith
Higdon, Hal 1931- 4
Higginbottom, David 1923- 87
  Earlier sketch in SATA 25
Higginbottom, J(effrey) Winslow 1945- 29
Higgins, Joanna 1945- 125
Higgins, Simon (Richard) 1958- 105
Higginsen, Vy 79
High, Linda Oatman 1958- 188
  Autobiography Feature 188
  Earlier sketches in SATA 94, 145
High, Philip E. 1914- 119
High, Philip Empson
  See High, Philip E.
Higham, David (Michael) 1949- 50
Higham, Jon Atlas
  See Higham, Jonathan Huw
Higham, Jonathan Huw 1960- 59
Highet, Helen
  See MacInnes, Helen (Clark)
Hightman, Jason 1971(?)- 189
Hightman, J.P.
  See Hightman, Jason
Hightower, Florence Cole 1916-1981 4
  Obituary 27
Highwater, Jamake (Mamake)
  1942(?)-2001 69
  Brief entry 30
  Earlier sketch in SATA 32
  See also CLR 17
Hilb, Nora 1953- 178
Hildebrandt, Greg 1939- 172
  Brief entry 33
  Earlier sketch in SATA 55
Hildebrandt, Tim 1939-2006 55
  Brief entry 33
Hildebrandt, Timothy
  See Hildebrandt, Tim
Hildebrandts, The
  See Hildebrandt, Greg
  and Hildebrandt, Tim
Hilder, Rowland 1905-1993 36
  Obituary 77
Hildick, E. W.
  See Hildick, Wallace
Hildick, Wallace 1925-2001 68
  Earlier sketch in SATA 2
  See also SAAS 6
Hilgartner, Beth 1957- 58
Hill, Alexis
  See Craig, Mary (Francis) Shura
  and Glick, Ruth (Burtnick)
Hill, Anthony R. 1942- 164
  Earlier sketch in SATA 91
Hill, Anthony Robert
  See Hill, Anthony R.
Hill, David 1942- 152
  Earlier sketch in SATA 103
Hill, Donna (Marie) 1921- 124
  Earlier sketch in SATA 24

Hill, Douglas 1935-2007 78
  Earlier sketch in SATA 39
Hill, Douglas Arthur
  See Hill, Douglas
Hill, Elizabeth Starr 1925- 143
  Earlier sketch in SATA 24
Hill, Eric 1927- 133
  Brief entry 53
  Earlier sketch in SATA 66
  See also CLR 13
Hill, Gordon
  See Eldin, Peter
Hill, Grace Brooks 67
  Earlier sketch in SATA 1
Hill, Grace Livingston 1865-1947
  See YABC 2
Hill, Helen M(orey) 1915- 27
Hill, John
  See Koontz, Dean
Hill, Johnson
  See Kunhardt, Edith
Hill, Judy I. R.
  See Roberts, Judy I.
Hill, Kathleen Louise 1917- 4
Hill, Kay
  See Hill, Kathleen Louise
Hill, Kirkpatrick 1938- 188
  Earlier sketches in SATA 72, 126
Hill, Laban
  See Hill, Laban Carrick
Hill, Laban Carrick 170
Hill, Lee Sullivan 1958- 96
Hill, Lorna 1902-1991 12
Hill, Margaret (Ohler) 1915- 36
Hill, Meg
  See Hill, Margaret (Ohler)
Hill, Meredith
  See Craig, Mary (Francis) Shura
Hill, Monica
  See Watson, Jane Werner
Hill, Pamela Smith 1954- 112
Hill, Ralph Nading 1917-1987 65
Hill, Robert W(hite) 1919-1982 12
  Obituary 31
Hill, Ruth A.
  See Viguers, Ruth Hill
Hill, Ruth Livingston
  See Munce, Ruth Hill
Hill, Stuart 1958- 186
Hill, Susan 1942- 183
Hill, Susan Elizabeth
  See Hill, Susan
Hill, Susanna Leonard 1965- 193
Hill, Thomas 1960- 82
Hillcourt, William 1900-1992 27
Hillenbrand, Will 1960- 210
  Earlier sketches in SATA 84, 147
Hiller, Ilo (Ann) 1938- 59
Hillerman, Anthony Grove
  See Hillerman, Tony
Hillerman, Tony 1925-2008 6
  Obituary 198
Hillert, Margaret 1920- 91
  Earlier sketch in SATA 8
Hilliard, Richard 183
Hillman, Ben 1957- 202
Hillman, Elizabeth 1942- 75
Hillman, John 1952- 120
Hillman, Martin
  See Hill, Douglas
Hillman, Priscilla 1940- 48
  Brief entry 39
Hillman, Shane 200
Hills, C.A.R. 1955- 39
Hills, Charles Albert Reis
  See Hills, C.A.R.
Hills, Tad 173
Hilton, Irene Pothus -1979 7
Hilton, James 1900-1954 34

Hilton, Margaret Lynette 1946- 105
  Earlier sketch in SATA 68
  See also CLR 25
  See also SAAS 21
Hilton, Nette
  See Hilton, Margaret Lynette
Hilton, Ralph 1907-1982 8
Hilton, Suzanne 1922- 4
Hilton-Bruce, Anne
  See Hilton, Margaret Lynette
Him, George 1937-1982
  Obituary 30
Himelblau, Linda -2005 179
Himelstein, Shmuel 1940- 83
Himler, Ann 1946- 8
Himler, Ronald 1937- 183
  Earlier sketches in SATA 6, 92, 137
Himler, Ronald Norbert
  See Himler, Ronald
Himmelman, John C(arl) 1959- 159
  Earlier sketches in SATA 47, 94
Hinckley, Helen
  See Jones, Helen Hinckley
Hind, Dolores (Ellen) 1931- 53
  Brief entry 49
Hindin, Nathan
  See Bloch, Robert (Albert)
Hindley, Judy 1940- 179
  Earlier sketch in SATA 120
Hinds, P(atricia) Mignon 98
Hine, Sesyle Joslin 1929- 2
Hines, Anna Grossnickle 1946- 209
  Brief entry 45
  Earlier sketches in SATA 51, 95, 141
  See also SAAS 16
Hines, Gary (Roger) 1944- 136
  Earlier sketch in SATA 74
Hinojosa, Maria (de Lourdes) 1961- 88
Hinton, Nigel 1941- 166
Hinton, S. E. 1950- 160
  Earlier sketches in SATA 19, 58, 115
  See also CLR 23
Hinton, Sam 1917-2009 43
Hinton, Susan Eloise
  See Hinton, S. E.
Hintz, Martin 1945- 128
  Brief entry 39
  Earlier sketch in SATA 47
Hintz, Stephen V. 1975- 129
Hippopotamus, Eugene H.
  See Kraus, (Herman) Robert
Hirano, Cathy 1957- 68
Hirao, Amiko 203
Hirsch, Karen 1941- 61
Hirsch, Odo 157
  Earlier sketch in SATA 111
Hirsch, Phil 1926- 35
Hirsch, S. Carl 1913-1990 2
  See also SAAS 7
Hirschfelder, Arlene B. 1943- 138
  Earlier sketch in SATA 80
Hirschi, Ron 1948- 192
  Earlier sketches in SATA 56, 95
Hirschmann, Linda (Ann) 1941- 40
Hirsh, Marilyn 1944-1988 7
  Obituary 58
Hirshberg, Al(bert Simon) 1909-1973 38
Hiscock, Bruce 1940- 204
  Earlier sketches in SATA 57, 137
Hiser, Constance 1950- 71
Hiser, Iona Seibert -1998 4
Hislop, Julia Rose Catherine 1962- 74
Hissey, Jane 1952- 130
  Autobiography Feature 130
  Earlier sketches in SATA 58, 103
Hissey, Jane Elizabeth
  See Hissey, Jane
Hitchcock, Alfred (Joseph) 1899-1980 27
  Obituary 24
Hite, Sid 1954- 175
  Earlier sketches in SATA 75, 136

Hitte, Kathryn 1919- *16*
Hitz, Demi
  See Demi
Hitzeroth, Deborah L. 1961- *78*
Hnizdovsky, Jacques 1915- *32*
Ho, Louise *185*
Ho, Minfong 1951- *151*
  Earlier sketches in SATA *15, 94*
  See also CLR *28*
Hoagland, Edward (Morley) 1932- *51*
Hoare, Robert J(ohn) 1921-1975 .... *38*
Hoban, Lillian 1925-1998 .... *69*
  Obituary *104*
  Earlier sketch in SATA *22*
  See also CLR *67*
Hoban, Russell 1925- *136*
  Earlier sketches in SATA *1, 40, 78*
  See also CLR *139*
Hoban, Russell Conwell
  See Hoban, Russell
Hoban, Tana 1917(?)-2006 .... *104*
  Obituary *173*
  Earlier sketches in SATA *22, 70*
  See also CLR *76*
  See also SAAS *12*
Hobart, Lois (Elaine) *7*
Hobbie, Holly 1944- *178*
  See also CLR *88*
Hobbie, Jocelyn *190*
Hobbie, Nathaniel *196*
Hobbs, Leigh 1953- *166*
Hobbs, Valerie 1941- *193*
  Autobiography Feature *145*
  Earlier sketches in SATA *93, 145*
  See also CLR *148*
Hobbs, Will 1947- *177*
  Autobiography Feature *127*
  Earlier sketches in SATA *72, 110*
  See also CLR *59*
Hobbs, William Carl
  See Hobbs, Will
Hoberman, Mary Ann 1930- *158*
  Earlier sketches in SATA *5, 72, 111*
  See also CLR *22*
  See also SAAS *18*
Hobson, Bruce 1950- *62*
Hobson, Burton (Harold) 1933- *28*
Hobson, Laura Z(ametkin) 1900-1986 .... *52*
Hobson, Sally 1967- *172*
  Earlier sketch in SATA *84*
Hoce, Charley E. *174*
Hochman, David *202*
Hochschild, Arlie Russell 1940- *11*
Hockaby, Stephen
  See Mitchell, Gladys (Maude Winifred)
Hockenberry, Hope
  See Newell, Hope Hockenberry
Hodge, Deborah 1954- *163*
  Earlier sketch in SATA *122*
Hodge, P. W.
  See Hodge, Paul W(illiam)
Hodge, Paul W(illiam) 1934- *12*
Hodgell, P(atricia) C(hristine) 1951- *42*
Hodges, C. Walter 1909-2004 .... *2*
  Obituary *158*
Hodges, Carl G. 1902-1964 .... *10*
Hodges, Cyril Walter
  See Hodges, C. Walter
Hodges, Elizabeth Jamison *1*
Hodges, Margaret 1911-2005 .... *167*
  Obituary *172*
  Earlier sketches in SATA *1, 33, 75, 117*
  See also SAAS *9*
Hodges, Margaret Moore
  See Hodges, Margaret
Hodgetts, Blake Christopher 1967- *43*
Hodgkins, Fran 1964- *199*
Hodgkinson, Leigh 1975- *202*
Hodgman, Ann 1956- *198*
Hodgson, Harriet (W.) 1935- *84*
Hoehne, Marcia 1951- *89*

Hoellwarth, Cathryn Clinton
  See Clinton, Cathryn
Hoestlandt, Jo 1948- *94*
Hoestlandt, Jocelyne
  See Hoestlandt, Jo
Hoexter, Corinne K. 1927- *6*
Hoeye, Michael 1947- *136*
Hoff, Carol 1900-1979 .... *11*
Hoff, Mary (King) 1956- *157*
  Earlier sketch in SATA *74*
Hoff, Syd(ney) 1912-2004 .... *138*
  Obituary *154*
  Earlier sketches in SATA *9, 72*
  See also CLR *83*
  See also SAAS *4*
Hoffman, Edwin D. *49*
Hoffman, Elizabeth P(arkinson) 1921-2003
  Obituary *153*
Hoffman, Mary 1945- *211*
  Earlier sketches in SATA *59, 97, 144*
  See also SAAS *24*
Hoffman, Mat 1972- *150*
Hoffman, Nina Kiriki 1955- *160*
Hoffman, Phyllis M(iriam) 1944- *4*
Hoffman, Rosekrans 1926- *15*
Hoffmann, E(rnst) T(heodor) A(madeus)
  1776-1822 .... *27*
  See also CLR *133*
Hoffmann, Felix 1911-1975 .... *9*
Hoffmann, Heinrich 1809-1894
  See CLR *122*
Hoffmann, Margaret Jones 1910- *48*
Hoffmann, Peggy
  See Hoffmann, Margaret Jones
Hofher, Catherine Baxley 1954- *130*
Hofher, Cathy
  See Hofher, Catherine Baxley
Hofmeyr, Dianne (Louise) *138*
Hofsepian, Sylvia A. 1932- *74*
Hofsinde, Robert 1902-1973 .... *21*
Hogan, Bernice Harris 1929- *12*
Hogan, Inez 1895-1973 .... *2*
Hogan, James P(atrick) 1941- *81*
Hogan, Jamie *192*
Hogan, Linda 1947- *132*
Hogan, Mary 1957- *210*
Hogarth, Burne 1911-1996 .... *89*
  Earlier sketch in SATA *63*
Hogarth, Grace (Weston Allen) 1905-1995 .. *91*
Hogarth, Jr.
  See Kent, Rockwell
Hogarth, (Arthur) Paul 1917-2001 .... *41*
Hogg, Garry 1902-1976 .... *2*
Hogg, Gary 1957- *172*
  Earlier sketch in SATA *105*
Hogner, Dorothy Childs *4*
Hogner, Nils 1893-1970 .... *25*
Hogrogian, Nonny 1932- *74*
  Autobiography Feature *127*
  Earlier sketch in SATA *7*
  See also CLR *95*
  See also SAAS *1*
Hoh, Diane 1937- *102*
  Brief entry *48*
  Earlier sketch in SATA *52*
Hoke, Helen
  See Watts, Helen L. Hoke
Hoke, Helen L.
  See Watts, Helen L. Hoke
Hoke, John (Lindsay) 1925- *7*
Hokenson, Terry 1948- *193*
Hol, Coby 1943- *126*
Holabird, Katharine 1948- *213*
  Earlier sketches in SATA *62, 135*
Holaday, Bobbie 1922- *153*
Holbeach, Henry
  See Rands, William Brighty
Holberg, Ruth L(angland) 1889-1984 .... *1*
Holbrook, Kathy 1963- *107*
Holbrook, Peter
  See Glick, Carl (Cannon)

Holbrook, Sabra
  See Erickson, Sabra Rollins
Holbrook, Sara *131*
Holbrook, Stewart Hall 1893-1964 .... *2*
Holcomb, Jerry (Leona) Kimble 1927- *113*
Holcomb, Nan
  See McPhee, Norma H.
Holden, Elizabeth Rhoda
  See Lawrence, Louise
Holding, James (Clark Carlisle, Jr.)
  1907-1997 .... *3*
Hole, Stian 1969- *204*
Holeman, Linda 1949- *136*
  Autobiography Feature *136*
  Earlier sketch in SATA *102*
Holinger, William (Jacques) 1944- *90*
Holisher, Desider 1901-1972 .... *6*
Holl, Adelaide Hinkle 1910- *8*
Holl, Kristi D(iane) 1951- *51*
Holland, Gay W. 1941- *128*
Holland, Isabelle (Christian) 1920-2002 .... *70*
  Autobiography Feature *103*
  Obituary *132*
  Earlier sketch in SATA *8*
  See also CLR *57*
Holland, Janice 1913-1962 .... *18*
Holland, John L(ewis) 1919- *20*
Holland, Joyce
  See Morice, Dave
Holland, Julia 1954- *106*
Holland, Lynda (H.) 1959- *77*
Holland, Lys
  See Gater, Dilys
Holland, Marion 1908-1989 .... *6*
  Obituary *61*
Hollander, John 1929- *13*
Hollander, Nicole 1940(?)- *101*
Hollander, Paul
  See Silverberg, Robert
Hollander, Phyllis 1928- *39*
Hollander, Zander 1923- *63*
Holldobler, Turid 1939- *26*
Holliday, Joe
  See Holliday, Joseph
Holliday, Joseph 1910- *11*
Holling, Holling C(lancy) 1900-1973 .... *15*
  Obituary *26*
  See also CLR *50*
Hollingsworth, Alvin C(arl) 1930- *39*
Hollingsworth, Mary 1947- *166*
  Earlier sketch in SATA *91*
Holloway, Teresa (Bragunier) 1906- *26*
Hollyer, Belinda *204*
Holm, (Else) Anne (Lise) 1922-1998 .... *1*
  See also CLR *75*
  See also SAAS *7*
Holm, Jennifer L. 1968(?)- *183*
  Earlier sketches in SATA *120, 163*
Holm, Matthew 1974- *174*
Holm, Sharon Lane 1955- *114*
  Earlier sketch in SATA *78*
Holman, Felice 1919- *82*
  Earlier sketch in SATA *7*
  See also SAAS *17*
Holm and Hamel
  See Holm, Jennifer L.
Holmberg, Bo R. 1945- *203*
Holme, Bryan 1913-1990 .... *26*
  Obituary *66*
Holmes, Barbara Ware 1945- *127*
  Earlier sketch in SATA *65*
Holmes, Elizabeth 1957- *191*
Holmes, Elizabeth Ann
  See Holmes, Elizabeth
Holmes, John
  See Souster, (Holmes) Raymond
Holmes, Marjorie (Rose) 1910-2002 .... *43*
Holmes, Martha 1961- *72*
Holmes, Mary Tavener 1954- *199*
Holmes, Mary Z(astrow) 1943- *80*
Holmes, Oliver Wendell 1809-1894 .... *34*

Author Index

Holmes, Peggy 1898- 60
Holmes, Raymond
  See Souster, (Holmes) Raymond
Holmes, Rick
  See Hardwick, Richard Holmes, Jr.
Holmes, Sara Lewis 186
Holmgren, Helen Jean 1930- 45
Holmgren, Sister George Ellen
  See Holmgren, Helen Jean
Holmgren, Virginia C(unningham) 1909- 26
Holmquist, Eve 1921- 11
Holt, Kimberly Willis 1960- 179
  Earlier sketch in SATA *122*
Holt, Margaret 1937- 4
Holt, Margaret Van Vechten (Saunders)
  1899-1963 32
Holt, Michael (Paul) 1929- 13
Holt, Rackham
  See Holt, Margaret Van Vechten (Saunders)
Holt, Rochelle L.
  See DuBois, Rochelle Holt
Holt, Stephen
  See Thompson, Harlan
Holt, Victoria
  See Hibbert, Eleanor Alice Burford
Holtei, Christa 1953- 214
Holton, Leonard
  See Wibberley, Leonard
Holtz, Thomas R., Jr. 1965- 203
Holtze, Sally Holmes 1952- 64
Holtzman, Jerome 1926-2008 57
  Obituary 194
Holub, Joan 1956- 149
  Earlier sketch in SATA *99*
Holub, Josef 1926- 175
Holubitsky, Katherine 1955- 165
  Earlier sketch in SATA *121*
Holyer, Erna Maria 1925- 22
Holyer, Ernie
  See Holyer, Erna Maria
Holz, Loretta (Marie) 1943- 17
Homel, David 1952- 97
Homze, Alma C. 1932- 17
Honey, Elizabeth 1947- 137
  Autobiography Feature 137
  Earlier sketch in SATA *112*
Honeycutt, Natalie 1945- 97
Hong, Lily Toy 1958- 76
Hong, Maxine Ting Ting
  See Kingston, Maxine Hong
Honig, Donald 1931- 18
Honness, Elizabeth H. 1904- 2
Hoobler, Dorothy 1941- 161
  Earlier sketches in SATA *28, 109*
Hoobler, Thomas 161
  Earlier sketches in SATA *28, 109*
Hood, Joseph F. 1925- 4
Hood, Robert E. 1926- 21
Hood, Sarah
  See Killough, (Karen) Lee
Hook, Brendan 1963- 105
Hook, Frances 1912-1983 27
Hook, Geoffrey R(aynor) 1928- 103
Hook, Jeff
  See Hook, Geoffrey R(aynor)
Hook, Martha 1936- 27
Hooker, Richard
  See Heinz, W. C.
Hooker, Ruth 1920-1998 21
hooks, bell 1952(?)- 170
  Earlier sketch in SATA *115*
Hooks, William H(arris) 1921- 94
  Earlier sketch in SATA *16*
Hoon, Patricia Easterly 1954- 90
Hooper, Byrd
  See St. Clair, Byrd Hooper
Hooper, Mary 1948- 205
  Earlier sketch in SATA *160*
Hooper, Maureen Brett 1927- 76
Hooper, Meredith 1939- 159
  Earlier sketches in SATA *28, 101*

Hooper, Meredith Jean
  See Hooper, Meredith
Hooper, Patricia 1941- 95
Hoopes, Lyn Littlefield 1953- 49
  Brief entry 44
Hoopes, Ned E(dward) 1932- 21
Hoopes, Roy 1922-2009 11
Hoose, Phillip 1947- 215
  Earlier sketch in SATA *137*
Hoover, H(elen) M(ary) 1935- 132
  Brief entry 33
  Earlier sketches in SATA *44, 83*
  See also SAAS *8*
Hoover, Helen (Drusilla Blackburn)
  1910-1984 12
  Obituary 39
Hope, Christopher 1944- 62
Hope, Christopher David Tully
  See Hope, Christopher
Hope, Laura Lee
  See Goulart, Ron
  and Stanley, George Edward
Hope Simpson, Jacynth 1930- 12
Hopf, Alice (Martha) L(ightner) 1904-1988 ... 5
  Obituary 55
Hopkins, A. T.
  See Turngren, Annette
Hopkins, C. M.
  See Hopkins, Cathy
Hopkins, Cathy 1953- 165
Hopkins, Cathy M.
  See Hopkins, Cathy
Hopkins, Clark 1895-1976
  Obituary 34
Hopkins, Ellen 1955- 128
  See Hopkins, Ellen L.
Hopkins, Ellen L.
  See Hopkins, Ellen
Hopkins, Jackie
  See Hopkins, Jackie Mims
Hopkins, Jackie Mims 1952- 178
  Earlier sketch in SATA *92*
Hopkins, Joseph G(erard) E(dward) 1909- ... 11
Hopkins, (Hector) Kenneth 1914-1988
  Obituary 58
Hopkins, Lee Bennett 1938- 215
  Earlier sketches in SATA *3, 68, 125, 168*
  See also CLR *44*
  See also SAAS *4*
Hopkins, Lyman
  See Folsom, Franklin (Brewster)
Hopkins, Marjorie 1911-1999 9
Hopkins, Mary R(ice) 1956- 97
Hopkinson, Amanda 1948- 84
Hopkinson, Deborah 1952- 180
  Autobiography Feature 180
  Earlier sketches in SATA *76, 108, 159*
  See also CLR *118*
Hopman, Philip 1961- 177
Hoppe, Joanne 1932- 42
Hoppe, Matthias 1952- 76
Hoppe, Paul 209
Hopper, Nancy J. 1937- 38
  Brief entry 35
Hopping, Lorraine Jean
  See Egan, Lorraine Hopping
Horacek, Judy 1961- 211
Horaek, Petr 214
  Earlier sketch in SATA *163*
Horenstein, Henry 1947- 108
Horgan, Paul (George Vincent O'Shaughnessy)
  1903-1995 13
  Obituary 84
Horlak, E.E.
  See Tepper, Sheri S.
Horler, Sydney 1888-1954 102
Horn, Sandra Ann 1944- 154
Hornblow, Arthur, Jr. 1893-1976 15
Hornblow, Leonora 1920-2005 18
  Obituary 171

Hornblow, Leonora Schinasi
  See Hornblow, Leonora
Horne, Constance 1927- 149
Horne, Richard 1960-2007 169
  Obituary 180
  Earlier sketch in SATA *111*
Horne, Richard Henry Hengist
  1802(?)-1884 29
Horner, Althea (Jane) 1926- 36
Horner, Dave 1934- 12
Horner, Jack 1946- 106
Horner, John R.
  See Horner, Jack
Horner, John Robert
  See Horner, Jack
Hornik, Laurie Miller 159
Horniman, Joanne 1951- 167
  Earlier sketch in SATA *98*
Hornos, Axel 1907-1994 20
Hornstein, Reuben Aaron 1912- 64
Horowitz, Anthony 1955- 195
  Earlier sketch in SATA *137*
Horowitz, Dave 1970- 204
  Earlier sketch in SATA *172*
Horowitz, Ruth 1957- 136
Horrocks, Anita 1958- 169
Horse, Harry
  See Horne, Richard
Horsfield, Alan 1939- 153
Hort, Lenny 179
Horton, James O. 1943- 173
Horton, James Oliver
  See Horton, James O.
Horton, Madelyn (Stacey) 1962- 77
Horvath, Betty 1927- 4
Horvath, David 1972(?)- 192
Horvath, Polly 1957- 194
  Earlier sketches in SATA *85, 140*
  See also CLR *90*
Horwich, Frances R(appaport) 1908-2001 11
  Obituary 130
Horwitz, Elinor Lander 45
  Brief entry 33
Horwood, William 1944- 85
Hosford, Dorothy (Grant) 1900-1952 22
Hosford, Jessie 1892-1990 5
Hoshi, Shin'ichi 1926- 101
Hoshino, Felicia 1968- 189
Hoskyns-Abrahall, Clare (Constance
  Drury) 13
Hosler, Danamarie 1978- 184
Hossack, Sylvia 1939- 83
Hossack, Sylvie Adams
  See Hossack, Sylvia
Hosseini, Khaled 1965- 156
Hossell, Karen Price
  See Price, Karen
Hosta, Dar 192
Hostetler, Marian 1932- 91
Houck, Carter 1924- 22
Hough, Charlotte 1924-2008 9
  Obituary 202
Hough, Helen Charlotte
  See Hough, Charlotte
Hough, Judy Taylor 1932- 63
  Brief entry 51
  Earlier sketch in SATA *56*
Hough, Richard (Alexander) 1922-1999 17
Houghton, Eric 1930- 7
Houk, Randy 1944- 97
Houlehen, Robert J. 1918- 18
Houlton, Peggy Mann 1925(?)-1990 6
Household, Geoffrey (Edward West)
  1900-1988 14
  Obituary 59
Housman, Laurence 1865-1959 25
Houston, Dick 1943- 74
Houston, Gloria 138
  Autobiography Feature 138
  Earlier sketch in SATA *81*

Houston, James A(rchibald) 1921-2005 74
   Obituary 163
   Earlier sketch in SATA 13
   See also CLR 3
   See also SAAS 17
Houston, James D. 1933-2009 78
   Obituary 203
Houston, James Dudley
   See Houston, James D.
Houston, James Dudley
   See Houston, James D.
Houston, Jeanne Toyo Wakatsuki
   See Houston, Jeanne Wakatsuki
Houston, Jeanne Wakatsuki 1934- 168
   Autobiography Feature 168
   Earlier sketch in SATA 78
Houston, Juanita C. 1921- 129
Houton, Kathleen
   See Kilgore, Kathleen
Houts, Amy F. 164
Hovey, Kate 158
Howard, Alan 1922- 45
Howard, Alyssa
   See Buckholtz, Eileen (Garber)
   and Glick, Ruth (Burtnick)
   and Titchener, Louise
Howard, Arthur 1948- 212
   Earlier sketch in SATA 165
Howard, Arthur Charles
   See Howard, Arthur
Howard, Elizabeth Fitzgerald 1927- 119
   Earlier sketch in SATA 74
Howard, Ellen 1943- 184
   Earlier sketches in SATA 67, 99
Howard, Jane R(uble) 1924- 87
Howard, Norman Barry 1949- 90
Howard, P. M.
   See Howard, Pauline Rodriguez
Howard, Paul 1967- 190
   Earlier sketch in SATA 118
Howard, Pauline Rodriguez 1951- 124
Howard, Prosper
   See Hamilton, Charles (Harold St. John)
Howard, Robert West 1908-1988 5
Howard, Todd 1964- 135
Howard, Tristan
   See Currie, Stephen
Howard, Vernon (Linwood) 1918-1992 40
   Obituary 73
Howard, Warren F.
   See Pohl, Frederik
Howarth, Daniel 188
Howarth, David (Armine) 1912-1991 6
   Obituary 68
Howarth, Lesley 1952- 94
Howe, Deborah 1946-1978 29
Howe, James 1946- 161
   Earlier sketches in SATA 29, 71, 111
   See also CLR 9
Howe, John F. 1957- 79
Howe, Norma 1930- 126
Howe, Peter 1942- 214
Howell, Pat 1947- 15
Howell, S.
   See Styles, (Frank) Showell
Howell, Simmone 1971- 214
Howell, Virginia
   See Ellison, Virginia H(owell)
Howes, Barbara 1914-1996 5
Howie, Betsy 1962- 215
Howie, Diana 1945- 122
Howie, Diana Melson
   See Howie, Diana
Howker, Janni 1957- 72
   Brief entry 46
   See also CLR 14
   See also SAAS 13
Howland, Ethan 1963- 131
Hoy, Linda 1946- 65
Hoy, Nina
   See Roth, Arthur J(oseph)

Hoyle, Geoffrey 1942- 18
Hoyt, Ard 190
Hoyt, Edwin P(almer), Jr. 1923- 28
Hoyt, Erich 1950- 140
   Earlier sketch in SATA 65
Hoyt, Olga
   See Gruhzit-Hoyt, Olga (Margaret)
Hrdlitschka, Shelley 1956- 167
   Earlier sketch in SATA 111
Hrdlitschka, Shelley Joanne
   See Hrdlitschka, Shelley
Htin Aung, U.
   See Aung, (Maung) Htin
Hu, Ying-Hwa 173
Huang, Benrei 1959- 86
Hubalek, Linda K. 1954- 111
Hubbard, Crystal 209
Hubbard, Margaret Ann
   See Priley, Margaret (Ann) Hubbard
Hubbard, Michelle Calabro 1953- 122
Hubbard, Patricia 1945- 124
Hubbard, Woodleigh Marx 160
   Earlier sketch in SATA 98
Hubbell, Patricia 1928- 186
   Earlier sketches in SATA 8, 132
Hubery, Julia 195
Hubley, Faith Elliot 1924-2001 48
   Obituary 133
Hubley, John 1914-1977 48
   Obituary 24
Huck, Charlotte S. 1922- 136
   Earlier sketch in SATA 82
Hudak, Michal 1956- 143
Hudson, Cheryl Willis 1948- 160
   Earlier sketch in SATA 81
Hudson, Jan 1954-1990 77
   See also CLR 40
Hudson, Jeffery
   See Crichton, Michael
Hudson, Jeffrey
   See Crichton, Michael
Hudson, (Margaret) Kirsty 1947- 32
Hudson, Margaret
   See Shuter, Jane (Margaret)
Hudson, W(illiam) H(enry) 1841-1922 35
Hudson, Wade 1946- 162
   Earlier sketch in SATA 74
Huelsmann, Eva 1928- 16
Huerlimann, Bettina 1909-1983 39
   Obituary 34
Huerlimann, Ruth 1939- 32
   Brief entry 31
Huff, Barbara A. 1929- 67
Huff, Tanya 1957- 171
   Earlier sketch in SATA 85
Huff, Tanya Sue
   See Huff, Tanya
Huff, T.S.
   See Huff, Tanya
Huff, Vivian 1948- 59
Huffaker, Sandy 1943- 10
Huffman, Tom 24
Huggins, Nathan Irvin 1927-1989 63
Huggins, Peter 1951- 178
Hughes, Carol 1955- 108
Hughes, Dean 1943- 139
   Earlier sketches in SATA 33, 77
   See also CLR 76
Hughes, Eden
   See Griffin, W.E.B.
Hughes, Edward James
   See Hughes, Ted
Hughes, James Langston
   See Hughes, Langston
Hughes, Langston 1902-1967 33
   Earlier sketch in SATA 4
   See also CLR 17
Hughes, Libby 71
Hughes, Matilda
   See MacLeod, Charlotte (Matilda)

Hughes, Monica 1925-2003 162
   Earlier sketches in SATA 15, 70, 119
   See also CLR 60
   See also SAAS 11
Hughes, Monica Ince
   See Hughes, Monica
Hughes, Pat 197
Hughes, Richard (Arthur Warren)
   1900-1976 8
   Obituary 25
Hughes, Sara
   See Saunders, Susan
Hughes, Shirley 1927- 159
   Earlier sketches in SATA 16, 70, 110
   See also CLR 15
Hughes, Ted 1930-1998 49
   Brief entry 27
   Obituary 107
   See also CLR 131
Hughes, Thomas 1822-1896 31
Hughes, Virginia
   See Campbell, Hope
Hughes, Walter (Llewellyn) 1910-1993 26
Hughey, Roberta 1942- 61
Hugo, Pierre Brackers de
   See Brackers de Hugo, Pierre
Hugo, Victor 1802-1885 47
Hugo, Victor Marie
   See Hugo, Victor
Huline-Dickens, Frank William 1931- 34
Huling, Jan 172
Huliska-Beith, Laura 175
Hull, Eleanor (Means) 1913- 21
Hull, Eric Traviss
   See Harnan, Terry
Hull, H. Braxton
   See Jacobs, Helen Hull
Hull, Jesse Redding
   See Hull, Jessie Redding
Hull, Jessie Redding 1932- 51
Hull, Katharine 1921-1977 23
Hull, Lise (E.) 1954- 148
Hull, Maureen 1949- 142
Hulme, Joy N. 1922- 161
   Earlier sketches in SATA 74, 112
Hults, Dorothy Niebrugge 1898-2000 6
Humble, Richard 1945- 60
Hume, Lachie 189
Hume, Lotta Carswell 7
Hume, Ruth Fox 1922-1980 26
   Obituary 22
Hume, Stephen Eaton 1947- 136
Hummel, Berta 1909-1946 43
Hummel, Sister Maria Innocentia
   See Hummel, Berta
Hummon, Marcus 1960- 213
Humphrey, Carol Sue 1956- 167
Humphrey, Henry (III) 1930- 16
Humphrey, Kate
   See Forsyth, Kate
Humphrey, Sandra McLeod 1936- 95
Humphreys, Martha 1943- 71
Humphreys, Susan L.
   See Lowell, Susan
Hundal, Nancy 1957- 128
Huneck, Stephen 1949- 183
   Earlier sketch in SATA 129
Hungerford, Hesba Fay
   See Brinsmead, H(esba) F(ay)
Hungerford, Pixie
   See Brinsmead, H(esba) F(ay)
Hunkin, Timothy Mark Trelawney 1950- 53
Hunt, Angela Elwell 1957- 159
   Earlier sketch in SATA 75
Hunt, Bernice 1920- 4
Hunt, Charlotte Dumaresq
   See Demi
Hunt, Francesca
   See Holland, Isabelle (Christian)

Hunt, Irene 1907-2001 .... *91*
    Earlier sketch in SATA *2*
    See also CLR *1*
Hunt, Janie Louise 1963- *102*
Hunt, Jonathan 1966- *84*
Hunt, Joyce 1927- *31*
Hunt, Linda 1940- *39*
Hunt, Lisa B(ehnke) 1967- *84*
Hunt, Mabel Leigh 1892-1971 .... *1*
    Obituary *26*
Hunt, Morton M(agill) 1920- *22*
Hunt, Nigel
    See Greenbank, Anthony Hunt
Hunt, Peter (Leonard) 1945- *76*
Hunter, Anne B. 1966- *118*
Hunter, Bernice Thurman 1922-2002 .... *85*
    Brief entry *45*
Hunter, Bobbi Dooley 1945- *89*
Hunter, Captain Marcy
    See Ellis, Edward S.
Hunter, Chris
    See Fluke, Joanne
Hunter, Clingham M.D.
    See Adams, William Taylor
Hunter, Edith Fisher 1919- *31*
Hunter, Erin
    See Cary, Kate
Hunter, Evan 1926-2005 .... *25*
    Obituary *167*
Hunter, George E.
    See Ellis, Edward S.
Hunter, Hilda 1921- *7*
Hunter, Jana
    See Hunter, Jana Novotny
Hunter, Jana Novotny *190*
Hunter, Jim 1939- *65*
Hunter, Kristin
    See Lattany, Kristin Hunter
Hunter, Leigh
    See Etchison, Birdie L(ee)
Hunter, Lieutenant Ned
    See Ellis, Edward S.
Hunter, Mel 1927-2004 .... *39*
Hunter, Mollie 1922- *139*
    Autobiography Feature *139*
    Earlier sketches in SATA *2, 54, 106*
    See also CLR *25*
    See also SAAS *7*
Hunter, Ned
    See Ellis, Edward S.
Hunter, Norman (George Lorimer)
    1899-1995 .... *84*
    Earlier sketch in SATA *26*
Hunter, Ryan Ann
    See Greenwood, Pamela D.
    and Macalaster, Elizabeth G.
Hunter, Sara Hoagland 1954- *98*
Hunter Blair, Pauline
    See Clarke, Pauline
Huntington, Amy 1956- *180*
    Earlier sketch in SATA *138*
Huntington, Geoffrey *145*
Huntington, Harriet E(lizabeth) 1909- *1*
Huntsberry, William E(mery) 1916- *5*
Hurd, Clement (G.) 1908-1988 .... *64*
    Obituary *54*
    Earlier sketch in SATA *2*
    See also CLR *49*
Hurd, Edith Thacher 1910-1997 .... *64*
    Obituary *95*
    Earlier sketch in SATA *2*
    See also CLR *49*
    See also SAAS *13*
Hurd, (John) Thacher 1949- *94*
    Autobiography Feature *123*
    Brief entry *45*
    Earlier sketch in SATA *46*
Hurley, Jo
    See Dower, Laura
Hurley, Tonya *207*

Hurlimann, Bettina
    See Huerlimann, Bettina
Hurlimann, Ruth
    See Huerlimann, Ruth
Hurmence, Belinda 1921- *77*
    See also CLR *25*
    See also SAAS *20*
Hurst, Carol Otis 1933-2007 .... *185*
    Earlier sketch in SATA *130*
Hurt-Newton, Tania 1968- *84*
Hurwin, Davida Wills 1950- *180*
Hurwitz, Johanna 1937- *175*
    Earlier sketches in SATA *20, 71, 113*
    See also SAAS *18*
Hurwood, Bernhardt J. 1926-1987 .... *12*
    Obituary *50*
Husain, Shahrukh 1950- *108*
Huser, Glen 1943- *151*
Hutchens, Paul 1902-1977 .... *31*
Hutchins, Carleen M.
    See Hutchins, Carleen Maley
Hutchins, Carleen Maley 1911-2009 .... *9*
    Obituary *206*
Hutchins, Hazel J. 1952- *175*
    Brief entry *51*
    Earlier sketches in SATA *81, 135*
    See also SAAS *24*
Hutchins, Pat 1942- *178*
    Earlier sketches in SATA *15, 70, 111*
    See also CLR *20*
    See also SAAS *16*
Hutchins, Ross Elliott 1906- *4*
Hutchison, Linda 1942- *152*
Huthmacher, J. Joseph 1929- *5*
Hutto, Nelson (Allen) 1904-1985 .... *20*
Hutton, Kathryn 1915- *89*
Hutton, Sam
    See Jones, Allan Frewin
Hutton, Warwick 1939-1994 .... *20*
    Obituary *83*
    See also SAAS *17*
Huxley, Aldous 1894-1963 .... *63*
    See also CLR *151*
Huxley, Aldous Leonard
    See Huxley, Aldous
Huxley, Elspeth (Josceline Grant)
    1907-1997 .... *62*
    Obituary *95*
Hyde, Catherine R.
    See Hyde, Catherine Ryan
Hyde, Catherine Ryan 1955- *141*
Hyde, Dayton O(gden) *9*
Hyde, Hawk
    See Hyde, Dayton O(gden)
Hyde, Jeannette
    See Eyerly, Jeannette
Hyde, Margaret O. 1917- *139*
    Earlier sketches in SATA *1, 42, 76*
    See also CLR *23*
    See also SAAS *8*
Hyde, Margaret Oldroyd
    See Hyde, Margaret O.
Hyde, Shelley
    See Reed, Kit
Hyde, Wayne Frederick 1922- *7*
Hylander, Clarence J(ohn) 1897-1964 .... *7*
Hyman, Miles 1962- *210*
Hyman, Paula Chase
    See Chase, Paula
Hyman, Robin P(hilip) 1931- *12*
Hyman, Trina Schart 1939-2004 .... *95*
    Obituary *158*
    Earlier sketches in SATA *7, 46*
    See also CLR *50*
Hymes, Lucia M(anley) 1907-1998 .... *7*
Hyndman, Jane Andrews Lee 1912-1978 ..... *46*
    Obituary *23*
    Earlier sketch in SATA *1*
Hyndman, Robert Utley 1906-1973 .... *18*
Hynes, Pat *98*

I

Iannone, Jeanne
    See Balzano, Jeanne (Koppel)
Ibatoulline, Bagram 1965(?)- *174*
Ibbitson, John Perrie 1955- *102*
Ibbotson, Eva 1925- *156*
    Earlier sketches in SATA *13, 103*
Ibbotson, M. C(hristine) 1930- *5*
Icenoggle, Jodi 1967- *168*
Icenoggle, Jodi O.
    See Icenoggle, Jodi
Ichikawa, Satomi 1949- *208*
    Brief entry *36*
    Earlier sketches in SATA *47, 78, 146*
    See also CLR *62*
Iggulden, Hal 1972- *196*
Ignoffo, Matthew 1945- *92*
Igus, Toyomi 1953- *112*
    Earlier sketch in SATA *76*
Ihimaera, Witi (Tame) 1944- *148*
Ikeda, Daisaku 1928- *77*
Ilowite, Sheldon A. 1931- *27*
Ilsey, Dent
    See Chapman, John Stanton Higham
Ilsley, Dent
    See Chapman, John Stanton Higham
Ilsley, Velma (Elizabeth) 1918- *12*
Imai, Ayano 1980- *190*
Imai, Miko 1963- *90*
Imershein, Betsy 1953- *62*
Immel, Mary Blair 1930- *28*
Immell, Myra H. 1941- *92*
Impey, Rose 1947- *152*
    Earlier sketch in SATA *69*
Ingelow, Jean 1820-1897 .... *33*
Ingermanson, Randall 1958- *134*
Ingermanson, Randy
    See Ingermanson, Randall
Ingersoll, Norman 1928- *79*
Ingham, Colonel Frederic
    See Hale, Edward Everett
Ingman, Bruce 1963- *182*
    Earlier sketch in SATA *134*
Ingman, Nicholas 1948- *52*
Ingold, Jeanette *128*
Ingpen, Robert 1936- *166*
    Earlier sketch in SATA *109*
Ingpen, Robert Roger
    See Ingpen, Robert
Ingraham, Erick 1950- *145*
Ingraham, Leonard W(illiam) 1913-2003 .... *4*
Ingram, Scott 1948- *167*
    Earlier sketch in SATA *92*
Ingram, W. Scott
    See Ingram, Scott
Ingrams, Doreen 1906-1997 .... *97*
    Earlier sketch in SATA *20*
Ingrid, Charles
    See Salsitz, Rhondi Vilott
Ingves, Gunilla (Anna Maria Folkesdotter)
    1939- *101*
Inkpen, Mick 1952- *154*
    Earlier sketch in SATA *99*
Innes, (Ralph) Hammond
    See Hammond Innes, Ralph
Innes, Ralph Hammond
    See Hammond Innes, Ralph
Innocenti, Roberto 1940- *159*
    Earlier sketch in SATA *96*
    See also CLR *126*
Innocenti and Gallaz
    See Gallaz, Christophe
    and Innocenti, Roberto
Inns, Chris *212*
Inyart, Gene
    See Namovicz, Gene Inyart
Ionesco, Eugene 1909-1994 .... *7*
    Obituary *79*

Ipcar, Dahlov (Zorach) 1917- *147*
  Autobiography Feature *147*
  Earlier sketches in SATA *1, 49*
  See also SAAS *8*
Ireland, Karin *151*
  Earlier sketch in SATA *101*
Ironside, Jetske 1940- *60*
Irvin, Fred 1914- *15*
Irvine, Georgeanne 1955- *72*
Irvine, Joan 1951- *80*
Irving, Alexander
  See Hume, Ruth Fox
Irving, Robert
  See Adler, Irving
Irving, Washington 1783-1859
  See YABC *2*
  See also CLR *97*
Irwin, Ann(abelle Bowen) 1915-1998 .... *89*
  Brief entry *38*
  Obituary *106*
  Earlier sketch in SATA *44*
  See also CLR *40*
  See also SAAS *14*
Irwin, Constance (H.) Frick 1913-1995 .... *6*
Irwin, Hadley
  See Hadley, Lee
  and Irwin, Ann(abelle Bowen)
Irwin, Keith Gordon 1885-1964 .... *11*
Isaac, Joanne 1934- *21*
Isaacs, Anne 1949- *185*
  Earlier sketch in SATA *90*
Isaacs, Jacob
  See Kranzler, George G(ershon)
Isaacson, Philip M(arshal) 1924- *87*
Isadora, Rachel 1953(?)- *204*
  Brief entry *32*
  Earlier sketches in SATA *54, 79, 121, 165*
  See also CLR *7*
Isbell, Rebecca T(emple) 1942- *125*
Isham, Charlotte H(ickock) 1912- *21*
Ishida, Jui *176*
Ish-Kishor, Judith 1892-1972 .... *11*
Ish-Kishor, Sulamith 1896-1977 .... *17*
Ishmael, Woodi 1914-1995 .... *31*
  Obituary *109*
Isle, Sue 1963- *105*
Israel, Elaine 1945- *12*
Israel, Marion Louise 1882-1973
  Obituary *26*
Iterson, S(iny) R(ose) Van
  See Van Iterson, S(iny) R(ose)
Ivanko, John D. 1966- *111*
Ivanko, John Duane
  See Ivanko, John D.
Iversen, Jeremy 1980(?)- *174*
Iversen, Jeremy Watt
  See Iversen, Jeremy
Iverson, Carol (L.) 1941- *145*
Iverson, Diane 1950- *122*
Iverson, Eric G.
  See Turtledove, Harry
Ivery, Martha M. 1948- *124*
Ives, David 1951- *173*
Ives, Morgan
  See Bradley, Marion Zimmer
Ives, Penny 1956- *215*
Iwai, Melissa *183*
Iwamatsu, Jun Atsushi 1908-1994 .... *81*
  Earlier sketch in SATA *14*
  See also CLR *4*
Iwamura, Kazuo 1939- *213*
Iwasaki (Matsumoto), Chihiro 1918-1974
  See CLR *18*

J

Jabar, Cynthia *210*
Jablonski, Carla *184*
Jac, Lee
  See Morton, Lee Jack, Jr.
Jacka, Martin 1943- *72*
Jackson, Alison 1953- *160*
  Earlier sketches in SATA *73, 108*
Jackson, Anne 1896(?)-1984
  Obituary *37*
Jackson, Barry
  See Jackson, Barry E.
Jackson, Barry E. *200*
Jackson, C(aary) Paul 1902-1991 .... *6*
Jackson, Caary
  See Jackson, C(aary) Paul
Jackson, Charlotte E. (Cobden) 1903(?)-1989
  Obituary *62*
Jackson, Dave
  See Jackson, J. David
Jackson, Donna M. 1959- *206*
Jackson, Ellen 1943- *214*
  Earlier sketches in SATA *75, 115, 167*
  See Jackson B., Ellen
Jackson, Garnet Nelson 1944- *87*
Jackson, Geoffrey (Holt Seymour) 1915-1987
  Obituary *53*
Jackson, Gina
  See Fluke, Joanne
Jackson, Guida M. 1930- *71*
Jackson, J. David 1944- *91*
Jackson, Jacqueline 1928- *65*
Jackson, Jacqueline Dougan
  See Jackson, Jacqueline
Jackson, Jesse 1908-1983 .... *29*
  Obituary *48*
  Earlier sketch in SATA *2*
  See also CLR *28*
Jackson, Marjorie 1928- *127*
Jackson, Melanie 1956- *141*
Jackson, Mike 1946- *91*
Jackson, Neta J. 1944- *91*
Jackson, O. B.
  See Jackson, C(aary) Paul
Jackson, Rob 1961- *176*
Jackson, Robert B(lake) 1926- *8*
Jackson, Robert Bradley
  See Jackson, Rob
Jackson, Sally
  See Kellogg, Jean (Defrees)
Jackson, Shirley 1919-1965 .... *2*
Jackson, Woody 1948- *92*
Jackson B., Ellen *214*
  See Jackson, Ellen
Jackson Issa, Kai *205*
Jacob, Helen Pierce 1927- *21*
Jacobin
  See Bisson, Terry
Jacobs, Deborah Lynn *187*
Jacobs, Flora Gill 1918-2006 .... *5*
  Obituary *178*
Jacobs, Francine 1935- *150*
  Brief entry *42*
  Earlier sketch in SATA *43*
Jacobs, Frank 1929- *30*
Jacobs, Helen Hull 1908-1997 .... *12*
Jacobs, Joseph 1854-1916 .... *25*
Jacobs, Judy 1952- *69*
Jacobs, Laurie A. 1956- *89*
Jacobs, Leah
  See Gellis, Roberta
Jacobs, Leland Blair 1907-1992 .... *20*
  Obituary *71*
Jacobs, Linda
  See Altman, Linda Jacobs
Jacobs, Lou(is), Jr. 1921- *2*
Jacobs, Shannon K. 1947- *77*
Jacobs, Susan
  See Quinn, Susan

Jacobs, William Jay 1933- *89*
  Earlier sketch in SATA *28*
Jacobsen, Laura *177*
Jacobson, Daniel 1923- *12*
Jacobson, Jennifer
  See Jacobson, Jennifer Richard
Jacobson, Jennifer Richard 1958- *170*
Jacobson, Morris K(arl) 1906- *21*
Jacobson, Rick *170*
Jacopetti, Alexandra
  See Hart, Alexandra
Jacques, Brian 1939- *176*
  Earlier sketches in SATA *62, 95, 138*
  See also CLR *21*
Jacques, Robin 1920-1995 .... *32*
  Brief entry *30*
  Obituary *86*
  See also SAAS *5*
Jaekel, Susan M. 1948- *89*
Jaffe, Michele *179*
Jaffe, Michele Sharon
  See Jaffe, Michele
Jaffee, Al(lan) 1921- *66*
  Earlier sketch in SATA *37*
Jagendorf, Moritz (Adolf) 1888-1981 .... *2*
  Obituary *24*
Jahn, Joseph Michael
  See Jahn, Michael
Jahn, Michael 1943- *28*
Jahn, Mike
  See Jahn, Michael
Jahn-Clough, Lisa 1967- *193*
  Earlier sketches in SATA *88, 152*
Jahsmann, Allan Hart 1916- *28*
Jakes, John 1932- *62*
Jakes, John William
  See Jakes, John
James, Andrew
  See Kirkup, James
James, Ann 1952- *168*
  Earlier sketches in SATA *82, 117*
James, Betsy *183*
James, B.J.
  See James, Brian
James, Brian 1976- *212*
  Earlier sketch in SATA *140*
James, Bronte
  See Nash, Renea Denise
James, Captain Lew
  See Stratemeyer, Edward L.
James, Charlie 1961- *185*
James, Curtis E. *182*
James, Dynely
  See Mayne, William
James, Edwin
  See Gunn, James E.
James, Elizabeth 1942- *97*
  Earlier sketches in SATA *39, 45, 52*
James, Emily
  See Standiford, Natalie
James, Gordon C. 1973- *195*
James, Harry Clebourne 1896-1978 .... *11*
James, J. Alison 1962- *146*
  Earlier sketch in SATA *83*
James, Josephine
  See Sterne, Emma Gelders
James, Mary
  See Meaker, Marijane
James, Matt *201*
James, Philip
  See del Rey, Lester
  and Moorcock, Michael
James, Robin 1953- *50*
James, Robin Irene
  See James, Robin
James, Simon *202*
  See Kunen, James Simon
James, T. F.
  See Fleming, Thomas
James, Tegan
  See Odgers, Sally Farrell

James, Will(iam Roderick) 1892-1942 .... *19*
Jameson, W. C. 1942- *93*
Jamieson, Ian R.
  See Goulart, Ron
Jamiolkowski, Raymond M. 1953- *81*
Jane, Mary Childs 1909- *6*
Jane, Pamela *158*
Janeczko, Paul B(ryan) 1945- *155*
  Earlier sketches in SATA *53, 98*
  See also CLR *47*
  See also SAAS *18*
Janes, Edward C. 1908-1984 .... *25*
Janes, J(oseph) Robert 1935- *148*
  Brief entry *50*
  Earlier sketch in SATA *101*
Janeway, Elizabeth (Hall) 1913-2005 .... *19*
Janger, Kathleen N. 1940- *66*
Jango-Cohen, Judith 1955- *208*
Janice
  See Brustlein, Janice Tworkov
Janisch, Heinz 1960- *181*
Janosch
  See Eckert, Horst
Janover, Caroline (Davis) 1943- *141*
  Earlier sketch in SATA *89*
Janovitz, Marilyn *194*
Jansen, Jared
  See Cebulash, Mel
Janson, Dora Jane (Heineberg) 1916- *31*
Janson, H(orst) W(oldemar) 1913-1982 .... *9*
Jansson, Tove (Marika) 1914-2001 .... *41*
  Earlier sketch in SATA *3*
  See also CLR *125*
Janus, Grete
  See Hertz, Grete Janus
Jaques, Faith 1923-1997 .... *97*
  Earlier sketches in SATA *21, 69*
Jaquith, Priscilla 1908- *51*
Jaramillo, Mari-Luci 1928- *139*
Jarman, Julia 1946- *198*
  Earlier sketch in SATA *133*
Jarman, Rosemary Hawley 1935- *7*
Jarrell, Mary Von Schrader 1914- *35*
Jarrell, Randall 1914-1965 .... *7*
  See also CLR *111*
Jarrett, Clare 1952- *201*
Jarrett, Roxanne
  See Werner, Herma
Jarrow, Gail 1952- *185*
  Earlier sketch in SATA *84*
Jarvis, E.K.
  See Ellison, Harlan
  and Silverberg, Robert
Jarvis, Robin 1963- *181*
Jaskol, Julie 1958- *127*
Jasner, W. K.
  See Watson, Jane Werner
Jassem, Kate
  See Oppenheim, Joanne
Jauss, Anne Marie 1902(?)-1991 .... *10*
  Obituary *69*
Javernick, Ellen 1938- *89*
Javins, Marie 1966- *212*
Jay, Alison *196*
Jayne, Lieutenant R. H.
  See Ellis, Edward S.
Jaynes, Clare
  See Mayer, Jane Rothschild
Jeake, Samuel, Jr.
  See Aiken, Conrad
Jean-Bart, Leslie 1954- *121*
Jeapes, Ben 1965- *174*
Jecan, Gavriel 1962- *200*
Jefferds, Vincent H(arris) 1916- *59*
  Brief entry *49*
Jefferies, (John) Richard 1848-1887 .... *16*
Jeffers, Dawn *189*
Jeffers, Oliver 1977- *213*
  Earlier sketch in SATA *175*

Jeffers, Susan 1942- *202*
  Earlier sketches in SATA *17, 70, 129, 137*
  See also CLR *30*
Jefferson, Sarah
  See Farjeon, (Eve) Annabel
Jeffries, Roderic 1926- *4*
Jeffries, Roderic Graeme
  See Jeffries, Roderic
Jenkin-Pearce, Susie 1943- *80*
Jenkins, A. M. 1961- *174*
Jenkins, Amanda McRaney
  See Jenkins, A. M.
Jenkins, Debra Reid
  See Reid Jenkins, Debra
Jenkins, Emily 1967- *174*
  Earlier sketch in SATA *144*
Jenkins, Jean *98*
Jenkins, Jerry B. 1949- *149*
Jenkins, Jerry Bruce
  See Jenkins, Jerry B.
Jenkins, Leonard *189*
Jenkins, Marie M(agdalen) 1909- *7*
Jenkins, Patrick 1955- *72*
Jenkins, Steve 1952- *188*
  Earlier sketch in SATA *154*
Jenkins, William A(twell) 1922-1998 .... *9*
Jenkyns, Chris 1924- *51*
Jennewein, James *215*
Jennewein, Jim
  See Jennewein, James
Jennings, Christopher S. 1971(?)- *201*
Jennings, Coleman A(lonzo) 1933- *64*
Jennings, C.S.
  See Jennings, Christopher S.
Jennings, Dana Andrew 1957- *93*
Jennings, Elizabeth (Joan) 1926-2001 .... *66*
Jennings, Gary 1928-1999 .... *9*
  Obituary *117*
Jennings, Gary Gayne
  See Jennings, Gary
Jennings, Linda 1937- *211*
Jennings, Linda M.
  See Jennings, Linda
Jennings, Patrick 1962- *205*
  Earlier sketches in SATA *96, 160*
Jennings, Paul 1943- *165*
  Earlier sketch in SATA *88*
  See also CLR *40*
Jennings, Richard W. 1945- *185*
  Earlier sketch in SATA *136*
Jennings, Robert
  See Hamilton, Charles (Harold St. John)
Jennings, S. M.
  See Meyer, Jerome Sydney
Jennings, Sharon 1954- *95*
Jennings, Sharon Elizabeth
  See Jennings, Sharon
Jennison, C. S.
  See Starbird, Kaye
Jennison, Keith Warren 1911-1995 .... *14*
Jensen, Kathryn 1949- *81*
Jensen, Kristine Mary 1961- *78*
Jensen, Niels 1927- *25*
Jensen, Vickie (Dee) 1946- *81*
Jensen, Virginia Allen 1927- *8*
Jenson-Elliott, Cynthia L(ouise) 1962- *143*
Jeram, Anita 1965- *154*
  Earlier sketches in SATA *71, 102*
Jerman, Jerry 1949- *89*
Jernigan, E. Wesley 1940- *85*
Jernigan, Gisela (Evelyn) 1948- *85*
Jeschke, Susan 1942- *42*
  Brief entry *27*
Jessel, Camilla (Ruth) 1937- *143*
  Earlier sketch in SATA *29*
Jessell, Tim *177*
Jessey, Cornelia
  See Sussman, Cornelia Silver
Jewel
  See Kilcher, Jewel

Jewell, Nancy 1940- *109*
  Brief entry *41*
Jewett, Eleanore Myers 1890-1967 .... *5*
Jewett, Sarah Orne 1849-1909 .... *15*
Jewett, Theodora Sarah Orne
  See Jewett, Sarah Orne
Jezard, Alison 1919- *57*
  Brief entry *34*
Jiang, Cheng An 1943- *109*
Jiang, Ji-li 1954- *101*
Jiang, Zheng An
  See Jiang, Cheng An
Jiler, John 1946- *42*
  Brief entry *35*
Jimenez, Francisco 1943- *108*
Jinks, Catherine 1963- *207*
  Earlier sketches in SATA *94, 155*
Jobb, Jamie 1945- *29*
Jobling, Curtis *131*
Jocelyn, Ann Henning 1948- *92*
Jocelyn, Marthe 1956- *198*
  Earlier sketches in SATA *118, 163*
Joerns, Consuelo *44*
  Brief entry *33*
Joey D
  See Macaulay, Teresa (E.)
Johansen, Krista V.
  See Johansen, K.V.
Johansen, K.V 1968- *186*
Johansen, K.V. 1968- *186*
  Earlier sketch in SATA *129*
Johansson, Philip *163*
John, Antony 1972- *206*
John, Joyce *59*
Johns, Avery
  See Cousins, Margaret
Johns, Elizabeth 1943- *88*
Johns, Janetta
  See Quin-Harkin, Janet
Johns, Linda 1945- *173*
Johns, W(illiam) E(arle) 1893-1968 .... *55*
Johns, Captain W. E.
  See Johns, W(illiam) E(arle)
Johnson, A.
  See Johnson, Annabell
Johnson, A. E.
  See Johnson, Annabell
  and Johnson, Edgar (Raymond)
Johnson, Angela 1961- *188*
  Earlier sketches in SATA *69, 102, 150*
  See also CLR *33*
Johnson, Annabel
  See Johnson, Annabell
Johnson, Annabell 1921- *72*
  Earlier sketch in SATA *2*
Johnson, Art 1946- *123*
Johnson, B. F. 1920- *1*
Johnson, Benjamin F., of Boone
  See Riley, James Whitcomb
Johnson, Bettye 1858-1919
  See Rogers, Bettye
Johnson, Caryn
  See Goldberg, Whoopi
Johnson, Caryn E.
  See Goldberg, Whoopi
Johnson, Caryn Elaine
  See Goldberg, Whoopi
Johnson, Charles R. 1925- *11*
Johnson, Charlotte Buel
  See von Wodtke, Charlotte Buel Johnson
Johnson, Chuck
  See Johnson, Charles R.
Johnson, Crockett
  See Leisk, David (Johnson)
Johnson, D(ana) William 1945- *23*
Johnson, Daniel Shahid 1954- *73*
Johnson, David
  See Johnson, David A.
Johnson, David A. 1951- *191*
Johnson, D.B. 1944- *183*
  Earlier sketch in SATA *146*

Johnson, Dianne 1960- *130*
Johnson, Dinah
  See Johnson, Dianne
Johnson, Dolores 1949- *69*
Johnson, Donald B.
  See Johnson, D.B.
Johnson, Dorothy M(arie) 1905-1984 .... *6*
  Obituary *40*
Johnson, E(ugene) Harper *44*
Johnson, Edgar (Raymond) 1912-1990 .... *72*
  Earlier sketch in SATA *2*
Johnson, Eleanor Murdock 1892-1987
  Obituary *54*
Johnson, Elizabeth 1911-1984 .... *7*
  Obituary *39*
Johnson, Eric W(arner) 1918-1994 ....
  Obituary *82*
  Earlier sketch in SATA *8*
Johnson, Evelyne 1922- *20*
Johnson, Fred 19(?)-1982 .... *63*
Johnson, Gaylord 1884-1972 .... *7*
Johnson, Gerald White 1890-1980 .... *19*
  Obituary *28*
Johnson, Gillian 1963- *215*
Johnson, Harper
  See Johnson, E(ugene) Harper
Johnson, Harriett 1908-1987
  Obituary *53*
Johnson, James Ralph 1922- *1*
Johnson, James Weldon 1871-1938 .... *31*
  See also CLR *32*
Johnson, Jane 1951- *48*
Johnson, Joan J. 1942- *59*
Johnson, John E(mil) 1929- *34*
Johnson, Johnny 1901-1995
  See Johnson, (Walter) Ryerson
Johnson, Kathleen Jeffrie 1950- *186*
Johnson, La Verne B(ravo) 1925- *13*
Johnson, Layne *187*
Johnson, Lee Kaiser 1962- *78*
Johnson, Lissa H(alls) 1955- *65*
Johnson, Lois Smith 1894-1993 .... *6*
Johnson, Lois Walfrid 1936- *130*
  Earlier sketches in SATA *22, 91*
Johnson, Margaret S(weet) 1893-1964 .... *35*
Johnson, Marguerite Annie
  See Angelou, Maya
Johnson, Mary Frances K. 1929(?)-1979
  Obituary *27*
Johnson, Maud Battle 1918(?)-1985
  Obituary *46*
Johnson, Maureen 1973- *200*
Johnson, Meredith Merrell 1952- *104*
Johnson, Milton 1932- *31*
Johnson, Neil 1954- *135*
  Earlier sketch in SATA *73*
Johnson, Pamela 1949- *71*
Johnson, Patricia Polin 1956- *84*
Johnson, Paul Brett 1947- *132*
  Earlier sketch in SATA *83*
Johnson, Rebecca L. 1956- *147*
  Earlier sketch in SATA *67*
Johnson, Rick L. 1954- *79*
Johnson, (Walter) Ryerson 1901-1995 .... *10*
  Obituary *106*
Johnson, Scott 1952- *119*
  Earlier sketch in SATA *76*
Johnson, Sherrie 1948- *87*
Johnson, Shirley K(ing) 1927- *10*
Johnson, Siddie Joe 1905-1977
  Obituary *20*
Johnson, Spencer 1938- *145*
  Brief entry *38*
Johnson, Stacie
  See Myers, Walter Dean
Johnson, Stephen T. 1964- *189*
  Earlier sketches in SATA *84, 141*
Johnson, Steve 1960- *177*
Johnson, Sue Kaiser 1963- *78*

Johnson, Sylvia A. *166*
  Brief entry *52*
  Earlier sketch in SATA *104*
Johnson, William R. *38*
Johnson, William Weber 1909-1992 .... *7*
Johnson-Feelings, Dianne
  See Johnson, Dianne
Johnston, Agnes Christine
  See Dazey, Agnes J(ohnston)
Johnston, Annie Fellows 1863-1931 .... *37*
Johnston, Dorothy Grunbock 1915-1979 ...... *54*
Johnston, Ginny 1946- *60*
Johnston, H(ugh) A(nthony) S(tephen)
  1913-1967 .... *14*
Johnston, Janet 1944- *71*
Johnston, Jeffry W. *188*
Johnston, Johanna 1914(?)-1982 .... *12*
  Obituary *33*
Johnston, Julie 1941- *110*
  Autobiography Feature *128*
  Earlier sketch in SATA *78*
  See also CLR *41*
  See also SAAS *24*
Johnston, Lynn 1947- *118*
Johnston, Lynn Beverley
  See Johnston, Lynn
Johnston, Mark *194*
Johnston, Norma
  See St. John, Nicole
Johnston, Portia
  See Takakjian, Portia
Johnston, Susan Taylor 1942- *180*
  Earlier sketches in SATA *8, 83, 128*
Johnston, Tim(othy Patrick) 1962- *146*
Johnston, Tony
  See Johnston, Susan Taylor
Joinson, Carla *160*
Jolin, Paula *186*
Jonas, Ann 1932- *135*
  Brief entry *42*
  Earlier sketch in SATA *50*
  See also CLR *74*
Jonell, Lynne 1956- *196*
  Earlier sketch in SATA *109*
Jones, Adrienne 1915-2000 .... *82*
  Earlier sketch in SATA *7*
  See also SAAS *10*
Jones, Allan Frewin 1954- *204*
Jones, Annabel
  See Lewis, Mary
Jones, Betty Millsaps 1940- *54*
Jones, Carol 1942- *153*
  Earlier sketch in SATA *79*
Jones, Carrie 1971- *191*
Jones, Charles M.
  See Jones, Chuck
Jones, Charlotte Foltz 1945- *122*
  Earlier sketch in SATA *77*
Jones, Chuck 1912-2002 .... *53*
  Obituary *133*
Jones, Constance *112*
Jones, Constance A.
  See Jones, Constance
Jones, David 1956- *202*
Jones, Diana Wynne 1934- *160*
  Earlier sketches in SATA *9, 70, 108*
  See also CLR *120*
  See also SAAS *7*
Jones, Douglas B. *202*
Jones, Douglas C(lyde) 1924-1998 .... *52*
Jones, Elizabeth McDavid *155*
Jones, Elizabeth Orton 1910-2005 .... *18*
  Obituary *164*
Jones, Evan 1915-1996 .... *3*
Jones, Frewin
  See Jones, Allan Frewin
Jones, Geraldine
  See McCaughrean, Geraldine
Jones, Gillingham
  See Hamilton, Charles (Harold St. John)
Jones, Gwyneth A(nn) 1952- *159*

Jones, Harold 1904-1992 .... *14*
  Obituary *72*
Jones, Helen Hinckley 1903-1991 .... *26*
Jones, Helen L(ouise) 1903-1973
  Obituary *22*
Jones, Hettie 1934- *42*
  Brief entry *27*
Jones, Hortense P. 1918- *9*
Jones, J. Sydney 1948- *101*
Jones, Jasmine
  See Papademetriou, Lisa
Jones, Jennifer (Berry) 1947- *90*
Jones, Jessie Mae Orton 1887(?)-1983
  Obituary *37*
Jones, John R(obert) 1926- *76*
Jones, Jon Sydney
  See Jones, J. Sydney
Jones, Kimberly K. 1957- *187*
Jones, Marcia Thornton 1958- *115*
  Earlier sketch in SATA *73*
Jones, Martha T(annery) 1931- *130*
Jones, Mary Alice 1898(?)-1980 .... *6*
Jones, McClure *34*
Jones, Noah Z. *182*
Jones, Patrick 1961- *210*
  Earlier sketch in SATA *136*
Jones, Penelope 1938- *31*
Jones, Rebecca C(astaldi) 1947- *99*
  Earlier sketch in SATA *33*
Jones, Robin D(orothy) 1959- *80*
Jones, Sanford W.
  See Thorn, John
Jones, Sylvie *185*
Jones, Sylvie Michelle
  See Jones, Sylvie
Jones, Terence Graham Parry 1942- *127*
  Brief entry *51*
  Earlier sketch in SATA *67*
Jones, Terry
  See Jones, Terence Graham Parry
Jones, Tim Wynne
  See Wynne-Jones, Tim
Jones, Traci L. *186*
Jones, V. M. 1958- *147*
Jones, Veda Boyd 1948- *119*
Jones, Victoria Mary
  See Jones, V. M.
Jones, Volcano
  See Mitchell, Adrian
Jones, Weyman (B.) 1928- *4*
  See also SAAS *11*
Jones, William Glynne
  See Glynne-Jones, William
Jonk, Clarence 1906-1987 .... *10*
Jonsberg, Barry 1951- *168*
Joos, Francoise 1956- *78*
Joos, Frederic 1953- *78*
Joosse, Barbara M. 1949- *164*
  Earlier sketches in SATA *52, 96*
Joosse, Barbara Monnot
  See Joosse, Barbara M.
Jordan, Alexis Hill
  See Glick, Ruth (Burtnick)
  and Titchener, Louise
Jordan, Anne Devereaux 1943- *80*
Jordan, Chris
  See Philbrick, Rodman
Jordan, Deloris *191*
Jordan, Don
  See Howard, Vernon (Linwood)
Jordan, Hope Dahle 1905-1995 .... *15*
Jordan, Jael (Michal) 1949- *30*
Jordan, June 1936-2002 .... *136*
  Earlier sketch in SATA *4*
  See also CLR *10*
Jordan, June Meyer
  See Jordan, June
Jordan, Lee
  See Scholefield, Alan
Jordan, Martin George 1944- *84*
Jordan, Robert 1948-2007 .... *95*

Jordan, Robert K.
See Jordan, Robert
Jordan, Rosa 1939- 191
Jordan, Roslyn M. 189
Jordan, Sherryl 1949- 122
Earlier sketch in SATA 71
See also SAAS 23
Jordan, Shirley 1930- 154
Jordan, Tanis 1946- 84
Jorgensen, Ivar
See Ellison, Harlan
and Garrett, Randall
Jorgensen, Mary Venn -1995 36
Jorgensen, Norman 1954- 157
Jorgenson, Ivar
See Silverberg, Robert
Jorisch, Stephane 178
Joseph, Anne
See Coates, Anna
Joseph, James (Herz) 1924- 53
Joseph, Joan 1939- 34
Joseph, Joseph M(aron) 1903-1979 22
Joseph, Patrick
See O'Malley, Kevin
Josephs, Rebecca
See Talbot, Toby
Josephson, Judith Pinkerton 1943- 198
Josh
See Twain, Mark
Joshua, Peter
See Stone, Peter
Joslin, Mary 1953- 176
Joslin, Sesyle
See Hine, Sesyle Joslin
Joubert, Beverly 1957- 204
Joubert, Dereck 204
Journet, Mireille
See Marokvia, Mireille
Joyce, Bill
See Joyce, William
Joyce, J(ames) Avery 1902-1987 11
Obituary 50
Joyce, Peter 1937- 127
Joyce, William 1957- 118
Brief entry 46
Earlier sketch in SATA 72
See also CLR 26
Joyner, Jerry 1938- 34
Juan, Ana 1961- 179
Jubb, Sophie 210
Jubert, Herve 185
Juby, Susan 1969- 202
Earlier sketch in SATA 156
Jucker, Sita 1921- 5
Judah, Aaron 1923- 118
Judd, Cyril
See Kornbluth, C(yril) M.
and Merril, Judith
and Pohl, Frederik
Judd, Denis (O'Nan) 1938- 33
Judd, Frances K.
See Benson, Mildred
Jude, Conny 81
Judge, Lita 192
Judson, Clara Ingram 1879-1960 38
Brief entry 27
Judy, Stephen
See Tchudi, Stephen N.
Judy, Stephen N.
See Tchudi, Stephen N.
Juhasz, Victor 1954- 177
Jukes, Mavis 1947- 111
Brief entry 43
Earlier sketch in SATA 72
See also SAAS 12
Jules, Jacqueline 1956- 183
Earlier sketch in SATA 148
Julesberg, Elizabeth Rider Montgomery
1902-1985 34
Obituary 41
Earlier sketch in SATA 3

Julian, Jane
See Wiseman, David
Jumpp, Hugo
See MacPeek, Walter G.
Jungman, Ann 165
Jupo, Frank J. 1904-1981 7
Jurmain, Suzanne 1945- 169
Earlier sketch in SATA 72
Jurmain, Suzanne Tripp
See Jurmain, Suzanne
Juster, Norton 1929- 132
Earlier sketch in SATA 3
See also CLR 112
Justus, May 1898-1989 1
Obituary 106
Juvenilia
See Taylor, Ann

K

Kaaberbol, Lene
See Kaaberbol, Lene
Kaaberbol, Lene 1960- 159
Kabdebo, Tamas
See Kabdebo, Thomas
Kabdebo, Thomas 1934- 10
Kabibble, Osh
See Jobb, Jamie
Kacer, Kathy 1954- 184
Earlier sketch in SATA 142
Kaczman, James 156
Kadair, Deborah Ousley 184
Kadesch, Robert R(udstone) 1922- 31
Kadohata, Cynthia 1956(?)- 180
Earlier sketch in SATA 155
See also CLR 121
Kadohata, Cynthia L.
See Kadohata, Cynthia
Kaempfert, Wade
See del Rey, Lester
Kaestner, Erich 1899-1974 14
See also CLR 153
Kahl, Jonathan (D.) 1959- 77
Kahl, M(arvin) P(hilip) 1934- 37
Kahl, Virginia (Caroline) 1919-2004 48
Brief entry 38
Obituary 158
Kahn, Joan 1914-1994 48
Obituary 82
Kahn, Katherine Janus 1942- 167
Earlier sketch in SATA 90
Kahn, Peggy
See Katz, Bobbi
Kahn, Roger 1927- 37
Kahukiwa, Robyn 1940- 134
Kains, Josephine
See Goulart, Ron
Kaizuki, Kiyonori 1950- 72
Kajikawa, Kimiko 212
Kakimoto, Kozo 1915- 11
Kalashnikoff, Nicholas 1888-1961 16
Kalb, Jonah 1926- 23
Kalbacken, Joan 1925- 96
Kalechofsky, Roberta 1931- 92
Kaler, James Otis 1848-1912 15
Kalis, Jennifer 207
Kalish, Claire M. 1947- 92
Kallen, Stuart A(rnold) 1955- 126
Earlier sketch in SATA 86
Kallevig, Christine Petrell 1955- 164
Kalman, Bobbie 1947- 63
Kalman, Maira 1949- 137
Earlier sketch in SATA 96
See also CLR 32
Kalnay, Francis 1899-1992 7
Kaloustian, Rosanne 1955- 93
Kalow, Gisela 1946- 32
Kalstein, Dave 175
Kamara, Mariatu 214

Kamen, Gloria 1923- 98
Earlier sketch in SATA 9
Kamerman, Sylvia E.
See Burack, Sylvia K.
Kamm, Josephine (Hart) 1905-1989 24
Kammerman, Sylvia K.
See Burack, Sylvia K.
Kandel, Michael 1941- 93
Kandell, Alice S. 1938- 35
Kane, Bob 1916-1998 120
Kane, Henry Bugbee 1902-1971 14
Kane, L. A.
See Mannetti, Lisa
Kane, Robert W. 1910- 18
Kane, Wilson
See Bloch, Robert (Albert)
Kanefield, Teri 1960- 135
Kanell, Beth 215
Kaner, Etta 1947- 198
Earlier sketch in SATA 126
Kanetzke, Howard W(illiam) 1932- 38
Kangas, Juli 1958- 200
Kann, Elizabeth 180
Kann, Victoria 180
Kanninen, Barbara 196
Kanninen, Barbara J.
See Kanninen, Barbara
Kanoza, Muriel Canfield
See Canfield, Muriel
Kantner, Seth 1965- 179
Kanzawa, Toshiko
See Furukawa, Toshi
Kanzler, John 1963- 188
Kaplan, Andrew 1960- 78
Kaplan, Anne Bernays
See Bernays, Anne
Kaplan, Bess 1927- 22
Kaplan, Boche 1926- 24
Kaplan, Elizabeth 1956- 83
Kaplan, Elizabeth A.
See Kaplan, Elizabeth
Kaplan, Irma 1900- 10
Kaplan, Jean Caryl Korn 1926- 10
Kaplow, Robert 1954- 70
Karageorge, Michael
See Anderson, Poul
Karas, G. Brian 1957- 178
Karas, George Brian
See Karas, G. Brian
Karasz, Ilonka 1896-1981
Obituary 29
Karen, Ruth 1922-1987 9
Obituary 54
Kark, Nina Mary
See Bawden, Nina
Karl, Herb 1938- 73
Karl, Jean E(dna) 1927-2000 122
Earlier sketch in SATA 34
See also SAAS 10
Karlin, Bernie 1927- 68
Karlin, Eugene 1918- 10
Karlin, Nurit 103
Earlier sketch in SATA 63
Karnes, Frances A. 1937- 110
Karp, Naomi J. 1926- 16
Karpinski, J. Rick
See Karpinski, John Eric
Karpinski, John Eric 1952- 81
Karpinski, Rick
See Karpinski, John Eric
Karr, Kathleen 1946- 212
Earlier sketches in SATA 82, 127
Karr, Phyllis Ann 1944- 119
Karwoski, Gail 1949- 127
Karwoski, Gail Langer
See Karwoski, Gail
Kashiwagi, Isami 1925- 10
Kaslik, Ibi
See Kaslik, Ibolya Emma
Kaslik, Ibolya Emma 1973- 185

Kassem, Lou 1931- 62
  Brief entry 51
Kastel, Warren
  See Silverberg, Robert
Kastner, Erich
  See Kaestner, Erich
Kastner, Jill (Marie) 1964- 117
  Earlier sketch in SATA 70
Kasuya, Masahiro 1937- 51
Kasza, Keiko 1951- 191
  Earlier sketch in SATA 124
Kataphusin
  See Ruskin, John
Katchen, Carole 1944- 9
Katcher, Brian 1975- 203
Kathryn
  See Searle, Kathryn Adrienne
Kato, Aya 1982- 202
Katona, Robert 1949- 21
Katsarakis, Joan Harries
  See Harries, Joan
Katz, Alan 185
Katz, Avi 1949- 199
Katz, Avner 1939- 103
Katz, Bobbi 1933- 179
  Earlier sketch in SATA 12
Katz, Fred(eric Phillip) 1938- 6
Katz, Jane B(resler) 1934- 33
Katz, Karen 1947- 195
  Earlier sketch in SATA 158
Katz, Marjorie P.
  See Weiser, Marjorie P(hillis) K(atz)
Katz, Susan 1945- 156
Katz, Welwyn Wilton 1948- 96
  Autobiography Feature 118
  Earlier sketch in SATA 62
  See also CLR 45
Katz, William 1940- 98
Katz, William Loren 1927- 13
Kaufman, Bel 57
Kaufman, Jeff 1955- 84
Kaufman, Joe 1911-2001 33
Kaufman, Joseph
  See Kaufman, Joe
Kaufman, Mervyn D. 1932- 4
Kaufmann, Angelika 1935- 15
Kaufmann, John 1931- 18
Kaula, Edna Mason 1906-1987 13
Kaur Khalsa, Dayal
  See Khalsa, Dayal Kaur
Kavaler, Lucy 1930- 23
Kavanagh, Jack 1920- 85
Kavanagh, P(atrick) J(oseph Gregory)
  1931- 122
Kavanaugh, Ian
  See Webb, Jean Francis (III)
Kay, Alan N. 1965- 144
Kay, Elizabeth 1949- 165
Kay, Guy Gavriel 1954- 167
  Earlier sketch in SATA 121
Kay, Helen
  See Goldfrank, Helen Colodny
Kay, Jackie 1961- 165
  Earlier sketch in SATA 97
Kay, Jacqueline Margaret
  See Kay, Jackie
Kay, Julia 205
Kay, Mara 13
Kay, Verla 1946- 210
  Earlier sketch in SATA 120
Kaye, Danny 1913-1987
  Obituary 50
Kaye, Geraldine (Hughesdon) 1925- 85
  Earlier sketch in SATA 10
Kaye, Judy
  See Baer, Judy
Kaye, Marilyn 1949- 110
  Earlier sketch in SATA 56
Kaye, Mary Margaret
  See Kaye, M.M.

Kaye, M.M. 1908-2004 62
  Obituary 152
Kaye, Mollie
  See Kaye, M.M.
Kaye, Peggy 1948- 143
Keach, James P. 1950- 125
Keams, Geri 1951- 117
Keane, Bil 1922- 4
Keaney, Brian 1954- 188
  Earlier sketch in SATA 106
Kearney, Meg 1964- 178
Kearny, Jillian
  See Goulart, Ron
Keating, Bern
  See Keating, Leo Bernard
Keating, Frank 1944- 143
Keating, Lawrence A. 1903-1966 23
Keating, Leo Bernard 1915- 10
Keats, Emma 1899(?)-1979(?) 68
Keats, Ezra Jack 1916-1983 57
  Obituary 34
  Earlier sketch in SATA 14
  See also CLR 35
Keefer, Catherine
  See Ogan, George F.
  and Ogan, Margaret E. (Nettles)
Keefer, Janice Kulyk
  See Kulyk Keefer, Janice
Keegan, Marcia 1943- 104
  Earlier sketch in SATA 9
Keehn, Sally M. 1947- 165
  Earlier sketch in SATA 87
Keel, Frank
  See Keeler, Ronald F(ranklin)
Keeler, Patricia 183
Keeler, Patricia A.
  See Keeler, Patricia
Keeler, Ronald F(ranklin) 1913-1983 47
Keely, Jack 1951- 119
Keen, Martin L. 1913-1992 4
Keenan, Sheila 1953- 95
Keene, Ann T(odd) 1940- 86
Keene, Carolyn
  See Benson, Mildred
  and Goulart, Ron
  and Lerangis, Peter
  and McFarlane, Leslie
  and Stanley, George Edward
  and Stratemeyer, Edward L.
Keens-Douglas, Richardo 1953- 154
  Earlier sketch in SATA 95
Keep, Linda Lowery
  See Lowery, Linda
Keep, Richard 1949- 170
Keep, Richard Cleminson
  See Keep, Richard
Keeping, Charles (William James)
  1924-1988 69
  Obituary 56
  Earlier sketch in SATA 9
  See also CLR 34
Keeshan, Robert J. 1927-2004 32
  Obituary 151
Kehlenbeck, Angela 1959- 186
Kehret, Peg 1936- 212
  Autobiography Feature 149
  Earlier sketches in SATA 73, 108, 149
Keillor, Garrison 1942- 58
Keillor, Gary Edward
  See Keillor, Garrison
Keir, Christine
  See Pullein-Thompson, Christine
Keister, Douglas 1948- 88
Keith, Doug 1952- 81
Keith, Eros 1942- 52
Keith, Hal 1934- 36
Keith, Harold (Verne) 1903-1998 74
  Earlier sketch in SATA 2
Keith, Robert
  See Applebaum, Stan
Keleinikov, Andrei 1924- 65

Kelemen, Julie 1959- 78
Kelen, Emery 1896-1978 13
  Obituary 26
Kelleam, Joseph E(veridge) 1913-1975 31
Kelleher, Anne 1959- 97
Kelleher, Annette 1950- 122
Kelleher, Daria Valerian 1955- 79
Kelleher, Victor (Michael Kitchener)
  1939- 129
  Brief entry 52
  Earlier sketch in SATA 75
  See also CLR 36
Keller, Beverly L(ou) 91
  Earlier sketch in SATA 13
Keller, Charles 1942- 82
  Earlier sketch in SATA 8
Keller, Debra 1958- 94
Keller, Dick 1923- 36
Keller, Emily 96
Keller, Gail Faithfull
  See Faithfull, Gail
Keller, Holly 1942- 157
  Brief entry 42
  Earlier sketches in SATA 76, 108
  See also CLR 45
Keller, Irene (Barron) 1927-2002 36
  Obituary 139
Keller, Laurie 1961(?)- 196
Kelley, Ellen A. 185
Kelley, Ellen Chavez
  See Kelley, Ellen A.
Kelley, Gary 1945- 183
Kelley, Leo P(atrick) 1928- 32
  Brief entry 31
Kelley, Marty 1971- 211
Kelley, Patrick (G.) 1963- 129
Kelley, Patte 1947- 93
Kelley, True 1946- 179
Kelley, True (Adelaide) 1946- 130
  Brief entry 39
  Earlier sketches in SATA 41, 92
Kelley, True Adelaide
  See Kelley, True
Kellin, Sally Moffet 1932- 9
Kelling, Furn L. 1914-2000 37
Kellogg, Gene
  See Kellogg, Jean (Defrees)
Kellogg, Jean (Defrees) 1916-1978 10
Kellogg, Steven 1941- 177
  Earlier sketches in SATA 8, 57, 130
  See also CLR 6
Kellogg, Steven Castle
  See Kellogg, Steven
Kellow, Kathleen
  See Hibbert, Eleanor Alice Burford
Kelly, C. M. O.
  See Gibbs, (Cecilia) May
Kelly, Clint 1950- 140
Kelly, Eric P(hilbrook) 1884-1960
  See YABC 1
Kelly, Fiona
  See Coleman, Michael
  and Hendry, Frances Mary
  and Jones, Allan Frewin
  and Oldfield, Jenny
  and Welford, Sue
Kelly, Irene 1957- 210
  Earlier sketch in SATA 147
Kelly, Jeff
  See Kelly, Jeffrey
Kelly, Jeffrey 1946- 65
Kelly, Joanne (W.) 1934- 87
Kelly, Kate 1958- 91
Kelly, Kathleen M. 1964- 71
Kelly, Katy 1955- 215
  Earlier sketch in SATA 169
Kelly, Lauren
  See Oates, Joyce Carol
Kelly, Laurene 1954- 123
Kelly, Martha Rose 1914-1983 37

Kelly, Marty
  See Kelly, Martha Rose
Kelly, Mij 166
Kelly, Ralph
  See Geis, Darlene Stern
Kelly, Regina Z(immerman) 1898-1986 5
Kelly, Rosalie (Ruth) 43
Kelly, Tom 1961- 191
Kelly, Walt(er Crawford) 1913-1973 18
Kelsey, Alice Geer 1896-1982 1
Kelsey, Elin 1961- 159
Kemly, Kathleen 1958- 197
Kemnitz, Thomas Milton, Jr. 1984- 152
Kemnitz, Tom, Jr.
  See Kemnitz, Thomas Milton, Jr.
Kemp, Gene 1926- 75
  Earlier sketch in SATA 25
  See also CLR 29
Kempner, Mary Jean 1913-1969 10
Kempter, Christa 1945- 187
Kempton, Jean Welch 1914- 10
Kenah, Katharine 1949- 182
Kenda, Margaret 1942- 71
Kendall, Carol (Seeger) 1917- 74
  Earlier sketch in SATA 11
  See also SAAS 7
Kendall, Gideon 1966- 215
Kendall, Katherine
  See Applegate, Katherine
Kendall, Lace
  See Stoutenburg, Adrien (Pearl)
Kendall, Martha E. 87
Kendall, Russ 1957- 83
Kenealy, James P. 1927- 52
  Brief entry 29
Kenealy, Jim
  See Kenealy, James P.
Kennaway, Adrienne 1945- 171
  Earlier sketch in SATA 60
Kennedy, Anne 1955- 198
Kennedy, Anne Vittur
  See Kennedy, Anne
Kennedy, Brendan 1970- 57
Kennedy, Dana Forrest 1917- 74
Kennedy, Dorothy M(intzlaff) 1931- 53
Kennedy, Doug 1963- 189
  Earlier sketch in SATA 122
Kennedy, Frances 1937- 192
Kennedy, James 214
  See Monahan, James
Kennedy, John F. 1917-1963 11
Kennedy, John Fitzgerald
  See Kennedy, John F.
Kennedy, Joseph Charles 1929- 130
  Autobiography Feature 130
  Earlier sketches in SATA 14, 86
  See also CLR 27
  See also SAAS 22
  See Kennedy, X. J.
Kennedy, Kim 189
Kennedy, Marlane 1962- 210
Kennedy, Pamela (J.) 1946- 87
Kennedy, Paul E(dward) 1929- 113
  Earlier sketch in SATA 33
Kennedy, Richard (Pitt) 1910-1989
  Obituary 60
Kennedy, (Jerome) Richard 1932- 22
Kennedy, Robert 1938- 63
Kennedy, T.A. 1953- 42
  Brief entry 35
Kennedy, Teresa
  See Kennedy, T.A.
Kennedy, Teresa A.
  See Kennedy, T.A.
Kennedy, William 1928- 57
Kennedy, William Joseph
  See Kennedy, William
Kennedy, X. J.
  See CLR 27
  See also SAAS 22
  See Kennedy, Joseph Charles

Kennell, Ruth Epperson 1893-1977 6
  Obituary 25
Kennemore, Tim 1957- 133
Kennen, Ally 190
Kennett, David 1959- 206
  Earlier sketch in SATA 121
Kennison, Ruth 202
Kenny, Ellsworth Newcomb 1909-1971
  Obituary 26
Kenny, Herbert Andrew 1912-2002 13
Kenny, Jude
  See Daly, Jude
Kenny, Kathryn
  See Bowden, Joan Chase
  and Krull, Kathleen
  and Sanderlin, Owenita (Harrah)
  and Stack, Nicolete Meredith
Kenny, Kevin
  See Krull, Kathleen
Kensinger, George
  See Fichter, George S.
Kensington, Kathryn Wesley
  See Rusch, Kristine Kathryn
Kent, Alexander
  See Reeman, Douglas Edward
Kent, David
  See Lambert, David
Kent, Deborah Ann 1948- 155
  Brief entry 41
  Earlier sketches in SATA 47, 104
Kent, Jack
  See Kent, John Wellington
Kent, John Wellington 1920-1985 24
  Obituary 45
Kent, Lisa 1942- 90
Kent, Mallory
  See Lowndes, Robert A(ugustine) W(ard)
Kent, Margaret 1894- 2
Kent, Rockwell 1882-1971 6
Kent, Rose 188
Kent, Sherman 1903-1986 20
  Obituary 47
Kenward, Jean 1920- 42
Kenworthy, Leonard S. 1912-1991 6
Kenyon, Karen (Smith) 1938- 145
Kenyon, Kate
  See Adorjan, Carol (Madden)
  and Ransom, Candice F.
Kenyon, Ley 1913-1990 6
Keown, Elizabeth 78
Kepes, Juliet A(ppleby) 1919-1999 13
Kephart, Beth 1960- 196
Kerby, Mona 1951- 202
  Earlier sketch in SATA 75
Kerigan, Florence 1896-1984 12
Kerley, Barbara 1960- 191
  Earlier sketch in SATA 138
Kerman, Gertrude
  See Furman, Gertrude Lerner Kerman
Kerns, Thelma 1929- 116
Kerr, Anne Louise
  See Mackey, Weezie Kerr
Kerr, Bob 1951- 120
Kerr, Jessica 1901-1991 13
Kerr, (Anne-)Judith 1923-1970 24
Kerr, M. E.
  See Meaker, Marijane
Kerr, P.B.
  See Kerr, Philip
Kerr, Philip 1956- 168
Kerr, Phyllis Forbes 1942- 72
Kerr, Tom 1950- 77
Kerrin, Jessica Scott 174
Kerry, Frances
  See Kerigan, Florence
Kerry, Lois
  See Duncan, Lois
Kershen, (L.) Michael 1982- 82
Kerven, Rosalind 1954- 83

Ker Wilson, Barbara 1929- 121
  Earlier sketches in SATA 20, 70
  See also SAAS 18
Keselman, Gabriela 1953- 128
Kesey, Ken 1935-2001 66
  Obituary 131
Kesey, Ken Elton
  See Kesey, Ken
Kesler, Jay 1935- 65
Kessel, Joyce Karen 1937- 41
Kessler, Cristina 190
Kessler, Ethel 1922- 44
  Brief entry 37
Kessler, Leonard P. 1921- 14
Kessler, Liz 1966- 206
Kest, Kristin 1967- 168
  Earlier sketch in SATA 118
Kesteven, G. R.
  See Crosher, G. R.
Ketcham, Hank
  See Ketcham, Henry King
Ketcham, Henry King 1920-2001 28
  Brief entry 27
  Obituary 128
Ketcham, Sallie 1963- 124
Ketchum, Liza 1946- 132
  Earlier sketch in SATA 78
Ketner, Mary Grace 1946- 75
Kettelkamp, Larry (Dale) 1933- 2
  See also SAAS 3
Ketteman, Helen 1945- 167
  Earlier sketches in SATA 73, 115
Kettle, Peter
  See Glover, Denis (James Matthews)
Kevles, Bettyann Holtzmann 1938- 23
Key, Alexander (Hill) 1904-1979 8
  Obituary 23
Key, Samuel M.
  See de Lint, Charles
Key, Watt 1970- 189
Keyes, Daniel 1927- 37
Keyes, Diane 207
Keyes, Fenton 1915-1999 34
Keyes, Greg 1963- 116
Keyes, J. Gregory
  See Keyes, Greg
Keyser, Marcia 1933- 42
Keyser, Sarah
  See McGuire, Leslie (Sarah)
Khalid, Mohamed Nor
  See Lat
Khalsa, Dayal Kaur 1943-1989 62
  See also CLR 30
Khan, Hena 214
Khan, Rukhsana 1962- 165
  Earlier sketch in SATA 118
Khanshendel, Chiron
  See Rose, Wendy
Kheirabadi, Masoud 1951- 158
Khemir, Sabiha 87
Kherdian, David 1931- 74
  Autobiography Feature 125
  Earlier sketch in SATA 16
  See also CLR 24
Khing, T.T. 1933- 192
Kibbe, Pat (Hosley) 60
Kidd, Diana 1933-2000 150
Kidd, Richard 1952-2008 152
  Obituary 194
Kidd, Ronald 1948- 173
  Earlier sketches in SATA 42, 92
Kiddell, John 1922- 3
Kiddell-Monroe, Joan 1908-1972 55
Kidwell, Carl 1910- 43
Kiefer, Irene 1926- 21
Kiefer, Kathleen Balmes 1957- 142
Kiepper, Shirley Morgan 1933- 10
Kierstead, Vera M.
  See Kierstead-Farber, Vera M.
Kierstead-Farber, Vera M. 1913- 121

Kierstead-Farber, Vera May
  See Kierstead-Farber, Vera M.
Kiesel, Stanley 1925- 35
Kiesler, Kate (A.) 1971- 152
  Earlier sketch in SATA 90
Kihn, Greg 1952- 110
Kikukawa, Cecily H(arder) 1919- 44
  Brief entry 35
Kilcher, Jewel 1974- 109
Kile, Joan 1940- 78
Kilgore, Kathleen 1946- 42
Kilian, Crawford 1941- 35
Killdeer, John
  See Mayhar, Ardath
Killien, Christi 1956- 73
Killilea, Marie (Lyons) 1913-1991 2
Killingback, Julia 1944- 63
Killough, (Karen) Lee 1942- 64
Kilpatrick, Don 206
Kilreon, Beth
  See Walker, Barbara (Jeanne) K(erlin)
Kilworth, Garry 1941- 94
Kilworth, Garry D.
  See Kilworth, Garry
Kilworth, Garry Douglas
  See Kilworth, Garry
Kim, David 1977- 201
Kim, Helen 1899-1970 98
Kim, Joung Un 1970- 205
Kimball, Gayle 1943- 90
Kimball, Violet T(ew) 1932- 126
Kimball, Yeffe 1914-1978 37
Kimber, Murray 1964- 171
Kimble, Warren 176
Kimbrough, Emily 1899-1989 2
  Obituary 59
Kimeldorf, Martin 1948- 121
Kimeldorf, Martin R.
  See Kimeldorf, Martin
Kimenye, Barbara 1940(?)- 121
Kimmel, Elizabeth Cody 209
  Earlier sketch in SATA 170
Kimmel, Eric A. 1946- 208
  Earlier sketches in SATA 13, 80, 125, 176
Kimmel, Margaret Mary 1938- 43
  Brief entry 33
Kimmelman, Burt 1947- 180
Kimmelman, Leslie 1958- 211
  Earlier sketches in SATA 85, 156
Kincaid, Jamaica 1949-
  See CLR 63
Kincher, Jonni 1949- 79
Kindl, Patrice 1951- 128
  Earlier sketch in SATA 82
  See also CLR 132
Kindred, Wendy (Good) 1937- 7
Kinerk, Robert 199
Kines, Pat Decker 1937- 12
King, Adam
  See Hoare, Robert J(ohn)
King, Alison
  See Martini, Teri
King, (Maria) Anna 1964- 72
King, Billie Jean 1943- 12
King, Christopher (L.) 1945- 84
King, (David) Clive 1924- 144
  Earlier sketch in SATA 28
King, Colin 1943- 76
King, Cynthia 1925- 7
King, Daniel (John) 1963- 130
King, Daren 1972- 197
King, Elizabeth 1953- 83
King, Frank O. 1883-1969
  Obituary 22
King, Frank R. 1904-1999 127
King, Jane
  See Currie, Stephen
King, Jeanette (Margaret) 1959- 105
King, Larry L. 1929- 66
King, Laurie R. 1952- 88

King, Marian 1900(?)-1986 23
  Obituary 47
King, Martin Luther, Jr. 1929-1968 14
King, Mary Ellen 1958- 93
King, Paul
  See Drackett, Phil(ip Arthur)
King, Paula
  See Downing, Paula E.
King, Stephen 1947- 161
  Earlier sketches in SATA 9, 55
  See also CLR 124
King, Stephen Edwin
  See King, Stephen
King, Stephen Michael 157
King, Steve
  See King, Stephen
King, Thomas 1943- 96
King, Thomas Hunt
  See King, Thomas
King, Tony 1947- 39
King, Willie Christine
  See Farris, Christine King
Kingfisher, Rupert 209
Kingman, Dong (Moy Shu) 1911-2000 44
Kingman, Lee
  See Natti, Lee
Kingsland, Leslie William 1912- 13
Kingsley, Charles 1819-1875
  See YABC 2
  See also CLR 77
Kingsley, Emily Perl 1940- 33
Kingsley, Kaza 193
King-Smith, Dick 1922- 192
  Brief entry 38
  Earlier sketches in SATA 47, 80, 135
  See also CLR 40
Kingston, Maxine Hong 1940- 53
Kingston, Maxine Ting Ting Hong
  See Kingston, Maxine Hong
Kinney, C. Cle(land) 1915- 6
Kinney, Harrison 1921- 13
Kinney, Jean Stout 1912- 12
Kinney, Jeff 1971- 187
Kinsey, Elizabeth
  See Clymer, Eleanor
Kinsey, Helen 1948- 82
Kinsey-Warnock, Natalie 1956- 167
  Earlier sketches in SATA 71, 116
Kinzel, Dorothy 1950- 57
Kinzel, Dottie
  See Kinzel, Dorothy
Kipling, Joseph Rudyard
  See Kipling, Rudyard
Kipling, Rudyard 1865-1936 100
  See also YABC 2
  See also CLR 65
Kippax, Frank
  See Needle, Jan
Kirby, David 1944- 78
Kirby, David K.
  See Kirby, David
Kirby, David Kirk
  See Kirby, David
Kirby, Margaret
  See Bingley, Margaret (Jane Kirby)
Kirby, Susan E. 1949- 62
Kirk, Connie Ann 1957- 167
Kirk, Daniel 1952- 196
  Earlier sketches in SATA 107, 153
Kirk, David 1955- 161
  Earlier sketch in SATA 117
Kirk, Heather 1949- 166
Kirk, Ruth (Kratz) 1925- 5
Kirkham, Dinah
  See Card, Orson Scott
Kirkland, Will
  See Hale, Arlene
Kirkpatrick, Katherine (Anne) 1964- 113
Kirkup, James 1918-2009 12
Kirkus, Virginia
  See Glick, Virginia Kirkus

Kirkwood, Kathryn
  See Fluke, Joanne
Kirsch, Vincent X. 211
Kirshenbaum, Binnie 79
Kirshner, David S. 1958- 123
Kirtland, G. B.
  See Hine, Sesyle Joslin
  and Hine, Al(fred Blakelee)
Kirwan, Wednesday 198
Kish, Eleanor M(ary) 1924- 73
Kish, Ely
  See Kish, Eleanor M(ary)
Kishida, Eriko 1929- 12
Kisinger, Grace Gelvin (Maze) 1913-1965 .. 10
Kissel, Richard 209
Kissin, Eva H. 1923- 10
Kissinger, Rosemary K.
  See Updyke, Rosemary K.
Kistler, John M. 1967- 160
Kitamura, Satoshi 1956- 201
  Earlier sketches in SATA 62, 98, 143
  See also CLR 60
Kitchen, Bert
  See Kitchen, Herbert Thomas
Kitchen, Herbert Thomas 1940- 70
Kite, L. Patricia
  See Kite, Pat
Kite, Pat 1940- 78
Kitt, Tamara
  See de Regniers, Beatrice Schenk (Freedman)
Kittinger, Jo S(usenbach) 1955- 148
  Earlier sketch in SATA 96
Kituomba
  See Odaga, Asenath (Bole)
Kitzinger, Sheila 1929- 57
Kiwak, Barbara 1966- 103
Kjelgaard, James Arthur 1910-1959 17
  See also CLR 81
  See Kjelgaard, Jim
Kjelgaard, Jim
  See Kjelgaard, James Arthur
Kjelle, Marylou Morano 1954- 146
Klages, Ellen 1954- 196
Klagsbrun, Francine (Lifton) 36
Klaits, Barrie 1944- 52
Klam, Cheryl 191
Klaperman, Gilbert 1921- 33
Klaperman, Libby Mindlin 1921-1982 33
  Obituary 31
Klass, David 1960- 207
  Earlier sketches in SATA 88, 142
Klass, Morton 1927-2001 11
Klass, Sheila Solomon 1927- 99
  Autobiography Feature 126
  Earlier sketch in SATA 45
  See also SAAS 26
Klause, Annette Curtis 1953- 175
  Earlier sketch in SATA 79
  See also CLR 104
Klaveness, Jan O'Donnell 1939- 86
Kleberger, Ilse 1921- 5
Kleeberg, Irene (Flitner) Cumming 1932- 65
Klein, Aaron E. 1930-1998 45
  Brief entry 28
Klein, Bill 1945- 89
Klein, David 1919-2001 59
Klein, Frederick C. 1938- 154
Klein, Gerda Weissmann 1924- 44
Klein, H(erbert) Arthur 8
Klein, James 1932- 115
Klein, Leonore (Glotzer) 1916- 6
Klein, Lisa 1958- 211
Klein, Lisa M.
  See Klein, Lisa
Klein, Mina C(ooper) 1906-1979 8
Klein, Norma 1938-1989 57
  Earlier sketch in SATA 7
  See also CLR 19
  See also SAAS 1
Klein, Rachel S. 1953- 105

Klein, Robin 1936- *164*
  Brief entry *45*
  Earlier sketches in SATA *55, 80*
  See also CLR 21
Klemin, Diana *65*
Klemm, Barry 1945- *104*
Klemm, Edward G., Jr. 1910-2001 .... *30*
Klemm, Roberta K(ohnhorst) 1884-1975 ..... *30*
Kleven, Elisa 1958- *173*
  Earlier sketch in SATA *76*
  See also CLR 85
Klevin, Jill Ross 1935- *39*
  Brief entry *38*
Kliban, B(ernard) 1935-1990 .... *35*
  Obituary *66*
Klier, Kimberly Wagner *208*
Klimo, Kate *214*
Klimowicz, Barbara 1927- *10*
Kline, Christina Baker 1964- *101*
Kline, James
  See Klein, James
Kline, Jim
  See Kline, Jim
Kline, Lisa Williams 1954- *143*
Kline, Suzy 1943- *193*
  Autobiography Feature *193*
  Brief entry *48*
  Earlier sketches in SATA *67, 99, 152*
Kliros, Thea 1935- *106*
Klise, Kate *181*
Klise, M. Sarah 1961- *180*
  Earlier sketch in SATA *128*
Klots, Alexander Barrett 1903-1989
  Obituary *62*
Klug, Ron(ald) 1939- *31*
Knaak, Richard A. 1961- *166*
  Earlier sketch in SATA *86*
Knaak, Richard Allen
  See Knaak, Richard A.
Knapman, Timothy *200*
Knapp, Edward
  See Kunhardt, Edith
Knapp, Ron 1952- *34*
Knebel, Fletcher 1911-1993 .... *36*
  Obituary *75*
Kneeland, Linda Clarke 1947- *94*
Knickerbocker, Diedrich
  See Irving, Washington
Knifesmith
  See Cutler, Ivor
Knigge, Robert (R.) 1921(?)-1987 .... *50*
Knight, Anne (Katherine) 1946- *34*
Knight, Brenda *112*
Knight, Christopher G. 1943- *96*
Knight, Damon (Francis) 1922-2002 .... *9*
  Obituary *139*
Knight, David C(arpenter) 1925-1984 .... *14*
  See also CLR 38
Knight, Eric 1897-1943 .... *18*
Knight, Eric Mowbray
  See Knight, Eric
Knight, Francis Edgar 1905- *14*
Knight, Frank
  See Knight, Francis Edgar
Knight, Hilary 1926- *132*
  Earlier sketches in SATA *15, 69*
Knight, Joan (MacPhail) *159*
  Earlier sketch in SATA *82*
Knight, Joan
  See Knight, Joan (MacPhail)
Knight, Kathryn Lasky
  See Lasky, Kathryn
Knight, Mallory T.
  See Hurwood, Bernhardt J.
Knight, Ruth Adams 1898-1974
  Obituary *20*
Knight, Theodore O. 1946- *77*
Knobloch, Dorothea 1951- *88*
Knoepfle, John (Ignatius) 1923- *66*
Knorr, Laura 1971- *200*

Knott, Bill
  See Knott, William C(ecil, Jr.)
Knott, William C(ecil, Jr.) 1927- *3*
Knotts, Howard (Clayton, Jr.) 1922- *25*
Knowles, Anne 1933- *37*
Knowles, Jo 1970- *197*
Knowles, Johanna Beth
  See Knowles, Jo
Knowles, John 1926-2001 .... *89*
  Obituary *134*
  Earlier sketch in SATA *8*
  See also CLR 98
Knox, Calvin M.
  See Silverberg, Robert
Knox, (Mary) Eleanor Jessie 1909-2000 ...... *59*
  Earlier sketch in SATA *30*
Knox, Elizabeth 1959- *176*
Knox, Elizabeth Fiona
  See Knox, Elizabeth
Knox, James
  See Brittain, William
Knox, Jolyne 1937- *76*
Knudsen, James 1950- *42*
Knudsen, Michelle 1974- *171*
Knudson, Mike 1965- *209*
Knudson, R. R.
  See Knudson, Rozanne
Knudson, Richard L(ewis) 1930- *34*
Knudson, Rozanne 1932-2008 .... *79*
  Earlier sketch in SATA *7*
  See also SAAS 18
Knutson, Barbara 1959-2005 .... *166*
Knutson, Kimberley *115*
Knye, Cassandra
  See Disch, Thomas M.
Kobayashi, Masako Matsuno 1935- *6*
Kober, Shahar 1979- *213*
Koch, Dorothy Clarke 1924- *6*
Koch, Kenneth 1925-2002 .... *65*
Koch, Kenneth Jay
  See Koch, Kenneth
Koch, Phyllis (Mae) McCallum 1911- *10*
Kochalka, James 1967- *196*
Kocsis, J. C.
  See Paul, James
Koda-Callan, Elizabeth 1944- *140*
  Earlier sketch in SATA *67*
Kodman, Stanislawa *201*
Koehler, Phoebe 1955- *85*
Koehler-Pentacoff, Elizabeth 1957- *160*
  Earlier sketch in SATA *96*
Koehn, Ilse
  See Van Zwienen, Ilse Charlotte Koehn
Koeller, Carol *192*
Koenig, Viviane 1950- *80*
Koering, Ursula 1921-1976 .... *64*
Koerner, W(illiam) H(enry) D(avid)
  1878-1938 .... *21*
Koertge, Ron 1940- *209*
  Earlier sketches in SATA *53, 92, 131*
Koestler-Grack, Rachel A. 1973- *156*
Koff, Richard Myram 1926- *62*
Koffinke, Carol 1949- *82*
Kogan, Deborah
  See Kogan Ray, Deborah
Kogan Ray, Deborah 1940- *203*
  Earlier sketches in SATA *8, 50, 161*
Kogawa, Joy 1935- *99*
Kogawa, Joy Nozomi
  See Kogawa, Joy
Kogler, Jennifer Anne 1982(?)- *174*
Kohara, Kazuno *207*
Kohl, Herbert 1937- *47*
Kohl, Herbert R.
  See Kohl, Herbert
Kohl, MaryAnn F(aubion) 1947- *144*
  Earlier sketch in SATA *74*
Kohler, Julilly H(ouse) 1908-1976
  Obituary *20*
Kohn, Bernice
  See Hunt, Bernice

Kohn, Rita (T.) 1933- *89*
Kohner, Frederick 1905-1986 .... *10*
  Obituary *48*
Koide, Tan 1938-1986 .... *50*
Koike, Kay 1940- *72*
Koja, Kathe 1960- *199*
  Earlier sketch in SATA *155*
Koja, Stephan *198*
Kolar, Bob 1960(?)- *206*
Kolb, Larry J. 1953- *175*
Kolba, St. Tamara *22*
Kolibalova, Marketa
  See Kolibalova, Marketa
Kolibalova, Marketa 1953- *126*
Koller, Jackie French 1948- *157*
  Earlier sketches in SATA *72, 109*
  See also CLR 68
Kolodny, Nancy J. 1946- *76*
Kolosov, Jacqueline 1967- *199*
Komaiko, Leah 1954- *164*
  Earlier sketch in SATA *97*
Komisar, Lucy 1942- *9*
Komoda, Beverly 1939- *25*
Komoda, Kiyo 1937- *9*
Kompaneyets, Marc 1974- *169*
Komroff, Manuel 1890-1974 .... *2*
  Obituary *20*
Konigsberg, Bill 1970- *207*
Konigsburg, E.L. 1930- *194*
  Earlier sketches in SATA *4, 48, 94, 126*
  See also CLR 81
Konigsburg, Elaine Lobl
  See Konigsburg, E.L.
Koning, Hans 1921-2007 .... *5*
  Obituary *182*
Koningsberger, Hans
  See Koning, Hans
Konkle, Janet Everest 1917- *12*
Kono, Erin Eitter 1973- *177*
Konzak, Burt 1946- *151*
Koob, Theodora (J. Foth) 1918- *23*
Kooiker, Leonie
  See Kooyker-Romijn, Johanna Maria
Koons, James
  See Pernu, Dennis
Koontz, Dean 1945- *165*
  Earlier sketch in SATA *92*
Koontz, Dean R.
  See Koontz, Dean
Koontz, Dean Ray
  See Koontz, Dean
Koontz, Robin Michal 1954- *136*
  Earlier sketch in SATA *70*
Kooyker, Leonie
  See Kooyker-Romijn, Johanna Maria
Kooyker-Romijn, Johanna Maria 1927- *48*
Kooyker-Romyn, Johanna Maria
  See Kooyker-Romijn, Johanna Maria
Kopelke, Lisa 1963- *154*
Kopper, Lisa (Esther) 1950- *105*
  Brief entry *51*
Koppes, Steven N. 1957- *169*
Koppes, Steven Nelson
  See Koppes, Steven N.
Korach, Mimi 1922- *9*
Koralek, Jenny 1934- *215*
  Earlier sketches in SATA *71, 140*
Korczak, Janusz
  See Goldszmit, Henryk
Koren, Edward (Benjamin) 1935- *148*
  Earlier sketch in SATA *5*
Koren, Edward 1935- *206*
Korinets, Iurii Iosifovich
  See Korinetz, Yuri (Iosifovich)
Korinetz, Yuri (Iosifovich) 1923- *9*
  See also CLR 4
Korman, Bernice 1937- *78*
Korman, Gordon 1963- *167*
  Brief entry *41*
  Earlier sketches in SATA *49, 81, 119*
  See also CLR 25

Korman, Gordon Richard
  See Korman, Gordon
Korman, Justine 1958- 70
Kornblatt, Marc 1954- 147
  Earlier sketch in SATA 84
Kornprobst, Jacques 1937- 177
Korte, Gene J. 1950- 74
Korthues, Barbara 1971- 203
Korty, Carol 1937- 15
Koscielniak, Bruce 1947- 153
  Earlier sketches in SATA 67, 99
Koshin, Alexander (A.) 1952- 86
Kositsky, Lynne 1947- 158
Koskenmaki, Rosalie
  See Maggio, Rosalie
Koss, Amy Goldman 1954- 158
  Earlier sketch in SATA 115
Kossin, Sandy (Sanford) 1926- 10
Kossman, Nina 1959- 84
Kostecki-Shaw, Jenny Sue 203
Kostick, Conor 1964- 186
Kotzwinkle, William 1938- 146
  Earlier sketches in SATA 24, 70
  See also CLR 6
Kouhi, Elizabeth 1917- 54
  Brief entry 49
Kouts, Anne 1945- 8
Koutsky, Jan Dale 1955- 146
Kovacs, Deborah 1954- 132
  Earlier sketch in SATA 79
Kovalski, Maryann 1951- 175
  Earlier sketches in SATA 58, 97
  See also CLR 34
  See also SAAS 21
Kowalski, Kathiann M. 1955- 151
  Earlier sketch in SATA 96
Koz, Paula G.
  See Goodman Koz, Paula
Kozjan, Drazen 209
Kraft, Betsy Harvey 1937- 157
Kraft, Erik P. 193
Krahn, Fernando 1935- 49
  Brief entry 31
  See also CLR 3
Krakauer, Hoong Yee Lee 1955- 86
Krakauer, Jon 1954- 108
Kramer, George
  See Heuman, William
Kramer, Nora 1896(?)-1984 26
  Obituary 39
Kramer, Remi (Thomas) 1935- 90
Krantz, Hazel (Newman) 12
Kranzler, George G(ershon) 1916- 28
Kranzler, Gershon
  See Kranzler, George G(ershon)
Krasilovsky, Phyllis 1926- 38
  Earlier sketch in SATA 1
  See also CLR 83
  See also SAAS 5
Krasne, Betty
  See Levine, Betty K(rasne)
Krasner, Steven 1953- 154
Krasno, Rena 1923- 104
Kratman, Tom 175
Kraus, Joanna Halpert 1937- 87
Kraus, (Herman) Robert 1925-2001 93
  Obituary 130
  Earlier sketches in SATA 4, 65
  See also SAAS 11
Krauss, Ruth (Ida) 1911-1993 30
  Obituary 75
  Earlier sketch in SATA 1
  See also CLR 42
Krautter, Elisa (Bialk) 1912(?)-1990 1
  Obituary 65
Krautwurst, Terry 1946- 79
Kray, Robert Clement 1930- 82
Krech, Bob 1956- 185
Krech, Robert
  See Krech, Bob
Kredel, Fritz 1900-1973 17

Kreikemeier, Gregory Scott 1965- 85
Kreloff, Elliot 189
Krementz, Jill 1940- 134
  Earlier sketches in SATA 17, 71
  See also CLR 5
  See also SAAS 8
Kremer, Marcie
  See Sorenson, Margo
Krenina, Katya 1968- 101
Krensky, Stephen 1953- 188
  Brief entry 41
  Earlier sketches in SATA 47, 93, 136
Krensky, Stephen Alan
  See Krensky, Stephen
Kresh, Paul 1919-1997 61
  Obituary 94
Kress, Nancy 1948- 147
  Autobiography Feature 147
  Earlier sketch in SATA 85
Kricher, John C. 1944- 113
Krieger, Melanie 96
Krinitz, Esther Nisenthal 1927-2001 194
Kripke, Dorothy Karp 30
Krisher, Trudy 1946- 160
  Earlier sketch in SATA 86
Krisher, Trudy B.
  See Krisher, Trudy
Krishnaswami, Uma 1956- 182
  Earlier sketch in SATA 144
Kristiansen, Teddy 1964- 210
Kristiansen, Teddy H.
  See Kristiansen, Teddy
Kristof, Jane 1932- 8
Kroeber, Theodora (Kracaw) 1897-1979 1
Kroeger, Mary Kay 1950- 92
Krohn, Katherine E(lizabeth) 1961- 125
  Earlier sketch in SATA 84
Kroll, Francis Lynde 1904-1973 10
Kroll, Steven 1941- 212
  Autobiography Feature 135
  Earlier sketches in SATA 19, 66, 125, 135
  See also SAAS 7
Kroll, Virginia L. 1948- 168
  Earlier sketches in SATA 76, 114
Kroll, Virginia Louisa
  See Kroll, Virginia L.
Kromhout, Rindert 1958- 189
Krommes, Beth 1956- 208
  Earlier sketches in SATA 128, 181
Kronenwetter, Michael 1943- 62
Kroniuk, Lisa
  See Berton, Pierre (Francis de Marigny)
Kropp, Paul 1948- 38
  Brief entry 34
  See also CLR 96
Kropp, Paul Stephan
  See Kropp, Paul
Krosoczka, Jarrett J. 1977- 200
  Earlier sketch in SATA 155
Krovatin, Christopher 1985- 171
Krudop, Walter
  See Krudop, Walter Lyon
Krudop, Walter Lyon 1966- 210
Kruess, James
  See Kruss, James
Kruglik, Gerald 187
Krull, Kathleen 1952- 184
  Autobiography Feature 106
  Brief entry 39
  Earlier sketches in SATA 52, 80, 149
  See also CLR 44
Krumgold, Joseph (Quincy) 1908-1980 48
  Obituary 23
  Earlier sketch in SATA 1
Krupinski, Loretta 1940- 161
  Earlier sketches in SATA 67, 102
Krupnick, Karen 1947- 89
Krupp, E(dwin) C(harles) 1944- 123
  Earlier sketch in SATA 53
Krupp, Robin Rector 1946- 53
Krush, Beth 1918- 18

Krush, Joe 1918-
  See Krush, Joseph P.
Krush, Joseph P. 1918- 18
Kruss, James 1926-1997 8
  See also CLR 9
Kruusval, Catarina 1951- 201
Krykorka, Vladyana 1945- 96
Krystoforski, Andrej 1943- 196
Kubick, Dana 212
Kubie, Eleanor Gottheil
  See Kubie, Nora Gottheil Benjamin
Kubie, Nora Benjamin
  See Kubie, Nora Gottheil Benjamin
Kubie, Nora Gottheil Benjamin 1899-1988 . 39
  Obituary 59
Kubinyi, Laszlo 1937- 94
  Earlier sketch in SATA 17
Kudlinski, Kathleen V. 1950- 213
  Earlier sketch in SATA 150
Kuehnert, Stephanie 1979- 205
Kuenstler, Morton 1927- 10
Kuh, Charlotte 1892(?)-1985
  Obituary 43
Kuharski, Janice 1947- 128
Kuhn, Dwight 199
Kuijer, Guus 1942- 179
Kujoth, Jean Spealman 1935-1975
  Obituary 30
Kuklin, Susan 1941- 163
  Earlier sketches in SATA 63, 95
  See also CLR 51
Kulikov, Boris 1966- 205
  Earlier sketch in SATA 170
Kulka, Joe 188
Kulling, Monica 1952- 89
Kullman, Harry 1919-1982 35
Kulyk Keefer, Janice 1952- 132
Kumin, Maxine 1925- 12
Kumin, Maxine Winokur
  See Kumin, Maxine
Kunhardt, Dorothy (Meserve) 1901-1979 53
  Obituary 22
Kunhardt, Edith 1937- 67
Kunjufu, Jawanza 1953- 73
Kunstler, Morton
  See Kuenstler, Morton
Kuntz, J(ohn) L. 1947- 91
Kuntz, Jerry 1956- 133
Kupferberg, Herbert 1918-2001 19
Kuratomi, Chizuko 1939- 12
  See also CLR 32
Kurczok, Belinda 1978- 121
Kurelek, William 1927-1977 8
  Obituary 27
  See also CLR 2
Kurian, George 1928- 65
Kurjian, Judi(th M.) 1944- 127
Kurland, Gerald 1942- 13
Kurland, Michael 1938- 118
  Earlier sketch in SATA 48
Kurland, Michael Joseph
  See Kurland, Michael
Kuroi, Ken 1947- 120
Kurokawa, Mitsuhiro 1954- 88
Kurten, Bjorn (Olof) 1924-1988 64
Kurtz, Jane 1952- 139
  Earlier sketch in SATA 91
  See also CLR 123
Kurtz, Katherine 1944- 182
  Earlier sketches in SATA 76, 126
Kurtz, Katherine Irene
  See Kurtz, Katherine
Kurz, Rudolf 1952- 95
Kushner, Donn (J.) 1927- 52
  See also CLR 55
Kushner, Ellen 1955- 202
  Earlier sketch in SATA 98
Kushner, Ellen Ruth
  See Kushner, Ellen
Kushner, Jill Menkes 1951- 62

Kushner, Lawrence 1943- *169*
  Earlier sketch in SATA *83*
Kushner, Tony 1956- *160*
Kuskin, Karla 1932-2009 .... *164*
  Obituary *206*
  Earlier sketches in SATA *2, 68, 111*
  See also CLR *4*
  See also SAAS *3*
Kuskin, Karla Seidman
  See Kuskin, Karla
Kusugak, Michael 1948- *143*
Kusugak, Michael Arvaarluk
  See Kusugak, Michael
Kutner, Merrily 1948- *196*
Kuttner, Paul 1922- *18*
Kuyper, Sjoerd 1952- *177*
Kuzma, Kay 1941- *39*
Kvale, Velma R(uth) 1898-1979 .... *8*
Kvasnosky, Laura McGee 1951- *182*
  Earlier sketches in SATA *93, 142*
Kwasney, Michelle D. 1960- *162*
Kyle, Benjamin
  See Gottfried, Theodore Mark
Kyle, Elisabeth
  See Dunlop, Agnes M. R.
Kyte, Kathy S. 1946- *50*
  Brief entry *44*

L

L., Barry
  See Longyear, Barry B(rookes)
L., Tommy
  See Lorkowski, Thomas V(incent)
Labatt, Mary 1944- *215*
Labouisse, Eve Curie
  See Curie, Eve
Labouisse, Eve Denise
  See Curie, Eve
Lace, William W. 1942- *126*
Lacey, Joshua
  See Doder, Josh
Lachner, Dorothea
  See Knobloch, Dorothea
Lachtman, Ofelia Dumas 1919- *179*
Lackey, Mercedes R. 1950- *127*
  Earlier sketch in SATA *81*
Lackey, Mercedes Ritchie
  See Lackey, Mercedes R.
Lacoe, Addie *78*
Lacombe, Benjamin 1982- *198*
Lacome, Julie 1961- *174*
  Earlier sketch in SATA *80*
Lacy, Leslie Alexander 1937- *6*
Ladd, Cheryl (Jean) 1951- *113*
Ladd, London 1972(?)- *206*
Ladd, Louise 1943- *97*
Ladd, Veronica
  See Miner, Jane Claypool
Laden, Nina 1962- *148*
  Earlier sketch in SATA *85*
Lader, Lawrence 1919-2006 .... *6*
  Obituary *178*
LaDoux, Rita C. 1951- *74*
Lady, A
  See Taylor, Ann
Lady Mears
  See Tempest, Margaret Mary
Lady of Quality, A
  See Bagnold, Enid
La Farge, Oliver 1901-1963 .... *19*
La Farge, Oliver Hazard Perry
  See La Farge, Oliver
La Farge, Phyllis *14*
LaFave, Kim *196*
LaFaye, A. 1970- *156*
  Earlier sketch in SATA *105*
LaFaye, Alexandria R.T.
  See LaFaye, A.

LaFevers, R.L. *191*
LaFevers, Robin L.
  See LaFevers, R.L.
Laffin, John (Alfred Charles) 1922- *31*
LaFontaine, Bruce 1948- *176*
  Earlier sketch in SATA *114*
La Fontaine, Jean de 1621-1695 .... *18*
Lafrance, Marie 1955- *197*
Lager, Claude
  See Lapp, Christiane (Germain)
Lager, Marilyn 1939- *52*
Lagercrantz, Rose (Elsa) 1947- *39*
Lagerloef, Selma
  See Lagerlof, Selma
Lagerlof, Selma 1858-1940 .... *15*
  See also CLR *7*
Laguna, Sofie 1968- *158*
LaHaye, Tim F. 1926- *149*
LaHaye, Timothy F.
  See LaHaye, Tim F.
Laidlaw, Rob *205*
Laiken, Deirdre S(usan) 1948- *48*
  Brief entry *40*
Laimgruber, Monika 1946- *11*
Lain, Anna
  See Lamb, Nancy
Laing, Alexander (Kinnan) 1903-1976 .... *117*
Laing, Martha 1951- *39*
Laird, Christa 1944- *108*
  Autobiography Feature *120*
  See also SAAS *26*
Laird, Elizabeth (Mary Risk) 1943- *159*
  Earlier sketches in SATA *77, 114*
  See also CLR *65*
Laird, Jean E(louise) 1930- *38*
Laite, Gordon 1925- *31*
Lake, Harriet
  See Taylor, Paula (Wright)
Lakeman, Victoria
  See Forester, Victoria
Lakin, Patricia 1944- *190*
Laklan, Carli 1907-1988 .... *5*
Laliberte, Louise-Andree 1958- *169*
Lalicki, Barbara *61*
Lalicki, Tom 1949- *186*
Lally, Soinbhe 1945- *119*
LaMarche, Jim *162*
Lamb, Albert *187*
Lamb, Beatrice Pitney 1904-1997 .... *21*
Lamb, Charles 1775-1834 .... *17*
Lamb, Elizabeth Searle 1917- *31*
Lamb, G(eoffrey) F(rederick) *10*
Lamb, Harold (Albert) 1892-1962 .... *53*
Lamb, Lynton (Harold) 1907-1977 .... *10*
Lamb, Mary Ann 1764-1847 .... *17*
Lamb, Nancy 1939- *80*
Lamb, Robert (Boyden) 1941- *13*
Lamba, Marie *195*
Lambert, David 1932- *84*
  Brief entry *49*
Lambert, David Compton
  See Lambert, David
Lambert, Janet 1895(?)-1973 .... *25*
Lambert, Martha L. *113*
Lambert, Saul 1928- *23*
Lambert, Stephen *174*
Lamburn, Richmal Crompton 1890-1969 .... *5*
Lamensdorf, Len 1930- *120*
Lamensdorf, Leonard
  See Lamensdorf, Len
Laminack, Lester L. 1956- *163*
  Earlier sketch in SATA *120*
Lammle, Leslie 1965- *213*
Lamont, Priscilla *200*
Lamorisse, Albert (Emmanuel) 1922-1970 ... *23*
Lampert, Emily 1951- *52*
  Brief entry *49*
Lamplugh, Lois 1921- *17*
Lampman, Evelyn Sibley 1907-1980 .... *87*
  Obituary *23*
  Earlier sketch in SATA *4*

Lamprey, Louise 1869-1951
  See YABC *2*
Lampton, Chris
  See Lampton, Christopher F.
Lampton, Christopher
  See Lampton, Christopher F.
Lampton, Christopher F. *67*
  Brief entry *47*
Lamstein, Sarah 1943- *174*
  Earlier sketch in SATA *126*
Lamstein, Sarah Marwil
  See Lamstein, Sarah
Lanagan, Margo 1960- *201*
  Earlier sketch in SATA *163*
Lancaster, Bruce 1896-1963 .... *9*
Lancaster, Matthew 1973(?)-1983
  Obituary *45*
Lance, Kathryn 1943- *76*
Land, Barbara (Neblett) 1923- *16*
Land, Jane
  See Borland, Kathryn Kilby
  and Speicher, Helen Ross S(mith)
Land, Myrick (Ebben) 1922-1998 .... *15*
Land, Ross
  See Borland, Kathryn Kilby
  and Speicher, Helen Ross S(mith)
Landau, Elaine 1948- *141*
  Earlier sketches in SATA *10, 94*
Landau, Jacob 1917- *38*
Landeck, Beatrice 1904-1978 .... *15*
Landin, Les 1923- *2*
Landis, J(ames) D(avid) 1942- *60*
  Brief entry *52*
Landis, James D.
  See Landis, J(ames) D(avid)
Landis, Jill Marie 1948- *101*
Landman, Tanya *207*
Landmann, Bimba 1968- *176*
Landon, Dena 1978(?)- *168*
Landon, Lucinda 1950- *56*
  Brief entry *51*
Landon, Margaret (Dorothea Mortenson)
  1903-1993 .... *50*
Landowne, Youme 1970- *211*
Landry, Leo *202*
Landshoff, Ursula 1908-1989 .... *13*
Landstrom, Lena 1943- *206*
  Earlier sketch in SATA *146*
Landstrom, Olof 1943- *146*
Landy, Derek 1974- *210*
Lane, Alison Hoffman *215*
Lane, Carolyn 1926-1993 .... *10*
Lane, Connie
  See Laux, Constance
Lane, Dakota 1959- *166*
  Earlier sketch in SATA *105*
Lane, Jerry
  See Martin, Patricia Miles
Lane, John (Richard) 1932- *15*
Lane, Leena *199*
Lane, Margaret 1907-1994 .... *65*
  Brief entry *38*
  Obituary *79*
Lane, Rose Wilder 1887-1968 .... *29*
  Brief entry *28*
Lanes, Selma Gordon 1929- *3*
Lanfredi, Judy 1964- *83*
Lang, Andrew 1844-1912 .... *16*
  See also CLR *101*
Lang, Aubrey *169*
Lang, Lang 1982- *208*
Lang, Paul 1948- *83*
Lang, Susan S. 1950- *68*
Lang, T.T.
  See Taylor, Theodore
Langart, Darrell T.
  See Garrett, Randall
Langdo, Bryan 1973- *191*
  Earlier sketch in SATA *138*
Lange, John
  See Crichton, Michael

Lange, Karen E. *190*
Lange, Suzanne 1945- *5*
Langley, Andrew 1949- *166*
  Earlier sketch in SATA *104*
Langley, Charles P(itman) III 1949- *103*
Langley, Jonathan 1952- *122*
Langley, Noel 1911-1980
  Obituary *25*
Langley, Wanda *173*
Langner, Nola
  See Malone, Nola Langner
Langone, John (Michael) 1929- *46*
  Brief entry *38*
Langreuter, Jutta 1944- *122*
Langrish, Katherine *177*
Langsen, Richard C. 1953- *95*
Langstaff, John 1920-2005 .... *68*
  Obituary *172*
  Earlier sketch in SATA *6*
  See also CLR *3*
Langstaff, John Meredith
  See Langstaff, John
Langstaff, Launcelot
  See Irving, Washington
Langston, Laura 1958- *186*
Langton, Jane 1922- *200*
  Autobiography Feature *140*
  Earlier sketches in SATA *3, 68, 129, 140*
  See also CLR *33*
  See also SAAS *5*
Lanier, Sidney 1842-1881 .... *18*
Lanier, Sterling E. 1927-2007 .... *109*
Lanier, Sterling Edmund
  See Lanier, Sterling E.
Lanino, Deborah 1964- *123*
Lankford, Mary D. 1932- *112*
  Earlier sketch in SATA *77*
Lannin, Joanne 1951- *121*
Lannin, Joanne A.
  See Lannin, Joanne
Lansdale, Joe R. 1951- *116*
Lansdale, Joe Richard
  See Lansdale, Joe R.
Lansing, Alfred 1921-1975 .... *35*
Lansing, Karen E. 1954- *71*
Lansky, Vicki 1942- *177*
Lanthier, Jennifer 1964- *204*
Lantier-Sampon, Patricia 1952- *92*
Lantz, Fran
  See Lantz, Francess L(in)
Lantz, Francess L(in) 1952-2004 .... *153*
  Autobiography Feature *153*
  Obituary *159*
  Earlier sketches in SATA *63, 109*
Lantz, Paul 1908- *45*
Lantz, Walter 1900-1994 .... *37*
  Obituary *79*
Lanza, Barbara 1945- *101*
Lapp, Christiane (Germain) 1948- *74*
Lappin, Peter 1911-1999 .... *32*
Larbalestier, Justine *178*
Lardy, Philippe 1963- *168*
LaReau, Jenna *181*
LaReau, Kara *181*
Larios, Julie 1949- *178*
Larios, Julie Hofstrand
  See Larios, Julie
Larkin, Amy
  See Burns, Olive Ann
Larkin, Maia
  See Wojciechowska, Maia (Teresa)
Larkspur, Penelope
  See Wyatt, Valerie
Laroche, Giles 1956- *126*
  Earlier sketch in SATA *71*
LaRochelle, David 1960- *171*
  Earlier sketch in SATA *115*
Larom, Henry V. 1903(?)-1975
  Obituary *30*
LaRose, Linda *125*
Larrabee, Lisa 1947- *84*

Larrecq, John M(aurice) 1926-1980 .... *44*
  Obituary *25*
Larrick (Crosby), Nancy 1910-2004 .... *4*
Larsen, Anita 1942- *78*
Larsen, Egon 1904- *14*
Larsen, Rebecca 1944- *54*
Larson, Eve
  See St. John, Wylly Folk
Larson, Gary 1950- *57*
Larson, Hope 1982- *205*
Larson, Ingrid D(ana) 1965- *92*
Larson, Jean Russell 1930- *121*
Larson, Kirby 1954- *181*
  Earlier sketch in SATA *96*
Larson, Norita D(ittberner) 1944- *29*
Larson, William H. 1938- *10*
Larsson, Carl (Olof) 1853-1919 .... *35*
LaSalle, Charles A.
  See Ellis, Edward S.
LaSalle, Charles E.
  See Ellis, Edward S.
Lasell, Elinor H. 1929- *19*
Lasell, Fen H.
  See Lasell, Elinor H.
Lasenby, Jack 1931- *172*
  Earlier sketches in SATA *65, 103*
Laser, Michael 1954- *117*
Lash, Joseph P. 1909-1987 .... *43*
Lasher, Faith B. 1921- *12*
Lasker, David 1950- *38*
Lasker, Joe
  See Lasker, Joseph Leon
Lasker, Joseph Leon 1919- *83*
  Earlier sketch in SATA *9*
  See also SAAS *17*
Laski, Marghanita 1915-1988 .... *55*
Laskin, Pamela L. 1954- *75*
Lasky, Kathryn 1944- *210*
  Earlier sketches in SATA *13, 69, 112, 157*
  See also CLR *140*
Lasky Knight, Kathryn
  See Lasky, Kathryn
Lass, Bonnie *131*
Lassalle, C. E.
  See Ellis, Edward S.
Lassiter, Mary
  See Hoffman, Mary
Lassiter, Rhiannon 1977- *157*
Lat 1951- *196*
Latham, Barbara 1896- *16*
Latham, Frank B(rown) 1910-2000 .... *6*
Latham, Jean Lee 1902-1995 .... *68*
  Earlier sketch in SATA *2*
  See also CLR *50*
Latham, Mavis
  See Clark, Mavis Thorpe
Latham, Philip
  See Richardson, Robert S(hirley)
Lathrop, Dorothy P(ulis) 1891-1980 .... *14*
  Obituary *24*
Lathrop, Francis
  See Leiber, Fritz (Reuter, Jr.)
Latimer, Jim 1943- *80*
Latta, Rich
  See Latta, Richard
Latta, Richard 1946- *113*
Latta, Sara L. 1960- *174*
Lattany, Kristin
  See Lattany, Kristin Hunter
Lattany, Kristin (Eggleston) Hunter 1931- . *154*
  Autobiography Feature *154*
  Earlier sketch in SATA *132*
Lattany, Kristin Hunter 1931- *132*
  Earlier sketch in SATA *12*
  See also CLR *3*
  See also SAAS *10*
Lattimore, Eleanor Frances 1904-1986 .... *7*
  Obituary *48*
Lattin, Ann
  See Cole, Lois Dwight

Lauber, Patricia (Grace) 1924- *138*
  Earlier sketches in SATA *1, 33, 75*
  See also CLR *16*
Laugesen, Malene *207*
Laugesen, Malene Reynolds
  See Laugesen, Malene
Laugesen, Mary E(akin) 1906-1995 .... *5*
Laughbaum, Steve 1945- *12*
Laughlin, Florence Young 1910-2001 .... *3*
Laughlin, Rosemary 1941- *123*
Launder, Sally *206*
Laure, Ettagale
  See Blauer, Ettagale
Laure, Jason 1940- *50*
  Brief entry *44*
Laurence, Ester Hauser 1935- *7*
Laurence, Jean Margaret Wemyss
  See Laurence, Margaret
Laurence, Margaret 1926-1987
  Obituary *50*
Laurie, Rona 1916- *55*
Laurin, Anne
  See McLaurin, Anne
Lauritzen, Jonreed 1902-1979 .... *13*
Lauscher, Hermann
  See Hesse, Hermann
Lauture, Denize 1946- *86*
Laux, Connie
  See Laux, Constance
Laux, Constance 1952- *97*
Laux, Dorothy 1920- *49*
Lavallee, Barbara 1941- *166*
  Earlier sketch in SATA *74*
Lavender, David (Sievert) 1910-2003 .... *97*
  Obituary *145*
  Earlier sketch in SATA *64*
Lavender, William D. 1921- *143*
Laverne, Christine *175*
Lavert, Gwendolyn Battle 1951-
  See Battle-Lavert, Gwendolyn
Laverty, Donald
  See Blish, James
  and Knight, Damon (Francis)
Lavigne, Louis-Dominique *107*
Lavine, David 1928- *31*
Lavine, Sigmund Arnold 1908-1986 .... *82*
  Earlier sketch in SATA *3*
  See also CLR *35*
Lavond, Paul Dennis
  See Kornbluth, C(yril) M.
  and Lowndes, Robert A(ugustine) W(ard)
  and Pohl, Frederik
Lawford, Paula Jane 1960- *57*
  Brief entry *53*
Lawhead, Stephen R. 1950- *109*
Lawhead, Steve
  See Lawhead, Stephen R.
Lawlor, Laurie 1953- *137*
  Earlier sketch in SATA *80*
Lawlor, William
  See Lawlor, William T.
Lawlor, William T. 1951- *183*
Lawrence, Ann (Margaret) 1942-1987 .... *41*
  Obituary *54*
Lawrence, Caroline 1954- *203*
Lawrence, Iain 1955- *183*
  Earlier sketch in SATA *135*
Lawrence, J. T.
  See Rowland-Entwistle, (Arthur) Theodore
  (Henry)
Lawrence, Jerome 1915-2004 .... *65*
Lawrence, John 1933- *30*
Lawrence, Josephine 1890(?)-1978
  Obituary *24*
Lawrence, Louise 1943- *119*
  Earlier sketches in SATA *38, 78*
Lawrence, Louise de Kiriline 1894-1992 ..... *13*
Lawrence, Lynn
  See Garland, Sherry
Lawrence, Margery H. 1889-1969 .... *120*
Lawrence, Michael 1943- *132*

Lawrence, Mildred Elwood 1907-1997 .... *3*
Lawrence, R(onald) D(ouglas) 1921- *55*
Lawrinson, Julia 1969- *141*
Lawson, Amy
  See Gordon, Amy
Lawson, Carol (Antell) 1946- *42*
Lawson, Don(ald Elmer) 1917-1990 .... *9*
Lawson, Joan 1906- *55*
Lawson, Julie 1947- *126*
  Earlier sketch in SATA *79*
  See also CLR *89*
Lawson, Marion Tubbs 1896-1994 .... *22*
Lawson, Robert 1892-1957 .... *100*
  See also YABC *2*
  See also CLR *73*
Lawton, Clive A. 1951- *145*
Laxdal, Vivienne 1962- *112*
Laybourn, Emma *193*
Laycock, George (Edwin) 1921- *5*
Layne, Laura
  See Knott, William C(ecil, Jr.)
Layne, Steven L. *171*
Layson, Annelex Hofstra 1938(?)- *211*
Layton, Neal 1971- *187*
  Earlier sketch in SATA *152*
Layton, Neal Andrew
  See Layton, Neal
Lazare, Gerald John 1927- *44*
Lazare, Jerry
  See Lazare, Gerald John
Lazarevich, Mila 1942- *17*
Lazarus, Keo Felker 1913-1993 .... *21*
  Obituary *129*
Lea, Alec 1907- *19*
Lea, Bob 1952- *203*
Lea, Joan
  See Neufeld, John (Arthur)
Leach, Maria 1892-1977 .... *39*
  Brief entry *28*
Leacock, Elspeth 1946- *131*
Leacroft, Helen (Mabel Beal) 1919- *6*
Leacroft, Richard (Vallance Becher) 1914- *6*
Leaf, Margaret P. 1909(?)-1988
  Obituary *55*
Leaf, (Wilbur) Munro 1905-1976 .... *20*
  See also CLR *25*
Leaf, VaDonna Jean 1929- *26*
Leah, Devorah
  See Devorah-Leah
Leakey, Richard E(rskine Frere) 1944- *42*
Leander, Ed
  See Richelson, Geraldine
Lear, Edward 1812-1888 .... *100*
  Earlier sketch in SATA *18*
  See also CLR *75*
Lears, Laurie 1955- *127*
Leasor, James 1923-2007 .... *54*
Leasor, Thomas James
  See Leasor, James
Leavitt, Jerome E(dward) 1916- *23*
Leavitt, Martine 1953- *170*
LeBar, Mary E(velyn) 1910-1982 .... *35*
LeBlanc, Annette M. 1965- *68*
LeBlanc, L(ee) 1913- *54*
LeBox, Annette 1943- *145*
Lebrun, Claude 1929- *66*
Le Cain, Errol (John) 1941-1989 .... *68*
  Obituary *60*
  Earlier sketch in SATA *6*
Lechner, Jack *201*
Lechner, John 1966- *200*
Lecourt, Nancy (Hoyt) 1951- *73*
Ledbetter, Suzann 1953- *119*
Leder, Jane Mersky 1945- *61*
  Brief entry *51*
Lederer, Muriel 1929- *48*
Lederer, William J. 1912-2009 .... *62*
Lederer, William Julius
  See Lederer, William J.

Lee, Amanda
  See Baggett, Nancy
  and Buckholtz, Eileen (Garber)
  and Glick, Ruth (Burtnick)
Lee, Benjamin 1921- *27*
Lee, Betsy 1949- *37*
Lee, Carol
  See Fletcher, Helen Jill
Lee, Carol Ann 1969- *185*
Lee, Chinlun *182*
Lee, Cora
  See Anderson, Catherine Corley
Lee, Dennis (Beynon) 1939- *102*
  Earlier sketch in SATA *14*
  See also CLR *3*
Lee, Dom 1959- *146*
  Autobiography Feature *121*
  Earlier sketch in SATA *83*
  See also SAAS *26*
Lee, Doris Emrick 1905-1983 .... *44*
  Obituary *35*
Lee, Edward
  See Lee, J. Edward
Lee, Elizabeth Rogers 1940- *90*
Lee, Harper 1926- *11*
Lee, Hector Viveros 1962- *115*
Lee, Howard N.
  See Goulart, Ron
Lee, Huy Voun 1969- *129*
Lee, Insu *213*
Lee, J. Edward 1953- *130*
Lee, Jared 1943- *215*
Lee, Jared D.
  See Lee, Jared
Lee, Jeanne M. 1943- *138*
Lee, John R(obert) 1923-1976 .... *27*
Lee, Jordan
  See Scholefield, Alan
Lee, Joseph Edward
  See Lee, J. Edward
Lee, Julian
  See Latham, Jean Lee
Lee, Linda
  See Eyerly, Jeannette
Lee, Liz
  See Lee, Elizabeth Rogers
Lee, Lucy
  See Talbot, Charlene Joy
Lee, Lyn 1953- *128*
Lee, Manning de Villeneuve 1894-1980 ...... *37*
  Obituary *22*
Lee, Marian
  See Clish, (Lee) Marian
Lee, Marie G. 1964- *178*
  Earlier sketches in SATA *81, 130*
Lee, Marie Myung-Ok
  See Lee, Marie G.
Lee, Mary Price 1934- *82*
  Earlier sketch in SATA *8*
Lee, Mildred
  See Scudder, Mildred Lee
Lee, Nelle Harper
  See Lee, Harper
Lee, Richard S. 1927- *82*
Lee, Robert C. 1931- *20*
Lee, Robert Edwin 1918-1994 .... *65*
  Obituary *82*
Lee, Robert J. 1921- *10*
Lee, Roy
  See Hopkins, Clark
Lee, Sally 1943- *67*
Lee, Suzy *193*
Lee, Tammie
  See Townsend, Thomas L.
Lee, Tanith 1947- *185*
  Earlier sketches in SATA *8, 88, 134*
Lee, Virginia 1976- *208*
Leech, Ben
  See Bowkett, Stephen
Leeds, Contance *188*

Leedy, Loreen 1959- *175*
  Brief entry *50*
  Earlier sketches in SATA *54, 84, 128*
Leedy, Loreen Janelle
  See Leedy, Loreen
Lee-Hostetler, Jeri 1940- *63*
Leekley, Thomas B(riggs) 1910-2001 .... *23*
Leeming, Jo Ann
  See Leeming, Joseph
Leeming, Joseph 1897-1968 .... *26*
Leemis, Ralph B. 1954- *72*
Leese, Jennifer L.B. 1970- *163*
Leeson, Muriel 1920- *54*
Leeson, R. A.
  See Leeson, Robert (Arthur)
Leeson, Robert (Arthur) 1928- *76*
  Earlier sketch in SATA *42*
Lee Tae-Jun 1904-1956(?) *194*
Lee-Tai, Amy 1964- *189*
Leffland, Ella 1931- *65*
Leffler, Silke *197*
Lefler, Irene (Whitney) 1917- *12*
LeFrak, Karen *182*
Le Gallienne, Eva 1899-1991 .... *9*
  Obituary *68*
Legg, Gerald 1947- *143*
Legg, Sarah Martha Ross Bruggeman (?)-1982
  Obituary *40*
LeGrand
  See Henderson, LeGrand
Le Guin, Ursula K. 1929- *194*
  Earlier sketches in SATA *4, 52, 99, 149*
  See also CLR *91*
Le Guin, Ursula Kroeber
  See Le Guin, Ursula K.
Legum, Colin 1919-2003 .... *10*
Lehman, Barbara 1963- *170*
  Earlier sketch in SATA *115*
Lehman, Bob *91*
Lehman, Elaine *91*
Lehmann, Debra Lynn
  See Vanasse, Deb
Lehn, Cornelia 1920- *46*
Lehne, Judith Logan 1947- *93*
Lehr, Delores 1920- *10*
Lehr, Norma 1930- *71*
Leiber, Fritz (Reuter, Jr.) 1910-1992 .... *45*
  Obituary *73*
Leibold, Jay 1957- *57*
  Brief entry *52*
Leichman, Seymour 1933- *5*
Leick, Bonnie *205*
Leigh, Nila K. 1981- *81*
Leigh, Tom 1947- *46*
Leigh-Pemberton, John 1911-1997 .... *35*
Leighton, Clare (Veronica Hope)
  1899-1989 .... *37*
Leighton, Margaret (Carver) 1896-1987 .... *1*
  Obituary *52*
Leiner, Al(an) 1938- *83*
Leiner, Katherine 1949- *93*
Leipold, L. Edmond 1902-1983 .... *16*
Leisk, David (Johnson) 1906-1975 .... *30*
  Obituary *26*
  Earlier sketch in SATA *1*
  See also CLR *98*
Leister, Mary 1917- *29*
Leitch, Patricia 1933- *98*
  Earlier sketch in SATA *11*
Leitner, Isabella 1924- *86*
Lekich, John *202*
Leland, Bob 1956- *92*
Leland, Robert E.
  See Leland, Bob
Lematre, Pascal 1967- *176*
Lember, Barbara Hirsch 1941- *92*
LeMieux, A.C. 1954- *125*
  Earlier sketch in SATA *90*
LeMieux, Anne
  See LeMieux, A.C.

Author Index

LeMieux, Anne Connelly
  See LeMieux, A.C.
Lemieux, Michele 1955- 139
Lemke, Horst 1922- 38
Lenain, Thierry 1959- 201
Lenanton, Carola Mary Anima Oman
  See Oman, Carola (Mary Anima)
Lenard, Alexander 1910-1972
  Obituary 21
Lendroth, Susan 207
L'Engle, Madeleine 1918-2007 128
  Obituary 186
  Earlier sketches in SATA 1, 27, 75
  See also CLR 57
  See also SAAS 15
L'Engle, Madeleine Camp Franklin
  See L'Engle, Madeleine
Lengyel, Cornel Adam 1915- 27
Lengyel, Emil 1895-1985 3
  Obituary 42
Lennon, John 1940-1980 114
Lennon, John Ono
  See Lennon, John
Leno, Jay 1950- 154
LeNoir, Janice 1941- 89
Lens, Sidney 1912-1986 13
  Obituary 48
Lenski, Lois 1893-1974 100
  Earlier sketches in SATA 1, 26
  See also CLR 26
Lent, Blair 1930-2009 133
  Obituary 200
  Earlier sketch in SATA 2
Lent, Henry Bolles 1901-1973 17
Lent, John 1948- 108
Leodhas, Sorche Nic
  See Alger, Leclaire (Gowans)
Leokum, Arkady 1916(?)- 45
Leon, Carol Boyd 212
Leon, Sharon 1959- 79
Leonard, Alison 1944- 70
Leonard, Anna
  See Gilman, Laura Anne
Leonard, Constance (Brink) 1923- 42
  Brief entry 40
Leonard, Dutch
  See Leonard, Elmore
Leonard, Elmore 1925- 163
Leonard, Elmore John, Jr.
  See Leonard, Elmore
Leonard, Jonathan N(orton) 1903-1975 36
Leonard, Laura 1923- 75
Leonard, Tom 1955- 207
Leonetti, Mike 1958- 202
Leong, Gor Yun
  See Ellison, Virginia H(owell)
Leonhardt, Alice 1950- 152
Lerangis, Peter 1955- 171
  Earlier sketch in SATA 72
Lerman, Josh 215
Lerner, Aaron 1920-2007 35
  Obituary 179
Lerner, Aaron Bunsen
  See Lerner, Aaron
Lerner, Carol 1927- 86
  Earlier sketch in SATA 33
  See also CLR 34
  See also SAAS 12
Lerner, Gerda 1920- 65
Lerner, Harriet 1944- 101
Lerner, Marguerite Rush 1924-1987 11
  Obituary 51
Lerner, Sharon (Ruth) 1938-1982 11
  Obituary 29
Leroe, Ellen W(hitney) 1949- 99
  Brief entry 51
  Earlier sketch in SATA 61
Leroux, Gaston 1868-1927 65
Leroux-Hugon, Helene 1955- 132
LeRoy, Gen 52
  Brief entry 36

Lerrigo, Marion Olive 1898-1968
  Obituary 29
LeShan, Eda J(oan) 1922-2002 21
  See also CLR 6
LeSieg, Theo.
  See Dr. Seuss
Lesinski, Jeanne M. 1960- 120
Leslie, Robert Franklin 1911-1990 7
Leslie, Roger 1961- 168
Leslie, Roger James
  See Leslie, Roger
Leslie, Sarah
  See McGuire, Leslie (Sarah)
LeSourd, Catherine
  See Marshall, (Sarah) Catherine (Wood)
Lessac, Frane
  See Lessac, Frane
Lessac, Frane 1954- 209
  Earlier sketches in SATA 61, 148
Lessem, Dino Don
  See Lessem, Don
Lessem, Don 1951- 182
  Earlier sketches in SATA 97, 155
Lesser, Margaret 1899(?)-1979
  Obituary 22
Lesser, Rika 1953- 53
Lester, Alison 1952- 129
  Earlier sketches in SATA 50, 90
Lester, Helen 1936- 189
  Earlier sketches in SATA 46, 92, 145
Lester, Julius 1939- 157
  Earlier sketches in SATA 12, 74, 112
  See also CLR 143
Lester, Julius Bernard
  See Lester, Julius
Lester, Mike 1955- 206
  Earlier sketch in SATA 131
Le Sueur, Meridel 1900-1996 6
Leszczynski, Diana 211
Lethcoe, Jason 191
Le Tord, Bijou 1945- 95
  Earlier sketch in SATA 49
Letts, Billie 1938- 121
Letts, Elizabeth
  See Alalou, Elizabeth
Leuck, Laura 1962- 192
  Earlier sketches in SATA 85, 146
Leutscher, Alfred (George) 1913- 23
Levai, Blaise 1919- 39
Levchuk, Lisa 215
Levenkron, Steven 1941- 86
Leverich, Kathleen 1948- 103
LeVert, (William) John 1946- 55
Levert, Mireille 1956- 211
Levete, Sarah 1961- 153
Levin, Betty 1927- 201
  Earlier sketches in SATA 19, 84, 137
  See also SAAS 11
Levin, Ira 1929-2007 66
  Obituary 187
Levin, Ira Marvin
  See Levin, Ira
Levin, Marcia Obrasky 1918- 13
Levin, Meyer 1905-1981 21
  Obituary 27
Levin, Miriam (Ramsfelder) 1962- 97
Levine, Abby 1943- 54
  Brief entry 52
Levine, Anna 212
Levine, Betty K(rasne) 1933- 66
Levine, David 1926-2009 43
  Brief entry 35
Levine, Edna S(imon) 35
Levine, Ellen 1939- 190
Levine, Evan 1962- 77
  Earlier sketch in SATA 74
Levine, Gail Carson 1947- 195
  Earlier sketches in SATA 98, 161
  See also CLR 85
Levine, I(srael) E. 1923-2003 12
  Obituary 146

Levine, Joan Goldman 11
Levine, Joseph 1910- 33
Levine, Kristin 1974- 213
Levine, Marge 1934- 81
Levine, Rhoda 14
Levine, Sarah 1970- 57
Levine, Shar 1953- 131
Levine-Freidus, Gail
  See Provost, Gail Levine
Levinson, Nancy Smiler 1938- 211
  Earlier sketches in SATA 33, 80, 140
Levinson, Riki 99
  Brief entry 49
  Earlier sketch in SATA 52
Levithan, David 1972- 166
Levitin, Sonia 1934- 192
  Autobiography Feature 131
  Earlier sketches in SATA 4, 68, 119, 131
  See also CLR 53
  See also SAAS 2
Levitt, Sidney (Mark) 1947- 68
Levon, O. U.
  See Kesey, Ken
Levoy, Myron 49
  Brief entry 37
Levy, Barrie 112
Levy, Constance 1931- 140
  Earlier sketch in SATA 73
  See also SAAS 22
Levy, Elizabeth 1942- 169
  Earlier sketches in SATA 31, 69, 107
  See also SAAS 18
Levy, Janice 172
Levy, Marilyn 1937- 67
Levy, Nathan 1945- 63
Levy, Robert 1945- 82
Lewees, John
  See Stockton, Francis Richard
Lewin, Betsy 1937- 169
  Autobiography Feature 115
  Earlier sketches in SATA 32, 90
Lewin, Hugh 1939- 72
  Brief entry 40
  See also CLR 9
Lewin, Ted 1935- 195
  Autobiography Feature 115
  Earlier sketches in SATA 21, 76, 119, 165
Lewis, Alice C. 1936- 46
Lewis, Alice Hudson 1895(?)-1971
  Obituary 29
Lewis, Amanda 1955- 80
Lewis, Anthony 1927- 27
Lewis, Anthony 1966- 120
Lewis, Barbara A. 1943- 73
Lewis, Beverly 1949- 80
Lewis, Brenda Ralph 1932- 72
Lewis, Brian 1963- 128
Lewis, C. S. 1898-1963 100
  Earlier sketch in SATA 13
  See also CLR 109
Lewis, Claudia (Louise) 1907-2001 5
Lewis, Clive Staples
  See Lewis, C. S.
Lewis, Cynthia Copeland 1960- 111
Lewis, E. M. 123
  Earlier sketch in SATA 20
Lewis, Earl Bradley
  See Lewis, E.B.
Lewis, E.B. 1956- 211
  Earlier sketches in SATA 93, 124, 168
Lewis, Elizabeth Foreman 1892-1958 121
  See also YABC 2
Lewis, Francine
  See Wells, Helen
Lewis, Harry Sinclair
  See Lewis, Sinclair
Lewis, Hilda (Winifred) 1896-1974
  Obituary 20
Lewis, J. Patrick 1942- 205
  Earlier sketches in SATA 69, 104, 162
Lewis, Jack P(earl) 1919- 65

Lewis, Jean 1924- *61*
Lewis, Jon Samuel
  See Lewis, J.S.
Lewis, Joseph Anthony
  See Lewis, Anthony
Lewis, J.S. 1972- *203*
Lewis, Julinda
  See Lewis-Ferguson, Julinda
Lewis, Kevin *173*
Lewis, Kim 1951- *136*
  Earlier sketch in SATA *84*
Lewis, Linda (Joy) 1946- *67*
Lewis, Lucia Z.
  See Anderson, Lucia (Lewis)
Lewis, Marjorie 1929- *40*
  Brief entry *35*
Lewis, Mary 1907(?)-1988 .... *64*
  Obituary *56*
Lewis, Mervyn
  See Frewer, Glyn (M.)
Lewis, Michael
  See Untermeyer, Louis
Lewis, Naomi 1911-2009 .... *144*
  Earlier sketch in SATA *76*
Lewis, Paeony 1960- *173*
Lewis, Paul
  See Gerson, Noel Bertram
Lewis, Richard 1935- *3*
Lewis, Richard 1956- *209*
Lewis, Rob 1962- *72*
Lewis, Roger
  See Zarchy, Harry
Lewis, Rose *209*
Lewis, Rose A.
  See Lewis, Rose
Lewis, Shannon
  See Llywelyn, Morgan
Lewis, Shari 1934-1998 .... *35*
  Brief entry *30*
  Obituary *104*
Lewis, Sylvan R.
  See Aronson, Virginia
Lewis, Thomas P(arker) 1936- *27*
Lewis, Wendy A. 1966- *150*
Lewis-Ferguson, Julinda 1955- *85*
Lewison, Wendy Cheyette *177*
Lewiton, Mina 1904-1970 .... *2*
Lew-Vriethoff, Joanne *186*
Lexau, Joan M. *130*
  Earlier sketches in SATA *1, 36*
Ley, Willy 1906-1969 .... *2*
Leydon, Rita (Floden) 1949- *21*
Leyland, Eric (Arthur) 1911- *37*
L'Hommedieu, Dorothy Keasley 1885-1961
  Obituary *29*
Li, Xiao Jun 1952- *86*
Liao, Jimmy 1958- *202*
Liatsos, Sandra Olson 1942- *103*
Libby, Alisa M. *189*
Libby, Barbara M. *153*
Libby, Bill
  See Libby, William M.
Libby, William M. 1927-1984 .... *5*
  Obituary *39*
Liberty, Gene 1924- *3*
Lichtenheld, Tom *208*
  Earlier sketch in SATA *152*
Lichtman, Wendy 1946- *193*
Liddell, Kenneth 1912-1975 .... *63*
Lidz, Jane *120*
Lieberman, E(dwin) James 1934- *62*
Liebers, Arthur 1913-1984 .... *12*
Lieblich, Irene 1923- *22*
Liers, Emil E(rnest) 1890-1975 .... *37*
Lies, Brian 1963- *190*
  Earlier sketch in SATA *131*
Liestman, Vicki 1961- *72*
Lietz, Gerald S. 1918- *11*
Life, Kay (Guinn) 1930- *83*
Lifton, Betty Jean *118*
  Earlier sketch in SATA *6*

Lifton, Robert Jay 1926- *66*
Lightburn, Ron 1954- *91*
Lightburn, Sandra 1955- *91*
Lightner, A. M.
  See Hopf, Alice (Martha) L(ightner)
Lightner, Alice
  See Hopf, Alice (Martha) L(ightner)
Lignell, Lois 1911- *37*
Liles, Maurine Walpole 1935- *81*
Lillegard, Dee *184*
Lilley, Stephen R. 1950- *97*
Lilley, Stephen Ray
  See Lilley, Stephen R.
Lillington, Kenneth (James) 1916-1998 .... *39*
Lilly, Nate *182*
Lilly, Ray
  See Curtis, Richard
Lim, John 1932- *43*
Liman, Ellen (Fogelson) 1936- *22*
Limb, Sue 1946- *203*
  Earlier sketch in SATA *158*
Limburg, Peter R(ichard) 1929- *13*
Lin, Grace 1974- *198*
  Earlier sketches in SATA *111, 162*
Lincoln, C(harles) Eric 1924-2000 .... *5*
Lincoln, Christopher 1952- *208*
Lincoln, Hazel *187*
Lincoln, James
  See Bates, Katharine Lee
Lindbergh, Anne
  See Sapieyevski, Anne Lindbergh
Lindbergh, Anne Morrow 1906-2001 .... *33*
  Obituary *125*
Lindbergh, Anne Spencer Morrow
  See Lindbergh, Anne Morrow
Lindbergh, Charles A(ugustus, Jr.)
  1902-1974 .... *33*
Lindbergh, Reeve 1945- *163*
  Earlier sketch in SATA *116*
Lindblom, Steven (Winther) 1946- *94*
  Brief entry *39*
  Earlier sketch in SATA *42*
Linde, Gunnel 1924- *5*
Lindenbaum, Pija 1955- *183*
  Earlier sketches in SATA *77, 144*
Lindgren, Astrid (Anna Emilia Ericsson)
  1907-2002 .... *38*
  Obituary *128*
  Earlier sketch in SATA *2*
  See also CLR *119*
Lindgren, Barbro 1937- *207*
  Brief entry *46*
  Earlier sketches in SATA *63, 120*
  See also CLR *86*
Lindman, Maj (Jan) 1886-1972 .... *43*
Lindop, Edmund 1925- *5*
Lindquist, Jennie Dorothea 1899-1977 .... *13*
Lindquist, Rowena Cory 1958- *98*
Lindquist, Willis 1908-1988 .... *20*
Lindsay, Nicholas Vachel
  See Lindsay, Vachel
Lindsay, Norman Alfred William
  1879-1969 .... *67*
  See also CLR *8*
Lindsay, Vachel 1879-1931 .... *40*
Lindsey, Kathleen D(orothy) 1949- *153*
Line, David
  See Davidson, Lionel
Line, Les 1935-2010 .... *27*
Lines, Kathleen Mary 1902-1988
  Obituary *61*
Linfield, Esther *40*
Lingard, Joan (Amelia) 1932- *130*
  Autobiography Feature *130*
  Earlier sketches in SATA *8, 74, 114*
  See also CLR *89*
  See also SAAS *5*
Link, Martin 1934- *28*
Linn, Margot
  See Ziefert, Harriet
Linnea, Sharon 1956- *82*

Lion, Melissa 1976- *176*
Lionni, Leo(nard) 1910-1999 .... *72*
  Obituary *118*
  Earlier sketch in SATA *8*
  See also CLR *71*
Lipinsky de Orlov, Lino S. 1908- *22*
Lipkind, William 1904-1974 .... *15*
Lipman, David 1931-2008 .... *21*
Lipman, Matthew 1923- *14*
Lipp, Frederick *204*
Lippincott, Bertram 1898(?)-1985
  Obituary *42*
Lippincott, Gary A. 1953- *119*
  Earlier sketch in SATA *73*
Lippincott, Joseph W(harton) 1887-1976 ..... *17*
Lippincott, Sarah Lee 1920- *22*
Lippman, Peter J. 1936- *31*
Lipsyte, Robert 1938- *198*
  Earlier sketches in SATA *5, 68, 113, 161*
  See also CLR *76*
Lipsyte, Robert Michael
  See Lipsyte, Robert
Lisandrelli, Elaine Slivinski 1951- *94*
Lisker, Sonia O. 1933- *44*
Lisle, Holly 1960- *208*
  Earlier sketch in SATA *98*
Lisle, Janet Taylor 1947- *150*
  Brief entry *47*
  Earlier sketches in SATA *59, 96*
  See also SAAS *14*
Lisle, Rebecca *162*
Lisle, Seward D.
  See Ellis, Edward S.
Lisowski, Gabriel 1946- *47*
  Brief entry *31*
Liss, Howard 1922-1995 .... *4*
  Obituary *84*
Lissiat, Amy
  See Thompson, Colin
Lisson, Deborah 1941- *110*
  Earlier sketch in SATA *71*
List, Ilka Katherine 1935- *6*
Liston, Robert A. 1927- *5*
Litchfield, Ada B(assett) 1916-1999 .... *5*
Litchfield, Jo 1973- *116*
Lithgow, John 1945- *145*
Lithgow, John Arthur
  See Lithgow, John
Litowinsky, Olga (Jean) 1936- *26*
Littke, Lael J. 1929- *140*
  Earlier sketches in SATA *51, 83*
Little, A. Edward
  See Klein, Aaron E.
Little, Douglas 1942- *96*
Little, (Flora) Jean 1932- *149*
  Earlier sketches in SATA *2, 68, 106*
  See also CLR *4*
  See also SAAS *17*
Little, Lessie Jones 1906-1986 .... *60*
  Obituary *50*
Little, Mary E. 1912-1999 .... *28*
Littlechild, George 1958- *85*
Littledale, Freya (Lota) 1929-1992 .... *74*
  Earlier sketch in SATA *2*
Littlefield, Bill 1948- *83*
Littlefield, Holly 1963- *97*
Littlesugar, Amy 1953- *176*
  Earlier sketch in SATA *122*
Littleton, Mark R. 1950- *142*
  Earlier sketch in SATA *89*
Littlewood, Karin *211*
Littman, Sarah Darer *175*
Litty, Julie 1971- *181*
Litzinger, Rosanne 1948- *196*
Lively, Penelope 1933- *164*
  Earlier sketches in SATA *7, 60, 101*
  See also CLR *7*
Lively, Penelope Margaret
  See Lively, Penelope
Liverakos, L. A.
  See Gilman, Laura Anne

Liversidge, (Henry) Douglas 1913- 8
Livesey, Claire (Warner) 1927- 127
Livingston, Carole 1941- 42
Livingston, (M.) Irene 1932- 150
Livingston, Myra Cohn 1926-1996 68
    Obituary 92
    Earlier sketch in SATA 5
    See also CLR 7
    See also SAAS 1
Livingston, Richard R(oland) 1922- 8
Livo, Norma J. 1929- 76
Liwska, Renata 199
Ljungkvist, Laura 180
Llerena Aguirre, Carlos 1952- 19
Llerena Aguirre, Carlos Antonio
    See Llerena Aguirre, Carlos
Llewellyn, Claire 1954- 196
    Earlier sketches in SATA 77, 143
Llewellyn, Grace 1964- 110
Llewellyn, Richard
    See Llewellyn Lloyd, Richard Dafydd Vivian
Llewellyn, Sam 1948- 185
    Earlier sketch in SATA 95
Llewellyn Lloyd, Richard Dafydd Vivian
    1906-1983 11
    Obituary 37
Llewelyn, T. Harcourt
    See Hamilton, Charles (Harold St. John)
Lloyd, Alan
    See Lloyd, A.R.
Lloyd, Alan Richard
    See Lloyd, A.R.
Lloyd, A.R. 1927- 168
    Earlier sketch in SATA 97
Lloyd, David
    See Lloyd, David T.
Lloyd, David T. 1954- 167
Lloyd, E. James
    See James, Elizabeth
Lloyd, Errol 1943- 22
Lloyd, Hugh
    See Fitzhugh, Percy Keese
Lloyd, James
    See James, Elizabeth
Lloyd, Megan 1958- 189
    Earlier sketches in SATA 77, 117
Lloyd, Norman 1909-1980
    Obituary 23
Lloyd, (Mary) Norris 1908-1993 10
    Obituary 75
Lloyd, Sam 183
Lloyd-Jones, Sally 1960- 179
Lloyd Webber, Andrew 1948- 56
Llywelyn, Morgan 1937- 109
Lo, Ginnie 165
Lo, Virginia M.
    See Lo, Ginnie
Lobato, Jose Bento Monteiro 1882-1948 ... 114
Lobel, Anita (Kempler) 1934- 162
    Earlier sketches in SATA 6, 55, 96
Lobel, Arnold (Stark) 1933-1987 55
    Obituary 54
    Earlier sketch in SATA 6
    See also CLR 5
Lobel, Gillian 181
Lobsenz, Amelia 12
Lobsenz, Norman M(itchell) 1919- 6
Lochak, Michele 1936- 39
Lochlons, Colin
    See Jackson, C(aary) Paul
Locke, Clinton W. 1
Locke, Elsie (Violet) 1912-2001 87
Locke, Gary 1963- 197
Locke, Lucie 1904-1989 10
Locke, Robert 1944- 63
    See also CLR 39
Locker, Thomas 1937- 109
    Earlier sketch in SATA 59
    See also CLR 14
Lockhart, E.
    See Jenkins, Emily

Lockridge, Hildegarde (Dolson)
    1908-1981 121
    Earlier sketch in SATA 5
Lockwood, Mary
    See Spelman, Mary
Lodge, Bernard 1933- 215
    Earlier sketches in SATA 33, 107
Lodge, Jo 1966- 173
    Earlier sketch in SATA 112
Loeb, Jeffrey 1946- 57
Loeb, Robert H., Jr. 1917- 21
Loefgren, Ulf 1931- 3
Loehfelm, Bill 1969- 153
Loehr, Mallory 184
Loehr, Patrick 1968(?)- 194
Loeper, John J(oseph) 1929- 118
    Earlier sketch in SATA 10
Loescher, Ann Dull 1942- 20
Loescher, Gil(burt Damian) 1945- 20
Loewer, Jean Jenkins
    See Jenkins, Jean
Loewer, (Henry) Peter 1934- 98
LoFaro, Jerry 1959- 77
Lofo
    See Heimann, Rolf
Lofthouse, Liz 199
Lofting, Hugh (John) 1886-1947 100
    Earlier sketch in SATA 15
    See also CLR 143
Lofts, Norah (Robinson) 1904-1983 8
    Obituary 36
Logan, Jake
    See Knott, William C(ecil, Jr.)
    and Krepps, Robert W(ilson)
    and Pearl, Jacques Bain
    and Riefe, Alan
    and Rifkin, Shepard
    and Smith, Martin Cruz
Logan, Mark
    See Nicole, Christopher (Robin)
Logan, Rochelle 1954- 169
Logston, Anne 1962- 112
Logue, Christopher 1926- 23
Logue, Mary 1952- 161
    Earlier sketch in SATA 112
Logue, Mary Louise
    See Logue, Mary
Loh, Morag 1935- 73
Lohans, Alison 1949- 101
Loizeaux, William 185
Loken, Newton Clayton 1919- 26
Lomas, Steve
    See Brennan, Joseph Lomas
Lomask, Milton (Nachman) 1909-1991 20
Lombard, Jenny 178
Lombino, Salvatore
    See Hunter, Evan
LoMonaco, Palmyra 1932- 102
London, Jack 1876-1916 18
    See also CLR 108
London, Jane
    See Geis, Darlene Stern
London, John Griffith
    See London, Jack
London, Jonathan (Paul) 1947- 157
    Earlier sketches in SATA 74, 113
Lonergan, (Pauline) Joy (MacLean) 1909- ... 10
Lonette, Reisie (Dominee) 1924- 43
Long, Cathryn J. 1946- 89
Long, Earlene (Roberta) 1938- 50
Long, Emmett
    See Leonard, Elmore
Long, Ethan 1968(?)- 182
Long, Helen Beecher 1
Long, Judith Elaine 1953- 20
Long, Judy
    See Long, Judith Elaine
Long, Kim 1949- 69
Long, Laura Mooney 1892-1967
    Obituary 29
Long, Laurel 203

Long, Loren 1966(?)- 188
    Earlier sketch in SATA 151
Long, Melinda 1960- 152
Long, Sylvia 1948- 179
    Earlier sketch in SATA 120
Longbeard, Frederick
    See Longyear, Barry B(rookes)
Longfellow, Henry Wadsworth 1807-1882 ... 19
    See also CLR 99
Longfellow, Layne 1937- 102
Longfellow, Layne A.
    See Longfellow, Layne
Longman, Harold S. 1919- 5
Longsworth, Polly 1933- 28
Longtemps, Kenneth 1933- 17
Longway, A. Hugh
    See Lang, Andrew
Longyear, Barry B(rookes) 1942- 117
Look, Lenore 180
Loomans, Diane 1955- 90
Loomis, Christine 160
    Earlier sketch in SATA 113
Loomis, Jennifer A. 1942- 101
Loomis, Robert D. 5
Lopez, Angelo (Cayas) 1967- 83
Lopez, Barry 1945- 67
Lopez, Barry Holstun
    See Lopez, Barry
Lopez, Jack 1950- 178
Lopez, Loretta 1963- 190
Lopez, Lorraine 1956- 181
Lopez, Lorraine M.
    See Lopez, Lorraine
Lopez, Rafael 1961(?)- 198
Lopshire, Robert M(artin) 1927- 6
Loraine, Connie
    See Reece, Colleen L.
Lorbiecki, Marybeth 1959- 172
    Earlier sketch in SATA 121
Lord, Athena V. 1932- 39
Lord, Beman 1924-1991 5
    Obituary 69
Lord, Bette Bao 1938- 58
    See also CLR 151
Lord, Cynthia 182
Lord, Doreen Mildred Douglas
    See Lord, Douglas
Lord, Douglas 1904-1992 12
Lord, Janet 204
Lord, John Vernon 1939- 21
Lord, Michele 201
Lord, Nancy
    See Titus, Eve
Lord, Patricia C. 1927-1988
    Obituary 58
Lord, Walter 1917-2002 3
Lorde, Diana
    See Reno, Dawn E(laine)
Lorenz, Albert 1941- 115
Lorenzini, Carlo
    See Collodi, Carlo
Lorey, Dean 1967- 193
Lorimer, Janet 1941- 60
Loring, Emilie (Baker) 1864(?)-1951 51
Lorkowski, Thomas V(incent) 1950- 92
Lorkowski, Tom
    See Lorkowski, Thomas V(incent)
Lorraine, Walter (Henry) 1929- 16
Lorrimer, Claire
    See Clark, Patricia Denise
Loss, Joan 1933- 11
Lothrop, Harriet Mulford Stone 1844-1924 . 20
Lottridge, Celia Barker 1936- 157
    Earlier sketch in SATA 112
LoTurco, Laura 1963- 84
Lotz, Wolfgang 1912-1981 65
Loughridge, Stuart 1978- 214
Louie, Ai-Ling 1949- 40
    Brief entry 34
Louis, Catherine 1963- 186

Louis, Pat
    See Francis, Dorothy
Louisburgh, Sheila Burnford
    See Burnford, Sheila (Philip Cochrane Every)
Louise, Anita
    See Riggio, Anita
Louise, Tina 1934- 191
Lourie, Helen
    See Storr, Catherine (Cole)
Lourie, Peter 1952- 183
    Earlier sketches in SATA 82, 142
Lourie, Peter King
    See Lourie, Peter
Love, Ann 1947- 168
    Earlier sketch in SATA 79
Love, D. Anne 1949- 180
    Earlier sketches in SATA 96, 145
Love, Douglas 1967- 92
Love, Judith Dufour
    See Love, Judy
Love, Judy 188
Love, Katherine (Isabel) 1907- 3
Love, Kathleen Ann
    See Love, Ann
Love, Sandra (Weller) 1940- 26
Lovejoy, Jack 1937- 116
Lovelace, Delos Wheeler 1894-1967 7
Lovelace, Maud Hart 1892-1980 2
    Obituary 23
Lovell, Ingraham
    See Bacon, Josephine Dodge (Daskam)
Lovelock, Brian 1956- 214
Loverseed, Amanda (Jane) 1965- 75
Lovett, Margaret (Rose) 1915- 22
Low, Alice 1926- 156
    Earlier sketches in SATA 11, 76
Low, Elizabeth Hammond 1898-1991 5
Low, Joseph 1911-2007 14
Low, Penelope Margaret
    See Lively, Penelope
Low, William 177
Lowe, Helen 1961- 206
Lowe, Jay, Jr.
    See Loeper, John J(oseph)
Lowell, Pamela 187
Lowell, Susan 1950- 206
    Earlier sketches in SATA 81, 127
Lowenstein, Dyno 1914-1996 6
Lowenstein, Sallie 1949- 116
Lowery, Linda 1949- 151
    Earlier sketch in SATA 74
Lowitz, Anson C. 1901(?)-1978 18
Lowitz, Sadyebeth Heath 1901-1969 17
Lowndes, Robert A(ugustine) W(ard)
    1916-1998 117
Lowrey, Janette Sebring 1892-1986 43
Lowry, Lois 1937- 177
    Autobiography Feature 127
    Earlier sketches in SATA 23, 70, 111
    See also CLR 72
    See also SAAS 3
Lowry, Lois Hammersberg
    See Lowry, Lois
Lowry, Peter 1953- 7
Lowther, George F. 1913-1975
    Obituary 30
Loyie, Larry 1933- 150
Lozansky, Edward D. 1941- 62
Lozier, Herbert 1915- 26
Lubar, David 1954- 190
    Earlier sketch in SATA 133
Lubell, Cecil 1912-2000 6
Lubell, Winifred (A. Milius) 1914- 6
Lubin, Leonard
    See Lubin, Leonard B.
Lubin, Leonard B. 1943-1994 45
    Brief entry 37
Lubka, S. Ruth 1948- 154
Lubner, Susan 185
Luby, Thia 1954- 124
Lucado, Max (Lee) 1955- 104

Lucas, Cedric 1962- 101
Lucas, David 1966- 208
Lucas, E(dward) V(errall) 1868-1938 20
Lucas, Eileen 1956- 113
    Earlier sketch in SATA 76
Lucas, George 1944- 56
Lucas, Jerry 1940- 33
Lucas, Margeaux 186
Lucas, Victoria
    See Plath, Sylvia
Lucashenko, Melissa 1967- 104
Luccarelli, Vincent 1923- 90
Luce, Celia (Geneva Larsen) 1914- 38
Luce, Willard (Ray) 1914-1990 38
Lucht, Irmgard 1937- 82
Lucke, Deb 202
Luckett, Dave 1951- 167
    Earlier sketch in SATA 106
Luckhardt, Mildred Corell 1898-1990 5
Ludden, Allen (Ellsworth) 1918(?)-1981
    Obituary 27
Ludel, Jacqueline 1945- 64
Ludlow, Geoffrey
    See Meynell, Laurence Walter
Ludlum, Mabel Cleland
    See Widdemer, Mabel Cleland
Ludwig, Helen 33
Ludwig, Lyndell 1923- 63
Ludwig, Trudy 1959- 209
    Earlier sketch in SATA 166
Luebs, Robin 1949- 212
Lueders, Edward (George) 1923- 14
Luenn, Nancy 1954- 79
    Earlier sketch in SATA 51
Lufkin, Raymond H. 1897- 38
Lugard, Flora Louisa Shaw 1852-1929 21
Luger, Harriett Mandelay 1914- 23
Luhrmann, Winifred B(ruce) 1934- 11
Luis, Earlene W. 1929- 11
Lujan, Jorge 201
Luke, Pauline 178
Luke, Pauline R.
    See Luke, Pauline
Lum, Peter
    See Crowe, (Bettina) Peter Lum
Lumry, Amanda (R.) 159
Lund, Deb 157
Lund, Doris Herold 1919- 12
Lunde, Darrin 202
Lundebrek, Amy 1975- 213
Lung, Chang
    See Jordan, Robert
Lunge-Larsen, Lise 1955- 184
    Earlier sketch in SATA 138
Lunn, Carolyn (Kowalczyk) 1960- 67
Lunn, Janet (Louise Swoboda) 1928- 110
    Earlier sketches in SATA 4, 68
    See also CLR 18
    See also SAAS 12
Lunsford, Cin Forshay
    See Forshay-Lunsford, Cin
Lupica, Michael
    See Lupica, Mike
Lupica, Michael Thomas
    See Lupica, Mike
Lupica, Mike 1952- 177
Lupoff, Dick
    See Lupoff, Richard A(llen)
Lupoff, Richard A(llen) 1935- 60
Lurie, Alison 1926- 112
    Earlier sketch in SATA 46
Lurie, Morris 1938- 72
Lussert, Anneliese 1929- 101
Lusted, Marcia Amidon 1962- 143
Lustig, Arnost 1926- 56
Lustig, Loretta 1944- 46
Lutes, Jason 1967- 210
Luthardt, Kevin 1973- 172
Luther, Frank 1905-1980
    Obituary 25
Luther, Rebekah (Lyn) S(tiles) 1960- 90

Luttmann, Gail
    See Damerow, Gail
Luttrell, Guy L. 1938- 22
Luttrell, Ida (Alleene) 1934- 91
    Brief entry 35
    Earlier sketch in SATA 40
Luttrell, William (J. III) 1954- 149
Lutz, John 1939- 180
Lutz, John Thomas
    See Lutz, John
Lutz, Norma Jean 1943- 122
Lutzeier, Elizabeth 1952- 72
Lutzker, Edythe 1904-1991 5
Luxbacher, Irene M. 1970- 153
Luzadder, Patrick 1954- 89
Luzzati, Emanuele 1921-2007 7
Luzzatto, Paola Caboara 1938- 38
Ly, Many 1977- 208
Lybbert, Tyler 1970- 88
Lydon, Michael 1942- 11
Lyfick, Warren
    See Reeves, Lawrence F.
Lyle, Katie Letcher 1938- 8
Lynch, Chris 1962- 209
    Earlier sketches in SATA 95, 131, 171
    See also CLR 58
Lynch, Jay 1945- 204
Lynch, Lorenzo 1932- 7
Lynch, Marietta 1947- 29
Lynch, Patricia (Nora) 1898-1972 9
Lynch, Patrick James
    See Lynch, P.J.
Lynch, P.J. 1962- 213
    Earlier sketches in SATA 79, 122
Lynds, Dennis 1924-2005 47
    Brief entry 37
Lyne, Alison Davis 188
Lyngseth, Joan
    See Davies, Joan
Lynn, Elizabeth A(nne) 1946- 99
Lynn, Mary
    See Brokamp, Marilyn
Lynn, Patricia
    See Watts, Mabel Pizzey
Lynn, Tracy 175
Lyon, Elinor 1921-2008 6
    Obituary 192
Lyon, Elinor Bruce
    See Lyon, Elinor
Lyon, George Ella 1949- 207
    Autobiography Feature 148
    Earlier sketches in SATA 68, 119, 148
Lyon, Lea 1945- 212
Lyon, Lyman R.
    See de Camp, L. Sprague
Lyons, Dorothy M(arawee) 1907-1997 3
Lyons, Grant 1941- 30
Lyons, Marcus
    See Blish, James
Lyons, Mary E. 1947- 195
    Autobiography Feature 195
    Earlier sketches in SATA 93, 142
Lyons, Mary Evelyn
    See Lyons, Mary E.
Lystad, Mary (Hanemann) 1928- 11
Lytle, Elizabeth Stewart 1949- 79
Lytle, Robert A. 1944- 119
Lyttle, Richard B(ard) 1927- 23
Lytton of Knebworth, Baron
    See Bulwer-Lytton, Edward

M

Ma, Wenhai 1954- 84
Maar, Leonard (Frank, Jr.) 1927- 30
Maartens, Maretha 1945- 73
Maas, Selve -1997 14
Maass, Robert 195

Mabie, Grace
  See Mattern, Joanne
Mac
  See MacManus, Seumas
  and Maccari, Ruggero
Macalaster, Elizabeth G. 1951- *115*
MacAlister, Katie *159*
MacAlister, V. A.
  See McKernan, Victoria
MacAllan, Andrew
  See Leasor, James
MacAodhagain, Eamon
  See Egan, E(dward) W(elstead)
MacArthur-Onslow, Annette Rosemary
  1933- *26*
Macaulay, David (Alexander) 1946- *137*
  Brief entry *27*
  Earlier sketches in SATA *46, 72*
  See also CLR *14*
Macaulay, Teresa (E.) 1947- *95*
Macavinta, Courtney *176*
MacBeth, George (Mann) 1932-1992 .... *4*
  Obituary *70*
MacBride, Roger Lea 1929-1995 .... *85*
MacCarter, Don 1944- *91*
MacClintock, Dorcas 1932- *8*
MacCready, Robin Merrow 1959(?)- *190*
MacCullough, Carolyn *174*
MacDonald, Alan 1958- *192*
MacDonald, Amy 1951- *156*
  Autobiography Feature *156*
  Earlier sketches in SATA *76, 136*
MacDonald, Anne Elizabeth Campbell Bard
  -1958
  See MacDonald, Betty
MacDonald, Anson
  See Heinlein, Robert A.
MacDonald, Betty 1908-1958
  See YABC *1*
Macdonald, Blackie
  See Emrich, Duncan (Black Macdonald)
Macdonald, Caroline 1948- *86*
  Obituary *111*
  See also CLR *60*
Macdonald, Dwight 1906-1982 .... *29*
  Obituary *33*
MacDonald, George 1824-1905 .... *100*
  Earlier sketch in SATA *33*
  See also CLR *67*
MacDonald, Golden
  See Brown, Margaret Wise
Macdonald, Guy *195*
Macdonald, James D. 1954- *67*
  Earlier sketches in SATA *81, 114, 165, 1*
Macdonald, Marcia
  See Hill, Grace Livingston
MacDonald, Margaret Read 1940- *194*
  Earlier sketches in SATA *94, 164*
Macdonald, Marianne 1934- *113*
Macdonald, Mary
  See Gifford, Griselda
Macdonald, Maryann 1947- *189*
  Earlier sketch in SATA *72*
MacDonald, Ross 1957- *201*
Macdonald, Shelagh 1937- *25*
MacDonald, Suse 1940- *193*
  Brief entry *52*
  Earlier sketches in SATA *54, 109*
Macdonald, Zillah K(atherine) 1885-1979 ... *11*
MacDonnell, Megan
  See Stevens, Serita
MacDougal, John
  See Blish, James
Mace, Elisabeth 1933- *27*
Mace, Varian 1938- *49*
MacEachern, Stephen *206*
MacEwen, Gwendolyn (Margaret)
  1941-1987 .... *50*
  Obituary *55*
Macfarlan, Allan A. 1892-1982 .... *35*
MacFarlane, Iris 1922- *11*

MacGill-Callahan, Sheila 1926-2000 .... *78*
MacGregor, Carol Lynn *153*
MacGregor, Ellen 1906-1954 .... *39*
  Brief entry *27*
MacGregor-Hastie, Roy (Alasdhair Niall)
  1929- *3*
MacGrory, Yvonne 1948- *142*
Machado, Ana Maria 1941- *150*
MacHale, D.J. 1956- *175*
MacHale, Donald James
  See MacHale, D.J.
Machetanz, Frederick 1908- *34*
Machin, Sue
  See Williams, Sue
Machin Goodall, Daphne (Edith) *37*
Macht, Norm
  See Macht, Norman L.
Macht, Norman L. 1929- *122*
Macht, Norman Lee
  See Macht, Norman L.
Macht, Norman Lee
  See Macht, Norman L.
MacInnes, Helen (Clark) 1907-1985 .... *22*
  Obituary *44*
Macintosh, Brownie 1950- *98*
MacIntyre, Elisabeth 1916- *17*
MacIntyre, Rod
  See MacIntyre, R.P.
MacIntyre, R.P. 1947- *203*
MacIntyre, R.P. 1947- *203*
MacIntyre, Wendy 1947- *196*
Mack, Jeff *194*
Mack, L.V.
  See Kimmelman, Burt
Mack, Stan(ley) *17*
Mack, Todd *168*
Mack, Tracy 1968- *183*
  Earlier sketch in SATA *128*
Mackall, Dandi D.
  See Mackall, Dandi Daley
Mackall, Dandi Daley 1949- *182*
  Earlier sketches in SATA *118, 177*
Mackay, Claire 1930- *97*
  Autobiography Feature *124*
  Earlier sketch in SATA *40*
  See also CLR *43*
Mackay, Constance D'Arcy (?)-1966 .... *125*
Mackay, Donald 1914-2005 .... *81*
  Obituary *173*
Mackay, Donald Alexander
  See Mackay, Donald
MacKaye, Percy (Wallace) 1875-1956 .... *32*
Mackel, Kathryn 1950- *162*
Mackel, Kathy
  See Mackel, Kathryn
MacKellar, William 1914- *4*
Macken, JoAnn Early 1953- *201*
Macken, Walter 1915-1967 .... *36*
Mackenzie, Anna 1963- *212*
MacKenzie, Jill (Kelly) 1947- *75*
Mackenzie, Robert 1974- *204*
Mackey, Ernan
  See McInerny, Ralph
Mackey, Weezie Kerr *188*
Mackie, Maron
  See McNeely, Jeannette
Mackin, Edward
  See McInerny, Ralph
MacKinnon, Bernie 1957- *69*
MacKinnon Groomer, Vera 1915- *57*
MacKinstry, Elizabeth 1879-1956 .... *42*
Mackler, Carolyn 1973- *156*
MacLachlan, Emily
  See Charest, Emily MacLachlan
MacLachlan, Patricia 1938- *168*
  Brief entry *42*
  Earlier sketches in SATA *62, 107*
  See also CLR *14*
MacLane, Jack
  See Crider, Bill

MacLean, Alistair 1922(?)-1987 .... *23*
  Obituary *50*
MacLean, Alistair Stuart
  See MacLean, Alistair
Maclean, Art
  See Shirreffs, Gordon D(onald)
MacLean, Christine Kole 1962- *177*
MacLean, Glynne 1964- *150*
MacLean, Jill 1941- *211*
MacLeod, Beatrice 1910- *162*
  Earlier sketch in SATA *10*
MacLeod, Beatrice Beach
  See MacLeod, Beatrice
MacLeod, Charlotte (Matilda) 1922-2005 .... *28*
  Obituary *160*
MacLeod, Doug 1959- *201*
  Earlier sketch in SATA *60*
MacLeod, Elizabeth *184*
  Earlier sketch in SATA *158*
MacLeod, Ellen Jane (Anderson) 1916- *14*
MacManus, James
  See MacManus, Seumas
MacManus, Seumas 1869-1960 .... *25*
MacMaster, Eve (Ruth) B(owers) 1942- *46*
MacMillan, Annabelle
  See Quick, Annabelle
MacMillan, Dianne M(arie) 1943- *125*
  Earlier sketch in SATA *84*
Macnaughton, Tina *182*
Macneill, Janet
  See McNeely, Jeannette
MacPeek, Walter G. 1902-1973 .... *4*
  Obituary *25*
MacPhail, Catherine 1946- *197*
  Earlier sketch in SATA *130*
MacPherson, Margaret 1908-2001 .... *9*
  See also SAAS *4*
MacPherson, Thomas George 1915-1976
  Obituary *30*
MacPherson, Winnie 1930- *107*
MacRae, Tom 1980- *181*
Macrae, Travis
  See Feagles, Anita M(acRae)
MacRaois, Cormac 1944- *72*
Macumber, Mari
  See Sandoz, Mari(e Susette)
Macy, Sue 1954- *134*
  Earlier sketch in SATA *88*
Madaras, Lynda 1947- *151*
Madden, Don 1927- *3*
Madden, Kerry 1961- *168*
Madden-Lunsford, Kerry
  See Madden, Kerry
Maddern, Eric 1950- *166*
Maddigan, Beth 1967- *174*
Maddison, Angela Mary 1923- *10*
  See also CLR *24*
Maddock, Reginald (Bertram) 1912-1994 .... *15*
Madenski, Melissa (Ann) 1949- *77*
Madian, Jon 1941- *9*
Madison, Alan *182*
Madison, Arnold 1937- *6*
Madison, Winifred *5*
Madonna 1958- *149*
Madsen, Gunnar *171*
Madsen, Jim 1964- *202*
Madsen, Ross Martin 1946- *82*
Madsen, Susan A. 1954- *90*
Madsen, Susan Arrington
  See Madsen, Susan A.
Maehlqvist, Stefan 1943- *30*
Maestro, Betsy (Crippen) 1944- *106*
  Brief entry *30*
  Earlier sketch in SATA *59*
  See also CLR *45*
Maestro, Giulio 1942- *106*
  Earlier sketches in SATA *8, 59*
  See also CLR *45*
Maeterlinck, Maurice 1862-1949 .... *66*
Magee, Doug 1947- *78*
Magee, Wes 1939- *64*

Maggio, Rosalie 1943- 69
Magid, Ken(neth Marshall) 65
Magnus, Erica 1946- 77
Magoon, Kekla 1980- 213
Magoon, Scott 182
Magorian, James 1942- 92
    Earlier sketch in SATA 32
Magorian, Michelle 1947- 128
    Earlier sketch in SATA 67
Magorian, Michelle Jane
    See Magorian, Michelle
Magovern, Peg 103
Magsamen, Sandra 1959- 213
Maguire, Anne
    See Nearing, Penny
Maguire, Gregory 1954- 200
    Autobiography Feature 200
    Earlier sketches in SATA 28, 84, 129
    See also SAAS 22
Maguire, Gregory Peter
    See Maguire, Gregory
Maguire, Jack 1920-2000 74
Maguire, Jesse
    See Smith, Sherwood
Maguire, Jessie
    See Smith, Sherwood
Maher, Ramona 1934- 13
Mahlqvist, Stefan
    See Maehlqvist, Stefan
Mahon, Julia C(unha) 1916- 11
Mahony, Elizabeth Winthrop
    See Winthrop, Elizabeth
Mahood, Kenneth 1930- 24
Mahy, Margaret 1936- 171
    Earlier sketches in SATA 14, 69, 119
    See also CLR 78
Mahy, Margaret May
    See Mahy, Margaret
Maiden, Cecil (Edward) 1902-1981 52
Maidoff, Ilka
    See List, Ilka Katherine
Maifair, Linda Lee 1947- 83
Maik, Henri
    See Hecht, Henri Joseph
Maillu, David G(ian) 1939- 111
Maine, Trevor
    See Catherall, Arthur
Mains, Randolph P. 1946- 80
Maione, Heather 189
Maiorano, Robert 1946- 43
Maisner, Heather 1947- 89
Maison, Della
    See Katz, Bobbi
Maitland, Antony Jasper 1935- 25
Maitland, Barbara 102
Mai-Wyss, Tatjana 1972- 187
Maizels, Jennie 210
Major, Kevin (Gerald) 1949- 134
    Earlier sketches in SATA 32, 82
    See also CLR 11
Majure, Janet 1954- 96
Makhijani, Pooja 188
Makie, Pam 1943- 37
Makowski, Silk
    See Sullivan, Silky
Makowski, Silvia Ann
    See Sullivan, Silky
Malam, John 1957- 152
    Earlier sketch in SATA 89
Maland, Nick 195
Malcolm, Dan
    See Silverberg, Robert
Malcolm, Jahnna N.
    See Beecham, Jahnna
Malcolmson, Anne
    See von Storch, Anne B.
Malcolmson, David 1899-1978 6
Maletta, Dr. Arlene
    See Feltenstein, Arlene
Maley, Carleen
    See Hutchins, Carleen Maley

Mali, Jane Lawrence 1937-1995 51
    Brief entry 44
    Obituary 86
Malkin, Nina 1959(?)- 179
Mallett, Jerry J. 1939- 76
Malley, Gemma 198
Malley, G.R.
    See Malley, Gemma
Mallory, Kenneth 1945- 185
    Earlier sketch in SATA 128
Mallowan, Agatha Christie
    See Christie, Agatha
Malmberg, Carl 1904-1979 9
Malmgren, Dallin 1949- 65
Malo, John W. 1911-2000 4
Malone, James Hiram 1930- 84
Malone, Nola Langner 1930-2003 8
    Obituary 151
Malone, Patricia 1932- 155
Malone, Peter 1953- 191
Maloney, Pat
    See Markun, Patricia Maloney
Malory, Sir Thomas 1410(?)-1471(?) 59
    Brief entry 33
Maltese, Michael 1909(?)-1981
    Obituary 24
Malvasi, Meg Greene 143
Malvern, Corinne 1905-1956 34
Malvern, Gladys (?)-1962 23
Mama G.
    See Davis, Grania
Mammano, Julie 1962- 202
    Earlier sketch in SATA 107
Mamonova, Tatyana 1943- 93
Manchel, Frank 1935- 10
Manchess, Gregory 1955- 203
Manchester, William (Raymond)
    1922-2004 65
Mandabach, Brian 1962(?)- 197
Mandel, Brett H. 1969- 108
Mandel, Peter 1957- 87
Mandel, Sally (Elizabeth) 1944- 64
Mandell, Muriel (Hortense Levin) 1921- 63
Manders, John 1957- 175
Manes, Stephen 1949- 99
    Brief entry 40
    Earlier sketch in SATA 42
Manfred, Frederick (Feikema) 1912-1994 30
Mangin, Marie France 1940- 59
Mangione, Gerlando 1909-1998 6
    Obituary 104
Mangione, Jerre
    See Mangione, Gerlando
Mango, Karin N. 1936- 52
Mangurian, David 1938- 14
Mania, Cathy 1950- 102
Mania, Robert 1952- 102
Mania, Robert C., Jr.
    See Mania, Robert
Maniatty, Taramesha 1978- 92
Maniscalco, Joseph 1926- 10
Manley, Deborah 1932- 28
Manley, Seon 1921- 15
    See also CLR 3
    See also SAAS 2
Mann, Elizabeth 1948- 153
Mann, Josephine
    See Pullein-Thompson, Josephine (Mary
    Wedderburn)
Mann, Kenny 1946- 91
Mann, Pamela 1946- 91
Mann, Patrick
    See Waller, Leslie
Mann, Peggy
    See Houlton, Peggy Mann
Mannetti, Lisa 1953- 57
    Brief entry 51
Mannheim, Grete (Salomon) 1909-1986 10
Manniche, Lise 1943- 31
Manning, Jane K. 185

Manning, Maurie
    See Manning, Maurie J.
Manning, Maurie J. 211
Manning, Maurie Jo
    See Manning, Maurie J.
Manning, Mick 1959- 176
Manning, Rosemary 1911-1988 10
Manning, Sarra 162
Manning-Sanders, Ruth (Vernon)
    1895(?)-1988 73
    Obituary 57
    Earlier sketch in SATA 15
Mannion, Diane
    See Paterson, Diane
Mannis, Celeste Davidson 173
Mannon, Warwick
    See Hopkins, (Hector) Kenneth
Manos, Helen 199
Mansir, A. Richard 1932- 170
Manson, Ainslie Kertland 1938- 115
Manson, Beverlie 1945- 57
    Brief entry 44
Manthorpe, Helen 1958- 122
Mantinband, Gerda (B.) 1917- 74
Manton, Jo
    See Gittings, Jo (Grenville) Manton
Manuel, Lynn 1948- 179
    Earlier sketch in SATA 99
Manushkin, Fran 1942- 205
    Earlier sketches in SATA 7, 54, 93, 166
Manushkin, Frances
    See Manushkin, Fran
Man Without a Spleen, A
    See Chekhov, Anton
Many, Paul 1947- 210
Many, Paul A.
    See Many, Paul
Manzano, Sonia 1950- 167
Mapes, Mary A.
    See Ellison, Virginia H(owell)
Maple, Marilyn 1931- 80
Mappin, Strephyn 1956- 109
Mara, Barney
    See Roth, Arthur J(oseph)
Mara, Jeanette
    See Cebulash, Mel
Mara, Rachna
    See Gilmore, Rachna
Marais, Josef 1905-1978
    Obituary 24
Marasmus, Seymour
    See Rivoli, Mario
Marbach, Ethel
    See Pochocki, Ethel (Frances)
Marcal, Annette B.
    See Callaway, Bernice (Anne)
Marcelino
    See Agnew, Edith J(osephine)
Marcellino, Fred 1939-2001 118
    Obituary 127
    Earlier sketch in SATA 68
March, Carl
    See Fleischman, Sid
Marchant, Bessie 1862-1941
    See YABC 2
Marchant, Catherine
    See Cookson, Catherine (McMullen)
Marcher, Marion Walden 1890-1987 10
Marchesi, Stephen 1951- 114
Marchesi, Steve
    See Marchesi, Stephen
    and Older, Effin
    and Older, Jules
Marchetta, Melina 1965- 170
Marciano, John Bemelmans 1970- 167
    Earlier sketch in SATA 118
    See also CLR 93
Marco, Lou
    See Gottfried, Theodore Mark
Marcus, Leonard S. 1950- 187
    Earlier sketch in SATA 133

Marcus, Paul 1953- 82
Marcus, Rebecca B(rian) 1907- 9
Marcuse, Aida E. 1934- 89
Marek, Margot L. 1934(?)-1987
  Obituary 54
Maren, Julie 1970- 199
Margaret, Karla
  See Andersdatter, Karla M(argaret)
Margolin, Harriet
  See Ziefert, Harriet
Margolis, Jeffrey A. 1948- 108
Margolis, Leslie 187
Margolis, Richard J(ules) 1929-1991 86
  Obituary 67
  Earlier sketch in SATA 4
Margolis, Vivienne 1922- 46
Mariana
  See Foster, Marian Curtis
Marie, Geraldine 1949- 61
Mariner, Scott
  See Pohl, Frederik
Marino, Dorothy Bronson 1912- 14
Marino, Jan 1936- 114
Marino, Nick
  See Deming, Richard
Marino, Peter 1960- 179
Mario, Anna
  See Odgers, Sally Farrell
Marion, Henry
  See del Rey, Lester
Maris, Ron 71
  Brief entry 45
Mark, Jan 1943-2006 164
  Obituary 173
  Earlier sketches in SATA 22, 69, 114
  See also CLR 11
Mark, Janet Marjorie
  See Mark, Jan
Mark, Joan T. 1937- 122
Mark, Pauline (Dahlin) 1913-1997 14
Mark, Polly
  See Mark, Pauline (Dahlin)
Mark, Ted
  See Gottfried, Theodore Mark
Markel, Michelle 169
Marker, Sherry 1941- 76
Markert, Jennifer 1965- 83
Markert, Jenny
  See Markert, Jennifer
Markey, Kevin 1965- 215
Markham, Lynne 1947- 102
Markham, Marion M. 1929- 60
Markham, Wendy
  See Staub, Wendy Corsi
Markins, W. S.
  See Jenkins, Marie M(agdalen)
Markle, Sandra L. 1946- 185
  Brief entry 41
  Earlier sketches in SATA 57, 92, 148
Markle, Sandra Lee
  See Markle, Sandra L.
Marklew, Gilly 211
Marko, Katherine D(olores) 28
Markoosie
  See Patsauq, Markoosie
Marks, Alan 1957- 187
  Earlier sketches in SATA 77, 151
Marks, Burton 1930- 47
  Brief entry 43
Marks, Graham 158
Marks, Hannah K.
  See Trivelpiece, Laurel
Marks, J.
  See Highwater, Jamake (Mamake)
Marks, J(ames) M(acdonald) 1921- 13
Marks, Laurie J. 1957- 68
Marks, Margaret L. 1911(?)-1980
  Obituary 23
Marks, Mickey Klar -1986 12
Marks, Peter
  See Smith, Robert Kimmel

Marks, Rita 1938- 47
Marks, Stan(ley) 14
Marks-Highwater, J.
  See Highwater, Jamake (Mamake)
Markun, Patricia Maloney 1924- 15
Markusen, Bruce (Stanley Rodriguez)
  1965- 141
Marley, Louise 1952- 173
  Earlier sketch in SATA 120
Marlin, Hilda
  See Van Stockum, Hilda
Marlow, Layne 204
Marlow, Max
  See Nicole, Christopher (Robin)
Marlow, Susan K. 1953- 178
Marlowe, Amy Bell 67
  Earlier sketch in SATA 1
Marlowe, Jack
  See Deary, Terry
Marney, Dean 1952- 90
Marokvia, Artur 1909- 31
Marokvia, Mireille 1908-2008 5
  Obituary 197
Marokvia, Mireille Journet
  See Marokvia, Mireille
Marol, Jean-Claude 1946- 125
Marr, John S(tuart) 1940- 48
Marr, Melissa 1972- 189
Marric, J. J.
  See Butler, William Vivian
  and Creasey, John
Marrin, Albert 1936- 193
  Brief entry 43
  Earlier sketches in SATA 53, 90, 126
  See also CLR 53
Marriott, Alice Lee 1910-1992 31
  Obituary 71
Marriott, Janice 1946- 134
Marriott, Pat(ricia) 1920- 35
Marroquin, Patricio
  See Markun, Patricia Maloney
Mars, W. T.
  See Mars, Witold Tadeusz J.
Mars, Witold Tadeusz J. 1912-1985 3
Marsden, Carolyn 1950- 212
  Autobiography Feature 212
  Earlier sketches in SATA 140, 175
Marsden, John 1950- 146
  Earlier sketches in SATA 66, 97
  See also CLR 34
  See also SAAS 22
Marsh, Carole 1946- 127
Marsh, Dave 1950- 66
Marsh, J. E.
  See Marshall, Evelyn
Marsh, James 1946- 73
Marsh, Jean
  See Marshall, Evelyn
Marsh, Joan F. 1923- 83
Marsh, Paul
  See Hopkins, (Hector) Kenneth
Marsh, Valerie 1954- 89
Marshall, Anthony D(ryden) 1924- 18
Marshall, Bonnie C. 1941- 141
  Earlier sketch in SATA 18
Marshall, Bridget M(ary) 1974- 103
Marshall, (Sarah) Catherine (Wood)
  1914-1983 2
  Obituary 34
Marshall, Douglas
  See McClintock, Marshall
Marshall, Edmund
  See Hopkins, (Hector) Kenneth
Marshall, Edward
  See Marshall, James
Marshall, Evelyn 1897-1991 11
Marshall, Felicity 1950- 116
Marshall, Garry 1934- 60
Marshall, H. H.
  See Jahn, Michael

Marshall, James 1942-1992 75
  Earlier sketches in SATA 6, 51
  See also CLR 21
Marshall, James Edward
  See Marshall, James
Marshall, James Vance
  See Payne, Donald Gordon
Marshall, Janet (Perry) 1938- 97
Marshall, Jeff
  See Laycock, George (Edwin)
Marshall, Kim
  See Marshall, Michael (Kimbrough)
Marshall, Michael (Kimbrough) 1948- 37
Marshall, Percy
  See Young, Percy M(arshall)
Marshall, S(amuel) L(yman) A(twood)
  1900-1977 21
Marsoli, Lisa Ann 1958- 101
  Brief entry 53
Marsten, Richard
  See Hunter, Evan
Marston, Elsa 1933- 156
Marston, Hope Irvin 1935- 127
  Earlier sketch in SATA 31
Marszalek, John F. 1939- 167
Marszalek, John Francis, Jr.
  See Marszalek, John F.
Marszalek, John Francis 1939-
  See Marszalek, John F.
Martchenko, Michael 1942- 154
  Earlier sketches in SATA 50, 95
Martel, Aimee
  See Thurlo, Aimee
  and Thurlo, David
Martel, Suzanne 1924- 99
Martignoni, Margaret E. 1908(?)-1974
  Obituary 27
Martin, Ann M. 1955- 192
  Brief entry 41
  Earlier sketches in SATA 44, 70, 126
  See also CLR 32
Martin, Bill, Jr. 1916-2004 145
  Brief entry 40
  Earlier sketches in SATA 40, 67
  See also CLR 97
Martin, Charles E(lmer)
  See Mastrangelo, Charles E(lmer)
Martin, Christopher
  See Hoyt, Edwin P(almer), Jr.
Martin, C.K. Kelly 207
Martin, Claire 1933- 76
Martin, Courtney Autumn 1984- 205
Martin, David Stone 1913-1992 39
Martin, Del 1921-2008 47
Martin, Donald
  See Honig, Donald
Martin, Dorothy
  See Martin, Del
Martin, Dorothy L.
  See Martin, Del
Martin, Eugene 1
Martin, Eva M. 1939- 65
Martin, Frances M(cEntee) 1906-1998 36
Martin, Francesca 1947- 101
Martin, Fred 1948- 119
Martin, Fredric
  See Christopher, Matt(hew Frederick)
Martin, George Raymond Richard
  See Martin, George R.R.
Martin, George R.R. 1948- 118
Martin, J(ohn) P(ercival) 1880(?)-1966 15
Martin, Jacqueline Briggs 1945- 188
  Earlier sketches in SATA 98, 149
Martin, Jane Read 1957- 84
Martin, Jeremy
  See Levin, Marcia Obrasky
Martin, Les
  See Schulman, L(ester) M(artin)
Martin, Linda 1961- 82
Martin, Lynne 1923- 21

Martin, Marcia
See Levin, Marcia Obrasky
Martin, Marvin 1926- *126*
Martin, Melanie
See Pellowski, Michael (Joseph)
Martin, Nancy
See Salmon, Annie Elizabeth
Martin, Patricia *200*
Martin, Patricia A.
See Martin, Patricia
Martin, Patricia Miles 1899-1986 .... *43*
Obituary *48*
Earlier sketch in SATA *1*
Martin, Peter
See Chaundler, Christine
Martin, Rafe 1946- *175*
Martin, Rene 1891-1977 .... *42*
Obituary *20*
Martin, Rupert (Claude) 1905- *31*
Martin, S. R.
See Mappin, Strephyn
Martin, Stefan 1936- *32*
Martin, Vicky
See Storey, Victoria Carolyn
Martin, Webber
See Silverberg, Robert
Martin, Wendy
See Martini, Teri
Martin, William Ivan, Jr.
See Martin, Bill, Jr.
Martineau, Diane 1940- *178*
Martineau, Harriet 1802-1876
See YABC *2*
Martinet, Jeanne 1958- *80*
Martinez, Agnes *167*
Martinez, Arturo O. 1933- *192*
Martinez, Claudia Guadalupe 1978- *214*
Martinez, Ed(ward) 1954- *98*
Martinez, Elizabeth Coonrod 1954- *85*
Martinez, Victor 1954- *95*
Martini, Teri 1930- *3*
Martini, Therese
See Martini, Teri
Martino, Alfred C. 1964- *174*
Martinson, Janis
See Herbert, Janis
Marton, Jirina 1946- *144*
Earlier sketch in SATA *95*
Marton, Pierre
See Stone, Peter
Martson, Del
See Lupoff, Richard A(llen)
Martyr, Paula (Jane)
See Lawford, Paula Jane
Maruki, Toshi 1912-2000 .... *112*
See also CLR *19*
Marvin, Isabel R(idout) 1924- *84*
Marx, Patricia Windschill
See Marx, Trish
Marx, Robert F(rank) 1936- *24*
Marx, Trish 1948- *202*
Earlier sketches in SATA *112, 160*
Marzani, Carl (Aldo) 1912-1994 .... *12*
Marzollo, Jean 1942- *190*
Autobiography Feature *190*
Earlier sketches in SATA *29, 77, 130*
See also SAAS *15*
Masefield, John (Edward) 1878-1967 .... *19*
Masiello, Ralph 1961- *214*
Masoff, Joy 1951- *118*
Mason, Adrienne 1962- *163*
Mason, Cherie *170*
Mason, Edwin A. 1905-1979
Obituary *32*
Mason, Ernst
See Pohl, Frederik
Mason, F(rancis) van Wyck 1901-1978 .... *3*
Obituary *26*
Mason, Frank W.
See Mason, F(rancis) van Wyck
Mason, George Frederick 1904-2000 .... *14*

Mason, Miriam E(vangeline) 1900-1973 .... *2*
Obituary *26*
Mason, Prue *195*
Mason, Simon 1962- *178*
Mason, Tally
See Derleth, August (William)
Mason, Van Wyck
See Mason, F(rancis) van Wyck
Mass, Wendy 1967- *196*
Earlier sketch in SATA *158*
Mass, William
See Gibson, William
Masselman, George 1897-1971 .... *19*
Massey, Misty *212*
Massie, Dianne Redfield 1938- *125*
Earlier sketch in SATA *16*
Massie, Elizabeth *108*
Massini, Sarah *213*
Masson, Sophie 1959- *179*
Earlier sketch in SATA *133*
Masters, Anthony (Richard) 1940-2003 .... *112*
Obituary *145*
Masters, Kelly R(ay) 1897-1987 .... *3*
Masters, Mildred 1932- *42*
Masters, William
See Cousins, Margaret
Masters, Zeke
See Bensen, Donald R.
and Goulart, Ron
Mastrangelo, Charles E(lmer) 1910-1995 ..... *70*
Earlier sketch in SATA *69*
Masuda, Takeshi 1944- *56*
Matas, Carol 1949- *194*
Autobiography Feature *112*
Earlier sketch in SATA *93*
See also CLR *52*
Matchette, Katharine E. 1941- *38*
Math, Irwin 1940- *42*
Mathabane, Mark 1960- *123*
Mather, Kirtley F(letcher) 1888-1978 .... *65*
Mathers, Petra 1945- *176*
Earlier sketch in SATA *119*
See also CLR *76*
Matheson, Richard (Christian) 1953- *119*
Matheson, Shirlee Smith 1942- *155*
Mathews, Eleanor
See Mathews, Ellie
Mathews, Ellie 1946(?)- *193*
Mathews, Janet 1914-1992 .... *41*
Mathews, Judith
See Goldberger, Judith M.
Mathews, Louise
See Tooke, Louise Mathews
Mathiesen, Egon 1907-1976
Obituary *28*
Mathieu, Joe 1949- *185*
Brief entry *36*
Earlier sketches in SATA *43, 94*
Mathieu, Joseph P.
See Mathieu, Joe
Mathis, Sharon Bell 1937- *58*
Earlier sketch in SATA *7*
See also CLR *147*
See also SAAS *3*
Matlin, Marlee 1965- *181*
Matlin, Marlee Beth
See Matlin, Marlee
Matloff, Gregory 1945- *73*
Matott, Justin 1961- *109*
Matranga, Frances Carfi 1922- *78*
Matray, James I. 1948- *161*
Matray, James Irving
See Matray, James I.
Matson, Emerson N(els) 1926- *12*
Matsui, Tadashi 1926- *8*
Matsuno, Masako
See Kobayashi, Masako Matsuno
Matsuoka, Mei 1981- *192*
Matte, (Encarnacion) L'Enc 1936- *22*
Mattern, Joanne 1963- *122*
Mattheson, Jenny *180*

Matthew, James
See Barrie, J. M.
Matthews, Aline
See De Wire, Elinor
Matthews, Andrew 1948- *138*
Matthews, Caitlin 1952- *122*
Matthews, Downs 1925- *71*
Matthews, Elizabeth 1978- *194*
Matthews, Ellen
See Bache, Ellyn
Matthews, Ellen 1950- *28*
Matthews, Harold Downs
See Matthews, Downs
Matthews, Jacklyn Meek
See Meek, Jacklyn O'Hanlon
Matthews, John (Kentigern) 1948- *116*
Matthews, Laura S.
See Matthews, L.S.
Matthews, Liz
See Pellowski, Michael (Joseph)
Matthews, L.S. *183*
Matthews, Morgan
See Pellowski, Michael (Joseph)
Matthews, Nicola
See Browne, N.M.
Matthews, Patricia 1927-2006 .... *28*
Matthews, Patricia Anne
See Matthews, Patricia
Matthews, Tina 1961- *190*
Matthews, Tom L.
See Lalicki, Tom
Matthews, William Henry III 1919- *45*
Brief entry *28*
Matthiessen, Peter 1927- *27*
Mattingley, Christobel (Rosemary) 1931- *85*
Earlier sketch in SATA *37*
See also CLR *24*
See also SAAS *18*
Matulay, Laszlo 1912- *43*
Matus, Greta 1938- *12*
Maugham, W. S.
See Maugham, W. Somerset
Maugham, W. Somerset 1874-1965 .... *54*
Maugham, William S.
See Maugham, W. Somerset
Maugham, William Somerset
See Maugham, W. Somerset
Maurer, Diane Philippoff
See Maurer-Mathison, Diane V(ogel)
Maurer, Diane Vogel
See Maurer-Mathison, Diane V(ogel)
Maurer-Mathison, Diane V(ogel) 1944- *89*
Mauser, Pat Rhoads
See McCord, Patricia
Mauser, Patricia Rhoads
See McCord, Patricia
Maves, Mary Carolyn 1916- *10*
Maves, Paul B(enjamin) 1913-1994 .... *10*
Mavor, Salley 1955- *125*
Mawicke, Tran 1911- *15*
Max 1906-1989
See Diop, Birago (Ismael)
Max, Peter 1939- *45*
Maxon, Anne
See Best, (Evangel) Allena Champlin
Maxwell, Arthur S. 1896-1970 .... *11*
Maxwell, B.E. 1957- *211*
Maxwell, Bruce E.
See Maxwell, B.E.
Maxwell, Edith 1923- *7*
Maxwell, Gavin 1914-1969 .... *65*
Maxwell, Katie
See MacAlister, Katie
Maxwell, William (Keepers, Jr.) 1908-2000
Obituary *128*
Maxwell-Hyslop, Miranda 1968- *154*
May, Charles Paul 1920- *4*
May, Elaine Tyler 1947- *120*
May, J. C.
See May, Julian
May, Julian 1931- *11*

May, Robert Lewis 1905-1976
  Obituary 27
May, Robert Stephen 1929-1996 46
May, Robin
  See May, Robert Stephen
Mayall, Beth 171
Mayberry, Florence V(irginia) Wilson 10
Maybury, Richard J. 1946- 72
Maybury, Rick
  See Maybury, Richard J.
Mayer, Agatha
  See Maher, Ramona
Mayer, Albert Ignatius, Jr. 1906-1994
  Obituary 29
Mayer, Ann M(argaret) 1938- 14
Mayer, Bill 200
Mayer, Danuta 1958- 117
Mayer, Hannelore Valencak 1929- 42
Mayer, Jane Rothschild 1903-2001 38
Mayer, Marianna 1945- 132
  Earlier sketches in SATA *32, 83*
Mayer, Mercer 1943- 137
  Earlier sketches in SATA *16, 32, 73, 129*
  See also CLR *11*
Mayerson, Charlotte Leon 36
Mayerson, Evelyn Wilde 1935- 55
Mayfield, Katherine 1958- 118
Mayfield, Sue 1963- 146
  Earlier sketch in SATA *72*
Mayhar, Ardath 1930- 38
Mayhew, James 1964- 204
  Earlier sketches in SATA *85, 149*
Maynard, Olga 1920- 40
Mayne, William 1928-2010 122
  Earlier sketches in SATA *6, 68*
  See also CLR *123*
  See also SAAS *11*
Mayne, William James Carter
  See Mayne, William
Maynes, J. O. Rocky, Jr.
  See Maynes, J. Oscar, Jr.
Maynes, J. Oscar, Jr. 1929- 38
Mayo, Gretchen Will 1936- 163
  Earlier sketch in SATA *84*
Mayo, Margaret 1935- 165
  Earlier sketches in SATA *38, 96*
Mayo, Margaret Mary
  See Mayo, Margaret
Mayr, Diane 1949- 197
Mays, Lucinda L(a Bella) 1924- 49
Mays, (Lewis) Victor (Jr.) 1927- 5
Mazellan, Ron 210
Mazer, Anne 1953- 192
  Earlier sketches in SATA *67, 105*
Mazer, Harry 1925- 167
  Earlier sketches in SATA *31, 67, 105*
  See also CLR *16*
  See also SAAS *11*
Mazer, Norma Fox 1931-2009 198
  Earlier sketches in SATA *24, 67, 105, 168*
  See also CLR *23*
  See also SAAS *1*
Mazille, Capucine 1953- 96
Mazza, Adriana 1928- 19
Mazzio, Joann 1926- 74
Mbugua, Kioi Wa 1962- 83
McAfee, Carol 1955- 81
McAllister, Amanda
  See Dowdell, Dorothy (Florence) Karns
  and Hager, Jean
  and Meaker, Eloise
McAllister, Angela 182
McAllister, Margaret I. 1956- 169
  Earlier sketch in SATA *117*
McAllister, M.I.
  See McAllister, Margaret I.
McArdle, Paula 1971- 198
McArthur, Nancy 96
McAvoy, Jim 1972- 142
McBain, Ed
  See Hunter, Evan

McBain, Georgina 189
McBratney, Sam 1943- 203
  Earlier sketches in SATA *89, 164*
  See also CLR *44*
McBrier, Michael
  See Older, Effin
  and Older, Jules
McCafferty, Jim 1954- 84
McCaffery, Janet 1936- 38
McCaffrey, Anne 1926- 152
  Autobiography Feature 152
  Earlier sketches in SATA *8, 70, 116*
  See also CLR *130*
  See also SAAS *11*
McCaffrey, Anne Inez
  See McCaffrey, Anne
McCaffrey, Mary
  See Szudek, Agnes S(usan) P(hilomena)
McCain, Becky Ray 1954- 138
McCain, Murray (David, Jr.) 1926-1981 7
  Obituary 29
McCall, Bruce 1935(?)- 209
McCall, Edith (Sansom) 1911- 6
McCall, Virginia Nielsen 1909-2000 13
McCall, Wendell
  See Pearson, Ridley
McCall Smith, Alexander
  See Smith, Alexander McCall
McCallum, Phyllis
  See Koch, Phyllis (Mae) McCallum
McCallum, Stephen 1960- 91
McCampbell, Darlene Z. 1942- 83
McCann, Edson
  See del Rey, Lester
  and Pohl, Frederik
McCann, Gerald 1916- 41
McCann, Helen 1948- 75
McCannon, Dindga 41
McCants, William D. 1961- 82
McCarter, Neely Dixon 1929- 47
McCarthy, Agnes 1933- 4
McCarthy, Colin (John) 1951- 77
McCarthy, Mary 1951- 203
McCarthy, Meghan 199
  Earlier sketch in SATA *168*
McCarthy, Ralph F. 1950- 139
McCarthy-Tucker, Sherri N. 1958- 83
McCarty, Peter 1966- 182
McCarty, Rega Kramer 1904-1986 10
McCaslin, Nellie 1914-2005 12
McCaughrean, Geraldine 1951- 173
  Earlier sketches in SATA *87, 139*
  See also CLR *38*
McCaughren, Tom 1936- 75
McCauley, Adam 1965- 209
  Earlier sketch in SATA *128*
McCay, (Zenas) Winsor 1869-1934 134
  Earlier sketch in SATA *41*
McClafferty, Carla Killough 1958- 137
McClary, Jane Stevenson 1919-1990
  Obituary 64
McCleery, Patsy R. 1925- 133
  Earlier sketch in SATA *88*
McClelland, Susan 214
McClements, George 196
McClintock, Barbara 1955- 213
  Earlier sketches in SATA *57, 95, 146*
McClintock, Marshall 1906-1967 3
McClintock, May Garelick
  See Garelick, May
McClintock, Mike
  See McClintock, Marshall
McClintock, Norah 178
McClintock, Theodore 1902-1971 14
McClinton, Leon 1933- 11
McCloskey, Kevin 1951- 79
McCloskey, (John) Robert 1914-2003 100
  Obituary 146
  Earlier sketches in SATA *2, 39*
  See also CLR *7*
McCloy, James F(loyd) 1941- 59

McClung, Robert M(arshall) 1916- 135
  Earlier sketches in SATA *2, 68*
  See also CLR *11*
  See also SAAS *15*
McClure, Gillian Mary 1948- 31
McColley, Kevin 1961- 80
  See also SAAS *23*
McConduit, Denise Walter 1950- 89
McConnell, James Douglas Rutherford
  1915-1988 40
  Obituary 56
McCord, Anne 1942- 41
McCord, David (Thompson Watson)
  1897-1997 18
  Obituary 96
  See also CLR *9*
McCord, Jean 1924- 34
McCord, Pat Mauser
  See McCord, Patricia
McCord, Patricia 1943- 159
  Earlier sketch in SATA *37*
McCord, Patricia Sue Rhoads Mauser
  See McCord, Patricia
McCormick, Brooks
  See Adams, William Taylor
McCormick, Dell J. 1892-1949 19
McCormick, (George) Donald (King)
  1911-1998 14
McCormick, Edith (Joan) 1934- 30
McCormick, Kimberly A. 1960- 153
McCormick, Patricia 1956- 181
  Earlier sketch in SATA *128*
McCourt, Edward (Alexander) 1907-1972
  Obituary 28
McCourt, Lisa 1964- 214
  Earlier sketches in SATA *117, 159*
McCourt, Malachy 1931- 126
McCoy, Glenn 1965- 212
McCoy, Iola Fuller 3
McCoy, J(oseph) J(erome) 1917- 8
McCoy, Karen Kawamoto 1953- 82
McCoy, Lois (Rich) 1941- 38
McCrady, Lady 1951- 16
McCrea, James (Craig, Jr.) 1920- 3
McCrea, Ruth (Pirman) 1921- 3
McCreigh, James
  See Pohl, Frederik
McCrumb, Sharyn 1948- 109
McCue, Lisa 1959- 212
  Earlier sketches in SATA *65, 177*
McCue, Lisa Emiline
  See McCue, Lisa
McCullen, Andrew
  See Arthur, Robert, (Jr.)
McCullers, Carson 1917-1967 27
McCullers, Lula Carson Smith
  See McCullers, Carson
McCulloch, Derek (Ivor Breashur) 1897-1967
  Obituary 29
McCulloch, John Tyler
  See Burroughs, Edgar Rice
McCulloch, Sarah
  See Ure, Jean
McCullough, David 1933- 62
McCullough, David Gaub
  See McCullough, David
McCullough, Frances Monson 1938- 8
McCullough, Sharon Pierce 1943- 131
McCully, Emily Arnold 210
  See Arnold, Emily
McCune, Dan
  See Haas, Dorothy F.
McCunn, Ruthanne Lum 1946- 63
McCurdy, Michael (Charles) 1942- 147
  Earlier sketches in SATA *13, 82*
McCutcheon, Elsie (Mary Jackson) 1937- ... 60
McCutcheon, John 1952- 97
McDaniel, Becky Bring 1953- 61
McDaniel, Lurlene 1944- 146
  Earlier sketch in SATA *71*
McDaniels, Pellom III 1968- 121

McDaniels, Preston 1952- *192*
McDearmon, Kay *20*
McDermott, Beverly Brodsky 1941- *11*
McDermott, Eleni *156*
McDermott, Gerald (Edward) 1941- *163*
 Earlier sketches in SATA *16, 74*
 See also CLR *9*
McDermott, Michael 1962- *76*
McDevitt, Jack 1935- *155*
 Earlier sketch in SATA *94*
McDevitt, John Charles
 See McDevitt, Jack
McDole, Carol
 See Farley, Carol (J.)
McDonald, Collin 1943- *79*
McDonald, Gerald D(oan) 1905-1970 .... *3*
McDonald, Jamie
 See Heide, Florence Parry
McDonald, Janet 1953-2007 .... *204*
 Earlier sketch in SATA *148*
McDonald, Jill (Masefield) 1927-1982 .... *13*
 Obituary *29*
McDonald, Joyce 1946- *164*
 Earlier sketch in SATA *101*
McDonald, Lucile Saunders 1898-1992 .... *10*
McDonald, Mary Ann 1956- *84*
McDonald, Megan 1958- *202*
 Autobiography Feature *151*
 Earlier sketches in SATA *67, 99, 148, 151*
 See also CLR *94*
McDonald, Meme 1954- *112*
McDonald, Mercedes 1956- *169*
 Earlier sketch in SATA *97*
McDonald, Rae A. 1952- *201*
McDonell, Chris 1960- *138*
McDonnell, Christine 1949- *115*
 Earlier sketch in SATA *34*
McDonnell, Flora (Mary) 1963- *146*
 Earlier sketch in SATA *90*
McDonnell, Kathleen 1947- *186*
McDonnell, Lois Eddy 1914-2001 .... *10*
McDonnell, Patrick 1956- *179*
McDonough, Yona Zeldis 1957- *73*
McElligott, Matt 1968- *196*
 Earlier sketch in SATA *135*
McElligott, Matthew
 See McElligott, Matt
McElmeel, Sharron L. 1942- *128*
McElmurry, Jill *198*
 Earlier sketch in SATA *159*
McElrath, William N. 1932- *65*
McElrath-Eslick, Lori 1960- *204*
 Earlier sketch in SATA *96*
McEntee, Dorothy (Layng) 1902- *37*
McEvoy, Anne *214*
McEwen, Katherine *183*
McEwen, Robert (Lindley) 1926-1980
 Obituary *23*
McFadden, Kevin Christopher
 See Pike, Christopher
McFall, Christie 1918- *12*
McFall, Gardner 1952- *183*
McFarlan, Donald M(aitland) 1915- *59*
McFarland, Henry "Hammer"
 See McFarland, Henry O.
McFarland, Henry O. 1934- *143*
McFarland, Kenton D(ean) 1920- *11*
McFarland, Martha
 See Smith-Ankrom, M. E.
McFarlane, Leslie 1902-1977 .... *100*
 Earlier sketches in SATA *31, 1, 65, 67*
 See also CLR *118*
McFarlane, Leslie Charles
 See McFarlane, Leslie
McFarlane, Peter (William) 1940- *95*
McFarlane, Sheryl P. 1954- *86*
McFarlane, Todd 1961- *117*
McGaw, Jessie Brewer 1913-1997 .... *10*
McGee, Barbara 1943- *6*
McGee, Marni *163*
McGhee, Alison 1960- *196*

McGiffin, (Lewis) Lee (Shaffer) 1908-1978 ... *1*
McGill, Alice *159*
McGill, Ormond 1913- *92*
McGinley, Jerry 1948- *116*
McGinley, Phyllis 1905-1978 .... *44*
 Obituary *24*
 Earlier sketch in SATA *2*
McGinnis, Lila S(prague) 1924- *44*
McGinty, Alice B. 1963- *202*
 Earlier sketch in SATA *134*
McGivern, Justin 1985- *129*
McGivern, Maureen Daly
 See Daly, Maureen
McGivern, Maureen Patricia Daly
 See Daly, Maureen
McGough, Elizabeth (Hemmes) 1934- *33*
McGovern, Ann 1930- *132*
 Earlier sketches in SATA *8, 69, 70*
 See also CLR *50*
 See also SAAS *17*
McGowen, Thomas E. 1927- *109*
 Earlier sketch in SATA *2*
McGowen, Tom
 See McGowen, Thomas E.
McGrady, Mike 1933- *6*
McGrath, Barbara Barbieri 1953- *169*
 Earlier sketch in SATA *108*
McGrath, Robin 1949- *121*
McGrath, Thomas (Matthew) 1916-1990 ..... *41*
 Obituary *66*
McGraw, Eloise Jarvis 1915-2000 .... *67*
 Obituary *123*
 Earlier sketch in SATA *1*
 See also SAAS *6*
McGraw, William Corbin 1916-1999 .... *3*
McGreal, Elizabeth
 See Yates, Elizabeth
McGregor, Barbara 1959- *82*
McGregor, Craig 1933- *8*
McGregor, Iona 1929- *25*
McGrory, Anik *193*
McGuffey, Alexander Hamilton 1816-1896 . *60*
McGuigan, Mary Ann 1949- *106*
McGuire, Edna 1899- *13*
McGuire, Leslie (Sarah) 1945- *94*
 Brief entry *45*
 Earlier sketch in SATA *52*
McGuire, Robert *187*
McGuirk, Leslie (A.) 1960- *152*
McGurk, Slater
 See Roth, Arthur J(oseph)
McHargue, Georgess 1941- *77*
 Earlier sketch in SATA *4*
 See also CLR *2*
 See also SAAS *5*
McHenry, E.B. 1963(?)- *193*
McHugh, (Berit) Elisabet 1941- *55*
 Brief entry *44*
McIlvaine, Jane
 See McClary, Jane Stevenson
McIlwraith, Maureen Mollie Hunter
 See Hunter, Mollie
McInerney, Judith W(hitelock) 1945- *49*
 Brief entry *46*
McInerny, Ralph 1929-2010 .... *93*
McInerny, Ralph Matthew
 See McInerny, Ralph
McKaughan, Larry (Scott) 1941- *75*
McKay, Donald 1895- *45*
McKay, Hilary 1959- *208*
 Earlier sketches in SATA *92, 145*
 See also SAAS *23*
McKay, Hilary Jane
 See McKay, Hilary
McKay, Lawrence, Jr. 1948- *114*
McKay, Robert W. 1921- *15*
McKay, Sharon E. 1954- *165*
McKay, Simon
 See Nicole, Christopher (Robin)
McKean, Dave 1963- *197*

McKean, David Jeff
 See McKean, Dave
McKeating, Eileen 1957- *81*
McKee, David (John) 1935- *158*
 Earlier sketches in SATA *70, 107*
 See also CLR *38*
McKee, Tim 1970- *111*
McKeever, Marcia
 See Laird, Jean E(louise)
McKellar, Danica 1975- *213*
McKelvey, Carole A. 1942- *78*
McKelvy, Charles 1950- *124*
McKendrick, Melveena (Christine) 1941- *55*
McKendry, Joe 1972- *170*
McKenna, Colleen O'Shaughnessy 1948- .. *136*
 Earlier sketch in SATA *76*
McKenzie, Dorothy Clayton 1910-1981
 Obituary *28*
McKenzie, Ellen Kindt 1928- *80*
McKernan, Victoria 1957- *171*
McKie, Robin *112*
McKillip, Patricia A. 1948- *174*
 Earlier sketches in SATA *30, 80, 126*
McKillip, Patricia Anne
 See McKillip, Patricia A.
McKim, Audrey Margaret 1909-1999 .... *47*
McKimmie, Chris *194*
McKinley, Jennifer Carolyn Robin
 See McKinley, Robin
McKinley, Robin 1952- *195*
 Brief entry *32*
 Earlier sketches in SATA *50, 89, 130*
 See also CLR *127*
McKinney, Barbara Shaw 1951- *116*
McKinney, Nadine 1938- *91*
McKinty, Adrian *186*
McKissack, Fredrick L. 1939- *162*
 Brief entry *53*
 Earlier sketches in SATA *73, 117*
 See also CLR *55*
McKissack, Fredrick Lemuel
 See McKissack, Fredrick L.
McKissack, Patricia C. 1944- *195*
 Earlier sketches in SATA *51, 73, 117, 162*
 See also CLR *129*
McKissack, Patricia L'Ann Carwell
 See McKissack, Patricia C.
McKissack and McKissack
 See McKissack, Fredrick L.
 and McKissack, Patricia C.
McKown, Robin (?)-1976 .... *6*
McKy, Katie 1956- *184*
McLaren, Chesley *213*
McLaren, Clemence 1938- *158*
 Earlier sketch in SATA *105*
McLaughlin, Frank 1934- *73*
McLaughlin, Lauren *209*
McLaurin, Anne 1953- *27*
McLean, Andrew 1946- *172*
 Earlier sketch in SATA *113*
McLean, J. Sloan
 See Gillette, Virginia M(ary)
 and Wunsch, Josephine (McLean)
McLean, Jacqueline
 See Kolosov, Jacqueline
McLean, Janet 1946- *113*
McLean, Kathryn (Anderson) 1909-1966 .... *9*
McLean, Virginia Overton 1946- *90*
McLean-Carr, Carol 1948- *122*
McLeish, Kenneth 1940-1997 .... *35*
McLenighan, Valjean 1947- *46*
 Brief entry *40*
McLennan, Connie *171*
McLennan, Will
 See Wisler, G(ary) Clifton
McLeod, Bob 1951- *173*
McLeod, Chum 1955- *95*
McLeod, Emilie Warren 1926-1982 .... *23*
 Obituary *31*
McLeod, Kirsty
 See Hudson, (Margaret) Kirsty

McLeod, Margaret Vail
  See Holloway, Teresa (Bragunier)
McLerran, Alice 1933- 137
  Earlier sketch in SATA 68
McLimans, David 1949- 182
McLoughlin, John C. 1949- 47
McMahon, Bob 1956- 208
McManus, Patrick F. 1933- 46
McManus, Patrick Francis
  See McManus, Patrick F.
McMeekin, Clark
  See McMeekin, Isabel McLennan
McMeekin, Isabel McLennan 1895-1973 3
McMenemy, Sarah 1965- 156
McMillan, Bruce 1947- 192
  Earlier sketches in SATA 22, 70, 129
  See also CLR 47
McMillan, Naomi
  See Grimes, Nikki
McMorey, James L.
  See Moyer, Terry J.
McMorrow, Annalisa 1969- 104
McMullan, Jim 1934- 150
  Earlier sketch in SATA 87
McMullan, K. H.
  See McMullan, Kate
McMullan, Kate 1947- 189
  Brief entry 48
  Earlier sketches in SATA 52, 87, 132
McMullan, Kate Hall
  See McMullan, Kate
McMullan, Margaret 1960- 203
McMurtrey, Martin A(loysias) 1921- 21
McNabb, Linda 1963- 147
McNair, Kate 3
McNair, Sylvia 1924-2002 74
McNamara, Margaret C(raig) 1915-1981
  Obituary 24
McNaught, Harry 32
McNaughton, Colin 1951- 211
  Earlier sketches in SATA 39, 92, 134
  See also CLR 54
McNaughton, Janet 1953- 162
  Earlier sketch in SATA 110
McNeal, Laura 194
McNeal, Tom 194
McNeely, Jeannette 1918- 25
McNeer, May (Yonge) 1902-1994 81
  Earlier sketch in SATA 1
McNeese, Tim 1953- 139
McNeill, Janet
  See Alexander, Janet
McNicholas, Shelagh 191
McNickle, D'Arcy 1904-1977
  Obituary 22
McNickle, William D'Arcy
  See McNickle, D'Arcy
McNicoll, Sylvia (Marilyn) 1954- 113
  See also CLR 99
McNulty, Faith 1918-2005 168
  Earlier sketches in SATA 12, 84, 139
McPhail, David 1940- 183
  Brief entry 32
  Earlier sketches in SATA 47, 81, 140
McPhail, David M.
  See McPhail, David
McPhail, David Michael
  See McPhail, David
McPhee, Norma H. 1928- 95
McPhee, Peter 1957- 214
McPhee, Richard B(yron) 1934- 41
McPherson, James M. 1936- 141
  Earlier sketch in SATA 16
McPherson, James Munro
  See McPherson, James M.
McQueen, Lucinda 1950- 58
  Brief entry 48
McQueen, Mildred Hark 1908-1978 12
McQuillan, Mary 200
McRae, Russell (William) 1934- 63
McShean, Gordon 1936- 41

Mc Swigan, Marie 1907-1962 24
McTavish, Sandy
  See Eyerly, Jeannette
McVeity, Jen 148
McVey, Vicki 1946- 80
McVicker, Charles (Taggart) 1930- 39
McVicker, Chuck
  See McVicker, Charles (Taggart)
McWhirter, A(lan) Ross 1925-1975 37
  Obituary 31
McWhirter, Norris (Dewar) 1925-2004 37
McWilliams, Karen 1943- 65
Mdurvwa, Hajara E. 1962- 92
Meacham, Margaret 1952- 203
  Earlier sketch in SATA 95
Meachum, Virginia 1918- 133
  Earlier sketch in SATA 87
Mead, Alice 1952- 146
  Earlier sketch in SATA 94
Mead, Margaret 1901-1978
  Obituary 20
Mead, Russell (M., Jr.) 1935- 10
Mead, Stella (?)-1981
  Obituary 27
Meade, Ellen
  See Roddick, Ellen
Meade, Holly 207
Meade, Marion 1934- 127
  Earlier sketch in SATA 23
Meader, Stephen W(arren) 1892-1977 1
Meadmore, Susan
  See Sallis, Susan (Diana)
Meadow, Charles T(roub) 1929- 23
Meadowcroft, Enid LaMonte
  See Wright, Enid Meadowcroft (LaMonte)
Meadows, Graham (W.) 1934- 161
Meadows, Michelle 202
Meaker, M. J.
  See Meaker, Marijane
Meaker, Marijane 1927- 160
  Autobiography Feature 111
  Earlier sketches in SATA 20, 61, 99
  See also CLR 29
  See also SAAS 1
Meaker, Marijane Agnes
  See Meaker, Marijane
Means, Florence Crannell 1891-1980 1
  Obituary 25
  See also CLR 56
Mearian, Judy Frank 1936- 49
Mecca, Judy Truesdell 1955- 127
Mechling, Lauren 1978(?)- 194
Mechling, Lauren 1978(?)- 194
Mechner, Jordan 1964- 205
Medary, Marjorie 1890-1980 14
Meddaugh, Susan 1944- 176
  Earlier sketches in SATA 29, 84, 125
Medearis, Angela Shelf 1956- 123
  Earlier sketch in SATA 72
Medearis, Mary 1915- 5
Medina, Jane 1953- 167
  Earlier sketch in SATA 122
Medina, Meg 1963- 212
Medina, Nico 1982- 193
Medlicott, Mary 1946- 88
Mee, Charles L., Jr. 1938- 72
  Earlier sketch in SATA 8
Meehl, Brian 204
Meek, Jacklyn O'Hanlon 1933- 51
  Brief entry 34
Meek, S(terner St.) P(aul) 1894-1972
  Obituary 28
Meeker, Clare Hodgson 1952- 96
Meeker, Oden 1919(?)-1976 14
Meeker, Richard
  See Brown, Fornan
Meeks, Esther MacBain 1
Meggs, Libby Phillips 1943- 130
Mehdevi, Alexander (Sinclair) 1947- 7
Mehdevi, Anne (Marie) Sinclair 1947- 8
Meidell, Sherry 1951- 73

Meier, Minta 1906- 55
Meighan, Donald Charles 1929- 30
Meigs, Cornelia Lynde 1884-1973 6
  See also CLR 55
Meilach, Dona Z(weigoron) 1926- 34
Meilman, Philip W(arren) 1951- 79
Meinstereifel, Ronald L. 1960- 134
Meisel, Paul 184
Meister, Cari 204
Melanson, Luc 198
Melcher, Daniel 1912-1985
  Obituary 43
Melcher, Frederic Gershom 1879-1963
  Obituary 22
Melcher, Marguerite Fellows 1879-1969 10
Meldrum, Christina 206
Melendez, Francisco 1964- 72
Melhuish, Eva 199
Melin, Grace Hathaway 1892-1973 10
Mellersh, H(arold) E(dward) L(eslie)
  1897- 10
Melling, David 186
Melmed, Laura Krauss 212
Melmoth, Sebastian
  See Wilde, Oscar
Melnikoff, Pamela (Rita) 97
Meltzer, Amy 1968- 202
Meltzer, Milton 1915-2009 201
  Autobiography Feature 124
  Earlier sketches in SATA 1, 50, 80, 128
  See also CLR 13
  See also SAAS 1
Melville, Anne
  See Potter, Margaret
Melville, Herman 1819-1891 59
Melwood, Mary
  See Lewis, E. M.
Melzack, Ronald 1929- 5
Memling, Carl 1918-1969 6
Menchin, Scott 188
Mendel, Jo
  See Bond, Gladys Baker
  and Gilbertson, Mildred Geiger
Mendelson, Steven T. 1958-1995 86
Mendelson-Stevens, Serita Deborah
  See Stevens, Serita
Mendes, Valerie 1939- 157
Mendez, Raymond A. 1947- 66
Mendez, Simon 1975- 215
Mendonca, Susan
  See Smith, Susan Vernon
Mendoza, George 1934- 41
  Brief entry 39
  See also SAAS 7
Menendez, Shirley (C.) 1937- 146
Meng, Cece 194
Meng, Heinz (Karl) 1924- 13
Mennen, Ingrid 1954- 85
Menotti, Gian Carlo 1911-2007 29
  Obituary 180
Menuhin, Sir Yehudi 1916-1999 40
  Obituary 113
Menville, Douglas 1935- 64
Menzel, Barbara Jean 1946- 63
Menzel, Peter 1948- 207
Mercati, Cynthia 164
Mercati, Cynthia J.
  See Mercati, Cynthia
Mercer, Charles (Edward) 1917-1988 16
  Obituary 61
Mercer, Jessie 21
Mercer, Sienna 192
Meredith, Arnold
  See Hopkins, (Hector) Kenneth
Meredith, David William
  See Miers, Earl Schenck
Meringoff, Laurene Krasny
  See Brown, Laurene Krasny
Meriwether, Louise 1923- 52
  Brief entry 31

Merlin, Arthur
See Blish, James
Merlin, Christina
See Heaven, Constance (Christina)
Merriam, Eve 1916-1992 73
Earlier sketches in SATA 3, 40
See also CLR 14
Merrill, Jane 1946- 42
Merrill, Jane Merrill
See Merrill, Jane
Merrill, Jean (Fairbanks) 1923- 82
Earlier sketch in SATA 1
See also CLR 52
Merrill, Phil
See Merrill, Jane
Merriman, Alex
See Silverberg, Robert
Merriman, Rachel 1971- 149
Earlier sketch in SATA 98
Merrit, Elizabeth
See Goudge, Eileen
Merski, Patricia K.
See Merski, P.K.
Merski, P.K. 172
Mertz, Barbara
See Peters, Elizabeth
Mertz, Barbara Gross
See Peters, Elizabeth
Merveille, David 200
Merz, Jennifer J. 196
Meschel, Susan V. 1936- 83
Meserve, Jessica 211
Messenger, Charles (Rynd Milles) 1942- 59
Messick, Dale 1906-2005 64
Brief entry 48
Messier, Claire 1956- 103
Messieres, Nicole de
See de Messieres, Nicole
Messinger, Carla 198
Messmer, Otto 1892(?)-1983 37
Mesta, Gabriel
See Moesta, Rebecca
Metaxas, Eric 1963- 211
Metcalf, Doris H(unter) 91
Metcalf, Suzanne
See Baum, L. Frank
Metos, Thomas H(arry) 1932- 37
Metter, Bert(ram Milton) 1927- 56
Metzenthen, David 1958- 167
Earlier sketch in SATA 106
Meunier, Brian 1954- 195
Meyer, Barbara 1939- 77
Meyer, Carolyn 1935- 142
Autobiography Feature 142
Earlier sketches in SATA 9, 70, 118
See also SAAS 9
Meyer, Carolyn Mae
See Meyer, Carolyn
Meyer, Edith Patterson 1895-1993 5
Meyer, F(ranklyn) E(dward) 1932- 9
Meyer, Jean Shepherd 11
Meyer, Jerome Sydney 1895-1975 3
Obituary 25
Meyer, June
See Jordan, June
Meyer, Kerstin 1966- 190
Meyer, L. A.
See Meyer, Louis A(lbert), Jr.
Meyer, Louis A(lbert), Jr. 1942- 144
Earlier sketch in SATA 12
Meyer, Renate 1930- 6
Meyer, Stephenie 1973- 193
See also CLR 142
Meyer, Susan E. 1940- 64
Meyerhoff, Jenny 1972- 208
Meyers, Susan 1942- 164
Earlier sketches in SATA 19, 108
Meynell, Laurence Walter 1899-1989
Obituary 61
Meynier, Yvonne (Pollet) 1908- 14
Mezey, Robert 1935- 33

Micale, Albert 1913- 22
Michael, James
See Scagnetti, Jack
Michael, Livi 1960- 172
Michael, Manfred
See Winterfeld, Henry
Michael, Olivia
See Michael, Livi
Michaelis, Antonia 1979- 215
Michaels, Barbara
See Peters, Elizabeth
Michaels, Jamie 195
Michaels, Joanne Louise
See Teitelbaum, Michael
Michaels, Kristin
See Williams, Jeanne
Michaels, Molly
See Untermeyer, Louis
Michaels, Neal
See Teitelbaum, Michael
Michaels, Rune 194
Michaels, Ski
See Pellowski, Michael (Joseph)
Michaels, Steve 1955- 71
Michaels, William M. 1917- 77
Michel, Anna 1943- 49
Brief entry 40
Michel, Francois 1948- 82
Michelin, Linda 183
Michelson, Richard 198
Earlier sketch in SATA 173
Micich, Paul 74
Mickelson, Scott 1963- 213
Micklish, Rita 1931- 12
Micklos, John, Jr. 1956- 173
Earlier sketch in SATA 129
Micklos J., John, Jr. 1956-
See Micklos, John, Jr.
Micucci, Charles (Patrick, Jr.) 1959- 144
Earlier sketch in SATA 82
Middleton, Haydn 1955- 152
Earlier sketch in SATA 85
Miers, Earl Schenck 1910-1972 1
Obituary 26
Migdale, Lawrence 1951- 89
Miglio, Paige 1966- 201
Mikaelsen, Ben 1952- 173
Earlier sketches in SATA 73, 107
Mikaelsen, Benjamin John
See Mikaelsen, Ben
Miklowitz, Gloria D. 1927- 129
Earlier sketches in SATA 4, 68
See also SAAS 17
Mikolaycak, Charles 1937-1993 78
Obituary 75
Earlier sketch in SATA 9
See also SAAS 4
Mild, Warren (Paul) 1922- 41
Milelli, Pascal 1965- 135
Miles, Betty 1928- 78
Earlier sketch in SATA 8
See also SAAS 9
Miles, Miska
See Martin, Patricia Miles
Miles, (Mary) Patricia 1930- 29
Miles, Patricia A.
See Martin, Patricia Miles
Miles, Victoria 1966- 188
Milgrim, David 187
Earlier sketch in SATA 158
Milgrom, Harry 1912-1978 25
Milhous, Katherine 1894-1977 15
Milich, Zoran 174
Milios, Rita 1949- 79
Militant
See Sandburg, Carl
Millais, Raoul 1901- 77
Millar, Barbara F. 1924- 12
Millar, Margaret (Ellis Sturm) 1915-1994 61
Obituary 79
Millard, Glenda 203

Millard, Kerry 204
Millbank, Captain H. R.
See Ellis, Edward S.
Millen, C(ynthia) M. 1955- 114
Miller, Albert G(riffith) 1905-1982 12
Obituary 31
Miller, Alice Ann 1958- 150
Miller, Alice P(atricia McCarthy) 22
Miller, Christopher 1976- 215
Miller, Debbie 1951- 160
Earlier sketch in SATA 103
Miller, Debbie S.
See Miller, Debbie
Miller, Deborah Uchill 1944- 61
Miller, Don 1923- 15
Miller, Doris R.
See Mosesson, Gloria R(ubin)
Miller, Eddie
See Miller, Edward
Miller, Edna Anita 1920- 29
Miller, Edward 1905-1974 8
Miller, Edward 1964- 183
Miller, Elizabeth 1933- 41
Miller, Ellanita 1957- 87
Miller, Eugene 1925- 33
Miller, Frances A. 1937- 52
Brief entry 46
Miller, Heather Lynn 1971- 214
Miller, Helen M(arkley) -1984 5
Miller, Helen Topping 1884-1960
Obituary 29
Miller, Jane (Judith) 1925-1989 15
Miller, Jewel 1956- 73
Miller, John
See Samachson, Joseph
Miller, Judi 117
Miller, Karen 1949- 210
Miller, Karen Hokanson
See Miller, Karen
Miller, Kate 1948- 193
Miller, Kirsten 1973- 185
Miller, Louise (Rolfe) 1940- 76
Miller, M. L. 85
Miller, Madge 1918- 63
Miller, Margaret J.
See Dale, Margaret J(essy) Miller
Miller, Marilyn (Jean) 1925- 33
Miller, Marvin 65
Miller, Mary
See Northcott, (William) Cecil
Miller, Mary Beth 1942- 9
Miller, Mary Beth 1964- 185
Miller, Maryann 1943- 73
Miller, Natalie 1917-1976 35
Miller, Pat 1951- 214
Miller, Robert H. 1944- 91
Miller, Ron 1947- 185
Miller, Ruth White
See White, Ruth C.
Miller, Sandra
See Miller, Sandy
Miller, Sandra Peden
See Miller, Sandy
Miller, Sandy 1948- 41
Brief entry 35
Miller, Sarah 1969- 175
Miller, Virginia
See Austin, Virginia
Miller, William R. 1959- 116
Miller Brothers
See Miller, Christopher
Milligan, Bryce 1953- 170
Milligan, Spike
See Milligan, Terence Alan
Milligan, Terence Alan 1918-2002 29
Obituary 134
See also CLR 92
Millington, Ada
See Deyneka, Anita
Millman, Isaac 1933- 140

Mills, Adam
  See Stanley, George Edward
Mills, Claudia 1954- *191*
  Brief entry *41*
  Earlier sketches in SATA *44, 89, 145*
Mills, Elaine (Rosemary) 1941- *72*
Mills, G. Riley *196*
Mills, Joyce C. 1944- *102*
Mills, Judith Christine 1956- *130*
Mills, Yaroslava Surmach 1925- *35*
Millspaugh, Ben P. 1936- *77*
Millstead, Thomas E. *30*
Millward, Gwen *202*
Milne, A. A. 1882-1956 .... *100*
  See also YABC *1*
  See also CLR *108*
Milne, Alan Alexander
  See Milne, A. A.
Milne, Lorus J. *5*
  See also CLR *22*
  See also SAAS *18*
Milne, Margery *5*
  See also CLR *22*
  See also SAAS *18*
Milne, Terry
  See Milne, Theresa Ann
Milne, Theresa Ann 1964- *84*
Milnes, Irma McDonough 1924- *101*
Milonas, Rolf
  See Myller, Rolf
Milone, Karen
  See Dugan, Karen
Milone-Dugan, Karen
  See Dugan, Karen
Milord, Susan 1954- *200*
  Earlier sketches in SATA *74, 147*
Milotte, Alfred G(eorge) 1904-1989 .... *11*
  Obituary *62*
Milstein, Linda 1954- *80*
Milton, Ann *134*
Milton, Hilary (Herbert) 1920- *23*
Milton, John R(onald) 1924- *24*
Milton, Joyce 1946- *101*
  Brief entry *41*
  Earlier sketch in SATA *52*
Milverton, Charles A.
  See Penzler, Otto
Milway, Alex 1978- *215*
Milway, Katie Smith 1960- *203*
Minahan, John A. 1956- *92*
Minar, Barbra (Goodyear) 1940- *79*
Minard, Rosemary 1939- *63*
Minarik, Else Holmelund 1920- *127*
  Earlier sketch in SATA *15*
  See also CLR *33*
Miner, Jane Claypool 1933- *103*
  Brief entry *37*
  Earlier sketch in SATA *38*
Miner, Lewis S. 1909-1971 .... *11*
Mines, Jeanette 1948- *61*
Mines, Jeanette Marie
  See Mines, Jeanette
Minier, Nelson
  See Stoutenburg, Adrien (Pearl)
Minnitt, Ronda Jacqueline
  See Armitage, David
Minor, Wendell 1944- *199*
  Earlier sketches in SATA *78, 109, 164*
Minter, Daniel 1961- *176*
Mintonye, Grace *4*
Miranda, Anne 1954- *109*
  Earlier sketch in SATA *71*
Miranda, Inaki 1983(?)- *207*
Mirocha, Paul *192*
Mirsky, Jeannette 1903-1987 .... *8*
  Obituary *51*
Mirsky, Reba Paeff 1902-1966 .... *1*
Misako Rocks! *192*
Mishica, Clare 1960- *91*
Miskovits, Christine 1939- *10*

Miss Frances
  See Horwich, Frances R(appaport)
Miss Read
  See Saint, Dora Jessie
Mister Rogers
  See Rogers, Fred McFeely
Mitchard, Jacquelyn 1956- *168*
  Earlier sketch in SATA *98*
Mitchell, Adrian 1932-2008 .... *166*
  Obituary *200*
  Earlier sketch in SATA *104*
Mitchell, Allison
  See Griffin, W.E.B.
Mitchell, Betty Jo
  See Mitchell, B.J.
Mitchell, B.J. 1931- *120*
Mitchell, Clyde
  See Ellison, Harlan
  and Silverberg, Robert
Mitchell, Cynthia 1922- *29*
Mitchell, (Sibyl) Elyne (Keith) 1913- *10*
Mitchell, Gladys (Maude Winifred)
  1901-1983 .... *46*
  Obituary *35*
Mitchell, Jay
  See Roberson, Jennifer
Mitchell, Joyce Slayton 1933- *142*
  Brief entry *43*
  Earlier sketch in SATA *46*
Mitchell, K. L.
  See Lamb, Elizabeth Searle
Mitchell, Kathy 1948- *59*
Mitchell, Lori 1961- *128*
Mitchell, Margaree King 1953- *84*
Mitchell, Marianne 1947- *145*
Mitchell, Rhonda *89*
Mitchell, Stephen 1943- *199*
Mitchell, Susan
  See Mitchell, Susan K.
Mitchell, Susan K. 1972- *210*
Mitchell, Todd 1974- *191*
Mitchell, Yvonne 1925-1979
  Obituary *24*
Mitchelson, Mitch
  See Mitchelson, Peter Richard
Mitchelson, Peter Richard 1950- *104*
Mitchison, Naomi (Margaret Haldane)
  1897-1999 .... *24*
  Obituary *112*
Mitchnik, Helen 1901-1982 .... *41*
  Brief entry *35*
Mitchum, Hank
  See Knott, William C(ecil, Jr.)
  and Murray, Stuart A. P.
  and Newton, D(wight) B(ennett)
  and Sherman, Jory (Tecumseh)
Mitgutsch, Ali 1935- *76*
Mitsuhashi, Yoko *45*
  Brief entry *33*
Mitton, Jacqueline 1948- *162*
  Earlier sketches in SATA *66, 115*
Mitton, Simon 1946- *66*
Mitton, Tony 1951- *203*
  Earlier sketches in SATA *104, 149*
Miura, Taro 1968- *181*
Mizner, Elizabeth Howard 1907- *27*
Mizumura, Kazue *18*
Mlynowski, Sarah 1977(?)- *180*
Mobin-Uddin, Asma *172*
Mobley, Joe A. 1945- *91*
Moche, Dinah (Rachel) L(evine) 1936- *44*
  Brief entry *40*
Mochi, Ugo (A.) 1889-1977 .... *38*
Mochizuki, Ken 1954- *146*
  Earlier sketch in SATA *81*
  See also SAAS *22*
Modarressi, Mitra 1967- *200*
  Earlier sketch in SATA *126*
Modell, Frank B. 1917- *39*
  Brief entry *36*

Modesitt, Jeanne 1953- *143*
  Earlier sketch in SATA *92*
Modesitt, L.E., Jr. 1943- *164*
  Earlier sketch in SATA *91*
Modesitt, Leland Exton, Jr.
  See Modesitt, L.E., Jr.
Modrell, Dolores 1933- *72*
Moe, Barbara 1937- *20*
Moe, Jorgen (Ingebretsen) 1813-1882
  See CLR *104*
Moed-Kass, Pnina *169*
Moerbeek, Kees 1955- *98*
Moeri, Louise 1924- *93*
  Earlier sketch in SATA *24*
  See also SAAS *10*
Moesta, Rebecca 1956- *182*
Moffett, Jami 1952- *84*
Moffett, Mark W. 1957(?)- *203*
Moffett, Martha (Leatherwood) 1934- *8*
Mogensen, Suzanne A(ncher) 1946- *129*
Mohammed, Khadra *197*
Mohn, Peter B(urnet) 1934- *28*
Mohn, Viola Kohl 1914- *8*
Mohr, Nicholasa 1938- *97*
  Autobiography Feature *113*
  Earlier sketch in SATA *8*
  See also CLR *22*
  See also SAAS *8*
Mok, Esther 1953- *93*
Molan, Christine 1943- *84*
Molarsky, Osmond 1909- *16*
Moldon, Peter L(eonard) 1937- *49*
Mole, John 1941- *103*
  Earlier sketch in SATA *36*
  See also CLR *61*
Molesworth, Mary Louisa 1839-1921 .... *98*
Molin, Charles
  See Mayne, William
Molina, Silvia 1946- *97*
Molk, Laurel 1957- *162*
  Earlier sketch in SATA *92*
Mollel, Tololwa M. 1952- *88*
Molloy, Anne Baker 1907-1999 .... *32*
Molloy, Michael (John) 1940- *162*
Molloy, Paul (George) 1924- *5*
Moloney, James 1954- *202*
  Autobiography Feature *144*
  Earlier sketches in SATA *94, 144*
Molski, Carol *215*
Momaday, N. Scott 1934- *48*
  Brief entry *30*
Momaday, Navarre Scott
  See Momaday, N. Scott
Monaco, Octavia 1963- *169*
Monagle, Bernie 1957- *121*
Moncure, Jane Belk 1926- *23*
Monjo, F(erdinand) N(icholas III)
  1924-1978 .... *16*
  See also CLR *2*
Monk, Isabell 1952- *136*
Monks, Lydia *189*
Monroe, Lyle
  See Heinlein, Robert A.
Monroe, Marion
  See Cox, Marion Monroe
Monroy, Manuel 1970- *196*
Monsell, Helen Albee 1895-1971 .... *24*
Monson-Burton, Marianne 1975- *139*
Montana, Bob 1920-1975
  Obituary *21*
Montanari, Eva 1977- *209*
Montecalvo, Janet *177*
Montenegro, Laura Nyman 1953- *95*
Montero, Gloria 1933- *109*
Montes, Marisa 1951- *144*
Montgomerie, Norah (Mary) 1913- *26*
Montgomery, Constance
  See Cappel, Constance
Montgomery, Elizabeth
  See Julesberg, Elizabeth Rider Montgomery

Montgomery, Elizabeth Rider
   See Julesberg, Elizabeth Rider Montgomery
Montgomery, Hugh (Edward) 1962- *146*
Montgomery, L. M. 1874-1942 .... *100*
   See also YABC *1*
   See also CLR *145*
Montgomery, Lucy Maud
   See Montgomery, L. M.
Montgomery, Michael G. 1952- *208*
Montgomery, Raymond A. (Jr.) 1936- *39*
Montgomery, Rutherford George 1894-1985 . *3*
Montgomery, Sy 1958- *184*
   Autobiography Feature *132*
   Earlier sketches in SATA *114, 132*
Montgomery, Vivian *36*
Monthei, Betty *179*
Montijo, Rhode *179*
Montileaux, Donald F. 1948- *183*
Montpetit, Charles 1958- *101*
Montresor, Beni 1926-2001 .... *38*
   Earlier sketch in SATA *3*
   See also SAAS *4*
Montserrat, Pep *181*
Monty Python
   See Chapman, Graham
   and Cleese, John (Marwood)
   and Gilliam, Terry
   and Idle, Eric
   and Jones, Terence Graham Parry
   and Palin, Michael
Moodie, Craig 1956- *172*
Moodie, Fiona 1952- *133*
Moody, Minerva
   See Alcott, Louisa May
Moody, Ralph Owen 1898-1982 .... *1*
Moon, Carl 1879(?)-1948 .... *25*
Moon, Grace (Purdie) 1877(?)-1947 .... *25*
Moon, Lily
   See Warnes, Tim
Moon, Nicola 1952- *147*
   Earlier sketch in SATA *96*
Moon, Pat 1946- *113*
Moon, Sheila 1910-1991 .... *5*
   Obituary *114*
Moon, Sheila Elizabeth
   See Moon, Sheila
Mooney, Bel 1946- *95*
Mooney, Bill 1936- *122*
Mooney, Elizabeth C(omstock) 1918-1986
   Obituary *48*
Mooney, William
   See Mooney, Bill
Moor, Emily
   See Deming, Richard
Moorcock, Michael 1939- *166*
   Earlier sketch in SATA *93*
Moorcock, Michael John
   See Moorcock, Michael
Moorcock, Michael John
   See Moorcock, Michael
Moore, Anne Carroll 1871-1961 .... *13*
Moore, Cheri
   See Ladd, Cheryl (Jean)
Moore, Clement Clarke 1779-1863 .... *18*
Moore, Cyd 1957- *186*
   Earlier sketches in SATA *83, 133*
Moore, Don W. 1905(?)-1986
   Obituary *48*
Moore, Elaine 1944- *86*
Moore, Eva 1942- *103*
   Earlier sketch in SATA *20*
Moore, Ishbel (Lindsay) 1954- *140*
Moore, Jack (William) 1941- *46*
   Brief entry *32*
Moore, Janet Gaylord 1905-1992 .... *18*
Moore, Jim 1946- *42*
Moore, John Travers 1908- *12*
Moore, Lilian 1909-2004 .... *137*
   Obituary *155*
   Earlier sketch in SATA *52*
   See also CLR *15*

Moore, Liz
   See Moore, M. Elizabeth
Moore, M. Elizabeth 1959- *156*
Moore, Margaret R(umberger) 1903- *12*
Moore, Margie *176*
Moore, Marianne 1887-1972 .... *20*
Moore, Marianne Craig
   See Moore, Marianne
Moore, Patrick (Alfred Caldwell) 1923- *49*
   Brief entry *39*
   See also SAAS *8*
Moore, Patrick 1959- *184*
Moore, Perry *193*
Moore, Peter 1963- *175*
Moore, Peter G.
   See Moore, Peter
Moore, Raina 1970- *212*
Moore, Ray (S.) 1905(?)-1984
   Obituary *37*
Moore, Regina
   See Dunne, Mary Collins
Moore, Rosalie (Gertrude) 1910-2001 .... *9*
Moore, Ruth (Ellen) 1908-1989 .... *23*
Moore, Ruth Nulton 1923- *38*
Moore, S(arah) E. *23*
Moore, Sarah Margaret
   See Hodges, Margaret
Moore, Stephanie Perry 1969(?)- *214*
Moore, Tara 1950- *61*
Moore, Yvette 1958- *154*
   Earlier sketches in SATA *69, 70*
Moores, Dick
   See Moores, Richard (Arnold)
Moores, Richard (Arnold) 1909-1986
   Obituary *48*
Mooser, Stephen 1941- *75*
   Earlier sketch in SATA *28*
Mora, Francisco X(avier) 1952- *90*
Mora, Pat 1942- *186*
   Earlier sketches in SATA *92, 134*
   See also CLR *58*
Mora, Patricia
   See Mora, Pat
Morais, Flavio *207*
Morales, Yuyi *180*
   Earlier sketch in SATA *154*
Moran, Tom 1943- *60*
Moranville, Sharelle Byars *196*
   Earlier sketch in SATA *152*
Moray Williams, Ursula 1911-2006 .... *3*
   Obituary *177*
   See also SAAS *9*
Morden, Simon 1966(?)- *211*
Mordvinoff, Nicolas 1911-1973 .... *17*
More, Caroline
   See Cone, Molly (Lamken)
   and Strachan, Margaret Pitcairn
Moreno, Rene King *190*
Moreton, Andrew Esq.
   See Defoe, Daniel
Morey, Charles
   See Fletcher, Helen Jill
Morey, Walt(er Nelson) 1907-1992 .... *51*
   Obituary *70*
   Earlier sketch in SATA *3*
   See also SAAS *9*
Morgan, Alfred P(owell) 1889-1972 .... *33*
Morgan, Alison (Mary) 1930- *85*
   Earlier sketch in SATA *30*
Morgan, Anne 1954- *121*
Morgan, Christopher 1956- *199*
Morgan, Clay 1950- *198*
Morgan, Douglas
   See Macdonald, James D.
Morgan, Ellen
   See Bumstead, Kathleen Mary
Morgan, Geoffrey 1916- *46*
Morgan, Helen (Gertrude Louise)
   1921-1990 .... *29*

Morgan, Jane
   See Cooper, James Fenimore
   and Franklin, Jane (Morgan)
   and Moren, Sally M(oore)
Morgan, Lenore H. 1908-1976 .... *8*
Morgan, Mary 1957- *213*
   Earlier sketches in SATA *81, 114*
Morgan, McKayla
   See Basile, Gloria Vitanza
Morgan, Michaela
   See Basile, Gloria Vitanza
Morgan, Nicola 1961- *161*
Morgan, Nina 1953- *110*
Morgan, Pierr 1952- *122*
   Earlier sketch in SATA *77*
Morgan, Robin (Evonne) 1941- *80*
Morgan, Roxanne
   See Gentle, Mary
Morgan, Sarah (Nicola) 1959- *68*
Morgan, Shirley
   See Kiepper, Shirley Morgan
Morgan, Stacy T(owle) 1959- *104*
Morgan, Stevie
   See Davies, Nicola
Morgan, Tom 1942- *42*
Morgan, Wendy
   See Staub, Wendy Corsi
Morgan-Vanroyen, Mary
   See Morgan, Mary
Morgenstern, Susie Hoch 1945- *133*
Mori, Hana 1909-1990(?) *88*
Mori, Kyoko 1957- *122*
   Autobiography Feature *126*
   See also CLR *64*
   See also SAAS *26*
Moriarty, Jaclyn *162*
Moriarty, William J. 1930- *127*
Morice, Dave 1946- *93*
Morin, Isobel V. 1928- *110*
Morine, Hoder
   See Conroy, John Wesley
Morley, Taia *199*
Morley, Wilfred Owen
   See Lowndes, Robert A(ugustine) W(ard)
Morningstar, Mildred (Whaley) 1912-1997 .. *61*
   Obituary *114*
Morozumi, Atsuko *110*
Morpurgo, Michael 1943- *184*
   Earlier sketches in SATA *93, 143*
   See also CLR *51*
Morrah, Dave
   See Morrah, David Wardlaw, Jr.
Morrah, David Wardlaw, Jr. 1914-1991 .... *10*
Morreale-de la Garza, Phyllis
   See De la Garza, Phyllis
Morressy, John 1930-2006 .... *23*
Morrill, Leslie H(olt) 1934-2003 .... *48*
   Brief entry *33*
   Obituary *148*
   See also SAAS *22*
Morris, Carla *210*
Morris, Carla D.
   See Morris, Carla
Morris, Chris(topher Crosby) 1946- *66*
Morris, Deborah 1956- *91*
Morris, Desmond 1928- *14*
Morris, Desmond John
   See Morris, Desmond
Morris, Don 1954- *83*
Morris, Gerald 1963- *207*
   Earlier sketches in SATA *107, 150*
Morris, Gerald Paul
   See Morris, Gerald
Morris, Gilbert (Leslie) 1929- *104*
Morris, Jackie *202*
   Earlier sketch in SATA *151*
Morris, Janet (Ellen) 1946- *66*
Morris, Jay
   See Tatham, Julie Campbell
Morris, (Margaret) Jean 1924- *98*
Morris, Jeffrey B(randon) 1941- *92*

Morris, Jennifer E. 1969- *179*
Morris, Jill 1936- *165*
  Earlier sketch in SATA *119*
Morris, Juddi *85*
Morris, Judy K. 1936- *61*
Morris, Oradel Nolen *128*
Morris, Robert A(da) 1933- *7*
Morris, William 1913-1994 .... *29*
Morrison, Bill 1935- *66*
  Brief entry *37*
Morrison, Chloe Anthony Wofford
  See Morrison, Toni
Morrison, Dorothy Nafus *29*
Morrison, Frank 1971- *185*
Morrison, Gordon 1944- *183*
  Earlier sketches in SATA *87, 128*
Morrison, Joan 1922- *65*
Morrison, Lillian 1917- *108*
  Earlier sketch in SATA *3*
Morrison, Lucile Phillips 1896- *17*
Morrison, Martha A. 1948- *77*
Morrison, Meighan 1966- *90*
Morrison, P.R. *196*
Morrison, Richard
  See Lowndes, Robert A(ugustine) W(ard)
Morrison, Robert
  See Lowndes, Robert A(ugustine) W(ard)
Morrison, Roberta
  See Webb, Jean Francis (III)
Morrison, Susan Dudley
  See Gold, Susan Dudley
Morrison, Taylor 1971- *187*
  Earlier sketches in SATA *95, 159*
Morrison, Toni 1931- *144*
  Earlier sketch in SATA *57*
  See also CLR *99*
Morrison, Velma Ford 1909- *21*
Morrison, Wilbur Howard 1915- *64*
Morrison, William
  See Samachson, Joseph
Morriss, James E(dward) 1932- *8*
Morrissey, Dean *183*
Morrow, Barbara Olenyik 1952- *167*
Morrow, Betty
  See Bacon, Elizabeth
Morse, C. Scott
  See Morse, Scott
Morse, Carol
  See Yeakley, Marjory Hall
Morse, C.S.
  See Morse, Scott
Morse, Dorothy B(ayley) 1906-1979
  Obituary *24*
Morse, Flo 1921- *30*
Morse, Scott 1973- *200*
Morse, Tony 1953- *129*
Mort, Vivian
  See Cromie, Alice Hamilton
Mortensen, Denise Dowling *179*
Mortimer, Anne 1958- *206*
  Earlier sketch in SATA *116*
Mortimer, Mary H.
  See Coury, Louise Andree
Morton, Alexandra (Hubbard) 1957- *144*
Morton, Anthony
  See Arthur, Robert, (Jr.)
Morton, Christine
  See Morton-Shaw, Christine
Morton, Jane 1931- *50*
Morton, Joseph C. 1932- *156*
Morton, Lee Jack, Jr. 1928- *32*
Morton, Miriam 1918(?)-1985 .... *9*
  Obituary *46*
Morton-Shaw, Christine 1957- *211*
Mosatche, Harriet 1949- *122*
Mosatche, Harriet S.
  See Mosatche, Harriet
Moscow, Alvin 1925- *3*
Mosel, Arlene (Tichy) 1921-1996 .... *7*
Moseley, James W(illett) 1931- *139*
Moseng, Elisabeth 1967- *90*

Moser, Barry 1940- *185*
  Earlier sketches in SATA *56, 79, 138*
  See also CLR *49*
  See also SAAS *15*
Moser, Don(ald Bruce) 1932- *31*
Moser, Laura *194*
Moser, Lisa *192*
Moses, Sheila P. 1961- *168*
Moses, Will 1956- *178*
  Earlier sketch in SATA *120*
Mosesson, Gloria R(ubin) *24*
Mosher, Richard 1949- *120*
Moskin, Marietta D(unston) 1928- *23*
Moskof, Martin Stephen 1930- *27*
Mosley, Francis 1957- *57*
Moss, Don(ald) 1920- *11*
Moss, Elaine (Dora) 1924- *57*
  Brief entry *31*
Moss, Jeff(rey) 1942-1998 .... *73*
  Obituary *106*
Moss, Marissa 1959- *163*
  Earlier sketches in SATA *71, 104*
  See also CLR *134*
Moss, Miriam 1955- *202*
  Earlier sketches in SATA *76, 140*
Moss, Thylias 1954- *108*
Moss, Thylias Rebecca Brasier
  See Moss, Thylias
Most, Bernard 1937- *134*
  Brief entry *40*
  Earlier sketches in SATA *48, 91*
Mosz, Gosia 1972- *194*
Mott, Evelyn Clarke 1962- *133*
  Earlier sketch in SATA *75*
Motz, Lloyd 1909-2004 .... *20*
Mould, Chris *205*
Mould, Edwin
  See Whitlock, Ralph
Moulton, Mark Kimball *212*
Mouly, Francoise *155*
Mountain, Robert
  See Montgomery, Raymond A. (Jr.)
Mountfield, David
  See Grant, Neil
Mourlevat, Jean-Claude 1952- *187*
Mourning, Tuesday *206*
Moussard, Jacqueline 1924- *24*
Mowat, Claire 1933- *123*
Mowat, Claire Angel Wheeler
  See Mowat, Claire
Mowat, Farley 1921- *55*
  Earlier sketch in SATA *3*
  See also CLR *20*
Mowat, Farley McGill
  See Mowat, Farley
Mowll, Joshua 1970(?)- *188*
Mowry, Jess 1960- *131*
  Autobiography Feature *131*
  Earlier sketch in SATA *109*
  See also CLR *65*
Moxley, Sheila 1966- *96*
Moyer, Terry J. 1937- *94*
Moyes, Patricia
  See Haszard, Patricia Moyes
Moyler, Alan (Frank Powell) 1926- *36*
Mozelle, Shirley *179*
Mozley, Charles 1915- *43*
  Brief entry *32*
Mphahlele, Es'kia 1919-2008 .... *119*
  Obituary *198*
Mphahlele, Ezekiel
  See Mphahlele, Es'kia
Mphahlele, Zeke
  See Mphahlele, Es'kia
Mr. McGillicuddy
  See Abisch, Roslyn Kroop
Mr. Sniff
  See Abisch, Roslyn Kroop
Mr. Tivil
  See Lorkowski, Thomas V(incent)

Mr. Wizard
  See Herbert, Don
Mrs. Fairstar
  See Horne, Richard Henry Hengist
Muchamore, Robert 1972- *175*
Muchmore, Jo Ann 1937- *103*
Mude, O.
  See Gorey, Edward (St. John)
Mudgeon, Apeman
  See Mitchell, Adrian
Mueller, Jorg 1942- *67*
  See also CLR *43*
Mueller, Miranda R. *201*
Mueller, Virginia 1924- *28*
Muggs
  See Watkins, Lois
Muir, Diana
  See Appelbaum, Diana Muir Karter
Muir, Frank (Herbert) 1920-1998 .... *30*
Muir, Helen 1937- *65*
Mukerji, Dhan Gopal 1890-1936 .... *40*
  See also CLR *10*
Mulcahy, Lucille Burnett *12*
Mulford, Philippa G. 1948- *112*
  Earlier sketch in SATA *43*
Mulford, Philippa Greene
  See Mulford, Philippa G.
Mulgan, Catherine 1931- *24*
Mulila, Vigad G.
  See Maillu, David G(ian)
Mull, Brandon 1974- *190*
Mullen, Michael 1937- *122*
Muller, Billex
  See Ellis, Edward S.
Muller, Birte 1973- *214*
Muller, Jorg
  See Mueller, Jorg
Muller, (Lester) Robin 1953- *86*
Mullin, Caryl Cude 1969- *130*
Mullins, Edward S(wift) 1922- *10*
Mullins, Hilary 1962- *84*
Mulock, Dinah Maria
  See Craik, Dinah Maria (Mulock)
Mulvihill, William Patrick 1923- *8*
Mumford, Ruth
  See Dallas, Ruth
Mumy, Bill 1954- *112*
Mun
  See Leaf, (Wilbur) Munro
Munari, Bruno 1907-1998 .... *15*
  See also CLR *9*
Munce, Ruth Hill 1898- *12*
Mundy, Simon 1954- *64*
Mundy, Simon Andrew James Hainault
  See Mundy, Simon
Munger, Nancy *170*
Munowitz, Ken 1935-1977 .... *14*
Munoz, Claudio *208*
Munoz, William 1949- *92*
  Earlier sketch in SATA *42*
Munro, Alice 1931- *29*
Munro, Alice Anne
  See Munro, Alice
Munro, Eleanor 1928- *37*
Munro, Roxie 1945- *184*
  Earlier sketches in SATA *58, 136*
Munsch, Bob
  See Munsch, Robert (Norman)
Munsch, Robert (Norman) 1945- *120*
  Brief entry *48*
  Earlier sketches in SATA *50, 83*
  See also CLR *19*
Munsinger, Lynn 1951- *177*
  Earlier sketches in SATA *33, 94*
Munson, Derek 1970- *139*
Munson, R. W.
  See Karl, Jean E(dna)
Munson-Benson, Tunie 1946- *15*
Munsterberg, Peggy 1921- *102*
Muntean, Michaela *182*
Munthe, Nelly 1947- *53*

Munves, James (Albert) 1922- *30*
Munzer, Martha E. 1899-1999 .... *4*
Murawski, Darlyne A. *193*
Murch, Mel
 See Manes, Stephen
Murdoch, David H(amilton) 1937- *96*
Murdoch, Patricia 1957- *192*
Murdock, Catherine Gilbert *185*
Murhall, J(acqueline) J(ane) 1964- *143*
Murphy, Barbara Beasley 1933- *130*
 Earlier sketch in SATA *5*
Murphy, Claire Rudolf 1951- *137*
 Earlier sketch in SATA *76*
Murphy, E(mmett) Jefferson 1926- *4*
Murphy, Elizabeth Ann Maureen
 See Murphy, Liz
Murphy, Jill 1949- *214*
 Earlier sketches in SATA *37, 70, 142*
 See also CLR *39*
Murphy, Jill Frances
 See Murphy, Jill
Murphy, Jim 1947- *185*
 Brief entry *32*
 Earlier sketches in SATA *37, 77, 124*
 See also CLR *53*
Murphy, Joseph E., Jr. 1930- *65*
Murphy, Kelly 1977- *190*
 Earlier sketch in SATA *143*
Murphy, Liz 1964- *210*
Murphy, Louise 1943- *155*
Murphy, Mary 1961- *196*
Murphy, Pat
 See Murphy, E(mmett) Jefferson
Murphy, Patricia J. 1963- *132*
Murphy, Rita *180*
Murphy, Robert (William) 1902-1971 .... *10*
Murphy, Shirley Rousseau 1928- *126*
 Earlier sketches in SATA *36, 71*
 See also SAAS *18*
Murphy, Stuart J. 1942- *157*
 Earlier sketch in SATA *115*
Murphy, Thomas Basil, Jr. 1935- *191*
Murphy, Tim
 See Murphy, Jim
Murphy, Tom
 See Murphy, Thomas Basil, Jr.
Murray, John 1923- *39*
Murray, Kirsty 1960- *165*
 Earlier sketch in SATA *108*
Murray, Marguerite 1917- *63*
Murray, Marian *5*
Murray, Martine 1965- *125*
Murray, (Judith) Michele (Freedman)
 1933-1974 .... *7*
Murray, Ossie 1938- *43*
Murray, Peter
 See Hautman, Pete
Murrow, Liza Ketchum
 See Ketchum, Liza
Musgrave, Florence 1902-1999 .... *3*
Musgrove, Margaret W(ynkoop) 1943- *124*
 Earlier sketch in SATA *26*
Musgrove, Marianne *207*
Mussey, Virginia Howell
 See Ellison, Virginia H(owell)
Mussey, Virginia T.H.
 See Ellison, Virginia H(owell)
Mussi, Sarah *206*
Mutel, Cornelia F. 1947- *74*
Muth, Jon J. *206*
 Earlier sketch in SATA *165*
Mutz
 See Kuenstler, Morton
Mwangi, Meja 1948- *174*
My Brother's Brother
 See Chekhov, Anton
Myers, Anna *160*
Myers, Arthur 1917- *91*
 Earlier sketch in SATA *35*
Myers, Bernice *81*
 Earlier sketch in SATA *9*

Myers, Caroline Elizabeth Clark
 1887-1980 .... *28*
Myers, Christopher 1975- *183*
 See also CLR *97*
Myers, Edward 1950- *172*
 Earlier sketch in SATA *96*
Myers, Elisabeth P(erkins) 1918- *36*
Myers, (Mary) Hortense (Powner)
 1913-1987 .... *10*
Myers, Jack 1913-2006 .... *83*
 Obituary *178*
Myers, Jack Edgar
 See Myers, Jack
Myers, Lou 1915-2005 .... *81*
 Obituary *171*
Myers, Louis
 See Myers, Lou
Myers, R.E. 1924- *119*
Myers, Robert Eugene
 See Myers, R.E.
Myers, Tim 1953- *176*
 Earlier sketch in SATA *147*
Myers, Timothy Joseph
 See Myers, Tim
Myers, Walter Dean 1937- *193*
 Brief entry *27*
 Earlier sketches in SATA *41, 71, 109, 157*
 See also CLR *110*
 See also SAAS *2*
Myers, Walter M.
 See Myers, Walter Dean
Myller, Rolf 1926-2006 .... *27*
 Obituary *175*
Myra, Harold L(awrence) 1939- *46*
 Brief entry *42*
Myracle, Lauren 1969- *204*
 Earlier sketch in SATA *162*
Myrus, Donald (Richard) 1927- *23*
Mysterious Traveler, The
 See Arthur, Robert, (Jr.)

N

Na, An *149*
Naaslund, Goorel Kristina 1940- *170*
Nadel, Laurie 1948- *74*
Naden, Corinne J. 1930- *166*
 Earlier sketch in SATA *79*
Nadimi, Suzan *188*
Nagda, Ann Whitehead *199*
Nagel, Andreas Fischer
 See Fischer-Nagel, Andreas
Nagel, Heiderose Fischer
 See Fischer-Nagel, Heiderose
Nagle, Shane *176*
Nahoko, Uehashi
 See Uehashi, Nahoko
Naidoo, Beverley 1943- *180*
 Earlier sketches in SATA *63, 135*
 See also CLR *29*
Nails, Jennifer *213*
Nakae, Noriko 1940- *59*
Nakata, Hiroe *205*
Nakatani, Chiyoko 1930-1981 .... *55*
 Brief entry *40*
 See also CLR *30*
Nally, Susan W. 1947- *90*
Namioka, Lensey 1929- *157*
 Autobiography Feature *116*
 Earlier sketches in SATA *27, 89*
 See also CLR *48*
 See also SAAS *24*
Namovicz, Gene Inyart 1927- *6*
Nance, Andrew *210*
Nanji, Shenaaz 1954- *204*
 Earlier sketch in SATA *131*
Nanogak Agnes 1925- *61*
Napier, Mark
 See Laffin, John (Alfred Charles)

Napoli, Donna Jo 1948- *190*
 Earlier sketches in SATA *92, 137*
 See also CLR *51*
 See also SAAS *23*
Napp, Daniel 1974- *204*
Narahashi, Keiko 1959- *115*
 Earlier sketch in SATA *79*
Narayan, R. K. 1906-2001 .... *62*
Narayan, Rasipuram Krishnaswami
 See Narayan, R. K.
Nascimbene, Yan 1949- *173*
 Earlier sketch in SATA *133*
Nash, Bruce M(itchell) 1947- *34*
Nash, Fredric Ogden
 See Nash, Ogden
Nash, Linell
 See Smith, Linell Nash
Nash, Mary (Hughes) 1925- *41*
Nash, Ogden 1902-1971 .... *46*
 Earlier sketch in SATA *2*
Nash, Renea Denise 1963- *81*
Nast, Elsa Ruth
 See Watson, Jane Werner
Nast, Thomas 1840-1902 .... *51*
 Brief entry *33*
Nastick, Sharon 1954- *41*
Natale, Vince *196*
Natarajan, Srividya *187*
Nathan, Adele (Gutman) 1900(?)-1986
 Obituary *48*
Nathan, Amy *155*
 Earlier sketch in SATA *104*
Nathan, Dorothy (Goldeen) (?)-1966 .... *15*
Nathan, Robert (Gruntal) 1894-1985 .... *6*
 Obituary *43*
Nathanson, Laura Walther 1941- *57*
Natti, Lee 1919- *67*
 Earlier sketch in SATA *1*
 See also SAAS *3*
Natti, Susanna 1948- *125*
 Earlier sketch in SATA *32*
Nau, Thomas *186*
Naughtie, Eleanor
 See Updale, Eleanor
Naughton, Bill
 See Naughton, William John (Francis)
Naughton, James Franklin 1957- *85*
Naughton, Jim
 See Naughton, James Franklin
Naughton, William John (Francis)
 1910-1992 .... *86*
Navarra, John Gabriel 1927- *8*
Naylor, Penelope 1941- *10*
Naylor, Phyllis 1933-
 See Naylor, Phyllis Reynolds
Naylor, Phyllis Reynolds 1933- *209*
 Autobiography Feature *152*
 See also CLR *135*
 See also SAAS *10*
Nazarian, Nikki
 See Nichols, Cecilia Fawn
Nazaroff, Alexander I(vanovich) 1898-1981 .. *4*
Nazoa, Aquiles 1920-1976 .... *198*
Neal, Harry Edward 1906-1993 .... *5*
 Obituary *76*
Neal, Michael
 See Teitelbaum, Michael
Nearing, Penny 1916- *47*
 Brief entry *42*
Nebel, Gustave E. *45*
 Brief entry *33*
Nebel, Mimouca
 See Nebel, Gustave E.
Nee, Kay Bonner *10*
Needham, Kate 1962- *95*
Needle, Jan 1943- *98*
 Earlier sketch in SATA *30*
 See also CLR *43*
 See also SAAS *23*
Needleman, Jacob 1934- *6*
Neel, David 1960- *82*

Neel, Preston 1959- 93
Negri, Rocco 1932- 12
Negrin, Fabian 1963- 189
Neidigh, Sherry 1956- 204
Neier, Aryeh 1937- 59
Neigoff, Anne 13
Neigoff, Mike 1920- 13
Neilan, Eujin Kim 1969- 200
Neilson, Frances Fullerton (Jones)
　1910-2001 14
Neimark, Anne E. 1935- 145
　Earlier sketch in SATA 4
Neimark, Paul G. 1934- 80
　Brief entry 37
Neitzel, Shirley 1941- 134
　Earlier sketch in SATA 77
Nell
　See Hanna, Nell(ie L.)
Nelscott, Kris
　See Rusch, Kristine Kathryn
Nelson, Blake 1960- 177
Nelson, Catherine Chadwick 1926- 87
Nelson, Cordner 1918-2009 54
　Brief entry 29
Nelson, Cordner Bruce
　See Nelson, Cordner
Nelson, D.A. 1970- 215
Nelson, Dawn Ann
　See Nelson, D.A.
Nelson, Drew 1952- 77
Nelson, Esther L. 1928- 13
Nelson, Jim A.
　See Stotter, Mike
Nelson, Julie L. 1970- 117
Nelson, Kadir 213
　Earlier sketches in SATA 154, 181
Nelson, Kris
　See Rusch, Kristine Kathryn
Nelson, Lawrence E(rnest) 1928-1977
　Obituary 28
Nelson, Marilyn 1946- 60
　Autobiography Feature 180
Nelson, Mary Carroll 1929- 23
Nelson, O. Terry 1941- 62
Nelson, Peter N. 1953- 73
Nelson, R. A. 197
Nelson, Richard K(ing) 1941- 65
Nelson, Robin Laura 1971- 141
Nelson, Roy Paul 1923- 59
Nelson, S.D. 181
Nelson, Sharlene (P.) 1933- 96
Nelson, Suzanne 1976- 184
Nelson, Ted (W.) 1931- 96
Nelson, Theresa 1948- 143
　Autobiography Feature 143
　Earlier sketch in SATA 79
Nemeth, Sally 187
Neri, G. 197
Neri, Greg
　See Neri, G.
Neri, Gregory
　See Neri, G.
Nerlove, Miriam 1959- 53
　Brief entry 49
Nesbit, E. 1858-1924 100
　See also YABC 1
　See also CLR 70
Nesbit, Edith
　See Nesbit, E.
Nesbit, Troy
　See Folsom, Franklin (Brewster)
Nespojohn, Katherine V(eronica) 1912-1975 . 7
Ness, Evaline (Michelow) 1911-1986 26
　Obituary 49
　Earlier sketch in SATA 1
　See also CLR 6
　See also SAAS 1
Ness, Patrick 1971- 207
Nestor, Larry 1940- 149
Nestor, William P(rodromos) 1947- 49
Nethery, Mary 93

Neubecker, Robert 214
　Earlier sketch in SATA 170
Neuberger, Julia (Babette Sarah) 1950- 142
　Earlier sketch in SATA 78
Neufeld, John (Arthur) 1938- 131
　Autobiography Feature 131
　Earlier sketches in SATA 6, 81
　See also CLR 52
　See also SAAS 3
Neuhaus, David 1958- 83
Neumeyer, Peter F(lorian) 1929- 13
Neurath, Marie (Reidemeister) 1898-1986 1
Neuschwander, Cindy 1953- 157
　Earlier sketch in SATA 107
Neusner, Jacob 1932- 38
Neville, Charles
　See Bodsworth, (Charles) Fred(erick)
Neville, Emily Cheney 1919- 1
　See also SAAS 2
Neville, Mary
　See Woodrich, Mary Neville
Nevins, Albert (Francis) J(erome)
　1915-1997 20
Nevius, Carol 1955- 186
Newberger, Devra
　See Speregen, Devra Newberger
Newberry, Clare Turlay 1903-1970 1
　Obituary 26
Newbery, John 1713-1767 20
　See also CLR 147
Newbery, Linda 1952- 184
　Earlier sketch in SATA 142
Newbigging, Martha 198
Newbold, Greg 199
Newcomb, Ellsworth
　See Kenny, Ellsworth Newcomb
Newcombe, Eugene A. 1923-1990 45
　Brief entry 33
Newcombe, Jack
　See Newcombe, Eugene A.
Newcome, Robert 1955- 91
Newcome, Zita 1959- 88
Newell, Crosby
　See Bonsall, Crosby Barbara (Newell)
Newell, Edythe W(eatherford) 1910-1989 11
Newell, Hope Hockenberry 1896-1965 24
Newfeld, Frank 1928- 26
Newgarden, Mark 1959- 194
Newlon, (Frank) Clarke 1905(?)-1982 6
　Obituary 33
Newman, Barbara Johansen 191
Newman, C.J.
　See Newman, Coleman J.
Newman, Coleman J. 1935- 82
Newman, Daisy 1904-1994 27
　Obituary 78
Newman, Gerald 1939- 46
　Brief entry 42
Newman, Jerry
　See Newman, Coleman J.
Newman, Leslea 1955- 134
　Earlier sketches in SATA 71, 128
Newman, Margaret
　See Potter, Margaret
Newman, Marjorie 146
Newman, Matthew (Harrison) 1955- 56
Newman, Nanette 1934- 162
Newman, Robert (Howard) 1909-1988 87
　Obituary 60
　Earlier sketch in SATA 4
Newman, Shirlee P(etkin) 144
　Earlier sketches in SATA 10, 90
Newsom, Carol 1948- 92
　Earlier sketch in SATA 40
Newsom, Tom 1944- 80
Newth, Mette 1942- 140
Newton, David E(dward) 1933- 67
Newton, James R(obert) 1935- 23
Newton, Jill 1964- 200
Newton, Robert 1965- 191

Newton, Suzanne 1936- 77
　Earlier sketch in SATA 5
Newton, Vanessa
　See Newton, Vanessa Brantley
Newton, Vanessa Brantley 1962(?)- 206
Ney, John 1923- 43
　Brief entry 33
Nez, John 155
Ng, Franklin 82
Nguyen, Vincent 187
Nichol, B(arrie) P(hillip) 1944-1988 66
Nicholas, Louise D.
　See Watkins, Dawn L.
Nicholls, Judith (Ann) 1941- 61
Nicholls, Sally 1983- 209
Nichols, Cecilia Fawn 1906-1987 12
Nichols, Grace 1950- 164
　Earlier sketch in SATA 98
Nichols, Janet (Louise) 1952- 67
Nichols, Judy 1947- 124
Nichols, Leigh
　See Koontz, Dean
Nichols, Michael 1952- 215
Nichols, Michael Nick
　See Nichols, Michael
Nichols, Paul
　See Hawks, Robert
Nichols, Peter
　See Youd, Samuel
Nichols, (Joanna) Ruth 1948- 15
　See also CLR 149
Nichols, Travis 206
Nicholson, C. R.
　See Nicole, Christopher (Robin)
Nicholson, Christina
　See Nicole, Christopher (Robin)
Nicholson, Joyce Thorpe 1919- 35
Nicholson, Lois P. 1949- 88
Nicholson, Robin
　See Nicole, Christopher (Robin)
Nicholson, William 180
Nicholson, William 1872-1949
　See CLR 76
Nickel, Barbara 1966- 188
Nickell, Joe 1944- 167
　Earlier sketch in SATA 73
Nickelsburg, Janet 1893-1983 11
Nickerson, Betty 1922- 14
Nickerson, Elizabeth
　See Nickerson, Betty
Nickl, Barbara (Elisabeth) 1939- 56
Nicklaus, Carol 62
　Brief entry 33
Nickle, John 181
Nickless, Will 1902-1979(?) 66
Nic Leodhas, Sorche
　See Alger, Leclaire (Gowans)
Nicol, Ann
　See Turnbull, Ann
Nicolas
　See Mordvinoff, Nicolas
Nicolay, Helen 1866-1954
　See YABC 1
Nicole, Christopher (Robin) 1930- 5
Nicoll, Helen 1937- 87
Nicolson, Cynthia Pratt 1949- 141
Ni Dhuibhne, Eilis 1954- 91
Niehaus, Paddy Bouma
　See Bouma, Paddy
Nields, Nerissa 1967- 166
Nielsen, Kay (Rasmus) 1886-1957 16
　See also CLR 16
Nielsen, Laura F. 1960- 93
Nielsen, Laura Farnsworth
　See Nielsen, Laura F.
Nielsen, Nancy J. 1951- 77
Nielsen, Susin 1964- 195
Nielsen, Virginia
　See McCall, Virginia Nielsen
Nielsen-Fernlund, Susin
　See Nielsen, Susin

Niemann, Christoph 1970- *191*
Nieuwsma, Milton J(ohn) 1941- *142*
Nightingale, Sandy 1953- *76*
Nikolajeva, Maria 1952- *127*
Nikola-Lisa, W. 1951- *180*
  Earlier sketch in SATA *71*
Niland, Deborah 1951- *172*
  Earlier sketch in SATA *27*
Niland, Kilmeny *75*
Nilsen, Anna 1948- *174*
  Earlier sketch in SATA *96*
Nilsson, Eleanor 1939- *117*
  Earlier sketch in SATA *81*
  See also SAAS *23*
Nilsson, Per 1954- *159*
Nimmo, Jenny 1944- *144*
  Earlier sketch in SATA *87*
  See also CLR *44*
Nishimura, Kae *196*
Niven, Larry 1938- *171*
  Earlier sketch in SATA *95*
Niven, Laurence VanCott
  See Niven, Larry
Nivola, Claire A. 1947- *208*
  Earlier sketches in SATA *84, 140*
Nix, Garth 1963- *210*
  Earlier sketches in SATA *97, 143*
  See also CLR *68*
Nixon, Hershell Howard 1923- *42*
Nixon, Joan Lowery 1927-2003 .... *115*
  Obituary *146*
  Earlier sketches in SATA *8, 44, 78*
  See also CLR *24*
  See also SAAS *9*
Nixon, K.
  See Nixon, Kathleen Irene (Blundell)
Nixon, Kathleen Irene (Blundell)
  1894-1988(?) *14*
  Obituary *59*
Nobati, Eugenia 1968- *201*
Nobisso, Josephine 1953- *121*
  Earlier sketch in SATA *78*
Noble, Iris (Davis) 1922-1986 .... *5*
  Obituary *49*
Noble, Marty 1947- *125*
  Earlier sketch in SATA *97*
Noble, Trinka Hakes 1944- *197*
  Brief entry *37*
  Earlier sketch in SATA *123*
Nobleman, Marc Tyler 1972- *203*
Noda, Takayo 1961- *168*
Nodelman, Perry 1942- *101*
Nodset, Joan L.
  See Lexau, Joan M.
Noel Hume, Ivor 1927- *65*
Noestlinger, Christine
  See Nostlinger, Christine
Noguere, Suzanne 1947- *34*
Nolan, Dennis 1945- *166*
  Brief entry *34*
  Earlier sketches in SATA *42, 92*
Nolan, Han 1956- *157*
  Earlier sketch in SATA *109*
Nolan, Janet 1956- *191*
  Earlier sketch in SATA *145*
Nolan, Jeannette Covert 1897-1974 .... *2*
  Obituary *27*
Nolan, Lucy *215*
Nolan, Paul T(homas) 1919- *48*
Nolan, William F. 1928- *88*
  Brief entry *28*
Nolan, William Francis
  See Nolan, William F.
Nolen, Jerdine 1953- *157*
  Earlier sketch in SATA *105*
Noll, Sally 1946- *82*
Noonan, Brandon 1979- *184*
Noonan, Diana 1960- *146*
Noonan, Julia 1946- *148*
  Earlier sketches in SATA *4, 95*
Norac, Carl 1960- *166*

Norcross, John
  See Conroy, John Wesley
Nordan, Robert W(arren) 1934-2004 .... *133*
Nordhoff, Charles Bernard 1887-1947 .... *23*
Nordlicht, Lillian *29*
Nordstrom, Ursula 1910-1988 .... *3*
  Obituary *57*
Nordtvedt, Matilda 1926- *67*
Norling, Beth 1969- *149*
Norman, Charles 1904-1996 .... *38*
  Obituary *92*
Norman, Howard
  See Norman, Howard A.
Norman, Howard A. 1949- *81*
Norman, James
  See Schmidt, James Norman
Norman, Jay
  See Arthur, Robert, (Jr.)
Norman, Lilith 1927- *120*
  Earlier sketch in SATA *86*
Norman, Mary 1931- *36*
Norman, Steve
  See Pashko, Stanley
Norment, Lisa 1966- *91*
Norris, Gunilla Brodde 1939- *20*
North, Andrew
  See Norton, Andre
North, Anthony
  See Koontz, Dean
North, Captain George
  See Stevenson, Robert Louis
North, Captain George
  See Stevenson, Robert Louis
North, Howard
  See Trevor, Elleston
North, Joan 1920- *16*
North, Milou
  See Erdrich, Louise
North, Robert
  See Withers, Carl A.
North, Sara
  See Bonham, Barbara Thomas
  and Hager, Jean
North, Sherry *201*
North, Sterling 1906-1974 .... *45*
  Obituary *26*
  Earlier sketch in SATA *1*
Northcott, (William) Cecil 1902-1987
  Obituary *55*
Northeast, Brenda V(ictoria) 1948- *106*
Northmore, Elizabeth Florence 1906-1974 . *122*
Norton, Alice Mary
  See Norton, Andre
Norton, Andre 1912-2005 .... *91*
  Earlier sketches in SATA *1, 43*
  See also CLR *50*
Norton, Browning
  See Norton, Frank R. B(rowning)
Norton, Frank R. B(rowning) 1909-1989 ..... *10*
Norton, Mary 1903-1992 .... *60*
  Obituary *72*
  Earlier sketch in SATA *18*
  See also CLR *140*
Nosredna, Trebor
  See Anderson, Bob
Nostlinger, Christine 1936- *162*
  Brief entry *37*
  Earlier sketch in SATA *64*
  See also CLR *12*
Nourse, Alan E(dward) 1928-1992 .... *48*
  See also CLR *33*
Novak, Matt 1962- *204*
  Brief entry *52*
  Earlier sketches in SATA *60, 104, 165*
Novelli, Luca 1947- *61*
Novgorodoff, Danica 1982(?)- *215*
Nowell, Elizabeth Cameron *12*
Noyes, Deborah 1965- *194*
  Earlier sketch in SATA *145*
Nugent, Cynthia 1954- *205*
Nugent, Nicholas 1949- *73*

Numeroff, Laura 1953- *206*
  Earlier sketches in SATA *28, 90, 142*
  See also CLR *85*
Numeroff Joffe, Laura
  See Numeroff, Laura
Nunes, Lygia Bojunga 1932- *154*
  Earlier sketch in SATA *75*
Nunn, Laura (Donna) Silverstein 1968- *124*
Nurenberg, Thelma
  See Greenhaus, Thelma Nurenberg
Nurnberg, Maxwell 1897-1984 .... *27*
  Obituary *41*
Nussbaumer, Paul (Edmund) 1934- *16*
Nutt, Ken 1951- *163*
  Earlier sketch in SATA *97*
Nuttall-Smith, Margaret Emily Noel 1919- .. *26*
Nuygen, Mathieu 1967- *80*
Nuzum, K. A. *195*
Nuzum, Kathy A.
  See Nuzum, K. A.
Nyberg, (Everett Wayne) Morgan 1944- *87*
Nyce, (Nellie) Helene von Strecker
  1885-1969 .... *19*
Nyce, Vera 1862-1925 .... *19*
Nye, Naomi Shihab 1952- *198*
  Earlier sketches in SATA *86, 147*
  See also CLR *59*
Nye, Robert 1939- *6*
Nyeu, Tao *206*
Nyikos, Stacy A. 1969- *164*
Nystrom, Carolyn 1940- *130*
  Earlier sketch in SATA *67*

O

O. Henry
  See Henry, O.
Oakes, Elizabeth H. 1964- *132*
Oakes, Vanya 1909-1983 .... *6*
  Obituary *37*
Oakley, Don(ald G.) 1927- *8*
Oakley, Graham 1929- *84*
  Earlier sketch in SATA *30*
  See also CLR *7*
Oakley, Helen (McKelvey) 1906- *10*
Oana, Katherine 1929- *53*
  Brief entry *37*
Oates, Eddie H. 1943- *88*
Oates, Joyce Carol 1938- *159*
Oates, Stephen B(aery) 1936- *59*
Obed, Ellen Bryan 1944- *74*
Oberle, Joseph 1958- *69*
Oberman, Sheldon 1949-2004 .... *85*
  Autobiography Feature *114*
  Obituary *153*
  See also CLR *54*
  See also SAAS *26*
Obligado, Lilian (Isabel) 1931- *61*
  Brief entry *45*
Obrant, Susan 1946- *11*
O'Brian, E.G.
  See Clarke, Arthur C.
O'Brien, Anne Sibley 1952- *213*
  Brief entry *48*
  Earlier sketches in SATA *53, 80*
O'Brien, E.G.
  See Clarke, Arthur C.
O'Brien, Esse Forrester 1895(?)-1975
  Obituary *30*
O'Brien, Patrick 1960- *193*
O'Brien, Robert C.
  See Conly, Robert Leslie
O'Brien, Thomas C(lement) 1938- *29*
O'Callaghan, Julie 1954- *113*
O'Callahan, Jay 1938- *88*
O'Carroll, Ryan
  See Markun, Patricia Maloney
Ochiltree, Dianne 1953- *117*

Ockham, Joan Price
  See Price, Joan
O'Connell, Margaret F(orster) 1935-1977 30
  Obituary 30
O'Connell, Peg
  See Ahern, Margaret McCrohan
O'Connell, Rebecca 1968- 212
  Earlier sketch in SATA 130
O'Connor, Barbara 1950- 193
  Earlier sketch in SATA 154
O'Connor, Francine M(arie) 1930- 90
O'Connor, Genevieve A. 1914- 75
O'Connor, George 183
O'Connor, Ian 1965- 188
O'Connor, Jane 1947- 186
  Brief entry 47
  Earlier sketches in SATA 59, 103, 150
O'Connor, Karen 1938- 89
  Earlier sketch in SATA 34
O'Connor, Patrick
  See Wibberley, Leonard
O'Connor, Richard 1915-1975
  Obituary 21
O'Conor, Jane 1958- 78
Odaga, Asenath (Bole) 1937- 130
  Earlier sketch in SATA 67
  See also SAAS 19
O Danachair, Caoimhin
  See Danaher, Kevin
Odanaka, Barbara 159
O'Daniel, Janet 1921- 24
O'Day, Cathy
  See Crane, Barbara (Joyce)
O'Dell, Scott 1898-1989 134
  Earlier sketches in SATA 12, 60
  See also CLR 126
Odenwald, Robert P(aul) 1899-1965 11
Odgers, Sally
  See Odgers, Sally Farrell
Odgers, Sally Farrell 1957- 139
  Earlier sketch in SATA 72
Odone, Jamison 1980- 209
O'Donnell, Dick
  See Lupoff, Richard A(llen)
  and Thompson, Don(ald Arthur)
O'Donnell, Liam 1970- 209
Odriozola, Elena 186
Oechsli, Kelly 1918-1999 5
Oesterle, Virginia Rorby
  See Rorby, Ginny
Ofek, Uriel 1926- 36
  See also CLR 28
Ofer, Avi 1975- 207
Offenbacher, Ami 1958- 91
Offill, Jenny 1968- 211
Offit, Sidney 1928- 10
Ofosu-Appiah, L(awrence) H(enry) 1920- ... 13
Ogan, George F. 1912-1983 13
Ogan, M. G.
  See Ogan, George F.
  and Ogan, Margaret E. (Nettles)
Ogan, Margaret E. (Nettles) 1923-1979 13
Ogburn, Charlton (Jr.) 1911-1998 3
  Obituary 109
Ogburn, Jacqueline K. 162
Ogilvie, Elisabeth May 1917-2006 40
  Brief entry 29
  Obituary 176
Ogilvy, Gavin
  See Barrie, J. M.
Ogilvy, Ian 1943- 177
Ogilvy, Ian Raymond
  See Ogilvy, Ian
Ogle, Lucille Edith 1904-1988
  Obituary 59
Ogletree, Charles J. 1952- 175
O'Green, Jennifer
  See Roberson, Jennifer
O'Green, Jennifer Roberson
  See Roberson, Jennifer
O'Hagan, Caroline 1946- 38

O'Hanlon, Jacklyn
  See Meek, Jacklyn O'Hanlon
O'Hara, Elizabeth
  See Ni Dhuibhne, Eilis
O'Hara, Kenneth
  See Morris, (Margaret) Jean
O'Hara, Mary
  See Alsop, Mary O'Hara
O'Hara (Alsop), Mary
  See Alsop, Mary O'Hara
O'Hare, Jeff(rey A.) 1958- 105
Ohi, Ruth 1964- 95
Ohiyesa
  See Eastman, Charles A(lexander)
Ohlsson, Ib 1935- 7
Ohmi, Ayano 1959- 115
Ohtomo, Yasuo 1946- 37
o huigin, sean 1942- 138
  See also CLR 75
Oiseau
  See Moseley, James W(illett)
Oke, Janette 1935- 97
O'Keefe, Susan Heyboer 176
  Earlier sketch in SATA 133
O'Keeffe, Frank 1938- 99
O'Kelley, Mattie Lou 1908-1997 97
  Earlier sketch in SATA 36
Okimoto, Jean Davies 1942- 103
  Earlier sketch in SATA 34
Okomfo, Amasewa
  See Cousins, Linda
olafsdottir, Gudrun Elin
  See Gunnella
Olaleye, Isaac O. 1941- 96
  See also SAAS 23
Olcott, Frances Jenkins 1872(?)-1963 19
Old, Wendie C(orbin) 1943- 154
Old Boy
  See Hughes, Thomas
Oldenburg, E(gbert) William 1936-1974 35
Older, Effin 1942- 114
Older, Jules 1940- 156
  Earlier sketch in SATA 114
Oldfield, Jenny 1949- 140
Oldfield, Margaret J(ean) 1932- 56
Oldfield, Pamela 1931- 86
Oldham, June 70
Oldham, Mary 1944- 65
Olds, Elizabeth 1896-1991 3
  Obituary 66
Olds, Helen Diehl 1895-1981 9
  Obituary 25
Oldstyle, Jonathan
  See Irving, Washington
O'Leary, Brian (Todd) 1940- 6
O'Leary, Chris 208
O'Leary, Patsy B(aker) 1937- 97
Oleynikov, Igor 1953- 202
Oliphant, B.J.
  See Tepper, Sheri S.
Oliver, Burton
  See Burt, Olive Woolley
Oliver, Chad
  See Oliver, Symmes C.
Oliver, John Edward 1933- 21
Oliver, Lin 202
Oliver, Marilyn Tower 1935- 89
Oliver, Mark 214
  See Tyler-Whittle, Michael Sidney
Oliver, Narelle 1960- 197
  Earlier sketch in SATA 152
Oliver, Shirley (Louise Dawkins) 1958- 74
Oliver, Symmes C. 1928-1993 101
Oliviero, Jamie 1950- 84
Olmsted, Lorena Ann 1890-1989 13
Olney, Ross R. 1929- 13
Olschewski, Alfred (Erich) 1920- 7
Olsen, Barbara 148
Olsen, Carol 1945- 89
Olsen, Ib Spang 1921- 81
  Earlier sketch in SATA 6

Olsen, Violet (Mae) 1922-1991 58
Olson, Arielle North 1932- 67
Olson, David J. 1974- 198
Olson, Gene 1922- 32
Olson, Gretchen 187
Olson, Helen Kronberg 48
Olson, Kay Melchisedech 1948- 175
Olson, Marianne
  See Mitchell, Marianne
Olson-Brown, Ellen 1967- 183
Olten, Manuela 1970- 197
Olugebefola, Ademole 1941- 15
Oluonye, Mary N(kechi) 1955- 111
Om
  See Gorey, Edward (St. John)
O'Malley, Donough 208
O'Malley, Kevin 1961- 191
  Earlier sketch in SATA 157
Oman, Carola (Mary Anima) 1897-1978 35
O'Mara, Carmel 1965- 166
O'Mara-Horwitz, Carmel
  See O'Mara, Carmel
O'Meara, Walter (Andrew) 1897-1989 65
Ommanney, F(rancis) D(ownes) 1903-1980 . 23
O Mude
  See Gorey, Edward (St. John)
Oneal, Elizabeth 1934- 82
  Earlier sketch in SATA 30
  See also CLR 13
O'Neal, Katherine Pebley 1957- 204
O'Neal, Reagan
  See Jordan, Robert
O'Neal, Regan
  See Jordan, Robert
Oneal, Zibby
  See Oneal, Elizabeth
O'Neill, Amanda 1951- 111
O'Neill, Catharine 203
O'Neill, Gerard K(itchen) 1927-1992 65
O'Neill, Judith (Beatrice) 1930- 34
O'Neill, Mary L(e Duc) 1908(?)-1990 2
  Obituary 64
O'Neill, Reagan
  See Jordan, Robert
Onslow, Annette Rosemary MacArthur
  See MacArthur-Onslow, Annette Rosemary
Onslow, John 1906-1985
  Obituary 47
Onyefulu, Ifeoma 1959- 157
  Earlier sketches in SATA 81, 115
Opie, Iona (Margaret Balfour) 1923- 118
  Earlier sketches in SATA 3, 63
  See also SAAS 6
Opie, Peter (Mason) 1918-1982 118
  Obituary 28
  Earlier sketches in SATA 3, 63
Oppel, Kenneth 1967- 199
  Earlier sketches in SATA 99, 153
Oppel, Kenneth Kerry
  See Oppel, Kenneth
Oppenheim, Joanne 1934- 174
  Earlier sketches in SATA 5, 82, 136
Oppenheim, Shulamith Levey 1928- 177
Oppenheimer, Joan L(etson) 1925- 28
Oppong, Joseph Ransford 1953- 160
Optic, Oliver
  See Adams, William Taylor
  and Stratemeyer, Edward L.
Oram, Hiawyn 1946- 101
  Earlier sketch in SATA 56
Orbach, Ruth Gary 1941- 21
Orback, Craig 197
Orczy, Emma
  See Orczy, Baroness Emmuska
Orczy, Emma Magdalena Rosalia Maria Josefa
  See Orczy, Baroness Emmuska
Orczy, Emmuska
  See Orczy, Baroness Emmuska
Orczy, Baroness Emmuska 1865-1947 40
Orde, A.J.
  See Tepper, Sheri S.

O'Reilly, Jackson
  See Jordan, Robert
Orenstein, Denise Gosliner 1950- *157*
Orgad, Dorit 1936- *199*
Orgel, Doris 1929- *148*
  Earlier sketches in SATA *7, 85*
  See also CLR *48*
  See also SAAS *19*
Orgill, Roxane *198*
Oriolo, Joe
  See Oriolo, Joseph D.
Oriolo, Joseph D. 1913-1985
  Obituary *46*
Orlean, Susan 1955- *209*
Orleans, Ilo 1897-1962 .... *10*
Orlev, Uri 1931- *135*
  Earlier sketch in SATA *58*
  See also CLR *30*
  See also SAAS *19*
Ormai, Stella *57*
  Brief entry *48*
Ormerod, Jan 1946- *210*
  Brief entry *44*
  Earlier sketches in SATA *55, 70, 132*
  See also CLR *20*
Ormerod, Janette Louise
  See Ormerod, Jan
Ormes, Jackie
  See Ormes, Zelda J.
Ormes, Zelda J. 1914-1986
  Obituary *47*
Ormondroyd, Edward 1925- *14*
Ormsby, Virginia H(aire) 1906-1990 .... *11*
Orona-Ramirez, Kristy 1964- *189*
Orozco, Jose-Luis 1948- *179*
Orr, Katherine S(helley) 1950- *72*
Orr, Wendy 1953- *206*
  Earlier sketches in SATA *90, 141*
Orris
  See Ingelow, Jean
Orth, Richard
  See Gardner, Richard (M.)
Ortiz Cofer, Judith
  See Cofer, Judith Ortiz
Orwell, George 1903-1950 .... *29*
  See also CLR *68*
Orwin, Joanna 1944- *141*
Osborn, Elinor 1939- *145*
Osborn, Jacob 1981(?)- *215*
Osborn, Kathy 1955(?)- *199*
Osborn, Lois D(orothy) 1915- *61*
Osborne, Charles 1927- *59*
Osborne, Chester G(orham) 1915-1987 .... *11*
Osborne, David
  See Silverberg, Robert
Osborne, George
  See Silverberg, Robert
Osborne, Leone Neal 1914-1996 .... *2*
Osborne, Linda Barrett 1949- *215*
Osborne, Mary Pope 1949- *144*
  Earlier sketches in SATA *41, 55, 98*
  See also CLR *88*
Osceola
  See Blixen, Karen
Osgood, William E(dward) 1926- *37*
O'Shaughnessy, Darren
  See Shan, Darren
O'Shaughnessy, Ellen Cassels 1937- *78*
O'Shea, Catherine Patricia Shiels
  See O'Shea, Pat
O'Shea, Pat 1931-2007 .... *87*
  See also CLR *18*
Osmond, Edward 1900- *10*
Ossoli, Sarah Margaret
  See Fuller, Margaret
Ostendorf, (Arthur) Lloyd, (Jr.) 1921-2000 .. *65*
  Obituary *125*
Ostow, Micol 1976- *170*
Otfinoski, Steven 1949- *116*
  Earlier sketch in SATA *56*

Otis, James
  See Kaler, James Otis
O'Toole, Thomas 1941- *71*
O'Trigger, Sir Lucius
  See Horne, Richard Henry Hengist
Otten, Charlotte
  See Otten, Charlotte F.
Otten, Charlotte F. 1926- *98*
Otten, Charlotte Fennema
  See Otten, Charlotte F.
Ottley, Matt 1962- *171*
  Earlier sketch in SATA *102*
Ottley, Reginald Leslie 1909-1985 .... *26*
  See also CLR *16*
Otto, Margaret Glover 1909-1976
  Obituary *30*
Otto, Svend
  See Soerensen, Svend Otto
Oughton, Jerrie (Preston) 1937- *131*
  Earlier sketch in SATA *76*
Oughton, (William) Taylor 1925- *104*
Ouida
  See De La Ramee, Marie Louise
Ousley, Odille 1896-1976 .... *10*
Outcalt, Todd 1960- *123*
Overmyer, James E. 1946- *88*
Overton, Jenny (Margaret Mary) 1942- *52*
  Brief entry *36*
Owen, Ann
  See Qualey, Marsha
Owen, Annie 1949- *75*
Owen, Caroline Dale
  See Snedeker, Caroline Dale (Parke)
Owen, Clifford
  See Hamilton, Charles (Harold St. John)
Owen, Dilys
  See Gater, Dilys
Owen, (Benjamin) Evan 1918-1984 .... *38*
Owen, (John) Gareth 1936-2002 .... *162*
  Earlier sketch in SATA *83*
  See also CLR *31*
  See also SAAS *14*
Owen, James A. *185*
Owens, Bryant 1968- *116*
Owens, Dana Elaine
  See Queen Latifah
Owens, Gail 1939- *54*
Owens, Mary Beth *191*
Owens, Thomas S(heldon) 1960- *86*
Owens, Tom
  See Owens, Thomas S(heldon)
Oxenbury, Helen 1938- *149*
  Earlier sketches in SATA *3, 68*
  See also CLR *70*
Oxendine, Bess Holland 1933- *90*
Oz, Frank (Richard) 1944- *60*
Ozer, Jerome S. 1927- *59*

P

Paananen, Eloise (Katherine) 1923-1993 .... *9*
Pace, Lorenzo 1943- *131*
Pace, Mildred Mastin 1907- *46*
  Brief entry *29*
Pachter, Hedwig (?)-1988 .... *63*
Pack, Janet 1952- *77*
Pack, Robert 1929- *118*
Packard, Edward 1931- *148*
  Earlier sketches in SATA *47, 90*
Packer, Kenneth L. 1946- *116*
Packer, Vin
  See Meaker, Marijane
Pad, Peter
  See Stratemeyer, Edward L.
Page, Eileen
  See Heal, Edith
Page, Eleanor
  See Coerr, Eleanor (Beatrice)
Page, Gail 1950- *205*

Page, Jake 1936- *81*
Page, James Keena, Jr.
  See Page, Jake
Page, Lou Williams 1912-1997 .... *38*
Page, Mary
  See Heal, Edith
Page, Robin 1943- *154*
Pagliarulo, Antonio 1977(?)- *212*
Pagnucci, Susan 1944- *90*
Pahlen, Kurt 1907-2003
  Obituary *147*
Pahz, Cheryl
  See Pahz, Cheryl Suzanne
Pahz, Cheryl Suzanne 1949- *11*
Pahz, James Alon 1943- *11*
Paice, Margaret 1920- *10*
Paige, Harry W(orthington) 1922- *41*
  Brief entry *35*
Paige, Richard
  See Koontz, Dean
Paige, Robin
  See Albert, Susan Wittig
Paine, Penelope Colville 1946- *87*
Paine, Roberta M. 1925- *13*
Paisley, Tom 1932- *11*
  See also CLR *3*
Palatini, Margie *207*
  Earlier sketches in SATA *134, 174*
Palazzo, Anthony D.
  See Palazzo, Tony
Palazzo, Tony 1905-1970 .... *3*
Palder, Edward L. 1922- *5*
Palecek, Josef 1932- *56*
Palecek, Libuse 1937- *89*
Palen, Debbie *195*
Palin, Michael 1943- *67*
Palin, Michael Edward
  See Palin, Michael
Palladini, David (Mario) 1946- *40*
  Brief entry *32*
Pallas, Norvin 1918-1983 .... *23*
Pallister, John C(lare) 1891-1980
  Obituary *26*
Pallotta, Gerard Larry
  See Pallotta, Jerry
Pallotta, Jerry 1953- *186*
Pallotta-Chiarolli, Maria 1960- *117*
Palmer, Bernard (Alvin) 1914-1998 .... *26*
Palmer, C. Everard 1930- *14*
Palmer, (Ruth) Candida 1926- *11*
Palmer, Cyril Everard
  See Palmer, C. Everard
Palmer, Don
  See Benson, Mildred
Palmer, Hap 1942- *68*
Palmer, Heidi 1948- *15*
Palmer, Helen Marion
  See Geisel, Helen
Palmer, Jessica 1953- *120*
Palmer, Judd 1972- *153*
Palmer, Juliette 1930- *15*
Palmer, Kate Salley 1946- *97*
Palmer, Maria
  See Strachan, Ian
Palmer, Maria
  See Brennan, Herbie
Palmer, Robin 1909-2000 .... *43*
Palmero Caceres, Ana *198*
Palmisciano, Diane *202*
Paltrowitz, Donna 1950- *61*
  Brief entry *50*
Paltrowitz, Donna Milman
  See Paltrowitz, Donna
Paltrowitz, Stuart 1946- *61*
  Brief entry *50*
Pamela, Todd 1950- *124*
Pamintuan, Macky *214*
  Earlier sketch in SATA *178*
Panagopoulos, Janie Lynn *149*
Panati, Charles 1943- *65*
Panchyk, Richard 1970- *138*

Panetta, George 1915-1969 .... *15*
Panetta, Joseph N. 1953- *96*
Pang, YaWen Ariel *206*
Panik, Sharon 1952- *82*
Panowski, Eileen Thompson 1920- *49*
Pansy
　See Alden, Isabella (Macdonald)
Pantell, Dora (Fuchs) *39*
Panter, Carol 1936- *9*
Paolini, Christopher 1983- *157*
　See also CLR 102
Papademetriou, Lisa *175*
Paparone, Pam *185*
Paparone, Pamela
　See Paparone, Pam
Papas, Bill
　See Papas, William
Papas, William 1927-2000 .... *50*
Papashvily, George 1898-1978 .... *17*
Papashvily, Helen (Waite) 1906-1996 .... *17*
Pape, D. L.
　See Pape, Donna (Lugg)
Pape, Donna (Lugg) 1930- *82*
　Earlier sketch in SATA *2*
Paperny, Myra (Green) 1932- *51*
　Brief entry *33*
Papp, Robert 1967- *205*
Paradis, Adrian A(lexis) 1912- *67*
　Earlier sketch in SATA *1*
　See also SAAS *8*
Paradis, Marjorie Bartholomew
　1886(?)-1970 .... *17*
Paradiz, Valerie 1963- *176*
Paratore, Coleen
　See Paratore, Coleen Murtagh
Paratore, Coleen Murtagh 1958- *200*
Pardo DeLange, Alex *211*
Parenteau, Shirley 1935- *199*
　Brief entry *40*
　Earlier sketch in SATA *47*
Parish, Margaret 1927-1988 .... *73*
　Obituary *59*
　Earlier sketch in SATA *17*
　See also CLR *22*
Parish, Margaret Holt
　See Holt, Margaret
Parish, Peggy
　See Parish, Margaret
Park, Barbara 1947- *123*
　Brief entry *35*
　Earlier sketches in SATA *40, 78*
　See also CLR *34*
Park, Bill
　See Park, W(illiam) B(ryan)
Park, Frances 1955- *171*
Park, Ginger *173*
Park, Janie Jaehyun *150*
Park, Jordan
　See Kornbluth, C(yril) M.
　and Pohl, Frederik
Park, Linda Sue 1960- *200*
　Earlier sketches in SATA *127, 173*
　See also CLR *84*
Park, Nick 1958- *113*
Park, (Rosina) Ruth (Lucia) 1923(?)- *93*
　Earlier sketch in SATA *25*
　See also CLR *51*
Park, W(illiam) B(ryan) 1936- *22*
Parke, Marilyn 1928- *82*
Parker, Barbara Keevil 1938- *157*
Parker, Daniel
　See Ehrenhaft, Daniel
Parker, Elinor Milnor 1906- *3*
Parker, Julie F. 1961- *92*
Parker, Kim 1963- *174*
Parker, Kristy 1957- *59*
Parker, Lois M(ay) 1912-1996 .... *30*
Parker, Margot M. 1937- *52*
Parker, Marjorie Blain 1960- *205*
　Earlier sketch in SATA *145*
Parker, Mary Jessie 1948- *71*

Parker, Nancy Winslow 1930- *132*
　Earlier sketches in SATA *10, 69*
　See also SAAS *20*
Parker, Richard 1915-1990 .... *14*
Parker, Robert
　See Boyd, Waldo T.
　and Parker, Robert Andrew
Parker, Robert Andrew 1927- *200*
Parker, Steve 1954- *213*
Parker, Tom S. *215*
Parker, Toni Trent 1947-2005 .... *142*
　Obituary *169*
Parker-Rees, Guy *193*
Parker-Rock, Michelle *214*
Parkes, Lucas
　See Harris, John (Wyndham Parkes Lucas)
　Beynon
Parkhill, John
　See Cox, William R(obert)
Parkins, David 1955- *176*
Parkinson, Ethelyn M(inerva) 1906-1999 ..... *11*
Parkinson, Kathryn N. 1954- *71*
Parkinson, Kathy
　See Parkinson, Kathryn N.
Parkinson, Siobhan
　See Parkinson, Siobhan
Parkinson, Siobhan 1954- *178*
Parks, Deborah A. 1948- *133*
　Earlier sketch in SATA *91*
Parks, Edd Winfield 1906-1968 .... *10*
Parks, Gordon 1912-2006 .... *108*
　Obituary *175*
　Earlier sketch in SATA *8*
Parks, Gordon Roger Alexander
　See Parks, Gordon
Parks, Peggy J. 1951- *143*
Parks, PJ
　See Parks, Peggy J.
Parks, Rosa 1913-2005 .... *83*
　Obituary *169*
Parks, Rosa Louise Lee
　See Parks, Rosa
Parks, Van Dyke 1943- *62*
Parley, Peter
　See Goodrich, Samuel Griswold
Parlin, John
　See Graves, Charles Parlin
Parme, Fabrice 1966- *191*
Parnall, Peter 1936- *69*
　Earlier sketch in SATA *16*
　See also SAAS *11*
Paros, Jennifer *210*
Parotti, Phillip (Elliott) 1941- *109*
Parr, Ann 1943- *144*
Parr, Danny
　See Parr, Ann
Parr, Letitia (Evelyn) 1906-1985(?) *37*
Parr, Lucy 1924- *10*
Parr, Todd *179*
　Earlier sketch in SATA *134*
Parrish, Anne 1888-1957 .... *27*
Parrish, Mary
　See Cousins, Margaret
Parrish, Maxfield
　See Parrish, (Frederick) Maxfield
Parrish, (Frederick) Maxfield 1870-1966 ..... *14*
Parry, Marian 1924- *13*
Parry, Rosanne *212*
Parson Lot
　See Kingsley, Charles
Parsons, Alexandra 1947- *92*
Parsons, Ellen
　See Dragonwagon, Crescent
Parsons, Garry *197*
Parsons, Martin 1951- *116*
Parsons, Martin Leslie
　See Parsons, Martin
Parsons, Tom
　See MacPherson, Thomas George
Parsons-Yazzi, Evangeline *172*

Partch, Virgil Franklin II 1916-1984 .... *39*
　Obituary *39*
Parton, Dolly 1946- *94*
Parton, Dolly Rebecca
　See Parton, Dolly
Partridge, Benjamin W., Jr. 1915-2005 .... *28*
　Obituary *163*
Partridge, Benjamin Waring, Jr.
　See Partridge, Benjamin W., Jr.
Partridge, Cora Cheney
　See Cheney, Cora
Partridge, Elizabeth *134*
Partridge, Jenny (Lilian) 1947- *52*
　Brief entry *37*
Pasachoff, Naomi 1947- *147*
Pascal, David 1918- *14*
Pascal, Francine 1938- *143*
　Brief entry *37*
　Earlier sketches in SATA *51, 80*
　See also CLR *25*
Paschal, Nancy
　See Trotter, Grace V(iolet)
Paschkis, Julie 1957- *177*
Pascudniak, Pascal
　See Lupoff, Richard A(llen)
Pashko, Stanley 1913-1982 .... *29*
Passailaigue, Thomas E.
　See Paisley, Tom
Pastel, Elyse *201*
Pateman, Robert 1954- *84*
Patent, Dorothy Hinshaw 1940- *162*
　Autobiography Feature *162*
　Earlier sketches in SATA *22, 69, 120*
　See also CLR *19*
　See also SAAS *13*
Paterson, A(ndrew) B(arton) 1864-1941 .... *97*
Paterson, Banjo
　See Paterson, A(ndrew) B(arton)
Paterson, Diane 1946- *177*
　Brief entry *33*
　Earlier sketch in SATA *59*
Paterson, John (Barstow) 1932- *114*
Paterson, Katherine 1932- *204*
　Earlier sketches in SATA *13, 53, 92, 133*
　See also CLR *127*
Paterson, Katherine Womeldorf
　See Paterson, Katherine
Patience, John 1949- *90*
Patneaude, David 1944- *159*
　Earlier sketch in SATA *85*
Paton, Alan 1903-1988 .... *11*
　Obituary *56*
Paton, Alan Stewart
　See Paton, Alan
Paton, Jane (Elizabeth) 1934- *35*
Paton, Priscilla 1952- *98*
Paton Walsh, Gillian
　See Paton Walsh, Jill
Paton Walsh, Jill 1937- *190*
　Autobiography Feature *190*
　Earlier sketches in SATA *4, 72, 109*
　See also CLR *128*
　See also SAAS *3*
Patricelli, Leslie *207*
Patrick, Susan
　See Clark, Patricia Denise
Patron, Susan 1948- *182*
　Earlier sketch in SATA *76*
Patsauq, Markoosie 1942-
　See CLR *23*
Patschke, Steve 1955- *125*
Patten, Brian 1946- *152*
　Earlier sketch in SATA *29*
Patterson, Charles 1935- *59*
Patterson, Geoffrey 1943- *54*
　Brief entry *44*
Patterson, James 1947- *197*
　Earlier sketch in SATA *164*
Patterson, James B.
　See Patterson, James

Patterson, Lillie G. -1999 88
Earlier sketch in SATA *14*
Patterson, Nancy Ruth 1944- 148
Earlier sketch in SATA *72*
Pattison, Darcy (S.) 1954- 126
Earlier sketch in SATA *72*
Pattou, Edith *164*
Patz (Blaustein), Nancy *154*
Paul, Aileen 1917- *12*
Paul, Alison *196*
Paul, Ann Whitford 1941- *209*
Earlier sketches in SATA *76, 110, 168*
Paul, David (Tyler) 1934-1988
Obituary 56
Paul, Dominique 1973- *184*
Paul, Elizabeth
See Crow, Donna Fletcher
Paul, Hamish Vigne Christie 1951- *151*
See also CLR *87*
Paul, James 1936- *23*
Paul, Korky
See Paul, Hamish Vigne Christie
Paul, Robert
See Roberts, John G(aither)
Paul, Tessa 1944- *103*
Pauley, Kimberly 1973- *208*
Pauli, Hertha (Ernestine) 1909-1973 .... *3*
Obituary 26
Paull, Grace A. 1898- *24*
Paulsen, Gary 1939- *189*
Earlier sketches in SATA *22, 50, 54, 79, 111, 158*
See also CLR *82*
Paulson, Jack
See Jackson, C(aary) Paul
Pauquet, Gina Ruck
See Ruck-Pauquet, Gina
Pausacker, Jenny 1948- *72*
See also SAAS *23*
Pausewang, Gudrun 1928- *165*
Earlier sketch in SATA *104*
Pavel, Frances 1907- *10*
Paver, Michelle *215*
Earlier sketch in SATA *170*
Paxton, Thomas R. 1937- *70*
Paxton, Tom
See Paxton, Thomas R.
Paye, Won-Ldy *185*
Payne, Alan
See Jakes, John
Payne, Bernal C., Jr. 1941- 60
Payne, C. Douglas
See Payne, C.D.
Payne, C.D. 1949- *133*
Payne, C.F. 1956- *179*
Payne, Chris Fox
See Payne, C.F.
Payne, Donald Gordon 1924- 37
Payne, Emmy
See West, Emily Govan
Payne, Nina *135*
Payne, Rachel Ann
See Jakes, John
Payson, Dale 1943- 9
Payzant, Charles *18*
Paz, A.
See Pahz, James Alon
Paz, Natalia Toledo
See Toledo, Natalia
Paz, Zan
See Pahz, Cheryl Suzanne
Peace, Mary
See Finley, Mary Peace
Peacock, Louise *210*
Peacock, Shane 1957- *192*
Peake, Mervyn 1911-1968 .... *23*
Peale, Norman Vincent 1898-1993 .... *20*
Obituary 78
Pearce, Ann Philippa
See Pearce, Philippa
Pearce, Emily Smith 1975- *199*

Pearce, Jacqueline 1962- *146*
Pearce, Margaret *104*
Pearce, Philippa 1920-2006 .... *129*
Obituary *179*
Earlier sketches in SATA *1, 67*
See also CLR *9*
Peare, Catherine Owens 1911- 9
Pearle, Ida *207*
Pearsall, Shelley 1966- *190*
Pearson, Gayle 1947- *119*
Earlier sketch in SATA *53*
Pearson, Jean Mary
See Gardam, Jane
Pearson, Kit 1947- 77
Autobiography Feature *117*
See also CLR *26*
Pearson, Mary E. 1955- *211*
Earlier sketch in SATA *134*
Pearson, Ridley 1953- *182*
Pearson, Susan 1946- *166*
Brief entry 27
Earlier sketches in SATA *39, 91*
Pearson, Tracey Campbell 1956- *155*
Earlier sketch in SATA *64*
Pease, (Clarence) Howard 1894-1974 .... *2*
Obituary 25
Peavy, Linda 1943- 54
Peck, Anne Merriman 1884-1976 .... *18*
Peck, Beth 1957- *190*
Earlier sketch in SATA *79*
Peck, Jan *159*
Peck, Jeanie J. 1967- *147*
Peck, Marshall III 1951- 92
Peck, Richard 1934- *190*
Autobiography Feature *110*
Earlier sketches in SATA *18, 55, 97, 110, 158*
See also CLR *142*
See also SAAS *2*
Peck, Richard Wayne
See Peck, Richard
Peck, Robert Newton 1928- *156*
Autobiography Feature *108*
Earlier sketches in SATA *21, 62, 111*
See also CLR *45*
See also SAAS *1*
Peck, Sylvia 1953- *133*
Peck-Whiting, Jeanie J.
See Peck, Jeanie J.
Peddicord, Jane Ann *199*
Pedersen, Janet *193*
Pederson, Sharleen
See Collicott, Sharleen
Pedler, Caroline *197*
Peebles, Anne
See Galloway, Priscilla
Peek, Merle 1938- 39
Peel, John 1954- 79
Peel, Norman Lemon
See Hirsch, Phil
Peeples, Edwin A(ugustus, Jr.) 1915-1994 ..... *6*
Peers, Judi 1956- *119*
Peers, Judith May West
See Peers, Judi
Peet, Bill
See Peet, William Bartlett
Peet, Creighton B. 1899-1977 30
Peet, Mal *171*
Peet, Malcolm
See Peet, Mal
Peet, William Bartlett 1915-2002 .... *78*
Obituary *137*
Earlier sketches in SATA *2, 41*
See also CLR *12*
Peguero, Leone *116*
Pelaez, Jill 1924- *12*
Pelham, David 1938- 70
Pell, Ed(ward) 1950- *157*
Pelletier, Andrew T. *195*
Pelletier, Andrew Thomas
See Pelletier, Andrew T.
Pellowski, Anne 1933- 20

Pellowski, Michael (Joseph) 1949- *151*
Brief entry 48
Earlier sketch in SATA *88*
Pellowski, Michael Morgan
See Pellowski, Michael (Joseph)
Pelta, Kathy 1928- *18*
Peltier, Leslie C(opus) 1900-1980 .... *13*
Pemberton, Bonnie *191*
Pemberton, John Leigh
See Leigh-Pemberton, John
Pembury, Bill
See Groom, Arthur William
Pemsteen, Hans
See Manes, Stephen
Pendennis, Arthur Esquir
See Thackeray, William Makepeace
Pender, Lydia Podger 1907- 61
Pendery, Rosemary (Schmitz) 7
Pendle, Alexy 1943- 29
Pendle, George 1906-1977
Obituary 28
Pendleton, Don
See Cunningham, Chet
and Garside, Jack
and Jagninski, Tom
and Krauzer, Steven M(ark)
and Obstfeld, Raymond
Pendleton, Thomas 1965- *206*
Pendziwol, Jean E. 1965- *177*
Pene du Bois, William (Sherman)
1916-1993 .... *68*
Obituary 74
Earlier sketch in SATA *4*
See also CLR *1*
Penn, Audrey 1947- *212*
Penn, Audrey 1950- *22*
Penn, Ruth Bonn
See Rosenberg, Eth Clifford
Pennac, Daniel 1944- *155*
Pennage, E. M.
See Finkel, George (Irvine)
Penner, Fred 1946- *169*
Earlier sketch in SATA *67*
Penner, Frederick Ralph Cornelius
See Penner, Fred
Penney, Grace Jackson 1904-2000 35
Penney, Ian 1960- 76
Penney, Sue 1957- *152*
Earlier sketch in SATA *102*
Pennington, Eunice 1923- 27
Pennington, Lillian Boyer 1904-2003 45
Pennypacker, Sara 1951- *187*
Penrose, Gordon 1925- 66
Penson, Mary E. 1917- 78
Penzler, Otto 1942- 38
Pepe, Phil 1935- 20
Pepe, Philip
See Pepe, Phil
Peppe, Rodney (Darrell) 1934- *74*
Earlier sketch in SATA *4*
See also SAAS *10*
Pepper, Frank S. 1910-1988
Obituary 61
Percy, Charles Henry
See Smith, Dorothy Gladys
Percy, Rachel 1930- 63
Perdrizet, Marie-Pierre 1952- 79
Perenyi, Constance 1954- 93
Perenyi, Constance Marie
See Perenyi, Constance
Perera, Hilda 1926- *105*
Perera, Thomas Biddle 1938- *13*
Peretti, Frank E. 1951- *141*
Earlier sketch in SATA *80*
Perez, L. King 1940- *199*
Perez, Lana
See Perez, Marlene
Perez, Lucia Angela 1973- *182*
Perez, Marlene *170*
Pericoli, Matteo 1968- *178*
Perkins, Al(bert Rogers) 1904-1975 30

Perkins, Lucy Fitch 1865-1937 72
Perkins, Lynne Rae 1956- 212
  Earlier sketches in SATA *131, 172*
Perkins, (Richard) Marlin 1905-1986 21
  Obituary 48
Perkins, Mitali 1963- 188
  Earlier sketch in SATA *88*
Perks, Anne-Marie 1955- 122
Perl, Erica S. 188
Perl, Lila 72
  Earlier sketch in SATA *6*
Perl, Susan 1922-1983 22
  Obituary 34
Perlman, Rhea 1948- 183
Perlmutter, O(scar) William 1920-1975 8
Pernu, Dennis 1970- 87
Perrault, Charles 1628-1703 25
  See also CLR *134*
Perret, Delphine 1980- 190
Perret, Gene (Richard) 1937- 76
Perriman, Cole
  See Perrin, Pat
Perriman, Cole
  See Coleman, Wim
Perrin, Pat 212
Perrine, Mary 1913-1976 2
Perrins, Lesley 1953- 56
Perrow, Angeli 1954- 121
Perry, Andrea 1956- 190
  Earlier sketch in SATA *148*
Perry, Barbara Fisher
  See Fisher, Barbara
Perry, Elizabeth 1959- 174
Perry, Elizabeth Goodwin
  See Perry, Elizabeth
Perry, Marie Fritz 165
Perry, Patricia 1949- 30
Perry, Phyllis J(ean) 1933- 152
  Earlier sketches in SATA *60, 101*
Perry, Ritchie (John Allen) 1942- 105
Perry, Roger 1933- 27
Perry, Steve(n Carl) 1947- 76
Pershall, Mary K. 1951- 172
  Earlier sketch in SATA *70*
Pershing, Marie
  See Schultz, Pearle Henriksen
Perske, Robert 1927- 57
Persun, Morgan Reed
  See Watkins, Dawn L.
Perversi, Margaret 213
Petach, Heidi 149
Peter
  See Stratemeyer, Edward L.
Peters, Alexander
  See Hollander, Zander
Peters, Andrew Fusek 1965- 169
  Earlier sketch in SATA *107*
Peters, Bernadette 1948- 212
Peters, Caroline
  See Betz, Eva Kelly
Peters, David
  See David, Peter
Peters, Elizabeth 1927- 49
Peters, Emma
  See Price, Karen
Peters, Gabriel
  See Matott, Justin
Peters, Julie Anne 1952- 197
  Earlier sketches in SATA *82, 128*
Peters, Linda
  See Catherall, Arthur
Peters, Lisa Westberg 1951- 161
  Earlier sketches in SATA *74, 115*
Peters, Patricia 1953- 84
Peters, Russell M. 1929- 78
Peters, S. H.
  See Henry, O.
  and Proffitt, Nicholas
Petersen, David 1946- 109
  Earlier sketch in SATA *62*
Petersen, Gwenn Boardman 1924- 12

Petersen, P(eter) J(ames) 1941- 118
  Brief entry 43
  Earlier sketches in SATA *48, 83*
Petersen, Palle 1943- 85
Petersham, Maud 1890-1971 17
  See also CLR *24*
Petersham, Maud Sylvia Fuller
  See Petersham, Maud
Petersham, Miska 1888-1960 17
  See also CLR *24*
Peterson, Cris 1952- 174
  Earlier sketches in SATA *84, 145*
Peterson, Dawn 1934- 86
Peterson, Esther (Allen) 1934- 35
Peterson, Hans 1922- 8
Peterson, Harold L(eslie) 1922-1978 8
Peterson, Helen Stone 1910- 8
Peterson, Jean Sunde 1941- 108
Peterson, Jeanne Whitehouse 1939- 159
  Earlier sketch in SATA *29*
Peterson, Kathleen B. 1951- 119
Peterson, Lorraine 1940- 56
  Brief entry 44
Peterson, Mary 215
Peterson, Shelley 1952- 146
Peterson, Will
  See Cocks, Peter
Petie, Haris
  See Petty, Roberta
Petricic, Dusan 1946- 176
Petrides, Heidrun 1944- 19
Petrie, Catherine 1947- 52
  Brief entry 41
Petrone, Valeria 186
Petrosino, Tamara 193
Petroski, Catherine (Ann Groom) 1939- 48
Petrovich, Michael B(oro) 1922- 40
Petrovskaya, Kyra
  See Wayne, Kyra Petrovskaya
Petruccio, Steven James 1961- 67
Petrucha, Stefan 1959- 213
Petry, Ann 1908-1997 5
  Obituary 94
  See also CLR *12*
Petry, Ann Lane
  See Petry, Ann
Pettit, Jayne 1932- 108
Petty, J.T. 1977- 189
Petty, Kate 1951-2007 204
Petty, Roberta 1915- 10
Pevsner, Stella 131
  Earlier sketches in SATA *8, 77*
  See also SAAS *14*
Peyo
  See Culliford, Pierre
Peyton, K. M.
  See Peyton, Kathleen Wendy
Peyton, Kathleen Wendy 1929- 157
  Earlier sketches in SATA *15, 62*
  See also CLR *3*
  See also SAAS *17*
Pfanner, (Anne) Louise 1955- 68
Pfeffer, Susan Beth 1948- 180
  Earlier sketches in SATA *4, 83*
  See also CLR *11*
  See also SAAS *17*
Pfeffer, Wendy 1929- 204
  Earlier sketches in SATA *78, 142*
Pfeiffer, Janet (B.) 1949- 96
Pfister, Marcus 207
  Earlier sketches in SATA *83, 150*
  See also CLR *42*
Pfitsch, Patricia Curtis 1948- 148
Pflieger, Pat 1955- 84
Pham, LeUyen 1973- 201
  Earlier sketch in SATA *175*
Phelan, Mary Kay 1914- 3
Phelan, Matt 1970- 215
  Earlier sketch in SATA *172*
Phelan, Terry Wolfe 1941- 56
Phelps, Ethel Johnston 1914-1984 35

Philbrick, Rodman 1951- 163
Philbrick, W. Rodman
  See Philbrick, Rodman
Philbrick, W.R.
  See Philbrick, Rodman
Philbrook, Clem(ent E.) 1917- 24
Phillips, Aileen Paul
  See Paul, Aileen
Phillips, Betty Lou
  See Phillips, Elizabeth Louise
Phillips, Bob 1940- 95
Phillips, Douglas A. 1949- 161
Phillips, Elizabeth Louise 58
  Brief entry 48
Phillips, Irv(ing W.) 1905-2000 11
  Obituary 125
Phillips, Jack
  See Sandburg, Carl
Phillips, Leon
  See Gerson, Noel Bertram
Phillips, Loretta (Hosey) 1893-1987 10
Phillips, Louis 1942- 102
  Earlier sketch in SATA *8*
Phillips, Mark
  See Garrett, Randall
  and Janifer, Laurence M(ark)
Phillips, Mary Geisler 1881-1964 10
Phillips, Michael
  See Nolan, William F.
Phillips, (Woodward) Prentice 1894-1981 10
Phillpotts, Eden 1862-1960 24
Phin
  See Thayer, Ernest Lawrence
Phipson, Joan
  See Fitzhardinge, Joan Margaret
Phiz
  See Browne, Hablot Knight
Phleger, Fred B. 1909-1993 34
Phleger, Marjorie Temple 1908(?)-1986 1
  Obituary 47
Piaget, Jean 1896-1980
  Obituary 23
Piatti, Celestino 1922- 16
Picard, Barbara Leonie 1917- 89
  Earlier sketch in SATA *2*
  See also SAAS *10*
Pichon, Liz 174
Pickard, Charles 1932- 36
Pickering, James Sayre 1897-1969 36
  Obituary 28
Pickering, Jimmy 195
Pickering, Robert B. 1950- 93
Pielichaty, Helena 1955- 142
Pienkowski, Jan (Michal) 1936- 131
  Earlier sketches in SATA *6, 58*
  See also CLR *6*
Pierce, Edith Gray 1893-1977 45
Pierce, Katherine
  See St. John, Wylly Folk
Pierce, Meredith Ann 1958- 127
  Brief entry 48
  Earlier sketch in SATA *67*
  See also CLR *20*
Pierce, Ruth (Ireland) 1936- 5
Pierce, Sharon
  See McCullough, Sharon Pierce
Pierce, Tamora 1954- 187
  Brief entry 49
  Earlier sketches in SATA *51, 96, 153*
Pierce, Terry 178
Pierik, Robert 1921- 13
Piernas-Davenport, Gail 199
Piers, Robert
  See Anthony, Piers
Pig, Edward
  See Gorey, Edward (St. John)
Pike, Bob
  See Pike, Robert W.
Pike, Christopher 1954(?)- 156
  Earlier sketch in SATA *68*
  See also CLR *29*

Pike, Deborah 1951- 89
Pike, E(dgar) Royston 1896-1980 22
    Obituary 56
Pike, R. William 1956- 92
Pike, Robert
    See Pike, Robert W.
Pike, Robert W. 1931- 102
Pike, Robert Wilson
    See Pike, Robert W.
Pilarski, Laura 1926- 13
Pilgrim, Anne
    See Allan, Mabel Esther
Pilkey, Dav 1966- 166
    Earlier sketches in SATA *68, 115*
    See also CLR *48*
Pilkey, David Murray, Jr.
    See Pilkey, Dav
Pilkington, Francis Meredyth 1907-1993 .... *4*
Pilkington, Roger (Windle) 1915-2003 .... *10*
    Obituary 144
Pilutti, Deb 208
Pin, Isabel 1975- 183
Pinchot, David 1914(?)-1983
    Obituary 34
Pincus, Harriet 1938- 27
Pinczes, Elinor J(ane) 1940- 81
Pine, Nicholas 1951- 91
Pine, Tillie S(chloss) 1896-1999 13
Pini, Richard (Alan) 1950- 89
Pini, Wendy 1951- 89
Pinkerton, Kathrene Sutherland (Gedney)
    1887-1967
    Obituary 26
Pinkett, Jada
    See Smith, Jada Pinkett
Pinkney, Andrea Davis 1963- 160
    Earlier sketch in SATA *113*
Pinkney, Brian 1961- 206
    Earlier sketches in SATA *74, 148*
    See also CLR *54*
Pinkney, Gloria Jean 1941- 212
    Earlier sketch in SATA *85*
Pinkney, J. Brian
    See Pinkney, Brian
Pinkney, Jerry 1939- 198
    Autobiography Feature 198
    Brief entry 32
    Earlier sketches in SATA *41, 71, 107, 151*
    See also CLR *43*
    See also SAAS *12*
Pinkney, John 97
Pinkney, Sandra L. 193
    Earlier sketch in SATA *128*
Pinkwater, D. Manus
    See Pinkwater, Daniel
Pinkwater, Daniel 1941- 210
    Earlier sketches in SATA *8, 46, 76, 114, 158*
    See also CLR *4*
    See also SAAS *3*
Pinkwater, Daniel M.
    See Pinkwater, Daniel
Pinkwater, Daniel Manus
    See Pinkwater, Daniel
Pinkwater, Jill 188
Pinkwater, Manus
    See Pinkwater, Daniel
Pinner, Joma
    See Werner, Herma
Pinto, Sara 200
Pioneer
    See Yates, Raymond F(rancis)
Piowaty, Kim Kennelly 1957- 49
Piper, Roger
    See Fisher, John
Pirner, Connie White 1955- 72
Piro, Richard 1934- 7
Pirot, Alison Lohans
    See Lohans, Alison
Pirotta, Saviour 184
Pirsig, Robert M(aynard) 1928- 39

Pita
    See Rendon, Maria
Pitcher, C.
    See Pitcher, Caroline
Pitcher, Caroline 1948- 214
    Earlier sketch in SATA *128*
Pitcher, Caroline Nell
    See Pitcher, Caroline
Pitman, (Isaac) James 1901-1985
    Obituary 46
Pitre, Felix 1949- 84
Pitrone, Jean Maddern 1920- 4
Pittman, Helena Clare 1945- 71
Pitz, Henry C(larence) 1895-1976 4
    Obituary 24
Pitzer, Susanna 1958- 181
Piven, Hanoch 1963- 173
Pixley, Marcella 194
Pizer, Vernon 1918- 21
Place, Marian T(empleton) 1910- 3
Place, Robin (Mary) 1926- 71
Plaidy, Jean
    See Hibbert, Eleanor Alice Burford
Plain, Belva 1919- 62
Plaine, Alfred R. 1898(?)-1981
    Obituary 29
Plant, Andrew 214
Plath, Sylvia 1932-1963 96
Platt, Chris 1959- 185
Platt, Kin 1911- 86
    Earlier sketch in SATA *21*
    See also SAAS *17*
Platt, Randall 1948- 95
Platt, Randall Beth
    See Platt, Randall
Platt, Richard 1953- 166
    Earlier sketch in SATA *120*
Playfellow, Robin
    See Ellis, Edward S.
Playsted, James
    See Wood, James Playsted
Plecas, Jennifer 1966- 149
    Earlier sketch in SATA *84*
Plimpton, George 1927-2003 10
    Obituary 150
Plimpton, George Ames
    See Plimpton, George
Plomer, William Charles Franklin
    1903-1973 24
Plotz, Helen Ratnoff 1913-2000 38
Plourde, Lynn 1955- 168
    Earlier sketch in SATA *122*
Plowden, David 1932- 52
Plowden, Martha Ward 1948- 98
Plowhead, Ruth Gipson 1877-1967 43
Plowman, Stephanie 1922- 6
Pluckrose, Henry (Arthur) 1931- 141
    Earlier sketch in SATA *13*
Plum, J.
    See Wodehouse, P. G.
Plum, Jennifer
    See Kurland, Michael
Plumb, Charles P. 1900(?)-1982
    Obituary 29
Plume, Ilse 170
    Brief entry 43
Plumme, Don E.
    See Katz, Bobbi
Plummer, Margaret 1911- 2
Plum-Ucci, Carol 184
Pochocki, Ethel (Frances) 1925- 76
Podendorf, Illa (E.) 1903(?)-1983 18
    Obituary 35
Podwal, Mark 1945- 160
    Earlier sketch in SATA *101*
Podwal, Mark H.
    See Podwal, Mark
Poe, Edgar Allan 1809-1849 23
Poe, Ty (Christopher) 1975- 94
Pogany, William Andrew 1882-1955 44
    Brief entry 30

Pogany, Willy
    See Pogany, William Andrew
Pohl, Frederik 1919- 24
Pohlmann, Lillian (Grenfell) 1902-1997 11
Pohrt, Tom 1953- 195
    Earlier sketches in SATA *67, 152*
Pointon, Robert
    See Rooke, Daphne
Points, Larry G. 1945- 177
    Earlier sketch in SATA *133*
Points, Larry Gene
    See Points, Larry G.
Pokeberry, P.J.
    See Mitchell, B.J.
POLA
    See Watson, Pauline
Polacco, Patricia 1944- 212
    Earlier sketches in SATA *74, 123, 180*
    See also CLR *40*
Polacco, Patricia Ann
    See Polacco, Patricia
Polak, Monique 1960- 178
Polatnick, Florence T. 1923- 5
Polcovar, Jane 1948- 211
Polder, Markus
    See Kruss, James
Polese, Carolyn 1947- 58
Polese, James 1914- 87
Polette, Nancy (Jane) 1930- 42
Polhamus, Jean Burt 1928- 21
Polhemus, Coleman 210
Policoff, Stephen Phillip 1948- 77
Polikoff, Barbara G. 1929- 162
    Earlier sketch in SATA *77*
Polikoff, Barbara Garland
    See Polikoff, Barbara G.
Polisar, Barry Louis 1954- 134
    Earlier sketch in SATA *77*
Politi, Leo 1908-1996 47
    Obituary 88
    Earlier sketch in SATA *1*
    See also CLR *29*
Polking, Kirk 1925- 5
Pollack, Jill S. 1963- 88
Pollack, Merrill S. 1924-1988
    Obituary 55
Polland, Barbara K(ay) 1939- 44
Polland, Madeleine A(ngela Cahill) 1918- ... 68
    Earlier sketch in SATA *6*
    See also SAAS *8*
Pollema-Cahill, Phyllis 1958- 123
Pollock, Bruce 1945- 46
Pollock, Mary
    See Blyton, Enid
Pollock, Penny 1935- 137
    Brief entry 42
    Earlier sketch in SATA *44*
Pollowitz, Melinda Kilborn 1944- 26
Polner, Murray 1928- 64
Polonsky, Arthur 1925- 34
Polseno, Jo 17
Pomaska, Anna 1946- 117
Pomerantz, Charlotte 1930- 177
    Earlier sketches in SATA *20, 80*
Pomeroy, Pete
    See Roth, Arthur J(oseph)
Pond, Alonzo W(illiam) 1894-1986 5
Pontiflet, Ted 1932- 32
Poole, Gray Johnson 1906- 1
Poole, Josephine
    See Helyar, Jane Penelope Josephine
Poole, (Jane Penelope) Josephine
    See Helyar, Jane Penelope Josephine
Poole, Lynn 1910-1969 1
Poole, Peggy 1925- 39
Poortvliet, Rien 1932- 65
    Brief entry 37
Pope, Elizabeth Marie 1917-1992 38
    Brief entry 36
Pope, Kevin 1958- 183

Popescu, Christine
  See Pullein-Thompson, Christine
Poploff, Michelle 1956- 67
Popp, K. Wendy 91
Poppel, Hans 1942- 71
Porfirio, Guy 1958- 197
Portal, Colette 1936- 6
Porte, Barbara Ann 1943- 152
  Brief entry 45
  Earlier sketches in SATA 57, 93
Porter, A(nthony) P(eyton) 1945- 68
Porter, Connie (Rose) 1959(?)- 129
  Earlier sketch in SATA 81
Porter, Donald Clayton
  See Gerson, Noel Bertram
Porter, Eleanor H(odgman) 1868-1920
  See CLR 110
Porter, Gene Stratton
  See Stratton-Porter, Gene
Porter, Janice Lee 1953- 108
  Earlier sketch in SATA 68
Porter, Katherine Anne 1890-1980 39
  Obituary 23
Porter, Kathryn
  See Swinford, Betty (June Wells)
Porter, Pamela 1956- 193
Porter, Sheena 1935- 24
  See also SAAS 10
Porter, Sue
  See Limb, Sue
Porter, Sue 1951- 213
  Earlier sketch in SATA 76
Porter, Tracey 191
Porter, William Sydney
  See Henry, O.
Portis, Antoinette 189
Porto, Tony 1960- 153
Portteus, Eleanora Marie Manthei (?)-1983
  Obituary 36
Posada, Mia 187
Posell, Elsa Z(eigerman) -1995 3
Posten, Margaret L(ois) 1915- 10
Posthuma, Sieb 1960- 150
Postier, Jim 1965- 202
Potok, Chaim 1929-2002 106
  Obituary 134
  Earlier sketch in SATA 33
  See also CLR 92
Potok, Herbert Harold
  See Potok, Chaim
Potok, Herman Harold
  See Potok, Chaim
Potter, Beatrix 1866-1943 132
  Earlier sketch in SATA 100
  See also YABC 1
  See also CLR 73
Potter, Giselle 187
  Earlier sketch in SATA 150
Potter, Helen Beatrix
  See Potter, Beatrix
Potter, Margaret 1926-1998 21
  Obituary 104
Potter, Marian 1915- 9
Potter, Miriam Clark 1886-1965 3
Poulin, Stephane 1961- 98
  See also CLR 28
Poulton, Kimberly 1957(?)- 136
Pournelle, Jerry (Eugene) 1933- 161
  Earlier sketches in SATA 26, 91
Povelite, Kay 1955- 102
Pow, Tom 1950- 163
Powe-Allred, Alexandra
  See Allred, Alexandra Powe
Powell, A. M.
  See Morgan, Alfred P(owell)
Powell, Consie 174
Powell, E. Sandy 1947- 72
Powell, E.S.
  See Powell, E. Sandy
Powell, Pamela 1960- 78
Powell, Patricia Hruby 1951- 136

Powell, Randy 1956- 118
Powell, Richard Stillman
  See Barbour, Ralph Henry
Powell, Robert (Stephenson Smyth) Baden
  See Baden-Powell, Robert (Stephenson Smyth)
Powell, Stephanie 1953- 93
Power, Margaret (M.) 1945- 125
  Earlier sketch in SATA 75
Powers, Anne
  See Schwartz, Anne Powers
Powers, Bill 1931- 52
  Brief entry 31
Powers, Daniel 1959- 164
Powers, J. L. 195
Powers, Jessica
  See Powers, J. L.
Powers, Jessica Lynn
  See Powers, J. L.
Powers, Margaret
  See Heal, Edith
Powers, Tim 1952- 107
Powers, Timothy Thomas
  See Powers, Tim
Powledge, Fred 1935- 37
Poydar, Nancy 190
Poynter, Margaret 1927- 27
Prachaticka, Marketa
  See Kolibalova, Marketa
Prachatika, Marketa
  See Kolibalova, Marketa
Prager, Arthur 44
Prager, Ellen J. 1962- 136
Prange, Beckie 172
Prap, Lila 1955- 177
Praprotnik-Zupancic, Lilijana
  See Prap, Lila
Pratchett, Terence David John
  See Pratchett, Terry
Pratchett, Terry 1948- 185
  Earlier sketches in SATA 82, 139
  See also CLR 64
Prater, John 1947- 149
  Earlier sketches in SATA 72, 103
Prato, Rodica 184
Pratt, Christine Joy 214
Pratt, (Murray) Fletcher 1897-1956 102
Pratt, Kristin Joy 1976- 87
Pratt, Pierre 1962- 208
  Earlier sketches in SATA 95, 166
Preiss, Byron 1953-2005 166
  Brief entry 42
  Earlier sketch in SATA 47
Preiss, Byron Cary
  See Preiss, Byron
Preller, James 1961- 209
  Earlier sketch in SATA 88
Prelutsky, Jack 1940- 171
  Earlier sketches in SATA 22, 66, 118
  See also CLR 115
Prentice, Amy
  See Kaler, James Otis
Prescott, Casey
  See Morris, Chris(topher Crosby)
Presnall, Judith (Ann) Janda 1943- 96
Pressler, Mirjam 1940- 155
Preston, Douglas 1956- 113
Preston, Edna Mitchell 40
Preston, Lillian Elvira 1918- 47
Preus, Margi 209
Preussler, Otfried 1923- 24
Prevert, Jacques (Henri Marie) 1900-1977
  Obituary 30
Prevost, Guillaume 1964- 192
Prevost, Mikela 203
Price, Beverley Joan 1931- 98
Price, Charlie 187
Price, Christine (Hilda) 1928-1980 3
  Obituary 23
Price, Garrett 1896-1979
  Obituary 22

Price, Jennifer
  See Hoover, Helen (Drusilla Blackburn)
Price, Joan 1931- 124
Price, Jonathan (Reeve) 1941- 46
Price, Karen 1957- 125
Price, Kathy Z. 1957- 172
Price, Lucie Locke
  See Locke, Lucie
Price, Olive 1903-1991 8
Price, Susan 1955- 128
  Earlier sketches in SATA 25, 85
Price, Willard 1887-1983 48
  Brief entry 38
Price-Groff, Claire 127
Priceman, Marjorie 1958- 168
  Earlier sketches in SATA 81, 120
Prichard, Katharine Susannah 1883-1969 66
Prideaux, Tom 1908-1993 37
  Obituary 76
Priestley, Alice 1962- 95
Priestley, Chris 1958- 198
Priestley, Lee (Shore) 1904-1999 27
Priestly, Doug 1954- 122
Priestly, Douglas Michael
  See Priestly, Doug
Prieto, Mariana Beeching 1912-1999 8
Priley, Margaret (Ann) Hubbard 1909-1992
  Obituary 130
Primavera, Elise 1954- 185
  Brief entry 48
  Earlier sketches in SATA 58, 109
Prime, Derek (James) 1931- 34
Prince, Alison (Mary) 1931- 86
  Earlier sketch in SATA 28
Prince, April Jones 1975- 180
Prince, J(ack) H(arvey) 1908- 17
Prince, Joshua 188
Prince, Maggie 102
Prineas, Sarah 204
Pringle, Eric 138
Pringle, Laurence 1935- 201
  Autobiography Feature 201
  Earlier sketches in SATA 4, 68, 104, 154
  See also CLR 57
  See also SAAS 6
Pringle, Laurence Patrick
  See Pringle, Laurence
Prinz, Yvonne 1960- 175
Prior, Natalie Jane 1963- 106
Pritchett, Elaine H(illyer) 1920- 36
Pritchett, Laura 1971- 178
Pritchett, Laura Rose
  See Pritchett, Laura
Pritts, Kim Derek 1953- 83
Prochazkova, Iva 1953- 68
Proctor, Everitt
  See Montgomery, Rutherford George
Proeysen, Alf 1914-1970 67
  See also CLR 24
Professor Scribbler
  See Hollingsworth, Mary
Proimos, James 1955- 173
Prose, Francine 1947- 198
  Earlier sketches in SATA 101, 149
Protopopescu, Orel 186
Protopopescu, Orel Odinov
  See Protopopescu, Orel
Provensen, Alice 1918- 147
  Earlier sketches in SATA 9, 70
  See also CLR 11
Provensen, Martin 1916-1987 70
  Obituary 51
  Earlier sketch in SATA 9
  See also CLR 11
Provensen, Martin Elias
  See Provensen, Martin
Provenzo, Eugene (F., Jr.) 1949- 142
  Earlier sketch in SATA 78
Provist, d'Alain 1906-1989
  See Diop, Birago (Ismael)
Provost, Gail Levine 1944- 65

Provost, Gary (Richard) 1944-1995 66
Proysen, Alf
 See Proeysen, Alf
Pruett, Candace (J.) 1968- 157
Pryor, Bonnie H. 1942- 69
Pryor, Boori (Monty) 1950- 112
Pryor, Helen Brenton 1897-1972 4
Pryor, Michael 1957- 153
Pucci, Albert John 1920- 44
Pudney, John (Sleigh) 1909-1977 24
Pugh, Ellen (Tiffany) 1920- 7
Pullein-Thompson, Christine 1925-2005 82
 Obituary 172
 Earlier sketch in SATA 3
Pullein-Thompson, Diana
 See Farr, Diana
Pullein-Thompson, Joanna Maxwell
 1898-1961 82
Pullein-Thompson, Josephine (Mary
 Wedderburn) 82
 Earlier sketch in SATA 3
Pullen, Zachary 189
Pullman, Philip 1946- 198
 Earlier sketches in SATA 65, 103, 150
 See also CLR 84
 See also SAAS 17
Pullman, Philip Nicholas
 See Pullman, Philip
Pulver, Harry, Jr. 1960- 129
Pulver, Robin 1945- 208
 Earlier sketches in SATA 76, 133
Puner, Helen W(alker) 1915-1989 37
 Obituary 63
Purdy, Carol 1943- 120
 Earlier sketch in SATA 66
Purdy, Susan G(old) 1939- 8
Purkiss, Diane 1961- 194
Purmell, Ann 1953- 206
 Earlier sketch in SATA 147
Purnell, Idella 1901-1982 120
Purscell, Phyllis 1934- 7
Purtill, Richard L. 1931- 53
Pushker, Gloria 1927- 162
 Earlier sketch in SATA 75
Pushker, Gloria Teles
 See Pushker, Gloria
Pushkin, Aleksandr Sergeevich
 See Pushkin, Alexander
Pushkin, Alexander 1799-1837 61
Putnam, Alice 1916- 61
Putnam, Arthur Lee
 See Alger, Horatio, Jr.
Putnam, Peter B(rock) 1920-1998 30
 Obituary 106
Puttapipat, Niroot 199
Puttock, Simon 178
Puvilland, Alex 205
Puvilland, Alexandre
 See Puvilland, Alex
Puybaret, Eric 1976- 195
Pyle, Howard 1853-1911 100
 Earlier sketch in SATA 16
 See also CLR 117
Pyle, Katharine 1863-1938 66
Pyne, Mable Mandeville 1903-1969 9
Pyrnelle, Louise-Clarke 1850-1907 114

Q

Quackenbush, Robert M(ead) 1929- 133
 Autobiography Feature 133
 Earlier sketches in SATA 7, 70
 See also CLR 122
 See also SAAS 7
Qualey, Marsha 1953- 124
 Earlier sketch in SATA 79
Qualls, Sean 177
Quammen, David 1948- 7

Quark, Jason
 See Eldin, Peter
Quarles, Benjamin 1904-1996 12
Quarles, Benjamin Arthur
 See Quarles, Benjamin
Quatermass, Martin
 See Carpenter, John
Quattlebaum, Mary 1958- 185
 Earlier sketches in SATA 88, 134
Quay, Emma 173
 Earlier sketch in SATA 119
Queen, Ellery
 See Deming, Richard
 and Dannay, Frederic
 and Davidson, Avram (James)
 and Fairman, Paul W.
 and Flora, Fletcher
 and Holding, James (Clark Carlisle, Jr.)
 and Hoch, Edward D.
 and Kane, Henry
 and Lee, Manfred B.
 and Marlowe, Stephen
 and Powell, (Oval) Talmage
 and Sheldon, Walter J(ames)
 and Sturgeon, Theodore (Hamilton)
 and Tracy, Don(ald Fiske)
 and Vance, Jack
Queen Latifah 1970- 185
Quennell, Marjorie Courtney 1884-1972 29
Quentin
 See Sheldon, David
Quentin, Brad
 See Bisson, Terry
Quest, (Edna) Olga W(ilbourne) Hall
 See Hall-Quest, (Edna) Olga W(ilbourne)
Quick, Annabelle 1922-1986 2
Quigg, Jane (Hulda) (?)-1986
 Obituary 49
Quill, Monica
 See McInerny, Ralph
Quin-Harkin, Janet 1941- 165
 Earlier sketches in SATA 18, 90, 119
Quin-Harkin, Janet Elizabeth
 See Quin-Harkin, Janet
Quinlan, Susan E. 1954- 88
Quinlan, Susan Elizabeth
 See Quinlan, Susan E.
Quinn, Elisabeth 1881-1962 22
Quinn, Pat 1947- 130
Quinn, Patrick 1950- 73
Quinn, Rob 1972- 138
Quinn, Susan 1940- 30
Quinn, Susan Taft
 See Quinn, Susan
Quinn, Theodora K.
 See Kroeber, Theodora (Kracaw)
Quinn, Vernon
 See Quinn, Elisabeth
Quirk, Anne (E.) 1956- 99
Quixley, Jim 1931- 56
Quyth, Gabriel
 See Jennings, Gary

R

Ra, Carol F. 1939- 76
Raab, Evelyn 1951- 129
Rabb, Margo 1972- 188
Rabb, M.E.
 See Rabb, Margo
Rabe, Berniece (Louise) 1928- 148
 Autobiography Feature 148
 Earlier sketch in SATA 7, 77
 See also SAAS 10
Rabe, Olive H(anson) (?)-1968 13
Rabin, Staton 1958- 162
 Earlier sketch in SATA 84
Rabinowich, Ellen 1946- 29

Rabinowitz, Sandy 1954- 52
 Brief entry 39
Rachlin, Carol K(ing) 1919- 64
Rachlin, Harvey 1951- 47
Rachlin, Harvey Brant
 See Rachlin, Harvey
Rachlin, Nahid 64
Rachlis, Eugene (Jacob) 1920-1986
 Obituary 50
Rackham, Arthur 1867-1939 100
 Earlier sketch in SATA 15
 See also CLR 57
Racoma, Robin Yoko 1953- 207
Raczka, Bob 1963- 191
 Earlier sketch in SATA 163
Radencich, Marguerite C. 1952-1998 79
Rader, Laura 197
Radford, Ruby L(orraine) 1891-1971 6
Radin, Ruth Yaffe 1938- 107
 Brief entry 52
 Earlier sketch in SATA 56
Radlauer, David 1952- 28
Radlauer, Edward 1921- 15
Radlauer, Ruth Shaw 1926- 98
 Earlier sketch in SATA 15
Radley, Gail 1951- 112
 Earlier sketch in SATA 25
Radunsky, Vladimir 177
Radzinski, Kandy 1948- 212
Rae, Gwynedd 1892-1977 37
Raebeck, Lois 1921- 5
Rael, Elsa Okon 1927-
 See CLR 84
Raffi
 See Cavoukian, Raffi
Raftery, Gerald (Bransfield) 1905-1986 11
Ragan-Reid, Gale 1956- 90
Rahaman, Vashanti 1953- 98
Rahn, Joan Elma 1929- 27
Rai, Bali 1971- 152
Raible, Alton (Robert) 1918- 35
Raiff, Stan 1930- 11
Raines, Shirley C(arol) 1945- 128
Rainey, W. B.
 See Blassingame, Wyatt Rainey
Rake, Jody 1961- 157
Rallison, Janette 1966- 183
Ralston, Jan
 See Dunlop, Agnes M. R.
Rama, Sue 190
Ramal, Walter
 See de la Mare, Walter (John)
Ramanujan, A(ttipat) K(rishnaswami)
 1929-1993 86
Rame, David
 See Divine, Arthur Durham
Ramirez, Jose 1967- 198
Ramirez, Orlando L. 1972- 194
Ramos, Jorge 1958- 205
Ramstad, Ralph L. 1919- 115
Ramthun, Bonnie 214
Rana, Indi
 See Rana, Indira Higham
Rana, Indira Higham 1944- 82
Rana, J.
 See Bhatia, Jamunadevi
Ranadive, Gail 1944- 10
Rand, Ann (Binkley) 30
Rand, Gloria 1925- 156
 Earlier sketch in SATA 101
Rand, Paul 1914-1996 6
Randall, Carrie
 See Ransom, Candice F.
Randall, David 1972- 167
Randall, Florence Engel 1917-1997 5
Randall, Janet
 See Young, Janet Randall
 and Young, Robert W(illiam)
Randall, Robert
 See Garrett, Randall
 and Silverberg, Robert

Randall, Ruth (Elaine) Painter 1892-1971 ..... *3*
Randell, Beverley
  See Price, Beverley Joan
Randle, Kristen D. 1952- *92*
  Autobiography Feature *119*
  See also SAAS *24*
Randle, Kristen Downey
  See Randle, Kristen D.
Randolph, Boynton M.D.
  See Ellis, Edward S.
Randolph, Ellen
  See Rawn, Melanie
Randolph, Geoffrey
  See Ellis, Edward S.
Randolph, J. H.
  See Ellis, Edward S.
Randolph, Lieutenant J. H.
  See Ellis, Edward S.
Rands, William Brighty 1823-1882 .... *17*
Raney, Ken 1953- *74*
Rankin, Joan 1940- *212*
  Earlier sketches in SATA *88, 148*
Rankin, Laura 1953(?)- *176*
Ranney, Agnes V. 1916-1985 .... *6*
Ransom, Candice F. 1952- *183*
  Brief entry *49*
  Earlier sketches in SATA *52, 89, 135*
Ransom, Jeanie Franz 1957- *187*
Ransome, Arthur (Michell) 1884-1967 .... *22*
  See also CLR *8*
Ransome, James E. 1961- *178*
  Earlier sketches in SATA *76, 123*
  See also CLR *86*
Rant, Tol E.
  See Longyear, Barry B(rookes)
Raphael, Elaine
  See Bolognese, Elaine
Raposo, Joseph Guilherme 1938-1989
  Obituary *61*
Rapp, Adam 1968- *148*
Rappaport, Doreen *211*
  Earlier sketch in SATA *151*
Rappaport, Eva 1924- *6*
Rappoport, Ken 1935- *167*
  Earlier sketch in SATA *89*
Rarick, Carrie 1911-2002 .... *41*
Raschka, Chris 1959- *207*
  Earlier sketches in SATA *80, 117, 166*
Raschka, Christopher
  See Raschka, Chris
Rascol, Sabina I. *159*
Rash, Andy *162*
Raskin, Edith Lefkowitz 1908-1987 .... *9*
Raskin, Ellen 1928-1984 .... *139*
  Earlier sketches in SATA *2, 38*
  See also CLR *12*
Raskin, Joseph 1897-1982 .... *12*
  Obituary *29*
Rathjen, Carl Henry 1909-1984 .... *11*
Rathmann, Peggy 1953- *157*
  Earlier sketch in SATA *94*
  See also CLR *77*
Ratliff, Thomas M. 1948- *118*
Ratner, Sue Lynn
  See Alexander, Sue
Rattigan, Jama Kim 1951- *99*
Ratto, Linda Lee 1952- *79*
Rattray, Simon
  See Trevor, Elleston
Ratz de Tagyos, Paul 1958- *198*
  Earlier sketch in SATA *76*
Rau, Dana Meachen 1971- *167*
  Earlier sketch in SATA *94*
Rau, Margaret 1913- *168*
  Earlier sketch in SATA *9*
  See also CLR *8*
Rauch, Mabel Thompson 1888-1972
  Obituary *26*
Raucher, Herman 1928- *8*
Raude, Karina *199*

Rauh, Sherry
  See North, Sherry
Raum, Elizabeth 1949- *155*
Raven, Margot Theis *184*
RavenWolf, Silver 1956- *155*
Ravielli, Anthony 1916-1997 .... *3*
  Obituary *95*
Ravilious, Robin 1944- *77*
Ravishankar, Anushka 1961- *200*
Rawding, F(rederick) W(illiam) 1930- *55*
Rawlings, Marjorie Kinnan 1896-1953 ...... *100*
  See also YABC *1*
  See also CLR *63*
Rawlins, Donna 1956- *206*
Rawlinson, Julia *212*
  Earlier sketch in SATA *175*
Rawls, (Woodrow) Wilson 1913-1984 .... *22*
  See also CLR *81*
Rawlyk, George Alexander 1935- *64*
Rawn, Melanie 1954- *98*
Rawn, Melanie Robin
  See Rawn, Melanie
Rawson, Katherine 1955- *190*
Ray, Carl 1943-1978 .... *63*
Ray, Deborah
  See Kogan Ray, Deborah
Ray, Delia 1963- *179*
  Earlier sketch in SATA *70*
Ray, Irene
  See Sutton, Margaret Beebe
Ray, Jane 1960- *196*
  Earlier sketches in SATA *72, 152*
Ray, JoAnne 1935- *9*
Ray, Mary (Eva Pedder) 1932- *127*
  Earlier sketch in SATA *2*
Ray, Mary Lyn 1946- *154*
  Earlier sketch in SATA *90*
Rayban, Chloe 1944- *167*
Rayevsky, Robert 1955- *190*
  Earlier sketch in SATA *81*
Raymond, James Crossley 1917-1981
  Obituary *29*
Raymond, Robert
  See Alter, Robert Edmond
Rayner, Catherine *204*
Rayner, Hugh *151*
Rayner, Mary 1933- *87*
  Earlier sketch in SATA *22*
  See also CLR *41*
Rayner, Shoo
  See Rayner, Hugh
Rayner, William 1929- *55*
  Brief entry *36*
Raynor, Dorka *28*
Rayson, Steven 1932- *30*
Razzell, Arthur (George) 1925- *11*
Razzell, Mary (Catherine) 1930- *102*
Razzi, James 1931- *10*
Read, Elfreida 1920- *2*
Read, Nicholas 1956- *146*
Read, Piers Paul 1941- *21*
Reade, Deborah 1949- *69*
Reader, Dennis 1929- *71*
Reading, Richard P(atrick) 1962- *161*
Readman, Jo 1958- *89*
Ready, Kirk L(ewis) 1943- *39*
Reaney, James 1926-2008 .... *43*
Reaney, James Crerar
  See Reaney, James
Reardon, Joyce
  See Pearson, Ridley
Reaver, Chap 1935-1993 .... *69*
  Obituary *77*
Reaver, Herbert R.
  See Reaver, Chap
Reaves, J. Michael
  See Reaves, (James) Michael
Reaves, (James) Michael 1950- *99*
Reber, Deborah *189*
Recorvits, Helen *191*
Redding, Robert Hull 1919- *2*

Redekopp, Elsa *61*
Redlich, Ben 1977- *181*
Redsand, Anna 1948- *184*
Redway, Ralph
  See Hamilton, Charles (Harold St. John)
Redway, Ridley
  See Hamilton, Charles (Harold St. John)
Reece, Colleen L. 1935- *116*
Reece, Gabrielle 1970- *108*
Reed, Betty Jane 1921- *4*
Reed, Dallas
  See Pendleton, Thomas
Reed, E.
  See Evans, Mari
Reed, Gwendolyn E(lizabeth) 1932- *21*
Reed, Kit 1932- *184*
  Autobiography Feature *184*
  Earlier sketches in SATA *34, 116*
Reed, Lynn Rowe *215*
  Earlier sketch in SATA *171*
Reed, Mike 1951- *211*
Reed, Neil 1961- *99*
Reed, Talbot Baines 1852-1893
  See CLR *76*
Reed, Thomas (James) 1947- *34*
Reed, William Maxwell 1871-1962 .... *15*
Reeder, Carolyn 1937- *97*
  Earlier sketch in SATA *66*
  See also CLR *69*
Reeder, Colin (Dawson) 1938- *74*
Reeder, Colonel Red
  See Reeder, Russell P(otter), Jr.
Reeder, Russell P(otter), Jr. 1902-1998 .... *4*
  Obituary *101*
Reeder, Stephanie Owen 1951- *102*
Reed-Jones, Carol 1955- *112*
Reef, Catherine 1951- *189*
  Earlier sketches in SATA *73, 128*
Reekie, Jocelyn (Margaret) 1947- *145*
Reeman, Douglas Edward 1924- *63*
  Brief entry *28*
Rees, Celia 1949- *124*
Rees, David (Bartlett) 1936-1993 .... *69*
  Obituary *76*
  Earlier sketch in SATA *36*
  See also SAAS *5*
Rees, Douglas 1947- *169*
Rees, Ennis (Samuel, Jr.) 1925- *3*
Rees, (George) Leslie (Clarence)
  1905-(2000) *105*
  Obituary *135*
Reese, Bob
  See Reese, Robert A.
Reese, Carolyn Johnson 1938- *64*
Reese, Della 1931(?)- *114*
Reese, Lyn
  See Reese, Carolyn Johnson
Reese, Robert A. 1938- *60*
  Brief entry *53*
Reese, (John) Terence 1913-1996 .... *59*
Reeve, Joel
  See Cox, William R(obert)
Reeve, Kirk 1934- *117*
Reeve, Philip *201*
  Earlier sketch in SATA *170*
Reeve, Rosie *188*
  Earlier sketch in SATA *186*
Reeves, Faye Couch 1953- *76*
Reeves, James
  See Reeves, John Morris
Reeves, Jeni 1947- *111*
Reeves, John Morris 1909-1978 .... *87*
  Earlier sketch in SATA *15*
Reeves, Joyce 1911- *17*
Reeves, Lawrence F. 1926- *29*
Reeves, Ruth Ellen
  See Ranney, Agnes V.
Regan, Dian Curtis 1950- *149*
  Autobiography Feature *149*
  Earlier sketches in SATA *75, 133*
Regehr, Lydia 1903-1991 .... *37*

Reger, James P. 1952- *106*
Reggiani, Renee 1925- *18*
Rehm, Karl M. 1935- *72*
Reibstein, Mark *211*
Reich, Ali
  See Katz, Bobbi
Reich, Susanna 1954- *214*
  Earlier sketch in SATA *113*
Reiche, Dietlof 1941- *159*
Reichert, Edwin C(lark) 1909-1988
  Obituary *57*
Reichert, Mickey Zucker
  See Reichert, Miriam Zucker
Reichert, Miriam Zucker 1962- *85*
Reichert, Renee *172*
Reichhold, Jane(t E.) 1937- *147*
Reid, Alastair 1926- *46*
Reid, Barbara 1922- *21*
Reid, Barbara (Jane) 1957- *93*
  See also CLR *64*
Reid, Desmond
  See Moorcock, Michael
  and McNeilly, Wilfred (Glassford)
Reid, Eugenie Chazal 1924- *12*
Reid, John Calvin *21*
Reid, (Thomas) Mayne 1818-1883 .... *24*
Reid, Meta Mayne 1905-1991 .... *58*
  Brief entry *36*
Reid, Robin (Nicole) 1969- *145*
Reid Banks, Lynne 1929- *165*
  Earlier sketches in SATA *22, 75, 111*
  See also CLR *86*
Reider, Katja 1960- *126*
Reid Jenkins, Debra 1955- *87*
Reiff, Stephanie Ann 1948- *47*
  Brief entry *28*
Reig, June 1933- *30*
Reigot, Betty Polisar 1924- *55*
  Brief entry *41*
Reilly, Joan *195*
Reim, Melanie (K.) 1956- *104*
Reinach, Jacquelyn (Krasne) 1930-2000 .... *28*
Reiner, Carl 1922- *151*
Reiner, William B(uck) 1910-1976 .... *46*
  Obituary *30*
Reinfeld, Fred 1910-1964 .... *3*
Reinhardt, Dana 1971- *175*
Reinhart, Matthew 1971- *197*
  Earlier sketch in SATA *161*
Reiniger, Lotte 1899-1981 .... *40*
  Obituary *33*
Reinsma, Carol 1949- *91*
Reinstedt, Randall A. 1935- *101*
Reinstedt, Randy
  See Reinstedt, Randall A.
Reisberg, Mira 1955- *82*
Reisberg, Veg
  See Reisberg, Mira
Reiser, Lynn 1944- *180*
  Earlier sketches in SATA *81, 138*
Reiser, Lynn Whisnant
  See Reiser, Lynn
Reisgies, Teresa (Maria) 1966- *74*
Reiss, Johanna (de Leeuw) 1929(?)- *18*
  See also CLR *19*
Reiss, John J. *23*
Reiss, Kathryn 1957- *144*
  Earlier sketch in SATA *76*
Reit, Seymour Victory 1918-2001 .... *21*
  Obituary *133*
Reit, Sy
  See Reit, Seymour Victory
Relf, Patricia 1954- *134*
  Earlier sketch in SATA *71*
Remi, Georges 1907-1983 .... *13*
  Obituary *32*
  See also CLR *114*
Remington, Frederic S(ackrider)
  1861-1909 .... *41*
Remkiewicz, Frank 1939- *152*
  Earlier sketch in SATA *77*

Rempt, Fiona 1973- *198*
Remy, Georges
  See Remi, Georges
Renaud, Anne 1957- *211*
Renaud, Bernadette 1945- *66*
Renault, Mary 1905-1983 .... *23*
  Obituary *36*
Rendell, Joan *28*
Rendina, Laura (Jones) Cooper 1902- *10*
Rendon, Marcie R. 1952- *97*
Rendon, Maria 1965- *116*
Renee, Janina 1956- *140*
Renfro, Ed 1924- *79*
Renick, Marion (Lewis) 1905-1983 .... *1*
Renier, Aaron 1977- *202*
Renken, Aleda 1907- *27*
Renlie, Frank H. 1936- *11*
Rennert, Richard Scott 1956- *67*
Rennison, Louise 1951- *149*
Reno, Dawn E(laine) 1953- *130*
Rensie, Willis
  See Eisner, Will
Renton, Cam
  See Armstrong, Richard
Renvoize, Jean *5*
Resau, Laura 1973- *190*
Resciniti, Angelo G. 1952- *75*
Resnick, Michael David
  See Resnick, Mike
Resnick, Mike 1942- *159*
  Earlier sketches in SATA *38, 106*
Resnick, Seymour 1920- *23*
Retla, Robert
  See Alter, Robert Edmond
Rettig, Liz *199*
Rettstatt, Chris
  See Ashland, Monk
Reuter, Bjarne (B.) 1950- *142*
  Earlier sketch in SATA *68*
Reuter, Carol (Joan) 1931- *2*
Revena
  See Wright, Betty Ren
Revsbech, Vicki
  See Liestman, Vicki
Rex, Adam *186*
Rex, Michael *191*
Rey, H. A. 1898-1977 .... *100*
  Earlier sketches in SATA *1, 26, 69*
  See also CLR *93*
Rey, Hans Augusto
  See Rey, H. A.
Rey, Luis V. 1955- *201*
Rey, Margret 1906-1996 .... *86*
  Obituary *93*
  Earlier sketch in SATA *26*
  See also CLR *93*
Rey, Margret Elisabeth
  See Rey, Margret
Reyher, Becky
  See Reyher, Rebecca Hourwich
Reyher, Rebecca Hourwich 1897-1987 .... *18*
  Obituary *50*
Reynold, Ann
  See Bernardo, Anilu
Reynolds, Aaron 1970- *197*
Reynolds, Adrian 1963- *192*
Reynolds, C. Buck 1957- *107*
Reynolds, Dickson
  See Reynolds, Helen Mary Greenwood Campbell
Reynolds, Helen Mary Greenwood Campbell
  1884-1969
  Obituary *26*
Reynolds, Jan 1956- *180*
Reynolds, John
  See Whitlock, Ralph
Reynolds, Madge
  See Whitlock, Ralph
Reynolds, Malvina 1900-1978 .... *44*
  Obituary *24*

Reynolds, Marilyn 1935- *121*
  See also SAAS *23*
Reynolds, Marilyn M.
  See Reynolds, Marilyn
Reynolds, Marilynn 1940- *141*
  Earlier sketch in SATA *80*
Reynolds, Pamela 1923- *34*
Reynolds, Peter H. 1961- *128*
Reynolds, Peter J. 1961- *179*
Reynolds, Susan *179*
Rhine, Richard
  See Silverstein, Alvin
  and Silverstein, Virginia B.
Rhoades, Diane 1952- *90*
Rhodes, Bennie (Loran) 1927- *35*
Rhodes, Donna McKee 1962- *87*
Rhodes, Frank Harold Trevor 1926- *37*
Rhue, Morton
  See Strasser, Todd
Rhyne, Nancy 1926- *66*
Rhynes, Martha E. 1939- *141*
Ribbons, Ian 1924- *37*
  Brief entry *30*
  See also SAAS *3*
Ricciuti, Edward R(aphael) 1938- *10*
Rice, Alice (Caldwell) Hegan 1870-1942 .... *63*
Rice, Bebe Faas 1932- *89*
Rice, Charles D(uane) 1910-1971
  Obituary *27*
Rice, Dale R. 1948- *42*
Rice, Dale Richard
  See Rice, Dale R.
Rice, Dick
  See Rice, R. Hugh
Rice, Earle (Wilmont), Jr. 1928- *151*
  Earlier sketch in SATA *92*
Rice, Edward 1918-2001 .... *47*
  Brief entry *42*
Rice, Elizabeth 1913-1976 .... *2*
Rice, Eve 1951- *91*
  Earlier sketch in SATA *34*
Rice, Eve Hart
  See Rice, Eve
Rice, Inez 1907- *13*
Rice, James 1934- *93*
  Earlier sketch in SATA *22*
Rice, John F. 1958- *82*
Rice, R. Hugh 1929- *115*
Rice, Richard H.
  See Rice, R. Hugh
Rich, Anna 1956- *212*
Rich, Barbara
  See Graves, Robert
Rich, Elaine Sommers 1926- *6*
Rich, Josephine Bouchard 1912- *10*
Rich, Louise Dickinson 1903-1991 .... *54*
  Obituary *67*
Richard, Adrienne 1921- *5*
  See also SAAS *9*
Richard, James Robert
  See Bowen, Robert Sydney
Richards, Chuck 1957- *170*
Richards, Frank
  See Hamilton, Charles (Harold St. John)
Richards, Hilda
  See Hamilton, Charles (Harold St. John)
Richards, Jackie 1925- *102*
Richards, Jean 1940- *135*
Richards, Justin *169*
Richards, Kay
  See Baker, Susan (Catherine)
Richards, Laura E(lizabeth Howe) 1850-1943
  See YABC *1*
  See also CLR *54*
Richards, Leigh
  See King, Laurie R.
Richards, Marlee
  See Brill, Marlene Targ
Richards, Norman 1932- *48*

Richards, R(onald) C(harles) W(illiam)
1923- *59*
  Brief entry *43*
Richards, Walter Alden (Jr.) 1907-1988
  Obituary *56*
Richardson, Andrew (William) 1986- *120*
Richardson, Carol 1932- *58*
Richardson, Frank Howard 1882-1970
  Obituary *27*
Richardson, Grace Lee
  See Dickson, Naida
Richardson, Jean (Mary) *59*
Richardson, Judith Benet 1941- *77*
Richardson, Nigel 1957- *187*
Richardson, Robert S(hirley) 1902-1981 .... *8*
Richardson, Sandy 1949- *116*
Richardson, V.A. *189*
Richardson, Willis 1889-1977 .... *60*
Richelson, Geraldine 1922- *29*
Richemont, Enid 1940- *82*
Richler, Mordecai 1931-2001 .... *98*
  Brief entry *27*
  Earlier sketch in SATA *44*
  See also CLR *17*
Richman, Sophia 1941- *142*
Rich-McCoy, Lois
  See McCoy, Lois (Rich)
Richmond, Robin 1951- *75*
Richoux, Pat(ricia) 1927- *7*
Richter, Alice 1941- *30*
Richter, Conrad (Michael) 1890-1968 .... *3*
Richter, Hans Peter 1925-1993 .... *6*
  See also CLR *21*
  See also SAAS *11*
Richter, Jutta 1955- *184*
Rickard, Graham 1949- *71*
Rico, Don(ato) 1917-1985
  Obituary *43*
Riddell, Chris 1962- *166*
  Earlier sketch in SATA *114*
Riddell, Christopher Barry
  See Riddell, Chris
Riddell, Edwina 1955- *82*
Ridden, Brian 1934- *123*
  See Ridden, Brian John
Riddle, Tohby 1965- *151*
  Earlier sketch in SATA *74*
Riddleburger, Sam *202*
Riddles, Libby 1956- *140*
Rideout, Sandy *194*
Ridge, Antonia (Florence) (?)-1981 .... *7*
  Obituary *27*
Ridge, Martin 1923-2003 .... *43*
Ridley, Philip *171*
  Earlier sketch in SATA *88*
Ridlon, Marci
  See Balterman, Marcia Ridlon
Riedman, Sarah R(egal) 1902-1995 .... *1*
Riehecky, Janet 1953- *164*
Ries, Lori *185*
Riesenberg, Felix, Jr. 1913-1962 .... *23*
Rieu, E(mile) V(ictor) 1887-1972 .... *46*
  Obituary *26*
Riffenburgh, Beau 1955- *175*
Rigg, Sharon
  See Creech, Sharon
Riggenbach, Holly
  See Black, Holly
Riggio, Anita 1952- *148*
  Earlier sketch in SATA *73*
Riggs, Shannon *190*
Riggs, Sidney Noyes 1892-1975
  Obituary *28*
Riggs, Stephanie 1964- *138*
Riglietti, Serena 1969- *189*
Rigney, James Oliver, Jr.
  See Jordan, Robert
Rikhoff, Jean 1928- *9*
Rikki
  See Ducornet, Erica
Riley, James A. 1939- *97*

Riley, James Whitcomb 1849-1916 .... *17*
Riley, Jocelyn 1949- *60*
  Brief entry *50*
Riley, Jocelyn Carol
  See Riley, Jocelyn
Riley, Linda Capus 1950- *85*
Riley, Martin 1948- *81*
Rimbauer, Steven
  See Pearson, Ridley
Rimes, (Margaret) LeAnn 1982- *154*
Rinaldi, Ann 1934- *202*
  Brief entry *50*
  Earlier sketches in SATA *51, 78, 117, 161*
  See also CLR *46*
Rinard, Judith E(llen) 1947- *140*
  Earlier sketch in SATA *44*
Rinck, Maranke 1976- *214*
Rinder, Lenore 1949- *92*
Ring, Elizabeth 1920- *79*
Ringdalh, Mark
  See Longyear, Barry B(rookes)
Ringgold, Faith 1930- *187*
  Earlier sketches in SATA *71, 114*
  See also CLR *30*
Ringi, Kjell (Arne Soerensen) 1939- *12*
Rinkoff, Barbara Jean (Rich) 1923-1975 .... *4*
  Obituary *27*
Rinn, Miriam 1946- *127*
Riordan, James 1936- *95*
Riordan, Rick *208*
  Earlier sketch in SATA *174*
Rios, Tere
  See Versace, Marie Teresa Rios
Ripken, Cal, Jr. 1960- *215*
  Earlier sketch in SATA *114*
Ripken, Calvin Edward, Jr.
  See Ripken, Cal, Jr.
Ripley, Catherine 1957- *82*
Ripley, Elizabeth Blake 1906-1969 .... *5*
Ripper, Charles L(ewis) 1929- *3*
Ripper, Chuck
  See Ripper, Charles L(ewis)
Riq
  See Atwater, Richard (Tupper)
Rish, David 1955- *110*
Riskind, Mary 1944- *60*
Rissinger, Matt 1956- *93*
Rissman, Art
  See Sussman, Susan
Rissman, Susan
  See Sussman, Susan
Ritchie, Barbara Gibbons *14*
Ritter, Felix
  See Kruss, James
Ritter, John H. 1951- *215*
  Earlier sketches in SATA *129, 137*
Ritter, Lawrence S(tanley) 1922-2004 .... *58*
  Obituary *152*
Ritthaler, Shelly 1955- *91*
Ritts, Paul 1920(?)-1980
  Obituary *25*
Ritz, Karen 1957- *202*
  Earlier sketch in SATA *80*
Rivera, Geraldo (Miguel) 1943- *54*
  Brief entry *28*
Rivers, Elfrida
  See Bradley, Marion Zimmer
Rivers, Karen 1970- *131*
Riverside, John
  See Heinlein, Robert A.
Rivkin, Ann 1920- *41*
Rivoli, Mario 1943- *10*
Roach, Marilynne K. 1946- *9*
Roach, Marilynne Kathleen
  See Roach, Marilynne K.
Roach, Portia
  See Takakjian, Portia
Robb, Don 1937- *194*
Robb, Laura 1937- *95*
Robberecht, Thierry 1960- *182*

Robbins, Frank 1917-1994(?) *42*
  Brief entry *32*
Robbins, Ken 1945- *147*
  Brief entry *53*
  Earlier sketch in SATA *94*
Robbins, Raleigh
  See Hamilton, Charles (Harold St. John)
Robbins, Ruth 1917(?)- *14*
Robbins, Tony
  See Pashko, Stanley
Robbins, Wayne
  See Cox, William R(obert)
Robel, S. L.
  See Fraustino, Lisa Rowe
Roberson, Jennifer 1953- *72*
Roberson, John R(oyster) 1930- *53*
Robert, Adrian
  See St. John, Nicole
Roberts, Bethany *202*
  Earlier sketch in SATA *133*
Roberts, Bruce (Stuart) 1930- *47*
  Brief entry *39*
Roberts, Charles G(eorge) D(ouglas)
1860-1943 .... *88*
  Brief entry *29*
  See also CLR *33*
Roberts, David
  See Cox, John Roberts
Roberts, David 1970- *191*
Roberts, Diane 1937- *184*
Roberts, Elizabeth 1944- *80*
Roberts, Elizabeth Madox 1886-1941 .... *33*
  Brief entry *27*
  See also CLR *100*
Roberts, Jim
  See Bates, Barbara S(nedeker)
Roberts, John G(aither) 1913-1993 .... *27*
Roberts, Judy I. 1957- *93*
Roberts, Katherine 1962- *152*
Roberts, M. L.
  See Mattern, Joanne
Roberts, Marion 1966- *212*
Roberts, Nancy Correll 1924- *52*
  Brief entry *28*
Roberts, Priscilla 1955- *184*
Roberts, Terence
  See Sanderson, Ivan T(erence)
Roberts, Willo Davis 1928-2004 .... *150*
  Autobiography Feature *150*
  Obituary *160*
  Earlier sketches in SATA *21, 70, 133*
  See also CLR *95*
  See also SAAS *8*
Robertson, Barbara (Anne) 1931- *12*
Robertson, Don 1929-1999 .... *8*
  Obituary *113*
Robertson, Dorothy Lewis 1912- *12*
Robertson, Ellis
  See Ellison, Harlan
  and Silverberg, Robert
Robertson, James I., Jr. 1930- *182*
Robertson, James Irvin
  See Robertson, James I., Jr.
Robertson, Janet (E.) 1935- *68*
Robertson, Jennifer Sinclair 1942-1998 .... *12*
Robertson, Jenny
  See Robertson, Jennifer Sinclair
Robertson, Keith (Carlton) 1914-1991 .... *85*
  Obituary *69*
  Earlier sketch in SATA *1*
  See also SAAS *15*
Robertson, Mark
  See Robertson, M.P.
Robertson, M.P. 1965- *197*
Robertson, Stephen
  See Walker, Robert W.
Robertus, Polly M. 1948- *212*
  Earlier sketch in SATA *73*
Robeson, Kenneth
  See Dent, Lester
  and Goulart, Ron

Robeson, Kenneth
  See Johnson, (Walter) Ryerson
Robinet, Harriette Gillem 1931- *104*
  Earlier sketch in SATA *27*
  See also CLR *64*
Robins, Deri 1958- *166*
  Earlier sketch in SATA *117*
Robins, Patricia
  See Clark, Patricia Denise
Robins, Rollo, Jr.
  See Ellis, Edward S.
Robins, Seelin
  See Ellis, Edward S.
Robinson, Adjai 1932- *8*
Robinson, Aminah Brenda Lynn 1940- *159*
  Earlier sketch in SATA *77*
Robinson, Barbara (Webb) 1927- *84*
  Earlier sketch in SATA *8*
Robinson, C(harles) A(lexander), Jr.
  1900-1965 .... *36*
Robinson, Charles 1870-1937 .... *17*
Robinson, Charles 1931- *6*
Robinson, Dorothy W. 1929- *54*
Robinson, Elizabeth Keeler 1959- *204*
Robinson, Eve
  See Tanselle, Eve
Robinson, Glen 1953- *92*
Robinson, Glendal P.
  See Robinson, Glen
Robinson, Jan M. 1933- *6*
Robinson, Jean O. 1934- *7*
Robinson, Joan (Mary) G(ale Thomas)
  1910-1988 .... *7*
Robinson, Kim Stanley 1952- *109*
Robinson, Lee 1948- *110*
Robinson, Lloyd
  See Silverberg, Robert
Robinson, Lynda S(uzanne) 1951- *107*
Robinson, Marileta 1942- *32*
Robinson, Maudie Millian Oller 1914- *11*
Robinson, Maurice R(ichard) 1895-1982
  Obituary *29*
Robinson, Nancy K(onheim) 1942-1994 ...... *91*
  Brief entry *31*
  Obituary *79*
  Earlier sketch in SATA *32*
Robinson, Ray 1920- *23*
Robinson, Raymond Kenneth
  See Robinson, Ray
Robinson, Shari
  See McGuire, Leslie (Sarah)
Robinson, Sharon 1950- *197*
  Earlier sketch in SATA *162*
Robinson, Spider 1948- *118*
Robinson, Sue
  See Robinson, Susan Maria
Robinson, Susan Maria 1955- *105*
Robinson, Susan Patricia
  See Gates, Susan
Robinson, Suzanne
  See Robinson, Lynda S(uzanne)
Robinson, T(homas) H(eath) 1869-1950 ...... *17*
Robinson, Tim 1963- *205*
Robinson, (Wanda) Veronica 1926- *30*
Robinson, W(illiam) Heath 1872-1944 .... *17*
Robison, Bonnie 1924- *12*
Robison, Nancy L(ouise) 1934- *32*
Robles, Harold E. 1948- *87*
Robottom, John 1934- *7*
Robson, Eric 1939- *82*
Roca, Francois 1971- *200*
Rocco, John 1967- *188*
Roche, A. K.
  See Abisch, Roslyn Kroop
  and Kaplan, Boche
Roche, Denis 1967- *196*
  Earlier sketch in SATA *99*
Roche, Denis Mary
  See Roche, Denis
Roche, Luane 1937- *170*

Roche, P(atricia) K. 1935- *57*
  Brief entry *34*
Roche, Terry
  See Poole, Peggy
Rochman, Hazel 1938- *105*
Rock, Lois
  See Joslin, Mary
Rock, Maxine 1940- *108*
Rocker, Fermin 1907- *40*
Rocklin, Joanne 1946- *134*
  Earlier sketch in SATA *86*
Rockwell, Anne F. 1934- *194*
  Earlier sketches in SATA *33, 71, 114, 162*
  See also SAAS *19*
Rockwell, Anne Foote
  See Rockwell, Anne F.
Rockwell, Bart
  See Pellowski, Michael (Joseph)
Rockwell, Harlow 1910-1988 .... *33*
  Obituary *56*
Rockwell, Lizzy 1961- *185*
Rockwell, Norman (Percevel) 1894-1978 .... *23*
Rockwell, Thomas 1933- *70*
  Earlier sketch in SATA *7*
  See also CLR *6*
Rockwood, Joyce 1947- *39*
Rockwood, Roy
  See McFarlane, Leslie
  and Stratemeyer, Edward L.
Rodanas, Kristina 1952- *155*
Rodari, Gianni 1920-1980
  See CLR *24*
Rodd, Kathleen Tennant
  See Rodd, Kylie Tennant
Rodd, Kylie Tennant 1912-1988 .... *57*
  Obituary *55*
  Earlier sketch in SATA *6*
Rodda, Emily 1948- *146*
  Earlier sketch in SATA *97*
  See also CLR *32*
Roddenberry, Eugene Wesley 1921-1991 ..... *45*
  Obituary *69*
Roddenberry, Gene
  See Roddenberry, Eugene Wesley
Roddick, Ellen 1936- *5*
Roddie, Shen *153*
Roddy, Lee 1921- *57*
Rodenas, Paula *73*
Rodgers, Frank 1944- *69*
Rodgers, Mary 1931- *130*
  Earlier sketch in SATA *8*
  See also CLR *20*
Rodman, Emerson
  See Ellis, Edward S.
Rodman, Eric
  See Silverberg, Robert
Rodman, Maia
  See Wojciechowska, Maia (Teresa)
Rodman, Mary Ann *185*
Rodman, (Cary) Selden 1909-2002 .... *9*
Rodowsky, Colby 1932- *164*
  Earlier sketches in SATA *21, 77, 120*
  See also SAAS *22*
Rodowsky, Colby F.
  See Rodowsky, Colby
Rodriguez, Alejo 1941- *83*
Rodriguez, Alex 1975- *189*
Rodriguez, Christina 1981- *177*
Rodriguez, Edel 1971- *196*
Rodriguez, Luis J. 1954- *125*
Rodriguez, Rachel *180*
Rodriguez, Rachel Victoria
  See Rodriguez, Rachel
Roeder, Virginia Marsh 1926- *98*
Roehrig, Catharine H. 1949- *67*
Roennfeldt, Robert 1953- *78*
Roessel-Waugh, C. C.
  See Waugh, Carol-Lynn Rossel
  and Waugh, Charles G(ordon)
Roets, Lois F. 1937- *91*
Roever, J(oan) M(arilyn) 1935- *26*

Rofes, Eric 1954-2006 .... *52*
Rofes, Eric Edward 1954-2006
  See Rofes, Eric
Roffey, Maureen 1936- *33*
Rogak, Lisa 1962- *80*
Rogak, Lisa Angowski
  See Rogak, Lisa
Rogan, S. Jones *199*
Rogan, Sally Jones
  See Rogan, S. Jones
Rogasky, Barbara 1933- *144*
  Earlier sketch in SATA *86*
Rogers, (Thomas) Alan (Stinchcombe)
  1937- *81*
  Earlier sketch in SATA *2*
Rogers, Bettye 1858-1919 .... *103*
Rogers, Cindy 1950- *89*
Rogers, Emma 1951- *74*
Rogers, Frances 1888-1974 .... *10*
Rogers, Fred McFeely 1928-2003 .... *33*
  Obituary *138*
Rogers, Gregory 1957- *211*
Rogers, Hal
  See Sirimarco, Elizabeth
Rogers, Jacqueline 1958- *213*
Rogers, Jean 1919- *55*
  Brief entry *47*
Rogers, Matilda 1894-1976 .... *5*
  Obituary *34*
Rogers, Pamela 1927- *9*
Rogers, Paul 1950- *98*
  Earlier sketch in SATA *54*
Rogers, Robert
  See Hamilton, Charles (Harold St. John)
Rogers, Sherry *193*
Rogers, W(illiam) G(arland) 1896-1978 .... *23*
Rohan, M. S.
  See Rohan, Michael Scott
Rohan, Michael Scott 1951- *98*
Rohan, Mike Scott
  See Rohan, Michael Scott
Rohmann, Eric 1957- *171*
  See also CLR *100*
Rohmer, Harriet 1938- *56*
Rohrer, Doug 1962- *89*
Rojan
  See Rojankovsky, Feodor (Stepanovich)
Rojankovsky, Feodor (Stepanovich)
  1891-1970 .... *21*
Rojany, Lisa *94*
Rokeby-Thomas, Anna E(lma) 1911- *15*
Roland, Albert 1925-2002 .... *11*
Roland, Mary
  See Lewis, Mary
Roleff, Tamara L. 1959- *143*
Rolerson, Darrell A(llen) 1946- *8*
Roll, Winifred 1909-1998 .... *6*
Rollins, Charlemae Hill 1897-1979 .... *3*
  Obituary *26*
Rollock, Barbara T(herese) 1924- *64*
Rolston, Steve 1978- *209*
Romack, Janice Reed
  See LeNoir, Janice
Romain, Trevor *134*
Romanenko, Vitaliy 1962- *101*
Romano, Christy
  See Romano, Christy Carlson
Romano, Christy Carlson 1984- *210*
Romano, Clare 1922- *111*
  Earlier sketch in SATA *48*
Romano, Louis G. 1921- *35*
Romano, Melora A. 1966- *118*
Romano, Ray 1957- *170*
Romano, Raymond
  See Romano, Ray
Romijn, Johanna Maria Kooyker
  See Kooyker-Romijn, Johanna Maria
Romyn, Johanna Maria Kooyker
  See Kooyker-Romijn, Johanna Maria
Rong, Yu 1970- *174*
Rongen, Bjoern 1906- *10*

Rongen, Bjorn
    See Rongen, Bjoern
Ronson, Mark
    See Alexander, Marc
Rood, Ronald (N.) 1920- *12*
Rook, Sebastian
    See Jeapes, Ben
Rooke, Daphne 1914-2009 .... *12*
Rooke, Daphne Marie
    See Rooke, Daphne
Rooney, Ronnie 1970- *212*
Roop, Connie 1951- *167*
    Brief entry *49*
    Earlier sketches in SATA *54, 116*
Roop, Constance Betzer
    See Roop, Connie
Roop, Peter 1951- *167*
    Brief entry *49*
    Earlier sketches in SATA *54, 116*
Roop, Peter G.
    See Roop, Peter
Roop, Peter Geiger
    See Roop, Peter
Roos, Stephen 1945- *128*
    Brief entry *41*
    Earlier sketches in SATA *47, 77*
Roose-Evans, James 1927- *65*
Roosevelt, Eleanor 1884-1962 .... *50*
Root, Barry *182*
Root, Betty *84*
Root, Kimberly Bulcken *192*
Root, Phyllis 1949- *184*
    Brief entry *48*
    Earlier sketches in SATA *55, 94, 145*
Root, Shelton L., Jr. 1923-1986
    Obituary *51*
Roper, Laura (Newbold) Wood 1911-2003 .. *34*
    Obituary *150*
Roper, Robert 1946- *142*
    Earlier sketch in SATA *78*
Roraback, Robin (Ellan) 1964- *111*
Rorby, Ginny 1944- *94*
Rorer, Abigail 1949- *85*
Rosaler, Maxine *208*
Rosamel, Godeleine de 1968- *151*
Roscoe, D(onald) T(homas) 1934- *42*
Rose, Anne *8*
Rose, Deborah Lee 1955- *185*
    Earlier sketches in SATA *71, 124*
Rose, Elizabeth (Jane Pretty) 1933- *68*
    Brief entry *28*
Rose, Florella
    See Carlson, Vada F.
Rose, Gerald (Hembdon Seymour) 1935- *68*
    Brief entry *30*
Rose, Malcolm 1953- *168*
    Earlier sketch in SATA *107*
Rose, Nancy A.
    See Sweetland, Nancy A(nn)
Rose, Ted 1940- *93*
Rose, Wendy 1948- *12*
Rosen, Elizabeth 1961- *205*
Rosen, Lillian (Diamond) 1928- *63*
Rosen, Marvin 1933- *161*
Rosen, Michael 1946- *181*
    Brief entry *40*
    Earlier sketches in SATA *48, 84, 137*
    See also CLR *45*
Rosen, Michael J. 1954- *199*
    Earlier sketch in SATA *86*
Rosen, Michael Wayne
    See Rosen, Michael
Rosen, Sidney 1916- *1*
Rosen, Winifred 1943- *8*
Rosenbaum, Maurice 1907-1987 .... *6*
Rosenberg, Amye 1950- *74*
Rosenberg, Dorothy 1906- *40*
Rosenberg, Eth Clifford 1915- *92*
    See also SAAS *22*
Rosenberg, Jane 1949- *58*

Rosenberg, Liz 1958- *129*
    Earlier sketch in SATA *75*
Rosenberg, Maxine B(erta) 1939- *93*
    Brief entry *47*
    Earlier sketch in SATA *55*
Rosenberg, Nancy (Sherman) 1931- *4*
Rosenberg, Sharon 1942- *8*
Rosenberry, Vera 1948- *144*
    Earlier sketch in SATA *83*
Rosenblatt, Arthur
    See Rosenblatt, Arthur S.
Rosenblatt, Arthur S. 1938- *68*
    Brief entry *45*
Rosenblatt, Lily 1956- *90*
Rosenbloom, Joseph 1928- *21*
Rosenblum, Richard 1928- *11*
Rosenburg, John M. 1918- *6*
Rosenfeld, Dina 1962- *99*
Rosenstiehl, Agnes 1941- *203*
Rosenthal, Amy Krouse 1965- *177*
Rosenthal, Betsy R. 1957- *178*
Rosenthal, Harold 1914-1999 .... *35*
Rosenthal, M(acha) L(ouis) 1917-1996 .... *59*
Rosenthal, Marc 1949- *193*
Rosenthal, Mark A(lan) 1946- *64*
Rosing, Norbert 1953- *196*
Rosman, Steven M 1956- *81*
Rosman, Steven Michael
    See Rosman, Steven M
Rosoff, Meg 1956- *209*
    Earlier sketch in SATA *160*
Ross, Alan
    See Warwick, Alan R(oss)
Ross, Christine 1950- *172*
    Earlier sketch in SATA *83*
Ross, Clare
    See Romano, Clare
Ross, Dana Fuller
    See Cockrell, Amanda
    and Gerson, Noel Bertram
Ross, Dave
    See Ross, David
Ross, David 1896-1975 .... *49*
    Obituary *20*
Ross, David 1949- *133*
    Earlier sketch in SATA *32*
Ross, Deborah J.
    See Wheeler, Deborah
Ross, Diana
    See Denney, Diana
Ross, Edward S(hearman) 1915- *85*
Ross, Eileen 1950- *115*
Ross, Frank (Xavier), Jr. 1914- *28*
Ross, Jane 1961- *79*
Ross, John 1921- *45*
Ross, Judy 1942- *54*
Ross, Katharine Reynolds
    See Ross, Kathy
Ross, Kathy 1948- *169*
    Earlier sketch in SATA *89*
Ross, Kent 1956- *91*
Ross, Lillian Hammer 1925- *72*
Ross, Michael Elsohn 1952- *170*
    Earlier sketches in SATA *80, 127*
Ross, Pat(ricia Kienzle) 1943- *53*
    Brief entry *48*
Ross, Ramon R(oyal) 1930- *62*
Ross, Stewart 1947- *134*
    Earlier sketch in SATA *92*
    See also SAAS *23*
Ross, Tom 1958- *84*
Ross, Tony 1938- *176*
    Earlier sketches in SATA *17, 65, 130*
Ross, Wilda 1915- *51*
    Brief entry *39*
Rossel, Seymour 1945- *28*
Rossell, Judith 1953- *187*
Rossel-Waugh, C. C.
    See Waugh, Carol-Lynn Rossel
Rossetti, Christina 1830-1894 .... *20*
    See also CLR *115*

Rossetti, Christina Georgina
    See Rossetti, Christina
Rossi, Joyce 1943- *116*
Rossotti, Hazel Swaine 1930- *95*
Rostkowski, Margaret I. 1945- *59*
Roth, Arnold 1929- *21*
Roth, Arthur J(oseph) 1925-1993 .... *43*
    Brief entry *28*
    Obituary *75*
    See also SAAS *11*
Roth, David 1940- *36*
Roth, Julie Jersild *180*
Roth, Matthue 1978(?)- *174*
Roth, Roger *190*
Roth, Stephanie *202*
Roth, Susan L. *181*
    Earlier sketch in SATA *134*
Rothberg, Abraham 1922- *59*
Roth-Hano, Renee 1931- *85*
Rothkopf, Carol Z. 1929- *4*
Rothman, Joel 1938- *7*
Rotner, Shelley 1951- *169*
    Earlier sketch in SATA *76*
Rottman, S.L. 1970- *157*
    Earlier sketch in SATA *106*
Rottman, Susan Lynn
    See Rottman, S.L.
Roueche, Berton 1911-1994 .... *28*
Roughsey, Dick 1921(?)-1985 .... *35*
    See also CLR *41*
Roughsey, Goobalathaldin
    See Roughsey, Dick
Rounds, Glen (Harold) 1906-2002 .... *112*
    Obituary *141*
    Earlier sketches in SATA *8, 70*
Rourke, Constance Mayfield 1885-1941
    See YABC *1*
Rouss, Sylvia *211*
Rovetch, Gerda 1925(?)- *202*
Rovetch, L. Bob
    See Rovetch, Lissa
Rovetch, Lissa *201*
Rowan, Deirdre
    See Williams, Jeanne
Rowe, Jennifer
    See Rodda, Emily
Rowe, John A. 1949- *198*
    Earlier sketch in SATA *146*
Rowe, Viola Carson 1903-1969
    Obituary *26*
Rowh, Mark 1952- *90*
Rowland, Florence Wightman 1900-1997 ...... *8*
    Obituary *108*
Rowland-Entwistle, (Arthur) Theodore (Henry)
    1925- *94*
    Earlier sketch in SATA *31*
Rowling, J.K. 1965- *174*
    Earlier sketch in SATA *109*
    See also CLR *112*
Rowling, Joanne Kathleen
    See Rowling, J.K.
Rowsome, Frank (Howard), Jr. 1914-1983 .. *36*
Roy, Gabrielle 1909-1983 .... *104*
Roy, Jacqueline 1954- *74*
Roy, Jennifer
    See Roy, Jennifer Rozines
Roy, Jennifer Rozines 1967- *178*
Roy, Jessie Hailstalk 1895-1986
    Obituary *51*
Roy, Liam
    See Scarry, Patricia (Murphy)
Roy, Ron(ald) 1940- *110*
    Brief entry *35*
    Earlier sketch in SATA *40*
Roybal, Laura 1956- *85*
Roybal, Laura Husby
    See Roybal, Laura
Royds, Caroline 1953- *55*
Royston, Angela 1945- *169*
    Earlier sketch in SATA *120*
Rozakis, Laurie E. 1952- *84*

Rozen, Anna 1960- 206
Rubel, Nicole 1953- 181
  Earlier sketches in SATA *18, 95, 135*
Rubin, Eva Johanna 1925- 38
Rubin, Susan Goldman 1939- 182
  Earlier sketches in SATA *84, 132*
Rubin, Vicky 1964- 193
Rubinetti, Donald 1947- 92
Rubinstein, Gillian 1942- 158
  Autobiography Feature 116
  Earlier sketches in SATA *68, 105*
  See also CLR *35*
  See also SAAS *25*
Rubinstein, Gillian Margaret
  See Rubinstein, Gillian
Rubinstein, Patricia -2003
  See Forest, Antonia
Rubinstein, Patricia Giulia Caulfield Kate
  See Forest, Antonia
Rubinstein, Robert E(dward) 1943- 49
Rublowsky, John M(artin) 1928- 62
Rubright, Lynn 1936- 171
Ruby, Laura 181
  Earlier sketch in SATA *155*
Ruby, Lois 1942- 184
  Autobiography Feature 105
  Brief entry 34
  Earlier sketches in SATA *35, 95*
Ruby, Lois F.
  See Ruby, Lois
Ruchlis, Hy(man) 1913-1992 3
  Obituary 72
Ruckdeschel, Liz 214
Rucker, Mike 1940- 91
Ruckman, Ivy 1931- 93
  Earlier sketch in SATA *37*
Ruck-Pauquet, Gina 1931- 40
  Brief entry 37
Ruddell, Deborah 1949- 210
Ruditis, Paul 190
Rudley, Stephen 1946- 30
Rudolph, Marguerita 1908- 21
Rudomin, Esther
  See Hautzig, Esther Rudomin
Rue, Leonard Lee III 1926- 142
  Earlier sketch in SATA *37*
Rueda, Claudia 183
Ruedi, Norma Paul
  See Ainsworth, Norma
Ruelle, Karen Gray 1957- 209
  Earlier sketches in SATA *84, 126*
Ruemmler, John D(avid) 1948- 78
Ruepp, Krista 1947- 143
Ruffell, Ann 1941- 30
Ruffins, Reynold 1930- 125
  Earlier sketch in SATA *41*
Rugg, Jim 206
Rugoff, Milton 1913- 30
Ruhen, Olaf 1911-1989 17
Rukeyser, Muriel 1913-1980
  Obituary 22
Rumbaut, Hendle 1949- 84
Rumford, James 1948- 193
  Earlier sketch in SATA *116*
Rumsey, Marian (Barritt) 1928- 16
Rumstuckle, Cornelius
  See Brennan, Herbie
Runnerstroem, Bengt Arne 1944- 75
Runyan, John
  See Palmer, Bernard (Alvin)
Runyon, Catherine 1947- 62
Ruoff, A. LaVonne Brown 1930- 76
Rupp, Rebecca 185
Rusch, Elizabeth 1966- 198
Rusch, Kris
  See Rusch, Kristine Kathryn
Rusch, Kristine Kathryn 1960- 113
Rush, Alison 1951- 41
Rush, Peter 1937- 32
Rushdie, Ahmed Salman
  See Rushdie, Salman

Rushdie, Salman 1947-
  See CLR *125*
Rushford, Patricia H(elen) 1943- 134
Rushmore, Helen 1898-1994 3
Rushmore, Robert (William) 1926-1986 8
  Obituary 49
Ruskin, Ariane
  See Batterberry, Ariane Ruskin
Ruskin, John 1819-1900 24
Russ, Lavinia (Faxon) 1904-1992 74
Russell, Charlotte
  See Rathjen, Carl Henry
Russell, Ching Yeung 1946- 107
Russell, Don(ald Bert) 1899-1986
  Obituary 47
Russell, Franklin (Alexander) 1926- 11
Russell, Gertrude Barrer
  See Barrer-Russell, Gertrude
Russell, Helen Ross 1915- 8
Russell, James 1933- 53
Russell, Jim
  See Russell, James
Russell, Joan Plummer 1930- 139
Russell, P(hilip) Craig 1951- 162
  Earlier sketch in SATA *80*
Russell, Patrick
  See Sammis, John
Russell, Paul (Gary) 1942- 57
Russell, Sarah
  See Laski, Marghanita
Russell, Sharman Apt 1954- 123
Russell, Solveig Paulson 1904-1985 3
Russo, Marisabina 1950- 188
  Earlier sketches in SATA *106, 151*
Russo, Monica J. 1950- 83
Russo, Susan 1947- 30
Russon, Penni 1974- 179
Rutgers van der Loeff, An
  See Rutgers van der Loeff-Basenau, An(na)
  Maria Margaretha
Rutgers van der Loeff-Basenau, An(na) Maria
  Margaretha 1910- 22
Ruth, Rod 1912-1987 9
Rutherford, Douglas
  See McConnell, James Douglas Rutherford
Rutherford, Meg 1932- 34
Ruthin, Margaret
  See Catherall, Arthur
Rutledge, Jill Zimmerman 1951- 155
Rutz, Viola Larkin 1932- 12
Ruurs, Margriet 1952- 215
  Earlier sketches in SATA *97, 147*
Ruzicka, Rudolph 1883-1978
  Obituary 24
Ruzzier, Sergio 1966- 210
  Earlier sketch in SATA *159*
, Ryan
  See Ryan, John
Ryan, Betsy
  See Ryan, Elizabeth (Anne)
Ryan, Cheli Duran 20
Ryan, Darlene 1958- 176
Ryan, Elizabeth (Anne) 1943- 30
Ryan, Jeanette
  See Mines, Jeanette
Ryan, John 1921-2009 22
Ryan, Margaret 1950- 166
  Earlier sketch in SATA *78*
Ryan, Mary E. 1953- 61
Ryan, Mary Elizabeth
  See Ryan, Mary E.
Ryan, Pam Munoz 1951- 197
  Earlier sketch in SATA *134*
Ryan, Patrick 1957- 138
Ryan, Peter (Charles) 1939- 15
Ryan-Lush, Geraldine 1949- 89
Rybakov, Anatoli (Naumovich) 1911-1998 .. 79
  Obituary 108
Rybakov, Anatolii (Naumovich)
  See Rybakov, Anatoli (Naumovich)
Rybolt, Thomas R. 1954- 62

Rybolt, Thomas Roy
  See Rybolt, Thomas R.
Rybolt, Tom
  See Rybolt, Thomas R.
Rydberg, Ernest E(mil) 1901-1993 21
Rydberg, Lou(isa Hampton) 1908- 27
Rydell, Katy 1942- 91
Rydell, Wendell
  See Rydell, Wendy
Rydell, Wendy 4
Ryden, Hope 91
  Earlier sketch in SATA *8*
Ryder, Joanne (Rose) 1946- 163
  Brief entry 34
  Earlier sketches in SATA *65, 122*
  See also CLR *37*
Ryder, Pamela
  See Lamb, Nancy
Rye, Anthony
  See Youd, Samuel
Rylant, Cynthia 1954- 195
  Brief entry 44
  Earlier sketches in SATA *50, 76, 112, 160*
  See also CLR *86*
  See also SAAS *13*
Rymer, Alta May 1925- 34
Rymond, Lynda Gene 199

                              S

S. L. C.
  See Twain, Mark
S., Svend Otto
  See Soerensen, Svend Otto
Saaf, Donald W(illiam) 1961- 124
Saal, Jocelyn
  See Sachs, Judith
Sabbeth, Carol (Landstrom) 1957- 125
Saberhagen, Fred 1930-2007 89
  Obituary 184
  Earlier sketch in SATA *37*
Saberhagen, Fred T.
  See Saberhagen, Fred
Saberhagen, Fred Thomas
  See Saberhagen, Fred
Saberhagen, Frederick Thomas
  See Saberhagen, Fred
Sabin, Edwin L(egrand) 1870-1952
  See YABC *2*
Sabin, Francene 27
Sabin, Lou
  See Sabin, Louis
Sabin, Louis 1930- 27
Sabre, Dirk
  See Laffin, John (Alfred Charles)
Sabuda, Robert (James) 1965- 120
  Earlier sketch in SATA *81*
Sabuda, Robert 1965- 170
Sabuda, Robert James
  See Sabuda, Robert
Sachar, Louis 1954- 154
  Brief entry 50
  Earlier sketches in SATA *63, 104*
  See also CLR *79*
Sachs, Elizabeth-Ann 1946- 48
Sachs, Judith 1947- 52
  Brief entry 51
Sachs, Marilyn 1927- 164
  Autobiography Feature 110
  Earlier sketches in SATA *3, 68*
  See also CLR *2*
  See also SAAS *2*
Sachs, Marilyn Stickle
  See Sachs, Marilyn
Sackett, S(amuel) J(ohn) 1928- 12
Sackson, Sid 1920- 16
Sacre, Antonio 1968- 152
Saddler, Allen
  See Richards, R(onald) C(harles) W(illiam)

Saddler, K. Allen
  See Richards, R(onald) C(harles) W(illiam)
Sadie, Stanley 1930-2005 .... *14*
Sadie, Stanley John
  See Sadie, Stanley
Sadiq, Nazneen 1944- *101*
Sadler, Catherine Edwards 1952- *60*
  Brief entry *45*
Sadler, Marilyn (June) 1950- *79*
Sadler, Mark
  See Lynds, Dennis
Saffer, Barbara *144*
Sagan, Carl 1934-1996 .... *58*
  Obituary *94*
Sagan, Carl Edward
  See Sagan, Carl
Sage, Angie 1952- *197*
Sage, Juniper
  See Brown, Margaret Wise
  and Hurd, Edith Thacher
Sagsoorian, Paul 1923- *12*
Said, S.F. 1967- *174*
Saidman, Anne 1952- *75*
Saint, Dora Jessie 1913- *10*
St. Anthony, Jane *175*
St. Antoine, Sara L. 1966- *84*
St. Clair, Byrd Hooper 1905-1976
  Obituary *28*
Saint-Exupery, Antoine de 1900-1944 .... *20*
  See also CLR *142*
Saint-Exupery, Antoine Jean Baptiste Marie
  Roger de
  See Saint-Exupery, Antoine de
St. George, Judith 1931- *161*
  Earlier sketches in SATA *13, 99*
  See also CLR *57*
  See also SAAS *12*
St. George, Judith Alexander
  See St. George, Judith
St. James, Blakely
  See Gottfried, Theodore Mark
  and Platt, Charles
St. James, Blakely
  See Griffin, W.E.B.
St. James, Sierra
  See Rallison, Janette
Saint James, Synthia 1949- *152*
  Earlier sketch in SATA *84*
St. John, Lauren 1966- *214*
St. John, Nicole *143*
  Autobiography Feature *143*
  Earlier sketches in SATA *29, 89*
  See also CLR *46*
  See also SAAS *7*
St. John, Patricia Mary 1919-1993
  Obituary *79*
St. John, Philip
  See del Rey, Lester
St. John, Wylly Folk 1908-1985 .... *10*
  Obituary *45*
St. Max, E. S.
  See Ellis, Edward S.
St. Meyer, Ned
  See Stratemeyer, Edward L.
St. Mox, E. A.
  See Ellis, Edward S.
St. Myer, Ned
  See Stratemeyer, Edward L.
St. Tamara
  See Kolba, St. Tamara
Saito, Michiko
  See Fujiwara, Michiko
Sakai, Komako 1966- *213*
Sakaki, Ichiro 1969- *192*
Sakamoto, Miki *198*
Sakers, Don 1958- *72*
Sakharnov, S.
  See Sakharnov, Svyatoslav
Sakharnov, Svyatoslav 1923- *65*
Sakharnov, Svyatoslav Vladimirovich
  See Sakharnov, Svyatoslav

Saksena, Kate *148*
Sakurai, Gail 1952- *153*
  Earlier sketch in SATA *87*
Salamanca, Lucy
  See del Barco, Lucy Salamanca
Salassi, Otto R(ussell) 1939-1993 .... *38*
  Obituary *77*
Salat, Cristina *82*
Saldana, Rene, Jr. *186*
Saldutti, Denise 1953- *39*
Sale, Tim 1956- *153*
Salem, Kay 1952- *92*
Salerno, Steven *176*
Salinger, J.D. 1919-2010 .... *67*
  See also CLR *18*
Salinger, Jerome David
  See Salinger, J.D.
Salisbury, Graham 1944- *195*
  Earlier sketches in SATA *76, 108, 161*
Salisbury, Joyce E(llen) 1944- *138*
Salkey, (Felix) Andrew (Alexander)
  1928-1995 .... *118*
  Earlier sketch in SATA *35*
Salley, Coleen *166*
Sallis, Susan (Diana) 1929- *55*
Salmieri, Daniel 1983- *208*
Salmon, Annie Elizabeth 1899- *13*
Salonen, Roxane Beauclair 1968- *184*
Salsi, Lynn 1947- *130*
Salsitz, R. A. V.
  See Salsitz, Rhondi Vilott
Salsitz, Rhondi Vilott *115*
Salten, Felix
  See Salzmann, Siegmund
Salter, Cedric
  See Knight, Francis Edgar
Saltman, Judith 1947- *64*
Saltzberg, Barney 1955- *194*
  Earlier sketch in SATA *135*
Saltzman, David (Charles Laertes)
  1967-1990 .... *86*
Salvadori, Mario (George) 1907-1997 .... *97*
  Earlier sketch in SATA *40*
Salwood, F.K.
  See Kilworth, Garry
Salzer, L. E.
  See Wilson, Lionel
Salzman, Marian 1959- *77*
Salzmann, Siegmund 1869-1945 .... *25*
Samachson, Dorothy (Mirkin) 1914-1997 ...... *3*
Samachson, Joseph 1906-1980 .... *3*
  Obituary *52*
Sammis, John 1942- *4*
Sampson, Emma (Keats) Speed 1868-1947 . *68*
Sampson, Fay (Elizabeth) 1935- *151*
  Brief entry *40*
  Earlier sketch in SATA *42*
Sampson, Michael 1952- *143*
  Earlier sketch in SATA *95*
Samson, Anne S(tringer) 1933- *2*
Samson, Joan 1937-1976 .... *13*
Samson, Suzanne M. 1959- *91*
Samuels, Barbara *199*
Samuels, Charles 1902-1982 .... *12*
Samuels, Cynthia K(alish) 1946- *79*
Samuels, Gertrude 1910(?)-2003 .... *17*
  Obituary *147*
Sanborn, Duane 1914-1996 .... *38*
Sancha, Sheila 1924- *38*
Sanchez, Alex 1957- *151*
Sanchez, Anita 1956- *209*
Sanchez, Sonia 1934- *136*
  Earlier sketch in SATA *22*
  See also CLR *18*
Sanchez-Silva, Jose Maria 1911- *132*
  Earlier sketch in SATA *16*
  See also CLR *12*
Sand, George X. *45*
Sandak, Cass R(obert) 1950-2001 .... *51*
  Brief entry *37*
Sandberg, (Karin) Inger 1930- *15*

Sandberg, Karl C. 1931- *35*
Sandberg, Lasse (E. M.) 1924- *15*
Sandburg, Carl 1878-1967 .... *8*
  See also CLR *67*
Sandburg, Carl August
  See Sandburg, Carl
Sandburg, Charles
  See Sandburg, Carl
Sandburg, Charles A.
  See Sandburg, Carl
Sandburg, Helga 1918- *3*
  See also SAAS *10*
Sandell, Lisa Ann 1977- *175*
Sandemose, Iben 1950- *211*
Sander, Heather L. 1947- *157*
Sanderlin, George 1915- *4*
Sanderlin, Owenita (Harrah) 1916- *11*
Sanders, Betty Jane
  See Monthei, Betty
Sanders, Nancy I. 1960- *141*
  Earlier sketch in SATA *90*
Sanders, Scott Russell 1945- *109*
  Earlier sketch in SATA *56*
Sanders, Winston P.
  See Anderson, Poul
Sanderson, Irma 1912- *66*
Sanderson, Ivan T(erence) 1911-1973 .... *6*
Sanderson, Margaret Love
  See Keats, Emma
  and Sampson, Emma (Keats) Speed
Sanderson, Ruth 1951- *172*
  Earlier sketches in SATA *41, 109*
Sanderson, Ruth L.
  See Sanderson, Ruth
Sand-Eveland, Cyndi *211*
Sandin, Joan 1942- *197*
  Earlier sketches in SATA *12, 94, 153*
Sandison, Janet
  See Cameron, Elizabeth Jane
Sandler, Martin W. *160*
Sandom, J. Gregory
  See Welsh, T.K.
Sandom, J.G.
  See Welsh, T.K.
Sandoz, Mari(e Susette) 1900-1966 .... *5*
Sanford, Agnes (White) 1897-1976 .... *61*
Sanford, Doris 1937- *69*
Sanford, Rose
  See Simmonds, Posy
Sanger, Amy Wilson 1967- *205*
Sanger, Marjory Bartlett 1920- *8*
San Jose, Christine 1929- *167*
Sankey, Alice (Ann-Susan) 1910- *27*
San Souci, Daniel *192*
  Earlier sketch in SATA *96*
San Souci, Robert D. 1946- *158*
  Earlier sketches in SATA *40, 81, 117*
  See also CLR *43*
Santamaria, Benjamin 1955- *184*
Santat, Dan *188*
Santesson, Hans Stefan 1914(?)-1975
  Obituary *30*
Santiago, Esmeralda 1948- *129*
Santopolo, Jill *214*
Santore, Charles 1935- *200*
Santos, Helen
  See Griffiths, Helen
Santrey, Louis
  See Sabin, Louis
Santucci, Barbara 1948- *130*
Sapergia, Barbara 1943- *181*
Sapet, Kerrily 1972- *214*
Sapieyevski, Anne Lindbergh 1940-1993 ..... *81*
  Brief entry *32*
  Earlier sketches in SATA *35, 78*
Saport, Linda 1954- *123*
Sapp, Allen 1929- *151*
Sarac, Roger
  See Caras, Roger A(ndrew)
Sarah, Duchess of York
  See Ferguson, Sarah

Sarasin, Jennifer
  See Sachs, Judith
Sarcone-Roach, Julia 215
Sardinha, Rick 192
Sarg, Anthony Frederick
  See Sarg, Tony
Sarg, Tony 1882-1942
  See YABC *1*
Sargent, Pamela 1948- 78
  Earlier sketch in SATA *29*
Sargent, Robert 1933- 2
Sargent, Sarah 1937- 44
  Brief entry 41
Sargent, Shirley 1927-2004 11
Sarnoff, Jane 1937- 10
Saroff, Phyllis V. 202
Saroyan, William 1908-1981 23
  Obituary 24
Sarton, Eleanor May
  See Sarton, May
Sarton, May 1912-1995 36
  Obituary 86
Sasaki, Chris 182
Sasaki, Ellen Joy 206
Saseen, Sharon (Dillon) 1949- 59
Sasek, Miroslav 1916-1980 16
  Obituary 23
  See also CLR *4*
Sasso, Sandy Eisenberg 1947- 162
  Earlier sketches in SATA *86, 116*
Sathre, Vivian 1952- 133
  Earlier sketch in SATA *79*
Satterfield, Charles
  See del Rey, Lester
  and Pohl, Frederik
Sattgast, L. J.
  See Sattgast, Linda J.
Sattgast, Linda J. 1953- 91
Sattler, Helen Roney 1921-1992 74
  Earlier sketch in SATA *4*
  See also CLR *24*
Sauer, Julia Lina 1891-1983 32
  Obituary 36
Sauerwein, Leigh 1944- 155
Saul, Carol P. 1947- 117
  Earlier sketch in SATA *78*
Saul, John III
  See Saul, John
Saul, John 1942- 98
Saul, John W.
  See Saul, John
Saul, John W. III
  See Saul, John
Saul, John Woodruff III
  See Saul, John
Saul, (Ellen) Wendy 1946- 42
Saulnier, Karen Luczak 1940- 80
Saunders, Caleb
  See Heinlein, Robert A.
Saunders, Dave 1939- 85
Saunders, Julie 1939- 85
Saunders, (William) Keith 1910-1994 12
Saunders, Rubie (Agnes) 1929- 21
Saunders, Steven
  See Jones, Allan Frewin
Saunders, Susan 1945- 96
  Brief entry 41
  Earlier sketch in SATA *46*
Saunders-Smith, Gail 1952- 169
Sauvain, Philip Arthur 1933- 111
Savadier, Elivia 1950- 164
  Earlier sketch in SATA *79*
Savage, Alan
  See Nicole, Christopher (Robin)
Savage, Blake
  See Goodwin, Harold L(eland)
Savage, Candace 1949- 142
Savage, Deborah 1955- 76
Savage, Jeff 1961- 97
Savage, Katharine James 1905-1989
  Obituary 61

Savage, Stephen 1965- 194
Savage, Thomas 1915-2003
  Obituary 147
Savageau, Cheryl 1950- 96
Savery, Constance (Winifred) 1897-1999 .... *1*
Saville, Andrew
  See Taylor, Andrew
Saville, (Leonard) Malcolm 1901-1982 23
  Obituary 31
Saviozzi, Adriana
  See Mazza, Adriana
Savitt, Sam 1917-2000 8
  Obituary 126
Savitz, Harriet May 1933- 72
  Earlier sketch in SATA *5*
  See also SAAS *26*
Sawicki, Mary 1950- 90
Sawyer, (Frederick) Don(ald) 1947- 72
Sawyer, Kem Knapp 1953- 84
Sawyer, Robert J. 1960- 149
  Earlier sketch in SATA *81*
Sawyer, Robert James
  See Sawyer, Robert J.
Sawyer, Ruth 1880-1970 17
  See also CLR *36*
Saxby, H.M.
  See Saxby, (Henry) Maurice
Saxby, (Henry) Maurice 1924- 71
Saxon, Andrew
  See Arthur, Robert, (Jr.)
Saxon, Antonia
  See Sachs, Judith
Say, Allen 1937- 161
  Earlier sketches in SATA *28, 69, 110*
  See also CLR *135*
Sayers, Frances Clarke 1897-1989 3
  Obituary 62
Sayles, Elizabeth 1956- 163
  Earlier sketch in SATA *108*
Saylor-Marchant, Linda 1963- 82
Sayre, April Pulley 1966- 191
  Earlier sketches in SATA *88, 131*
Sazer, Nina 1949- 13
Scabrini, Janet 1953- 13
Scagell, Robin 1946- 107
Scagnetti, Jack 1924- 7
Scaletta, Kurtis 1968- 215
Scamander, Newt
  See Rowling, J.K.
Scamell, Ragnhild 1940- 180
  Earlier sketch in SATA *77*
Scanlon, Marion Stephany 11
Scannel, John Vernon
  See Scannell, Vernon
Scannell, Vernon 1922-2007 59
  Obituary 188
Scarborough, Elizabeth
  See Scarborough, Elizabeth Ann
Scarborough, Elizabeth Ann 1947- 171
  Earlier sketch in SATA *98*
Scarf, Maggi
  See Scarf, Maggie
Scarf, Maggie 1932- 5
Scariano, Margaret M. 1924- 86
Scarlett, Susan
  See Streatfeild, Noel
Scarry, Huck
  See Scarry, Richard McClure, Jr.
Scarry, Patricia (Murphy) 1924- 2
Scarry, Patsy
  See Scarry, Patricia (Murphy)
Scarry, Richard (McClure) 1919-1994 75
  Obituary 90
  Earlier sketches in SATA *2, 35*
  See also CLR *41*
Scarry, Richard McClure, Jr. 1953- 35
Schachner, Judith Byron 1951- 178
  Earlier sketch in SATA *88*
Schachner, Judy
  See Schachner, Judith Byron
Schachtel, Roger 1949- 38

Schachtel, Roger Bernard
  See Schachtel, Roger
Schade, Susan 189
Schaedler, Sally 116
Schaefer, Carole Lexa 173
Schaefer, Jack (Warner) 1907-1991 66
  Obituary 65
  Earlier sketch in SATA *3*
Schaefer, Lola M. 1950- 183
  Earlier sketches in SATA *91, 144*
Schaeffer, Mead 1898- 21
Schaeffer, Susan Fromberg 1941- 22
Schaer, Brigitte 1958- 112
Schaller, George
  See Schaller, George B.
Schaller, George B. 1933- 30
Schaller, George Beals
  See Schaller, George B.
Schanzer, Rosalyn (Good) 1942- 138
  Earlier sketch in SATA *77*
Schatell, Brian 66
  Brief entry 47
Schechter, Betty (Goodstein) 1921- 5
Schechter, Simone
  See Elkeles, Simone
Schecter, Ellen 1944- 85
Scheeder, Louis 1946- 141
Scheer, Julian (Weisel) 1926-2001 8
Scheffer, Victor B(lanchard) 1906- 6
Scheffler, Axel 1957- 180
Scheffler, Ursel 1938- 81
Scheffrin-Falk, Gladys 1928- 76
Scheidl, Gerda Marie 1913- 85
Scheier, Michael 1943- 40
  Brief entry 36
Schell, Mildred 1922- 41
Schell, Orville (Hickok) 1940- 10
Scheller, Melanie 1953- 77
Schellie, Don 1932- 29
Schembri, Jim 1962- 124
Schembri, Pamela 1969- 195
Schemm, Mildred Walker 1905-1998 21
  Obituary 103
Schenker, Dona 1947- 133
  Earlier sketch in SATA *68*
Scher, Paula 1948- 47
Scherer, Jeffrey 194
Scherf, Margaret 1908-1979 10
Schermer, Judith (Denise) 1941- 30
Schertle, Alice 1941- 192
  Earlier sketches in SATA *36, 90, 145*
Schick, Alice 1946- 27
Schick, Eleanor 1942- 144
  Earlier sketches in SATA *9, 82*
Schick, Joel 1945- 31
  Brief entry 30
Schields, Gretchen 1948- 75
Schiff, Ken(neth Roy) 1942- 7
Schiller, Andrew 1919- 21
Schiller, Barbara (Heyman) 1928- 21
Schiller, Pamela (Byrne) 127
Schindel, John 1955- 213
  Earlier sketches in SATA *77, 115*
Schindelman, Joseph 1923- 67
  Brief entry 32
Schindler, S.D. 1952- 198
  Brief entry 50
  Earlier sketches in SATA *75, 118, 171*
Schindler, Steven D.
  See Schindler, S.D.
Schinto, Jeanne 1951- 93
Schisgall, Oscar 1901-1984 12
  Obituary 38
Schlaepfer, Gloria G. 1931- 154
Schlee, Ann 1934- 44
  Brief entry 36
Schleichert, Elizabeth 1945- 77
Schlein, Miriam 1926-2004 130
  Obituary 159
  Earlier sketches in SATA *2, 87*
  See also CLR *41*

Schlesinger, Arthur M., Jr. 1917-2007 .... *61*
  Obituary *181*
  See Schlesinger, Arthur Meier
Schlesinger, Arthur Meier 1888-1965
Schlessinger, Laura (Catherine) 1947- *160*
  Earlier sketch in SATA *110*
Schlitz, Laura Amy *184*
Schloat, G. Warren, Jr. 1914-2000 .... *4*
Schmatz, Pat *197*
Schmid, Eleonore 1939- *126*
  Earlier sketches in SATA *12, 84*
Schmid, Susan Maupin *208*
Schmiderer, Dorothy 1940- *19*
Schmidt, Annie M. G. 1911-1995 .... *67*
  Obituary *91*
  See also CLR 22
Schmidt, C.A. *196*
Schmidt, Diane 1953- *70*
Schmidt, Elizabeth 1915- *15*
Schmidt, Gary D. 1957- *193*
  Earlier sketches in SATA *93, 135*
Schmidt, James Norman 1912-1983 .... *21*
Schmidt, Karen Lee 1953- *185*
  Earlier sketch in SATA *94*
Schmidt, Lynette 1952- *76*
Schmitz, Tamara *207*
Schneider, Antonie 1954- *167*
  Earlier sketch in SATA *89*
Schneider, Christine M. 1972(?)- *171*
  Earlier sketch in SATA *120*
Schneider, Dick
  See Schneider, Richard H.
Schneider, Elisa
  See Kleven, Elisa
Schneider, Herman 1905-2003 .... *7*
  Obituary *148*
Schneider, Howie -2007 .... *181*
Schneider, Josh 1980- *196*
Schneider, Laurie
  See Adams, Laurie
Schneider, Nina 1913-2007 .... *2*
  Obituary *186*
Schneider, Nina Zimet
  See Schneider, Nina
Schneider, Rex 1937- *44*
Schneider, Richard H. 1922- *171*
Schneider, Richard Henry
  See Schneider, Richard H.
Schneider, Robyn 1986- *187*
Schnirel, James R. 1931- *14*
Schnitter, Jane T. 1958- *88*
Schnitzlein, Danny *134*
Schnur, Steven 1952- *144*
  Earlier sketch in SATA *95*
Schnurre, Wolfdietrich 1920-1989
  Obituary *63*
Schoberle, Cecile 1949- *80*
Schock, Pauline 1928- *45*
Schoell, William 1951- *160*
Schoen, Barbara (Taylor) 1924-1993 .... *13*
Schoenherr, Ian *177*
Schoenherr, John 1935-2010 .... *66*
  Earlier sketch in SATA *37*
  See also SAAS *13*
Schoenherr, John Carl
  See Schoenherr, John
Schofield, Sandy
  See Rusch, Kristine Kathryn
Scholastica, Sister Mary
  See Jenkins, Marie M(agdalen)
Scholefield, A. T.
  See Scholefield, Alan
Scholefield, Alan 1931- *66*
Scholefield, Edmund O.
  See Griffin, W.E.B.
Scholey, Arthur 1932- *28*
Scholz, Jackson Volney 1897-1986
  Obituary *49*
Schone, Virginia *22*

Schongut, Emanuel 1936- *184*
  Brief entry *36*
  Earlier sketch in SATA *52*
Schoonover, Frank (Earle) 1877-1972 .... *24*
Schoor, Gene 1921- *3*
Schories, Pat 1952- *164*
  Earlier sketch in SATA *116*
Schorr, Melissa 1972- *194*
Schorr, Melissa Robin
  See Schorr, Melissa
Schott, Jane A. 1946- *172*
Schotter, Roni *190*
  Earlier sketches in SATA *105, 149*
Schraff, Anne E(laine) 1939- *92*
  Earlier sketch in SATA *27*
Schram, Peninnah 1934- *119*
Schrank, Joseph 1900-1984
  Obituary *38*
Schrecengost, Maity 1938- *118*
Schrecengost, S. Maitland
  See Schrecengost, Maity
Schreck, Karen
  See Schreck, Karen Halvorsen
Schreck, Karen Halvorsen 1962- *185*
Schrecker, Judie 1954- *90*
Schreiber, Elizabeth Anne (Ferguson)
  1947- *13*
Schreiber, Ralph W(alter) 1942- *13*
Schreiner, Samuel A(gnew), Jr. 1921- *70*
Schroades, John *214*
Schroeder, Alan 1961- *98*
  Earlier sketch in SATA *66*
Schroeder, Binette
  See Nickl, Barbara (Elisabeth)
Schroeder, Russell (K.) 1943- *146*
Schroeder, Ted 1931(?)-1973
  Obituary *20*
Schubert, Dieter 1947- *101*
  Earlier sketch in SATA *62*
Schubert, Leda 1950(?)- *181*
Schubert-Gabrys, Ingrid 1953- *101*
  Earlier sketch in SATA *62*
Schuelein-Steel, Danielle
  See Steel, Danielle
Schuelein-Steel, Danielle Fernande
  See Steel, Danielle
Schuerger, Michele R. *110*
Schuett, Stacey 1960- *168*
  Earlier sketch in SATA *75*
Schulke, Flip Phelps Graeme 1930- *57*
Schulman, Arlene 1961- *105*
Schulman, Janet 1933- *208*
  Earlier sketches in SATA *22, 137*
Schulman, L(ester) M(artin) 1934- *13*
Schulte, Elaine L(ouise) 1934- *36*
Schultz, Betty K(epka) 1932- *125*
Schultz, Gwendolyn *21*
Schultz, James Willard 1859-1947
  See YABC *1*
Schultz, Pearle Henriksen 1918- *21*
Schulz, Charles M. 1922-2000 .... *10*
  Obituary *118*
Schulz, Charles Monroe
  See Schulz, Charles M.
Schumacher, Julie 1958- *191*
Schumaker, Ward 1943- *96*
Schuman, Michael A. 1953- *134*
  Earlier sketch in SATA *85*
Schur, Maxine
  See Schur, Maxine Rose
Schur, Maxine Rose 1948- *135*
  Autobiography Feature *135*
  Brief entry *49*
  Earlier sketches in SATA *53, 98*
Schurfranz, Vivian 1925- *13*
Schutzer, A. I. 1922- *13*
Schuyler, Pamela R. 1948- *30*
Schwabach, Karen *185*
Schwager, Tina 1964- *110*
Schwandt, Stephen (William) 1947- *61*
Schwark, Mary Beth 1954- *51*

Schwartz, Alvin 1927-1992 .... *56*
  Obituary *71*
  Earlier sketch in SATA *4*
  See also CLR 89
Schwartz, Amy 1954- *189*
  Brief entry *41*
  Earlier sketches in SATA *47, 83, 131*
  See also CLR 25
  See also SAAS *18*
Schwartz, Anne Powers 1913-1987 .... *10*
Schwartz, Carol 1954- *77*
Schwartz, Charles W(alsh) 1914- *8*
Schwartz, David M. 1951- *110*
  Earlier sketch in SATA *59*
Schwartz, David Martin
  See Schwartz, David M.
Schwartz, Elizabeth Reeder 1912- *8*
Schwartz, Ellen 1949- *117*
Schwartz, Jerome L.
  See Lawrence, Jerome
Schwartz, Joel L. 1940- *54*
  Brief entry *51*
Schwartz, Joyce R. 1950- *93*
Schwartz, Julius 1907-2004 .... *45*
Schwartz, Perry 1942- *75*
Schwartz, Sheila (Ruth) 1929- *27*
Schwartz, Stephen (Lawrence) 1948- *19*
Schwartz, Virginia Frances 1950- *184*
  Earlier sketch in SATA *131*
Schwarz, Silvia Tessa Viviane
  See Schwarz, Viviane
Schwarz, Viviane 1977- *204*
Schwarz, (Silvia Tessa) Viviane 1977- *141*
Schweitzer, Byrd Baylor
  See Baylor, Byrd
Schweitzer, Iris *59*
  Brief entry *36*
Schweninger, Ann 1951- *168*
  Earlier sketches in SATA *29, 98*
Schwerin, Doris H(alpern) 1922- *64*
Schy, Yael *197*
Scieszka, Jon 1954- *199*
  Earlier sketches in SATA *68, 105, 160*
  See also CLR 107
Scillian, Devin *199*
  Earlier sketch in SATA *128*
Scioscia, Mary (Hershey) 1926- *63*
Sciurba, Katie 1957- *196*
Scofield, Penrod 1933- *62*
  Obituary *78*
Scoggin, Margaret C(lara) 1905-1968 .... *47*
  Brief entry *28*
Scoltock, Jack 1942- *141*
  Earlier sketch in SATA *72*
Scoppettone, Sandra 1936- *92*
  Earlier sketch in SATA *9*
Scot, Michael
  See Rohan, Michael Scott
Scot-Bernard, P.
  See Bernard, Patricia
Scotland, Jay
  See Jakes, John
Scott, Alastair
  See Allen, Kenneth S.
Scott, Ann Herbert 1926- *140*
  Autobiography Feature *140*
  Brief entry *29*
  Earlier sketches in SATA *56, 94*
Scott, Bill
  See Scott, William N(eville)
Scott, Bill 1920(?)-1985
  Obituary *46*
Scott, Cora Annett (Pipitone) 1931- *11*
Scott, Dan
  See Barker, S. Omar
Scott, Elaine 1940- *198*
  Earlier sketches in SATA *36, 90, 164*
Scott, Elizabeth 1972- *194*

Scott, Jack Denton 1915-1995 83
  Earlier sketch in SATA 31
  See also CLR 20
  See also SAAS 14
Scott, Jane (Harrington) 1931- 55
Scott, Jessica
  See De Wire, Elinor
Scott, John 1912-1976 14
Scott, John Anthony 1916- 23
Scott, John M(artin) 1913- 12
Scott, Mary
  See Mattern, Joanne
Scott, Melissa 1960- 109
Scott, Michael 1959- 211
Scott, Mike
  See Scott, Michael
Scott, Richard
  See Rennert, Richard Scott
Scott, Roney
  See Gault, William Campbell
Scott, Sally 1909-1978 43
Scott, Sally 1948- 44
Scott, Sally Elisabeth
  See Scott, Sally
Scott, W. N.
  See Scott, William N(eville)
Scott, Sir Walter 1771-1832
  See YABC 2
Scott, Warwick
  See Trevor, Elleston
Scott, William N(eville) 1923- 87
Scotti, Anna
  See Coates, Anna
Scotton, Rob 1960- 214
  Earlier sketch in SATA 177
Scribner, Charles, Jr. 1921-1995 13
  Obituary 87
Scribner, Joanne L. 1949- 33
Scribner, Kimball 1917- 63
Scrimger, Richard 1957- 164
  Earlier sketch in SATA 119
Scrimsher, Lila Gravatt 1897-1974
  Obituary 28
Scroder, Walter K. 1928- 82
Scroggs, Kirk 187
Scruggs, Sandy 1961- 89
Scudder, Brooke 1959- 154
Scudder, Mildred Lee 1908- 6
  See also SAAS 12
Scull, Marie-Louise 1943-1993 77
Scuro, Vincent 1951- 21
Seabrooke, Brenda 1941- 148
  Earlier sketches in SATA 30, 88
Seaman, Augusta Huiell 1879-1950 31
Seamands, Ruth 1916- 9
Searcy, Margaret Zehmer 1926- 54
  Brief entry 39
Searight, Mary W(illiams) 1918- 17
Searle, Kathryn Adrienne 1942- 10
Searle, Ronald (William Fordham) 1920- 70
  Earlier sketch in SATA 42
Sears, Stephen W. 1932- 4
Seaskull, Cecil
  See Castellucci, Cecil
Sebastian, Lee
  See Silverberg, Robert
Sebestyen, Igen
  See Sebestyen, Ouida
Sebestyen, Ouida 1924- 140
  Earlier sketch in SATA 39
  See also CLR 17
  See also SAAS 10
Sebrey, Mary Ann 1951- 62
Sechrist, Elizabeth Hough 1903-1991 2
Sederman, Marty 211
Sedges, John
  See Buck, Pearl S.
Sedgwick, Marcus 1968- 197
  Earlier sketch in SATA 160

Seed, Cecile Eugenie 1930- 86
  Earlier sketch in SATA 8
  See also CLR 76
Seed, Jenny
  See Seed, Cecile Eugenie
Seed, Sheila Turner 1937(?)-1979
  Obituary 23
Seeger, Elizabeth 1889-1973
  Obituary 20
Seeger, Laura Vaccaro 200
  Earlier sketch in SATA 172
Seeger, Pete 1919- 139
  Earlier sketch in SATA 13
Seeger, Peter R.
  See Seeger, Pete
Seeley, Laura L. 1958- 71
Seever, R.
  See Reeves, Lawrence F.
Sefozo, Mary 1925- 82
Sefton, Catherine
  See Waddell, Martin
Segal, John 178
Segal, Joyce 1940- 35
Segal, Lore 1928- 163
  Earlier sketches in SATA 4, 66
  See also SAAS 11
Segal, Lore Groszmann
  See Segal, Lore
Segar, E(lzie) C(risler) 1894-1938 61
Segovia, Andres 1893(?)-1987
  Obituary 52
Seguin, Marilyn W(eymouth) 1951- 91
Seguin-Fontes, Marthe 1924- 109
Seibold, J. Otto 1960- 196
  Earlier sketches in SATA 83, 149
  See also SAAS 22
Seidel, Ross 95
Seidelman, James Edward 1926- 6
Seiden, Art(hur) 107
  Brief entry 42
Seidensticker, John 1944- 200
Seidler, Ann (G.) 1925- 131
Seidler, Tor 1952- 149
  Brief entry 46
  Earlier sketches in SATA 52, 98
Seidman, Karla
  See Kuskin, Karla
Seidman, Laurence Ivan 1925- 15
Seigel, Kalman 1917-1998 12
  Obituary 103
Seignobosc, Francoise 1897-1961 21
Seinfeld, Jerry 1954- 146
Seitz, Jacqueline 1931- 50
Seixas, Judith S. 1922- 17
Sejima, Yoshimasa 1913- 8
Selberg, Ingrid (Maria) 1950- 68
Selden, George
  See Thompson, George Selden
Selden, Neil R(oy) 1931- 61
Self, Margaret Cabell 1902-1996 24
Selfors, Suzanne 1963- 193
Selick, Henry 1952- 183
Selig, Sylvie 1942- 13
Selkirk, Jane
  See Chapman, John Stanton Higham
Sellers, Naomi
  See Flack, Naomi John White
Sellier, Marie 1953- 212
Selman, LaRue W. 1927- 55
Selsam, Millicent E(llis) 1912-1996 29
  Obituary 92
  Earlier sketch in SATA 1
  See also CLR 1
Seltzer, Meyer 1932- 17
Seltzer, Richard 1946- 41
Seltzer, Richard Warren, Jr.
  See Seltzer, Richard
Selvadurai, Shyam 1965(?)- 171
Selway, Martina 1940- 169
  Earlier sketch in SATA 74
Selzer, Adam 1980- 192

Selznick, Brian 1966- 210
  Earlier sketches in SATA 79, 117, 171
Semel, Nava 1954- 107
Semloh
  See Holmes, Peggy
Sendak, Jack 1924(?)-1995 28
Sendak, Maurice 1928- 165
  Earlier sketches in SATA 1, 27, 113
  See also CLR 131
Sendak, Maurice Bernard
  See Sendak, Maurice
Sender, Ruth M(insky) 1926- 62
Sengler, Johanna 1924- 18
Senisi, Ellen B. 1951- 116
Senisi, Ellen Babinec
  See Senisi, Ellen B.
Senn, J(oyce) A(nn) 1941- 115
Senn, Steve 1950- 60
  Brief entry 48
Sensel, Joni 1962- 204
Serafini, Frank 201
Serage, Nancy 1924- 10
Seredy, Kate 1899-1975 1
  Obituary 24
  See also CLR 10
Serfozo, Mary 1925- 194
Seroff, Victor I(ilyitch) 1902-1979 12
  Obituary 26
Serra, Sebastia 1966- 202
Serraillier, Ian (Lucien) 1912-1994 73
  Obituary 83
  Earlier sketch in SATA 1
  See also CLR 2
  See also SAAS 3
Serros, Michele 175
Serros, Michele M.
  See Serros, Michele
Servello, Joe 1932- 10
Service, Pamela F. 1945- 64
Service, Robert
  See Service, Robert W.
Service, Robert W. 1874(?)-1958 20
Serwadda, W(illiam) Moses 1931- 27
Serwer-Bernstein, Blanche L(uria)
  1910-1997 10
Sescoe, Vincent E. 1938- 123
Seskin, Steve 1953- 211
Seth, Mary
  See Lexau, Joan M.
Seton, Anya 1904(?)-1990 3
  Obituary 66
Seton, Ernest (Evan) Thompson 1860-1946 . 18
  See also CLR 59
Seton-Thompson, Ernest
  See Seton, Ernest (Evan) Thompson
Seuling, Barbara 1937- 193
  Earlier sketches in SATA 10, 98, 145
  See also SAAS 24
Seuss, Dr.
  See Dr. Seuss
Severn, Bill
  See Severn, William Irving
Severn, David
  See Unwin, David S.
Severn, William Irving 1914- 1
Sewall, Marcia 1935- 119
  Earlier sketches in SATA 37, 69
Seward, Prudence 1926- 16
Sewell, Anna 1820-1878 100
  Earlier sketch in SATA 24
  See also CLR 17
Sewell, Helen (Moore) 1896-1957 38
Sexton, Anne 1928-1974 10
Sexton, Anne Harvey
  See Sexton, Anne
Seymour, Alta Halverson 10
Seymour, Jane 1951- 139
Seymour, Tres 1966- 164
  Earlier sketch in SATA 82
Sfar, Joann 1971- 182
Shachtman, Tom 1942- 49

Shackleton, C.C.
  See Aldiss, Brian W.
Shader, Rachel
  See Sofer, Barbara
Shadow, Jak
  See Sutherland, Jon
Shadyland, Sal
  See Cooper, Louise
Shafer, Audrey 183
Shafer, Robert E(ugene) 1925- 9
Shaffer, Terea 1968- 79
Shahan, Sherry 1949- 134
  Earlier sketch in SATA 92
Shahn, Ben(jamin) 1898-1969
  Obituary 21
Shahn, Bernarda Bryson
  See Bryson, Bernarda
Shaik, Fatima 114
Shalant, Phyllis 1949- 150
Shan, Darren 1972- 199
  Earlier sketches in SATA 129, 168
Shan, D.B.
  See Shan, Darren
Shanahan, Lisa 199
Shanberg, Karen
  See Shragg, Karen (I.)
Shane, Harold Gray 1914-1993 36
  Obituary 76
Shange, Ntozake 1948- 157
Shanks, Ann Zane (Kushner) 10
Shannon, David 1959- 152
  Earlier sketch in SATA 107
  See also CLR 87
Shannon, George 1952- 202
  Earlier sketches in SATA 35, 94, 143
Shannon, George William Bones
  See Shannon, George
Shannon, Jacqueline 63
Shannon, Margaret
  See Silverwood, Margaret Shannon
Shannon, Monica 1905(?)-1965 28
Shannon, Terry
  See Mercer, Jessie
Shannon, Terry Miller 1951- 148
Shapiro, Irwin 1911-1981 32
Shapiro, Jody Fickes 1940- 193
Shapiro, Karen Jo 1964- 186
Shapiro, Michelle 1961- 196
Shapiro, Milton J. 1926- 32
Shapiro, Tricia
  See Andryszewski, Tricia
Shapiro, Zachary 1970- 213
Shapp, Charles M(orris) 1906-1989
  Obituary 61
Shapp, Martha Glauber 1910- 3
Sharenow, Robert 193
Sharfman, Amalie 14
Sharkey, Niamh 213
Sharma, Partap 1939- 15
Sharma, Rashmi
  See Singh, Rashmi Sharma
Sharman, Alison
  See Leonard, Alison
Sharmat, Marjorie Weinman 1928- 133
  Earlier sketches in SATA 4, 33, 74
Sharmat, Mitchell 1927- 127
  Earlier sketch in SATA 33
Sharp, Anne Wallace 1947- 144
Sharp, Luke
  See Alkiviades, Alkis
Sharp, Margery 1905-1991 29
  Obituary 67
  Earlier sketch in SATA 1
  See also CLR 27
Sharp, Zerna A. 1889-1981
  Obituary 27
Sharpe, Jon
  See Duncan, Alice
  and Knott, William C(ecil, Jr.)
  and Messman, Jon
Sharpe, Mitchell R(aymond) 1924- 12

Sharpe, Susan 1946- 71
Sharratt, Nick 1962- 199
  Earlier sketches in SATA 104, 153
Shasha, Mark 1961- 80
Shattuck, Roger 1923-2005 64
  Obituary 174
Shattuck, Roger Whitney
  See Shattuck, Roger
Shaw, Arnold 1909-1989 4
  Obituary 63
Shaw, Carolyn V. 1934- 91
Shaw, Charles (Green) 1892-1974 13
Shaw, Evelyn S. 1927- 28
Shaw, Flora Louisa
  See Lugard, Flora Louisa Shaw
Shaw, Janet 1937- 146
  Earlier sketch in SATA 61
  See also CLR 96
Shaw, Janet Beeler
  See Shaw, Janet
Shaw, Lisa
  See Rogak, Lisa
Shaw, Margret 1940- 68
Shaw, Mary 1965- 180
Shaw, Nancy 1946- 162
  Earlier sketch in SATA 71
Shaw, Ray 7
Shaw, Richard 1923- 12
Shawn, Frank S.
  See Goulart, Ron
Shay, Art
  See Shay, Arthur
Shay, Arthur 1922- 4
Shay, Lacey
  See Shebar, Sharon Sigmond
Shea, Bob 188
Shea, George 1940- 54
  Brief entry 42
Shea, Pegi Deitz 1960- 172
  Earlier sketches in SATA 77, 137
Shearer, Alex 1949- 204
Shearer, John 1947- 43
  Brief entry 27
  See also CLR 34
Shearer, Ted 1919- 43
Shearing, Leonie 1972- 184
Sheban, Chris 182
Shebar, Sharon Sigmond 1945- 36
Shecter, Ben 1935- 16
Shedd, Warner 1934- 147
  Earlier sketch in SATA 87
Sheedy, Alexandra Elizabeth 1962- 39
  Earlier sketch in SATA 19
Sheehan, Ethna 1908-2000 9
Sheehan, Patty 1945- 77
Sheehan, Sean 1951- 154
  Earlier sketch in SATA 86
Sheen, Barbara 1949- 143
Shefelman, Janice 1930- 205
  Earlier sketches in SATA 58, 129
Shefelman, Janice Jordan
  See Shefelman, Janice
Shefelman, Tom 1927- 204
  Earlier sketch in SATA 58
Sheffer, H. R.
  See Abels, Harriette S(heffer)
Sheffield, Charles 1935-2002 109
Sheffield, Janet N. 1926- 26
Sheikh, Nazneen
  See Sadiq, Nazneen
Sheinkin, Steve 1968- 204
Sheinmel, Courtney 1977- 211
Shekerjian, Regina Tor 16
Shelby, Anne 1948- 85
  Autobiography Feature 121
  See also SAAS 26
Sheldon, Ann
  See Antle, Nancy
Sheldon, Ann 67
  Earlier sketch in SATA 1
Sheldon, Aure 1917-1976 12

Sheldon, David 185
Sheldon, Deyan 181
Sheldon, John
  See Bloch, Robert (Albert)
Sheldon, Muriel 1926- 45
  Brief entry 39
Shell, Barry 1951- 176
Shelley, Frances
  See Wees, Frances Shelley
Shelley, John 1959- 202
Shelley, Mary
  See Shelley, Mary Wollstonecraft
Shelley, Mary Wollstonecraft 1797-1851 29
  See also CLR 133
Shelton, William Roy 1919-1995 5
  Obituary 129
Shemie, Bonnie (Jean Brenner) 1949- 96
Shemin, Margaretha (Hoeneveld) 1928- 4
Shen, Michele 1953- 173
Shenker, Michele
  See Shen, Michele
Shenton, Edward 1895-1977 45
Shepard, Aaron 1950- 187
  Earlier sketches in SATA 75, 113
Shepard, Ernest Howard 1879-1976 100
  Obituary 24
  Earlier sketches in SATA 3, 33
  See also CLR 27
Shepard, James R.
  See Shepard, Jim
Shepard, Jim 1956- 164
  Earlier sketch in SATA 90
Shepard, Mary
  See Knox, (Mary) Eleanor Jessie
Shepard, Esther 1891-1975 5
  Obituary 26
Shepherd, Amanda 201
Shepherd, Donna Walsh
  See Walsh Shepherd, Donna
Shepherd, Elizabeth 4
Shepherd, Irana 173
Shepherd, Roni
  See Shepherd, Irana
Sheppard, Kate 195
Shepperson, Rob 178
Sherburne, Zoa (Lillian Morin) 1912-1995 3
  See also SAAS 18
Sherk-Savage, Candace
  See Savage, Candace
Sherlock, Patti 71
Sherman, D(enis) R(onald) 1934- 48
  Brief entry 29
Sherman, Diane (Finn) 1928- 12
Sherman, Elizabeth
  See Friskey, Margaret (Richards)
Sherman, Harold (Morrow) 1898-1987 37
  Obituary 137
Sherman, Josepha 163
  Earlier sketch in SATA 75
Sherman, Michael
  See Lowndes, Robert A(ugustine) W(ard)
Sherman, Nancy
  See Rosenberg, Nancy (Sherman)
Sherman, Pat 174
Sherman, Peter Michael
  See Lowndes, Robert A(ugustine) W(ard)
Sherrard, Valerie (Anne) 1957- 141
Sherrod, Jane
  See Singer, Jane Sherrod
Sherry, Clifford J. 1943- 84
Sherry, (Dulcie) Sylvia 1932- 122
  Earlier sketch in SATA 8
Sherwan, Earl 1917- 3
Sherwood, Jonathan
  See London, Jonathan (Paul)
Sheth, Kashmira 186
Shetterly, Will 1955- 78
  Autobiography Feature 106
Shetterly, William Howard
  See Shetterly, Will
Shiefman, Vicky 1942- 22

Shields, Brenda Desmond (Armstrong) 1914- 37
Shields, Carol Diggory 174
Shields, Charles 1944- 10
Shields, Gillian 203
Shiels, Barbara
   See Adams, Barbara Johnston
Shiffman, Lena 1957- 101
Shiina, Makoto 1944- 83
Shimin, Symeon 1902-1984 13
Shimko, Bonnie 1941- 191
Shine, Andrea 1955- 104
Shine, Deborah 1932- 71
Shinn, Everett 1876-1953 21
Shinn, Sharon 1957- 164
   Earlier sketch in SATA *110*
Shippen, Katherine B(inney) 1892-1980 .... *1*
   Obituary 23
   See also CLR *36*
Shippey, T. A. 1943- 143
Shippey, Thomas Alan
   See Shippey, T. A.
Shipton, Eric Earle 1907-1977 10
Shipton, Jonathan 1948- 215
Shipton, Paul 1963- 196
Shiraz, Yasmin 173
Shirer, William L(awrence) 1904-1993 45
   Obituary 78
Shirley, Debra 203
Shirley, Gayle C 1955- 96
Shirley, Gayle Corbett
   See Shirley, Gayle C
Shirley, Jean 1919- 70
Shirreffs, Gordon D(onald) 1914-1996 11
Shirts, Morris A(lpine) 1922- 63
Shlichta, Joe 1968- 84
Shmurak, Carole B. 1944- 118
Sholokhov, Mikhail 1905-1984
   Obituary 36
Sholokhov, Mikhail Aleksandrovich
   See Sholokhov, Mikhail
Shore, Diane Z. 215
   Earlier sketch in SATA *179*
Shore, Diane ZuHone
   See Shore, Diane Z.
Shore, June Lewis 30
Shore, Nancy 1960- 124
Shore, Robert 1924- 39
Short, Michael 1937- 65
Short, Roger
   See Arkin, Alan
Shortall, Leonard W. 19
Shortt, Tim(othy Donald) 1961- 96
Shotwell, Louisa Rossiter 1902-1993 3
Shoup, Barbara 1947- 156
   Earlier sketch in SATA *86*
   See also SAAS *24*
Shoveller, Herb 184
Showalter, Jean B(reckinridge) 12
Showell, Ellen Harvey 1934- 33
Showers, Paul C. 1910-1999 92
   Obituary 114
   Earlier sketch in SATA *21*
   See also CLR *6*
   See also SAAS *7*
Shpakow, Tanya 1959(?)- 94
Shpitalnik, Vladimir 1964- 83
Shragg, Karen (I.) 1954- 142
Shreeve, Elizabeth 1956- 156
Shreve, Susan
   See Shreve, Susan Richards
Shreve, Susan Richards 1939- 152
   Brief entry 41
   Earlier sketches in SATA *46, 95*
Shriver, Jean Adair 1932- 75
Shriver, Maria 1955- 134
Shriver, Maria Owings
   See Shriver, Maria
Shrode, Mary
   See Hollingsworth, Mary
Shtainmets, Leon 32

Shub, Elizabeth 1915(?)-2004 5
Shuken, Julia 1948- 84
Shulevitz, Uri 1935- 165
   Earlier sketches in SATA *3, 50, 106*
   See also CLR *61*
Shulman, Alix Kates 1932- 7
Shulman, Dee 1957- 146
Shulman, Irving 1913-1995 13
Shulman, Lisa 202
Shulman, Mark 1962- 184
Shulman, Max 1919-1988
   Obituary 59
Shulman, Milton 1913-2004
   Obituary 154
Shulman, Neil B(arnett) 1945- 89
Shumsky, Zena
   See Collier, Zena
Shura, Mary Francis
   See Craig, Mary (Francis) Shura
Shusterman, Neal 1962- 201
   Autobiography Feature 140
   Earlier sketches in SATA *85, 121, 140*
Shuter, Jane (Margaret) 1955- 151
   Earlier sketch in SATA *90*
Shuttlesworth, Dorothy Edwards 3
Shwartz, Susan (Martha) 1949- 94
Shyer, Christopher 1961- 98
Shyer, Marlene Fanta 13
Siberell, Anne 29
Sibley, Don 1922- 12
Siburt, Ruth 1951- 121
Siculan, Daniel 1922- 12
Siddon, Barbara
   See Bradford, Barbara Taylor
Sidgwick, Ethel 1877-1970 116
Sidjakov, Nicolas 1924- 18
Sidman, Joyce 1956- 181
   Earlier sketch in SATA *145*
Sidney, Frank
   See Warwick, Alan R(oss)
Sidney, Margaret
   See Lothrop, Harriet Mulford Stone
Siebert, Diane 1948- 189
Siegal, Aranka 1930- 88
   Brief entry 37
Siegel, Beatrice 36
Siegel, Helen
   See Siegl, Helen
Siegel, Robert 1939- 39
Siegel, Robert Harold
   See Siegel, Robert
Siegel, Siena Cherson 1967(?)- 185
Siegelson, Kim L. 1962- 114
Sieger, Ted 1958- 189
Siegl, Helen 1924- 34
Siepmann, Mary Aline
   See Wesley, Mary (Aline)
Sierra, Judy 1945- 195
   Earlier sketches in SATA *104, 162*
Sieswerda, Paul L. 1942- 147
Sievert, Terri
   See Dougherty, Terri (L.)
Sigsawa, Keiichi 1972- 211
Silas
   See McCay, (Zenas) Winsor
Silcock, Sara Lesley 1947- 12
Silin-Palmer, Pamela 184
Sill, Cathryn 1953- 141
   Earlier sketch in SATA *74*
Sill, John 1947- 140
   Earlier sketch in SATA *74*
Sillitoe, Alan 1928-2010 61
Sills, Leslie (Elka) 1948- 129
Silly, E. S.
   See Kraus, (Herman) Robert
Silsbe, Brenda 1953- 73
Silva, Joseph
   See Goulart, Ron
Silver, Ruth
   See Chew, Ruth

Silverberg, Robert 1935- 91
   Autobiography Feature 104
   Earlier sketch in SATA *13*
   See also CLR *59*
Silverman, Erica 1955- 165
   Earlier sketches in SATA *78, 112*
Silverman, Janis L. 1946- 127
Silverman, Mel(vin Frank) 1931-1966 9
Silverman, Robin L. 1954- 96
Silverman, Robin Landew
   See Silverman, Robin L.
Silverstein, Alvin 1933- 124
   Earlier sketches in SATA *8, 69*
   See also CLR *25*
Silverstein, Herma 1945- 106
Silverstein, Robert Alan 1959- 124
   Earlier sketch in SATA *77*
Silverstein, Shel 1932-1999 92
   Brief entry 27
   Obituary 116
   Earlier sketch in SATA *33*
   See also CLR *96*
Silverstein, Sheldon Allan
   See Silverstein, Shel
Silverstein, Virginia B. 1937- 124
   Earlier sketches in SATA *8, 69*
   See also CLR *25*
Silverstein, Virginia Barbara Opshelor
   See Silverstein, Virginia B.
Silverthorne, Elizabeth 1930- 35
Silverwood, Margaret Shannon 1966- 137
   Earlier sketch in SATA *83*
Silvey, Diane F. 1946- 135
Sim, David 1953- 162
Sim, Dorrith M. 1931- 96
Simak, Clifford D(onald) 1904-1988
   Obituary 56
Simard, Remy 1959- 168
Simmie, Lois (Ann) 1932- 106
Simmonds, Posy 1945- 130
   See also CLR *23*
Simmonds, Rosemary Elizabeth
   See Simmonds, Posy
Simmons, Andra 1939- 141
Simmons, Elly 1955- 134
Simmons, Michael 1970- 185
Simms, Laura 1947- 117
Simner, Janni Lee 113
Simon, Charlie May
   See Fletcher, Charlie May Hogue
Simon, Francesca 1955- 111
Simon, Gabriel 1972- 118
Simon, Hilda Rita 1921- 28
   See also CLR *39*
Simon, Howard 1903-1979 32
   Obituary 21
Simon, Joe
   See Simon, Joseph H.
Simon, Joseph H. 1913- 7
Simon, Martin P(aul William) 1903-1969 12
Simon, Mina Lewiton
   See Lewiton, Mina
Simon, Norma (Feldstein) 1927- 129
   Earlier sketches in SATA *3, 68*
Simon, Seymour 1931- 202
   Earlier sketches in SATA *4, 73, 138*
   See also CLR *63*
Simon, Shirley (Schwartz) 1921- 11
Simon, Solomon 1895-1970 40
Simonetta, Linda 1948- 14
Simonetta, Sam 1936- 14
Simons, Barbara B(rooks) 1934- 41
Simont, Marc 1915- 126
   Earlier sketches in SATA *9, 73*
Simpson, Colin 1908-1983 14
Simpson, Harriette
   See Arnow, Harriette (Louisa) Simpson
Simpson, Jacynth Hope
   See Hope Simpson, Jacynth
Simpson, Lesley 1963- 150
Simpson, Margaret 1943- 128

Simpson, Myrtle L(illias) 1931- *14*
Sims, Blanche *168*
    Earlier sketch in SATA *75*
Sims, Blanche L.
    See Sims, Blanche
Simundsson, Elva 1950- *63*
Sinclair, Clover
    See Gater, Dilys
Sinclair, Emil
    See Hesse, Hermann
Sinclair, Jeff 1958- *77*
Sinclair, Olga 1923- *121*
Sinclair, Rose
    See Smith, Susan Vernon
Sinclair, Upton 1878-1968 .... *9*
Sinclair, Upton Beall
    See Sinclair, Upton
Singer, A.L.
    See Lerangis, Peter
Singer, Arthur 1917-1990 .... *64*
Singer, Isaac
    See Singer, Isaac Bashevis
Singer, Isaac Bashevis 1904-1991 .... *27*
    Obituary *68*
    Earlier sketch in SATA *3*
    See also CLR *1*
Singer, Jane Sherrod 1917-1985 .... *4*
    Obituary *42*
Singer, Julia 1917- *28*
Singer, Kurt D. 1911-2005 .... *38*
    Obituary *172*
Singer, Marilyn 1948- *201*
    Autobiography Feature *158*
    Brief entry *38*
    Earlier sketches in SATA *48, 80, 125, 158*
    See also CLR *48*
    See also SAAS *13*
Singer, Muff 1942-2005 .... *104*
    Obituary *160*
Singer, Nicky 1956- *194*
Singer, Susan (Mahler) 1941- *9*
Singh, Rashmi Sharma 1952- *90*
Singleton, Linda Joy 1957- *166*
    Earlier sketch in SATA *88*
Singleton, L.J.
    See Singleton, Linda Joy
Singleton, Sarah 1966- *214*
Sinykin, Sheri
    See Sinykin, Sheri Cooper
Sinykin, Sheri Cooper 1950- *142*
    Autobiography Feature *142*
    Earlier sketches in SATA *72, 133*
Sinykin, Sheril Terri Cooper
    See Sinykin, Sheri Cooper
Sipiera, Paul P., (Jr.) 1948- *144*
    Earlier sketch in SATA *89*
Siracusa, Catherine (Jane) 1947- *82*
Sirett, Dawn (Karen) 1966- *88*
Sirimarco, Elizabeth 1966- *158*
Sirof, Harriet 1930- *94*
    Earlier sketch in SATA *37*
Sirois, Allen L. 1950- *76*
Sirvaitis (Chernyaev), Karen (Ann) 1961- ... *79*
Sis, Peter 1949- *192*
    Earlier sketch in SATA *149*
    See also CLR *110*
Sisson, Rosemary Anne 1923- *11*
Sister Mary Terese
    See Donze, Mary Terese
Sita, Lisa 1962- *87*
Sitarski, Anita 1958- *200*
Sitomer, Alan Lawrence *174*
Sitomer, Harry 1903-1985 .... *31*
Sitomer, Mindel 1903-1987 .... *31*
Sittenfeld, Curtis 1975(?)- *164*
Sive, Helen R(obinson) 1951- *30*
Sivulich, Sandra (Jeanne) Stroner 1941- *9*
Siy, Alexandra *193*
Skarmeta, Antonio 1940- *57*
Skeers, Linda 1958- *207*
Skelly, James R(ichard) 1927- *17*

Skelton, Matthew 1971- *185*
Skinner, Constance Lindsay 1877-1939
    See YABC *1*
Skinner, Cornelia Otis 1901-1979 .... *2*
Skipper, G. C. 1939- *46*
    Brief entry *38*
Sklansky, Amy E. 1971- *204*
Sklansky, Amy E(dgar) 1971- *145*
Skofield, James *95*
    Brief entry *44*
Skold, Betty Westrom 1923- *41*
Skorpen, Liesel Moak 1935- *3*
Skott, Maria
    See Nikolajeva, Maria
Skrypuch, Marsha Forchuk 1954- *134*
Skultety, Nancy Laney 1960- *175*
Skurzynski, Gloria 1930- *145*
    Autobiography Feature *145*
    Earlier sketches in SATA *8, 74, 122*
    See also SAAS *9*
Skurzynski, Gloria Joan
    See Skurzynski, Gloria
Skutch, Robert 1925- *89*
Skye, Maggie
    See Werner, Herma
Skye, Obert *200*
    Earlier sketch in SATA *170*
Slack, Michael 1969- *189*
Slackman, Charles B. 1934- *12*
Slade, Arthur G. 1967- *149*
    Earlier sketch in SATA *106*
Slade, Arthur Gregory
    See Slade, Arthur G.
Slade, Christian 1974- *193*
Slade, Richard 1910-1971 .... *9*
Slangerup, Erik Jon 1969- *130*
Slate, Joseph 1928- *174*
    Earlier sketches in SATA *38, 122*
Slate, Joseph Frank
    See Slate, Joseph
Slater, Dashka 1963- *179*
Slater, David Michael 1970- *212*
Slater, Ray
    See Lansdale, Joe R.
Slaughter, Hope 1940- *84*
Slaughter, Jean
    See Doty, Jean Slaughter
Slaughter, Tom 1955- *152*
Slavicek, Louise Chipley 1956- *144*
Slavin, Bill 1959- *199*
    Earlier sketches in SATA *76, 148*
Slaymaker, Melissa Eskridge 1958- *158*
Sleator, William 1945- *208*
    Earlier sketches in SATA *3, 68, 118, 161*
    See also CLR *128*
Sleator, William Warner III
    See Sleator, William
Slegers, Liesbet 1975- *154*
Sleigh, Barbara 1906-1982 .... *86*
    Obituary *30*
    Earlier sketch in SATA *3*
Slepian, Jan 1921- *85*
    Brief entry *45*
    Earlier sketch in SATA *51*
    See also SAAS *8*
Slepian, Janice B.
    See Slepian, Jan
Slicer, Margaret O. 1920- *4*
Slier, Debby
    See Shine, Deborah
Sloan, Brian 1966- *172*
Sloan, Carolyn 1937- *116*
    Earlier sketch in SATA *58*
Sloan, Glenna 1930- *120*
Sloan, Glenna Davis
    See Sloan, Glenna
Sloane, Eric 1910(?)-1985 .... *52*
    Obituary *42*
Sloane, Todd 1955- *88*
Sloat, Teri 1948- *164*
    Earlier sketches in SATA *70, 106*

Slobodkin, Florence Gersh 1905-1994 .... *5*
    Obituary *107*
Slobodkin, Louis 1903-1975 .... *26*
    Earlier sketch in SATA *8*
Slobodkina, Esphyr 1908-2002 .... *1*
    Obituary *135*
    See also SAAS *8*
Sloggett, Nellie 1851-1923 .... *44*
Slonim, David 1966- *207*
Sloss, Lesley Lord 1965- *72*
Slote, Alfred 1926- *72*
    Earlier sketch in SATA *8*
    See also CLR *4*
    See also SAAS *21*
Slote, Elizabeth 1956- *80*
Small, Charlie
    See Ward, Nick
Small, David 1945- *183*
    Brief entry *46*
    Earlier sketches in SATA *50, 95, 126*
    See also CLR *53*
Small, Ernest
    See Lent, Blair
Small, Mary 1932- *165*
Small, Terry 1942- *75*
Smallcomb, Pam 1954- *159*
Smallman, Steve *197*
Smalls, Irene
    See Smalls-Hector, Irene
Smalls-Hector, Irene 1950- *146*
    Earlier sketch in SATA *73*
    See also CLR *103*
Smallwood, Norah (Evelyn) 1910(?)-1984
    Obituary *41*
Smaridge, Norah (Antoinette) 1903-1994 ...... *6*
Smath, Jerry 1933- *198*
Smee, Nicola 1948- *167*
    Earlier sketch in SATA *76*
Smiley, Virginia Kester 1923- *2*
Smit, Noelle 1972- *199*
Smith, Alexander McCall 1948- *179*
    Earlier sketch in SATA *73*
Smith, Andrew 1959- *209*
Smith, Andrew Anselmo
    See Smith, Andrew
Smith, Andy J. 1975- *207*
Smith, Anne Warren 1938- *41*
    Brief entry *34*
Smith, Barry (Edward Jervis) 1943- *75*
Smith, Beatrice S(chillinger) *12*
Smith, Betsy Covington 1937- *55*
    Earlier sketch in SATA *43*
Smith, Betty (Wehner) 1904-1972 .... *6*
Smith, Bradford 1909-1964 .... *5*
Smith, Brenda 1946- *82*
Smith, C. Pritchard
    See Hoyt, Edwin P(almer), Jr.
Smith, Caesar
    See Trevor, Elleston
Smith, Cat Bowman 1939- *201*
Smith, Charles R., Jr. 1969- *203*
    Earlier sketch in SATA *159*
Smith, Craig 1955- *172*
    Earlier sketches in SATA *81, 117*
Smith, Cynthia Leitich 1967- *215*
    Earlier sketch in SATA *152*
Smith, Datus C(lifford), Jr. 1907-1999 .... *13*
    Obituary *116*
Smith, Debra 1955- *89*
Smith, Derek 1943- *141*
Smith, Dick King
    See King-Smith, Dick
Smith, Dodie
    See Smith, Dorothy Gladys
Smith, Doris Buchanan 1934-2002 .... *75*
    Obituary *140*
    Earlier sketch in SATA *28*
    See also SAAS *10*
Smith, Dorothy Gladys 1896-1990 .... *82*
    Obituary *65*
Smith, Dorothy Stafford 1905- *6*

Smith, Duane 1974- *202*
Smith, E(lmer) Boyd 1860-1943
  See YABC *1*
Smith, E(dric) Brooks 1917- *40*
Smith, Elwood H. 1941- *203*
Smith, Emily Wing 1980- *215*
Smith, Emma 1923- *52*
  Brief entry *36*
Smith, (Katherine) Eunice (Young)
  1902-1993 .... *5*
Smith, Frances C(hristine) 1904-1986 .... *3*
Smith, Gary R. 1932- *14*
Smith, Geof 1969- *102*
Smith, George Harmon 1920- *5*
Smith, Gordon 1951- *184*
Smith, Greg Leitich *152*
Smith, H(arry) Allen 1907-1976
  Obituary *20*
Smith, Helene 1937- *142*
Smith, Hope Anita *202*
Smith, Howard E(verett), Jr. 1927- *12*
Smith, Hugh L(etcher) 1921-1968 .... *5*
Smith, Imogene Henderson 1922- *12*
Smith, Jacqueline B. 1937- *39*
Smith, Jada Pinkett 1971- *161*
Smith, James D. 1955- *176*
Smith, James Noel 1950- *193*
Smith, Janet (Buchanan) Adam
  See Adam Smith, Janet (Buchanan)
Smith, Janice Lee 1949- *155*
  Earlier sketch in SATA *54*
Smith, Jean
  See Smith, Frances C(hristine)
Smith, Jean Pajot 1945- *10*
Smith, Jeff 1958- *161*
  Earlier sketch in SATA *93*
Smith, Jeff Allen
  See Smith, Jeff
Smith, Jenny 1963- *90*
Smith, Jessie
  See Kunhardt, Edith
Smith, Jessie Willcox 1863-1935 .... *21*
  See also CLR *59*
Smith, Joan (Mary) 1933- *54*
  Brief entry *46*
Smith, Johnston
  See Crane, Stephen
Smith, Jos A. 1936- *181*
  Earlier sketches in SATA *73, 120*
Smith, Joseph Arthur
  See Smith, Jos A.
Smith, Judie R. 1936- *80*
Smith, Kirsten 1970- *210*
Smith, Lafayette
  See Higdon, Hal
Smith, Lane 1959- *179*
  Earlier sketches in SATA *76, 131*
  See also CLR *47*
Smith, Lee
  See Albion, Lee Smith
Smith, Lendon H(oward) 1921- *64*
Smith, Lillian H(elena) 1887-1983
  Obituary *32*
Smith, Linda 1949- *177*
Smith, Linell Nash 1932- *2*
Smith, Lucia B. 1943- *30*
Smith, Maggie 1965- *190*
Smith, Margaret Emily Noel Nuttall
  See Nuttall-Smith, Margaret Emily Noel
Smith, Marion Hagens 1913- *12*
Smith, Marion Jaques 1899-1987 .... *13*
Smith, Mary Ellen *10*
Smith, Marya 1945- *78*
Smith, Mike
  See Smith, Mary Ellen
Smith, Nancy Covert 1935- *12*
Smith, Norman F. 1920- *70*
  Earlier sketch in SATA *5*
Smith, Patricia Clark 1943- *96*
Smith, Pauline C.
  See Arthur, Robert, (Jr.)

Smith, Pauline C(oggeshall) 1908-1994 .... *27*
Smith, Philip Warren 1936- *46*
Smith, R. Alexander McCall
  See Smith, Alexander McCall
Smith, Rebecca 1946- *123*
Smith, Robert Kimmel 1930- *77*
  Earlier sketch in SATA *12*
Smith, Robert Paul 1915-1977 .... *52*
  Obituary *30*
Smith, Roland 1951- *193*
  Earlier sketches in SATA *115, 161*
Smith, Rosamond
  See Oates, Joyce Carol
Smith, Ruth Leslie 1902- *2*
Smith, Samantha 1972-1985
  Obituary *45*
Smith, Sandra Lee 1945- *75*
Smith, Sarah Stafford
  See Smith, Dorothy Stafford
Smith, Sharon 1947- *82*
Smith, Sherri L. 1971- *156*
Smith, Sherwood 1951- *206*
  Autobiography Feature *206*
  Earlier sketches in SATA *82, 140*
Smith, Shirley Raines
  See Raines, Shirley C(arol)
Smith, Susan Carlton 1923- *12*
Smith, Susan Mathias 1950- *43*
  Brief entry *35*
Smith, Susan Vernon 1950- *48*
  Brief entry *45*
Smith, Tim(othy R.) 1945- *151*
Smith, Ursula 1934- *54*
Smith, Vian (Crocker) 1920-1969 .... *11*
Smith, Wanda VanHoy 1926- *65*
Smith, Ward
  See Goldsmith, Howard
Smith, William A. 1918- *10*
Smith, William Jay 1918- *154*
  Autobiography Feature *154*
  Earlier sketches in SATA *2, 68*
  See also SAAS *22*
Smith, Winsome 1935- *45*
Smith, Z.Z.
  See Westheimer, David
Smith-Ankrom, M. E. 1942- *130*
Smith-Griswold, Wendy 1955- *88*
Smith-Rex, Susan J. 1950- *94*
Smithsen, Richard
  See Pellowski, Michael (Joseph)
Smits, Teo
  See Smits, Theodore R(ichard)
Smits, Theodore R(ichard) 1905-1996 .... *45*
  Brief entry *28*
Smolinski, Dick 1932- *86*
Smothers, Ethel Footman 1944- *149*
  Earlier sketch in SATA *76*
Smucker, Anna Egan 1948- *209*
Smucker, Barbara 1915-2003 .... *130*
  Earlier sketches in SATA *29, 76*
  See also CLR *10*
  See also SAAS *11*
Smucker, Barbara Claassen
  See Smucker, Barbara
Smyth, Iain 1959- *105*
Snedeker, Caroline Dale (Parke) 1871-1956
  See YABC *2*
Sneed, Brad *191*
Sneider, Marian 1932-2005 .... *197*
Snell, Nigel (Edward Creagh) 1936- *57*
  Brief entry *40*
Snellgrove, L(aurence) E(rnest) 1928- *53*
Snelling, Dennis (Wayne) 1958- *84*
Sneve, Virginia Driving Hawk 1933- *95*
  Earlier sketch in SATA *8*
  See also CLR *2*
Snicket, Lemony 1970- *215*
  Earlier sketches in SATA *126, 187*
  See also CLR *79*
Sniegoski, Thomas E. *195*

Sniegoski, Tom
  See Sniegoski, Thomas E.
Snodgrass, Mary Ellen 1944- *75*
Snodgrass, Quentin Curtius
  See Twain, Mark
Snodgrass, Thomas Jefferson
  See Twain, Mark
Snook, Barbara (Lillian) 1913-1976 .... *34*
Snow, Alan 1959- *190*
Snow, Carol 1965- *208*
Snow, Donald Clifford 1917-1979 .... *16*
Snow, Dorothea J(ohnston) 1909- *9*
Snow, Richard F(olger) 1947- *52*
  Brief entry *37*
Snyder, Anne 1922-2001 .... *4*
  Obituary *125*
Snyder, Bernadette McCarver 1930- *97*
Snyder, Carol 1941- *35*
Snyder, Gerald S(eymour) 1933- *48*
  Brief entry *34*
Snyder, Jerome 1916-1976
  Obituary *20*
Snyder, Laurel 1974- *209*
Snyder, Midori 1954- *106*
Snyder, Paul A. 1946- *125*
Snyder, Zilpha Keatley 1927- *163*
  Autobiography Feature *163*
  Earlier sketches in SATA *1, 28, 75, 110*
  See also CLR *121*
  See also SAAS *2*
Snyderman, Reuven K. 1922- *5*
So, Meilo *162*
Sobel, June 1950- *149*
Soble, Jennie
  See Cavin, Ruth (Brodie)
Sobol, Donald J. 1924- *132*
  Earlier sketches in SATA *1, 31, 73*
  See also CLR *4*
Sobol, Harriet Langsam 1936- *47*
  Brief entry *34*
Sobol, Richard *211*
Sobol, Rose 1931- *76*
Sobott-Mogwe, Gaele 1956- *97*
Soderlind, Arthur E(dwin) 1920- *14*
Soentpiet, Chris K. 1970- *159*
  Earlier sketch in SATA *97*
Soerensen, Svend Otto 1916- *67*
Sofer, Barbara 1949- *109*
Sofer, Rachel
  See Sofer, Barbara
Softly, Barbara Frewin 1924- *12*
Sogabe, Aki *207*
Soglow, Otto 1900-1975
  Obituary *30*
Sohl, Frederic J(ohn) 1916- *10*
Sohr, Daniel 1973- *190*
Sokol, Bill
  See Sokol, William
Sokol, William 1923- *37*
Sokolov, Kirill 1930- *34*
Solbert, Romaine G. 1925- *2*
Solbert, Ronni
  See Solbert, Romaine G.
Solheim, James *133*
Solomon, Heather M. *188*
Solomon, Joan 1930- *51*
  Brief entry *40*
Solomons, Ikey Esquir
  See Thackeray, William Makepeace
Solonevich, George 1915-2003 .... *15*
Solot, Mary Lynn 1939- *12*
Soman, David 1965- *200*
Somerlott, Robert 1928-2001 .... *62*
Somers, Kevin *205*
Somervill, Barbara A(nn) 1948- *140*
Sommer, Angela
  See Sommer-Bodenburg, Angela
Sommer, Carl 1930- *175*
  Earlier sketch in SATA *126*
Sommer, Elyse 1929- *7*
Sommer, Robert 1929- *12*

Sommer-Bodenburg, Angela 1948- *113*
  Earlier sketch in SATA *63*
Sommerdorf, Norma 1926- *131*
Sommerdorf, Norma Jean
  See Sommerdorf, Norma
Sommerfelt, Aimee 1892-1975 .... *5*
Son, John *160*
Sones, Sonya *131*
Sonneborn, Ruth (Cantor) 1899-1974 .... *4*
  Obituary *27*
Sonnenblick, Jordan 1969- *185*
  See also CLR *144*
Sonnenmark, Laura A. 1958- *73*
Soo, Kean *201*
Sopko, Eugen 1949- *58*
Sorel, Edward 1929- *126*
  Brief entry *37*
  Earlier sketch in SATA *65*
Sorensen, Henri 1950- *115*
  Earlier sketch in SATA *77*
Sorensen, Svend Otto
  See Soerensen, Svend Otto
Sorensen, Virginia 1912-1991 .... *2*
  Obituary *72*
  See also SAAS *15*
Sorenson, Jane 1926- *63*
Sorenson, Margo 1946- *96*
Sorley Walker, Kathrine *41*
Sorra, Kristin *185*
Sorrells, Walter *177*
Sorrentino, Joseph N. 1937- *6*
Sortor, June Elizabeth 1939- *12*
Sortor, Toni
  See Sortor, June Elizabeth
Sosa, Hernan 1977- *203*
Soskin, V. H.
  See Ellison, Virginia H(owell)
Soto, Gary 1952- *174*
  Earlier sketches in SATA *80, 120*
  See also CLR *38*
Sotomayor, Antonio 1902-1985 .... *11*
Souci, Robert D. San
  See San Souci, Robert D.
Soudley, Henry
  See Wood, James Playsted
Souhami, Jessica *176*
Soule, Gardner (Bosworth) 1913-2000 .... *14*
Soule, Jean Conder 1919- *10*
Souster, (Holmes) Raymond 1921- *63*
South, Sheri Cobb 1959- *82*
Southall, Ivan 1921-2008 .... *134*
  Autobiography Feature *134*
  Earlier sketches in SATA *3, 68*
  See also CLR *2*
  See also SAAS *3*
Southall, Ivan Francis
  See Southall, Ivan
Southey, Robert 1774-1843 .... *54*
Southgate, Vera *54*
Souza, Janet
  See Tashjian, Janet
Sovak, Jan 1953- *115*
Sowden, Celeste
  See Walters, Celeste
Sowter, Nita *69*
Spafford, Suzy 1945- *160*
Spagnoli, Cathy 1950- *134*
  Earlier sketch in SATA *79*
Spain, Sahara Sunday 1991- *133*
Spain, Susan Rosson *185*
Spalding, Andrea 1944- *150*
  Earlier sketch in SATA *101*
Spalenka, Greg 1958- *198*
Spanfeller, James J. 1930- *19*
  See also SAAS *8*
Spanfeller, Jim
  See Spanfeller, James J.
Spangenberg, Judith Dunn 1942- *5*
Spangler, Brie *212*
Spanyol, Jessica 1965- *206*
  Earlier sketch in SATA *137*

Spar, Jerome 1918- *10*
Sparks, Barbara 1942- *78*
Sparks, Beatrice (Mathews) 1918- *44*
  Brief entry *28*
  See also CLR *139*
Sparks, Mary W. 1920- *15*
Spaulding, Douglas
  See Bradbury, Ray
Spaulding, Leonard
  See Bradbury, Ray
Spaulding, Norma *107*
Speare, Elizabeth George 1908-1994 .... *62*
  Obituary *83*
  Earlier sketch in SATA *5*
  See also CLR *8*
Spearing, Judith (Mary Harlow) 1922- *9*
Spears, Rick *182*
Speck, Katie *196*
Speck, Nancy 1959- *104*
Specking, Inez 1890-1960(?) *11*
Speed, Nell
  See Keats, Emma
  and Sampson, Emma (Keats) Speed
Speed, Nell (Ewing) 1878-1913 .... *68*
Speer, Bonnie Stahlman 1929- *113*
Speer-Lyon, Tammie L. 1965- *89*
Speicher, Helen Ross S(mith) 1915- *8*
Speir, Nancy 1958- *210*
  Earlier sketch in SATA *81*
Spellman, John W(illard) 1934- *14*
Spellman, Roger G.
  See Cox, William R(obert)
Spelman, Cornelia Maude 1946- *144*
  Earlier sketch in SATA *96*
Spelman, Mary 1934- *28*
Spelvin, George
  See Lerangis, Peter
  and Phillips, David Atlee
Spence, Cynthia
  See Eble, Diane
Spence, Eleanor (Rachel) 1928- *21*
  See also CLR *26*
Spence, Geraldine 1931- *47*
Spencer, Ann 1918- *10*
Spencer, Britt *206*
Spencer, Cornelia
  See Yaukey, Grace S(ydenstricker)
Spencer, Donald D(ean) 1931- *41*
Spencer, Elizabeth 1921- *14*
Spencer, Leonard G.
  See Garrett, Randall
  and Silverberg, Robert
Spencer, William 1922- *9*
Spencer, Zane A(nn) 1935- *35*
Sper, Emily 1957- *142*
Speregen, Devra Newberger 1964- *84*
Sperling, Dan(iel Lee) 1949- *65*
Sperry, Armstrong W. 1897-1976 .... *1*
  Obituary *27*
Sperry, Raymond
  See Garis, Howard R.
Sperry, Raymond, Jr. *1*
Spetter, Jung-Hee 1969- *134*
Spicer, Dorothy Gladys -1975 .... *32*
Spiegel, Beth *184*
Spiegelman, Art 1948- *158*
  Earlier sketch in SATA *109*
Spiegelman, Judith M. *5*
Spielberg, Steven 1947- *32*
Spier, Peter (Edward) 1927- *54*
  Earlier sketch in SATA *4*
  See also CLR *5*
Spilhaus, Athelstan (Frederick) 1911-1998 .. *13*
  Obituary *102*
Spilka, Arnold 1917- *6*
Spillane, Frank Morrison
  See Spillane, Mickey
Spillane, Mickey 1918-2006 .... *66*
  Obituary *176*
Spinelli, Eileen 1942- *186*
  Earlier sketches in SATA *38, 101, 150*

Spinelli, Jerry 1941- *195*
  Earlier sketches in SATA *39, 71, 110, 158*
  See also CLR *82*
Spink, Reginald (William) 1905-1994 .... *11*
Spinka, Penina Keen 1945- *72*
Spinner, Stephanie 1943- *132*
  Earlier sketches in SATA *38, 91*
Spinossimus
  See White, William, Jr.
Spiotta-DiMare, Loren *173*
Spires, Ashley 1978- *183*
Spires, Elizabeth 1952- *215*
  Earlier sketches in SATA *71, 111*
Spiridellis, Gregg 1971(?)- *199*
Spirin, Gennadii
  See Spirin, Gennady
Spirin, Gennadij
  See Spirin, Gennady
Spirin, Gennady 1948- *204*
  Earlier sketches in SATA *95, 134*
  See also CLR *88*
Spiro, Ruth *208*
Spivak, Dawnine *101*
Spizman, Robyn Freedman *194*
Spohn, David 1948- *72*
Spohn, Kate 1962- *147*
  Earlier sketch in SATA *87*
Spollen, Christopher 1952- *12*
Spooner, Michael (Tim) 1954- *92*
Spowart, Robin 1947- *177*
  Earlier sketch in SATA *82*
Spradlin, Michael P. *204*
Sprague, Gretchen 1926-2003 .... *27*
Spranger, Nina 1969- *203*
Sprengel, Artie
  See Lerangis, Peter
Sprigge, Elizabeth (Miriam Squire)
  1900-1974 .... *10*
Spring, (Robert) Howard 1889-1965 .... *28*
Springer, Margaret 1941- *78*
Springer, Marilyn Harris 1931- *47*
Springer, Nancy 1948- *172*
  Earlier sketches in SATA *65, 110*
Springstubb, Tricia 1950- *78*
  Brief entry *40*
  Earlier sketch in SATA *46*
Spudvilas, Anne 1951- *199*
  Earlier sketch in SATA *94*
Spurll, Barbara 1952- *78*
Spurr, Elizabeth *172*
Spykman, E(lizabeth) C(hoate) 1896-1965 .. *10*
  See also CLR *35*
Spyri, Johanna (Heusser) 1827-1901 .... *100*
  Earlier sketch in SATA *19*
  See also CLR *115*
Squires, Janet *215*
Squires, Phil
  See Barker, S. Omar
Srba, Lynne *98*
Sreenivasan, Jyotsna 1964- *101*
S-Ringi, Kjell
  See Ringi, Kjell (Arne Soerensen)
Staake, Bob 1957- *209*
Stacey, Cherylyn 1945- *96*
Stacy, Donald
  See Pohl, Frederik
Stadler, John *204*
Stadtler, Bea 1921- *17*
Stafford, Jean 1915-1979
  Obituary *22*
Stafford, Liliana 1950- *141*
Stafford, Paul 1966- *116*
Stahl, Ben(jamin) 1910-1987 .... *5*
  Obituary *54*
Stahl, Hilda 1938-1993 .... *48*
  Obituary *77*
Stahler, David, Jr. *162*
Staines, Bill 1949- *213*
Stainton, Sue *187*
Stair, Gobin (John) 1912- *35*
Stalder, Valerie *27*

Stamaty, Mark Alan 1947- *12*
Stambler, Irwin 1924- *5*
Stampler, Ann Redisch *209*
Standiford, Natalie 1961- *169*
  Earlier sketch in SATA *81*
Stanek, Lou Willett 1931- *63*
Stang, Judit 1921-1977 .... *29*
Stang, Judy
  See Stang, Judit
Stangl, (Mary) Jean 1928- *67*
Stanhope, Eric
  See Hamilton, Charles (Harold St. John)
Stankevich, Boris 1928- *2*
Stanley, Diane 1943- *213*
  Brief entry *32*
  Earlier sketches in SATA *37, 80, 115, 164*
  See also CLR *46*
  See also SAAS *15*
Stanley, Elizabeth 1947- *206*
Stanley, George Edward 1942- *67*
  Earlier sketches in SATA *53, 111, 157, 1*
Stanley, Jerry 1941- *127*
  Earlier sketch in SATA *79*
Stanley, Mandy *165*
Stanley, Robert
  See Hamilton, Charles (Harold St. John)
Stanley, Sanna 1962- *145*
Stanli, Sue
  See Meilach, Dona Z(weigoron)
Stanstead, John
  See Groom, Arthur William
Stanton, Karen 1960- *190*
Stanton, Schuyler
  See Baum, L. Frank
Staples, Suzanne Fisher 1945- *207*
  Earlier sketches in SATA *70, 105, 151*
  See also CLR *137*
Stapleton, Marjorie (Winifred) 1932- *28*
Stapp, Arthur D(onald) 1906-1972 .... *4*
Starbird, Kaye 1916- *6*
  See also CLR *60*
Stark, Evan 1942- *78*
Stark, James
  See Goldston, Robert (Conroy)
Stark, Ken 1943- *199*
Stark, Ulf 1944- *124*
Starke, Ruth (Elaine) 1946- *129*
Starkey, Marion L(ena) 1901-1991 .... *13*
Starr, Ward
  See Manes, Stephen
Starret, William
  See McClintock, Marshall
Starr Taylor, Bridget 1959- *99*
Stasiak, Krystyna *49*
Staub, Frank 1949- *116*
Staub, Frank Jacob
  See Staub, Frank
Staub, Wendy Corsi 1964- *114*
Stauffacher, Sue 1961- *199*
  Earlier sketch in SATA *155*
Stauffer, Don
  See Berkebile, Fred D(onovan)
Staunton, Schuyler
  See Baum, L. Frank
Staunton, Ted 1956- *167*
  Earlier sketch in SATA *112*
Stead, Judy *210*
Stead, Rebecca 1968(?)- *188*
Steadman, Ralph 1936- *123*
  Earlier sketch in SATA *32*
Steadman, Ralph Idris
  See Steadman, Ralph
Stearman, Kaye 1951- *118*
Stearns, Monroe (Mather) 1913-1987 .... *5*
  Obituary *55*
Steckler, Arthur 1921-1985 .... *65*
Steding, Laurie 1953- *119*
Steel, Danielle 1947- *66*
Steel, Danielle Fernande
  See Steel, Danielle

Steele, Addison II
  See Lupoff, Richard A(llen)
Steele, Alexander 1958- *116*
Steele, Henry Maxwell
  See Steele, Max
Steele, Mary 1930- *94*
Steele, Mary Q(uintard Govan) 1922-1992 .. *51*
  Obituary *72*
  Earlier sketch in SATA *3*
Steele, Max 1922-2005 .... *168*
  Earlier sketch in SATA *10*
Steele, Philip 1948- *140*
  Earlier sketch in SATA *81*
Steele, William O(wen) 1917-1979 .... *51*
  Obituary *27*
  Earlier sketch in SATA *1*
Steelhammer, Ilona 1952- *98*
Steelsmith, Shari 1962- *72*
Stefanik, Alfred T. 1939- *55*
Steffanson, Con
  See Cassiday, Bruce (Bingham)
  and Goulart, Ron
Steffens, Bradley 1955- *166*
  Earlier sketch in SATA *77*
Steffensmeier, Alexander 1977- *195*
Stegeman, Janet Allais 1923- *49*
  Brief entry *49*
Steggall, Susan 1967- *182*
Steig, William 1907-2003 .... *111*
  Obituary *149*
  Earlier sketches in SATA *18, 70*
  See also CLR *103*
Steig, William H.
  See Steig, William
Stein, David Ezra *211*
  Earlier sketch in SATA *180*
Stein, M(eyer) L(ewis) 1920- *6*
Stein, Mathilde 1969- *195*
Stein, Mini *2*
Stein, R(ichard) Conrad 1937- *154*
  Earlier sketches in SATA *31, 82*
Stein, Wendy 1951- *77*
Steinbeck, John 1902-1968 .... *9*
Steinbeck, John Ernst
  See Steinbeck, John
Steinberg, Alfred 1917-1995 .... *9*
Steinberg, David 1962- *200*
Steinberg, D.J.
  See Steinberg, David
Steinberg, Fannie 1899-1990 .... *43*
Steinberg, Fred J. 1933- *4*
Steinberg, Phillip Orso 1921- *34*
Steinberg, Rafael (Mark) 1927- *45*
Steinberg, Saul 1914-1999 .... *67*
Steincrohn, Maggie
  See Davis, Maggie S.
Steiner, Barbara A(nnette) 1934- *83*
  Earlier sketch in SATA *13*
  See also SAAS *13*
Steiner, Charlotte 1900-1981 .... *45*
Steiner, George 1929- *62*
Steiner, Joan *199*
  Earlier sketch in SATA *110*
Steiner, Jorg
  See Steiner, Jorg
Steiner, Jorg 1930- *35*
Steiner, K. Leslie
  See Delany, Samuel R., Jr.
Steiner, Stan(ley) 1925-1987 .... *14*
  Obituary *50*
Steins, Richard 1942- *79*
Stem, Jacqueline 1931- *110*
Stemple, Heidi E.Y. 1966- *214*
Stemple, Jason *179*
Steneman, Shep 1945- *132*
Stengel, Joyce A. 1938- *158*
Stephanie, Gordon
  See Gordon, Stephanie Jacob
Stephens, Alice Barber 1858-1932 .... *66*
Stephens, Casey
  See Wagner, Sharon B.

Stephens, Henrietta Henkle 1909-1993 .... *6*
Stephens, J.B.
  See Lynn, Tracy
Stephens, Mary Jo 1935- *8*
Stephens, Rebecca 1961- *141*
Stephens, Reed
  See Donaldson, Stephen R.
Stephens, Suzanne
  See Kirby, Susan E.
Stephens, William M(cLain) 1925- *21*
Stephensen, A. M.
  See Manes, Stephen
Stephenson, Lynda 1941- *179*
Stephenson, Lynda A.
  See Stephenson, Lynda
Stepp, Ann 1935- *29*
Stepto, Michele 1946- *61*
Steptoe, Javaka 1971- *213*
  Earlier sketch in SATA *151*
Steptoe, John (Lewis) 1950-1989 .... *63*
  Earlier sketch in SATA *8*
  See also CLR *12*
Sterling, Brett
  See Bradbury, Ray
  and Hamilton, Edmond
  and Samachson, Joseph
Sterling, Dorothy 1913-2008 .... *83*
  Autobiography Feature *127*
  Obituary *200*
  Earlier sketch in SATA *1*
  See also CLR *1*
  See also SAAS *2*
Sterling, Helen
  See Watts, Helen L. Hoke
Sterling, Philip 1907-1989 .... *8*
  Obituary *63*
Sterling, Shirley (Anne) 1948- *101*
Stern, Ellen Norman 1927- *26*
Stern, Judith M. 1951- *75*
Stern, Madeleine
  See Stern, Madeleine B.
Stern, Madeleine B. 1912-2007 .... *14*
Stern, Madeleine Bettina
  See Stern, Madeleine B.
Stern, Maggie 1953- *156*
Stern, Philip Van Doren 1900-1984 .... *13*
  Obituary *39*
Stern, Simon 1943- *15*
Sterne, Emma Gelders 1894- *6*
Steurt, Marjorie Rankin 1888-1978 .... *10*
Stevens, April 1963- *208*
Stevens, Bryna 1924- *65*
Stevens, Carla M(cBride) 1928- *13*
Stevens, Chambers 1968- *128*
Stevens, Diane 1939- *94*
Stevens, Franklin 1933- *6*
Stevens, Greg
  See Cook, Glen
Stevens, Gwendolyn 1944- *33*
Stevens, Helen *209*
Stevens, Jan Romero 1953- *95*
Stevens, Janet 1953- *193*
  Earlier sketches in SATA *90, 148*
Stevens, Kathleen 1936- *49*
Stevens, Leonard A. 1920- *67*
Stevens, Lucile Vernon 1899-1994 .... *59*
Stevens, Margaret Dean
  See Aldrich, Bess Streeter
Stevens, Patricia Bunning 1931- *27*
Stevens, Peter
  See Geis, Darlene Stern
Stevens, Serita 1949- *70*
Stevens, Serita Deborah
  See Stevens, Serita
Stevens, Serita Mendelson
  See Stevens, Serita
Stevens, Shira
  See Stevens, Serita
Stevenson, Anna (M.) 1905- *12*
Stevenson, Augusta 1869(?)-1976 .... *2*
  Obituary *26*

Stevenson, Burton Egbert 1872-1962 .... *25*
Stevenson, Drew 1947- *60*
Stevenson, Emma *207*
Stevenson, Harvey 1960- *148*
  Earlier sketch in SATA *80*
Stevenson, James 1929- *195*
  Brief entry *34*
  Earlier sketches in SATA *42, 71, 113, 161*
  See also CLR *17*
Stevenson, Janet 1913- *8*
Stevenson, Robert Louis 1850-1894 .... *100*
  See also YABC *2*
  See also CLR *107*
Stevenson, Robert Louis Balfour
  See Stevenson, Robert Louis
Stevenson, Sucie
  See Stevenson, Sucie
Stevenson, Sucie 1956- *194*
  Earlier sketch in SATA *104*
Stewart, A(gnes) C(harlotte) *15*
Stewart, Amber *181*
Stewart, Chantal 1945- *173*
  Earlier sketch in SATA *121*
Stewart, Charles
  See Zurhorst, Charles (Stewart, Jr.)
Stewart, Eleanor
  See Porter, Eleanor H(odgman)
Stewart, Elisabeth J(ane) 1927- *93*
Stewart, Elizabeth Laing 1907- *6*
Stewart, Gail B. 1949- *141*
Stewart, George Rippey 1895-1980 .... *3*
  Obituary *23*
Stewart, Jennifer J. 1960- *128*
Stewart, Jennifer Jenkins
  See Stewart, Jennifer J.
Stewart, Joel *211*
  Earlier sketch in SATA *151*
Stewart, John 1920- *14*
Stewart, Mary (Florence Elinor) 1916- *12*
Stewart, Mary Rainbow
  See Stewart, Mary (Florence Elinor)
Stewart, Melissa 1968- *209*
  Earlier sketches in SATA *111, 167*
Stewart, Paul 1955- *199*
  Earlier sketches in SATA *114, 163*
Stewart, Robert Neil 1891-1972 .... *7*
Stewart, Sarah *143*
Stewart, Scott
  See Zaffo, George J.
Stewart, W(alter) P. 1924- *53*
Stewart, Whitney 1959- *167*
  Earlier sketch in SATA *92*
Stewig, John Warren 1937- *162*
  Earlier sketches in SATA *26, 110*
Stickler, Soma Han 1942- *128*
Stidworthy, John 1943- *63*
Stiegemeyer, Julie *180*
Stier, Catherine *198*
Stiles, Martha Bennett *108*
  Earlier sketch in SATA *6*
Still, James 1906-2001 .... *29*
  Obituary *127*
Stille, Darlene R. 1942- *170*
  Earlier sketch in SATA *126*
Stille, Darlene Ruth
  See Stille, Darlene R.
Stillerman, Marci *104*
Stillerman, Robbie 1947- *12*
Stilley, Frank 1918- *29*
Stilton, Geronimo *158*
Stimpson, Gerald
  See Mitchell, Adrian
Stimson, James 1964- *213*
Stine, Catherine *165*
Stine, G(eorge) Harry 1928-1997 .... *136*
  Earlier sketch in SATA *10*
Stine, Jovial Bob
  See Stine, R.L.
Stine, R.L. 1943- *194*
  Earlier sketches in SATA *31, 76, 129*
  See also CLR *111*

Stine, Robert Lawrence
  See Stine, R.L.
Stinetorf, Louise (Allender) 1900-1992 .... *10*
Stinson, Kathy 1952- *98*
Stirling, Arthur
  See Sinclair, Upton
Stirling, Ian 1941- *77*
Stirling, Nora B(romley) 1900-1997 .... *3*
Stirnweis, Shannon 1931- *10*
Stobbs, William 1914-2000 .... *17*
  Obituary *120*
Stock, Carolmarie 1951- *75*
Stock, Catherine 1952- *214*
  Earlier sketches in SATA *65, 114, 158*
Stockdale, Susan 1954- *206*
  Earlier sketch in SATA *98*
Stockham, Peter (Alan) 1928- *57*
Stockton, Francis Richard 1834-1902 .... *44*
  Brief entry *32*
Stockton, Frank R.
  See Stockton, Francis Richard
Stockwell-Moniz, Marc J. 1954- *164*
Stoddard, Edward G. 1923- *10*
Stoddard, Hope 1900-1987 .... *6*
Stoddard, Sandol 1927- *98*
  Earlier sketch in SATA *14*
Stoehr, Shelley 1969- *107*
Stoeke, Janet Morgan 1957- *202*
  Earlier sketches in SATA *90, 136*
Stohner, Anu 1952- *179*
Stoiko, Michael 1919- *14*
Stojic, Manya 1967- *156*
Stoker, Abraham
  See Stoker, Bram
Stoker, Bram 1847-1912 .... *29*
Stokes, Cedric
  See Beardmore, George
Stokes, Jack (Tilden) 1923- *13*
Stokes, Olivia Pearl 1916- *32*
Stolarz, Laurie Faria *203*
Stolz, Mary 1920-2006 .... *133*
  Obituary *180*
  Earlier sketches in SATA *10, 71*
  See also SAAS *3*
Stolz, Mary Slattery
  See Stolz, Mary
Stone, Alan
  See Svenson, Andrew E(dward)
Stone, David K(arl) 1922- *9*
Stone, David Lee 1978- *166*
Stone, Eugenia 1879-1971 .... *7*
Stone, Gene
  See Stone, Eugenia
Stone, Helen V(irginia) *6*
Stone, Idella Purnell
  See Purnell, Idella
Stone, Ikey
  See Purnell, Idella
Stone, Irving 1903-1989 .... *3*
  Obituary *64*
Stone, Jeff *178*
Stone, Jon 1931-1997 .... *39*
  Obituary *95*
Stone, Josephine Rector
  See Dixon, Jeanne
Stone, Kyle M. 1972- *202*
Stone, Lesley
  See Trevor, Elleston
Stone, Peter 1930-2003 .... *65*
  Obituary *143*
Stone, Phoebe *205*
  Earlier sketch in SATA *134*
Stone, Raymond *1*
Stone, Rosetta
  See Dr. Seuss
Stone, Tanya Lee 1965- *182*
Stonehouse, Bernard 1926- *140*
  Earlier sketches in SATA *13, 80*
Stones, (Cyril) Anthony 1934- *72*
Stong, Phil(ip Duffield) 1899-1957 .... *32*

Stoops, Erik D(aniel) 1966- *142*
  Earlier sketch in SATA *78*
Stoppelmoore, Cheryl Jean
  See Ladd, Cheryl (Jean)
Stops, Sue 1936- *86*
Storace, Patricia *193*
Storad, Conrad J. 1957- *119*
Storey, Margaret 1926- *9*
Storey, Victoria Carolyn 1945- *16*
Stork, Francisco
  See Stork, Francisco X.
Stork, Francisco X. 1953- *210*
Storme, Peter
  See Stern, Philip Van Doren
Storr, Catherine (Cole) 1913-2001 .... *87*
  Obituary *122*
  Earlier sketch in SATA *9*
Story, Josephine
  See Loring, Emilie (Baker)
Stotko, Mary-Ann 1960- *154*
Stott, Dorothy (M.) 1958- *99*
  Earlier sketch in SATA *67*
Stott, Dot
  See Stott, Dorothy (M.)
Stotter, Mike 1957- *108*
Stout, William 1949- *132*
Stoutenburg, Adrien (Pearl) 1916-1982 .... *3*
Stoutland, Allison 1963- *130*
Stover, Allan C(arl) 1938- *14*
Stover, Jill (Griffin) 1958- *82*
Stover, Marjorie Filley 1914- *9*
Stowe, Harriet Beecher 1811-1896
  See YABC *1*
  See also CLR *131*
Stowe, Harriet Elizabeth Beecher
  See Stowe, Harriet Beecher
Stowe, Leland 1899-1994 .... *60*
  Obituary *78*
Stowe, Rosetta
  See Ogan, George F.
  and Ogan, Margaret E. (Nettles)
Stower, Adam *195*
Strachan, Bruce 1959- *205*
Strachan, Ian 1938- *85*
Strachan, Linda *167*
Strachan, Margaret Pitcairn 1908-1998 .... *14*
Strahinich, H. C.
  See Strahinich, Helen C.
Strahinich, Helen C. 1949- *78*
Strait, Treva Adams 1909-2002 .... *35*
Strand, Mark 1934- *41*
Strange, Philippa
  See Coury, Louise Andree
Stranger, Joyce
  See Wilson, Joyce M.
Strangis, Joel 1948- *124*
Strannigan, Shawn 1956- *93*
Strannigan, Shawn Alyne
  See Strannigan, Shawn
Strasser, Todd 1950- *215*
  Earlier sketches in SATA *41, 45, 71, 107, 153*
  See also CLR *11*
Stratemeyer, Edward L. 1862-1930 .... *100*
  Earlier sketches in SATA *1, 67*
  See Adams, Harrison
Stratford, Philip 1927- *47*
Stratton, Allan 1951- *178*
Stratton, J. M.
  See Whitlock, Ralph
Stratton, Thomas
  See Coulson, Robert S(tratton)
  and DeWeese, Thomas Eugene
Stratton-Porter, Gene 1863-1924 .... *15*
  See also CLR *87*
Strauss, Gwen 1963- *77*
Strauss, Joyce 1936- *53*
Strauss, Linda Leopold 1942- *127*
Strauss, Susan (Elizabeth) 1954- *75*
Strayer, E. Ward
  See Stratemeyer, Edward L.
Streano, Vince(nt Catello) 1945- *20*

Streatfeild, Mary Noel
See Streatfeild, Noel
Streatfeild, Noel 1897(?)-1986 20
Obituary 48
See also CLR 83
Street, Janet Travell 1959- 84
Street, Julia Montgomery 1898-1993 11
Streissguth, Thomas 1958- 116
Strelkoff, Tatiana 1957- 89
Stren, Patti 1949- 88
Brief entry 41
See also CLR 5
Strete, Craig Kee 1950- 96
Earlier sketch in SATA 44
Stretton, Barbara (Humphrey) 1936- 43
Brief entry 35
Strickland, Brad 1947- 200
Earlier sketches in SATA 83, 137, 142
Strickland, Craig (A.) 1956- 102
Strickland, Dorothy S(alley) 1933- 89
Strickland, Michael R. 1965- 144
Earlier sketch in SATA 83
Strickland, Shadra 209
Strickland, Tessa 173
Strickland, William Bradley
See Strickland, Brad
Striegel, Jana 1955- 140
Striegel-Wilson, Jana
See Striegel, Jana
Striker, Lee
See Clark, Margaret (D.)
Striker, Susan 1942- 63
Stringer, Lauren 1957- 183
Earlier sketch in SATA 129
Stroeyer, Poul 1923- 13
Stromoski, Rick 1958- 111
Strong, Charles
See Epstein, Beryl
and Epstein, Samuel
Strong, David
See McGuire, Leslie (Sarah)
Strong, Jeremy 1949- 175
Earlier sketches in SATA 36, 105
Strong, J.J.
See Strong, Jeremy
Strong, Pat
See Hough, Richard (Alexander)
Strong, Stacie 1965- 74
Stroud, Bettye 1939- 165
Earlier sketch in SATA 96
Stroud, Jonathan 1970- 213
Earlier sketches in SATA 102, 159
See also CLR 134
Stroyer, Poul
See Stroeyer, Poul
Strug, Kerri 1977- 108
Stryer, Andrea Stenn 1938- 192
Stryker, Daniel
See Morris, Chris(topher Crosby)
and Stump, Jane Barr
Stuart, David
See Hoyt, Edwin P(almer), Jr.
Stuart, Derek
See Foster, John L(ouis)
Stuart, Forbes 1924- 13
Stuart, Ian
See MacLean, Alistair
Stuart, Jesse (Hilton) 1906-1984 2
Obituary 36
Stuart, Ruth McEnery 1849(?)-1917 116
Stuart, Sheila
See Baker, Mary Gladys Steel
Stuart-Clark, Christopher (Anthony) 1940- .. 32
Stubis, Talivaldis 1926- 5
Stubley, Trevor (Hugh) 1932- 22
Stuchner, Joan Betty 209
Stucky, Naomi R. 1922- 72
Stuceley, Elizabeth
See Northmore, Elizabeth Florence
Stultifer, Morton
See Curtis, Richard

Sture-Vasa, Mary
See Alsop, Mary O'Hara
Sturges, Philemon 174
Sturtevant, Katherine 1950- 180
Earlier sketch in SATA 130
Sturton, Hugh
See Johnston, H(ugh) A(nthony) S(tephen)
Sturtzel, Howard A(llison) 1894-1985 1
Sturtzel, Jane Levington 1903-1996 1
Stutley, D(oris) J(ean) 1959- 142
Stutson, Caroline 1940- 104
Stuve-Bodeen, Stephanie
See Bodeen, S. A.
Stux, Erica 1929- 140
Styles, (Frank) Showell 1908- 10
Stynes, Barbara White 133
Suarez, Maribel 1952- 201
Suba, Susanne 4
Suber, Melissa 213
Subond, Valerie
See Grayland, Valerie (Merle Spanner)
Sudbery, Rodie 1943- 42
Sudyka, Diana 208
Sue, Majella Lue 209
Suen, Anastasia 1956(?)- 157
Sufrin, Mark 1925- 76
Sugarman, Joan G. 1917- 64
Sugarman, Tracy 1921- 37
Sugita, Yutaka 1930- 36
Suhl, Yuri (Menachem) 1908-1986 8
Obituary 50
See also CLR 2
See also SAAS 1
Suhr, Joanne 129
Suid, Murray 1942- 27
Sullivan, Edward T. 206
Sullivan, George (Edward) 1927- 147
Earlier sketches in SATA 4, 89
Sullivan, Jacqueline Levering 203
Sullivan, Jody
See Rake, Jody
Sullivan, Kathryn A. 1954- 141
Sullivan, Mary Ann 1954- 63
Sullivan, Mary W(ilson) 1907- 13
Sullivan, Pat
See Messmer, Otto
Sullivan, Paul 1939- 106
Sullivan, Sarah G. 1953- 179
Sullivan, Silky 1940- 101
Sullivan, Sue
See Sullivan, Susan E.
Sullivan, Susan E. 1962- 123
Sullivan, Thomas Joseph, Jr. 1947- 16
Sullivan, Tom
See Sullivan, Thomas Joseph, Jr.
Sully, Tom 1959- 104
Sumichrast, Jozef 1948- 29
Sumiko
See Davies, Sumiko
Summerforest, Ivy B.
See Kirkup, James
Summers, Barbara 1944- 182
Summers, Cassia Joy
See Cowley, Joy
Summers, James L(evingston) 1910-1973 57
Brief entry 28
Summertree, Katonah
See Windsor, Patricia
Summy, Barrie 208
Sun, Chyng Feng 1959- 90
Sunderlin, Sylvia (S.) 1911-1997 28
Obituary 99
Sung, Betty Lee 26
Supeene, Shelagh Lynne 1952- 153
Supplee, Suzanne 204
Supraner, Robyn 1930- 101
Earlier sketch in SATA 20
Supree, Burt(on) 1941-1992 73
Surface, Mary Hall 1958- 126
Surge, Frank 1931- 13
Susac, Andrew 1929- 5

Susi, Geraldine Lee 1942- 98
Sussman, Cornelia Silver 1914-1999 59
Sussman, Irving 1908-1996 59
Sussman, Susan 1942- 48
Sutcliff, Rosemary 1920-1992 78
Obituary 73
Earlier sketches in SATA 6, 44
See also CLR 138
Sutcliffe, Jane 1957- 138
Sutherland, Colleen 1944- 79
Sutherland, Efua (Theodora Morgue)
1924-1996 25
Sutherland, Jon 1958- 167
Sutherland, Jonathan D.
See Sutherland, Jon
Sutherland, Jonathan David
See Sutherland, Jon
Sutherland, Margaret 1941- 15
Sutherland, Zena Bailey 1915-2002 37
Obituary 137
Suttles, Shirley (Smith) 1922- 21
Sutton, Ann (Livesay) 1923- 31
Sutton, Eve(lyn Mary) 1906-1992 26
Sutton, Felix 1910(?)-1973 31
Sutton, Jane 1950- 52
Brief entry 43
Sutton, Larry M(atthew) 1931- 29
Sutton, Margaret Beebe 1903-2001 1
Obituary 131
Sutton, Myron Daniel 1925- 31
Sutton, Roger 1956- 93
Sutton, Sally 1973- 214
Suzanne, Jamie
See Hawes, Louise
and Lantz, Francess L(in)
and Singleton, Linda Joy
and Zach, Cheryl (Byrd)
Suzuki, David 1936- 138
Suzuki, David Takayoshi
See Suzuki, David
Svendsen, Mark 1962- 181
Earlier sketch in SATA 120
Svendsen, Mark Nestor
See Svendsen, Mark
Svenson, Andrew E(dward) 1910-1975 2
Obituary 26
Swaab, Neil 1978- 191
Swaim, Jessica 1950- 202
Swain, Carol 1962- 172
Swain, Gwenyth 1961- 134
Earlier sketch in SATA 84
Swain, Ruth
See Swain, Ruth Freeman
Swain, Ruth Freeman 1951- 161
Earlier sketch in SATA 119
Swain, Su Zan (Noguchi) 1916- 21
Swallow, Pamela Curtis 178
Swamp, Jake 1941- 98
Swan, Susan 1944- 108
Earlier sketch in SATA 22
Swann, Brian (Stanley Frank) 1940- 116
Swann, E.L.
See Lasky, Kathryn
Swann, Ruth Rice 1920- 84
Swanson, Diane 1944- 203
Swanson, Helen M(cKendry) 1919- 94
Swanson, June 1931- 76
Swanson, Susan Marie 209
Swanson, Wayne 1942- 167
Swarner, Kristina 1965- 215
Swarthout, Glendon (Fred) 1918-1992 26
Swarthout, Kathryn 1919- 7
Swayne, Sam(uel F.) 1907- 53
Swayne, Zoa (Lourana) 1905- 53
Sweat, Lynn 1934- 168
Earlier sketch in SATA 57
Swede, George 1940- 67
Sweeney, James B(artholomew) 1910-1999 . 21
Sweeney, Joyce 1955- 167
Earlier sketches in SATA 65, 68, 108

Sweeney, Joyce Kay
  See Sweeney, Joyce
Sweeney, Karen O'Connor
  See O'Connor, Karen
Sweeney, Matthew (Gerard) 1952- 156
Sweet, Melissa 1956- 211
  Earlier sketch in SATA 172
Sweet, Sarah C.
  See Jewett, Sarah Orne
Sweetland, Nancy A(nn) 1934- 48
Swenson, Allan A(rmstrong) 1933- 21
Swenson, May 1919-1989 15
Swentzell, Rina 1939- 79
Swiatkowska, Gabi 1971(?)- 180
Swift, Bryan
  See Knott, William C(ecil, Jr.)
Swift, David
  See Kaufmann, John
Swift, Hildegarde Hoyt 1890(?)-1977
  Obituary 20
Swift, Jonathan 1667-1745 19
  See also CLR 53
Swift, Merlin
  See Leeming, Joseph
Swiger, Elinor Porter 1927- 8
Swinburne, Laurence (Joseph) 1924- 9
Swinburne, Stephen R. 1952- 188
  Earlier sketch in SATA 150
Swinburne, Steve
  See Swinburne, Stephen R.
Swindells, Robert (Edward) 1939- 150
  Brief entry 34
  Earlier sketches in SATA 50, 80
  See also SAAS 14
Swinford, Betty (June Wells) 1927- 58
Swinford, Bob
  See Swinford, Betty (June Wells)
Swithen, John
  See King, Stephen
Switzer, Ellen 1923- 48
Swope, Sam 156
Swope, Samuel
  See Swope, Sam
Sybesma, Jetske
  See Ironside, Jetske
Sydney, Frank
  See Warwick, Alan R(oss)
Sydor, Colleen 1960- 207
Sykes, Julie 1963- 202
Sylvada, Peter 1964- 202
Sylvester, Natalie G(abry) 1922- 22
Syme, (Neville) Ronald 1913-1992 87
  Earlier sketch in SATA 2
Symes, R. F. 77
Symes, Ruth Louise 1962- 179
Symons, (Dorothy) Geraldine 1909- 33
Symons, Stuart
  See Stanley, George Edward
Symynkywicz, Jeffrey B. 1954- 87
Symynkywicz, Jeffrey Bruce
  See Symynkywicz, Jeffrey B.
Synge, (Phyllis) Ursula 1930- 9
Sypher, Lucy Johnston 1907- 7
Szasz, Suzanne (Shorr) 1915-1997 13
  Obituary 99
Szekeres, Cyndy 1933- 157
  Autobiography Feature 157
  Earlier sketches in SATA 5, 60, 131
  See also SAAS 13
Szekessy, Tanja 98
Szpura, Beata 1961- 93
Szudek, Agnes S(usan) P(hilomena) 57
  Brief entry 49
Szulc, Tad 1926-2001 26
Szydlow, Jarl
  See Szydlowski, Mary Vigliante
Szydlowski, Mary Vigliante 1946- 94
Szymanski, Lois 1957- 91

T

Taback, Simms 1932- 170
  Brief entry 36
  Earlier sketches in SATA 40, 104
  See also CLR 100
Taber, Gladys (Bagg) 1899-1980
  Obituary 22
Tabor, Nancy Maria Grande 1949- 161
  Earlier sketch in SATA 89
Tabrah, Ruth Milander 1921- 14
Tacang, Brian 213
Tackach, James 1953- 123
Tackach, James M.
  See Tackach, James
Tadgell, Nicole 1969- 177
Tafuri, Nancy 1946- 192
  Autobiography Feature 192
  Earlier sketches in SATA 39, 75, 130
  See also CLR 74
  See also SAAS 14
Tagg, Christine Elizabeth 1962- 138
Tagliaferro, Linda 173
Taha, Karen T(erry) 1942- 156
  Earlier sketch in SATA 71
Tai, Sharon O. 1963- 153
Tait, Douglas 1944- 12
Takabayashi, Mari 1960- 156
  Earlier sketch in SATA 115
Takahashi, Hideko 209
Takahashi, Rumiko 1957- 163
Takakjian, Portia 1930- 15
Takashima, Misako
  See Misako Rocks!
Takashima, Shizuye 1928- 13
Takayama, Sandi 1962- 106
Takeda, Pete(r M.) 1964- 148
Tal, Eve 1947- 176
Talbert, Marc (Alan) 1953- 154
  Autobiography Feature 154
  Earlier sketches in SATA 68, 99
Talbot, Charlene Joy 1928- 10
Talbot, Toby 1928- 14
Talbott, Hudson 1949- 212
  Earlier sketches in SATA 84, 131
Taliaferro, Dorothy L.
  See Martin, Del
Talifero, Gerald 1950- 75
Talker, T.
  See Rands, William Brighty
Tallarico, Tony 1933- 116
Tallcott, Emogene 10
Tallec, Olivier 1970- 197
Tallis, Robyn
  See Smith, Sherwood
Tallon, Robert 1939- 43
  Brief entry 28
Talmadge, Marian 14
Tamaki, Jillian 1980- 201
Tamar, Erika 1934- 150
  Earlier sketches in SATA 62, 101
Tamarin, Alfred H. 1913-1980 13
Tamburine, Jean 1930- 12
Tames, Richard (Lawrence) 1946- 102
  Earlier sketch in SATA 67
Tamminga, Frederick W(illiam) 1934- 66
Tammuz, Benjamin 1919-1989
  Obituary 63
Tan, Amy 1952- 75
Tan, Amy Ruth
  See Tan, Amy
Tan, Shaun 1974- 198
Tanaka, Beatrice 1932- 76
Tanaka, Shelley 214
  Earlier sketch in SATA 136
Tanaka, Yoko 1947- 215
Tang, Charles 1948- 81
Tang, Greg 172
Tang, You-Shan 1946- 53
Tania B.
  See Blixen, Karen

Tankard, Jeremy 1973- 191
Tannen, Mary 1943- 37
Tannenbaum, Beulah Goldstein 1916- 3
Tannenbaum, D(onald) Leb 1948- 42
Tanner, Jane 1946- 74
Tanner, Louise S(tickney) 1922-2000 9
Tanobe, Miyuki 1937- 23
Tanselle, Eve 1933- 125
Tapio, Pat Decker
  See Kines, Pat Decker
Tapp, Kathy Kennedy 1949- 88
  Brief entry 50
Tarbescu, Edith 1939- 107
Tarkington, (Newton) Booth 1869-1946 17
Tarpley, Natasha A(nastasia) 1971- 147
Tarr, Judith 1955- 149
  Earlier sketch in SATA 64
Tarry, Ellen 1906- 16
  See also CLR 26
  See also SAAS 16
Tarshis, Jerome 1936- 9
Tarshis, Lauren 187
Tarsky, Sue 1946- 41
Taschek, Karen 1956- 185
Tashjian, Janet 1956- 151
  Earlier sketch in SATA 102
Tashjian, Virginia A. 1921-2008 3
Tasker, James 1908- 9
Tate, Don(ald E.) 159
Tate, Eleanora E. 1948- 191
  Earlier sketches in SATA 38, 94
  See also CLR 37
Tate, Eleanora Elaine
  See Tate, Eleanora E.
Tate, Ellalice
  See Hibbert, Eleanor Alice Burford
Tate, Joan 1922- 86
  Earlier sketch in SATA 9
  See also SAAS 20
Tate, Mary Anne
  See Hale, Arlene
Tate, Nikki 134
Tate, Richard
  See Masters, Anthony (Richard)
Tate, Suzanne 1930- 91
Tatham, Betty 142
Tatham, Campbell
  See Elting, Mary
Tatham, Julie
  See Tatham, Julie Campbell
Tatham, Julie Campbell 1908-1999 80
Tavares, Matt 198
  Earlier sketch in SATA 159
Tavares, Victor 1971- 176
Taves, Isabella 1915- 27
Tayleur, Karen 1961- 213
Taylor, Alastair 1959- 130
Taylor, Andrew 1951- 70
Taylor, Andrew John Robert
  See Taylor, Andrew
Taylor, Ann 1782-1866 41
  Brief entry 35
Taylor, Audilee Boyd 1931- 59
Taylor, Barbara J. 1927- 10
Taylor, Ben
  See Strachan, Ian
Taylor, Brooke 205
Taylor, Carl 1937-2010 14
Taylor, Cheryl Munro 1957- 96
Taylor, Cora (Lorraine) 1936- 103
  Earlier sketch in SATA 64
  See also CLR 63
Taylor, Dave 1948- 78
Taylor, David
  See Taylor, Dave
Taylor, David 1900-1965 10
Taylor, Debbie A. 1955- 169
Taylor, Eleanor 1969- 206
Taylor, Elizabeth 1912-1975 13
Taylor, Florance Walton 9

Taylor, Florence M(arian Tompkins)
  1892-1983 9
Taylor, Gage 1942-2000 87
Taylor, Geoff 1946- 204
Taylor, G.P. 1958(?)- 156
Taylor, Graham Peter
  See Taylor, G.P.
Taylor, Herb(ert Norman, Jr.) 1942-1987 22
  Obituary 54
Taylor, J. David
  See Taylor, Dave
Taylor, Jane 1783-1824 41
  Brief entry 35
Taylor, Jerry D(uncan) 1938- 47
Taylor, John Robert
  See Taylor, Andrew
Taylor, Judy
  See Hough, Judy Taylor
Taylor, Kenneth N. 1917-2005 26
Taylor, Kenneth Nathaniel
  See Taylor, Kenneth N.
Taylor, Kim 180
Taylor, L(ester) B(arbour), Jr. 1932- 27
Taylor, Lois Dwight Cole
  See Cole, Lois Dwight
Taylor, Louise Todd 1939- 47
Taylor, Margaret 1950- 106
Taylor, Mark 1927- 32
  Brief entry 28
Taylor, Mildred D. 1943- 135
  See also CLR 144
  See also SAAS 5
Taylor, Mildred Delois
  See Taylor, Mildred D.
Taylor, Paula (Wright) 1942- 48
  Brief entry 33
Taylor, Peter Lane 210
Taylor, Robert Lewis 1912-1998 10
Taylor, Sean 1965- 192
Taylor, Sydney (Brenner) 1904(?)-1978 28
  Obituary 26
  Earlier sketch in SATA 1
Taylor, Theodore 1921-2006 128
  Obituary 177
  Earlier sketches in SATA 5, 54, 83
  See also CLR 30
  See also SAAS 4
Taylor, William 1938- 164
  Earlier sketches in SATA 78, 113
  See also CLR 63
Tazewell, Charles 1900-1972 74
Tchana, Katrin
  See Tchana, Katrin Hyman
Tchana, Katrin H.
  See Tchana, Katrin Hyman
Tchana, Katrin Hyman 1963- 177
  Earlier sketch in SATA 125
Tchekhov, Anton
  See Chekhov, Anton
Tchen, Richard 120
Tchudi, Stephen N. 1942- 55
Teague, Bob
  See Teague, Robert
Teague, Mark 1963- 205
  Earlier sketches in SATA 68, 99, 170
Teague, Mark Christopher
  See Teague, Mark
Teague, Robert 1929- 32
  Brief entry 31
Teal, Val 1902-1997 10
  Obituary 114
Teal, Valentine M.
  See Teal, Val
Teale, Edwin Way 1899-1980 7
  Obituary 25
Teasdale, Sara 1884-1933 32
Tebbel, John (William) 1912-2004 26
Teckentrup, Britta 1969- 200
Tedesco, P.R.
  See Naylor, Phyllis Reynolds

Teensma, Lynne Bertrand
  See Bertrand, Lynne
Tee-Van, Helen Damrosch 1893-1976 10
  Obituary 27
Tegner, Bruce 1928- 62
Teitelbaum, Michael 1953- 116
  Earlier sketch in SATA 59
Tejima
  See Tejima, Keizaburo
Tejima, Keizaburo 1931- 139
  See also CLR 20
Telander, Todd (G.) 1967- 88
Teleki, Geza 1943- 45
Telemaque, Eleanor Wong 1934- 43
Telescope, Tom
  See Newbery, John
Tellis, Annabel 1967- 191
Temkin, Sara Anne Schlossberg 1913-1996 . 26
Temko, Florence 13
Tempest, Margaret Mary 1892-1982
  Obituary 33
Templar, Maurice
  See Groom, Arthur William
Temple, Arthur
  See Northcott, (William) Cecil
Temple, Charles 1947- 79
Temple, Frances (Nolting) 1945-1995 85
Temple, Herbert 1919- 45
Temple, Paul
  See McConnell, James Douglas Rutherford
Temple, William F(rederick) 1914-1989 107
Tenggren, Gustaf 1896-1970 18
  Obituary 26
Tennant, Kylie
  See Rodd, Kylie Tennant
Tennant, Veronica 1947- 36
Tenneshaw, S.M.
  See Beaumont, Charles
  and Garrett, Randall
  and Silverberg, Robert
Tenniel, John 1820-1914 74
  Brief entry 27
  See also CLR 146
Tepper, Sheri S. 1929- 113
Terada, Alice M. 1928- 90
Terban, Marvin 1940- 54
  Brief entry 45
Teresi, Judith M.
  See Goldberger, Judith M.
ter Haar, Jaap 1922- 6
  See also CLR 15
Terhune, Albert Payson 1872-1942 15
Terkel, Susan N(eiburg) 1948- 103
  Earlier sketch in SATA 59
Terlouw, Jan (Cornelis) 1931- 30
Terrell, John Upton 1900-1988
  Obituary 60
Terrill, Beth 198
Terrill, Elizabeth
  See Terrill, Beth
Terris, Susan 1937- 77
  Earlier sketch in SATA 3
Terry, Luther L(eonidas) 1911-1985 11
  Obituary 42
Terry, Margaret
  See Dunnahoo, Terry Janson
Terry, Walter 1913-1982 14
Terry, Will 1966- 205
Terzian, James P. 1915- 14
Tessendorf, K(enneth) C(harles) 1925-2003 . 75
  Obituary 142
Tessler, Manya 200
Tessler, Stephanie Gordon
  See Gordon, Stephanie Jacob
Testa, Dom 208
Tester, Sylvia Root 1939- 64
  Brief entry 37
Tether, (Cynthia) Graham 1950- 46
  Brief entry 36
Tetzner, Lisa 1894-1963 169
Thach, James Otis 1969- 195

Thacher, Mary McGrath 1933- 9
Thackeray, William Makepeace 1811-1863 .. 23
Thaler, Michael C.
  See Thaler, Mike
Thaler, Mike 1936- 215
  Brief entry 47
  Earlier sketches in SATA 56, 93
Thaler, Shmuel 1958- 126
  Earlier sketch in SATA 72
Thamer, Katie 1955- 42
Thane, Elswyth 1900-1984(?) 32
Tharp, Louise (Marshall) Hall 1898-1992 3
  Obituary 129
Tharp, Tim 1957- 189
Thayer, Ernest Lawrence 1863-1940 60
Thayer, Jane
  See Woolley, Catherine
Thayer, Marjorie 1908-1992 74
  Brief entry 37
Thayer, Peter
  See Wyler, Rose
Thelwell, Norman 1923-2004 14
Themerson, Stefan 1910-1988 65
Thermes, Jennifer 1966- 155
Theroux, Paul 1941- 109
  Earlier sketch in SATA 44
Theroux, Paul Edward
  See Theroux, Paul
Thesman, Jean 124
  Earlier sketch in SATA 74
The Tjong-Khing
  See Khing, T.T.
Thieda, Shirley Ann 1943- 13
Thiele, Colin 1920-2006 125
  Earlier sketches in SATA 14, 72
  See also CLR 27
  See also SAAS 2
Thiele, Colin Milton
  See Thiele, Colin
Thiesing, Lisa 1958- 159
  Earlier sketch in SATA 95
Thimmesh, Catherine 189
Thiry, Joan (Marie) 1926- 45
Thistlethwaite, Miles 1945- 12
Thollander, Earl 1922- 22
Thomas, Abigail 1941- 112
Thomas, Andrea
  See Hill, Margaret (Ohler)
Thomas, Art(hur Lawrence) 1952- 48
  Brief entry 38
Thomas, Carroll
  See Ratliff, Thomas M.
  and Shmurak, Carole B.
Thomas, Dylan 1914-1953 60
Thomas, Dylan Marlais
  See Thomas, Dylan
Thomas, Egbert S.
  See Ellis, Edward S.
Thomas, Estelle Webb 1899-1982 26
Thomas, Frances 1943- 171
  Earlier sketch in SATA 92
Thomas, Garen 213
Thomas, H. C.
  See Keating, Lawrence A.
Thomas, Ianthe 1951- 139
  Brief entry 42
  See also CLR 8
Thomas, J. F.
  See Fleming, Thomas
Thomas, Jan 1958- 197
Thomas, Jane Resh 1936- 171
  Earlier sketches in SATA 38, 90
Thomas, Jerry D. 1959- 91
Thomas, Joan Gale
  See Robinson, Joan (Mary) G(ale Thomas)
Thomas, Joyce Carol 1938- 210
  Autobiography Feature 137
  Earlier sketches in SATA 40, 78, 123, 137
  See also CLR 19
  See also SAAS 7

Thomas, Lee
  See Floren, Lee
  and Pendleton, Thomas
Thomas, Lowell Jackson, Jr. 1923- *15*
Thomas, Margaret
  See Thomas, Peggy
Thomas, Meredith 1963- *119*
Thomas, Michael
  See Wilks, Michael Thomas
Thomas, Middy 1931- *191*
Thomas, Patricia 1934- *199*
  Earlier sketch in SATA *51*
Thomas, Peggy *174*
Thomas, Rob 1965- *97*
Thomas, Scott 1959- *147*
Thomas, Velma Maia 1955- *171*
Thomas, Vernon (Arthur) 1934- *56*
Thomas, Victoria
  See DeWeese, Thomas Eugene
  and Kugi, Constance Todd
Thomasma, Kenneth R. 1930- *90*
Thomason, Mark *215*
Thomassie, Tynia 1959- *92*
Thompson, Brenda 1935- *34*
Thompson, Carol 1951- *189*
  Earlier sketch in SATA *85*
Thompson, China
  See Lewis, Mary
Thompson, Colin 1942- *198*
  Earlier sketches in SATA *95, 163*
Thompson, David H(ugh) 1941- *17*
Thompson, Eileen
  See Panowski, Eileen Thompson
Thompson, George Selden 1929-1989 .... *73*
  Obituary *63*
  Earlier sketch in SATA *4*
  See also CLR *8*
Thompson, Harlan 1894-1987 .... *10*
  Obituary *53*
Thompson, Hilary 1943- *56*
  Brief entry *49*
Thompson, Joanna Maxwell Pullein
  See Pullein-Thompson, Joanna Maxwell
Thompson, Julian F(rancis) 1927- *155*
  Brief entry *40*
  Earlier sketches in SATA *55, 99*
  See also CLR *24*
  See also SAAS *13*
Thompson, K(athryn Carolyn) Dyble
  1952- *82*
Thompson, Kate 1956- *204*
Thompson, Kay 1912(?)-1998 .... *16*
  See also CLR *22*
Thompson, Lauren 1962- *200*
  Earlier sketches in SATA *132, 174*
Thompson, Lauren Stevens
  See Thompson, Lauren
Thompson, Megan Lloyd
  See Lloyd, Megan
Thompson, Richard 1951- *184*
Thompson, Ruth Plumly 1891-1976 .... *66*
Thompson, Sharon 1952- *119*
Thompson, Sharon Elaine
  See Thompson, Sharon
Thompson, Stith 1885-1976 .... *57*
  Obituary *20*
Thompson, Vivian L(aubach) 1911- *3*
Thomson, Bill 1963- *187*
Thomson, Celia
  See Lynn, Tracy
Thomson, David (Robert Alexander)
  1914-1988 .... *40*
  Obituary *55*
Thomson, Melissa 1979- *205*
Thomson, Pat 1939- *122*
  Earlier sketch in SATA *77*
Thomson, Peggy 1922- *31*
Thomson, Sarah L. *212*
  Earlier sketch in SATA *178*
Thon, Melanie Rae 1957- *132*
Thong, Roseanne *174*

Thorburn, John
  See Goldsmith, John Herman Thorburn
Thorn, John 1947- *59*
Thorndyke, Helen Louise
  See Benson, Mildred
Thorne, Ian
  See May, Julian
Thorne, Jean Wright
  See May, Julian
Thornhill, Jan 1955- *148*
  Earlier sketch in SATA *77*
Thornton, Hall
  See Silverberg, Robert
Thornton, W. B.
  See Burgess, Thornton Waldo
Thornton, Yvonne S(hirley) 1947- *96*
Thorpe, E(ustace) G(eorge) 1916- *21*
Thorpe, J. K.
  See Nathanson, Laura Walther
Thorvall, Kerstin 1925- *13*
Thorvall-Falk, Kerstin
  See Thorvall, Kerstin
Thrasher, Crystal (Faye) 1921- *27*
Threadgall, Colin 1941- *77*
Three Little Pigs
  See Lantz, Francess L(in)
Thum, Gladys 1920- *26*
Thum, Marcella *28*
  Earlier sketch in SATA *3*
Thundercloud, Katherine
  See Witt, Shirley Hill
Thurber, James 1894-1961 .... *13*
Thurber, James Grover
  See Thurber, James
Thurlo, Aimee *161*
Thurlo, David *161*
Thurman, Judith 1946- *33*
Thurman, Mark (Gordon Ian) 1948- *63*
Thwaite, Ann (Barbara Harrop) 1932- *14*
Tibbetts, Peggy *127*
Tibbles, Jean-Paul 1958- *115*
Tibo, Gilles 1951- *107*
  Earlier sketch in SATA *67*
Tiburzi, Bonnie 1948- *65*
Ticheburn, Cheviot
  See Ainsworth, William Harrison
Tichenor, Tom 1923-1992 .... *14*
Tichnor, Richard 1959- *90*
Tichy, William 1924- *31*
Tickle, Jack
  See Chapman, Jane
Tiegreen, Alan F. 1935- *94*
  Brief entry *36*
Tierney, Frank M. 1930- *54*
Tierney, Tom 1928- *113*
Tiffault, Benette W. 1955- *77*
Tildes, Phyllis Limbacher 1945- *210*
Tiller, Ruth L. 1949- *83*
Tilley, Debbie *190*
Tillman, Nancy *211*
Tilly, Nancy 1935- *62*
Tilton, Madonna Elaine 1929- *41*
Tilton, Rafael
  See Tilton, Madonna Elaine
Timberlake, Amy *156*
Timberlake, Carolyn
  See Dresang, Eliza (Carolyn Timberlake)
Timmers, Leo 1970- *190*
Timmins, William F(rederick) *10*
Tinbergen, Niko(laas) 1907-1988
  Obituary *60*
Tincknell, Cathy *194*
Tiner, John Hudson 1944- *32*
Tingle, Dolli (?)-
  See Brackett, Dolli Tingle
Tingle, Rebecca *174*
Tingle, Tim *208*
Tingum, Janice 1958- *91*
Tinkelman, Murray 1933- *12*
Tinkham, Kelly A. *188*
Tinkle, (Julien) Lon 1906-1980 .... *36*

Tinling, Marion (Rose) 1904- *140*
Tipene, Tim 1972- *141*
Tippett, James S(terling) 1885-1958 .... *66*
Tirone Smith, Mary-Ann 1944- *143*
Titlebaum, Ellen *195*
Titler, Dale M(ilton) 1926- *35*
  Brief entry *28*
Titmarsh, Michael Angelo
  See Thackeray, William Makepeace
Titus, Eve 1922- *2*
Tjia, Sherwin 1975- *204*
Tjong Khing, The 1933- *76*
Tobias, Katherine
  See Gottfried, Theodore Mark
Tobias, Tobi 1938- *82*
  Earlier sketch in SATA *5*
  See also CLR *4*
Todd, Anne Ophelia
  See Dowden, Anne Ophelia Todd
Todd, Barbara 1961- *173*
Todd, Barbara K(eith) 1917- *10*
Todd, Chuck *195*
Todd, H(erbert) E(atton) 1908-1988 .... *84*
  Earlier sketch in SATA *11*
Todd, Loreto 1942- *30*
Todd, Pamela *212*
Todd, Peter
  See Hamilton, Charles (Harold St. John)
Toews, Miriam 1964- *165*
Tofel, Richard J. 1957- *140*
Toft, Kim Michelle 1960- *170*
Tokunbo, Dimitrea *187*
Tolan, Stephanie S. 1942- *142*
  Earlier sketches in SATA *38, 78*
Toland, John (Willard) 1912-2004 .... *38*
Tolbert, Steve 1944- *143*
Toledo, Francisco 1940- *198*
Toledo, Natalia 1967- *197*
Tolkien, J. R. R. 1892-1973 .... *100*
  Obituary *24*
  Earlier sketches in SATA *2, 32*
  See also CLR *152*
Tolkien, John Ronald Reuel
  See Tolkien, J. R. R.
Toll, Emily
  See Cannon, Eileen E(mily)
Toll, Nelly S. 1935- *78*
Tolland, W. R.
  See Heitzmann, William Ray
Tolles, Martha 1921- *76*
  Earlier sketch in SATA *8*
Tolliver, Ruby C(hangos) 1922- *110*
  Brief entry *41*
  Earlier sketch in SATA *55*
Tolmie, Kenneth Donald 1941- *15*
Tolstoi, Lev
  See Tolstoy, Leo
Tolstoy, Leo 1828-1910 .... *26*
Tolstoy, Count Leo
  See Tolstoy, Leo
Tolstoy, Leo Nikolaevich
  See Tolstoy, Leo
Tomalin, Ruth *29*
Tomaselli, Rosa
  See Pausacker, Jenny
Tomecek, Steve *172*
Tomes, Margot (Ladd) 1917-1991 .... *70*
  Brief entry *27*
  Obituary *69*
  Earlier sketch in SATA *36*
Tomey, Ingrid 1943- *77*
Tomfool
  See Farjeon, Eleanor
Tomic, Tomislav 1977- *202*
Tomkins, Jasper
  See Batey, Tom
Tomline, F. Latour
  See Gilbert, W(illiam) S(chwenck)
Tomlinson, Heather *192*
Tomlinson, Jill 1931-1976 .... *3*
  Obituary *24*

Tomlinson, Reginald R(obert) 1885-1979(?)
  Obituary 27
Tomlinson, Theresa 1946- 165
  Earlier sketch in SATA 103
  See also CLR 60
Tommaso, Rich 1970(?)- 200
Tompert, Ann 1918- 139
  Earlier sketches in SATA 14, 89
Tompkins, Troy
  See Cle, Troy
Toner, Raymond John 1908-1986 10
Tong, Gary S. 1942- 66
Tong, Paul 188
Took, Belladonna
  See Chapman, Vera (Ivy May)
Tooke, Louise Mathews 1950- 38
Tooke, Susan 173
Toonder, Martin
  See Groom, Arthur William
Toothaker, Roy Eugene 1928- 18
Tooze, Ruth (Anderson) 1892-1972 4
Topaz, Ksenia 212
Topek, Susan Remick 1955- 78
Topping, Audrey R(onning) 1928- 14
Tor, Regina
  See Shekerjian, Regina Tor
Torbert, Floyd James 1922- 22
Torgersen, Don Arthur 1934- 55
  Brief entry 41
Torley, Luke
  See Blish, James
Torrecilla, Pablo 1967- 206
Torres, Andres Segovia
  See Segovia, Andres
Torres, Daniel 1958- 102
Torres, John A. 1965- 163
  Earlier sketch in SATA 94
Torres, John Albert
  See Torres, John A.
Torres, Laura 1967- 146
  Earlier sketch in SATA 87
Torres, Leyla 1960- 155
Torrey, Rich
  See Torrey, Richard
Torrey, Richard 189
Torrie, Malcolm
  See Mitchell, Gladys (Maude Winifred)
Toten, Teresa 1955- 99
Totham, Mary
  See Breinburg, Petronella
Touponce, William F. 1948- 114
Tournier, Michel 1924- 23
Tournier, Michel Edouard
  See Tournier, Michel
Towle, Wendy 1963- 79
Towne, Mary
  See Spelman, Mary
Townley, Rod
  See Townley, Roderick
Townley, Roderick 1942- 177
Townsend, Brad W. 1962- 91
Townsend, John Rowe 1922- 132
  Autobiography Feature 132
  Earlier sketches in SATA 4, 68
  See also CLR 2
  See also SAAS 2
Townsend, Michael 1981- 194
Townsend, Sue 1946- 93
  Brief entry 48
  Earlier sketch in SATA 55
Townsend, Susan Lilian
  See Townsend, Sue
Townsend, Thomas L. 1944- 59
Townsend, Tom
  See Townsend, Thomas L.
Townsend, Wendy 1962- 201
Townson, Hazel 134
Toye, William Eldred 1926- 8
Traherne, Michael
  See Watkins-Pitchford, Denys James

Trahey, Jane 1923-2000 36
  Obituary 120
Trapani, Iza 1954- 214
  Earlier sketches in SATA 80, 116
Trapp, Maria Augusta von
  See von Trapp, Maria Augusta
Travers, P(amela) L(yndon) 1899-1996 100
  Obituary 90
  Earlier sketches in SATA 4, 54
  See also CLR 93
  See also SAAS 2
Travis, Lucille 133
  Earlier sketch in SATA 88
Treadgold, Mary 1910- 49
Trease, (Robert) Geoffrey 1909-1998 60
  Obituary 101
  Earlier sketch in SATA 2
  See also CLR 42
  See also SAAS 6
Treat, Lawrence 1903-1998 59
Tredez, Alain 1926- 17
Tredez, Denise 1930- 50
Treece, Henry 1912-1966 2
  See also CLR 2
Tregarthen, Enys
  See Sloggett, Nellie
Tregaskis, Richard 1916-1973 3
  Obituary 26
Treherne, Katie Thamer 1955- 76
Trell, Max 1900-1996 14
  Obituary 108
Tremain, Ruthven 1922- 17
Trembath, Don 1963- 168
  Earlier sketch in SATA 96
Tremens, Del
  See MacDonald, Amy
Trent, Robbie 1894-1988 26
Trent, Timothy
  See Malmberg, Carl
Treseder, Terry Walton 1956- 68
Tresilian, (Cecil) Stuart 1891-(?) 40
Tresselt, Alvin 1916-2000 7
  See also CLR 30
Trevino, Elizabeth B(orton) de 1904- 29
  Earlier sketch in SATA 1
  See also SAAS 5
Trevor, Elleston 1920-1995 28
Trevor, Frances
  See Teasdale, Sara
Trevor, Glen
  See Hilton, James
Trevor, (Lucy) Meriol 1919-2000 113
  Obituary 122
  Earlier sketch in SATA 10
Trewellard, J.M. 195
Trewellard, Juliet
  See Trewellard, J.M.
Trez, Alain
  See Tredez, Alain
Trez, Denise
  See Tredez, Denise
Trezise, Percy 1923-
  See CLR 41
Trezise, Percy James
  See Trezise, Percy
Triggs, Tony D. 1946- 70
Trimble, Marshall I(ra) 1939- 93
Trimby, Elisa 1948- 47
  Brief entry 40
Tring, A. Stephen
  See Meynell, Laurence Walter
Tripp, Eleanor B(aldwin) 1936- 4
Tripp, Janet 1942- 108
Tripp, Jenny 188
Tripp, John
  See Moore, John Travers
Tripp, Nathaniel 1944- 101
Tripp, Paul 1916-2002 8
  Obituary 139
Tripp, Valerie 1951- 168
  Earlier sketch in SATA 78

Tripp, Wallace (Whitney) 1940- 31
Trivelpiece, Laurel 1926- 56
  Brief entry 46
Trivett, Daphne Harwood 1940- 22
Trivizas, Eugene 1946- 84
Trnka, Jiri 1912-1969 43
  Brief entry 32
Trollope, Anthony 1815-1882 22
Trost, Lucille W(ood) 1938- 149
  Earlier sketch in SATA 12
Trott, Betty 1933- 91
Trotter, Deborah W. 184
Trotter, Grace V(iolet) 1900-1991 10
Trottier, Maxine 1950- 175
  Earlier sketch in SATA 131
Troughton, Joanna (Margaret) 1947- 37
Trout, Kilgore
  See Farmer, Philip Jose
Trout, Richard E. 123
Trudeau, Garretson Beekman
  See Trudeau, G.B.
Trudeau, Garry
  See Trudeau, G.B.
Trudeau, Garry B.
  See Trudeau, G.B.
Trudeau, G.B. 1948- 168
  Earlier sketch in SATA 35
Trueit, Trudi
  See Trueit, Trudi Strain
Trueit, Trudi Strain 1963- 179
Trueman, Matthew 183
Trueman, Terry 1947- 178
  Earlier sketch in SATA 132
Truesdell, Judy
  See Mecca, Judy Truesdell
Truesdell, Sue 212
  See Truesdell, Susan G.
Truesdell, Susan G. 108
  Brief entry 45
  See Truesdell, Sue
Trumbauer, Lisa (Trutkoff) 1963- 149
Truss, Jan 1925- 35
Truss, Lynne 1955(?)- 194
Tryon, Leslie 194
  Earlier sketch in SATA 139
Tubb, Jonathan N. 1951- 78
Tubb, Kristin O'Donnell 1971- 209
Tubby, I. M.
  See Kraus, (Herman) Robert
Tucker, Caroline
  See Nolan, Jeannette Covert
Tudor, Edward
  See Browne, Anthony
Tudor, Tasha 1915-2008 160
  Obituary 205
  Earlier sketches in SATA 20, 69
  See also CLR 13
Tuerk, Hanne 1951- 71
Tugeau, Jeremy 199
Tulloch, Richard 1949- 180
  Earlier sketch in SATA 76
Tulloch, Richard George
  See Tulloch, Richard
Tulloch, Shirley 169
Tully, John (Kimberley) 1923- 14
Tumanov, Vladimir A. 1961- 138
Tung, Angela 1972- 109
Tunis, Edwin (Burdett) 1897-1973 28
  Obituary 24
  Earlier sketch in SATA 1
  See also CLR 2
Tunis, John R(oberts) 1889-1975 37
  Brief entry 30
Tunnell, Michael
  See Tunnell, Michael O.
Tunnell, Michael O. 1950- 157
  Earlier sketch in SATA 103
Tunnell, Michael O'Grady
  See Tunnell, Michael O.
Tunnicliffe, C(harles) F(rederick)
  1901-1979 62

Turck, Mary C. 1950- *144*
Turk, Hanne
  See Tuerk, Hanne
Turk, Ruth 1917- *82*
Turkle, Brinton 1915- *79*
  Earlier sketch in SATA *2*
Turlington, Bayly 1919-1977 .... *5*
  Obituary *52*
Turnbull, Agnes Sligh 1888-1982 .... *14*
Turnbull, Ann 1943- *160*
  Earlier sketch in SATA *18*
Turnbull, Ann Christine
  See Turnbull, Ann
Turner, Alice K. 1940- *10*
Turner, Ann 1945- *188*
  Autobiography Feature *188*
  Earlier sketches in SATA *14, 77, 113, 178*
Turner, Ann Warren
  See Turner, Ann
Turner, Bonnie 1932- *75*
Turner, Elizabeth 1774-1846
  See YABC *2*
Turner, Glennette Tilley 1933- *183*
  Earlier sketch in SATA *71*
Turner, Josie
  See Crawford, Phyllis
Turner, Megan Whalen 1965- *174*
  Earlier sketch in SATA *94*
Turner, Pamela S. 1957- *211*
Turner, Philip (William) 1925- *83*
  Earlier sketch in SATA *11*
  See also CLR *89*
  See also SAAS *6*
Turner, Robyn 1947- *77*
Turner, Sheila R.
  See Seed, Sheila Turner
Turngren, Annette 1902(?)-1980
  Obituary *23*
Turngren, Ellen (?)-1964 .... *3*
Turska, Krystyna (Zofia) 1933- *31*
  Brief entry *27*
Turteltaub, H.N.
  See Turtledove, Harry
Turtledove, Harry 1949- *166*
  Earlier sketch in SATA *116*
Turtledove, Harry Norman
  See Turtledove, Harry
Tusa, Tricia 1960- *207*
  Earlier sketches in SATA *72, 111*
Tusiani, Joseph 1924- *45*
Twain, Mark 1835-1910 .... *100*
  See also YABC *2*
  See also CLR *66*
Tweit, Susan J 1956- *94*
Tweit, Susan Joan
  See Tweit, Susan J
Tweton, D. Jerome 1933- *48*
Twinem, Neecy 1958- *92*
Twohill, Maggie
  See Angell, Judie
Tworkov, Jack 1900-1982 .... *47*
  Obituary *31*
Tyche
  See Papademetriou, Lisa
Tyers, Jenny 1969- *89*
Tyers, Kathy 1952- *82*
Tyler, Anne 1941- *173*
  Earlier sketches in SATA *7, 90*
Tyler, Linda
  See Tyler, Linda W(agner)
Tyler, Linda W(agner) 1952- *65*
Tyler, Vicki 1952- *64*
Tyne, Joel
  See Schembri, Jim
Tyrrell, Frances 1959- *107*

U

Ubell, Earl 1926-2007 .... *4*
  Obituary *182*
Uchida, Yoshiko 1921-1992 .... *53*
  Obituary *72*
  Earlier sketch in SATA *1*
  See also CLR *56*
  See also SAAS *1*
Udall, Jan Beaney 1938- *10*
Uden, (Bernard Gilbert) Grant 1910- *26*
Uderzo, Albert 1927-
  See CLR *37*
Udovic, David 1950- *189*
Udry, Janice May 1928- *152*
  Earlier sketch in SATA *4*
Uegaki, Chieri 1969- *211*
  Earlier sketch in SATA *153*
Uehashi, Nahoko 1962- *215*
Ueno, Noriko
  See Nakae, Noriko
Ugliano, Natascia *196*
Uhlberg, Myron *174*
Uhlig, Richard 1970- *195*
Uhlig, Susan 1955- *129*
Ulam, S(tanislaw) M(arcin) 1909-1984 .... *51*
Ullman, Barb Bentler *210*
Ullman, James Ramsey 1907-1971 .... *7*
Ulm, Robert 1934-1977 .... *17*
Ulmer, Louise 1943- *53*
Ulmer, Wendy K. 1950- *201*
Ulrich, Maureen 1958- *206*
Ulriksen, Mark 1957- *210*
Ulyatt, Kenneth 1920- *14*
Umansky, Kaye 1946- *188*
  Earlier sketch in SATA *158*
Unada
  See Gliewe, Unada (Grace)
Uncle Carter
  See Boucher, (Clarence) Carter
Uncle Eric
  See Maybury, Richard J.
Uncle Gus
  See Rey, H. A.
Uncle Mac
  See McCulloch, Derek (Ivor Breashur)
Uncle Ray
  See Coffman, Ramon Peyton
Uncle Shelby
  See Silverstein, Shel
Underhill, Alice Mertie (Waterman)
  1900-1971 .... *10*
Underhill, Liz 1948- *53*
  Brief entry *49*
Underwood, Deborah 1962- *206*
Unger, Harlow G. 1931- *75*
Unger, Harlow Giles
  See Unger, Harlow G.
Unger, Jim 1937- *67*
Ungerer, (Jean) Thomas 1931- *106*
  Earlier sketches in SATA *5, 33*
  See also CLR *77*
Ungerer, Tomi 1931-
  See Ungerer, (Jean) Thomas
Unkelbach, Kurt 1913-1992 .... *4*
Unnerstad, Edith (Totterman) 1900-1982 ...... *3*
  See also CLR *36*
Unobagha, Uzo *139*
Unrau, Ruth 1922- *9*
Unstead, R(obert) J(ohn) 1915-1988 .... *12*
  Obituary *56*
Unsworth, Walt(er) 1928- *4*
Untermeyer, Bryna Ivens 1909-1985 .... *61*
Untermeyer, Louis 1885-1977 .... *37*
  Obituary *26*
  Earlier sketch in SATA *2*
Unwin, David S. 1918-2010 .... *14*
Unwin, David Storr
  See Unwin, David S.
Unwin, Nora S(picer) 1907-1982 .... *3*
  Obituary *49*

Unzner, Christa 1958- *141*
  Earlier sketch in SATA *80*
Unzner-Fischer, Christa
  See Unzner, Christa
Updale, Eleanor 1953- *175*
Updyke, Rosemary K. 1924- *103*
Upitis, Alvis *109*
Urbain, Cat 1956- *211*
Urbain, Catherine
  See Urbain, Cat
Urban, Helle (Denise) 1957- *149*
Urban, Linda *199*
Urbanovic, Jackie *189*
Urbigkit, Cat 1965- *196*
Urdahl, Catherine *215*
Ure, Jean 1943- *192*
  Autobiography Feature *192*
  Earlier sketches in SATA *48, 78, 129*
  See also CLR *34*
  See also SAAS *14*
U'Ren, Andrea 1968- *213*
  Earlier sketch in SATA *142*
Uris, Leon 1924-2003 .... *49*
  Obituary *146*
Uris, Leon Marcus
  See Uris, Leon
Ursu, Anne *177*
Ury, Allen B. 1954- *98*
Uschan, Michael V. 1948- *129*
Usher, Margo Scegge
  See McHargue, Georgess
Uslan, Michael E. 1951- *169*
Uston, Ken(neth Senzo) 1935-1987 .... *65*
Uttley, Alice Jane 1884-1976 .... *88*
  Obituary *26*
  Earlier sketch in SATA *3*
Uttley, Alison
  See Uttley, Alice Jane
Utz, Lois (Marie) 1932-1986 .... *5*
  Obituary *50*

V

Vaeth, J. Gordon 1921- *17*
Vaeth, Joseph Gordon
  See Vaeth, J. Gordon
Vagin, Vladimir (Vasilevich) 1937- *142*
Vail, Rachel 1966- *201*
  Earlier sketches in SATA *94, 163*
Vainio, Pirkko 1957- *123*
  Earlier sketch in SATA *76*
Valen, Nanine 1950- *21*
Valencak, Hannelore
  See Mayer, Hannelore Valencak
Valens, Amy 1946- *70*
Valens, E(vans) G(ladstone), Jr. 1920-1992 ... *1*
Valentine, Johnny *72*
Valerio, Geraldo 1970- *180*
Valgardson, W. D. 1939- *151*
  Earlier sketch in SATA *101*
Valgardson, William Dempsey
  See Valgardson, W. D.
Valleau, Emily 1925- *51*
Vamos, Samantha R. *215*
Van Abbe, Salaman 1883-1955 .... *18*
Van Allsburg, Chris 1949- *156*
  Earlier sketches in SATA *37, 53, 105*
  See also CLR *113*
Van Anrooy, Francine 1924- *2*
Van Anrooy, Frans
  See Van Anrooy, Francine
Vanasse, Deb 1957- *170*
Van Buren, David *203*
Vance, Cynthia *207*
Vance, Eleanor Graham 1908-1985 .... *11*
Vance, Gerald
  See Garrett, Randall
  and Silverberg, Robert
Vance, Marguerite 1889-1965 .... *29*

Vance-Abrams, Cynthia
  See Vance, Cynthia
VanCleave, Janice 1942- *116*
  Autobiography Feature *123*
  Earlier sketch in SATA *75*
Vandenburg, Mary Lou 1943- *17*
Vander Boom, Mae M. *14*
Vander-Els, Betty 1936- *63*
van der Heide, Iris 1970- *183*
van der Linde, Laurel 1952- *78*
van der Linden, Martijn 1979- *214*
van der Meer, Ron 1945- *98*
van de Ruit, John 1975- *199*
Van der Veer, Judy 1912-1982 .... *4*
  Obituary *33*
Vanderwerff, Corrine 1939- *117*
Vander Zee, Ruth *199*
  Earlier sketch in SATA *159*
Vande Velde, Vivian 1951- *211*
  Earlier sketches in SATA *62, 95, 141*
  See also CLR 145
Vandivert, Rita (Andre) 1905-1986 .... *21*
Van Draanen, Wendelin *207*
  Earlier sketch in SATA *122*
Van Dusen, Chris *173*
Van Duyn, Janet 1910- *18*
Van Dyne, Edith
  See Baum, L. Frank
  and Sampson, Emma (Keats) Speed
  and van Zantwijk, Rudolf (Alexander
    Marinus)
Vane, Mitch
  See Vane, Mitchelle
Vane, Mitchelle *176*
van Frankenhuyzen, Gijsbert 1951- *132*
Van Genechten, Guido 1957- *165*
van Haeringen, Annemarie *193*
Van Hook, Beverly 1941- *99*
Van Hook, Beverly H.
  See Van Hook, Beverly
Van Hook, Beverly Hennen
  See Van Hook, Beverly
Van Horn, William 1939- *43*
van Hout, Mies 1962- *178*
Van Iterson, S(iny) R(ose) *26*
Van Kampen, Vlasta 1943- *163*
  Earlier sketch in SATA *54*
Van Laan, Nancy 1939- *214*
  Earlier sketch in SATA *105*
van Lawick-Goodall, Jane
  See Goodall, Jane
Van Leeuwen, Jean 1937- *211*
  Autobiography Feature *141*
  Earlier sketches in SATA *6, 82, 132, 141*
  See also SAAS 8
van Lhin, Erik
  See del Rey, Lester
van Lieshout, Maria *201*
Van Loon, Hendrik Willem 1882-1944 .... *18*
van Ommen, Sylvia 1978- *186*
VanOosting, James 1951- *170*
Van Orden, M(erton) D(ick) 1921- *4*
Van Patter, Bruce *183*
Van Reek, Wouter *204*
Van Rensselaer, Alexander (Taylor Mason)
  1892-1962 .... *14*
Van Riper, Guernsey, Jr. 1909-1995 .... *3*
van Rossum, Heleen 1962- *174*
Van Rynbach, Iris 1952- *102*
Vansant, Rhonda Joy Edwards 1950- *92*
Van Steenwyk, Elizabeth (Ann) 1928- *89*
  Earlier sketch in SATA *34*
Van Stockum, Hilda 1908-2006 .... *5*
  Obituary *179*
van Straaten, Harmen 1961- *195*
Van Tuyl, Barbara 1940- *11*
van Vogt, A(lfred) E(lton) 1912-2000 .... *14*
  Obituary *124*
Van Wassenhove, Sue 1951- *202*
Van Woerkom, Dorothy (O'Brien)
  1924-1996 .... *21*

Van Wormer, Joe
  See Van Wormer, Joseph Edward
Van Wormer, Joseph Edward 1913-1998 ...... *35*
Van Wright, Cornelius *173*
Van Zwienen, Ilse Charlotte Koehn
  1929-1991 .... *34*
  Brief entry *28*
  Obituary *67*
Van Zyle, Jon 1942- *176*
  Earlier sketch in SATA *84*
Varela, Barry *180*
Varga, Judy
  See Stang, Judit
Varley, Dimitry V. 1906-1984 .... *10*
Varley, Susan 1961- *134*
  Earlier sketch in SATA *63*
Varon, Sara *195*
Vasileva, Tatiana
  See Wassiljewa, Tatjana
Vasiliev, Valery 1949- *80*
Vasilieva, Tatiana
  See Wassiljewa, Tatjana
Vasiliu, Mircea 1920- *2*
Vass, George 1927- *57*
  Brief entry *31*
Vaughan, Carter A.
  See Gerson, Noel Bertram
Vaughan, Harold Cecil 1923- *14*
Vaughan, Marcia (K.) 1951- *159*
  Earlier sketches in SATA *60, 95*
Vaughan, Richard 1947- *87*
Vaughan, Sam(uel) 1928- *14*
Vaughn, Ruth 1935- *14*
Vaught, Susan 1965- *195*
Vaupel, Robin *198*
Vautier, Ghislaine 1932- *53*
Vavra, Robert James 1935- *8*
Vecsey, George Spencer 1939- *9*
Vedral, Joyce L(auretta) 1943- *65*
Vega, Denise *174*
Vega, Denise B.
  See Vega, Denise
Vega, Diego
  See Adkins, Jan
Veglahn, Nancy (Crary) 1937- *5*
Vejjajiva, Jane 1963- *189*
Velasquez, Eric *192*
Velasquez, Gloria 1949-
  See Velasquez, Gloria
Velasquez, Gloria 1949- *113*
Velthuijs, Max 1923-2005 .... *110*
  Obituary *160*
  Earlier sketch in SATA *53*
Venable, Alan (Hudson) 1944- *8*
Venezia, Mike 1945- *150*
Ventura, Anthony
  See Pellowski, Michael (Joseph)
Ventura, Piero (Luigi) 1937- *61*
  Brief entry *43*
  See also CLR 16
Vequin, Capini
  See Quinn, Elisabeth
Verba, Joan Marie 1953- *78*
Verboven, Agnes 1951- *103*
verDorn, Bethea (Stewart) 1952- *76*
Vere, Ed *197*
Verissimo, Erico (Lopes) 1905-1975 .... *113*
Verne, Jules 1828-1905 .... *21*
  See also CLR 88
Verne, Jules Gabriel
  See Verne, Jules
Verner, Gerald 1897(?)-1980
  Obituary *25*
Verney, John 1913-1993 .... *14*
  Obituary *75*
Verniero, Joan C. 1949- *181*
Vernon, (Elda) Louise A(nderson) 1914- *14*
Vernon, Rosemary
  See Smith, Susan Vernon
Vernon, Ursula *204*

Vernor, D.
  See Casewit, Curtis W(erner)
Verr, Harry Coe
  See Kunhardt, Edith
Verral, Charles Spain 1904-1990 .... *11*
  Obituary *65*
Verrillo, Erica 1953- *199*
Verrillo, Erica F.
  See Verrillo, Erica
Verrone, Robert J. 1935(?)-1984
  Obituary *39*
Versace, Marie Teresa Rios 1917- *2*
Vertreace, Martha M(odena) 1945- *78*
Vesey, A(manda) 1939- *62*
Vesey, Mark (David) 1958- *123*
Vesey, Paul
  See Allen, Samuel W(ashington)
Vess, Charles 1951- *215*
Vestergaard, Hope *178*
Vestly, Anne-Cath(arina) 1920- *14*
  See also CLR 99
Vevers, (Henry) Gwynne 1916-1988 .... *45*
  Obituary *57*
Viator, Vacuus
  See Hughes, Thomas
Viau, Nancy *208*
Vicar, Henry
  See Felsen, Henry Gregor
Vick, Helen Hughes 1950- *88*
Vicker, Angus
  See Felsen, Henry Gregor
Vickers, Sheena 1960- *94*
Vickery, Kate
  See Kennedy, T.A.
Victor, Edward 1914- *3*
Victor, Joan Berg 1942- *30*
Vidrine, Beverly Barras 1938- *188*
  Earlier sketch in SATA *103*
Vieceli, Emma 1979- *210*
Viereck, Ellen K. 1928- *14*
Viereck, Phillip 1925- *3*
Viertel, Janet 1915- *10*
Vigliante, Mary
  See Szydlowski, Mary Vigliante
Vigna, Judith 1936- *102*
  Earlier sketch in SATA *15*
Viguers, Ruth Hill 1903-1971 .... *6*
Vila, Laura *207*
Villareal, Ray *187*
Villasenor, Edmund
  See Villasenor, Victor E.
Villasenor, Edmundo
  See Villasenor, Victor E.
Villasenor, Victor
  See Villasenor, Victor E.
Villasenor, Victor E. 1940- *171*
Villasenor, Victor Edmundo
  See Villasenor, Victor E.
Villiard, Paul 1910-1974 .... *51*
  Obituary *20*
Villiers, Alan (John) 1903-1982 .... *10*
Vilott, Rhondi
  See Salsitz, Rhondi Vilott
Vincent, Amy
  See Gray, Claudia
Vincent, Eric Douglas 1953- *40*
Vincent, Erin 1969- *188*
Vincent, Felix 1946- *41*
Vincent, Gabrielle 1928-2000 .... *121*
  Earlier sketch in SATA *61*
  See also CLR 13
Vincent, Mary Keith
  See St. John, Wylly Folk
Vincent, William R.
  See Heitzmann, William Ray
Vinegar, Tom
  See Gregg, Andrew K.
Vinest, Shaw
  See Longyear, Barry B(rookes)
Vinge, Joan (Carol) D(ennison) 1948- *113*
  Earlier sketch in SATA *36*

Vining, Elizabeth Gray 1902-1999 6
   Obituary *117*
Vinson, Kathryn 1911-1995 .... *21*
Vinton, Iris 1906(?)-1988 .... *24*
   Obituary *55*
Viola, Herman J(oseph) 1938- *126*
Viorst, Judith 1931- *172*
   Earlier sketches in SATA *7, 70, 123*
   See also CLR *90*
Vip
   See Partch, Virgil Franklin II
Vipont, Charles
   See Foulds, Elfrida Vipont
Vipont, Elfrida
   See Foulds, Elfrida Vipont
Viramontes, Helena Maria 1954-
   See CLR *285*
Viscott, David S(teven) 1938-1996 .... *65*
Visser, W(illem) F(rederik) H(endrik)
   1900-1968 .... *10*
Vitale, Stefano 1958- *180*
   Earlier sketch in SATA *114*
Vivas, Julie 1947- *96*
Vivelo, Jackie 1943- *63*
Vivelo, Jacqueline J.
   See Vivelo, Jackie
Vivelo, Jacqueline Jean
   See Vivelo, Jackie
Vivian, Siobhan 1979(?)- *215*
Vizzini, Ned 1981- *179*
   Earlier sketch in SATA *125*
Vlahos, Olivia 1924- *31*
Vlasic, Bob
   See Hirsch, Phil
Voake, Charlotte *180*
   Earlier sketch in SATA *114*
Voake, Steve 1961- *178*
Vo-Dinh, Mai 1933- *16*
Vogel, Carole Garbuny 1951- *105*
   Earlier sketch in SATA *70*
Vogel, Ilse-Margret 1918- *14*
Vogel, John H., Jr. 1950- *18*
Vogt, Esther Loewen 1915-1999 .... *14*
Vogt, Gregory L. *94*
Vogt, Marie Bollinger 1921- *45*
Vohwinkel, Astrid 1969- *207*
Voight, Virginia Frances 1909-1989 .... *8*
Voigt, Cynthia 1942- *160*
   Brief entry *33*
   Earlier sketches in SATA *48, 79, 116*
   See also CLR *141*
Voigt, Erna 1925- *35*
Voigt-Rother, Erna
   See Voigt, Erna
Vojtech, Anna 1946- *108*
   Earlier sketch in SATA *42*
Vollstadt, Elizabeth Weiss 1942- *121*
Volponi, Paul *175*
Volting, Dr. R.E.
   See Lerangis, Peter
Von Ahnen, Katherine 1922- *93*
von Buhler, Cynthia *185*
Vondra, J. Gert
   See Vondra, Josef
Vondra, Josef 1941- *121*
Vondra, Josef Gert
   See Vondra, Josef
Von Gunden, Kenneth 1946- *113*
Von Hagen, Victor Wolfgang 1908-1985 ...... *29*
von Klopp, Vahrah
   See Malvern, Gladys
von Schmidt, Eric 1931-2007 .... *50*
   Brief entry *36*
   Obituary *181*
von Storch, Anne B. 1910- *1*
von Trapp, Maria Augusta 1905-1987 .... *16*
von Wodtke, Charlotte Buel Johnson
   1918-1982 .... *46*
von Ziegesar, Cecily 1970- *161*

Vos, Ida 1931-2006 .... *121*
   Earlier sketch in SATA *69*
   See also CLR *85*
Vosburgh, Leonard (W.) 1912- *15*
Votaw, Carol 1961- *201*
Voyle, Mary
   See Manning, Rosemary
Vrettos, Adrienne Maria *187*
Vriens, Jacques 1946- *151*
Vugteveen, Verna Aardema
   See Aardema, Verna
Vulture, Elizabeth T.
   See Gilbert, Suzie
Vuong, Lynette Dyer 1938- *110*
   Earlier sketch in SATA *60*

W

Waas, Uli
   See Waas-Pommer, Ulrike
Waas-Pommer, Ulrike 1949- *85*
Waber, Bernard 1924- *155*
   Brief entry *40*
   Earlier sketches in SATA *47, 95*
   See also CLR *55*
Wachtel, Shirley Russak 1951- *88*
Wachter, Oralee (Roberts) 1935- *61*
   Brief entry *51*
Waddell, Evelyn Margaret 1918- *10*
Waddell, Martin 1941- *129*
   Autobiography Feature *129*
   Earlier sketches in SATA *43, 81, 127*
   See also CLR *31*
   See also SAAS *15*
Waddy, Lawrence (Heber) 1912-2010 .... *91*
Wade, Mary Dodson 1930- *151*
   Earlier sketch in SATA *79*
Wade, Suzanne
   See Kirby, Susan E.
Wade, Theodore E., Jr. 1936- *37*
Wademan, Peter John 1946- *122*
Wademan, Spike
   See Wademan, Peter John
Wadsworth, Ginger 1945- *157*
   Earlier sketch in SATA *103*
Wagenheim, Kal 1935- *21*
Wagner, Michele R. 1975- *157*
Wagner, Sharon B. 1936- *4*
Wagoner, David (Russell) 1926- *14*
Wahl, Jan (Boyer) 1933- *132*
   Earlier sketches in SATA *2, 34, 73*
   See also SAAS *3*
Wahl, Mats 1945- *186*
Waide, Jan 1952- *29*
Wainscott, John Milton 1910-1981 .... *53*
Wainwright, Richard M. 1935- *91*
Wainwright, Ruth
   See Symes, Ruth Louise
Wait, Lea 1946- *137*
Waite, Judy *174*
Waite, Judy Bernard
   See Bernard, Patricia
Waite, Michael
   See Waite, Michael P.
Waite, Michael P. 1960- *101*
Waite, P(eter) B(usby) 1922- *64*
Waites, Joan C. *187*
Waitley, Douglas 1927- *30*
Wakefield, Jean L.
   See Laird, Jean E(louise)
Wakin, Daniel (Joseph) 1961- *84*
Wakin, Edward 1927- *37*
Wakiyama, Hanako 1966- *192*
Walck, Henry Z. 1908(?)-1984
   Obituary *40*
Walden, Amelia Elizabeth *3*
Walden, Mark *188*
Waldherr, Kris 1963- *76*
Waldman, Bruce 1949- *15*

Waldman, Neil 1947- *203*
   Earlier sketches in SATA *51, 94, 142*
Waldrep, Richard *198*
Waldron, Ann Wood 1924- *16*
Waldron, Kathleen Cook *176*
Wales, Dirk 1931- *205*
Walgren, Judy 1963- *118*
Walker, Addison
   See Walker, (Addison) Mort
Walker, Alice 1944- *31*
Walker, Alice Malsenior
   See Walker, Alice
Walker, Barbara (Jeanne) K(erlin) 1921- *80*
   Earlier sketch in SATA *4*
Walker, Barbara M(uhs) 1928- *57*
Walker, (James) Braz(elton) 1934-1983 .... *45*
Walker, David 1965- *197*
Walker, David G(ordon) 1926- *60*
Walker, David Harry 1911-1992 .... *8*
   Obituary *71*
Walker, Diana 1925- *9*
Walker, Diane Marie Catherine
   See Walker, Kate
Walker, Dick
   See Pellowski, Michael (Joseph)
Walker, Frank 1931-2000 .... *36*
Walker, Holly Beth
   See Bond, Gladys Baker
Walker, Kate 1950- *165*
   Earlier sketch in SATA *82*
Walker, Kathrine Sorley
   See Sorley Walker, Kathrine
Walker, Lou Ann 1952- *66*
   Brief entry *53*
Walker, Louise Jean 1891-1976
   Obituary *35*
Walker, Mary Alexander 1927- *61*
Walker, Mildred
   See Schemm, Mildred Walker
Walker, (Addison) Mort 1923- *8*
Walker, Pamela 1948- *142*
   Earlier sketch in SATA *24*
Walker, Paul Robert 1953- *154*
Walker, Robert W. 1948- *66*
Walker, Sally M(acArt) 1954- *135*
Walker, Stephen J. 1951- *12*
Walker-Blondell, Becky 1951- *89*
Wallace, Barbara Brooks 1922- *136*
   Earlier sketches in SATA *4, 78*
   See also CLR *150*
   See also SAAS *17*
Wallace, Beverly Dobrin 1921- *19*
Wallace, Bill 1947- *169*
   Brief entry *47*
   Earlier sketches in SATA *53, 101*
Wallace, Daisy
   See Cuyler, Margery
Wallace, Ian 1950- *141*
   Earlier sketches in SATA *53, 56*
   See also CLR *37*
Wallace, John 1966- *155*
   Earlier sketch in SATA *105*
Wallace, John A(dam) 1915-2004 .... *3*
   Obituary *155*
Wallace, Karen 1951- *188*
   Earlier sketches in SATA *83, 139*
Wallace, Nancy Elizabeth 1948- *186*
   Earlier sketch in SATA *141*
Wallace, Nigel
   See Hamilton, Charles (Harold St. John)
Wallace, Paula S. *153*
Wallace, Rich 1957- *196*
   Earlier sketches in SATA *117, 158*
Wallace, Robert 1932-1999 .... *47*
   Brief entry *37*
Wallace, Ruby Ann 1923(?)- *77*
Wallace, William Keith
   See Wallace, Bill
Wallace-Brodeur, Ruth 1941- *169*
   Brief entry *41*
   Earlier sketches in SATA *51, 88*

Wallenta, Adam 1974- *123*
Waller, Leslie 1923-2007 .... *20*
Walley, Byron
  See Card, Orson Scott
Wallis, Diz 1949- *77*
Wallis, G. McDonald
  See Campbell, Hope
Wallner, Alexandra 1946- *156*
  Brief entry *41*
  Earlier sketches in SATA *51, 98*
Wallner, John C. 1945- *133*
  Earlier sketches in SATA *10, 51*
Wallower, Lucille *11*
Walrod, Amy 1973(?)- *182*
Walsh, Ann 1942- *176*
  Earlier sketch in SATA *62*
Walsh, Ellen Stoll 1942- *194*
  Earlier sketches in SATA *49, 99, 147*
Walsh, George Johnston 1889-1981 .... *53*
Walsh, Gillian Paton
  See Paton Walsh, Jill
Walsh, Jill Paton
  See Paton Walsh, Jill
Walsh, Joanna 1970- *182*
Walsh, Lawrence 1942- *170*
Walsh, Marissa 1972- *195*
Walsh, Mary Caswell 1949- *118*
Walsh, Mitzy
  See Walsh, Marissa
Walsh, Suella *170*
Walsh, V. L.
  See Walsh, Vivian
Walsh, Vivian 1960- *120*
Walsh Shepherd, Donna 1948- *78*
Walter, Frances V. 1923- *71*
Walter, Mildred Pitts 1922- *133*
  Brief entry *45*
  Earlier sketch in SATA *69*
  See also CLR *61*
  See also SAAS *12*
Walter, Villiam Christian
  See Andersen, Hans Christian
Walter, Virginia
  See Walter, Virginia A.
Walter, Virginia A. *134*
Walters, Audrey 1929- *18*
Walters, Celeste 1938- *126*
Walters, Eric 1957- *205*
  Earlier sketches in SATA *99, 155*
Walters, Eric Robert
  See Walters, Eric
Walters, Gregory 1964- *213*
Walters, Helen B. (?)-1987
  Obituary *50*
Walters, Hugh
  See Hughes, Walter (Llewellyn)
Walther, Thomas A. 1950- *31*
Walther, Tom
  See Walther, Thomas A.
Waltner, Elma 1912-1987 .... *40*
Waltner, Willard H. 1909- *40*
Walton, Darwin McBeth 1926- *119*
Walton, Fiona L. M. 1959- *89*
Walton, Richard J. 1928- *4*
Walton, Rick 1957- *204*
  Earlier sketches in SATA *101, 151*
Waltrip, Lela (Kingston) 1904-1995 .... *9*
Waltrip, Mildred 1911- *37*
Waltrip, Rufus (Charles) 1898-1988 .... *9*
Walworth, Nancy Zinsser 1917- *14*
Wang, Gabrielle *212*
Wangerin, Walter, Jr. 1944- *98*
  Brief entry *37*
  Earlier sketch in SATA *45*
Waniek, Marilyn Nelson 1946-
  See Nelson, Marilyn
Wannamaker, Bruce
  See Moncure, Jane Belk
Warbler, J. M.
  See Cocagnac, Augustin Maurice(-Jean)

Warburg, Sandol Stoddard
  See Stoddard, Sandol
Ward, David 1967- *213*
Ward, E. D.
  See Gorey, Edward (St. John)
  and Lucas, E(dward) V(errall)
Ward, Ed
  See Stratemeyer, Edward L.
Ward, Helen 1962- *206*
  Earlier sketches in SATA *72, 144*
Ward, Jay 1920-1989
  Obituary *63*
Ward, Jennifer 1963- *146*
Ward, John (Stanton) 1917- *42*
Ward, Jonas
  See Ard, William
  and Cox, William R(obert)
  and Garfield, Brian (Francis Wynne)
Ward, Lynd (Kendall) 1905-1985 .... *36*
  Obituary *42*
  Earlier sketch in SATA *2*
Ward, Martha (Eads) *5*
Ward, Melanie
  See Curtis, Richard
  and Lynch, Marilyn
Ward, Nicholas John
  See Ward, Nick
Ward, Nick 1955- *190*
Ward, Tom
  See Stratemeyer, Edward L.
Wardell, Dean
  See Prince, J(ack) H(arvey)
Wardlaw, Lee 1955- *115*
  Earlier sketch in SATA *79*
Ware, Cheryl 1963- *101*
Ware, Chris 1967- *140*
Ware, Leon (Vernon) 1909-1976 .... *4*
Wargin, Kathy-jo 1964- *210*
  Earlier sketch in SATA *145*
Warhola, James 1955- *187*
Warner, Frank A. *67*
  Earlier sketch in SATA *1*
Warner, Gertrude Chandler 1890-1979 .... *9*
  Obituary *73*
Warner, J(ohn) F. 1929- *75*
Warner, Lucille Schulberg *30*
Warner, Matt
  See Fichter, George S.
Warner, Oliver (Martin Wilson) 1903-1976 . *29*
Warner, Sally 1946- *214*
  Earlier sketch in SATA *131*
Warner, Sunny (B.) 1931- *108*
Warnes, Tim 1971- *166*
  Earlier sketch in SATA *116*
Warnes, Timothy
  See Warnes, Tim
Warnick, Elsa 1942- *113*
Warren, Andrea 1946- *98*
Warren, Betsy
  See Warren, Elizabeth Avery
Warren, Billy
  See Warren, William Stephen
Warren, Cathy 1951- *62*
  Brief entry *46*
Warren, Elizabeth
  See Supraner, Robyn
Warren, Elizabeth Avery 1916- *46*
  Brief entry *38*
Warren, Jackie M. 1953- *135*
Warren, Joshua P(aul) 1976- *107*
Warren, Joyce W(illiams) 1935- *18*
Warren, Mary Phraner 1929- *10*
Warren, Robert Penn 1905-1989 .... *46*
  Obituary *63*
Warren, Scott S. 1957- *79*
Warren, William Stephen 1882-1968 .... *9*
Warrick, Patricia Scott 1925- *35*
Warriner, John 1907(?)-1987
  Obituary *53*
Warsh
  See Warshaw, Jerry

Warshaw, Jerry 1929- *30*
Warshaw, Mary 1931- *89*
Warshofsky, Fred 1931- *24*
Warshofsky, Isaac
  See Singer, Isaac Bashevis
Wartski, Maureen (Ann Crane) 1940- *50*
  Brief entry *37*
Warwick, Alan R(oss) 1900-1973 .... *42*
Wa-Sha-Quon-Asin
  See Belaney, Archibald Stansfeld
Wa-sha-quon-asin
  See Belaney, Archibald Stansfeld
Washburn, Bradford 1910-2007 .... *38*
  Obituary *181*
Washburn, Henry Bradford, Jr.
  See Washburn, Bradford
Washburn, Jan(ice) 1926- *63*
Washburn, Lucia *193*
Washburne, Carolyn Kott 1944- *86*
Washburne, Heluiz Chandler 1892-1970 ..... *10*
  Obituary *26*
Washington, Booker T. 1856-1915 .... *28*
Washington, Donna L. 1967- *159*
  Earlier sketch in SATA *98*
Wasserman, Robin 1978- *207*
Wasserstein, Wendy 1950-2006 .... *94*
  Obituary *174*
Wassiljewa, Tatjana 1928- *106*
Watanabe, Shigeo 1928- *131*
  Brief entry *32*
  Earlier sketch in SATA *39*
  See also CLR *8*
Waters, John F(rederick) 1930- *4*
Waters, Summer
  See Sykes, Julie
Waters, Tony 1958- *75*
Waterton, Betty 1923- *99*
  Brief entry *34*
  Earlier sketch in SATA *37*
Waterton, Betty Marie
  See Waterton, Betty
Watkins, Dawn L. *126*
Watkins, Gloria Jean
  See hooks, bell
Watkins, Lis
  See Watkins, Liselotte
Watkins, Liselotte 1971- *215*
Watkins, Lois 1930- *88*
Watkins, Peter 1934- *66*
Watkins, Yoko Kawashima 1933- *93*
Watkins-Pitchford, Denys James
  1905-1990 .... *87*
  Obituary *66*
  Earlier sketch in SATA *6*
  See also SAAS *4*
Watling, James 1933- *117*
  Earlier sketch in SATA *67*
Watson, Aldren A(uld) 1917- *42*
  Brief entry *36*
Watson, Amy Zakrzewski 1965- *76*
Watson, B. S.
  See Teitelbaum, Michael
Watson, Carol 1949- *78*
Watson, C.G. *193*
Watson, Clyde 1947- *68*
  Earlier sketch in SATA *5*
  See also CLR *3*
Watson, Helen Orr 1892-1978
  Obituary *24*
Watson, James 1936- *106*
  Earlier sketch in SATA *10*
Watson, Jane Werner 1915- *54*
  Earlier sketch in SATA *3*
Watson, Jesse Joshua *199*
Watson, John H.
  See Farmer, Philip Jose
Watson, Mary 1953- *117*
Watson, N. Cameron 1955- *81*
Watson, Nancy Dingman *32*
Watson, Pauline 1925- *14*

Watson, Richard F.
  See Silverberg, Robert
Watson, Richard Jesse 1951- *211*
  Earlier sketch in SATA *62*
Watson, Sally (Lou) 1924- *3*
Watson, Sasha *211*
Watson, Wendy (McLeod) 1942- *142*
  Earlier sketches in SATA *5, 74*
Watson Taylor, Elizabeth 1915- *41*
Watt, Melanie 1975- *193*
  Earlier sketch in SATA *136*
Watt, Thomas 1935- *4*
Wattenberg, Jane *174*
Watterson, Bill 1958- *66*
Watt-Evans, Lawrence 1954- *121*
Watts, (Anna) Bernadette 1942- *103*
  Earlier sketch in SATA *4*
Watts, Ephraim
  See Horne, Richard Henry Hengist
Watts, Franklin (Mowry) 1904-1978 .... *46*
  Obituary *21*
Watts, Helen L. Hoke 1903-1990
  Obituary *65*
Watts, Irene N(aemi) 1931- *111*
  Earlier sketch in SATA *56*
Watts, Isaac 1674-1748 .... *52*
Watts, James K(ennedy) M(offitt) 1955- *59*
Watts, Jeri Hanel 1957- *170*
Watts, Julia 1969- *103*
Watts, Leander 1956- *146*
Watts, Leslie Elizabeth 1961- *168*
Watts, Mabel Pizzey 1906-1994 .... *11*
Watts, Nigel 1957-1999 .... *121*
Waugh, C. C. Roessel
  See Waugh, Carol-Lynn Rossel
  and Waugh, Charles G(ordon)
Waugh, Carol-Lynn Rossel 1947- *41*
Waugh, Dorothy -1996 .... *11*
Waugh, Sylvia 1935- *169*
Waugh, Virginia
  See Sorensen, Virginia
Wax, Wendy A. 1963- *163*
  Earlier sketch in SATA *73*
Wayland, April Halprin 1954- *143*
  Earlier sketch in SATA *78*
  See also SAAS *26*
Wayland, Patrick
  See O'Connor, Richard
Wayne, (Anne) Jenifer 1917-1982 .... *32*
Wayne, Kyra Petrovskaya 1918- *8*
Wayne, Richard
  See Decker, Duane
Wayshak, Deborah Noyes
  See Noyes, Deborah
Waystaff, Simon
  See Swift, Jonathan
Weales, Gerald (Clifford) 1925- *11*
Weary, Ogdred
  See Gorey, Edward (St. John)
Weatherford, Carole Boston 1956- *181*
  Earlier sketch in SATA *138*
Weatherill, Cat *203*
Weatherly, Lee 1967- *192*
Weatherly, Myra 1926- *130*
Weatherly, Myra S.
  See Weatherly, Myra
Weaver, Harriett E. 1908-1993 .... *65*
Weaver, John L. 1949- *42*
Weaver, Robyn
  See Conley, Robyn
Weaver, Robyn M.
  See Conley, Robyn
Weaver, Tess *197*
Weaver, Ward
  See Mason, F(rancis) van Wyck
Weaver, Will 1950- *161*
  Earlier sketches in SATA *88, 109*
Weaver, William Weller
  See Weaver, Will
Weaver-Gelzer, Charlotte 1950- *79*

Webb, Christopher
  See Wibberley, Leonard
Webb, Jacqueline
  See Pearce, Margaret
Webb, Jacqueline
  See Pearce, Margaret
  and Pearce, Margaret
Webb, Jean Francis (III) 1910-1991 .... *35*
Webb, Kaye 1914- *60*
Webb, Lois Sinaiko 1922- *82*
Webb, Margot 1934- *67*
Webb, Sharon 1936-2010 .... *41*
Webb, Sophie 1958- *135*
Webber, Andrew Lloyd
  See Lloyd Webber, Andrew
Webber, Desiree Morrison 1956- *170*
Webber, Irma E(leanor Schmidt)
  1904-1995 .... *14*
Weber, Alfons 1921- *8*
Weber, Bruce 1942- *120*
  Earlier sketch in SATA *73*
Weber, Debora 1955- *58*
Weber, EdNah New Rider 1919(?)- *168*
Weber, Jill 1950- *209*
  Earlier sketch in SATA *127*
Weber, Judith E(ichler) 1938- *64*
Weber, Ken(neth J.) 1940- *90*
Weber, Lenora Mattingly 1895-1971 .... *2*
  Obituary *26*
Weber, Michael 1945- *87*
Weber, Sandra 1961- *158*
Weber, William J(ohn) 1927- *14*
Webster, Alice Jane Chandler 1876-1916 ..... *17*
Webster, David 1930- *11*
Webster, Frank V. *67*
  Earlier sketch in SATA *1*
Webster, Gary
  See Garrison, Webb B(lack)
Webster, James 1925-1981 .... *17*
  Obituary *27*
Webster, Jean
  See Webster, Alice Jane Chandler
Wechsler, Doug *189*
Wechsler, Herman J. 1904-1976
  Obituary *20*
Wechter, Nell (Carolyn) Wise 1913-1989 .. *127*
  Earlier sketch in SATA *60*
Weck, Thomas L. 1942- *62*
Wedd, Kate
  See Gregory, Philippa
Weddle, Ethel Harshbarger 1897-1996 .... *11*
Wedekind, Annie *204*
Weeks, Sarah *194*
  Earlier sketch in SATA *158*
Weems, David B(urnola) 1922- *80*
Wees, Frances Shelley 1902-1982 .... *58*
Weevers, Peter 1944- *59*
Wegen, Ronald 1946-1985 .... *99*
Wegman, William (George) 1943- *135*
  Earlier sketches in SATA *78, 129*
Wegner, Fritz 1924- *20*
Weidhorn, Manfred 1931- *60*
Weidt, Maryann N. 1944- *85*
Weigel, Jeff 1958- *170*
Weigelt, Udo 1960- *201*
  Earlier sketch in SATA *168*
Weihs, Erika 1917- *107*
  Earlier sketch in SATA *15*
Weik, Mary Hays 1898(?)-1979 .... *3*
  Obituary *23*
Weil, Ann Yezner 1908-1969 .... *9*
Weil, Lisl 1910- *7*
Weilerstein, Sadie Rose 1894-1993 .... *3*
  Obituary *75*
Weill, Cynthia 1959- *167*
Wein, Elizabeth E. 1964- *151*
  Earlier sketch in SATA *82*
Wein, Elizabeth Eve
  See Wein, Elizabeth E.
Weinberg, Larry
  See Weinberg, Lawrence (E.)

Weinberg, Lawrence (E.) *92*
  Brief entry *48*
Weinberger, Tanya 1939- *84*
Weiner, Sandra 1922- *14*
Weingarten, Violet (Brown) 1915-1976 .... *3*
  Obituary *27*
Weingartner, Charles 1922- *5*
Weinheimer, Beckie 1958- *186*
Weinstein, Ellen Slusky 1959- *200*
Weinstein, Muriel Harris *215*
Weinstein, Nina 1951- *73*
Weinstock, Robert 1967- *204*
Weir, Bob 1947- *76*
Weir, Diana (R.) Loiewski 1958- *111*
Weir, Joan S(herman) 1928- *99*
Weir, LaVada *2*
Weir, Rosemary (Green) 1905-1994 .... *21*
Weir, Wendy 1949- *76*
Weis, Margaret 1948- *164*
  Earlier sketches in SATA *38, 92*
Weisberger, Bernard A(llen) 1922- *21*
Weisburd, Stefi 1957- *202*
Weiser, Marjorie P(hillis) K(atz) 1934- *33*
Weisgard, Leonard (Joseph) 1916-2000 .... *85*
  Obituary *122*
  Earlier sketches in SATA *2, 30*
  See also SAAS *19*
Weiss, Adelle 1920- *18*
Weiss, Ann E(dwards) 1943- *69*
  Earlier sketch in SATA *30*
  See also SAAS *13*
Weiss, Edna
  See Barth, Edna
Weiss, Ellen 1953- *44*
Weiss, Harvey 1922- *76*
  Earlier sketches in SATA *1, 27*
  See also CLR *4*
  See also SAAS *19*
Weiss, Jaqueline Shachter 1926- *65*
Weiss, Malcolm E. 1928- *3*
Weiss, Margaret Edith
  See Weis, Margaret
Weiss, Miriam
  See Schlein, Miriam
Weiss, Mitch 1951- *183*
  Earlier sketch in SATA *123*
Weiss, Nicki 1954- *86*
  Earlier sketch in SATA *33*
Weiss, Renee Karol 1923- *5*
Weissberger, Ela 1930- *181*
Weissberger, Ela Stein
  See Weissberger, Ela
Weissenborn, Hellmuth 1898-1982
  Obituary *31*
Weitzman, David L. 1936- *172*
  Earlier sketch in SATA *122*
Wekesser, Carol A. 1963- *76*
Welber, Robert *26*
Welch, Amanda (Jane) 1945- *75*
Welch, D'Alte Aldridge 1907-1970
  Obituary *27*
Welch, Holly *206*
Welch, Jean-Louise
  See Kempton, Jean Welch
Welch, Pauline
  See Bodenham, Hilda Morris
Welch, Ronald
  See Felton, Ronald Oliver
Welch, Sheila Kelly 1945- *130*
Welch, Willy 1952- *93*
Weldin, Frauke 1969- *188*
Welford, Sue 1942- *75*
Weller, George 1907-2002 .... *31*
  Obituary *140*
Weller, George Anthony
  See Weller, George
Welling, Peter J. 1947- *135*
Wellington, Monica 1957- *157*
  Earlier sketches in SATA *67, 99*
Wellman, Alice 1900-1984 .... *51*
  Brief entry *36*

Wellman, Manly Wade 1903-1986 6
  Obituary 47
Wellman, Paul I. 1898-1966 3
Wellman, Paul Iselin
  See Wellman, Paul I.
Wellman, Sam 1939- 122
Wellman, Samuel
  See Wellman, Sam
Wells, H. G. 1866-1946 20
  See also CLR 133
Wells, Helen
  See Campbell, Hope
Wells, Helen 1910-1986 49
  Earlier sketch in SATA 2
Wells, Herbert George
  See Wells, H. G.
Wells, J. Wellington
  See de Camp, L. Sprague
Wells, June
  See Swinford, Betty (June Wells)
Wells, Robert
  See Welsch, Roger L(ee)
Wells, Robert E. 184
Wells, Rosemary 1943- 207
  Earlier sketches in SATA 18, 69, 114, 156
  See also CLR 69
  See also SAAS 1
Wells, Susan (Mary) 1951- 78
Wels, Byron G(erald) 1924-1993 9
Welsbacher, Anne 1955- 89
Welsch, Roger L(ee) 1936- 82
Welsh, David
  See Hills, C.A.R.
Welsh, Mary Flynn 1910(?)-1984
  Obituary 38
Welsh, T.K. 1956- 184
Weltner, Linda R(iverly) 1938- 38
Welton, Jude 1955- 143
  Earlier sketch in SATA 79
Welty, S. F.
  See Welty, Susan F.
Welty, Susan F. 1905- 9
Wemmlinger, Raymond 190
Wendelin, Rudolph 1910-2000 23
Weninger, Brigitte 1960- 189
Wentworth, Robert
  See Hamilton, Edmond
Werlin, Nancy 1961- 161
  Earlier sketches in SATA 87, 119
Werner, Elsa Jane
  See Watson, Jane Werner
Werner, Herma 1926- 47
  Brief entry 41
Werner, Jane
  See Watson, Jane Werner
Werner, K.
  See Casewit, Curtis W(erner)
Wersba, Barbara 1932- 58
  Autobiography Feature 103
  Earlier sketch in SATA 1
  See also CLR 78
  See also SAAS 2
Werstein, Irving 1914(?)-1971 14
Werth, Kurt 1896-1983 20
Wesley, Alison
  See Barnes, Michael
Wesley, Kathryn
  See Rusch, Kristine Kathryn
Wesley, Mary (Aline) 1912-2002 66
Wesley, Valerie Wilson 1947- 168
  Earlier sketch in SATA 106
West, Andrew
  See Arthur, Robert, (Jr.)
West, Anna 1938- 40
West, Barbara
  See Price, Olive
West, Betty 1921- 11
West, Bruce 1951- 63
West, C. P.
  See Wodehouse, P. G.

West, Dorothy
  See Benson, Mildred
West, Emily Govan 1919- 38
West, Emmy
  See West, Emily Govan
West, James
  See Withers, Carl A.
West, Jerry
  See Svenson, Andrew E(dward)
West, (Mary) Jessamyn 1902-1984
  Obituary 37
West, John
  See Arthur, Robert, (Jr.)
West, Owen
  See Koontz, Dean
West, Ward
  See Borland, Harold Glen
Westall, Robert (Atkinson) 1929-1993 69
  Obituary 75
  Earlier sketch in SATA 23
  See also CLR 13
  See also SAAS 2
Westaway, Jane 1948- 121
Westcott, Nadine Bernard 1949- 130
Westera, Marleen 1962- 187
Westerberg, Christine 1950- 29
Westerduin, Anne 1945- 105
Westerfeld, Scott 1963- 161
Westervelt, Virginia Veeder 1914-2005 10
Westheimer, David 1917-2005 14
  Obituary 170
Westheimer, David Kaplan
  See Westheimer, David
Westmacott, Mary
  See Christie, Agatha
Westman, Barbara 70
Westman, Paul (Wendell) 1956- 39
Westmoreland, William C. 1914-2005 63
Westmoreland, William Childs
  See Westmoreland, William C.
Weston, Allen
  See Hogarth, Grace (Weston Allen)
  and Norton, Andre
Weston, Carol 1956- 135
Weston, Carrie 190
Weston, John (Harrison) 1932- 21
Weston, Martha 1947- 119
  Earlier sketch in SATA 53
Weston, Robert Paul 209
Westphal, Arnold Carl 1897- 57
Westrup, Hugh 102
Westwood, Jennifer 1940-2008 10
  Obituary 192
Wexler, Jerome (LeRoy) 1923- 14
Weyland, Jack 1940- 81
Weyn, Suzanne 1955- 164
  Earlier sketches in SATA 63, 101
Weyr, Garret
  See Freymann-Weyr, (Rhoda) Garret
  (Michaela)
Wezyk, Joanna 1966- 82
Whaley, Joyce Irene 1923- 61
Whalin, W. Terry 1953- 93
Wharf, Michael
  See Weller, George
Wharmby, Margot 63
Wharton, Edith 1862-1937
  See CLR 136
Wharton, Edith Newbold Jones
  See Wharton, Edith
Whatley, Bruce 1954- 213
  Earlier sketch in SATA 177
Wheatley, Arabelle 1921- 16
Wheatley, Nadia 1949- 147
Wheeler, Cindy 1955- 49
  Brief entry 40
Wheeler, Deborah 1947- 83
Wheeler, Janet D. 1
Wheeler, Jill C. 1964- 136
  Earlier sketch in SATA 86

Wheeler, Jody 1952- 148
  Earlier sketch in SATA 84
Wheeler, Lisa 1963- 200
  Earlier sketch in SATA 162
Wheeler, Opal 1898- 23
Whelan, Elizabeth M(urphy) 1943- 14
Whelan, Gloria 1923- 178
  Earlier sketches in SATA 85, 128
  See also CLR 90
Whelan, Gloria Ann
  See Whelan, Gloria
Whipple, A(ddison) B(eecher) C(olvin)
  1918- 64
Whipple, Cal
  See Whipple, A(ddison) B(eecher) C(olvin)
Whisp, Kennilworthy
  See Rowling, J.K.
Whistler, Reginald John 1905-1944 30
Whistler, Rex
  See Whistler, Reginald John
Whitaker, Zai 183
Whitcher, Susan (Godsil) 1952- 96
Whitcomb, Jon 1906-1988 10
  Obituary 56
Whitcomb, Laura 1958- 214
  Earlier sketch in SATA 171
White, Anne Terry 1896-1980 2
White, Bessie (Felstiner) 1892(?)-1986
  Obituary 50
White, Carolyn 1948- 130
White, Dale
  See Place, Marian T(empleton)
White, Dori 1919- 10
White, E. B. 1899-1985 100
  Obituary 44
  Earlier sketches in SATA 2, 29
  See also CLR 107
White, Eliza Orne 1856-1947
  See YABC 2
White, Elwyn Brooks
  See White, E. B.
White, Florence M(eiman) 1910- 14
White, Laurence B(arton), Jr. 1935- 10
White, Lee 176
White, Martin 1943- 51
White, Nancy 1942- 126
White, Ramy Allison 67
  Earlier sketch in SATA 1
White, Robb 1909-1990 83
  Earlier sketch in SATA 1
  See also CLR 3
  See also SAAS 1
White, Ruth C. 1942- 186
  Autobiography Feature 186
  Earlier sketches in SATA 39, 117, 165
White, T(erence) H(anbury) 1906-1964 12
  See also CLR 139
White, Tekla N. 1934- 115
White, Timothy (Thomas Anthony)
  1952-2002 60
White, Tom 1923- 148
White, William, Jr. 1934- 16
Whitehead, Don(ald) F. 1908-1981 4
Whitehead, Jenny 1964- 191
Whitehead, Kathy 1957- 176
Whitehouse, Arch
  See Whitehouse, Arthur George Joseph
Whitehouse, Arthur George Joseph
  1895-1979 14
  Obituary 23
Whitehouse, Elizabeth S(cott) 1893-1968 35
Whitehouse, Jeanne
  See Peterson, Jeanne Whitehouse
Whitelaw, Nancy 1933- 166
  Earlier sketch in SATA 76
Whitesel, Cheryl Aylward 162
Whiting, Sue 1960- 205
Whiting, Susan Allana
  See Whiting, Sue
Whitinger, R. D.
  See Place, Marian T(empleton)

Whitley, Mary Ann
  See Sebrey, Mary Ann
Whitley, Peggy 1938- *140*
Whitlock, Pamela 1921(?)-1982
  Obituary *31*
Whitlock, Ralph 1914-1995 35
Whitman, Alice
  See Marker, Sherry
Whitman, Candace 1958- *208*
Whitman, Sylvia (Choate) 1961- *135*
  Earlier sketch in SATA *85*
Whitman, Walt 1819-1892 20
Whitman, Walter
  See Whitman, Walt
Whitmore, Arvella 1922- *125*
Whitmore, Benette 1955- *203*
Whitney, Alex(andra) 1922- *14*
Whitney, David C(harles) 1921- 48
  Brief entry 29
Whitney, Kim Ablon *162*
Whitney, Phyllis A. 1903-2008 30
  Obituary *189*
  Earlier sketch in SATA *1*
  See also CLR 59
Whitney, Phyllis Ayame
  See Whitney, Phyllis A.
Whitney, Sharon 1937- 63
Whitney, Thomas P. 1917-2007 25
  Obituary *189*
Whitney, Thomas Porter
  See Whitney, Thomas P.
Whittington, Mary K(athrine) 1941- 75
Whitworth, John 1945- *123*
Whybrow, Ian *202*
  Earlier sketch in SATA *132*
Whyte, Mal(colm Kenneth, Jr.) 1933- 62
Whyte, Mary 1953- *148*
  Earlier sketch in SATA *94*
Whyte, Ron 1942(?)-1989
  Obituary 63
Whytock, Cherry *177*
Wiater, Stanley 1953- 84
Wibbelsman, Charles J(oseph) 1945- 59
Wibberley, Leonard 1915-1983 45
  Obituary 36
  Earlier sketch in SATA *2*
  See also CLR *3*
Wibberley, Leonard Patrick O'Connor
  See Wibberley, Leonard
Wiberg, Harald (Albin) 1908- 93
  Brief entry 40
Wick, Walter 1953- *148*
Wickberg, Susan
  See Rottman, S.L.
Wickens, Elaine 86
Wicker, Ireene 1905(?)-1987
  Obituary 55
Wickstrom, Sylvie 1960- *169*
Wickstrom, Thor 1960- *200*
Widdemer, Mabel Cleland 1902-1964 5
Widener, Terry 1950- *209*
  Earlier sketch in SATA *105*
Widerberg, Siv 1931- *10*
Wiebe, Rudy 1934- *156*
Wiebe, Rudy Henry
  See Wiebe, Rudy
Wieler, Diana (Jean) 1961- *109*
Wiener, Lori 1956- 84
Wier, Ester (Alberti) 1910-2000 .... *3*
Wiese, Kurt 1887-1974 36
  Obituary 24
  Earlier sketch in SATA *3*
  See also CLR *86*
Wiesner, Portia
  See Takakjian, Portia

Wiesner, William 1899-1984 5
Wiggers, Raymond 1952- 82
Wiggin, Eric E. 1939- *167*
  Earlier sketch in SATA *88*
Wiggin, Eric Ellsworth 1939-
  See Wiggin, Eric E.
Wiggin (Riggs), Kate Douglas (Smith)
  1856-1923
  See YABC *1*
  See also CLR *52*
Wiggins, VeraLee (Chesnut) 1928-1995 89
Wight, James Alfred
  See Herriot, James
Wignell, Edel 1936- 69
Wijnberg, Ellen 85
Wikland, Ilon 1930- 93
  Brief entry 32
Wikler, Madeline 1943- *114*
Wilber, Donald N(ewton) 1907-1997 35
Wilbur, C. Keith 1923- 27
Wilbur, Frances 1921- *107*
Wilbur, Helen L. 1948- *204*
Wilbur, Richard 1921- *108*
  Earlier sketch in SATA *9*
Wilbur, Richard Purdy
  See Wilbur, Richard
Wilburn, Kathy 1948- 68
Wilcox, Charlotte 1948- 72
Wilcox, Leah 1975(?)- *207*
Wilcox, R(uth) Turner 1888-1970 36
Wilcox, Roger
  See Collins, Paul
Wild, Jocelyn 1941- 46
Wild, Kate 1954- *192*
Wild, Margaret 1948- *197*
  Earlier sketch in SATA *151*
Wild, Robin (Evans) 1936- 46
Wild, Robyn 1947- *117*
Wilde, D. Gunther
  See Hurwood, Bernhardt J.
Wilde, Oscar 1854(?)-1900 24
  See also CLR *114*
Wilde, Oscar Fingal O'Flahertie Willis
  See Wilde, Oscar
Wilder, Buck
  See Smith, Tim(othy R.)
Wilder, Laura Elizabeth Ingalls
  See Wilder, Laura Ingalls
Wilder, Laura Ingalls 1867-1957 .... *100*
  Earlier sketches in SATA *15, 29*
  See also CLR *111*
Wildsmith, Brian 1930- *124*
  Earlier sketches in SATA *16, 69*
  See also CLR *52*
  See also SAAS *5*
Wiles, Deborah *171*
Wilhelm, Doug 1952- *190*
Wilhelm, Hans 1945- *196*
  Autobiography Feature *196*
  Earlier sketches in SATA *58, 135*
  See also CLR *46*
  See also SAAS *21*
Wilkie, Katharine E(lliott) 1904-1980 .... *31*
Wilkin, Eloise 1904-1987 49
  Obituary 54
Wilkins, Frances 1923- *14*
Wilkins, Kim *147*
Wilkins, Marilyn (Ruth) 1926- 30
Wilkins, Marne
  See Wilkins, Marilyn (Ruth)
Wilkins, Mary Huiskamp 1926- *2*
  See also CLR *42*
Wilkins, Mary Huiskamp Calhoun
  See Wilkins, Mary Huiskamp
Wilkins, Rose *180*
Wilkinson, (Thomas) Barry 1923- 50
  Brief entry 32
Wilkinson, Beth 1925- 80
Wilkinson, Brenda 1946- 91
  Earlier sketch in SATA *14*
  See also CLR *20*

Wilkinson, (John) Burke 1913-2000 4
Wilkinson, Carole 1950- *210*
Wilkinson, Sylvia 1940- 56
  Brief entry 39
Wilkon, Jozef 1930- *133*
  Earlier sketches in SATA *31, 71*
Wilkowski, Sue *193*
Wilks, Michael Thomas 1947- 44
Wilks, Mike
  See Wilks, Michael Thomas
Will
  See Lipkind, William
Willard, Barbara (Mary) 1909-1994 74
  Earlier sketch in SATA *17*
  See also CLR *2*
  See also SAAS *5*
Willard, Elizabeth Kimmel
  See Kimmel, Elizabeth Cody
Willard, Mildred Wilds 1911-1978 .... *14*
Willard, Nancy 1936- *191*
  Brief entry 30
  Earlier sketches in SATA *37, 71, 127*
  See also CLR *5*
Willcox, Isobel 1907-1996 42
Willems, Mo *180*
  Earlier sketch in SATA *154*
  See also CLR *114*
Willett, Edward 1959- *115*
Willett, Edward C.
  See Willett, Edward
Willey, Bee *184*
Willey, Margaret 1950- 86
Willey, Robert
  See Ley, Willy
Willhoite, Michael A. 1946- 71
William, Kate
  See Armstrong, Jennifer
Williams, Alex 1969- *209*
Williams, Arlene *171*
Williams, Barbara 1925- *107*
  Earlier sketch in SATA *11*
  See also CLR *48*
  See also SAAS *16*
Williams, Barbara 1937- 62
Williams, Beryl
  See Epstein, Beryl
Williams, Brian (Peter) 1943- 54
Williams, Carol Lynch 1959- *212*
  Earlier sketch in SATA *110*
Williams, Charles
  See Collier, James Lincoln
Williams, Clyde C. 1881-1974 8
  Obituary 27
Williams, Coe
  See Harrison, C(hester) William
Williams, Colleen Madonna Flood 1963- .. *156*
Williams, Cynthia G. 1958- *123*
Williams, Dar 1967- *168*
Williams, Donna Reilly 1945- 83
Williams, Dorothy
  See Williams, Marcia
Williams, Dorothy Snowden
  See Williams, Dar
Williams, Eric (Ernest) 1911-1983 .... *14*
  Obituary 38
Williams, Ferelith Eccles
  See Eccles Williams, Ferelith
Williams, Frances B.
  See Browin, Frances Williams
Williams, Garth (Montgomery) 1912-1996 .. 66
  Obituary 90
  Earlier sketch in SATA *18*
  See also CLR *57*
  See also SAAS *7*
Williams, Guy R(ichard) 1920- *11*
Williams, Hawley
  See Heyliger, William
Williams, Helen 1948- 77
Williams, J. R.
  See Williams, Jeanne

Williams, J. Walker
   See Wodehouse, P. G.
Williams, Jay 1914-1978 .... *41*
   Obituary *24*
   Earlier sketch in SATA *3*
   See also CLR *8*
Williams, Jeanne 1930- *5*
Williams, Jenny 1939- *60*
Williams, Karen Lynn 1952- *99*
   Earlier sketch in SATA *66*
Williams, Kit 1946(?)- *44*
   See also CLR *4*
Williams, L. E.
   See Williams, Laura E.
Williams, Laura E.
   See Williams, Laura Ellen
Williams, Laura Ellen *180*
Williams, Leslie 1941- *42*
Williams, Linda 1948- *59*
Williams, Louise Bonino 1904(?)-1984
   Obituary *39*
Williams, Lynn
   See Hale, Arlene
Williams, Marcia 1945- *159*
   Earlier sketches in SATA *71, 97*
Williams, Marcia Dorothy
   See Williams, Marcia
Williams, Margery
   See Bianco, Margery Williams
Williams, Mark
   See Arthur, Robert, (Jr.)
Williams, Mark London 1959- *140*
Williams, Maureen 1951- *12*
Williams, Michael
   See St. John, Wylly Folk
Williams, Patrick J.
   See Griffin, W.E.B.
Williams, Pete
   See Faulknor, Cliff(ord Vernon)
Williams, S. P.
   See Hart, Virginia
Williams, Sam *177*
   Earlier sketch in SATA *124*
Williams, Selma R(uth) 1925- *14*
Williams, Sherley Anne 1944-1999 .... *78*
   Obituary *116*
Williams, Sheron 1955- *77*
Williams, Shirley
   See Williams, Sherley Anne
Williams, Slim
   See Williams, Clyde C.
Williams, Sophy 1965- *135*
Williams, Sue 1948-2007 .... *208*
Williams, Susan
   See Beckhorn, Susan Williams
Williams, Suzanne
   See Williams, Suzanne Morgan
Williams, Suzanne 1953- *202*
   Earlier sketch in SATA *71*
Williams, Suzanne M.
   See Williams, Suzanne Morgan
Williams, Suzanne Morgan 1949- *207*
Williams, Ursula Moray
   See Moray Williams, Ursula
Williams, Vera B(aker) 1927- *102*
   Brief entry *33*
   Earlier sketch in SATA *53*
   See also CLR *9*
Williams-Andriani, Renee 1963- *98*
Williams-Ellis, (Mary) Amabel (Nassau
   Strachey) 1894-1984 .... *29*
   Obituary *41*
Williams-Garcia, Rita 1957- *160*
   Earlier sketch in SATA *98*
   See also CLR *36*
Williamson, Gwyneth 1965- *109*
Williamson, Henry (William) 1895-1977 ..... *37*
   Obituary *30*
Williamson, Joanne S(mall) 1926- *122*
   Earlier sketch in SATA *3*
Williamson, Kate T. 1979- *215*

Williamson, Melanie *196*
Willis, Charles
   See Clarke, Arthur C.
Willis, Connie 1945- *110*
   See also CLR *66*
Willis, Cynthia Chapman *215*
Willis, Jeanne 1959- *195*
   Earlier sketches in SATA *61, 123*
Willis, Jeanne Mary
   See Willis, Jeanne
Willis, Meredith Sue 1946- *101*
Willis, Nancy Carol 1952- *139*
   Earlier sketch in SATA *93*
Willis, Paul J. 1955- *113*
Willms, Russ *95*
Willoughby, Lee Davis
   See Avallone, Michael (Angelo, Jr.)
   and Brandner, Gary (Phil)
   and Deming, Richard
   and DeAndrea, William L(ouis)
   and Laymon, Richard (Carl)
   and Streib, Dan(iel Thomas)
   and Toombs, John
   and Webb, Jean Francis (III)
Willson, Robina Beckles
   See Beckles Willson, Robina
Wilma, Dana
   See Faralla, Dana
Wilsdorf, Anne 1954- *191*
Wilson, April *80*
Wilson, Barbara Ker
   See Ker Wilson, Barbara
Wilson, Beth P(ierre) *8*
Wilson, Budge 1927- *55*
   Brief entry *51*
Wilson, Carletta 1951- *81*
Wilson, Carter 1941- *6*
Wilson, Charles Morrow 1905-1977 .... *30*
Wilson, Christopher B. 1910(?)-1985
   Obituary *46*
Wilson, Darryl B(abe) 1939- *90*
Wilson, Diane Lee *172*
Wilson, Dirk
   See Pohl, Frederik
Wilson, Dorothy Clarke 1904-2003 .... *16*
Wilson, Edward A(rthur) 1886-1970 .... *38*
Wilson, Ellen (Janet Cameron) (?)-1976 ...... *9*
   Obituary *26*
Wilson, Eric (H.) 1940- *34*
   Brief entry *32*
Wilson, Erica *51*
Wilson, Forrest 1918- *27*
Wilson, Gahan 1930- *35*
   Brief entry *27*
Wilson, Gina 1943- *85*
   Brief entry *34*
   Earlier sketch in SATA *36*
Wilson, (Leslie) Granville 1912- *14*
Wilson, Hazel (Hutchins) 1898-1992 .... *3*
   Obituary *73*
Wilson, J(erry) M. 1964- *121*
Wilson, Jacqueline 1945- *199*
   Brief entry *52*
   Earlier sketches in SATA *61, 102, 153*
Wilson, John 1922- *22*
Wilson, John 1951- *182*
Wilson, John Alexander
   See Wilson, John
Wilson, Johnniece Marshall 1944- *75*
Wilson, Jonathan 1950- *181*
Wilson, Joyce M. *84*
   Earlier sketch in SATA *21*
   See also SAAS *24*
Wilson, Karma *174*
Wilson, Leslie 1952- *166*
Wilson, Linda Miller 1936- *116*
Wilson, Lionel 1924-2003 .... *33*
   Brief entry *31*
   Obituary *144*
Wilson, Marjorie
   See Wilson, Budge

Wilson, Martin 1973- *205*
Wilson, Maurice (Charles John) 1914- *46*
Wilson, Nancy Hope 1947- *138*
   Earlier sketch in SATA *81*
Wilson, Nathan D.
   See Wilson, N.D.
Wilson, N.D. 1978- *194*
Wilson, Nick
   See Ellis, Edward S.
Wilson, Phil 1948- *181*
Wilson, Ron(ald William) 1941- *38*
Wilson, Sarah 1934- *208*
   Earlier sketches in SATA *50, 142*
Wilson, Tom 1931- *33*
   Brief entry *30*
Wilson, Troy 1970- *169*
Wilson, Walt(er N.) 1939- *14*
Wilson-Max, Ken 1965- *170*
   Earlier sketch in SATA *93*
Wilton, Elizabeth 1937- *14*
Wilton, Hal
   See Pepper, Frank S.
Wilwerding, Walter Joseph 1891-1966 .... *9*
Wimmer, Mike 1961- *194*
   Earlier sketch in SATA *70*
Winborn, Marsha (Lynn) 1947- *75*
Winch, John 1944- *165*
   Earlier sketch in SATA *117*
Winchester, James H(ugh) 1917-1985 .... *30*
   Obituary *45*
Winchester, Stanley
   See Youd, Samuel
Windawi, Thura al- 1983(?)- *165*
Winders, Gertrude Hecker -1987 .... *3*
Windham, Basil
   See Wodehouse, P. G.
Windham, Kathryn T(ucker) 1918- *14*
Windham, Sophie *184*
Windling, Terri 1958- *151*
Windrow, Martin
   See Windrow, Martin Clive
Windrow, Martin C.
   See Windrow, Martin Clive
Windrow, Martin Clive 1944- *68*
Windsor, Claire
   See Hamerstrom, Frances
Windsor, Linda 1950- *124*
Windsor, Patricia 1938- *78*
   Earlier sketch in SATA *30*
   See also SAAS *19*
Wineman-Marcus, Irene 1952- *81*
Winer, Yvonne 1934- *120*
Winerip, Michael *175*
Winfield, Arthur M.
   See Stratemeyer, Edward L.
Winfield, Edna
   See Stratemeyer, Edward L.
Winfield, Julia
   See Armstrong, Jennifer
Wing, Natasha 1960- *200*
   Earlier sketch in SATA *82*
Wingerter, Linda S. 1973(?)- *207*
Winget, Susan *211*
Winick, Judd 1970- *124*
Winks, Robin William 1930-2003 .... *61*
Winn, Alison
   See Wharmby, Margot
Winn, Chris 1952- *42*
Winn, Janet Bruce 1928- *43*
Winn, Marie 1936(?)- *38*
Winnick, Karen B. 1946- *211*
Winnick, Karen B(eth) B(inkoff) 1946- *51*
Winn-Lederer, Ilene *198*
Winslow, Barbara 1947- *91*
Winstead, Rosie *180*
Winston, Clara 1921-1983 .... *54*
   Obituary *39*
Winston, Richard 1917-1979 .... *54*
Winston, Sherri 1964(?)- *201*
Winter, Janet 1926- *126*

Winter, Jeanette 1939- *184*
Earlier sketch in SATA *151*
Winter, Jonah 1962- *179*
Winter, Milo (Kendall) 1888-1956 .... *21*
Winter, Paula Cecelia 1929- *48*
Winter, R. R.
See Winterbotham, R(ussell) R(obert)
Winter, Susan *182*
Winterbotham, R(ussell) R(obert)
1904-1971 .... *10*
Winterbotham, Russ
See Winterbotham, R(ussell) R(obert)
Winterfeld, Henry 1901-1990 .... *55*
Winters, J. C.
See Cross, Gilbert B.
Winters, Jon
See Cross, Gilbert B.
Winters, Katherine
See Winters, Kay
Winters, Kay 1936- *153*
Earlier sketch in SATA *103*
Winters, Nina 1944- *62*
Winters, Paul A. 1965- *106*
Winterson, Jeanette 1959- *190*
Winterton, Gayle
See Adams, William Taylor
Winthrop, Elizabeth 1948- *164*
Autobiography Feature *116*
Earlier sketches in SATA *8, 76*
See also CLR *89*
Winton, Ian (Kenneth) 1960- *76*
Winton, Tim 1960- *98*
Wintz-Litty, Julie
See Litty, Julie
Wirt, Ann
See Benson, Mildred
Wirt, Mildred A.
See Benson, Mildred
Wirtenberg, Patricia Z. 1932-2007 .... *10*
Wirtenberg, Patricia Zarrella
See Wirtenberg, Patricia Z.
Wirth, Beverly 1938- *63*
Wirths, Claudine (Turner) G(ibson)
1926-2000 .... *104*
Earlier sketch in SATA *64*
Wise, Bill 1958- *191*
Wise, Lenny
See Wise, Leonard
Wise, Leonard 1940- *167*
Wise, Leonard A.
See Wise, Leonard
Wise, Leonard Allan
See Wise, Leonard
Wise, William 1923- *163*
Earlier sketch in SATA *4*
Wise, Winifred E. *2*
Wiseman, Ann (Sayre) 1926- *31*
Wiseman, B(ernard) 1922-1995 .... *4*
Wiseman, David 1916- *43*
Brief entry *40*
Wiseman, Eva 1947- *210*
Wishinsky, Frieda 1948- *166*
Earlier sketches in SATA *70, 112*
Wisler, G(ary) Clifton 1950- *103*
Brief entry *46*
Earlier sketch in SATA *58*
Wismer, Donald (Richard) 1946- *59*
Wisner, Bill
See Wisner, William L.
Wisner, William L. 1914(?)-1983 .... *42*
Wisnewski, David 1953-2002
See Wisniewski, David
Wisniewski, David 1953-2002 .... *95*
Obituary *139*
See also CLR *51*
Wister, Owen 1860-1938 .... *62*
Witham, (Phillip) Ross 1917- *37*
Withers, Carl A. 1900-1970 .... *14*
Withers, Pam 1956- *182*
Withrow, Sarah 1966- *199*
Earlier sketch in SATA *124*

Witt, Dick 1948- *80*
Witt, Shirley Hill 1934- *17*
Wittanen, Etolin 1907- *55*
Wittels, Harriet Joan 1938- *31*
Wittig, Susan
See Albert, Susan Wittig
Wittlinger, Ellen 1948- *189*
Autobiography Feature *128*
Earlier sketches in SATA *83, 122*
Wittman, Sally (Anne Christensen) 1941- *30*
Witty, Paul 1898-1976 .... *50*
Obituary *30*
Wodehouse, P. G. 1881-1975 .... *22*
Wodehouse, Pelham Grenville
See Wodehouse, P. G.
Wodge, Dreary
See Gorey, Edward (St. John)
Woelfle, Gretchen 1945- *145*
Wohlberg, Meg 1905-1990 .... *41*
Obituary *66*
Wohlrabe, Raymond A. 1900-1977 .... *4*
Wohnoutka, Mike *195*
Wojciechowska, Maia (Teresa) 1927-2002 ... *83*
Autobiography Feature *104*
Obituary *134*
Earlier sketches in SATA *1, 28*
See also CLR *1*
See also SAAS *1*
Wojciechowski, Susan *126*
Earlier sketch in SATA *78*
Wojnarowski, Adrian 1970- *190*
Wojtusik, Elizabeth *208*
Wolcott, Patty 1929- *14*
Wold, Allen L. 1943- *64*
Wold, Jo Anne 1938- *30*
Woldin, Beth Weiner 1955- *34*
Wolf, Allan 1963- *192*
Wolf, Bernard 1930- *102*
Brief entry *37*
Wolf, Erica (Van Varick) 1978- *156*
Wolf, Gita 1956- *101*
Wolf, J. M.
See Wolf, Joan M.
Wolf, Janet 1957- *78*
Wolf, Joan M. 1966- *193*
Wolf, Sallie 1950- *205*
Earlier sketch in SATA *80*
Wolfe, Art 1952- *76*
Wolfe, Burton H. 1932- *5*
Wolfe, Gene 1931- *165*
Earlier sketch in SATA *118*
Wolfe, Gene Rodman
See Wolfe, Gene
Wolfe, Gillian *199*
Wolfe, Louis 1905-1985 .... *8*
Obituary *133*
Wolfe, Rinna (Evelyn) 1925- *38*
Wolfenden, George
See Beardmore, George
Wolfer, Dianne 1961- *167*
Autobiography Feature *117*
Earlier sketch in SATA *104*
Wolff, Alexander (Nikolaus) 1957- *137*
Earlier sketch in SATA *63*
Wolff, Ashley 1956- *203*
Earlier sketches in SATA *50, 81, 155*
Wolff, Diane 1945- *27*
Wolff, Ferida 1946- *164*
Earlier sketch in SATA *79*
Wolff, Jason 1972- *213*
Wolff, Jennifer Ashley
See Wolff, Ashley
Wolff, Nancy *202*
Wolff, Robert Jay 1905-1977 .... *10*
Wolff, Sonia
See Levitin, Sonia
Wolff, Virginia Euwer 1937- *137*
Earlier sketch in SATA *78*
See also CLR *62*
Wolfman, Judy 1933- *138*
Wolfson, Evelyn 1937- *62*

Wolitzer, Hilma 1930- *31*
Wolkoff, Judie (Edwards) *93*
Brief entry *37*
Wolkstein, Diane 1942- *138*
Earlier sketches in SATA *7, 82*
Wollheim, Donald A(llen) 1914-1990
Obituary *69*
Wolny, P.
See Janeczko, Paul B(ryan)
Wolters, Richard A. 1920-1993 .... *35*
Wondriska, William 1931- *6*
Wong, Jade Snow 1922-2006 .... *112*
Obituary *175*
Wong, Janet S. 1962- *210*
Earlier sketches in SATA *98, 148*
See also CLR *94*
Wong, Nicole *214*
Woo, Howie 1974- *207*
Wood, Anne (Savage) 1937- *64*
Wood, Audrey *198*
Brief entry *44*
Earlier sketches in SATA *50, 81, 139*
See also CLR *26*
Wood, Catherine
See Etchison, Birdie L(ee)
Wood, David 1944- *212*
Earlier sketch in SATA *87*
Wood, Don 1945- *50*
Brief entry *44*
See also CLR *26*
Wood, Douglas 1951- *180*
Earlier sketches in SATA *81, 132*
Wood, Douglas Eric
See Wood, Douglas
Wood, Edgar A(llardyce) 1907-1998 .... *14*
Wood, Esther
See Brady, Esther Wood
Wood, Frances Elizabeth *34*
Wood, Frances M. 1951- *97*
Wood, Jacqueline
See Wood, Jakki
Wood, Jakki 1957- *211*
Wood, James Playsted 1905- *1*
Wood, Jenny 1955- *88*
Wood, John Norris 1930- *85*
Wood, June Rae 1946- *120*
Earlier sketch in SATA *79*
See also CLR *82*
Wood, Kerry
See Wood, Edgar A(llardyce)
Wood, Kim Marie *134*
Wood, Laura N.
See Roper, Laura (Newbold) Wood
Wood, Linda C(arol) 1945- *59*
Wood, Marcia 1956- *80*
Wood, Marcia Mae
See Wood, Marcia
Wood, Nancy
See Wood, Nancy C.
Wood, Nancy C. 1936- *178*
Earlier sketch in SATA *6*
Wood, Nuria
See Nobisso, Josephine
Wood, Owen 1929- *64*
Wood, Phyllis Anderson 1923- *33*
Brief entry *30*
Wood, Richard 1949- *110*
Wood, Tim(othy William Russell) 1946- *88*
Wood, Wallace 1927-1981
Obituary *33*
Woodard, Carol 1929- *14*
Woodburn, John Henry 1914- *11*
Woodbury, David Oakes 1896-1981 .... *62*
Woodford, Peggy 1937- *25*
Woodhouse, Barbara (Blackburn)
1910-1988 .... *63*
Woodhull, Ann Love *194*
Wooding, Chris 1977- *166*
Wooding, Sharon
See Wooding, Sharon L(ouise)
Wooding, Sharon L(ouise) 1943- *66*

Woodman, Allen 1954- 76
Woodrich, Mary Neville 1915- 2
Woodruff, Elvira 1951- 211
    Earlier sketches in SATA 70, 106, 162
Woodruff, Joan Leslie 1953- 104
Woodruff, Liza 1971(?)- 182
Woodruff, Marian
    See Goudge, Eileen
Woodruff, Noah 1977- 86
Woods, George A(llan) 1926-1988 30
    Obituary 57
Woods, Geraldine 1948- 111
    Brief entry 42
    Earlier sketch in SATA 56
Woods, Harold 1945- 56
    Brief entry 42
Woods, Lawrence
    See Lowndes, Robert A(ugustine) W(ard)
Woods, Margaret 1921- 2
Woods, Nat
    See Stratemeyer, Edward L.
Woods, Titania
    See Weatherly, Lee
Woodson, Jack
    See Woodson, John Waddie Jr.
Woodson, Jacqueline 1964- 189
    Earlier sketches in SATA 94, 139
    See also CLR 49
Woodson, Jacqueline Amanda
    See Woodson, Jacqueline
Woodson, John Waddie Jr. 1913- 10
Woodtor, Dee
    See Woodtor, Delores Parmer
Woodtor, Dee Parmer 1945(?)-2002
    See Woodtor, Delores Parmer
Woodtor, Delores Parmer 1945-2002 93
Wood-Trost, Lucille
    See Trost, Lucille W(ood)
Woodward, (Landon) Cleveland 1900-1986 . 10
    Obituary 48
Woodworth, Chris 1957- 168
Woodworth, Viki 1952- 127
Woody, Regina Jones 1894-1983 3
Woodyadd, Charlotte
    See Hough, Charlotte
Woog, Adam 1953- 125
    Earlier sketch in SATA 84
Wooldridge, Connie Nordhielm 1950- 143
    Earlier sketch in SATA 92
Wooldridge, Frosty 1947- 140
Wooldridge, Rhoda 1906-1988 22
Wooley, Susan Frelick 1945- 113
Woolf, Paula 1950- 104
Woolfe, Angela 1976- 169
Woolley, Catherine 1904-2005 3
    Obituary 166
Woolman, Steven 1969-2004 163
    Earlier sketch in SATA 90
Woolsey, Janette 1904-1989 3
    Obituary 131
Worcester, Donald E(mmet) 1915- 18
Word, Reagan 1944- 103
Work, Virginia 1946- 57
    Brief entry 45
Worline, Bonnie Bess 1914- 14
Wormell, Christopher 1955- 154
    Earlier sketch in SATA 103
Wormell, Mary 1959- 96
Wormser, Richard 1933- 106
    Autobiography Feature 118
    See also SAAS 26
Wormser, Sophie 1897-1979 22
Worth, Richard 1945- 59
    Brief entry 46
Worth, Valerie 1933-1994 81
    Earlier sketches in SATA 8, 70
    See also CLR 21
Worthington, Leonie 1956- 200
Wortis, Avi
    See Avi

Wortis, Edward Irving
    See Avi
Wosmek, Frances 1917- 29
Woychuk, Denis 1953- 71
Wrede, Patricia C(ollins) 1953- 146
    Earlier sketch in SATA 67
Wriggins, Sally Hovey 1922- 17
Wright, Alexandra 1979- 103
Wright, Betty Ren 1927- 109
    Brief entry 48
    Earlier sketch in SATA 63
Wright, Cliff 1963- 168
    Earlier sketch in SATA 76
Wright, Courtni
    See Wright, Courtni C(rump)
Wright, Courtni C(rump) 1950- 84
Wright, Courtni Crump
    See Wright, Courtni C(rump)
Wright, Dare 1914(?)-2001 21
    Obituary 124
Wright, David K. 1943- 112
    Earlier sketch in SATA 73
Wright, Elinor
    See Lyon, Elinor
Wright, Enid Meadowcroft (LaMonte)
    1898-1966 3
Wright, Esmond 1915-2003 10
Wright, Frances Fitzpatrick 1897-1982 10
Wright, J. B.
    See Barkan, Joanne
Wright, Judith 1915-2000 14
    Obituary 121
Wright, Judith Arundell
    See Wright, Judith
Wright, Katrina
    See Gater, Dilys
Wright, Kenneth
    See del Rey, Lester
Wright, Kit 1944- 87
Wright, Leslie B(ailey) 1959- 91
Wright, Michael 1954- 198
Wright, Nancy Means 38
Wright, R(obert) H(amilton) 1906- 6
Wright, Rachel 134
Wright, Susan Kimmel 1950- 97
Wrightfrierson
    See Wright-Frierson, Virginia (Marguerite)
Wright-Frierson, Virginia (Marguerite)
    1949- 110
    Earlier sketch in SATA 58
Wrightson, Alice Patricia
    See Wrightson, Patricia
Wrightson, Patricia 1921-2010 112
    Obituary 215
    Earlier sketches in SATA 8, 66
    See also CLR 14
    See also SAAS 4
Wroble, Lisa A. 1963- 134
Wrongo, I.B.
    See Katz, Alan
Wronker, Lili
    See Wronker, Lili Cassel
Wronker, Lili Cassel 1924- 10
Wryde, Dogear
    See Gorey, Edward (St. John)
Wu, Donald 212
Wu, Elizabeth
    See Wu, Liz
Wu, Liz 184
Wu, Norbert 1961- 155
    Earlier sketch in SATA 101
Wulf, Linda Press 205
Wulffson, Don 1943- 155
    Earlier sketches in SATA 32, 88
Wulffson, Don L.
    See Wulffson, Don
Wummer, Amy 1955- 201
Wunderli, Stephen 1958- 79
Wunsch, Josephine (McLean) 1914- 64
Wunsch, Marjory 1942- 82

Wuorio, Eva-Lis 1918- 34
    Brief entry 28
Wurts, Janny 1953- 98
Wyatt, B. D.
    See Robinson, Spider
Wyatt, David 1968- 185
Wyatt, Jane
    See Bradbury, Bianca (Ryley)
Wyatt, Melissa 1963- 177
Wyatt, Valerie 209
Wyeth, Betsy James 1921- 41
Wyeth, N(ewell) C(onvers) 1882-1945 17
    See also CLR 106
Wyler, Rose 1909-2000 18
    Obituary 121
Wylie, Betty Jane 48
Wylie, Laura
    See Matthews, Patricia
Wylie, Laurie
    See Matthews, Patricia
Wyllie, Stephen 86
Wyman, Andrea 75
Wyman, Carolyn 1956- 83
Wymer, Norman (George) 1911- 25
Wynard, Talbot
    See Hamilton, Charles (Harold St. John)
Wyndham, John
    See Harris, John (Wyndham Parkes Lucas)
    Beynon
Wyndham, Lee
    See Hyndman, Jane Andrews Lee
Wyndham, Robert
    See Hyndman, Robert Utley
Wynne, Patricia J. 210
Wynne-Jones, Tim 1948- 186
    Autobiography Feature 136
    Earlier sketches in SATA 67, 96, 136
    See also CLR 58
Wynne-Jones, Timothy
    See Wynne-Jones, Tim
Wynter, Edward (John) 1914- 14
Wynyard, Talbot
    See Hamilton, Charles (Harold St. John)
Wyss, Johann David Von 1743-1818 29
    Brief entry 27
    See also CLR 92
Wyss, Thelma Hatch 1934- 202
    Earlier sketches in SATA 10, 140

                            X

Xavier, Father
    See Hurwood, Bernhardt J.
Xuan, YongSheng 1952- 116
    Autobiography Feature 119

                            Y

Yaccarino, Dan 192
    Earlier sketch in SATA 141
Yadin, (Rav-Aloof) Yigael 1917-1984 55
Yaffe, Alan
    See Yorinks, Arthur
Yagher, Kevin 1962- 143
Yakovetic, (Joseph Sandy) 1952- 59
Yakovetic, Joe
    See Yakovetic, (Joseph Sandy)
Yamada, Utako 1963- 188
Yamaguchi, Marianne (Illenberger) 1936- 7
Yamaka, Sara 1978- 92
Yamanaka, Lois-Ann 1961- 166
Yamasaki, Katie 206
Yancey, Diane 1951- 138
    Earlier sketch in SATA 81
Yancey, Richard 193
Yancey, Rick
    See Yancey, Richard
Yang, Belle 1960- 170

Yang, James 1960- *190*
Yang, Jay 1941- *12*
Yang, Mingyi 1943- *72*
Yarbrough, Camille 1938- *79*
  See also CLR *29*
Yarbrough, Ira 1910(?)-1983
  Obituary *35*
Yaroslava
  See Mills, Yaroslava Surmach
Yarrow, Peter 1938- *195*
Yashima, Taro
  See Iwamatsu, Jun Atsushi
Yates, Elizabeth 1905-2001 .... *68*
  Obituary *128*
  Earlier sketch in SATA *4*
  See also SAAS *6*
Yates, Janelle K(aye) 1957- *77*
Yates, John 1939- *74*
Yates, Kelly 1971- *208*
Yates, Philip 1956- *212*
Yates, Philip 1958- *149*
  Earlier sketch in SATA *92*
Yates, Raymond F(rancis) 1895-1966 .... *31*
Yaukey, Grace S(ydenstricker) 1899-1994 ... *80*
  Earlier sketch in SATA *5*
Yazzie, Johnson 1946- *205*
Ye, Ting-xing 1952- *106*
Yeahpau, Thomas M. 1975- *187*
Yeakley, Marjory Hall 1908- *21*
Yeatman, Linda 1938- *42*
Yeatts, Tabatha 1970- *215*
Yee, Brenda Shannon *133*
Yee, Lisa 1959- *160*
Yee, Paul 1956- *211*
  Earlier sketches in SATA *67, 96, 143*
  See also CLR *44*
Yee, Tammy *206*
Yee, Wong Herbert 1953- *172*
  Earlier sketches in SATA *78, 115*
Yeh, Chun-Chan 1914- *79*
Ye Junjian
  See Yeh, Chun-Chan
Yelchin, Eugene 1956- *196*
Yenawine, Philip 1942- *85*
Yensid, Retlaw
  See Disney, Walt(er Elias)
Yeo, Wilma (Lethem) 1918-1994 .... *81*
  Earlier sketch in SATA *24*
Yeoman, John 1934- *80*
  Earlier sketch in SATA *28*
  See also CLR *46*
Yep, Kathleen S. *203*
Yep, Laurence 1948- *213*
  Earlier sketches in SATA *7, 69, 123, 176*
  See also CLR *132*
Yep, Laurence Michael
  See Yep, Laurence
Yepsen, Roger B(ennet), Jr. 1947- *59*
Yerian, Cameron John *21*
Yerian, Margaret A. *21*
Yerxa, Leo 1947- *181*
Yetska
  See Ironside, Jetske
Yezerski, Thomas F. 1969- *190*
Yin *194*
Ylvisaker, Anne 1965(?)- *172*
Yoder, Carolyn P. 1953- *149*
Yoder, Carolyn Patricia
  See Yoder, Carolyn P.
Yoder, Dorothy Meenen 1921- *96*
Yoder, Dot
  See Yoder, Dorothy Meenen
Yoder, Walter D. 1933- *88*
Yolen, Jane 1939- *194*
  Autobiography Feature *111*
  Earlier sketches in SATA *4, 40, 75, 112, 158*
  See also CLR *149*
  See also SAAS *1*
Yolen, Jane Hyatt
  See Yolen, Jane
Yonezu, Yusuke *196*

Yonge, Charlotte 1823-1901 .... *17*
Yonge, Charlotte Mary
  See Yonge, Charlotte
Yoo, Paula 1969(?)- *174*
Yoo, Taeeun *191*
Yoon, Salina 1972- *204*
Yorinks, Adrienne 1956- *171*
Yorinks, Arthur 1953- *200*
  Earlier sketches in SATA *33, 49, 85, 144*
  See also CLR *20*
York, Alison
  See Nicole, Christopher (Robin)
York, Andrew
  See Nicole, Christopher (Robin)
York, Carol Beach 1928- *77*
  Earlier sketch in SATA *6*
York, Rebecca
  See Buckholtz, Eileen (Garber)
  and Glick, Ruth (Burtnick)
York, Simon
  See Heinlein, Robert A.
Yoshida, Toshi 1911- *77*
Yoshikawa, Sachiko *181*
Yost, Edna 1889-1971
  Obituary *26*
Youd, C. S.
  See Youd, Samuel
Youd, Samuel 1922- *135*
  Brief entry *30*
  Earlier sketch in SATA *47*
  See also CLR *2*
  See also SAAS *6*
Youme
  See Landowne, Youme
Young, Amy L. *185*
Young, Anne Mortimer
  See Mortimer, Anne
Young, Bob
  See Young, Robert W(illiam)
  and Young, James Robert
Young, Carol 1945- *102*
Young, Catherine
  See Olds, Helen Diehl
Young, Clarence
  See Garis, Howard R.
  and Stratemeyer, Edward L.
Young, Collier
  See Bloch, Robert (Albert)
Young, Dan 1952- *126*
Young, Dianne 1959- *88*
Young, Dorothea Bennett 1924- *31*
Young, Ed 1931- *211*
  Earlier sketches in SATA *10, 74, 122, 173*
  See also CLR *27*
Young, Ed Tse-chun
  See Young, Ed
Young, Edward
  See Reinfeld, Fred
Young, Elaine L.
  See Schulte, Elaine L(ouise)
Young, James
  See Graham, Ian
Young, Jan
  See Young, Janet Randall
Young, Janet 1957- *188*
Young, Janet Randall 1919-1994 .... *3*
Young, Janet Ruth
  See Young, Janet
Young, Jeff C. 1948- *132*
Young, John
  See Macintosh, Brownie
Young, Judy 1956- *207*
  Earlier sketch in SATA *155*
Young, Judy (Elaine) Dockrey 1949- *72*
Young, Karen Romano 1959- *168*
  Earlier sketch in SATA *116*
Young, Ken 1956- *86*
Young, Lois Horton 1911-1981 .... *26*
Young, Louisa *161*
Young, Louise B. 1919- *64*
Young, Margaret B. 1922-2009 .... *2*

Young, Margaret Buckner
  See Young, Margaret B.
Young, Mary 1940- *89*
Young, Miriam 1913-1974 .... *7*
Young, Noela 1930- *89*
Young, (Rodney Lee) Patrick (Jr.) 1937- *22*
Young, Percy M(arshall) 1912-2004 .... *31*
  Obituary *154*
Young, Richard Alan 1946- *72*
Young, Robert W(illiam) 1916-1969 .... *3*
Young, Ross B. 1955- *150*
Young, Ruth 1946- *67*
Young, Sara
  See Pennypacker, Sara
Young, Scott A. 1918-2005 .... *5*
Young, Scott Alexander
  See Young, Scott A.
Young, Selina 1971-2006 .... *201*
Young, Vivien
  See Gater, Dilys
Younger, Barbara 1954- *108*
Youngs, Betty 1934-1985 .... *53*
  Obituary *42*
Younkin, Paula 1942- *77*
Yount, Lisa (Ann) 1944- *124*
  Earlier sketch in SATA *74*
Yourgrau, Barry *179*
Yuditskaya, Tatyana 1964- *75*
Yum, Hyewon *211*
Yumoto, Kazumi 1959- *153*

Z

Zach, Cheryl (Byrd) 1947- *98*
  Brief entry *51*
  Earlier sketch in SATA *58*
  See also SAAS *24*
Zacharias, Gary L. 1946- *153*
Zaffo, George J. (?)-1984 .... *42*
Zagarenski, Pamela 1969(?)- *183*
Zagwyn, Deborah Turney 1953- *138*
  Earlier sketch in SATA *78*
Zahares, Wade *193*
Zahn, Timothy 1951- *156*
  Earlier sketch in SATA *91*
Zaid, Barry 1938- *51*
Zaidenberg, Arthur 1908(?)-1990 .... *34*
  Obituary *66*
Zalben, Jane Breskin 1950- *170*
  Earlier sketches in SATA *7, 79, 120*
  See also CLR *84*
Zallinger, Jean (Day) 1918- *115*
  Earlier sketches in SATA *14, 80*
Zallinger, Peter Franz 1943- *49*
Zambreno, Mary Frances 1954- *140*
  Earlier sketch in SATA *75*
Zanderbergen, George
  See May, Julian
Zappa, Ahmet 1974- *180*
Zappa, Ahmet Emuukha Rodan
  See Zappa, Ahmet
Zappler, Lisbeth 1930- *10*
Zarchy, Harry 1912-1987 .... *34*
Zarin, Cynthia 1959- *192*
  Earlier sketch in SATA *108*
Zaring, Jane (Thomas) 1936- *40*
Zarins, Joyce Audy
  See dos Santos, Joyce Audy
Zaslavsky, Claudia 1917- *36*
Zaugg, Sandra L. 1938- *118*
Zaugg, Sandy
  See Zaugg, Sandra L.
Zaunders, Bo 1939- *137*
Zawadzki, Marek 1958- *97*
Zebra, A.
  See Scoltock, Jack
Zebrowski, George 1945- *67*
Zebrowski, George T.
  See Zebrowski, George

Zecca, Katherine 207
Zeck, Gerald Anthony 1939- 40
Zeck, Gerry
  See Zeck, Gerald Anthony
Zed, Dr.
  See Penrose, Gordon
Zei, Alki 1925- 24
  See also CLR 6
Zeier, Joan T(heresa) 1931- 81
Zeinert, Karen 1942-2002 137
  Earlier sketch in SATA 79
Zeises, Lara M. 1976- 184
  Earlier sketch in SATA 145
Zelazny, Roger 1937-1995 57
  Brief entry 39
Zelazny, Roger Joseph
  See Zelazny, Roger
Zeldis, Malcah 1931- 146
  Earlier sketch in SATA 86
Zelinsky, Paul O. 1953- 154
  Brief entry 33
  Earlier sketches in SATA 49, 102
  See also CLR 55
Zellan, Audrey Penn
  See Penn, Audrey
Zemach, Harve
  See Fischtrom, Harvey
Zemach, Kaethe 1958- 149
  Brief entry 39
  Earlier sketch in SATA 49
Zemach, Margot 1931-1989 70
  Obituary 59
  Earlier sketch in SATA 21
Zemach-Bersin, Kaethe
  See Zemach, Kaethe
Zeman, Ludmila 1947- 153
Zepeda, Gwendolyn 1971- 206
Zephaniah, Benjamin 1958- 189
  Earlier sketches in SATA 86, 140
Zephaniah, Benjamin Obadiah Iqbal
  See Zephaniah, Benjamin
Zephaniah, Benjamin Pbadiah Iqubal
  See Zephaniah, Benjamin
Zerman, Melvyn Bernard 1930-2010 46
Zettner, Pat 1940- 70
Zevin, Gabrielle 176
Zhang, Christopher Zhong-Yuan 1954- 91
Zhang, Song Nan 1942- 170
  Earlier sketch in SATA 85

Ziefert, Harriet 1941- 205
  Earlier sketches in SATA 101, 154
Ziegler, Jack (Denmore) 1942- 60
Ziemienski, Dennis (Theodore) 1947- 10
Ziliox, Marc
  See Fichter, George S.
Zillah
  See Macdonald, Zillah K(atherine)
Zim, Herbert S(pencer) 1909-1994 30
  Obituary 85
  Earlier sketch in SATA 1
  See also CLR 2
  See also SAAS 2
Zim, Sonia Bleeker 1909-1971 2
  Obituary 26
Zima, Gordon 1920- 90
Zimelman, Nathan 1921- 65
  Brief entry 37
Zimmer, Dirk 1943- 147
  Earlier sketch in SATA 65
Zimmer, Tracie Vaughn 169
Zimmerman, Andrea 1950- 192
  Earlier sketch in SATA 123
Zimmerman, Andrea Griffing
  See Zimmerman, Andrea
Zimmerman, H. Werner 1951- 101
Zimmerman, Heinz Werner
  See Zimmerman, H. Werner
Zimmerman, Naoma 1914-2004 10
Zimmermann, Arnold E. 1909- 58
Zimmermann, Karl 1943- 211
Zimmermann, Karl R.
  See Zimmermann, Karl
Zimmett, Debbie
  See Becker, Deborah Zimmett
Zimmy
  See Stratemeyer, Edward L.
Zimnik, Reiner 1930- 36
  See also CLR 3
Zindel, Bonnie 1943- 34
Zindel, Lizabeth 187
Zindel, Paul 1936-2003 102
  Obituary 142
  Earlier sketches in SATA 16, 58
  See also CLR 85
Ziner, Feenie
  See Ziner, Florence
Ziner, Florence 1921- 5
Zingara, Professor
  See Leeming, Joseph

Zinger, Yitskhok
  See Singer, Isaac Bashevis
Zion, Eugene 1913-1975 18
Zion, Gene
  See Zion, Eugene
Zoehfeld, Kathleen Weidner 1954- 193
Zohorsky, Janet R. 1958- 148
Zolkower, Edie Stoltz 171
Zolkowski, Cathy (A.) 1969- 121
Zollars, Jaime 191
Zolotow, Charlotte 1915- 138
  Earlier sketches in SATA 1, 35, 78
  See also CLR 77
Zolotow, Charlotte Gertrude Shapiro
  See Zolotow, Charlotte
Zolotow, Ellen
  See Dragonwagon, Crescent
Zonderman, Jon 1957- 92
Zonia, Dhimitri 1921- 20
Zonta, Pat 1951- 143
Zubrowski, Bernard 1939- 90
  Earlier sketch in SATA 35
Zubrowski, Bernie
  See Zubrowski, Bernard
Zucker, Miriam S.
  See Reichert, Miriam Zucker
Zuckerman, Linda 190
Zudeck, Darryl 1961- 61
Zug, Mark 204
Zupa, G. Anthony
  See Zeck, Gerald Anthony
Zupancic, Lilijana Praprotnik
  See Prap, Lila
Zurbo, Matt(hew) 1967- 98
Zurhorst, Charles (Stewart, Jr.) 1913-1989 .. 12
Zurlo, Tony 1941- 145
Zuromskis, Diane
  See Stanley, Diane
Zuromskis, Diane Stanley
  See Stanley, Diane
Zusak, Markus 1975- 149
Zwahlen, Diana 1947- 88
Zweifel, Frances W. 1931- 14
Zwerger, Lisbeth 1954- 194
  Earlier sketches in SATA 66, 130
  See also CLR 46
  See also SAAS 13
Zwinger, Ann (H.) 1925- 46
Zymet, Cathy Alter 1965- 121